TABLE II

Present Value of $1 Due in n Periods

$$PV = A\left[\frac{1}{(1+i)^n}\right] = A(PVF_{\overline{n}|\,i})$$

n	2%	3%	4%	5%	6%	8%	10%	12%	16%	20%
1	0.9804	0.9709	0.9615	0.9524	0.9434	0.9259	0.9091	0.8929	0.8621	0.8333
2	0.9612	0.9426	0.9246	0.9070	0.8900	0.8573	0.8264	0.7972	0.7432	0.6944
3	0.9423	0.9151	0.8890	0.8638	0.8396	0.7938	0.7513	0.7118	0.6407	0.5787
4	0.9238	0.8885	0.8548	0.8227	0.7921	0.7350	0.6830	0.6355	0.5523	0.4823
5	0.9057	0.8626	0.8219	0.7835	0.7473	0.6806	0.6209	0.5674	0.4761	0.4019
6	0.8880	0.8375	0.7903	0.7462	0.7050	0.6302	0.5645	0.5066	0.4104	0.3349
7	0.8706	0.8131	0.7599	0.7107	0.6651	0.5835	0.5132	0.4523	0.3538	0.2791
8	0.8535	0.7894	0.7307	0.6768	0.6274	0.5403	0.4665	0.4039	0.3050	0.2326
9	0.8368	0.7664	0.7026	0.6446	0.5919	0.5002	0.4241	0.3606	0.2630	0.1938
10	0.8203	0.7441	0.6756	0.6139	0.5584	0.4632	0.3855	0.3220	0.2267	0.1615
11	0.8043	0.7224	0.6496	0.5847	0.5268	0.4289	0.3505	0.2875	0.1954	0.1346
12	0.7885	0.7014	0.6246	0.5568	0.4970	0.3971	0.3186	0.2567	0.1685	0.1122
13	0.7730	0.6810	0.6006	0.5303	0.4688	0.3677	0.2897	0.2292	0.1452	0.0935
14	0.7579	0.6611	0.5775	0.5051	0.4423	0.3405	0.2633	0.2046	0.1252	0.0779
15	0.7430	0.6419	0.5553	0.4810	0.4173	0.3152	0.2394	0.1827	0.1079	0.0649
16	0.7284	0.6232	0.5339	0.4581	0.3936	0.2919	0.2176	0.1631	0.0930	0.0541
17	0.7142	0.6050	0.5134	0.4363	0.3714	0.2703	0.1978	0.1456	0.0802	0.0451
18	0.7002	0.5874	0.4936	0.4155	0.3503	0.2502	0.1799	0.1300	0.0691	0.0376
19	0.6864	0.5703	0.4746	0.3957	0.3305	0.2317	0.1635	0.1161	0.0596	0.0313
20	0.6730	0.5537	0.4564	0.3769	0.3118	0.2145	0.1486	0.1037	0.0514	0.0261
25	0.6095	0.4776	0.3751	0.2953	0.2330	0.1460	0.0923	0.0588	0.0245	0.0105
30	0.5521	0.4120	0.3083	0.2314	0.1741	0.0994	0.0573	0.0334	0.0116	0.0042
40	0.4529	0.3066	0.2083	0.1420	0.0972	0.0460	0.0221	0.0107	0.0026	0.0007
50	0.3715	0.2281	0.1407	0.0872	0.0543	0.0213	0.0085	0.0035	0.0006	0.0001

INTERMEDIATE ACCOUNTING

Second Canadian Edition

John R. E. Parker, MBA, CA
Professor of Accounting
Dalhousie University

Harry Simons, MA, CPA
Professor Emeritus of Accounting
University of California, Los Angeles

Jay M. Smith, Jr., PhD, CPA
Professor of Accounting
Brigham Young University

K. Fred Skousen, PhD, CPA
Professor of Accounting
Brigham Young University

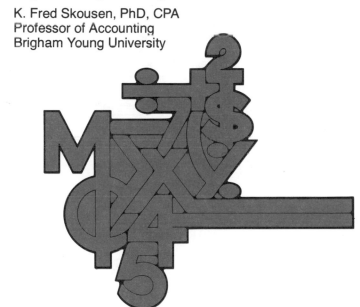

 **gage** PUBLISHING LIMITED
TORONTO ONTARIO CANADA

Canadian Cataloguing in Publication Data

Main entry under title:
Intermediate accounting

First Canadian ed.: Simons, Harry, 1912-   Intermediate accounting.
ISBN 0-7715-5776-0

1. Accounting. I. Simons, Harry, 1912-   Intermediate accounting. II. Parker, John R. E., 1931-

HF5635.S55 1981   657'.044   C81-094240-2

Co-ordinating Editor: Joan Kerr
Editor: Geraldine Kikuta
Cover Design: Jack Steiner

3 4 5 6 7 8 9 BP   85 84

Printed and bound in Canada.

PREFACE

The Second Canadian Edition of *Intermediate Accounting* is based on its highly successful American predecessors initially authored by Wilbert E. Karrenbrock and Harry Simons and first published in 1949. Over the years, several editions of both comprehensive and standard volumes of *Intermediate Accounting* have been published in the United States, the most recent being the seventh edition of the comprehensive volume by Jay M. Smith, Jr. and K. Fred Skousen, published in 1981. The foundation for this Canadian Edition is therefore an established book with proven performance over a period of over 30 years. On the one hand, the Canadian Edition retains the format and structure of its American predecessors; at the same time, this edition has been carefully adapted for Canadian use and includes up-to-date coverage of the Canadian Business Corporations Act and applicable Research Recommendations issued by committees of the Canadian Institute of Chartered Accountants through December 31, 1980.

As indicated by its title, *Intermediate Accounting* presupposes the completion of an introductory course or courses in financial accounting. In addition, the book is designed to articulate with *Accounting Principles*, Second Canadian Edition, by John R. E. Parker, C. Rollin Niswonger and Philip E. Fess.

Designed for a full-year course to follow the introductory study of accounting, *Intermediate Accounting* seeks to serve the needs of two groups: (1) economics, business, or management students who do not plan to go beyond the intermediate course and (2) accounting students who expect to continue study at an advanced level. Each group must be familiar with the objectives of accounting and the principles that have evolved in response to stated objectives. They must also possess a full understanding of the nature of basic accounting statements and the limitations inherent in their preparation. With such a background, the student who does not specialize in accounting can properly interpret the statements and reports that emerge from the accounting process. Likewise, the accounting major can make important progress in the study of accounting and can look forward to achieving admission into the accounting profession.

In this edition, emphasis is placed on a blending of theory and current practice. For each topic, the currently accepted position of the profession is clearly presented with numerous examples to illustrate the essentials of the topic. Alternative views to the generally accepted position are explored and evaluated, and the dynamic nature of accounting is emphasized throughout.

Specific changes in this edition are described in the following paragraphs.

One new chapter has been included — chapter 12, "Consolidation and Equity Accounting." Traditionally, the subject matter of chapter 12 has been deferred for coverage in advanced accounting classes. However, both consolidation and equity accounting have been included at the intermediate level as methods of accounting for long-term investments. The intent of chapter 12 is to encourage a more thorough treatment of long-term investments in intermediate accounting.

While not new, three chapters have been so extensively revised that they almost qualify as new. Chapter 14, "Accounting for Income Tax," now includes a new methodology and comprehensive coverage of losses, including the complexities of loss carryforwards. The material on leases in chapter 15 is now based on Section 3065 of the *Accounting Recommendations*. Chapter 21, "Financial Reporting and Changing Prices," has been completely rewritten to keep pace with the evolving nature of this important topic. The chapter now emphasizes current value accounting, and covers recent pronouncements and the Canadian Exposure Draft "Current Cost Accounting." An appendix at the end of chapter 21 provides a comprehensive two-year illustration of general price level accounting.

An appendix has also been added to chapter 20, "The Statement of Changes in Financial Position." This appendix presents the T account method of preparing the statement of changes.

To make room for the new chapter 12 and for the expanded coverage of deferred income tax and inflation accounting, it has been necessary to delete financial statement analysis. This topic is usually covered in both introductory accounting and finance, and is often integrated throughout intermediate accounting rather than being treated as a separate topic. Financial statement analysis is also the subject of a chapter in *Accounting Principles*, Second Canadian Edition.

Obviously, the preceding description of changes is not exhaustive. Modifications have been made throughout the book to make this revision as up-to-date as possible. Each chapter concludes with a broad selection of new and revised questions, exercises, and problems. The questions provide a review of theory, while the exercises and problems offer practice in the application of theory to business-like situations. The exercises are relatively brief and require the application of the theory presented in the chapter, whereas the problems are comprehensive and require the application of the theory presented to date. Almost all of the chapters conclude with problems adapted from the examinations of professional accounting organizations. Such problems have been selected because they represent a strong challenge and at the same time contribute importantly to accounting growth and maturity.

Since accounting principles reflect the interaction of theory and practice with environmental influences the principles in use in Canada are not necessarily the same as those that operate in the United States. Differences in generally accepted accounting principles in Canada and the United States can be classified as (1) areas where additional disclosures may be required in the United States, (2) areas where practices other than those acceptable in the United States may be permissible in Canada, and

(3) areas of conflict. Where conflicts exist, the Canadian position, without exception, is the subject of expanded coverage. Examples of important areas of conflict include extraordinary items, earnings per share, accounting changes, and long-term investments. In all cases where Canadian GAAP differs from that of the United States, the Canadian position is subjected to in-depth coverage.

A separate publication, *Decision Problems in Intermediate Accounting*, by Joan E. D. Conrod and John R. E. Parker, is recommended for use with *Intermediate Accounting*, Second Canadian Edition. *Decision Problems in Intermediate Accounting* includes over forty short cases, many of which are multi-subject. The cases have been designed to integrate the topics commonly included in intermediate accounting.

ACKNOWLEDGEMENTS

Professor John H. Scheibelhut, Director, School of Business Administration, Dalhousie University, provided the type of encouragement that really matters — limited committee and other internal assignments that can be so time-consuming. The suggestion to include a chapter on consolidation and the equity method of accounting originated with Professor Robert H. Crandall, Queen's University.

The contributions of Brian J. Thompson, partner, Price Waterhouse and Co., acknowledged in the previous Canadian edition, are also very apparent in this edition. More specifically, several of the problems in chapter 14 were originally prepared by Brian Thompson for use at the Ontario Institute School of Accountancy.

User comments have indeed been very helpful, especially the detailed written comments of Professor Harvey Babiak, Scarborough College, University of Toronto; Professor Brian Duggan, University of Manitoba; and Professor Rashmi Thakkar, University of Calgary. A very high percentage of their comments have been acted upon in the preparation of this edition.

A general acknowledgement is also due to the accounting faculty at Dalhousie University. In particular, two colleagues at Dalhousie, Donald C. Cherry and Joan E. D. Conrod, have been very helpful, especially with assignment material, the manual, and other supporting materials. Mrs. Conrod prepared the revised material on leases included in chapter 15. Professor G. Richard Chesley has also contributed far more than he may realize simply as a result of our numerous discussions over a period of many years.

Numerous exercises and problems have been adapted from the examinations of professional accounting organizations and are identified in the text as follows:

Uniform CPA examinations	AICPA adapted
Uniform final examinations (CA)	CICA adapted
CGA examinations	CGA adapted
SMA examinations (RIA)	SMA adapted
Ontario Institute School of Accountancy	OISA adapted

There are numerous references to publications of the Canadian Institute of Chartered Accountants, especially to the *Accounting Recommendations* and the *Auditing*

Recommendations. Because of their influence in Canada, there are also various references to pronouncements issued in the United States and the United Kingdom, especially those of the Financial Accounting Standards Board and its predecessor, the Accounting Principles Board. It is a pleasure to thank the Canadian Institute of Chartered Accountants for their permission to reprint material from the *CICA Handbook* and other Institute publications. The permission to quote from pronouncements and other publications of the American Accounting Association, the American Institute of Certified Public Accountants, and the Financial Accounting Standards Board, together with permission to adapt examination materials of the American Institute of Certified Public Accountants, the Canadian Certified General Accountants Association, the Canadian Institute of Chartered Accountants, the Institute of Chartered Accountants of Ontario and the Society of Management Accountants of Canada is gratefully acknowledged. And finally, the book itself owes its existence to the dedicated work of the people at Gage, especially the editorial work of Geraldine Kikuta and the persistent encouragement of Joan Kerr.

John R. E. Parker
Halifax, Nova Scotia
March, 1981

CONTENTS

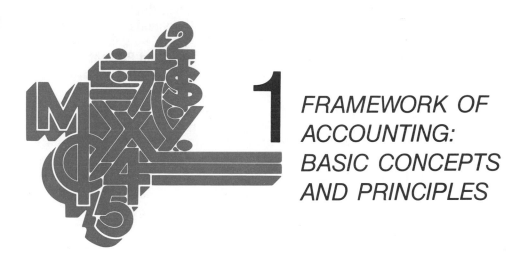

1 FRAMEWORK OF ACCOUNTING: BASIC CONCEPTS AND PRINCIPLES

The basic economic problem facing each individual or business entity is the allocation of scarce resources among competing alternative uses. Because resources are limited and because there is uncertainty as to which alternative use of resources is best, each business entity is required to make decisions which have important economic consequences. As indicated in the following quotation, accounting assists in providing information which can be used in the decision process.

> Accounting is a service activity. Its function is to provide quantitative information, primarily financial in nature, about economic entities that is intended to be useful in making economic decisions — in making reasoned choices among alternative courses of action.[1]

Several important concepts are included in this definition of accounting. Accounting is a *service activity*. It is intended to fulfil a *useful function* in our society by offering to provide service to various segments of society that are involved directly or indirectly with economic entities. It is primarily concerned with *quantitative financial information* describing the activities of an entity, rather than qualitative, judgmental evaluations of those activities. The output of the accounting system is intended to serve as an aid to users who must make *decisions* between alternative actions available to them. To

---

[1]*Statements of the Accounting Principles Board, No. 4*, "Basic Concepts and Accounting Principles Underlying Financial Statements of Business Enterprises" (New York: American Institute of Certified Public Accountants, 1970), par. 40.

the extent accounting information fulfils these goals, the accounting system is fulfilling its major purpose. Accounting is *utilitarian in nature*. It has developed to meet the needs of society. Accounting is also *dynamic*. As the needs of society and environmental conditions change, the techniques, concepts, and to some extent even the basic objectives of accounting must also change.

To ensure that changes are orderly and in the right direction, it is important to consider questions such as the following: What is the nature and purpose of accounting? Who are the primary users of accounting information and what are their needs? What should be the reporting objectives underlying financial statement presentation? What is the essential nature of assets, liabilities, and equities? What valuation and measurement bases should be used in accounting? To what extent should the accounting model reflect current value changes?

The impression should not be left that these and similar questions have not been considered in the past, nor that the traditional accounting model is not without considerable merit. Overall, accounting has served society well. However, continual modification and improvement of accounting is needed in order to keep pace with a changing business world.

This chapter provides an overview of the basic elements of accounting. The remaining chapters in the book not only consider how to apply basic accounting concepts and principles, but also explain the theoretical issues relating to the concepts, although some of the issues are not fully resolved.

USERS OF ACCOUNTING INFORMATION

Users of accounting information may be divided into two major categories: external users and internal users. *External users* are those groups or individuals who are not directly concerned with the day-to-day operations of the entity, but who are indirectly related to it. As listed by the Financial Accounting Standards Board (FASB) users include "owners, lenders, suppliers, potential investors and creditors, employees, management, directors, customers, financial analysts and advisors, brokers, underwriters, stock exchanges, lawyers, economists, taxing authorities, regulatory authorities, legislators, financial press and reporting agencies, labor unions, trade associations, business researchers, teachers and students, and the public."[2] *Internal users* include all levels of management personnel within an entity who are responsible for the planning and control of operations.

Several branches of accounting have evolved to meet the needs of these groups. Two of the most important branches have been identified as financial

---

[2]*Statement of Financial Accounting Concepts, No. 1*, "Objectives of Financial Reporting by Business Enterprises" (Stamford, Conn.: Financial Accounting Standards Board, 1978), par. 24.

accounting and managerial accounting. *Financial accounting* systems are primarily designed to provide financial statements to external users for their decision processes, although internal users also have access to the statements and use them in many of their decisions. *Managerial accounting* systems are primarily designed to supplement the financial accounting information for internal users, thus assisting them in reaching certain operating decisions. As businesses have become more complex, the availability of relevant information provided on a timely basis has become highly important to both classes of users. In order to meet these informational needs, companies have found it necessary to establish improved information systems. The increasing availability and use of business computers have resulted in vastly improved information systems that can provide more relevant and timely data than was possible heretofore.

This book is primarily concerned with financial accounting and thus places particular emphasis on the needs of external users.

GENERAL OBJECTIVES OF FINANCIAL ACCOUNTING

Financial accounting has been described as a system providing "a continual history quantified in money terms of economic resources and obligations of a business enterprise and of economic activities that change these resources and obligations."[3] This history has become increasingly important to the external user as the complexities of organizations and operations have made it more difficult to determine the position of a company and the results of its operations. The corporate form of business organization has contributed to this difficulty.

By its very nature the corporate form calls for extended and accurate accounting. It has permitted the accumulation of large amounts of resources by a single entity. In large corporations the investment and management groups are separated. Ownership interests are liquid and readily transferable. The number of investors having any first-hand knowledge of the activities of the companies in which they have an interest is small. Accounting becomes a major source of information concerning corporate financial status and progress for the investor. Accounting also becomes an indispensable source of information for a variety of purposes, including a report of stewardship accountability, for other absentee groups interested in an entity's activities.

If important economic decisions must be made by absentee owners, creditors, and other external users from statements produced by the financial accounting system, these statements should meet several general objectives. They should:

---

[3]*Statements of the Accounting Principles Board, No. 4, op. cit.*, par. 41.

1. Provide information useful for making economic decisions.
2. Serve primarily those users who have limited authority, ability, or resources to obtain information and who rely on financial statements as their principal source of information about an enterprise's economic activities.
3. Provide information useful to investors and creditors for predicting, comparing, and evaluating potential cash flows in terms of amount, timing, and related uncertainty.
4. Provide users with information for predicting, comparing, and evaluating enterprise earning power.
5. Supply information useful in judging management's ability to utilize enterprise resources effectively in achieving primary enterprise goals.
6. Provide factual and interpretive information about transactions and other events which is useful for predicting, comparing, and evaluating enterprise earning power. Basic underlying assumptions with respect to matters subject to interpretation, evaluation, prediction, or estimation should be disclosed.[4]

More recently the FASB has stated one key objective of financial reporting as follows:

> Financial reporting should provide information that is useful to present and potential investors and creditors and other users in making rational investment, credit and similar decisions. The information should be comprehensible to those who have a reasonable understanding of business and economic activities and are willing to study the information with reasonable diligence.[5]

Two important points merit emphasis: (1) present and potential investors and creditors are singled out as the most obvious prominent external users of financial reporting, and (2) the user is assumed to be sufficiently competent to comprehend the information content of financial reporting. User groups, such as investors and creditors are, however, defined to include those intermediaries who advise or represent them. In addition, the definition of financial reporting encompasses not only annual reports, prospectuses and SEC filings, but also the financial and nonfinancial information contained in "news releases, management's forecasts or other descriptions of its plans or expectations, and descriptions of an enterprise's social or environmental impact."[6] The information derived from these sources that is included within financial reporting "relates, directly or indirectly, to the information provided by the accounting system."[7] It should also be recognized that the more common examples of financial reporting, such as annual reports and prospectuses, also include both financial and nonfinancial information.

Satisfying these objectives requires continual study of the needs of external users. Financial statements designed to meet the needs of the external user and the objectives listed above are frequently referred to as *general*

---

[4]Adapted from *Objectives of Financial Statements, Report of the Study Group on the Objectives of Financial Statements* (New York: American Institute of Certified Public Accountants, 1973), pp. 61-63; see also *Tentative Conclusions on Objectives of Financial Statements of Enterprises* (Stamford, Conn.: Financial Accounting Standards Board, 1976).
[5]*Statement of Financial Accounting Concepts, No. 1, op. cit.*, par. 34.
[6]*Ibid.*, par. 7.
[7]*Ibid.*

purpose statements. They include statements disclosing financial position, the balance sheet; results of operations, the income statement; and changes in financial position, the funds statement.

ACCOUNTING AND THE ATTEST FUNCTION

A special responsibility of some accountants is to attest to the reliability and fairness of accounting statements prepared for external users by other accountants. Some persons regard this as the most important role accountants can assume, a role giving them professional status. Accountants performing this role are called *auditors*. They examine and review the statements prepared under the direction of management and issue an opinion as to how fairly the data in the statements are presented. The auditor thus adds some greater degree of confidence to the various segments of the business community which utilize and rely on such statements.

THE NEED FOR ACCOUNTING PRINCIPLES

If accounting data were used only within a company, management could prescribe the rules and procedures to be followed. If the rules and procedures were consistently and accurately applied, the resulting information could be used in the decision process without change. But many external users of financial statements use accounting reports in a comparative way. Company A is compared with Company B; Industry X is compared with Industry Y. As a result of this use, standards and guidelines are necessary so that accounting information can be compiled and reported in a manner that will enable comparisons to be made. These standards and guidelines are referred to most commonly as *generally accepted accounting principles*.

Accounting principles are not static or unchanging. Many of them do not have universal acceptance, and there are frequently alternative procedures for recording identical events. Before accountants can either prepare financial statements for external use or engage in audits of management's external statements, they must have an in-depth knowledge of these generally accepted accounting principles. Persons who rely on the financial statements in making decisions also need to understand these principles so they can better understand the nature of the statements as well as their limitations.

ORGANIZATIONS INFLUENCING ACCOUNTING PRINCIPLES

There have been several attempts by individuals and by professional and governmental organizations to establish fundamental accounting concepts and principles. These efforts have met with varying degrees of success. Before discussing some of the more important of these attempts, reference to the several accounting bodies who share the responsibility for the development of accounting principles is in order.

In Canada, the regulation of professions is essentially a matter within provincial jurisdiction. While there are certainly provincial differences, two distinct types of legislation provide the legal framework for regulation: (1) enabling legislation which serves to establish professional accounting organizations, grant legal recognition to a specific designation, and restrict the use of that designation, and (2) regulatory legislation which serves to restrict the practice of public accounting, usually by licensing those who have met established criteria. It should be noted that regulation only applies to public accounting as defined in the legislation and therefore regulation is often restricted to auditing services. In general, regulatory legislation does not encompass such services as bookkeeping and income tax.

The accounting profession in Canada encompasses three well-established organizations: the Certified General Accountants' Associations (CGA's), the Institutes of Chartered Accountants (CA's), and the Societies of Management Accountants (RIA's).[8] While the chartered accountants predominate in public practice, members of all three bodies are employed by industrial and commercial firms, by governments, and by non-profit organizations. Excluding students, who otherwise are included in CGA and RIA membership statistics, there are approximately 28,000 CA's in Canada, 10,000 RIA's and 7,000 CGA's.

Each of the provinces has acted uniformly by granting legislative recognition to both the CA's and RIA's. In addition, the CGA's are established by Act of Incorporation in New Brunswick, Prince Edward Island, Quebec, Manitoba, and British Columbia, and provincially under applicable corporate legislation in the other Canadian provinces. All three organizations are also incorporated federally and, in addition, have affiliated organizations in such jurisdictions as the Yukon, Northwest Territories, and Bermuda.

Legislation regulating the practice of public accounting was first introduced in Canada by Quebec in 1946, followed by Prince Edward Island in 1949, and Ontario in 1950. In both Prince Edward Island and Quebec the enabling and regulatory legislation are essentially combined, while in other Canadian jurisdictions regulation is provided for by a separate act. The practice of public accounting is also regulated in Newfoundland, Nova Scotia, and in British Columbia where audit opinions on the financial statements of "public" companies and credit unions are subject to statutory regulation under the Companies Act and the Credit Unions Act.

Where only enabling legislation exists, at present in New Brunswick, Manitoba, Saskatchewan, and Alberta, anyone, regardless of qualifications,

---

[8]Under recent legislation in the Province of Quebec, the names of professional accounting organizations have been changed as follows: The Corporation of Certified General Accountants of Quebec, The Corporation of Management Accountants of Quebec, and The Order of Chartered Accountants of Quebec.

may practise public accounting. In British Columbia, anyone may practise subject to the restrictions that apply to the audit of "public" companies and credit unions.

It must be emphasized that accounting principles are man-made; moreover, they are not developed in a vacuum. Thus, a number of organizations other than accounting bodies impact upon the development of accounting principles. Certainly governments play a role, especially such agencies as the provincial securities commissions. In addition, both accounting theory and practice in Canada are influenced by developments elsewhere, most importantly by those that take place in the United States.

Canadian Institute of Chartered Accountants (CICA)

The Canadian Institute of Chartered Accountants is the national body of chartered accountants in Canada. There are also provincial and territorial organizations of CA's which are called Institutes, except in Quebec, where the name Order is used. In 1973, the Institute in Bermuda became affiliated with the CICA. Membership in a provincial or territorial Institute, the Bermuda Institute, or the Order carries with it membership in the national body. At the present time there are over 28,000 CA's in Canada, about 46% of whom are engaged in public accounting practice.

In Canada, the history of the accounting profession began with the immigration of Scottish and English accountants. The first professional accounting body in Canada, the Quebec Institute/Order, was established in Montreal in 1880. The Institute of Chartered Accountants of Ontario was founded in 1879 and subsequently incorporated in 1883, followed by the Manitoba Institute in 1886 and the Nova Scotia Institute in 1900. The CICA was incorporated in 1902 as the Dominion Association of Chartered Accountants; the name change took place in 1949.

The CICA, as a service organization, provides important services to the accounting profession at both the national and international levels, and to the public and private sectors in Canada, especially by way of its input to the legislative process in such key areas as taxation, company law, and securities regulation. In general, the major activities of the CICA are concerned with standards of education and examination, professional development, public relations, research, publications, and a range of other activities which are primarily aimed at assisting members to better serve their clients or employers.

Research and publications are probably the most visible CICA activities. *CA Magazine*, formerly the *Canadian Chartered Accountant*, has been published continuously since 1911, and on a monthly basis since 1932. For a period of more than 30 years, duly authorized CICA committees, acting on their own responsibility, have been promulgating accounting and auditing standards, initially in the form of bulletins, but more recently as *Accounting Recommendations* and as *Auditing Recommendations*. Since 1968, these recommendations have formed the major part of the *CICA Handbook*. In addition to research pronouncements, a series of *Research Studies* and *Audit Technique Studies* have been published under the general authority of the research committees.

In 1973, the CICA reorganized the structure of its research and pronouncement activities. Two separate committees, the Accounting Research Committee and the Auditing Standards Committee, replaced the former Accounting and Auditing Research Committee. More importantly, the membership rules of the Accounting Research Committee were revised to require only a minimum of two-thirds of the Committee's 22 members to be CA's. It has thus been possible to include as members of the Accounting Research Committee representatives of the Canadian Council of Financial Analysts, the Financial Executives Institute Canada, the General Accountants Associations, and the Society of Management Accountants. On the other hand, all 16 members of the Auditing Standards Committee must be CA's, a minimum of ten of whom must be engaged in public accounting practice. The appointment in 1974 of an Accounting Research Advisory Board provides a direct input into the setting of research priorities by representatives of the various groups — small business, commerce and industry, government, labor, education, the financial press, accounting practice, and other professions — that have a stake in financial reporting.

Society of Management Accountants of Canada (SMA)

The Society of Management Accountants of Canada is the national organization of registered industrial accountants. There are also provincial SMA bodies in all ten provinces, in the territories and elsewhere. The Society is essentially a professional organization of management accountants, a fact which is attested to by the name change in 1977 from the Society of Industrial Accountants to the Society of Management Accountants of Canada.

As stated previously, the SMA is represented on the CICA's Accounting Research Committee. In 1973, the Society established an Accounting Principles and Practices Committee to: (1) research topics of concern to management accountants, (2) analyse and comment on official documents issued by other accounting bodies, (3) develop guidelines on accounting principles and practices for the profession, and (4) interpret the impact of legislation affecting all areas of accounting and the business community. The work of this Committee commonly results in the publication of *Research Monographs*, many of which are very relevant to financial accounting. The Society also publishes a journal, *Cost and Management*, established in 1926, and has published an *SMA Special Study* series.

While the primary interests of the SMA concern the internal use of accounting information, many RIA's are deeply involved in financial accounting and external reporting. This involvement stems from the fact that the responsibilities of some RIA's include the preparation of financial statements for external reporting purposes. Also, some RIA's are engaged in public accounting practice as permitted by applicable regulatory legislation, or, in some cases, as CA's because the practitioner has qualified for membership in both organizations.

Canadian Certified General Accountants' Association (CCGAA)

Although the organizations discussed have traditionally exercised considerable influence upon the establishment of accounting principles, the influence of other groups has also been felt, in particular that of the Canadian Certified General Accountants' Association, established in 1913, as the national body of certified general accountants. The Association publishes the monthly journal *CGA Magazine*, and, as previously noted, is represented on the CICA's Accounting Research Committee. Although the Association's interests encompass both financial and managerial accounting, most CGA's are employees of industrial or commercial firms, governments, and non-profit organizations. Again, as may be the case with some RIA's, CGA's are engaged in public accounting practice as permitted by applicable regulatory legislation or as the result of some CGA's also holding the CA designation.

The Association's research activities include its active participation in work of the CICA's Accounting Research Committee. In addition, the Association, through a separate Research Foundation, is engaged in the sponsoring of research projects, for the most part projects conducted by academic accountants. Although CGA sponsorship of research projects is of recent origin, the Foundation plans to publish the results of the research it sponsors in the form of a *CCGAA Research Monograph* series.[9]

Provincial Securities Commissions

In Canada, securities regulation is primarily a matter of provincial jurisdiction. Each of the ten provinces has a securities act which is administered by a provincial securities commission or, in a few instances, by a branch or division of the provincial attorney general's department. The companies or corporations acts, which include both federal statutes and separate acts in each province, may also affect securities regulation, as does the federal Criminal Code in matters concerning fraud.

The primary concern of securities regulation is "full, true, and plain disclosure," which, of course, is basic to the communication aspect of accounting. According to the late Howard Ross, "the whole attention of the accounting profession and of government regulatory bodies has been con-

---

[9]Ahmed Belkaoui and Alfred Kahl, "Corporate Financial Disclosure in Canada," *CCGAA Research Monograph #1*, (Vancouver: The Canadian Certified General Accountants' Association, 1978).

centrated on the prevention of fraudulent or misleading statements. This important battle has been in fair measure won."[10]

In order to offer securities for public distribution, a corporation must file a prospectus or offering circular, including financial statements and other required information which is satisfactory to the regulatory body in each province in which the securities are to be offered. While this process sounds cumbersome, it works with reasonable efficiency because of the co-operation between provincial regulatory bodies, especially at the administrative level.

The adoption of policy statements by the provincial securities administrators, starting in 1971, has stimulated co-operation in the administration of securities legislation. Although there are three classes of policy statements: (1) National Policies, (2) Uniform Act Policies, and (3) Ontario Securities Commission Policies, the National Policy Statements have the widest application. On rare occasions the policy statements have impinged on questions concerning accounting principles. In general, however, regulatory bodies in Canada have relied upon the CICA's Accounting Research Committee for the development of accounting principles.

American Institute of Certified Public Accountants (AICPA)

The American Institute of Certified Public Accountants is the professional organization of practising certified public accountants (CPA's) in the United States. The organization was formed in 1887, and originally was known as the American Institute of Accountants. A monthly publication, the *Journal of Accountancy*, has been published by the Institute since 1905.

The range of functions performed by the AICPA are generally similar to those performed by the CICA. One point of contrast is that membership in the AICPA is neither automatic upon certification as a CPA, nor is it required. In general, there are two groups within the states that assume responsibility for the professional activites of CPA's: (1) state boards and (2) state societies. The members of a *state board of accountancy* are normally appointed by the governor of the state. The state board is responsible for determining and regulating the admission requirements of new members into the profession. Once a state board has approved issuance of a certificate, it must further determine that the appropriate regulations governing the use of the certificate are followed by those who are recognized as CPA's. These boards, therefore, have the power to issue and to revoke the CPA certificate.

The *state societies of certified public accountants* are responsible for meeting the professional organizational needs of the members in each state. Although state societies are independent organizations, they maintain close relationships with the staff of the AICPA. National committee assignments of the Institute, for example, are generally initiated by the state societies.

---

[10]Howard Ross, *The Elusive Art of Accounting* (New York: The Ronald Press Company, 1966), p. 7.

Neither the Institute nor the state societies can issue or revoke a certificate. They may admit and suspend members from their respective organizations based upon their own rules and regulations; however, they cannot prevent one from using the "CPA" designation.

For a period of over 40 years, duly appointed committees of the AICPA have played a leading role in the development of accounting and auditing standards, not only in the United States, but indirectly in Canada and elsewhere. A discussion of the development of accounting principles by the AICPA is presented in a later section of this chapter.

Financial Accounting Standards Board (FASB)

The Financial Accounting Standards Board is an independent accounting-principles-making body. It is an organization representing not only accountants but also other members of the business community, such as financial analysts and business executives who have a stake in the accounting-standards-setting process. The FASB is comprised of seven persons who serve as full-time, paid members of the Board. The Board members are assisted by an Advisory Council, by various task forces selected for each major project undertaken, and by a full-time research staff.

The FASB is charged with the responsibility of establishing and improving financial accounting standards and reporting practices. It held its first official meeting in March, 1973, replacing the Accounting Principles Board (APB) as the chief accounting-standards-setting body for the private sector in the United States.

All of the members of the predecessor, APB, became members of the AICPA; they continued their previous affiliations and served the latter part time and without pay. In contrast, where originally four members of the FASB were drawn from public practice, now all are required to resign from the firms or institutions with which they have been affiliated; they serve full time and receive a six-figure salary.

The organization and structure of the FASB is in sharp contrast with that of the CICA's Accounting Research Committee. The latter being relatively large, part time, and unpaid, more closely resembles the disbanded APB. The establishment of the FASB in 1973 marks the first time the professions in Canada and the United States have undertaken to organize their development of accounting principles in uniquely different ways.

American Accounting Association (AAA)

The American Accounting Association was known as the American Association of University Instructors in Accounting from 1918 until 1935, when its name was changed to its present designation. The AAA is primarily an organization for accounting educators, although others may join. The membership of the AAA includes accounting educators from Canada, other Canadians, and members from a long list of other countries. In Canada, there is also a national organization known as the Canadian Academic Accounting Association (CAAA) that meets annually.

The AAA publishes a quarterly journal, *The Accounting Review*. Articles in *The Accounting Review* generally discuss matters of accounting theory as compared with articles in the *Journal of Accountancy* that are primarily concerned with matters of accounting practice. AAA committee reports and discussions of these reports are communicated to members through *The Accounting Review Supplement*. Selected research projects are published by the AAA in an accounting research monograph series.

Securities and Exchange Commission (SEC)

The Securities and Exchange Commission in the United States was created by an act of Congress in 1934. Its primary role is to regulate the issuance and trading of securities by corporations to the general public. The Commission's intent is not to prevent the trading of speculative securities, but to insist that investors have adequate information. Thus, the SEC's objective is to insure *full, true and fair* disclosure of all material facts concerning securities offered for public investment. The SEC may use its statutory authority to prescribe accounting and reporting requirements for all corporations falling within its jurisdiction. This includes most major companies in the United States and a significant number of Canadian corporations. For example, Canadian companies whose shares are listed on stock exchanges in the United States come under SEC jurisdiction.

The regulations of the SEC require independent audits of annual financial statements. The SEC reviews both the reports and supporting verification to ascertain compliance with the law. Although the SEC has the power to issue regulations declaring how corporations should report financial matters to shareholders, it has, for the most part, relied upon the accounting profession, through the AICPA and FASB, to perform this function. In recent years, the SEC has taken some actions that have motivated the profession to accelerate its efforts to improve accounting practices and to achieve greater uniformity in reporting.[11]

Other Organizations

The Financial Executives Institute (FEI), formerly the Controllers' Institute, a national and international organization with constituent bodies

---

[11] For additional information on the nature and workings of the SEC, see K. Fred Skousen, *An Introduction to the SEC* (Cincinnati: South-Western Publishing Co., 1976).

in both Canada and the United States, is composed primarily of financial executives employed by large corporations. The FEI membership includes treasurers, controllers, and financial vice-presidents, among others. The FEI publishes a monthly journal, *The Financial Executive*, and has sponsored several research projects relating to financial reporting problems.

Several societies of financial analysts have been formed in Canada and the United States. The most prominent of these groups is the Financial Analysts Federation. Admittance to this group is based upon a qualifying examination. Because financial analysts are a major user of external accounting reports, they are very much concerned with the present status of financial reporting. Members of this group have often been quite critical of corporate financial reporting practices and have continued to request increased disclosure of pertinent financial data.

The Canadian Organizations of both the financial executives and the financial analysts are represented on the CICA's Accounting Research Committee.

The National Association of Accountants (NAA) in the United States in many respects resembles the Society of Management Accountants of Canada. The NAA is more concerned with the use of accounting information within the enterprise than with external reporting, and thus has directed its research primarily toward cost accounting and information systems. Its monthly publication, *Management Accounting*, has traditionally dealt mainly with problems involving information systems and the use of accounting data within the organization. Because the corporation's information system can provide information for both internal and external users, the NAA is concerned about the relationship of accounting principles for internal reporting to those for external reporting.

Although membership in the Society of Management Accountants of Canada encompasses both student and general members, much of the Society's energies have been devoted to the educational program leading to the RIA designation. In the United States, the NAA now conducts, through a separate foundation, examinations leading to the CMA designation.

The Cost Accounting Standards Board (CASB) in the United States is another important standards-setting body. The CASB was established in 1970 by act of Congress and charged with the responsibility of setting cost accounting standards to be followed by contractors in negotiated defence contracts. The CASB has issued standards; however, because of their restricted focus, to date these standards have had limited impact upon financial accounting in general.

DEVELOPMENT OF ACCOUNTING PRINCIPLES

Over 40 years ago, accounting was defined by the Committee on Terminology of the AICPA as follows:

> Accounting is the art of recording, classifying, and summarizing in a significant manner and in terms of money, transactions and events which are, in part at least, of a financial character, and interpreting the results thereof.[12]

The reference to accounting as an art does not rule out the fact that an accountant's work is practised within a framework of fundamental doctrine. This body of doctrine consists of certain concepts, principles, and practices that have won acceptance within the profession because of both their logic and their established utility. These principles, in effect, represent the response of the accounting profession to the needs and expectations of the various user groups requiring financial information. Again it should be emphasized that when reference is made to accounting principles, the term is not used to suggest natural laws of universal applicability but rather the body of standards that are currently considered to be good accounting practice. This concept is well described in APB Statement No. 4 as follows:

> Present generally accepted accounting principles are the result of an evolutionary process that can be expected to continue in the future. Changes may occur at any level of generally accepted accounting principles. . . . Generally accepted accounting principles change in response to changes in economic and social conditions, to new knowledge and technology, and to demands of users for more serviceable financial information. The dynamic nature of financial accounting — its ability to change in response to changed conditions — enables it to maintain and increase the usefulness of the information it provides.[13]

The evolutionary process followed and the primary groups involved in the development of accounting principles are described in the following sections.

Development of Principles by the CICA

The CICA began its role of leadership in the development of accounting principles in Canada by establishing a Terminology Committee in 1936. Ten years later in October, 1946, the Accounting and Auditing Research Committee was both created and vested with the authority, on its own responsibility, to promulgate accounting and auditing standards. Over a period of 27 years, the Accounting and Auditing Research Committee issued bulletins and other pronouncements that now form major portions of the Accounting Recommendations and the Auditing Recommendations contained in the *CICA Handbook*. In 1973, as previously mentioned, the Accounting and Auditing Research Committee was superseded by two separate committees, the Accounting Research Committee and the Auditing Standards Committee.

The pronouncements of the AICPA have always had a significant impact on the development of accounting principles in Canada. At one time, it might not have been a gross exaggeration to view Canadian pronouncements as

---

[12]*Accounting Research and Terminology Bulletins — Final Edition*, "Accounting Terminology Bulletins, No. 1, Review and Résumé" (New York: American Institute of Certified Public Accountants, 1961), par. 9.
[13]*Statements of the Accounting Principles Board, No. 4, op. cit.*, pars. 208 and 209.

AICPA pronouncements with appropriate changes as required by legal differences. This is no longer even a subject for argument; several sections of the *Accounting Recommendations* are uniquely different from their counterpart pronouncements of United States origin. Examples include Section 1580, *Business Combinations*; Section 1600, *Consolidated Financial Statements and the Equity Method of Accounting*; Section 3500, *Earnings per Share*, and many points of difference in numerous other sections of the *Handbook*.

Since at least 1970, the *Accounting Recommendations* and the *Auditing Recommendations* issued by the CICA have gradually proposed more Canadian solutions to financial reporting problems. During the period that APB Opinions and FASB Statements increasingly specified detailed rules, the *Accounting Recommendations*, in particular, while providing necessary guidance, continued to rely on professional judgment. Thus, the gap in generally accepted accounting principles between Canada and the United States has been widening, in part as a result of Canadian trends which many might encourage. These trends, however, may or may not continue. Except for uniquely Canadian problems, it may be very difficult to reject the conclusions of the FASB. This opinion rests on two propositions: (1) the FASB will have an international impact, and (2) this impact will be felt most in Canada.

It must be emphasized that the *Accounting Recommendations* and the *Auditing Recommendations* do not have legal sanction, except to the extent that their content is parallelled by applicable statutory requirements. Thus, in the context of compliance, in some jurisdictions the recommendations not parallelled in statute law are primarily dependent on their persuasiveness. At the same time, three significant events have had a positive impact on the increasing acceptance and authoritative status of the CICA's research recommendations: (1) National Policy Statement No. 27, issued in December, 1972, by Canada's securities administrators, states that where the term "generally accepted accounting principles" is used in companies and securities legislation the research recommendations contained in the *CICA Handbook* will be regarded as generally accepted accounting principles, (2) Rule 206.3 of the Rules of Professional Conduct of the Institute of Chartered Accountants of Ontario imposes on members a specific requirement relating to conformity with the "accounting standards of the profession,"[14] and (3) Regulation 44 under the Canada Business Corporations Act makes compliance with the *Accounting Recommendations* and the *Auditing Recommendations* the basic legal requirement applicable to the financial statements required of companies incorporated under the Act.[15] As a result of these

---

[14]The Ontario example has encouraged similar action by other provincial institutes. It should be noted that failure to comply with rules of professional conduct exposes members to disciplinary action that could result in suspension or expulsion. There is, however, an important proviso; departures from generally accepted accounting standards are allowed, if they can be justified in the particular circumstances.

[15]The Canada Business Corporations Act has provided the basis for new or revised corporate statutes in Manitoba.

developments, the research recommendations are very widely applied in the financial reporting of Canadian companies.

The general question of compliance with the research recommendations is reported on biennially in the CICA publication, *Financial Reporting in Canada*, now in its thirteenth edition. This publication surveys the financial reporting practices of 325 Canadian companies, and reports on such matters as the types of financial statements presented, the form and terminology used, the accounting treatment of transactions and items reflected in the statements, and the form and content of the auditors' report.

In addition to the research recommendations, the *CICA Handbook* also contains Accounting Guidelines and Auditing Guidelines. The subject matter of the guidelines can be classified as follows: (1) subjects that have been approved for study by either the Accounting Research Committee or the Auditing Standards Committee as a possible recommendation but on which an interim position is needed, (2) subjects on which some clarification or interpretation is needed with respect to either an Accounting Recommendation or an Auditing Recommendation, and (3) subjects considered too narrow or specific in detail to justify release as research recommendations. It should be noted that the guidelines do not have the authoritative status of the research recommendations.

In 1972, the CICA published *Accounting Principles: A Canadian Viewpoint* by Ross M. Skinner, the culmination of a study initiated by the Accounting and Auditing Research Committee. Part I of Skinner's study traces the historical development of accounting principles, explains the logic underlying their development, and describes the solved and unsolved problems in present accounting practice, including consistent principles and incompatible accounting treatments. Part II of the study contemplates the process of change and development of accounting principles. This publication is a very complete statement of generally accepted accounting principles in the context of Canadian accounting practice. There have, of course, been further developments of accounting principles in Canada since Skinner's book was published.

Development of Principles by the AICPA

The AICPA began to play a significant role in the development of financial accounting principles in the early 1930's. From 1932 to 1934, an Institute committee worked with the New York Stock Exchange in an attempt to establish some basic standards. From this committee came a short list of "accepted accounting principles" designed to improve financial reporting. The Institute continued to study financial reporting through various committees, and in the late thirties formed the Committee on Accounting Procedure. The primary responsibility of this committee was to prepare Accounting Research Bulletins (ARB's) establishing more detailed guidelines for reporting corporate financial activity. Between 1939 and 1958, fifty-one bulletins were issued. These bulletins covered a variety of matters. In some instances, the conclusions of newly released bulletins were not consistent with those issued in the past. Furthermore, no serious attempt was made to relate the various topics studied into an integrated theory of accounting, although a consolidation of the first 42 bulletins was issued in 1953 as Bulletin No. 43.

During this same time period, a subcommittee of the Committee on Accounting Procedure continued to examine the terminology used in financial statements. The first terminology committee had been formed in 1920 by the Institute. Several of the ARBs issued between 1939 and 1952 dealt primarily with terminology. When the Accounting Research Bulletins were consolidated in 1953, the terminology bulletins were also consolidated into Terminology Bulletin No. 1. Between 1953 and 1958, three additional terminology bulletins were issued.

The progress of the AICPA in improving reporting practices through almost 20 years of publishing bulletins was not regarded by all parties as entirely satisfactory. Critics, both inside and outside of the profession, felt there was a lack of sufficient research and documentation in the study and deliberations of the committees leading to the publication of the bulletins. Many of the bulletins, it was claimed, were either overly permissive or overly vague, which permitted the accountant wide discretion in applying the position taken in the bulletins. Some members of the profession preferred this flexibility; in fact, some felt it was absolutely necessary. Other members were of the opinion that the lack of a strong theoretical foundation and the resulting large number of alternative principles regarded as equally acceptable tended to seriously undermine the potential usefulness of financial statements.

The critics' voices became more influential, and a new organization was initiated by the AICPA in 1959. In place of the Committee on Accounting Procedure, the Institute adopted a dual approach in the development of accounting principles. One part of the program created the Accounting Research Division with a full-time director of accounting research. Research projects were developed by the staff and others who were asked to assist the staff. The results of the research projects were published in a series of *Accounting Research Studies* (ARS). The second part of the program provided that these studies were to be used by the profession as a whole and more specifically by a special board of the AICPA, the Accounting Principles Board. The APB consisted primarily of practising accountants who reviewed all evidence available on a given subject and were authorized to issue Opinions that served to establish accounting standards and to supplement or replace positions stated in preceding bulletins.

The influence of the Accounting Principles Board was enhanced in 1964 when the Council of the Institute unanimously adopted a set of recommendations which stated, in effect, that departures from the APB Opinions must be disclosed either in the notes to the financial statements or in the audit reports prepared by members of the AICPA. In 1972, this recommendation was effectively incorporated in the rules of conduct of the AICPA's Code of Professional Ethics.[16] As a result, official pronouncements are applied almost universally to financial reporting.

The Board, in some situations, authorized the issuance of Statements. These Statements did not carry the authority of an Opinion. Statements were considered necessary when the Board felt it did not have sufficient evidence to recommend specific action but believed certain analyses or observations on accounting matters should be stated. For example, Statement No. 4, "Basic Concepts and Accounting Principles Underlying Financial Statements of Business Enterprises" had as its objectives (1) "to provide a basis for enhanced understanding of the broad fundamentals of financial accounting," and (2) "to provide a basis for guiding the future development of financial accounting."[17]

Statement No. 4 was the first publication of the Board that attempted to establish a broad framework for the development of generally accepted accounting principles. In this statement the APB defined the environment of accounting as faced by the profession, and divided the basic concepts of accounting into (1) objectives, (2) basic features, (3) basic elements, (4) pervasive principles, (5) modifying conventions, (6) broad operating principles, and (7) detailed accounting principles. Members of the Board who prepared the statement benefited from earlier research studies of the Accounting Research Division and from publications of the American Accounting Association.[18] Many of the definitions, terms, and concepts contained in Statement No. 4 are incorporated into the material presented in the remainder of this book.

During the spring of 1971, the president of the AICPA appointed two important committees. The first, known as the Wheat Committee, was charged with examining the process of establishing accounting principles. The committee was specifically directed to examine the organization and operation of the APB to determine whether it could be improved or whether a new approach was needed. The recommendations of this committee resulted in the replacement of the APB by the FASB.

The second committee, chaired by the late Robert M. Trueblood, was established to refine the objectives of financial statements. The study group

---

[16] See Rule 203, Restatement of the *Code of Professional Ethics* (New York: American Institute of Certified Public Accountants, 1972). A generally similar departure disclosure was incorporated into the *CICA Handbook* in 1969.

[17] *Statements of the Accounting Principles Board, No. 4, op. cit.*, par. 2.

[18] Special credit was given by the Accounting Principles Board to ARS No. 1, *The Basic Postulates of Accounting* by Moonitz, ARS No. 3, *A Tentative Set of Broad Accounting Principles* by Sprouse and Moonitz, and ARS No. 7, *Inventory of Generally Accepted Accounting Principles for Business Enterprises* by Grady.

considered such questions as: Who needs financial statements? What information is needed? How much of the information can be provided by accounting? The basic objectives of financial statements presented on page 3 are adapted from *The Trueblood Report*.

With the dissolution of the APB and the establishment of the FASB, the AICPA formed its Accounting Standards Executive Committee (AcSEC). This is the Institute's senior technical committee authorized to speak for the AICPA in the area of financial reporting.[19] AcSEC is comprised of 15 CPA's. It issues Statements of Position (SOP's) which are more advisory than authoritative. Whatever support these statements receive is attained from general acceptance by the profession. Unlike FASB statements, they have no official status.

Recently, AcSEC has devoted most of its attention to emerging problems. In effect, AcSEC serves as a screening device for the FASB. As a problem arises, AcSEC considers it and makes a recommendation as to whether the FASB should add the project to its agenda. If the FASB does not add to its agenda, AcSEC has the option to issue a SOP on the topic. In general, SOP's are issued with the objective of influencing the development of accounting standards and of providing guidance where none may otherwise exist.

Because of expressed concerns that AcSEC was evolving into a competing standards-setting body, the FASB proposed to rewrite SOP's into FASB style and format and to establish a new series of FASB Technical Bulletins. In 1979, FASB Statement 32 designated a large number of SOP's and Guides on accounting and auditing as containing preferable principles for justification of a change in accounting principles. Also, in 1978, the FASB initiated a new series of Invitations to Comment, which have not been deliberated by the Board and have no authoritative status. Nonetheless, if after exposure the comment appears to have been formulated satisfactorily, a standard might be issued.

Development of Principles by the FASB

As indicated, the FASB is now the official advocate in the U.S. for the accounting profession in the private sector. The FASB issues "Statements of Financial Accounting Standards," "Statements of Financial Accounting Concepts," and "Interpretations." The statements establish new standards or modify existing ones; the interpretations provide explanations and clarification for previously issued pronouncements, including those of the FASB's predecessors. The statements of concepts set forth fundamentals on which financial accounting and reporting standards will be based. Unlike a statement of standards, the statements of concepts do not establish GAAP and do not invoke the AICPA code of professional ethics.

---

[19]The Auditing Standards Executive Committee (AudSEC) is the AICPA's senior technical committee in terms of auditing standards.

The FASB's standards-setting process emphasizes due process and usually involves: (1) the distribution of a *discussion memorandum* which analyses the issues involved in a particular project; (2) the holding of a *public hearing* on the subject; (3) the issuance of an *exposure draft* of a proposed statement; and (4) the adoption of a final *statement of financial accounting standard.* FASB meetings are open to the public and adoption of FASB pronouncements requires only a majority vote of the seven-member Board. FASB Statements, APB Opinions, and ARB's which have not been superseded are among those authoritative pronouncements forming the basis for generally accepted accounting principles and reporting practices in the U.S.

In a relatively short period of time, the FASB has issued over thirty-six standards, two statements of concepts, numerous interpretations, and has a full agenda of important topics under consideration. Many feel the leadership to be given by the FASB during the next few years is critical to the maintenance of a standards-setting body in the private sector. The success of the FASB may also be significant to the future role of the profession in standard setting in Canada.

Development of Principles by the AAA

The American Accounting Association has also had as one of its major objectives the development of accounting principles. The general approach of the executive committee of the Association has been to establish broad basic principles upon which financial reporting should be based. Six basic statements, under a variety of titles, have been issued by special committees appointed by the AAA. These statements have not attempted to cover all possible aspects of accounting theory. Rather, they have directed attention to areas where the committees have felt serious objections could be raised to existing practices. The statements were issued in 1936, 1941, 1948, 1957, 1966, and 1978. A number of statements of a supplementary nature were issued relative to both the 1948 and 1957 statements. Although each of the AAA statements made some impact upon the profession, frequently their conclusions were regarded by many accountants as too theoretical for practical use.

The 1966 statement, *A Statement of Basic Accounting Theory*, broke tradition from the earlier statements. Not only was it much longer and broader in scope, but it purported to develop a more cohesive framework underlying accounting data. The members of the committee preparing the statement attempted to specify what constituted accounting data. They established four standards that, in their opinion, should be found in all accounting information: (1) relevance; (2) verifiability; (3) freedom from bias; and (4) quantifiability.[20] Using these standards as a foundation, they also proposed

---

[20]*A Statement of Basic Accounting Theory* (Evanston, Illinois: American Accounting Association, 1966), p. 8.

certain communication guidelines and indicated how accounting information for both internal and external use could be developed in terms of these standards. A number of the concepts introduced in this statement were incorporated in Statement No. 4 of the Accounting Principles Board. The 1978 statement, *Statement on Accounting Theory and Theory Acceptance*, emphasizes the difficulty of developing a theoretical structure for accounting.

Development of Principles by the SEC

The Securities and Exchange Commission has made extensive contributions to the development and the expression of accounting doctrine in the United States, by issuing rules and regulations relating to the reports to be filed by registrants, and by rendering opinions on matters of theory and practice in its official decisions, reports, and its Accounting Series Releases (ASR's). The issuance of Accounting Series Releases by the Commission is intended to provide opinions on accounting principles for the purpose of contributing to the development of uniform standards and practices in major accounting questions.

To date there have been over 250 Accounting Series Releases issued. Their major role has been to point out problems requiring some action by the accounting profession and to encourage research in establishing more universally acceptable accounting principles. In late 1975, the SEC began the practice of issuing staff accounting bulletins (SAB's), now numbering over twenty-five. The purpose of the staff bulletins is to provide unofficial interpretations of SEC releases and to describe practices followed in administering SEC disclosure requirements.

Summary of Developments of Accounting Principles

The progress made in defining the body of doctrine applicable to contemporary reporting has been highly important both to the accounting profession and to those who use the services offered by the profession. Practitioners, aware of standards having general support, are afforded guidance as well as a sense of security in their performance. The product of accounting is improved, and at the same time tends to achieve greater uniformity and comparability. The reader of financial statements, familiar with the standards applied in their preparation, can view them with added confidence and within established limits compare them with other reports within a common framework.

GENERALLY ACCCEPTED ACCOUNTING CONCEPTS AND PRINCIPLES

Major objectives of this book include presenting the theory underlying current accounting practice, explaining the alternative methods presently acceptable for recording transactions, and developing the analytical ability required for one to evaluate the strengths and weaknesses of both present and proposed accounting alternatives. The theory in support of specific accounting procedures is discussed in the appropriate sections of the text. However, there are a number of basic concepts and principles that should be understood before the different classes and types of transactions are reviewed. These basic concepts and principles have had alternative terms applied to them: assumptions, standards, conventions, basic features, objectives, postulates, and axioms. Several frameworks of theory have been prepared attempting to classify concepts and principles into various categories. The first serious attempt by the Accounting Principles Board to do this resulted in the publication of Statement No. 4. The FASB is currently engaged in a major conceptual foundations project which has resulted in two statements of financial accounting concepts. Although differences exist, in several of these frameworks some concepts and principles are identified as being more basic than others. The APB referred to the primary factors that financial accounting should possess as *qualitative objectives*.[21] Other accounting concepts and principles are descriptive of conventions developed over time and partly dictated by the environment in which accounting functions.

In the remaining pages of this chapter, the rationale for several of the more important concepts and principles will be presented. The discussion is divided into: (1) *basic qualitative objectives* as outlined in Statement No. 4; and (2) *other basic concepts and principles*. The concepts and principles discussed in the second category are presented in alphabetical sequence to avoid any implication of priority in the theoretical framework.

Basic Qualitative Objectives

In order for accounting information to be useful, it must have certain qualities or characteristics. Seven qualities were identified by the APB in Statement No. 4 as being basic if financial accounting is to fulfil its service objectives. These qualities are:

1. Relevance
2. Understandability
3. Verifiability
4. Neutrality
5. Timeliness
6. Comparability
7. Completeness

---

[21]Similar concepts were labelled "standards" by the special committee of the American Accounting Association in *A Statement of Basic Accounting Theory*.

The objectives listed are related to the broad ethical goals of society; goals of truth, justice, and fairness. These objectives must be achieved in financial reporting if the statements generated by the accounting system are to achieve maximum usefulness.[22]

Relevance. The Accounting Principles Board identified relevance as the primary qualitative objective. Information must be relevant to its intended use. If it is not relevant, it is useless regardless of how well it meets the other objectives. The objective of relevance is to select methods of measuring and reporting that will aid those individuals who rely upon financial statements to make decisions. Many critics of financial statements have argued that traditionally prepared statements are irrelevant to many decisions that must be made. An increasing amount of research is being conducted to evaluate this criticism. What information is required by those who must make a decision? How can current practice be changed to improve the relevance, and thus the usefulness, of accounting information?

In its statement in 1966, the American Accounting Association commented on the importance of the concept of relevance as follows:

> The accounting function should, under many circumstances, provide information with a high degree of relevance to a specific intended use although it may have little relevance to any other. When this is done, care must be taken to disclose the limitations of the information to prevent the possible assumption of universal relevance. To have information used for purposes for which it has no relevance is likely to be worse than having no information at all. Not only may decisions be influenced wrongly, but the user may be diverted from an effort to acquire relevant information.[23]

Understandability. In order for financial information to be useful in a decision process, it must be expressed in terminology that is understandable to the user. Business transactions and activities have become increasingly complex. It is not always possible to describe complex transactions in simple terms; therefore, the user of the statements must attain a minimum level of competence in understanding the terminology used in accounting statements. However, the accountant has a basic responsibility to describe business transactions clearly and concisely.

Verifiability. Accountants seek to base their findings on facts that are determined objectively and that can be verified by other trained accountants. The APB in listing verifiability as an objective stated, "verifiable financial accounting information provides results that would be substantially duplicated by independent measurers using the same measurement methods.'[24]

All accounting measurements, however, cannot be completely free from

---

[22]*Statements of the Accounting Principles Board, No. 4, op. cit.,* pars. 85 and 86.
[23]*A Statement of Basic Accounting Theory, op. cit.,* p. 9.
[24]*Statements of the Accounting Principles Board, No. 4, op. cit.,* par. 90.

subjective opinions and judgments. Cash receipts and disbursements can be adequately supported by vouchers, and cash on hand is determined by count; full support and verification for this element and its changes are available. Findings here can be readily verified. Purchases of goods and services, as well as sales, are also generally well supported by evidence and subject to verification. There are a number of areas in accounting, however, where determinations must be based in part upon judgment, estimate, and other subjective factors. The recognition of depreciation is an example of the latter. But the degree of estimate can be minimized by the attempt to develop evidence lending objective support to conclusions. Verifiable determinations are encouraged as a means of reducing possible error, bias, or intentional distortion, and achieving an accounting that can be accepted with confidence.

Neutrality. Financial statements should not be biassed in favor of one group to the detriment of another. This objective may conflict with the basic objective of relevance; however, the presumption of the Accounting Principles Board was that external financial reports are general purpose statements meeting the common needs of a wide variety of users. Specialized needs must be met in other ways. The qualitative objective of neutrality is similar in concept to the American Accounting Association standard "freedom from bias" and to the all-encompassing principle of "fairness."

The following observations were made concerning freedom from bias in the AAA statement:

> The standard of freedom from bias is advocated because of the many users accounting serves and the many uses to which it may be put. . . . It is conceivable that biased information could properly be introduced if it would aid one group without injuring the position of any other, but this conclusion cannot be reached with certainty in external reporting, where all potential users must be considered. Thus, bias should be avoided in external general purpose reports.[25]

Neutrality, freedom from bias, and fairness to all parties are terms that together describe an important qualitative objective of financial accounting information.

Timeliness. The meaning of the qualitative objective of timeliness is almost self-evident. However, it is so vital to the concept of usefulness that it must be explicitly included. Information furnished after a decision has been made is of no value. All accounting systems should be established to provide information to all users in a timely manner. In meeting this objective, financial statements must be prepared prior to the time an accountant can be absolutely certain as to the results of an entity's operations. The entity is an ongoing enterprise with many interacting activities. Thus, any attempt to measure the success of an entity at some point in time before its dissolution

---

[25]*A Statement of Basic Accounting Theory, op. cit.*, p. 11.

must rely heavily on estimates. Unless such estimates are made and reported, it is not possible for users to judge the success or failure of the entity during a given period. Decisions by investors, creditors, governmental authorities, managements, and others rely on these estimates. By convention, the year has been established as the normal period for reporting. Annual statements, as well as statements covering shorter intervals, such as quarters, have been provided by entities to satisfy the needs of those requiring financial information.[26]

Comparability. Comparability may be regarded as intra-comparability, or comparability within a single enterprise, and inter-comparability, or comparability between enterprises.

Consistency is an important ingredient of intra-comparability. In view of variations, such as the different procedures for cost allocation in measuring depreciation, the different approaches for pricing inventories in developing cost of goods sold, and the different forms and classifications for the presentation of operating and financial data, methods adopted should be consistently employed if there is to be continuity and comparability in the accounting presentations. In analysing statements one constantly seeks to identify and evaluate the changes and trends within the enterprise. Conclusions concerning financial position and operations may be materially in error if, for example, accelerated depreciation is applied against the revenue of one year and straight-line depreciation against the revenue of the next year, or if securities are reported under long-term investments in one year and under current assets in the following year. Consistency in the application of accounting procedures is also recognized as a means of insuring integrity in financial reporting; the use of alternate procedures in succeeding periods opens the doors to manipulation of net income and asset and equity measurements.

This is not to suggest that methods once adopted should not be changed. A continuing analysis of the business activities, as well as changing conditions, may suggest changes in accounting methods and presentations leading to more informative statements. These changes should be incorporated in the accounting system and statements. But the financial statements should be accompanied by a clear explanation of the nature of the changes and their effects, where they are material, so current reporting can be properly interpreted and related to past reporting.

Inter-comparability, or comparability between enterprises, is more difficult to achieve than comparability within a single enterprise. A primary objective of external financial accounting reports is to provide information permitting a comparison of one company with another. This concept of

---

[26]There is a definite trend toward increased disclosure of information in interim reports. See, for example, Securities and Exchange Commission, *Accounting Series Release No. 177*, "Adoption of Article 11A of Regulation S-X" (Washington: U.S. Government Printing Office, 1975).

comparability requires that like things be accounted for in the same manner on the financial statements. Basic similarities and differences in the activities of companies should be clearly apparent from the financial statements. They should not be influenced by selection and use of different accounting methods.

One of the greatest unsolved problems in accounting is the present acceptance of alternative accounting methods under situations that do not appear to be sufficiently different to warrant different practices. Much current research in accounting is directed toward identifying circumstances justifying the use of a given method of accounting. If this research is successful, alternative methods can be eliminated where circumstances are found to be the same. In the meantime, current practice requires disclosure of the accounting methods used, as well as the impact of changes in methods used when a change is made. Although this disclosure does not generally provide enough information for a user to convert published financial information from one accounting method to another, it does provide information that will assist the user to determine the degree of inter-company comparability. The Accounting Principles Board recognized the importance of comparability and its related concept of consistency, and in Statement No. 4 declared:

> The Board ranks comparability among the most important of the objectives of financial accounting, . . . and is attempting to narrow areas of difference in accounting practices that are not justified by differences in circumstances.[27]

Completeness. The last qualitative objective enumerated by the Accounting Principles Board was completeness. This requires all financial accounting data meeting the other six qualitative objectives to be reported. This objective is frequently referred to in accounting literature as *full disclosure*. Completeness, however, does not mean disclosure of just any data. Too much data may be valueless to users if it does not meet the basic requirements of relevance, understandability, verifiability, neutrality, timeliness, and comparability. Excessive detail, descriptions, and qualifications may actually serve to obscure certain significant facts and relationships and thus impair financial presentations. A better term for full disclosure is *adequate disclosure* — disclosure meeting the needs and purposes of the users.

The objective of completeness calls not only for disclosure of all financial facts but also for the presentation of such facts in a manner leading to their proper interpretation. Care should be taken in developing data classifications, arrangements, and summaries, and in employing exhibits and supporting and supplementary schedules.

It may be possible to provide all significant financial information within the body of the financial statements through the use of descriptive account

---

[27]*Statements of the Accounting Principles Board, No. 4, op. cit.*, par. 105.

titles and supporting data developed in parenthetical form. Frequently, however, certain matters can better be handled by means of (1) special notes to accompany the statements, or (2) explanations in the auditor's report accompanying the statements. Whenever the data are not included in the statements, the statements should refer to such supporting material as representing an integral part of financial reporting.

Other Concepts and Principles of Accounting

A number of other concepts and principles of accounting have become widely accepted. These have not been regarded as being as basic as the qualitative objectives just discussed. They are frequently found to be the result of a combination of both theory and practice. As further knowledge is gained concerning the purposes and uses of accounting statements, new concepts and principles may become accepted. This is the evolving process characterizing the art of accounting.

The following accounting concepts and principles are discussed in the remaining pages of this chapter:

1. Conservatism
2. Continuity of life — the going concern
3. Entity
4. Historical cost
5. Income measurement
6. Materiality
7. Quantifiability
8. Stable monetary measure

Conservatism. Alternative approaches may frequently be indicated in resolving certain problems relative to the measurement of financial position and progress. When alternatives exist, accountants have generally felt they can serve business best by adopting a conservative approach — choosing the alternative with the least favorable effect upon owners' equity.

The doctrine of conservatism is illustrated in the application of practices such as the following: increases in the values of assets and anticipated gains are normally ignored until realized by means of sale; declines in asset values and anticipated losses, however, are normally recognized before a sale occurs. Inventories, for example, are normally valued at cost or market, whichever is lower. A market value in excess of cost is ignored or shown only parenthetically, recognition of the gain awaiting realization through sale; a decrease in market value, however, although not yet incurred through sale, is recognized. Again, certain expenditures are charged in full against a current revenue despite the possibility of future benefits. For example, a large-scale advertising campaign may contribute to future revenues; however, in view of the indeterminate character of the contribution, conservatism would suggest no deferral but rather the recognition of the entire amount as expense.

A conservative approach in the measurement process may be desirable. However, the deliberate and arbitrary understatement of asset values or overstatement of liabilities simply to achieve conservatism on the balance sheet is hardly the appropriate application of this concept. There are instances when, as a means of arriving at conservative appraisals of business worth or business debt-paying ability, inventories have been deliberately understated, property and intangible assets have been reported at nominal amounts, and allowances for possible losses and future contingencies have been established and reported among the liabilities. Conservatism expressed in this manner results in financial statements that no longer serve to report a revenue-expense matching process. The understatement of inventories to achieve a conservative working capital position carries with it an understatement of current income; the current understatement of inventories results further in the understatement of cost of goods sold and the overstatement of net income in the next period. The arbitrary reduction of property items to report a conservative asset position results in the understatement of depreciation charges and in the overstatement of net incomes in subsequent periods; balance sheet conservatism here has been accompanied by a contrary effect on subsequent income statements. The recognition of fictitious liabilities to achieve a conservative owners' equity results in the misrepresentation of financial position until such balances are cancelled; if payment of expenses in the future is applied against such liability balances, net incomes of these periods will be overstated. Departures from sound measurement procedures to accomplish balance sheet conservatism serve to distort net income and net asset and owners' equity measurements. Conservatism should be accepted only as a moderating and refining influence to be applied carefully to the matching process as a whole.

Continuity of Life — the Going Concern. When the future is unpredictable, one can only assume a continuity of existence and a business environment to follow similar to that in which the enterprise finds itself currently. The business unit is viewed as a *going concern* in the absence of evidence to the contrary. The continuity assumption is support for the preparation of a balance sheet reporting costs assignable to future activities rather than realizable values that would attach to properties in the event of voluntary liquidation or forced sale. The continuity assumption calls for the preparation of an income statement reporting only such portions of costs as are allocable to current activities. Obviously, the assumption of a going concern may be invalidated by future experience. Financial statements, then, should be regarded as of a provisional nature, with support for their conclusions still to be found in the events of the future. If business termination were anticipated, a *quitting concern* or *liquidation* assumption would be called for; the implications of such change of status would then require recognition.

In applying the assumption of continuity, the intent of management must frequently be recognized in problems of valuation and presentation. For example, if it is the policy of management to trade in automotive equipment at three-year intervals even though such equipment may have a materially longer life, the intent of management governs the allocation of cost. Or if management has taken steps to replace a currently maturing bond issue with a new issue, the maturing issue continues to be reported as non-current since it will make no claim upon current assets.

Entity. Accountants normally view the business enterprise as a specific entity separate and distinct from its owners and any other business unit. It is the entity and its activities that assume the focus of attention. The unit owns resources contributed by creditors and by its owners, whether sole proprietor, partners, or shareholders. The boundaries of the accounting equity may not be the same as the legal boundaries. The entity concept is most directly in conflict with the proprietorship concept under which the individual owner receives the focus of attention, and the owner's personal assets are not legally separated from the assets invested in the business venture.

Historical Cost. Accounting, as it is practised today, is founded upon the *cost valuation principle*. The amount of money actually exchanged in a transaction is the amount used as a basis for the recognition of goods or services acquired. Cost represents a value regarded as definite and immediately determinable, and thus also satisfies the objectives of verifiability and neutrality. Its use is supported as a means of closing the doors to possible error, bias, or even intentional misstatement, and achieving an accounting that can be accepted with confidence.

The exclusive use of cost as opposed to alternative current value measurements has been questioned with increasing frequency in recent years. Several committees of the American Accounting Association have suggested that supplementary statements be provided to reflect current values for items such as inventory and long-term assets. In its 1966 statement, the AAA recommended the multivalued reports be adopted providing both historical cost data that had been verified by market transactions and current values that went beyond completed transactions to reflect the effects of the environment and possessed a high degree of relevance.[28] Advocacy of the current value approach has not been limited to committees of the American Accounting Association. The SEC in its recent ASR No. 190 adopted requirements for supplementary disclosure of selected current replacement cost information. In the United Kingdom, there are current proposals for an even more extensive departure from historical cost to a current value basis for accounting and reporting. Individual practitioners and some of the large

---

[28]*A Statement of Basic Accounting Theory, op. cit.*, pp. 30 and 31.

public accounting firms have also recently become more vocal in maintaining adequate disclosures cannot be made unless current value information is presented.[29]

It is conceivable that in the relatively near future, the accounting profession will forsake the historical cost valuation principle in favor of some form of current value reporting. Before that happens, however, several important issues will have to be carefully thought through and many implementation problems resolved.

Income Measurement. As has been previously emphasized, one of the chief functions of financial statements is to provide information that will aid users in evaluating the effectiveness of an entity in meeting its objectives. The income statement has been increasingly used to provide information assisting in this evaluation. The income statement is divided into two main categories: net inflows of resources from the profit-directed activities of an enterprise, referred to as *revenues*; and net outflows of resources from the profit-directed activities of an enterprise, referred to as *expenses*. The difference between these two categories yields the *income before extraordinary items*; net income is the residual after the addition or deduction of extraordinary items. In general, extraordinary items are non-operating and non-recurring items unrelated to the profit-directed activities of the entity.

The revenue for a period is generally determined independently from expense by application of the concept of *revenue realization*. Essentially, the realization of revenue is a timing problem. Revenue could be recognized at a number of points during the production and sales cycle of a product. The realization principle, however, provides that before revenue is realized (1) the earning process must be complete or virtually complete, and (2) an arms-length market exchange must have taken place.[30] Based upon these criteria, revenue is generally recognized at *the point of sale*, that is, at the point when an arms-length transaction between two willing and competent parties has been completed. Other points in the cycle are sometimes used because of the special nature of the transactions.

Expenses for a period are determined by their recognition either directly against revenue or indirectly against revenue by association with the time period involved. This process has frequently been referred to as *the matching process*. Many allocations of cost are arbitrary because of the artificiality of attaching a cost to each unit of revenue and because of the uncertainty that remaining unallocated costs will contribute to the realization of future revenue.

---

[29] For example, Howard Ross, a practitioner and partner in Touche, Ross, & Co., published a book in 1969 entitled *Financial Statements — A Crusade for Current Values*. In this book, Mr. Ross is in agreement with the multivalued statement approach advocated by the 1966 AAA Statement. More recently, Touche, Ross, & Co. has published a booklet entitled "Economic Reality in Financial Reporting" which provides a program for experimenting with a current value accounting model

[30] *Statements of the Accounting Principles Board, No. 4, op. cit.*, par. 150.

It should be emphasized that since the point in time for the recognition of revenue and expense is identical with the point in time that changes in assets and liabilities are recognized, income determination is directly interrelated with asset valuation. Because of the importance attached to net income, a more detailed discussion of income determination is included in Chapter 4.

Materiality. Financial reporting is concerned only with information affecting the decisions to be made by users of the financial statements. Contrary to the belief of many readers of financial statements, the amounts reported in the statements are often not exact. For many decisions such exactness is not required. There is, of course, a point at which information that is incomplete or inexact does affect a decision. This point defines the boundary between information that is material and information that is immaterial. At the present time, there are few guidelines to assist the accountant in applying the concept of materiality. The accountant must exercise judgment as to whether a failure to disclose inexact amounts or certain incomplete data will affect the decisions of the users of financial statements.

The American Accounting Association Committee on Concepts and Standards Underlying Corporate Financial Statements comments on materiality and offers a criterion for judging materiality in the following statement:

> In the selection of classifications, in planning the extent of summarization, in giving emphasis to or omitting information, and in determining periodic net income, materiality is often a deciding factor. Materiality, as used in accounting, may be described as a state of relative importance. The materiality of an item may depend on its size, its nature, or a combination of both. An item should be regarded as material if there is reason to believe that knowledge of it would influence the decisions of an informed investor.[31]

Additional research is presently being conducted by the FASB to assist in defining and applying the materiality concept to situations encountered by accountants in their practice.[32]

Quantifiability. There are many kinds of information of interest to a person who wishes to be fully informed about a business. This information includes not only matters that can be readily measured, such as the number of machines in operation, the wages paid to employees, and the amount of raw materials used, but also more subjective facts, such as the attitudes of the employees about their employer and their work, the motivation of management to achieve previously stated objectives, and the effectiveness of the research department. What types of information, or parts thereof,

---

[31]*Accounting and Reporting Standards for Corporate Financial Statements and Preceding Statements and Supplements* (Madison, Wisconsin: American Accounting Association, 1957), p. 8.
[32]See the FASB Discussion Memorandum, "Criteria for Determining Materiality" (Stamford, Conn.: Financial Accounting Standards Board, 1975).

should be measured and presented by accountants if they are to fulfil their responsibility?

Generally, accounting attempts to reduce information to a common denominator so facts may be conveniently summarized. The monetary measure has traditionally been accepted as that common unit and is generally used in most financial reporting. The statement by the American Accounting Association in 1966 urged the money concept be broadened to include non-monetary information that could be quantified. Measurements in terms of pounds, yards, and months could also be included as accounting information if they meet the other prescribed standards. However, if the information is to be included in the body of the financial statements, the data must be converted to monetary terms to permit aggregation. Parenthetical remarks and notes, however, may contain data measured in non-monetary units and, indeed, must be provided if the principle of full disclosure is to be realized.

Stable Monetary Measure. The dollar is the common money denominator of financial accounting in Canada. Value changes in the dollar have traditionally been assumed to be unimportant. Accounting systems are designed to account for the use of given units of money, that is, their inflow and their outflow. Thus, the accounting systems tend to produce statements that summarize stewardship functions of management. Changes in the value of the monetary unit fail to assume importance when a historical cost principle is adopted that regards only the accounting for original dollars as important. However, many accountants have felt uncomfortable about the relevance of accounting information that is insensitive to changes in the value of the measuring unit. Although all accounts shown on the balance sheet are labelled dollars, they are not dollars of equal purchasing power. Accountants add these various dollars together as though the monetary units were stable. But when the value of the dollar fluctuates greatly over time, the stable monetary unit assumption obviously loses its validity.

Some countries, recognizing the need for reporting a stable unit, have adopted some form of *price-level accounting*. Although price-level accounting has been proposed from time to time by accountants in Canada and the United States, a strong movement to require price-level adjusted data has not materialized. In 1969, the Accounting Principles Board issued Statement No. 3 in which it concluded that statements adjusted for changes in the purchasing power of the dollar should be provided as supplements to the conventional financial statements. However, this recommendation has not been followed in practice. As indicated earlier, there is a current movement toward current value accounting which may or may not be coupled with general price-level adjustments. The nature of the problems involved are presented in Chapter 21.

Qualitative Characteristics of Accounting Information

Statement of Financial Accounting Concepts, No. 2, "Qualitative Characteristics of Accounting Information," issued in 1980, examines the characteristics that make accounting information useful. Why? Because these characteristics are the qualities to be sought when accounting choices have to be made. The Statement presents a hierarchy of accounting qualities that identify *usefulness* for decision making as being pre-eminent — without usefulness there would be no benefits to offset the costs of information. *Understandability* is considered to be a user-specific quality while *relevance* and *reliability* are identified as primary decision-specific qualities, both of which can be further analysed into components. The chart on page 34 diagrams the hierarchy presented in *Statement of Financial Accounting Concepts, No. 2*.[33]

The terms used in the chart have been defined in the Statement as follows:[34]

Comparability. The quality of information that enables users to identify similarities in and differences between two sets of economic phenomena.

Consistency. Conformity from period to period with unchanging policies and procedures.

Feedback Value. The quality of information that enables users to confirm or correct prior expectations.

Materiality. The magnitude of an omission or misstatement of accounting information that, in the light of surrounding circumstances, makes it probable that the judgment of a reasonable person relying on the information would have been changed or influenced by the omission or misstatement.

Neutrality. Absence in reported information of bias intended to attain a predetermined result or to induce a particular mode of behavior.

Predictive Value. The quality of information that helps users to increase the likelihood of correctly forecasting the outcome of past or present events.

Relevance. The capacity of information to make a difference in a decision by helping users to form predictions about the outcomes of past, present, and future events or to confirm or correct prior expectations.

Reliability. The quality of information that assures that information is reasonably free from error and bias and faithfully represents what it purports to represent.

Representational Faithfulness. Correspondence or agreement between a measure or description and the phenomenon that it purports to represent (sometimes called validity).

Timeliness. Having information available to a decision maker before it loses its capacity to influence decisions.

[33]*Statement of Financial Accounting Concepts, No. 2*, "Qualitative Characteristics of Accounting Information" (Stamford, Conn.: Financial Accounting Standards Board, 1980), p. 15.
[34]*Ibid.*, p. xv, xvi.

A HIERARCHY OF ACCOUNTING QUALITIES

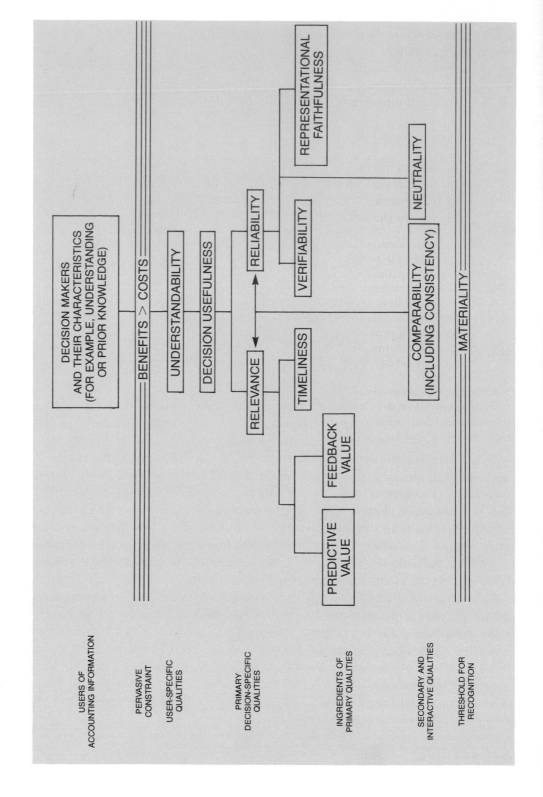

Understandability. The quality of information that enables users to perceive its significance.

Verifiability. The ability through consensus among measurers to ensure that information represents what it purports to represent or that the chosen method of measurement has been used without error or bias.

CHALLENGES FOR THE FUTURE

The accounting profession has been criticized because of the alleged weaknesses of current financial statements and the lack of conceptual accounting framework. Among the major deficiencies attributed to financial statements are the following:

1. The balance sheet presents only historical costs; it does not reflect the current financial position or worth of a business, although increasingly supplementary disclosures, as may be required or as voluntarily provided, are providing current value information.
2. The income statement tends to match current revenues and historical costs (expenses) rather than current costs; again, supplementary disclosures are alleviating this problem.
3. The income statement does not reflect those increases in net asset values that are not considered realized, e.g., increases in securities or land values held as investments.
4. Financial statements do not show the impact of inflation.
5. Because alternative accounting procedures are often equally acceptable, financial statements do not always present comparable data for similar reporting entities.

Some accountants argue that most, if not all, of the above deficiencies of financial statements are the result of not having an established conceptual framework which is accepted by the accounting and business community. Such a framework should define: (1) the objectives of financial statements, i.e., their purpose and to whom they are directed; (2) the various accounting elements, i.e., assets, liabilities, capital, revenue, and expense; (3) the accounting valuation basis, i.e., historical entry value, market value, present value of future cash flows, or expected exit value; and (4) the extent and comparability of disclosures required by reporting entitles. The framework should provide a basis for resolving many of the issues facing accountants today and should help strengthen the usefulness of financial information presented by business enterprises.[35]

Establishing a generally accepted accounting framework will not be easy nor necessarily provide a panacea for all accounting problems. Meeting user needs for financial information in an increasingly complex environment will

---

[35]The CICA has a research study in progress on *Corporate Reporting* which is to examine objectives and underlying concepts, and recommend the form of financial reporting required. A project entitled *Conceptual Framework for Accounting and Reporting* is receiving the priority attention of the FASB in the United States. This project has already resulted in two Statements of Financial Accounting Concepts and a third Statement, "Elements of Financial Statements of Business Enterprises," is expected shortly.

continue to be a major problem for accounting professionals. Increasing governmental control and regulation of business and accounting is another challenge to be faced. Furthermore, accountants are being asked to assume additional responsibilities, e.g., the detection of fraud or the reporting of the social impact of enterprise activity. And these responsibilities must be performed in a manner which will maintain high professional standards and thus avoid legal difficulties.

The challenges facing the accounting profession are significant. They provide an exciting opportunity for future accountants to make important contributions to their profession and to society. Resolution of problems may not be easy, but it will be rewarding and it will certainly make a career in accounting interesting.

QUESTIONS

1. How may accounting help in solving the basic economic problem of allocating scarce resources among alternative uses?

2. For whom should general purpose external financial statements be prepared? What kinds of decisions are made on the basis of financial statements?

3. Describe the nature of information that general-purpose financial statements should provide.

4. Why is an attest function necessary in our economic environment?

5. The owner of a business, planning to sell, has requested a CA to prepare statements for the information of prospective buyers. "Don't use your regular statements," the owner instructs the CA, "because I want to get as much as I can. Make the business look as good as possible." Would it be proper for the CA to prepare statements that are different from those ordinarily prepared for the client at the end of the year? If so, what form would they take?

6. M. Lowe, president of Lowe Enterprises Ltd., has read much in the business literature about the controversies over accounting principles. Lowe does not understand why the development of principles is important. Explain why it is important for the accounting profession to have a set of principles.

7. "Prescribed principles are hindrances to creative and flexible financial reporting. More misleading information is likely to be communicated as the rules of accounting become more rigid." Comment upon these thoughts.

8. Summarize the essential differences between the methods used by each of the following organizations in formulating accounting principles: (a) the AAA, (b) the AICPA, (c) the CICA, (d) the FASB, (e) the SEC.

9. Why is relevance considered the most basic of the qualitative objectives?

10. How can the quality of verifiability be measured?

11. What is the difference between consistency and comparability?

12. Some accountants have suggested that budgets and profit plans should be reported to external users. Evaluate this type of forecast statement in terms of each of the seven qualitative objectives.

13. Which of the qualitative objectives is most likely violated by each of the following situations? (Briefly support your answers.)

  (a) A prospective purchaser of a company receives only the conventional financial statements.
  (b) An investor examines the published annual reports of all companies in the steel industry for the purpose of investing in the most profitable one.
  (c) A company uses the prefix "reserve" for a contra asset, a liability, and a retained earnings appropriation.
  (d) A company reports all of its land, buildings, and equipment on the basis of a recent appraisal.
  (e) Management elects to change its method of inventory valuation in order to overcome an unprofitable year from operations. This change enables the company to report a gradual growth in earnings.

14. Why is the concept of conservatism considered to have both favorable and unfavorable connotations?

15. If the entity concept were not applied, how would financial reporting differ for a sole proprietorship?

16. The historical cost concept has been seriously challenged. What deficiencies does it have, and what alternative measurement methods have been proposed to overcome these weaknesses?

17. What conditions must exist before revenue is recognized as having been earned?

18. Why is the materiality concept a difficult one to apply?

19. Identify the accounting principle or principles that are applied in each situation:

  (a) A company uses the lower of cost or market for valuation of its physical inventory.   *Conservatism*
  (b) An inventory delivery on the last day of the year was omitted from the physical inventory. No adjustment was made in the accounts for the omission.   *Materiality*
  (c) During the year, inflation of 5% took place. No adjustment for this change is made in the accounts.   *Stable Monetary Measure*
  (d) Product development costs are deferred as assets to be written off against future income.   *Income determination*
  (e) Albert Haws owns a laundry, a restaurant, and a bookstore. He has separate financial statements prepared for each business.   *Entity concept*
  (f) The Metropolitan Construction Company prepares an annual statement reflecting the profitability of its contracts in process.   *Going concern Income determination*

20. What is needed to give direction to the development of accounting principles and practices?

1-1. Mr. Fence, a sole proprietor of a small store and an equipment rental shop, prepared the following income statement for 1981:

Sales	$40,000
Expenses	30,000
Net income	$10,000

An examination of the records of both operations showed that store sales were $30,000 and rent revenues were $10,000. Expenses consisted of the following:

Cost of goods sold (store)	$15,000
Other expenses (store)	2,000
Expenses (rental operations)	8,000
Living expenses of the Fence family	5,000
Total expenses	$30,000

(a) Indicate what changes, if any, you would make in reporting income for 1981.

(b) Give theoretical support for your conclusions.

1-2. Jane Roxey is impressed with her accountant's defence of conservatism in accounting and therefore suggests that the accountant currently make the adjustments indicated below. State your position on each item and give theoretical support for your position.

(a) Inventories are reported at a cost of $56,000. Roxey would report these at the lower of cost or market, $52,500.

(b) Goods that have been unsalable for a five-year period have been excluded from the inventory and have been set aside in the warehouse with the hope that someone might buy them. They are carried at $5,000 and Roxey would write them off.

(c) An account receivable for $1,080 is carried with a customer that Roxey has not seen for more than a year. Roxey would write this balance off.

(d) Leasehold improvements of $15,000 were made by Roxey. However, these improvements will ultimately revert to the owner of the property on termination of the lease, and Roxey would write off the $15,000 currently.

(e) Cash surrender value on life insurance with a balance of $4,930 is reported among the assets. Since Roxey does not expect to make any claim on the policy until maturity, she believes this balance should be written off.

(f) Goodwill of $45,000 had been recorded on the books currently when Roxey acquired a branch unit and paid this amount in excess of tangible assets acquired because of exceptionally high earnings of the branch unit. Roxey believes this asset is one that cannot be sold and therefore should be written off.

(g) Roxey is being sued for breach of contract in the amount of $8,500. No liability has yet been established in the accounts for this item. Although the court has not yet rendered a final decision, Roxey believes that the statements should reflect this potential liability. Roxey's attorney is uncertain as to the outcome of the suit.

(h) All goods are sold with a warranty for repairs and replacements for a six-month period. In the past, expenses for repairs and replacements were recorded at the time they were incurred. Roxey estimates that expenses for repairs and replacements still to be incurred on goods sold during the last half of the year will total $5,000 and believes that a liability for this amount should be reported.

1-3. The following items were reported in the machinery account of the Barns Company in 1981. What position would you take on each item? Give theoretical support for your conclusions.

Date		Description	Debit	Credit
January	3	Costs of dismantling and removing old machine ..	$ 1,000	
January	5	Proceeds from disposal of old machine		$4,500
January	10	Invoice price of new machine	40,000	
January	16	Freight charges paid on delivery of new machine .	1,200	
February	12	Costs of installing new machine	8,500	
February	12	Costs of labor, spoilage, etc., in test runs prior to actual use of machine......................	1,500	

1-4. The President of Allied Industries Ltd. received an income statement from his controller. The statement covered the calendar year 1981. "Mort," said the President, "this statement indicates that a net income of only $275,700 was earned last year. You know the value of the company is much more than it was this time last year. In fact, I estimate it to be over a million dollars more."

"You're probably right," replied the controller. "You see, there are factors in accounting which sometimes keep reported operating results from reflecting the change in the fair value of the company."

Present a detailed explanation of the accounting principles and practices to which the controller referred. Include justification to the extent possible for the generally used accounting principles and methods. (SMA adapted)

PROBLEMS

✓**1-1A.** For each of the circumstances enumerated below, give the letter item indicating the accounting objective attained or the principle applied.

(a) Understandability
(b) Verifiability
(c) Timeliness
(d) Comparability
(e) Completeness
(f) Conservatism
(g) Continuity of life — the going concern
(h) Entity
(i) Historical cost
(j) Income measurement
(k) Quantifiability
(l) Materiality

b, f (1) Goodwill is only recorded in the accounts when it arises from the purchase of another entity at a price higher than the fair market value of the purchased entity's tangible assets.

e (2) A note describing the company's possible liability in a lawsuit is included with the financial statements even though no formal liability exists at the balance sheet date.

l (3) All payments out of petty cash are debited to Miscellaneous Expense.

a (4) Fixed assets are classified separately as land and buildings, with an accumulated depreciation account for buildings.

c (5) A retail store uses estimates rather than a complete physical count of its inventory for purposes of preparing monthly financial statements.

f (6) Marketable securities are valued at the lower of cost or market.

$\overset{\iota}{}$ (7) Marketable securities are valued at cost.

$\overset{\jmath}{}$ (8) An advance payment of insurance premiums is reported as an asset.

$\overset{b}{}$ (9) A voucher system is used to account for all cash disbursements.

$\overset{\iota}{}$ (10) Small tools used by a large manufacturing firm are recorded as an expense when purchased.

$\overset{h}{}$ (11) Periodic payments of $1,000 per month for services of J. Roy, who owns all of the shares of the company, are reported as salary; additional amounts paid to Roy are reported as dividends.

✓ **1-2A.** J. L. Wood opened a retail store at the beginning of 1980. From informal records maintained, a comparative income statement for 1981 and 1980 was prepared as shown below.

	Year Ended	
	Dec. 31, 1981	Dec. 31, 1980
Sales	$ 81,200	$ 65,000
Cost of goods sold	46,500	52,500
Gross profit	$ 34,700	$ 12,500
Selling and general expenses	26,500	24,000
Net income (loss)	$ 8,200	$ (11,500)

You are called in to review Wood's records, and in the course of your review you find the following:

(a) Wood has included in sales only amounts collected from customers. Receivables from customers on December 31, 1980, were $1,650 and on December 31, 1981, $2,600.

(b) Wood has reported all purchases of goods for resale each year as cost of goods sold. No inventory was taken at year-end since the amounts would be approximately the same. You determine that the inventories had a cost of approximately $18,000 at the end of 1980 and at the end of 1981.

(c) Advertising charges were assigned to the year in which the specific charges were incurred. Advertising charges totalled $6,000 of which $4,500 was incurred in the first year to cover heavy promotion to announce the store opening.

(d) Acquisitions of furniture and fixtures were recognized as debits to general expense each year, since Wood believed that acquisitions would be more or less continuous during the life of the business. Furniture and fixtures acquisitions were $4,500 in 1980 and $3,600 in 1981. Furniture and fixtures had an estimated life of 10 years.

(e) Wood withdrew $400 per month in 1980 and $500 per month in 1981 and debited general expenses for such drawings. Wood insisted that the time and effort spent in the business were worth double the amounts withdrawn and that such charges were very conservative.

(f) Wood contributed certain supplies to the business that had been salvaged from a previous operation. These supplies had an original acquisition cost of approximately $800, had a replacement cost as of the beginning of 1980 of $1,200, but since the expenditure had been made prior to 1980, Wood had recognized no charge on the transfer to the new business. The supplies had been fully consumed in approximately equal amounts in 1980 and 1981.

Instructions:

Prepare a corrected comparative income statement. In supporting schedules for each balance, indicate any changes made and the accounting concept or principle you would use to support such changes.

1-3A. The Fader Company does not maintain a formal set of accounting records. However, a description of all transactions is kept in chronological order. For the month of June the following summary of transactions was provided by management to their public accountant:

(a) Total sales $75,000.

(b) Cash receipts totalled $82,500, including $58,000 from customers, $6,000 from rent received in advance (July-October) on a warehouse owned by the company, and the balance of a loan from the bank on a six-month note.

(c) Purchases of merchandise on account, $70,000.

(d) A physical inventory of merchandise at June 30 disclosed a value of $23,000, an increase of $6,000 from the beginning of the month.

(e) Cash disbursements for the month were listed as follows:

    (1) Payments for purchases of merchandise on account, $45,000.

    (2) Payment of a one-year fire insurance policy dated June 1, $2,400.

    (3) Payments for supplies, $6,200 (60% of these supplies are on hand on June 30).

    (4) Payments for salaries, $1,850. An additional $300 is owed at June 30.

Instructions:

(1) Prepare an income statement from the above list of transactions. What accounting concepts and principles are illustrated by the preparation of this statement?

(2) What additional information would be necessary to more completely apply the income measurement principle?

1-4A. G. M. Money has drawn up a financial statement on December 31, 1981, employing valuation procedures as follows:

Cash $20,000	(includes cash in the bank, $15,000, and customers' cheques that could not be cashed, but that Money feels will ultimately be recoverable, $5,000.)	Cash 15,000 A/R 5,000
Marketable securities $45,000	(represents the value on December 31 of securities reported at the beginning of 1981 at a cost of $34,500.)	
Value of insurance policy .. $15,000	(the sum of the payments made on a life insurance policy that requires further payments through 1991. The cash surrender value of the policy at the end of 1981 is $5,000.)	
Furniture and fixtures ..... $45,000 Less accumulated depreciation .... 45,000 Book value .... $ 0	(represents furniture and fixtures acquired in 1974 that have been fully depreciated although they are still in use.)	

Intangible assets . . . . $40,000 (recorded in 1981 when a competitor offered to pay Money this amount for the lease entered into when the company was formed and which still has 5 years to run at a rental that is 5% of net sales.)

Sundry payables . . . . $1 (recorded as a result of a suit of $50,000 against Money for breach of contract; the attorney for Money has offered to pay $15,000 in settlement of the suit but this has been rejected; it is the opinion of the attorney that the suit can be settled by payment of $25,000.)

25,000

Instructions:

Indicate what change, if any, you would make in reporting each of the items listed above. In each case disclose any theoretical failure indicated in the present reporting and the theoretical support for the suggested change.

2 OVERVIEW OF THE ACCOUNTING PROCESS

Certain procedures must be established by every business entity to provide the data to be reported on financial statements. These procedures are frequently referred to as the *accounting process.*

The accounting process consists of two interrelated parts: (1) the *recording phase* and (2) the *summarizing phase.* During the fiscal period it is necessary to engage in a continuing activity — the recording of transactions in the various journals and ledgers. At the end of the fiscal period, the recorded data are brought up to date through adjustments, are summarized, and financial statements are prepared. The recording and summarizing phases of the accounting process are reviewed and illustrated in this chapter. Data from a hypothetical manufacturing company, the Jensen Corporation, are used to illustrate the various procedures involved. The form and content of the basic financial statements are discussed and illustrated in Chapters 3 and 4.

The accounting process generally includes the following steps, in a well-defined sequence:

Recording Phase
1. *Appropriate business documents are prepared or received.* This documentation provides the basis for making an initial record of each transaction.
2. *Transactions are recorded.* Based upon the supporting documents from Step 1, each transaction is recorded in chronological order in journals which are books of original entry.

3. *Transactions are posted.* Each transaction, as classified and recorded in the journals, is posted to the appropriate accounts in the general and subsidiary ledgers.

Summarizing Phase

4. *A trial balance of the accounts in the general ledger is taken.* The trial balance, usually prepared on a work sheet (Step 6), offers a summary of the information as classified in the ledger, as well as a general check on the accuracy of recording and posting.
5. *The data required to bring the accounts up to date are compiled.* Before financial statements can be prepared, all of the accountable information that has not been recorded must be determined. Often adjustments are first made on a work sheet (Step 6), then they are formally recorded and posted (Step 8).
6. *A work sheet is prepared.* By means of the work sheet, data in Steps 4 and 5 are summarized and classified. This step is not essential, but it facilitates statement preparation.
7. *Financial statements are prepared.* Statements summarizing operations and showing financial condition are prepared from the information provided on the work sheet.
8. *Accounts are adjusted and closed.* Accounts in the ledger are brought up to date by journalizing and posting adjusting entries. Balances in the inventory and *nominal* (temporary) *accounts* are then closed into appropriate summary accounts.[1] As determined in summary accounts, the results of operations are transferred to the appropriate owners' equity accounts.
9. *A post-closing trial balance is taken.* A trial balance is taken to determine the equality of the debits and credits after posting the adjusting and closing entries.
10. *Accounts are reversed.* Accrued and prepaid balances that were established by adjusting entries are returned to the nominal accounts that are to be used in recording and summarizing activities involving these items in the new period. This last step is not required but is often desirable as a means of facilitating recording and adjusting routines in the succeeding period.

RECORDING PHASE

Accurate statements can be prepared only if transactions have been properly recorded. A *transaction* is an action resulting in a change in the assets, the liabilities, or the owners' equity of a business. There are two general classes of transactions requiring accounting recognition: (1) *business transactions,* or transactions entered into with outsiders; and (2) *internal transactions,* or accountable transfers of costs within the business. For example, among the latter in manufacturing activities are the transfer of materials, labor, and manufacturing overhead costs to work in process and transfers of work in process to finished goods.

---

[1]The process of recording the proper inventory account balance may be treated as part of the adjusting process or as part of the closing process. This text will illustrate it as part of the closing process.

Accounting Records

The accounting records of a business consist of: (1) the original source materials evidencing the transactions, called *business documents*; (2) the records for classifying and recording the transactions, known as *books of original entry* or *journals*; and (3) the records for summarizing the effects of transactions upon individual asset, liability, and owners' equity accounts, known as the *ledgers*.

The manner in which the accounting records are organized and employed within a business is referred to as its *accounting system*. The exact form the accounting records take depends on the complexity and degree of mechanization of the system. The various recording routines in each system are developed to meet the special needs of the business entity. Recording processes must be designed to provide accurate information on a timely and efficient basis, while they must also serve as effective controls in preventing mistakes and guarding against dishonesty.

Business Documents. Normally a business document prepared or received is the first record of each transaction. Such a document offers detailed information concerning the transaction and also fixes responsibility by naming the parties involved. The business documents provide the data to be recorded in books of original entry. Copies of *sales invoices* or *cash register tapes*, for example, are the evidence in support of the sales record; *purchase invoices* support the purchase or invoice record; *debit* and *credit memorandums* support adjustments in debtor and creditor balances; *cheque stubs* or *duplicate cheques* provide data concerning cash disbursements; the corporation *minute book* supports entries authorized by action of the board of directors; *journal vouchers* prepared and approved by appropriate officers are a source of data for adjustments or corrections that are to be reported in the accounts. Documents underlying each recorded transaction provide a means of verifying the accounting records and thus form a vital part of the information and control system.

Books of Original Entry. Transactions are analysed from the information provided on business documents. They are then recorded in chronological order in the appropriate books of original entry. Transactions are analysed in terms of accounts to be maintained for (1) assets, (2) liabilities, (3) owners' equity, (4) revenues, and (5) expenses. Classes (4) and (5) are nominal or temporary owners' equity accounts summarizing income data for the current period. The analysis is expressed in terms of *debit* and *credit*. Asset and expense accounts have left-hand or debit balances and are decreased by entries on the right-hand or credit side. Liabilities, owners' equity, and revenue accounts have credit balances and are decreased by entries on the debit side.

Although it would be possible to record every transaction in a single book of original entry, this is rarely done. Whenever a number of transactions of the same character take place, special journals can be designed in which the transactions can be conveniently entered and summarized. Special journals eliminate much of the repetitive work involved in recording routine transactions. In addition, they permit the recording function to be divided among accounting personnel, each individual being responsible for a separate record. This specialization often results in greater efficiency as well as a higher degree of control.

Some examples of special journals are the *sales journal*, the *purchases journal*, the *cash receipts journal*, the *cash disbursements journal*, the *payroll register*, and, as an alternative to the purchases journal, the *voucher register*. Some of these journals are used by the Jensen Corporation and are illustrated later in this chapter. Regardless of the number and nature of special journals, certain transactions cannot appropriately be recorded in the special journals and are recorded in the *general journal*.

Sales on account are recorded in the sales journal. The subsequent collections on account, as well as other transactions involving the receipt of cash, including cash sales, are recorded in the cash receipts journal. Merchandise purchases on account are entered in the purchases journal. Subsequent payments on account, as well as other transactions involving the payment of cash, are recorded in the cash disbursements journal or in the *cheque register*. A *payroll record* may be employed to accumulate payroll information, including special payroll withholdings for taxes and other purposes.

Column headings in the various journals specify the accounts to be debited or credited; account titles and explanations may therefore be omitted in recording routine transactions. A Sundry column is usually provided for transactions that are relatively infrequent and account titles are specifically designated in recording such transactions.

The use of special columns facilitates recording and also serves to summarize the effects of a number of transactions upon individual account balances. The subsequent transfer of information from the journals is thus simplified as this process is performed with the aggregates of many transactions rather than with separate data for each transaction. Certain data must be transferred individually — data affecting individual accounts receivable and accounts payable and data reported in the Sundry columns — but the volume of transcription is substantially reduced.

Transactions not occurring frequently enough to justify a special journal are recorded in the general journal. The general journal provides debit and credit columns and space for designating account titles; thus, it can be used in recording any transaction. A particular business entity may not need certain special journals, but it must have a general journal.

The Voucher System. A relatively large organization ordinarily provides for the control of purchases and cash disbursements through adoption of some form of a *voucher system*. With the use of a voucher system, cheques may be drawn only upon a written authorization in the form of a *voucher* approved by some responsible official.

A voucher is prepared, not only in support of each payment to be made for goods and services purchased on account, but also for all other transactions calling for payment by cheque, including cash purchases, retirement of debt, replenishment of petty cash funds, payrolls, and dividends. The voucher identifies the person authorizing the expenditure, explains the nature of the transaction, and names the accounts affected by the transaction. Vouchers related to purchase invoices should be compared with receiving reports. Upon verification, the voucher and the related business documents are submitted to the appropriate official for final approval. Upon approval, the voucher is numbered and recorded in a *voucher register*. The voucher register is a book of original entry and takes the place of a purchases journal. Charges on each voucher are classified and summarized in appropriate Debit columns and the amount to be paid is listed in an Accounts Payable or Vouchers Payable column. After a voucher is entered in the register, it is placed in an unpaid vouchers file together with its supporting documents.

Cheques are written in payment of individual vouchers. The cheques are recorded in a cheque register as debits to Accounts Payable or Vouchers Payable and credits to Cash. Charges to the various asset, liability, or expense accounts, having been recognized when the payable was recorded in the voucher register, need not be listed in the payments record. When a cheque is issued, payment of the voucher is reported in the voucher register by entering the cheque number and the payment date. Paid vouchers and invoices are removed from the unpaid vouchers file, marked "paid," and placed in a separate paid vouchers file. The balance of the payable account, after the credit for total vouchers issued and the debit for total vouchers paid, should be equal to the sum of the unpaid vouchers as reported in the voucher register and as found in the unpaid vouchers file. The voucher register, while representing a book of original entry, also provides the detail in support of the accounts or vouchers payable total. Thus, the need for a separate record reporting the individual payable accounts is eliminated.

Posting to the Ledger Accounts. Information as reported on a business document and analysed, classified, and summarized in terms of debits and credits in the journals is transferred to accounts in the ledger. This transfer is referred to as *posting*. The accounts then summarize the full effects of the transactions upon assets, liabilities, and owners' equity and are used for preparing the financial statements.

Accounts are sometimes referrred to as *real* (or *permanent*) accounts and *nominal* (or *temporary*) accounts. The balance sheet accounts are referred to as real accounts; the income statement accounts are referred to as nominal accounts. If during the course of the accounting period a balance sheet or an income statement account balance represents both real and nominal elements, it may be described as a *mixed account*. For example, the store supplies account before adjustment is composed of two elements: (1) the store supplies used, and (2) the store supplies still on hand. There is no need to analyse mixed accounts until financial statements are prepared. At this time the real and nominal portions of each mixed account must be determined.

When accounts are set up to record subtractions from related accounts reporting positive balances, such accounts are termed *offset* or *contra accounts*. Allowance for Doubtful Accounts is a contra account to Accounts Receivable. Sales Returns and Allowances is a contra account to Sales. Certain accounts relate to others and when added to them on the statements are referred to as *adjunct accounts*. Examples of these are Freight In that is added to the Purchases balance and Bond Premium that should be added to the Bonds Payable balance for financial statement purposes.

The real and nominal accounts required by a business entity vary depending upon the nature of the business, its properties and activities, the information to be provided on the financial statements, and the controls to be employed in carrying out the accounting functions. The accounts to be maintained by a particular business are usually expressed in the form of a *chart of accounts*. This chart lists the accounts in a systematic manner with identifying numbers or symbols that are to form the framework for summarizing the events and transactions of the entity.

It is often desirable to establish separate ledgers for detailed information in support of balance sheet or income statement items. The *general ledger* carries summaries of all of the accounts appearing on the financial statements, while separate *subsidiary ledgers* afford additional detail in support of general ledger balances. For example, a single accounts receivable account is usually carried in the general ledger, and individual customers' accounts are shown in a subsidiary *accounts receivable ledger*; the capital stock account in the general ledger is normally supported by individual shareholders' accounts in a subsidiary *shareholders' ledger*; selling and general and administrative expenses may be summarized in a single general ledger account, individual expenses being carried in a subsidiary *expense ledger*. The general ledger account that summarizes the detailed information reported elsewhere is known as a *control account*. The accounts receivable account from a general ledger and excerpts from the corresponding accounts receivable subsidiary ledger are shown opposite.

Whenever possible, individual postings to subsidiary accounts are made directly from the business document evidencing the transaction. This practice saves time and avoids errors that might arise in summarizing and transferring this information. A business document also provides the basis

GENERAL LEDGER

ACCOUNT Accounts Receivable **ACCOUNT NO.** 113

DATE		ITEM	POST. REF.	DEBIT	CREDIT	BALANCE	
						DEBIT	CREDIT
1981 Oct.	3	Balance	√			5,260	
	13		J18		25	5,235	
	28		J18		65	5,170	

ACCOUNTS RECEIVABLE LEDGER

NAME Allen Company
ADDRESS 436 Monroe St., Burnaby, British Columbia V5M 1B2

DATE		ITEM	POST. REF.	DEBIT	CREDIT	BALANCE
1981 Oct.	10		S35	750		750
	13		J18		25	725

NAME King & Co.
ADDRESS 48 Converse Rd., Vancouver, British Columbia V7B 2T4

DATE		ITEM	POST. REF.	DEBIT	CREDIT	BALANCE
1981 Oct.	24		S35	1,502		1,502
	28		J18		65	1,437

for the journal entry authorizing the postings to the control account in the general ledger. In many instances business documents themselves are used to represent a book of original entry. When this is done, business documents are assembled and summarized, and the summaries are transferred directly to the appropriate control accounts as well as to the other accounts affected in the general ledger. Whatever the procedure may be, if postings to the subsidiary records and to the control accounts are made accurately, the sum of the detail in a subsidiary record will agree with the balance in the control account. A reconciliation of each subsidiary record with its related control account should be made periodically, and any discrepancies found should be investigated and corrected.

The use of subsidiary records results in a number of advantages: (1) the number of accounts in the general ledger is reduced, thus making the general ledger more useful as a basis for preparing reports; (2) errors in the general ledger are minimized because of fewer accounts and fewer postings; (3) the accuracy of the posting to a large number of subsidiary accounts may be tested by comparing the total of the balances of the accounts with the balance of one account in the general ledger; (4) totals relating to various items are readily obtained; (5) specialization of accounting duties and individual accounting responsibilities is made possible; and (6) daily posting is facilitated for accounts that must be kept up to date, such as customer and creditor accounts.

Illustration of Journals and Posting. The Jensen Corporation maintains the following books of original entry: sales journal, cash receipts journal, voucher register, cash disbursements journal, and general journal.[2]

Sales Journal. The sales journal as summarized at the end of the month appears as follows:

	SALES JOURNAL		
DATE	DESCRIPTION	ACCOUNTS RECEIVABLE DR.	SALES CR.
31	Sales on Account for day	2,100	2,100
31	Total	40,150	40,150
		(116)	(41)

One entry is made to record the sales on account for each day. Accounts Receivable is debited; Sales is credited. Debits are posted to the individual customer's account in the accounts receivable ledger directly from the sales invoices. The numbers in parentheses at the bottom of the journal refer to the accounts to which the total is posted.

Cash Receipts Journal. The cash receipts journal appears as follows:

			CASH RECEIPTS JOURNAL				
CASH DR.	SALES DISCOUNTS DR.	DATE	DESCRIPTION	POST. REF.	SUNDRY CR.	SALES CR.	ACCOUNTS RECEIVABLE CR.
8,565		31	Notes Receivable	113	8,500		
			Interest Revenue	72	65		
1,960	40	31	Collection on accounts ..	✓			2,000
2,250		31	Cash Sales	✓		2,250	
151,550	395	31	Total		106,245	9,800	35900
(111)	(42)				(✓)	(41)	(116)

One entry is made each day for the total amount collected on accounts receivable. In this entry Cash and Sales Discounts are debited and Accounts

---

[2]The format of a particular journal must satisfy the needs of the individual business entity. Those presented here are illustrative only. For example, a multi-column sales journal is used by some companies instead of a one-column sales journal like the one illustrated.

Receivable is credited. Credits are posted to the individual customer's account in the accounts receivable subsidiary ledger from a separate list of receipts on account maintained by the cashier.

One entry is also made for the cash sales for each day. In this entry Cash is debited and Sales is credited. Since the cash receipts journal is intended to provide a complete record of all cash received, a Sundry credit column is required to record miscellaneous and infrequent items such as the note transaction in the illustration. A (√) under the Sundry column indicates that the amounts in this column are posted individually and not in total. In this illustration, $8,500 was posted to Notes Receivable (account number 113), and $65 was posted to Interest Revenue (account number 72).

Voucher Register. The voucher register takes the place of a purchase journal, providing a record of all authorized payments to be made by cheque. The voucher register appears below. For illustrative purposes, separate debit columns are provided for two accounts — raw materials purchases and payroll. Other items are recorded in the Sundry Dr. column. Additional separate columns could be added for other items, such as advertising, if desired. The total amount of each column is posted to the corresponding account, with the exception of the Sundry Dr. and Cr. columns which are posted individually.

VOUCHER REGISTER

DATE	VOU. NO.	PAYEE	PAID DATE	PAID CH. NO.	ACCOUNTS PAYABLE CR.	RAW MATERIALS PURCHASES DR.	PAYROLL DR.	SUNDRY ACCOUNT	SUNDRY POST. REF.	SUNDRY AMOUNT DR.	SUNDRY AMOUNT CR.
31	7132	First Canada Bank	12/31	3106	9,120			Notes Payable	211	9,120	
31	7133	Payroll	12/31	3107	1,640		2,130	Payroll Taxes Payable .	215		90
								Income Tax Payable ..	214		400
31	7134	Far Fabrications ...			3,290	3,290					
31	7135	Midland Mining ...			1,500	1,500					
31	7136	Nyland Supply Co.			5,550	5,550					
31		Total			55,375	24,930	2,130			33,645	5,330
					(213)	(51)	(620)			(√)	(√)

Cash Disbursements Journal. The cash disbursements journal is illustrated at the top of page 52. It accounts for all of the cheques issued during the period. Cheques are issued only in payment of properly approved vouchers. The payee is designated together with the number of the voucher authorizing the payment. The cash disbursements record when prepared in this form is frequently called a *cheque register*.

CASH DISBURSEMENTS JOURNAL

DATE	CHEQUE NO.	PAYEE	VOU. NO.	ACCOUNTS PAYABLE DR.	PURCHASE DISCOUNTS CR.	CASH CR.
31	3106	First Canada Bank	7132	9,120		9,120
31	3107	Payroll	7133	1,640		1,640
31	3108	Pat Bunnell	7005	1,500	30	1,470
31		Total		61,160	275	60,885
				(213)	(52)	(111)

General Journal. The general journal, with illustrative entries for the month of December, is given below. This general journal is prepared in three-column form. A pair of columns is provided for the entries that are to be made to the general ledger accounts. A detail column is provided for the individual debits and credits to subsidiary records that accompany entries affecting general ledger control accounts.

GENERAL JOURNAL

DATE	DESCRIPTION	POST. REF.	DETAIL	DEBIT	CREDIT
1981 Dec. 1	Notes Receivable	113		8,000	
	Accounts Receivable	116			8,000
	M. E. Scott	AR	8,000		
	Received note from customer.				
13	Allowance for Doubtful Accounts	0116		1,270	
	Accounts Receivable	116			1,270
	W. G. Haag	AR	1,270		
	To write off uncollectible account.				
31	Payroll Taxes Expense	625		250	
	Payroll Taxes Payable				250
	To record employer's payroll taxes for month.				

From Manual Operations to Electronic Data Processing

As a business grows in size and complexity, the recording process becomes more involved and means are sought for improving efficiency and reducing costs. Some business entities may find that a system involving primarily manual operations is adequate in meeting their needs. Others may find that recording requirements can be handled effectively only through mechanical devices, elaborate electronic data processing equipment, or computer systems.

In a manual accounting system all operations are performed by hand. Original source materials — invoices, cheques, and other business documents are written out, and the data they contain are transferred by hand to the journals, the ledgers, and the trial balance. Many small businesses rely solely on manual methods of processing accounting data.

As the volume of record keeping expands, machines may be added to the system. Machines to supplement manual operations, often include posting machines, accounting machines, and billing machines. By using special multi-part forms, these machines are able to prepare original documents and journal and ledger records at one time, thus saving the work of transferring data. They also can perform a few routine arithmetic operations, such as adding journal columns and computing ledger balances.

Companies requiring great speed and accuracy in processing large amounts of accounting data may utilize an electronic computer system capable of storing and recalling vast quantities of data, performing many mathematical functions, and making certain routine decisions based on mathematical comparisons. These systems normally include various other machines that can "read" data from magnetic tapes or punched cards and print information in a variety of forms, all under the control of the computer.

Despite their tremendous capabilities, electronic systems cannot replace skilled accountants. In fact, their presence places increased demands on the accountant in directing the operations of the system to assure the use of appropriate procedures. Although all arithmetical operations can be assumed to be done accurately by the computer, the validity of the output data depends upon the adequacy of the instructions given it. Unlike a human accountant, a computer cannot think for itself but must be given explicit instructions in performing each operation. This has certain advantages in that the accountant can be sure every direction will be carried out precisely. On the other hand, this places a great responsibility on the accountant to anticipate any unusual situations requiring special consideration or judgment. Particular techniques must also be developed for checking and verifying data recorded in electronic form.

The remainder of this chapter is concerned with the summarizing activities required in preparing periodic financial statements. The exact manner in which these activities are carried out may vary somewhat, depending upon the degree of mechanization of the particular accounting system. The underlying objectives of these procedures are the same, however, whether the operations are performed manually or with a high-speed computer.

SUMMARIZING PHASE

The accounting routine at the close of the fiscal period is frequently referred to as the *periodic summary*. The steps in the process were outlined earlier; they are described in more detail in the following sections.

Preparing a Trial Balance

After all transactions for the period have been posted to the ledger accounts, the balance for each account is determined. Every account will have either a debit, credit, or zero balance. A trial balance is a list of each account balance and it, therefore, indicates whether in total the debits equal the credits. Thus, a trial balance helps provide a check on the accuracy of the recording and posting. It does not, however, guarantee that the recording and posting have been done correctly. Errors, such as posting an amount to the wrong account, are of course possible even though the trial balance does balance.

Compiling Adjusting Data

Division of the life of a business into periods of arbitrary length creates many problems for the accountant who must summarize the financial operations for the designated period and report on the financial position at the end of that period. Transactions during the period have been recorded in real and nominal accounts. At the end of the period, accounts with mixed balances require adjustment. At this time, too, other financial data, not recognized currently, must be recorded to bring the accounts up to date. This is done by analysing individual accounts and various source documents.

In order to illustrate this part of the accounting process, the adjusting data from Jensen Corporation are presented in the following sections. The data are classified according to the typical areas requiring updating at the end of a designated time period, in this case the year 1981. The adjusting data must be combined with the information on the trial balance in bringing the accounts up to date. The trial balance data for Jensen Corporation are listed in the first two amount columns of the work sheet on pages 58 to 59. It is found that the accounts of Jensen Corporation do not reflect the following information.[3]

Asset Depreciation and Cost Amortization
(a) Buildings and equipment depreciation, 5% a year.
(b) Office furniture and fixtures depreciation, 10% a year.
(c) Patent amortization for the year, $2,900.

Doubtful Accounts
(d) The allowance for doubtful accounts is to be increased by $1,100.

Accrued Expenses
(e) Salaries and wages:
    Direct labor, $1,700.
    Indirect labor, $450.
(f) Interest on bonds payable, $5,000.

Accrued Revenue
(g) Interest on notes receivable, $250.

Prepaid Expenses
(h) Prepaid insurance, $3,800.

---

[3]The adjusting data are coded to correspond to the letters given on the work sheet on pages 58 to 59.

Deferred Revenues
(i) Royalties received in advance, $475.

Provision for Income Tax
(j) Provision of $8,000 to be made for federal and provincial income taxes.

The expenses associated with buildings and equipment, insurance, and taxes (exclusive of income tax) are to be distributed 85% to manufacturing operations and 15% to general and administrative operations. Ending inventory balances are: raw materials, $22,350; goods in process, $26,500; and finished goods, $51,000.

Asset Depreciation and Cost Amortization. Charges to operations for the use of buildings and equipment and intangible assets must be recorded at the end of the period. In recording asset depreciation or amortization, operations are charged with a portion of the asset cost and the carrying value of the asset is reduced by that amount. A reduction in an asset for depreciation is usually recorded by a credit to a contra account. Adjustments at the end of the year for depreciation and amortization for Jensen Corporation are as follows:

(a) Depreciation Expense — Buildings and Equipment	7,800	
Accumulated Depreciation — Buildings and Equipment . .		7,800
To record depreciation on buildings and equipment.		
(b) Depreciation Expense — Office Furniture and Fixtures	1,900	
Accumulated Depreciation — Office Furniture and Fixtures		1,900
To record depreciation on office furniture and fixtures.		
(c) Amortization of Patents	2,900	
Patents		2,900
To record amortization of patents.		

Doubtful Accounts. Provision is ordinarily made for the probable expense resulting from failure to collect receivables. In recognizing the probable expense arising from the policy of granting credit to customers, operations are charged with the estimated expense, and receivables are reduced by means of a contra account. When there is positive evidence that receivables are uncollectible, receivables are written off against the contra account. To illustrate, the adjustment for Jensen Corporation at the end of the year assumes the allowance account is to be increased by $1,100. The adjustment is as follows:

(d) Doubtful Accounts Expense	1,100	
Allowance for Doubtful Accounts		1,100
To provide for doubtful accounts.		

Accrued Expenses. During the period, certain expenses may have been incurred although payment is not to be made until a subsequent period. At the end of the period, it is necessary to determine and record the expenses not yet recognized. In recording an accrued expense, an expense account is debited and a liability account is credited. The adjusting entries to record accrued expenses for Jensen Corporation are:

(e) Direct Labor	1,700	
Indirect Labor	450	
Salaries and Wages Payable		2,150
To record accrued salaries and wages.		
(f) Interest Expense	5,000	
Interest Payable		5,000
To record accrued interest on bonds.		

At the beginning of the new period, adjustments for accrued expenses may be reversed to make it possible to record expense payments during the new period in the usual manner. The nature of reversing entries is explained more fully later in the chapter.

Accrued Revenues. During the period, certain amounts may have been earned although collection is not to be made until a subsequent period. At the end of the period, it is necessary to determine and record the earnings not yet recognized. In recording accrued revenue, an asset account is debited and a revenue account is credited. The illustrative entry recognizing the accrued revenues for the year for Jensen Corporation is shown below:

(g) Interest Receivable	250	
Interest Revenue		250
To record accrued interest on notes receivable.		

Prepaid Expenses. During the period, charges may have been recorded on the books for commodities or services that are not to be received or used up currently. At the end of the period it is necessary to determine the portions of such charges that are applicable to subsequent periods and hence require recognition as assets.

The method of adjusting for prepaid expenses depends upon how the expenditures were originally entered in the accounts. The charges for the commodities or services may have been recorded as debits to (1) an expense account or (2) an asset account.

Original Debit to an Expense Account. If an expense account was originally debited, the adjusting entry requires that an asset account be debited for the expense applicable to the future period and the expense account be credited. The expense account then remains with a debit balance representing the amount applicable to the current period. The adjusting entry may be reversed at the beginning of the new period as is explained later in the chapter.

Original Debit to an Asset Account. If an asset account was originally debited, the adjusting entry requires that an expense account be debited for the amount applicable to the current period and the asset account be credited. The asset account remains with a debit balance that shows the amount applicable to future periods. In this instance, no reversing entry is needed. An adjusting entry for prepaid insurance for Jensen Corporation illustrates this situation as follows:

```
(h)  Insurance Expense .....................................  4,200
        Prepaid Insurance ....................................          4,200
            To record expired insurance ($8,000 − $3,800 = $4,200).
```

Since the asset account Prepaid Insurance was originally debited, the amount of the prepayment must be reduced to reflect only the $3,800 that remains unexpired.

Deferred Revenues. During the period, cash or other assets may have been received from customers in advance of fulfilment of the company's obligation to deliver goods or services. In recording these transactions, assets are debited and accounts reporting such receipts are credited. The latter balances must be analysed at the end of the period to determine the portions that are applicable to future periods and hence require recognition as liabilities.

The method of adjusting for deferred revenues depends upon how the receipts for undelivered goods or services were originally entered in the accounts. The receipts may have been recorded as credits to (1) a revenue account or (2) a liability account.

Original Credit to a Revenue Account. If a revenue account was originally credited, this account is debited and a liability account is credited for the revenue applicable to a future period. The revenue account remains with a credit balance representing the earnings applicable to the current period. Again, this adjustment may be reversed as is explained later.

Assuming the credit was made originally to the revenue account, the entry to record royalties received in advance for Jensen Corporation is as follows:

```
(i)  Royalty Revenue ......................................  475
        Royalties Received in Advance .....................          475
            To record royalties received in advance.
```

Original Credit to a Liability Account. If a liability account was originally credited, this account is debited and a revenue account is credited for the amount applicable to the current period. The liability account remains with a credit balance that shows the amount applicable to future periods. In this instance, no reversing entry is needed.

Provision for Income Tax. When a corporation reports earnings, provision must be made for federal and provincial income taxes. Income Tax is

	ACCOUNT TITLE	TRIAL BALANCE		ADJUSTMENTS		
		DEBIT	CREDIT	DEBIT	CREDIT	
1	Cash	83,110				1
2	Notes Receivable	28,000				2
3	Accounts Receivable	106,500				3
4	Allowance for Doubtful Accounts		1,610		(d) 1,100	4
5	Raw Materials	21,350				5
6	Work in Process	29,400				6
7	Finished Goods	45,000				7
8	Prepaid Insurance	8,000			(h) 4,200	8
9	Land	114,000				9
10	Buildings and Equipment	156,000				10
11	Accumulated Depreciation — Buildings and					11
12	Equipment		19,300		(a) 7,800	12
13	Office Furniture and Fixtures	19,000				13
14	Accumulated Depreciation — Office Furniture					14
15	and Fixtures		1,600		(b) 1,900	15
16	Patents	55,400			(c) 2,900	16
17	Accounts Payable		37,910			17
18	Payroll Taxes Payable		5,130			18
19	Dividends Payable		3,400			19
20	8% First-Mortgage Bonds		250,000			20
21	Common Stock, $20 par		150,000			21
22	Contributed Surplus		50,000			22
23	Retained Earnings		113,610			23
24	Dividends	13,600				24
25	Sales		533,000			25
26	Sales Discounts	3,500				26
27	Raw Materials Purchases	107,500				27
28	Purchase Discounts		3,290			28
29	Freight In	5,100				29
30	Direct Labor	95,150		(e) 1,700		30
31	Indirect Labor	67,300		(e) 450		31
32	Factory Heat, Light, and Power	27,480				32
33	Payroll Taxes Expense	13,300				33
34	Miscellaneous Factory Overhead	12,610				34
35	Sales Salaries and Commissions	31,000				35
36	Advertising Expense	13,200				36
37	Administrative Salaries	87,300				37
38	Miscellaneous General Expense	14,700				38
39	Interest Revenue		1,100		(g) 250	39
40	Royalty Revenue		2,550	(i) 475		40
41	Interest Expense	15,000		(f) 5,000		41
42	Doubtful Accounts Expense			(d) 1,100		42
43	Depreciation Expense — Buildings and Equipment			(a) 7,800		43
44	Depreciation Expense — Office Furniture					44
45	and Fixtures			(b) 1,900		45
46	Amortization of Patents			(c) 2,900		46
47	Salaries and Wages Payable				(e) 2,150	47
48	Interest Payable				(f) 5,000	48
49	Insurance Expense			(h) 4,200		49
50	Interest Receivable			(g) 250		50
51	Royalties Received in Advance				(i) 475	51
52	Provision for Income Tax			(j) 8,000		52
53	Income Tax Payable				(j) 8,000	53
54		1,172,500	1,172,500	33,775	33,775	54
55	Cost of Goods Manufactured					55
56						56
57	Net Income					57
58						58
59						59

Corporation
Sheet
December 31, 1981

| | MANUFACTURING SCHEDULE | | INCOME STATEMENT | | BALANCE SHEET | | |
	DEBIT	CREDIT	DEBIT	CREDIT	DEBIT	CREDIT	
1					83,110		1
2					28,000		2
3					106,500		3
4						2,710	4
5	21,350	22,350			22,350		5
6	29,400	26,500			26,500		6
7			45,000	51,000	51,000		7
8					3,800		8
9					114,000		9
10					156,000		10
11							11
12						27,100	12
13					19,000		13
14							14
15						3,500	15
16					52,500		16
17						37,910	17
18						5,130	18
19						3,400	19
20						250,000	20
21						150,000	21
22						50,000	22
23						113,610	23
24					13,600		24
25				533,000			25
26			3,500				26
27	107,500						27
28		3,290					28
29	5,100						29
30	96,850						30
31	67,750						31
32	27,480						32
33	11,305		1,995				33
34	12,610						34
35			31,000				35
36			13,200				36
37			87,300				37
38			14,700				38
39				1,350			39
40				2,075			40
41			20,000				41
42			1,100				42
43	6,630		1,170				43
44							44
45			1,900				45
46	2,900						46
47						2,150	47
48						5,000	48
49	3,570		630				49
50					250		50
51						475	51
52			8,000				52
53						8,000	53
54	392,445	52,140					54
55		340,305	340,305				55
56	392,445	392,445	569,800	587,425	676,610	658,985	56
57			17,625			17,625	57
58			587,425	587,425	676,610	676,610	58
59							59

debited and Income Tax Payable is credited. The entry to record estimated tax payable for Jensen Corporation is as follows:

(j) Provision for Income Tax 8,000
    Income Tax Payable   8,000
      To record estimated income tax payable.

Preparing a Work Sheet

The adjusting data must be combined with the information on the trial balance to bring the accounts up to date. This may be done and the financial statements developed through the preparation of a work sheet. In the construction of a work sheet, trial balance data are listed in the first two amount columns. The adjusting entries are listed in the second pair of columns. Sometimes a third pair of columns is included to show the trial balance after adjustment or the adjusted trial balance. Account balances as adjusted are carried to the appropriate statement columns. A work sheet for a manufacturing enterprise usually includes a pair of columns for (1) manufacturing schedule accounts, (2) income statement accounts, and (3) balance sheet accounts. Two columns for retained earnings may be placed between the Income Statement and Balance Sheet columns if sufficient transactions to this account warrant it. A similar work sheet form may be used for a merchandising enterprise except for the absence of Manufacturing Schedule columns. There are no columns for the statement of changes in financial position because this statement involves a rearrangement of information included in the balance sheet and income statement. A discussion of the preparation of the statement of changes in financial position is deferred to Chapter 20.

The work sheet for Jensen Corporation is shown on pages 58 to 59. All adjustments previously illustrated are included. The simple procedure for reporting the ending inventory balances should be noted. Beginning balances are transferred as debits to the Manufacturing Schedule or Income Statement columns, while ending balances are entered directly as credits in the Manufacturing Schedule or Income Statement columns and as debits in the Balance Sheet columns.[4]

It was indicated earlier that expenses associated with buildings and equipment, insurance, and taxes (exclusive of income tax) are allocated 85% to manufacturing activities and 15% to general and administrative activities. These percentages were developed by analysing the expenses during the period. The percentages are then applied to the appropriate items on the work sheet.

---

[4]An alternative procedure is to adjust the inventory balances in the Adjustments column by crediting the beginning balance and debiting the ending balance. Corresponding amounts are closed through Cost of Goods Sold or Income Summary to the Income Statement columns and the ending inventory balances transferred to the Balance Sheet columns.

Preparing Financial Statements

The financial statements are prepared using the work sheet as the basic source of data for the presentations. The basic financial statements are illustrated in the next two chapters. They include the balance sheet, the income statement, and the statement of changes in financial position.

Adjusting and Closing the Inventory Accounts

When perpetual or book inventory records are not maintained, physical inventories must be taken at the end of the period to determine the inventory to be reported on the balance sheet and the cost of goods sold to be reported on the income statement. When perpetual or book inventories are maintained, the ending inventory and the cost of goods sold balances appear in the ledger and an adjustment should not be required. The closing procedures are described in the following paragraphs.

Physical Inventories — The Merchandising Enterprise. In a merchandising enterprise, the beginning inventory and the purchases account may be closed into the income summary account. The ending inventory is then recorded by a debit to the inventory account and a credit to the income summary account. The asset account now reports the inventory balance at the end of the period; the income summary account shows the cost of goods sold.

Physical Inventories — The Manufacturing Enterprise. In a manufacturing enterprise, three inventories are recognized: raw materials, work in process, and finished goods. If cost of goods manufactured is to be summarized separately, beginning and ending raw materials and work in process inventories are recorded in a manufacturing summary account, and beginning and ending finished goods inventories are recorded in the income summary account. To illustrate, assume the following data from Jensen Corporation:

Inventories, January 1, 1981: Raw materials, $21,350; Work in process, $29,400; Finished goods, $45,000.
Charges incurred during 1981: Raw materials purchases, $107,500; Direct labor, $96,850; Manufacturing overhead, $134,005.[5]
Inventories, December 31, 1981: Raw materials, $22,350; Work in process, $26,500; Finished goods, $51,000.

The entries to close the beginning inventories and to record the ending inventories follow:

---

[5]For purposes of this illustration, manufacturing overhead includes all amounts shown on the Manufacturing Schedule of the Jensen Corporation work sheet, except net purchases and direct labor.

OVERVIEW OF THE ACCOUNTING PROCESS

To close the beginning inventories:	Manufacturing Summary	21,350	
	Raw Materials		21,350
	Manufacturing Summary	29,400	
	Work in Process		29,400
	Income Summary	45,000	
	Finished Goods		45,000
To record the ending inventories:	Raw Materials	22,350	
	Manufacturing Summary		22,350
	Work in Process	26,500	
	Manufacturing Summary		26,500
	Finished Goods	51,000	
	Income Summary		51,000

After manufacturing costs are closed into the manufacturing summary account, the balance in this account summarizes the cost of goods manufactured. The cost of goods manufactured is transferred to the income summary account and the latter then reports cost of goods sold. Inventory and summary accounts will appear as shown here.

Raw Materials

Beginning inventory	21,350	To Manufacturing Summary	21,350
Ending inventory	22,350		

Work in Process

Beginning inventory	29,400	To Manufacturing Summary	29,400
Ending inventory	26,500		

Finished Goods

Beginning inventory	45,000	To Income Summary	45,000
Ending inventory	51,000		

Manufacturing Summary

Beginning Raw Materials Inventory	21,350	Ending Raw Materials Inventory	22,350
Beginning Work in Process Inventory	29,400	Ending Work in Process Inventory	26,500
Raw Materials Purchases	107,500	Cost of Goods Manufactured to Income Summary	340,305
Direct Labor	96,850		
Manufacturing Overhead	134,055		
	389,155		389,155

Income Summary

Beginning Finished Goods Inventory	45,000	Ending Finished Goods Inventory	51,000
Cost of Goods Manufactured	340,305		

(Balance: Cost of goods sold, $334,305)

Perpetual Inventories — The Merchandising Enterprise. When a perpetual inventory is maintained, a separate purchases account is not used. The inventory account is charged whenever goods are acquired. When a sale takes place, two entries are required: (1) the sale is recorded in the usual manner, and (2) the merchandise sold is recorded by a debit to Cost of Goods Sold and a credit to the inventory account. Subsidiary records for inventory items are normally maintained. Detailed increases and decreases in the various inventory items are reported in the subsidiary accounts, and the costs of goods purchased and sold are summarized in the inventory control account. At the end of the period, the inventory account reflects the inventory on hand; the cost of goods sold account is closed into Income Summary.

Perpetual Inventories — The Manufacturing Enterprise. When perpetual inventories are maintained by a manufacturing enterprise, materials purchases are recorded by a debit to Raw Materials. Materials removed from stores for processing are recorded by debits to Work in Process and credits to Raw Materials. Labor and manufacturing overhead costs, also, are debited to Work in Process. Finished Goods is debited and Work in Process is credited for the cost of goods completed and transferred into the finished goods stock. The entry to record a sale is accompanied by an entry to record the cost of goods sold, Cost of Goods Sold being debited and Finished Goods being credited. At the end of the period, inventory accounts report the balance of goods on hand; Cost of Goods sold is closed into Income Summary. Normally raw materials, work in process, and finished goods inventory accounts are control accounts, individual changes in the various inventory items being reported in the respective subsidiary ledgers. Frequently such procedures are maintained as a part of a system designed to offer detailed information concerning costs.

Even if the perpetual inventory system is not used, a closing procedure similar to the foregoing may be preferred. The raw materials purchases account can be closed into the raw materials inventory account. The inventory account would then be reduced to the ending inventory balance, and Work in Process would be debited. Direct labor and manufacturing overhead accounts are closed into Work in Process. Work in Process is then reduced to the ending inventory figure and Finished Goods is debited. Finished Goods is finally reduced to its ending balance and a cost of goods sold account is opened and debited for the inventory decrease. Cost of Goods Sold is closed into Income Summary.

Closing the Nominal Accounts

Upon completing the work sheet and statements, entries are made in the general journal to bring all accounts up to date and to close the accounts. The procedures for closing the inventory accounts were just described. Before closing the inventory and the nominal accounts, any correcting and adjusting entries are recorded. Although such entries usually have been prepared on the work sheet, these are now entered formally in the general journal. Closing entries may be conveniently prepared by using as a basis for the entries the balances as shown in the Manufacturing Schedule and Income Statement columns of the work sheet. The following entries, including those needed to adjust and close inventories, are required for Jensen Corporation.

Closing Entries
December 31, 1981

Manufacturing Summary	340,305	
Raw Materials	22,350	
Work in Process	26,500	
Purchase Discounts	3,290	
Raw Materials		21,350
Work in Process		29,400
Raw Materials Purchases		107,500
Freight In		5,100
Direct Labor		96,850
Indirect Labor		67,750
Factory Heat, Light, and Power		27,480
Payroll Taxes Expense		11,305
Miscellaneous Factory Overhead		12,610
Depreciation Expense — Buildings and Equipment		6,630
Amortization of Patents		2,900
Insurance Expense		3,570
To close manufacturing accounts into Manufacturing Summary.		
Sales	533,000	
Interest Revenue	1,350	
Royalty Revenue	2,075	
Income Summary		536,425
To close revenue accounts into Income Summary.		
Income Summary	518,800	
Finished Goods	51,000	
Finished Goods		45,000
Manufacturing Summary		340,305
Sales Discounts		3,500
Payroll Taxes Expense		1,995
Sales Salaries and Commissions		31,000
Advertising Expense		13,200
Administrative Salaries		87,300
Miscellaneous General Expense		14,700
Interest Expense		20,000
Doubtful Accounts Expense		1,100
Depreciation Expense — Buildings and Equipment		1,170
Depreciation Expense — Office Furniture and Fixtures		1,900
Insurance Expense		630
Income Tax		8,000
To close expense accounts into Income Summary.		

Income Summary	17,625	
Retained Earnings		17,625
To transfer the balance in Income Summary to Retained Earnings.		
Retained Earnings	13,600	
Dividends		13,600
To close Dividends into Retained Earnings.		

Preparing a Post-Closing Trial Balance

After the adjusting and closing entries are posted, a post-closing trial balance is prepared to verify the equality of the debits and credits. The post-closing trial balance for Jensen Corporation is given below:

Jensen Corporation Post-Closing Trial Balance December 31, 1981		
Cash	83,110	
Notes Receivable	28,000	
Accounts Receivable	106,500	
Allowance for Doubtful Accounts		2,710
Interest Receivable	250	
Raw Materials	22,350	
Work in Process	26,500	
Finished Goods	51,000	
Prepaid Insurance	3,800	
Land...	114,000	
Buildings and Equipment	156,000	
Accumulated Depreciation — Buildings and Equipment		27,100
Office Furniture and Fixtures	19,000	
Accumulated Depreciation — Office Furniture and Fixtures		3,500
Patents	52,500	
Accounts Payable		37,910
Income Tax Payable		8,000
Payroll Taxes Payable		5,130
Salaries and Wages Payable		2,150
Interest Payable		5,000
Dividends Payable		3,400
8% First-Mortgage Bonds		250,000
Royalties Received in Advance		475
Common Shares, $20 par		150,000
Contributed Surplus		50,000
Retained Earnings		117,635
	663,010	663,010

Reversing the Accounts

At the beginning of a new period, the adjusting entries for accrued expenses, accrued revenues, prepaid expenses when the original debit was to an expense account, and deferred revenues when the original credit was to a revenue account may be reversed. Reversing entries are not necessary, but they make it possible to record the expense payments or revenue receipts in the new period in the usual manner. If a reversing entry is not made, for example, for accrued expenses, the expense payments would have to be analysed as to (1) the amount representing payment of the accrued liability, and (2) the amount representing the expense of the current period. Alternatively, the accrued and deferred accounts could be left unadjusted until the close of the subsequent reporting period when they would be adjusted to their correct balances.

To illustrate accounting for an accrued expense when (1) reversing entries are made and (2) reversing entries are not made, assume that accrued salaries on December 31, 1981, are $350 and on December 31, 1982, are $500. Payment of salaries for the period ending January 4, 1982, is $1,000. Adjustments are made and the books are closed annually on December 31. The possible entries are shown below:

	(1) ASSUMING LIABILITY ACCOUNT IS REVERSED	(2) ASSUMING LIABILITY ACCOUNT IS NOT REVERSED	
		(a) Transaction in Next Period is Analysed.	(b) Transaction in Next Period is Not Analysed. Adjustment at Close of Next Reporting Period.
December 31, 1981 Adjusting entry to record accrued salaries.	Salaries .... 350 Salaries Payable 350	Salaries .... 350 Salaries Payable 350	Salaries .... 350 Salaries Payable 350
December 31, 1981 Closing entry to transfer expense to the income summary account.	Income Summary ...... xxx Salaries xxx	Income Summary ...... xxx Salaries xxx	Income Summary ...... xxx Salaries xxx
January 1, 1982 Reversing entry to transfer balance to the account that will be charged when payment is made.	Salaries Payable .... 350 Salaries 350	No entry	No entry
January 4, 1982 Payment of salaries for period ending Jan. 4, 1982.	Salaries ....1,000 Cash 1,000	Salaries Payable .... 350 Salaries .... 650 Cash 1,000	Salaries ....1,000 Cash 1,000
December 31, 1982 Adjusting entry to record accrued salaries.	Salaries .... 500 Salaries Payable 500	Salaries .... 500 Salaries Payable 500	Salaries .... 150 Salaries Payable 150

The adjustments establishing accrued and prepaid balances for Jensen Corporation were illustrated earlier in the chapter. The appropriate reversing entries are shown here.

Reversing Entries
January 1, 1982

Salaries and Wages Payable	2,150	
Direct Labor		1,700
Indirect Labor		450
Interest Payable	5,000	
Interest Expense		5,000
Interest Revenue	250	
Interest Receivable		250
Royalties Received in Advance	475	
Royalty Revenue		475

FROM TRANSACTION TO STATEMENTS

The preceding chapter discussed the accounting concepts and principles underlying the financial statements and stressed the importance of financial reports in a modern economic society. The usual procedures for recording transactions and the sequence of events incident to the preparation of such reports have been briefly reviewed in this chapter. The treatment applied to these transactions and events was referred to as the accounting process.

The accounting process includes the entire field of analysing, classifying, recording, summarizing, and reporting. It includes the successive steps that constitute the accounting cycle. It starts with the first written record of the transactions of the business unit and concludes with the final summarized financial statements.

The significance of the accounting process and its applicability to every business entity, regardless of size, in our economic society must be appreciated. Although the procedures may be modified to meet special conditions, the process reviewed here is basic in accounting for every business entity.

---

1. Distinguish between the recording phase and the summarizing phase of the accounting process.

2. List and describe the procedures in the accounting process. Why is each step necessary?

3. What is the accounting function of: (a) the business document, (b) a book of original entry, (c) the ledger?

4. Distinguish between: (a) real and nominal accounts, (b) general journal and special journals, (c) general ledger and subsidiary ledgers.

5. What advantages are provided through the use of: (a) special journals, (b) subsidiary ledgers, and (c) the voucher system?

6. The Isom Co. maintains a sales journal, a voucher register, a cash receipts journal, a cash disbursements journal, and a general journal. For each account listed below and on page 69 indicate the most common journal sources of debits and credits.

Cash
Marketable Securities
Notes Receivable
Accounts Receivable
Allowance for Doubtful Accounts
Merchandise Inventory
Land and Buildings
Accumulated Depreciation
Notes Payable
Vouchers Payable
Capital Stock
Retained Earnings
Sales
Sales Discounts
Purchases
Freight In
Purchase Returns and Allowances
Purchase Discounts
Salaries
Depreciation

7. As Robinson Company's auditor, you find that the company accountant posts adjusting and closing entries directly to the ledger without formal entries in the general journal. How would you evaluate this procedure in your report to management?

8. Define a mixed account. Should any accounts remain mixed after the adjusting entries have been posted? Explain.

9. Explain the nature and the purpose of (a) adjusting entries, (b) closing entries, and (c) reversing entries.

10. Give three common examples of contra accounts; explain why contra accounts are used.

11. What are the major advantages of electronic data processing as compared with manual processing of accounting data?

12. One of your clients overheard a computer manufacturer sales representative saying the computer will make the accountant obsolete. How would you respond to this comment?

13. What are the implications of electronic data processing for the accountant?

14. Payment of insurance in advance may be recorded in either (a) an expense account or (b) an asset account. Which method would you recommend? What periodic entries are required under each method?

15. The receipt of rentals in advance may be recorded in either (a) a revenue account or (b) a liability account. Which method would you recommend? What periodic entries would be required under each of these methods?

16. The bookkeeper for the Florence Co. does not reverse accrued and prepaid balances at the beginning of the period. At the end of the period debits or credits are made to these accounts to bring them to the appropriate balances as of the end of the fiscal period, and the offsetting debits and credits are made to the related revenue and expense accounts. Revenue and expense accounts at the end of the year thus report receipts and disbursements and the adjustments resulting from variations in the accrued and prepaid balances. Evaluate this procedure.

17. The bookkeeper for the Sterling Corporation does not adjust the revenue and expense accounts at the end of the period but makes closing entries in the usual manner, leaving certain revenue accounts with debit balances and certain expense accounts with credit balances. The bookkeeper claims this saves the effort required in adjusting and reversing accounts, adjusting, closing, and reversing being accomplished at the same time. Do you agree?

18. What columns might be used on a work sheet for: (a) a merchandising company; (b) a manufacturing company; (c) a departmentalized business, the gross profit to be ascertained for each department; (d) a manufacturing organization with retail sales departments, an operating income to be determined for each department?

19. When would work sheets with columns reporting an adjusted trial balance be recommended?

20. The accountant for the Slater Co. in adjusting the accounts on the work sheet debits or credits the beginning inventory to adjust it to the ending balance, with an offsetting credit or debit to an inventory variation balance. The inventory as adjusted is carried to the Balance Sheet column and the variation balance is carried to the appropriate Income Statement column. Appraise this procedure.

21. Distinguish between closing the inventory account for a merchandising enterprise using a physical inventory system and one using a perpetual inventory system.

22. The accountant for the D. A. Anderton Store, after completing all adjustments except for the merchandise inventory, makes the entry reported below to close the beginning inventory, to set up the ending inventory, to close all nominal accounts, and to report the net result of operations in the capital account.

Mdse. Inv., Dec. 31, 1981	22,500	
Sales	250,000	
Purchase Discounts	2,500	
Mdse. Inv., Jan. 1, 1981		25,000
Purchases		175,000
Selling Expense		25,000
General and Admin. Expense		18,750
Interest Expense		1,875
D. A. Anderton, Capital		29,375

(a) Would you regard this procedure as being acceptable?
(b) What alternate procedure could you have followed in adjusting and closing the accounts?

2-1. The Commercial Refining Corporation, a manufacturer, engaged in the following transactions during April 1981. Commercial Refining Corporation records inventory on the perpetual system.

1981
Apr. 1 Purchased a factory building and land for $100,000 in cash and a 30-year mortgage payable for $500,000. The land was appraised at $200,000 and the buildings at $600,000.
      4 Sold finished goods to the Arnaud Company for $9,000; terms 2/10, n/30, FOB shipping point. Arnaud paid $150 freight on the goods. Finished goods cost $5,580.
      5 Received raw materials worth $15,000; terms, n/30.
      7 Received payment from Arnaud for goods shipped April 4.
     15 The payroll for the first half of April was $16,000.
     18 Traded in a truck that cost $6,000 with a net book value of $1,000 for a machine with a fair market value of $8,700. A trade-in allowance of $800 is allowed on the old truck.
     22 Declared a dividend at $1.15 per share on the common stock. Common stock outstanding is 45,500 shares.

Record the above transactions in general journal form.

2-2. Using sales and cash receipts journals, as illustrated previously in the text, record the following transactions:
(a) A sale on account is made to J. A. Wells for $900.
(b) A cheque for $882 is received from Wells representing payment of the invoice less a sales discount of $18.
(c) Cash sales for the day are $1,315.
(d) Cash of $1,200 is received on a 60-day, 8% note for this amount issued to the bank.
(e) A dividend cheque for $80 is received on shares of stock owned.

2-3. In analysing the accounts of Gerry Garner, the adjusting data listed below are determined on December 31, the end of an annual fiscal period. (1) Give the adjusting entry for each item. (2) What reversing entries would be appropriate? (3) What sources would provide the information for each adjustment?
(a) The prepaid insurance account shows a debit of $900, representing the cost of a 3-year fire insurance policy dated July 1.
(b) On October 1, Rental Revenue was credited for $1,200, representing income from subrental for a 4-month period beginning on that date.
(c) Purchase of advertising materials for $800 during the year was recorded in the advertising expense account. On December 31 advertising materials of $175 are on hand.
(d) On November 1, $750 was paid as rent for a 6-month period beginning on that date. The expense account, Rent, was debited.
(e) Miscellaneous Office Expense was debited for office supplies of $450 purchased during the year. On December 31 office supplies of $95 are on hand.
(f) Interest of $65 is accrued on notes payable.

2-4. The following information is taken from the records of the Basil Company:

	Balance January 1, 1981	Balance December 31, 1981	Transactions During 1981
Accruals:			
Interest receivable	$270	$325	
Wages payable	550	575	
Interest payable	400	225	
Cash receipts and payments:			
Interest on notes receivable			$ 620
Wages..............................			32,000
Interest on notes payable			465

Compute the interest revenue, the wages expense, and the interest expense for the year.

2-5. Nelson Mobile Homes has a fiscal year ending December 31. For the year ended in 1982 the Company originally reported a profit of $12,070. The owner, however, has some doubt about this figure and has asked you to review his accounting records. Your review uncovers the following information:

(a) Items charged to insurance expense include premiums in that account totalling $340 which pertain to 1983.

(b) Maintenance supplies and parts on hand at December 31, 1982 were valued at $570. These had been charged to expense.

(c) The annual provision for depreciation had been overlooked. There was no change in fixed assets during 1982. Nelson Mobile Homes uses a trailer for an office. Original cost was $12,000. Estimated salvage value is $2,000 and estimated life is 10 years. Office equipment annual depreciation should have been $150.

(d) The owner had financed the cost of installing various utility services. Annual payments are called for each June 30 until the loan is repaid. Principal and interest had been paid in full to June 30, 1982. The outstanding principal according to the general ledger was $5,000.00 at December, 1982 and no entries had been made since the June payment. Interest is payable at 10% per annum.

(e) Certain tenants pay their monthly rent in advance and there is an account in the liability section of the ledger showing a credit balance of $500 for Rentals Received in Advance. All of this amount pertains to 1983 rentals.

(f) One tenant owes $200 in rental arrears at December 31, 1982. Although the owner has written the tenant on several occasions, nothing had been set up in the accounting records. There is no doubt the amount will eventually be collected.

Prepare journal entries without narratives to adjust any omissions which have to be corrected as a result of your review.

Prepare a brief statement to give to the owner showing the revised profit or loss figure for the year ended December 31, 1982. (SMA adapted).

2-6. Upon inspecting the books and records for the Bombay Manufacturing Co. for the year ended December 31, 1981, you find the following data. What entries are required to bring the accounts up to date?

(a) A receivable of $450 from R. W. Brown is determined to be uncollectible. The company maintains no allowance for such losses.

(b) A creditor, the Arne Co., has just been awarded damages of $3,200 as a result of breach of contract during the current year by Bombay Manufacturing Co. Nothing appears in the accounts in connection with this matter.

(c) A fire destroyed part of a branch office. Furniture and fixtures that cost $17,000 and had a book value of $13,000 at the time of the fire were completely destroyed. The insurance company has agreed to pay $10,000 under the provision of the fire insurance policy.

(d) Advances of $2,000 to salespersons have been recorded as Sales Salaries.

(e) Machinery at the end of the year shows a balance of $34,500. It is discovered that additions to this account during the year totalled $8,000, but of this amount $4,500 should have been recorded as repairs. Depreciation is to be recorded at 10% on machinery owned throughout the year, but at one half this rate on machinery purchased or sold during the year.

2-7. Accounts of Modern Products Co. at the end of the first year of operations show the following balances:

Cash	$ 13,600	
Investments	16,000	
Machinery	40,000	
Factory Buildings	64,000	
Land	32,000	
Accounts Payable		$ 24,000
Common Stock		160,000
Premium on Common Stock		32,000
Sales		240,000
Raw Materials Purchases	112,000	
Direct Labor	80,000	
Manufacturing Overhead	58,000	
Operating Expenses	41,600	
Investment Revenue		1,200
	$457,200	$457,200

At the end of the year physical inventories are: raw materials, $32,000; work in process, $24,000; finished goods, $24,000. Prepaid operating expenses are $1,200 and accrued manufacturing overhead is $400. Investment revenue receivable is $240. Depreciation for the year on buildings is $1,600, apportioned $1,200 to the factory and $400 to general operations. Depreciation of machinery is $2,000. Federal and provincial income taxes for the year are estimated at $8,000. Give the entries to adjust and close the accounts.

2-8. Account balances before and after adjustment of December 31 follow. Give the adjustment that was made for each account.

	Before Adjustment		After Adjustment	
Account Title	Debit	Credit	Debit	Credit
(a) Merchandise Inventory	$33,500		$38,000	
(b) Allowance for Doubtful Accounts	1,750			$ 7,000
(c) Accumulated Depreciation		$18,000		21,500
(d) Sales Salaries	32,200		32,950	
(e) Provision for Income Tax	5,500		6,350	
(f) Royalty Revenue		9,000		11,500
(g) Interest Revenue		650		875

2-9. On May 16, 1981, Susan Young paid insurance for a three-year period beginning June 1. She recorded the payment as follows:

Prepaid Insurance	1,512	
Cash		1,512

    (a) What adjustment is required on December 31? What reversing entry, if any, would you make?

    (b) What nominal account could be debited instead of Prepaid Insurance? What adjustment would then be necessary? What reversing entry, if any, would you make?

2-10. Ed Warnick received $14,400 for rent of an office suite for one year beginning May 1. He recorded the receipt as a deferred revenue.

    (a) What adjustment is required on December 31? If a reversing entry is appropriate, what is the entry?

    (b) If he had credited a nominal account, what adjustment would now be necessary? If a reversing entry is appropriate, what is the entry?

2-11. The data listed below were obtained from an analysis of the accounts of Bradford Publishing Company as of March 31, 1981, in preparation of the annual report. Bradford records current transactions in nominal accounts and does not reverse adjusting entries. What are the appropriate adjusting entries?

    (a) Prepaid Insurance has a balance of $9,400. Bradford has the following policies in force.

Policy	Date	Term	Cost	Coverage
A	1/1/81	2 years	$2,400	Shop equipment
B	12/1/80	6 months	1,200	Delivery equipment
C	7/1/80	3 years	8,000	Office and factory buildings

    (b) Subscriptions Received in Advance has a balance of $37,500. The following subscriptions were included in the balance.

Inception	Amount		Term
July 1, 1980	$18,000		1 year
October 1, 1980	14,000		1 year
January 1, 1981	19,200		1 year
April 1, 1981	13,800		1 year

    (c) Interest Payable has a balance of $550. Bradford owes an 8%, 90-day note for $30,000 dated March 1, 1981.

    (d) Supplies has a balance of $1,460. An inventory of supplies revealed a total of $940.

    (e) Salaries Payable has a balance of $6,500. The payroll for the 5-day workweek ended April 3, totalled $7,500.

2-12. Some of the accounts appearing in the ledger of the Thorn Manufacturing Co. on November 30, the end of a fiscal year, follow:

Finished Goods	$84,000	Sales	$1,080,000
Work in Process	48,000	Operating Expense	180,000
Raw Materials	72,000		

(a) Prepare closing entries given the following information. Physical inventories on November 30 are: raw materials, $70,000; work in process, $40,000; finished goods, $45,000. Raw materials puchases are $340,000; direct labor is $156,000; and manufacturing overhead is $120,000.

(b) Assuming that on a perpetual basis, cost of goods sold totals $665,000, close the accounts.

2-13. An accountant for the Sandell Stamping Co., a manufacturing enterprise, has just finished posting all the year-end adjusting entries to the ledger accounts and now wishes to close the ledger balances in preparation for the new period.

For each of the accounts listed below indicate whether the year-end balance should be: (1) carried forward to the new period, (2) closed by debiting the account, or (3) closed by crediting the account. If the account is to be closed, identify into which summary account it will be closed.

(a) Cash	(k) Manufacturing Summary
(b) Sales	(l) Accounts Receivable
(c) Dividends	(m) Prepaid Insurance
(d) Finished Goods — Beginning Inventory	(n) Interest Receivable
(e) Selling Expense	(o) Raw Materials — Beginning Inventory
(f) Capital Stock	(p) Freight In
(g) Income Summary	(q) Interest Revenue
(h) Direct Labor	(r) Factory Supervision
(i) Dividends Payable	(s) Retained Earnings
(j) Raw Materials Purchases	(t) Accumulated Depreciation

2-14. The Oster Sales Co. shows a credit balance in the income summary account of $32,400 after the revenue and expense items have transferred to this account at the end of a fiscal year. Give the remaining entries to close the books, assuming:

(a) The business is a sole proprietorship: the owner, P. B. Oster, has made withdrawals of $9,000 during the year and this is reported in a drawing account.

(b) The business is a partnership: the owners, P. B. Oster and T. Z. Oster, share profits 5:3; they have made withdrawals of $12,000 and $9,600 respectively, and these amounts are reported in drawing accounts.

(c) The business is a corporation: the ledger reports capital stock, $200,000, and retained earnings, $50,000; during the year dividends of $14,000 were charged to a dividends account.

PROBLEMS

2-1A. J. Ellis, a fruit wholesaler, records his business transactions in the following books of original entry: general journal (GJ); voucher register (VR); cheque register (CHR); sales journal (SJ); and cash receipts journal (CRJ). Ellis uses a voucher system. At the close of business on April 18, Ellis recorded and filed the following business documents:

(a) Sales invoices for sales on account totalling $2,300.
(b) The day's cash register tape showing receipts for cash sales at $350.
(c) A list of cash received on various customer accounts totalling $1,485. Sales discounts taken were $15.
(d) The telephone bill for $30 payable in one week.
(e) Vendor's invoices for $2,500 worth of fruit received.
(f) Cheque stub for payment of last week's purchases from All-Growers Farms, $2,970. Terms of 1/10, net 30 were taken.
(g) Cheque stub for repayment of a $5,000, 90-day note to Commerce Bank, $5,100.
(h) A letter notifying Ellis that Littex Markets, a customer, has declared bankruptcy. All creditors will receive 10 cents on every dollar due. Littex owes Ellis $650.

Instructions:
(1) Indicate the books of original entry in which Ellis recorded each of the business documents. (Use the designated abbreviations.)
(2) Record the debits and credits for each entry as though only a general journal were used. Use account titles implied by the voucher system.

2-2A. A fire destroyed Rodriquez Company's journals. However, the general ledger and accounts receivable subsidiary ledger were saved. An inspection of the ledgers reveals the information shown below.

General Ledger

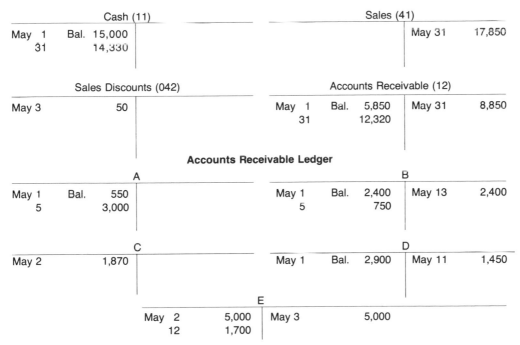

Rodriquez's credit policy is 1/10, n/30.

Instructions: Reconstruct the sales and cash receipts journals from the information given above.

2-3A. The trial balance of Dennis Ltd., shows among other items the following balances on December 31, 1981, the end of a fiscal year.

Accounts Receivable	90,000	
9% Century City Bonds	60,000	
Buildings	120,000	
Accumulated Depreciation — Buildings		34,650
Land	110,000	
8% First-Mortgage Bonds Payable		120,000
Rental Revenue		28,600
Office Expense	3,000	

The following facts are ascertained on this date upon inspection of the company's records.

(a) It is estimated that approximately 2% of accounts receivable may prove uncollectible. The Allowance for Doubtful Accounts has a zero balance on December 31, 1981 (before adjustments).

(b) Interest is receivable semi-annually on the Century City bonds on March 1 and September 1.

(c) Buildings are depreciated at $2^{1}/_{2}$% a year; however, there were building additions of $20,000 during the year. The company computes depreciation on asset acquisitions during the year at one half the annual rate.

(d) Interest on the first-mortgage bonds is payable semi-annually on February 1 and August 1.

(e) Rental revenue includes $1,500 that was received on November 1, representing rent on part of the buildings for the period November 1, 1981, to October 31, 1982.

(f) Office supplies of $800 are on hand on December 31. Purchases of office supplies were debited to the office expense account.

Instructions:

(1) Prepare the journal entries to adjust the accounts on December 31, 1981.

(2) Give the reversing entries that may appropriately be made at the beginning of 1982.

2-4A. The bookkeeper for the Boyer Co. is preparing an income statement for the year ended December 31, 1981, reporting income from operations as $110,900. Accounts have not yet been closed, and a review of the books disclosed the need for the following adjustments:

(a) The account, Office Expense, shows the cost of all purchases of office supplies for the year. At the end of 1981 there are supplies of $600 on hand.

(b) The allowance for doubtful accounts shows a debit balance of $200. It is estimated that 3% of the accounts receivable as of December 31 will prove uncollectible. The accounts receivable balance on this date is $29,100.

(c) The ledger shows a balance for accrued salaries and wages of $1,800 as of December 31, 1980, which was left unchanged during 1981. No recognition was made in the accounts at the end of 1981 for accrued salaries and wages which amounted to $1,950.

(d) The ledger shows a balance for interest receivable of $375 as of December 31, 1980, which was left unchanged during 1981. No recognition was made in the accounts at the end of 1981 for accrued interest which amounted to $440.

(e) The prepaid insurance account was debited during the year for amounts paid for insurance and shows a balance of $1,200 at the end of 1981. The unexpired portions of the policies on December 31, 1981 total $560.

(f) A portion of a building was subleased for three months, November 1, 1981, to February 1, 1982. Unearned Rental Revenue was credited for $1,200 and no adjustment was made in this account at the end of 1981.

(g) The interest expense account was charged for all interest charges incurred during the year and shows a balance of $1,900. However, of this amount, $250 represents charges applicable to notes due in 1982.

(h) Provision for income taxes for 1981 is to be computed at a 45% rate.

Instructions:

Give the entries that are required on December 31, 1981, to bring the accounts up to date. (In recording income tax, provide a schedule to show how the corrected income subject to tax was determined.)

2-5A. The bookkeeper for the Barry Co. prepares no reversing entries and records all revenue and expense items in nominal accounts during the period. The following balances, among others, are listed on the trial balance at the end of the fiscal period, December 31, 1981, before accounts have been adjusted:

Accounts Receivable	38,000
Allowance for Doubtful Accounts	250
Interest Receivable	700
Discount on Notes Payable	75
Prepaid Real Estate and Personal Property Taxes	450
Salaries and Wages Payable	1,000
Discount on Notes Receivable	700
Unearned Rental Revenue	375

Inspection of the company's records reveals the following as of December 31, 1981:

(a) Uncollectible accounts are estimated at 3% of the accounts receivable balance.

(b) The accrued interest on investments totals $600.

(c) The company borrows cash by discounting its own notes at the bank. Discount on notes payable at the end of 1981 is $400.

(d) Prepaid real estate and personal property taxes are $450, the same as at the end of 1980.

(e) Accrued salaries and wages are $1,075.

(f) The company accepts notes from the customers giving its customers credit for the face of the note less a charge for interest. At the end of each period any interest applicable to the succeeding period is reported as a discount. Discount on notes receivable at the end of 1981 is $375.

(g) Part of the company's properties had been sublet on September 15, 1980, at a rental of $750 per month. The arrangement was terminated at the end of one year.

Instructions:

Give the adjusting entries required to bring the accounts up to date.

2-6A. The income statement for the Marble Electric Co. for the year ended December 31, 1981, was as follows:

Marble Electric Co.
Income Statement
For Year Ended December 31, 1981

Sales			$1,200,000
Cost of goods sold:			
Materials purchased	$360,000		
Add decrease in materials inventory	20,000	$380,000	
Direct labor		110,000	
Manufacturing overhead		140,000	
Add decrease in work in process inventory		$630,000	
		20,000	
		$650,000	
Deduct increase in finished goods inventory		15,000	635,000
Gross profit on sales			$565,000
Selling and general expenses			205,000
Income before income tax and extraordinary item			$360,000
Deduct income tax (income tax, $165,000 plus credit applicable to extraordinary loss, $10,000)			175,000
Income before extraordinary item			$185,000
Less loss on sale of investments acquired for resale (net of $10,000 income tax credit)			40,000
Net income			$145,000

Instructions:
Give the journal entries to close the accounts at the end of 1981.

2-7A. Account balances taken from the ledger of the Jones Supply Corporation on December 31, 1981, follow:

Accounts Payable	$ 36,000	Land	$ 69,600
Accounts Receivable	67,200	Long-Term Investments	12,600
Advertising	4,800	Mortgage Payable	48,000
Accumulated Depreciation —		Notes Payable — Short Term	15,000
Buildings	19,800	Office Expense	16,080
Allowance for Doubtful Accounts	1,380	Purchases	138,480
Buildings	72,000	Purchase Discounts	1,140
Capital Stock, $10 par	180,000	Retained Earnings, Dec. 31, 1980	14,040
Cash	24,000	Sales	246,000
Dividends	14,400	Sales Discounts	5,400
Freight In	3,600	Sales Returns	3,360
Insurance Expense	1,440	Selling Expense	49,440
Interest Expense	2,640	Supplies Expense	4,200
Interest Revenue	660	Taxes — Real Estate,	
Inventory, Dec. 31, 1980	64,800	Payroll, and Other	7,980

Adjustments on December 31 are required as follows:

(a) The inventory on hand is $90,720.
(b) The allowance for doubtful accounts is to be increased to a balance of $3,000.
(c) Buildings are depreciated at the rate of $3^1/_3$% per year.
(d) Accrued selling expenses are $3,840.
(e) There are supplies of $780 on hand.
(f) Prepaid insurance relating to 1982 and 1983 totals $720.
(g) Accrued interest on long-term investments is $240.
(h) Accrued real estate, payroll and other taxes are $900.
(i) Accrued interest on the mortgage is $480.
(j) Income tax is estimated to be 45% of the income before income tax.

Instructions:
(1) Prepare an eight-column work sheet.
(2) Prepare adjusting, closing, and reversing entries.

2-8A. The following account balances are taken from the accounts of the Hales Manufacturing Co. Ltd. on December 31, 1981.

Cash	$ 30,875	Retained Earnings	$ 15,850
Accounts Receivable	92,800	Sales	590,000
Allowance for Doubtful Accounts	650	Raw Materials Purchases	245,700
Raw Materials	30,000	Freight In	7,000
Work in Process	12,000	Direct Labor	105,000
Finished Goods	28,000	Indirect Labor	25,500
Factory Supplies	1,200	Heat, Light, and Power	10,500
Office Supplies	700	Factory Insurance Expense	1,000
Prepaid Rent	2,000	Factory Supplies Expense	1,200
Prepaid Factory Insurance	2,500	Maintenance and Repairs	7,200
Land	50,000	Miscellaneous Factory Overhead	3,500
Buildings and Equipment	205,000	Office Rent	15,000
Accumulated Depreciation —		Sales Salaries and Commissions	24,000
Buildings and Equipment	25,000	Advertising	18,000
Accounts Payable	86,000	Office Salaries	19,500
Wages and Salaries Payable	7,000	Office Supplies Expense	700
Interest Payable	4,500	Miscellaneous Selling and	
9% Bonds Payable	150,000	Administrative Expense	26,625
Common Stock, $20 par	100,000	Interest Expense	13,500

The following information was supplied by management.

(a) Inventories Dec. 31, 1981:

Raw Materials	$22,000	Finished goods	$26,000
Work in Process	14,000	Factory supplies	500
		Office supplies	250

(b) Provision for doubtful accounts, 1% of annual sales of finished product.
(c) Depreciation, 8%, applied to manufacturing operations.
(d) Accrued wages and salaries:

12/31/81		12/31/80	
Direct labor	$4,200	Direct labor	$5,400
Indirect labor	500	Indirect labor	900
Sales salaries	300	Sales salaries	700

(e) A dividend of $1 per share had been declared December 28, 1981, and is payable January 10, 1982.

(f) Bond interest payment dates are March 1 and September 1.

(g) Rent paid, applicable to 1982, is $1,800.

(h) Insurance paid, applicable to 1982, is $500.

(i) Income tax for 1981 is estimated at $13,000.

Instructions:

(1) Prepare a ten-column work sheet.

(2) Prepare the adjusting and closing entries.

2-9A. The account balances taken from the ledger of Frank Arnold and Vern Bradshaw at the end of the first year's operations on December 31, 1981, and the data for adjustments are given below:

Accounts Payable	$12,600	Personal — Frank Arnold (debit)	$ 2,400
Accounts Receivable	3,100	Personal — Vern Bradshaw (debit)	900
Capital — Frank Arnold	10,000	Purchases	82,000
Capital — Vern Bradshaw	8,150	Purchase Discounts	2,300
Cash	9,650	Purchase Ret. and Allow	1,650
Interest Expense	500	Sales	85,000
Interest Revenue	350	Sales Salaries	8,000
Miscellaneous General Expense	12,600	Store Furniture	3,700
Notes Payable	6,000	Store Supplies	600
Notes Receivable	2,000	Taxes	600

Data for adjustments, year ended December 31, 1981.

(a) Inventories: merchandise, $24,100; store supplies, $280.

(b) Depreciation of store furniture, 10% a year. Additions to store furniture were recorded on March 1 costing $900.

(c) Accrued advertising, $95.

(d) Taxes paid in advance, $200.

(e) Accrued taxes, $215.

(f) Accrued interest on notes payable, $75.

(g) Accrued interest on notes receivable, $105.

(h) 5% of the accounts receivable are expected to prove uncollectible.

(i) Arnold and Bradshaw divide earnings in the ratio 3:2.

Instructions:

(1) Prepare an eight-column work sheet.

(2) Prepare adjusting, closing, and reversing entries.

2-10A. The following account balances are taken from the general ledger of the James Manufacturing Co. Ltd. on December 31, 1981, the end of its fiscal year. The corporation was organized January 2, 1975:

Cash on Hand and in Banks	$ 36,125	Buildings	$125,000
Notes Receivable	18,500	Accumulated Depreciation —	
Accounts Receivable	56,000	Buildings	18,000
Allowance for Doubtful		Machinery and Equipment	160,000
Accounts	650	Accumulated Depreciation —	
Finished Goods — January 1,		Machinery and Equipment	30,000
1981	40,500	Office Furniture and Fixtures	15,000
Work in Process — January 1		Accumulated Depreciation —	
1981	42,000	Office Furniture and Fixtures	9,000

Raw Materials — January 1, 1981	24,000	Shipping Department Equipment	12,000
Factory Supplies	17,000	Accumulated Depreciation — Shipping Department Equipment	7,200
Shipping Supplies	8,500		
Office Supplies	6,200		
Land	20,000	Patterns and Dies	30,000
Tools	20,000	Maintenance and Repairs of Machinery	7,000
Patents	27,500		
Notes Payable	20,000	Heat, Light, and Power (Factory)	11,000
Accounts Payable	45,700	Taxes	10,200
9% First-Mortgage Bonds	100,000	Miscellaneous Factory Overhead	3,600
6% Preferred Shares, $100 par	100,000	Sales Salaries	35,000
Common Shares, $100 par	100,000	Sales Commissions	12,300
Premium on Common Shares	10,000	Traveling Expense	8,500
Retained Earnings	125,000	Advertising Expense	23,125
Sales	560,000	Shipping Department Salaries	6,000
Sales Returns and Allowances	10,000	Miscellaneous Shipping Department Expense	1,000
Sales Discounts	7,000		
Raw Materials Purchases	107,950	Officers Salaries	25,000
Freight In	8,800	Office Salaries	14,000
Purchase Returns and Allowances	3,000	Insurance Expense	8,500
Purchase Discounts	3,400	Postage, Telephone, and Telegraph	1,400
Direct Labor	108,000	Miscellaneous Office Expense	1,500
Indirect Labor	32,000	Interest Revenue	800
Plant Superintendence	20,000	Interest Expense — Bonds	5,250
Maintenance and Repairs of Buildings	6,300	Interest Expense — Other	1,000

Data for adjustments at December 31, 1981, are as follows:

(a) Inventories:
   Finished goods, $49,500; work in process, $60,200; raw materials, $36,600; factory supplies, $2,700; shipping supplies, $2,500; office supplies, $1,000.
(b) Depreciation and amortization:
   Shipping department equipment, $12\frac{1}{2}\%$.
   Office furniture and fixtures, 10%.
   Machinery and equipment, 5%. New machinery and equipment costing $60,000 was installed on March 1, 1981.
   Buildings, 4%. Additions to the buildings costing $50,000 were completed June 30, 1981.
   Patents were acquired on January 2, 1975. A charge for patent amortization for 1981 is to be made at $\frac{1}{17}$ of the original patents cost.
   A charge for patterns and dies amortization for 1981 is to be made at 15% of the balance in the patterns and dies account.
   A charge for tools used during the year is to be made at 25% of the balance in the tools account.
(c) The allowance for doubtful accounts is to be increased to a balance of $3,200.
(d) Accrued expenses:
   Salaries and wages: direct labor, $1,400; indirect labor, $300; sales salaries, $400; shipping department salaries, $200.
   Interest on bonds is payable semi-annually on February 1 and August 1.
   Interest on notes payable, $50.
   Property tax, $2,000.

(e) Prepaid expenses: insurance, $2,500.

(f) Accrued revenue: interest on notes receivable, $500.

(g) The following information is also to be recorded:

  (1) It is discovered that sales commissions of $1,200 were charged in error to the account Shipping Department Salaries.

  (2) On December 30 the board of directors declared a quarterly dividend on preferred stock and a dividend of $1.50 on common stock, payable January 25, 1982, to shareholders of record January 15, 1982.

  (3) Income tax for 1981 is estimated at $30,000.

Taxes, expired insurance, and building expenses are to be distributed as follows: manufacturing operations, 60%; selling operations, 25%; general operations, 15%. The only charges to retained earnings during the year resulted from the declaration of the regular quarterly dividends on preferred shares.

Instructions:

  (1) Prepare a ten-column work sheet. There should be a pair of columns for trial balance, adjustments, manufacturing schedule, income statement, and balance sheet.

  (2) Prepare all of the journal entries necessary to give effect to the foregoing information and to adjust and close the accounts of the corporation.

  (3) Prepare the reversing entries that may appropriately be made.

2-11A. The Forbes Company commenced operations on July 1, 1981. The following shows the gross debits and credits in each account of the ledger as of December 31, 1981, except for work in process and finished goods inventory accounts. The company uses a cost system for its manufacturing operations.

	Transactions		Trial Balance December 31, 1981	
	Debit	Credit	Debit	Credit
Cash	$464,000	$370,000	94,000	
Notes Receivable	20,000	12,000	8,000	
Accounts Receivable	340,000	302,000	38,000	
Finished Goods	compute	compute	30,000	
Work in Process	compute	compute	14,000	
Raw Materials	125,000	118,000	7,000	
Supplies	18,000	14,000	4,000	
Prepaid Insurance	1,900	1,500	400	
Land, Buildings, and Equipment	95,000	0	95,000	
Mortgage Payable	0	50,000		50,000
Interest Payable	0	750		750
Wages Payable	145,100	147,000		1,900
Vouchers Payable	325,000	365,500		40,500
Capital Stock	0	150,000		150,000
Sales	0	360,000		360,000
Cost of Goods Sold	250,000	0	250,000	
Selling Expense	27,500	0	27,500	
Administrative Expense	29,000	0	29,000	
Financial Expense	6,250	0	6,250	
			603,150	603,150

You are also given the following information:

(a) The ending goods in process inventory consists of the following: materials, $6,000; direct labor, $4,500; and manufacturing overhead, $3,500.

(b) Insurance premiums apply two thirds to the factory and one third to the office.

(c) The cost of the finished product is made up of: materials, 40%; labor, 40%; and manufacturing overhead, 20%.

Instructions:

Set up skeleton ledger "T" accounts. Show therein the entries making up the transactions included in the figures shown on the trial balance. Key each entry (debit and offsetting credit) by use of a number, and on a separate sheet give an explanation and support for each entry. (AICPA adapted)

3 FINANCIAL STATEMENTS — THE BALANCE SHEET

The principles and techniques applied in the preparation of financial statements have been summarized in the preceding chapters. Accounting systems are established to provide the various reports and analyses for internal and external use. Traditionally, however, only one set of statements has been made available externally. This set normally consists of (1) a *balance sheet* reporting the financial position of the business at a certain date; (2) an *income statement* presenting the results of operations of an entity for the reporting period, i.e., the changes in owners' equity arising from operations since the position of the enterprise was last stated; and (3) a *statement of changes in financial position* describing the changes in the financial resources that have occurred during the last reporting period of the business. When the change in owners' equity is not fully explained by the income statement, a supplemental statement referred to as the *statement of changes in owners' equity,* or for a corporation, the *retained earnings statement*, is usually provided.

This set of financials has become accepted as general purpose statements. They are intended to be relevant to a broad variety of external users. Although there has been some discussion about the need to prepare special purpose statements directed to specific external users, there has been no significant movement toward this in practice.

The balance sheet is discussed in this chapter. The essential nature of the statement of changes in financial position is also introduced in this chapter, but is explained in more detail in Chapter 20. The income statement will be discussed in Chapter 4. Items relating to these primary financial statements, as well as a number of supplementary analytical statements, are described in later chapters.

CONTENT OF THE BALANCE SHEET

The *balance sheet*, also called the *statement of financial position*, reports the assets, liabilities, and owners' equity of a business entity as of a given date. The *financial position* is the cumulative result of all transactions of a business from its inception. Since the balance sheet is basically historical, only a thorough understanding of the principles and practices followed in the recording process offers an appreciation of the nature of reporting the balance sheet position resulting from a series of recorded transactions. Some of the basic concepts of balance sheet content, form, and presentation are considered in this chapter. Discussions of the individual asset, liability, and owners' equity items in later chapters will serve to develop more fully the nature of the balance sheet.

The balance sheet is an expansion of the basic accounting equation, Assets = Equities. The character and the amount of the assets are exhibited. Equities — the liabilities and owners' equity — normally bear no relationship to specific assets and hence are presented as balances related to the assets as a whole.

For accounting purposes, assets include those costs that have not been applied to revenues in the past and are considered to afford economic utility in the production of revenues in the future. Assets, then, include both monetary assets, such as cash, marketable securities, and receivables, and those costs recognized as recoverable and hence properly assignable to revenues of future periods, such as inventories, prepaid insurance, equipment, and patents.[1] A 1979 FASB Exposure Draft (Revised), "Elements of Financial Statements of Business Enterprises" defines assets as "probable future economic benefits obtained or controlled by a particular enterprise as a result of past transactions or events affecting the enterprise."[2]

Liabilities measure the economic obligations of the enterprise to the creditor group. The method for settlement of liabilities varies. Liabilities may call for settlement by cash payment or settlement through goods to be

---

[1]The authors of Accounting Research Study No. 3 define assets as ". . . expected future economic benefits, rights to which have been acquired by the enterprise as a result of some current or past transaction." Robert T. Sprouse and Maurice Moonitz, A *Tentative Set of Broad Accounting Principles for Business Enterprises*, Accounting Research Study No. 3 (New York: American Institute of Certified Public Accountants, 1962), p. 8. The Accounting Principles Board defined assets as ". . . economic resources of an enterprise that are recognized and measured in conformity with generally accepted accounting principles." *Statements of the Accounting Principles Board, No. 4*. "Basic Concepts and Accounting Principles Underlying Financial Statements of Business Enterprises" (New York: American Institue of Certified Public Accountants, 1970), par. 132.

[2]*Statement of Financial Accounting Concepts No. 3*, "Elements of Financial Statements of Business Enterprises" (Stamford, Conn.: Financial Accounting Standards Board, 1980), par. 19.

delivered or services to be performed.[3] Again, the FASB Exposure Draft referred to above defines liabilities as "probable future sacrifices of economic benefits stemming from present legal, equitable, or constructive obligations of a particular enterprise to transfer assets or provide services in the future as a result of past transactions or events affecting the enterprise."[4]

Owners' equity measures the interest of the ownership group in the total resources of the enterprise. This interest arises from investments by owners, and the equity increase or decrease from the change in net assets resulting from operations. An ownership equity does not call for settlement on a certain date: in the event of business dissolution, it represents a claim on assets only after creditors have been paid in full. The method of reporting the owners' equity varies with the form of the business unit. Business units are typically divided into three categories: (1) *proprietorships*, (2) *partnerships*, and (3) *corporations*.

Balance sheet items are generally classified in a manner to facilitate analysis and interpretation of financial data. Information of primary concern to all parties is the business unit's liquidity and solvency — its ability to meet current and long-term obligations. Accordingly, assets and liabilities are classified as (1) *current* or *short-term* items and (2) *non-current, long-term*, or *fixed* items. When assets and liabilities are classified, the difference between current assets and current liabilities may be determined. This is referred to as the company's *working capital* — the liquid buffer available in meeting financial demands and contingencies of the future.[5]

Current Assets and Current Liabilities

The position of the Accounting Research Committee on current assets and current liabilities is stated in Section 1510 of the *Accounting Recommendations*.[6]

> As a balance sheet classification, current assets should include those assets ordinarily realizable within one year from the date of the balance sheet or within the normal operating cycle, where that is longer than a year.
>
> Current assets should be segregated as between the main classes, e.g., cash, temporary investments, accounts and notes receivable, inventories, prepaid expenses and deferred income taxes.
>
> As a balance sheet classification, current liabilities should include amounts payable within one year from the date of the balance sheet or within the normal

---

[3]Liabilities are defined by Sprouse and Moonitz in ARS No. 3 as ". . . obligations to convey assets or perform services, such obligations resulting from past or current transactions and requiring settlement in the future." *loc. cit.* The Accounting Principles Board defined liabilities as ". . . economic obligations of an enterprise that are recognized and measured in conformity with generally accepted accounting principles." *Statements of the Accounting Principles Board*, No. 4, *loc. cit.*

[4]*Ibid.*, par. 28.

[5]"Working Capital" is used in this text to denote the excess of current assets over current liabilities. Sometimes this excess is referred to as "net working capital."

[6]*CICA Handbook: Accounting Recommendations, Section 1510*, "Current Assets and Current Liabilities" (Toronto: Canadian Institute of Chartered Accountants, 1968), par. .01, .02, .03, and .07.

operating cycle, where this is longer than a year (the normal operating cycle should correspond with that used for current assets).

Current liabilities should be segregated as between the main classes, e.g., bank loans, trade creditors and accrued liabilities, loans payable, taxes payable, dividends payable, deferred revenues, current payments on long-term debt and deferred income taxes. Amounts owing on loans from directors, officers and shareholders, amounts owing to subsidiaries not consolidated, whether on account of a loan or otherwise, and amounts owing to parent and other affiliated companies, whether on account of a loan or otherwise, should be shown separately.

The *normal operating cycle* referred to is the time required for cash to be converted into inventories, inventories into receivables, and receivables ultimately into cash. In effect, the committee suggests a one-year period be used as a basis for the current classification in those instances when the average operating cycle is less than twelve months. When the operating cycle exceeds twelve months, as in the case of tobacco, distillery, and lumber industries, the Committee suggests that the longer period be used.

The position of the American Institute of Certified Public Accountants' Committee on Accounting Procedure on current assets is essentially the same as the Canadian position but it nonetheless merits quotation because it contains more extensive descriptions of individual classes of current assets.

> For accounting purposes, the term *current* assets is used to designate cash and other assets or resources commonly identified as those which are reasonably expected to be realized in cash or sold or consumed during the normal operating cycle of the business. Thus the term comprehends in general such resources as (a) cash available for current operations and items which are the equivalent of cash; (b) inventories of merchandise, raw materials, goods in process, finished goods, operating supplies, and ordinary maintenance material and parts; (c) trade accounts, notes, and acceptances receivable; (d) receivables from officers, employees, affiliates, and others, if collectible in the ordinary course of business within a year; (e) installment or deferred accounts and notes receivable if they conform generally to normal trade practices and terms within the business; (f) marketable securities representing the investment of cash available for current operations; and (g) prepaid expenses such as insurance, interest, rents, taxes, unused royalties, current paid advertising service not yet received, and operating supplies. <u>Prepaid expenses are not current assets in the sense that they will be converted into cash but in the sense that, if not paid in advance, they would require the use of current assets during the operating cycle.[7]</u>

Current liabilities are described by the AICPA as follows:

> The term *current liabilities* is used principally to designate obligations whose liquidation is reasonably expected to require the use of existing resources properly classifiable as current assets, or the creation of other current liabilities.

---

[7]*Accounting Research and Terminology Bulletins — Final Edition*, "No. 43, Restatement and Revision of Accounting Research Bulletins" (New York: American Institute of Certified Public Accountants, 1961), Ch. 3, Sec. A. par. 4.

As a balance sheet category, the classification is intended to include obligations for items which have entered into the operating cycle, such as payables incurred in the acquisition of materials and supplies to be used in the production of goods or in providing services to be offered for sale; collections received in advance of the delivery of goods or performance of services; and debts which arise from operations directly related to the operating cycle, such as accruals for wages, salaries, commissions, rentals, royalties, and income and other taxes. Other liabilities whose regular and ordinary liquidation is expected to occur within a relatively short period of time, usually twelve months, are also intended for inclusion, such as short-term debts arising from the acquisition of capital assets, serial maturities of long-term obligations, amounts required to be expended within one year under sinking fund provisions, and agency obligations arising from the collection or acceptance of cash or other assets for the account of third persons.[8]

With respect to short-term obligations which normally would come due within the operating cycle but which are expected to be refinanced, i.e., discharged by means of the issuance of new obligations in their place, the Financial Accounting Standards Board (FASB) has concluded such obligations should be excluded from current liabilities if the following conditions are met:

1. The intent of the company is to refinance the obligations on a long-term basis, and
2. The company's intent is supported by an ability to consummate the refinancing as evidenced by a post-balance-sheet-date issuance of long-term obligations or equity securities or an explicit financing agreement.[9]

In effect, the FASB is recognizing that certain short-term obligations will not require the use of working capital during a period even though they are scheduled to mature during that period. Thus, they should not be classified as current liabilities.

Current assets are normally listed on the balance sheet in the order of their liquidity. These assets, with the exception of marketable securities and inventories, are usually reported at their estimated realizable values. Thus, current receivable balances are reduced by an allowance for doubtful accounts. Marketable equity securities preferably should be reported at the lower of aggregate cost or market.[10] Inventories may be reported at cost or on the basis of "market" if this amount is lower than cost.

Few problems are generally found in the valuation of current liabilities. Payables can usually be determined accurately, even though some items may

---

[8]*Ibid.*, par. 7.

[9]*Statement of Financial Accounting Standards No. 6*, "Classification of Short-Term Obligations Expected to Be Refinanced" (Stamford, Conn.: Financial Accounting Standards Board, 1975), par. 9-11.

[10]*Statement of Financial Accounting Standards No. 12*, "Accounting for Certain Marketable Securities" (Stamford, Conn.: Financial Accounting Standards Board, 1975), par 8. In Canada, marketable securities still are carried most commonly at cost. However, Section 3010 of the *Accounting Recommendations*, "Temporary Investments," states that "when the market value of temporary investments has declined below the carrying value, they should be carried at market value."

require estimates as to the amounts ultimately to be paid. These claims, however determined, if payable currently, must be included under the current heading.

The importance of an adequate working capital position cannot be over-emphasized. A business may not be able to survive in the absence of a satisfactory relationship between current assets and current liabilities. Furthermore, its ability to prosper is largely determined by the composition of the current asset pool. There must be a proper balance between liquid assets in the form of cash and temporary investments, and receivables and inventories. Activities of the business are centred on these assets. Cash and temporary investments, representing immediate purchasing power, are used to meet current claims and purchasing, payroll, and expense requirements; receivables are the outgrowth of sales effort and provide cash in the course of operations; merchandise is also a source of cash as well as the means of achieving revenue. Management, in setting policies with respect to selling, purchasing, financing, expansion, and dividends, must work within the limitations set by the company's working capital position.

Non-current Assets and Non-current Liabilities

Assets and liabilites not qualifying for presentation under the current headings are classified under a number of non-current headings. Non-current assets, often referred to as *fixed assets*, may be listed under separate headings, such as "Long-term investments," "Land, buildings, and equipment," "Intangible assets," and "Other long-term assets." Non-current liabilities are generally listed under separate headings, such as "Long-term liabilities," "Deferred revenues," and "Other long-term liabilities."

Long-Term Investments. Investments held for such long-term purposes as regular income, appreciation, or ownership control are reported under the heading "Long-term investments." Examples of items properly reported under this heading are long-term shares, bonds, and mortgage holdings; securities of affiliated companies including unconsolidated subsidiaries, as well as advances to such companies; sinking fund assets consisting of cash and securities held for the redemption of bonds or shares, the replacement of buildings, or the payment of pensions; land held for future use or sale; the cash surrender value of life insurance; and other miscellaneous investments not used directly in the operations of the business. Although many long-term investments are reported at cost, there are required modifications to the valuation of some long-term investments which will be discussed in later chapters.

Land, Buildings, and Equipment. Properties of a tangible and relatively permanent character that are used in the normal business operations are reported under the heading "Land, buildings, and equipment." Land, buildings, equipment, machinery, tools, furniture, fixtures, and vehicles are included under this heading. The rights to the use of assets obtained under capital leases are also included under this heading. Buildings and equipment items are normally reported at cost less accumulated depreciation.

Intangible Assets. The long-term rights and privileges of a non-physical character acquired for use in business operations are reported under the heading "Intangible assets." Included in this class are such items as goodwill, patents, trademarks, franchises, copyrights, formulas, leaseholds, and organization costs. Intangible assets are normally reported at cost less amounts amortized to date.

Other Long-Term Assets. Those non-current or fixed assets not suitably reported under any of the previous classifications may be listed under the general heading "Other long-term assets" or may be listed separately under special descriptive headings. Such assets include cash funds representing deposits received from customers on returnable containers, deposits made with vendors to secure contracts, and long-term advances to officers.

Prepayments for services or benefits to be received over a number of periods are properly regarded as non-current. Among these are such items as plant rearrangement costs and developmental and improvement costs. These long-term prepayments are frequently reported under a "Deferred costs" or "Deferred charges" heading. However, objection can be raised to a deferred cost category since this designation could be applied to all costs assignable to future periods including inventories, buildings and equipment, and intangible assets. The deferred costs heading may be avoided by reporting long-term prepayments within the other long-term assets section or under separate descriptive headings.

Contingent Assets. Circumstances at the balance sheet date may indicate the existence of certain rights or claims that could materialize as valuable assets depending upon the favorable outcome of certain events. In the absence of a legal right to the properties at that time, these can be viewed only as *contingent assets*. Contingencies that might result in gains are not usually recorded in the accounts; they may be disclosed in notes to the financial statements by appropriate comment under a separate "Contingencies" heading. Tax claims, insurance claims, and claims against merchandise creditors may warrant such treatment. Reference to contingent assets in the balance sheet is rare in practice.

Long-Term Liabilities. Long-term notes, bonds, mortgages, and similar obligations not requiring the use of current funds for their retirement are generally reported on the balance sheet under the heading "Long-term liabilities."

When an amount borrowed is not the same as the amount ultimately required in settlement of the debt, and the debt is stated in the accounts at its maturity amount, a debt discount or premium is reported. The discount or premium should be related to the debt item: a discount, then, should be subtracted from the amount reported for the debt, and a premium should be added to the amount reported for the debt. The debt is thus reported at its present value as measured by the proceeds from its issuance. Amortization of the discount or premium brings the obligation to the maturity amount by the end of its normal term. When a note, a bond issue, or a mortgage formerly classified as a long-term obligation becomes payable within a year, it should be reclassified and presented as a current liability, except when the obligation is expected to be refinanced or is to be paid out of a sinking fund.

Deferred Revenues. Cash may be received or other assets recognized for goods and services to be supplied in future periods. Such transactions are recognized in the accounts by debits to assets and credits to liability accounts reporting the advance payments. The latter balance is properly carried forward until the company meets its responsibilities through the delivery of goods or the performance of services. If, in subsequent periods, the expenses of providing the goods and services are less than the obligations that are discharged thereby, earnings will be recognized; on the other hand, if expenses are greater than the obligations that are discharged, losses will be incurred. Examples of transactions that call for revenue deferral and recognition as long-term obligations include fees received in advance on long-term service contracts, and long-term lease-hold and rental prepayments. These prepayments are normally reported on the balance sheet under the heading of "Deferred revenues."

All revenues received in advance for goods and services are frequently reported under the "Deferred revenues" heading, including those calling for settlement in the near future. However, the non-current classification is appropriate only when an item represents no significant claim upon current assets. When significant costs are involved in satisfying a claim and these costs will be met from the company's current assets, the prepayment should be recognized as a current liability. The obligation arising from the receipt of cash in advance on magazine subscriptions, for example, is properly recognized as a current liability in view of the claim it makes upon current assets.

Other Long-Term Liabilities. Those non-current liabilities not suitably reported under the "Long-term liabilities" or "Deferred revenues" headings may be listed under the general heading "Other long-term liabilities" or may be listed separately under special descriptive headings. Such liabilities include obligations to customers in the form of long-term refundable deposits on returnable containers, long-term obligations to company officers or affiliated companies, matured by unclaimed bond principal and interest obligations, and long-term liabilities under pension plans.

Deferred Income Tax is sometimes shown under "Other long-term liabilities" or may be reported separately. Income taxes are deferred when taxes are paid on a taxable income that is less than the income reported on the financial statements. The difference, may be a temporary one caused by a timing difference which has resulted in postponing income taxes until a later period. Timing differences may occur, for example, in recognizing different amounts of depreciation for accounting and for tax purposes and also in recognizing revenue on instalment sales and on long-term construction contracts. A matching of income tax expense with revenue requires that postponed taxes be deferred and recognized as a subtraction from tax paid in the period when the item is ultimately recognized for tax purposes.

Contingent Liabilities. Past activities or circumstances may have given rise to possible future liabilities, although legal obligations do not exist on the date of the balance sheet. These possible claims are known as *contingent liabilities.* They are potential obligations involving uncertainty as to possible losses. As future events occur or fail to occur, this uncertainty will be resolved. Thus, a contingent liability is distinguishable from an *estimated liability.* The latter is a definite obligation with only the amount of the obligation in question and subject to estimation at the balance sheet date. There may not be any doubt as to the amount of a contingent liability, but there is considerable uncertainty as to whether the obligation will actually materialize.

Traditionally, contingent liabilities have not been recorded in the accounts and, therefore, have not been presented on the face of the balance sheet. Typically, when they have been disclosed, it has been in notes to the financial statements. However, Section 3290 of the *Accounting Recommendations* requires that "the amount of a contingent loss should be accrued in the financial statements by a charge to income when both of the following conditions are met: (a) it is likely that a future event will confirm that an asset had been impaired or a liability incurred at the date of the financial statements; and (b) the amount of the loss can be reasonably estimated."[11] Footnote disclosure continues to apply to any other contingencies, including contingent gains, the accrual of which would violate the realization concept.

Owners' Equity

In the case of a proprietorship, the owner's equity in assets is reported by means of a single capital account. The balance in this account is the cumula-

---

[11]*Accounting Recommendations, Section 3290,* "Contingencies" (Toronto: Canadian Institute of Chartered Accountants, 1978), par. .12.

tive result of the owner's investments and withdrawals as well as past earnings and losses. In a partnership, capital accounts are established for each partner. Capital account balances summarize the investments and withdrawals and shares of past earnings and losses of each partner, and thus measure the partners' individual equities in partnership assets.

In a business corporation, the difference between assets and liabilities is referred to as *shareholders' equity, stockholders' equity,* or simply, *capital.* In presenting the shareholders' equity on the balance sheet, sub-headings are used to distinguish such components as share capital, contributed surplus, and retained earnings. The equity originating from shareholders' investments, to the extent it constitutes legal capital, is reported as *share capital.* Amounts received from shareholders that do not constitute legal capital, together with capital received from other sources, are reported as *contributed surplus.* The equity originating from earnings is reported as *retained earnings.* Sometimes the term *surplus* is applied to corporate capital balances other than share capital. Thus retained earnings may occasionally be designated *earned surplus.*

Shares outstanding having a par value are shown on the balance sheet at par. Shares without nominal or par value are generally stated at the amount received on original issue or at some other value as stipulated by law or as assigned by action of the board of directors of the corporation. When more than a single class of shares have been issued and are outstanding, the details of each class are reported separately. *Treasury shares,* which are shares issued but subsequently reacquired by the corporation, are subtracted from total shareholders' equity. The share capital balance is the *legal capital* or *permanent capital* of the corporation.

A premium received on the sale of par-value shares is recognized as contributed surplus which may also arise from the acquisition of property as a result of a donation, or from the sale of treasury shares at more than cost. In the very limited number of cases where shares may be legally sold at less than par, share capital is shown at par and the discount is reported as a subtraction item in arriving at the amount of contributed surplus.

The amount of undistributed earnings of past periods is reported as *retained earnings.* The amount thus shown does not represent cash available for payment as dividends; it is simply another source of assets. An excess of dividends and losses over earnings results in a negative retained earnings balance called a *deficit.* The balance of retained earnings is added to the balances in share capital and contributed surplus in summarizing shareholders' equity; a deficit is subtracted.

Portions of retained earnings are sometimes reported as restricted and unavailable as a basis for dividends. Restricted earnings may be designated as *appropriations* or *reserves.* Appropriations are frequently made for such purposes as sinking funds, plant expansion, loss contingencies, and the reacquisition of share capital. When appropriations have been made, retained earnings on the balance sheet consists of an amount designated as *Appropriated* and a balance designated as *Unappropriated* or *Free*.

Offsets on the Balance Sheet

A number of balance sheet items are frequently reported at gross amounts calling for the recognition of offset balances in arriving at proper valuations. Such offset balances are found in contra asset, liability, and owners' equity categories. In the case of assets, for example, an allowance for doubtful accounts is subtracted from the sum of the customers' accounts in reporting the net amount estimated collectible; accumulated depreciation is subtracted from the related buildings and equipment balances in reporting the costs of the assets still assignable to future revenues. In the case of liabilities, bonds reacquired, or *treasury bonds*, are subtracted from bonds issued in reporting the amount of bonds outstanding; a bond discount is subtracted from the face value of bonds outstanding in reporting the net amount of the debt. In the case of shareholders' equity in the corporation, a discount on par value shares is subtracted in the determination of contributed surplus; a deficit is subtracted in the determination of total shareholders' equity.

The types of offsets described above, utilizing contra accounts, are required for proper reporting of particular balance sheet items. Offsets are improper, however, if applied to different asset and liability balances or to asset and owners' equity balances even when there is some relationship between the items. For example, a company may accumulate cash in a special fund to discharge certain tax liabilities; but as long as control of the cash is retained and the liabilities are still outstanding, the company should continue to report both the asset and the liabilities. Or a company may accumulate cash in a special fund for the redemption of preferred shares outstanding; but until the cash is applied to the reacquisition of the shares, the company must continue to report the asset as well as the owners' equity item. A company may have made advances to certain salespersons while at the same time reporting accrued amounts payable to others; but a net figure cannot be justified here, just as a net figure cannot be justified for the offset of trade receivables against trade payables. In the latter case, however, receivable and payable balances with the same customer/supplier are commonly netted.

Balance Sheet Terminology

The accounting profession has engaged in a continuing effort to define appropriate terms for use in accounting. It has also directed attention to those terms that have been subject to misinterpretation and inappropriate use. Such efforts have been accompanied by a movement to modify terminology where modification might contribute to a better understanding of accounting.

Net Worth and Surplus. The use of *net worth* to designate shareholders' equity has been challenged on the grounds that a balance sheet does not purport to reflect and could not usefully reflect the value of the enterprise or of equity interests therein. The need for designations emphasizing *investment* rather than *value* is recognized. The use of the term *surplus* is also objectionable because its popular use to indicate excess, residue, or that which remains when use or need has been satisfied, is hardly in agreement with its accounting use. As indicated earlier, *surplus,* as employed in an accounting sense, is used with reference to contributed surplus, and accumulated earnings are sometimes reported as earned surplus. To clarify financial reporting, the Accounting Research Committee stops just short of recommending discontinuance of the term *surplus* in the balance sheet presentation of shareholders' equity. The Committee appears to favor substitution of terms clearly indicating the sources from which surplus was derived.[12]

Reserves. The term *reserve* has been employed in the following conflicting ways on the balance sheet.

1. As a contra account — Reserve for Bad Debts, for example, to reduce a receivable balance to the estimated amount collectible, or Inventory Reserve, for example, to reflect an adjustment for lifo inventory changes.
2. As a liability the amount of which is uncertain — Reserve for Income Tax, for example, to indicate the amount of income tax estimated to be payable.
3. As an appropriation of retained earnings — Reserve for Bond Retirement Fund, for example, to represent an appropriation of retained earnings corresponding to the assets that have been segregated and that are to be used for bond retirement.

Since the generally accepted meaning of the term *reserve* relates only to appropriations of retained earnings, the Accounting Research Committee recommended its use be limited to items within this category.[13] Contra asset accounts should be referred to by more descriptive titles, such as Allowance for Doubtful Accounts and Accumulated Depreciation. Liabilities involving estimates should be reported as estimated liabilities.

Use of the term "reserve" in the context of a contra asset, liability, or owners' equity account should be discouraged. Even more objectionable is the practice of listing such diverse reserve elements under a common heading "Reserves," usually reported between the liabilities and owners' equity sections on the balance sheet. This practice results in a distortion of asset, liability, and owners' equity balances, making necessary a full analysis of the reserves and their identification with the appropriate balance sheet

---

[12]*CICA Handbook: Accounting Recommendations, Section 3250,* "Surplus" (Toronto: Canadian Institute of Chartered Accountants, 1968), par. .03.

[13]*CICA Handbook: Accounting Recommendations, Section 3260,* "Reserves" (Toronto: Canadian Institute of Chartered Accountants, 1968), par. .01. See also par. .04.

Assets

Current assets:

Cash in bank and on hand		$ 36,500	
Marketable securities (reported at cost; market value, $71,500)		70,000	
Notes receivable, trade debtors (Note 2)	$ 15,000		
Accounts receivable	50,000		
	$ 65,000		
Less allowance for doutful accounts	5,000	60,000	
Claim for income tax refund		9,000	
Creditors' accounts with debit balances		750	
Advances to employees		1,250	
Interest receivable		250	
Inventories (Note 1a)		125,000	
Prepaid expenses:			
Supply inventories	$ 3,000		
Insurance	4,250	7,250	$310,000

Long-term investments:

Investment in land and unused facilities (Note 1d)		$ 22,500	
Cash surrender value of officers' life insurance policies ..		9,000	31,500

Land, buildings, and equipment (Note 1b):

	Cost	Accumulated Depreciation	Book Value	
Land	$ 80,000		$ 80,000	
Buildings	150,000	$ 35,000	115,000	
Equipment	100,000	45,000	55,000	
	$330,000	$ 80,000		250,000

Intangible assets (Note 1c):

Patents		$ 70,000	
Goodwill		18,500	88,500

Other long-term assets:

Advances to officers		20,000
Total assets		$700,000

See accompanying notes to financial statements.

section in arriving at a summary of assets and related equities. Further, the use of such titles as Miscellaneous Reserves, General Reserves, and Contingency Reserves within a reserves section frequently makes accurate identification of the reserve item impossible.

The term *net worth* is rarely found in modern practice. However, the terms *surplus* and *reserve* are still used, although not extensively. Most of the illustrations in the text employ the statement forms and terminology recommended by leading accounting authorities. However, alternate forms

Corporation
Sheet
31, 1981

Liabilities

Current liabilities:

Notes payable, trade creditors		$ 14,250	
Accounts payable		12,500	
Dividends payable		5,000	
Advances from customers		5,750	
Income tax payable		27,000	
Other liabilities:			
Salaries and wages payable	$1,000		
Taxes payable	1,500	2,500	$ 67,000
Long-term liabilities:			
8% First-mortgage bonds due December 31, 2001 (Note 3)		$100,000	
Less unamortized bond discount		5,000	95,000
Other long-term liabilities:			
Liability under pension plan (Note 4)			65,000
Deferred revenues:			
Unearned lease income (Note 1d)			20,000
Deferred income tax			3,000
Total liabilities			$250,000

Shareholders' Equity

Share capital:

Common stock, $5 par value, 100,000 shares authorized,		
50,000 shares issued and outstanding	$250,000	
Contributed Surplus	45,000	
Retained earnings	155,000	
Total shareholders' equity		450,000
Total liabilities and shareholders' equity		$700,000

Account Form
Balance Sheet

and terms are used in some text questions, exercises, and problems, since these are still encountered in practice. It must be pointed out that in the communication aspects of accounting, movement toward more readily understood terminology is only one phase of the problem. The person who uses the statement must be educated to understand the nature of accounting, the service it can legitimately perform, the limitations to which it is subject, and the kind of analysis and interpretation appropriate under these circumstances.

Form of the Balance Sheet

The form of the balance sheet varies in practice. Its form may be influenced by the nature and size of the business, by the character of the business properties, and by legal requirements in companies and securities acts. The balance sheet is generally prepared in *account form*, assets being reported on the left-hand side and liabilities and owners' equity on the right-hand side. It may also be prepared in *report form*, with assets, liabilities, and owners' equity sections appearing in vertical arrangement.

The order of asset and liability classifications may vary, but usually emphasis is placed upon a company's working capital position and liquidity, with asset and liability groups, as well as the items within such groups, presented in the order of liquidity. A balance sheet in account form with financial data reported in the order of liquidity is illustrated on pages 96 and 97.

When the report form is used, liability and owners' equity totals may be added together to constitute an amount equal to the asset total. In other instances, total liabilities are subtracted from total assets, and owners' equity is reported as the difference. A variation of the report form referred to as the *financial position form* emphasizes the current position and reports a working capital balance. The financial position form is illustrated on page 99. (Individual assets and liabilities are omitted in the example.)

Related balance sheet items are frequently combined so the balance sheet may be prepared in condensed form. For example, land, buildings, and equipment may be reported as a single item; raw materials, work in process, and finished goods inventories may be combined; and the presentation of receivables may be condensed. Consolidation of similar items within reasonable limits may actually serve to clarify the business position and data relationships. Supporting detail for individual items, when considered of particular significance or when required by law, may be supplied by means of notes to the financial statements or by special summaries referred to as *supplementary schedules.*

Balance sheet data are generally presented in comparative form. With comparative reports for two or more dates or with five- or ten-year summaries commonly included in corporate annual reports, information is made available concerning the nature and trend of financial changes taking place within the periods between balance sheet dates. When a statement is presented in a special form, the heading should designate the nature of the form that is provided, as for example, "Condensed Balance Sheet," or "Comparative Balance Sheet."

Notes to the Financial Statements

Along with the movement toward more descriptive terminology have come attempts to improve the manner of presentation and the extent of disclosure of financial data. Notes to the financial statements are an integral part of any formal financial statement presentation. They are essential in explaining the basic financial data and should be prepared and read with care.[14]

Summary of Significant Accounting Policies

In addition to the other notes, a summary of the significant accounting policies followed should be presented with the financial statements. In this regard, the Accounting Research Committee concluded in Section 1505 of the *Accounting Recommendations:*

A clear and concise description of the significant accounting policies of an enterprise should be included as an integral part of the financial statements.[15]

The Committee further stated:

As a minimum, disclosure of information on accounting policies should be provided in the following situations:

Andersen Corporation
Statement of Financial Position
December 31, 1981

Current assets		$310,000
Less current liabilities		67,000
Working capital		$243,000
Add:		
Long-term investments		30,000
Land, buildings, and equipment		250,000
Intangible assets		25,000
Other long-term assets		20,000
Total assets less current liabilities		$568,000
Deduct:		
Long-term liabilities less unamortized bond discount	$95,000	
Deferred revenues	20,000	
Deferred income tax payable	3,000	118,000
Net assets		$450,000
Shareholders' equity:		
Share capital		$250,000
Contributed surplus		45,000
Retained earnings		155,000
Total shareholders' equity		$450,000

Financial Position Form of Balance Sheet

---

[14]The required disclosures for each balance sheet item are of such detail that they cannot be completely discussed in Chapters 3 and 4. Therefore, the notes to the financial statements illustrated in this chapter and in the end-of-chapter material do not provide complete disclosure, but are only illustrative of the general nature and content of the notes which are included in financial statements. Notes to financial statements in end-of-chapter material need only be prepared when specifically required by the problem.

[15]*CICA Handbook: Accounting Recommendations, Section 1505,* "Disclosure of Accounting Policies" (Toronto: Canadian Institute of Chartered Accountants, 1974) par. .04.

ANDERSEN CORPORATION

**NOTES TO FINANCIAL STATEMENTS — YEAR ENDED
DECEMBER 31, 1981**

1. Summary of Significant Accounting Policies:
   (a) Inventories are valued at cost or market, whichever is lower. Cost is calculated by the first-in, first-out method.
   (b) Depreciation is computed for both the books and tax return by the declining balance method.
   (c) Intangible assets are being amortized over the period of their estimated useful lives: patents, 10 years, and goodwill, 20 years.
   (d) The company leased Market Street properties for a 15-year period ending January 1, 1988. Leasehold payment received in advance is being recognized as revenue over the life of the lease.

2. The company is contingently liable on guaranteed notes and accounts totalling $40,000. Also, various suits are pending on which the ultimate payment cannot be determined. In the opinion of counsel and management, such liability, if any, will not be material.

3. Bonds may be called at the option of the board of directors at 105 plus accrued interest on or before December 31, 1983, and at gradually reduced amounts but at not less than 102$\frac{1}{2}$ plus accrued interest after January 1, 1989.

4. The pension plan covers all employees. The company funds all pension costs accrued. The liability under the company pension plan has been calculated on the basis of actuarial studies.

   (a) where a selection has been made from alternative acceptable accounting principles, methods and procedures;
   (b) where there are accounting principles, methods and procedures used which are peculiar to an industry in which an enterprise operates, even if such accounting principles, methods and procedures are predominantly followed in that industry.[16]

Examples of disclosure of accounting policies required by this opinion would include, among others, those relating to depreciation methods, amortization of intangible assets, the recognition of profit on long-term construction-type contracts, and the recognition of revenue from franchising and leasing operations.[17]

[16]*Ibid*., par. .09.
[17]*Ibid*., par. .10.

The exact format for reporting the summary of accounting policies was not specified by the Committee. However, the Committee recommended such disclosure be included as the initial note or as a separate summary preceding the notes to the financial statements. As an illustration, the notes to the financial statements for the Andersen Corporation, including a summary of accounting policies followed, are shown at the top of page 100.

Careful classification of items under descriptive headings, appropriate explanatory notes, and the presentation of data in comparative form provides more meaningful statements. Presentations in condensed forms and the rounding of numbers to the nearest dollar, hundred or thousands of dollars clarify relationships and facilitate analysis. A variety of different balance sheet forms is found in practice.[18]

OVERVIEW OF THE STATEMENT OF CHANGES IN FINANCIAL POSITION

The statement of changes in financial position, also commonly referred to as the *funds statement,* may be characterized as a condensed report of how the activities of a business have been financed and how the financial resources have been used. It is a flow statement, emphasizing the inflows and outflows of resources related to the significant financial events of a business entity during a reporting period.

Although based on the same data as the balance sheet and the income statement, the statement of changes in financial position helps to answer questions not readily apparent from cursory examination of either or both of the other two statements. For example, the funds statement helps the reader answer questions, such as Where did the earnings go? Why were dividends not larger? How can dividends be distributed in excess of current earnings, or when there was a reported loss? Why are current assets decreasing when the results of operations are positive? How was the plant expansion financed? and What use was made of the proceeds from the sale of shares?

By helping to answer questions such as these, the statement of changes in financial position serves an important function. Its purposes and the techniques used in its preparation are discussed more fully in Chapter 20. An illustration of a simple funds statement, presented on a working capital basis, is provided at the top of the following page.

---

[18]Illustrative financial statements complete with applicable notes are provided in Appendix A of this textbook.

Andersen Corporation
Statement of Changes in Financial Position — Working Capital Basis
For Year Ended December 31, 1981

Working capital was provided by:			
Operations:			
Income before extraordinary items		$25,000	
Add items not requiring working capital:			
Depreciation	$10,000		
Amortization of patents and goodwill	10,600	20,600	
Working capital provided by operations		$45,600	
Issuance of bonds		95,000	
Issuance of common shares to acquire land		70,000	$210,600
Working capital was applied to:			
Dividends		$20,000	
Retirement of long-term debt		80,000	
Acquisition of land by issuance of common shares		70,000	170,000
Increase in working capital*			$40,600

*Details of increase in working capital are not given. The above figures are illustrative only. They cannot be derived from the financial statements presented because comparative statements are not provided.

QUESTIONS

1. Which accounting statements are considered general purpose financial statements?

2. What is the composition of the balance sheet? How is it related to the income statement and the statement of changes in financial position?

3. What is the balance sheet equation? Define each of the elements of that equation.

4. Why is the distinction between current and non-current assets and liabilities so important?

5. What criteria would you use (a) in classifying assets as current or non-current? (b) in classifying liabilities as current or non-current?

6. (a) Give examples of expense prepayments properly reported as (1) current items and (2) non-current items. What factors govern in the determination of the appropriate classification? (b) Give examples of unearned revenues properly reported as (1) current items and (2) non-current items. What factors govern here?

7. Farnley's Ltd. reports the cash surrender value of life insurance on company officials as a current asset in view of its immediate convertibility into cash. Do you support this treatment?

8. Indicate under what circumstances each of the following can be considered non-current: (a) cash, (b) receivables, (c) inventories, (d) collections received in advance of the delivery of goods.

9. Under what circumstances may bonds payable in six months be reported as a long-term liability, even though they will not be liquidated from accumulated non-current funds?

10. What objections can be made to the use of the heading "Deferred costs?"

11. What justification is there for treating intangible items as assets on the balance sheet?

12. Why should a premium or discount on bonded indebtedness be reported as an addition to or subtraction from the face value of the bond liability?

13. Give an example of (a) a contingent asset and (b) a contingent liability.

14. Distinguish between the following: (a) contingent liabilites and estimated liabilites, (b) appropriated retained earnings and free retained earnings.

15. What are the major classifications of (a) assets, (b) liabilities, and (c) owners' equity items? Indicate the nature of the items reported within each major classification.

16. Under what circumstances may offset balances be properly recognized on the balance sheet?

17. (a) What objections are raised to the use of the terms (1) reserve, (2) net worth, and (3) surplus? (b) What suggestions have been made with respect to these terms in attempts to improve financial reporting?

18. What information is emphasized by use of the financial position form of the balance sheet?

19. Indicate those balance sheet items that may require the disclosure of significant accounting policies or other parenthetical remarks or notes if the reader of the statement is to be adequately informed.

20. What is the basic purpose of the statement of changes in financial position? What kind of information does this statement provide that is not readily available from the other general purpose statements?

3-1. A balance sheet contains the following classifications: **EXERCISES**

(a) Current assets	(g) Long-term liabilities
(b) Long-term investments	(h) Deferred revenues
(c) Land, buildings, and equipment	(i) Capital share
(d) Intangible assets	(j) Contributed surplus
(e) Other long-term assets	(k) Retained earnings
(f) Current liabilities	

Indicate by letter how each of the following accounts would be classified. Place a minus sign (−) after all accounts representing offset or contra balances.

    ____ (1) Discount on Bonds Payable   ____ (3) 7% Bonds Payable (due in six
    ____ (2) Shares of Subsidiary Corporation   months)

_____ (4) Government Treasury Notes
_____ (5) Income Tax Payable
_____ (6) Sales Tax Payable
_____ (7) Estimated Claims Under Guarantees for Service and Replacements
_____ (8) Accounts Payable (debit balance)
_____ (9) Unearned Rental Revenue (three years in advance)
_____ (10) Accumulated Depletion

_____ (11) Interest Receivable
_____ (12) Preferred Shares Retirement Fund
_____ (13) Trademarks
_____ (14) Allowance for Doubtful Accounts
_____ (15) Dividends Payable
_____ (16) Accumulated Depreciation
_____ (17) Petty Cash Fund
_____ (18) Prepaid Rent
_____ (19) Prepaid Interest
_____ (20) Organization Costs

3-2. State how each of the following accounts should be classified on the balance sheet.

(a) Accumulated Patent Amortization
(b) Retained Earnings
(c) Vacation Pay
(d) Retained Earnings Appropriated for Loss Contingencies
(e) Allowance for Doubtful Accounts
(f) Liability for Pension Payments
(g) Marketable Securities
(h) Premium from Sale of Shares at More Than Par Value
(i) Unamortized Bond Issue Costs
(j) Goodwill
(k) Receivables — Government Contracts
(l) Advances to Salespersons
(m) Customers Accounts with Credit Balances

(n) Raw Materials
(o) Cash Representing Refundable Deposits on Returnable Containers
(p) Unclaimed Payroll Cheques
(q) Employees Income Tax Payable
(r) Subscription Revenue Received in Advance
(s) Interest Payable
(t) Deferred Income Tax (debit balance)
(u) Tools
(v) Deferred Income Tax (credit balance)
(w) Loans to Officers
(x) Leasehold Improvements
(y) Patents

3-3. Indicate how each of the following items should be classified on the balance sheet:

(a) Cash surrender value of life insurance.
(b) Sinking fund cash for retirement of bonds.
(c) Bonds payable in six months out of sinking fund cash.
(d) Note receivable that will be collected in 10 annual instalments.
(e) Cash deposited with broker on option to buy real estate.
(f) Land held as future plant site.
(g) Warehouse in process of construction.
(h) Cash fund representing customers' deposits on returnable containers.
(i) Cash fund representing sales tax collections.
(j) Goods in process that will require more than one year for completion.

3-4. The bookkeeper for Can-Co Ltd., submitted the following balance sheet as of Dec. 31, 1981.

Can-Co Ltd.
Balance Sheet
December 31, 1981

Cash	$ 15,000	Accounts payable — trade	$ 25,000
Accounts receivable — trade	25,000	Salaries payable	10,000
Inventories	40,000	Shareholders' equity	70,000
Machinery	10,000		
Goodwill	15,000		
	$105,000		$105,000

Reference to the records of the company indicated the following:

(a) Cash included:

Petty Cash	$ 500
Payroll account	5,000
Savings account for cash to be used for building remodeling	5,000
General account	4,500
	$15,000

(b) Municipal taxes of $1,200 were accrued on December 31. However, $1,200 had been deposited in a special cash account to be used to pay these and neither cash nor the accrued taxes were reported on the balance sheet.

(c) Twenty-five per cent of Can-Co Ltd.'s inventory is rapidly becoming obsolete. The obsolete portion of the inventory as of the balance sheet date was worth only one half of what Can-Co. Ltd. paid for it.

(d) Goods costing $1,500 were shipped to customers on December 30 and 31, at a sales price of $2,200. Goods shipped were not included in the inventory as of December 31. However, receivables were not recognized for the shipment since invoices were not sent out until January 3.

(e) One of Can-Co Ltd.'s machines costing $4,000 is located on the Autonomous Island Republic, Tropicana. The dictator of Tropicana nationalized several foreign businesses during 1981 and is threatening to expropriate Can-Co Ltd.'s machinery for personal use. All machinery was acquired in July of 1981 and will not be depreciated this year.

(f) The corporation had been organized on January 1, 1981, by exchanging 5,500 shares of stock with a par value of $10 per share for the net assets of the partnership Canfield and Collins.   *55,000 Par*

Prepare a corrected balance sheet as of December 31, 1981.

3-5. From the following chart of accounts, prepare a balance sheet in account form showing all balance sheet items properly classified. (No monetary amounts are to be recognized.)

Accounts Payable
Accounts Receivable
Accumulated Depreciation — Building
Accumulated Depreciation — Equipment
Advertising Expense
Allowance for Decline in Value of Market- able Securities
Allowance for Doubtful Accounts
Bond Fund
Bonds Payable
Buildings
Cash in Bank
Cash on Hand
Common Shares
Contributed Surplus Capital from Sale of Common Shares at More Than Stated Value

Contributed Surplus Capital from Sale of Treasury Shares
Cost of Goods Sold
Deferred Income Tax
Depreciation Expense — Buildings
Dividends
Dividends Payable
Doubtful Accounts Expense
Equipment
Estimated Warranty Expense Payable
Gain on Sale of Land
Gain on Sale of Marketable Securities
Goodwill
Income Summary
Income Tax
Income Tax Payable
Interest Receivable

Interest Revenue
Inventory
Investment in Bonds
Land
Land Improvements
Leasehold Improvements
Loss on Purchase Commitments
Marketable Securities
Miscellaneous General Expense
Notes Payable
Notes Receivable
Notes Receivable Discounted
Patents
Payroll Taxes Payable
Pension Fund

Petty Cash
Premium on Bonds Payable
Prepaid Insurance
Prepaid Taxes
Property Tax
Purchases
Purchase Discounts
Retained Earnings
Retained Earnings Appropriated for Loss
    Contingencies
Salaries Payable
Sales
Sales Salaries
Travel Expense

PROBLEMS

3-1A. Kennedy Realty Ltd., a dealer in land, is searching for funds for a long-term expansion program. Kennedy must maintain a working capital balance of $4,000,000 to be in a favorable position for borrowing. The post-closing trial balance as of December 31, 1981, is as follows:

Accounts Payable — Trade		1,226,000
Accounts Receivable	5,232,000	
Accumulated Depreciation — Office Buildings		8,000,000
Advances to Affiliates	550,000	
Allowance for Doubtful Accounts		63,000
Bonds (payable in instalments of $500,000 on June 1 of each year)		7,500,000
Cash Surrender Value of Life Insurance	15,000	
Common Shares, $10 par		5,000,000
Contributed Surplus		7,500,000
Deferred Income Tax Payable		750,000
First Canada Bank Fund for Construction of Office Building	800,000	
First Canada Bank — General Account	622,000	
Income Tax Payable		485,000
Land	14,000,000	
Loans on Life Insurance Policies		10,000
Marketable Securities	3,000,000	
Notes Payable to Bank		2,000,000
Office Building	12,000,000	
Office Supplies	75,000	
Organization Costs	2,000	
Prepaid Insurance	25,000	
Retained Earnings		2,087,000
Retained Earnings Appropriated for Loss Contingencies		500,000
Salaries and Wages Payable		150,000
Unearned Lease Revenue		50,000

Additional investigation revealed:

(a) Accounts receivable consists of:

Due in six months from vice-president of finance	$ 232,000
Employee advances — long-term	500,000
Due in 1983 from sale of old office building	1,250,000
Instalment notes receivable — trade	2,500,000
Accounts receivable — trade	650,000
Dividends receivable	100,000
	$5,232,000

(b) Land includes several parcels purchased for $5,000,000, which have become subject to severe flooding, thus lowering the value to $250,000. All the land is for sale except the $5,300,000 site for Kennedy's new office building.

(c) Kennedy purchased 25% of the voting shares of a savings and loan company for $2,500,000 and included the acquisition in marketable securities.

(d) Kennedy received $50,000 in advance for next year's lease payments by tenants of Kennedy's office building.

(e) The loans on the life insurance policies come due in 18 months; the bank notes fall due in 8 months.

Instructions:

Show whether Kennedy Realty Ltd. is in a favorable position for borrowing money by preparing the first portion of a balance sheet in financial position form: current assets less current liabilities equal working capital. Because of the nature of the business, land for sale is considered inventory.

3-2A. Below is a list of account titles and balances for the Compiano Sales Corp. as of March 31, 1981.

Accounts Payable	$ 42,900	Investment in Shares of Subsidiary Company	$125,000
Accounts Receivable	53,000		
Accumulated Depreciation—		Investment in Undeveloped	
Buildings	70,000	Properties	106,000
Accumulated Depreciation —		Land	65,000
Machinery and Equipment	20,000	Machinery and Equipment	72,000
Advances from Customers on		Misc. Supplies Inventories	3,100
Contracts in Progress	6,500	Notes Payable (current)	34,630
Allowance for Doubtful Notes		Notes Payable (due 1986)	25,000
and Accounts	2,100	Notes Receivable	11,200
Buildings	150,000	Preferred Shares, $5 par	150,000
Cash in Banks	53,650	Premium on Common Shares ...	30,000
Cash on Hand	4,440	Prepaid Insurance	2,250
Cash Surrender Value of Life		Property Tax Payable	2,100
Insurance	8,500	Raw Materials	16,900
Claim for Income Tax Refund ...	2,500	Retained Earnings (debit balance)	63,470
Common Shares, $20 par	300,000		
Employees Income Tax Payable .	1,820	Salaries and Wages Payable	3,700
Finished Goods	21,000	8% Serial Bonds Payable (due	
Franchises	21,000	March 1, 1982)	50,000
Work in Process	39,400	8% Serial Bonds Payable (due	
Income Tax Payable	12,300	in 1983 and thereafter)	150,000
Interest Payable	1,000	Temporary Investments in Marketable Securities	78,440
Interest Receivable	200		
		Tools	5,000

Instructions:
Prepare a properly classified balance sheet.

3-3A. Account balances and supplemental information for the Padden Corporation, as of December 31, 1981, are given below:

Accounts Payable	$ 32,160	Furniture, Fixtures, and Store	
Accounts Receivable — Trade	57,731	Equipment	$769,000
Accumulated Depreciation —		Inventory	201,620
Leasehold Improvements and		Investment in Unconsolidated	
Equipment	579,472	Subsidiary	80,000
Allowance for Doubtful Accounts	1,731	Insurance Claims Receivable	120,000
Automotive Equipment	132,800	Land	6,000
Cash	30,600	Leasehold Improvements	65,800
Cash Surrender Value of Life		5¹/₂-10% Mortgage Notes	200,000
Insurance	3,600	Notes Payable — Banks	17,000
Common Shares	200,000	Notes Payable — Trade	63,540
Contributed Surplus	100,000	Patent Licences	57,402
Deferred Income Tax	45,000	Prepaid Insurance	5,500
Dividends Payable	37,500	Profit Sharing, Payroll and Vaca-	
Franchises	12,150	tion Payable	40,000
		Retained Earnings	225,800

Supplemental information:

(a) Depreciation is provided by the straight-line method over the estimated useful lives of the assets.

(b) Common stock is $5 par, and 40,000 of the 100,000 authorized shares were issued and are outstanding.

(c) The cost of an exclusive franchise to import a foreign company's ball bearings and a related patent licence are being amortized on the straight-line method over their remaining lives: franchise, 10 years; patents, 15 years.

(d) Inventories are stated at the lower of cost or market: cost was determined by the specific identification method.

(e) Insurance claims based upon the opinion of an independent insurance adjustor are for property damages at the central warehouse. These claims are estimated to be one-half collectible in the following year and one-half collectible thereafter.

(f) The company leases all of its buildings from various lessors. Estimated fixed lease obligations are $50,000 per year for the next ten years.

(g) The company is currently in litigation over a claimed overpayment of income tax of $13,000. In the opinion of counsel, the claim is valid. The company is contingently liable on guaranteed notes worth $17,000.

Instructions:
Prepare a properly classified balance sheet in account form. Include all notes and parenthetical notations necessary to properly disclose the essential financial data.

3-4A. The following balance sheet was prepared by the accountant for Canada Fabrics Ltd.

Canada Fabrics Ltd.
Balance Sheet
June 30, 1981

Assets

Cash	$ 25,500
Marketable securities (includes 25% ownership of shares of Town Textiles Ltd., at	
cost of $250,000)	332,000
Inventories (net of amount still due suppliers of $75,980)	624,600
Prepaid expenses (includes a deposit of $10,000 made on inventories to be	
delivered in 18 months)	32,100
Fixed assets (excluding $50,000 of equipment still in use, but fully depreciated)	220,000
Goodwill (based upon estimate of President of Canada Fabrics Ltd.)	100,000
Total assets	$1,334,200

Liabilities and Shareholders' Equity

Notes payable ($75,000 due in 1983)	$ 135,000
Accounts payable (not including amount due to suppliers of inventory — see above) .	142,000
Long-term liability under pension plan	80,000
Reserve for building expansion	75,000
Reserve for depreciation — fixed assets	73,000
Taxes payable	44,500
Bonds payable (net of discount of $30,000)	270,000
Reserve for deferred income tax	83,000
Common stock (25,000 shares @ $10 par)	250,000
Premium on common shares	50,500
Reserve for loss contingencies	15,000
Retained earnings — unappropriated	116,200
Total liabilities and shareholders' equity	$1,334,200

Instructions:
Prepare a corrected statement in good form using account titles that meet the accounting standards of the profession in Canada.

3-5A. Ranchero Limited summarizes its financial position in the following letter to their accountant.

January 20, 1982

Dear Harold:

The following information should be of value to you in preparing the balance sheet for Ranchero Limited as of December 31, 1981. The balance of cash as of December 31 as reported on the bank statement was $43,825. There were still outstanding cheques of $9,320 that had not cleared the bank and cash on hand of $3,640 was not deposited until January 4, 1982.

Customers owed the company $40,500 at December 31. We estimated 5% of this amount will never be collected. We owe suppliers $32,000 for poultry feed purchased in November and December. About 80% of this feed was used before December 31.

Because we think the price of grain will rise in 1982, we are holding 10,000 bushels of wheat and 5,000 bushels of oats until spring. The market value at December 31 was $3.50 per bushel of wheat and $1.50 per bushel of oats. We estimate that both prices will increase 10% by selling time. We are not able to estimate the cost of raising this product.

Ranchero Limited owns 1,850 acres of land. Two separate purchases of land were made as follows: 1,250 acres at $200 per acre in 1963, and 600 acres at $400 per acre in 1969. Similar land is currently selling for $800 per acre. The balance of the mortgage on the two parcels of land is $270,000 at December 31; 10% of this mortgage must be paid in 1982.

Our farm buildings and equipment cost us $176,400 and on the average are 50% depreciated. If we were to replace these buildings and equipment at today's prices, we believe we would be conservative in estimating a cost of $300,000.

We have not paid property tax of $5,500 for 1982 billed us in late November. Our estimated income tax for 1981 is $18,500. A refund claim for $2,800 has been filed relative to the 1979 income tax return. The claim arose because of an error made on the 1979 return.

The operator of the ranch will receive a bonus of $7,000 for 1981 operations. It will be paid when the entire grain crop has been sold.

As you will recall, we issued 14,000 shares of $10 par stock upon incorporation. The ranch received $255,000 as net proceeds from the stock issue. Dividends of $45,000 were declared last month and will be paid on February 1, 1982.

The new year appears to hold great promise. Thanks for your help in preparing this statement.

Sincerely

Alice Mahle
President — Ranchero Limited

Instructions:

Based upon this information, prepare a properly classified balance sheet as of December 31, 1981.

3-6A. The bookkeeper for the Toni Corporation prepares the following condensed balance sheet.

Toni Corporation
Balance Sheet
December 31, 1981

Current assets	$116,830
Less current liabilities	68,000
Working capital	$ 48,830
Add other assets	120,880
	$169,710
Deduct other liabilities	7,200
Investment in business	$162,510

A review of the account balances disclosed the data listed below:

(a) An analysis of the current asset grouping revealed the following:

Cash	$ 19,200
Trade accounts receivable (fully collectible)	25,000
Notes receivable (notes of customer who has been declared bankrupt and is unable to pay anything on the obligations)	2,000
Marketable securities, at cost (market value, $5,150)	8,500
Inventory	57,930
Cash surrender value of insurance on officers' lives	4,200
Total current assets	$116,830

The inventory account was found to include the cost of supplies of $850, a delivery truck acquired at the end of 1981 at a cost of $4,200, and fixtures at a depreciated value of $20,800. The fixtures had been acquired in 1978 at a cost of $25,000.

(b) The total for other assets was determined as follows:

Land and buildings, at cost of acquisition on July 1, 1979	$154,000
Less balance due on mortgage, $32,000, and accrued interest on mortgage, $1,120 (mortgage is payable in annual instalments of $8,000 on July 1 of each year together with interest for the year at that time at 7%	33,120
Total other assets	$120,880

It was estimated that the land, at the time of purchase, was worth $60,000. Buildings as of December 31, 1981 were estimated to have a remaining life of $17\frac{1}{2}$ years.

(c) Current liabilities represented balances that were payable to trade creditors. Other liabilities consisted of withholding, payroll, real estate, and other taxes payable to the governments. However, no recognition was given to the accrued salaries, utilities, and other miscellaneous items totalling $700.

(d) The company was originally organized in 1977 when 10,000 shares of stock with a par value of $5 per share were issued in exchange for business assets that were recognized on the books at their fair market value of $110,000.

Instructions:
Prepare a corrected balance sheet in financial position form with the items properly classified.

3-7A. The bookkeeper for the Maple Corporation submits the following condensed balance sheet.

Maple Corporation
Balance Sheet
June 30, 1981

Current assets	$252,150	Current liabilities	$136,550
Other assets	638,400	Other liabilities	90,000
		Capital	664,000
	$890,550		$890,550

A review of the account balances reveals the data listed below and on page 112.

(a) An analysis of current assets discloses the following:

Cash	$ 49,250
Marketable securities held as temporary investment	60,000
Trade accounts receivable	57,400
Inventories, including advertising supplies of $2,500	85,500
	$252,150

(b) Other assets include:

Land, buildings, and equipment, cost $665,000, depreciated value	$549,000
Deposit with a supplier for merchandise ordered for August delivery	2,000
Goodwill recorded on the books to cancel losses incurred by the company in prior years	87,400
	$638,400

(c) Current liabilities include:

Payrolls payable	$ 7,650
Taxes payable	4,000
Rent payable..	12,000
Trade accounts payable, $90,400, less a $1,500 debit balance reported in the account of a vendor to whom merchandise had been returned after the account had been paid in full	88,900
Notes payable	24,000
	$136,550

(d) Other liabilities include:

9% mortgage on land, buildings and equipment, payable in semi-annual instalments of $9,000 through June 30, 1986	$ 90,000

(e) Capital includes:

20,000 shares of preferred stock, $20 par	$400,000
160,000 shares of common stock	264,000
	$664,000

(f) Common shares were originally issued for a total consideration of $400,000, but the losses of the company for past years were charged against the common stock balance.

Instructions:
Using the balance sheet and the related data, prepare a corrected balance sheet in report form showing individual asset, liability, and capital balances properly classified.

√ **3-8A.** The balance sheet below is submitted to you for inspection and review.

Baylor Corporation
Balance Sheet
December 31, 1981

Assets		Liabilities and Shareholders' Equity	
Cash	$ 50,000	Miscellaneous liabilities	$ 2,500
Accounts receivable	180,000	Loan payable	56,250
Inventories	220,000	Accounts payable	146,250
Prepaid insurance	12,500	Capital share	250,000
Land, buildings, and equipment	325,000	Contributed surplus	332,500
	$787,500		$787,500

In the course of the review you find the data listed below:

(a) The possibility of uncollectible accounts on accounts receivable has not been considered. It is estimated that uncollectible accounts will total $5,000.

(b) $50,000 representing the cost of a large-scale newspaper advertising campaign completed in 1981 has been added to the inventories, since it is believed that this campaign will benefit sales of 1982. It is also found that inventories include merchandise of $16,250 received on December 31 that has not yet been recorded as a purchase.

(c) Prepaid insurance consists of $1,000, the cost of fire insurance for 1982, and $11,500, the cash surrender value on officers' life insurance policies.

(d) The accounts show that land, buildings, and equipment have a cost of $525,000 with depreciation of $200,000 recognized in prior years. However, these balances include fully depreciated equipment of $75,000 that has been scrapped and is no longer on hand.

(e) Miscellaneous liabilities of $2,500 represent salaries payable of $7,500, less non-current advances of $5,000 made to company officials.

(f) Loan payable represents a loan from the bank that is payable in regular quarterly instalments of $6,250.

(g) Tax liabilities shown are estimated at $11,250.

(h) Deferred income tax credit arising from timing differences in recognizing income totals $23,750. This tax was not included on the balance sheet.

(i) Capital Share consists of 6,250 shares of preferred 6% stock, par $20, and 12,500 shares of common stock, par value $10.

(j) Capital Share had been issued for a total consideration of $312,500, the amount received in excess of the par value of the shares being reported as contributed surplus.

Instructions:
Prepare a corrected balance sheet in report form with accounts properly classified.

3-9A. George Jenkins incorporated his cement manufacturing operations on January 1, 1981, by issuing 10,000 shares of $10 par common stock to himself. The following balance sheet for the new corporation was prepared.

Cement Corporation
Balance Sheet
January 1, 1981

Cash	$ 10,000	Accounts payable — suppliers .	$ 45,000
Accounts receivable	45,000	Capital Share, $10 par	100,000
Inventory	75,000	Premium on Capital Share	100,000
Equipment	115,000		
	$245,000		$245,000

During 1977, Cement Corporation engaged in the following transactions:

(a) Cement Corporation produced cement costing $270,000. Cement costs consisted of $200,000, raw materials purchases; $25,000, labor; and $45,000, overhead. Cement Corporation paid the $45,000 owed to suppliers as of January 1, and $130,000 on the $200,000 of raw materials purchased during the year. All labor, except for $1,500, and recorded overhead were paid for in cash during the year. Other operating expenses of $15,000 were incurred and paid in 1981.

(b) Cement costing $300,000 was sold during 1981 for $425,000. All sales were made on credit, and collections on receivables were $365,000.

(c) Cement Corporation purchased machinery (fair market value = $190,000) by trading in old equipment costing $50,000 and paying $140,000 in cash. There is no accumulated depreciation on the old equipment as it was revalued when the new corporation was formed.

(d) Cement Corporation issued an additional 4,000 shares of common stock for $25 per share and declared a dividend of $4 per share to all shareholders of record as of December 31, 1981, payable on January 15, 1982.

(e) Depreciation expense for 1981 was $27,000. The allowance for doubtful accounts after year-end adjustments is $2,500.

Instructions:

Prepare a properly classified balance sheet in report form for the Cement Corporation as of December 31, 1981.

4 FINANCIAL STATEMENTS — THE INCOME STATEMENT

The *income statement*, also variously called the *earnings statement*, the *statement of profit and loss*, and the *statement of operations*, summarizes business activities for a given period and reports the resulting net income or loss for the period covered by the statement. The close relationship between the income statement, balance sheet, and statement of changes in financial position should be recognized. For example, a change in valuation of marketable securities on the balance sheet will alter reported net income, and the amount of income from operations is a major item on the statement of changes in financial position. The importance of measuring and reporting income, as well as the nature and the content of the income statement, is described in the following sections.

IMPORTANCE OF MEASURING AND REPORTING INCOME

The measuring and reporting of business income has acquired steadily increasing importance and, at present, accountants generally regard this as one of their most important responsiblities.[1] Reference is made to the income statement by many different groups who need to evaluate the results of

---

[1]For example, APB Statement No. 4 states: "The information presented in an income statement is usually considered the most important information provided by financial accounting because profitability is a paramount concern to those interested in the economic activities of the enterprise." *Statements of the Accounting Principles Board, No. 4*, "Basic Concepts and Accounting Principles Underlying Financial Statements of Business Enterprises" (New York: American Institute of Certified Public Accountants, 1970), par. 12.

business activities. Reference is also made to this statement by those who desire to determine the value of a business entity, for it is earnings which ultimately validate asset values. Proper measurement of income helps capital flow to the most profitable and presumably the most efficient enterprises, thus providing for the optimal allocation of scarce economic resources.

The measurement of income has presented many problems to accountants because of the absence of a precise definition for *income*, and because of the need to exercise judgment on a great many matters in arriving at such measurement. Thus, considerable research has been directed toward the matter of *income measurement*.

A number of factors have contributed to the importance of the income statement. Primary factors have been the income tax laws, the absentee ownership of corporations, and the increased internal use of accounting information.

Income Tax Laws

In Canada, federal taxes on income were first introduced as a temporary war measure in 1917. The existence of provincial income taxes preceded the federal levies, however, at rates that were modest. Particularly since the end of World War II, taxes on income at both federal and provincial levels have become increasingly significant. This has emphasized the need for every business entity to establish a system for the measurement of income. Moreover, income tax laws have become increasingly specific as to what constitutes income for tax purposes. In the majority of cases these laws follow practices currently being applied by accountants in preparing general purpose financial statements. However, differences between tax laws and established accounting practices exist, in part because of the important role of taxation in the fiscal policy of governments. While tax laws have influenced the development of accounting principles, serious questions can be raised when income tax methods become accepted for financial accounting purposes.

Absentee Ownership of Corporations

The growth of the corporate form of ownership has created a large group of absentee owners. There are millions of shareholders of corporations, most of whom have very little contact with the operations of the companies in which they have holdings except through the published reports they receive periodically. Although they can attend annual shareholders' meetings, very few of them actually do. The shareholders regard their involvement as a financial one and evaluate their investment in comparison with other financial alternatives. Because of these conditions, the average shareholder requires financial data to assist in the evaluation of investments. Both the income before extraordinary items and the net income amounts, as well as related income or earnings per share data, are widely reported in newspapers and financial services. Although there is much theorizing among observers of the stock market as to the degree to which the market value of shares is affected by periodic reports of earnings, it is clear that the shareholder is interested and does pay close attention to this measure of profitability. Stockbrokers often refer to the relationship between share prices and current earnings (price/earnings ratio) and use the multiple of price times earnings to reflect the profitability and growth potential of the entity.

Increased Internal Use of Accounting Information

Not only has there been increased interest in the income statement by outside users, but the same can also be said for the primary internal user — management. Years ago, proprietors often could acquire an intuitive feel as to how well things were going in an enterprise; but, today, in most situations, the complexity of modern business makes this impossible. Managements of large and growing corporate enterprises, dealing in many different product areas, need to have profitability information to answer questions relating to past, present, and projected programs. Questions arise such as: How effective was our past advertising policy? Should we make or buy certain component parts for our end-line products? Should we add to our product line? Information systems within the enterprise must be prepared to answer these and related questions and often do so in the context of some version of an income report.

NATURE OF INCOME

With the increasing attention being given to reporting the results of operations, it is only natural that certain questions have been raised: What purpose should the measurement of income serve in our economy? How can it best serve this purpose? Is our function limited to that of a historian reporting on the past? Or are we trying to provide the best guide for estimating future earning power?[2] All of these questions are appropriate ones; however, all of the answers may not be provided by the same income statement. Some of the purposes, perhaps, are being satisfied better by present accounting methods than others. Before examining the concepts underlying

---

[2]As indicated in Chapter 1, the general objectives of financial accounting that were enumerated by the APB in Statement No. 4 include both of these general concepts. Objective 2 emphasizes the provision of reliable information about changes in net resources that result from profit-directed activities, and objective 3 emphasizes the provision of financial information that assists in estimating the earning potential of the enterprise. *Ibid.*, par. 78 and 79. More recently, the *Report of the Study Group on the Objectives of Financial Statements* has been published by the AICPA. It states "an objective of financial statements is to provide users with information for predicting, comparing, and evaluating enterprise earning power." *Report of the Study Group on the Objectives of Financial Statements* (New York: American Institute of Certified Public Accountants, October, 1973).

present income measurement and reporting, some of the other concepts suggested by accounting and economic literature deserve attention.

It should also be noted that the amount of net income can be determined by an analysis of the change in owners' equity between successive balance sheet dates. Under the conventional accounting model or GAAP, net income can be determined by use of the following equation where OE^E is owners' equity at end of period, OE^B is owners' equity at beginning of period, I is additional investment during the period, if any, and D is dividends declared, if any.

Net Income = $OE^E - OE^B - I + D$

The income statement provides a detailed report of the revenues, gains, expenses, and losses including extraordinary items, if any, that result in the period's net income. Its amount, but not its detail, can be obtained from the above equation.

The Valuation (Indirect) Method of Income Determination

As suggested earlier, a business entity commences activities in the attempt to increase its net assets through profitable operations. This increase in net assets is referred to by many economists as a change in the *well-offness* of the entity, alternately referred to as the *income* of the firm. This is indeed an appealing concept. It suggests, as noted above, that one way to determine income is to value the net assets of an entity at two different points in time and compute the change that has occurred. If the change is positive after adjustment for any investment or withdrawal of assets by the owners, there has been *income*. If the change is negative, there has been a *loss*. Because income is determined by comparing net assets at two different dates, this method is referred to as the *asset-liability viewpoint, valuation method*, or *indirect method*. It is obviously dependent upon the methods used to value net assets or simply on the asset valuation rule. Under GAAP, the asset valuation rule, with occasional exceptions, relies on historic cost valuations.

The asset-liability viewpoint is most commonly used by economists in their discussion of income. One of the most quoted economists in accounting literature, J. R. Hicks, defined income as the maximum value which an entity can distribute during a period and still expect to be as well-off.[3] Although the measurement of net assets is accepted as the key indicator, it is necessary to arrive at a precise definition of the meaning of *value of net assets*. Is it the historical cost of the net assets reduced by some amount for their use? Is it the current value of the net assets determined by replacement or market values? Is it the historical cost of the net assets adjusted for the change in price levels since original acquisitions? All of these, as well as other concepts,

---

[3]J. R. Hicks, *Value and Capital* (2d ed.; Oxford University Press, 1946).

may be regarded as satisfying the general term, value of net assets. Another question that must be resolved is what is to be included in net assets. Should intangible items, such as goodwill, patents, and leaseholds be included in assets? Should human resources be reported as an asset? Should estimated payments relating to warranties and pensions be included in liabilites?

For many years economists, and recently some accountants, have approached these difficult questions by attempting to define net assets in terms of the present value of the cash benefits that net assets are expected to provide. These parties maintain that we should arrive at *future cash flows* in amount and time, and with the use of appropriate discount rates determine the present worth of these streams of future benefits. Net assets as thus computed can be compared as of different time intervals in arriving at income.

Although this concept has theoretical merit, it has had minor influence upon practice primarily because of the measurement problems involved. These measurement problems encompass both the amounts and timing of future cash flows. We live in an uncertain world with limited knowledge of future cash flows. Expectations as to these future flows vary among those individuals with an interest in the company. Also, with limited knowledge of the future, what should be accepted as the appropriate discount rates to apply to cash flows in arriving at asset values? Because of these uncertainties the accountant has turned to more direct ways of defining income.

The Matching (Direct) Method of Income Determination

The method of income determination that has proved most acceptable to the accountant has been the *revenue-expense viewpoint*, the *matching method*, or *direct method*. This method involves the determination of the amount of revenue earned by an entity during a given period and the amount of expired costs applicable to that revenue. The difference between these two items is recognized as *net income*. If users were willing to wait until the end of the life of a business entity for the full results of its operations, it would be an easy matter to compute the total revenue and total expense of the business and the resulting net income or loss. However, users of income statements, seeking to judge the progress of an entity, need periodic measurements of business profitability. In fact, users seem increasingly interested in receiving financial statements more frequently than at the traditional annual intervals. To satisfy the need, interim statements are also required of most large companies. Thus, the element of timing, both for revenue and expense, becomes ever more significant. Rather than concentrating on asset valuations, the centre of attention is thus transferred to a discussion of *revenue realization* and *expense recognition*. It should be recognized, however, that because the financial statements are fundamentally interrelated, the point in time at which revenues and expenses are recognized is also the time when changes in amounts of net assets are recognized.[4]

Nature of Revenues

The Accounting Principles Board has defined *revenues* as follows:

> . . . gross increases in assets or gross decreases in liabilities recognized and measured in conformity with generally accepted accounting principles that result from those types of profit-directed activities of an enterprise that can change owners' equity[5]

Similarly, the Financial Accounting Standards Board in Statement of Financial Accounting Concepts No. 3 defines revenues as:

> . . . inflows or other enhancements of assets of an entity or settlements of its liabilities (or a combination of both) during a period from delivering or producing goods, rendering services or other activities that constitute the entity's ongoing major or central operations[6]

Generally, revenues are derived from three main activities:

1. Selling products.
2. Rendering services and permitting others to use enterprise resources, which result in interest, rent, royalties, fees, and the like.
3. Disposing of resources other than products — for example, plant and equipment or investments in other entities[7]

Revenues do not include assets acquired by purchase, proceeds from borrowing, investments by owners, or adjustments of revenue of prior periods.

Although this description of revenue defines the activities that produce revenue, it does not specify the time period in which revenue should be recorded and recognized in the income statement. A general realization rule has evolved stating that revenue should be recorded when two conditions are met: (1) the earnings process is complete or virtually so; and (2) an exchange transaction has taken place. These criteria have led to the conventional recognition of revenue at a specific point in the earnings process — when assets are sold or services are rendered[8] However, some accountants would argue that an exchange does not necessarily have to occur for recognition of revenue. What is critical is that objective measurement is possible, whether or not an exchange has taken place, in addition to the earning process being substantially complete. There are sufficient deviations from the general rule to justify a closer look into the nature of revenue.

---

[4]This interrelatedness is recognized and described in *Statements of the Accounting Principles Board, No. 4, op. cit.*, par. 136 and 147.

[5]*Ibid.*, par. 134.

[6]*Statement of Financial Accounting Concepts No. 3*, "Elements of Financial Statements of Business Enterprises" (Stamford, Conn.: Financial Accounting Standards Board, 1980), par. 63.

[7]*Statements of the Accounting Principles Board, No. 4, op. cit.*, par. 134 and 148.

[8]*Ibid.*, par. 150 and 151.

The first type of activity described as producing revenue is the sale of products. The cycle of revenue-producing goods as they pass through an entity can be a long one. The beginning point is not well defined, but assume it begins with the development of proposals for a certain product by an individual or by the research and development department of a business entity. From the idea stage, the future product is carefully described in plans and engineering specifications. Bills of material are prepared, a production schedule is agreed upon, and raw materials are ordered, delivered, and placed into production. Labor and factory overhead are added to the raw materials as the product proceeds through the manufacturing process. Once completed, the product is transferred to finished goods inventory. The product is listed in company catalogues, it is promoted in advertising campaigns, and it moves through the company's distribution system to the final sale. Frequently sales are on a credit basis, and, after a period of time, collections are made on the accounts. The product may be sold with a warranty for necessary repairs or replacements. The cycle thus extends from the original idea to the end of the warranty period. All these steps are involved in the realization of the sales revenue. If there is a failure at any step, revenue may be seriously curtailed or possibly completely eliminated. And yet, there is only one aggregate revenue amount for the entire cycle, the sale price of the goods. The question then is: When should revenue by recognized?

Answers to the question of when revenue should be recognized can be divided into two broad categories: (1) at one specific point in the cycle, or (2) at two or more points in the cycle.[9] The prevailing practice provides for recognition of revenue at one specific point in the cycle. Of course, determining the specific point presents a problem. Applying the previously mentioned guidelines, revenue from sale of products is recognized at the *point of sale*, usually interpreted to mean the time of delivery to customers. It is felt that prior to the sale, there has not been an arm's-length transaction to establish the market value of the goods. This makes any objective measure of revenue subject to dispute. In addition, most accountants feel that the critical event is the sale of an item, and that the earning process is not complete until the sales commitment has been substantially fulfilled. The same guidelines dictate that revenue from services is recognized *when services have been performed and are billable*, and that revenue from permitting others to use enterprise resources by way of rent is recognized *as resources are used* or *as time passes*.

There are two notable exceptions to the general rule. One exception to the rule of recognition of revenue at the point of sale is found, for example, when market values are firmly established and the marketability of a given prod-

---

[9]This subject was considered by a special AAA Committee on Realization which was established in 1964 and published its conclusions in 1966. Some of their comments on the point of revenue realization are included in this section. *Accounting Review* (Evanston, Illinois: American Accounting Association, April 1965), pp. 312-322.

uct is assured. Revenue in such instances is recognized at the *point of completed production*. Farm products with assured sales prices meet these criteria. In other instances, when uncertainty exists as to the collectibility of a receivable arising from the sale of goods or services, recognition of revenue may be deferred to the *point of actual cash collection*. The *instalment sales method* of accounting is an example of the application of this practice. Although the instalment sales method of deferring revenue beyond the point of sale is accepted as an alternate method for purposes of income taxation, it should not be accepted for financial statement purposes "unless the circumstances are such that the collection of the sale price is not reasonably assured."[10]

The second exception is found when revenue is recognized at two or more points in the cycle. Although conceptually one can maintain that revenue is being earned continuously throughout the cycle, the measurement of revenue under this concept may become impractical. It also raises special questions, such as: Should revenue of an equal amount be assigned to each phase of the cycle? Or should revenue be recognized in proportion to the costs incurred in each phase of the cycle? In certain cases, however, the production phase of the cycle extends over more than one accounting period and some allocation of revenue over the periods involved is considered essential to meaningful statements. Construction contracts for buildings, roads, and dams requiring several periods to complete are often of this nature. The *percentage-of-completion* method of accounting is used to meet these special conditions. This method requires a firm contract for sale prior to construction and an ability to estimate with reasonable accuracy the costs remaining to be incurred on the project. Portions of the total estimated revenue are recognized as the project progresses.

Thus, revenue recognition occurs at certain specifically defined points in the revenue-producing cycle. Prior to these points, valuations are stated in terms of cost. After these points, use is made of *estimated* or *actual realizable values*. Discussion will certainly continue within the accounting profession as to the validity and acceptability of alternative points of revenue recognition. However, regardless of the point of revenue recognition selected, the relationship that has been defined between revenues and expenses will still hold.

Nature of Expenses

In Statement No. 4, the Accounting Principles Board defined *expenses* as:

> . . . gross decreases in assets or gross increases in liabilities recognized and
> measured in conformity with generally accepted accounting principles that

---

[10]*Opinions of the Accounting Principles Board, No. 10*, "Omnibus Opinion — 1966" (New York: American Institute of Certified Public Accountants, 1966), par. 12.

result from those types of profit-directed activities of an enterprise that can change owners' equity.[11]

The APB stated further that expenses are:

> . . . costs that are associated with the revenue of the period, often directly but frequently indirectly through association with the period to which the revenue has been assigned.[12]

The Financial Accounting Standards Board in Statement of Financial Accounting Concepts No. 3 defines expenses as follows:

> Expenses are outflows or other using up of assets or incurrences of liabilities (or a combination of both) during a period from delivering or producing goods, rendering services, or carrying out other activities that constitute the entity's ongoing major or central operations.[13]

Some costs are not charged currently to the income statement because they relate to future revenues and, therefore, are shown as assets on the balance sheet. If the future service potential has expired, the costs are either associated with current revenues and reported as expenses or, in rare circumstances, associated with past revenues and charged to retained earnings as prior period adjustments. Expenses are classified in Statement No. 4 as follows:

1. Costs directly associated with the revenue of the period.
2. Costs associated with the period on some basis other than a direct relationship with revenue (such as time, for example).
3. Costs that cannot, as a practical matter, be associated with any other period.[14]

The Accounting Principles Board used the terminology of *gains* and *losses* to refer to the results of transactions involving revenues and expenses from other than sales of product, merchandise, or service. Expenses, of course, do not include repayments of borrowing, expenditures to acquire assets, or distributions to owners (including the acquisition of treasury shares).

A primary difficulty in income determination is the decision as to how various expenses are, in fact, to be associated with revenues. It has not been possible to prescribe exact rules for *association* or *matching*.[15] Certain guidelines for the matching of expenses with revenues in arriving at net income or loss have evolved through time. When an accountant is faced with an absence of guidelines, judgment must be exercised. Three expense recognition principles have been noted as being of special significance: (1) *associating cause and effect*; (2) *systematic and rational allocation*; and (3) *immediate recognition*.[16]

Associating Cause and Effect. Some costs can be associated directly with

---

[11]*Statement of the Accounting Principles Board, No. 4, op. cit.*, par. 134.

[12]*Ibid.*, par. 155.

[13]*Statement of Financial Accounting Concepts No. 3, op. cit.*, par 65.

[14]*Statement of the Accounting Principles Board, No. 4, op. cit.*, par. 155.

[15]Recent accounting pronouncements have been more specific in establishing guidelines for making these associations. Critics of this trend have stated their fear that accounting may become a set of rigid rules if such a trend continues.

[16]*Statement of the Accounting Principles Board, No. 4, op. cit.*, par. 157-160.

specific revenues. When this association is possible, the cost is recognized as an expense of the period in which the revenue is recognized. Thus, if an inventory item on hand at the end of a period represents a source of future revenue under the point of sale principle, the cost of producing the item is deferred to a future period and it is reported as an asset. Certain costs, such as labor and materials, usually can be directly related to the cost of producing the inventory item. Other costs, such as manufacturing overhead, may be assumed to be associated with an inventory item on some logical basis such as the number of labor hours or the number of machine hours required to produce the item. Judgment plays an increasingly more important part as the association becomes less direct.

Care must be taken to assure that proper recognition is made of all costs already incurred, as well as those yet to be incurred relative to any revenue currently recognized.

Systematic and Rational Allocation. In the absence of a direct cause and effect relationship, a different basis for expense recognition is commonly used. Here the attempt is made to associate costs in a systematic and rational manner with the products or the periods benefited. In arriving at period expense recognition, estimates must be made of the timing pattern of the benefits received from the individual costs and systematic allocation methods developed. The methods adopted should appear reasonable to an unbiased observer and should be followed consistently.

Some of the costs allocated to a period become expenses immediately and are associated with current revenue. Other costs *attach* to inventories and other similar assets on some logical basis, and thus are associated with future revenue by being deferred as assets. Examples of costs that are associated with periods in a systematic way include costs of buildings and equipment, insurance, and taxes.

While accounting allocations may be unavoidable, they are by nature essentially arbitrary. Moreover, these allocations have an impact on both financial position and operating results.

Immediate Recognition. Those costs that cannot be related to revenue either by associating cause and effect or by systematic and rational allocation, must be recognized as expenses or losses of the current period or written off as prior period adjustments. Because of specific restrictions on the items that qualify as prior period adjustments, most of the asset balances or costs currently incurred are recognized as expenses in the period when no discernible future revenues can be associated with them, and their deferral cannot be supported.[17]

---

[17]Previously, some development stage companies deferred many costs without regard to recoverability or matching on the basis that they were not yet a fully operating enterprise. In Statement No. 7, the FASB indicates this practice is no longer acceptable. Development stage enterprises must follow the same generally acceptable accounting principles that apply to established operating enterprises. *Statement of Financial Accounting Standards No. 7*, "Accounting and Reporting by Development Stage Enterprises" (Stamford, Conn.: Financial Accounting Standards Board, 1975), par. 10.

EFFECTS OF CHANGING PRICES

Thus far, reference has been made to the use of historical cost association. There is nothing in income measurement requiring use of historical costs. When the current costs of replacing the goods and services of an entity differ from historical transaction-based costs, such current costs could be matched against currently generated revenues. This approach was suggested by Sprouse and Moonitz in Accounting Research Study No. 3 and was also implicit in the recommendations of the American Accounting Association in their *Statement of Basic Accounting Theory*. In the latter publication, the study committee advocated the use of multivalued statements: both the balance sheet and the income statement would show in one column historical costs, and in a second column, current values. When it is maintained that the primary purpose of the income statement is to enable the user to predict future income, it should follow that current values will more closely suggest the costs expected to be experienced in the future.

In recent years there has been increasing discussion of the use of current value accounting.[18] In both Canada and the United States, while accountants generally do not appear ready to move completely away from the more traditional and objective historical cost structure, requirements for supplementary disclosures already exist in the United States and are imminent in Canada.

One of the principal causes of deviation between historical costs and current values is the steady decline in the purchasing power of the dollar. As indicated in Chapter 1, accountants operate on the *as if* assumption. They account for activities as if the value of the dollar were stable. To the extent this assumption is not valid, effects will be far-reaching on all financial statements. Particular care is necessary in interpreting comparative statements. With changing price levels, income statements comparing operations for several years may lead to inacurrate conclusions: reported sales increases may, in real terms, represent decreases.

In some countries general price-level adjustments are regularly made on the financial statements to reflect changes in the *general price index*. Such adjustments are applied to historical costs, and, therefore, are not usually measures of current value. On the other hand, disclosures of current values, which may or may not be adjusted for changes in the general price level, are becoming more popular and in some countries are even required.[19]

SPECIAL PROBLEMS IN THE PREPARATION OF THE INCOME STATEMENT

The importance of the revenue-expense relationships and the significance

---

[18]Discussion Paper, "Current Value Accounting" (Toronto: Canadian Institute of Chartered Accountants, 1976) and Exposure Draft, "Current Cost Accounting" (Toronto: Canadian Institute of Chartered Accountants, 1979.)

[19]For further discussion, see Chapter 21.

attached to the earnings and earning power of the entity for the user of the income statement have been described in the first part of this chapter. In view of the importance attached to these matters, the question continually arises: How can these matters be expressed on the income statement in the most informative and useful form?

Reporting Results of Operations on an All-Inclusive Basis

Historically, there have been two generally accepted forms that could be used for income statement presentation, and the selection of the form determined the manner in which the business entity chose to recognize extraordinary items. One form, referred to as the *current operating performance income statement*, provided for reporting only normal and recurring operating items; extraordinary items and prior period adjustments were recorded directly in retained earnings and reported on an accompanying statement that summarized all changes in retained earnings for the period. An alternative form, known as the *all-inclusive income statement*, provided for the presentation of extraordinary items on the face of the income statement, usually after reporting normal operating items. In employing the first form, the final amount was generally designated as net income; in the second form the final amount was designated by some as net income and by others as net income after extraordinary items. Because both of these income statement forms were being used in practice, there was a lack of consistency in income reporting and thus a real danger of misinterpretation of the results of operations by statement users.

Since 1969, the *Accounting Recommendations* have required extraordinary items to be excluded from the results of normal business activities and, with suitable descriptions of their nature, shown separately as a determinant of net income.[20] Assuming the reporting of extraordinary items, the income statement should conclude with the following captions: (1) income before extraordinary items, (2) extraordinary items, less applicable income tax, and (3) net income. Although this format is essentially a compromise between the current operating performance and all-inclusive concepts, the *Accounting Recommendations* clearly favor the latter.

According to the *Accounting Recommendations*, a gain or loss may be classified as extraordinary if it is (1) *not typical of the normal business activities of the enterprise*, (2) *not expected to occur regularly over a period of years*, and (3) *not considered as a recurring factor in any evaluation of the ordinary operations of the enterprise*.[21] For example, a material gain or loss on the sale of an entire plant or other significant segment of a business would be an

---

[20]*CICA Handbook: Accounting Recommendations*, Section 3480, "Extraordinary Items" (Toronto: Canadian Institute of Chartered Accountants, 1969), par. 02.

[21]Ibid., par. 05.

extraordinary item. Similarly, the sale of an investment not acquired for resale, or the loss of assets from floods, earthquakes, or other catastrophes not ordinarily covered by insurance, would also be classified as extraordinary. On the other hand, gains or losses on the disposal of fixed assets, or the write-down of inventory because of obsolescence, would not be extraordinary regardless of size. In the event such items are material in amount, they require separate disclosure in the income statement, but not the segregation accorded to extraordinary items.

The Accounting Research Committee recognized that the distinction between ordinary operating items and extraordinary items would require the use of judgment. From the viewpoint of practice, however, it can be argued that the criteria for distinguishing extraordinary items are at best difficult to apply, or perhaps may even be unworkable. It is indeed possible for companies that have experienced seemingly similar, unusual and infrequent events and transactions to report significantly different amounts of income before extraordinary items. Thus, what was at one time a problem in reporting net income is perhaps now a problem in reporting income before extraordinary items!

In the United States, *extraordinary items*, according to APB Opinion No. 30, are "events and transactions that are distinguished by their unusual nature *and* by the infrequence of their occurrence."[22] Thus, to qualify as extraordinary, an item must "possess a high degree of abnormality and be of a type clearly unrelated to or only incidentally related to the ordinary and typical activities of the entity . . . [and] be of a type that would not reasonably be expected to reoccur in the foreseeable future."[23] In addition, the item must be material in amount. Thus, the overall effect of APB Opinion No. 30 is to restrict the items that can be classified as extraordinary.

On the other hand, according to the FASB, at least one item — gains or losses from extinguishment of debt — is to be reported as an extraordinary item regardless of the criteria stated in APB Opinion No. 30.[24]

Prior period adjustments have also been the subject of much discussion in connection with the current operating performance and all-inclusive approaches. Prior period adjustments were usually handled in the same manner as extraordinary items and reported either in the retained earnings statement or in the income statement. Since 1969, however, the *Accounting Recommendations* have included specific criteria for the recognition of items as prior period adjustments and in addition, have required their exclusion from the current period's income statement. An item treated as a prior adjustment is therefore reported as a restatement of the balance of retained

---

[22]*Opinions of the Accounting Principles Board, No. 30*, "Reporting the Results of Operations" (New York: American Institute of Certified Public Accountants, 1973), par. 20.

[23]*Ibid.*

[24]*Statement of Financial Accounting Standards No. 4*, "Reporting Gains and Losses from Extinguishment of Debt" (Stamford, Conn.: Financial Accounting Standards Board, 1975).

earnings at the beginning of the period in which the adjustment is made. To justify exclusion from the current income statement as a prior period adjustment, the adjustments must meet all four of the following characteristics:

(1) Specifically identified with and directly related to the business activities of particular prior periods.
(2) Not attributable to economic events occurring subsequent to the date of the financial statements for such periods.
(3) Depend primarily on decisions and determinations by persons other than management or owners.
(4) Could not reasonably be estimated prior to such decisions or determinations.[25]

It should be noted that prior period adjustments are intended to be rare. The *Accounting Recommendations* provide only two examples (1) non-recurring adjustments or settlements of income taxes, and (2) settlements of claims resulting from litigation.[26] However, the retroactive application of a change in accounting principles, and corrections of errors are treated in the same manner as prior period adjustments even though they do not meet the above-noted criteria.[27]

Accounting Changes

The term "accounting changes" encompasses both changes in accounting principles, including the methods of their application, and changes in accounting estimates. A key question involved in reporting changes is whether the effects of the change should be applied retroactively, with or without restatement of prior periods, or prospectively. If retroactive treatment with restatement is followed, the change should be reported by restating the financial statements of prior periods. However, the restatement of prior period financial statements for some changes is frequently difficult, if not impossible, because of the unavailability of data. In addition, a policy of restating prior period statements may confuse the reader and may also erode public confidence in financial reporting. On the other hand, if the effects of the change are reported prospectively, trend summaries of operations and other analytical computations could be misleading to statement users.

If an accounting change is given retroactive application, it is reported in essentially the same manner as a prior period adjustment. Retroactive application with no restatement applies the new policy to events and transactions from their inception but uses a cumulative adjustment in the period of change to reflect the retroactivity. Two different treatments of the cumula-

---

[25]*Accounting Recommendations, Section 3600*, "Prior Period Adjustments" (Toronto: Canadian Institute of Chartered Accountants, 1971), par. 04.

[26]*Ibid*,, par. 02.

[27]*CICA Handbook: Accounting Recommendations, Section 1506*, "Accounting Changes" (Toronto: Canadian Institute of Chartered Accountants, 1980).

tive adjustment have been proposed: (1) an item in net income, or (2) an adjustment of the opening balance of retained earnings.[28] Retroactive application with restatement, primarily for comparative purposes, applies the change as applicable to the financial statements of each prior period presented and the balance of the cumulative effect of the change is presented as a restatement of the balance of retained earnings at the beginning of the earliest period presented.[29] The only alternative is to account for the change prospectively, which means that the new principle is used in the future but the historical record remains unchanged. In general, changes in accounting principles should be reported retroactively with restatement. However, a change in an accounting estimate, such as the useful life of fixed assets, should be accounted for prospectively.

In Canadian accounting practice, retroactive application of a change in accounting principles generally contemplates the restatement of previously issued financial statements. In particular, it is important to note the treatment of any retroactive application related to the income of the immediately preceding period. If financial statements are presented in comparative form, which is often required and certainly preferable, the income for the preceding period should be restated to reflect the portion, if any, of the prior period adjustment applicable thereto, and the fact that it has been restated should be disclosed. The balance of the prior period adjustment not applied as a restatement of the previous year's income is disclosed as an adjustment of the retained earnings balance as at the beginning of the preceding period. Retroactive application and the resulting restatement of reported incomes, also arises in the preparation of the five- or ten-year earnings summaries that frequently appear in corporate annual reports.

To illustrate, a statement of retained earnings is presented which includes as a restatement of opening retained earnings balances the retroactive application of a change from the taxes payable to the allocation method of accounting for corporate income taxes. An explanatory note in support of this change in accounting principles is also presented.

OVERVIEW OF CONTENT OF THE INCOME STATEMENT

The income statement is an array of revenues, expenses, gains and losses, including extraordinary items, if any, the precise format of which is not specified. Generally the income statement consists of a series of sections developing the net income or loss for the period. As mentioned earlier, all elements of income, except for prior period adjustments, are to be included. However, a distinction should be made between the results of normal operations and of any extraordinary items affecting net income. Major categories

---

[28] *Ibid.*, par. .06 (b).
[29] *Ibid.*, par. .06 (c).

AMR Limited
Statement of Retained Earnings
For Years Ended August 31, 1981, and 1980

	1981	1980
Balance at beginning of year:		
As previously reported	$2,790,000	$2,300,000
Adjustment of prior year's income taxes (Note 9)	250,000	210,000
As restated	$2,540,000	$2,090,000
Net income for the year (1980 as restated, Note 9)	860,000	750,000
	$3,400,000	$2,840,000
Cash dividends declared	300,000	300,000
Balance at end of year	$3,100,000	$2,540,000

Note 9. During 1981 the company changed its method of accounting for income taxes from the taxes payable basis to the tax allocation basis. As a result, the balance of retained earnings at August 31, 1980 has been restated from the amount previously reported to show a retroactive charge of $250,000, representing the cumulative amount by which income taxes had been reduced at August 31, 1980. In the amount of $250,000 is $40,000 applicable to the year ended Auust 31, 1980 which has been charged to earnings and is included in deferred income taxes in that year. The remainder ($210,000) is applicable to years prior to September 1, 1979 and has been charged to retained earnings at that date.

included within the normal operations section are: (1) revenues from the sale of goods and service; (2) cost of goods sold and expenses of providing goods and/or services; (3) operating expenses; (4) other revenue and expense items; and (5) income tax relative to income from normal operations. Extraordinary items, if any, are shown separately net of their tax effect. Illustrative statements, in more detail than is customary for external reporting purposes, are presented on pages 134 and 135.

On the income statement for a corporation, the summary of net income may be followed by the presentation of earnings per share for the period. Earnings per share is computed by dividing income before extraordinary items after deduction of applicable preferred dividends, if any, by the weighted average number of common shares outstanding. For example, the Andersen Corporation income statement illustrated on page 134 shows earnings per share of 50¢ for income before extraordinary items and 70¢ for net income. These figures are derived by dividing the respective amounts in the income categories by the 50,000 shares of common stock outstanding during the period.

Sales

Revenue from sales reports the total sales to customers for the period. This total should not include additions to billings for sales and excise taxes that the business is required to collect on behalf of governments. These billing increases are properly recognized as current liabilites. Sales returns and allowances and sales discounts should be subtracted from gross sales in arriving at net sales revenue. When the sale price is increased to cover the cost of freight to the customer and the customer is billed accordingly, freight charges paid by the company should also be subtracted from sales in arriving at net sales. Freight charges not absorbed by the buyer are recognized as selling expenses.

Cost of Goods Sold

When merchandise is acquired from outsiders, the cost of goods relating to sales of the period must be determined. *Cost of merchandise available for sale* is first determined. This is the sum of the beginning inventory, purchases, and all other buying, freight, and storage costs relating to the acquisition of goods. A net purchases balance is developed by subtracting purchase returns and allowances and purchase discounts from gross purchases. *Cost of goods sold* is calculated by subtracting the ending inventory from the cost of merchandise available for sale.

When the goods are manufactured by the seller, the *cost of goods manufactured* must first be calculated. Cost of goods manufactured replaces purchases in the summary just described. The determination of cost of goods manufactured begins with the cost of goods in process at the beginning of the period. To this is added the cost of materials put into production, the cost of labor applied to material conversions, and all of the other costs for services and facilities utilized in manufacturing, including factory superintendence, indirect labor, depreciation and other costs relating to factory buildings and equipment, factory supplies used, patent amortization, and factory light, heat, and power. The total thus obtained represents the cost of goods completed and goods still in production. The goods in process inventory at the end of the period is subtracted from this total in arriving at the cost of the goods finished and made available for sale. In Canada, disclosure of cost of goods sold is not required. The *Accounting Recommendations* list cost of goods sold as additional desirable information.[30]

Operating Expenses

Operating expenses are generally reported in two categories: (1) selling expenses and (2) general and administrative expenses. Selling expenses in-

---

[30]*CICA Handbook, Accounting Recommendations*, Section 1520, "Income Statement" (Toronto: Canadian Institute of Chartered Accountants, 1968), par. 02.

clude such items as sales salaries and commissions and related payroll taxes, advertising and store displays, store supplies used, depreciation of store furniture and equipment, and delivery expenses. General and administrative expenses include officers and office salaries and related payroll taxes, office supplies used, depreciation of office furniture and fixtures, telephone, postage, business licences and fees, legal and accounting services, contributions, and similar items. Charges related to the use of buildings, such as rent, depreciation, taxes, insurance, light, heat, and power, should be allocated in some equitable manner to manufacturing activities and to selling and general and administrative activities. In the case of the merchandising concern, charges relating to buildings are generally reported in full in the general and administrative category.

Other Revenue and Expense Items

Other revenue and expense items include items identified with financial management and other miscellaneous recurring items not related to major or central operations. Other revenue includes earnings in the form of interest and dividends, and miscellaneous earnings from rentals, royalties, and service fees. Other expense includes interest expense and other expenses related to the miscellaneous revenue items reported.

Income Tax Relative to Income from Normal Operations

The provision for income tax or income tax expense should report the tax on revenue and expense transactions included in pretax ordinary income from normal operations. This will require application of income tax allocation procedures described in Chapter 14. In reporting the provision, its current and deferred components should be disclosed.

While the above detailed breakdown of income statement items may be desirable, income statements presented in corporate annual reports are usually very much condensed. For example, cost of goods sold and operating expenses are often combined and presented as a single amount, usually on the grounds that competitive disadvantages may result from more detailed disclosures. As previously noted, the *Accounting Recommendations* acknowledge this viewpoint by listing the amounts for cost of goods sold and other major operating expenses as "additional desirable information."[31]

FORM OF THE INCOME STATEMENT

The income statement traditionally has been prepared in either multiple-step or single-step form. An example of an income statement in multiple-step

---

[31]*Ibid.*

form is presented on page 134 and in condensed single-step form on page 135. In each example, the presentation is made in accordance with the *Accounting Recommendations* discussed earlier and, in particular, illustrates the treatment of extraordinary items.

In the *multiple-step* form, the ordinary operations are first summarized and designated as "Income before income tax." The income tax related to ordinary operations is computed and deducted. The title of the remaining figure varies depending upon whether there are any extraordinary gains or losses to be added or deducted to arrive at the final net income figure. Of course, extraordinary items are shown net of their tax effect.

Revenue and expense items are grouped to provide different income measurements as follows:

1. *Gross profit on sales* (or *gross margin*) — the difference between sales and the costs directly related to such sales.
2. *Operating income* — gross profit on sales less operating expenses.
3. *Income before income tax* — operating income increased by other revenue items and decreased by other expense items.
4. *Income from normal operations* (or *Income before extraordinary items*) — income less the income tax applicable to ordinary income.
5. *Net income* — income from normal operations plus or minus any extraordinary items net of applicable income tax.
6. *Earnings per common share* — the presentation of earnings per common share for income before extraordinary items and for net income.[32]

The *single-step form* is in reality a modified single-step form because of the required separation of ordinary and extraordinary items. However, as illustrated, all ordinary revenue and expense items are listed and summarized without separate headings for cost of goods sold, gross profit, and other revenue and expense items. In practice, the single-step form may also be modified so as to present the income tax expense related to income before taxes and extraordinary items, if any, as a separate item.

Many accountants have raised objections to the multiple-step income statement form. They point out that the various income designations have no universal meaning and may prove a source of confusion to the reader. Quoting such designations in the absence of a complete income statement may prove ambiguous or actually misleading. They further maintain that multiple-step presentation implies certain cost priorities and an order for cost recoveries. But there is no such order and there can be no earnings unless all costs are recovered. These persons support the single-step form that minimizes sectional labelling. However, recent accounting pronouncements seem to be requiring greater sectionalization of the income statement or at least modification of the single-step format.

[32]Section 3500 of the *Accounting Recommendations* permits footnote disclosure of earnings per share. If the corporation's capital structure includes potentially dilutive securities, it may also be necessary to report earnings per share on a fully diluted basis. Earnings per share is treated in detail in Chapter 18.

Andersen Corporation
Income Statement
For Year Ended December 31, 1981

Revenue from sales:			
Sales		$510,000	
Less: Sales returns and allowances	$ 7,500		
Sales discounts	2,500	10,000	$500,000
Cost of goods sold:			
Merchandise inventory, January 1, 1981		$ 95,000	
Purchases	$320,000		
Freight in	15,000		
Delivered cost of purchases	$335,000		
Less: Purchase returns and allowances $1,000			
Purchase discounts 4,000	5,000	330,000	
Merchandise available for sale		$425,000	
Less merchandise inventory, December 31, 1981		125,000	300,000
Gross profit on sales			$200,000
Operating expenses:			
Selling expenses:			
Sales salaries	$ 30,000		
Advertising expense	15,000		
Depreciation expense — selling and delivery equipment	5,000		
Miscellaneous selling expense	10,000	$ 60,000	
General and administrative expenses:			
Officers and office salaries	$ 48,000		
Taxes and insurance	20,000		
Miscellaneous supplies expense	5,000		
Depreciation expense — office furniture and fixtures	5,000		
Doubtful accounts expense	2,500		
Amortization expense	10,600		
Miscellaneous general expense	4,400	95,500	155,500
Operating income			$ 44,500
Other revenue and expense items:			
Interest revenue	$ 3,000		
Dividend revenue	5,000		
Gain on sale of investment	5,000	$ 13,000	
Interest expense		7,500	5,500
Income before income tax			$ 50,000
Income tax:			
Current tax charge, $32,000 less $10,000 applicable to gain on extinguishment of debt reported below		$ 22,000	
Deferred tax charge arising from timing difference in computing depreciation		3,000	25,000
Income before extraordinary items			$ 25,000
Extraordinary items:			
Gain on extinguishment of debt		$ 20,000	
Less applicable income tax		10,000	10,000
Net income			$ 35,000
Earnings per common share:*			
Income before extraordinary items			$ .50
Net income			$ .70

Multiple-Step
Income
Statement

*$25,000 ÷ 50,000 shares = $.50; $35,000 ÷ 50,000 shares = $.70

Andersen Corporation
Income Statement
For Year Ended December 31, 1981

Revenues:		
Net sales	$500,000	
Other revenue — interest and dividends	13,000	$513,000
Expenses:		
Cost of goods sold	$300,000	
Selling expense	60,000	
General and administrative expense	95,500	
Interest expense	7,500	
Income tax (including deferred tax of $3,000)	25,000	488,000
Income before extraordinary items		$ 25,000
Extraordinary gain on extinguishment of debt (net of income tax		
of $10,000)		10,000
Net income		$ 35,000
Earnings per common share: *		
Income before extraordinary items		$ .50
Net income		$ .70

*$25,000 ÷ 50,000 shares = $.50; $35,000 ÷ 50,000 shares = $.70

Condensed
Single-Step
Income
Statement

The income statement is frequently prepared in condensed form and simply reports totals for certain classes of items, such as cost of goods sold, selling expenses, general expenses, other revenue and expense, and extraordinary items. Additional detail may be provided by the use of supporting schedules and notes to the financial statements.

It may be observed that the use of condensed income statements by large units engaged in a number of diversified activities has been severely criticized. There have been numerous mergers of companies with a large diversity of products and services provided by each entity. Income statements prepared in condensed form may tend to disguise the important trends operating within the individual segments of a diversified company. Because of this, some corporations acts require disclosure of at least sales information by major segments of a company. Segmented Information is the subject matter of Section 1700 of the *Accounting Recommendations*.

When goods are manufactured by the seller, the cost of the goods manufactured must be determined before the cost of goods sold can be computed. If a summary of cost of goods manufactured is to accompany the financial statements, it should be presented as a schedule in support of the amount reported on the income statement. Assuming the merchandise available for sale in the example on page 134 was obtained by manufacture rather than by purchase, cost of goods sold on the income statement would be presented as shown at the top of the next page. The supporting schedule immediately follows the presentation.

Andersen Corporation
Manufacturing Schedule
For Year Ended December 31, 1981

Work in process inventory, January 1, 1981			$ 25,000
Raw materials:			
Inventory, January 1, 1981		$ 30,000	
Purchases	$105,000		
Freight in	10,000		
Delivered cost of raw materials	$115,000		
Less: Purchase returns and allowances .. $1,000			
Purchase discounts 4,000	5,000	110,000	
Total cost of raw materials available for use		$140,000	
Less inventory, December 31, 1981		40,000	100,000
Direct labor			140,000
Manufacturing overhead:			
Indirect labor		$ 20,000	
Factory superintendence		14,500	
Depreciation expense — factory buildings			
and equipment		12,000	
Light, heat, and power		10,000	
Factory supplies expense		8,500	
Miscellaneous factory overhead		15,000	80,000
Total work in process during 1981			$345,000
Less work in process inventory,			
December 31, 1981			35,000
Cost of goods manufactured			$310,000

Andersen Corporation
Retained Earnings Statement
For Year Ended December 31, 1981

Retained earnings, January 1, 1981	$149,000
Deduct — correction of inventory overstatement, net of income tax refund of	
$9,000	9,000
Adjusted retained earnings, January 1, 1981	$140,000
Add net income per income statement	35,000
	$175,000
Deduct dividends declared	20,000
Retained earnings, December 31, 1981	$155,000

Frequently, only the cost of goods sold is reported on the income statement. If a schedule of the cost of goods sold is to be provided, it should summarize the cost of goods manufactured as well as the change in finished goods inventories. Instead of reporting beginning and ending inventories, it is possible simply to report inventory variations for the period in arriving at the cost of materials used, cost of goods manufactured, or cost of goods sold. For example, an increase in the finished goods inventory would be subtracted from the cost of goods manufactured in arriving at the cost of goods sold; a decrease in the finished goods inventory would be added to the cost of goods manufactured in arriving at the cost of goods sold.

Cost of good sold:		
Finished goods inventory, January 1, 1981	$ 40,000	
Add cost of goods manufactured per manufacturing schedule	310,000	
Merchandise available for sale	$350,000	
Less finished goods inventory, December 31, 1981	50,000	$300,000

THE STATEMENT OF CHANGES IN OWNERS' EQUITY

When the only change in the owners' equity arises from earnings for the period, the balance sheet prepared at the end of the period may report in the owners' equity section the balance of the equity at the beginning of the period, the change arising from earnings for the period, and the resulting balance at the end of the period. Normally, however, more than the earnings must be recognized in explaining the change in equity, and a *statement of changes in the owners' equity* may be prepared to accompany the financial statements. In the case of a corporation, if transactions affecting the shareholders' equity have been limited to changes in retained earnings, a *retained earnings statement* is prepared. This statement reports the beginning balance for retained earnings, any prior period adjustments shown net of tax to arrive at the adjusted retained earnings at the beginning of the period, earnings for the period, and dividend declarations. A retained earnings statement to accompany the income statement prepared on page 134 is shown opposite.

The income statement and retained earnings statement may be prepared in *combined* form. In preparing the combined statement, net income data are first listed and summarized. The net earnings for the period is then combined with the retained earnings balance at the beginning of the period or the adjusted balance due to prior period adjustments. This total is adjusted for dividend declarations in arriving at the retained earnings balance at the end of the period. Data can be presented in either multiple-step or single-step form. The combined statement listing data in single-step form can be pre-

Combined
Income and
Retained
Earnings
Statement

Andersen Corporation
Income and Retained Earnings Statement
For Year Ended December 31, 1981

Revenues		$513,000
Expenses		488,000
Income before extraordinary item		$ 25,000
Extraordinary gain on extinguishment of debt (net of income tax of $10,000)		10,000
Net income		$ 35,000
Adjusted retained earnings, January 1, 1981:		
Retained earnings, January 1, 1981	$149,000	
Deduct prior period adjustment — correction of inventory over-		
statement, net of income refund of $9,000	9,000	140,000
		$175,000
Deduct dividends declared		20,000
Retained earnings, December 31, 1981		$155,000

pared in the above form (details for revenues and expenses have been omitted).

Prior to the issuance of Section 3480 of the *Accounting Recommendations*, the combined income and retained earnings statement was frequently prepared because it offered a means of reporting both ordinary operations and extraordinary items on the same statement while still offering a clear distinction between the two classes of data. Now that the extraordinary items are clearly set forth on the income statement, the popularity of this form may decline. However, the combined statement may still be preferable when prior period adjustments are reported.

QUESTIONS

1. An article in a financial journal was titled "What are Earnings? The Growing Creditability Gap." What do you think was meant by this title?

2. What reasons can you offer for the increased importance of the income statement?

3. What are the major differences between the valuation and matching methods of income measurement?

4. What concepts of the "value of net assets" might be applied in the valuation method of income measurement? Which do you prefer and why?

5. What factors determine the timing of revenue recognition?

6. A manufacturer of farm implements sells its products to dealers who in turn sell them to farmers. To induce dealers to carry an adequate stock, the dealer is not required to pay for merchandise received until 30 days after sale to the customer. In addition, dealers are permitted to return unsold merchandise at any time within nine months from the time it is received. Dealers hold title to the merchandise while it is in their hands. In some years, the returns were low; in others years they have amounted to 25% of the shipments. Bad debts are low. No interest is charged dealers on the balances in their accounts. At what point should the manufacturer recognize revenue?

7. At harvest time, a wheat producer moves the wheat to a grain elevator and receives a warehouse receipt for it. The decision to sell wheat is based on the need for cash and on the forecast of the market. At what point should the producer recognize revenue?

8. Why is the process of matching costs with revenues in income measurement so difficult?

9. Do you think matching expenses with revenues is more difficult to apply in a machine assembly plant than in a CA firm? Why?

10. What guidelines are used to match costs with revenues in measuring income?

11. Small loan companies often experience operating losses in the operation of newly opened branch loan offices. Such results can usually be anticipated by management prior to making a decision on expansion. It has been recommended that the operating losses of newly opened branches should be reported as deferred charges during the first twelve months of operation or until the first profitable month occurs. Such deferred charges would then be amortized over a five-year period. Would you support this recommendation?

12. A construction contractor classifies all revenues and expenses by project, each project being considered a separate venture. All revenue from uncompleted projects is treated as unearned revenue and all expenses applicable to each uncompleted project as "work in process" inventory. The income statement for the year includes only the revenues and expenses related to the projects completed during the year. (a) Evaluate the practice described. (b) What alternative approach can you suggest for the above described practice?

13. What items on the income statement are most significantly affected by changing prices?

14. How does the all-inclusive form of the income statement differ from the current operating performance form?

15. How would you distinguish between ordinary items and extraordinary items for income statement presentation? Where should extraordinary items be presented on the income statement?

16. What factors determine whether an item may be reported as a prior period adjustment?

17. (a) What objections can be made to the multiple-step income statement? (b) What objections can be made to the single-step statement?

18. What information not found in the income statement or the balance sheet is disclosed in the retained earnings statement?

4-1. Changes in account balances for the Sanchez Sales Co. during 1981 were as follows:

	Increase (Decrease)
Cash	$ 45,000
Accounts Receivable	5,000
Merchandise Inventory	40,000
Buildings and Equipment (net)	120,000
Accounts Payable	(35,000)
Bonds Payable	100,000
Share Capital	75,000
Contributed Surplus	15,000

Dividends paid during 1981 were $25,000. Calculate the net income for the year assuming there were no transactions affecting retained earnings other than the dividend payment.

4-2. The Coleman Company Ltd. declared and paid cash dividends of $10,000 during 1981. The company's accounts show the following changes in account balances during 1981:

	Increase	Decrease
Cash	$40,000	
Accounts receivable		$1,000
Merchandise inventory	15,000	
Equipment (net)	18,000	
Building (net)	30,000	
Accounts payable		8,000
Notes payable	50,000	
Common shares	30,000	
Premium on common shares	10,000	

Assuming there were no transactions affecting retained earnings except the cash dividend, calculate the net income for 1981.

4-3. Indicate which of the following items involves the realization of revenue or gain. Give reasons for your answers.

(a) Land acquired in 1952 at $15,000 is now conservatively appraised at $100,000.

(b) Timberlands show a growth in timber valued at $40,000 for the year.

(c) An addition to a building was self-constructed at a cost of $3,600 after two offers from private contractors for the work at $4,650 and $5,000.

(d) Certain valuable franchise rights were received from a city on payment of annual licensing fees.

(e) A customer owing $4,600, which was delinquent for one year, gave securities valued at $5,000 in settlement of the obligation.

(f) Merchandise, cost $1,000, is sold for $1,600 with a 50% down payment on a conditional sales contract, title to the merchandise being retained by the seller until the full contract price is collected.

(g) Cash is received on the sale of gift certificates redeemable in merchandise in the following period.

4-4. How would you report each of the following items on the financial statements?

(a) Plant shut-down and start-up costs due to a strike.

(b) Loss on sale of the fertilizer production division of a lawn supplies manufacturer.

(c) Material penalties arising from early payment of a mortgage.

(d) Gain resulting from changing asset balances to adjust for the effect of excessive depreciation charged in error in prior years.

(e) Loss resulting from excessive accrual in prior years of estimated revenues from long-term contracts.

(f) Costs incurred to purchase a valuable patent.

(g) Cost of rearranging plant machinery into a more efficient order.

(h) Error made in capitalizing advertising expense.

(i) Gain on sale of land to the government.

(j) Loss from destruction of crops by a hail storm.

(k) Additional depreciation resulting from a change in the estimated useful life of the asset.

(l) Gain on sale of long-term investments.

(m) Loss from spring flooding.

(n) Sale of obsolete inventory at less than book value.

(o) Additional federal income tax assessment for prior years.

4-5. Where in the income or retained earnings statement would each item be reported?

(a) Gain on sale of land.

(b) Purchase discounts.

(c) Charge for doubtful accounts in anticipation of failure to collect receivables.

(d) Loss from long-term investments written off as worthless.

(e) Loss from a strike.

(f) Error in prior period of recording revenue.

(g) Loss from inventory price decline.

(h) Depletion.

(i) Sales discounts.

(j) Dividends received on long-term investments.

(k) Income tax for current period.

(l) Charge for omission of depreciation in prior periods.

(m) Collection of life insurance policy upon death of officer.

(n) Vacation pay of employees.

(o) Payment in settlement of damage suit for breach of contract arising in current period.

4-6. Using proper headings, prepare a manufacturing schedule in good form selecting the proper accounts from the following:

Purchases	$100,000	Beginning Inventory — Work in Process	$13,000
Purchase Returns and Allowances	10,000	Beginning Inventory — Finished Goods	20,000
Beginning Inventory — Raw Materials	15,000	Factory Labor	26,000
Accounts Receivable	85,000	Factory Overhead	15,000
Equipment	26,000	Ending Inventory — Raw Materials	18,000
Depreciation of Factory Equipment	2,500	Ending Inventory — Work in Process	12,000
Depreciation of Factory Building	2,000	Ending Inventory — Finished Goods	16,000
Selling Expenses	18,000	Cash	11,000

4-7. The selling expenses of Caven Ltd. for 1981 are 10% of sales. General expenses, excluding doubtful accounts, are 25% of cost of goods sold but only 15% of sales. Doubtful accounts are 2% of sales. The beginning merchandise inventory was $62,000 and it decreased 25% during the year. Income for the year before income tax of 45% is $52,000. Prepare an income statement, including earnings per share data, showing supporting computations. Caven Ltd. has 104,000 shares of common stock outstanding.

4-8. From the chart of accounts presented below, prepare a multistep income statement in good form showing all appropriate items properly classified, including disclosure of earnings per share data. Assume a supporting manufacturing statement has been prepared. (No monetary amounts are to be recognized.)

Accounts Payable
Accumulated Depreciation — Buildings
Accumulated Depreciation — Delivery
  Equipment
Accumulated Depreciation — Office
  Furniture and Fixtures
Advertising Expense
Allowance for Doubtful Accounts
Amortization of Patents
Cash
Common Stock, $20 par (10,000 shares
  outstanding)
Delivery Salaries
Depreciation Expense — Buildings
Depreciation Expense — Delivery
  Equipment
Depreciation Expense — Office
  Furniture and Fixtures
Depreciation Expense — Tools
Direct Labor
Dividend Revenue
Dividends Payable
Dividends Receivable
Doubtful Accounts Expense
Extraordinary Loss (net of tax savings)
Factory Heat, Light, and Power
Factory Superintendence
Factory Supplies
Factory Supplies Used
Finished Goods
Freight In
Federal UI Payable
Work in Process

Goodwill
Income Tax
Income Tax Payable
Insurance Expense
Interest Expense — Bonds
Interest Expense — Other
Interest Payable
Interest Receivable
Interest Revenue
Miscellaneous Delivery Expense
Miscellaneous Factory Overhead
Miscellaneous General Expense
Miscellaneous Selling Expense
Office Salaries
Office Supplies
Office Supplies Used
Officers' Salaries
Patents
Purchase Discounts
Raw Materials
Raw Materials Purchases
Raw Materials Returns and Allowances
Retained Earnings
Royalties Received in Advance
Royalty Revenue
Salaries and Wages Payable
Sales
Sales Discounts
Sales Returns and Allowances
Sales Salaries and Commissions
Sales Tax Payable
Taxes
Tools

4-1A. Selected account balances of the Jensen Company along with additional information as of December 31, 1981, are as follows:

Contribution to Employees Pension Fund	$290,000	Loss on Sale of Marketable Securities	$ 50,000
Delivery Expense	425,000	Loss from Write-Down of Obsolete Inventory	125,000
Depreciation Expense — Delivery Trucks	29,000	Merchandise Inventory, Jan. 1, 1981	900,000
Depreciation Expense — Office Buildings and Equipment	35,000	Miscellaneous General Expense	45,000
Depreciation Expense — Store Equipment	25,000	Miscellaneous Selling Expense	50,000
Dividends	150,000	Officers and Office Salaries	950,000
Dividend Revenue	5,000	Purchase Discounts	47,700
Doubtful Accounts Expense	22,000	Purchases	4,633,200
Federal Income Tax, 1981 (applicable to income from operations)	315,000	Retained Earnings, Jan. 1, 1981	550,000
		Sales	8,350,000
Freight In	145,000	Sales Discounts	55,000
Gain on Sale of Office Equipment	10,000	Sales Returns and Allowances	95,000
Interest Revenue	1,500	Sales Salaries	601,000
		Provincial and Local Taxes	100,000
		Store Supplies Expense	50,000

(a) Inventory at year-end was valued at $750,000 — $875,000 cost less the $125,000 write-down of obsolete inventory.
(b) Jensen Company made an error in understanding depreciation expense in the year 1975 by $125,000. (Ignore any tax implications.)
(c) Jensen Company has 100,000 shares of common stock outstanding.

Instructions:
Prepare a combined statement of income and retained earnings for the year ended December 31, 1981. (Use a multiple-step form.)

4-2A. The Lane Co. on July 1, 1980, reported a retained earnings balance of $762,500. The accounts of the company showed the following account balances on June 30, 1981:

Sales	$1,250,000
Inventory: July 1, 1980	80,000
June 30, 1981	82,500
Sales Returns and Allowances	15,000
Purchases	768,000
Purchase Discounts	12,000
Gain from Extinguishment of Debt	40,000
Dividends	130,000
Selling and General Expenses	125,000
Income Tax: Applicable to ordinary income	99,750
Applicable to gain from extinguishment of debt	20,000
Overstatement of depreciation erroneously recorded in prior years (Ignore tax implications)	26,000

Instructions:
Prepare a single-step income statement accompanied by a retained earnings statement. The Lane Company has 200,000 shares of common stock outstanding.

4-3A. Fidelity Investment Company purchased 100 shares of Durham Ltd. and 100 shares of Hoyt Stores Ltd. on January 1, 1981. Data on these investments on a per share basis are as follows:

	Durham	Hoyt
Cost	$60.50	$82.25
Net income reported — 1981	7.00	7.50
Dividend paid — 1981	6.00	5.00
Market value — December 31, 1981	54.25	79.75

Fundamental Investment Company and Canadian Shores Ltd. each purchased 100 shares of Hume Manufacturing Co. and 100 shares of Kovar Electronics Ltd. on January 1, 1981. Data on these investments, also on a per share basis, are as follows:

	Hume	Kovar
Cost	$50.75	$90.25
Net income reported — 1981	4.00	6.00
Dividend paid — 1981	3.00	none
Market value — 12/31/81	56.25	94.00

Canadian Shores Ltd. sold its shares of Kovar Electronics Ltd. on December 31, 1981, at the market value shown above. At the same time it purchased 200 shares of Magnatronics Ltd. for $9,350. The other companies continued to hold their original investment.

Instructions:
(1) Compute the revenues for the three companies, using each of the following approaches to revenue recognition for each company (no expenses are to be recognized in computing your answers):
   (a) Dividends received (plus gain on sales, if any).
   (b) Net income reported by company whose shares are owned.
   (c) Dividends received adjusted by any change in the market value of the shares.
(2) Evaluate each of the approaches as to its informational value to investors.

4-4A. The Emerson Company Limited has released the following condensed financial statements for 1979 and 1980 and has prepared the following proposed statements for 1981.

Emerson Company Limited
Comparative Balance Sheet
December 31

	1981	1980	1979
Assets			
Current assets	$ 83,000	$ 73,000	$ 55,000
Land	20,000	15,000	10,000
Equipment	50,000	50,000	50,000
Accumulated depreciation — equipment	(15,000)	(10,000)	(5,000)
Total assets	$138,000	$128,000	$110,000

Liabilities and Shareholders' Equity

Current liabilities	$ 59,000	$ 59,000	$ 49,000
Common shares	20,000	20,000	20,000
Retained earnings	59,000	49,000	41,000
Total liabilities and shareholders' equity	$138,000	$128,000	$110,000

Emerson Company Limited
Comparative Income Statement
For Years Ended December 31

	1981	1980	1979
Sales	$105,000	$100,000	$ 85,000
Cost of goods sold	$ 80,000	$ 75,000	$ 63,000
Other expenses except depreciation	10,000	12,000	11,000
Depreciation expense — equipment	5,000	5,000	5,000
Total costs	$ 95,000	$ 92,000	$ 79,000
Net income	$ 10,000	$ 8,000	$ 6,000

The Emerson Company Limited acquired the equipment for $50,000 on January 1, 1979, and began depreciating the equipment over a ten-year estimated useful life with no salvage value, using the straight-line method of depreciation. The declining balance method of depreciation, (double the straight-line rate) under the same assumptions, would have required the following depreciation expense:

$$1979 = 20\% \times \$50,000 = \$10,000$$
$$1980 = 20\% \times \$40,000 = \$ 8,000$$
$$1981 = 20\% \times \$32,000 = \$ 6,400$$

Instructions:
In comparative format, prepare a balance sheet and a combined statement of income and retained earnings (including earnings per share data) for 1981, giving effect to the following changes. Ignore any income tax effect. Emerson Company Limited has 10,000 shares of common stock outstanding. The following situations are independent of each other.

(1) For justifiable reasons, Emerson Company Limited changed to the declining balance method of depreciation (double the straight-line rate) in 1981.
(2) During 1981, Emerson Company Limited found the equipment was fast becoming obsolete and decided to change the estimated useful life from ten years to five years. The accounts for 1981 had not yet been closed.
(3) During 1981, Emerson Company Limited found additional equipment, also acquired on January 1, 1979, costing $8,000, had been recorded in the land account and had not been depreciated. This error should be corrected using straight-line depreciation over a 10-year period.

4-5A. The Norway Supply Co. Ltd. prepares a multiple-step income statement. The statement is supported by (1) a manufacturing schedule, (2) a selling expense schedule, and (3) a general and administrative expense schedule. You are supplied the data shown at the top of the next page.

Income tax for the current year was as follows:

Applicable to ordinary income	$18,925
Applicable to extraordinary items	5,000
Total income tax	$23,925

Inventory balances at the end of the fiscal period as compared with balances at the beginning of the fiscal period were as follows:

Finished goods	$20,000 decrease
Goods in process	4,500 increase
Raw materials	10,000 decrease

Other account balances include the following:

Advertising Expense	$ 15,000	Indirect Labor	74,000
Delivery Expense	23,000	Interest Expense	10,200
Depreciation Exp. — Mach.	5,600	Miscellaneous Factory Costs	10,500
Direct Labor	184,000	Miscellaneous General Expense .	3,200
Dividend Revenue	300	Miscellaneous Selling Expense ..	2,150
Dividends	30,000	Officers Salaries	116,200
Doubtful Accounts Expense	1,600	Office Salaries	70,000
Extraordinary Gain	10,400	Office Supplies Expense	3,200
Factory Heat, Light, and Power ..	26,990	Raw Materials Purchases	196,900
Factory Maintenance	15,000	Raw Materials Returns	2,000
Factory Superintendence	60,000	Royalty Revenue	2,700
Factory Supplies Expense	14,000	Sales	989,800
Factory Taxes	14,000	Sales Discounts	8,000
Freight In on Raw Materials	10,000	Sales Returns and Allowances ..	6,500
Gain on Sale of Land	8,000	Sales Salaries	65,000

Norway Supply Co. Ltd. has 50,000 shares of common stock outstanding.

Instructions:

Prepare an income statement with supporting schedules using the data for the year ended April 30, 1981, listed above.

4-6A. The Ellis Corporation was organized on March 21, 1981, 15,000 shares of no-par stock being issued in exchange for land, buildings and equipment valued at $60,000 and cash of $15,000. Data below summarize activities for the initial fiscal period ending December 31, 1981:

(a) Net income for the period ending December 31, 1981, was $15,000.
(b) Raw materials on hand on December 31 were equal to 25% of raw materials purchased in 1981.
(c) Manufacturing costs in 1981 were distributed as follows:
Materials used 50%
Direct labor 30%
Manufacturing overhead ..... 20% (includes depreciation of building, $2,500)
(d) Work in process remaining in the factory on December 31 was equal to $33^{1}/_3$% of the goods finished and transferred to stock.
(e) Finished goods remaining in stock were equal to 25% of the cost of goods sold.

(f) Operating expenses were 30% of sales.

(g) Cost of goods sold was 150% of the operating expenses total.

(h) Ninety per cent of sales were collected in 1981; the balance was considered collectable in 1982.

(i) Seventy-five per cent of the raw materials purchased were paid for; there were no expense accruals or prepayments at the end of the year.

Instructions:

(1) Prepare a balance sheet, an income statement, and a supporting manufacturing schedule. (Disregard income tax.)

(2) Prepare a summary of cash receipts and disbursements to support the cash balance reported on the balance sheet.

4-7A. Kwik-Bild Corporation sells and erects shell houses. These are frame structures completely finished on the outside but unfinished on the inside except for flooring, partition studding, and ceiling joists. Shell houses are sold chiefly to customers who are handy with tools and who have time to do the interior wiring, plumbing, wall completion and finishing, and other work necessary to make the shell houses livable dwellings.

Kwik-Bild buys shell houses from a manufacturer in unassembled packages consisting of all lumber, roofing, doors, windows, and similar materials necessary to complete a shell house. Upon commencing operations in a new area, Kwik-Bild buys or leases land as a site for its local warehouse, field office, and display houses. Sample display houses are erected at a total cost of from $3,000 to $7,000 including the cost of the unassembled packages. The chief element of cost of the display houses is the unassembled packages, since erection is a short low-cost operation. Old sample models are torn down or altered into new models every three to seven years. Sample display houses have little salvage value because dismantling and moving costs amount to nearly as much as the cost of an unassembled package.

Instructions:

(1) A choice must be made between (a) expensing the costs of sample display houses in the period in which the expenditure is made, and (b) spreading the costs over more than one period. Discuss the advantages of each method.

(2) Would it be preferable to amortize the cost of display houses on the basis of (a) the passage of time or (b) the number of shell houses sold? Explain. (AICPA adapted)

4-8A. John McPherson, the president of Powell Company Ltd., sent a letter to one of his friends, Arthur McArthur, an accountant:

Dear Arthur:

Last month, our company engaged a new accountant who has followed a three-year accounting course. At the end of the fiscal year of the company, he prepared the financial statements. I and the other directors of the company have examined these financial statements but we are not sure that the presentation is in accordance with generally accepted accounting principles. Would you please examine them and send us your comments.

Enclosed is a copy of the financial statements and a list of items which might be useful to you.

Yours very truly,

John

Powell Company Ltd.
Balance Sheet
For Year Ended December 31, 1981

Assets

Current assets:

Accounts receivable	$1,541,817	
Inventories, at the lower of cost or market value	817,991	
Prepaid expenses	14,023	$2,373,831
Long-term investments		117,431
Fixed assets		976,841
Goodwill		25,000
		$3,493,103

Liabilities

Current liabilities:

Bank loan	$1,623,465	
Account payable and accrued charges	562,390	
Income and other taxes	64,993	$2,250,848
Long-term debt:		
Mortgage, 8%		300,000
		$2,550,848

Shareholders' Equity

Capital share, authorized, issued, and fully paid:

100,000 preferred shares	100,000	
500,000 common shares	500,000	
	600,000	
Retained earnings	342,255	942,255
		$3,493,103

Powell Company Ltd.
Statement of Retained Earnings
For Year Ended December 31, 1981

Balance — beginning of the year	$292,064
Premium on preferred shares issued during the year	50,000
	342,064
Net income for the year	20,191
	362,255
Dividends	20,000
Balance — end of the year	$342,255

Powell Company Ltd.
Income Statement
For Year Ended December 31, 1981

Sales		$6,329,411
Cost of sales		5,888,899
Gross profit		440,512
Selling expenses	$ 99,417	
Administration expenses	116,391	
Financial expenses	182,213	398,021
Income before taxes		42,491
Income taxes		22,300
Net income for the year	$	20,191

Other Information

(a) There are *absolutely* no notes attached to the financial statements.
(b) The inventories include finished goods, work in process, and raw materials.
(c) The figure for long-term investments represents the cost of shares of various companies. The market value of the shares has declined: their market value is now lower than their cost by $25,000. A survey of the market shows that it will be a permanent decline.
(d) The bank loan is secured by accounts receivable and inventories.
(e) The mortgage is repayable by annual principal instalments of $50,000 each, payable on December 31 of each year.
(f) During the year, the company issued for cash the 100,000 preferred shares. These shares with a par value of $1 were issued for $1.50 each.
(g) During the year, the directors decided to create a reserve of $100,000 for any possible loss.
(h) From the current administration expenses the accountant deducted an extraordinary profit of $40,200. This amount is net of Income taxes of $45,300.
(i) Financial expenses include interest on bank loan and on mortgage, bank charges, and cash discounts on sales and on purchases.

Instructions:
On the basis of the financial statements and the information provided,
 (i) list all errors of presentation in the financial statements;
(ii) explain clearly, with figures where possible, what should be the appropriate presentation for all errors found in (i). (SMA adapted.)

5 CASH, TEMPORARY INVESTMENTS, AND RECEIVABLES

At this point a foundation has been established for a careful analysis of the specific balance sheet classifications. The order of presentation begins with the most liquid assets — cash, temporary investments, and receivables, and proceeds with inventories, long-term assets, current and long-term liabilities, and owners' equity.

CASH

Cash is obviously the most active item on the balance sheet. It is involved in most business transactions. This is due to the nature of business transactions which include a price and conditions calling for settlement in terms of a medium of exchange. For example, purchases of goods and services normally result in cash payments; sales normally result in cash receipts.

In striking contrast to the activity of cash is its unproductive nature. Since cash is a measure of value, it cannot expand or grow unless it is converted into other asset forms. Excessive balances of cash on hand are often referred to as *idle cash*. Efficient cash management requires available cash to be continuously working in one of several ways — e.g., as part of the operating cycle or as a short-term or long-term investment.

Composition of Cash

Cash includes commercial and savings deposits in banks and elsewhere available upon demand, and money items on hand that can be used as a medium of exchange or that are acceptable for deposit at face value by a bank. Cash on hand would include petty cash funds, change funds, and other regularly used and unexpended monetary funds, together with such items as personal cheques, travellers' cheques, cashiers' cheques, bank drafts, and money orders.

"Acceptance at face value on deposit" is a satisfactory test in classifying items as cash. Since the concept of cash embodies a standard of value, no valuation problem is encountered in reporting those items qualifying as cash.

It is assumed that deposits in a bank are made regularly and that deposits become the basis for disbursements by the depositor. Post-dated cheques are in effect notes receivable and should not be recognized as cash until the time they can be deposited. Cheques deposited but returned by the bank because of insufficient funds in the debtor's account are receivables. Cash-due memorandums (IOU's) for money advanced to officers and employees are receivable items, in some instances less satisfactory receivables than those of trade customers. Paper left at a bank for collection represents a receivable until collection is made and the amount is added to the depositor's account.

Deposits in foreign banks subject to immediate and unrestricted withdrawal qualify as cash. Such balances should be converted into their Canadian dollar equivalents as of the date of the balance sheet. However, cash in foreign banks blocked or otherwise restricted as to use or withdrawal should be designated as claims or receivables of a current or non-current character and should be reported subject to allowances for losses on their realization.

Cash restricted as to use by agreement should be separately designated and reported. Restricted cash should be reported as a current item only if it is to be applied to some current purpose or obligation. Classification of the cash balance as current or non-current should parallel the classification applied to the related liability or obligation.

Cash balances not available for current purposes require separate designation and classification under a non-current heading on the balance sheet. The non-current classification applies to items such as the following: time deposits not currently available as a result of withdrawal restrictions; cash deposits on bids or options that may be applied to the acquisition of non-current assets; and cash funds held by trustees for plant acquisitions, bond retirement, and pension payments.

A credit balance in the cash account resulting from the issuance of cheques in excess of the amount on deposit is known as a *bank overdraft* and should be reported as a current liability. An overdraft may not necessarily embarrass a company if a number of cheques are outstanding and deposits are made to cover the cheques before clearance. When a company has two or more balances with a single bank, there can be no objection to the offsetting of the overdraft against accounts with positive balances. However, when a company has accounts with two different banks and there is a positive balance in one account and an overdraft in the other, both an asset balance and a liability balance should be recognized.

Control of Cash

The term *internal control* has been broadly defined as ". . . the plan of organization and all of the coordinate methods and measures adopted within a business to safeguard its assets, check the accuracy and reliability of its accounting data, promote operational efficiency, and encourage adherence to prescribed managerial policies."[1] This definition may be considered to embrace both *accounting controls* and *administrative controls*. Accounting controls dealing with the safeguarding of assets and the reliability of records are expressed in the form of systems of authorization and approval, separation of duties concerned with record keeping and reporting from those concerned with operations and asset custody, physical controls over assets, and internal auditing. Administrative controls dealing with operational efficiency and adherence to managerial policies are expressed in the form of statistical analyses, time and motion studies, performance reports, employee training programs, and quality controls.[2]

Obviously, the system of internal control must be developed with appropriate regard to the size and nature of the particular entity to be served. Its design should provide the maximum contributions practicable considering any special risks faced as well as the cost of providing controls.

In any system of internal accounting control, special emphasis must be placed on the procedures for handling and accounting for cash.

Problems in Cash Control. Because of the characteristics of cash — its small bulk, its lack of owner identification, and its immediate transferability — it is the asset most subject to misappropriation, intentional or otherwise. Losses can be avoided only by careful control of cash from the time it is received until the time it is spent.

Control over business cash normally requires as a minimum the separation of cash custodial functions and cash recording functions. When the same persons have access to cash and also to cash records, the business becomes vulnerable to the misappropriation of cash and to the manipulation or falsification of cash records. The following are representative of practices found under these circumstances: (1) cash receipts from sales, from recoveries of accounts previously written off, from refunds on invoice overpayments, and from other sources are understated, the unrecorded cash being pocketed; (2) receivables are not entered on the books and cash collected on these

---

[1]*Statement on Auditing Standards No. 1*, "Codification of Auditing Standards and Procedures" (New York: American Institute of Certified Public Accountants, 1973), par. 320.09.

[2]*Ibid.*, par. 320.10.

receivables is withheld; (3) customers' accounts are credited for remittances but Sales Returns or Allowance for Doubtful Accounts is debited and the cash is withheld; (4) cheques for personal purposes are debited to business expense; (5) invoices, vouchers, receipts, payroll records, or vouchers once approved and paid are used in support of fictitious charges, and endorsements on cheques issued in payment of these charges are subsequently forged; (6) the cash balance is misstated by erroneous footings in the cash receipts and disbursement records, cash equivalent to the misstatement being withheld. Two additional practices, cheque kiting and lapping, may be found when those who handle cash also maintain the cash records of the business.

Cheque kiting occurs when at the end of a month a transfer of funds is made by cheque from one bank to another to cover a cash shortage, and the entry to record the issue of the cheque is held over until the beginning of the new period. A cash increase in the customer's balance is recognized by the second bank in the current month as a result of the receipt of the cheque, but a corresponding decrease in the customer's balance is not recognized by the first bank because the cheque has not yet been presented for payment. When the bank statements are received, the balance in the bank in which the cheque was deposited shows an increase. At the same time, the balance shown in the bank on which the cheque was drawn remains unchanged. A cash shortage is thus temporarily concealed.

Lapping occurs when a customer's remittance is misappropriated, the customer's account being credited when cash is collected from another customer at a later date. This process may be continued with further misappropriations and increasing delays in postings. To illustrate lapping, assume that on successive days cash is received from customers A, B, and C in amounts of $75, $125, and $120. A's payment is misappropriated. A is subsequently credited with $75 out of B's payment and the difference, $50, is misappropriated. B is credited for $125 upon C's $120 payment and $5 is returned on the amounts originally *borrowed*. The shortage at this point is $120, the unrecorded credit to C's account.

Attributes of Cash Control Systems. A system of accounting control over cash funds should serve to disclose cash discrepancies as well as to fix responsibility for any possible misappropriations or mistakes in handling and recording cash. When misuse of funds or errors are indicated, it is only fair to members of an organization to determine the causes and to fix the responsibility so that innocent parties may be spared any embarrassment. Responsibilities for the handling and recording functions should be specifically defined and scrupulously observed and carried out.

The system for the control of cash must be adapted to a particular business. It is not feasible to attempt to describe all of the features and techniques employed in businesses of various kinds and sizes. In general, however, systems of cash control deny access to the records to those who handle cash. The misappropriation of cash is greatly reduced if two or more employees must conspire in the embezzlement. Further, systems normally provide for separation of the receiving and paying functions. The basic characteristics of a cash control system are listed below:

1. Specifically assigned responsibility for handling cash receipts.
2. Separation of handling and recording cash receipts.
3. Daily deposit of all cash received.
4. Voucher system to control cash payments.
5. Internal audit at irregular intervals.

Specifically Assigned Responsibility for Handling Cash Receipts. A fundamental principle in controlling any asset is that the responsibility be specifically assigned to one person. This principle is especially vital in the area of cash. If more than one person must have access to the same cash fund at different times, a reconciliation of the cash on hand should be made each time the responsibility is shifted. Any shortage or questionable transaction can then be identified with a particular person.

Separation of Handling and Recording Cash Receipts. An adequate control system normally requires that cash from sales and cash remittances from customers be made available directly to the treasurer or the cashier for deposit, while records related to these transactions, as well as records related to bank deposits, be made available directly to the accounting department. It is also desirable that comparisons of bank deposits with the accounting records of cash be made regularly by a third party who is engaged neither in the cash handling nor in the cash recording functions. Frequently, for example, a clerk opens the mail, prepares lists of remittances in duplicate, and then sends the cash and one copy of the list of remittances to the cashier and the second copy of the list to the accounting department. Readings of cash registers are made by some responsible individual other than the cashier at the end of the day. The cash, together with a summary of the receipts, is sent to the cashier; a summary of the receipts is also sent to the accounting department. Although deposits in the bank are made by the cashier or treasurer, entries in the accounts are made from lists of remittances and register readings prepared by individuals not otherwise involved in handling or recording cash. Members of the accounting or auditing staff compare periodic bank statements with related data in the accounts to determine whether the data are in agreement. If customers' remittances are not listed and the cash is misused, statements to customers will report excessive amounts and protests will lead to sources of the discrepancies; if cash receipts listed are not deposited properly, the bank record will not agree with cash records.

Daily Deposit of All Cash Received. The daily deposit of all cash received prevents sums of cash from lying around the office and being used for other than business purposes. Moreover, the bank now protects company funds and releases these only upon proper company authorization. When the full receipts are deposited daily, the bank's record of deposits must agree with the depositor's record of cash receipts. This double record provides an automatic check over cash receipts.

Voucher System to Control Cash Payments. The use of a voucher system to control cash payments is a desirable feature of cash control. Vouchers authorizing disbursements of cash by cheque are made at the time goods or services are received and found acceptable. Cheques are also prepared and are sent, together with documents supporting the disbursements, to the person specifically authorized to make payment. This person signs and issues cheques only after careful inspection of the vouchers supporting and authorizing payments. Thus, receiving and paying functions of the business are maintained as two separate systems. In each instance, custodial and recording activities are exercised by different parties.

Internal Audit at Irregular Intervals. Internal audits at irregular and unannounced intervals may be made a part of the system of cash control. A member of the internal auditing staff verifies the records and checks on the activities of those employees handling cash to make sure the procedures of the system are being followed.

Double Record of Cash. The preceding section listed the daily deposit of all cash received as an important factor in the control of cash. If all cash receipts are deposited daily, then the bank record of deposits will agree with the depositor's record of cash receipts. As a complementary device, all cash payments should be made by cheque; the bank's record for cheques should agree with the depositor's record for cash payments. Two complete cash summaries are thus available, one in the cash account and the other on the monthly bank statement.

Maintenance of this double record of cash involves two special business and accounting procedures described in the following sections: (1) the adoption of a system of cash disbursements from a petty cash fund, and (2) reconciliation of the bank balance with the cash account balance at regular intervals.

Imprest System of Cash Funds. Immediate cash payments and payments too small to be made by cheque may be made from a petty cash fund. Under the *imprest system*, the petty cash fund is created by drawing a cheque to Petty Cash for the amount of the fund. In recording the establishment of the fund, Petty Cash Fund is debited and Cash is credited. The cash is then turned over to a cashier or some person who is solely responsible for payments out of the fund. The cashier should require a signed receipt (which may be printed in prenumbered form) for all payments made. Frequently, a bill, invoice, or other memorandum is submitted when a payment is requested.

Whenever the amount of cash in the fund runs low and also at the end of each fiscal period, the fund is replenished by writing a cheque equal to the payments made. In recording replenishment, expenses and other appropriate accounts are debited for petty cash disbursements and Cash is credited. Replenishment is necessary whenever statements are to be prepared since petty cash disbursements are recognized in the accounts only when the fund is replenished.

The cashier of the petty cash fund is held accountable for the total amount of the fund. The person responsible must have on hand at all times cash and signed receipts equal in amount to the original balance of the fund.

The imprest system may be employed not only for petty cash but for other cash funds in a large organization. For example, a branch office or agency may be allowed a fund subsequently replenished for amounts equal to disbursements out of the fund. Evidence concerning payments out of the fund is submitted with the request for replenishment, and fund disbursements are recorded in the accounts at the time of fund replenishment.

Reconciliation of Bank Balances. A comparison of the bank balance with the balance reported in the accounts is usually made monthly by means of a summary known as a *bank reconciliation statement*. The bank reconciliation statement is prepared to disclose any errors or irregularities existing in either the records of the bank or the records of the business entity. It is developed in a form that points out the reasons for discrepancies in the two balances. It should be prepared by an individual who neither handles nor records cash. Any discrepancies should be brought to the immediate attention of appropriate company officials.

An understanding of the reciprocal relationship existing between the records of the depositor and of the bank is necessary in the preparation of the reconciliation statement. All debits to the bank in the accounts of the depositor should be matched by credits to the depositor in the accounts of the bank; all credits to the bank in the accounts of the depositor should be matched by debits to the depositor in the accounts of the bank.

When the two records are compared, certain items may appear on one record and not on the other, resulting in a difference in the two balances. Most of these differences result from timing lags, and are thus normal. The differences in depositor and bank balances may be classified as follows:

1. *Debits on the depositor's records without corresponding credits on the bank records.* For example, a deposit recognized on the depositor's records on the last day of the month may have been mailed, put into an after-hours depository, or held for transfer to the bank on the next day, and does not appear on the bank statement. This item is referred to as a *deposit in-transit.*

2. *Credits on the depositor's records without corresponding debits on the bank records.* For example, cheques drawn and recognized on the depositor's records may not have cleared and do not appear on the bank statement. This item is referred to as an *outstanding cheque.*
3. *Debits on the bank records without corresponding credits on depositor's records.* For example, the bank may have charged the depositor's account for bank services, chequebooks, interest, returned customers' cheques, and other items, but the depositor has not been notified of these charges before receiving a bank statement and these do not appear in the depositor's accounts.
4. *Credits on the bank records without corresponding debits on the depositor's records.* For example, the bank may have credited the depositor's account for collections, but the depositor has not been notified of these before receiving a bank statement and these do not appear in the depositor's accounts.

If, after considering the items mentioned, the balances according to the bank statement and the depositor's records cannot be reconciled, a detailed analysis of both the bank's records and the depositor's accounts may be necessary to determine whether errors or other irregularities exist on the records of either party.

After preparing the reconciliation, the depositor should record any items appearing on the bank statement and requiring recognition on the company's accounts as well as any corrections for errors discovered in its own records. The bank should be notified immediately of any bank errors.

The bank reconciliation is frequently expanded to incorporate a proof of both receipts and disbursements as separate steps in the reconciliation process. This is often referred to as a *four-column reconciliation* or a *proof of cash* and is widely used by auditors when there is any question of possible discrepancies in the handling of cash. Two reconciliation forms may be employed; one form develops corrected balances for both receipts and disbursements of the bank and the depositor, as illustrated on page 158. The other form, as illustrated at the top of page 159, reports the items accounting for the discrepancies in receipts and disbursement balances on the two sets of records.

Opening balances, increases, decreases, and closing balances as reported on both the bank statement and the depositor's records are first listed. A reconciliation as of the end of the preceding period is then provided in the first column. Receipts are reconciled in the second column and disbursements in the third column. With proof of receipt and disbursement data, adjustments relating to ending balances may now be reported in the final column and the closing bank and general ledger balances proved.

In order to complete this type of reconciliation, each adjustment must be carefully analysed. Two columns are always affected for each adjustment. For example, receipts of $515.40 on October 31, 1981, were received by the bank in November and are therefore included in the total bank receipts of $21,212.40 for November. However, the deposit was recorded in the accounts

Caughman Ltd.
Reconciliation of Receipts, Disbursements, and Bank Balance
November 30, 1981

	Beginning Reconciliation October 31	Receipts	Disburse-ments	Ending Reconciliation November 30
Balance per bank statement	$5,895.42	$21,212.40	$24,128.10	$2,979.72
Receipts not deposited:				
October 31	515.40	(515.40)		
November 30		658.50		658.50
Outstanding cheques:				
October 31	(810.50)		(810.50)	
November 30			703.83	(703.83)
Charge for interest made by bank in error			(12.50)	12.50
Corrected bank balance	$5,600.32	$21,355.50	$24,008.93	$2,946.89
Balance per general ledger	$5,406.22	$21,057.00	$23,910.73	$2,552.49
Bank service charges:				
October	(5.90)		(5.90)	
November			3.16	(3.16)
Customer's cheque deposited November 25 found to be uncollectible			118.94	(118.94)
Drafts collected by bank:				
October	200.00	(200.00)		
November		498.50		498.50
Cheque No. 1116 for $46 recorded by depositor at $64 in error			(18.00)	18.00
Corrected general ledger balance	$5,600.32	$21,355.50	$24,008.93	$2,946.89

as a receipt in October and is not included in the receipts of $21,057 for November. The reconciliation accounts for this by deducting the in-transit receipt from the total bank receipts.

The parentheses in the disbursements column may be reversed; thus the total disbursement is shown with parentheses to indicate a deduction when adding horizontally. Using this reverse procedure requires a careful analysis of the reconciling items because whenever an item is to be added vertically to the disbursement total it must be enclosed in parentheses, while an item to be deducted is not enclosed in parentheses.

This expanded reconciliation procedure normally reduces the time and effort required to find errors made by either the bank or the depositor. In developing comparisons of both receipts and disbursements, the areas in which errors have been made, as well as the amounts of the discrepancies within each area, are immediately identified and checking procedures can be directed and narrowed accordingly.

Caughman Ltd.
Reconciliation of Receipts, Disbursements, and Bank Balance
November 30, 1981

	Beginning Reconciliation October 31	Receipts	Disbursements	Ending Reconciliation November 30
Balance per bank statement	$5,895.42	$21,212.40	$24,128.10	$2,979.72
Receipts not deposited:				
October 31	515.40	(515.40)		
November 30		658.50		658.50
Outstanding cheques:				
October 31	(810.50)		(810.50)	
November 30			703.83	(703.83)
Bank service charges:				
October........................	5.90		5.90	
November			(3.16)	3.16
Customer's cheque deposited November 25 found to be uncollectible			(118.94)	118.94
Drafts collected by bank:				
October........................	(200.00)	200.00		
November		(498.50)		(498.50)
Charge for interest made by bank in error			(12.50)	12.50
Cheque No. 1116 for $46 recorded by depositor at $64 in error			18.00	(18.00)
Balance per general ledger	$5,406.22	$21,057.00	$23,910.73	$2,552.49

Reconciliation of Bank Balance to General Ledger Balance

Misrepresentation of Current Condition. Certain practices designed to present a more favorable financial condition than is actually the case may be encountered. Such practices are sometimes referred to as *window dressing*. For example, cash records may be held open for a few days after the close of a fiscal period and cash received from customers during this period reported as receipts of the preceding period. An improved cash position is thus reported. If this balance is then used as a basis for drawing predated cheques in payment of accounts payable, the ratio of current assets to current liabilities is improved. For example, if current assets are $30,000 and current liabilities are $20,000 providing a current ratio of 1.5 to 1, recording payment to creditors of $10,000 will produce balances of $20,000 and $10,000, a current ratio of 2 to 1. In addition, the current position, as well as earnings and owner's equity, is overstated by predating sales made at the beginning of the new period. A careful review of the records will disclose whether improper practices have been employed. If such practices are discovered, the accounts should be corrected.

TEMPORARY INVESTMENTS

A company with excess cash temporarily available may deposit these funds as a time deposit, a certificate of deposit at a bank, or it may purchase securities. As a result, revenue will be produced that would not otherwise be available if cash were left idle. Investments made during seasonal periods of low activity can be converted into cash in periods of expanding operations. Asset items arising from temporary conversions of cash are commonly reported in the "Current assets" section of the balance sheet as "Temporary investments."

Criteria for Reporting Securities as Temporary Investments

Investments in securities qualify for reporting as temporary investments as long as (1) there is a ready market for converting such securities into cash, and (2) it is management's intention to sell them if the need for cash arises.

Securities are considered marketable when a day-to-day market exists and when they can be sold on short notice. The volume of trading in the securities should be sufficient to absorb a company's holdings without materially affecting the market price. Generally, marketable securities include such items as listed shares, high-grade bonds, and first-mortgage notes. Government securities, despite their relatively low yield, are also a highly favored form of marketable security because of their stable prices and wide market. Securities having a limited market and which fluctuate widely in price are not suitable for temporary investments.

Marketable securities may be converted into cash shortly after being acquired or they may be held for some time. In either case, however, they are properly classified as temporary investments as long as management intends to sell them when the need for cash arises. The deciding factor is management's intent, not the length of time the securities are held.

Recording Purchase and Sale of Marketable Securities

Shares and bonds acquired as temporary investments are recorded at cost, which includes brokers' fees, taxes, and other charges incurred in their acquisition. Shares are normally quoted at a price per single share; bonds are quoted at a price per $100 face value.

When bonds are acquired between interest payment dates, the bond price is increased by a charge for accrued interest to the date of purchase. This charge should not be reported as part of investment cost. Two assets have been acquired — bonds and accrued interest — and the purchase price should be reported in two separate asset accounts. Upon the receipt of bond interest, the accrued interest account is closed and Interest Revenue is credited for any excess. Instead of recording the interest as an asset, Interest Revenue may be debited for the accrued interest paid. The subsequent collection of interest would then be credited in full to Interest Revenue. The latter procedure is usually more convenient.

When bonds are acquired at a higher or lower price than their maturity value and it is expected that they will be held until maturity, periodic amortization of the premium or accumulation of the discount with corresponding adjustments to interest revenue is appropriate. However, when bonds are acquired as a temporary investment and it is not likely the bonds will be held until maturity, such procedures are normally not necessary.

When a temporary investment is sold, the difference between the sales proceeds and the cost or carrying value of the securities is reported as a gain or loss on the sale.

Valuation of Marketable Securities

Three different methods for the valuation of marketable securities have been advanced: (1) cost, (2) cost or market, whichever is lower, and (3) market.

Cost. Valuation of marketable securities at cost refers to the original acquisition price of a marketable security including all related fees, unless there has been recognition previously of a permanent impairment of value and a new cost basis has been assigned to the marketable security. When this method is strictly applied, the recognition of either gain or loss is deferred until the asset is sold, at which time investment cost is matched against investment proceeds.

Cost or Market, Whichever is Lower. When using the lower of cost or market method, if market is lower than cost, security values are written down to the lower value; if market is higher than cost, securities are maintained at cost, gains awaiting confirmation through sale.

Traditionally, the lower of cost or market method has been used only when market was considered substantially lower than cost, and the decline was not considered temporary. The *Accounting Recommendations*, however, state "when the market value of temporary investments has declined below the carrying value, they should be carried at market value."[3]

Significant fluctuations of the stock market in recent years have created many more situations where market values are lower than cost. After due consideration of the issues involved, the FASB, in December of 1975, issued Statement No. 12 concerning accounting for certain marketable securities. This statement requires that marketable equity securities (primarily com-

---

[3]*CICA Handbook: Accounting Recommendations, Section 3010*, "Temporary Investments" (Toronto: Canadian Institute of Chartered Accountants, 1973), par. 06.

mon shares) be carried at the lower of aggregate cost or market value.[4] Other marketable securities, such as bonds, still may be carried at cost unless there is a decline that is substantial in amount and is not due to temporary conditions.[5]

In accounting for marketable equity securities, it should be noted that FASB Statement No. 12 requires use of the lower of aggregate cost or market value. An important factor in choosing the aggregate basis is that many companies consider their marketable securities portfolios as collective assets. Further, the Board felt that applying the lower of cost or market procedure on an individual security basis would be unduly conservative.

Market. Market value refers to the current market price of the marketable security. Their use in accounting rests on the premise that market provides an objective basis for the valuation of marketable securities. Securities on the balance sheet are reported at their current values whether higher or lower than cost.

In applying market, it would be possible to recognize changes in security values by reporting the gain or the loss on the income statement. However, if it is felt that any increase in income, caused by market values in excess of cost, should await the sale of securities, a separate capital account, such as Unrealized Appreciation in Valuation of Marketable Securities, may be credited.

To illustrate the procedure that may be followed, assume at the end of 1981 securities costing $50,000 have quoted values of $60,000. The securities are sold in 1982 for $62,000. Unrealized appreciation is reported at the end of 1981. This is cancelled when the securities are sold in 1982 and the effect of the sale is reported in the income statement. The entries are:

December 31, 1981

Marketable Securities — Increase to Current Market Value	10,000	
Unrealized Appreciation in Valuation of Marketable Securities ...		10,000

March 5, 1982

Cash	62,000	
Unrealized Appreciation in Valuation of Marketable Securities	10,000	
Marketable Securities (at cost)		50,000
Marketable Securities — Increase to Current Market Value		10,000
Gain on Sale of Marketable Securities		12,000

In the above illustration, instead of recording the valuation change on the balance sheet, it is possible to reflect the change on the income statement by crediting Unrealized Gain on Marketable Securities instead of the unrealized appreciation account.

---

[4]*Statement of Financial Accounting Standards No. 12*, "Accounting for Certain Marketable Securities" (Stamford, Conn.: Financial Accounting Standards Board, 1975), par. 8. There is no comparable Canadian pronouncement.

[5]While FASB Statement No. 12 deals only with marketable equity securities and does not require the lower of aggregate cost or market for other marketable securities, it seems logical to treat all short-term marketable securities similarly. In the illustrations and end-of-chapter material for this chapter, the lower of cost or market rule is used for all marketable securities, whether shares or bonds.

Evaluation of Methods

Valuation at cost finds support on the grounds that it is an extension of the cost principle; the asset is carried at cost until a sale or exchange provides an alternative asset and confirms a gain or loss.

However, certain objections to cost can be raised. The use of cost means investments may be carried at amounts differing from values objectively determinable at the balance sheet date, and the integrity of both balance sheet and income statement measurements can be challenged. The use of cost also means identical securities may be reported at different values because of purchases at different prices. A further objection is that management, in controlling the sale of securities, can determine the periods in which gains or losses are to be recognized even though these changes may have accrued over a number of periods.

The use of market value is advocated on the basis that there is evidence of the net realizable value of the marketable securities held at the balance sheet date and therefore any changes from previous carrying values should be recognized as gains or losses in the current period. Assuming marketable securities are defined as having a readily available sales price, this method is objective and relatively simple to apply. The major objection to this method is that gains or losses may be recognized prior to realization, i.e., prior to the actual sale of the securities. Market is also challenged as a departure from the cost principle and as lacking in conservatism.

The lower of cost or market procedure provides for recognizing market declines and serves to prevent potential mistakes arising in analysing statements when these declines are not reported. The lower of cost or market is supported as a conservative procedure. This approach may be challenged on the basis that it may be the most complicated method to apply, and it fails to provide consistency in valuation — cost at the end of one period may be replaced by a lower market at the end of the next. Furthermore, if applied to individual securities, the lower of cost or market procedure may be overly conservative, providing valuation less than the aggregate lower market.

RECEIVABLES

Receivables are composed of two classes: (1) those supported by formal promises to pay in the form of notes, referred to as *notes receivable*, and (2) those not so supported, and commonly referred to as *accounts receivable*. Accounts receivable may be divided into groupings as follows: (a) receivables from customers; (b) receivables from others; and (c) accrued receivables. Receivables are established in the accounts only when supportable claims exist and it can be assumed the claims will be realized.

Notes Receivable

A note is an unconditional written promise by one party to another to pay a certain sum of money at a specified time. The term *notes* is used to include not only promisory notes but also time drafts and trade acceptances. If time drafts and trade acceptances are material in amount, they may be summarized separately.

The notes receivable designation for reporting purposes should be limited to negotiable short-term instruments acquired from trade debtors and not yet due. When a written instrument fails to meet these requirements, it should be reported separately under an appropriately descriptive title. For example, notes arising from loans to customers, officers, employees, and affiliated companies should be reported separately.

Accounts Receivable

As previously indicated, accounts receivable broadly include all receivables other than those supported by some form of commercial paper. Although it would be appropriate to refer to open accounts with customers arising from the sale of goods and services as Trade Debtors or Trade Receivables to distinguish these from other receivables, it has become established practice to use the designation Accounts Receivable to represent these claims.

A receivable arising from the sale of goods is generally recognized when the title to goods passes to the buyer. Because the point at which title passes may vary with the terms of the sale, it is general practice to recognize the receivable when goods are shipped to the customer. Receivables should not be recognized for goods shipped on approval where the shipper retains title to the goods until there is a formal acceptance, or for goods shipped on consignment where the shipper retains title to the goods until they are sold by the consignee.

Receivables for services to customers are properly recognized when the services are performed. When work under a contract has not been completed at the end of the period, the amount due as of the balance sheet date will have to be calculated. Receivables should be recognized for the portion of work completed under construction contracts and for reimbursable costs and accrued fees on cost-plus-fixed-fee contracts.

Ordinarily, detailed accrued fees of customer transactions and customers' balances are carried in subsidiary records. Entries to subsidiary records may be made from original business documents evidencing the transactions. With machine methods, subsidiary records are frequently maintained simultaneously with the preparation of invoices and remittance records.

Non-trade receivables may be summarized in appropriately titled accounts and should be reported separately. The following are examples of the receivables that should be carried separately: claims arising from the sale of securities or property other than goods or services; advances to shareholders, directors, officers, employees, and affiliated companies; deposits with creditors, utilities, and other agencies; purchase prepayments; deposits to guarantee contract performance or expense payment; claims for losses or damages; claims for rebates and tax refunds; dividends receivable; and in some jurisdictions, subscriptions for capital stock.

Certain revenues for services or goods accrue with the passage of time and are most conveniently recognized when collections are made. At the end of the period, it is necessary to calculate the amounts accrued since the last collections and to establish appropriate accrued receivables. Accrued interest is recognized on assets, such as bank deposits, notes, bonds, and annuities. Rentals may accrue on real estate holdings. Royalties and patent fees may accrue on certain rights and properties. For some business entities, accrued receivables may be small in total; for others, they may involve significant amounts.

It was indicated in an earlier chapter that the "Current assets" classification as broadly conceived comprehends all receivables identified with the normal operating cycle. Instalment and other deferred collection contracts are current regardless of their terms. But receivables arising outside of the inventory-to-cash cycle qualify as current only if they are expected to be collected within one year. Non-current receivables are reported under the "Long-term Investments" or "Other long-term assets" caption, whichever may be considered appropriate.

Amounts due from officers, directors, and major shareholders arising out of sales and subject to the usual credit terms are normally considered current; however, when claims have arisen from transactions other than sales and current recovery is not assured, such items are properly classified as non-current. Sales to affiliated companies give rise to current claims, but advances are generally regarded as long-term in nature.

Subscriptions for capital stock are current only if they are currently collectible; when current collection is not probable or when payments may be deferred indefinitely, such balances are reported as non-current assets, or in some instances more appropriately as subtractions from capital balances so that no more than the amount actually paid in by shareholders and subscribers is reported as capital.[6]

Creditor and customer accounts with contra balances require special attention. These balances are found by an analysis of subsidiary ledger detail. For example, assume the accounts payable control account reports a balance of $10,000. Inspection of subsidiary account detail reveals accounts with credit balances of $10,500 and accounts with debit balances of $500. The nature of the debit balances should be investigated. If the debit balances

---

[6]Subscriptions for capital stock may be permitted or excluded depending upon the companies or corporations act of the incorporating jurisdiction.

have arisen as a result of overpayments or returns and allowances after payment, they are reportable as current assets in view of the claims they represent for cash or merchandise from vendors. Such balances are properly reported under a title, such as Creditors Accounts with Debit Balances or Sundry Claims. If debit balances represent advance payments on the purchase of raw materials or merchandise, these too are current assets reportable under some descriptive title, such as Advances on Purchase Contracts. In either case, Accounts Payable is reported at $10,500. Although both an asset and a liability are reported, no adjustment to the control account or the subsidiary ledger detail is required.

Customer ledger detail needs similar analysis. Customers' accounts with credit balances may result from overpayments, from customer returns after full payment, or from advance payments by customers. Such credits should be recognized as current liabilities, and accounts receivable should be reported at the sum of the debit balances in the subsidiary ledger.

When contra balances in customer and creditor accounts are not material in amount, they are frequently disregarded and only the net receivable or payable balance is reported on the balance sheet.

VALUATION OF RECEIVABLES

Theoretically, receivables arising from the sale of property, goods, or services should be reported at their net realizable or cash value. This would suggest that receivables should be reduced by any interest implicit in their face amount, unearned finance or interest charges reported in their face amounts, and uncollectible items anticipated in the course of their collection.

Reporting Receivables at Present Values

When a sale is made at an amount that is collectible at some future date, the amount collectible may be regarded as consisting of both a sales price and a charge for interest for the period of the payment deferral. In the absence of an established exchange or sales price, the *present value* of the receivable should be determined by reducing the face amount of the receivable by an interest rate regarded as appropriate under the circumstances for the period that payment is deferred. The interest rate approximated for this period is generally referred to as the *imputed rate*; the process of arriving at the present value of the sum is generally referred to as *discounting* the sum. The difference between the face value of the receivable and its present value is recognized as a discount.[7] This discount is amortized as a credit to Interest

---

[7]An interest rate provided by terms of the receivable that is higher or lower than a rate regarded as appropriate under the circumstances would call for similar analysis and the recognition of a premium or discount on the receivable.

Revenue over the life of the receivable; in preparing a balance sheet, any unamortized discount is reported as a direct subtraction from the face amount of the receivable.

To illustrate, assume on January 1, 1981, Alpha Corporation sells used equipment with a book value of $600 receiving a note for $1,000 due in two years with no stated interest. If the equipment had an established sales price, the difference between the sales price and the face amount of the notes would be considered the charge for interest to be recognized over the two years. However, in this case, the value of the equipment is unknown but the interest rate for this type of note is estimated to be 10%. The following entry is made to record the sale:

Notes Receivable	1,000.00	
Equipment		600.00
Gain on Sale of Equipment		226.40
Discount on Notes Receivable		173.60

Computation:
Discount on notes receivable:
$1,000 note discounted for two years at 10% ($1,000 × .8264 = $826.40): $1,000.00 − $826.40 = $173.60[8]

The amount of the discount amortized each year is found by applying the imputed interest rate to the net balance or carrying value of the note (the face value less unamortized discount). Amortization for the two years is as shown in the schedule below:

Year	(1) Face Amount of Note	(2) Unamoritzed Discount	(3) Net Amount (1) − (2)	(4) Discount Amortization 10% × (3)
1	$1,000	$173.60	$826.40	$ 82.64
2	1,000	90.96	909.04	90.96*
				$173.60

*The 6¢ discrepancy is due to rounding.

The entry for the first year's amortization would be:

Discount on Notes Receivable	82.64	
Interest Revenue		82.64

Although the proper valuation of receivables calls for the procedure just described, exceptions to this procedure may be appropriate because of materiality or practical considerations. In the United States, the Accounting Principles Board in Opinion No. 21 provided guidelines for the recognition of interest on receivables and payables and the accounting subsequently to be

[8]The present value of $1 due in two years at an interest rate of 10% is $0.8264. This is found in Table II which is located on the inside of the front cover.

employed. However, the Board indicated that this process is not to be regarded as applicable under all circumstances. Among the exceptions are the following important groups:

> . . . receivables and payables arising from transactions with customers or suppliers in the normal course of business which are due in customary trade terms not exceeding approximately one year.[9]

In Canada, the *Accounting Recommendations* do not, as yet, include any corresponding pronouncement. Thus, in Canadian practice interest is rarely imputed for accounting purposes because such is not required under Canadian GAAP. Given the obvious theoretical merit of the method, the recognition of interest on receivables and payables by discounting should be encouraged in Canadian accounting practice.

Estimated Uncollectible Accounts

Almost invariably some of the receivables arising from sales will prove uncollectible. Uncollectible amounts will have to be anticipated if the charge for them is to be related to the period of the sale and receivables are to be stated at their estimated realizable amounts.

The amount of receivables estimated uncollectible is recorded by a debit to expense and a credit to an allowance account. The charge for doubtful accounts may be reported as a deduction from sales on the theory that it is net sales — sales after uncollectibles — that must cover current charges and yield a profit. Instead of being treated as a contra-sales balance, however, the expense item is usually regarded as emerging from a failure of management, and, hence, is reported as a selling, general and administrative, or financial charge, depending upon the division held responsible for approving credit sales. The allowance account is then reported as a subtraction from accounts receivable.

When positive evidence is available concerning the partial or complete worthlessness of an account, the allowance account is debited and the receivable is credited. Positive evidence of worthlessness is found in the bankruptcy, death, or disappearance of a debtor, failure to enforce collection legally, or a barring of collection by the statute of limitations. Write-offs should be supported by evidence of the uncollectibility of the accounts and should be authorized in writing by appropriate company officers.

Bases for Estimating Charge for Doubtful Accounts

The estimate for doubtful accounts may be based upon (1) the amount of sales or (2) the amount of receivables. When sales are used as the basis for

---

[9]*Opinions of the Accounting Principles Board, No. 21*, "Interest on Receivables and Payables" (New York: American Institute of Certified Public Accountants, 1972), par. 3(a). It may be noted that the primary objective of the Opinion was not to suggest new principles but simply to clarify and refine the manner of applying existing principles.

calculation, the problem of estimating the charge for doubtful accounts is viewed as one involving primarily the proper measurement of income. When receivables are used as the basis for calculation, the problem is viewed as one involving primarily the proper valuation of receivables.

If the sales basis is used, the periodic charge for bad debts is strictly related to sales of the current period. Any previous balance in the allowance account resulting from past period charges is disregarded. For example, if 2% of sales are considered doubtful in terms of collection and sales for the period are $100,000, the charge for doubtful accounts expense would be 2% of the current period's sales, or $2,000, regardless of the carryover balance in the allowance account. On the other hand, if the amount of receivables is used as a basis for estimating the charge for doubtful accounts, a corrected allowance figure is established each period by adjusting the existing balance. For example, if it is determined that the allowance for doubtful accounts should be $1,500 and the current credit balance in the allowance account is $600, the debit to Doubtful Accounts Expense and corresponding credit to the allowance account would be $900.

Adjustment for Doubtful Accounts Based on Sales. The charges for doubtful accounts of recent periods are related to the sales of these periods in developing a percentage of the charge for doubtful accounts to sales. This percentage may be modified by expectations in the light of current experience. Since doubtful accounts occur only with credit sales, it would seem logical to develop a percentage of doubtful accounts to charge sales of past periods. This percentage would be applied to charge sales of the current period. However, since extra work may be required in maintaining records of cash and credit sales or in analysing sales data, the percentage is frequently developed in terms of total sales. Unless there is considerable fluctuation in the proportion of cash and credit sales periodically, the total sales method will give satisfactory results.

The *sales percentage method* for anticipating doubtful accounts is widely used in practice because it is sound in theory and simple to apply. Although normally offering a satisfactory approach to income measurement by providing equitable charges to periodic revenue, the method may not offer a "cash realizable" valuation for receivables. This shortcoming can be overcome by analysing receivables at different intervals and correcting the allowance for any significant excess or deficiency.

Adjustment for Doubtful Accounts Based on Receivables. There are two methods of establishing and maintaining an allowance for doubtful accounts when receivables are used as the basis for the adjustment:

1. The allowance is adjusted to a certain percentage of receivables.
2. The allowance is adjusted to an amount determined by ageing the accounts.

Under the first method, the uncollectible accounts experiences of recent periods are related to accounts outstanding in these periods and the data are considered in terms of special current conditions. An estimate of the probable uncollectibles is developed and Doubtful Accounts Expense is debited and Allowance for Doubtful Accounts credited for an amount bringing the allowance to the desired balance. To illustrate, assume receivables of $60,000 and a credit balance of $200 in the allowance account at the end of the period. Doubtful accounts are estimated at 2% of accounts receivable, or $1,200. The following entry brings the allowance to the desired amount:

| Doubtful Accounts Expense | 1,000 | |
| Allowance for Doubtful Accounts | | 1,000 |

Although this method provides a satisfactory approach to the valuation of receivables, it may fail to provide equitable period charges to revenue. This is particularly true in view of the irregular determinations of actual uncollectibles as well as the lag in their recognition. After the first year, periodic provisions are directly affected by the current reductions in the allowance resulting from a recognition of uncollectible accounts originating in prior periods.

The most commonly used method for establishing an allowance in terms of receivables involves *ageing* receivables. Individual accounts are analysed to determine those not yet due and those past due. Past-due accounts are classified in terms of the length of the period past due. An analysis sheet used in ageing accounts receivable is shown below.

Baker and Pope Analysis of Receivables — December 31, 1981								
Customer	Amount	Not Yet Due	Not More Than 30 Days Past Due	31-60 Days Past Due	61-90 Days Past Due	91-180 Days Past Due	181-365 Days Past Due	More Than One Year Past Due
A. B. Andrews	$ 450			$ 450				
B. T. Brooks	300				$ 100	$ 200		
B. Bryant	200		$ 200					
L. B. Devine	2,100	$ 2,100						
K. Martineau	200							$ 200
M. A. Young	1,400	1,000			100	300		
Total	$47,550	$40,000	$3,000	$1,200	$ 650	$ 500	$ 800	$1,400

It is desirable to review each overdue balance with an appropriate company official and to arrive at estimates concerning the degree of collectibility of each item listed. An alternative procedure is to develop a series of estimated loss percentages and apply these to the different receivable classifications. The calculation of the allowance on the latter basis is illustrated below.

Baker and Pope Estimated Amount of Uncollectible Accounts — December 31, 1981			
Classification	Balances	Uncollectible Accounts Experience Percentage	Estimated Amount of Uncollectible Accounts
Not yet due	$40,000	2%	$ 800
Not more than 30 days past due	3,000	5%	150
31-60 days past due	1,200	10%	120
61-90 days past due	650	20%	130
91-180 days past due	500	30%	150
181-365 days past due	800	50%	400
More than one year past due	1,400	80%	1,120
	$47,550		$2,870

Doubtful Accounts Expense is debited and Allowance for Doubtful Accounts is credited for an amount bringing the allowance account to the required balance. Assuming uncollectibles estimated at $2,870 as shown in the tabulation and a credit balance of $620 in the allowance before adjustment, the following entry would be made:

Doubtful Accounts Expense	2,250	
Allowance for Doubtful Accounts		2,250

The ageing method provides the most satisfactory approach to the valuation of receivables at their cash realizable amounts. Furthermore, data developed through ageing receivables may be quite useful to management for purposes of credit analysis and control. On the other hand, application of this method may require considerable time and may prove expensive.

Corrections in Allowance for Doubtful Accounts

As previously indicated, the allowance for doubtful accounts balance is established and maintained by means of adjusting entries at the close of each accounting period. If the allowance provisions are too large, the allowance account balance will be unnecessarily inflated and earnings will be understated; if the allowance provisions are too small, the allowance account balance will be inadequate and earnings will be overstated.

When the uncollectible accounts experience approximates the anticipation of the losses, the allowance procedure may be considered satisfactory and no adjustment is required. When it appears there has been a failure to estimate uncollectible accounts satisfactorily, resulting in an allowance balance clearly inadequate or excessive, an adjustment is in order. Such an adjustment should be reported as an ordinary item on the income statement, usually as an addition to or subtraction from Doubtful Accounts Expense.

The recognition of current period receivables as uncollectible by debits to the allowance and credits to the receivable accounts may result in a debit balance in the allowance account. A debit balance arising in this manner does not indicate the allowance is inadequate; debits to the allowance simply predate the current provision for uncollectible accounts, and the adjustment at the end of the period should cover uncollectibles already determined as well as those yet to be recognized.

Occasionally, accounts that have been charged off as uncollectible are collected. Assuming an account of $1,500 was determined to be uncollectible but was subsequently collected, the entries would be as follows:

Accounts Receivable	1,500	
Allowance for Doubtful Accounts		1,500
To reinstate account written off.		
Cash	1,500	
Accounts Receivable		1,500
To record collection of account.		

Many businesses may feel that the accounting refinement to be gained by anticipating uncollectibles hardly warrants the additional work required. Instead of anticipating uncollectible accounts, these businesses may prefer simply to recognize them in the periods in which accounts are determined to be uncollectible (direct write-off method). When the loss is not anticipated by the establishment of an allowance, uncollectible accounts are written off by a debit to Uncollectible Accounts Expense or Bad Debts and a credit to the customer's account. Because the loss is now certain, and the write-off is made directly to the customer's account rather than to an allowance, the term Doubtful Accounts Expense is not appropriate.

The recognition of uncollectibles in the period of their discovery is practised because of its simplicity and convenience. However, the matching concept supports the anticipation of uncollectibles so that current revenue may carry its full burden of expenses.

Anticipation of Discounts and Other Charges in Valuation of Receivables

The foregoing discussion has been restricted to the provision for uncollectible items. Conditions of sales and collections may suggest the anticipation of other charges that will emerge in the realization of accounts receivable and hence would properly be matched against current revenue. These charges and the procedures for handling them are equally applicable to notes receivable and to trade accounts receivable.

For example, if customers generally take cash discounts in making remittances, it may be argued that reporting revenue and receivables in terms of customer billings involves some overstatement of these balances. Under these circumstances, it may be desirable to anticipate the discounts by a debit to Sales Discounts and a credit to Allowance for Sales Discounts. Allowance for Sales Discounts would be subtracted from Accounts Receivable so that receivables are reported at their estimated cash realizable value.

Similar recognition may be suggested for probable allowances yet to be made to customers for shipment shortages and defects, for price adjustments, and also for probable losses on sales returns. Customer's claims for freight charges paid on the receipt or return of goods may call for consideration. Probable future expenses involved in the realization of accounts, such as billing and collection expenses and attorneys' fees may likewise warrant consideration. The anticipation of charges for the items just mentioned is seldom found in practice and is not allowed for income tax purposes.

USE OF RECEIVABLES IN CASH PLANNING

A business may require cash for current purposes exceeding the amount on hand and the amount to become available in the normal course of operations. The business may use accounts receivable or notes receivable as a basis for a cash advance from a bank or a finance company. These procedures are described in the following sections.

Customers' Accounts as a Source of Cash

In order to obtain immediate cash, accounts receivable owned by the business may be (1) pledged, (2) assigned, or (3) sold.

Pledge of Accounts Receivable. Advances are frequently obtained from banks or other lending institutions by pledging accounts receivable as security on a loan. Ordinarily, collections are made by the borrower who is required to use this cash in meeting the obligation to the lender. The lender may be given access to the borrower's records to determine whether remittances are being properly made on pledged accounts.

Assignment of Accounts Receivable. Banks and finance companies may agree to advance cash over a period of time as accounts receivable are assigned to them. The assignments carry a guarantee on the part of the assignor to make up any deficiency if the accounts fail to realize required amounts. Assignments thus represent, in effect, sale of accounts on a *recourse* basis. The cash advanced by the bank or the finance company is normally less than the assigned accounts by a percentage considered adequate to cover uncollectible items, returns and allowances, offsets, and amounts subject to dispute. When amounts actually recovered on assigned accounts exceed the sum of the advance and the assignee's charges, such excess accrues to the assignor. Charges frequently consist of a commission on the amount advanced, plus interest on the unrecovered balance of the advance computed on a daily basis. Assignments are usually made on a *non-notification basis*, customers remaining uninformed concerning the assignment; customers, then, make their payments to the assignor who is then required to turn the collections over to the assignee. When assignments are made on a *notification basis*, customers are instructed to make their payments directly to the assignee.

Sale of Accounts Receivable. Certain dealers or finance companies purchase accounts receivable outright on a *without recourse* basis. This is known as accounts receivable *factoring*, and the buyer is referred to as a *factor*. Customers are notified that their bills are payable to the factor, and this party assumes the burden of billing and collecting accounts. In many instances, factoring may involve more than simply the purchase and collection of accounts receivable. Factoring frequently involves a continuing agreement whereby a financing institution assumes the credit function as well as the collection function. Under such an arrangement, the factor grants or denies credit, handles the accounts receivable accounting, bills customers, and makes collections. The business entity is relieved of all these activities. The sale of goods provides immediate cash for business use. Because the factor absorbs the losses from bad accounts and frequently assumes credit and collection responsibilities, the charge made exceeds the interest charge involved in borrowing cash or the commission and interest charges involved in the assignment of receivables.

Accounting Procedures for Accounts Receivable Financing. No special accounting problems are encountered in the pledge or the sale of receivables. When receivables are pledged, the accounts simply report the loan and the subsequent settlement. Disclosure should be made on the balance sheet by parenthetical comment or note of the receivables pledged to secure the obligation to the lending agency. When receivables are sold outright, Cash is debited, receivables and related allowance balances are closed, and an expense account is debited for factoring charges. If part of the purchase price is withheld by the factor, a receivable is established pending final settlement.

The accounting treatment required for assignment of accounts receivable is illustrated by the following example. Assume the Bronson Co. on March 1 assigns accounts receivable of $25,000 to the Weber Finance Co. and receives $19,500 representing an advance of 80% of receivables less a commission on the advance of $2^1/2\%$. Collections are to be made by the assignor who is to deposit such receipts intact to the equity of the assignee. The entries in the accounts of the assignor and assignee are given on page 175.

It will be observed that the assignor makes two entries at the time of

TRANSACTION	ENTRIES IN ASSIGNOR'S ACCOUNTS (BRONSON COMPANY)		ENTRIES IN ASSIGNEE'S ACCOUNTS (WEBER FINANCE CO.)	
March 1 Bronson Co. assigned accounts receivable of $25,000 to Weber Finance Co. receiving $19,500 representing an advance of 80% of receivables less a commission on the advance of $2\frac{1}{2}$%.	Accounts Receivable Assigned .... 25,000 Accounts Receivable .... Cash .... 19,500 Assignment Expense .. 500 Equity of Weber Finance Co. in Assigned Accounts ..	25,000 20,000	Bronson Co. Accounts .... 25,000 Equity of Bronson Co. in Assigned Accounts .... Commission Revenue .... Cash	5,000 500 19,500
March 31 Bronson Co. collected $15,000 on assigned accounts. This amount together with interest at 12% for one month on this amount, or $150, was remitted to Weber Finance Co.	Cash .... 15,000 Accounts Receivable Assigned .... Equity of Weber Finance Co. in Assigned Accounts .... 15,000 Interest Expense ...... 150 Cash	15,000 15,150	Cash .... 15,150 Bronson Co. Accounts .... Interest Revenue ..	15,000 150
March 31 Sales returns and allowances granted by Bronson Co. on assigned accounts during March totalled $1,000.	Sales Returns and Allowance .... 1,000 Accounts Receivable Assigned	1,000	Equity of Bronson Co. in Assigned Accounts 1,000 Bronson Co. Accounts	1,000
May 31 Bronson Co. collected $8,500 on assigned accounts. Balance due, $5,000, together with interest at 12% for three months on this amount or, $150, was remitted to Weber Finance Co. in final settlement; $3,500 was retained. Remaining account balances relative to assignment were closed.	Cash .... 8,500 Accounts Receivable Assigned .... Equity of Weber Finance Co. in Assigned Accounts .... 5,000 Interest Expense ...... 150 Cash .... Accounts Receivable .. 500 Accounts Receivable Assigned	8,500 5,150 500	Cash .... 5,150 Bronson Co. Accounts ...... Interest Revenue .. Equity of Bronson Co. in Assigned Accounts 4,000 Bronson Co. Accounts	5,000 150 4,000

assignment: one entry sets the assigned accounts receivable apart under separate control; a second entry establishes a credit representing the equity in the receivables of the assignee, accompanied by debits to Cash for the cash received, and to Assignment Expense for the charges made by the assignee. Thereafter, as cash is collected on assigned accounts, the assigned receivables balance is reduced and cash is permitted to reduce the assignee's equity. Entries are made to reduce the assigned receivables balance for such items as returns, allowances, and write-offs. Upon final settlement with the assignee, any balance in Accounts Receivable Assigned is returned to the unassigned accounts control. The equity of the assignor in the accounts is always the remaining balance in the assigned accounts less the equity of the assignee.

In the accounts of the assignee, the advance of cash is recorded by a debit to an asset account for the total receivables assigned, a credit to an account with an assignor for the latter's equity in this total, a credit to Commission Revenue for the charges made, and a credit to Cash for the cash paid. As cash is received, Cash is debited and the assigned accounts and Interest Revenue are credited. Reductions in assigned accounts involving charges to be absorbed by the assignor are recognized by reductions in the assignor's equity. Upon final settlement, any balance remaining in the assignor's equity in assigned accounts is offset against the assigned receivables balance.

If a balance sheet is prepared before the finance company has received full payment, the assignor recognizes the difference between the total accounts assigned and the portion required to cover the claim of the finance company as an asset. Disclosure is also made of the responsibilities to the finance company if assigned accounts do not realize enough to liquidate the loan. The assignee in preparing a balance sheet would report the interest in assigned accounts as an asset.

To illustrate, if in the preceding example balance sheets are prepared on March 31, information relating to assigned accounts may be reported as shown below.

Bronson Co. (Assignor)

Current assets:		
Accounts receivable — unassigned		$50,000
Company's equity in assigned accounts receivable:		
Assigned accounts $9,000		
Less equity of Weber Finance Co. in assigned		
accounts (company is contingently liable as guar-		
antor of assigned accounts) 5,000	4,000	
Total accounts receivable		$54,000

Weber Finance Co. (Assignee)

Current assets:		
Bronson Co. accounts	$9,000	
Less equity of Bronson Co. in assigned accounts	4,000	$ 5,000

When collections are made by the finance company, procedures similar to those illustrated can still be employed. In these instances, however, entries are made by the assignor when information is received from the finance company concerning collections, interest charges, and the return of accounts in excess of claims.

Managements may employ accounts receivable financing as a temporary or emergency matter after exhausting the limited line of unsecured credit available from a lending institution. On the other hand, managements may engage in accounts receivable financing as a continuing policy. Recent years have witnessed an increasing number of factoring arrangements involving the full delegation of credit and collection responsibilities to specialists.

Financial assistance to business through the factoring of open accounts today amounts to billions of dollars.

Customers' Notes as a Source of Cash

Cash may be obtained by selling customers' notes to a bank or to some other agency willing to accept such instruments. If a customer's note is non-interest-bearing, cash is received for the face value of the note less a charge for interest, known as *discount*, for the period from the date the note is discounted to the date of its maturity. If the note is interest-bearing, the maturity value of the note is first determined. The amount received from the bank is the maturity value of the note less a discount calculated on this maturity value from the date the note is discounted to its maturity.

Except for notes payable on demand, the legal due date for a note or draft is three days after the indicated date of payment. The three days to be added to the term of a note for the purpose of determining its legal due date are called *days of grace*. When the term of a note is expressed in days, the due date is the specified number of days after its issuance plus three days of grace.

To illustrate entries for a non-interest-bearing note, assume a 90-day, $1,000 note dated December 1 is received from a customer; the note, due on March 4 is discounted on December 21 at 10%. The following entries are made:

Dec. 1 Notes Receivable	1,000.00	
Accounts Receivable		1,000.00
Dec. 21 Cash	980.00	
←Interest Expense	20.00	
Notes Receivable		1,000.00

Computation:
Interest: $1,000 × .10 × 73/365 = $20.00

To illustrate the accounting for an interest-bearing note, assume the note received from a customer in the previous example provides for the payment of interest at 10% at its maturity and it is discounted at the bank at 10%. Under these circumstances, the following entries would be appropriate:

Dec. 1 Notes Receivable	1,000.00	
Accounts Receivable		1,000.00
Dec. 21 Cash	1,004.97	
Notes Receivable		1,000.00
Interest Revenue		4.97

Computation:
Maturity value of note:
$1,000 + interest ($1,000 × .10 × 93/365) = $1,025.48
Discount: ~ 20.51
$1,025.48 × .10 × 73/365 = $20.51
                                              ‾‾‾‾‾‾
                                              1004.97

A note endorsed "without recourse" relieves the endorser of any liability for the inability of the maker of the note or any prior endorser to pay the note upon its maturity. When a note is endorsed without making any qualification, the endorser becomes liable to subsequent holders of the note if it is not paid at maturity. However, if the endorser is held liable on the note, that person has the right to recover amounts paid from the maker of the note or prior endorsers who failed to comply with its terms.

Normally, endorsement without qualification is required in discounting a note, and the endorser becomes contingently liable on the note. Under these circumstances Notes Receivable Discounted instead of Notes Receivable may be credited when the note is discounted. A separate account for Notes Receivable Discounted facilitates accounting for the accompanying contingent liability. When the person who holds the note at maturity receives payment from the maker, all contingencies are ended, and Notes Receivable Discounted can be applied against Notes Receivable.

Since data concerning the contingent liability are of concern only on the balance sheet date and these can be determined readily at the end of the period from an examination of the detailed record of notes discounted, the extra work involved in maintaining a notes receivable discounted account may not be warranted. When a notes receivable discounted balance is carried in the accounts, this balance is subtracted from Notes Receivable in reporting the notes receivable balance. When a notes receivable discounted account is not used, information concerning the contingent liability is provided on the balance sheet by means of a parenthetical remark or by a note to the financial statements.

If a note is not paid when it is due, the holder of the note must give the endorser prompt notice of such dishonor. The endorser is then required to make payment to the holder. Payment consists of the face value of the note plus interest and plus any fees and costs relating to collection. The full amount paid is recoverable from the maker of the note, and Accounts Receivable, Notes Receivable Dishonored, or Notes Receivable Past Due may be debited. If Notes Receivable Discounted were credited at the time the note was discounted, this balance, together with the original notes receivable balance, should be cancelled. Subsequent recovery on the note is recorded by a debit to Cash and a credit to the account with the debtor; failure to recover any portion of the balance due would call for writing off the unpaid balance.

To illustrate, assume in the preceding example Notes Receivable Discounted instead of Notes Receivable was credited when the note was discounted. The following entry would be made when the note is paid at maturity.

Notes Receivable Discounted	1,000	
Notes Receivable		1,000

If the note was not paid at maturity and the bank charged the endorser with a $2.50 protest fee, an entry would be made as follows:

Accounts Receivable	1,027.98	
Notes Receivable Discounted	1,000.00	
Cash		1,027.98
Notes Receivable		1,000.00

Computation:
Maturity value of note, $1,025.48 + $2.50 protest fee = $1,027.98

Protest fee passed on to customer

Subsequent payment from the customer is recorded as follows:

Cash	1,027.98	
Accounts Receivable		1,027.98

PRESENTATION OF CASH, TEMPORARY INVESTMENTS, AND RECEIVABLES ON THE BALANCE SHEET

Since current assets are normally reported in the order of their liquidity cash is listed first, followed by temporary investments, and receivables. For statement purposes, cash is usually reported as a single item. Both temporary investments and receivables usually require a variety of detailed disclosures that alternatively may be provided on the face of the balance sheet, or by note.

The basis of valuation of temporary investments should be indicated and, where the holdings are significant, their market value as well as their carrying value should be disclosed. When temporary investments are pledged, the nature and the purpose of the pledge should be disclosed.

Normally, the receivables qualifying as current items are grouped for presentation in the following classes: (1) notes — trade debtors, (2) accounts — trade debtors, (3) other receivables, and (4) accrued receivables. Reporting should disclose non-negotiable notes. The detail reported for other receivables depends upon the relative significance of the various items included. When trade accounts or instalment contracts are properly reported as current but involve collections beyond one year, particulars of such deferred collections should be provided. Valuation accounts are deducted from the individual receivable balances or combined balances to which they relate. Notes receivable may be reported gross with notes receivable discounted shown as a deduction from this balance, or notes may be reported net with appropriate disclosure of the contingent liability arising from notes discounted. Accounts receivable assigned may be reported gross with the interest of the assignee in such balance shown as a subtraction item, or the company's interest in receivables may be reported net; here too, appropriate reference would be made to the contingent liability involved. When receivables are supported by pledges of collateral to assure their collectibility, the nature of the pledge and the fact that the receivables are wholly or partly secured should be disclosed. On the other hand, when receivables have been pledged or otherwise hypothecated on obligations of the company, these facts, too, should be disclosed and reference made to the obligation thus secured.

Cash, temporary investments, and receivables, as they might appear on the balance sheet, are shown below. An alternative to the parenthetical disclosures would be to present supplementary information in notes to the financial statements:

Current assets:

Cash on hand and demand deposits in banks			$ 46,000
Special cash deposits (to pay interest and dividends).			24,000
Temporary investments:			
Certificates of deposit		$100,000	
Marketable securities:			
Canadian Government obligations (reported at cost; market, $158,500; $50,000 in bonds has been pledged as security on short-term bank loan)	$150,000		
Other shares and bonds (reported at cost; market, $44,200)	35,000	185,000	285,000
Receivables:			
Trade notes and drafts receivable (notes of $20,000 have been pledged to secure bank borrowing) . .	$ 39,500		
Less discount on notes receivable	1,500	$ 38,000	
Trade accounts receivable (including instalment contracts of approximately $30,000 not due for 12-18 months)	$112,000		
Less allowance for doubtful accounts and repossession charges	2,500	109,500	
Miscellaneous notes and accounts, including short-term loans to employees of $6,500		12,000	
Accrued receivables		4,500	$164,000

QUESTIONS

1. Why is cash on hand both necessary and yet potentially unproductive?

2. The following items were included as Cash on the balance sheet for the Lawrence Co. How should each of the items have been reported?

   (a) Customers' cheques returned by the bank marked "Not Sufficient Funds."
   (b) Customers' postdated cheques.

(c) Cashier's note with no due date.

(d) Postal money orders from customers awaiting deposit.

(e) Receipts for expense advances to buyers.

(f) Change funds.

(g) Notes receivable in the hands of the bank for collection.

(h) Special bank account in which sales tax collections are deposited.

(i) Customers' cheques not yet deposited.

3. (a) Explain cheque kiting and lapping. (b) Mention at least six other practices resulting in misappropriations of cash in the absence of an adequate system of internal control. (c) What is the basic principle of cash control making fraudulent practices extremely difficult?

4. The Riverside Country Club maintained a $1,500 change fund. It was used to cash members' cheques and to pay miscellaneous bills under $50. The fund was used by any of four persons in the office (including the accountant), depending upon which one was free when a need arose. At the close of each day, all cash collected from the cash registers in the club was merged with the fund and with collections on account received from members. All cheques and sufficient cash to equal daily receipts were deposited, and the remainder was returned to the fund. (a) What system weaknesses do you observe? (b) How would you correct them?

5. How may the differences between depositor and bank balances be classified? Give an example of each type of difference.

6. (a) What purposes are served by preparing a four-column reconciliation of receipts and disbursements? (b) Why would this form be used by auditors?

7. The Phelps Co. engaged in the following practices at the end of a fiscal year:

(a) Sales on account from January 1–January 5 were predated as of the month of December.

(b) Cheques in payment of accounts were prepared on December 31 and were entered on the books, but they were placed in the safe awaiting instructions for mailing.

(c) Customers' cheques returned by the bank and marked "Not Sufficient Funds" were ignored for statement purposes.

(d) Amounts owed company officers were paid off on December 31 and reborrowed on January 2.

Explain what is wrong with each of the practices mentioned and give the entries that are required to correct the accounts.

8. Define *temporary investments*. What criteria must be met for a security to be considered a temporary investment?

9. The Canning Co. reports marketable securities on the balance sheet at the lower of cost or market. What adjustments are required on the books at the end of the year in each situation below:

(a) Securities are purchased early in 1979 and at the end of 1979 their market value is more than cost.

(b) At the end of 1980 the market value of the securities is less than cost.

(c) At the end of 1981 the market value of the securities is greater than at the end of 1980 but is still less than cost.

(d) At the end of 1982 the market value of the securities is more than the amount originally paid.

10. The Philips Corporation shows on its balance sheet one receivable balance including the following items: (a) advances to officers, (b) deposits on machinery and equipment being produced by various companies for the Philips Corporation, (c) advances for traveling expenses, (d) damage claims against transportation companies approved by such companies, (e) estimated federal income tax refunds, (f) accrued interest on notes receivable, (g) overdue notes, (h) receivables from a foreign subsidiary company, (i) subscriptions receivable on a new bond issue, and (j) creditor overpayments. Suggest the proper treatment of each item.

11. The Aldwin Manufacturing Co. ships merchandise on a consignment basis to customers, title to such goods passing only at the time the goods are sold by the consignees. The Aldwin Manufacturing Co. debits accounts receivable for the cost of the goods shipped until sales are reported, when it increases the receivable accounts with the consignee to the regular billing price. Goods on consignment appear on the balance sheet as receivables. (a) Would you approve such practice? (b) Suggest an alternative procedure.

12. (a) Give three methods for the establishment and the maintenance of an allowance for doubtful accounts. (b) What are the advantages and disadvantages of each method?

13. How would the percentages used in estimating uncollectible accounts be determined under any of the methods of maintaining an allowance for doubtful accounts?

14. (a) What entries are necessary when an account previously written off is collected? (b) Why would the collection of an account written off in a previous year not be a prior period adjustment?

15. An analysis of the accounts receivable balance of $8,702 on the records of Books Ltd. on December 31 reveals the following:

Accounts from sales of last three months (appear to be fully collectible)	$7,460
Accounts from sales prior to October 1 (of doubtful value)	1,312
Accounts known to be worthless	320
Dishonored notes charged back to customers' accounts	800
Credit balances in customers' accounts	1,190

(a) What adjustments are required?
(b) How should the various balances be shown on the balance sheet?

16. How do the accounting procedures for recognizing uncollectible accounts in the period of discovery (direct write-off) differ from those of anticipating uncollectible accounts?

17. (a) Distinguish between the practices of (1) pledging, (2) assigning, and (3) selling accounts receivable. (b) Describe the accounting procedure to be followed in each instance.

18. The Barker Co. enters into a continuing agreement with Mercantile Finance Inc., whereby the latter company buys without recourse all of the trade receivables as they arise and assumes all credit and collection functions. Describe the advantages that may accrue to the Barker Co. as a result of the factoring agreement.

19. A. B. Crowell, who has been recording a contingent liability on notes receivable discounted, has noticed that he has been held liable on nearly as many customers' cheques as he has on notes. He suggests setting up a "cheques endorsed" account to show his contingent liability on cheques. Is this advisable? Why?

20. Indicate several methods for presenting information on the balance sheet relating to (a) notes receivable discounted, and (b) accounts receivable assigned.

5-1. An examination on the morning of January 2 by the auditor for the Valley Hardware Company discloses the following items in the petty cash drawer:

Currency and coin		$ 35.22
IOU's from members of the office staff		45.00
An envelope containing collections for a football pool, with office staff names attached		15.00
Petty cash vouchers for:		
Typewriter repairs	$ 8.00	
Stamps	15.00	
Telegram charges	9.50	32.50
Employee's cheque postdated January 15		50.00
Employee's cheque marked "N.S.F."		70.00
Cheque drawn by Valley Hardware Company to Petty Cash		115.00
		$362.72

The ledger account discloses a $350 balance for Petty Cash. (a) What adjustments should be made on the auditor's working papers so petty cash may be correctly stated on the balance sheet? (b) What is the correct amount of petty cash for the balance sheet? (c) How could the practice of borrowing by employees from the fund be discouraged?

5-2. The following data are assembled in the course of reconciling the bank balance as of Decembr 31, 1981, for Hinton Tool Co. What cash balance will be found in the company accounts, assuming no errors on the part of the bank and the depositor?

Balance per bank statement	$1,215.60
Cheques outstanding	1,760.00
December 31 receipts recorded but not deposited	350.00
Bank charges for December not recognized in accounts	7.50
Draft collected by bank but not recognized in accounts	550.00

5-3. The following information was included in the bank reconciliation for Near Corporation for June. What was the total of the outstanding cheques at the beginning of June? Assume all other reconciling items are listed below:

Cheques and charges returned by bank in June, including a June service charge of $15	$32,869
Service charge made by bank in May and recorded in June	10
Total of credits to Cash in all journals during June	38,583
Customer's N.S.F. cheque returned as a bank charge in June (no entry made in accounts)	200
Customer's N.S.F. cheque returned in May and redeposited in June (no entry made in accounts in either May or June)	500
Outstanding cheques at June 30	16,119
Deposit in transit at June 30	1,200

5-4. Give the entries necessary to record the following transactions of the Greely Corporation during 1981:

(a) Purchased $25,000 Government of Canada 8% bonds, paying 102$\frac{1}{2}$ plus accrued interest of $750. Broker's fees were $185. Greely Corp. uses the revenue approach to record accrued interest on purchased bonds.

(b) Purchased 1,000 shares of Fails Co. Ltd. common shares at 64 plus brokerage fees of $300.

(c) Received semi-annual interest on the Government bonds.
(d) Sold 300 shares of Fails Co. Ltd. common shares at 65¼.
(e) Sold $15,000 of Government bonds at 103 plus accrued interest of $200.
(f) Purchased a $5,000, six-month certificate of deposit.

5-5. Grotto Corp. acquires marketable securities in 1980 at a cost of $75,000. Market values of the securities at the end of each year are as follows: 1980, $70,000; 1981, $73,000; 1982, $80,000. Give the entries at the end of 1980, 1981, and 1982 indicating how the securities would be reported on the balance sheet at the end of each year under each of the following assumptions:

(a) Securities are reported at cost.
(b) Securities are reported at the lower of cost or market on an aggregate basis.
(c) Securities are reported at market.

5-6. Lakeside Trading Co. keeps subsidiary ledgers for receivables and payables with a controlling account for each in the general ledger.

On March 31, 1981 the company Balance Sheet contained the following data:

Cash	$15,000
Accounts Receivable	58,000
Inventory at Cost	60,000
Accounts Payable	35,000
Notes Payable	5,000

The following additional information for the month of April, 1981 is available:

Credit sales	$56,000
Cash sales	1,600
Sales returns and allowances (credit sales)	1,100
Sales discounts allowed	1,000
Cash received from customers	49,000
Trade discounts granted	14,000
Sales salaries	3,000
Uncollectible receivable written off	500
Credit purchases	27,000
Cash purchases	400
Purchase returns and allowances (credit sales)	300
Purchase discounts received	900
Cheques issued to trade creditors	44,100
Freight-in paid in cash	200
Note payable due and paid	5,000
Notes payable accepted re purchase of fixed asset	2,500

From the relevant information provided above, prepare the Accounts Receivable and Accounts Payable Control Accounts for April, 1981. (SMA adapted)

5-7. Transcoma Furniture Company sells direct to retail customers and also to wholesalers. Accounts Receivable and an Allowance for Bad Debts are maintained separately for each division. At January 1, 1982 the balance of the Retail Accounts Receivable was $209,000.

The following information regarding credit sales, bad debts written off and bad debt recoveries for the past three years is available:

	Credit Sales	Bad Debts Written Off	Bad Debts Recoveries
1979	$1,110,000	$ 26,000	$ 2,150
1980	1,225,000	29,500	3,750
1981	1,465,000	30,000	3,600
	$3,800,000	$ 85,500	$ 9,500

Bad debts are provided for as a percentage of credit sales. The accountant calculates the percentage annually by using the experience of the three years prior to the current year. The formula is Bad Debts written off less recoveries expressed as a percentage of the credit sales for the same period.

Retail credit sales for 1982	$1,500,000
Allowance for bad debts January 1, 1982 with respect to retail customers	7,600 Cr.
Bad debt recoveries in 1982 (Retail)	4,200
Bad debts written off in 1982 (Retail)	31,000
Cash receipts in 1982 from credit sales to retail customers	1,380,200

The Allowance for Bad Debts on the wholesale accounts has been calculated up to December 31, 1981 as a percentage of net sales.

January 1, 1982 Balance in the Allowance account	$17,200 Cr.
Bad debt recoveries in 1982 (Wholesale)	2,800
Bad debt written off in 1982 (Wholesale)	23,500

It is decided to provide for bad debts on Wholesale Accounts commencing with the December 31, 1982 adjusting entry on the basis of an analysis of the age of the receivables.

The following schedule was prepared:

	Amount	Per cent Estimated Uncollectible
Not yet due	$170,000	Nil
1 – 30 days past due	120,000	5
31 – 60 days past due	10,000	25
61 – 90 days past due	15,000	50
Over 90 days past due	12,000	
Additional accounts to be written off .	3,000	
	$330,000	

For the Retail Accounts Receivable (a) calculate the percentage to be used to compute the allowance for bad debts at December 31, 1982; (b) prepare the adjusting journal entry for the bad debts provision at December 31, 1982 (narrative not required); (c) prepare in summary form the Accounts Receivable Control Account and the Allowance for Bad Debts Account for 1982.

For the Wholesale Accounts Receivable (d) calculate the estimated bad debts in the December 31, 1982 receivables; (e) prepare the adjusting journal entry for the bad debts provision at December 31, 1982 (narrative not required). (SMA adapted)

5-8. The accounts receivable control account for the Arlo Co. shows a debit balance of $96,950; the Allowance for Doubtful Accounts shows a credit balance of $3,800. Subsidiary ledger detail reveals the following:

Trade accounts receivable — assigned (Finance Co. equity in assigned accounts is $8,000)	$10,000
Subscriptions receivable for common shares due in 60 days	50,000
Interest receivable on bonds	2,500
Instalment receivables, due 1 – 18 months hence (including unearned finance charges of $500)	3,500
Trade receivables from officers, due currently	1,250
Customers' accounts reporting credit balances arising from sales returns ..	250
Advance payments to creditors on purchase orders	$ 3,000
Advance payments to creditors on orders for machinery	5,000
Customers' accounts reporting credit balances arising from advance payments	1,000
Accounts known to be worthless	450
Trade accounts on which postdated cheques are held (no entries were made on receipt of cheques)	500
Advances to affiliated companies	10,000
Other trade accounts receivable — unassigned	12,000

Show how this information would be reported on the balance sheet.

5-9. Prior to 1982, the James Company followed the percentage-of-sales method of estimating doubtful accounts. The following data are gathered by the accounting department.

	1978	1979	1980	1981
Total sales	$350,000	$600,000	$1,200,000	$2,100,000
Charge sales	200,000	320,000	650,000	1,200,000
Accounts receivable (end-of-year balance)	62,000	78,000	120,000	250,000
Allowance for doubtful accounts (end-of-year credit balance)	2,000	6,000	4,000	22,000
Accounts written off	9,000	2,000	14,000	3,000

(a) What amount was debited to expense for 1979, 1980, and 1981?
(b) Compute the balance in the valuation account at the beginning of 1978 assuming there has been no change in the percentage of sales used over the four-year period.
(c) What explanation can be given for the fluctuating amount of write-off?
(d) Why do the actual write-offs fail to give the correct charge to expense?

5-10. Yewchuk Sales Co. assigns accounts of $60,000 to the Warren Finance Co. guaranteeing these accounts and receiving an 80% advance less a flat commission of 2% on the amount of the advance. Accounts of $45,000 are collected and remittance is made to the finance company. Uncollectible accounts of $2,000 are written off against an allowance for doubtful accounts; remaining accounts are collected and settlement is made with the finance company together with payment of $1,200 for interest. What entries are required in the accounts of Yewchuk Sales Co. and in the accounts of Warren Finance Co. to record the assignment and the subsequent transactions?

5-11. The Plow Co. decides to use the accounts receivable as a basis for financing. Its current position at this time is as follows:

Accounts receivable	$30,000	Cash overdraft	$ 550
Inventories	35,000	Accounts payable	28,000

Prepare a statement of its current position, assuming cash is obtained as indicated in each case at the top of page 187.

(a) Cash of $20,000 is borrowed on short-term notes and $15,000 is applied to the payment of creditors; accounts of $25,000 are pledged to secure the loan.

(b) Cash of $20,000 is advanced to the company by High Finance Co., the advance representing 80% of accounts assigned to it; assignment is made on a with-recourse basis, and amounts collected in excess of the loan balance and charges accrued to the Plow Co.

(c) Cash of $20,000 is received on the sale of accounts receivable of $22,500 on a no-recourse basis.

5-12. Mike Owne received from Joe Last, a customer, a 90-day, 8% note for $3,000, dated November 6, 1980. On November 26, Owne had Last's note discounted at 7% and recorded the contingent liability. The bank protested non-payment of the note and charged the endorser with protest fees of $3.00 in addition to the amount of the note. On February 28, 1981, the note was collected plus interest at 10% from the maturity date on the face value of the note. What entries would appear on Owne's books as a result of the foregoing?

5-1A. Analysis of the December bank statement for Trost Tractors Ltd. discloses the following information:

(a) Statement balance at December 31, 1981, was $16,675.

(b) Cheque issued by Transpo-Matic Ltd. for $315 was charged to Trost Tractors Ltd. in error.

(c) December bank charges were $30.

(d) Deposit of $700 was erroneously credited to Trost Tractors Ltd. account by the bank.

(e) Outstanding cheques at December 31, 1981, were $5,280. They included a $300 cheque outstanding for eight months to Amco Products which was cancelled in December and a new cheque issued. No entry was made for the cancellation.

(f) Receipts on December 31 were $4,500. Receipts were deposited on January 2.

(g) An error in addition was made on the December 23 deposit slip. This slip showed a total of $2,120. The correct balance as credited to our accounts by the bank was $2,020. A count of cash on hand showed an overage of $100 as of December 31.

(h) The Cash in Bank balance in the general ledger as of December 31, 1981 was $15,640.

Instructions:

(1) Prepare a bank reconciliation statement which reconciles the bank balance with the balance per accounts.

(2) Give all entries required in the accounts at December 31, 1981.

5-2A. The following information is related to Dolan Ltd.:

	1981	
	August	September
Bank statement balance — at month end	$ 4,830	$ 5,570
Cash account balance — at month end	3,910	4,549
Bank charges for N.S.F. cheque returned (normally written off in month following return)	75	160
Outstanding cheques — at month end	1,200	1,930
Deposits in transit — at month end	600	940
Bank service charges (normally recorded in month following bank charge)	5	9
Drafts collected by bank (not recorded by company until month following collection)	400	300
Total credits to cash account	29,705	35,961
Total deposits on bank statement		36,160

Cheque #411 was erroneously recorded in the company chequebook and journal as $286; the correct amount is $186. (This cheque was not outstanding on September 30.)

The outstanding cheques on September 30 include a company cheque for $200 certified by the bank on September 18.

All disbursements were made by cheque.

Instructions:

Prepare a four-column bank reconciliation for the month of September, 1981. Use the form where both bank and accounts balances are brought to a corrected cash balance.

5-3A. The following information concerning the cash accounts of Penetration Company is available:

(a) Balance per bank:

November 30, 1981	$18,570
December 31, 1981	19,362

(b) Balance per accounts:

November 30, 1981	$12,368
December 31, 1981	18,808

(c) Outstanding cheques:

November 30, 1981	$ 6,352
December 31, 1981	7,504

(d) December deposits, per bank statement, $135,040.

(e) December cash receipts, per cash receipts journal, $170,510.

(f) N.S.F. cheques returned by the bank are recorded as a reduction in the cash receipts journal. Those redeposited are recorded as regular cash receipts. Data regarding N.S.F. cheques are as follows:

(1) Returned by bank in November and recorded by company as a reduction in cash receipts in December, $150.

(2) Returned by bank in December and recorded by company as a reduction in cash receipts in December, $1,350.

(3) Returned by the bank in December and recorded by company as a reduction in cash receipts in January, $230.

(4) Redeposited by company during December, $800.

(g) According to the repayment terms of a large loan with the bank, the bank credits the company's chequing account with 80% of the amount presented for deposit. The remaining 20% is applied to reduce the unpaid balance of the loan. The following summary entries, recorded in the cash receipts and cash disbursements journals, for December indicate the company's treatment of the deposits and resulting loan reductions:

Cash in Bank	172,010	
Cash on Hand		172,010
Bank Loan	34,402	
Cash in Bank		34,402

(h) The above summary entries include one deposit in transit on December 31, in the amount of $3,210. There were no deposits in transit on November 30, 1981. There was no undeposited cash on hand on December 31, 1981.

(i) Interest on the bank loan for the month of December was charged by the bank against the chequing account, $1,829.

(j) On December 31, 1981, a $2,323 cheque of Precision Company was charged to the company's account in error.

Instructions:

(1) Prepare a four-column reconciliation of receipts, disbursements, and bank balance for December 31, 1981. Use the form where both bank and account balances are brought to a corrected cash balance.

(2) Give the December 31, 1981 adjusting entries relating to the cash accounts of Penetration Company.

5-4A. Lexicon Corporation reports the following on their December 31, 1980 balance sheet:

Marketable securities (at cost)	$225,850	
Less allowance for decline in value of marketable securities	2,260	$223,590

Supporting records of Lexicon's temporary holdings show marketable securities as follows:

	Cost	Market
200 shares of Lampex Co. common	$ 25,450	$ 24,300
$80,000 Government of Canada 7% bonds	79,650	77,400
$120,000 Government of Canada 7½% bonds	120,750	121,890
	$225,850	$223,590

Interest dates on the government bonds are January 1 and July 1. Lexicon Corporation makes reversing entries and uses the revenue approach to recording the purchase of bonds with accrued interest.

During 1981 and 1982, Lexicon Corporation completed the following transactions related to their temporary investments:

1981

Jan. 1 Received semi-annual interest on government bonds. (The entry to reverse the interest accrual at the end of the last year has already been made.)

Apr. 1 Sold $60,000 of the 7½% government bonds at 102 plus accrued interest. Brokerage fees were $200.

May 21 Received dividends of 25 cents per share on the Lampex Co. common stock. The dividend had not been recorded on the declaration date.

July 1 Received semi-annual interest on government bonds, then sold the 7% government bonds at 97^1/$_2$. Brokerage fees were $250.

Aug. 15 Purchased 100 shares of Norris Nets Ltd. common stock at 116 plus brokerage fees of $50.

Nov. 1 Purchased $50,000 of 8% government bonds at 101 plus accrued interest. Brokerage fees were $125. Interest dates are January 1 and July 1.

Dec. 31 Market prices of securities were: Lampex Co. common, 110; 7^1/$_2$% government bonds, 101^3/$_4$; 8% government bonds, 101; Norris Nets Ltd. common, 116^3/$_4$. Lexicon Corporation reports all marketable securities at the lower of aggregate cost or market.

1982

Jan. 2 Recorded the receipt of semi-annual interest on the government bonds.

Feb. 1 Sold the 7^1/$_2$% government bonds at 101 plus accrued interest. Brokerage fees were $300.

Instructions:

(1) Prepare journal entries for the foregoing transactions and accrue required interest on December 31. Give computations in support of your entries.

(2) Show how marketable securities would be presented on the December 31, 1981, balance sheet.

5-5A. The balance sheet of Rector and Towle Ltd. shows the following balances for cash and temporary investments within its "Current assets" section as of December 31, 1981:

Current assets:		
Cash	$ 76,429	
Temporary investments	173,291	$249,720

In examining the accounts, the following information is revealed with respect to the current assets:

Cash consists of a demand deposit of $16,337 at the Bank of Commerce; a time deposit of $5,500 that cannot be withdrawn until after April 1, 1983, customers' cheques not yet deposited, $500, and customers' returned N.S.F. cheques, $200; a demand deposit of $9,184, which is unavailable, being in a bank in a foreign country at war; an overdraft of $192 in the Merchants Bank; a time deposit of $4,500 in a closed building and loan savings association; advances of $1,675 to officers; sinking funds cash of $16,525; a pension fund of $22,000 for employees; and a petty cash fund of $200, of which $65 is cash, $45 is in the form of employee's IOU's and $90 is supported by the receipts for expenses paid out of the fund.

The following securities are included under the temporary investments heading:

	Cost	Market Value (Including Accrued Interest)
Rector and Towle Ltd. treasury shares	$ 6,920	$ 7,358
Eastern Corporation common shares (temporary holding)	3,490	3,250
Prairie Company, 8% bonds (interest payable March 1 and Sept. 1). Face value, $9,000. Acquired on Sept. 1, 1981 (temporary holding)	9,190	9,140

		Market Value (Including
	Cost	Accrued Interest)

	Cost	Market Value (Including Accrued Interest)
7% Government of Canada bonds (interest payable on March 1 and September 1). Face value, $30,000. Purchased with pension sinking fund cash. Acquired September 1, 1981	30,600	30,750
Golns Co. common shares (temporary holding)	7,235	5,500
Tonka Co. common shares (shares of subsidiary company).......................................	112,000	106,300
ACC Corp. preferred shares (temporary holding) ...	4,900	6,300

Instructions:

Show cash and temporary investments as these items should properly appear in the "Current assets" section of the balance sheet. Provide schedules to indicate how foregoing balances are determined and what disposition is to be made of items not appropriately shown under the cash and temporary investment headings. Assume that marketable securities are reported at cost or aggregate market, whichever is lower, by means of a valuation account.

5-6A. Accounts receivable for the Tool Co. were reported on the balance sheet prepared at the end of 1981 as follows:

Accounts receivable		$62,400	
Less: Allowance for doubtful accounts	$2,630		
Allowance for sales discounts	870	3,500	$58,900

The company sells goods on terms of 3/10, n/30. At the end of the year accounts receivable are aged and the following percentages are applied in arriving at an estimate of the charge for doubtful accounts:

	Estimated Loss
Accounts not more than two months overdue	8%
Accounts more than two months but not more than six months overdue	25%
Accounts more than six months but not more than one year overdue	60%
Accounts more than one year overdue	100%

At the end of the year the company also anticipates sales discounts on all receivables not yet due for payment.

In 1982, the following transactions took place:

Sales on account...	$426,582
Cash collected on account	408,970
Cash discounts allowed	5,862
Sales returns and allowances	2,320
Accounts written off	1,950
Accounts previously written off but recovered	430

At the end of the year overdue accounts are as follows:

Accounts not more than two months overdue	$6,500
Accounts more than two months but not more than six months overdue	3,100
Accounts more than six months but not more than one year overdue	1,200
Accounts more than one year overdue	1,380

Instructions:
(1) Give the entries required to record the transactions listed above and also to adjust the accounts.
(2) Calculate the balances for accounts receivable and the related allowances as at December 31, 1981, and show these as they will appear on the balance sheet.

5-7A. Ross Enterprises prepared a bank reconciliation every month. At December 31, 1981 the following information was available:

Balance at November 30, 1981 when the bank balance was last reconciled and verified.

General Ledger balance after adjustments	$11,300
Bank Statement balance	11,800

There were no outstanding deposits at November 30th.

The general ledger account for Cash contained the following details:

1981		Debit	Credit	Balance
November 30	Balance			$11,300
Decmeber 31	C. R. J. 16	$7,300		
December 31	C. P. J. 12		$8,450	

The December 31, 1981 bank statement when checked showed the following:

Cheques charged in December totalled $9,280.00,

(i) A cheque for $70.00 issued in December was the only one outstanding.
(ii) Included in the cheques charged total was a cheque actually drawn on Ross Sales Co. bank account, but which had been charged to Ross Enterprises in error.

Deposits recorded by the bank during December totalled $7,000.00

Bank charges not recorded by company include (i) Collection fee, $4.00; (ii) N.S.F. cheque returned, $76.00. Additional credits on bank statement not recorded by the company include (i) Note Receivable collected, $500.00; (ii) Interest on investments, $100.00.

Instructions:
(1) Prepare a bank reconciliation table as of December 31, 1981.
(2) Prepare any required journal entries (SMA adapted).

5-8A. You have completed your examination of the cash on hand and in banks in your audit of the Carrier Company's financial statements for the year ended December 31, 1981, and note the following:

(a) The company maintains a general bank account at the First Canada Bank and an imprest payroll bank account at The Royal Bank. All cheques are signed by the company president, Carolyn Carrier.
(b) Data and reconciliations prepared by Donald Hume, the company accountant, on November 30, 1981, indicated that the payroll account had a $1,000 general ledger and bank balance with no in-transit or outstanding items, and the general bank account had a $12,405 general ledger balance with cheques outstanding aggregating $918 (#1202 for $575 and #1205 for $343) and one deposit of $492 in transit.
(c) Your surprise cash count on Tuesday January 5, 1982, revealed customers'

cheques totalling $540 and a First Canada Bank deposit slip for that amount dated December 30, 1981, were in the company safe and that no cash was in transit to the bank at that time. Your examination of the general account chequebook had revealed cheque #1219 to be the first unused cheque.

(d) Company general ledger accounts are prepared on a posting machine and all transactions are posted in chronological sequence. The ledger card for the general bank account is reproduced below.

LEDGER

General Bank Account

First Canada Bank

DATE	FOLIO	DEBITS	CREDITS	BALANCE
30/11/81			BALANCE FORWARD →	12,405
01/12/81		496		12,901
05/12/81	1206		1,675	11,226
06/12/81	1207		645	10,581
06/12/81		832		11,413
08/12/81	1208		1,706	9,707
08/12/81		975		10,682
08/12/81	1209		2,062	8,620
08/12/81	1210		3,945	4,675
11/12/81	1211		6,237	(1,562)
12/12/81		8,045		6,483
15/12/81		9,549		16,032
15/12/81	1212		1,845	14,187
21/12.81	RT		241	13,946
21/12/81	1213		350	13,596
21/12/81	1214		2,072	11,524
22/12/81		1,513		13,037
23/12/81	1215		2,597	10,440
27/12/81	1216		1,739	8,701
29/12/81		540		9,241
29/12/81		942		10,183
29/12/81	1217		1,987	8,196
04/01/82	1218		1,120	7,076
		22,892	28,221	

(e) The December statements from both banks were delivered unopened to you. The Royal Bank statement contained deposits for $1,675; $1,706; $1,845; and $2,597; and seventy-two paid cheques totalling $7,823. The First Canada Bank statement is reproduced below.

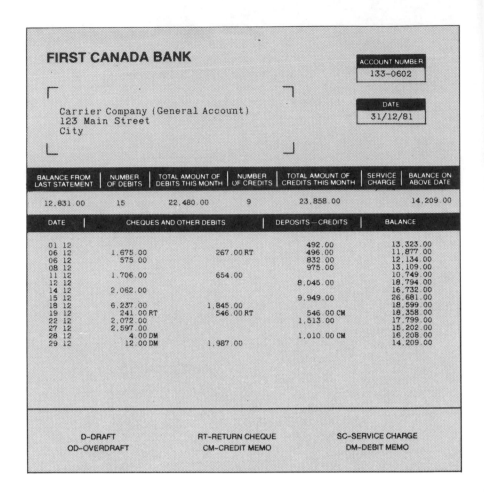

FIRST CANADA BANK

ACCOUNT NUMBER
133–0602

Carrier Company (General Account)
123 Main Street
City

DATE
31/12/81

BALANCE FROM LAST STATEMENT	NUMBER OF DEBITS	TOTAL AMOUNT OF DEBITS THIS MONTH	NUMBER OF CREDITS	TOTAL AMOUNT OF CREDITS THIS MONTH	SERVICE CHARGE	BALANCE ON ABOVE DATE
12,831.00	15	22,480.00	9	23,858.00		14,209.00

DATE	CHEQUES AND OTHER DEBITS		DEPOSITS — CREDITS	BALANCE
01 12			492.00	13,323.00
06 12	1,675.00	267.00 RT	496.00	11,877.00
06 12	575.00		832.00	12,134.00
08 12			975.00	13,109.00
11 12	1,706.00	654.00		10,749.00
12 12			8,045.00	18,794.00
14 12	2,062.00			16,732.00
15 12			9,949.00	26,681.00
18 12	6,237.00	1,845.00		18,599.00
19 12	241.00 RT	546.00 RT	546.00 CM	18,358.00
22 12	2,072.00		1,513.00	17,799.00
27 12	2,597.00			15,202.00
28 12	4.00 DM		1,010.00 CM	16,208.00
29 12	12.00 DM	1,987.00		14,209.00

D–DRAFT	RT–RETURN CHEQUE	SC–SERVICE CHARGE
OD–OVERDRAFT	CM–CREDIT MEMO	DM–DEBIT MEMO

(f) A special bank statement was secured by you personally from both banks on January 8, 1982, and the First Canada Bank statement is reproduced below.

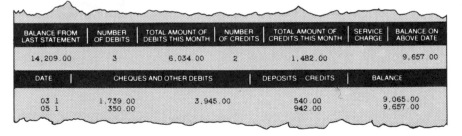

BALANCE FROM LAST STATEMENT	NUMBER OF DEBITS	TOTAL AMOUNT OF DEBITS THIS MONTH	NUMBER OF CREDITS	TOTAL AMOUNT OF CREDITS THIS MONTH	SERVICE CHARGE	BALANCE ON ABOVE DATE
14,209.00	3	6,034.00	2	1,482.00		9,657.00

DATE	CHEQUES AND OTHER DEBITS		DEPOSITS — CREDITS	BALANCE
03 1	1,739.00	3,945.00	540.00	9,065.00
05 1	350.00		942.00	9,657.00

(g) You determine the bank statements are correct except that the First Canada Bank incorrectly charged a returned cheque on December 19 but credited the account the same day.

(h) On December 28 a $1,000 note plus interest of $10 was collected by the First Canada Bank for Carrier for a $4 collection fee.

(i) The $12 debit memo from the First Canada Bank was a charge for printed cheques.

(j) Cheque #1213 was issued to replace cheque #1205 when the latter was reported not received by a vendor. Because of the delay in paying this account Carrier Company was no longer entitled to the 2% cash discount it had taken in preparing the original cheque.

Instructions:

Prepare a proof of cash for December for Carrier's general bank account in the First Canada Bank. Your proof of cash should show the computation of the adjusted balances for both the bank statement and the general ledger account of the First Canada Bank for cash in bank November 30, December receipts, December disbursements, and cash in bank December 31. The following column headings are recommended:

Description	Beginning Reconciliation November 30	December Receipts	December Disbursements	Ending Reconciliation December 31

(AICPA adapted)

5-9A. The balance sheet for the Valentine Co. on December 31, 1981, includes the following receivable balances:

Interest receivable		$ 300
Notes receivable . ,,,,,.................................	$32,500	
Less notes receivable discounted	15,500	17,000
Accounts receivable	$75,000	
Less allowance for doubtful accounts	3,750	71,250

Transactions during 1982 included the following:

(a) Sales on account were $642,200.

(b) Cash collected on accounts totalled $492,000, which included accounts of $104,000 on which cash discounts of 2% were allowed.

(c) Notes received in payment of accounts totalled $83,000.

(d) Notes receivable discounted as of December 31, 1981, were paid at maturity with the exception of one $8,000 note on which the company has to pay $8,090, which included interest and protest fees. It is expected that recovery will be made on this note in 1982.

(e) Customers' notes of $50,000 were discounted during the year, proceeds from their sale being $48,500. Of this total, $34,500 matured during the year without notice of protest.

(f) Customers' accounts of $9,610 were written off during the year as worthless.

(g) Recoveries of doubtful accounts written off in prior years were $740.

(h) Notes receivable collected during the year totalled $18,000 and interest collected was $1,200.

(i) On December 31, accrued interest on notes receivable was $580.

(j) Uncollectible accounts are estimated to be 5% of the December 31, 1982, Accounts Receivable balance.

(k) Cash of $20,000 was borrowed from the bank, accounts receivable of $25,000 being pledged on the loan. Collections of $13,000 had been made on these receivables (included in the total given in transaction [b]) and this amount was applied on December 31, 1982, to payment of accrued interest on the loan of $400, and the balance to partial payment of the loan.

Instructions:

(1) Prepare journal entries summarizing the transactions and information given above.

(2) Prepare a summary of current receivables for balance sheet presentation.

5-10A. The Mosher Company completed the following transactions during 1981 related to accounts receivable.

Apr. 1 Assigned accounts of $60,000 to Farns Finance Co. for a cash advance of 80% of receivables less a commission on the advance of $1^1/_2$%.

Apr. 30 Collections during April on assigned accounts were $22,440. This amount plus 10% interest for one month on the amount owed was remitted to Farns Finance Co.

Apr. 30 Wrote off against the allowance account, $3,500 of uncollectible accounts of which $2,000 were assigned accounts.

May 31 Collections during May on assigned accounts were $24,000. This amount plus 10% interest for one month on the amount owed was remitted to Farns Finance Co.

May 31 Granted sales returns of $5,000 on assigned accounts during May.

June 30 Collections during June on assigned accounts were $500. Balance due Farns Finance Co. plus 10% interest for one month on the amount owed was remitted. Remaining account balances relative to assignment were closed.

Instructions:

(1) Give the entries required to record the above transactions in the Mosher Company's accounts.

(2) Give the entries required to record the same transactions in the accounts of the Farns Finance Company.

5-11A. The Hallock Fur Company has run into financial difficulties. It decides to improve its cash position by factoring one third of its accounts receivable and assigning one half of the remaining receivables to the local bank. Details of these arrangements were as follows:

Accounts receivable, Dec. 31, 1981 . . . . $240,000 (before financing)
Allowance for doubtful accounts,
   Dec. 31, 1981 . . . . 1,500 (credit)
Estimated uncollectibles, Dec. 31, 1981   2% of accounts receivable balance
Factor discount rate . . . . 15% of gross receivables financed
Assignment withholding rate . . . . 10% of gross receivables financed
Assignment service charge rate . . . . 2% of amount advanced

Instructions:

(1) Prepare the journal entries to record the receipt of cash from (a) factoring, and (b) assigning the accounts receivable.

(2) Prepare the journal entry to record the necessary adjustment to Allowance for Doubtful Accounts.

(3) Prepare the accounts receivable section of the balance sheet as it would appear after these transactions.

(4) What entry would be made in the company accounts of the Hallock Fur Company when factored accounts have been collected?

5-12A. Current assets for the Klein Company are listed as follows on the balance sheet prepared on December 31, 1981:

Current assets:

Cash	$ 11,600
Marketable securities	32,575
Notes receivable	16,900
Accounts receivable	74,485
Merchandise inventory	82,300
	$217,860

An examination of the books revealed the following information concerning the current assets:

(a) Cash included:

Petty cash funds (of which $490 is cash, $130 is in the form of employees' IOU's, and $30 is in the form of postage stamps)	$ 650
Customers' cheques not yet deposited	2,100
Demand deposit at the First Canadian Bank	8,200
An overdraft at the Central Bank	(300)
Customer's non-interest-bearing note (due January 2, 1982) deposited at the First Canada Bank for collection	950
	$11,600

(b) Marketable securities included:

Glendale Company Common (a subsidiary company), reported at cost	$16,155
Klein Company Preferred (treasury shares), reported at cost	12,100
9% Hamilton Company Bonds (interest payable January 1 and July 1), $4,000 face value, purchased September 1, 1981, as a temporary investment, reported at cost plus accrued interest to date of purchase	4,320
	$32,575

(c) Notes receivable included:

Customers' notes (due in 1982)	$ 8,750
Glendale Company note (due March 1, 1982)	6,000
Note receivable from sale of equipment (due July 1, 1983)	6,150
Notes receivable discounted (customers' notes)	(4,000)
	$16,900

(d) Accounts receivable included:

Creditor's accounts with debit balances	$ 1,000
Customers' accounts (regular)	37,770
Dividends receivable on investments	500
Deposit on equipment (ordered for delivery in December, 1983)	1,000
Instalment accounts receivable ($17,800 due in 1982; $9,200 due in 1983)	27,000
Interest receivable on bond investment	120
Interest receivable on notes	270
Receivables from consignees (representing the merchandise at cost transferred to consignees and still unsold on December 31, 1981)	2,100
Refundable income taxes of prior periods (believed to be collectible in 1982)	1,250
Travel advances to employees	975
Subscriptions receivable on capital stock (due in 1983)	4,500
Allowance for doubtful accounts (on regular and instalment accounts)	(2,000)
	$74,485

(e) Merchandise inventory (representing a physical count of goods on hand),

at cost $82,300

Instructions:

Revise the "Current assets" section of the balance sheet presenting individual items appropriately included therein in a proper manner. Prepare schedules stating what disposition was made of those items excluded in the revised presentation.

5-13A. The Eastern Gas Company follows the practice of cycle billing in order to minimize peak work loads for its clerical employees. All customers are billed monthly on various dates, except in those cases when the meter readers are unable to enter the premises to obtain a reading.

The company presents the following information for the year ended September 30, 1981.

Cycle	Billing Period	Number	Amount	Customers Not Billed
		Customers Billed		
1	Aug. 7 – Sept. 5 (inclusive)	2760	$13,800.00	324
2	Aug. 12 – Sept. 10 (inclusive)	3426	13,704.00	411
3	Aug. 17 – Sept. 15 (inclusive)	3265	14,692.50	335
4	Aug. 22 – Sept. 20 (inclusive)	2630	12,492.50	370
5	Aug. 27 – Sept. 25 (inclusive)	3132	13,311.00	468

You are further advised that all customers have been billed for prior periods and that the company's experience shows that charges for those customers whose meters were not read average the same amount as the charges for the customers billed in their cycle. In addition, the company assumes that the customers' usage will be uniform from month to month.

Instructions:

Compute the unbilled revenues of the company as of September 30, 1981, arising from cycles no. 1 and no. 3. *(Do not* compute revenues from cycles 2, 4 and 5.) (AICPA adapted)

5-14A. The Comity Loan Company is engaged in the consumer finance business. Prior to 1981 the company followed the direct write-off method of recording uncollectible loans. The company also provided a reserve for uncollectible loans by an appropriation of retained earnings.

During 1981 the Comity Loan Company decided to change to the allowance method of recognizing losses due to uncollectible loans. Permission was received to use this method for income tax purposes. The accounts, however, were continued on the write-off method for the full year of 1981. An analysis of the company's loss experience showed that 4% of the loans receivable at the end of each year prove uncollectible and are written off in the following year.

The following are condensed trial balances:

The Comity Loan Company
Trial Balances
December 31, 1981 and 1980

	December 31, 1981		December 31, 1980 (Post-closing)	
Cash	49,300		86,500	
Loans receivable	712,500		687,500	
Other assets	27,000		25,000	
Liabilities other than income tax		520,700		543,500
Income tax payable		19,170		20,000
Capital stock		100,000		100,000
Retained earnings		108,000		108,000
Reserve for uncollectible loans		27,500		27,500
Dividends paid	10,000			
Interest revenue		165,000		
Operating expenses	49,500			
Uncollectible loans written off	13,400			
Interest expense	59,500			
Income tax	19,170			
	940,370	940,370	799,000	799,000

Instructions:

(Assume that the current income tax rate is 45%).

(1) Prepare the formal journal entries at December 31, 1981, to record the change in accounting method for 1981.

(2) Prepare an income and retained earnings statement for the year ended December 31, 1981. (AICPA adapted)

5-15A. Hoffman Factors Ltd. was incorporated December 31, 1980. The share capital of the company consists of 100,000 shares of $10 par value each, all of which were paid in at par. The company was organized for the purpose of factoring the accounts receivable of various businesses requiring this service.

Hoffman Factors Ltd. charges a commission to its client of 2% of all receivables factored and assumes all credit risks. Besides the commission, an additional 10% of gross receivables is withheld on all purchases and is credited to Client Retainer. This retainer is used for merchandise returns, etc., made by customers of the clients for which a credit memo would be due. Payments are made to the clients by Hoffman Factors Ltd. at the end of each month to adjust the retainer so that it equals 10% of the unpaid receivables at the month's end.

Based on the collection experience of other factoring companies in this area, officials of Hoffman Factors Ltd. have decided to make monthly provisions to Allowance for Doubtful Accounts based on $1/4$% of all receivables purchased during the month.

The company also decided to recognize commission revenue on only the factored receivables which have been collected; however, for bookkeeping simplicity all commissions are originally credited to Commission Revenue and an adjustment is made to Unearned Commissions at the end of each quarter based on 2% of receivables then outstanding.

Operations of the company during the first quarter of 1981 resulted in the following:
Accounts receivable factored:

January	$200,000
February	400,000
March	300,000
	900,000

Collections on the above receivables totalled $700,000.
General and administrative expenses paid during the period:

Salaries	$5,000
Office rent	900
Advertising	500
Equipment rent	1,600
Miscellaneous	1,000
	9,000

On February 1, 1981, a three-month 10% bank loan was obtained for $500,000 with interest payable at maturity.

For the first three months of the year, the company rented all of its office furniture and equipment; however, on March 31, 1981, it purchased various equipment at a cost of $5,000, liability for which had not been recorded as of March 31.

Instructions:

(1) Give all of the entries necessary to record the above transactions and to close the books as of March 31, 1981. (Disregard all taxes.)

(2) Prepare a balance sheet and an income statement as of March 31, 1981. (AICPA adapted)

6 INVENTORIES — COST PROCEDURES

The term *inventories* is a designation for goods held for sale in the normal course of business, as well as for goods in production or to be placed in production. Practically all tangible items fall into this classification at one time or another somewhere in the universe of accounting entities. In addition, the sale of inventories normally provides a business with its chief source of revenue.

Inventories represent one of the most active elements in business operations, being continuously acquired, converted, and resold. A large part of a company's resources is frequently invested in goods purchased or manufactured. The cost of goods must be recorded, grouped, and summarized during the period. At the end of the period, costs must be allocated to current activities and to future activities. This allocation normally occupies a central role in the measurement of income as well as in the determination of financial position. Failure to allocate costs properly can result in serious distortions of both financial position and operating results.

Accounting for inventory costs presents a number of theoretical and practical problems. This chapter and the next chapter consider these problems.

CLASSES OF INVENTORIES

The term *merchandise inventory* is generally applied to goods held by a merchandising concern, either wholesale or retail, when such goods have been acquired in a condition for resale. The terms *raw materials*, *work in process*, and *finished goods* refer to the inventories of a manufacturing concern. The latter items require description.

Raw Materials

Raw materials are those tangible goods acquired for use in the productive process. Raw materials are normally acquired from other companies and represent the finished products of the companies from which they were purchased. For example, newsprint is the finished product of a paper mill but represents raw material to the printer who acquires it.

Although the term raw materials can be used broadly to cover all of the materials used in manufacturing, this designation is frequently restricted to materials that will be physically incorporated in the products being manufactured. The term *factory supplies*, or *manufacturing supplies*, is then used to refer to auxiliary materials, that is, materials that although necessary in the productive process are not directly incorporated in the products. Oils, fuels, cleaning supplies, etc., fall into this grouping since these items are not incorporated in a product but simply facilitate production as a whole; paint, nails, bolts, etc., although physically embodied in the final product, are normally of such minor significance as to warrant inclusion within the auxiliary grouping. Raw materials directly associated with the production of goods are frequently referred to as *direct materials*; factory supplies, then, are referred to as *indirect materials*.

Although factory supplies may be summarized separately, they should be reported as a part of a company's inventories since they will ultimately be applied in the productive process. Factory supplies should be distinguished from other supplies that make contributions to the delivery, sales, and general administrative functions of the enterprise. Such other supplies should not be reported as part of inventories. They are prepaid expenses.

Work in Process

Work in process, alternately referred to as *goods in process*, consists of materials partly processed and requiring further work before they can be sold. This inventory is considered to be made up of three cost elements: (1) *direct materials*, (2) *direct labor*, and (3) *manufacturing overhead* or *burden*. The cost of materials that can be directly identified with the goods in production is included under (1). The cost of labor that can be directly identified with goods in production is included under (2). The portion of manufacturing overhead assignable to goods still in production forms the third element of cost.

Manufacturing overhead consists of all manufacturing costs other than direct materials and direct labor. It includes factory supplies and labor not directly identified with the production of specific products. It also includes general manufacturing costs such as depreciation, maintenance, repairs, property taxes, insurance, and light, heat, and power, as well as a reasonable share of the managerial costs other than those relating solely to the selling and administrative functions of the business. Overhead may be designated as *fixed, variable* and *semifixed* or *semivariable*. Overhead charges that remain constant in amount regardless of the volume of production are referred to as fixed. Depreciation, insurance, rent, and property taxes normally fall into this category. Charges that fluctuate in proportion to the volume of production are called variable. Indirect materials and indirect labor often vary with production. Some charges vary, but the variations are not in direct proportion to the volume. These charges have both fixed and variable components and are designated as semifixed or semivariable items. For example, factory supervision is a semivariable item because it is fixed within a certain range of production but changes when production is not within this range.

Finished Goods

Finished goods are the manufactured products awaiting sale. The cost of the finished product consists of the direct materials, direct labor, and manufacturing overhead costs assigned to it. Finished parts purchased and used in the production of the finished product are normally classified as raw materials; finished parts held for purposes of sale may be reported as finished goods.

INVENTORIES IN THE MEASUREMENT OF INCOME

When goods purchased or manufactured are sold within a fiscal period, the determination of the gross profit on sales is a simple matter. The total cost of goods purchased or manufactured is also the cost of goods sold properly chargeable to revenue. Such a situation, however, is seldom found in practice. Normally a part of the goods acquired remains on hand at the end of the period. A value must be assigned to these goods. This value is subtracted from the total merchandise acquisition costs and is carried into the subsequent period to be charged against future revenue. Adequate records are required in providing cost data for financial statement purposes. These records are also required for proper internal control of goods on hand.

Two classes of questions arise in the determination of the inventory to be reported on the statements: (1) What items are properly included in inventory? and (2) What values are to be assigned to such items?

INVENTORY SYSTEMS

Quantities of inventories on hand are ascertained either through a *periodic system* requiring *physical inventories* at the end of each period, or a *perpetual system* requiring *perpetual* or *book inventories.*

The periodic system requires the taking of a physical inventory by counting, measuring, or weighing goods at the end of the period to determine the quantities on hand. Values are then assigned to such quantities to determine the portion of the recorded costs to be carried forward.

The perpetual inventory system requires the maintenance of records that offer a continuous summary of inventory items on hand. Individual accounts are kept for each class of goods. Inventory increases and decreases are recorded in the individual accounts, the resulting balances representing the amounts on hand. In a manufacturing organization, a perpetual system applied to inventories requires recording the full movement of goods through individual accounts for raw materials, work in process, and finished goods. Perpetual records may be kept in terms of quantities only or in terms of both quantities and costs.

When the perpetual system is employed, physical counts of the units on hand should be made at least once a year to confirm the balances recorded in the accounts. The frequency of physical inventories will vary depending upon the nature of the goods, their rate of turnover, and the degree of internal control. A plan for continuous counting of inventory items on a rotation basis is frequently employed. Variations between the perpetual record and the amounts actually on hand resulting from errors in recording, shrinkage, breakage, theft, and other causes should be recognized, and the recorded inventories should be brought into agreement with the physical count with offsetting debits and credits to an inventory adjustment account. The explanation for the discrepancy will determine whether the inventory adjustment balance should be regarded as an adjustment to cost of goods sold or as an operating expense. Normal adjustments for shrinkage and breakage are recorded as adjustments to cost of goods sold. Abnormal shortages or thefts, if material, should probably be reported separately as operating expenses.

Practically all large trading and manufacturing enterprises, as well as many relatively small organizations, have adopted the perpetual inventory system as an integral part of their record keeping and internal control. This system offers a continuous check and control over inventories as well as immediate data concerning inventory position. Purchasing and production planning are facilitated, adequate supplies on hand are assured, and losses incurred through damage and theft are determinable. The additional costs of maintaining such a system are usually well repaid by the benefits provided to management through its adoption.

ITEMS TO BE INCLUDED IN INVENTORY

As a general rule, goods should be included in the inventory of the party holding title. The passing of title is a legal term designating the point at which ownership changes. There are instances where the legal rule may be waived for practical reasons or because of certain limitations found in its application. When the circumstances are such that the rule of passing of title does not need to be observed, there should be appropriate disclosure on the statements of the special practice followed and the factors supporting such practice. Application of the legal test under a number of special circumstances is described in the following paragraphs.

Goods in Transit

When terms of sale are *FOB (free on board) shipping point*, title passes to the buyer with the loading of goods at the point of shipment. Application of the legal rule to a year-end shipment calls for recognition of a sale and an accompanying decrease in goods on hand in the accounts of the vendor. On the other hand, the buyer should recognize such *goods in transit* as a purchase and an accompanying inventory increase even though there is no physical possession. A determination of the goods in transit at year-end is made by a review of the incoming orders during the early part of the next fiscal period. The purchase records may be kept open beyond the fiscal period to permit the recognition of goods in transit as of the end of the period, or goods in transit may be recorded by means of an adjusting entry. Although no objection to the application of the legal rule can be raised by a vendor, the buyer, in the interests of expediency, may prefer to ignore such a rule and employ receipt as a basis for the recognition of a purchase and the related inventory increase. The latter approach is not objectionable when amounts in transit are not material and the inclusion of such items before their receipt and acceptance offers practical difficulties.

When terms of a sale are *FOB destination*, application of the legal test calls for no recognition of the transaction until goods are received by the buyer. In this case, it is the vendor who may prefer to ignore the legal rule and employ shipment as a basis for recording a sale and the accompanying inventory decrease. In view of the difficulties involved in ascertaining whether goods have reached their destination at year-end, application of a shipment rule is not objectionable under normal circumstances.

Segregated Goods

When goods are prepared on special order and segregated for shipment, title may pass with such segregation. When goods are segregated at the end of the period and title has passed, the vendor may properly recognize a sale and exclude *segregated goods* from the inventory, while the buyer may properly recognize both a purchase and an inventory increase. Frequently, one encounters practical problems in arriving at the portion of the inventory segregated as well as perplexing legal problems in defining their precise status. These difficulties normally result in the adoption of a policy whereby entries for both sale and purchase await formal shipment of goods by the vendor.

Goods on Consignment

Goods are frequently transferred to dealers on a consignment basis, the consignor retaining title to the goods until their sale by the consignee. Until the goods are sold and cash or a receivable can be recognized, the goods should continue to be reported as a part of the inventory of the consignor. *Consigned goods* are properly reported at the sum of their cost and the handling and shipping costs involved in their transfer to the consignee. The goods may be separately designated on the balance sheet as merchandise on consignment. The consignee does not own the consigned goods; hence neither consigned goods nor obligations for such goods are reported on the consignee's financial statements. Other merchandise owned by a business but in the possession of others, such as goods in the hands of salespersons and agents, goods held by customers on approval, and goods held by others for storage, processing, or shipment, should also be shown as a part of the owner's ending inventory.

Conditional and Instalment Sales

Conditional sales and instalment sales contracts may provide for a retention of title by the vendor until the sales price is fully recovered. Under these circumstances, the vendor, who retains title, may continue to show the goods, reduced by the buyer's equity in such goods as established by collections; the buyer, in turn, can report an equity in the goods accruing through payments made. However, in the usual case when the possibilites of returns and defaults are negligible, the test of passing of title should be relinquished and the transaction recorded in terms of the expected outcome: the vendor, anticipating completion of the contract and the ultimate passing of title, recognizes the transaction as a regular sale involving deferred collections; the buyer, intending to comply with the contract and acquire title, recognizes the transactions as a regular purchase.

INVENTORY VALUATION

In viewing the inventory in its dual position as (1) a value reported on the income statement representing charges properly applicable to current revenue and (2) a value reported on the balance sheet representing the charges properly assignable to future revenues, the profession has accepted cost as the primary basis for inventory valuation. A marked change in the value of the inventory between the purchase date and the inventory date raises the question as to whether some recognition should be given to current inventory replacement values. With a rise in prices, accountants generally answer this question in the negative, insisting that income must await sale of goods; with a decline in prices, however, there is wide support for recognizing such decline by applying the "cost or market, whichever is lower" valuation procedure.[1] In a few special instances the use of a sales price or a modified sales price basis, rather than the usual cost basis, is considered acceptable.

Income measurement rather than balance sheet valuation is generally regarded as the major criterion in accounting for inventories. Thus, the Accounting Research Committee has taken the position that "the method selected for determining cost should be one which results in the fairest matching of costs against revenues."[2]

In contrast with this position, and with that of the AICPA which is essentially the same, the American Accounting Association's Special Committee on Inventories recognized market value for inventories as being very important, and recommended preparing multi-column statements reporting both cost and market valuations. This view was also supported in the AAA's *A Statement of Basic Accounting Theory*.[3]

INVENTORY COST METHODS

The principal inventory valuation methods and their special applicabilities will be considered in detail. Attention is directed in this chapter to the measurement of cost when cost is required for inventory valuation as well as when cost is to be used as the first step in the development of a lower of cost or market value.

Determination of Cost

The determination of the cost of inventory may not be a simple matter. First, it involves determining the expenditures for the cost of the goods that

---

[1]The lower of cost or market valuation procedure is covered in Chapter 7.

[2]*CICA Handbook: Accounting Recommendations, Section 3030*, "Inventories" (Toronto: Canadian Institute of Chartered Accountants, 1968), par. 09.

[3]*A Statement of Basic Accounting Theory* (Evanston, Illinois: American Accounting Association, 1966), p. 11.

were acquired. Second, it involves applying a method for relating the different costs of the goods acquired to periodic revenue.

Inventory cost consists of all expenditures, both direct and indirect, relating to inventory acquisition, preparation, and placement for sale. In the case of raw materials or goods acquired for resale, cost includes, in addition to the purchase price, freight, receiving, storage, and all other expenditures incurred to the time goods are ready for sale. Certain expenditures can be traced to specific acquisitions or can be allocated to inventory items in some equitable manner. Other expenditures may be relatively small and difficult to allocate. Such items are normally excluded in the calculation of inventory cost and are thus charged in full against current revenue as *period costs* or *expense*.

The charges to be included in the cost of manufactured products have already been mentioned. Proper accounting for materials, labor, and manufacturing overhead items and their identification with work in process and finished goods inventories may be best achieved through adoption of a cost accounting system designed to meet the needs of the particular business entity. Certain costs relating to the acquisition or the manufacture of goods may be excluded in arriving at inventory cost. For example, costs arising from idle capacity, excessive spoilage, and reprocessing are often excluded from inventory cost and instead charged against current revenue. Only those portions of general and administrative costs that are clearly related to procurement of production should be included in inventory cost.

In practice, companies take different positions in classifying inventoriable costs. For example, costs of the purchasing department, costs of accounting for manufacturing activities, and costs of pensions for production personnel may be found either as part of the inventoriable costs or as direct deductions from revenue.

Discounts as Reductions in Cost

Discounts treated as a reduction of cost in recording the acquisition of goods should similarly be treated as a reduction in the cost assigned to the inventory. *Trade discounts* are discounts converting a printed price list to the prices actually charged to a buyer. Sometimes, trade discounts are stated in a series, e.g., 30/20/10 or 30%, then 20%, then 10%. Each discount is taken on the net invoice cost after taking the earlier discounts.[4]

---

[4]An equivalent composite discount rate may be computed as follows:

(1) Discount Rate	(2) Percentage of Original Invoice Cost	(3) Composite Discount Rate (1) × (2)
30%	100%	30.0%
20%	70% (100% − 30%)	14.0
10%	56% (100% − 44%)	5.6
		49.6%

Cost, then, is list price less the trade discount; purchases and inventory should be reported at such cost with no accounting recognition given to the discount. *Cash discounts* are reductions in prices allowed only upon payment of invoices within a limited period. Inventory treatment depends upon whether cash discounts are regarded as a reduction in cost or as a source of revenue. If cash discounts are treated as a subtraction from purchases, which is the more common practice, the inventory balance should be correspondingly reduced; if cash discounts are reported as other revenue, inventories should be at invoice cost without reference to the discounts taken. In practice, this treatment is rare. More importantly, it is not theoretically sound; cash discounts are not revenues.

Subtraction of purchase discounts from purchases recognizes discounts as an adjustment in the purchase price. When settlement is not made within the discount period, a failure on the part of financial management is indicated either through carelessness in considering payment alternatives or through financial inability to avoid the extra charge. The inefficiency of management can be disclosed by recording purchases net and recognizing any amounts paid in excess of these amounts as Purchase Discounts Lost, a financial management expense item. When such a practice is to be followed, two methods may be employed: (1) accounts payable may be reported at the invoice price net or (2) accounts payable may be reported at the gross invoice price with a payable offset balance or liability valuation account reporting the purchase discounts available. The two methods are illustrated at the top of page 210.

Although recording purchases net and recognizing cash discounts lost as an expense has obvious merit, it has failed to gain wide adoption. Chief objection is made on practical grounds. Use of this method required converting gross amounts into net amounts relating to individual acquisitions and using converted values throughout the accounting for inventories. This is normally less convenient than accounting in terms of gross invoice charges.

Specific Identification of Costs with Inventory Items

Revenue may be charged for goods sold on the basis of identified costs of the specific items sold. Such practice calls for the identification of a cost with each item acquired. When perpetual inventories are maintained, the sale of goods requires the transfer of articles and their identified costs to the cost of goods sold. When a system of physical inventories is maintained, goods on hand require identification with specific invoices. In each instance, costs related to units sold are reported as cost of goods sold and costs identified with goods on hand remain to be reported as the ending inventory.

Although such identification procedure may be considered a highly satis-

TRANSACTION	ACCOUNTS PAYABLE REPORTED NET		ACCOUNTS PAYABLE REPORTED GROSS	
Purchase of merchandise priced at $2,500 less trade discount of 30%/20% and a cash discount of 2%: $2,500 less 30% = $1,750 $1,750 less 20% = $1,400 $1,400 less 2% = $1,372	Purchases (or Inventory) .... 1,372 Accounts Payable .	1,372	Purchases (or Inventory) .... 1,372 Allowance for Purchase Discounts ... 28 Accounts Payable ...	1,400
(a) Assuming payment of the invoice within discount period.	Accounts Payable ... 1,372 Cash	1,372	Accounts Payable ..... 1,400 Allowance for Purchase Discounts Cash	28 1,372
(b) Assuming payment of the invoice after discount period.	Accounts Payable ... 1,372 Purchase Discounts Lost .... 28 Cash	1,400	Accounts Payable ..... 1,400 Cash .... Purchase Discounts Lost .... 28 Allowances for Purchase Discounts	1,400 28
(c) Required adjustment at the end of the period assuming that the invoice was not paid and the discount period has lapsed.	Purchase Discounts Lost .... 28 Accounts Payable..	28	Purchase Discounts Lost .... 28 Allowance for Purchase Discounts	28

factory approach because of objectivity and adherence to empirical fact,[5] the practice may be difficult or impossible to apply. When an inventory is composed of a great many items, some being similar items acquired at different times and at different prices, cost identification procedures may prove to be slow, burdensome, and costly. When identical items have been acquired at different times, their identities may be lost and cost identification thus denied. Furthermore, when units are identical and interchangeable, this method opens the doors to possible profit manipulation through the choice of particular units for delivery. Finally, marked changes in costs during a period may warrant charges to revenue on a basis other than past identifiable costs.

Nonetheless, specific identification should be considered where it is practicable. For example, serial numbers, permit its use for costing new and used car sales in an automobile dealership.

TRADITIONAL COST FLOW METHODS

When specific identification procedures are considered inappropriate,

---

[5]This point is stressed in Accounting Research Study No. 13 as follows: "There appears to be little theoretical argument against the use of specific identification of cost with units of product if that method of determining inventory costs is practicable." Horace G. Barden, *The Accounting Basis of Inventories*, Accounting Research Study No. 13 (New York: American Institute of Certified Public Accountants, 1973), p. 82.

it is necessary to adopt some assumption with respect to the flow of costs associated with the movement of goods. Three methods, each with a different assumption as to an orderly flow of costs, have achieved wide recognition in accounting practice. These are: (1) *first-in, first-out*, (2) *weighted average*, and (3) *last-in, first-out*.

First-In, First-Out Method

The first-in, first-out method (*fifo* method) is based on the assumption that costs should be charged to revenue in the order in which they are incurred. Inventories are thus stated in terms of the most recent costs incurred. To illustrate the application of this method, assume the following data:

Jan.	1 Inventory	200 units at $10	$ 2,000
	12 Purchase	400 units at 12	4,800
	26 Purchase	300 units at 11	3,300
	30 Purchase	100 units at 12	1,200
	Total	1,000	$11,300

A physical inventory on January 31 shows 300 units on hand. The inventory would be considered to be composed of the most recent costs as follows:

Most recent purchase, Jan. 30	100 units at $12	$1,200
Next most recent purchase, Jan. 26	200 units at 11	2,200
Total	300	$3,400

If the ending inventory is recorded at $3,400, cost of goods sold is $7,900 ($11,300 − $3,400), and revenue is charged with the earliest costs incurred.

When perpetual inventory accounts are maintained, a form similar to that illustrated at the top of page 213 is used to record the cost of units issued and the cost relating to the goods on hand. The columns show the quantities and values relating to goods acquired, goods issued, and balances on hand. It should be observed that identical values for physical and perpetual inventories are obtained when fifo is applied.

Fifo can be supported as a logical and realistic approach to the flow of costs when it is impractical or impossible to achieve specific cost identification. Fifo assumes a cost flow that should often closely parallel the actual physical flow of goods sold. Revenue is charged with costs considered applicable to those goods involved in the realization of revenue; ending inventories are reported in terms of most recent costs — costs fairly presenting the latest acquisitions and costs equitably assignable to revenues of the subsequent period. Fifo affords little opportunity for profit manipulation; assignment of costs against revenue is determined by the order in which costs are incurred.

Weighted Average Method

The weighted average method is based on the assumption that goods sold should be charged at an average cost, such average being influenced by the number of units acquired at each price. Inventories are stated at the same weighted average cost. Assuming the cost data in the preceding section, the weighted average cost of a physical inventory of 300 units on January 31 would be as follows:

Jan. 1	Inventory	200 units at $10	$2,000
12	Purchase	400 units at 12	4,800
26	Purchase	300 units at 11	3,300
30	Purchase	100 units at 12	1,200
	Total	1,000	$11,300

Weighted average cost . . . .$11,300 ÷ 1,000 = $11.30.
Ending inventory . . . . .300 units at $11.30 = $3,390.

If the ending inventory is recorded at a cost of $3,390, cost of goods sold is $7,910 ($11,300 − $3,390), and revenue is charged without a weighted average cost. Calculations above were made for costs of one month. Similar calculations could be developed in terms of data for a quarter or for a year.

When perpetual inventories are maintained but the costs of units issued are not recorded until the end of a period, a weighted average cost for the period may be calculated at that time and the accounts may be credited for the cost of total units issued. Frequently, however, costs relating to issues are recorded currently, and it is necessary to calculate costs on the basis of the weighted average on the date of issue. This requires calculating a new weighted average cost immediately after the receipt of each individual lot of merchandise. This method, involving successive average recalculations, is referred to as a *moving average method*. The use of this method is illustrated on the next page.

On January 12 the new unit cost of $11.33 was found by dividing $6,800, the total cost, by 600, the number of units on hand. Then on January 16, the dollar balance, $1,135, represented the previous balance, $6,800, less $5,665, the cost assigned to the 500 units issued on this date. New unit costs were calculated on January 26 and 30 when additional units were acquired.

With successive recalculations of cost and the use of such different costs during the period, the cost identified with the ending inventory will differ from that determined when cost is assigned to the ending inventory in terms of average cost for all goods available during the period. A physical inventory and use of the weighted average method resulted in a value for the ending inventory of $3,390; a perpetual inventory and use of the moving average method resulted in a value for the ending inventory of $3,417.

COMMODITY: X (fifo)

DATE	RECEIVED			ISSUED			BALANCE		
	QUANTITY	UNIT COST	TOTAL COST	QUANTITY	UNIT COST	TOTAL COST	QUANTITY	UNIT COST	TOTAL COST
Jan. 1							200	$10	$2,000
12	400	$12	$4,800				200	10	2,000
							400	12	4,800
16				200	$10	$2,000			
				300	12	3,600	100	12	1,200
26	300	11	3,300				100	12	1,200
							300	11	3,300
29				100	12	1,200			
				100	11	1,100	200	11	2,200
30	100	12	1,200				200	11	2,200
							100	12	1,200

COMMODITY: X (moving average)

DATE	RECEIVED			ISSUED			BALANCE		
	QUANTITY	UNIT COST	TOTAL COST	QUANTITY	UNIT COST	TOTAL COST	QUANTITY	UNIT COST	TOTAL COST
Jan. 1							200	$10.00	$2,000
12	400	$12	$4,800				600	11.33	6,800
16				500	$11.33	$5,665	100	11.35	1,135
26	300	11	3,300				400	11.09	4,405
29				200	11.09	2,218	200	11.09	2,217
30	100	12	1,200				300	11.39	3,417

The average cost approach can be supported as realistic and as parallel-ing the physical flow of goods, particularly where there is an intermingling of identical inventory units. Unlike the other inventory methods, the average approach provides the same cost for similar items of equal utility. The method does not permit profit manipulation. Limitations of the average method are inventory values that perpetually contain some degree of influence of earliest costs and inventory values that may lag significantly behind current prices in periods of rapidly rising or falling prices. In addition, the moving average method involves a considerable amount of clerical work and therefore is expensive to use.

Last-In, First-Out Method

It should be noted that use of the last-in, first-out (*lifo*) method is not permitted for income tax purposes in Canada.[6] It is therefore hardly surpris-

---

[6]*Minister of National Revenue v. Anaconda American Brass Co.* (1956), a case decided by the Judicial Committee of the Privy Council in the United Kingdom because the action originated before the Supreme Court of Canada became Canada's highest court of appeal. It is interestesting to note that the Privy Council decision in the Anaconda case overruled a Supreme Court of Canada decision that would have permitted use of the lifo for income tax purposes.

ing that lifo is rarely used in Canadian accounting practice. In contrast, the lifo method is widely used in the United States because it is recognized for income tax purposes ,under the Internal Revenue Code. The result is an excellent example of the influence income tax can have on the development of accounting principles. Thus, in the United States, lifo procedures have been refined to facilitate the method's widest possible application for income tax purposes. From the income tax viewpoint, refinement of the lifo method serves no useful purpose in Canada. From the accounting viewpoint, however, lifo is recognized in Section 3030 of the *Accounting Recommendations* as a generally accepted method for determining inventory cost. However, less than 5 per cent of the survey companies reported upon in the CICA publication, *Financial Reporting in Canada*, indicate use of the lifo. Moreover, in many instances use of lifo is restricted to United States subsidiaries.[7]

It should be noted that double digit inflation during the 1970s stimulated renewed interest in the lifo method. In spite of pressure from the business community, among others, recognition of lifo for income tax purposes is still not permitted. In 1978, however, the deduction of a 3 per cent inventory allowance based on opening inventories was introduced for tax purposes. For the time being at least, the possible use of lifo for income tax purposes in Canada appears to be a dead issue.

The last-in, first-out method is based on the assumption that the latest costs of a specific good be charged to cost of goods sold (*specific goods method*). Inventories are thus stated at earliest costs. Assuming the cost data in the preceding section, a physical inventory of 300 units on January 31 would have a cost as follows:

Earliest costs relating to goods, Jan. 1	200 units at $10	$2,000
Next earliest cost, Jan. 12	100 units at 12	1,200
Total	300	$3,200

If the ending inventory is recorded at a cost of $3,200, then cost of goods sold is $8,100 ($11,300 − $3,200), and revenue is charged with the most recently incurred costs.

When perpetual inventories are maintained but the cost of units issued is not recorded until the end of the period, the most recent cost relating to the total units issued for the period may be determined and the inventory account credited for cost. Cost, then, is the same as reported above. If costs relating to issues are recorded currently, it is necessary to calculate costs on a last-in, first-out basis using the cost data on the date of issue. This is illustrated on page 215.

It should be noted that in applying lifo, physical and perpetual inventory values are not usually the same. In the example, a cost of $3,200 was obtained

---

[7]*Financial Reporting in Canada* (13th ed.; Toronto: Canadian Institute of Chartered Accountants, 1979), p. 101.

COMMODITY: X (lifo)										
	RECEIVED			ISSUED			BALANCE			
DATE	QUANTITY	UNIT COST	TOTAL COST	QUANTITY	UNIT COST	TOTAL COST	QUANTITY	UNIT COST	TOTAL COST	
Jan. 1							200	$10	$2,000	
12	400	$12	$4,800				200	10	2,000	
							400	12	4,800	
16				400	$12	$4,800				
				100	10	1,000	100	10	1,000	
26	300	11	3,300				100	10	1,000	
							300	11	3,300	
29							100	10	1,000	
				200	11	2,200	100	11	1,100	
30	100	12	1,200				100	10	1,000	
							100	11	1,100	
							100	12	1,200	

for the periodic inventory, whereas $3,300 was obtained when costs were calculated as goods were issued. This difference results because it was necessary to charge out 100 units of the beginning inventory at $10 in the issue of January 16. The ending inventory thus reflects only 100 units of the beginning inventory.

These temporary liquidations of inventory frequently do occur during the year, especially for companies with seasonal business. These liquidations cause monthly reports prepared on the lifo basis to be unrealistic and meaningless, because the drawdown of opening inventory quantities may have to be costed at a price that differs significantly from current costs. Because of this, companies using lifo may maintain their internal records using other inventory methods, such as fifo or weighted average, and adjust the statements to lifo at the end of the year with a lifo allowance account.[8]

Specific-Goods Pools. With large and diversified inventories, application of the lifo procedures to specific goods has proved to be extremely burdensome. Because of the complexity and cost involved, companies frequently selected only a few very important inventory items, usually raw materials, for application of the lifo method. As a means of simplifying the valuation process, and extending its applicability to more items, an adaptation of the specific goods method was developed permitting the establishment of inventory pools of substantially identical goods. Under this adaptation, the total quantity of items in the pool and the total costs of these units are determined. Average unit costs for goods within each pool are calculated, units being regarded as having been acquired at the same time. At the end of a period, units in each pool equal to the beginning number are assigned the beginning

[8]Companies frequently refer to this account as the *lifo reserve* account. Because the profession has recommended that the word *reserve* not be used for asset valuation accounts, the term *allowance* is used in this text.

unit costs. As with all lifo applications, an increase in the number of units in an inventory pool during a period is regarded as an incremental layer, and such incremental layer is valued at current costs applied on the basis of (1) actual costs of earliest acquisitions within the period (lifo), (2) the average cost of acquisitions within the period, or (3) actual costs of the latest acquisitions within the period (fifo). Increments in subsequent periods form successive inventory layers. A decrease in the number of units in an inventory pool during a period is regarded as a reduction in the most recently added layer, then in successively lower layers, and finally in the original or base quantity. Once a specific layer is reduced or eliminated, it is not restored.

To illustrate the lifo valuation process, assume inventory pools and changes in pools as listed on page 217. The inventory calculations that follow the listing are based on the assumption average costs are used in valuing annual incremental layers.

A new layer was added to the inventory of Class A goods each year. Previously established layers were reduced in 1982 for Class B goods and in 1981 for Class C goods.

Dollar-Value Pools. Even the grouping of substantially identical items into quantity pools does not produce all the benefits desired from the use of the lifo method. Technological changes sometimes introduce new products thus requiring the elimination of inventory in old pools, and requiring the establishment of new pools for the new product that no longer qualifies as being substantially identical. For example, the introduction of synthetic fabrics to replace cotton meant that "cotton" pools were eliminated and new "synthetic fabric" pools established. This change resulted in the loss of lower lifo bases by companies changing the type of fabrics they used. To overcome this type of problem and to further simplify the clerical work involved, the dollar-value method was developed. Under this method, the unit of measurement is the dollar rather than the quantity of goods. All similar items, such as all raw materials for a given line of business, are grouped into a pool and layers are determined based upon total dollar changes, using index numbers to indicate price-level changes. The procedures to apply dollar-value lifo are discussed in Chapter 7.

Theoretical Arguments Concerning Lifo. The cost assignment resulting from the application of lifo cannot normally be considered in harmony with a movement of goods through the business. One would seldom encounter in practice priorities for the use or transfer of goods representing latest acquisitions. Sequences involved in the physical movement of goods are disregarded so that charges may be made to revenue in terms of most-current costs, that is, cost more nearly representative of the cost of replacing the inventory resulting from sales.[9]

[9]If the inventory turnover is slow, and if prices are rising or falling rapidly, current costs could differ significantly from lifo. Some accountants would go beyond lifo and charge revenue with the replacement cost of goods sold (next-in, first-out, or *nifo*) rather than with latest acquisition costs.

Inventory pool increments and liquidations:

	Class A Goods	Class B Goods	Class C Goods
Inv., Dec. 31, 1980	3,000 @ $6	3,000 @ $5	2,000 @ $10
Purchases — 1981	3,000 @ $7	2,000 @ $6	3,000 @ $11
	1,000 @ $9		
Sales — 1981	7,000	5,000	5,000
	3,000	1,000	3,500
Inv., Dec. 31, 1981	4,000	4,000	1,500
Purchases — 1982	1,000 @ $8	2,000 @ $6	3,000 @ $11
	3,000 @ $10		
Sales — 1982	8,000	6,000	4,500
	3,500	2,500	2,000
Inv., Dec. 31, 1982	4,500	3,500	2,500

Unit-lifo inventory valuations:

	Class A Goods		Class B Goods		Class C Goods	
Inv., Dec. 31, 1980	3,000 @ $6	$18,000	3,000 @ $5	$15,000	2,000 @ $10	$20,000
Inv., Dec. 31, 1981	3,000 @ $6	$18,000	3,000 @ $5	$15,000	1,500 @ $10	$15,000
	1,000 @ $7.50[1]	7,500	1,000 @ $6	6,000		
	4,000	$25,500	4,000	$21,000	1,500	$15,000
Inv., Dec. 31, 1982	3,000 @ $6	$18,000	3,000 @ $5	$15,000	1,500 @ $10	$15,000
	1,000 @ $7.50	7,500	500 @ $6	3,000	1,000 @ $11	11,000
	500 @ $9.50[2]	4,750				
	4,500	$30,250	3,500	$18,000	2,500	$26,000

[1] Cost of units acquired in 1981, $30,000, divided by number of units acquired, 4,000, or $7.50.
[2] Cost of units acquired in 1982, $38,000, divided by number of units acquired, 4,000, or $9.50.

The layer process for lifo inventories may be further illustrated in the following manner:

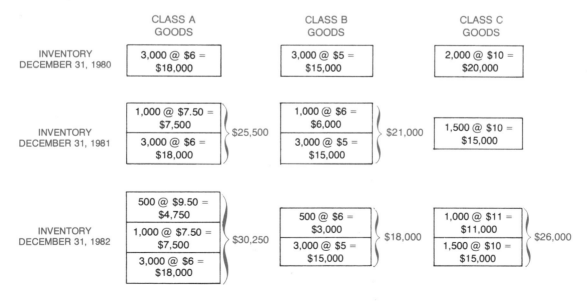

However, it is argued that lifo offers a more accurate statement of earnings accruing to the ownership group than alternate methods. When fifo is used in a period of rising prices, for example, earnings reported are not fully available to owners but rather must be applied in part or in whole to higher-cost inventory replacement; in a period of falling prices, reported earnings fail to show the full resources accruing to owners from sales activities plus the amounts made available through lower cost inventory replacement. Lifo, on the other hand, by charging revenue with latest costs, avoids the recognition of "paper gain or loss" on an inventory that the company must continue to hold as long as it operates as a going concern. This aspect of the measurement process may be illustrated as follows:

	Inventory Cost	Sales Price	Latest Purchase Price	Fifo "Profit"	Lifo "Profit"	Dollars Available After Unit Replacement at Latest Purchase Price
With rising prices:	$10	$15	$12	$5	$3	$3
With falling prices:	$10	$12	$ 8	$2	$4	$4

Under lifo, that portion of sales proceeds that is required for the replacement of the inventory at higher costs receives recognition as net income only when it is freed through a subsequent replacement of inventories at lower costs. Thus, so-called "inventory profits" do not emerge under lifo. Also for purposes of supplement disclosures of current cost information, cost of goods sold determined in accordance with lifo can be considered equivalent to the current or replacement cost of goods sold provided there has been no drawdown of lifo inventories.

Although arguments for lifo as a means of achieving satisfactory income measurement are impressive, one must consider the deficiencies of this method as applied to the recognition of inventory position for balance sheet purposes. The lifo inventory consists of an assembly of congealed costs or cost layers dating back to original acquisitions — costs often differing materially from current prices. Such inventory costs enter into the determination of working capital and may seriously distort this measurement. Inventory position is also a determinant of total assets and capital. Adoption of lifo in a period of rising prices results in inventory understatement, a practice that is normally rationalized as acceptable on conservative grounds. Adoption of lifo in a period of falling prices results in inventory overstatement; here, it is fair to assume, there would be strong pressure for special action to write down inventory balances to replacement cost.

In certain instances, the use of lifo may produce highly unrealistic operating results. Assume, for example, that circumstances make it necessary for a company to temporarily liquidate a significant part or an entire inventory carried at costs that are materially different from current costs. Under these circumstances, the lifo gross profit margin would not be the steady percentage offered by the recurring application of current costs to current revenues but instead a highly distorted figure resulting from the need to charge off original inventory costs. The following example should clarify this weakness.

Assume that a lumber company normally received its lumber by ship, but that at year-end orders were mishandled and a boat load was not received as planned. The company, in failing to record the boat load of lumber as a current year purchase, would have to apply older lifo costs against sales. The resulting profit could lead to conclusions that would not be justified by the facts.

To avoid the distortion caused by a temporary reduction of lifo layers at the end of a year, some accountants advocate establishing a replacement allowance that charges the current period for the extra replacement cost to be incurred in the subsequent period when the inventory is replenished. However, the use of an allowance for temporary liquidation of lifo layers is in reality an application of the base stock method, rather than lifo.

Lifo may also invite profit manipulation practices. For example, purchases, though required to maintain an inventory position, may be postponed at the end of the period so that costs of prior periods may be used in measuring net income. On the other hand, purchases may be made at the end of the period, though goods are not required, so that costs of the latest purchases may be used in arriving at net incomes.

Last-in, first-out has been advocated by some accountants because of its ability to smooth the profit curve in a period of steadily rising prices. However, it is not the effects of a procedure but its merits as a means of sound measurement that should determine its acceptance for general accounting purposes. Depreciation and amortization charges, for example, could be recorded in accordance with the ability of revenue to absorb such charges in smoothing the profit curve. Such practices would not lead to measurements of what actually took place; instead, they would serve to obscure measurements and thus contradict the aim of accounting to report financial activities fairly.

Effects of Traditional Cost Flow Procedures Compared

In using the first-in, first-out procedure, inventories are reported on the balance sheet at or near current costs. In using last-in, first-out, inventories not changing significantly in quantity are reported at more or less fixed amounts relating back to perhaps the date that lifo was adopted, or at least to the date of the earliest purchases. Use of the average method generally provides inventory values closely paralleling first-in, first-out values, since purchases during a period are normally several times the opening inventory balance and average costs are thus heavily influenced by current costs. When the prices paid for merchandise do not fluctuate significantly, alternative inventory methods may provide only minor financial statement differences.

However, in periods of steadily rising or falling prices, the alternative methods may produce material differences. Moreover, differences in inventory valuations on the balance sheet are accompanied by differences in earnings on the income statement for the period.

Use of first-in, first-out in a period of rising prices matches oldest low-cost inventory with rising sales prices, thus expanding the gross profit margin. In a period of declining prices, oldest high-cost inventory is matched with declining sales prices, thus narrowing the gross profit margin. On the other hand, use of last-in, first-out in a period of rising prices relates current high costs of acquiring goods with rising sales prices, and in a period of falling prices, low costs of acquiring goods with declining sales prices. Average methods that provide inventory costs closely comparable with first-in, first-out costs offer operating results approximating first-in, first-out results.

The application of the different methods in periods of rising and falling prices is illustrated in the following example. Assume that the Welch Sales Co. sells its goods at 50% in excess of prevailing costs from 1979 to 1982. The company sells its inventories and terminates activities at the end of 1982. Sales, costs, and gross profits using each of the three methods are shown in the tabulation below.

	FIFO			WEIGHTED AVERAGE¹			LIFO		
1979:									
Sales, 500 units @ $9			$4,500			$4,500			$4,500
Inventory, 200 units	@ $5	$1,000		200 @ $5	$1,000		200 @ $5	$1,000	
Purchases, 500 units	@ $6	3,000		500 @ $6	3,000		500 @ $6	3,000	
		$4,000			$4,000			$4,000	
Ending Inv., 200 units	@ $6	1,200	2,800	200 @ $5.71 ($4,000 ÷ 700)	1,142	2,858	200 @ $5	1,000	$3,000
Gross Profit on Sales			$1,700			$1,642			$1,500
1980:									
Sales, 450 units @ $12			$5,400			$5,400			$5,400
Inventory, 200 units	@ $6	$1,200		200 @ $5.71	$1,142		200 @ $5	$1,000	
Purchases, 500 units	@ $8	4,000		500 @ $8	4,000		500 @ $8	4,000	
		$5,200			$5,142			$5,000	
Ending Inv., 250 units	@ $8	2,000	3,200	250 @ $7.35 ($5,142 ÷ 700)	1,838	3,304	200 @ $5 / 50 @ $8	1,400	3,600
Gross Profit on Sales			$2,200			$2,096			$1,800
1981:									
Sales, 475 units @ $10.50			$4,988			$4,988			$4,988
Inventory, 250 units	@ $8	$2,000		250 @ $7.35	$1,838		200 @ $5 / 50 @ $8	$1,400	
Purchases, 450 units	@ $7	3,150		450 @ $7	3,150		450 @ $7	3,150	
		$5,150			$4,988			$4,550	
Ending Inv., 225 units	@ $7	1,575	3,575	225 @ $7.13 ($4,988 ÷ 700)	1,604	3,384	200 @ $5 / 25 @ $8	1,200	3,350
Gross Profit on Sales			$1,413			$1,604			$1,638
1982:									
Sales, 625 units @ $7.50			$4,688			$4,688			$4,688
Inventory, 225 units	@ $7	$1,575		225 @ $7.13	$1,604		200 @ $5 / 25 @ $8	$1,200	
Purchases, 400 units	@ $5	2,000	3,575	400 @ $5	2,000	3,604	400 @ $5	2,000	3,200
Gross Profit on Sales			$1,113			$1,084			$1,488

¹Totals in the illustration are calculated to the nearest dollar.

Although the different methods give the same total gross profit on sales for the four-year period, use of first-in, first-out resulted in increased gross profit percentages in periods of rising prices and a contraction of gross profit percentages in a period of falling prices, while last-in, first-out resulted in relatively steady gross profit percentages in spite of fluctuating prices. The weighted average method offered results closely comparable to those obtained by first-in, first-out. Assuming operating expenses at 30% of sales, use of last-in, first-out would result in a net income for each of the four years; first-in, first-out would result in larger net incomes in 1979 and 1980, but losses in 1981 and 1982. Inventory valuation on the last-in, first-out basis tends to smooth the peaks and fill the troughs of business fluctuations.

The foregoing transactions are summarized below:

Year	Sales	FIFO			WEIGHTED AVERAGE			LIFO		
		Cost of Goods Sold	Gross Profit on Sales	Gross Profit % to Sales	Cost of Goods Sold	Gross Profit on Sales	Gross Profit % to Sales	Cost of Goods Sold	Gross Profit on Sales	Gross Profit % to Sales
1979	$ 4,500	$ 2,800	$1,700	37.8%	$ 2,858	$1,642	36.5%	$ 3,000	$1,500	33.3%
1980	5,400	3,200	2,200	40.7	3,304	2,096	38.8	3,600	1,800	33.3
1981	4,988	3,575	1,413	28.3	3,384	1,604	32.2	3,350	1,638	32.8
1982	4,688	3,575	1,113	23.7	3,604	1,084	23.1	3,200	1,488	31.7
	$19,576	$13,150	$6,426	32.8%	$13,150	$6,426	32.8%	$13,150	$6,426	32.8%

OTHER COST PROCEDURES

The methods previously described for arriving at inventory cost are the ones most widely used. Several other procedures are sometimes encountered and deserve mention.

Cost of Latest Purchases

Sometimes goods are valued at cost of the latest purchase regardless of quantities on hand. When the inventory consists largely of recent purchases, this method may give results closely approximating those obtained through specific cost identification or first-in, first-out procedures with considerably less work. However, when the quantities of goods on hand are significantly in excess of the latest quantities purchased and major price changes have taken place, use of latest costs may result in significant cost misstatement.

Simple Average of Costs

Goods on hand are sometimes valued at a simple average of all of the costs for the period without regard to the number of units acquired on each purchase. With significant differences in quantities acquired, the disregard of the weight factor may result in unrepresentative costs.

Base Stock Method

This method assumes that a minimum inventory quantity is a normal and permanent requirement of the business; current purchases are intended to satisfy current sales requirements, and hence their cost is properly applicable to revenues. The base stock inventory is regarded as fixed as to both quantity and price. At the end of the period the amount of goods on hand is determined. The base stock quantity is priced at the lowest cost experienced since the adoption of the method. An amount in excess of the base stock quantity is regarded as a temporary inventory increase and is valued at current costs, applied on a first-in, first-out, average, or other basis. A reduction in the base stock quantity is viewed as an amount temporarily "borrowed" to meet sales requirements, and this is charged to sales at current replacement value in view of the cost to be incurred in restoring the inventory deficiency.

To illustrate use of the base stock method, assume a base stock of 100,000 units at $1 per unit that has increased to a total of 120,000 units. If the current cost is $1.60 per unit, the inventory is valued as follows:

Base stock	100,000 units @ $1.00	$100,000
Add base stock quantity		
excess at current cost	20,000 units @ $1.60	32,000
Inventory value	120,000 units	$132,000

Assume an inventory of only 90,000 units, and a current cost for units of $1.60. The inventory would be valued as follows:

Base stock	100,000 units @ $1.00	$100,000
Deduct base stock quantity		
deficiency at current cost ...	10,000 units @ $1.60	16,000
Inventory value	90,000 units	$ 84,000

Instead of reporting $84,000, the inventory may be left at $100,000 by establishing an allowance for the deficiency with a credit balance of $16,000 offset by a debit to Cost of Goods Sold. Initial purchases in the next period of $16,000 would be applied against the allowance to cancel this balance.

As indicated previously, the base stock is regarded as a permanent asset; operations are charged with the costs of maintaining the normal stock. Results obtained through the base stock method are closely comparable with those obtained by the last-in, first-out method and the arguments for and against last-in, first-out can be applied here. Charges to revenue are costs currently experienced. The inventory, normally reported at the lowest value in the experience of the user entity, may be seriously understated in terms of current prices. Use of the base stock method is not permitted for income tax purposes.

Standard Costs

Manufacturing inventories are frequently reported as *standard costs* — predetermined costs based upon representative or normal conditions of efficiency and volume of operations. Differences between actual costs and standard costs for materials, labor, and manufacturing overhead result in *standard cost variances* indicating favorable and unfavorable operational or cost experiences. When inventories are valued at standard cost the standard cost variances are charged against current revenue.

Standard costs are developed from a variety of sources. Past manufacturing experiences may be carefully analysed; time and motion studies, as well as job and process studies, may be undertaken; data from industry and economy-wide sources may be consulted. Standards should be reviewed at frequent intervals to determine whether they continue to offer reliable cost criteria. Changing conditions require adjustment in the standards so that, at the balance sheet date, standard costs may reasonably approximate actual costs.

The *Accounting Recommendations* take the position that standard costs may be used for financial accounting purposes only "if there is no significant variation between aggregate standard costs and aggregate actual costs properly applicable to the inventory."[10] Thus, actual cost is the primary basis of inventory costing; standards may be used if they are a reasonable approximation of actual cost. Otherwise, standard cost variances should be allocated to inventories and cost of sales so as to approximate actual costs.

Direct Costing

A practice widely debated for many years is referred to as *direct costing, marginal costing,* or *variable costing*. Inventories under direct costing are assigned only the variable costs incurred in production — direct materials, direct labor, and the variable components of manufacturing overhead. Fixed costs are treated as periodic charges and assigned to current revenue. Only costs directly related to output are assigned to goods and charged to the period in which the goods are sold; costs that are a function of time and that are continuing regardless of the volume of output — for example, supervisory salaries, depreciation, and property tax — are charged against revenue of the period in which they are incurred.

[10]*CICA Handbook: Accounting Recommendations, Section 3030,* "Inventories" *op. cit.,* par. 04.

These differences may be illustrated by the information given below.

	Full Costing		Direct Costing	
Sales		$200,000		$200,000
Variable cost of goods sold	$110,000		$110,000	
Fixed cost of goods sold	55,000		62,500	
Total cost of goods sold		165,000		172,500
Gross profit		$ 35,000		$ 27,500
Inventory value:				
Variable costs		$ 15,000		$ 15,000
Fixed costs		7,500		—
Total cost of inventory		$ 22,500		$ 15,000

With conventional *full costing* or *absorption costing* applied to inventories, a high gross profit may emerge in a period of high production even though sales are declining. With direct costing, cost of goods sold varies directly with sales and a high gross profit emerges in a period of high sales; changes in the volume of production have no effect upon gross profit. For example, assume in the illustration above that, although sales remained the same, production had been greater and as a result the ending inventory was double the amount shown. Variable costs identified with the inventory would amount to $30,000. Under full costing, a different allocation of fixed costs would be appropriate. Assuming that $12,500 in fixed costs is allocated to the inventory reducing the fixed costs assigned to operations by $5,000, the gross profit would increase to $40,000. Under direct costing, the gross profit would remain unchanged at $27,500.

Support for direct costing is made on the grounds that it provides more meaningful and useful data to management than full costing. Direct costing enables management to appraise the effects of sales fluctuations on net income. Sales, current and potential, can be evaluated in terms of out-of-pocket costs to achieve such sales. The direct costing approach becomes a valuable tool for planning and control and offers management highly useful approaches to cost, price, and volume relationships.

Although no objection can be raised to the use of direct costing when it is used for internal reporting and as a means for assisting management in decision-making, objection can be raised to the extension of direct costing procedures to the annual financial statements. The traditional position is that for purposes of measuring financial position and results of operations, inventories should carry their full costs including a satisfactory allocation of the fixed overhead costs. Fixed costs, no less than variable costs, are incurred in contemplation of future benefits and should be matched against the revenues ultimately produced through such efforts. When inventories are valued by direct costing procedures for internal reporting, they should be restated in terms of full costing whenever financial statements are to be prepared. At the same time, it must be acknowledged that restatement for external reporting purposes is neither a difficult nor time-consuming adjustment. In general, the direct costing net income is increased by the year-end amount of deferred fixed cost pertaining to inventories and reduced by the corresponding amount as at the beginning of the period to determine the absorption or full cost net income.

Cost Apportionment by Relative Sales Value Method

A special accounting problem arises when different commodities are purchased for a single lump sum. The apportionment of the cost to the units acquired must be made in some equitable manner. This cost apportionment should recognize the utility found in the different units. Ordinarily, the estimated sales value of the different units provides the best measure of respective utilities, and accordingly cost is allocated on the basis of such estimated sales value. This procedure is referred to as the *relative sales value method*. Costs derived through apportionment in terms of sales value are charged to revenue as units are sold.

To illustrate application of the relative sales value method, assume the purchase by a realty company of 60 acres of land for $220,000. The costs of grading, landscaping, streets, walks, water mains, lighting, and other improvements total $300,000. The property is divided into three groups of lots as follows: Class A, 100 lots to sell for $2,000 each; Class B, 200 lots to sell for $2,500 each; and Class C, 20 lots to sell for $5,000 each. The total cost of the inventory, $520,000, is apportioned to the lots on the basis of their relative sales values. The cost apportionment is made as follows:

Class A lots, 100 at $2,000	$200,000
Class B lots, 200 at $2,500	500,000
Class C lots, 20 at $5,000	100,000
Total sales value of Class A, B and C lots	$800,000

	Total	No. of Lots	Cost Assigned to Each Lot
Cost apportioned to Class A lots:			
200,000/800,000 × $520,000	$130,000	100	$1,300
Cost apportioned to Class B lots:			
500,000/800,000 × $520,000	325,000	200	$1,625
Cost apportioned to Class C lots:			
100,000/800,000 × $520,000	65,000	20	$3,250
Total	$520,000		

The sale of a lot of any class results in a constant gross profit of 35% of sales.[11] Sale of a Class A lot would be recorded as follows:

Contracts Receivable	2,000	
Real Estate — Lot A-56		1,300
Gross Profit on Sale of Real Estate		700

Products that are manufactured simultaneously by a common process are referred to as *joint products*. When it is impractical or perhaps impossible to identify raw material and processing costs with the individual products produced, such costs may be assigned to the different products in a manner similar to that just illustrated. The sales value of each product is determined, and total production costs are allocated according to the relative sales values of the respective products.

Products of relatively little value that are produced in the course of manufacturing the primary products are referred to as *by-products*. By-products are frequently valued at their sales prices or at sales prices less expenses of disposal, and costs identified with the primary products are reduced by the amounts assigned to the by-products. Total costs are thus identified with the entire output; earnings, however, emerge only upon the sale of the primary products.

UNCOMPLETED CONTRACTS — INCOME BASED ON THE DEGREE OF COMPLETION

A special inventory problem is encountered in those instances where a contractor engages in certain construction work requiring months or perhaps years for completion. In these instances, projects are in various degrees of completion at the end of the contractor's fiscal period.

It is possible for a contractor engaged in a long-term project to carry such work in process at cost until it is completed, accepted by the customer, and the full income can be calculated. This practice, referred to as the *completed-contract method*, is in conformity with the concept that revenue is not realized until a sale is completed and there can be formal recognition of new assets; revenue emerges from sales, not production.

However, the application of a sales basis concept of revenue for long-term contracts may lead to serious distortions of periodic achievement. If income recognition is to await contract completion, the full income will be related to the year the project is completed even though only a small part of the

---

[11]The same cost allocation can be developed by calculating the percentage of total cost to total estimated sales value, and applying such percentage to the sales price for the individual unit. In the example, cost is 65% of the total estimated sales value of the properties (520,000 ÷ 800,000). Each lot, then, is assigned a cost equal to 65% of its sales value: Class A lots have a cost of 65% of $2,000, or $1,300; Class B lots a cost of 65% of $2,500, or $1,625; Class C lots a cost of 65% of $5,000, or $3,250.

earnings may be attributable to productive effort in that period. Previous periods receive no credit for their productive efforts; as a matter of fact, they may be penalized through the absorption of selling, general and administrative, and other overhead costs relating to construction in progress but not considered chargeable to the construction inventory. Authorities are in general agreement that circumstances such as those described may justify departure from the sales standard as a basis for the recognition of revenue. Accordingly, they would support the accrual of income over the life of the contract in some equitable and systematic manner.

Periodic income recognition on long-term construction contracts may be achieved by use of the *percentage-of-completion method*. Use of the percentage-of-completion method calls for the selection of either of the following approaches to determine the degree of contract completion.

1. *Percentage-of-cost.* The degree of completion is developed by comparing costs already incurred with the most recent estimates as to total estimated costs to complete the project. The percentage that costs incurred bear to total estimated costs is applied to the estimated net income on the project in arriving at the earnings to date. Income is thus recognized in terms of a *percentage-of-cost completion*.

2. *Engineers' and Architects' Estimates.* Estimates of the progress of a project in terms of the work performed are obtained from qualified engineers and architects. Such estimates are applied to the estimated income in arriving at the earnings to date.

To illustrate the application of the percentage-of-completion method using the percentage-of-cost approach, assume that a dam is to be constructed over a two-year period commencing in September, 1980, at a contract price of $750,000. Summaries of construction progress and the estimated earnings for each year calculated on a degree of completion basis follow.

1980: Contract price		$750,000
Less estimated cost:		
Cost to date	$ 50,000	
Estimated cost to complete project	550,000	600,000
Estimated total income		$150,000
Percentage completed ($50,000/$600,000)		$8^{1}/_{3}$%
Estimated income — 1980:		
($150,000 × $8^{1}/_{3}$%)		$ 12,500*

---

*The same estimated earnings are developed if the relationship of cost incurred to total estimated cost is applied to the total contract price in arriving at the contract price considered earned, and this balance is then reduced by cost incurred to date. Calculations in the example would be:

Contract price considered earned: $50,000/$600,000 × $750,000	$62,500
Cost to date	50,000
Estimated income — 1980	$12,500

1981: Contract price		$750,000
Less estimated cost:		
Cost to date	$450,000	
Estimated cost to complete project	175,000	625,000
Estimated total income		$125,000
Percentage completed ($450,000/$625,000)		72%
Estimated income to date:		
($125,000 × 72%)		$ 90,000
Less income recognized in 1980		12,500
Estimated income — 1981		$ 77,500
1982: Contract price		$750,000
Less total cost:		
Cost of prior periods	$450,000	
Current cost to complete	167,500	617,500
Total income		$132,500
Less income recognized to date ($12,500 + $77,500)		90,000
Income — 1982		$ 42,500

The financing of long-term construction contracts usually requires progress billings by the contractor and advance payments by the customer on these billings. Generally, long-term construction contracts require inspection before final settlement is made. As a protection for the customer, the contract frequently provides for an amount to be held out from the progress payment. This retention is usually a percentage of the progress billings, 10% to 20%, and is paid upon final acceptance of the construction.

In the preceding example, recognition of income only upon project completion would have resulted in income of $132,500 in 1982. In the series of entries on page 229, recognition of income on the basis of degree of completion is compared with recognition of income only upon project completion based upon the facts in the example.

The practice of recognizing earnings on a job still in progress is a departure from normal accounting procedures. It should be applied only when there is a firm sales contract for the job, and when the estimate of either the remaining costs to be incurred or the degree of physical completion can be objectively determined. When reliable estimates cannot be obtained or when possible future contingencies may operate to reduce or cancel what appear to be accruing profits, conservatism requires the recognition of income only upon project completion. In the event that estimates indicate an ultimate loss on the contract, the full amount of the loss should be immediately recognized in the accounts. This is true regardless of which method of income recognition is used. Thus, income estimates must be made throughout the contract, even if the completed contract method is used.

In preparing the balance sheet, Progress Billings Receivable and the

TRANSACTION	INCOME RECOGNITION BY PERCENTAGE-OF-COMPLETION METHOD		INCOME RECOGNITION BY COMPLETED-CONTRACT METHOD	

1980
Cost of construction.
	Construction in
	Progress ....
	  Materials, Cash, etc.
		50,000
		
		50,000
			Construction in
			Progress ....
			  Materials, Cash, etc.
				50,000
				
				50,000

Progress billings.	Progress Billings
	Receivable ....
	  Progress Billings on
	  Construction
	  Contracts ....
		60,000
		
		60,000
			Progress Billings
			Receivable ....
			  Progress Billings on
			  Construction
			  Contracts ....
				60,000
				
				60,000

Payments from customer on contract. 10% retention.	Cash ....
	  Progress Billings
	  Receivable ....
		54,000
		
		54,000
			Cash ....
			  Progress Billings
			  Receivable ....
				54,000
				
				54,000

Recognition of income for year.	Construction in
	Progress ....
	  Income on Construc-
	  tion Contracts ......
		12,500
		
		12,500
			No entry.	

1981
Costs of construction.
	Construction in
	Progress ....
	  Materials, Cash, etc.
		400,000
		
		400,000
			Construction in
			Progress ....
			  Materials, Cash, etc.
				400,000
				
				400,000

Progress billings.	Progress Billings
	Receivable ....
	  Progress Billings on
	  Construction
	  Contracts ....
		425,000
		
		425,000
			Progress Billings
			Receivable ....
			  Progress Billings on
			  Construction
			  Contracts ....
				425,000
				
				425,000

Payments from customer on contract. 10% retention.	Cash ....
	  Progress Billings
	  Receivable ....
		382,500
		
		382,500
			Cash ....
			  Progress Billings
			  Receivable ....
				382,500
				
				382,500

Recognition of income for year.	Construction in Progress .... Income on Construction Contracts	77,500 77,500	No entry.	

1982
Cost of construction in completing contract.
	Construction in
	Progress ....
	  Materials, Cash, etc.
		167,500
		
		167,500
			Construction in
			Progress ....
			  Materials, Cash, etc.
				167,500
				
				167,500

Final billing.	Progress Billings
	Receivable ....
	  Progress Billings
	  on Construction
	  Contracts ....
		265,000
		
		265,000
			Progress Billings
			Receivable ....
			  Progress Billings
			  on Construction
			  Contracts ....
				265,000
				
				265,000

Completion of contract:
(a) Recognition of income for year.
	Construction in
	Progress ....
	  Income on Construc-
	  tion Contracts ......
		42,500
		
		42,500
			Construction in
			Progress ....
			  Income on Construc-
			  tion Contracts ......
				132,500
				
				132,500

(b) Final payment in settlement including retention.	Cash ....
	  Progress Billings
	  Receivable ....
		313,500
		
		313,500
			Cash ....
			  Progress Billings
			  Receivable ....
				313,500
				
				313,500

(c) Approval of completed projects by customer.	Progress Billings on
	Construction Contracts
	  Construction in
	  Progress ....
		750,000
		
		750,000
			Progress Billings on
			Construction Contracts
			  Construction in
			  Progress ....
				750,000
				
				750,000

account Construction in Progress summarizing construction costs and recorded income on construction to date are properly recognized as current assets. The credit balance in the account Progress Billings on Construction Contracts is properly reported as a subtraction from the construction in progress balance. An excess of progress billings over the balance in the asset account Construction in Progress should be recognized as a current liability. Any advances from customers representing loans or deposits should be reported as liabilities. Using the previous example for both the percentage-of-completion method and the completed-contract method the balance sheet at the end of 1980 would include the following accounts:

Percentage-of-completion method:
Current assets:

Progress billings receivable		$ 6,000
Construction in progress	$62,500	
Less progress billings on construction contracts	60,000	2,500

Completed-contract method:
Current assets:

Progress billings receivable		$ 6,000
Current liabilities:		
Progress billings on construction contracts	$60,000	
Less construction in progress	50,000	$10,000

Financial statements should disclose the method of income recognition on long-term construction contracts.[12] In addition, the use of different methods for accounting and for income tax purposes will require the application of interperiod tax allocation procedures.[13]

EFFECTS OF ERRORS IN RECORDING INVENTORY POSITION

Failures to report the inventory position accurately result in mistatements on both the balance sheet and the income statement. The effects of common inventory errors on the financial statements prepared at the end of the fiscal period are indicated in the summary that follows.

1. Overstatement of the ending inventory through errors in the count of goods on hand, pricing, or the inclusion in inventory of goods not owned or goods already sold:

   Current year:

   Income statement — overstatement of the ending inventory will cause the cost of goods sold to be understated and the net income to be overstated.
   Balance sheet — the inventory will be overstated and the owners' equity will be overstated.

---

[12]*CICA Handbook: Accounting Recommendations, Section 1505,* "Disclosure of Accounting Policies" (Toronto: Canadian Institute of Chartered Accountants, 1974), par. 10.

[13] See discussion in Chapter 14.

Succeeding year:
Income statement — overstatement of the beginning inventory will cause the cost of goods sold to be overstated and the net income to be understated.
Balance sheet — the error of the previous year will have been counterbalanced on the succeeding income statement and the balance sheet will be correctly stated.

2. Understatement of ending inventory through errors in the count of goods on hand, pricing, or the failure to include in inventory goods purchased or goods transferred but not yet sold:
Misstatements indicated in (1) above are reversed.

3. Overstatement of ending inventory accompanied by failure to recognize sales and corresponding receivables at end of period:
Current year:
Income statement — sales are understated by the sales price of the goods and cost of goods sold is understated by the cost of the goods relating to the sales; gross profit and net income are thus understated by the gross profit on the sales.
Balance sheet — receivables are understated by the sales price of the goods and the inventory is overstated by the cost of the goods that were sold; current assets and owners' equity are thus understated by the gross profit on the sales.
Succeeding year.
Income statement — sales of the preceding year are recognized in this year in sales and cost of sales; gross profit and net income, therefore, are overstated by the gross profit on such sales.
Balance sheet — the error of the previous year is counterbalanced on the succeeding income statement and the balance sheet will be correctly stated.

4. Understatement of ending inventory accompanied by failure to recognize purchases and corresponding payables at end of period:
Current year:
Income statement — purchases are understated, but this is counterbalanced by the understatement of the ending inventory; gross profit and net income are correctly stated as a result of the counterbalancing effect of the error.
Balance sheet — although owners' equity is reported correctly, both current assets and current liabilities are understated.
Succeeding year:
Income statement — the beginning inventory is understated, but this is counterbalanced by an overstatement of purchases, as purchases at the end of the prior year are recognized currently; gross profit and net income are correctly stated as a result of the counterbalancing effect of the error.
Balance sheet — the error of the previous year no longer affects balance sheet data.

Discoveries of inventory errors call for careful analyses of the effects of such errors and the preparation of entries to correct real and nominal accounts in order that both current and future activities may be accurately stated.

If the error is not discovered until a succeeding period, accounting standards require that inventory errors described in this section, if material, should be recorded as prior period adjustments. If trend statistics are included in the annual reports, prior years' balances should be adjusted to reflect the correction of the error. Because of present-day audit techniques, it is probable that material inventory counting and cut-off errors will occur only rarely.

QUESTIONS

1. (a) What are the three cost elements entering into work in process and finished goods? (b) What items enter into manufacturing overhead? (c) Define fixed overhead, variable overhead, and semifixed or semivariable overhead and give an example of each.

2. (a) What charges may be considered to compose the cost of raw material acquisitions? (b) Which of these charges are normally included as a part of raw material cost for inventory purposes? (c) Which of these are normally excluded? Why? What disposition would be made of such items?

3. What are the advantages of using the perpetual inventory system as compared with the periodic system?

4. Under what normal conditions is merchandise in transit reported as inventory?

5. Under what normal conditions would an accounting failure to recognize incoming merchandise in transit that was shipped FOB shipping point have no effect on the income statement?

6. The Miller Company has followed the practice of recording all consignment sales as current period sales and has not carried goods on consignment as inventory. Under what conditions would this practice have no effect upon income?

7. State how you would report each of the following items on the financial statements:
(a) Manufacturing supplies.
(b) Goods on hand received on a consignment basis.
(c) Materials of a customer held for processing.
(d) Goods received without an accompanying invoice.
(e) Goods on hand to be delivered to customers in subsequent periods.
(f) Goods in hands of agents and consignees.
(g) Deposits with vendors for merchandise to be delivered next period.
(h) Goods in hands of customers on approval.
(i) Defective goods requiring reprocessing.

8. (a) What are the theoretical arguments for recording purchases net of cash discounts? (b) What are the practical reasons for recording purchases gross rather than net?

9. What are the advantages of using the cost method of inventory valuation? Do you see any disadvantages?

10. Trade discounts are frequently used to avoid extra catalogue printing costs. Describe in what way trade discounts could affect these savings.

11. What objections can be raised to inventory valuation by specific cost identification procedures?

12. What is the difference between a weighted average and a moving average cost method? Which may be preferred and why?

13. The Wallace Co. decides to adopt specific goods lifo as of the beginning of 1981, and determines the cost of the different lines of merchandise carried as of this date. (a) What three different methods may be employed at the end of each period in assigning costs to quantity increases in specific lines? (b) What procedure is employed at the end of each period for quantity decreases in specific lines?

14. The auditor for Reliance Steel Co. recommends that the company change its method of inventory from fifo to lifo because of an increase in the rate of inflation. Evaluate this recommendation including the advantages and disadvantages of such a change in inventory methods.

15. (a) Describe the base stock method. (b) How does this method differ from inventory valuation by lifo?

16. (a) What type of company is likely to use standard costs? (b) What precautions are necessary in the use of standard costs?

17. J. M. Livasy, a building contractor, states, "I do not use the percentage-of-completion method. It is just too difficult to apply." What problems are associated with costing of inventories by the percentage-of-completion method? How can they be overcome?

18. How would the following accounts be classified on the financial statements? (a) Progress Billings Receivable, (b) Construction in Progress, (c) Income on Construction Contracts, (d) Progress Billings on Construction Contracts.

19. What effect would each of the following situations have upon the current year's net income for a company manufacturing a single product if it used direct costing to value its ending inventory rather than full costing? Assume fixed costs are the same for each year.
  - (a) Quantity of items produced and sold are the same for the year.
  - (b) Quantity of items produced exceeds the quantity sold.
  - (c) Quantity of items produced exceeds the quantity produced.

20. Under what circumstances would you recommend use of cost apportionment by the relative sales method?

21. State the effect of each of the following errors made by Cole, Ltd., upon the balance sheet and the income statement (1) of the current period and (2) of the succeeding period:
  - (a) The company fails to record a sale of merchandise on account; goods sold are excluded in recording the ending inventory.
  - (b) The company fails to record a sale of merchandise on account; the goods sold are included, however, in recording the ending inventory.
  - (c) The company fails to record a purchase of merchandise on account; goods purchased are included in recording the ending inventory.

(d) The company fails to record a purchase of merchandise on account; goods purchased are not recognized in recording the ending inventory.
(e) The ending inventory is understated as the result of a miscount of goods on hand.
(f) The ending inventory is overstated as the result of inclusion of goods held on a consignment basis and never recognized as a purchase.

22. The Carol Mfg. Co. reviewed its in-transit inventory and found the following items. Indicate which items should be included in the inventory balance at December 31, 1981. Give reasons for the treatment.

(a) Merchandise costing $2,350 was received on January 3, 1982, and the related purchase invoice recorded January 5. The invoice showed the shipment was made on December 29, 1981, FOB destination.
(b) Merchandise costing $625 was received on December 28, 1981, and the invoice was not recorded. You located it in the hands of the purchasing agent; it was marked on consignment.
(c) A packing case containing a product costing $816 was standing in the shipping room when the physical inventory was taken. It was not included in the inventory because it was marked "Hold for shipping instructions." Your investigation revealed that the customer's order was dated December 18, 1981, but that the case was shipped and the customer billed on January 10, 1982. The product was a stock item of your client.
(d) Merchandise received on January 6, 1982, costing $720 was entered in the purchase register on January 7, 1982. The invoice showed shipment was made FOB supplier's warehouse on December 3, 1981. Since it was not on hand at December 31, it was not included in inventory.
(e) A special machine, fabricated to order for a customer, was finished and in the shipping room on December 31, 1981. The customer was billed on that date and the machine excluded from inventory although it was shipped January 4, 1982. (AICPA adapted)

EXERCISES

6-1. Transactions of the McKinnon Co. relating to goods purchased during December are summarized below:

Purchases were $15,000, terms 2/10, n/30.
Accounts of $12,500 were paid, including accounts of $11,500 paid within the discount period.

Give the entries to record purchases and invoice payments in December, assuming that:

(a) Accounts payable are recorded at invoice price and purchase discounts earned are summarized in the accounts.
(b) Accounts payable are recorded net and purchase discounts lost are summarized in the accounts.
(c) Accounts payable are recorded at invoice price and purchase discounts lost are summarized in the accounts.

6-2. Minson Body and Paint Shop purchases its supplies from Rankin Auto Wholesale. Rankin gives Minson a trade discount of 5/20/15 with a cash discount of 2/10, n/30. During March, Minson purchased supplies with a list price of $70,000. Eighty per cent of the supplies bought were sold during March.

    (a) What is the cost of goods sold if purchases are recorded net?

    (b) What is the equivalent composite discount rate?

6-3. Yukon Merchandising company had a beginning inventory, valued at the lower of cost or replacement cost, of $20,000. During the fiscal period purchases were $100,000, subject to a 2% discount if paid within the discount period. Because of negligence, $500 of the available discounts were not taken. At the end of the period a physical count of inventory was taken and the value was determined as $18,000 (lower of cost or replacement cost). Not included in the physical count was a shipment in transit which was shipped f.o.b. shipping point. The invoice for the goods in transit ($6,000 gross) was recorded in the accounts and reflected in the $100,000 amount above.

    Assume that the value of the goods in transit approximated their replacement cost.

Instructions:
Prepare the cost of goods sold section of the income statement assuming that:
(a) purchases were recorded net, and
(b) purchases were recorded gross.

                                                        (CGA adapted)

6-4. Changes in Commodity X during March are:

Mar.	1	Balance 700 units @ $6	Mar. 10	Sale 600 units @ $12
	12	Purchase 150 units @ 8	30	Sale 150 units @ 14
	28	Purchase 300 units @ 9		

    (a) Assuming that perpetual inventories are maintained and that accounts are kept up to date currently, what is the cost of the ending inventory for Commodity X using: (1) fifo; (2) lifo; (3) average? (Carry your calculations to four places and round to three.)

    (b) Assuming that perpetual inventories are not maintained and that a physical count at the end of the month shows 400 units to be on hand, what is the cost of the ending inventory using each of the three methods listed in part (a)?

6-5. The Barker Store shows the following information relating to Commodity A which it handles:

Inventory, January 1	100 units @ $7.50
Purchases, January 10	300 units @ $8.00
Purchases, January 20	400 units @ $9.00
Sales, January 8	50 units
Sales, January 18	200 units
Sales, January 25	400 units

    What are the values of ending inventory under (1) perpetual and (2) periodic methods assuming the cost flows below? (Carry your calculations to four places and round to three.)

    (a) Fifo

    (b) Lifo

    (c) Average

6-6. The Andrews Wholesale Company record for Material No. 101-2 follows:

Mar.	1 Balance	150 units at $10			$1,500
	10 Received	200 units at	9		1,800
	20 Received	100 units at	12		1,200
	28 Received	100 units at	11		1,100

At the end of the month, 250 units are on hand. Give the cost of the ending inventory, assuming that it is calculated by each method listed below. (Carry your calculations to four places and round to three.)

(a) First-in, first-out.
(b) Weighted average.
(c) Last-in, first-out.
(d) Cost of latest purchase.
(e) Simple average of costs.

6-7. First-in, first-out has been used for inventory valuation by the Harper Co. since it was organized in 1978. Using the data that follow, redetermine the net incomes for each year on the assumption of inventory valuation on the last-in, first-out basis:

	1978	1979	1980	1981
Reported net income	$ 17,500	$ 30,000	$ 32,500	$ 45,000
Reported ending inventories — fifo basis	61,500	102,000	126,000	130,000
Inventories — lifo basis	59,000	75,100	95,000	105,000

6-8. Clement Corporation uses direct costing for internal reporting. It has been suggested that use of direct costing on the balance sheet would understate income because of the complete write-off of fixed costs. Information concerning the valuation of inventory for the year 1981 is as follows:

Inventory, January 1, 1981	20,000 units
Variable costs	$6.00 per unit
Fixed costs (if inventory valued at full costs)	$2.00 per unit
Units produced in 1981	140,000
Total fixed costs	$280,000
Inventory, December 31, 1981	25,000 units
Variable costs	$6.50 per unit

(a) Compute the effect on net income for 1981 of using direct costing to value the inventory as compared with full costing. Assume that there is no change in work in process between the beginning and the end of the year, and that the fifo cost flow method is used.
(b) What is the effect on net income if the ending inventory consisted of only 10,000 units?

6-9. The Hi-Land Realty Co. acquires land for $105,000 and incurs additional costs of $45,000 in improving the land. The land is divided into lots that are classified as follows:

Class	No. of Lots	Sales Price per Lot
100	20	$3,500
200	20	2,300
300	42	2,000

(a) What is the cost of each lot to the company?

(b) What entry should be made if five Class 200 lots are sold on contract?

6-10. Orsini Construction Co. has used the percentage-of-completion method of recognizing profits. Aldo Orsini recently died and his son, Rocco, has assumed leadership of the business. In reviewing the records, Rocco finds the following information regarding a recently completed building project for which the total contract was $500,000.

	1979	1980	1981
Income (loss)	$10,000	$35,000	$ (5,000)
Cost incurred in year	90,000	?	205,000

Rocco wants to know how effectively the company operated during the last three years on this project. Since the information is not complete, he has asked you to help him by answering the following questions:

(a) How much cost was incurred in 1980?

(b) What percentage of the project was completed by the end of 1980?

(c) What was the total estimated income on the project by the end of 1980?

(d) What was the estimated cost to complete the project at the end of 1980?

6-11. Wonder Builders Ltd., entered into a contract to construct an office building at a contract price of $10,000,000. Income is to be reported using the percentage-of-completion method as determined by estimates made by the architect. The data below summarizes the activities on the construction for the years 1980 through 1982. What entries are required to record this information?

Year	Cost Incurred	Estimated Cost to Complete	Architect's Estimate	Project Billings	Collections on Billings
1980	$3,200,000	$5,800,000	25%	$3,300,000	$3,100,000
1981	4,100,000	1,200,000	75%	4,200,000	4,000,000
1982	1,300,000	0	100%	2,500,000	2,900,000

6-12. Annual income for the Robinson Co. for the period 1977-1981 appears below. However, a review of the records for the company reveals inventory misstatements as listed. Calculate corrected net income for each year.

	1977	1978	1979	1980	1981
Reported net income (loss)	$19,500	$20,000	$1,500	$(7,500)	$15,000
Inventory overstatement, end of year	2,500		2,800		1,600
Inventory understatement, end of year				4,000	

6-1A. The Geneva Corporation uses raw material A in a manufacturing process. Information as to balances on hand, purchases, and requisitions of material A are given in the following table:

| | Quantities | | | |
Date	Received	Issued	Balance	Unit Price of Purchase
Jan. 11	—	—	100	$1.50
Jan. 24	300	—	400	1.72
Feb. 8	—	80	320	—
Mar. 16	—	140	180	—
June 10	150	—	330	1.75
Aug. 18	—	130	200	—
Sept. 6	—	110	90	—
Oct. 14	200	—	290	2.00
Dec. 29	—	120	170	—

Instructions:

What is the closing inventory under each of the following pricing methods? (Carry calculations to four places and round.)

(1) Perpetual fifo
(2) Perpetual lifo
(3) Moving average
(4) Periodic fifo
(5) Periodic lifo
(6) Weighted average

6-2A. Records of the Stratton Sales Co. show the following data relative to Commodity Z:

Jan. 1 Inventory......325 units at $25.50   Jan. 2 Sales......300 units at $37.50
3 Purchase .....300 units at 26.00   18 Sales......200 units at 35.70
12 Purchase .....350 units at 27.00   29 Sales......150 units at 36.00
24 Purchase ..... 75 units at 27.50

Instructions:

Calculate the inventory balance and the gross profit on sales for the month on each of the following bases:

(1) First-in, first-out. Perpetual inventories are maintained and costs are charged out currently.
(2) First-in, first-out. No perpetual inventory is maintained.
(3) Last-in, first-out. Perpetual inventories are maintained and costs are charged out currently.
(4) Last-in, first-out. No perpetual inventory is maintained.
(5) Moving average. Perpetual inventories are maintained and costs are charged out currently. (Carry calculations to four places and round to three.)
(6) Weighted average. No perpetual inventory is maintained.

6-3A. The Brown Mfg. Co. was organized in 1979 to produce a single product. Its production and sales records for the period 1979-1982 are summarized below:

| | Units Produced | | Sales | |
	No. of Units	Production Costs	No. of Units	Sales Revenue
1979	320,000	$ 86,400	200,000	$122,500
1980	310,000	130,200	290,000	175,000
1981	270,000	129,600	290,000	203,000
1982	220,000	99,000	200,000	150,000

Instructions:

Calculate the gross profit for each of the four years assuming that inventory balances are calculated in terms of:

(1) First-in, first-out.   (2) Last-in, first-out.

6-4A. Hoover's Ltd., sells a single commodity. Purchases, sales, and expenses for May, June, and July are summarized below.

| | | Purchases | |
		Units	Cost per Unit
May	1-15	2,000	$3.50
	16-31	3,000	3.75
June	1-15	1,500	4.25
	16-30	2,000	4.75
July	1-15	—	—
	16-31	2,000	4.25

| | Sales | | |
	Units	Sales Price per Unit	Operating Expenses
May	2,000	$6.75	$2,700
June	3,200	7.50	4,100
July	3,100	7.75	3,700

Instructions:

Prepare a comparative income statement summarizing operations for the months of May, June, and July for each case below:

(1) Assume that monthly inventories are calculated at cost on a first-in, first-out basis.

(2) Assume that monthly inventories are calculated at cost on a last-in, first-out basis.

(3) Assume that monthly inventories are calculated at cost on a weighted average basis. (Unit costs are calculated to the nearest cent.)

6-5A. The Bramble Products Company reports its inventories at lifo. Inventories are composed of three classes of goods. Values are assigned to each class as follows: units equal to the number on hand when lifo was adopted are assigned average costs as of this date; annual incremental layers thereafter are assigned the average cost for the period. Lifo was adopted in 1979. The inventory on January 1, 1982, and purchases and sales for 1982 were as follows:

Inventory, January 1, 1982

| | Model A | | | Model B | | | Model C | | |
	Quantity	Unit Cost	Total Cost	Quantity	Unit Cost	Total Cost	Quantity	Unit Cost	Total Cost
1979, Balance	40,000	$.10	$ 4,000	20,000	$ .60	$12,000	5,000	$3.00	$15,000
1980, Increment	20,000	.15	3,000	1,500	1.00	1,500			
1981, Increment	10,000	.17	1,700				2,000	3.25	6,500
Total	70,000		$ 8,700	21,500		$13,500	7,000		$21,500
1982, Purchase	250,000		$50,000	60,000		$61,200	12,500		$42,500
1982, Sales	265,000		79,500	64,500		96,750	12,000		48,000

Instructions:

Prepare a statement reporting sales, cost of goods sold (including purchases and inventory detail), and gross profits for each class of goods handled and for combined activities as of December 31, 1982. Provide supporting schedules to show how the ending inventory balances are developed for each class of goods.

6-6A. The Ames Construction Company purchased 50 acres of land in the suburbs of a large city with the intention of improving, subdividing, and selling it in one-acre lots. The purchase price for the tract of land was $210,000. The lots are given numbers and similar lots are grouped numerically. Lots 1-15 are choice lots and did not require extra improvements. They will sell for $8,000 each. Lots 16-30 required some extra improvements costing $34,000. They will sell for $7,000 each. Lots 31-50 required extensive drainage and clearing costing $40,000. They will sell for $6,500 each.

Instructions:

Using the relative sales method, allocate the purchase and improvement costs to the various lots.

6-7A. The Strasser Company's inventory record appears below and at the top of the next page.

	Purchases		Sales
	Quantity	Unit Cost	Quantity
1979	8,000	$5.60	5,500
1980	9,500	5.75	10,000
1981	7,200	5.80	5,000

The company uses a lifo cost flow assumption. It reported ending inventories as follows:

1979	$14,000
1980	11,500
1981	24,360

Instructions:

Determine if the Strasser Company has reported their inventory correctly. Assuming that 1981 accounts are not yet closed, make any necessary correcting entries.

6-8A. Tall Construction Co. signed a long-term construction contract in 1979. The contract price was $600,000 and the company expected to earn $90,000 on the contract. The following schedule summarizes the contract to its completion.

Year	Actual Cost	Estimated Cost to Complete	Billings on Contract	Collections on Contract
1979	$ 50,000	$450,000	$ 55,000	$ 48,000
1980	184,000	286,000	190,000	170,000
1981	280,000	0	355,000	382,000
	$514,000		$600,000	$600,000

Instructions:

(1) Prepare a schedule showing the income earned each year under the percentage-of-completion method.
(2) Prepare all journal entries required relative to the contract assuming the use of the percentage-of-completion method.

(3) Assuming proper entries have been made for 1979 and 1980, prepare journal entries for 1981 assuming the use of the completed-contract method.

6-9A. The Highcrest Bridge Company obtained a construction contract to build a highway and bridge over the Ottawa River. It estimated at the beginning of the contract that it would take three years to complete the project at an expected cost of $50,000,000. The contract price was $60,000,000. The project actually took four years, being accepted as completed late in 1981. The following information describes the status of the job as of the close of each production year.

	1978	1979	1980	1981	1982
Costs incurred	$12,000,000	$15,000,000	$18,000,0000	$10,000,000	
Estimated cost to complete	38,000,000	27,000,000	11,250,000		
Collections on contract ...	12,000,000	13,000,000	15,000,000	15,000,000	$5,000,000
Billings on contract	13,000,000	15,500,000	17,000,000	14,500,000	

Instructions:
(1) What is the income for each of the years 1978-1982 under (a) the percentage-of-completion method, (b) the completed-contract method?
(2) Give combined journal entries for each year assuming that the percentage-of-completion method is used.

6-10A. The Metro Constructions Company commenced doing business in January, 1981. Construction activities for the year 1981 are summarized as follows:

Project	Total Contract Price	Contract Expenditures to Dec. 31, 1981	Estimated Additional Costs to Complete Contracts	Cash Collections to Dec. 31, 1981	Billings to Dec. 31, 1981
A	$ 310,000	$187,500	$ 12,500	$155,000	$155,000
B	415,000	195,000	255,000	210,000	249,000
C	350,000	320,000	——	300,000	350,000
D	300,000	16,500	183,500	——	4,000
	$1,375,000	$719,000	$451,000	$665,000	$758,000

The company is your client. The president has asked you to compute the amounts of revenue for the year ended December 31, 1981, that would be reported under the completed-contract method and the percentage-of-completion method of accounting for long-term contracts.

The following information is available:
(a) All contracts are with different customers.
(b) Any work remaining to be done on the contracts is expected to be completed in 1982.
(c) The company's accounts have been maintained on the completed-contract method.

Instructions:
(1) Prepare a schedule computing the amount of income (loss) by project for the year ended December 31, 1981, to be reported under (a) the completed-contract method, and (b) the percentage-of-completion method. (Round to the nearest thousandths.)

(2) Prepare a schedule under the completed-contract method computing the amounts that would appear in the company's balance sheet at December 31, 1981, for (a) costs in excess of billings, and (b) billings in excess of costs.

(3) Prepare a schedule under the percentage-of-completion method that would appear in the company's balance sheet at December 31, 1981, for (a) costs and estimated earnings in excess of billings, and (b) billings in excess of costs and estimated earnings. (AICPA adapted)

6-11A. In 1981 the Sunset Construction Company Ltd. was awarded a contract for $3,150,000 to construct a building for Jay Manufacturing Ltd. There was an escalator clause which provided for including all increases in labor rates as an extra to the contract price. The contract price included an estimated profit of $150,000.

Since its contracts are generally long-term, Sunset Construction Company Ltd. recognizes income by the percentage-of-completion method. This method is based on the relationship between the cost incurred to date and the total estimated cost to complete the contract. The estimated cost to complete is based upon the most recent information available.

At December 31, 1981 the following information is available:

(1) Construction labor was originally estimated at 92,000 hours at an average rate of $3.25 per hour. To date 65,800 hours have been expended and it is estimated that an additional 65,000 hours will be needed to complete the job.

(2) Effective January 1, 1982, the construction force union contract provides for a 4% increase in the basic hourly rate.

(3) Material costs were originally estimated as $1,375,000. Purchase orders for 90% of the material have been placed at a total cost of $1,250,000. The remaining material will cost 7% more than originally estimated because of price increases.

(4) The electrical work estimated at $130,000 was subcontracted for $127,500.

(5) The Sunset Construction Company Ltd. has billed a total of $1,500,000 under the terms of the contract. Cash payments by the Jay Manufacturing Ltd. totaled $1,300,000. Total costs incurred to date are $1,605,000.

Instructions:

(a) Using the information available at December 31, 1981 calculate the total estimated profit or loss on the contract.

(b) How much of this profit or loss should be recognized in 1981?

(c) Calculate the amount which would appear on the balance sheet as at December 31, 1981 for construction in progress.

(SMA adapted)

6-12A. The errors listed below were made by the Scoll Sales Corporation in 1981.

(a) The company failed to record a sale on account of $210 at the end of 1981. The merchandise had been shipped and was not included in the ending inventory. The sale was recorded in 1982 when cash was collected from the customer.

(b) On January 2, 1982, the company received goods costing $780 which were shipped on December 30, 1981. The terms of the sale were FOB shipping point. The purchase was recorded and the merchandise was included in inventory when payment was made in 1982.

(c) The company included in its physical count of goods $560 for goods which had been custom built and are being held for the customer. The sale was recorded in 1982, sales value, $720.

(d) The company failed to make an entry for a purchase on account of $60 at the end of 1981, although it included this merchandise in the inventory count. The purchase was recorded when payment was made to the creditor in 1982.

(e) The company overlooked goods of $360 in the physical count of goods at the end of 1981.

(f) The company included goods of $270 in the physical count which were returned on January 2, 1982, by a consignee who was unable to sell them.

Instructions:

Give the entry required in 1982 to correct each error. Assume that the company arrives at its inventory position by physical count and that the books for 1981 have been closed. Assume that all amounts are material.

6-13A. The Brooksby Metal Products Co. adjusted and closed its accounts at the end of 1981, the summary of 1981 activities showing a loss of $8,000. The following errors, made in 1981, all regarded as material, are discovered upon an audit of the books of the company made in March, 1982.

(a) Merchandise, cost $3,000, was recorded as a purchase at the end of 1981 but was not included in the ending inventory since it was received on January 3, 1982. The merchandise was sent FOB shipping point.

(b) Merchandise, cost $700, was received in 1981 and included in the ending inventory; however, the entry recording the purchase was made on January 4, 1982, when the invoice was received.

(c) 800 units of Commodity Z, costing $5.36 per unit, were recorded at a per unit cost of $3.56 in summarizing the ending inventory.

(d) Goods in the hands of a consignee, cost $4,000, were included in the inventory; however, $2,400 of such goods had been sold as of December 31, 1981 and the sale was not recorded until January 3, 1982, when the consignee made a full remittance of $3,200 on this item.

(e) Merchandise, cost $600, sold for $760 and shipped on December 31, 1981, was not included in the ending inventory; however, the sale was not recorded until January 12, 1982, when the customer made payment on the sale.

Instructions:

(1) Compute the corrected net income or loss for 1981.

(2) Give the entries that are required in 1982 to correct the accounts assuming the company uses the periodic inventory method.

6-14A. You have been engaged for the audit of the Y Company for the year ended December 31, 1981. The Y Company is engaged in the wholesale chemical business and makes all sales at 25% over cost.

Portions of the client's sales and purchases accounts for the calendar year 1981 follow.

Sales

Date	Reference	Amount	Date	Reference	Amount
12/31	Closing entry	$699,860	Balance forward		$658,320
			12/27	SI# 965	5,195
			12/28	SI# 966	19,270
			12/28	SI# 967	1,302
			12/31	SI# 969	5,841
			12/31	SI# 970	7,922
			12/31	SI# 971	2,010
		$699,860			$699,860

		Purchases			
Date	Reference	Amount	Date	Reference	Amount
Balance forward		$360,300	12/31	Closing entry	$385,346
12/28	RR# 1059	3,100			
12/30	RR# 1061	8,965			
12/31	RR# 1062	4,861			
12/31	RR# 1063	8,120			
		$385,346			$385,346

RR = Receiving report.
SI = Sales invoice.

You observed the physical inventory of goods in the warehouse on December 31, 1981, and were satisfied that it was properly taken.

When performing a sales and purchases cutoff test, you found that at December 31, 1981, the last receiving report that had been used was No. 1063 and that no shipments had been made on any sales invoices with numbers larger than No. 968. You also obtained the following additional information:

(a) Included in the warehouse physical inventory at December 31, 1981, were chemicals that had been purchased and received on receiving report No. 1060 but for which an invoice was not received until 1982. Cost was $2,183.

(b) In the warehouse at December 31, 1981, were goods that had been sold and paid for by the customer but that were not shipped out until 1982. They were all sold on sales invoice No. 965 and were not inventoried.

(c) On the evening of December 31, 1981, there were two cars on the Y Company siding:
   1. Car #AR38162 was unloaded on Janury 2, 1982, and received on receiving report No. 1063. The freight was paid by the vendor.
   2. Car #BAE74123 was loaded and sealed on December 31, 1981, and was switched off the company's siding on January 2, 1982. The sales price was $12,700 and the freight was paid by the customer. This order was sold on sales invoice No. 968.

(d) Temporarily stranded at December 31, 1981, on a railroad siding were two cars of chemicals enroute to the Z Pulp and Paper Co. They were sold on sales invoice No. 966 and the terms were FOB destination.

(e) Enroute to the Y Company on December 31, 1981, was a truckload of material that was received on receiving report No. 1064. The material was shipped FOB destination and freight of $75 was paid by the Y Company. However, the freight was deducted from the purchase price of $975.

(f) Included in the physical inventory were chemicals exposed to rain in transit and deemed unsalable. Their invoice was $1,250, and freight charges of $350 had been paid on the chemicals.

Instructions:
(1) Compute the adjustments that should be made to the client's physical inventory at December 31, 1981.
(2) Prepare the adjusting entries that are required as of December 31, 1981. (AICPA adapted)

6-15A. You are engaged in an audit of The Wayne Mfg. Company for the year ended December 31, 1981. To reduce the work load at year end, the company took its annual physical inventory under your observation on November 30, 1981. The company's inventory account, which includes raw materials and work in process, is on a perpetual basis and the first-in, first-out method of pricing is used. There is no finished goods inventory. The company's physical inventory revealed that the perpetual inventory of $60,570 was understated by $3,000. To avoid distorting the interim financial statements, the company decided not to adjust the perpetual inventory until year end except for obsolete inventory items. Your audit revealed this information about the November 30th inventory:

(a) Pricing tests showed that the physical inventory was overpriced by $2,200.
(b) Footing and extension errors resulted in a $150 understatement of the physical inventory.
(c) Direct labor included in the physical inventory amounted to $10,000. Overhead was included at the rate of 200% of direct labor. You determined that the amount of direct labor was correct and the overhead rate was proper.
(d) The physical inventory included obsolete materials recorded at $250. During December these obsolete materials were removed from the inventory account by a charge to cost of sales.

Your audit also disclosed the following information about the December 31st inventory:

(e) Total debits to certain accounts during December are listed below:

	December
Purchases	$24,700
Direct labor	12,100
Manufacturing overhead expense	25,000
Cost of sales	68,600

(f) The cost of sales of $68,600 included direct labor of $13,800.
(g) Normal scrap loss on established product lines is negligible. However, a special order started and completed during December had excessive scrap loss of $800, which was charged to Manufacturing Overhead Expense.

Instructions:

(1) Compute the correct amount of the physical inventory at November 30, 1981.
(2) Without prejudice to your solution to part (1), assume that the correct amount of the inventory at November 30, 1981, was $57,700. Compute the amount of the inventory at December 31, 1981. (AICPA adapted)

7 INVENTORIES — ESTIMATION AND VALUATION PROCEDURES

Estimates are frequently employed in developing inventory quantities and inventory costs. Certain estimating procedures must be applied when inventories are lost by fire or other casualty. Estimating procedures are frequently employed in arriving at inventories of the mercantile enterprise when such procedures can offer satisfactory measurements without the counting and costing routines that would otherwise be necessary. Also, estimates of the impact of inflation on inventory values may be employed using dollar-value lifo techniques. Widely used estimating procedures and the circumstances under which they are employed are described in the first part of this chapter.

Although inventories are typically valued at their cost, there are situations in which deviations from cost may be warranted. Some of these deviations are regarded as generally accepted; others are under careful study within the profession. These valuation procedures are described and discussed in the latter part of this chapter.

GROSS PROFIT METHOD

Estimates of merchandise on hand may be developed by means of the *gross profit method*. In using the gross profit method, the company's gross profit percentage is applied to sales to determine cost of goods sold; cost of goods sold is subtracted from the cost of goods available for sale in arriving at an estimated inventory balance.

The gross profit method of arriving at an inventory is applicable:

1. When inventories are required for interim statements, or for the determination of the week-to-week or month-to-month inventory position, and the cost of taking physical inventories would be excessive for such purposes.
2. When an inventory has been destroyed by fire or other cause and the specific data required for its valuation are not available.
3. When it is desired to test or check on the validity of inventory figures determined by other means. Such application is referred to as the *gross profit test*.

The gross profit percentage in reducing sales to a cost of goods sold balance must be a reliable measure of current sales experience. In developing a reliable rate, reference is usually made to past rates and these are adjusted for variations considered to exist currently. For example, past gross profit rates may require adjustment when inventories are valued at last-in, first-out, and significant fluctuations in inventory position and in prices have affected gross profits in a manner not representative of current experiences. Current changes in cost-price relationships or in the sales mix of specific products further create a need for modifying past rates.

The calculation of cost of goods sold depends upon whether the gross profit percentage is developed and stated in terms of sales or in terms of cost. The procedures to be followed in each case are illustrated below:

Example 1 — Gross profit as a percentage of sales. Assume sales are $100,000 and goods are sold at a gross profit of 40% of sales.

If gross profit is 40% of sales then cost of goods sold must be 60% of sales:

Sales	100%		Sales	100%
Cost of goods sold	?	=	Cost of goods sold	60%
Gross profit	40%		Gross profit	40%

Cost of goods sold, then, is 60% of $100,000, or $60,000. Goods available for sale less the estimated cost of goods sold gives the estimated cost of the remaining inventory. Assuming the cost of goods available for sale is $85,000, this balance less the estimated cost of goods sold, $60,000, gives an estimated inventory of $25,000.

Example 2 — Gross profit as a percentage of cost. Assume sales are $100,000 and goods are sold at a gross profit that is 60% of their cost.

(a) If sales are made at a gross profit of 60% of cost, then sales must be equal to the sum of cost, considered 100%, and the gross profit on cost, 60%. Sales, then, are 160% of cost:

Sales	?		Sales	160%
Cost of goods sold	100%	=	Cost of goods sold	100%
Gross profit	60%		Gross profit	60%

To find cost, or 100%, sales may be divided by 160 and multiplied by 100, or sales may simply be divided by 1.60. Cost of goods sold, then, is $100,000 ÷ 1.60

= $62,500. This amount is subtracted from the cost of goods available for sale to determine the estimated inventory.

(b) The cost of goods sold can be developed through an alternate calculation. If sales are 60% above cost, then the cost relationship to sales must be 100/160, or 62.5%.

Sales	160%	But in terms		Sales	100.0%
Cost of goods sold ..	100%	of sales as	=	Cost of goods sold ..	62.5% (100/160)
Gross profit	60%	100%		Gross profit	37.5% (60/160)

Cost of goods sold, then, is 62.5% × $100,000 = $62,500.

Example 3 — Sales as a percentage increase above cost. Assume sales are $100,000 and goods are sold at 20% above cost. This is the same as saying that the gross profit is 20% of cost, and the answer would be developed as in Example 2 above. Sales, then, would be divided by 1.20, as in (a) above, or multiplied by .83⅓ (100/120), as in (b) above, in arriving at the estimated cost of goods sold.

When various lines of merchandise are sold at different gross profit rates, it may be possible to develop a reliable inventory value only by making separate calculations for each line. Under such circumstances, it is necessary to develop summaries of sales, goods available, and gross profit data for the different sections of the inventory.

Use of Gross Profit Method for Monthly Inventory Calculations

The gross profit method may be employed in developing a series of inventory values. For example, assume the merchandise turnover is to be determined for a retail store the gross profit of which is as follows:

Sales		$500,000
Cost of goods sold:		
Merchandise inventory, January 1	$ 20,000	
Purchases	310,000	
Merchandise available for sale	$330,000	
Merchandise inventory, December 31	30,000	
Cost of goods sold		300,000
Gross profit on sales		$200,000

If only these data are available, the average inventory is $25,000, the sum of the beginning and ending balances divided by 2. The merchandise turnover, the number of times the average inventory has been replenished during the fiscal period, is 12 times, calculated as follows:

$$\frac{\text{Cost of goods sold}}{\text{Average inventory (using year-end balances)}} = \frac{\$300,000}{\$ 25,000} = 12$$

A more representative average inventory may be obtained by analysing sales and purchases and computing monthly inventories by the gross profit method. These computations are given below.

| | A Purchases | B Sales | Cost of Goods Sold | | | E Inventory Increase or (Decrease) (A − D) | F Inventory (F + E) |
			C Cost as a Percentage of Sales	D Cost of Goods Sold (B × C)			
January 1						$ 20,000
January	$ 20,000	$ 30,000	60%	$ 18,000	$ 2,000	22,000
February	20,000	30,000	60	18,000	2,000	24,000
March	20,000	30,000	60	18,000	2,000	26,000
April	20,000	30,000	60	18,000	2,000	28,000
May	30,000	40,000	60	24,000	6,000	34,000
June	30,000	40,000	60	24,000	6,000	40,000
July	30,000	60,000	60	36,000	(6,000)	34,000
August	30,000	40,000	60	24,000	6,000	40,000
September	40,000	40,000	60	24,000	16,000	56,000
October	40,000	50,000	60	30,000	10,000	66,000
November	20,000	50,000	60	30,000	(10,000)	56,000
December	10,000	60,000	60	36,000	(26,000)	30,000
	$310,000	$500,000	60%	$300,000	$10,000	$476,000

The average inventory is calculated from the monthly inventory balances, and the merchandise turnover is determined as follows:

$$\frac{\text{Total of inventories}}{\text{Number of inventories}} = \frac{\$476,000}{13} = \$36,615$$

$$\text{Turnover} \frac{\text{Cost of goods sold}}{\text{Average inventory (using monthly balances)}} = \frac{\$300,000}{\$36,615} = \$8.2 \text{ times}$$

This figure is more accurate than the one developed on the basis of the year-end inventories which often may be low and unrepresentative.

Use of Gross Profit Method for Computation of Fire Loss

An important application of the gross profit method occurs when a physical count of an inventory is impossible because of its physical destruction. For example, assume that on October 31, 1981, a wholesale distributing company had a fire in a warehouse which totally destroyed the contents, including many accounting records. Remaining records indicated that the last physical inventory was taken on December 31, 1980, and that the inventory at that date was $329,500. Microfilm bank records of cancelled cheques disclosed that during 1981 payments to suppliers for inventory items were $1,015,000. Unpaid invoices at the beginning of 1981 amounted to $260,000, and circularization of suppliers indicated a balance due at the time of the fire of $315,000. Bank deposits for the ten months amounted to $1,605,000. All deposits came from customers for merchandise except for a loan of $100,000 obtained from the bank during the year. Accounts receivable at the beginning of the year were $328,000, and an analysis of the available records indicated that accounts receivable on October 31 totalled $275,000. Gross profit percentages on sales were computed for the preceding four years as follows:

1977	28%	1979	23%
1978	25%	1980	24%

From these facts, the inventory in the warehouse at the time of the fire could be estimated as follows:

Estimate of sales January 1 to October 31, 1981:

Collection of accounts receivable ($1,605,000 − $100,000)		$1,505,000
Add accounts receivable at October 31, 1981		275,000
		$1,780,000
Deduct accounts receivable at January 1, 1981		328,000
Estimate of sales January 1 to October 31, 1981		$1,452,000
Average gross profit percentage on sales for past 4 years		25%
Average cost percentage on sales for past 4 years		75%
Estimate of cost of goods sold to October 31, 1981 ($1,452,000 × 75%)		$1,089,000

Estimate of inventory on October 31, 1981:

Merchandise inventory January 1, 1981		$ 329,500
Add: Payments to suppliers — 1981	$1,015,000	
Amounts payable to suppliers, October 31, 1981	315,000	
	$1,330,000	
Deduct accounts payable to suppliers, January 1, 1981	260,000	
Estimate of purchases January 1 to October 31, 1981		1,070,000
Merchandise available for sale		$1,399,500
Estimate of cost of goods sold for 1981 (from above)		1,089,000
Estimated merchandise inventory, October 31, 1981		$ 310,500

RETAIL INVENTORY METHOD

The *retail inventory method* is widely employed by retail concerns, particularly by department stores, as a means of arriving at reliable estimates of the business unit's inventory position whenever desired. When this method is employed, records of goods purchased are maintained in terms of costs and also at marked retail prices. The goods on hand at retail may be calculated at any time by subtracting sales for the period from the total goods available at retail. Cost and retail pricings of goods available are used in developing the percentage that cost bears to retail, and this percentage is applied to the goods on hand at retail in arriving at the estimated cost of such goods.

The determination of a company's inventory at the end of a month by using the retail inventory method follows:

	Cost	Retail
Merchandise inventory, January 1	$30,000	$45,000
Purchases in January	20,000	35,000
Merchandise available for sale	$50,000	$80,000
Cost percentage ($50,000/$80,000) = $62\frac{1}{2}\%$		
Deduct sales for January		25,000
Merchandise inventory, January 31, at retail		$55,000
Merchandise inventory, January 31, at estimated cost ($55,000 × $62\frac{1}{2}\%$)	$34,375	

It should be observed that the effect of the above procedure is to provide an inventory valuation in terms of average cost. No cost sequence is recognized; the percentage of cost to retail for the ending inventory is the same as the percentage of cost to retail for goods sold.

Use of the retail inventory method offers the following advantages:

1. Estimated interim inventories can be obtained without a physical count.
2. When a physical inventory is actually taken for periodic statement purposes, it can be taken at retail and then converted to cost without reference to individual costs and invoices, thus saving time and expense.
3. Checks are afforded on the movement of goods, since physical counts at retail should compare closely with inventories calculated at retail.

A physical count of the inventory to be reported on annual statements is generally required at least once a year. Relatively significant discrepancies between a physical inventory and the inventory position as derived from retail-method calculations should be investigated. Such inquiry may lead to sources of inventory misappropriations. Retail inventory records should be adjusted for variations shown by the physical count so that records reflect the actual status of the inventory for purposes of future estimates and control.

Markups and Markdowns

The earlier inventory calculation assumed that after the goods were originally marked at retail prices, no further changes in such prices were made. Frequently, however, because of changes in the price level, changes in consumer demand, or other reasons, original retail prices are changed. The items listed below must ordinarily be considered in employing the retail method:

1. *Original retail* — the established sales price, including the original increase over cost variously referred to as the *markon* or *initial markup*.
2. *Additional markups* — increases that raise sales prices above original retail.
3. *Markup cancellations* — decreases in additional markups that do not reduce sales prices below original retail.
4. *Markdowns* — decreases that reduce sales prices below original retail.
5. *Markdown cancellations* — decreases in the markdowns that do not raise the sales prices above original retail.

The difference between cost and retail as adjusted for the described changes is referred to as the *maintained markup*.

To illustrate the use of the five terms, assume that goods originally placed for sale are marked at 50% above cost. Certain merchandise costing $4 a unit, then, is marked at $6, which is termed the original retail. This increase in cost is variously referred to as a "50% markon on cost" or a "33\frac{1}{2}% markon on sales price." In anticipation of a heavy demand for the article, the retail price of the goods is subsequently increased to $7.50. This represents an additional markup of $1.50. At a later date the price is reduced to $7. This is a markup cancellation of 50 cents and not a markdown since the retail price has not been reduced below the original sales price. But assume that goods originally marked to sell at $6 are subsequently marked down to $5. This represents a markdown of $1. At a later date the goods are marked to sell at $5.25. This is a markdown cancellation of 25 cents and not a markup since sales price does not exceed the original retail.

In determining the goods on hand without a physical inventory, a record of each of the foregoing adjustments is required. The beginning inventory and purchases at retail are increased by net markups to arrive at goods available for sale at retail. Subtractions from goods available at retail are then made for sales, net markdowns, inventory breakage, spoilage, and other losses. The ending inventory at retail may be reduced to cost by applying the percentage that cost bears to retail.

In obtaining the cost percentage, the cost of goods available for sale (including any freight in) is normally related to the original retail plus the net markups, without taking into account the net markdowns. Calculation of the inventory in this manner is illustrated below.

	Cost	Retail
Beginning inventory	$ 8,600	$ 14,000
Purchases	69,000	110,000
Freight in	3,100	
Additional markups		13,000
Markup cancellations		(2,500)
Goods available for sale	$80,700	$134,500

Cost percentage ($80,700 ÷ $134,500) = 60%

Deduct: Sales	$108,000
Markdowns	4,800
Markdown cancellations	(800)
	$112,000
Ending inventory at retail	$ 22,500

134,500 - 112,000

Ending inventory at estimated cost ($22,500 × 60%) ... $ 13,500

Excluding markdowns in calculating the cost percentage results in a lower percentage and consequently a lower inventory figure than would otherwise be obtained. This lower inventory figure represents a lower of average cost or market valuation. It is sometimes referred to as the *conventional retail inventory* method, and is the more common type of retail inventory method used.

Markdowns may be made for special sales or clearance purposes, or they may be made as a result of market fluctuations and a decline in the replacement cost of goods. In either case their omission in calculating the cost percentage is necessary in order to value the inventory at the lower of cost or market. This is illustrated in the two examples which follow:

Example 1 — Markdowns for special sales purposes. Assume that merchandise costing $50,000 is marked to sell for $100,000. To dispose of part of the goods immediately, one fourth of the stock is marked down $5,000 and is sold. The cost of the ending inventory is calculated as follows:

	Cost	Retail
Purchases	$ 50,000	$100,000
Cost percentage ($50,000 ÷ $100,000) = 50%		
Deduct: Sales		$ 20,000
Markdowns		5,000
		$ 25,000
Ending inventory at retail		$ 75,000

¼

Ending inventory at estimated cost ($75,000 × 50%) .... $ 37,500

If cost, $50,000, had been related to sales prices after markdowns, $95,000, a cost percentage of 52.6% would have been obtained, and the inventory, which is three fourths of the merchandise originally acquired, would have been reported at 52.6% of $75,000, or $39,450. The inventory would thus be stated above the $37,500 cost of the remaining inventory and cost of goods sold would be understated by $1,950. A markdown relating to goods no longer on hand would have been recognized in the development of a cost percentage to be applied to the inventory. Reductions in the goods available at sales prices resulting from shortages or damaged goods should likewise be disregarded in calculating the cost percentage.

Example 2 — Markdowns as a result of market declines. Assume that merchandise costing $50,000 is marked to sell for $100,000. With a drop in replacement cost of the merchandise to $40,000, sales prices are marked down to $80,000. One half of the merchandise is sold. The cost of the ending inventory is calculated as follows:

	Cost	Retail
Purchases	$50,000	$100,000
Cost percentage ($50,000 ÷ $100,000) = 50%		
Deduct: Sales .... 80,000 × .50		$ 40,000
Markdowns		20,000
		$ 60,000
Ending inventory at retail		$ 40,000
Ending inventory at estimated cost ($40,000 × 50%)	$ 20,000	

If cost, $50,000, had been related to sales price after markdowns, $80,000, a cost percentage of 62.5% would have been obtained and the inventory would have been reported at 62.5% of $40,000, or $25,000. The use of the 50% cost percentage in the example reduces the inventory to $20,000, a balance providing the usual gross profit in subsequent periods if current prices and relationships between cost and retail prices prevail.

Discounts, Returns, and Allowances

Purchases should be shown net of cash discounts and purchase returns and allowances. A purchase return affects both the cost and the retail computations, while a purchase allowance affects only the cost total unless a change in retail price is made as a result of the allowance. Sales returns and allowances are proper adjustments to gross sales; however, sales discounts are not deducted to determine the ending retail inventory since retail prices for goods purchased are recorded at gross amounts.

Limitations of Retail Method

The calculation of a cost percentage for all goods carried is valid only when goods on hand can be regarded as a representative slice of the total goods handled. Varying markon percentages and sales of high- and low-margin items in proportions that differ from purchases will require separate records and the development of separate cost percentages for the different classes of goods. For example, assume that a store operates three departments and that for July the following information pertains to these departments:

	Department A		Department B		Department C		Total	
	Cost	Retail	Cost	Retail	Cost	Retail	Cost	Retail
Beginning inventory	$20,000	$ 28,000	$10,000	$15,000	$16,000	$ 40,000	$ 46,000	$ 83,000
Net purchases	57,000	82,000	20,000	35,000	20,000	60,000	97,000	177,000
Goods available for sale	$77,000	$110,000	$30,000	$50,000	$36,000	$100,000	$143,000	$260,000
Cost percentage		70%		60%		36%		55%
Sales		80,000		30,000		40,000		150,000
Inventory at retail		$ 30,000		$20,000		$ 60,000		$110,000
Inventory at cost		$ 21,000		$12,000		$ 21,600		$ 60,500

($54,600)

Because of the range in cost percentages from 36% to 70% and the difference in mix of the purchases and ending inventory, the ending inventory balance, using an overall cost percentage, is $5,900 higher ($60,500 − $54,600), than when the departmental rates are used. When material variations exist in the cost percentages by departments, separate departmental rates should be computed and applied.

The retail method is acceptable for income tax purposes, provided the taxpayer maintains adequate and satisfactory records supporting inventory calculations and applies the method consistently on successive tax returns.

DOLLAR-VALUE LIFO PROCEDURES

Dollar-value lifo views all goods in the inventory or in the separate pools to which it is to be applied as though they were similar items. Physical inventories are taken in terms of current replacement prices. Beginning and ending inventory values are then converted by means of appropriate price indexes to base-year prices, i.e., prices existing at the time the lifo method was adopted. The difference between beginning and ending dollar balances as converted is regarded as a measure of the inventory quantity change for the year. An inventory increase is recognized as an inventory layer to be added to the beginning inventory, and such increase is converted at the current price index and added to the dollars identified with the beginning balance. An inventory decrease is recognized as a shrinkage to be applied to the most recent or top layer and to successively lower layers of the beginning inventory, and this decrease is converted at the price indexes applying to such layers and subtracted from the dollars identified with the beginning inventory.

The example presented on pages 256 and 257 illustrates dollar-value lifo calculations. The index numbers used follow:

Year	Index
December 31, 1977	100
December 31, 1978	120
December 31, 1979	132
December 31, 1980	140
December 31, 1981	125

January 1, 1978 — Date of adoption of dollar-value lifo.
January 1, 1978 inventory at base prices (cost) $38,000

December 31, 1978 — end of first year:
(a) December 31, 1978 inventory at year-end prices $54,000
(b) December 31, 1978 inventory at base prices (a ÷ 1.20)   45,000
(c) January 1, 1978 inventory at base prices   38,000
(d) 1978 inventory increase at base prices, $45,000 − $38,000 (b − c) .   7,000
(e) 1978 layer increase, $7,000 × 1.20   8,400
(f) December 31, 1978 inventory at dollar-value lifo, $38,000 + $8,400
(c + e)   46,400

Inventory composition:		Base Prices	Index	Cost
	1978 layer	$ 7,000	120	$ 8,400
	Base quantity . . .	38,000	100	38,000
		$45,000		$46,400

December 31, 1979 — end of second year:
(a) December 31, 1979 inventory at year-end prices $66,000
(b) December 31, 1979 inventory at base prices (a ÷ 1.32)   50,000
(c) January 1, 1979 inventory at base prices   45,000
(d) 1979 inventory increase at base prices, $50,000 − $45,000 (b − c) .   5,000
(e) 1979 layer increase, $5,000 × 1.32   6,600
(f) December 31, 1979 inventory at dollar-value lifo, $46,400 + $6,600
(1978 f + e)   53,000

Inventory composition:		Base Prices	Index	Cost
	1979 layer	$ 5,000	132	$ 6,600
	1978 layer	7,000	120	8,400
	Base quantity . . .	38,000	100	38,000
		$50,000		$53,000

December 31, 1980 — end of third year:
(a) December 31, 1980 inventory at year-end prices $56,000
(b) December 31, 1980 inventory at base prices (a ÷ 1.40)   40,000
(c) January 1, 1980 inventory at base prices   50,000
(d) 1980 inventory decrease at base prices, $50,000 − $40,000 (c − b)   10,000
(e) 1980 decrease: 1979 layer, $5,000 × 1.32 = $6,600
                    1980 layer,   5,000 × 1.20 =   6,000   12,600
(f) December 31, 1980 inventory at dollar-value lifo, $53,000 − $12,600
(1979 f − e)   40,400

		Base Prices	Index	Cost
Inventory composition:	1978 layer	$ 2,000	120	$ 2,400
	Base quantity ...	38,000	100	38,000
		$40,000		$40,400

December 31, 1981 — end of fourth year:
(a) December 31, 1981 inventory at year-end prices $55,000
(b) December 31, 1981 inventory at base prices (a ÷ 1.25) 44,000
(c) January 1, 1981 inventory at base prices 40,000
(d) 1981 inventory increase at base prices, $44,000 − $40,000 (b − c) . 4,000
(e) 1981 layer increase, $4,000 × 1.25 (d × e) 5,000
(f) December 31, 1981 inventory at dollar-value lifo, $40,400 + $5,000
(1980 f + e) 45,400

		Base Prices	Index	Cost
Inventory composition:	1981 layer	$ 4,000	125	$ 5,000
	1978 layer	2,000	120	2,400
	Base quantity ...	38,000	100	38,000
		$44,000		$45,400

This example can be illustrated by highlighting the layers as follows:

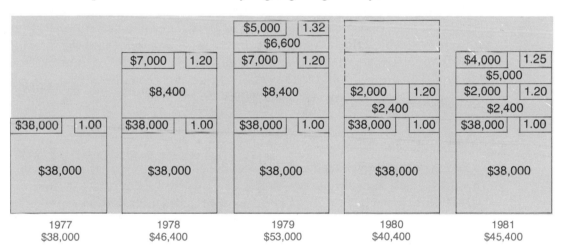

The amount of each layer is determined by multiplying together the amounts in the corner boxes. The amount in the upper left hand box is the base cost of the layer; the amount in the upper right hand box is the price index for the layer year.

The following items should be observed in the example:

December 31, 1978 — With an ending inventory of $45,000 in terms of base prices, the inventory has increased in 1978 by $7,000; however, the $7,000 increase is stated in terms of the pricing when lifo was adopted and

$7000 \times 1.20 = 8,400$

$5000 \times 1.32 = 6,600$

needs to be restated in terms of year-end prices which are 120% of the base level.

December 31, 1979 — With an ending inventory of $50,000 in terms of base prices, the inventory has increased in 1979 by another $5,000; however, the $5,000 increase is stated in terms of the pricing when lifo was adopted and needs to be restated in terms of year-end costs which are 132% of the base level.

December 31, 1980 — With an ending inventory of $40,000 in terms of base prices, the inventory has decreased in 1980 by $10,000; however, the $10,000 decrease is stated in terms of pricing when lifo was adopted and needs to be restated in terms of the pricing of the inventory layers that are eliminated or reduced. The decrease is applied first to elimination of the 1979 $5,000 layer and next to the reduction of the 1978 $7,000 layer; decreases are restated in terms of the percentages at which these layers were included in the inventory cost — for 1979, 132% of the base level, and for 1978, 120% of the base level.

December 31, 1981 — The ending inventory of $44,000 in terms of the base prices indicates an inventory increase for 1981 of $4,000; this increase requires restatement in terms of year-end prices which are 125% of the base level.

In the previous examples, it was assumed that the base year index was 100. If the base year index is not 100, a relative index can be computed from a fraction in which the numerator is the current year index and the denominator is the base year index. For example, assume that the current index is 140 and the base year is 112. The relative index for the current year conversions would therefore be $140 \div 112 = 125$.

Retail-Lifo Procedures

Dollar-value lifo procedures just described can be applied to the retail inventory method in developing inventory values reflecting a last-in, first-out valuation approach. *Retail lifo* requires that index numbers be applied to inventories stated at retail in arriving at the quantitative changes in inventories. When the quantitative changes have been developed, ending inventories are restated in terms of the retail base amounts, and the layers involved in their composition and related cost percentages are applied to such values.

The retail-lifo process calls for two modifications to the conventional retail procedures to determine a cost percentage.

1. Beginning inventory values are disregarded. The lifo inventory is composed of a base cost and subsequent cost layers that have not been assigned to revenues. With costs for prior periods to remain unchanged, only the cost of a current incremental layer requires calculation.
2. Markdowns, as well as markups, are recognized in calculating the cost

percentage applicable to goods stated at retail. Markdowns were not recognized in arriving at the cost percentage when the objective was to arrive at a lower of cost or market valuation. However, with lifo measurements requiring inventory valuation in terms of cost, the recognition of both markups and markdowns becomes appropriate.

Since lifo is rarely used in Canada, the retail-lifo procedures do not merit extended coverage. The following brief example illustrates the above-noted modifications in calculating cost percentages under retail-lifo procedures:

	Cost	Retail
Purchases	$63,000	$ 98,000
Purchase returns	(2,000)	(3,000)
Purchase discounts	(1,000)	
Freight in	2,220	
Markups, net of cancellations		8,000
Markdowns, net of cancellations		(1,000)
Total current period purchases adjusted for markups and markdowns	$62,220	$102,000

Cost percentage ($62,220 ÷ $102,000) = 61%

It is important to note that this cost percentage will be used only if an incremental layer is added to the inventory in the current period. If the inventory level has declined, previous inventory layers will be reduced using the price index and cost percentage applicable to the most recent layer(s) acquired.

INVENTORY VALUATION AT COST OR MARKET, WHICHEVER IS LOWER

One circumstance justifying a departure from cost occurs when replacement costs for goods on hand fall below original acquisition costs. Because wholesale and retail prices are generally related, declines in replacement costs usually indicate selling prices also have declined since the goods were purchased. However, the selling price of inventory may decline for other reasons. Perhaps an inventory item has been used as a demonstrator which reduces its marketability as a new product. Or perhaps an inventory item is damaged in storage or becomes shopworn through excessive handling. In each of these instances, a decline in utility is indicated, suggesting a departure from cost. The following statement from an AICPA publication provides support for this departure:

A departure from the cost basis of pricing the inventory is required when the utility of the goods is no longer as great as its cost. Where there is evidence that the utility of goods, in their disposal in the ordinary course of business, will be less than cost, whether due to physical deterioration, obsolescence, changes in price levels, or other causes, the difference should be recognized as a loss of the current period. This is generally accomplished by stating such goods at a lower level commonly designated as *market*.[1]

Recognition of a decline in the value of inventory identifies the loss with the period in which the loss occurred. This practice is referred to as *valuation at cost or market, whichever is lower*, or simply valuation at the *lower of cost or market*.

Definition of Market

The term "market" is subject to at least three interpretations: (1) replacement cost by purchase or manufacture, (2) net realizable value; the estimated sales proceeds less reasonably predictable costs of completion and sale, and (3) net realizable value less an allowance for a normal profit margin. In Canada, these interpretations all see some use because the *Accounting Recommendations* do not, as yet, define the term "market." Any resulting uncertainty as to how the term should be interpreted has seemingly had very little impact in Canadian accounting practice. The CICA publication, *Financial Reporting in Canada*, for example, states that "the most common basis of valuation, 'lower of cost or market,' was used by 92% of the survey companies in 1978 for all or part of their inventory."[2]

Since the Accounting Research Committee has not defined market, Canadian accountants would generally follow the pronouncements of either the American Institute of Certified Public Accountants or of the Institute of Chartered Accountants in England and Wales. While the pronouncements of both Institutes define market, each has done so differently.

In the United States, market is generally interpreted to be inventory replacement cost by purchase or manufacture. Replacement cost usually includes the purchase price of the product plus freight, duties, and other costs incidental to the acquisition of the goods. Replacement cost is sometimes referred to as *entry cost*. However, declines in entry cost are not always reflected immediately in the exit values, or selling prices. If there has been no decline in selling prices, no loss in utility has occurred and a write-down in inventory values is not justified. Thus, the entry cost definition of market must be modified to consider the utility of the inventory as measured by the selling prices. This modification is generally expressed in terms of the inventory's *net realizable value*, or estimated selling price less the cost of completion and disposal.

The American Institute of Certified Public Accountants has included this modification in their definition of market as follows:

---

[1] *Accounting Research and Terminology Bulletins — Final Edition*, "No. 43, Restatement and Revision of Accounting Research Bulletins" (New York: American Institute of Certified Public Accountants, 1961), Ch. 4, statement 5.

[2] *Financial Reporting in Canada* (13th ed.; Toronto: Canadian Institute of Chartered Accountants, 1979), p. 100.

AICPA

As used in the phrase *lower of cost or market*, the term *market* means current replacement cost (by purchase or by reproduction, as the case may be) except that:

(1) Market should not exceed the net realizable value (i.e., estimated selling price in the ordinary course of business less reasonably predictable costs of completion and disposal); and

(2) Market should not be less than net realizable value reduced by an allowance for an approximately normal profit margin.[3]

This definition establishes a ceiling for the market value at sales price less costs of completion and disposal and a floor for market at sales price less both the costs of completion and disposal and the normal profit margin. The ceiling limitation is applied so the inventory is not valued at more than its net realizable value. Failure to observe this limitation would result in charges to future revenue that exceed the utility carried forward and an ultimate loss on the sale of the inventory. The floor limitation is applied so the inventory is not valued at less than its net realizable value minus a normal profit. The concept of normal profit is a difficult one to measure objectively. Profits vary by item and over time. Records are seldom accurate enough to determine a normal profit by individual inventory item. Despite these difficulties, however, the use of a floor prevents a definition of market that would result in a write-down of inventory values in one period to create an abnormally high profit in future periods.

To illustrate, assume that a certain commodity sells for one dollar; selling expenses are twenty cents; the normal profit is 25% or twenty-five cents. The lower of cost or market as modified by the AICPA is developed in each case as shown in the illustration below.

CASE	COST	REPLACE-MENT COST	MARKET FLOOR (ESTIMATED SALES PRICE LESS SELLING EXPENSES AND NORMAL PROFIT)	MARKET CEILING (ESTIMATED SALES PRICE LESS SELLING EXPENSES)	MARKET (LIMITED BY FLOOR AND CEILING VALUES)	LOWER OF COST OR MARKET
A	$.65	$ .70 ✓ 1	$.55	$.80	$.70 1	$.65
B	.65	.60 ✓ 2	.55	.80	.60 2	.60
C	.65	.50	.55 ✓ 3	.80	.55 3	.55
D	.50	.45	.55 ✓ 4	.80	.55 4	.50
E	.75	.85	.55	.80 ✓ 5	.80 5	.75
F	.90	1.00	.55	.80 ✓ 6	.80 6	.80

A: Market is not limited by floor or ceiling; cost is less than market.
B: Market is not limited by floor or ceiling; market is less than cost.
C: Market is limited to floor; market is less than cost.
D: Market is limited to floor; cost is less than market.
E: Market is limited to ceiling; cost is less than market.
F: Market is limited to ceiling; market is less than cost.

---

[3]*Accounting Research and Terminology Bulletins — Final Edition*, op. cit., statement 6.

The dollar line below graphically illustrates the floor and ceiling range. B and A replacement costs clearly are within bounds and therefore are defined as market. D and C are below the floor and thus the market is the floor; E and F are above the ceiling and market therefore is the ceiling.

```
     D    C    x    B         A         x    E              F
  ───┼────┼────────┼────┼────┼────┼─────────┼────┼────┼────┼───
    .45  .50  .55  .60  .65  .70  .75  .80  .85  .90  .95  1.00
               (floor)                            (ceiling)
```

Replacement cost is abandoned as a test of subsequent utility as long as cost is recoverable in the selling price. It should also be noted that the market value is always the middle value of three amounts; replacement cost, floor, and ceiling.

The Institute of Chartered Accountants in England and Wales takes the position that market means net realizable value, except in circumstances where replacement cost may be the best available indicator of net realizable value. Under the ICAEW pronouncement the definition of net realizable value corresponds to the ceiling included in the AICPA definition. Excluding the possible use of replacement costs as a surrogate for net realizable value, the ICAEW position will on occasion produce a higher inventory value than would result under the AICPA approach. Conversely, the AICPA definition will never attribute a higher amount to inventory than the amount ICAEW position.

Differences in the interpretations of market are probably more noticeable in theory than in practice. The ICAEW position is based on the premise that if inventory could be replaced for less than cost it does not necessarily mean that a loss must result. All that can be said with certainty is that possible profits might have been better. Since a reduction of possible profits is not the same as a loss, the ICAEW recommends that inventory be valued at the lower of cost or net realizable value.

There is some evidence that Canadian practice may correspond more closely with the ICAEW position than it does with the AICPA definition of market.[4] A research study published by the CICA in 1963 concluded that the term "market" should normally be interpreted to mean net realizable value, except that, in the case of raw materials, replacement cost may, by reason of expedience and practicality, be substituted for net realizable value. This conclusion reflects the view that "this is the most reasonable interpretation from the point of both income measurement and balance sheet presentation."[5]

---

[4]*Financial Reporting in Canada* (13th ed.; Toronto: Canadian Institute of Chartered Accountants, 1979), p. 101.

[5]Gertrude Mulcahy, *Use and Meaning of 'Market' in Inventory Valuation* (Toronto: Canadian Institute of Chartered Accountants, 1963), p. 20.

	Quan-tities	Unit Cost	Market	Totals Cost	Totals Market	(1) If Applied to Individual Inventory Items	(2) If Applied to Inventory Classes	(3) If Applied to Inventory as a Whole
Material A	4,000	$1.20	$1.10	$ 4,800	$ 4,400	$ 4,400		
Material B	5,000	.50	.40	2,500	2,000	2,000		
Material C	2,000	1.00	1.10	2,000	2,200	2,000		
Total raw materials				$ 9,300	$ 8,600		$ 8,600	
Goods in Process D	10,000	1.60	1.40	$16,000	$14,000	14,000		
Goods in Process E	12,000	1.00	1.20	12,000	14,400	12,000		
Total goods in process				$28,000	$28,400		28,000	
Finished Goods F	3,000	2.00	1.70	$ 6,000	$ 5,100	5,100		
Finished Goods G	2,000	1.50	1.60	3,000	3,200	3,000		
Total finished goods				$ 9,000	$ 8,300		8,300	
				$46,300	$45,300			$45,300
Inventory valuation						$42,500	$44,900	$45,300

Methods of Applying Lower of Cost or Market Procedure

The lower of cost or market procedure may be applied to each inventory item, to the major classes or categories of inventory items, or to the inventory as a whole. Application of this procedure to the individual inventory items will result in the lowest inventory value. However, application to inventory groups or to the inventory as a whole may provide a sufficiently conservative valuation with considerably less effort. For example, assume that balanced stocks of raw materials are on hand, some of which have gone down and others have gone up. When raw materials are used as components of a single finished product, a loss in the value of certain materials may be considered to be counterbalanced by the gains that are found in other materials, and the lower of cost or market applied to this category as a whole may provide an adequate measure of the utility of the goods.

The illustration at the top of this page shows the valuation procedure applied to (1) individual inventory items, (2) independent classes of the inventory, and (3) inventory as a whole.

In valuing manufacturing inventories, raw materials declines are applicable to the raw materials inventory and also to raw materials costs in goods in process and finished goods inventories. Declines in direct labor and manufacturing overhead costs also affect the values of goods in process and finished goods, but these are usually ignored when they are relatively minor.

The method that is chosen for reducing an inventory to a lower value should be applied consistently in successive valuations. When valuing inventories by individual items, a lower market value assigned to goods at the end of a period is considered to be its cost for purposes of inventory valuation in subsequent periods; cost reductions once made, then, are not restored in subsequent inventory determinations. This restriction does not apply to inventories valued by major classes or as a whole when a record of the individual price changes is not maintained.

Application of Lower of Cost or Market in the Accounts

When an inventory value decline takes place, the decline may be reflected directly in the inventory account and thus cost is not reported separately on the balance sheet. When this is done, the decline is included in the cost of goods sold and there is no separate recognition on the income statement of the effect of the price change. Because price changes may or may not recur, the effect of these changes should be reflected separately in the financial statements as price or holding gains or losses. This will provide readers with increased information to forecast operations and cash flows, information considered essential by the Trueblood Committee in their report on the *Objectives of Financial Statements.*[6]

This separation can be accomplished by using an inventory valuation or allowance account reflecting the reduction of the inventory from cost to market and a separate cost account adjusting the cost of goods sold to reflect the market decline in the inventory value. The allowance account serves as a contra asset on the balance sheet, and the cost account adjusts the cost of goods sold in the income statement to reflect the inventory valuation change. The allowance account is adjusted at the end of each year to reflect the net change that has occurred between the ending inventory at cost and the ending inventory at market. If the difference at the end of the year is greater than the difference at the beginning of the year, the difference is added to the cost of goods sold. If the difference at the end of the year is less than the difference at the beginning, a reduction in the cost of goods sold must be reported.

To illustrate these two alternative approaches to recording the decline in inventory valuation, assume the inventory values given below for a company using the periodic inventory method.

	Cost	Market
January 1, 1981	$50,000	$50,000
December 31, 1981	60,000	52,000
December 31, 1982	75,000	70,000

---

[6]*Objectives of Financial Statements* (New York: American Institute of Certified Public Accountants, 1973), p. 46.

The entries required for these two methods at the end of 1981 and 1982 and their effects upon the income statement would be as at the tops of pages 266 and 267.

In the first example, cost of goods sold each year reflects both goods sold and the effects of inventory declines. In the second example, cost of goods sold is reported in terms of original cost. Inventory price fluctuations are screened out of this section and the net effect of such price changes is reported separately as an adjustment to the cost of goods sold. This separation provides the user with more information to forecast future operating results. If the price changes are expected to continue at the same magnitude and in the same direction, the past can be extrapolated to the future. If conditions are expected to change, the effect of the change can be more easily determined.

Evaluation of Lower of Cost or Market Procedure

The lower of cost or market rule is an evidence of the concept of accounting conservatism. If selling prices for the inventory have declined and the decline is expected to hold until the inventory is sold, the adjustment of income in the period of the decline seems justified. The value of the inventory has been impaired which requires current adjustment. However, care must be taken in using this method not to manipulate income by allowing excessive charges against income in one period to be offset by excessive income in the next period.

Some accountants have argued against the use of lower of cost or market because it violates the cost concept. Market valuations are often subjective and based upon expectations. To the extent that these expectations are not realized, misleading financial statements will be produced. To illustrate, assume activities summarized in terms of cost provide the following results over a three-year period:

	1980		1981		1982	
Sales		$200,000		$225,000		$250,000
Cost of goods sold:						
Beginning inventory	$ 60,000		$ 80,000		$127,500	
Purchases	120,000		160,000		90,000	
	$180,000		$240,000		$217,500	
Less ending inventory	80,000	100,000	127,500	112,500	92,500	125,000
Gross profit on sales		$100,000		$112,500		$125,000
Operating expenses		80,000		90,000		100,000
Net income		$ 20,000		$ 22,500		$ 25,000
Rate of income to sales		10%		10%		10%

	(1) FAILURE TO RECOGNIZE SEPARATELY EFFECTS OF FLUCTUATIONS IN INVENTORY VALUE		(2) SEPARATE RECOGNITION OF EFFECT OF FLUCTUATIONS IN INVENTORY VALUE	
December 31, 1981 To close beginning inventory.	Income Summary ... 50,000 Merchandise Inventory	50,000	Income Summary .... 50,000 Merchandise Inventory	50,000
December 31, 1981 To record ending inventory.	Merchandise Inventory .... 52,000 Income Summary	52,000	Merchandise Inventory .... 60,000 Income Summary	60,000
December 31, 1981 To establish allowance account.	No entry		Loss on Reduction of Inventory to Market. ...... 8,000 Allowance for Inventory Decline to Market	8,000
Partial income statement for period ending Dec. 31, 1981.	Sales .... $240,000 Cost of goods sold: Merchandise inv., Jan. 1, 1981 .... $ 50,000 Purchases .... 130,000 Mdse. available for sale .... $180,000 Less mdse. inv., Dec. 31, 1981 (lower of cost or market) ...... 52,000 128,000 Gross profit on sales $112,000		Sales .... $240,000 Cost of goods sold: Merchandise inv., Jan. 1, 1981 .... $ 50,000 Purchases .... 130,000 Mdse. available for sale .... $180,000 Less mdse. inv., Dec. 31, 1981 (cost) .... 60,000 120,000 Gross profit on sales (cost) .... $120,000 Loss on reduction of inv. to market .... 8,000 Adjusted gross profit on sales $112,000	

Assume estimates as to the future utility of ending inventories indicated market values as follows:

1980	1981	1982
−5,000 $75,000	⌐17,500 $110,000	0 $92,500

If sales remained the same for three years, inventory valuation at the lower of cost or market would provide the results shown below.

	1980		1981		1982	
Sales		$200,000		$225,000		$250,000
Cost of goods sold:						
Beginning inventory	$ 60,000		$ 75,000		$100,000	
Purchases	120,000		160,000		90,000	
	$180,000		$235,000		$200,000	
Less ending inventory	75,000 ✓	105,000	110,000 ✓	125,000	92,500 ✓	107,500
Gross profit on sales		$ 95,000		$100,000		$142,500
Operating expenses		80,000		90,000		100,000
Net income		$ 15,000		$ 10,000		$ 42,500
Rate of income to sales		7.5%		4.4%		17.0%

	(1) FAILURE TO RECOGNIZE SEPARATELY EFFECTS OF FLUCTUATIONS IN INVENTORY VALUE	(2) SEPARATE RECOGNITION OF EFFECT OF FLUCTUATIONS IN INVENTORY VALUE
December 31, 1982 To close beginning inventory.	Income Summary ... 52,000 Merchandise Inventory 52,000	Income Summary .... 60,000 Merchandise Inventory 60,000
December 31, 1982 To record ending inventory.	Merchandise Inventory .... 70,000 Income Summary 70,000	Merchandise Inventory .... 75,000 Income Summary 75,000
December 31, 1982 To adjust allowance account.	No entry	Allowance for Inventory Decline to Market .... 3,000 Gain from Decrease in Inventory Allowance . 3,000
Partial income statement for period ending Dec. 31, 1982.	Sales .... $280,000 Cost of goods sold: Merchandise inv., Jan. 1, 1982 (lower of cost or market) .... $ 52,000 Purchases .... 163,000 Mdse. available for sale .... $215,000 Less mdse. inv., Dec. 31, 1982 (lower of cost or market) ...... 70,000 145,000 Gross profit on sales . $135,000	Sales .... $280,000 Cost of goods sold: Merchandise inv., Jan. 1, 1982 (cost) .... $ 60,000 Purchases .... 163,000 Mdse. available for sale .... $223,000 Less mdse. inv., Dec. 31, 1982 (cost) .... 75,000 148,000 Gross profit on sales (cost) .... $132,000 Gain from decrease in inv. allow .... 3,000 Adjusted gross profit on sales $135,000

Reduction of an inventory below cost reduces the net income of the period in which the reduction is made and increases the net income of a subsequent period. In the example just given, total net income for the three-year period is the same under either set of calculations. But the reduction of inventories to lower market values reduced the net income for 1980 and for 1981 and increased the net income for 1982. The fact that inventory reductions were not followed by decreases in the sales prices resulted in net income determinations that varied considerably from those that might reasonably have been expected from increasing sales and costs that normally vary with sales volume.

Objection to valuation at the lower of cost or market is also raised on the grounds that it produces inconsistencies in the measurements of both the financial position and the operations of the enterprise. Market decreases are recognized but increases are not because to do so would violate the conventional realization concept.

LOSSES ON PURCHASE COMMITMENTS

Commitments are frequently made for the future purchase of goods at fixed prices. When price declines take place subsequent to such commitments, it is considered appropriate to measure and recognize these losses in the accounts just as losses on goods on hand. A decline is recorded by a debit to a special loss account and a credit to an accrued liability account, such as Estimated Losses on Purchase Commitments. Acquisition of the goods in a subsequent period is recorded by a credit to Accounts Payable, a debit cancelling the accrued liability, and a debit to Purchases for the difference.

For example, assume that Travis Manufacturing Company entered into a purchase contract for $120,000 of materials to be delivered in March of the following year. At the end of the current year, the market price for this order had fallen to $100,000. The entry to record this decline and subsequent delivery of the materials would be as follows:

Dec. 31	Loss on Purchase Commitments	20,000	
	Estimated Loss on Purchase Commitments		20,000
Mar. 1	Estimated Loss on Purchase Commitments	20,000	
	Purchases	100,000	
	Accounts Payable		120,000

The loss is thus assigned to the period in which the decline took place, and a subsequent period is charged for no more than the economic utility of the goods it receives. Current loss recognition would not be appropriate when commitments can be cancelled, when commitments provide for price adjustments, when hedging transactions prevent losses, or when declines do not suggest reductions in sales prices. Losses expected to arise from future sales commitments are not normally recognized as a charge against income. They may be recognized by footnote disclosure or by an appropriation of retained earnings.

VALUATION AT MARKET

There has been increasing support, particularly in recent years, for reporting inventories on the financial statements at their net realizable values or current replacement costs. Such valuation would recognize gains as well as losses when market or replacement costs differ from the costs of purchase or production. Earnings would emerge in two stages: (1) part of the earnings would be related to the periods in which goods are acquired, processed, and held, and (2) the balance of the earnings would be related to the periods in which goods are sold. Supporters of valuation at market insist this is necessary if inventories and working capital are to be fairly stated on the balance sheet. They also maintain that valuation at market is necessary if net income is to be measured in a fair and consistent manner.

A strong appeal for inventory valuation at market was made by Robert T. Sprouse and Maurice Moonitz in Accounting Research Study No. 3, "A Tentative Set of Broad Accounting Principles for Business Enterprises." Two statements by committees of the American Accounting Association have also stressed the need for these values. The AAA Committee on Concepts and Standards for Inventory Measurement indicated that, although no single method for pricing inventory quantities had been found, the majority of Committee members felt replacement cost was the best of the several available measurements. They concluded that the best solution to current reporting was a "simultaneous presentation of statements based on historical (acquisition) cost and the best estimate of 'current value' in order to disclose adequately the status and progress of the enterprise.[7]

The special committee of the AAA authorized to produce a basic statement of accounting theory recommended the acceptance of multi-valued reports that included current replacement cost data. The committee also indicated means of obtaining current-cost data. The committee concluded by stating:

> . . . techniques presently used to determine current replacement cost produce information which is sufficiently verifiable, quantifiable, and free from bias to justify their use in stating inventories of merchandise, materials, and supplies at their current replacement cost.[8]

In 1976, the Securities and Exchange Commission in the United States issued a pronouncement that now requires larger companies to include supplementary disclosure of the current replacement cost of inventories at each fiscal year-end for which a balance sheet is provided.[9] More recently, in 1979, Financial Accounting Standards Board Statement No. 33, Financial Reporting and Changing Prices established supplementary disclosure requirements that have replaced the SEC requirements.[10]

Despite such support, there has been little general acceptance to date by practitioners of inventory valuation at market. This procedure has been challenged chiefly on the grounds it represents a departure from the cost concept and violates the accounting standards of verifiability and objectivity. In special instances, however, there is support for valuation of inventory at sales prices less costs to be incurred in their sale even though such values may exceed cost. This valuation is accepted only when it is a regular trade practice and arises from either (1) assured market conditions that make possible the immediate sale of the goods at stated prices, or (2) standard products, a ready market, plus the inability to arrive at a reasonable deter-

---

[7]"A Discussion of Various Approaches to Inventory Measurement, Supplementary Statement No. 2," *Accounting Review* (July, 1964), p. 700.

[8]*A Statement of Basic Accounting Theory* (Evanston, Illinois: American Accounting Association, 1966), p. 74.

[9]Securities and Exchange Commission, *Accounting Series Release No. 190*, "Disclosure of Replacement Cost Data" (Washington: U.S. Government Printing Office, 1976).

[10]Statement No. 33 is covered in Chapter 21.

mination of costs. Inventories, such as certain precious metals, may be accorded this exceptional treatment in view of their immediate marketability at a relatively fixed sales price. Similar treatment may be accorded a farmer's inventory in view of the difficulty of arriving at satisfactory costs. When inventories are reported at more than cost, the special valuation procedure must be disclosed in the financial statements.

VALUATION OF TRADE-INS AND REPOSSESSIONS

When goods are acquired in secondhand condition as a result of repossessions and trade-ins, they should be recorded at their estimated cash purchase price. However, when this is difficult or impossible to define, the consistent application of *floor values* — amounts which, after any increase for reconditioning charges, will permit the recognition of normal profits — would be appropriate. Sales efforts are required in the sale of repossessions and trade-ins just as in the sale of new items; recording the goods at floor values will permit the recognition of normal profits when goods are sold.

The accounting for trade-ins is illustrated by the following example: Daynes Department Store sells a new washing machine to a customer for $350 cash and a trade-in of an old washer. It is estimated that a realistic floor value for the trade-in is $50. Reconditioning costs of $30 are incurred after which the trade-in washer is sold for $120, an amount that provides a normal profit. Perpetual inventory records are maintained for trade-ins but not for the regular inventory. The entries shown below reflect these transactions:

Cash	350	
Trade-In Inventory	50	
Sales		400
Trade-In Inventory	30	
Cash		30
Cash	120	
Sales — Trade-Ins		120
Cost of Trade-Ins Sold	80	
Trade-In Inventory		80

Assume Daynes Department Store sold another washing machine on account for $350 plus interest on the unpaid balance. The customer made principal payments of $200 on the machine and then defaulted on the contract. The machine was repossessed and overhauled at a cost of $40. It was then sold for $150, a price that provided a normal profit of 50% on cost.

The following entries reflect the repossession and subsequent resale.

Loss on Repossession	90	
Repossessed Inventory	60	
Accounts Receivable		150

Computation:

Value of repossession established to permit 50% normal profit on cost. (33¹/₃% on selling price.)

Selling price	$150
Less profit at 33¹/₃%	50
Cost of repossessed goods sold	$100
Less cost of overhaul	40
Value of repossessed inventory	$ 60

[handwritten:] 50/100 = .50 ✓

Repossessed Inventory	40	
Cash		40
Cost to overhaul repossessed washing machine.		
Cash	150	
Sales — Repossessed Inventory		150
Sale of repossessed washing machine.		
Cost of Repossessed Goods Sold	100	
Repossessed Inventory		100
Cost of repossessed washing machine.		

INVENTORIES ON THE BALANCE SHEET

It is customary for business units to report trading as well as manufacturing inventories as current assets even though in some instances it may take considerable time before portions of such inventories are realized in cash. Among the items that are generally reported separately under the inventories heading are merchandise inventory or finished goods, work in process, raw materials, factory supplies, goods out on consignment, and goods in the hands of agents and salespersons. Inventories are normally listed in the order of their liquidity.

The valuation procedures employed should be disclosed in a note to the financial statements outlining all significant accounting policies.[11] The basis of valuation together with the method of arriving at cost should normally be indicated. In Canada it is customary to use only the term "cost" where the method of determining it has resulted in a figure which does not differ materially from recent cost. Otherwise, the method of determining cost should be disclosed. Because of uncertainty as to its meaning, use of the term "market" should be avoided in favor of more specific terminology such as "replacement cost" or "net realizable value." [12]

When the inventory method produces values that are materially less than market, however defined, disclosure of market values should be provided. The use of lifo, for example, may result in a serious distortion of working capital measurements. Data concerning market should be given if the reader of the statement is to be adequately informed on financial position.

---

[11] *Accounting Recommendations, Section 1505*, "Disclosure of Accounting Policies" (Toronto: Canadian Institute of Chartered Accountants, 1974), par. .09.

[12] *Accounting Recommendations, Section 3030*, "Inventories" (Toronto: Canadian Institute of Chartered Accountants, 1968), par. .11.

An inventory allowance to reduce an inventory to a lower of cost or market basis is reported as a subtraction from the inventory at cost. However, an appropriation of retained earnings to preserve earnings within the business for possible future market decline in the inventory value is reported as a part of the shareholders' equity. If the decline fails to materialize, the appropriation balance is no longer required and is returned to the retained earnings account. If the decline does materialize, the appropriation is still returned to the retained earnings account where it will absorb the inventory loss ultimately carried to the latter account through net income.

If significant inventory price declines take place between the balance sheet date and the date the statement is prepared, such declines should be disclosed by parenthetical remark or note. When relatively large orders for merchandise have been placed in a period of widely fluctuating prices, but the title to such goods has not yet passed, such commitments should be described by note. Information should also be provided concerning possible losses on purchase commitments. Similar information may be appropriate for possible losses on sales commitments.

When inventories or sections of an inventory have been pledged as security on loans from banks, finance companies, or factors, the amounts pledged should be disclosed parenthetically in the inventory section of the balance sheet or by note.

Inventory items may be reported as follows:

Inventories:			
Raw materials:			
On hand	$228,000		
Less allowance to reduce inventory from cost to net realizable value	18,000	$210,000	
In transit from supplier		30,000	$240,000
Work in process			300,000
Finished goods:			
On hand (goods of $100,000 have been pledged as security on loans of $75,000 from First Canada Bank)		$300,000	
On consignment		15,000	315,000
Factory supplies			12,000
Total inventories			$867,000

Alternative presentations are very common in practice. In particular, the information provided parenthetically in the illustration above is often disclosed in notes to the financial statements.

1. Give certain instances in which estimates of inventory costs are necessary or appropriate and state what procedure would be followed in developing satisfactory estimates of such costs.

2. Distinguish between: (a) gross profit as a percentage of cost and gross profit as a percentage of sales: (b) markup cancellation and markdown; (c) the gross profit method of calculating estimated inventory cost and the retail inventory method of calculating estimated inventory cost.

3. What effect would the use of the lifo inventory method have upon the applicability of the gross profit method of valuing inventory?

4. How can the retail inventory method be considered a perpetual inventory method?

5. Define (a) initial markup, (b) additional markup, (c) markup cancellation, (d) markdown, (e) markdown cancellation, and (f) maintained markup.

6. How should the cost percentage be calculated for the conventional retail inventory method?

7. How are sales discounts recognized in using the retail inventory method?

8. Describe the application of dollar-value lifo procedures.

9. What are the similarities between dollar-value lifo and retail-lifo?

10. (a) Describe retail-lifo. (b) What modifications in the conventional retail procedures are required in adopting and applying retail-lifo?

11. Under what circumstances would a decline in replacement cost of an item not justify a departure from the cost basis of valuing inventory?

12. Does normal profit in the AICPA definition of market refer to gross profit or some other profit? How is it determined?

13. Why is a ceiling and floor limitation on replacement cost considered necessary by the AICPA?

14. How does the ICAEW define market? How does this differ from the AICPA definition?

15. Why does the individual item inventory procedure result in a more conservative inventory valuation than either the inventory class or inventory as a whole procedure?

16. What arguments can be presented for separate reporting in the income statement of the effect of using the lower of cost or market procedure?

17. How does the accounting treatment for losses on purchase commitments differ between actual losses which have already occurred and losses which may occur in the future?

18. There has been increasing support for the use of market values in reporting inventories on the financial statements. What are the major arguments that are raised in supporting such use?

19. What is the justification for valuing trade-ins or repossessions so that a normal profit can be realized upon their sale?

20. The Berg Corporation began business on January 1, 1979. Information about inventories, as of December 31, under different valuation methods is shown below. Using this information you are to choose the phrase which best answers each of the following questions:

	Lifo Cost	Fifo Cost	Market	Lower of Cost or Market*
1979	$10,200	$10,000	$ 9,600	$ 8,900
1980	9,100	9,000	8,800	8,500
1981	10,300	11,000	12,000	10,900

*Fifo cost, item by item valuation.

(a) The inventory basis that would result in the highest net income for 1979 is: (1) Lifo cost, (2) Fifo cost, (3) Market, (4) Lower of cost or market.
(b) The inventory basis that would result in the highest net income for 1980 is: (1) Lifo cost, (2) Fifo cost, (3) Market, (4) Lower of cost or market.
(c) The inventory basis that would result in the lowest net income for the three years combined is: (1) Lifo cost, (2) Fifo cost, (3) Market, (4) Lower of cost or market.
(d) For the year 1980, how much higher or lower would net income be on the fifo cost basis than on the lower of cost or market basis? (1) $400 higher, (2) $400 lower, (3) $600 higher, (4) $600 lower, (5) $1,000 higher, (6) $1,000 lower, (7) $1,400 higher, (8) $1,400 lower.
(e) On the basis of the information given, it appears that the movement of prices for the items in the inventory was: (1) up in 1979 and down in 1981 (2) up in both 1979 and 1981, (3) down in 1980 and up in 1981, (4) down in both 1979 and 1981.

EXERCISES

7-1. Sales for a period are $100,000. What is the cost of goods sold under each assumption below?

(a) Gross profit on sales is 20%.
(b) Gross profit on cost of sales is 60%.
(c) Goods are marked up $1/4$ above cost.
(d) Gross profit on cost of sales is 150%.
(e) Goods are marked up 200% above cost.
(f) Gross profit on sales is 18%.
(g) Gross profit on cost is 18%.

7-2. The sales and purchases data for the Minton Co. follow:

	Sales	Purchases
January	$50,000	$40,000
February	60,000	45,000
March	65,000	50,000

The merchandise inventory at cost on January 1 was $30,000. Goods are sold at a gross profit of 20% on sales. Compute the monthly inventory balances for interim statement purposes.

7-3. M. Wilde requires an estimate of the cost of goods lost by fire on March 7. Merchandise on hand on January 1 was $60,000. Purchases since January 1 were $45,000; freight in, $5,000; purchase returns and allowances, $3,000. Sales are made at 20% above cost and totalled $48,000 to March 7. Goods costing $12,250 were left undamaged by the fire; remaining goods were destroyed. (a) What was the cost of goods destroyed? (b) What would your answer be if sales are made at a gross profit of 20% of sales?

7-4. Brucie Lovelace, the owner of Brucie's Boutique, has always carried fire insurance on his inventory. Under the terms of the policy, he is to collect from the insurance company 80% of any loss of inventory destroyed by fire.

On the morning of November 20, 1980, Brucie was burned out. The fixtures and inventory were a total loss, but the records for this year, kept in a fireproof safe, were saved.

The records disclose the following data:

Sales	$81,800
Rent expense	2,550
Freight in	1,500
Salaries expense	18,200
Purchases	59,500
Sales returns	280
Purchase returns	1,150
Sales discounts	1,520
Purchase discounts	1,850

Also found in the office was part of the Income Statement for the fiscal year, ending December 31, 1979. The following items were extracted from that Statement:

Cost of goods available for sale	$132,400
Total administrative and selling expenses	34,400
Purchases	115,000
Purchase returns & allowances	3,600
Transportation in	8,000
Sales — net	172,000
Purchase discounts	2,000
Cost of goods sold	120,400

Compute the amount that Brucie Lovelace may expect to collect from the insurance company.

7-5. Records for the Fox Department Store disclose the following data:

	Cost	Retail
Merchandise inventory, January 1	$ 30,000	$ 60,000
Purchases, January 1 — December 31	180,000	
Sales, January 1 — December 31		205,000
Sales returns, January 1 — December 31		5,000
Freight in, January 1 — December 31	12,500	
Purchase discounts taken, January 1 — December 31	2,500	

A physical inventory taken on December 31 shows merchandise on hand valued at retail at $120,000. Compute the estimated cost of ending inventory.

7-6. From the following information, compute the cost of inventory shortage for the

Brandenburg Discount Stores for 1977. The company uses conventional retail inventory procedures.

	Cost	Retail
Inventory, January 1, 1977 (cost ratio — 80%)	$ 9,600	
Purchases	59,000	$80,000

Total sales for the year amounted to $70,000. Markups were $6,000; markup cancellations were $1,500; markdowns, $3,000; freight in, $2,845; sales discounts, $2,000; and purchase discounts, $1,000. The physical inventory on December 31, 1981 was $20,000 (prices as shown on sales tags on items).

7-7. On the night of November 11, a Ford truck silently arrived at the warehouse of Jimmy Carter's Peanut Butter Plant and stole a number of cases of peanut butter.

Given the following data, what was the dollar value of the peanut butter stolen?

Sales Nov. 1 — Nov. 11	$325,000
Inventory Oct. 31	25,000
Manufacturing costs of goods finished Nov. 1 — Nov. 11	335,000
Jimmy prices his peanut butter 22% over cost	
Sales returns Nov. 1 — Nov. 11	20,000
Value of inventory count on Nov. 12	60,000

7-8. You assemble the following information for the Pratt Department Store which computes its inventory at retail-lifo.

	Cost	Retail
Inventory, January 1, 1981	$117,000	$150,000
Net purchases	208,000	250,000
Markups		10,000
Markdowns		5,000
Increase in price level for year		5%

Calculate the cost of the inventory on December 31, 1981, assuming that the inventory at retail is (a) $147,000, (b) $168,000.

7-9. Determine the proper carrying value of the inventory items below if priced in accordance with the recommendations of the AICPA on inventory pricing. Would any of these items be priced differently under the ICAEW definition of market? If yes, compute the proper inventory value.

Item	Cost	Replacement Cost	Sales Price	Cost of Completion	Normal Profit
A	$1.75	$1.80	$2.25	$.30	$.17
B	.68	.65	1.00	.30	.04
C	.29	.27	.50	.15	.05
D	.83	.83	1.05	.24	.05
E	.79	.74	.90	.11	.07
F	1.19	1.15	1.25	.13	.07

7-10. The Merrill Manufacturing Co. has the following items in its inventory on December 31, 1981.

	Units	Unit Cost	Unit Market
Raw Material A	2,000	$1.10	$1.00
Raw Material B	6,500	2.40	2.50
Raw Material C	6,000	3.00	3.20

Work in Process #1	8,000	3.75	3.80
Work in Process #2	4,000	5.20	5.10
Finished Goods X	3,000	7.00	7.20
Finished Goods Y	2,500	8.00	7.50

Calculate the value of the company's inventory using cost or market, whichever is lower, assuming that this valuation procedure is applied:

(a) To individual inventory items.
(b) To each class of inventory.
(c) To the inventory as a whole.

7-11. Ferris Ltd. sells two products, A and B, and values its inventory at the lower of cost or market value, using weighted average to determine the cost. The following data are available.

	Product A		Product B	
	Quantity	Cost	Quantity	Cost
Inventory Oct. 31, 1981	2,500	$18,500	400	$ 5,000
Purchases during November				
Purchase #1	3,000	13,300	200	2,800
#2	1,500	10,600	500	6,100
#3	900	7,700	300	4,200
#4	1,400	8,500	900	9,200
#5	1,600	12,250	300	4,300
#6			400	5,000
	10,900	$70,850	3,000	$36,600

	Product A	Product B
Inventory November 30, 1981	2,220 units	500 units
Unit selling price November 30, 1981	$9.00	$18.00
Unit replacement cost November 30, 1981	6.30	13.00
Unit selling expenses	2.00	2.00
Unit normal profit	1.00	1.50

Calculate the total inventory value at November 30, 1981, using the lower of cost or market. Show details of your calculation.

7-12. The Hubbard Products Co. entered into a 6-month, $800,000 purchase commitment for a supply of its major raw material on October 1, 1981. On December 31, 1981, the market value of this material has fallen so that current acquisition of the ordered quantity would cost $675,000. It is anticipated that a further decline will occur during the next three months and that market at date of delivery will be approximately $525,000. What entries would you make on December 31, 1981, to recognize these facts?

7-1A. The following information was taken from the records of the Lucky Company.

	1/1/80–31/12/80	1/1/81–30/9/81
Sales (net of returns)	$1,250,000	$750,000
Beginning inventory	210,000	365,000
Purchases	1,076,000	530,500
Freight in	58,000	36,000

	1/1/80–31/12/80	1/1/81–30/9/81
Purchase discounts	15,000	7,500
Purchase returns	20,000	6,500
Purchase allowances	4,000	2,500
Ending inventory	365,000	
Selling and general expenses	225,000	160,000

Instructions:
Compute by the gross-profit method the value to be assigned to the inventory as of September 30, 1981, and prepare an interim statement summarizing operations for the nine-month period ending on this date.

7-2A. In December, 1981, Target Merchandise Inc., had a significant portion of their inventory stolen. The company determined the cost of their inventory not stolen to be $31,705. The following information was taken from the records of the company.

	January 1, 1981 to Date of Theft	1980
Purchases	$129,045	$134,433
Purchase returns and allowances	6,021	7,017
Sales	196,677	203,317
Sales returns and allowances	2,402	2,167
Wages	17,743	18,356
Salaries	8,000	9,000
Taxes other than income	3,732	3,648
Rent	5,400	5,400
Insurance	967	982
Light, heat, and water	1,134	1,271
Advertising	4,250	2,680
Interest expense	2,755	3,020
Depreciation expense	1,255	1,280
Furniture and fixtures	10,065	10,570
Miscellaneous expense	6,634	6,877
Beginning inventory	47,880	49,200

Instructions:
Estimate the cost of the stolen inventory.

7-3A. The records of the appliance department for Bargain Basement Discount Store show the following data for the month of March:

Sales	$201,500	Purchase returns (at cost price)	$ 2,500
Sales returns	2,000	Purchase returns (at sales price).	3,400
Additional markups	17,900	Markup cancellations	4,000
Markdowns	24,000	Beginning inventory (at cost	
Markdown cancellations	3,500	price)	125,000
Freight on purchases	3,500	Beginning inventory (at sales	
Purchases (at cost price)	61,000	price)	170,000
Purchases (at sales price) ...	94,500		

Instructions:

Compute the inventory using the conventional retail inventory method.

7-4A. The following information was taken from the records of Gardens Inc., for the years 1980 and 1981.

	1981	1980
Sales	$173,250	$169,500
Sales discounts	2,300	1,500
Sales returns	2,250	2,000
Freight in	5,000	4,550
Purchases (at cost)	97,500	85,700
Purchases (at retail)	125,700	115,600
Purchase discounts	1,472	1,250
Beginning inventory (at cost)		82,000
Beginning inventory (at retail)		109,400

Instructions:

Compute the value of the inventory at the end of 1980 and 1981 using the conventional retail inventory method.

7-5A. Barnett Ltd. has operated a retail sporting goods store for several years. On January 31, 1980 the company opened its first branch store by purchasing an established business in another city. Management of Barnett Ltd. has decided to use the retail inventory method in the new branch for the company's fiscal year ended December 31, 1980.

The main store records show the following with respect to the branch:

(a) Inventory on hand purchased January 31, 1980; cost — $39,040; retail — $48,800;

(b) Purchases on behalf of branch to December 31, 1980: cost — $203,330; retail — $302,000;

(c) Freight prepaid on shipments to the branch — $3,780;

(d) Shipments back to the main store from the branch: cost — $4,650; retail — $6,200.

The branch records show:

(1) Sales for the 11 months — $278,150;

(2) Retail value of goods broken or stolen — $350;

(3) In April 1980, the branch put 70 pairs of skis on sale for 25% less than the normal retail price of $100 per pair. After the sale, the 18 pairs of skis remaining were returned to their original price;

(4) Forty tents were marked up $10 each in July, in response to an announced manufacturer's price increase.

Instructions:

(a) What are the advantages to a company of this kind using the retail method of accounting for inventories?

(b) Calculate the estimated branch inventory as at December 31, 1980 at retail and at lower of average cost or market.

7-6A. The records of Southam Sporting Goods Store provide the following data for the month of June:

Sales	$679,000
Return sales	8,000
Additional markups	16,500
Markup cancellations	6,500
Markdowns	6,500
Purchases:	
At retail	715,000
At cost	404,600
Purchase returns:	
At retail	5,000
At cost	2,900
Freight on purchases	9,000
Beginning inventory	
At cost	47,500
At retail	80,000
Employee discounts	1,000
Markdown cancellations	4,000

Instructions:

Estimate the lower of cost or market valuation of the closing inventory using the retail inventory method. (SMA adapted)

7-7A. The Cougar Sports Shop values its inventory on the retail-lifo basis. At December 31, 1980, the inventory was valued as follows:

Lifo Layer Year	Cost	Actual Retail	Price Index for Year	Retail at Base of 100
1974	$ 4,920	$ 8,200	100	$ 8,200
1976	3,160	4,515	105	4,300
1978	4,480	8,961	103	8,700
1979	1,500	2,000	110	1,818
	$14,060	$23,676		$23,018

The following data were also compiled.

December 31, 1980 inventory at 1980 retail prices	$ 25,780
Purchases — cost	145,200
Purchases — selling price	224,615
Freight in	3,300
Sales returns	3,740
Sales discounts	650
Markups	1,580
Markup cancellations	360
Markdowns	835
Gross sales	234,000
Price index for 1981	108

Instructions:

Based upon the above information for 1981, compute (1) the 1981 cost ratio, and (2) the inventory amount that would be reported on the balance sheet at December 31, 1981.

7-8A. The operation of a department of a retail store that uses the conventional retail method of inventory determination are given in the figures presented below:

Opening inventory — cost	$14,250
Opening inventory — sales price	19,105
Purchases — cost	33,771
Purchases — sales price	46,312
Purchase allowances	1,093
Freight in	845
Departmental transfers (debit) — cost	100
Departmental transfers (debit) — sales price	140
Additional markups	1,207
Markup cancellations	274
Inventory shortage — sales price	704
Sales (including sales of $4,460 of items that were marked down from $5,920)	37,246

Instructions:

Set up a computation showing the ending inventory at sales prices and at cost as determined by the conventional retail method. (AICPA adapted)

7-9A. The E.A.P. Company is engaged in manufacturing. Its products are made principally from one raw material, and in order to insure uninterrupted production, it normally maintains a substantial inventory of the raw material. Because of advancing prices, the company in 1965 adopted the last-in, first-out method of pricing out its material requisitions, and thereafter valued its inventory at the prices shown by its perpetual inventory records.

As of December 31, 1980, the inventory consisted of 380,000 pounds carried on its books at an average price of $.90 per pound. The market price on December 31, 1980, was $1.50 per pound. As of December 31, 1981, the inventory was 420,000 pounds with a market price of $1.60 per pound. This was carried at the prices shown on the stock records, 270,000 pounds of this being valued at $.90 per pound and the remainder at prices which averaged $1.54 per pound. The purchases during the year were also made at an average price of about $1.54 per pound.

The operating accounts for the year ended December 31, 1981, included the following:

Sales	$2,100,000
Goods in Process Inventory, 1/1/81	146,600
Finished Goods Inventory, 1/1/81	90,000
Direct Labor	344,000
Cost of Materials Used	1,217,000
Manufacturing Overhead	302,000
Goods in Process Inventory, 12/31/81	180,000
Finished Goods Inventory, 12/31/81	100,000

On March 30, 1982, the warehouse in which the raw material inventory was stored and badly damaged by fire. The stock records were destroyed, but from other records the following figures were obtained:

Sales to March 30	$820,000
Purchases of materials	551,425
Direct labor	132,405
Manufacturing overhead	117,604
Goods in process inventory, March 30	175,000
Finished goods inventory, March 30	105,000
Salvage value of damaged materials	25,000

The purchase price of raw material during the three months had averaged $1.61 per pound with the price on March 30, at $1.62 per pound. The sales price during the period had varied only with the current material, labor and overhead cost existing at date of acceptance of the order, as is normal in this business.

Instructions:

Calculate the amount of a claim for fire loss, assuming full insurance coverage. Show all computations to support the claim. (AICPA adapted)

7-10A. The President of X Co. Ltd. has asked you, the controller, to evaluate the inventory as at the year-end, December 31, 1981. The following information is available.

(1) Purchases:

1 Jan $16,050   15,000   1.07

Month		Quantity	Price/Unit
January	5,500	5,000	1.10
February	3,150	3,000	1.05
March	6,900	6,000	1.15
April	8,400	7,000	1.20
May	10,350	9,000	1.15
June	6,000	5,000	1.20
July	7,200	6,000	1.20
August	6,250	5,000	1.25
September	8,750	7,000	1.25
October	10,800	9,000	1.20
November	11,500	10,000	1.15
December	6,250	5,000	1.25

$91,050

(2) The January 1, 1981 inventory amounted to 15,000 units valued at a cost of $16,050.

(3) The partial income statement for last year appears below:

Sales	100%	$140,000
Cost of Goods Sold	60%	84,000
Gross Profit	40%	$ 56,000

The gross profit percentage for that year is representative of the gross profit of the last few years and of the one expected in the next year.

(4) The sales for the current year totalled $148,000.

(5) The normal cost of marketing of one unit is $0.20.

(6) The physical count of inventory for the current year-end reveals that there are 18,000 units on hand valued at a retail price of $35,000.

(7) It is expected that a 20% decrease in the purchase price will take effect in January of the coming year and that this price decrease will be permanent. However, retail prices are expected to drop only by about 10%.

Instructions:

(a) Calculate the cost of the closing inventory under four different inventory costing methods.

(b) Compare the results of your calculations with the market value and recommend the inventory value that should be used at the end of the year.

(c) Why is the inventory figure calculated under weighted average method normally between the figures obtained through the FIFO and LIFO method? (SMA adapted)

7-11A. Robinson Ltd. carries five items in their inventory. The following data are relative to such goods at the end of 1981:

			Per Unit			
	Units	Cost	Replacement Cost	Estimated Sales Price	Selling Cost	Normal Profit
Commodity A ..	1,000	$ 2.90	$ 3.05	$ 5.00	$1.50	$1.25
Commodity B ..	1,200	3.50	3.50	6.00	.80	1.00
Commodity C ..	2,000	5.50	5.00	8.00	.90	2.00
Commodity D ..	2,500	7.00	7.50	9.00	1.20	1.75
Commodity E ..	250	12.30	12.00	12.00	1.00	2.50

Instructions:

Calculate the value of the inventory under each of the following methods:

(1) Cost.

(2) The lower of cost or market without regard to market floor and ceiling limitations, applied to the individual inventory items.

(3) The lower of cost or market without regard to market floor and ceiling limitations applied to the inventory as a whole.

(4) The lower of cost or net realizable value applied to the individual inventory items.

(5) The lower of cost or market recognizing floor and ceiling limitations applied to the individual inventory items.

7-12A. The Taylor Company accounts for fluctuations in the valuation of inventory by using the lower of cost or market method with an allowance account. The following data summarized inventory data for the years 1978 through 1981.

	Cost	Replacement Cost	Sales Price	Selling Cost	Normal Profit
1978	$65,000	$60,000	$70,000	$15,000	$15,000
1979	68,000	60,000	65,000	3,000	9,000
1980	58,000	59,000	75,000	15,000	10,000
1981	70,000	59,000	82,000	15,000	5,000

Instructions:

Give the entries which would be required to recognize gains and losses due to changes in inventory value. Use the AICPA definition of market.

7-13A. The Scott Sales Co. sells three products. Inventories and purchases during February and the market prices of these goods on February 28 are as follows:

	Product A	Product B	Product C
Feb. 1 Inventory	200 units at $ 65	200 units at $110	60 units at $145
1–28 Purchases	60 units at 50	120 units at 105	60 units at 200
Total available for sale ...	260	320	120
Feb. 1–28 Sales..................	50 units at 95	40 units at 145	10 units at 220
	130 units at 100	110 units at 150	40 units at 210
Total sales	180	150	50
Feb. 28 Inventory	80	170	70
Feb. 28 Market values per unit $55	$95	$140

Selling, general, and administrative expenses for February were $15,300.

Instructions:
(1) Prepare an income statement for February, assuming that the ending inventory is valued at cost on a first-in, first-out basis.
(2) Prepare an income statement for February, assuming that the inventory is reduced to cost or market, whichever is lower, applied to individual products, and the inventory loss is reported separately on the income statement. (First-in, first-out is used in arriving at cost.)

7-14A. The Napa Appliance Company began business on January 1, 1980. The company decided from the beginning to grant allowances on merchandise traded in as part payment on new sales. During 1981 the company granted trade-in allowances of $42,690. The wholesale value of merchandise traded in was $27,250. Trade-ins recorded at $26,000 were sold for their wholesale value of $18,000 during the year.

The following summary entries were made to record annual sales and trade-in sales:

Accounts Receivable	293,260	
Trade-In Inventory	42,690	
Sales		335,950
Cash	18,000	
Loss on Trade-In Inventory	8,000	
Trade-In Inventory		26,000

When a customer defaults on the accounts receivable contract, the appliance is repossessed. During 1981 the following repossessions occurred:

	Original Sales Price	Unpaid Contract Balance
On 1980 contracts	$25,000	$13,500
On 1981 contracts	16,000	12,500

The wholesale value of these goods is estimated by the trade as follows:
(a) Goods repossessed during year of sale are valued at 50% of original sales price.
(b) Goods repossessed in later years are valued at 25% of original sales price.

Instructions:
(1) At what values should Napa Appliance report the trade-in and repossessed inventory at December 31, 1981?

(2) Give the entry that should have been made to record the repossession of 1977.

(3) Give the entry that is required to correct the trade-in summary entries.

7-15A. The Swenson Company, using the AICPA definition of market, values its perpetual inventory at the lower of fifo cost or market. The inventory accounts at December 31, 1980, had the following balances:

Raw Materials	$135,000
Allowance to Reduce Raw Material Inventory from Cost to Market	9,500
Work in Process	219,200
Finished Goods	342,000

The following are some of the transactions that affected the inventory of the Swenson Company during 1981:

Feb. 10   Purchased raw materials at an invoice price of $50,000; terms 3/15, n/30. Swenson Company uses the net method of valuing inventories.

Mar. 15   Swenson Company repossessed an inventory item from a customer who was overdue in making payment. The unpaid balance on the sale was $175. The repossessed merchandise is to be refinished and placed on sale. It is expected that the item can be sold for $250 after estimated refinishing cost of $50. The normal profit for this item is considered to be $40.

Apr. 1   Refinishing costs of $45 are incurred on the repossessed item.

Apr. 10   The repossessed item is resold for $230 on account; 20% down.

May 30   A sale on account is made of finished goods that have a list price of $740 and a cost of $480. A reduction from the list price of $100 is granted as a trade-in allowance. The trade-in item is to be priced to sell at $80 as is. The normal profit on this type of inventory is 25% of the sales price.

Nov. 30   Ordered materials to be delivered January 31, 1982, at a cost of $36,000. No discount terms were included.

Dec. 31   The following information was available to adjust the accounts for the annual statements:

    (a) The market value of the items ordered on November 30 had declined to $30,000.

    (b) The raw material inventory account had a cost balance of $184,000. Current market value was $169,000.

    (c) The finished goods inventory account had a cost balance of $296,000. Current market value was $315,000.

Instructions:
Record this information in journal entry form, including any required adjusting entries at December 31, 1981.

7.16A. Jesse Jones, a neighbour of yours, asks you to audit the accounts of a business he is negotiating to buy because he is concerned about the use of inconsistent inventory valuation methods. Jesse has agreed to a purchase price equal to the value of the total asset accounts less the current liabilities plus a premium of twice the 1980 net profit. This amounts to $820,000 as calculated from the statements presented on the next page.

Wiseman Enterprises
Income Statement
for the Year Ending December 31, 1980

Sales	$1,280,000
Less: Cost of goods sold	1,067,275
	$ 212,725
Operating expenses	32,725
Net profit	$ 180,000

Wiseman Enterprises
Balance Sheet
as at December 31, 1980

Assets	
Accounts receivable	$ 236,775
Inventory	133,225
	$ 370,000
Fixed assets (net)	250,000
Total assets	$ 620,000
Liabilities and Equity	
Accounts payable	$ 160,000
Owners' equity	460,000
Total liabilities and equity	$ 620,000

Your audit of Wiseman Enterprises, which was established January 1st, 1980, reveals the following inventory purchases:

	ITEM A			ITEM B			ITEM C		
Date	Quantity	Unit Price	Amount	Quantity	Unit Price	Amount	Quantity	Unit Price	Amount
Jan.	650	$20.00	$ 13,000	2200	$22.00	$ 48,400	300	$52.00	$ 15,600
Feb.	600	20.00	12,000	2300	23.00	52,900	400	51.00	20,400
Mar.	850	21.00	17,850	2300	24.00	55,200	400	51.00	20,400
Apr.	900	22.00	19,800	2400	24.00	57,600	400	50.00	20,000
May	800	22.00	17,600	2400	25.50	61,200	500	48.00	24,000
June	600	23.00	13,800	2300	27.00	62,100	500	47.00	23,500
July	600	24.00	14,400	2400	28.00	67,200	400	46.00	18,400
Aug.	500	23.00	11,500	2400	29.00	69,600	400	46.00	18,400
Sept.	800	22.00	17,600	2300	30.00	69,000	500	44.00	22,000
Oct.	900	21.50	19,350	2300	31.00	71,300	600	42.00	25,200
Nov.	650	20.00	13,000	2400	32.00	76,800	500	41.00	20,500
Dec.	750	20.00	15,000	2300	33.00	75,900	500	40.00	20,000
TOTAL	8600		$184,900	28000		$767,200	5400		$248,400

Closing Inventory Valuations:

Item	Quantity	Value
A	1,050	$ 22,575
B	2,500	82,300
C	550	28,350
		$133,225

There was no opening inventory.

Instructions:
(a) Determine how the closing inventory was valued.
(b) Determine the purchase price for the business based on the consistent use of each of the three most common methods of inventory valuation. (SMA adapted)

8
LAND, BUILDINGS, AND EQUIPMENT— ACQUISITION, USE, AND RETIREMENT

Land, buildings, and equipment is a classification heading for those tangible properties of a relatively permanent character used in the normal conduct of a business. Many other terms have been and are being used to describe such properties. *Fixed assets* is the term used by the Accounting Research Committee. However, it should be modified by *tangible* or *intangible* to distinguish between these two classes of assets. *Plant and equipment* is ambiguous because of the several connotations to the word *plant*. Plant could mean only the buildings, or perhaps buildings and land. *Property, plant and equipment* has been used frequently but it is also ambiguous. In this context, property means land, but in a more normal connotation, both plant and equipment are also property. The heading "Land, buildings, and equipment" is used throughout this text. "Property" is used as a general term referring to all three classes of items.

In common with other non-current assets, land, buildings, and equipment items do not turn over as frequently as current assets. Land, buildings, and equipment are acquired, used, and retired. Although these properties as a class remain as long as the business continues, the individual items, with the exception of land, have limited service lives. The costs of buildings and equipment are assigned to operations by means of periodic depreciation charges. When an item is no longer of economic benefit to the business, its costs should have been fully absorbed through these periodic charges.

COMPOSITION OF LAND, BUILDINGS, AND EQUIPMENT

Land refers to earth surface and includes building sites, yards, and parking areas. When natural resources in the form of mineral deposits, oil and gas wells, and timber are found on land, the aggregate acquisition, exploration, and development cost is frequently reported separately. Buildings refer to improvements permanently affixed to land and include not only structures in the form of factories, office buildings, storage quarters, and garages, but also structure facilities and appurtenances such as loading docks, heating and air conditioning systems, and walks and drives. Equipment consists of a wide variety of items including factory machines, hand and machine tools, patterns and dies, store and office equipment, and motor vehicles and other transport equipment. Items in the equipment group are frequently referred to as *personal property* or *personalty* as distinguished from the land and buildings group referred to as *real property* or *realty*.

CAPITAL AND REVENUE EXPENDITURES

The proper treatment of expenditures relative to the acquisition and use of property presents many accounting problems. Expenditures for property are made in anticipation of their favorable effects upon operations. In recording such expenditures, it must be determined whether favorable effects are limited to the current period or whether they extend into future periods. The underlying concept involved is the matching principle already described. An expenditure benefiting only the current period is called a *revenue expenditure* and is recorded as a period cost or expense. An expenditure benefiting operations beyond the current period is called a *capital expenditure* and is recorded as an asset. A property expenditure recorded as an asset is said to be *capitalized*.

Income cannot be fairly measured unless expenditures are properly identified and recorded as revenue or capital charges. For example, an incorrect debit to an equipment account instead of an expense results in the current overstatement of earnings on the income statement and the overstatement of assets and capital on the balance sheet. As the charge is assigned to operations in subsequent periods, earnings of such periods will be understated; assets and capital on the successive balance sheets will continue to be overstated, although by lesser amounts each year, until the asset is written off and the original error is fully counterbalanced. On the other hand, an incorrect debit to an expense instead of an equipment account results in the current understatement of earnings and the understatement of assets and capital. Earnings of subsequent periods will be overstated in the absence of debits for depreciation; assets and capital will continue to be understated, although by lesser amounts each year, until the original error is counterbalanced.

Although all property expenditures providing benefits beyond the current periods should be capitalized, companies frequently adopt an arbitrary practice of debiting to expense all expenditures not exceeding a certain amount, perhaps $50 or $100. This practice is adopted for the sake of expediency: the analysis of relatively small expenditures, as well as the application of depreciation procedures for them, is avoided. Adherence to such a practice is acceptable if it results in no material mistatement of property costs and periodic income.

VALUATION OF PROPERTY

Property items, just as all other facilities acquired by a business entity, are recognized initially at cost — the original bargained price. When payment for an asset is not made in the form of cash, the cash value of the consideration given in exchange must be established to arrive at cost. When it is not possible to arrive at a satisfactory cash value for the consideration transferred, the asset is reported at its present fair market value or, stated differently, the amount which would have been paid if it had been acquired in a cash transaction.[1] A similar procedure is followed for assets acquired through gift or discovery.

The cost of property includes not only the original purchase price or equivalent value, but also any other expenditures required in obtaining and preparing it for its intended use. Any taxes and duties, freight or cartage, and installation and other expenditures related to the acquisition should be added to the original outlay.

Property items are presented on the balance sheet at cost less the portion of cost assigned to past revenues. Land is normally considered to have an unlimited service life and, therefore, is reported at its original cost. In special cases where agricultural land may lose its fertility through use or erosion, or a building site may lose its utility through physical or environmental changes, reductions in cost to reflect the decline in asset usefulness may be appropriate. Natural resources are subject to exhaustion and are normally reported at cost less the portion of cost related to resources removed. This expired cost is referred to as *depletion*. All other property items are considered to have a limited service life and are normally reported at *cost less accumulated depreciation. Accumulated depreciation* is the portion of the asset cost written off by periodic depreciation charges since the acquisition of the asset. The difference between asset cost and accumulated depreciation is referred to as the asset *net book value*. Historically, no reference to market values or replace-

---

[1]*Opinions of the Accounting Principles Board, No. 29,* "Accounting for Nonmonetary Transactions" (New York: American Institute of Certified Public Accountants, 1973), par. 18.

ment values has been made in presenting property on the balance sheet. However, certain large corporations may be required, or otherwise voluntarily decide to disclose property items at their current values or at their costs adjusted for general price-level changes.[2]

ACQUISITION OF PROPERTY

There are a number of different ways in which property is acquired and each presents special problems relating to asset cost. The acquisition of properties is discussed under the following headings: (1) purchase for cash, (2) purchase on long-term contract, (3) exchange, (4) issuance of securities, (5) self-construction, and (6) donation or discovery.

Purchase for Cash

Property acquired for cash is recorded at the amount of the cash outlay, including all incidental outlays relating to its purchase or preparation for use.

As suggested in an earlier chapter, sound accounting theory requires discounts on purchases to be regarded as reductions in costs: earnings arise from sales, not from purchases. In applying this theory, any available discounts on property acquisitions should be treated as reductions to the asset cost. Failure to take such discounts should be reported as Discounts Lost or Interest Expense. The concept of materiality may serve to explain why this is not necessarily done in practice.

A number of property items may be acquired for one lump sum. Some of the assets may be depreciable, others non-depreciable. Depreciable assets may have different useful lives. If there is to be accountability for the assets on an individual basis, the total purchase price must be allocated among the individual assets. When part of a purchase price can be clearly identified with specific assets, such cost assignment should be made and the balance of the purchase price allocated among the remaining assets. When no part of the purchase price can be related to specific assets, the entire amount must be allocated among the different assets acquired. Appraisal values or similar evidence provided by a competent independent authority should be sought to support such allocation.

To illustrate the allocation of a joint asset cost, assume land, buildings, and equipment are acquired for $80,000. Assume further that assessed values for the individual assets as reported for property tax purposes are considered to provide an equitable basis for cost allocation. The allocation is made as shown at the top of the next page.

---

[2]These matters are discussed in Chapter 21.

	Assessed Values	Cost Allocation According to Relative Assessed Values	Cost Assigned to Individual Assets
Real properties:			
Land	$14,000	14,000/50,000 × $80,000	$22,400
Improvements (building)	30,000	30,000/50,000 × $80,000	48,000
Personal property (equipment)	6,000	6,000/50,000 × $80,000	9,600
	$50,000		$80,000

It is especially important that the value attributed to land be segregated, since land does not give rise to periodic depreciation charges.

An asset acquired in second-hand or used condition should be set up at its cost without reference to the balance found in the vendor's accounts. Expenditures to repair, recondition, or improve the asset before it is placed in use should be added to cost. It must be assumed that the buyer knew additional expenditures would be required when the purchase was made.

Purchase on Long-Term Contract

Real estate or other property is frequently acquired under contracts whereby payments are to be made over a number of years. Interest charged on the unpaid balance of the contract should be recognized as an expense. To illustrate the accounting for a long-term purchase contract, assume land is acquired for $100,000; $25,000 is paid at the time of purchase and the balance is to be paid in semi-annual instalments of $5,000, including interest on the unpaid principal at 8% per year. Entries for the purchase and for the first and second payments on the contract are shown on page 293.

In this example, the contract specified both a purchase price and interest at a stated rate on the unpaid balance. Sometimes, however, a contract may simply provide for a series of payments without reference to interest or may provide for a stated interest rate that is unreasonable in relation to market conditions. Although the Accounting Research Committee has yet to consider the issue, the Accounting Principles Board in the United States identified this type of contract in Opinion No. 21, "Interest on Receivables and Payables," and stated that:

> ... In these circumstances, the note, the sales price, and the cost of the property, goods, or service exchanged for the note should be recorded at the fair value of the property, goods or services or at an amount that reasonably approximates the market value of the note, whichever is the more clearly determinable. That amount may or may not be the same as its face amount, and any resulting discount or premium should be accounted for as an element of interest over the life of the note. In the absence of established exchange prices for the related property, goods, or service or evidence of the market value of the note, the

TRANSACTION	ENTRY

January 2, 1981 Purchased land for $100,000 paying $25,000 down, the balance to be paid in semi-annual payments of $5,000 including interest at 8%.	Land 100,000
	    Cash 25,000
	    Contract Payable . . 75,000

June 30, 1981 Made first payment:
 Amount of payment $5,000
 Amount representing interest, 4% of
   of unpaid balance of $75,000 . . .   3,000
 Balance — reduction in principal . . . $2,000
	Interest Expense 3,000
	 Contract Payable 2,000
	    Cash 5,000

December 31, 1981 Made second payment:
 Amount of payment $5,000
 Amount representing interest, 4% of
   unpaid balance of $73,000
   ($75,000 − $2,000)   2,920
 Balance — reduction in principal . $2,080
	Interest Expense . . 2,920
	 Contract Payable . . 2,080
	    Cash 5,000

present value of a note that stipulates either no interest or a rate of interest that is clearly unreasonable should be determined by discounting all future payments on the notes using an imputed rate of interest. . . .[3]

To illustrate the accounting for this type of long-term contract, assume that certain equipment is acquired at a price of $40,000; the down payment is $10,000, and the balance is payable in four equal annual instalments of $7,500. Assume further that, although there is no interest rate specified in the contract, it is fair to assume that the contract price involves implicit interest at 8%. The cost of the equipment, then, should be regarded as the discounted value at 8% of instalments of $7,500 due in one, two, three and four years, plus the down payment. The present value of the contract, including the down payment, is $34,840.75.[4] The obligation is recorded by a credit to Contract Payable for $30,000 and a debit to a discount on the payable for $5,159.25, or a net obligation of $24,840.75. The 8% rate is applied to the declining debt balance in subsequent periods in amortizing the debt discount. Entries for the acquisition of the property item, and the first periodic payment are as follows:

---

[3]*Opinions of the Accounting Principles Board, No. 21*, "Interest on Receivables and Payables" (New York: American Institute of Certified Public Accountants, 1971), par. 12.

[4]$PV_n = R(PVAF_{n|i})$

$PV_n = \$7,500$ (Table $IV_{4|8\%}$) $= \$7,500\ (3.3121) = \$24,840.75$. The total contract equals the down payment plus the present value of four instalments: ($10,000 + $24,840.75 = $34,840.75).

TRANSACTION	ENTRY

January 2, 1981
Purchased equipment at a price of $40,000 paying $10,000 down, the balance in four equal instalments of $7,500. It is assumed that interest at 8% is implicit in the purchase price and the obligation is recorded at its present value of $24,840.75 ($30,000.00 − $5,159.25).
	Equipment 34,840.75
	Discount on Equipment
	Contract Payable 5,159.25
	  Cash 10,000.00
	  Equipment Contract
	  Payable 30,000.00

December 31, 1981
Made first payment of $7,500.
Amortization of debt discount:
8% × $24,840.75 = $1,987.26.
	Equipment Contract
	Payable 7,500.00
	  Cash 7,500.00
	Interest Expense 1,987.26
	  Discount on Equipment
	  Contract Payable 1,987.26

Handwritten annotations:
$8\% \times (22,500 - 3171.99) = 1,546.24$
$\checkmark\ (15,000 - 1625.75) = 1,069.94$
$\checkmark\ (7,500 - 555.81)\qquad 555.54$
$.27$ rounding
$\underline{5159.25}$

When a cash price is quoted for a property item, this amount may be used in recording the property item and in recognizing the present value of the debt. In such instances, the debt discount may be amortized either by (1) calculating the effective or implicit interest rate and applying this to the declining debt balance as in the previous example, or (2) developing fractions expressing the dollar debt for the period to the dollar debt for the life of the contract and applying them to the debt discount, or (3) in Canadian practice, by means of the straight-line method of amortization.

To illustrate the second and third procedures, assume that in the preceding example the equipment is quoted at a cash price of $35,000. The equipment, then, would be reported at $35,000, cash would be credited for the down payment of $10,000, and a payable would be recognized for $30,000 less a discount of $5,000. Discount amortization may be calculated as follows:

Year	Liability Balance	Fraction of Discount to be Amortized	Annual Discount Amortization (Fraction × $5,000)	($5,000 ÷ 4)
1981	$30,000	300/750	$2,000	$1,250
1982	22,500	225/750	1,500	1,250
1983	15,000	150/750	1,000	1,250
1984	7,000	75/750	500	1,250
	$75,000	750/750	$5,000	$5,000

The only advantage of straight-line amortization is its simplicity. It lacks theoretical merit because it fails to recognize the year-by-year decline in the liability balance. Nonetheless, the method is generally accepted in Canada and, as a result, is widely used.

Property may be acquired under a conditional sales contract whereby legal title to the asset is retained by the vendor until payments are completed. The failure to acquire legal title may be disregarded by the buyer and the transaction recognized in terms of its substance — the acquisition of an asset and the assumption of a liability. The buyer has the possession and use of the asset and must absorb any decline in its value; title to the asset is retained by the vendor simply as a means of assuring payment of the purchase contract. In reporting the asset on the balance sheet prior to full settlement, there should be disclosure by parenthetical remark or note indicating legal title to the asset still remains with the vendor.

Acquisition by Exchange

When one non-monetary asset[5] is traded for another, the new asset generally should be recorded at the fair market value of the asset given up, or the fair market value of the asset received if its fair market value is more clearly evident.[6] If a used asset is surrendered for a new asset, the fair market value of the new asset is often more clearly evident than the market value of the old asset, and thus would be used to value the exchange. Care must be taken to determine the true market value of the new asset. Frequently, the quoted list price is not a good indicator of market because it may be higher than the actual cash price that would be paid for the new asset. The price for which the asset could be acquired in a strictly cash transaction is the fair market value that should be used.

Any difference between the fair market value assigned to the asset received and the net book value (carrying value) of the old asset should be recognized as a gain or loss on the exchange. If the exchange involves a monetary payment, the new asset should be recorded at the sum of the value of the monetary asset and the fair market value of the surrendered asset. Any trade-in allowance should be carefully examined to determine whether it measures fairly the value of the asset exchanged. The use of an inflated trade-in allowance as representative of the market value of the surrendered asset will result in the overstatement of the newly acquired asset and also in the subsequent overstatement of depreciation charges. The newly acquired asset should be recorded at no more than the cash price that would be paid in the absence of a trade-in.

To illustrate an exchange involving non-similar, non-monetary assets, assume equipment with an original cost of $5,000 and a net book value of $3,000 is accepted at a trade-in value of $2,600 in part payment on a truck

---

[5]*Monetary assets* are those whose amounts are fixed in terms of units of currency by contract or otherwise. Examples include cash and short or long-term accounts receivable. *Non-monetary assets* include all other assets, such as inventories, land, buildings, and equipment.

[6]*Opinions of the Accounting Principles Board, No. 29, op. cit.*, par. 18.

with a fair market value of $3,200. The difference of $600 is paid in cash. The following entry would be made to record the exchange:

Trucks	3,200	
Accumulated Depreciation — Equipment	2,000	
Loss on Exchange of Equipment	400	
Equipment		5,000
Cash		600

Computation:

Accumulated depreciation:
$5,000 cost − $3,000 net book value = $2,000 accumulated depreciation.
Loss:
$3,000 net book value − $2,600 trade-in allowance = $400 loss.

A loss of $400 is recognized because the net book value of $3,000 is greater than the trade-in allowance of $2,600.

If, in the above example, the truck could have been acquired at a cash price of $2,800, this value should have been used in recording the asset rather than the inflated trade-in allowance. Although the trade-in allowance on the old equipment was stated at $2,600, this asset apparently had an actual worth of no more than $2,200 ($2,800 − $600); the loss on the exchange was $800, the difference between the actual trade-in value of the surrendered asset, $2,200 and its net book value, $3,000.

In the example, the asset was assumed to have been exchanged at the beginning of a fiscal period. When a depreciable asset is exchanged during the fiscal period, depreciation should be recognized to the date of the exchange, and the entry to record the exchange should recognize the net book value of the asset at that date.

Acquisition by Issuance of Securities

A company may acquire property by issuing its own bonds or shares. When a market value for the securities can be determined, such value is assigned to the asset; in the absence of a market value for the securities, the fair market value of the asset would be sought. If bonds are selling at more or less than their face or par value, the asset should be reported at the current cash value; Bonds Payable should be credited at par and a premium or discount should be established for the difference. To illustrate, assume a company issues bonds of $100,000 in acquiring land; the bonds are currently selling on the market at 95. An entry should be made as follows:

Land...	95,000	
Discount on Bonds Payable	5,000	
Bonds Payable		100,000

Thus, the value of the securities is set as of the time of the issuance and at a price established by market conditions.

When securities do not have an established market value, appraisal of the assets by an independent authority may be required to arrive at an objective determination of their fair market value. If satisfactory market values cannot be obtained for either the securities issued or the assets acquired, values as established by the board of directors may have to be accepted for accounting purposes. For example, assume a corporation issues shares in payment for certain mining property. A market value cannot be established for the shares, and there are no means of arriving at a fair market value for the property received. If the board of directors values the property at $100,000, the property value and the issuing price of the shares are thereby set at this amount. Disclosure of the source of the valuation should be provided on the balance sheet. The assignment of values by the board of directors is normally not subject to challenge unless it can be shown that the board has acted fraudulently. Nevertheless, evidence should be sought to validate the fairness of original valuations, and if within a short time after an acquisition, the sale of shares or other information indicates that original valuations were erroneous, appropriate action should be taken to restate asset and owners' equity accounts.

Property is frequently acquired in exchange for securities pursuant to a corporate combination. When the combination is designated a purchase for accounting purposes, the acquired assets are reported at their cost to the new owner, that is, fair market value as at the date of combination. But, in the rare event the combination is designated a pooling of interests accounting authorities permit recording properties at the values shown in the accounts of the acquired company. Specific guidelines for distinguishing between a purchase and a pooling of interests are included in Section 1580 of the *Accounting Recommendations*.

Acquisition by Self-Construction

Sometimes buildings or equipment items are constructed by a company for its own use. This may be done to save on construction costs, to utilize idle facilities, or to achieve a higher quality of construction. When construction takes place, a number of special problems arise in arriving at asset cost.

Overhead Chargeable to Self-Construction. All costs that can be related to construction should be charged to the assets under construction. There is no question about the inclusion of material and labor charges directly attributable to the new construction. However, there is a difference of opinion regarding the amount of overhead properly assignable to the construction activity. Some accountants take the position that assets under construction should be charged with no more than the incremental overhead — the increase in a company's total overhead resulting from the special construction activity. Others maintain that overhead should be assigned to construction just as it is assigned to normal operations. This would call for the inclusion of not only the increase in overhead resulting from construction activities but also a pro rata share of the company's fixed overhead.

Those supporting charges for overhead limited to incremental amounts maintain that the cost of construction is actually no more than the extra costs incurred. Normal operations should receive no special favors as a result of construction. Management is aware of the cost of normal operations and decides to undertake a project on the basis of the anticipated added costs. Those taking the position that construction should carry a fair share of the fixed overhead maintain this must be done if the full cost of the asset is to be reported. It is their view that construction is entitled to no special favors, and this practice should be followed even though general operations are relieved of a portion of the overhead that they would normally carry; overhead has served a double purpose during the construction period and this is properly reflected in reduced operating costs. The latter argument may be particularly persuasive if construction takes place during a period of subnormal operations and utilizes what would otherwise represent idle capacity cost, or if construction restricts production or other regular business activities.

The assignment to construction of normal overhead otherwise chargeable to current operations will increase net income during the construction period. The recognition of a portion of overhead is postponed and related to subsequent periods through charges in the form of depreciation.

Companies have not been successful in coming to an agreement on this issue. Authors of a research study for the AICPA have suggested the following criterion to help resolve the issue.

> . . . in the absence of compelling evidence to the contrary, overhead costs considered to have "discernible future benefits" for the purpose of determining the cost of inventory should be presumed to have "discernible future benefits" for the purpose of determining the cost of a self-constructed depreciable asset.[7]

This criterion would charge both normal and incremental overhead costs to self-constructed fixed assets and have the advantage of providing consistency within a company in the treatment of overhead costs.

Saving or Loss on Self-Construction. When the cost of self-construction of an asset is less than the cost to acquire it through purchase or construction by outsiders, the difference for accounting purposes is not a profit but a *saving*. The construction is properly reported at its actual cost. The saving will emerge as income over the life of the asset as lower depreciation is charged against periodic revenue. Assume, on the other hand, the cost of self-construction is greater than bids originally received for the construction. There is generally no assurance that the asset under alternative arrange-

---

[7]Charles Lamden, Dale L. Gerboth, and Thomas McRae, "Accounting for Depreciable Assets," *Accounting Research Monograph No. 1* (New York: American Institute of Certified Public Accountants, 1975), p. 57.

ments might have been equal in quality to that which was self-constructed. In recording this transaction, just as in recording others, accounts should reflect those courses of action taken, not the alternatives that might have been selected. At the same time, if there is evidence indicating cost has been materially excessive because of certain construction inefficiencies or failures, the excess is properly recognized as a loss; subsequent periods should not be burdened with charges for depreciation arising from costs that could have been avoided.

Interest During Period of Construction. In public utility accounting, interest during a period of building construction is recognized as a part of asset cost. This practice applies both to interest actually paid and to an implicit interest charge if the public utility uses its own funds. Interest, then, emerges as a charge for depreciation in the periods in which the properties are income-producing. Service rates established by regulatory bodies are based upon current charges and may provide for a recovery of past interest in this manner.

The practice of capitalizing interest has sometimes been carried into accounting for industrial companies. Support for this practice is made on the grounds that interest is a cost of construction, and the proper matching of revenues and expenses suggests it be deferred and charged over the life of the constructed asset. It can also be argued that if buildings or equipment were acquired by purchase rather than by self-construction, a charge for interest during the construction period would be implicit in the purchase price.

Arguments advanced against this practice are:

1. It is difficult to follow cash once it is invested in a firm. Is the interest charge really related to the constructed asset, or is it a payment made to meet general financial needs? Even when a loan is made for specific purposes, it frees cash raised by other means to be used for other projects.
2. To be consistent, implicit interest on all funds used, not just borrowed funds, should be charged to the asset cost. This practice is followed in utility accounting and requires determining a cost of capital for internal funds used, a very difficult task.

Traditionally, non-utility companies have not capitalized interest. However, in the mid-1970s an increasing number of companies changed their accounting method to a policy of capitalizing interest, an action that tended to increase net income. In reaction to these changes, the Securities and Exchange Commission, in the United States, declared a moratorium on companies changing their methods of accounting for interest costs pending study of the issue by the Financial Accounting Standards Board.[8] FASB Statement No. 34, *Capitalization of Interest Costs*, issued in 1980, established

[8] Securities and Exchange Commission, *Accounting Series Release No. 163*, "Capitalization of Interest by Companies Other than Public Utilities" (Washington: U.S. Government Printing Office, 1974).

standards for interest capitalization where assets require a period of time before they can be used for their intended purpose and the effect of capitalization compared to expensing would be material.[9] Capitalization of interest has yet to emerge as an accounting issue.

Development Stage Expenditures

Some have maintained that all charges for interest, taxes, and general and administrative services during the development stage of a new company should be capitalized. Support for this procedure is based on the theory that future periods are benefited by necessary initial costs and it is unreasonable to assume losses have been incurred before sales activities begin. The Financial Accounting Standards Board reviewed this practice and concluded that accounting principles for companies in the organizational or developmental stage should be the same as for more mature companies. No special rules or principles should apply. Therefore, capitalization policies would not be different for these companies, and the above expenditures should be expensed in the period incurred.[10]

Acquisition by Gift or Discovery

When property is received by way of a gift there is no cost that can be used as a basis for its valuation. Even though certain expenditures may have to be made incident to the gift, these expenditures are generally considerably less than the value of the property. Since cost obviously fails to provide a satisfactory basis for asset accountability, as well as for future income measurement, property acquired through gift could be appraised and recorded as its fair market value. In such circumstances, one accounting method, known as the *capital approach*, would credit contributed surplus with the fair market value of the property acquired through donation. An alternative method, the *income approach*, is based on the premise that the donation confers a benefit which should be reflected in the measurement of income.

In practice, acquisition by gift or donation is part and parcel of accounting for governmental assistance. It is only on rare occasions that a corporation is likely to receive property through donation from a shareholder or shareholders. The more usual source of donation, or at least of assistance, comes from various levels of government. Some programs of government assistance are concerned with the acquisition of property; however, the term encompasses a broad range of government actions intended to influence business decisions on matters such as capital investment, employment, and location.

---

[9]*Statement of Financial Accounting Standards No. 34*, "Capitalization of Interest Costs" (Stamford, Conn.: Financial Accounting Standards Board, 1980).

[10]*Statement of Financial Accounting Standards No. 7*, "Accounting and Reporting by Development Stage Enterprises" (Stamford, Conn.: Financial Accounting Standards Board, 1975), par. 10.

Accounting for government assistance is the subject matter of Section 3800 of the *Accounting Recommendations*, issued in August, 1976. As between the capital and income approaches, the Accounting Research Committee concluded that the arguments in favor of the latter were more persuasive. Section 3800 describes the income approach as follows.[11]

> The income approach requires that government assistance be credited to income in the following ways, depending upon its nature:
> (a) direct increases in revenues, or reductions in expenses;
> (b) reduced depreciation and amortization charges based on reduced asset costs;
> (c) amortization of deferred credits.

In the context of property, therefore, government assistance should be either (1) deducted from the related fixed assets with depreciation determined on the net amount, or (2) deferred, and amortized to income on the same basis as the related property is being depreciated.[12]

In the rare event of property acquisition by way of shareholder(s) donation, the capital approach is still the generally accepted accounting method. To illustrate, if shareholders donate land and buildings appraised at $50,000 and $150,000 respectively, the entry in the accounts of the recipient would be:

Land	50,000	
Buildings	150,000	
Donated Capital		200,000

Depreciation of an asset acquired by gift should be recorded in the usual manner; the value assigned to the asset providing the basis for the depreciation charge. The credit to Donated Capital should be shown as contributed surplus for balance sheet purposes.

Occasionally, valuable resources are discovered on land already owned. The discovery greatly increases the value of the property. However, because the cost of the land is not affected by the discovery, it is common practice to ignore this increase in value. Similarly, the increase in value for assets that change over time, such as growing timber or ageing wine, is ignored in common practice. Failure to recognize these discovery or accretion values ignores the economic reality of the situation and tends to materially understate the assets of the entity. More meaningful decisions could probably be made if the user of the statements was aware of these changes in value.

Section 3060 of the *Accounting Recommendations* contains a provision that authorizes the valuation of property on the basis of an appraisal, and imposes disclosure requirements that within certain time periods such information as the name of the appraiser, the basis of the valuation, and the

---

[11]*CICA Handbook: Accounting Recommendations, Section 3800*, "Accounting for Government Assistance" (Toronto: Canadian Institute of Chartered Accountants, 1975), par. 08.
[12]*Ibid.*, par. 26.

disposition of the appraisal adjustments be disclosed.[13] In general the adjustments should show up in shareholders' equity where it should be shown separately as an appraisal increase credit.[14]

Since the valuation of property at appraised values is a departure from the cost concept, the practice is indeed rare. Section 3060 states that there may be instances where it is appropriate to reflect property at values which are different from historical costs. Only one example is cited — at appraised values assigned in a reorganization.[15] Certainly there is no valid basis for concluding that the *Accounting Recommendations* intend appraisals as a generally accepted method for reflecting value changes relating to either discovery or accretion.

Special Problems

Special accounting problems arise in recording the acquisition of certain property items. Attention is directed in the following sections to specific properties and their special problems.

Land. Rights to land arising from *purchase* should be distinguished from rights under *leaseholds* and under *easements*. With a purchase, the buyer acquires title and ownership *in fee simple*, and the property is properly recognized as an asset. A leasehold provides rights for the *possession and profits* of land for a certain period. An easement provides rights for the *use* of land as in the case of rights-of-way or other special privileges. Recognition of asset balances for leaseholds and easements is limited to prepayments of rents and fees to the owners of land for the acquired rights unless the leasehold or easement is in substance a purchase. In this case, the present value of future rental payments should be capitalized.[16]

When land is purchased, its cost includes not only the negotiated purchase price but also all other costs related to the acquisition including brokers' commissions, legal fees, title, recording, escrow, and surveying fees. Any existing unpaid taxes, interest, or other liens on the property assumed by the buyer are added to cost.

Costs of clearing, grading, subdividing, landscaping, or otherwise permanently improving the land after its acquisition should also be treated as increases in the cost of land. When a site secured for a new plant is already occupied by a building that must be torn down, the cost of removing the old structure less any recovery from salvage is added to land cost. If salvage exceeds the cost of razing buildings, the excess may be considered a reduc-

---

[13]*CICA Handbook: Accounting Recommendations*, Section 3060, "Fixed Assets" (Toronto: Canadian Institute of Chartered Accountants, 1968), par. 04.
[14]*CICA Handbook: Accounting Recommendations*, Section 3270, "Appraisal Increase Credits" (Toronto: Canadian Institute of Chartered Accountants, 1968), par. 02.
[15]*CICA Handbook: Accounting Recommendations*, Section 3060, *op. cit.*, par. 01.
[16]See Chapter 15 for discussion of capitalization of leases.

tion of land cost. Special assessments by governments for certain local benefits, such as streets and sidewalks, lighting, and sewers and drainage systems that will be maintained by the government, may be regarded as permanently improving land and are thus chargeable to this asset. When expenditures are incurred for land improvements having a limited life and requiring ultimate replacement as, for example, paving, fencing, and water and sewage systems, such costs should be summarized separately in an account entitled Land Improvements and depreciated over the estimated useful life of the improvements. The useful life of some improvements may be limited to the life of the buildings on the land; other improvements may have an independent service life.

Land qualifies for presentation in the land, buildings, and equipment category only when it is being used in the normal activities of the business. For example, land held for future use or for speculation should be reported under the long-term investments heading; land held for current sale should be reported as a current asset. A descriptive account title should be used to distinguish land not used in normal operations from land in use.

When land is acquired and held for future use or as a speculative venture, a question arises as to the proper treatment of the charges of carrying such property. Should expenditures for taxes and interest on mortgages, for example, be charged to periodic revenue or be added to the cost of the land? There is strong support for adding these charges to land. The buyer knows that costs will be involved in holding the land before it can be applied to the specific purpose for which it is acquired and makes the purchase with the expectation that the investment will yield benefits exceeding both the original cost and carrying charges. When carrying charges are capitalized, the full cost of the investment can be assigned to the purpose for which it is ultimately applied.

To illustrate, assume that in 1981 a company acquires land for expansion purposes although it does not expect to use the land until 1991. Cost of the land is $40,000; taxes and other carrying charges are estimated at $20,000 for the ten-year period. Under these circumstances, the company has actually made a decision to invest $60,000 in land instead of delaying action until some later date when efforts toward expansion might find circumstances less favorable. Or assume that in 1981 land is acquired as a speculative investment for $40,000 and that it is ultimately sold in 1991 for $75,000, carrying charges during the ten-year period having totalled $20,000. Here too, the investment in land may be regarded as $60,000 and the gain as $15,000. The land represented, in effect, work in process during the holding period; $75,000 is ultimately realized on an investment totalling $60,000. If carrying charges had been assigned to the periodic revenues, net income during the ten-year holding period would have been reduced by $20,000 and a gain of $35,000 would be reported on the sale of the property. The latter treatment fails to offer a satisfactory accounting for periodic earnings and for the gain emerging from the investment.

It is difficult to support capitalizing expenditures for carrying assets when market values fail to confirm increasing property values; here conservatism requires the treatment of such expenditures as charges against periodic revenues. The capitalization procedure is likewise inappropriate when land is used for such purposes as rental or farming and produces current revenue; expenditures under these circumstances should be treated as charges against such revenue.

Carrying charges on investments in land are sometimes recorded as expenses rather than as part of the cost of land. In reporting land held as a long-term investment on the balance sheet it is desirable to indicate parenthetically or in a note the cost procedure employed for the asset as well as its current fair market value when this can be supported by objective evidence.

Buildings. A purchase involving the acquisition of both land and buildings requires the cost to be allocated between the two assets. Allocable cost consists of the purchase price plus all charges incident to the purchase. The cost allocated to buildings is increased by expenditures for reconditioning and repairs in preparing the asset for use as well as by expenditures for improvements and additions.

When buildings are constructed, their cost consists of materials, labor, and overhead related to construction. Costs of excavation or grading and filing required for purposes of the specific project, rather than for making land usable, are charged to buildings. Charges for architects' fees, building permits and fees, workmen's compensation and accident insurance, fire insurance for the period of construction, and temporary buildings used for construction activities, form part of the total building cost. Taxes on property improvements, as well as financing costs during a period of construction, are generally capitalized as a cost of buildings.

It was suggested earlier that when land and buildings are acquired and buildings are immediately demolished, the cost of demolishing buildings is added to land as a cost of preparing land for its intended use. However, the cost of demolishing buildings that have been previously occupied by the company requires different treatment. This is a cost that should be identified with the life of the original buildings. The recovery of salvage upon asset retirement serves to reduce the cost arising from the use of an asset and is frequently anticipated in calculating periodic charges for depreciation; a cost arising from asset retirement serves to increase the cost of asset use but is seldom anticipated in developing periodic charges for depreciation.

In many instances, careful analysis is required in determining whether an expenditure should be recognized as buildings or whether it should be identified with the land or equipment categories. For example, expenditures for sidewalks and roads that are part of a building program are normally reported as buildings, but these would be properly reported as land improvements when they improve land regardless of its use; expenditures for items such as shelving, cabinets, or partitions in the course of building construction are normally reported as buildings, but these would be properly reported as equipment items when they are movable, can be used in different centres, and are considered to have independent lives. Particular care should be directed to charges against revenues under different classification and recording alternatives. Frequently alternative classifications can be supported and the ultimate choice will be a matter of judgment.

If depreciation on buildings is to be recognized satisfactorily, separate accounts should be maintained for each building with a different life as well as for those structural elements of a building requiring modification or replacement before the building is fully depreciated, such as loading and shipping quarters, storage facilities, and garages. Separate recording should also be extended to building equipment and appurtenances requiring replacement before the building is fully depreciated, such as boilers, heating and ventilating systems, plumbing and lighting systems, elevators, and wiring and piping installations. The latter items are frequently summarized in an account titled Building Equipment or Building Improvements, but detailed records will be required in support of this balance because of the different service lives of the individual items.

Equipment. Equipment covers a wide range of items that vary with the particular enterprise and its activities. The discussion in the following paragraphs is limited to machinery, tools, patterns and dies, furniture and fixtures, motor vehicles, and returnable containers.

Machinery of the manufacturing concern includes such items as lathes, stamping machines, ovens, and conveyor systems. The machinery account is debited for all expenditures identified with the acquisition and the preparation for use of factory machines. Machinery cost includes the purchase price, taxes, and duties on purchase, freight charges, insurance charges while in transit, installation charges, expenditures for testing and final preparation for use, and costs for reconditioning used equipment when purchased.

Two classes of tools are employed in productive activities: (1) machine tools, representing detachable parts of a machine, such as dies, drills, and punches; and (2) hand tools, such as hammers, wrenches, and saws. Both classes of tools are normally of small individual cost and are relatively short-lived as a result of wear, breakage, and loss. These factors frequently suggest that these items be accounted for as a single asset. Replacement of these small tools may then either be charged directly to expense or added to the single asset account and written off by reasonable annual amortization charges.

Patterns and dies are acquired for designing, stamping, cutting, or forging out a particular object. The cost of patterns and dies is either a purchase cost or a developmental cost composed of labor, materials, and overhead. When patterns and dies are used in normal productive activities, their cost is reported as an asset and the asset values are written off over the period of their usefulness. When the use of such items is limited to the manufacture of a single job, their cost is recognized as a part of the cost of that job.

Furniture and fixtures include such items as desks, chairs, carpets, showcases, and display fixtures. Acquisitions should be identified with production, selling, or general and administrative functions. Such classification makes it possible to assign depreciation accurately to the different business activities. Furniture and fixtures are recorded at cost, which includes purchase price, tax, freight, and installation charges.

Automobile and truck acquisitions should also be identified with production, selling, or general and administrative functions. Depreciation can then be accurately related to the different activities. Automotive equipment is recorded at its purchase price increased by any sales and excise tax and delivery charges paid. When payment for equipment includes charges for items, such as current licence fees, personal property tax, and insurance, these should be recognized separately as expenses relating to both the current and the future use of the equipment.

Goods are frequently delivered in containers to be returned and reused. Returnable containers consist of such items as tanks, drums, and barrels. Containers are depreciable assets used in the business and are included in the equipment group. Adjustments must be made periodically to reduce the asset account and its related accumulated depreciation for containers not expected to be returned. The reduction is reported as a current loss.

EXPENDITURES INCURRED DURING SERVICE LIFE OF PROPERTY ITEMS

During the lives of property items, regular as well as special expenditures are incurred. Certain expenditures are required to maintain and repair assets; others are incurred to increase their capacity or efficiency or to extend their useful lives. Each expenditure requires careful analysis to determine whether it should be assigned to revenue of the current period, hence charged to an expense account, or whether it should be assigned to revenue of more than one period, which calls for a debit to an asset account or to an accumulated depreciation account. In many cases the answer may not be clear, and the procedure chosen may be a matter of judgment.

The terms maintenance, repairs, betterments, improvements, additions, and rearrangements are used in describing expenditures made in the course of asset use. These are described in the following sections.

Maintenance

Expenditures to maintain assets in fit conditions are referred to as *maintenance*. Since maintenance items are ordinary and recurring and do not improve the asset or add to its life, they are recorded as expenses.

Repairs

Expenditures to restore assets to a fit condition upon their breakdown or to restore and replace broken parts are referred to as *repairs*. When these expenditures are ordinary and benefit only current operations, they are debited to expense. When they are extraordinary and extend the life of the asset, they may be debited to the accumulated depreciation account. The depreciation rate may then be redetermined in recognition of any changes in the asset value and estimated life. Debits for repairs extending the useful life of the asset are made against the accumulated depreciation account to avoid a build-up of gross asset values. The net book value of the asset will be the same whether the debit is made to the asset account directly or to the accumulated depreciation account.

Repairs involving the overhauling of certain assets are frequently referred to as *renewals*. Substitutions of parts or entire units are referred to as *replacements*. The cost of the replacement may be expensed or capitalized depending upon how the property unit is defined. For example, components of a major piece of equipment, such as the motor, the frame, and the attachments, may be considered separate property units, or the entire machine may be considered the property unit. If the component parts are the property units, replacement of a component requires entries canceling the net book value related to the old component and capitalizing the cost of the new equipment. If the property unit is the entire machine, the replacement of the component would be debited to an expense if it is considered to be a normal replacement, or debited to accumulated depreciation if it is considered to be an extraordinary replacement. General criteria as to what constitutes a property unit have not been developed by the profession. Companies have had to establish their own guidelines and consistently apply them. Research indicates that companies do not feel that this lack of guidelines has led to serious abuses in practice.[17]

Repairs arising from flood, fire, or other casualty require special analysis. An expenditure to restore an asset to its previous condition should be reported as a loss from casualties that should qualify for income statement presentation as an extraordinary item.

---

[17]Lamden, Berboth, and McRae, *op. cit.*, pp. 48-49.

Betterments or Impovements

Changes in assets designed to provide increased or improved services are referred to as *betterments* or *improvements*. Installation of improved lighting systems, heating systems, or sanitary systems represent betterments. Minor expenditures for betterments may be recorded as ordinary repairs. Major expenditures call for entries to cancel the net book value related to the old asset and to establish the new, or entries to reduce the accumulated depreciation related to the original asset. The latter method is sometimes required when the cost of the item replaced is not readily separable from the whole unit.

Additions

Enlargements and extensions of existing facilities are referred to as *additions*. A new plant wing, additional loading docks, or the expansion of a paved parking lot represent additions. These expenditures are capitalized, and the cost is written off over the service life of the addition.

Rearrangements

Movement of machinery and equipment items and reinstallations to secure economies or greater efficiencies are referred to as *rearrangements*. Costs related to rearrangements should be assigned to those periods benefiting from such changes. When more than one period is benefited, an asset account — appropriately designated to indicate the nature of the cost deferral — should be established and this balance allocated systematically to revenue. When rearrangements involve reinstallation costs, the portion of asset net book value related to an original installation should be cancelled; the cost of the new installation should be added to the asset and written off over its remaining life.

Establishment of Allowance for Repairs and Parts Replacements

When certain relatively large repair and parts replacement charges are expected at irregular intervals during the life of an asset, provision may be made to charge operations not only with a share of the original cost of the asset but also with a share of the total repair and replacement charges anticipated over the life of the asset. An expense account may be debited periodically and a repairs and replacements allowance account credited for the estimated repairs and replacements. If this is done, repairs and replacements, when incurred, are properly debited to the allowance. To illustrate, a new roof for a building does not increase the original estimated service life of the building, but it may represent a relatively heavy charge if made against the revenue of a single fiscal period. If an allowance for repairs and replacements has been set up by periodic charges to operations, the expenditure for the new roof can be debited to this allowance. Each period is thus charged with its share of the charges of this kind, and an unreasonably large charge against the revenue of a single period is avoided. In preparing the balance sheet, the building account would be reduced by both accumulated depreciation and the allowance for repairs and replacements. The allowance for repairs and replacements may be regarded as reflecting the above-normal depreciation of certain components of the property item.

If a business has many equipment items of different ages in service, total repairs and replacements charges may not vary significantly from period to period, and little may be gained by establishing an allowance. Charges for repairs and replacements are deductible for tax purposes only when the expenditures are made. Therefore, an allowance for repairs and replacements results in a timing difference between accounting income and taxable income and the recognition of deferred income taxes.[18]

It should be observed that irregular charges for major repairs and parts replacements are largely avoided when individual accounts are established for each separate component of an asset item deemed to have an independent life. Instead of a single depreciation rate applied to a composite asset, individual rates are applied to the separate asset components. Major expenditures during the life of the property item are reported as newly acquired asset components, and balances related to original components are cancelled. Although it may require considerable analysis and detailed records, this procedure has merit in achieving fairer assignments of expenses to revenue.

PROPERTY RETIREMENTS

Properties may be retired by sale, trade, scrapping and removal, or abandonment. When properties are disposed of, both property and accumulated depreciation accounts are cancelled and a gain or loss is recognized for the difference between the amount recovered on the asset and its net book value or carrying value.

In recording a disposal, it is necessary to follow the practice adopted by the entity for recognizing depreciation for fractional periods. Various practices are employed including the following:

1. Depreciation is recognized on the asset from the time it is acquired to the time it is retired.
2. Depreciation is recognized at the annual rate on the beginning-of-year balance in the asset account plus or minus depreciation at one half the annual rate on the net additions or subtractions in the account for the year. The

---

[18]Accounting for income tax is considered in detail in Chapter 14.

effect of this procedure is to recognize depreciation for one-half year on all acquisitions and all retirements.

3. Depreciation is recognized at the annual rate on the beginning-of-year balance in the asset account. Thus, no depreciation is recognized on acquisitions during the year but depreciation for a full year is recognized on retirements.
4. Depreciation is recogonized at the annual rate of the end-of-year-balance in the asset account. Thus, depreciation is recognized for a full year on acquisitions during the year but no depreciation is recognized on retirements.

Methods (2), (3), and (4) are attractive because of their simplicity. However, method (1) provides greatest accuracy and its use is assumed unless some alternate policy is specifically stated. In applying method (1), depreciation, rather than being recognized on as short a period as a day or a week, would normally be calculated to the nearest month: no charge would be made for an asset used for less than half a month; a charge for a full month would be recognized for an asset used for more than half of a month.

To illustrate the entries for asset retirement, assume it is decided to sell certain machinery. The machinery was originally acquired on November 20, 1972, for $10,000 and had been depreciated at 10% per year. The asset is sold on April 10, 1981, for $1,250. The entries to record depreciation for 1981 and sale of the property item follow:

Depreciation Expense — Machinery	250.00	
Accumulated Depreciation — Machinery		250.00
To record depreciation for three months in 1981.		

Computation:
$10,000 × 10% × 3/12 = $250.

Cash	1,250.00	
Accumulated Depreciation — Machinery	8,333.33	
Loss on Sale of Machinery	416.67	
Machinery		10,000.00
To record sale of machinery.		

Computation:

Cost		$10,000.00
Depreciation to date of sale:		
November 20, 1972 — April 10, 1981 (10% per year for		
8⁴/₁₂ years)		8,333.33
Asset net book value		$ 1,666.67
Proceeds from sale		1,250.00
Loss on sale		$ 416.67

The preceding entries can be combined in the form of a single compound entry as follows:

Cash	1,250.00	
Depreciation Expense — Machinery	250.00	
Accumulated Depreciation — Machinery	8,083.33	
Loss on Sale of Machinery	416.67	
Machinery		10,000.00

If a property item is scrapped or abandoned without cash recovery, a loss would be recognized equal to the asset net book value; if the full cost of the asset has been written off, the asset and its offset balances would simply be cancelled. If a property item is retired from active or standby service but is not immediately disposed of, asset and accumulated depreciation balances should be closed and the salvage value of the asset established as a separate asset.

Gains and losses on property retirements pertain to operations and are recurring. Therefore, the net amount of gain or loss would be reported as an ordinary income item in the year of asset disposition. Only in rare circumstances might the gain or loss qualify for presentation as an extraordinary item, perhaps only where it is part of a larger amount pertaining to the closing out of a division or segment of the entity.

Property Damage or Destruction

Special accounting problems arise when property is damaged or destroyed as a result of fire, flood, storm, or other casualty. When a company owns many properties and these are widely distributed, the company itself may assume the risk of loss. However, companies ordinarily carry insurance for casualties that may involve large sums.

When uninsured properties are partly or wholly destroyed, asset net book values should be reduced or cancelled and a loss recorded for such reductions. Generally, these losses will be classified as ordinary; however, they may be classified as extraordinary, if they meet the criteria as established in Section 3480 of the *Accounting Recommendations*. When property items are insured and these are damaged or destroyed, entries must be made in the accounts to report asset losses and also the insurance claims arising from such losses.

The most common casualty loss incurred by a business is that from fire. Of all of the various types of protection offered by insurance, fire is the risk most widely covered. Because of the importance of fire insurance and because of the special accounting problems that arise in the event of fire, the remaining pages of this chapter are devoted to a detailed discussion of this matter.

Fire Insurance

Fire insurance policies are usually written in $100 or $1,000 units for periods up to three years. Insurance premiums are normally paid in advance annually or for the entire three-year period. The amount of the premium is determined by the conditions prevailing in each case.

The insurance contract may be cancelled by either the insurer or the insured. When the insurance company cancels the policy, a refund is made on a pro rata basis. When the policyholder cancels the policy, a refund may be made on what is known as a short-rate basis that provides for a higher insurance premium for the shorter period of coverage.

A *co-insurance clause* is frequently written into a policy by the insurance companies to offset the tendency by the buyer to purchase only minimum insurance coverage. A business with assets worth $100,000 at fair market value, for example, may estimate that any single loss could not destroy more than one half of these assets and might consider itself adequately protected by insurance of $50,000. With an 80% co-insurance clause, however, the business would have to carry insurance equal to 80% of the fair market value of the property, or $80,000, to recover the full amount on claims up to the face of the policy. When less than this percentage is carried, the insured shares the risk with the insurer.

To illustrate the calculation of the amount recoverable on a policy failing to meet co-insurance requirements, assume the following: assets are insured for $70,000 under a policy containing an 80% co-insurance clause; on the date of a fire, assets have a fair market value of $100,000. Because insurance of only $70,000 is carried when co-insurance requirements are $80,000, any loss will be borne 7/8 by the insurance company and 1/8 by the policyholder; furthermore, whatever the loss, the maximum to be borne by the insurance company is $70,000, the face value of the policy. The amount recoverable from the insurance company if a fire loss is $50,000, for example, is calculated as follows:

$$\frac{70,000 \text{ (policy)}}{80,000 \text{ (co-insurance requirement)}} \times \$50,000 \text{ (loss)} = \$43,750$$

The same calculations are made when the loss is greater than the face of the policy. Assume the same facts given above, but asusme a fire loss of $75,000. The amount recoverable from insurance is calculated as follows:

$$\frac{70,000 \text{ (policy)}}{80,000 \text{ (co-insurance requirement)}} \times \$75,000 \text{ (loss)} = \$65,625$$

In the example above, application of the formula gives an amount still less than the face of the policy and hence fully recoverable. But if application of the formula results in an amount exceeding the face value of the policy, the claim is limited to the latter amount. If, for example, the loss is $90,000, the following calculation is made:

$$\frac{70,000 \text{ (policy)}}{80,000 \text{ (co-insurance requirement)}} \times \$90,000 \text{ (loss)} = \$78,750$$

Recovery from the insurance company, however, is limited to $70,000, the ceiling set by the face amount of the policy.

When the insurance coverage is equal to or greater than the percentage required by the co-insurance clause, the formula need not be applied since any loss is paid in full up to the face value of the policy. It is important to note that co-insurance requirements are based not on the cost or accounting value of the insured property but upon the actual market value of the property on the date of a fire. If co-insurance requirements are to be met, an increase in the value of insured assets requires that insurance coverage be increased.

The following general rules may be formulated:

1. In the absence of a co-insurance clause the amount recoverable is the lower of the loss or the face value of the policy.
2. When a policy includes a co-insurance clause, the amount recoverable is the lower of the loss as adjusted by the co-insurance formula or the face value of the policy.

Insurance policies normally include a *contribution clause* that provides that if other policies are carried on the same property, recovery of a loss on a policy shall be limited to the ratio which the face value of the policy bears to the total insurance carried. Such a limitation on the amount to be paid eliminates the possibility of recovery by the insured of amounts in excess of the actual loss. When co-insurance clauses are found in the different policies, the recoverable amount on each is limited to the ratio of the face value of the policy to the higher of (a) the total insurance carried, or (b) the total insurance required to be carried by the policy. To illustrate the limitations set by contribution clauses, assume a fire loss of $30,000 on property with a value of $100,000 on which policies are carried as follows: Co. A, $50,000; Co. B, $15,000; Co. C, $10,000.

1. Assuming policies have no co-insurance clauses, amounts that may be recovered from each company are as follows:

Co. A: $\dfrac{50,000 \text{ (policy)}}{75,000 \text{ (total policies)}} \times \$30,000 \text{ (loss)}$ $20,000

Co. B: $\dfrac{15,000 \text{ (policy)}}{75,000 \text{ (total policies)}} \times \$30,000 \text{ (loss)}$ 6,000

Co. C: $\dfrac{10,000 \text{ (policy)}}{75,000 \text{ (total policies)}} \times \$30,000 \text{ (loss)}$ 4,000

Total amount recoverable $30,000

2. Assuming each policy includes an 80% co-insurance clause, co-insurance requirements on each policy would exceed the total insurance carried and amounts recoverable from each company are as follows:

Co. A: $\dfrac{50,000 \text{ (policy)}}{80,000 \text{ (co-insurance requirement)}} \times \$30,000 \text{ (loss)}$ $18,750

Co. B: $\dfrac{15,000 \text{ (policy)}}{80,000 \text{ (co-insurance requirement)}} \times \$30,000 \text{ (loss)}$ 5,625

Co. C: $\dfrac{10,000 \text{ (policy)}}{80,000 \text{ (co-insurance requirement)}} \times \$30,000 \text{ (loss)}$ 3,750

Total amount recoverable $28,125

3. Assuming each policy includes a 70% co-insurance clause, total insurance carried exceeds co-insurance requirements on each policy and amounts recoverable from each company are the same as in (1).

4. Assuming that co-insurance requirements are Co. A — none, Co. B — 70%, and Co. C — 80%, recovery on each policy is based on its relationship to the total insurance carried or the co-insurance requirement where this is higher, as follows:

Co. A: $\dfrac{50,000 \text{ (policy)}}{75,000 \text{ (total policies)}} \times \$30,000 \text{ (loss)}$ $20,000

Co. B: $\dfrac{15,000 \text{ (policy)}}{75,000 \text{ (total policies)}} \times \$30,000 \text{ (loss)}$ 6,000

Co. C: $\dfrac{10,000 \text{ (policy)}}{80,000 \text{ (co-insurance requirement)}} \times \$30,000 \text{ (loss)}$ 3,750

Total amount recoverable $29,750

Accounting for Fire Losses

When a fire occurs and accounting records are destroyed, account balances to the date of the fire will have to be reconstructed from the best available evidence. As the first step in summarizing the fire loss, accounts as maintained or as reconstructed are adjusted as of the date of the fire. With accounts brought up to date, the loss may be summarized in a fire loss account. The fire loss account is debited for the net book value of properties destroyed, and it is credited for amounts recoverable from insurance companies and amounts recoverable from salvage. The balance of the account is normally recognized as an extraordinary item and is closed into the income summary account.

A number of special problems are encountered in arriving at the charges to be made to the fire loss account. When depreciable assets are destroyed, accumulated depreciation on the properties must be brought up to date and net book values in total or in part transferred to the fire loss account. When merchandise is destroyed, the estimated cost of the merchandise on hand at the time of the fire must be determined. If perpetual inventory records are available, the goods on hand may be obtained from this source. In the absence of such records, the inventory is generally calculated by the gross profit method. The inventory may be set up by a debit to the inventory account and a credit to the income summary account. The inventory total or portion destroyed may then be transferred to the fire loss account.

Insurance expired to the date of the fire is recorded as an expense. The balance in the unexpired insurance account is carried forward when policies continue in force and offer original protection on rehabilitated properties or newly acquired replacements. If a business does not plan to repair or replace the assets, it may cancel a part or all of a policy and recover cash on a short-rate basis. The difference between the unexpired insurance balance and the amount received on the short-rate basis is a loss from insurance cancellation brought about by the fire and is recorded as an addition to the fire loss balance.[19]

To illustrate the accounting for a fire loss, assume the following facts. J. J. Bailey, a retailer, suffers a fire loss after the close of business on March 31, 1981. Assets destroyed and amounts recoverable from insurance and salvage are summarized at the bottom of this page.

Entries for the fire loss are given on the following page. These are given in three groups: (1) entries that bring asset values up to date so that the loss may be determined, (2) entries that record the assets lost, and (3) entries that record the amounts recoverable from salvage and due from the insurance companies.

Entries to adjust the accounts and to record the fire loss may be transferred to the ledger, but nominal accounts may be left open and transactions for the remainder of the fiscal period recorded therein. At the end of the period, nominal accounts will reflect activities for the entire period and statements can be prepared summarizing activities in the usual manner. Any differences that are found during the period between amounts originally stated to be recoverable from insurance and amounts actually recovered should be debited or credited to the fire loss account, thus correcting this balance to the loss actually sustained.

ITEM	LOSSES		AMOUNT RECOVERABLE	
Inventory	Entire inventory, estimated to have a cost of $18,000.		Policy carried	$12,500
			Value of property at date of fire as agreed by insured and insurer	18,000
			Salvage goods valued at	1,400
			Amount recoverable from insurance company: Full amount of policy	12,500
Equipment	One third of equipment:		Policy carried	$ 6,000
	Cost of equipment	$15,000	Value of equipment at date of fire, as agreed by insured and insurer	7,800
	Accumulated depr., 1/1/81 . $9,000		Amount recoverable from insurance	
	Add depr. at 10%		company: $1/3 \times \$7,800$	2,600
	for 3 months 375	9,375		
	Asset net book value	$ 5,625		
	Net book value of portion lost:			
	$1/3 \times \$5,625$	$ 1,875		
Buildings	One fourth of buildings:		Policy carried	$35,000
	Cost of buildings	$32,000	Value of buildings at date of fire, as agreed by insured and insurer	32,000
	Accumulated depr., 1/1/81 . $4,000		Amount recoverable from insurance	
	Add depr. at $2^1/2\%$		company: $1/4 \times \$32,000$	8,000
	for 3 months 200	4,200		
	Asset net book value	$27,800		
	Net book value of portion lost:			
	$1/4 \times \$27,800$	$6 950		

[19]Under policies written in some jurisdictions, payment by the insurer on a policy may serve to cancel that portion of the policy paid by the insurer. When this is the case, any unexpired insurance balance applicable to the portion of the policy paid should be written off as an addition to the fire loss account.

(a)	Income Summary	12,250	
	Inventory[20]		12,250
(b)	Inventory	18,000	
	Income Summary		18,000
(c)	Depreciation Expense — Equipment	375	
	Accumulated Depreciation — Equipment		375
(d)	Depreciation Expense — Buildings	200	
	Accumulated Depreciation — Buildings		200

Entries to Record Assets Lost by Fire

(e)	Fire Loss	18,000	
	Inventory		18,000
(f)	Fire Loss	1,875	
	Accumulated Depreciation — Equipment	3,125	
	Equipment		5,000
(g)	Fire Loss	6,950	
	Accumulated Depreciation — Buildings	1,050	
	Buildings		8,000

Entries to Record Amounts Recoverable
from Salvage and Due from Insurance Companies

(h)	Salvage Receivable	1,400	
	Fire Loss		1,400
(i)	Recoverable from Insurance Companies	12,500	
	Fire Loss		12,500
(j)	Recoverable from Insurance Companies	2,600	
	Fire Loss		2,600
(k)	Recoverable from Insurance Companies	8,000	
	Fire Loss		8,000

The total amount recoverable from the insurance companies is $23,100 and this balance would be reported as a current asset if current settlement is anticipated. The fire loss account reports a debit balance of $2,325; this is the loss from the fire and should qualify for disclosure as an extraordinary item.

Because the insurance proceeds are based upon appraised values, insurance proceeds may exceed the carrying value of assets destroyed, resulting in a credit balance in the fire loss account. If the assets destroyed must be replaced at current market prices, the credit balance can hardly be viewed as indicating an economic gain. The credit balance may be designated for income statement reporting purposes as "Excess of Insurance and Salvage over Carrying Value of Assets Lost by Fire."

---

[20]It is assumed the opening inventory balance is $12,250; this balance is closed to Income Summary. The inventory on the date of the fire is recorded in entry (b) by a debit to the asset and a credit to Income Summary; the credit represents a subtraction item from goods available for the period in arriving at the cost of goods sold. The inventory balance as of the date of the fire is transferred to the fire loss account in entry (e).

1. Distinguish among the terms *plant, property, tangible fixed assets,* and *intangible fixed assets.*

2. Which of the following items are properly shown under the heading "Land, buildings, and equipment"?
   (a) Deposits on machinery not yet received.
   (b) Idle equipment awaiting sale.
   (c) Property held for investment purposes.
   (d) Land held for possible future plant site.

3. (a) Distinguish between capital expenditures and revenue expenditures. (b) Give five examples of each.

4. Which of the following items would be recorded as a revenue expenditure and which would be recorded as a capital expenditure?
   (a) Cost of installing machinery.
   (b) Cost of moving and reinstalling machinery.
   (c) Extensive repairs as a result of fire.
   (d) Cost of grading land.
   (e) Insurance on machinery in transit.
   (f) Bond discount amortization during construction period.
   (g) Cost of major overhaul on machinery.
   (h) Additional safety guards on machinery.
   (i) Commission on purchase of real estate.
   (j) Special tax assessment for street improvements.
   (k) Cost of repainting offices.

5. Indicate the effects of the following errors on the balance sheet and the income statement in the current year and in succeeding years:
   (a) The cost of a depreciable asset is incorrectly recorded as a revenue expenditure.
   (b) A revenue expenditure is incorrectly recorded as an addition to the cost of a depreciable asset.

6. What additional accounting problems are introduced when a company purchases equipment on a long-term contract rather than with cash?

7. What is meant by a business combination that is a *pooling of interests*? As regards fixed asset values, how does a pooling differ from a *purchase* combination?

8. Christie Ltd., decides to construct a building for itself and plans to use whatever plant facilities it has to further such construction. (a) What costs will enter into the cost of construction? (b) What two positions can the company take with respect to general overhead allocation during the period of construction? Evaluate each position and indicate your preference.

9. The Waters Co. decides to construct a piece of specialized machinery using personnel from the maintenance department. Personnel were instructed to schedule their work so that all overtime hours were charged to the machinery. Evaluate the practice as it relates to the resulting cost of the machine.

10. When the Boatman Corporation finds that the lowest bid it can get on the construction of an addition to its building is $40,000, it proceeds to erect the building with its own workers and equipment. (a) Assuming that the cost of construction is $35,000, how would you treat the savings? (b) Assuming the cost of construction is $50,000, how would you treat the excess cost?

11. Evaluate the practice of including interest as a cost of construction for (a) public utilities, (b) commercial utilities.

12. The Parkhurst Corporation acquires land and buildings valued at $250,000 as a gift from Industrial City. The president of the company maintains that since there was no cost for the acquisition, neither cost of the facilities nor depreciation needs to be recognized for financial statement purposes. Evaluate the president's position assuming (a) the gift is unconditional; (b) the gift is contingent upon the employment by the company of a certain number of employees for a ten-year period.

13. In the balance sheets of many companies, the largest classification of assets in amount is fixed assets. Name the items, in addition to the amount paid to the former owner or contractor, that may be properly included as part of the acquisition cost of the following property items: (a) land, (b) buildings, and (c) equipment.

14. Distinguish between (a) maintenance and repairs, (b) ordinary repairs and extraordinary repairs, (c) betterments and additions.

15. (a) What is a co-insurance clause and why is it found in policies? (b) What is a contribution clause? How does it affect recovery of a loss?

EXERCISES

8-1. Hillcrest Ltd., acquires a machine priced at $72,000. Payment of this amount may be made within 60 days; a 5% discount is allowed if cash is paid at time of purchase. Give the entry to record the acquisition, assuming:

(a) Cash is paid at time of purchase.
(b) Payment is to be made at the end of 60 days.
(c) A long-term contract is signed whereby a down payment of $12,000 is made with 12 payments of $6,000 to be made at monthly intervals thereafter.

8-2. The Webber Natralist Co. acquired land, buildings, and equipment items at a lump-sum price of $125,000. An appraisal of the assets at the time of acquisition disclosed the following values:

Land	$80,000
Buildings	70,000
Equipment	50,000

What cost should be assigned to each asset?

8-3. Timpanogas Ltd., purchases equipment costing $80,000 with a down payment of $20,000 and sufficient semi-annual instalments of $7,000 (including interest on the unpaid principal at 10% per year) to pay the balance. In accordance with APB Opinion No. 21:

(a) Give the entries to record the purchase and the first two semi-annual payments.
(b) Assume that there was no known cash price and ten semi-annual instalments were to be made. Give the entries to record the purchase and the first two semi-annual payments.

8-4. Concepcion Co. purchased a new milling machine. The following data relate to the purchase:

List price of new machine to Concepcion Co. — $55,000.
Cash price of new machine with no trade-in — $48,700.
The Concepcion Co. received a trade-in allowance of $15,000 on a dissimilar machine costing $25,000 new and having a present net book value of $12,000.
The Express Delivery Service charged Concepcion Co. $1,200 to deliver the machine.

Give the entry to record the acquisition of the new machine.

8-5. Espanola Company built a plant in Northern Ontario for which it received a 25% government assistance grant. The plant was completed early in January at a cost of $600,000. The plant was to be depreciated over a 20-year useful life on a straight-line basis with no salvage value.

Give the entries for depreciation using the two alternative methods of accounting for government assistance related to capital expenditures. (CGA adapted)

8-6. The Belmont Company acquired a new delivery truck, having a list price of $10,000 which was paid for by trading in an old truck and making a cash payment of $6,000 which included $150 for extra equipment and $200 for annual licence fees.

The following information concerning the trade-in is obtained from the Company's accounts:

Cost of old truck	$8,000
Accumulated depreciation	5,000
Fair market value of the old truck	3,600
Trade-in allowance	4,000

Prepare separate journal entries to illustrate three different methods of recording the new asset and the disposal of the old. (SMA adapted)

8-7. Assume Nebo Corporation has a machine that cost $12,000, has a net book value of $6,000, and has a fair market value of $10,000. For each of the following situations, indicate the value at which Nebo should record the new asset and why it should be recorded at that value.

(a) Nebo exchanged the machine for a truck with a list price of $11,000.
(b) Nebo exchanged the machine for a newer model machine with a list price of $14,000. Nebo paid $1,000 in the transaction.
(c) Nebo exchanged the machine and $750 cash for a similar machine from Quin Co. The newly acquired machine is carried in Quin's accounts at $15,000 with accumulated depreciation of $5,000; its fair market value is $10,750. In addition to determining the value, give the journal entries for both companies to record the exchange.

8-8. The Eagle Co. enters into a contract with the Taulbee Construction Co. for construction of an office building at a cost of $720,000. Upon completion of construction, the Taulbee Construction Co. agrees to accept in full payment of the contract price Eagle Co. 6% bonds with a face value of $400,000 and no par common shares with a market value of $340,000. Eagle Co. bonds are selling on the market at this time at 95. How would you recommend the building acquisition be recorded?

8-9. The Ross Company acquired land and an old building in exchange for 5,000 shares of its no par common shares, and cash of $25,000. The auditor ascertains that the company's shares were selling on the market at $12 when the purchase was made. The following additional costs were incurred to complete the transaction.

Escrow cost to complete transaction	$1,000
Property tax for previous year	500
Cost of building demolition	8,000
Salvage value of demolished building	4,000

What entry should be made to record the acquisition of the property?

8-10. The Hansen Corporation summarizes manufacturing and construction activities for 1981 as follows:

	Product Manufacture	Building Wing Construction
Materials	$150,000	$32,000
Direct labor	220,000	45,000

Overhead for 1980 was 80% of the direct labor cost. Overhead in 1981 related to both product manufacture construction activities totalled $199,810.

(a) Calculate the cost of the building addition, assuming manufacturing activities are to be charged with overhead at the rate experienced in 1980 and construction activities are to be charged with the excess.

(b) Calculate the cost of the addition if manufacturing and construction activities are to be charged with overhead at the same rate.

8-11. The following expenditures were incurred by the Watson Co. in 1981: purchase of land, $120,000; land survey, $1,500; fees for search of title on land, $350; building permit, $250; temporary quarters for construction crews, $2,750; payment to tenants of old building for vacating premises, $2,000; razing of old building, $2,000; excavation for basement, $10,000; special assessment taxes for street project, $2,000; dividends, $5,000; damages awarded for injuries sustained in construction, $4,200 (no insurance was carried; the cost of insurance would have been $200); costs of construction, $225,000; cost of paving parking lot adjoining building, $12,500; cost of shrubs, trees, and other landscaping, $1,500. What is the cost of the land and the cost of the building?

8-12. Stornetta's Dairy bills its customers for milk bottles. During July the total amount billed for milk and bottles was $78,350. Of this amount, $4,780 was for the bottles. Bottles were returned by customers and customers were given credit for $3,620 on these returns. The cost of bottles not returned was determined to be $750 and the accumulated depreciation on these bottles was $300. The cost of bottles is carried in a property account entitled Containers.

Give the entries to record the transactions for July.

8-13. One of the most difficult problems facing an accountant is the determination of which expenditures should be deferred as assets and which should be immediately charged off as expenses. What position would you take in each of the following instances?

(a) Painting of partitions in a large room recently divided into four sections.

(b) Labor cost of tearing down a wall to permit extension of assembly line.

(c) Replacement of motor on a machine. Life used to depreciate the machine is 8 years. The machine is 4 years old. Replacement of the motor was anticipated when the machine was purchased.

(d) Cost of grading land prior to construction.

(e) Assessment for street paving.

(f) Cost of moving and reinstalling equipment.

(g) Cost of tearing down an old building in preparation for new construction; old building is fully depreciated.

8-14. The Stoddard Company purchased a building for $120,000 on August 1, 1973. Depreciation was recorded at 3% a year. On October 31, 1981, 50% of the building was destroyed. On this date the building had a fair market value of $100,000. A policy for $60,000 was carried on the building, the policy containing an 80% co-insurance clause. What entries would be made to record (a) the loss from destruction of the building, and (b) the amount due from the insurance company? (Assume the company's fiscal period is the calendar year.)

8-15. Multiple choice: select the *best* choice for each of the following items.

(a) When fixed assets are acquired by shareholder gift or donation, the preferred accounting treatment is to:
   (i) make a memo entry wherein no amount is recorded;
   (ii) record them at the cost of taking title to them;
   (iii) record them at their fair market value at the time of the gift;
   (iv) recognize the transaction as a revenue transaction.

(b) B Company Ltd. bought fixed assets subject to a 2% discount if paid for promptly. The invoice price was $10,000. These assets should be recorded on B's books at:
   (i) $10,000 regardless of whether the discount is taken;
   (ii) $10,000 if this is the amount paid;
   (iii) $9,800 if this is the amount paid;
   (iv) $9,800 regardless of whether the discount is taken.

(c) T Corp. Ltd. acquired some machinery in exchange for 36 instalment notes of $200 each, payable over the next three years. In other words, one note matures on the first day of each of the next 36 months. No interest is mentioned in connection with the notes or the purchase contract. The machinery should be recorded in T's accounts at:
   (i) $7,200;
   (ii) an amount less than $7,200 equal to the implicit interest;
   (iii) an amount higher than $7,200 equal to the implicit interest;
   (iv) some other value.

(d) Under the construction period theory:
   (i) fixed assets under construction are not recognized on the books until completed;
   (ii) some interest costs may be capitalized;
   (iii) periods of less than one year are ignored;
   (iv) self-constructed assets are recorded at fair market value.

(e) Y Company Ltd. acquired some land in exchange for 20 shares of its stock which have a par value of $100 each. The stock is fairly widely traded and sold for $110 per share when exchanged for the land. The land is similar to other tracts which recently sold for $2,500. Y Ltd. should take up the land in its accounts at:
   (i) $2,000;
   (ii) $2,200;
   (iii) $2,500;
   (iv) some other value.

(CGA adapted)

8-1A. The following transactions were completed by the St. Helena Co. during 1981:

Mar. 1   Purchased real property for $178,925 which included a charge of $3,925 representing property tax for March 1-June 30 that had been prepaid by the vendor. Twenty per cent of the purchase price is deemed applicable to land and the balance to buildings. A mortgage of $125,000 was assumed by the St. Helena Co. on the purchase.

Mar. 2-30   Previous owners had failed to take care of normal maintenance and repair requirements on the building, necessitating current reconditioning at a cost of $8,300.

Apr. 1-May 15   Garages in the rear of the buildings were demolished, $1,500 being recovered on the lumber salvage. The company itself proceeded to construct a warehouse. The cost of such construction was $12,500 which was almost exactly the same as bids made on the construction by independent contractors. Upon completion of construction, city inspectors ordered extensive modifications in the buildings as a result of failure on the part of the company to comply with the Building Safety Code. Such modifications, which could have been avoided, cost $2,800.

Nov. 5-20   The company contracted for parking lots and landscaping at a cost of $15,000 and $3,200 respectively. The work was completed and billed on November 20.

Dec. 29-31   The business was closed to permit taking the year-end inventory. During this period, required redecorating and repairs were completed at a cost of $1,500.

Instructions:

Give journal entries to record each of the preceding transactions. (Disregard depreciation.)

8-2A. On December 31, 1981, the Danville Co. shows the following account for machinery it had assembled for its own use during 1981:

ACCOUNT Machinery (Job Order #62)

			BALANCE	
ITEM	DEBIT	CREDIT	DEBIT	CREDIT
Cost of dismantling old machine	3,120		3,120	
Cash proceeds from sale of old machine ...		2,500	620	
Raw materials used in construction of new machine............................	15,750		16,370	
Labor in construction of new machine	12,250		28,620	
Cost of installation	2,800		31,420	
Materials spoiled in machine trial runs	600		32,020	
Profit on construction	6,900		38,920	
Purchase of machine tools	3,600		42,520	
Depreciation for 1981, 10% of $42,520		4,252	38,268	

An analysis of the detail in the account discloses the following:

(a) The old machine, which was removed in the installation of the new one, had been fully depreciated.
(b) Cash discounts received on the payments for materials used in construction totalled $400 and these were recorded in the purchase discounts account.
(c) The factory overhead account shows a balance of $73,000 for the year ended December 31, 1981; this balance exceeds normal overhead on regular plant activities by approximately $3,700 and is attributable to machine construction.
(d) A profit was recognized on construction for the difference between costs incurred and the price at which the machine could have been purchased.
(e) Machine tools have an estimated life of 3 years; machinery has an estimated life of 10 years. The machinery was used for production beginning on September 1, 1981. (Depreciation should be computed to nearest month.)

Instructions:

(1) Determine the machiney and machine tools balances as of December 31, 1981.
(2) Give individual journal entries necessary to correct the accounts as of December 31, 1981, assuming the nominal accounts are still open.

8-3A. The Calistoga Wholesale Company incurred the following expenses in 1981 for their office building acquired on July 1, 1981, the beginning of the fiscal year:

Cost of land	$ 30,000
Cost of building	170,000
Remodeling and repairs prior to occupancy	27,000
Escrow fee	1,500
Landscaping	10,000
Unpaid property tax for period prior to acquisition	3,500
Real estate commission	6,000

The company signed a non-interest-bearing note for $200,000 on the acquisition. The implicit interest rate is 8%. Payments of $10,000 are to be made semi-annually beginning January 1, 1982, for 10 years.

Instructions:

In accordance with sound accounting theory give the required journal entries to record (1) the acquisition of the land and building (assume cash is paid to equalize the cost of the assets and the present value of the note), and (2) the first two semi-annual payments, including amortization of discount on notes payable.

8-4A. You are given the following information about equipment held by Woolley Manufacturing.

	Asset A	Asset B	Asset C
Cost	$25,000	$100,000	$78,000
Accumulated depreciation (12/31/80)	12,500	20,000	70,200
Fair market value	20,000	60,000	10,000
Depreciation (per year — straight-line)	10%	5%	10%

Asset A is exchanged on March 31, 1981, for a similar piece of equipment plus cash of $2,000. Assets B and C are sold for $80,000 on June 30, 1981.

Instructions:

Give the required journal entries to record the above transactions.

8-5A. The Thompson Company planned to open a new store. The company narrowed the possible sites to two lots and decided to take purchase options on both lots while they studied traffic densities in both areas. They paid $2,400 for the option on Lot A and $4,800 for the option on Lot B. After studying traffic densities, they decided to purchase Lot B. The company opened a single real estate account that shows the following:

Debits:	Option on Lot A	$ 2,400
	Option on Lot B	4,800
	Payment of balance on Lot B	40,000
	Title insurance	700
	Assessment for street improvements	1,700
	Recording fee for deed	100
	Cost of razing old building on Lot B	3,000
	Payment for erection of new building	100,000
Credit:	Sale of salvaged materials from old building	3,000

The salvage value of material obtained from the old building and used in the erection of the new building was $2,500. The depreciated value of the old building, as shown by the books of the company from which the purchase was made, was $18,000. The old building was razed immediately after the purchase.

Instructions:

(1) Determine the cost of the land, listing the items included in the total.

(2) Determine the cost of the new building, listing the items included in the total.

8-6A. The Pageant Corporation was organized in June, 1981. In auditing the accounts of the company, you find a land, buildings, and equipment account with the following detail:

ACCOUNT Land, Buildings, and Equipment

DATE		ITEM	DEBIT	CREDIT	BALANCE DEBIT	BALANCE CREDIT
1981						
June	8	Organization fees	2,500		2,500	
	16	Land site and old building	325,000		327,500	
	30	Corporate organization costs	2,500		330,000	
July	2	Title clearance fees	2,100		332,100	
Aug.	28	Cost of razing old building	4,000		336,100	
Sept.	1	Salaries of Pageant Corporation executives	15,000		351,100	
Dec.	12	Stock bonus to corporate promoters, 2,000 shares of common stock, $10 par	20,000		371,100	
	15	County real estate tax	3,600		374,700	
	15	Cost of new building completed and occupied on this date	620,000		994,700	

An analysis of the foregoing account and of other accounts disclosed the following additional information:

(a) The building acquired on June 16, 1981, was valued at $35,000.

(b) The company paid $4,000 for the demolition of the old building, then sold the scrap for $200 and credited the proceeds to Miscellaneous Revenue.

(c) The company executives did not participate in the construction of the new building.

(d) The county real estate tax was for the six-month period ended December 31, 1981, and was assessed by the county on the land.

Instructions:

Prepare journal entries to correct the books of the Pageant Corporation. Each entry should include an explanation.

8-7A. Newold Ltd. commenced construction of a new plant on July 1, 1980. All construction activities were completed by March 31, 1981 after which the plant went into operation.

Total cost incurred during the construction period included the following:

Cost of land (which includes the cost of an old building erected on it) ..	$	55,000 L

Engineering fees:
Analysis of the sub-soil		8,000 B
Construction supervision		50,000 B
Analysis of the electrical system		30,000 B
Planning of a new production process (required in order to use new equipment which will be installed in the new building)		45,000 R&D expense or machinery
↳ Research	$	133,000

Subcontractors' charges:
Demolition of the old building	$	3,000 L
Wages and materials, excluding landscaping		531,000 B
Landscaping		4,000 L
	$	538,000

Charges included in the company's operating accounts:
Wages of employees on construction site	$	325,000 B
Salaries of other employees attached to this project		135,000 B
Materials		839,000 B
Overhead applied on the same basis and the same rate as for regular production		428,000 B
Taxes and interest, payable in advance, for the *entire year* commencing July 1, 1980		18,000
	$1,745,000	

The company is to receive a government grant of $200,000 for having selected a recommended site as the actual location of the new plant.

Instructions:

(a) As Controller of Newold Ltd., you must determine which of the above costs should be properly included in the cost of the new plant. Indicate briefly why you would include or exclude each above mentioned cost item.

(b) Determine the total amount that should appear in the company's property, plant and equipment accounts. (SMA adapted)

8-8A. The Lucci Company completed a program of expansion and improvements of its plant during 1981. You are provided with the following information concerning its buildings account:

(a) On October 31, 1981, a 30-foot extension to the present factory building was completed at a contract cost of $72,000.

(b) During the course of construction, the following costs were incurred for the removal of the end wall of the building where the extension was being constructed:
  (1) Payroll costs during the month of April arising from employees' time spent in removal of the wall, $4,627.
  (2) Payments to a salvage company for removing unusual debris, $520.
(c) The cost of the original structure allocable to the end wall was estimated to be $17,600, with accumulated depreciation thereon of $7,400; $4,721 was received by Lucci Company from the construction company for windows and other assorted materials salvaged from the old wall.
(d) The old flooring was covered with a new long-lasting floor covering at a cost of $3,257.
(e) The interior of the plant was painted in new bright colors for a contract price of $3,250.
(f) New and improved shelving was installed at a cost of $572.
(g) Old electrical wiring was replaced at a cost of $6,812. Cost of the old wiring was determined to be $3,100 with accumulated depreciation to date of $1,370.
(h) New electrical fixtures using fluorescent bulbs were installed. The new fixtures were purchased on the instalment plan; the schedule of monthly payments showed total payments of $6,200, which included interest and carrying charges of $480. The old fixtures were carried at a cost of $1,860, with accumulated depreciation to date of $796. The old fixtures had no scrap value.

Instructions:
Prepare journal entries including explanations for the above information. Briefly justify the capitalization v. revenue decision for each item.

8-9A. On March 1, 1979, the Torrez Co. took out a $500,000, 4-year fire insurance policy on a building that was completed at a cost of $880,000 at the end of June, 1963. The insurance policy contains an 80% co-insurance clause. Depreciation is calculated at $2^{1}/_{2}\%$ annually. On July 5, 1981, the building was 50% destroyed by fire. The insurance company accepted a value for the property of $687,500 and agreed to make settlement on this basis. The fiscal period for the Torrez Co. is the calendar year.

Instructions:
Prepare the journal entries necessary as of July 5, 1981, to summarize the foregoing information in the fire loss account and to close the account to Income Summary.

8-10A. In your examination of the financial statements of Gaar Corporation at December 31, 1981, you observe the contents of certain accounts and other pertinent information as follows:

ACCOUNT Building

DATE		ITEM	POST. REF.	DEBIT	CREDIT	BALANCE DEBIT	BALANCE CREDIT
1980							
Dec.	31	Balance	X	100,000		100,000	
1981							
July	1	New boiler	CD	16,800	1,480	115,320	
Sept.	1	Insurance recovery	CR		2,000	113,320	

ACCOUNT Accumulated Depreciation — Building

DATE		ITEM	POST. REF.	DEBIT	CREDIT	BALANCE	
						DEBIT	CREDIT
1980 Dec.	31	Balance — 15 years at 4% of $100,000	X		60,000		60,000
1981 Dec.	31	Annual depreciation	GJ		4,440		64,440

You learn that on June 15 the company's old high-pressure boiler exploded. Damage to the building was insignificant but the boiler was replaced by a more efficient oil-burning boiler. The company received $2,000 as an insurance adjustment under terms of its policy for damage to the boiler.

The disbursement voucher charged to the building account on July 1, 1981, follows:

To: REX HEATING COMPANY
List price — new oil-burning boiler
  (including fuel oil tank and 5,000 gallons fuel oil) $16,000
Sales tax — 5% of $16,000   800

   Total $16,800
Less allowance for old coal-burning boiler in building — to be removed
  at the expense of the Rex Heating Company 1,480

   Total price $15,320

In vouching the expenditure you determine that the terms included a 2% cash discount which was properly computed and taken. The sales tax, fuel oil, and trade-in allowance are not subject to discount.

Your audit discloses that a voucher for $1,000 was paid to Emment Co. on July 2, 1981, and debited to the repair expense account. The voucher is adequately supported and is marked "installation costs for new oil-burning boiler."

The company's fuel oil supplier advises that fuel oil had a market price of 16¢ per gallon July 1 and 18¢ per gallon December 31. The fuel oil inventory at December 31 was 2,000 gallons.

A review of subsidiary property records discloses that the replaced coal-burning boiler was installed when the building was constructed and was recorded at a cost of $10,000. According to its manufacturers the new boiler should be serviceable for 15 years.

In computing depreciation for retirements Gaar Corporation consistently treats a fraction of a month as a full month.

Instructions:
Prepare the adjusting journal entries that you would suggest for the accounts of Gaar Corporation. The accounts have not been closed. Support your entries with computations in good form. (AICPA adapted)

8.11A. Ellford Corporation received a $400,000 low bid from a reputable manufacturer for the construction of special production equipment needed by Ellford in an expansion program. Because the company's own plant was not operating at capacity, Ellford decided to construct the equipment there and recorded the following production costs related to the construction:

Services of consulting engineer	$ 10,000
Work subcontracted	20,000
Materials	200,000
Plant labor normally assigned to production	65,000
Plant labor normally assigned to maintenance	100,000
Total	$395,000

Management prefers to record the cost of the equipment under the incremental cost method. Approximately 40% of the corporation's production is devoted to government supply contracts which are all based in some way on cost. The contracts require that any self-constructed equipment be allocated its full share of all costs related to the construction.

The following information is also available:

(a) The above production labor was for partial fabrication of the equipment in the plant. Skilled personnel were required and were assigned from other projects. The maintenace labor would have been idle time of non-production plant employees who would have been retained on the payroll whether or not their services were utilized.

(b) Payroll taxes and employee fringe benefits are approximately 30% of labor cost and are included in manufacturing overhead cost. Total manufacturing overhead for the year was $5,630,000 including the $100,000 maintenance labor used to construct the equipment.

(c) Manufacturing overhead is approximately 50% variable and is applied on the basis of production labor cost. Production labor cost for the year for the corporation's normal products totalled $6,810,000.

(d) General and administrative expenses include $22,500 of executive salary cost and $10,500 of postage, telephone, supplies, and miscellaneous expenses identifiable with this equipment construction.

Instructions:

(1) Prepare a schedule computing the amount that should be reported as the full cost of the constructed equipment to meet the requirements of the government contracts. Any supporting computations should be in good form.

(2) Prepare a schedule computing the incremental cost of the constructed equipment.

(3) What is the greatest amount that should be capitalized as the cost of the equipment? Why? (AICPA adapted)

8-12A. The ABC Corporation is a small manufacturing company producing a highly flammable cleaning fluid. On May 31, 1981, the company had a fire which completely destroyed the processing building and the in-process inventory; some of the equipment was saved.

The cost of the fixed assets destroyed and their related accumulated depreciation accounts at May 31, 1981 were as follows:

	Cost	Accumulated Depreciation
Buildings	$40,000	$24,667
Equipment	15,000	4,375

At present prices, the cost to replace the destroyed property would be: building, $80,000; equipment, $37,500. At the time of the fire, it was determined that the destroyed building was 62½% depreciated, and the destroyed equipment was 33⅓% depreciated. The insurable value of the building and equipment was determined to be $75,000.

After the fire a physical inventory was taken. The raw materials were valued at $30,000, the finished goods at $60,000, and supplies at $5,000.

The inventories on January 1, 1981, consisted of:

Raw materials	$ 15,000
Goods in process	50,000
Finished goods	70,000
Supplies	2,000
Total	$137,000

A review of the accounts showed that the sales and gross profit for the last five years were:

	Sales	Gross Profit
1976	$300,000	$ 86,200
1977	320,000	102,400
1978	330,000	108,900
1979	250,000	62,500
1980	280,000	84,000

The sales for the first five months of 1981 were $150,000. Raw materials purchases were $50,000. Freight on purchases was $5,000. Direct labor for the five months was $40,000; for the past five years manufacturing overhead was 50% of direct labor.

Insurance on the property and inventory was carried with three companies. Each policy included an 80% co-insurance clause. The amount of insurance carried with the various companies was:

	Buildings and Equipment	Inventories
Company A	$30,000	$38,000
Company B	20,000	35,000
Company C	15,000	35,000

The cost of cleaning up the debris was $7,000. The value of the scrap salvaged from the fire was $600.

Instructions:

(1) Compute the value of inventory lost.
(2) Compute the expected recovery from each insurance company. (AICPA adapted)

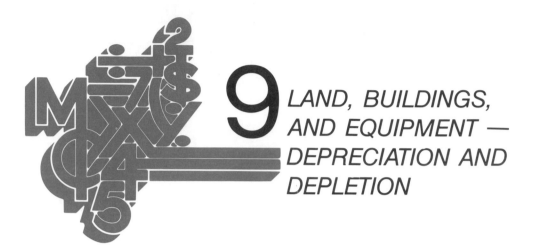

9 LAND, BUILDINGS, AND EQUIPMENT — DEPRECIATION AND DEPLETION

In spite of expenditures for maintenance and repairs, the time ultimately comes when all buildings and equipment items can no longer make a favorable contribution to business activities and must be retired. The costs of these assets must be allocated to revenues over the limited duration of the assets' usefulness. *Depreciation* represents an estimate of the decline in service potential of the asset occurring during the period.

The Committee on Terminology of the American Institute of Certified Public Accountants has defined depreciation accounting as follows:

> *Depreciation accounting* is a system of accounting which aims to distribute the cost or other basic value of tangible capital assets, less salvage (if any), over the estimated useful life of the unit (which may be a group of assets) in a systematic and rational manner. It is a process of allocation, not of valuation. *Depreciation for the year* is the portion of the total charge under such a system that is allocated to the year. Although the allocation may properly take into account occurrences during the year, it is not intended to be a measurement of the effect of all such occurrences.[1]

It should be noted that the term depreciation is used in a specialized sense in accounting. It is the systematic allocation of cost in recognition of the exhaustion of asset life and is applicable only to those tangible assets used by the business. Depreciation is not used to designate a decline in market value as the term is popularly employed. Nor is the term used to designate the

[1]*Accounting Research and Terminology Bulletins — Final Edition,* "Accounting Terminology Bulletins, No. 1, Review and Résumé" (New York: American Institute of Certified Public Accountants, 1961) par. 56.

physical change in an asset, for an asset may show little physical decline in the early years and may have significant physical utility even at the time of its retirement. It is not used to designate the charge for using wasting assets, which is termed *depletion*, nor to designate the allocation of costs over a period of time for limited-life intangible assets, which is termed *amortization*. Depreciation does not refer to a decrease in value assigned to marketable securities as a result of market decline, nor to a decrease in value assigned to inventories as a result of obsolescence, spoilage, or other deterioration.

FACTORS DETERMINING THE PERIODIC DEPRECIATION CHARGE

Four factors must be recognized in arriving at the periodic charge for the use of a depreciable property item: (1) *asset cost*, (2) *residual or salvage value*, (3) *useful life*, and (4) *pattern of use*.

Asset Cost

The *cost* of a property item includes all the expenditures relating to its acquisition and preparation for use as described in Chapter 8. Expenditures considered to be related to revenues of future periods are capitalized and form the base for depreciation charges.

Residual or Salvage Value

The *residual* or *salvage value* of a depreciable asset is the amount which can reasonably be expected to be realized upon retirement of an asset. This may depend upon the retirement policy of the company as well as market conditions and other factors. If, for example, the company normally uses equipment until it is physically exhausted and no longer serviceable, the residual value, represented by the scrap or junk that may be salvaged, may be only nominal. But if the company normally trades its equipment after a relatively short period of use, the residual value, represented by the value in trade, may be relatively high. In some cases the cost of dismantling and removing an asset may equal or exceed the residual value. From a theoretical point of view, any estimated residual value should be subtracted from cost in arriving at the depreciable cost of the asset; on the other hand, dismantling and removal costs expected to exceed the ultimate salvage value should be added to the cost in arriving at an asset's depreciable cost.

In practice, both salvage values and dismantling and removal costs are frequently ignored in developing periodic depreciation charges. Disregard of these items is not objectionable when they are relatively small and not subject to reasonable estimation and when it is doubtful whether greater accuracy will be gained through such refinement of the depreciation estimate.

Useful Life

Buildings and equipment items have a limited *useful life* as a result of certain *physical* and *functional* factors. The physical factors that move a property item towards its ultimate retirement are (1) *wear and tear*, (2) *deterioration and decay*, and (3) *damage or destruction*. Everyone is familiar with the processes of wear and tear that render an automobile, a typewriter, or furniture no longer usable. The deterioration and the decay of an asset through ageing, whether the asset is used or not, is also well known. Finally, fire, flood, earthquake, or accident may reduce or terminate the useful life of an asset.

The functional factors limiting the life of a property item are (1) *inadequacy* and (2) *obsolescence*. An asset may lose its usefulness when, as a result of altered business requirements, it can no longer carry the productive load and requires replacement. Although the asset is still usable, its inadequacy for present purposes has cut short its service life. An asset may also lose its usefulness as a result of consumer demand for new and different products or services or as a result of technological change and the availability of other assets that can be more economically employed. In such instances, obsolescence is the factor operating to limit service life.

Depreciation accounting calls for the recognition of both the physical and functional factors limiting the useful life of an asset. This recognition requires the estimation of future events and requires careful judgment on the part of the accountant.[2] Physical factors are more readily apparent than functional factors in predicting the asset life. But when certain functional factors are expected to hasten the retirement of an asset, these must also be recognized. Both physical and functional factors may operate gradually or may emerge in sudden fashion. Recognition of depreciation is usually limited to the conditions that operate gradually and are reasonably foreseeable. For example, a sudden change in demand for a certain product may make a property item worthless, or an accident may destroy a property item, but these are unforeseeable events to be recognized when they occur.

Since the service life of an asset is affected by maintenance and repairs, the policy operating with respect to these matters must be considered in estimating useful life. Low standards of maintenance and repair keep these charges at a minimum but may hasten the physical deterioration of the asset, thus requiring higher-than-normal allocations for depreciation. On the other hand, high standards of maintenance and repairs will mean higher charges for these items; but with a policy prolonging the usefulness of assets, allocations for depreciation may be reduced.

---

[2]Although the concept of useful life is generally recognized to be difficult to apply, there has been relatively little written on it in accounting literature. For a thorough discussion of the topic, see Charles Lamden, Dale L. Gerboth, and Thomas McRae, "Accounting for Depreciable Assets," *Accounting Research Monograph No. 1* (New York: American Institute of Certified Public Accountants, 1975), Chap. 5.

The useful life of a property item may be expressed in terms of either an estimated *time* factor or an estimated *use* factor. The time factor may be a period of months or years; the use factor may be a number of hours of service or a number of units of output. The cost of the property item flows into production in accordance with the lapse of time or degrees of use. The rate of cost flow may be modified by other factors, but basically depreciation must be measured on a time or use basis.

Pattern of Use

In arriving at the useful life of an asset, it is necessary to consider the *pattern of use* and focus upon how the asset's services are actually to be used over that life. Service cost is being matched against revenue. If the asset produces a varying revenue pattern, then the depreciation charges should vary in a corresponding manner. When depreciation is measured in terms of a time factor, the pattern of use must be estimated. Several somewhat arbitrary methods have come into common use. Each method represents a different pattern and is designed to make the time basis approximate the use basis.[3] The time factor is employed in two general classes of methods, *straight-line depreciation* and *decreasing-charge depreciation*. When depreciation is measured in terms of a use factor, the units of use must be estimated. The depreciation charge varies periodically in accordance with the services provided by the asset. The use factor is employed in *service-hours depreciation* and in *productive-output depreciation*.

RECORDING DEPRECIATION

Periodic depreciation could be recorded by a debit to operations and a credit to the property item. However, it is customary to report the reduction in a depreciable asset in a separate valuation or asset contra account. When cost allocation is reported in a separate account, original cost, as well as that part of the cost already allocated to revenues, can be provided on the balance sheet. This practice also serves to emphasize the estimates inherent in the allocation process.

A variety of titles are used to designate the valuation balance, such as Accumulated Depreciation, Allowance for Depreciation, and Depreciation Allocated to Past Operations. In the past the term Reserve for Depreciation had been widely used; now such terminology is considered objectionable because it may suggest the existence of a fund available for asset replacement.

A separate valuation account is maintained for each asset or class of

---

[3]The Cost Accounting Standards Board (CASB) has considered guidelines for accounting for depreciation on government contracts. Generally, the standard for depreciation requires that the method selected "shall reflect the expected consumption of services in each accounting period." ("Depreciation of Tangible Capital Assets," *Code of Federal Regulations*, Title 4, Chap. III, Part 409[3]).

assets requiring the use of a separate depreciation rate. When a subsidiary ledger is maintained for land, buildings, and equipment, such record normally provides for the accumulation of depreciation allocations on the individual assets. Separate debits relating to individual property items in the subsidiary ledger support the land, buildings, and equipment balance in the general ledger; separate credits representing individual property item cost allocations in the subsidiary ledger support the accumulated depreciation balance in the general ledger.

When a property item consists of a number of units or structural elements with varying lives and these units are recorded separately, depreciation is recognized in terms of the respective lives of the different units. Retirement of an individual unit and its replacement by a new unit requires the cancellation of cost and accumulated depreciation balances related to the old unit and recognition of the new.

METHODS OF COST ALLOCATION

As mentioned earlier, there are a number of different methods for allocating the costs of depreciable assets. The method used in any specific instance is a matter of judgment and should be selected to most closely approximate the actual pattern of use expected from the asset. The following methods are described in this chapter:

Time-Factor Methods
1. Straight-line depreciation
2. Decreasing-charge depreciation
    (a) Declining-balance method
    (b) Sum-of-the-years digits method

Use-Factor Methods
1. Service-hours method
2. Productive-output method

Group-Rate and Composite-Rate Methods
1. Group depreciation
2. Composite depreciation

Two other time-factor methods each providing for increasing charges, the *annuity method* and the *sinking fund method*, require the use of compound interest calculations. These methods are rarely encountered in practice except for some applications in the real estate development industry.

The examples that follow assume the acquisition of a machine at a cost of $10,000 with a salvage value at the end of its useful life of $500. The following symbols are employed in the formulas for the development of depreciation rates and charges:

C = Asset Cost
S = Estimated salvage value

n = Estimated life in years, hours of service, or units of output
r = Depreciation rate per period, per hour of service, or per unit of output
D = Annual depreciation charge

Straight-Line Depreciation

Straight-line depreciation relates cost allocation to the passage of time and recognizes equal periodic charges over the life of the asset. The depreciation charge assumes equal usefulness per time period, and in applying this assumption, the charge is not affected by asset productivity or efficiency variations. In developing the periodic charge, an estimate is made of the useful life of the asset in terms of months or years. The difference between the asset cost and salvage value is divided by the useful life of the asset in arriving at the cost assigned to each time unit.

Using data for the machine referred to earlier and assuming a 10-year life, annual depreciation is determined as follows:

$$D = \frac{C - S}{n} \text{ , or } \frac{\$10,000 - \$500}{10} = \$950$$

The depreciation rate is commonly expressed as a percentage to be applied periodically to asset cost. The depreciation rate in the example is calculated as follows: $(100\% - 5\%) \div 10 = 9.5\%$. This percentage applied to cost provides a periodic charge of $950. The rate may also be expressed as a percentage to be applied to depreciable cost — cost less residual value. Expressed in this way the rate is simply the reciprocal value of the useful life expressed in periods, or r (per period) = $1 \div n$. In the example, then, the annual rate would be $1 \div 10 = 10\%$, and this rate applied to depreciable cost, $9,500, gives an annual charge of $950. A table to summarize the process of cost allocation follows:

End of Year	Asset Cost Allocation — Straight-Line Method		
	Debit to Depreciation and Credit to Accumulated Depreciation	Balance of Accumulated Depreciation	Asset Book Value
			$10,000
1	$ 950	$ 950	9,050
2	950	1,900	8,100
3	950	2,850	7,150
4	950	3,800	6,200
5	950	4,750	5,250
6	950	5,700	4,300
7	950	6,650	3,350
8	950	7,600	2,400
9	950	8,550	1,450
10	950	9,500	500
	$9,500		

It was indicated earlier that residual value is frequently ignored when the amount is relatively minor. If this were done in the example, a ten-year life would call for the use of a 10% rate; depreciation, then, would be recognized at $1,000 per year instead of $950.

In using the straight-line method, depreciation is a constant or fixed charge for each period. Net income measurements become particularly sensitive to changes in the volume of business activity: with above-normal activity, there is no increase in the depreciation charge; with below-normal activity, revenue is still charged with the costs of assets standing ready to serve. When the life of a property item is affected primarily by the lapse of time rather than by the degree of use, recognition of depreciation as a constant charge is particularly appropriate.

The straight-line method of depreciation is widely used in practice. It is readily understood and frequently parallels asset deterioration. It has the advantage of simplicity and under normal property conditions offers a satisfactory means of cost allocation. Normal property conditions mean (1) properties that have been accumulated over a period of years so that the total of depreciation plus maintenance is comparatively even from period to period, and (2) properties whose service potentials are being steadily reduced by functional as well as physical factors. The absence of either of these conditions may suggest the use of some method other than the straight-line method.

Decreasing Charge Depreciation

Decreasing-charge or *accelerated depreciation methods* also relate charges for depreciation to time. However, they provide for the highest depreciation charge in the first year of asset use and declining depreciation charges in ensuing years. Such plans are based largely on the assumption that there will be reductions in asset efficiency, output, or other benefits as the asset ages. Such reductions may be accompanied by increased charges for maintenance and repairs. Charges for depreciation decline, then, as the economic advantages afforded through ownership of the asset decline.

Declining-Balance Method. The *declining-balance method* provides decreasing charges by applying a constant percentage rate to a declining asset book value. The theoretical rate to be applied to the declining book value in producing the estimated salvage value at the end of the useful life of the asset can be determined by the following formula:

$$r \text{ (rate per period applicable to declining book value)} = 1 - \sqrt[n]{S \div C}$$

Using the previous asset data and assuming a 10-year asset life, the depreciation rate is determined as follows:

$$1 - \sqrt[10]{500 \div 10,000} = 1 - \sqrt[10]{.05} = 1 - .74113 = .25887, \text{ or } 25.887\%$$

Dividing the estimated salvage value by cost in the preceding formula gives .05, the value that the salvage value at the end of 10 years should bear to cost. The tenth root of this value is .74113. Multiplying cost and the successive declining book values by .74113 ten times will reduce the asset to .05 of its cost. The difference between 1 and .74113, or .25887, then, is the rate of decrease to be applied successively in bringing the asset down to .05 of its original balance. Since it is impossible to bring a value down to zero by a constant multiplier, a residual value must be assigned to the asset in using the formula. In the absence of an expected residual value, a nominal value of $1 can be assumed for this purpose.

Depreciation calculated by application of the 25.887% rate to the declining book value is summarized in the following table:

Asset Cost Allocation — Declining-Balance Method

Year	Debit to Depreciation and Credit to Accumulated Depreciation		Balance of Accumulated Depreciation	Asset Book Value
				$10,000.00
1	(25.887% × $10,000.00)	$2,588.70	$2,588.70	7,411.30
2	(25.887% × 7,411.30)	1,918.56	4,507.26	5,492.74
3	(25.887% × 5,492.74)	1,421.91	5,929.17	4,070.83
4	(25.887% × 4,070.83)	1,053.82	6,982.99	3,017.01
5	(25.887% × 3,017.01)	781.01	7,764.00	2,236.00
6	(25.887% × 2,236.00)	578.83	8,342.83	1,657.17
7	(25.887% × 1,657.17)	428.99	8,771.82	1,228.18
8	(25.887% × 1,228.18)	317.94	9,089.76	910.24
9	(25.887% × 910.24)	235.63	9,325.39	674.61
10	(25.887% × 674.61)	174.61	9,500.00	500.00*
		$9,500.00		

*Discrepancy due to rounding.

Instead of developing an exact rate that will produce a salvage value of $500, it is usually more convenient to approximate a rate that will provide satisfactory cost allocation; since depreciation involves an estimate there is little assurance that rate refinement will produce more accurate results. In the previous illustration, the use of a rate of 25% is more convenient than 25.887%; differences are not material. In practice, capital cost allowance rates as prescribed for tax purposes are sometimes used in applying the declining-balance method of depreciation. Usually a residual value is not taken into account.

Sum-of-the-Years-Digits Method. The *sum-of-the-years-digits method* provides decreasing charges by applying a series of fractions, each of a smaller value, to depreciable asset cost. Fractions are developed in terms of the sum of the asset life periods. Weights for purposes of developing reducing fractions are the years-digits listed in reverse order. The denominator for the fraction is obtained by adding these weights; the numerator is the weight assigned to the specific year. The denominator for the fraction can be obtained by an alternate calculation: the sum of the digits for the first and last years can be divided by 2 and multiplied by the number of years of asset life. In the example, the denominator can be determined as follows: ($[10 + 1] \div 2) \times 10 = 55$. Periodic charges for depreciation using the sum-of-the-years-digits method for the asset previously described are developed as follows:

	Reducing Weights	Reducing Fractions
First year	10	10/55
Second year	9	9/55
Third year	8	8/55
Fourth year	7	7/55
Fifth year	6	6/55
Sixth year	5	5/55
Seventh year	4	4/55
Eighth year	3	3/55
Ninth year	2	2/55
Tenth year	1	1/55
	55	55/55

Depreciation computed by the application of reducing fractions to depreciable cost is summarized in the table below:

End of Year	Debit to Depreciation and Credit to Accumulated Depreciation		Balance of Accumulated Depreciation	Asset Book Value
				$10,000.00
1	(10/55 × $9,500)	$1,727.27	$1,727.27	8,272.73
2	(9/55 × 9,500)	1,554.55	3,281.82	6,718.18
3	(8/55 × 9,500)	1,381.82	4,663.64	5,336.36
4	(7/55 × 9,500)	1,209.09	5,872.73	4,127.27
5	(6/55 × 9,500)	1,036.36	6,909.09	3,090.91
6	(5/55 × 9,500)	863.64	7,772.73	2,227.27
7	(4/55 × 9,500)	690.91	8,463.64	1,536.36
8	(3/55 × 9,500)	518.18	8,981.82	1,018.18
9	(2/55 × 9,500)	345.45	9,327.27	672.73
10	(1/55 × 9,500)	172.73	9,500.00	500.00
		$9,500.00		

Asset Cost Allocation — Sum-of-the-Years-Digits Method

Evaluation of Decreasing-Charge Methods. Decreasing-charge methods can be supported as reasonable approaches to asset cost allocation when the benefits provided by a property item decline as it grows older. These methods, too, are suggested when a property item calls for increasing maintenance and repairs over its useful life.[4] When straight-line depreciation is employed, the combined charges for depreciation, maintenance, and repairs will increase over the life of the asset; when the decreasing-charge methods are used, the combined charges may tend to be equalized.

Other factors suggesting the use of a decreasing-charge method include: (1) the anticipation of a significant contribution to production or earnings in early periods of asset life; (2) the possibility that inadequacy or obsolescence may result in premature retirement of the asset. In the event of premature retirement, depreciation charges will have absorbed what would otherwise require recognition as a loss.

Capital cost allowance, which is the income tax counterpart of depreciation, is in effect an accelerated method that permits larger deductions for income tax purposes during the early years of asset life. Although total capital cost allowances over asset life are no greater, the recognition of higher deductions in the early years of an asset's life serves to postpone income tax and thus provides interest-free working capital. Canadian taxpayers have no alternative to the use of capital cost allowances for income tax purposes; however, many corporations use straight-line depreciation for accounting purposes. In such circumstances, income tax allocation adjustments are required because of timing differences in recognizing depreciation charges.[5]

Use-Factor Methods

Use-factor methods view asset exhaustion as related primarily to asset use or output and provide periodic charges varying with the degree of such service. Service life for certain assets can best be expressed in terms of hours of services; for others in terms of units of production.

Service-Hours Method. *Service-hours* depreciation is based on the theory that purchase of an asset represents the purchase of a number of hours of direct service. This method requires an estimate of the life of the asset in terms of service hours. Depreciable cost is divided by total service hours in arriving at the depreciation rate to be assigned for each hour of asset use. The use of the asset during the period is measured, and the number of service hours is multiplied by the depreciation rate in arriving at the depreciation charge. Depreciation charges fluctuate periodically according to the contribution the asset makes in service hours.

---

[4] The AICPA Committee on Accounting Procedure has stated, "The declining-balance method is one of those which meets the requirements of being 'systematic and rational.' In those cases where the expected productivity or revenue-earning power of the asset is relatively greater during the earlier years of its life, or where maintenance charges tend to increase during the later years, the declining-balance method may well provide the most satisfactory allocation of cost." The Committee would apply these conclusions to other decreasing-charge methods, including the sum-of-the-years-digits method, that produce substantially similar results. See *Accounting Research and Terminology Bulletins — Final Edition*, "No. 44 (Revised), Declining-Balance Depreciation" (New York: American Institute of Certified Public Accountants, 1961), par. 2.

[5] See discussion in Chapter 14.

Using asset data previously given and an estimated service life of 20,000 hours, the rate to be applied for each service hour is determined as follows:

$$r \text{ (per hour)} = \frac{C - S}{n}, \text{ or } \frac{\$10,000 - \$500}{20,000} = \$.475$$

Allocation of asset cost in terms of service hours is summarized in the table below:

		Asset Cost Allocation — Service-Hours Method			
Year	Service Hours	Debit to Depreciation and Credit to Accumulated Depreciation		Balance of Accumulated Depreciation	Asset Book Value
					$10,000.00
1	1,500	(1,500 × $.475)	$ 712.50	$ 712.50	9,287.50
2	2,500	(2,500 × .475)	1,187.50	1,900.00	8,100.00
3	2,500	(2,500 × .475)	1,187.50	3,087.50	6,912.50
4	2,000	(2,000 × .475)	950.00	4,037.50	5,962.50
5	1,500	(1,500 × .475)	712.50	4,750.00	5,250.00
6	1,500	(1,500 × .475)	712.50	5,462.50	4,537.50
7	3,000	(3,000 × .475)	1,425.00	6,887.50	3,112.50
8	2,500	(2,500 × .475)	1,187.50	8,075.00	1,925.00
9	2,000	(2,000 × .475)	950.00	9,025.00	975.00
10	1,000	(1,000 × .475)	475.00	9,500.00	500.00
	20,000		$9,500.00		

It is assumed that the original estimate of service hours is confirmed and the asset is retired after 20,000 hours are reached in the tenth year. Such precise confirmation would seldom be found in practice.

It should be observed that straight-line depreciation resulted in an annual charge of $950 regardless of fluctuations in productive activity. When asset life is affected directly by the degree of use, and when there are significant fluctuations in such use in successive periods, the service-hours method, which recognizes hours used instead of hours available for use, normally provides the more equitable charges to operations.

Productive-Output Method. *Productive-output* depreciation is based on the theory that an asset is acquired for the service it can provide in the form of production output. This method requires an estimate of the total unit output of the property item. Depreciable cost divided by the total output gives the equal depreciation debit to be assigned for each unit of output. The measured production for a period multiplied by the depreciation charge per unit gives the charge to be made for depreciation. Depreciation charges fluctuate periodically according to the contribution the asset makes in unit output.

Using the previous asset data and an estimated productive life of 2,500,000 units, the rate to be applied for each thousand units produced is determined as follows:

$$r \text{ (per thousand units)} = \frac{C - S}{n}, \text{ or } \frac{\$10,000 - \$500}{2,500} = \$3.80$$

Asset cost allocation in terms of productive output is summarized in the tabulation below:

		Asset Cost Allocation — Productive-Output Method			
Year	Unit Output	Debit to Depreciation and Credit to Accumulated Depreciation		Balance of Accumulated Depreciation	Asset Book Value
					$10,000
1	80,000	(80 × $3.80)	$ 304	$ 304	9,696
2	250,000	(250 × 3.80)	950	1,254	8,746
3	400,000	(400 × 3.80)	1,520	2,774	7,226
4	320,000	(320 × 3.80)	1,216	3,990	6,010
5	440,000	(440 × 3.80)	1,672	5,662	4,338
6	360,000	(360 × 3.80)	1,368	7,030	2,970
7	280,000	(280 × 3.80)	1,064	8,094	1,906
8	210,000	(210 × 3.80)	798	8,892	1,108
9	120,000	(120 × 3.80)	456	9,348	652
10	40,000	(40 × 3.80)	152	9,500	500
	2,500,000		$9,500		

Evaluation of Use-Factor Methods. When quantitative uses of depreciable properties can be reasonably estimated and readily measured, the use-factor methods provide highly satisfactory approaches to asset cost allocation. Depreciation is a fluctuating charge tending to follow the revenue curve: high depreciation charges are assigned to periods of high activity; low depreciation charges are assigned to periods of low activity. When the useful life of an asset is affected primarily by the degree of its use, recognition of depreciation as a variable charge is particularly appropriate.

However, certain limitations in the use-factor methods need to be pointed out. Asset performance in terms of service hours or productive output may be difficult to estimate. Measurement solely in terms of these factors could fail to recognize special conditions, such as increasing maintenance and repair costs as well as possible inadequacy and obsolescence. Furthermore, when service life expires even in the absence of use, a use-factor method may serve to conceal actual fluctuations in earnings; by relating periodic depreciation to the volume of operations; periodic operating results may be smoothed out, thus creating a false appearance of stability.

Group-Rate and Composite-Rate Methods

It was assumed in preceding discussions that depreciation is associated with individual property items and is applied to each separate unit. This practice is commonly referred to as *unit depreciation*. However, there may be certain advantages in associating depreciation with a group of properties and applying a single rate to the collective cost of the group. Group cost allocation procedures are referred to as *group depreciation* and *composite depreciations*.

Group Depreciation. When useful life is affected primarily by physical factors, a group of similar items purchased at one time should have the same expected life, but in fact some will probably remain useful longer than others. In recording depreciation on a unit basis, the sale or retirement of an asset before or after its anticipated life requires recognition of a gain or loss. Such gains and losses, however, can usually be attributed to normal variations in useful life rather than to unforeseen disasters and windfalls.

The *group-depreciation* procedure treats a collection of similar assets as a single group. Depreciation is accumulated in a single valuation account, and the depreciation rate is based on the average life of assets in the group. Because the accumulated depreciation account under the group procedure applies to the entire group of assets, it is not related to any specific asset. Thus, there are no fully depreciated assets and the depreciation rate is applied to the cost of all assets remaining in service, regardless of age, in arriving at the periodic depreciation charge.

When an item in the group is retired, no gain or loss is recognized; the asset account is credited with the cost of the item and the valuation account is debited for the difference between cost and any salvage. With normal variations in asset lives, the losses not recognized on early retirements are offset by the continued depreciation charges on those assets still in service after the average life has elapsed.

To illustrate, assume 100 similar machines having an average expected useful life of 5 years are purchased at a total cost of $200,000. Of this group, 30 machines are retired at the end of four years, 40 at the end of five years, and the remaining 30 at the end of the sixth year. Based on the average expected useful life of 5 years, a depreciation charge of 20% is reported on those assets in service each year. The charges for depreciation and the changes in the group asset and accumulated depreciation accounts are summarized at the top of the next page.

It should be noted that the depreciation charge is exactly $400 per machine-year. In each of the first four years, 100 machine-years of service are utilized, and the annual depreciation charge is $40,000. In the fifth year, when only 70 machines are in operation, the charge is $28,000. In the sixth year, when 30 units are still in service, a proportionate charge for such use of $12,000 is made. Under unit depreciation a loss of $12,000 would have been recognized at the end of the fourth year when 30 machines were scrapped prematurely. However, no charge for depreciation would have been recog-

	Debit to Depreciation (20% of Cost)	Asset Cost Allocation — Group Depreciation						
		Asset			Accumulated Depreciation			Asset Book Value
Year		Debit	Credit	Balance	Debit	Credit	Balance	
		$200,000		$200,000				$200,000
1	$ 40,000			200,000		$ 40,000	$ 40,000	$160,000
2	40,000			200,000		40,000	80,000	120,000
3	40,000			200,000		40,000	120,000	80,000
4	40,000		$ 60,000	140,000	$ 60,000	40,000	100,000	40,000
5	28,000		80,000	60,000	80,000	28,000	48,000	12,000
6	12,000		60,000	——	60,000	12,000	——	——
	$200,000	$200,000	$200,000		$200,000	$200,000		

nized in the sixth year when the 30 machines remaining in service would have been fully depreciated.[6]

Application of the group depreciation procedure under circumstances such as the foregoing provides an annual charge that is more closely related to the quantity of productive facilities being used. Gains and losses due solely to normal variations in asset lives are not recognized, and operating results are more meaningfully stated. The convenience of applying a uniform depreciation rate to a number of similar items may also represent a substantial advantage.

Composite Depreciation. The basic procedures employed under the group method for allocating the cost of substantially identical assets may be extended to include dissimilar assets. This special application of the group procedure is known as *composite depreciation*. The composite method retains the convenience of the group method, but because assets with varying service-lives are aggregated to determine an average life, it is unlikely to provide all the reporting advantages of the group method.

A composite rate is established by analysing the various assets or classes of assets in use and computing the depreciation as follows:

Asset	Cost	Residual Value	Depreciable Cost	Estimated Life in Years	Annual Depreciation
A	$ 2,000	$ 120	$ 1,880	4	$ 470
B	6,000	300	5,700	6	950
C	12,000	1,200	10,800	10	1,080
	$20,000	$1,620	$18,380		$2,500

Composite depreciation rate to be applied to cost: $2,500 ÷ $20,000 = 12.5%
Composite or average life of assets: $18,380 ÷ $2,500 = 7.35 years

[6]It should be observed that in the example the original estimates of an average useful life of 5 years is confirmed in the use of the assets. Such precise confirmation would seldom be the case. In instances where assets in a group are continued in use after their cost has been assigned to operations, no further depreciation charges would be recognized. On the other hand, where all of the assets in a group are retired before their cost has been assigned to operations, a special charge related to such retirement would have to be recognized.

It will be observed that a rate of 12.5% applied to the cost of the assets, $20,000, results in annual depreciation of $2,500. Annual depreciation of $2,500 will accumulate to a total of $18,380 in 7.35 years; hence 7.35 years may be considered the composite or average life of the assets. Composite depreciation would be reported in a single valuation account. Upon the retirement of an individual asset, the asset account is closed and the valuation account is debited with the difference between cost and residual value. As with the group procedure, no gains or losses are recognized at the time individual assets are retired.

After a composite rate has been set, it is ordinarily continued in the absence of significant changes in the lives of assets or asset additions and retirements having a material effect upon the rate. It is assumed in the preceding example that the assets are replaced with similar assets when retired. If they are not replaced, continuation of the 12.5% rate will misstate depreciation charges.

DEPRECIATION FOR PARTIAL PERIODS

The discussion thus far has assumed that assets were purchased or sold on the first day of a company's fiscal period. In reality, of course, asset transactions occur throughout the year. Company policy determines how partial periods will be handled for depreciation purposes. The following are some alternatives commonly followed:

1. Compute depreciation to the nearest whole month. Assets acquired on or before the 15th of the month are considered owned for the entire month; assets acquired after the 15th are not considered owned for any part of the month. Conversely, assets sold on or before the 15th of the month are not considered owned for any part of the month; assets sold after the 15th are considered owned for the entire month.
2. Compute depreciation to the nearest whole year. Assets acquired during the first six months are considered held for the entire year; assets acquired during the last six months are not considered in the depreciation computation. Conversely, no depreciation is recorded on assets sold during the first six months and a full year's depreciation is recorded on assets sold during the last six months.
3. One-half year's depreciation is taken on all assets purchased or sold during the year. A full year's depreciation is taken on all other assets.

If a company uses the sum-of-the-years-digits method of depreciation and recognizes partial year's depreciation on assets purchased or sold, each year's computation after the first year must be divided into two parts. The depreciation expense for each full year must be computed and then prorated over the partial periods. For example, assume the asset discussed on page 335 was acquired midway through a fiscal period. The computation of depreciation for the first two years recognizing partial period depreciation would be as follows:

First Year

Depreciation for first full year (see page 338)	$1,727.27	
One-half year's depreciation		$ 863.64

Second Year

Depreciation for balance of first year		$ 863.63
Depreciation for second full year (see page 338)	$1,554.55	
One-half year's depreciation		777.28
Total depreciation — second year		$1,640.91

DEPRECIATION ACCOUNTING FOR INCOME TAX PURPOSES

Strictly speaking the Income Tax Act does not permit the deduction of depreciation for income tax purposes. However, in lieu of depreciation, the capital cost allowance system provides as a deduction for income tax purposes an allowance for the capital cost invested in certain specified long-life assets. For practical purposes, therefore, capital cost allowance is the tax counterpart of depreciation.

Capital cost allowance is not merely an allocation of a past cost as is depreciation accounting. The critical event for capital cost allowance purposes is the investment itself rather than its service or use. In theory, of course, it is the service or use of property that underlies depreciation accounting.

The capital cost allowance system was initially introduced in 1949 primarily for administrative convenience. Over the years, however, the system has been used to provide a variety of tax incentives to encourage capital investment and the creation of jobs. As a result, the distinction between capital cost allowance and depreciation has expanded to the point where the two now have little in common.

For accounting purposes, some small businesses use the capital cost allowance system as the basis of recording depreciation. Since capital cost allowances and depreciation are becoming increasingly different, the former should not be used as a surrogate for the latter. According to the CICA publication, *Financial Reporting in Canada*, approximately 60 per cent of the survey companies that disclosed their depreciation method(s) for 1978 used the straight-line method, in a number of cases together with other methods. Diminishing balance ranked second, being used by 25 per cent of the survey companies.[7] Differences between depreciation for accounting purposes and

<hr>

[7]*Financial Reporting in Canada* (13th ed.; Toronto: Canadian Institute of Chartered Accountants, 1979), p. 170.

capital cost allowance give rise to timing differences that require the application of income tax allocation procedures.[8]

Capital cost allowance is normally determined by the declining-balance method applied on a group basis to each category or class of specified asset. The most common classes of assets and the related rates of capital cost allowance are as follows:

Frame buildings	Class 3	5%
Brick buildings	Class 6	10%
Equipment	Class 8	20%
Cars and trucks	Class 10	30%

In general, capital cost allowances are determined by applying prescribed rates to the year-end balance in each class of asset. It is important to note that capital cost allowances are computed on a group rather than individual asset basis. Additions are always added to the group or class no matter when they are acquired. Disposals are deducted in an amount equal to the lesser of the capital cost of the asset or the proceeds of disposal. This procedure in the case of disposals has the effect of excluding any capital gain from the undepreciated capital cost balance in the class. The foregoing can be summarized in the form of a schedule as follows:

Undepreciated capital cost at the beginning of the year	$xx
Add: Additions during the year	xx
	$xx
Deduct: Disposals during the year, the lesser of	
(a) the capital cost, or	
(b) the proceeds of disposal	xx
Undepreciated capital cost before allowance	$xx
Capital cost allowance for the year	xx
Undepreciated capital cost at the beginning of the next year	$xx

For income tax purposes, the deduction for capital cost allowance can be any amount from zero to the maximum permitted. The maximum is determined by aggregating, for each class of asset, amounts determined in the manner summarized in the preceding schedule. The decision to claim the maximum or some lesser amount rests with the taxpayer.[9] Exceptions, calculated on a straight-line basis, are provided for certain classes of assets as follows: (1) Class 13, leasehold improvements, (2) Class 14, limited life intangibles, and (3) Class 29, manufacturing equipment subject to accelerated

---

[8] See discussion in Chapter 14.

[9] In the circumstances of a loss for income tax purposes, the decision to claim capital cost allowance, thus increasing the amount of the loss, should be given careful consideration. For income tax purposes, the loss may be carried back one year and forward for a period of five years. At the end of five years, the potential benefit of the tax deductibility of the loss carry forward expires. Obviously the amount of a loss for income tax purposes should not be increased by a claim for capital cost allowance if future prospects cast doubt on the likelihood of being able to fully deduct the loss within the carry forward period.

capital cost allowance. Class 29 is an interesting example of capital cost allowance being used to encourage investment. Equipment in Class 29 qualifies for a capital cost allowance deduction of 50 per cent calculated on a straight-line basis. Although Class 29 was introduced as a temporary measure to encourage investment it is still in use with no indication of any proposal to terminate it.

A negative or credit year-end balance in a class of assets results in *recaptured capital cost allowance*, which the taxpayer must include in income in the year in which it arises. Recapture is based on the premise that past capital cost allowance claims were not really justified because the asset(s) in fact appreciated rather than depreciated. A positive or debit year-end balance in a class in which all assets have been disposed of is called a *terminal loss* and may be claimed as a deduction in the year in which it arises.

DEPRECIATION ACCOUNTING AND PROPERTY REPLACEMENT

There has been a tendency on the part of many readers of financial statements to interpret depreciation accounting as somehow related to the accumulation of a fund for asset replacement. The use of such terms as "provision for depreciation" and "reserve for depreciation" has contributed toward this misinterpretation. Also, the presentation of depreciation as a line item in the determination of funds provided by operations on the statement of changes in financial position has further contributed to this misunderstanding.

It is true that if property did not depreciate replacement might not be necessary. The charge for depreciation, however, originates from the recognition of the movement of a property item toward ultimate exhaustion. The nature of this charge is no different from those made to recognize the expiration of insurance premiums or patent rights. It is true that revenues equal to or in excess of expenses for a period result in a recovery of these expenses; salary expense is thus recovered by revenues, as is insurance expense, patent amortization, and charges for depreciation. But this does not mean that cash equivalent to the recorded depreciation will necessarily be segregated to use for property replacement. Resources from revenues may be applied to many uses: to the increase in receivables, inventories, or other working capital items; to the acquisition of new property or other non-current items; to the retirement of debt or the redemption of shares; or to the payment of dividends. If a special fund is to be available for the replacement of property, special authorization by management would be required. Such a fund is seldom found, however, because good financial management would require fund-earnings exceeding those accruing from alternative uses of the resources.

PROPERTY RECORDS

Data concerning individual property items are required in accounting for past activities, in planning future activities, and for insurance, tax, and other purposes. Data requirements can be met only by detailed records systematically and efficiently maintained. Such records are variously termed Unit Property Records, Property Ledger, and Fixed Asset Control Records. They usually involve the control account principle; property items being summarized in the general ledger, and detail being recorded in subsidiary ledgers.

Subsidiary records are commonly found in the form of a property register or a property file. When a property register is used, special sections are usually assigned to the assets of each department so depreciation charges may be accumulated departmentally. One line is provided for each asset, and significant information regarding the asset is reported in special columns. A register prepared in a form that summarizes periodic depreciation charges is generally referred to as a *lapsing schedule*. Individual assets are listed as they are acquired and periodic depreciation charges for the entire life of each depreciable asset are reported in a series of columns representing successive years. The charge for depreciation is readily determined by adding the debits appearing in the column for the particular years.

The use of a property file consisting of cards or separate sheets frequently provides a more flexible record than the register form since assets can be arranged in an order other than date of acquisition. One card or one sheet is provided for each asset on which all information with respect to the item is listed. For buildings and equipment, this information usually includes the name of the asset, location, name of the vendor, guarantee period, insurance carried, date acquired, original cost, transportation charges, installation cost, estimated life, estimated residual value, depreciation rate, depreciation to date, major expenditures for repairs and improvements, and proceeds from final disposal. Property files are frequently maintained on tabulating cards, magnetic tapes, or in the memory of an electronic computer. When the information is maintained and stored in this form, it may be easily sorted and used to make depreciation computations and accounting entries.

DISCLOSURE OF DEPRECIATION METHODS IN FINANCIAL STATEMENTS

Because of the alternative methods available to compute depreciation, the method used should be disclosed in the financial statements. Without disclosure, a user of the statements might be misled in trying to compare the financial results of one company with another. The *Accounting Recommendations* list both the methods and rates of depreciation as examples of items requiring disclosure of accounting policies.[10]

---

[10]*CICA Handbook: Accounting Recommendations, Section 1505*, "Disclosure of Accounting Policies" (Toronto: Canadian Institute of Chartered Accountants, 1974), par. 10.

DEPLETION

Natural resources, also called *wasting assets*, move toward exhaustion as the physical units representing these resources are removed and sold. The withdrawal of oil or gas, the cutting of timber, and the mining of coal, sulphur, iron, copper, or silver ore are examples of processes leading to the exhaustion of natural resources. The reduction in the cost or value of natural resources as a result of the withdrawal of resources is referred to as *depletion*.

Depletion may be distinguished from depreciation in the following respects:

1. Depletion is recognition of the quantitative exhaustion taking place in a natural resource, while depreciation is recognition of the service exhaustion taking place in a building or equipment item.
2. Related to (1), depletion is recognized as the cost of the material that becomes directly embodied in the product of the company; through depreciation, the cost of an asset may be allocated to production but the asset itself does not become a part of the finished product.
3. Depletion involves a distinctive asset that cannot be directly replaced in kind upon its exhaustion; depreciation involves an asset that can generally be replaced upon its exhaustion.

Income measurement calls for the recognition of depletion. If the natural resource is sold directly upon its emergence or withdrawal, the recognition of depletion is, in effect, the recognition of cost of goods sold; if the natural resource is processed and stored before sale, depletion is initially recognized as a part of inventory cost.

When natural resources are acquired together with land for a lump sum, the total cost of the property must be allocated to the two property items. Separate accounts may be established for land and for the resources. The cost of the latter asset divided by the estimated quantity of resources that can profitably be removed gives the charge to be recognized for each unit removed, or the *unit depletion charge*. Depletion for the period is computed in the same way as productive-output depreciation; i.e., the measured number of units removed during the period are multiplied by the unit depletion charge.

To illustrate, assume the following facts: Land containing natural resources is purchased at a cost of $5,500,000. The land has an estimated value after removal of the resources of $250,000; the natural resources supply is estimated at 1,000,000 tons. The unit depletion charge and the total depletion charge for the first year, assuming the withdrawal of 80,000 tons, are calculated as shown here.

Depletion charge per ton: ($5,500,00 − $250,000) ÷ 1,000,000 = $5.25
Depletion charge for the first year: 80,000 tons × $5.25 = $420,000

When developmental costs, such as costs of drilling, sinking mine shafts, and constructing roads, are related to the removal of the resource, these should be added to the original cost of the property in arriving at the total cost subject to depletion. These costs may be incurred before normal activities begin. On the other hand, they may be continuing and, therefore, may call for estimates in arriving at a depletion charge to be used uniformly for all recoverable units. It should be observed that the capitalization of developmental costs is an application of the matching process requiring that costs incurred in anticipation of subsequent revenue be deferred. In practice, however, in view of a variety of special situations encountered by companies with wasting assets, practices ranging from the full capitalization of periodic developmental expenditures to the full assignment to current revenue of such expenditures are encountered. Support for charging current revenue for developmental costs is made on the grounds this practice affords the conservatism required in view of the general uncertainty of the benefits the costs may provide. Because a number of companies report developmental costs as expenses, there is a need to review carefully the financial statements of companies with wasting assets if operating results are to be properly evaluated.[11] When costs will be required to restore land for use after the resources are exhausted, these should also be added to depletable cost.

The charge for resource exhaustion is recorded by a debit to Depletion Expense and a credit directly to the resource account or to Accumulated Depletion. If an accumulated depletion account is established, it should be subtracted from the resource account in reporting the asset.

The charge for depletion, increased by labor and overhead relating to removal and processing, is reported in the "Cost of goods sold" section of the income statement. If all of the units represented by the depletion charge are sold, depletion, labor, and overhead costs measure the cost of goods sold to be applied against revenue in arriving at gross profit on sales; if some of the units remain on hand, the total for depletion, labor, and overhead related to such units is recognized as inventory and subtracted from total costs in arriving at cost of goods sold. Depletion, therefore, is comparable to raw materials purchases.

When developmental costs differ significantly from original estimates and when estimates of the available unit supply change as a result of further discoveries or improved extraction processes, revisions in the unit depletion charge often become necessary. Revisions may also be required when changes in sales prices indicate changes in the number of units that can profitably be extracted.

In revising depletion charges, no adjustment would be made for past charges; the current annual charge would be established by dividing the resource cost balance as found at the end of the year by the estimated

---

[11] Neither Section 3450 of the *CICA Handbook: Accounting Recommendations*, nor the FASB Statement No. 2 dealing with research and development costs, nor the FASB Statement No. 5 dealing with development-stage companies included activities that are unique to entities in the extractive industries.

remaining recoverable units as of the beginning of the year (units recovered during the year plus the estimated recoverable units at the end of the year). To illustrate, assume in the preceding example that additional developmental costs of $525,000 are incurred in the second year and recoverable units are estimated at 950,000 tons after second-year withdrawals of 100,000 tons. The depletion charge for the second year is then determined as shown below:

Cost assignable to recoverable tons as of the beginning of the second year:	
Original costs applicable to depletable resources	$5,250,000
Add additional costs incurred in the second year	525,000
	$5,775,000
Deduct depletion charge for the first year	420,000
Balance of cost subject to depletion	$5,355,000
Estimated recoverable tons as of the beginning of the second year:	
Number of tons withdrawn in the second year	100,000
Estimated recoverable tons as of the end of the second year	950,000
Total recoverable tons at the beginning of the second year	1,050,000

Depletion charge per ton for the second year: $5,355,000 ÷ 1,050,000 = $5.10
Depletion charge for the second year: 100,000 × $5.10 = $510,000

When buildings and improvements are constructed in connection with the removal of natural resources and their usefulness is limited to the duration of the project, it is reasonable to recognize depreciation on such properties on an output basis consistent with the charges to be recognized for the natural resources themselves. For example, assume buildings are constructed at a cost of $250,000; the useful lives of the buildings are expected to terminate upon exhaustion of the natural resource consisting of 1,000,000 units. Under these circumstances, a depreciation charge of $.25 ($250,000 ÷ 1,000,000) should accompany the depletion charge recognized for each unit. When improvements provide benefits expected to terminate prior to the exhaustion of the natural resource, the cost of such improvements may be allocated on the basis of the units to be removed during the life of the improvements or on a time basis, whichever is considered more appropriate.

QUESTIONS

1. There are several different methods that may be used to allocate the cost of property items against revenue. Wouldn't it be better to require all companies to use the same method? Discuss briefly.

2. What factors must be considered to determine the periodic depreciation charges that should be made for a company's depreciable assets?

3. What rationale can be given for ignoring salvage or residual values when computing depreciation?

4. Distinguish between functional depreciation and physical depreciation of assets.

5. After reading an article on the allocation of costs, the controller for a client corporation asks you to explain the following excerpt.

Depreciation may be either a fixed cost or a variable cost, depending on the method used to compute it.

6. The president of the Vega Co. Ltd. recommends that no depreciation be recorded for 1981 since the depreciation rate is 5% per year and indexes show that prices during the year have risen by more than this figure. Evaluate this argument.

7. The policy of the Lyons Co. is to recondition its building and equipment each year so they may be maintained in perfect repair. In view of the extensive periodic costs involved in keeping the property in such condition, officials of the company feel the need for recognizing depreciation is eliminated. Evaluate this argument.

8. The Egnew Manufacturing Company purchased a new machine especially built to perform one particular function on their assembly line. A difference of opinion has arisen as to the method of depreciation to be used in connection with this machine. Three methods are now being considered:
  (a) The straight-line method.
  (b) The productive-output method.
  (c) The sum-of-the-years-digits method.
List separately the arguments for and against each of the proposed methods from both the theoretical and the practical viewpoints. In your answer, you need not express your preference and you are to disregard income tax considerations.

9. In what ways, if any, do accelerated methods of depreciation increase the flow of cash funds into a company?

10. From the theoretical viewpoint, briefly describe the arguments that support the use of decreasing charge or accelerated methods of depreciation.

11. The president of the Canter Co. Ltd. objects to the use of straight-line depreciation on the grounds that sale of the asset at the end of the first year of its life would result in a loss significantly greater than the depreciation charge. The vice-president objects to the use of the straight-line method on the grounds that an appraisal of the asset at the end of the first year would hardly show a physical decline equal to the depreciation charge. Evaluate each position.

12. The chartered accountant is frequently called upon by management for advice regarding methods of computing depreciation. Although the question arises less frequently, of comparable importance is whether the depreciation method should be based on the consideration of the property items as units, as groups, or as having a composite life.
  (a) Briefly describe the depreciation methods based on recognizing property items as (1) units, (2) groups, or (3) as having a composite life.
  (b) Present the arguments for and against the use of each of these methods.
  (c) Describe how retirements are recorded under each of these methods.

13. The recognition of depreciation has no essential relation to the problem of replacement. Do you agree?

14. The computer has greatly simplified accounting for buildings and equipment. In what ways has this simplification taken place?

15. (a) Define wasting assets. (b) Give five examples of wasting assets.

16. What are the similarities and the differences in recognizing depreciation on buildings and equipment and depletion on wasting assets?

17. What procedures must be followed when the estimate of recoverable wasting assets is changed due to subsequent developmental work?

9-1. A machine is purchased at the beginning of 1981 for $25,500. Its estimated life is 6 years. Freight in on the machine is $400. Installation costs are $300. The machine is estimated to have a residual value of $1,000, and a useful life of 40,000 hours. It was used 5,000 hours in 1981.

EXERCISES

    (a) What is the cost of the machine for accounting purposes?
    (b) Compare the depreciation charge for 1981 using (1) the straight-line method, and (2) the service-hours method.

9-2. The Atlantic Company purchased a $30,000 depreciable asset with a five-year life expectancy and no salvage value. Three alternative methods of depreciating this asset are presented below. Identify the method of depreciation and compute the depreciation expense for the third year under each depreciation method.

		DEPRECIATION	
Year	Method A	Method B	Method C
	$	$	$
1	6,000	10,000	12,000
2	6,000	8,000	7,200
3	—	—	—

(CGA adapted)

9-3. Sun Corp. purchased equipment costing $65,000 on June 30, 1979, having an estimated life of 5 years and a residual value of $5,000. The company uses the sum-of-the-years-digits method of depreciation, and takes one-half year's depreciation on assets in the year of purchase. The asset was sold on December 31, 1981 for $21,000. Give the entry to record the sale of the equipment.

9-4. The Piper Manufacturing Co. acquired a machine at a cost of $9,540 on March 1, 1975. The machine is estimated to have a life of 10 years except for a special unit that will require replacement at the end of 6 years. The asset is recorded in two accounts, $7,200 being assigned to the main unit, and $2,340 to the special unit. Depreciation is recorded by the straight-line method to the nearest month, salvage values being disregarded. On March 1, 1981, the special unit is scrapped and is replaced with a similar unit; the cost of the replacement at this time is $5,600, and it is estimated that the unit will have a residual value of approximately 25% of cost at the end of the useful life of the main unit. What are the depreciation charges to be recognized for the years 1975, 1981, and 1982?

9-5. Equipment was purchased at the beginning of 1978 for $100,000 with an estimated product life of 600,000 units. The equipment has a salvage value of $10,000. During 1978, 1979, and 1980, the unit production of the equipment was 80,000 units, 120,000 units, and 40,000 units respectively. The machine was damaged at the beginning of 1981, and the equipment was scrapped with no salvage value. (1) Determine depreciation taken during 1978, 1979, and 1980. (2) Give the entry to write off the equipment.

9-6. The Quartz Co. records show the following assets:

	Acquired	Cost	Salvage	Estimated Useful Life
Machinery	7/1/80	$70,000	$5,000	10 years
Equipment	1/1/81	22,000	1,000	7 years
Fixtures	1/1/81	30,000	3,000	4 years

What is (a) the composite depreciation rate to be applied to cost and (b) the composite life of the asset?

9-7. The Salvador Co. obtains a lease for 20 years on a piece of land upon which it erects a building at cost of $300,000 with an estimated life of 30 years. Buildings belong to the lessor at the end of the lease period. It also leases another piece of land for 30 years and erects a factory building at a cost of $262,500 with an estimated life of 25 years. What is the annual depreciation charge on each piece of property, assuming use of the straight-line method?

9-8. The Pitts Mining Company purchased a mine for $210,000. It was estimated that the land contained 800,000 tons of recoverable mineral deposit, and that after recovery of the deposits the land would have a salvage value of $10,000. During the first year, 60,000 tons were mined and 50,000 tons were sold. Labor and overhead costs were $100,000. Determine (a) the cost of goods sold and (b) the ending inventory valuation.

9-9. The Manitoban Mining Co. in 1978 paid $1,600,000 for property with a supply of natural resources estimated at 1,000,000 tons. The property was estimated to be worth $200,000 after removal of the natural resource. Developmental costs of $300,000 were incurred in 1979 before withdrawals of the resource could be made. In 1980, resources removed totalled 200,000 tons. In 1981 resources removed totalled 300,000 tons. During 1981 discoveries were made indicating that available resources subsequent to 1981 will total 1,500,000 tons. Additional developmental costs of $440,000 were incurred in 1981. What entries should be made to recognize depletion for 1980 and 1981?

9-10. On July 1, 1981, Miller Mining, a calendar-year corporation, purchased the rights to a copper mine. Of the total purchase price, $2,800,000 was appropriately allocable to the copper. Estimated reserves were 800,000 tons of copper. Miller expects to extract and sell 10,000 tons of copper per month. Production began immediately. The selling price is $25 per ton.

To aid production, Miller also purchased some new equipment on July 1, 1981. The equipment cost $76,000 and had an estimated useful life of 8 years. However, after all the copper is removed from this mine, the equipment will be of no use to Miller and will be sold for an estimated $4,000.

If sales and production conform to expectations, what is Miller's depletion expense on this mine and depreciation expense on the new equipment for financial accounting purposes for the calendar year 1981?

9-1A. An examination of the records of Graham Co. Ltd. for the year ending December 31, 1979 disclosed the following:

1. On July 1, 1979 a building was acquired in exchange for 5,000 shares of Graham Co. Ltd., $10 par value common stock. The new asset was recorded at the aggregate par values of the exchanged shares. On July 1, Graham Co. Ltd. common stock was trading on the market at $18 per share. 20% of the value was associated with the land although the total amount had been recorded in the building account. As at July 1, 1979 the building had an estimated remaining service life of 25 years.

2. On September 1, 1979 a machine constructed by Graham Co. Ltd. was placed in operation. The total cost of construction was $9,600. The company saved $2,400 by building its own machine and this amount was credited to Miscellaneous Income. The machine was estimated to have a total service life of 10 years.

Instructions:
a) Compute the amount at which the assets described above should have been recorded initially by Graham Co. Ltd.
b) Explain the accounting theory for the valuation to be placed on the machine.
c) Compute the net error in net income (ignore income tax) for 1979.

(SMA adapted)

9-2A. The Bacon Company purchased a machine for $60,000 on June 15, 1981. It is estimated that the machine will have a 10-year life and will have a salvage value of $6,000. Its working hours and production in units are estimated at 36,000 and 600,000 respectively. It is the company's policy to take a half-year's depreciation on all assets for which they use the straight-line or declining-balance depreciation method (at double the straight-line rate) in the year of purchase. During 1981, the machine was operated 4,050 hours and produced 67,000 units.

Instructions:
Which of the following methods will give the greatest depreciation expense for 1981: (1) declining balance; (2) productive-output; or (3) service-hours. (Show computations for all three methods.)

9-3A. A delivery truck was acquired by Big Bag, Ltd., for $5,000 on January 1, 1980. The truck was estimated to have a 3-year life and a trade-in value at the end of that time of $500. The following depreciation methods are being considered.

(a) Depreciation is to be calculated by the straight-line method.
(b) Depreciation is to be calculated by the sum-of-the-years-digits method.
(c) Depreciation is to be calculated by applying a fixed percentage to the declining book value of the asset that will reduce the asset book value to its residual value at the end of the third year. (The third root of .10 = .464.)
(d) Repair charges are estimated at $70 for the first year and are estimated to increase by $50 in each succeeding year; depreciation charges are to be made on a diminishing scale so that the sum of depreciation and estimated repairs is the same for each year over the life of the asset.

Instructions:
Prepare tables reporting periodic depreciation and asset book value over the 3-year period for each assumption listed above.

9-4A. In January of 1979, a company buys a machine for $4,800. The maintenance costs for the years 1979-1982 are as follows:

1979 .... $ 50
1980   55
1981 .... 1,274 (Includes $1,248 for cost of a new motor installed in December, 1981).
1982   70

Instructions:
(1) Assume the machine is recorded in a single account at a cost of $4,800. No record is kept of the cost of the component parts. Straight-line depreciation is used and the asset is estimated to have a useful life of 8 years. It is assumed there will be no residual value at the end of the useful life. What is the sum of the depreciation and maintenance charges for each of the first four years?
(2) Assume the cost of the frame of the machine was recorded in one account at a cost of $3,600 and the motor was recorded in a second account at a cost of $1,200. Straight-line depreciation is used with a useful life of 10 years for the frame and 4 years for the motor. Neither item is assumed to have any residual value at the end of its useful life. What is the sum of depreciation and maintenance charges for each of the first four years?
(3) Evaluate the two methods.

9-5A. The Boswell Company purchased machinery costing $220,000 in 1976. In 1977, $80,000 of machinery was purchased. All machinery has an estimated useful life of 20 years. The machinery purchased at $220,000 has an estimated salvage value of $40,000, and the machinery purchased for $80,000 has an estimated salvage value of $4,000. It is the company policy to take a full year's depreciation in the year of purchase. At the beginning of 1979, the company changed the method of depreciation on the 1976 purchase from declining balance (at double the straight-line rate) to sum-of-the-years-digits in order to fully depreciate the machinery. On December 31, 1980, the company sold machinery for $30,000 that cost $55,000 in 1976.

Instructions:
Determine the gain or loss on the sale of the machinery. (Round depreciation computations to the nearest dollar.)

9-6A. In 1979 the Winston Machine Co., having outgrown its original plant, decided to build a new plant to accommodate its increased production demand.
The new site was to be located on two acres of serviced land which was purchased from the City three years before at a cost of $25,000 per acre. It was paid for at the time by $10,000 cash and a 10% one year promissory note for the balance. Property taxes on the land were $1,200 in 1977, $1,500 in 1978 and $1,600 in 1979. Legal fees in respect of the acquisition were 3% of the purchase price. During 1979 the Company incurred the following costs in connection with the relocation:

Regrading and filling of site	$ 2,500
Design and engineering of building	70,000
Construction of building	400,000
Landscaping	3,000
Interest on construction financing	30,000
Moving cost	36,000
Property tax on new building	4,500

Upon moving, on June 30, 1979, the old plant was sold for $120,000 which was applied toward the cost of the new plant with the balance of the total relocation costs being met by a 10 year 9% mortgage.

The service life of the new plant is estimated to be 30 years with an estimated residual value of $50,000. The company uses the straight-line method of depreciation for plant and equipment.

The Company's Equipment Register as at June 30, 1979 revealed the following:

Equipment Description	Date of Purchase	Purchase Price	Service Life	Estimated Scrap Value
Machine A	Jan. 1, 1972	$30,000	10 Years	$5,000
Machine B	Jan. 1, 1975	42,000	6 Years	6,000
Machine C	June 30, 1977	28,000	5 Years	8,000
Machine D	Jan. 1, 1978	35,000	10 Years	5,000

During construction the Winston Company engineers designed and built a new Machine E to replace Machine A at a direct cost of $45,000. Winston's normal overhead rate on production is 20% of direct costs. Machine E has a service life of 10 years with an estimated residual value of $6,000. The market value of the new machine was estimated at $70,000.

Machine A was retained in a standby capacity.

On September 30, 1979 Machine B was traded in on a new Machine F priced at $65,000. A trade-in allowance of $15,000 was given with the balance paid in cash. At September 30th Machine B had an estimated market value of $10,000.

Machine F has a service life of 8 years and an estimated residual value of $8,000.

Instructions:

(a) Prepare the Fixed Asset & Other Assets Section of the Balance Sheet for Winston Machine Co. as of December 31, 1979. Include all calculations with your submission.

(b) Calculate the accounting gain or loss on Machine B.

(c) The treatment of interest costs on construction is a controversial question in accounting theory. Give your reasons for the manner in which you treated interest costs in your answer to part (a).

(SMA adapted)

9-7A. The Majestic Manufacturing Co. acquired 25 similar machines at the beginning of 1976 for $100,000. Machines have an average life of 5 years and no residual value. The group-depreciation method is employed in writing off the cost of the machines. Machines were retired as follows:

2 machines at the end of 1978   11 machines at the end of 1980
6 machines at the end of 1979   6 machines at the end of 1981

Instructions:

Give the entries to record the retirement of machines and the periodic depreciation for the years 1976-1981 inclusive.

9-8A. Machines are acquired by McEwan Ltd., on March 1, 1981, as follows:

	Cost	Estimated Salvage Value	Estimated Life in Years
Machine 101	$27,000	$6,000	6
102	10,000	1,000	8
103	1,000	400	8
104	9,000	850	10
105	3,500	None	10

Instructions:

(1) Calculate the composite depreciation rate for this group.
(2) Calculate the composite or average life in years for the group.
(3) Give the entry to record the depreciation for the year ending December 31, 1981.

9-9A. Head Steel Products Company uses a number of electric cranes, each consisting of a chassis, motor, and truck. The crane chassis has a normal service life of 10 years, the truck lasts 5 years and must be overhauled at the end of every 3 years, and the motor normally requires a major overhaul at the end of every 2 years and must be replaced every 4 years.

The operating history of crane No. 315 is as follows:

Jan. 1972   Purchased crane for $70,000. Estimated cost of components: chassis, $35,000; truck, $25,000; motor, $10,000.
Dec. 1973   Overhauled motor at cost of $1,000.
Dec. 1974   Overhauled truck at cost of $3,000.
Dec. 1975   Replaced motor at cost of $10,200.
Dec. 1976   Overhauled motor at cost of $700; replaced truck at cost of $28,000.
Dec. 1978   Overhauled truck at cost of $3,300; replaced motor at cost of $11,000.
Dec. 1979   Overhauled motor at cost of $1,100.
Dec. 1981   Scrapped crane; proceeds from scrap was equal to the cost of dismantling and removing the asset.

The company depreciates its cranes at an average straight-line rate of 15% per year. The cost of motor and truck overhauls is debited to expense, and the cost of replacing motors and trucks is debited to the accumulated depreciation account.

The assistant controller has suggested the company revise its accounting procedure as follows: separate property records would be maintained for motors, trucks, and chassis. Annual depreciation on each component would be computed by totalling the cost of the component and the estimated cost of the overhaul (in the case of motors and trucks) and dividing by the estimated service life. The cost of major overhauls would be debited to Accumulated Depreciation, and components would be retired from the property account with any gain or loss recorded at the time of replacement.

The controller feels this procedure would not make any significant difference in the pattern of operating charges and asks the assistant to prepare a comparative history, using crane No. 315 as an example, showing the results under the company's present policy and the results under the assistant's suggested procedure.

Instructions:

(1) Prepare a schedule summarizing the operating history of crane No. 315 if the company's present procedures are followed showing the total debit to expense for depreciation and repairs for each of the 10 years. Assume any difference between asset cost and accumulated depreciation is added to or deducted from the depreciation charged in the tenth year.
(2) Prepare a similar schedule summarizing the operating history of crane No. 315 assuming the company had followed the assistant's suggested procedure. Assume the cost of the first overhaul is estimated as follows: motor, $1,000; truck, $3,000. Subsequent overhauls are estimated at the cost actually incurred in making the last previous overhaul. Include supporting schedules showing the computation of revised depreciation charges after the replacement of a component and the gain or loss at the time of retirement.

(3) Evaluate the two procedures and explain why you would or would not recommend that the assistant's suggestion be adopted.

9-10A. The Gold Mining Company paid $1,800,000 in 1979 for property with a supply of natural resources estimated at 2,000,000 tons. The estimated cost of restoring the land for use after the resources are exhausted is $150,000. After the land is restored, it will have an estimated value of $375,000. Development costs,such as drilling and road construction, were $550,000. Buildings, such as bunk houses and mess hall, were constructed on the site for $75,000. The useful lives of the buildings are expected to terminate upon exhaustion of the natural resources. Operations were not begun until January 1, 1980. In 1980, resources removed totalled 600,000 tons. During 1981, an additional discovery was made indicating that available resources subsequent to 1981 will total 1,800,000 tons. Because of a strike, only 400,000 tons of resources were removed during 1981.

Instructions:
Compute the debits to Depletion Expense for 1979, 1980, and 1981. Depreciation on the buildings is to be included in Depletion Expense.

9-11A. The Squires Corp. was organized on January 2, 1981. It was authorized to issue 80,000 shares of common stock, par $50. On the date of organization it sold 20,000 shares at par and gave the remaining shares in exchange for certain land bearing recoverable ore deposits estimated by geologists at 800,000 tons. The property is deemed to have a value of $3,000,000.

During 1981 mine improvements totalled $45,000. Miscellaneous buildings and sheds were constructed at a cost of $99,000. During the year 50,000 tons were mined; 4,000 tons of this amount were on hand unsold on December 31, the balance of the tonnage being sold for cash at $16 per ton. Expenses incurred and paid for during the year, exclusive of depletion and depreciation, were as follows:

Mining	$151,750
Delivery	15,000
General and administrative	12,800

It is believed that buildings and sheds will be useful only over the life of the mine; hence depreciation is to be recognized in terms of the mine output.

Instructions:
Prepare an income statement and a balance sheet for 1981. Submit working papers showing the development of statement data.

9-12A. The Slick Oil Company Ltd. paid $3,900,000 for a tract of land containing oil and spent an additional $500,000 for developing the property during the first year prior to the extraction of oil. Company chemists estimated that the oil deposit would produce 4 million barrels of oil and it is assumed that the land will have a residual value of $400,000 after all the oil is extracted.

At the end of the Year 1 the Company has incurred the following capital costs:

Asset	Estimated Physical Life	Cost
Buildings	30 years	$ 200,000
Pipeline and drilling equipment	20 years	1,000,000
Miscellaneous equipment	10 years	200,000

The buildings, pipeline and drilling equipment cannot be economically moved to another oil drilling location, but the miscellaneous equipment can be moved and utilized at another location. All the long-term assets are depreciated or depleted on the straight-line method based on time and/or production.

Operations commenced in Year 2. The operations for Year 2 are summarized below:

Barrels of oil extracted .... 1,000,000 barrels
Barrels of oil sold, at $3.50 per barrel .... 950,000 barrels

Labor and other costs, not including depreciation or depletion
   (1/10 fixed costs) $1,000,000
Administrative and selling expenses .... $ 500,000

Instructions:

(a) Prepare an Income Statement for the Slick Oil Company Ltd. for Year 2, showing the computation of depletion and depreciation per barrel in supporting schedules in good form.

(b) Early in Year 3 a foreign firm is interested in purchasing 100,000 barrels of oil F.O.B. their country for $3.75 per barrel. The cost to ship the oil will be $1.25 per barrel. Would you recommend that the company accept this order? Include calculations to support your conclusions.

(SMA adapted)

9-13A. Thompson Corporation, a manufacturer of steel products, began operations on October 1, 1980. The accounting department of Thompson has started the fixed asset and depreciation schedule presented on page 361. You have been asked to assist in completing this schedule. In addition to ascertaining that the data already on the schedule are correct, you have obtained from the company's records and personnel the information shown below.

(a) Depreciation is computed from the first of the month of acquisition to the first of the month of disposition.

(b) Land A and Building A were acquired from a predecessor corporation. Thompson paid $812,500 for the land and building together. At the time of acquisition, the land had an appraised value of $72,000 and the building had an appraised value of $828,000.

(c) Land B was acquired on October 2, 1980, in exchange for 3,000 newly issued shares of Thompson's common stock. At the date of acquisition, the shares had a par value of $5 per share and a fair value of $25 per share. During October, 1980, Thompson paid $10,400 to demolish an existing building on this land so it could construct a new building.

(d) Construction of Building B on the newly acquired land began on October 1, 1981. By September 30, 1982, Thompson had paid $210,000 of the estimated total construction costs of $300,000. Estimated completion and occupancy are July, 1983.

(e) Certain equipment was donated to the corporation by a shareholder. An independent appraisal of the equipment when donated placed the fair value at $16,000 and the salvage value at $2,000.

(f) Machinery A's total cost of $110,000 includes installation expense of $550 and normal repairs and maintenance of $11,000. Salvage value is estimated at $5,500. Machinery A was sold on February 1, 1982.

(g) On October 1, 1981, Machinery B was acquired with a down payment of $4,000 and the remaining payments to be made in ten annual instalments of $4,000 each beginning October 1, 1982. The prevailing interest rate was 8%.

Thompson Corporation
Fixed Asset and Depreciation Schedule
For Years Ended September 30, 1981, and September 30, 1982

Assets	Acquisition Date	Cost	Salvage	Depreciation Method	Estimated Life in Years	Depreciation Expense Year Ended September 30,	
						1981	1982
Land A	October 1, 1980	$ (1)	N/A*	N/A	N/A	N/A	N/A
Building A.....	October 1, 1980	(2)	$47,500	Straight Line	(3)	$14,000	(4)
Land B	October 2, 1980	(5)	N/A	N/A	N/A	N/A	N/A
Building B.....	Under Construction	210,000 to date	—	Straight Line	30	—	(6)
Donated Equipment ..	October 2, 1980	(7)	2,000	15% Declining Balance	10	(8)	(9)
Machinery A ..	October 2, 1980	(10)	5,500	Sum-of-the Years-Digits	10	(11)	(12)
Machinery B ..	October 1, 1981	(13)	—	Straight Line	15	—	(14)

*N/A — Not Applicable

Instructions:

For each numbered item on the preceding schedule determine the correct amount. Round each answer to the nearest dollar.

(AICPA adapted)

9:14A. You are engaged in the examination of the financial statements of The Smoky Mountain Mfg. Company and are auditing the machinery and equipment account and the related depreciation accounts for the year ended December 31, 1981.

Your permanent file contains the following schedules:

Machinery and Equipment

Year	Balance 31/12/79	1980 Retirements	1980 Additions	Balance 31/12/80
1967-70	$ 8,000	$2,100	—	$ 5,900
1971	400	—	—	400
1972	—	—	—	—
1973	—	—	—	—
1974	3,900	—	—	3,900
1975	—	—	—	—
1976	5,300	—	—	5,300
1977	—	—	—	—
1978	4,200	—	—	4,200
1979	—	—	—	—
1980	—	—	$5,700	5,700
	$21,800	$2,100	$5,700	$25,400

Accumulated Depreciation

Year	Balance 31/12/79	1980 Retirements	1980 Provision	Balance 31/12/80
1967-70	$ 7,840	$2,100	$ 160	$ 5,900
1971	340	——	40	380
1972	——	——	——	——
1973	——	——	——	——
1974	2,145	——	390	2,535
1975	——	——	——	——
1976	1,855	——	530	2,385
1977	——	——	——	——
1978	630	——	420	1,050
1979	——	——	——	——
1980	——	——	285	285
	$12,810	$2,100	$1,825	$12,535

A transcript of the machinery and equipment account for 1981 follows:

Machinery and Equipment

Date	Item	Debit	Credit
1981			
Jan. 1	Balance forward	$25,400	
Mar. 1	Burnham grinder	1,200	
May 1	Air compressor	4,500	
June 1	Power lawnmower	600	
June 1	Lift truck battery	320	
Aug. 1	Rockwood saw		$ 150
Nov. 1	Electric spot welder	4,500	
Nov. 1	Baking oven	2,800	
Dec. 1	Baking oven	236	
		$39,556	$ 150
Dec. 31	Balance		39,406
		$39,556	$39,556

Your examination reveals the following information:

(a) The company uses a ten-year life for all machinery and equipment for depreciation purposes. Depreciation is computed by the straight-line method. Six months' depreciation is recorded in the year of acquisition or retirement. For 1981 the company recorded depreciation of $2,800 on machinery and equipment.

(b) The Burnham grinder was purchased for cash from a firm in financial distress. The chief engineer and a used machinery dealer agreed that the practically new machine was worth $2,100 in the open market.

(c) For production reasons the new air compressor was installed in a small building that was erected in 1981 to house the machine and will also be used for general storage. The cost of the building, which has a 25-year life, was $2,000 and is included in the $4,500 voucher for the air compressor.

(d) The power lawn mower was delivered to the home of the company president for personal use.

(e) On June 1 the battery in a battery-powered lift truck was accidentally damaged beyond repair. The damaged battery was included at a price of $600 in the $4,200 cost of the lift truck purchased on July 1, 1978. The company decided to rent a replacement battery rather than buy a new battery. The $320 expenditure is the annual rental for the battery paid in advance, net of a $40 allowance for the scrap value of the damaged battery that was returned to the battery company.

(f) The Rockwood saw sold on August 1 had been purchased on August 1, 1978, for $1,500. The saw was in use until it was sold.

(g) On September 1 the company determined that a production casting machine was no longer needed and advertised it for sale for $1,800 after determining from a used machinery dealer that this was its market value. The casting machine had been purchased for $5,000 on September 1, 1976.

(h) The company elected to exercise an option under a lease-purchase agreement to buy the electric spot welder. The welder had been installed on February 1, 1981, at a monthly rental of $100.

(i) On November 1 a baking oven was purchased for $10,000. A $2,800 downpayment was made and the balance will be paid in monthly instalments over a three-year period. The December 1 payment includes interest charges of $36. Legal title to the oven will not pass to the company until the payments are completed.

Instructions:

Prepare the adjusting journal entries required at December 31, 1981, for equipment and the related depreciation. (AICPA adapted)

9-15A. You are engaged in the examination of the financial statements of the Ute Corp. for the year ended December 31, 1981. Schedules for the land, buildings, and equipment and related accumulated depreciation accounts have been prepared by the client and are shown below. You have checked the opening balances to your prior year's audit working papers.

Assets

Description	Final 31/12/80	Additions	Retirements	31/12/81
Land	$ 22,500	$ 5,000		$ 27,500
Buildings	120,000	17,500		137,500
Machinery and equipment	385,000	40,400	$26,000	399,400
	$527,500	$62,900	$26,000	$564,400

Accumulated Depreciation

Description	Final 31/12/80	Additions*	Retirements	Per Books 31/12/81
Buildings	$ 60,000	$ 5,150		$ 65,150
Machinery and equipment	173,250	39,220		212,470
	$233,250	$44,370		$277,620

*Depreciation expense for the year.

Your examination reveals the following information:

(a) All equipment is depreciated on the straight-line basis (no salvage value taken into consideration) based on the following estimated lives: buildings, 25 years; all other items, 10 years. The company's policy is to take one-half year's depreciation on all asset acquisitions and disposals during the year.

(b) On April 1, the company entered into a ten-year lease contract for a die casting machine with annual rentals of $5,000 payable in advance every April 1. The lease is cancellable by either party (sixty days written notice is required) and there is no option to renew the lease or buy the equipment at the end of the lease. The estimated useful life of the machine is ten years with no salvage value. The company recorded the die casting machine in the machinery and equipment account at $40,400, the present discounted value at the date of the lease, and $2,020 applicable to the machine has been included in depreciation expense for the year.

(c) The company completed the construction of a wing on the plant building on June 30. The useful life of the building was not extended by this addition. The lowest construction bid received was $17,500, the amount recorded in the buildings account. Company personnel were used to construct the addition at a cost of $16,000 (materials, $7,500; labor, $5,500; and overhead, $3,000).

(d) On August 18, $5,000 was paid for paving and fencing a portion of land owned by the company and used as a parking lot for employees. The expenditure was accepted to the land account.

(e) The amount shown in the machinery and equipment asset retirement column represents cash received on September 5 upon dispoal of a machine purchased in July, 1974, for $48,000. The bookkeeper recorded depreciation expense of $3,500 on this machine in 1981.

(f) A shareholder donated land and building appraised at $10,000 and $40,000 respectively to the Ute Corporation for a plant. On September 1, the company began operating the plant. Since no costs were involved, the bookkeeper made no entry for the above transaction.

Instructions:

Prepare the formal adjusting journal entries that you would suggest at December 31, 1981, to adjust the accounts for the above transactions. Disregard income tax implications. The books have not been closed. Computations should be rounded off to the nearest dollar. (AICPA adapted)

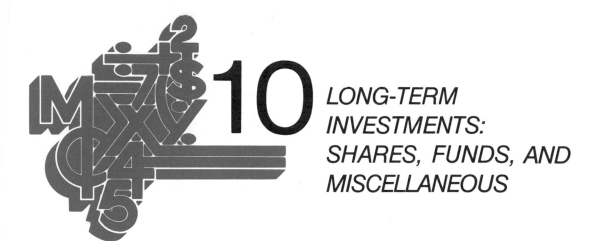

10 LONG-TERM INVESTMENTS: SHARES, FUNDS, AND MISCELLANEOUS

A company must invest funds in inventories, receivables, land, buildings and equipment, and other assets in order to engage in the sale of goods and services. But a portion of its available funds may be applied to assets not directly identified with primary activities. Assets that occupy an auxiliary relationship to central revenue-producing activities are referred to as *investments*. Investments are expected to contribute to the success of the business either by exercising certain favorable effects upon sales and operations generally, or by making an independent contribution to business earnings over the long term.

CLASSIFICATION OF INVESTMENTS

Investments are either temporary or long-term. As suggested earlier, investments are classified as current only where they are readily marketable and it is management's intent to use them in meeting current cash requirements. Investments not meeting these tests are considered *long-term* or *permanent investments* and are usually reported on the balance sheet under a separate non-current heading. The purpose to be served by the investment as well as its marketability govern its classification.

Long-term or permanent investments include a variety of items. For discussion purposes, long-term investments will be classified in four groups: (1) investments in shares, both preferred and common; (2) investments in bonds, mortgages, and similar debt instruments; (3) funds for bond retirement, share redemption, and other special purposes; and (4) miscellaneous investments including real estate held for appreciation or for future use, advances to affiliates, interests in life insurance contracts, ownership equities in partnership and joint ventures, and interests in trusts and estates.[1]

LONG-TERM INVESTMENT IN SHARES

An investment by one corporation, the *investor*, in the shares of another corporation, the *investee*, is commonly referred to as a *long-term intercorporate investment*. The essential characteristic that identifies an intercorporate investment is the presence of two separate legal entities: (1) an investor corporation, and (2) an investee corporation. The modifier "long term" is primarily dependent upon the intent of the investor corporation; thus some intercorporate investments may be transitional or current in nature.

Corporations invest in the common or preferred shares of other corporations for various reasons. Often these investments are made to permit the purchaser to exercise either control or significant influence over the operating and financial policies of the corporation whose shares were acquired. Ownership of shares may permit the purchaser to be guaranteed a supplier of a major raw material or a critical assembled part, or it may provide a sales outlet for finished products. In some cases, the investment may be strictly for income purposes. If the intent is generally to hold the shares for long-term purposes, the investment should be classified as a non-current asset.

The ability to exercise significant influence by share ownership may be indicated in several ways, such as representation on the board of directors, participation in policy-making processes, material intercompany transactions, interchange of managerial personnel, or technological dependency. Another important consideration is the extent of ownership by an investor in relation to the concentration of other shareholdings. If the investment represents more than 50% of the voting shares, a controlling interest obviously exists. Under these conditions, the company holding the shares is usually referred to as a *parent* company; the company controlled is referred to as a *subsidiary* company. However, control may effectively be achieved with an investment significantly lower than 50%. The Accounting Research Committee addressed this problem in Section 3050 of the *Accounting Recommendations*. They recognized that control factors will not always be clear and that judgment will be required in assessing the status of each investment. To achieve a reasonable degree of uniformity in the application of its position, the Committee set 20% as an ownership standard: the ownership of 20% or more of the voting shares of the company carries the presumption,

---

[1]Since accounting for investments in bonds, mortgages, and similar debt instruments should mirror the accounting for long-term liabilities, these topics are included in Chapter 13.

in the absence of evidence to the contrary, that an investor has the ability to exercise significant influence over that company. Conversely, ownership of less than 20% leads to the presumption that the investor does not have the ability to exercise significant influence unless such ability, can be demonstrated.[2] In such circumstances, the result is a portfolio investment. Ownership of more than 50 per cent of the investee's voting shares results in classification of the investee as a subsidiary. These classifications are summarized in Table 1.

Table 1: Investor's Percentage Ownership of Voting Shares

Continuum of Influence Relationships

The valuation of long-term intercorporate investments differs depending upon the relationship between the investor and investee corporations. On the basis of the relationship between the investor and the investee, the latter may be classified as (1) a subsidiary corporation, (2) an investment that enables the investor to exercise significant influence over the investee, (3) a corporate joint venture, or (4) a portfolio investment. If the investment represents less than 20% of the outstanding voting shares, it is generally presumed that no control exists and the investment is accounted for as a portfolio investment valued at either cost or, in the event of permanent decline in value, at the lower of cost or market. If the investment represents 20% or more of the outstanding voting shares, significant influence should be assumed and the investment should be carried at its original cost as adjusted by a portion of the acquired company's periodic net income or loss, and any distributions in the form of dividends to the shareholder. This procedure is referred to as the *equity method of accounting*. If the investee is a subsidiary corporation it is customary for the parent company to present *consolidated financial statements* that aggregate on a line-by-line basis the financial statements of one or more subsidiaries with those of the parent corporation as modified by the elimination of intercompany balances and transactions.[3]

The following discussions of investment in shares relates to both the cost and equity methods unless otherwise indicated.

Share Purchases

Shares of stock may be acquired on the Toronto Stock Exchange, or other exchanges in the different regions of the country. Shares not listed on the

[2]*CICA Handbook: Accounting Recommendations*, Section 3050, "Long-Term Investments" (Toronto: Canadian Institute of Chartered Accountants, 1973, revised 1978), par. .19.
[3]Chapter 12 provides an introduction to consolidated financial statements including their preparation.

exchanges are acquired over the counter through stockbrokers. Shares may also be acquired directly from the issuing corporation or from a private investor.

In the circumstances of a business combination that takes the form of a purchase of shares the transaction may proceed by way of a take-over bid. In Canada, take-over bids are regulated by provincial securities acts and federally by the Canada Business Corporations Act. In general, a take-over bid is simply an offer made by an offeror to shareholders of the offeree corporation to acquire their shares. Although the legislative requirements pertaining to take-over bids are detailed and complex, the rationale behind the legislation is that every shareholder of the offeree corporation must have an equal opportunity to accept or reject the bid. On this premise, take-over bid legislation prescribes such matters as the rules under which, and the time periods within which, the subject shares are to be deposited, or within which a shareholder may reconsider and withdraw his shares without further obligation. In the event more shares are deposited than the total covered by the bid, the offeror must take up and pay for shares on a pro rata basis. If an offeror increases the purchase price during the period the bid is outstanding, as is often the case with take-over bids, all shareholders accepting the bid must receive the increased price even if they had accepted before the price increase. The Canada Business Corporations Act requires the directors of an offeror corporation to approve both the take-over bid and the take-over bid circular. In addition, the Act requires the directors of the offeree corporation to send out a directors' circular commenting upon the bid.

It should also be noted that in the circumstances of a take-over bid an offeree corporation may be taken over in spite of objections raised in the directors' circular or by management. Two points are significant: (1) the price offered in the take-over bid is likely to be substantially above the existing market price, and (2) the decision to accept or reject the take-over bid rests with the individual shareholder, not the corporation. At the same time, there are a variety of defensive tactics that a potential target corporation can use to defend against a take-over bid, or to make itself less attractice to a potential bidder. Examples of these defensive tactics include (1) increasing dividends, (2) revaluation of assets, (3) seeking another bid or combination possibly, and (4) offering shareholders' rights to acquire additional shares.

When shares are purchased for cash, they are recorded at the amount paid, including brokers' commissions, taxes, and other fees incidental to the purchase. When shares are acquired *on margin*[4], the shares should be recorded at full cost and a liability should be recognized for the unpaid balance: to report only the amount invested would be, in effect, to offset the obligation to the broker against the investment account. An agreement or *subscription* entered into with a corporation for the purchase of shares is

---

[4]A deposit or advance by an investor with or to a broker representing a part payment on the purchase price of a security or commodity is defined as a purchase on margin.

recognized by a debit to an asset account for the security to be received and a credit to a liability account for the amount to be paid. A charge for interest on an obligation arising from a stock purchase should be reported as expense. When shares are acquired in exchange for properties or services, the fair market value of such considerations or the value at which the shares are currently selling, whichever may be more clearly determinable, should be used as a basis for recording the investment. In the absence of clearly defined values for assets or services exchanged or a market price for the security acquired, appraisals and estimates are required in arriving at cost.

When two or more securities are acquired for a lump-sum price, this cost should be allocated in some equitable manner to the different acquisitions. When market prices are available for each security, cost may be apportioned on the basis of the relative market prices. When there is a market price for one security but not for the other, it may be reasonable to assign the market price to the one and the cost excess to the other. When market prices are not available, it may be necessary to postpone cost apportionment until support for an equitable division becomes available. In certain instances it may be desirable to carry the two securities in a single account and to treat the proceeds from the sale of one as a subtraction from total cost, the residual cost then to be identified with the other. To illustrate these procedures, assume the purchase of 100 units of preferred and common shares at $75 per unit; each unit consists of one share of preferred and two shares of common. Market prices at the time the stock is acquired are $60 per share for preferred and $10 per share for common. The investment cost is recorded in terms of the relative market values of the securities, as follows:

Investment in Preferred Shares	5,625	
Investment in Common Shares	1,875	
Cash		7,500

Computation:

Value of preferred:	100 × $60 = $6,000
Value of common:	200 × $10 = 2,000
	$8,000

Cost assigned to preferred:	6,000/8,000 × $7,500 = $5,625.
Cost assigned to common:	2,000/8,000 × $7,500 = $1,875.

If there is no market value for the common shares, the investment may be recorded as follows:

Investment in Preferred Shares	6,000	
Investment in Common Shares	1,500	
Cash		7,500

Computation:

Cost of preferred and common	$7,500
Cost identified with preferred (market)	6,000
Remaining cost identified with common	$1,500

If the division of cost must be deferred, the following entry is made:

Investment in Preferred and Common Shares	7,500	
Cash		7,500

The joint investment balance may be eliminated when a basis for apportionment is established and costs can be assigned to individual classes.

When shares are subject to special calls or assessments and such payments are made to the corporation, these are recorded as additions to the costs of the holdings. Pro rata contributions by the shareholders to the corporation to eliminate a deficit, to retire bonds, or to effect a reorganization, are also treated as additions to investment cost.

Revenue from Long-Term Investment in Shares

The revenue recognized from an investment in shares depends upon whether the investment is considered to be of a magnitude to warrant use of the equity method as opposed to the cost method. As indicated earlier, ownership of 20% or more of voting shares provides a practical guideline to distinguish between long-term investments held in order to exercise significant influence and other long-term investments that are only portfolio investments.

Equity Method. The equity method of recognizing revenue reflects the economic substance of the relationship between the investor and investee corporations rather than the legal distinction of the separate entities. Although the earnings of the investee company are not legally available to shareholders until their distribution as dividends has been authorized by the board of directors, the timing of the distribution can be subject to significant influence. Failure to accrue income as earned would permit the investor to influence its income by the dividend distribution policy followed.

Under the equity method of accounting, a proportionate share of the earnings or losses to the investee is recognized by the investor in the year earned or incurred. The earnings are generally reflected in a single account unless the investee has extraordinary gains or losses. In this case, separate accounts should be used for both ordinary and extraordinary earnings or losses. The investment account is increased by the proportionate share of the earnings and decreased by the proportionate share of losses and the proportionate distribution of dividends.

For example, assume Probert Manufacturing Co. held a 40% interest in the common shares of Stewart, Ltd. In 1977, Stewart, Ltd., reported net income of $150,000, including an extraordinary gain of $30,000. Dividends of $70,000 were distributed to shareholders. The following entries would be made in the accounts of Probert Manufacturing Co. to record its share of the 1977 earnings of Stewart, Ltd.

Investment in Stewart, Ltd., Common Shares	60,000	
Share of Ordinary Income — Stewart, Ltd., Common Shares		48,000
Share of Extraordinary Income — Stewart, Ltd., Common Shares		12,000
To recognize 40% of the income earned by Stewart, Ltd., common shares.		

Cash	28,000	
Investment in Stewart, Ltd., Common Shares		28,000
To record receipt of cash dividend.		

Special adjustments are necessary in recognizing the proportionate share of the investee's income, if the amount paid for the shares exceeds the proportionate share of the investee's underlying assets at the date of purchase. The excess must either be attributed to an excess of fair value over carrying value of identifiable tangible and intangible assets, or to the intangible asset goodwill. If the assets involved have limited lives, an adjustment to the proportionate share of the income to be recognized must be made to reflect the depreciation of the fair value allocated to depreciable assets or the amortization of goodwill.

For example, assume the total shareholders' equity of Stewart, Ltd., was $500,000 at the time Probert Manufacturing Co. purchased 40% of its shares for $250,000. The implied value of the total shareholders' equity of Stewart, Ltd., would be $625,000 ($250,000 ÷ .40), or $125,000 in excess of the recorded shareholders' equity. Assume that review of the asset values discloses that the market value of depreciable properties with an average remaining life of ten years exceeds the carrying value of these assets by $50,000. The remaining $75,000 difference ($125,000 − $50,000) is attributed to goodwill. The adjustment to Stewart, Ltd.'s revenue to be recognized by Probert Manufacturing Co. would be a deduction of $2,000 for the proportionate depreciation of the excess market value on depreciable property, ($50,000 × .40) ÷ 10, and a deduction of $750 for the proportionate amortization of goodwill over a forty year period, ($75,000 × .40) ÷ 40. The entry for this adjustment would be as follows:

Share of Ordinary Income — Stewart, Ltd., Common Shares .	2,750	
Investment in Stewart, Ltd., Common Shares		2,750
To adjust share of ordinary income on Stewart, Ltd., common stock for proportionate depreciation on excess market value of depreciable property, $2,000, and for amortization of implied goodwill from acquisition, $750.		

In some cases, the cost may be less than the underlying book value at the time of acquisition. In this situation, it is assumed that specific assets of the investee are overvalued and an adjustment is necessary to reduce the depreciation or amortization taken by the investee. The journal entry to reflect this adjustment is the reverse of that just illustrated.

If the investor and the investee are engaged in intercompany revenue-producing activities, adjustments must also be made to eliminate unrealized intercompany gains and losses. These adjustments are similar to those made when consolidated statements are prepared for parent and subsidiary corporations.

Cost Method. When the investment in another company's shares does not involve either a controlling interest or significant influence, the revenue recognized is limited to the distribution of the dividends declared by the investee. The receipt of cash dividends by a shareholder is recorded by a debit to Cash and a credit to Dividend Revenue. Three dates are generally included in the formal dividend announcement: (1) date of declaration, (2) record date, and (3) date of payment. The formal dividend announcement may read somewhat as follows: "The Board of Directors at their meeting on November 5, 1980, declared a regular quarterly dividend on outstanding common stock of 50 cents per share payable on January 15, 1981, to shareholders of record at the close of business, December 29, 1980." The shareholder becomes aware of the dividend action upon its announcement. But if the holdings are sold and a new owner is recognized by the corporation prior to the record date, the dividend is paid to the new owner. If the shareholder retains the holdings until the record date, he or she will be entitled to the dividends when paid. After the record date, shares no longer carry a right to dividends and sell *ex-dividend*. Accordingly, a shareholder is justified in recognizing the corporate dividend action on the record date. At this time a receivable account may be debited and Dividend Revenue credited. Upon receipt of the dividend, Cash is debited and the receivable credited.

There are some who would accrue dividends in the same manner as interest when the declaration of a regular dividend at a certain date is virtually assured by the nature of the security, the position and earnings of the company, and the policies of the board of directors. The recognition of accrued dividends under such circumstances is not objectionable if disclosure is made on the statements that such special practice is followed.

Liquidating Dividends

Dividends are sometimes identified as liquidating dividends. A *liquidating dividend* involves a return of the invested capital of a corporation to its shareholders. Although liquidating dividends can occur in any company, they are most common in a company consuming natural resources in its operations. When natural resources are limited and irreplaceable, the company may choose to distribute full proceeds becoming available from operations. Dividends paid, then, represent in part a distribution of earnings and in part a distribution of invested capital. Distributions involving both earnings and invested capital may also be found when a corporation makes full distribution of the proceeds from the sale of certain properties, such as land or securities, or when a distribution represents the proceeds from business liquidation.

A shareholder, receiving a dividend consisting of both a distribution of earnings and return of invested capital, credits revenue for the amount representing earnings and the investment account for the amount representing invested capital. To illustrate, assume that Lucky Mines, Ltd., pays a dividend of $500,000, 60% representing a distribution of earnings and 40% representing a distribution of the cost recovery of certain wasting assets. A shareholder receiving a dividend of $1,200 makes the following entry:

Cash	1,200	
Dividend Revenue		720
Investment in Lucky Mines, Ltd., Common Shares		480
To record receipt of cash dividend; 40% liquidating dividend.		

Information regarding the portion of dividends representing earnings and the portion representing invested capital should be reported to the shareholder by the corporation making the distribution. This report may not accompany each dividend cheque but instead may be provided annually and may cover the total dividends paid during the year. If dividends have been recorded as revenue during the year, the revenue account is debited and the investment account is credited when notification is received of the amount to be recognized as a distribution of invested capital.

When liquidating dividends exceed investment costs, excess distributions are reported as a gain from the investment. If liquidation is completed and the investment cost is not fully recovered, the balance of the investment account should be written off as a loss.

Property Dividends

Dividends that are distributed in the form of assets other than cash are referred to as *property dividends*. In distributing earnings by means of a property dividend, the corporation credits the asset account for the cost of the asset distributed, debits Retained Earnings for the market value of the asset distributed, if determinable, and accounts for the difference as a gain or a loss. APB Opinion No. 29 defines this type of transaction as a non-reciprocal transfer to an owner.[5] The shareholder debits an asset account and credits Dividend Revenue. The shareholder also recognizes the dividend in terms of the market value of the property item at the date of its distribution. To illustrate these situations, assume that the Wells Corporations with 1,000,000

---

[5]*Opinions of the Accounting Principles Board, No. 29*, "Accounting for Nonmonetary Transactions" (New York: American Institute of Certified Public Accountants, 1973), par. 3. This matter is not yet the subject of an Accounting Recommendation.

shares of common stock outstanding distributes as a dividend its holdings of 50,000 shares of Barnes Co. stock acquired at a cost of $11 per share. The distribution of one share of Barnes Co. stock for every 20 shares of Wells Corporation held is made when Barnes Co. shares are selling at $16. Wells Corporation would record the dividend as follows:

Retained Earnings 800,000		
Investment in Barnes Co. Common Shares		550,000
Gain from Distribution of Barnes Co. Common Shares		250,000
To record distribution of 50,000 shares of Barnes Co. stock as a property dividend.		

A shareholder owning 100 shares of Wells Corporation stock would make the following entry in recording the receipt of the dividend:

Investment in Barnes Co. Common Shares	80	
Dividend Revenue		80
Received 5 shares of Barnes Co. common stock, market price $16 per share, as a dividend on 100 shares of Wells Corporation.		

Stock Dividends

A company may distribute a dividend in the form of additional shares that are the same as those held by its shareholders. Such a dividend does not affect company assets but simply results in the transfer of retained earnings to invested capital. The increase in total shares outstanding is distributed pro rata to individual shareholders. The receipt of additional shares by shareholders leaves their respective equities exactly as they were. Although the number of shares held by individual shareholders has gone up, there are now a greater number of shares outstanding and proportionate interests remain unchanged. The division of equities into a greater number of parts cannot be regarded as giving rise to revenue. To illustrate, assume that Eagle Corporation has 10,000 shares of common stock outstanding. The total of the shareholders' equity is $330,000; the book value per share is $33. If a 10% stock dividend is declared, an additional 1,000 shares will be issued and the book value per share will decline to $30. A shareholder who held 10 shares with a book value of $330 (10 × $33) will hold 11 shares after the stock dividend, with the book value remaining at $330 (11 × $30).

The market value of the shares may or may not react in a similar manner. Theoretically the same relative decrease should occur in the market value as occurred in the book value; however, there are many variables influencing the market price of securities. If the percentage of the stock dividend issued is comparatively low, under 20–25%, there is generally less than a pro rata immediate effect on the market price. This means that while a shareholder after receiving a stock dividend will have no greater interest in the company, the investment may have a greater market value.

Because there is no effect on the underlying book value of the investment, only a memorandum entry needs to be made by the shareholder in recognizing the receipt of additional shares. Original investment cost applies to a greater number of shares, and this cost is divided by the total shares now held in arriving at the cost per share to be used upon subsequent dispositon of holdings. The new per-share cost basis is indicated in the memorandum entry.

When shares have been acquired at different dates and at different costs, the stock dividend should be related to each different acquisition. Adjusted costs for shares comprising each lot held can then be developed. To illustrate, assume that H. C. De Soto owns shares of the Banner Corporation acquired as follows:

	Shares	Cost per Share	Total Cost
Lot 1	50	$120	$6,000
Lot 2	30	90	2,700

A stock dividend of 1 share for every 2 held is distributed by the Banner Corporation. A memorandum entry on De Soto's books to report the number of shares now held and the cost per share within each lot would be made as follows:

Received 40 shares of Banner Corporation stock, representing a 50% stock dividend on 80 shares held. Number of shares held and costs assigned to shares are now as follows:

	Shares	Total Cost	Revised Cost per Share
Lot 1	75 (50 + 25)	$6,000	$80 ($6,000 ÷ 75)
Lot 2	45 (30 + 15)	2,700	60 ($2,700 ÷ 45)

The number of shares to be issued as a stock dividend may include fractional shares. Usually a cash payment is made to the shareholder by the issuing company in lieu of issuing fractional shares.

When shares of a class different from that held are received as a stock dividend, such a dividend, too, should not be regarded as revenue. As in the case of a like dividend, a portion of the retained earnings relating to the original holdings is formally labelled invested capital. All owners of the shares on which the dividend is declared participate pro rata in the distribution and now own two classes of shares instead of a single class. A book value is now identified with the new shares, but this is accompanied by a corresponding decrease in the book value identified with the original holdings. A similar position can be taken when an investor receives dividends in the form of bonds or other contractual obligations of the corporation.

One difference between the receipt of shares of the same class and securities of a different class needs to be noted. When common stock is received on common, all shares are alike and original cost may be equitably assigned in terms of the total number of units held after the dividend. When different securities are received whose value is not the same as that of the shares originally held, it would not be proper to assign an equal amount of original cost to both old and new units. Instead, equitable apportionment of cost would require use of the relative market values of the two classes of securities. To illustrate, assume the ownership of 100 shares of Bell Co. common acquired at $100 per share. A stock dividend of 50 shares of $25 par preferred shares is received on the common. On the date of distribution the common shares are selling for $65 and the preferred for $20. The receipt of the dividend and the apportionment of cost is recorded as follows:

Investment in Bell Co. Preferred Shares 1,333.33
    Investment in Bell Co. Common Shares 1,333.33
        To record receipt of 50 shares of preferred stock
        as a dividend on 100 shares of common.

Computation:

Cost of common apportioned to common and preferred shares on the basis of relative market values of the two securities on the date of distribution:

Value of preferred: 50 × $20 = $1,000
Value of common: 100 × $65 =   6,500
                          $7,500

Cost assigned to preferred: 1,000/7,500 × $10,000 = $1,333.33
(Cost per share: $1,333.33 ÷ 50 = $26.67.)
Cost assigned to common: 6,500/7,500 × $10,000 = $8,666.67.
(Cost per share: $8,666.67 ÷ 100 = $86.67.)

Stock dividends may be reported as revenue if they are regarded as having been made in lieu of cash. The distribution may be regarded as having been made in lieu of cash if (1) it is made in discharge of preference dividends normally paid in cash, or (2) the shareholder is given the option of receiving cash or other property instead of shares.

Stock Splits

For corporations whose shares are publicly traded the price range within which their shares may trade is a matter of concern to management, especially if its shares are appreciating in market value. Over a period of perhaps several years the market value of a company's shares could increase to a price well beyond any notion of an established trading range. Thus, the potential market for the company's shares may be curtailed because the price is too high to support widely held ownership. A procedure known as a *stock split* or *stock split-up* is one way to maintain per share prices within an established trading range.

A corporation may effect a stock split by reducing the par value of its common shares and increasing accordingly the number of shares outstanding. For example, a corporation with 1,000,000 shares outstanding may decide to split its stock on a 3-for-1 basis. After the split the corporation will have 3,000,000 shares outstanding: each shareholder will have three shares for every share originally held. However, each share will now represent only one third of the interest previously represented; furthermore, each share can be expected to sell for approximately one third of its previous value.

The shareholders ledger is revised to show the increased number of shares identified with each shareholder and the reduced par value, if any. Accounting for a stock split in the accounts of the investor is the same as that for a stock dividend. With an increase in the number of shares, each share now carries only a portion of the original cost. When shares have been acquired at different dates and at different prices, the shares received in a split should be associated with the original acquisitions and per-share costs for each lot revised. A memorandum entry is made to report the increase in the number of shares and the allocation of cost to the shares held after the split.

Stock Rights

A corporation that wishes to raise cash by the sale of additional shares may be required to offer existing shareholders the right to subscribe to the new shares. This privilege attaching to shares is called the *pre-emptive right* and is designed to enable shareholders to retain their respective interest in the corporation. For example, assume that a shareholder owns 50% of a company's outstanding shares. If the number of shares is doubled and the additional shares are offered and sold to other parties, that shareholder's interest in the company would drop to 25%. With the right to subscribe to the pro rata share of any new offering, the shareholder can maintain the same proportionate interest in the corporation. Although the pre-emptive right is a general requirement in most corporation acts, the right may be nullified in the articles of incorporation of a company.

In order to make subscription privileges attractive and to insure sale of the shares, it is customary for corporations to offer the additional issues to its shareholders at less than the market price of the shares. Certificates known as *rights* or *warrants* are issued to shareholders enabling them to subscribe for shares in proportion to the holdings on which they are issued. One right is generally offered for each share held. But more than one right may be required in subscribing for each new share, in addition to any required cash payment. Rights may be sold by shareholders who do not care to exercise them.

As in the case of cash and other dividends, the directors of the corporation in declaring rights to subscribe for additional shares designate a record date that follows the declaration date. All shareholders on the record date are entitled to the rights. Up to the record date, shares sell *cum rights* or *rights-on*, since parties acquiring the shares will receive the rights when they are issued; after the record date, the shares will *ex-rights*, and the rights may be sold separately by those owning the rights as of the record date. A date on which the rights expire is also designated when the rights are declared. Rights not exercised are worthless beyond the expiration date. Generally, rights have a limited life of only a few weeks.

Accounting for Stock Rights. The receipt of stock rights is comparable to the receipt of a stock dividend. The corporation has made no asset distribution; shareholders' equities remain unchanged. However, the shareholders' investment is evidenced by shares originally acquired and rights that have a value of their own since they permit the purchase of shares at less than market price. These circumstances call for an allocation of cost between the original shares and the rights. Since the shares and the rights have different values, an apportionment should be made in terms of the relative market values as of the date the rights distribution is declared. A separate accounting for each class of security is subsequently followed. The accounting for stock rights is illustrated in the following example.

Assume that in 1973 Eva Montano acquired 100 shares of Superior Products no-par common at $180 per share. In 1977 the corporation issues rights to purchase 1 share of common at $100 for every 5 shares owned. Montano thus receives 100 rights — one right for each share owned. However, since 5 rights are required for the acquisition of a single share, the 100 rights enable her to subscribe for only 20 new shares. Montano's original investment of $18,000 now applies to two assets, the shares and the rights. This cost is apportioned on the basis of the relative market values of each security as of the date that the rights are distributed to the shareholders. The cost allocation may be expressed as follows:

$$\text{Cost assigned to rights: } \frac{\text{Market Value of Rights}}{\text{Market Value of Stock Ex-rights} + \text{Market Value of Rights}} \times \begin{array}{c}\text{Original}\\\text{Cost of}\\\text{Stock}\end{array}$$

$$\text{Cost assigned to stock: } \frac{\text{Market Value of Stock Ex-rights}}{\text{Market Value of Stock Ex-rights} + \text{Market Value of Rights}} \times \begin{array}{c}\text{Original}\\\text{Cost of}\\\text{Stock}\end{array}$$

Assume that Superior Products common is selling ex-rights at $121 per share and rights are selling at $4 each. The cost allocation would be made as follows:

To rights: $\dfrac{4}{121 + 4} \times \$18,000 = \$576$ ($576 ÷ 100 = $5.76, cost per right)

To shares (balance): $18,000 − $576 = $17,424 (17,424 ÷ 100 = $174.24, cost per share)

The following entry may be made at this time:

| Investment in Superior Products Stock Rights . . . . | 576 | |
| Investment in Superior Products Common Shares . . . . | | 576 |

Received 100 rights permitting the purchase of 20 shares at $100.
Cost of shares was apportioned on the basis of the relative market
values of the shares and rights on the date rights were distributed.

The cost apportioned to the rights is used in determining the gain or the loss arising from the sale of rights. Assume that the rights in the preceding example are sold at $4^1/_2$. The following entry would be made:

Cash	450	
Loss on Sale of Superior Products Stock Rights	126	
Investment in Superior Products Stock Rights		576

Sold 100 rights at $4^1/_2$.

If the rights are exercised, the cost of the new shares acquired consists of the cost assigned to the rights plus the cash that is paid on the exercise of the rights. Assume that, instead of selling the rights, Montano exercises her privilege to purchase 20 additional shares at $100. The following entry is made:

Investment in Superior Products Common Shares	2,576	
Investment in Superior Products Stock Rights		576
Cash		2,000

Exercised rights acquiring 20 shares at $100.

Upon exercising the rights, Montano's records show an investment balance of $20,000 consisting of two lots as follows:

Lot 1 (1977 acquisition) 100 shares:	
($17,424 ÷ 100 = $174.24, cost per share as adjusted)	$17,424
Lot 2 (1981 acquisition) 20 shares:	
($2,576 ÷ 20 = $128.80, cost per share acquired through rights) . .	2,576
Total	$20,000

These costs provide the basis for calculating gains or losses upon subsequent sales of the shares.

Frequently the receipt of rights includes one or more rights that cannot be used in the purchase of a whole share. For example, assume that the owner of 100 shares receives 100 rights; 6 rights are required for the purchase of 1 share. Here the holder uses 96 rights in purchasing 16 shares. Several options are available to the holder: allow the remaining 4 rights to lapse; sell the rights and report a gain or a loss on such sale; or supplement the rights held by the purchase of 2 more rights making possible the purchase of an additional share of stock.

If the owner of valuable rights allows them to lapse, it would appear that the cost assigned to such rights should be written off as a loss. This can be supported on the theory that the issuance of shares by the corportation at less than current market price results in some dilution in the equities identified with original holdings. However, when changes in the market price of the shares make the exercise of rights unattractive and none of the rights can be sold, no dilution has occurred and any cost of rights reported separately should be returned to the investment account.

Disposition of Shares

Long-term investments in shares may be disposed of by sale, redemption, or exchange for another type of security. It is necessary to maintain sufficient records so the carrying value of the shares can be determined.

Sale of Shares. If there is a difference between the sales proceeds and the carrying value of the investment, the sale of shares results in the recognition of a gain or loss. Because share certificates are identified by number, the carrying value can usually be specifically determined. In some cases, however, companies use the average carrying value method or the first-in, first-out method for shares sold from lots acquired at different dates and prices. The gain or loss on the sale of long-term investments is often recognized as ordinary income but may qualify for segregation as an extraordinary item.

Redemption of Shares. Shares, particularly preferred issues, may be called in for redemption and cancellation by the corporation under conditions set by the issue. The redemption or call price is ordinarily set at a figure higher than the price at which the shares were originally issued, but may be more or less than the cost to the holder who acquired shares from another person after their original issue. When shares are surrendered to the corporation, an entry is made debiting Cash and crediting the investment account. Any difference between the cash proceeds and the investment cost is recorded as a gain or a loss. For example, assume that an investor acquires 100 shares of Y Co. 6%, $100 par preferred shares at 97. These shares are subsequently called in at 105. The redemption is recorded in the shareholder's accounts by the following entry.

```
Cash ...............................................  10,500
    Investment in Y Co. 6% Preferred Shares ................         9,700
    Gain on Redemption of Y Co. Preferred Shares ...........           800
    Received $10,500 on call of Y Co. preferred, cost $9,700.
```

Exchange of Shares. When shares are exchanged for other securities, the investor opens an account for the newly acquired security and closes the account of the security originally held. The new securities should be recorded at their fair market value or at the fair market value of the shares given up, whichever may be more clearly determinable, and a gain or loss is recognized on the exchange for the difference between the value assigned to the securities acquired and the carrying value of the shares given up. In the absence of a market value for either old or new securities, the carrying value of the shares given up will have to be recognized as the cost of the new securities. To illustrate, assume that the Z Co. offers its preferred shareholders two shares of no-par common shares in exchange for each share of $100 par preferred. An investor exchanges 100 shares of preferred carried at a cost of $10,000 for 200 shares of common. Common shares are quoted on the market at the time of exchange at $65. The exchange is recorded in the accounts of the shareholder by the following entry:

Investment in Z Co. Common Shares	13,000	
Investment in Z Co. Preferred Shares		10,000
Gain on Conversion of Z Co. Preferred Shares		3,000
Acquired 200 shares of common valued at $65 per share in exchange for 100 shares of preferred costing $10,000.		

Recognition of a gain or a loss on a security exchange can be supported on the grounds that the exchange closes the transaction cycle relating to the original asset and a new cycle, the newly acquired asset requiring valuation in terms of current market.

Share Valuation at Lower of Cost or Market

Reference was made in Chapter 5 to the valuation of equity securities held as a temporary investment and included with current assets. In general, current marketable equity securities are valued at the lower of aggregate cost or market, with an allowance account used to reduce the cost to market. Any change in the allowance account is recognized in the income statement in the period of change.

When equity securities are classified as long term investments because management's intent is not to use the securities as a current source of cash, the advantages of market valuations are less certain. Market prices of shares can fluctuate greatly while the shares are being held, and if the investment is to be retained for long-term purposes, the impact of gains or losses on net income could be misleading. Accordingly, as stated in Section 3050 of the *Accounting Recommendations*, "where there has been a loss in value of an investment that is other than a temporary decline, the investment should be written down to recognize the loss. The write-down would be included in the determination of income and may or may not be an extraordinary item.[6]

When an investment is consolidated, Section 3050 suggests that "a decline in value that is other than temporary would be reflected by a reduction in the carrying values of specific tangible and intangible assets to the extent that such assets declined in value."[7] Such treatment, of course, will reduce

---

[6]*CICA Handbook: Accounting Recommendations, Section 3050, op. cit.*, par. .31.
[7]*Ibid.*, par. .30.

the amounts to be charged against investment income as a result of adjustments for depreciation and amortization. Section 3050 further states that "when either the equity method or the cost method is used, a decline in value that is other than temporary would be recognized by writing down the investment."[8] In the case of equity accounting, however, adjustments with respect to subsequent depreciation and amortization would be required for purposes of determining investment income.

In the United States, the Financial Accounting Standards Board in its Statement No. 12 recommended a different treatment for valuation of non-current equity investments than for current equity investments.[9] Unless the investment is accounted for under the equity method,[10] the lower of aggregated cost or market is to be used for valuation of the asset exactly as is recommended for equity securities classified as current assets. However, the offset entry does not affect current net income. Instead, a negative shareholders' equity account is created. This account, which in FASB Statement No. 12 is entitled Net Unrealized Loss on Non-current Marketable Equity Securities is to be deducted from the total shareholders' equity balance in the balance sheet. Both the allowance account that reduces the cost to market and the negative shareholders' equity account should have the same balance at all times. As the market price of the non-current equity security portfolio varies, these accounts will be adjusted to bring the valuation to the lower of aggregate cost or market. When equity securities are sold, the transaction is recorded on the historical cost basis and a gain or loss recognized. These transactions are illustrated in the following example.

A company carries a long-term investment equity portfolio that has a cost of $125,000. At December 31, 1981, the market value of the securities held has fallen to $110,000. There is no indication that the decline is necessarily permanent. The following entries would be required to reduce the securities valuation from cost to market.

Net Unrealized Loss in Non-current Marketable Equity Securities	15,000	
Allowance for Decline in Value of Non-current Marketable Equity Securities		15,000

At the end of 1982, the portfolio has increased to an original cost of $155,000. The market value of the portfolio is $148,000. The amount in the allowance account and in the negative equity account can now be reduced to $7,000 as follows:

Allowance for Decline in Value of Non-current Marketable Equity Securities	8,000	
Net Unrealized Loss in Non-current Marketable Equity Securities		8,000

---

[8]*Ibid.*

[9]*Statement of Financial Accounting Standards No. 12*, "Accounting for Certain Marketable Securities" (Stamford, Conn.: Financial Accounting Standards Board, 1975), par. 9.

[10]Statement No. 12 does not apply to investments accounted for by the equity method.

If the decline in market value is judged to be other than temporary, the cost basis of the property should be written down (no allowance), and the write-down should be accounted for as a realized loss. The new cost basis is not to be changed for subsequent increases in market value.

If the reduction in value at December 31, 1981, in the preceding example is judged to be permanent, the entry would be altered as follows:

Realized Loss from Permanent Decline in Market Value of Non-
    current Marketable Equity Securities 15,000
        Long-Term Investment in Marketable Securities 15,000

Assume the portfolio cost at the end of 1982, after adjusting for the permanent decline in securities at the end of 1981, was $140,000, and the market was still $148,000. In this situation, no entry would be necessary in 1982. The investment would continue to be carried at the new cost of $140,000.

If there is a change in the classification of a marketable equity security between current and non-current assets, the transfer should be made at the lower of cost or market at the date of the transfer, and the lower figure is defined as the new cost base with a loss being recorded in the current period.

LONG-TERM INVESTMENT IN FUNDS

Cash and other assets set apart for certain common purposes are called *funds*, *sinking funds*, or *redemption funds*. Some funds may be used for specified current purposes, such as the payment of expenses or the discharge of current obligations, and are appropriately reported as current assets. Examples of these are petty cash funds, payroll funds, interest funds, dividend funds, and withholding, social security, and other tax funds. Other funds are accumulated over a long term for such purposes as the acquisition or the replacement of properties, the retirement of long-term indebtedness, the redemption of share capital, the operation of a pension plan, or possible future contingencies. These funds are properly considered non-current and should be reported under the long-term investment heading.

Establishment of Funds

A fund may be established through the voluntary action of management or it may be established as a result of contractual requirements. It may arise from a single deposit or from a series of deposits, or it may be composed of the sum of the deposits plus the earnings identified with such deposits. The fund may be used for a single purpose, such as the redemption of preferred shares, or it may be used for several related purposes, such as the periodic payment of interest on bonds, the retirement of bonds at various intervals, and the ultimate retirement of the remaining bonded indebtedness.

When a fund is voluntarily created by management, control of the fund and its disposition is dependent upon the wishes of management. When a fund is created through some legal requirement, it must be administered and applied in accordance therewith. Such a fund may be administered by one or more independent trustees under an agreement known as a *trust indenture*. If the trustee assumes responsibility for the fulfilment of the requirement, such as may be true for a bond retirement or a pension program, the fund is not carried as an asset on the company's books. However, if the indenture does not free the company from further obligation, the fund must be accounted for as if there were no trustee.

Fund Accumulation

When a corporation is required by agreement to establish a fund for a certain purpose, such as the retirement of bonds or the redemption of shares, the agreement generally provides that fund deposits (1) shall be fixed amounts, or (2) shall vary according to gross revenue, net income, or units of product sold, or (3) shall be equal periodic sums which, together with earnings, will produce a certain amount at some future date. The latter arrangement is based on compound-interest factors, and compound-interest or annuity tables are used to determine the equal periodic deposits. In order to accumulate a fund of $100,000 by a series of 5 equal annual deposits at 8% compounded annually, a periodic deposit of $17,045.65 is required.[11] A schedule can be developed to show the planned fund accumulation through deposits and earnings. Such a schedule is illustrated below:

	Fund Accumulation Schedule			
Year	Earnings on Fund Balance for Year	Amount Deposited in Fund	Total Increase in Fund for Year	Accumulated Fund Total
1		$17,045.65	$17,045.65	$ 17,045.65
2	$1,363.65	17,045.65	18,409.30	35,454.95
3	2,836.40	17,045.65	19,882.05	55,337.00
4	4,426.96	17,045.65	21,472.61	76,809.61
5	6,144.74	17,045.65	23,190.39	100,000.00

Assuming deposits at the end of each year, the table shows a fund balance at the end of the first year of $17,045.65 resulting from the first deposit. At the end of the second year the fund is increased by (1) earnings at 8% on the investment in the fund during the year, $1,363.65, and (2) the second deposit to the fund, $17,045.65. The total in the fund at this time is $35,454.95. Fund

---

[11]This amount can be determined from Table III, on the inside back cover. The rent or annual payment for an annuity whose amount is $100,000 at 8% for 5 periods is computed as follows:

$$R \times \frac{FV_n}{FVAF_{n/i}} \times \frac{FV_n}{\text{Table III}_{5/8}} \times \frac{100,000}{5.8666} = \$17,045.65$$

earnings in the following year are based on a total investment of $35,454.95 as of the beginning of the year.

The schedule is developed on the assumption of annual earnings of 8%. However, various factors, such as fluctuations in the earnings rate and gains and losses on investments, may provide earnings that differ from the assumed amounts. If the fund is to be maintained in accordance with the accumulation schedule, deposits may be adjusted for earnings that differ from estimated amounts. Smaller deposits, then, can be made in periods when earnings exceed the assumed rate; larger deposits are necessary when earnings fail to meet the assumed rate.

Accounting for Funds

A fund is usually composed of cash and securities. The accounting for shares held in a fund is the same as that described earlier in this chapter except the securities are reported as part of the fund balance. The accounting for investments in bonds will be discussed in Chapter 13.

To illustrate the accounting for a fund held by a company, assume a preferred share redemption fund is established with annual payments to the fund of $20,000. The fund administrator invests 90% of its assets in shares and places the remainder in bank certificates of deposit paying 6% interest. Journal entries for the first year's transactions are as follows:

Share Redemption Fund Cash	20,000	
Cash		20,000
Annual fund contribution.		
Share Redemption Fund Securities	18,000	
Share Redemption Fund Cash		18,000
Investment of fund cash in securities.		
Share Redemption Fund Certificates of Deposit	2,000	
Share Redemption Fund Cash		2,000
Investment of fund cash in certificates of deposit.		
Share Redemption Fund Cash	1,400	
Share Redemption Fund Revenue		1,400
Dividends on fund securities.		
Share Redemption Fund Cash	120	
Share Redemption Fund Revenue		120
Interest on certificates of deposit.		
Share Redemption Fund Expenses	200	
Share Redemption Fund Cash		200
Expenses to operate fund.		

At the end of the year, the share redemption fund assets are as follows:

Share redemption fund cash	$ 1,320
Share redemption fund certificate of deposit	2,000
Share redemption fund securities	18,000
Total	$21,320

This total amount would be reported under the "Long-term investments" heading on the balance sheet.

Share redemption fund revenue for the year is $1,520 and share redemption fund expense is $200, resulting in a net income from the fund operation of $1,320. This amount is reported on the income statement as other revenue. When shares are redeemed, the payment is made from the Share Redemption Fund Cash after the securities are converted to cash.

CASH SURRENDER VALUE OF LIFE INSURANCE

Many business enterprises carry life insurance policies on the lives of their executives because the business has a definite stake in the continuing services of its officers. In some cases the insurance plan affords a financial cushion in the event of loss of such personnel. In other instances the insurance offers a means of purchasing a deceased owner's interest in the business, thus avoiding a transfer of such interest to some outside party or the need to liquidate the business in effecting settlement with the estate of the deceased.

Insurance premiums normally consist of an amount for insurance protection and the balance for a form of investment. The investment portion is manifest in a growing *cash surrender value* available to the insured in the event of policy surrender and cancellation. If this cash surrender value belongs to the business, it should be reported as a long-term investment. Insurance expense for a fiscal period is the difference between the insurance premium paid and the increase in the cash surrender value of the policy. The increase in the cash surrender value is relatively uniform after the first year of the policy. At the end of the first year there may be no cash surrender value, or, if there is such a value, it may be quite low because the insurance company must recover certain costs connected with selling and initiating the policy. The cost of life insurance to the business, then, may be considered higher during the first year of the policy than in later years because of the starting costs involved.

An insurance policy with a cash surrender value also has a *loan value*; this is the amount that the insurance company will permit the insured to borrow on the policy. When the insured uses the policy as a basis for a loan, the amount borrowed should be recorded as a liability and not as a reduction in the cash value. Such a loan may be liquidated by payments of principal and interest, or the loan may be continued and be applied against the insurance proceeds upon policy cancellation or ultimate settlement.

The loan an insurance company will make on a policy is normally limited to the policy cash surrender value at the end of the policy year less discount from the loan date to the cash surrender value date. For example, assume a cash surrender value of $3,000 at the end of a fifth policy year. The maximum loan value on the policy at the beginning of the fifth policy year, assuming the insurance premium for the fifth year is paid, is $3,000 discounted for one year. If the discount rate applied by the insurance company is 5%, the policy loan value is calculated as follows: $3,000 ÷ 1.05 = $2,857.14.

Although it is possible for the insured to recognize policy loan values instead of cash surrender values, the latter values are generally used.

The insured may authorize the insurance company to apply any dividends declared upon insurance policies to the reduction of the annual premium payment or to the increase in insurance cash surrender value, or the dividends may be collected in cash. Dividends should be viewed as a reduction in the cost of carrying insurance rather than as a source of supplementary revenue. Hence, if dividends are applied to the reduction of the annual premium, Insurance Expense is simply debited for the net amount paid. If the dividend is applied to the increase in the policy cash surrender value or if it is collected in cash, it should still be treated as an offset to the periodic expense of carrying the policy; the policy cash surrender value or Cash, then, is debited and Insurance Expense is credited. After a number of years, the periodic dividends plus increases in the cash surrender value may exceed the premium payments, thus resulting in revenue rather than expense on policy holdings.

Collection of a policy upon death of the insured requires cancellation of any cash surrender balance. The difference between the insurance proceeds and the balances relating to the insurance policy is recognized as a gain in the period of the death. The nature of the insurance policies carried and their coverage may be disclosed by footnote, but this would indeed be rare.

The entries to be made for an insurance contract are illustrated in the following example. The Andrews Manufacturing Company insured the life of its president, W. E. Andrews, on October 1, 1978. The amount of the policy was $50,000; the annual premiums were $2,100.

Year	Gross Premium	Dividend	Net Premium	Increase in Cash Value	Insurance Expense for Year
1	$2,100	——	$2,100	——	$2,100
2	2,100	——	2,100	$1,150	950
3	2,100	$272	1,828	1,300	528

The fiscal period for the company is the calendar year. Mr. Andrews died on July 1, 1981. The entries made in recording transactions relating to the insurance contract are shown on the next page.

Cash surrender value increases are recognized in the accounts whenever a premium is paid. The periodic insurance premium includes a charge for the increase in the policy cash surrender value but the increase actually becomes effective as of the end of the policy year. Hence, anticipation of the cash surrender value on the date of the premium payment needs to be accom-

TRANSACTION	ENTRY
October 1, 1978 Paid first annual premium, $2,100.	Prepaid Insurance .... 2,100.00 Cash 2,100.00

December 31, 1978
To record insurance expense for Oct. 1–Dec. 31:
  $^1/_4 \times \$2,100 = \$525$.
	Life Insurance Expense......... 525.00
	  Prepaid Insurance 525.00

October 1, 1979
Paid second annual premium, $2,100.
  Premium....................... $2,100
  Less cash surrender value 1,150
  Net insurance charge .... $ 950
	Cash Surrender Value of Life In-
	surance (as of Sept. 30, 1980) .. 1,150.00
	Prepaid Insurance 950.00
	  Cash 2,100.00

December 31, 1979
To record insurance expense for the year:
  $^3/_4 \times \$2,100$ (Jan. 1–Sept. 30) $1,575.00
  $^1/_4 \times \$950$ (Oct. 1–Dec. 31) 237.50
                                     $1,812.50
	Life Insurance Expense......... 1,812.50
	  Prepaid Insurance 1,812.50

October 1, 1980
Paid third annual premium, $2,100.
  Premium $2,100
  Less: Cash surrender value credit .. $1,300
          Dividend credit 272   1,572
  Net insurance charge .... $ 528
	Cash Surrender Value of Life In-
	surance (as of Sept. 30, 1981) .. 1,300.00
	Prepaid Insurance 528.00
	  Cash 1,828.00

December 31, 1980
To record insurance expense for the year:
  $^3/_4 \times \$950$ (Jan. 1–Sept. 30) $712.50
  $^1/_4 \times \$528$ (Oct. 1–Dec. 31) 132.00
                                  $844.50
	Life Insurance Expense......... 844.50
	  Prepaid Insurance 844.50

July 1, 1981
To record insurance expense for Jan. 1–July 1:
  $^1/_2 \times \$528 = \$264$.
 	
July 1, 1981
To record cancellation of policy upon death of insured:
  Amount recoverable on policy:
    Face of policy $50,000
    Premium rebate for period July 1-Oct. 1
    and current year dividend 735
                                  $50,735
  Cancellation of asset values:
    Cash surrender value .... $ 2,450
    Prepaid insurance 132
                                $ 2,582
  Gain on policy settlement $48,153
	Life Insurance Expense......... 264.00
	  Prepaid Insurance 264.00
	
	Receivable from Insurance
	Company 50,735.00
	  Cash Surrender Value of Life
	  Insurance 2,450.00
	  Prepaid Insurance 132.00
	  Gain on Settlement of Life
	  Insurance 48,153.00

panied by a notation as to its effective date. Anticipation of the cash surrender value should be disclosed in presenting this asset on the balance sheet. If loan values instead of cash surrender values were recognized, no notation would be required since the loan values become effective immediately upon meeting premium requirements for the policy year. Dividends in the example reduce the insurance charge of the period in which they are applied against a premium. Actually the dividend applied against the premium for the third year accrues at the end of the second year and could be considered as a correction in the expense of the second year. Dividends received in the period of policy termination are recognized as a part of policy proceeds in final settlement rather than as a correction of insurance expense. The procedures illustrated involve certain concessions in theoretical accuracy but are normally preferred because of their practicality.

INTERESTS IN REAL ESTATE

Improved property purchased for supplementary income and possible price appreciation or for future use is shown under the long-term investment heading. The expenses relating to such holdings should be deducted from any revenue produced by the property. Unimproved property is frequently acquired for possible future use or for sale. Land while unused makes no contribution to periodic revenue. Costs incident to holding the land should be added to the investment balance. When the land is used for construction purposes or is sold, its costs will include all expenditures incident to its acquisition and holding. Market or appraised values, when available, may be reported parenthetically.

MISCELLANEOUS LONG-TERM INVESTMENTS

Many assets could be named that are of an auxiliary character in terms of central business activities and are properly reportable under the "Long-term investments" heading. Long-term investments include such items as: advances to subsidiaries that are of a permanent nature; deposits made to guarantee contract performance; and equity interests in partnerships, trusts, and estates. Most of these assets produce either current revenue or have a favorable business effect in some other way. Although cost is the underlying basis for these miscellaneous investments, the accounting procedure varies according to the type of investment involved.

LONG-TERM INVESTMENTS ON THE BALANCE SHEET

Long-term investments are generally reported on the balance sheet following the current assets classification. The long-term investment section should not include temporary investments held as a ready source of cash.

Headings should be provided for the different long-term investment categories and individual long-term investments reported within such groupings. Detailed information relative to individual long-term investments may be provided in separate supporting schedules or in the notes. Long-term investment costs should be supplemented by market quotations, if available, provided in parenthetical or note form if market exceeds cost. Information concerning the pledge of long-term investments as collateral on loans should be provided. When long-term investments are carried at amounts other than cost, the valuation that is employed should be described.

In reporting funds to be applied to specific purposes or paid to specific parties, disclosure should be made by special note of the conditions relative to their establishment and ultimate application. A fund arrearage or other failure to meet contractual requirements should be pointed out; the demand to be made upon current assets by deposit requirements in the succeeding fiscal period should also be disclosed when material. Offset of a fund balance against a liability item is proper only when an asset transfer to a trustee is irrevocable and actually serves to discharge the obligation.

The "Long-term investments" section of a balance sheet might appear as follows:

Long-term investments:			
Affiliated companies:			
Investment in Wilson Co. common shares, reported by the equity method (Investment consists of 90,000 shares representing a 40% interest acquired on July 1, 1977, for $1,500,000. Retained earnings of the affiliate since date of acquisition have increased by $120,000; 40% of this amount, or $48,000, is identified with the investor company equity and has been recognized in the accounts.)	$1,548,000		
Advances to Wilson Co.	115,000	$1,663,000	
Miscellaneous investments in shares, at cost (shares have an aggregate quoted market value of $112,000; shares have been deposited as security on bank loan — refer to notes payable, contra)		100,000	
Share redemption fund, composed of:			
Cash	$ 15,000		
Shares and bonds, at cost (aggregate quoted market value, $420,000)	410,500		
Dividends and interest receivable	4,500	430,000	
Investment in land and unused facilities . .		125,000	
Cash surrender value of life insurance carried on officers' lives		12,500	
Total long-term investments			$2,330,500

1. Why would a manufacturing company invest funds in shares, bonds and other securities?

2. How should each of the following be classified on the balance sheet?
   (a) Shares held for purposes of controlling the activities of a subsidiary.
   (b) Listed stock rights to be sold.
   (c) Shares intended to be transferred to a supplier in cancellation of an amount owed.

3. (a) Define: (1) parent company, (2) subsidiary company. (b) How much share ownership is required to exercise control? to exercise significant influence?

4. How would you record the purchase of share and bond units acquired for a lump sum when (a) only one of the securities is quoted on the market? (b) both securities are quoted? (c) neither security is quoted?

5. R. S. Doug purchases 1,000 shares of Abbott Motors at $90 a share in November, paying his broker $65,000. The market value of the shares on December 31 is $125 a share; Doug has made no further payment to his broker. On this date he shows on his balance sheet Abbott Motors Shares, $100,000, the difference between marked value and the unpaid balance to the broker. Do you approve of this report? Explain.

6. What conflict, if any, exists between the equity method of reporting subsidiary company earnings on investor company statements and the entity theory?

7. When using the equity method, what special adjustments are necessary in recognizing the proportionate share of the investee's income?

8. What dates are significant in the declaration of a dividend?

9. Distinguish between the following types of dividends: (a) cash, (b) liquidating, (c) stock, (d) property.

10. What reasons may be offered for the infrequent use of property dividends by corporations?

11. B. A. Eliot receives $400 representing a dividend of $4 per share on Atlas Securities Co. common stock, accompanied by a statement that $1.56 represents a distribution of income and $2.44 represents a dividend in partial liquidation. (a) What is the meaning of this statement? (b) What entry should Eliot make in recording the dividend?

12. Some accounting writers have suggested that certain stock dividends should constitute revenue to the recipients. What is the basis for this view?

13. Distinguish between a stock dividend and a stock split.

14. If stock rights lapse and are not used, what disposition should be made of the investment cost allocated to the rights?

15. The Porter Co. accepts 2,000 shares of Murdock common stock in full payment of a claim of $12,000 against the latter company. State how this transaction would be recorded in the accounts of the Porter Co., assuming that (a) Murdock shares are closely held and no market value is available; (b) Murdock shares are quoted on the market at $5; (c) Murdock shares are quoted on the market at $6.50 bid, $7.50 asked.

16. Name and describe five funds that would be listed as current assets and five that would be listed as long-term investments.

17. The Duane Co. has made certain major modifications in property that was leased for a ten-year period. The leasehold contract provides that in addition to the payment of monthly rents Duane Co. was to make monthly deposits to a sinking fund that will be used to restore the properties to their original condition upon termination of the lease-hold. How would you record the payments required by the terms of the contract?

18. (a) Distinguish between life insurance cash surrender value and loan value. (b) How is the loan value on a life insurance policy calculated?

19. The Meadows Company collects in cash the dividends on the life insurance policies that it carries. The Nielson Company uses dividend credits to reduce the life insurance premium it pays. The Ogg Corporation authorizes the insurance companies to apply dividend credits to the increase of policy surrender value. What entries will each company make in recognizing dividends?

20. Name ten items properly reported under the "Long-term investments" heading on the balance sheet.

EXERCISES

10-1. The Leisure Life Co. acquired on margin 2,000 shares of Alloy, Ltd., preferred stock and 20,000 shares of Alloy, Ltd., common stock for $450,000 plus broker's commission of 1%. Market prices at the time the shares were acquired were $50 per share for preferred and $20 per share for common. Terms of the margin agreement provided for payment at acquisition date of 25% of the purchase price plus the broker's commission. The balance due the broker, plus 8% interest, must be paid within six months.

(a) What entry should have been made to record the purchase?
(b) What entry would be made to pay the balance due the broker three months after purchase?

10-2. The Crawford Co. holds shares of Russell Co. acquired as follows:

	Shares	Total Cost
1979	100	$5,600
1980	150	7,350
1981	50	2,410

Give the entries that would be made upon the sale of 150 shares in 1982 at $53 per share assuming that cost is determined by (a) the first-in, first-out method, (b) the average carrying value method, (c) identification of lot sold as the 1980 purchase.

10-3. In 1980, Fred Arthurs acquired 15,000 shares of Tropi-Cal & Co. for a cost of $375,000. He was also appointed chairman of the board of directors, a position that gave him significant influence over the affairs of the company. Tropi-Cal & Co. has 100,000 shares outstanding. What entries would be made by Arthurs in 1981 for the following events?

(a) Tropi-Cal & Co. announces net income of $45,000 for the first six months and pays a dividend of 6¢ per share.

(b) Arthurs acquires an additional 5,000 shares of Tropi-Cal & Co. at 15.

(c) Tropi-Cal & Co. announces ordinary income of $60,000 for the second six months and an extraordinary loss of $100,000.

10-4. On January 1, 1981, M. Wilde and Company purchased 20,000 shares of Storms Corporation common stock for $100,000. At that date there were 50,000 shares of Storms common authorized and outstanding. The net assets of Storms at January 1 were valued at $200,000. You determine that fixed assets with a remaining life of 15 years have a fair market value of $30,000 above their net book value, and that the remainder of the excess is attributed to goodwill to be straight-line amortized over 40 years.

What entries are required to report adjusted net income or loss for (a) 1982, reported proportionate share of income, $10,000; and (b) 2001, reported proportionate share of loss, $2,000?

10-5. During January 1981, Prairie Company purchased 1,000 of the outstanding 5,000 shares of B.C. Limited at $26 per share. At that date the following data was available for B.C. Limited.

	At book value	At fair market value
Assets not subject to depreciation	$ 80,000	$85,000
Assets subject to depreciation (ten-year remaining life)	50,000	56,000
	$130,000	
Liabilities	$ 20,000	
Share capital, common	75,000	
Retained earnings	35,000	
	$130,000	

At the end of 1981, B.C. Limited reported a net income of $18,000 and paid a cash dividend of $7,000. Assuming Prairie Company used the equity method to account for this investment (a) prepare the necessary entries pertaining to the investment at the end of 1981. (Assume goodwill, if any, is amortized over a ten-year period.) (b) What is the difference in amount that Prairie Company would recognize as investment income under the equity method, and the amount it would recognize if the cost method had been used? (CGA adapted)

10-6. During January 1981, Parent Ltd. purchased 30% of the 6,000 outstanding common shares of Kidd Limited at $50 per share. At that date the following data was available for Kidd Limited.

	At book value	At fair market value
Assets not subject to depreciation	$100,000	$102,000
Assets subject to depreciation (ten-year remaining life)	200,000	210,000
	$300,000	
Liabilities	40,000	40,000
Common shares (par value $20)	120,000	
Retained earnings	140,000	
	$300,000	

At the end of 1981, Kidd Limited reported a net income of $40,000 and declared dividends of $12,000. Prepare journal entries to be recorded in the accounts of Parent Ltd. assuming (a) the cost method is used; (b) the equity method is used. Goodwill, if any, is to be amortized over a twenty-year period. What effect, if any, might fair market value allocations to assets not subject to depreciation have on the measurement of investment income under the equity method? Explain. (CGA adapted)

10-7. Joseph Marr owns shares of Blackburn & Co. acquired in two lots as follows:

	Shares	Cost per Share	Total Cost
February 10, 1978	100	$45	$4,500
April 23, 1979	100	50	5,000

In 1980, a stock dividend of 50 shares was received. Because Joseph Marr needed cash, he sold the 50 shares at $32 per share and credited the proceeds to a revenue account, Gain on Sale of Blackburn Co. Shares. If the first-in, first-out method is used to record sales, what correction in the accounts is necessary assuming (a) the books are still open for 1980; (b) the error is not detected until 1981 after the 1980 financial reports were prepared?

10-8. On April 4, 1976, an investor purchased 100 shares of AEL Ltd. stock for $6,000. AEL Ltd. paid a 100% stock dividend on July 1, 1978 at which time the stock had a market price of $80.00 per share. On April 1, 1980, AEL Ltd. announced the issuance, to holders of record on May 5, 1980, of rights to subscribe to one new share at $40.00 for each four shares held. On May 6, 1980, the investor sold 40 rights at $5.00 and exercised the remainder. On May 18, 1982 the investor sold 20 old shares and 5 new shares, all at $72.00 per share. On May 6, 1980 the market price of the rights and of the stock ex-rights were $5.00 and $70.00 respectively.

Prepare journal entries to be recorded by the investor for all of the above transactions. (SMA adapted)

10-9. Jill Hagen owns 400 shares of Automat Co. common acquired at $50 per share. Give the cost basis per share for her investment holdings if:
   (a) She receives a common stock dividend of 1 for 4.
   (b) Common stock is exchanged in a 5-for-1 split.
   (c) She receives a preferred stock dividend of 1 share for every 4 shares of common held; common is selling ex-dividend at $75; preferred is selling at $200.
   (d) She receives a property dividend of 1 share of Jasper Co. common, market price $7, for every 5 shares held.

10-10. On March 1, R. Wallace purchased 1,000 shares of Alberta Corp. common stock, par $5, at $32. On May 3, Wallace received a stock dividend of 1 share for every 4 owned. On September 13, he received a cash dividend of 40¢ on the stock and was granted the right to purchase 1 share at $10 for every 4 shares held. On this date the market value of the shares ex-rights was $15, and each right had a value of $1; share cost was allocated on this basis. On November 15, Wallace sold 450 rights at $1.50 each and exercised the remaining rights. What entries will appear in Wallace's accounts as a result of the foregoing?

10-11. The Flavor Co. holds shares of Jarvis Ltd., acquired as follows:

	Shares	Total Cost
Lot A, 1979	100	$8,400
Lot B, 1980	50	4,300

In 1981, Flavor Co. receives 150 rights to purchase Jarvis Ltd., shares at $75 per share. Four rights are required to purchase one share. At issue date, rights had a market value of $5 each and each share was selling ex-rights at $95. Flavor Co. used rights to purchase 20 additional shares of Jarvis Ltd., and alllowed the unexercised rights to lapse. Assume use of the first-in, first-out method of identifying stock rights used. What entries are required to record the above events?

10-12. On March 1, 1977, Gilkes Corporation invested $75,000 share redemption fund cash in 8% preferred stock of Wilkens Inc., par value of $80,000. Wilkens normally declares and pays dividends on preferred semi-annually: May 1 and November 1. On April 1, 1978, Gilkes exchanged the shares with another investor for 2,000 shares of Simmons Corporation common stock. The market value of the common at the date of exchange was $42^{1}/_{2}$.

Give all the entries necessary to record the above transactions assuming semi-annual dividends were paid.

10-13. Sinking fund tables show that 5 annual deposits of $18,097.48 accruing interest at 5% compounded annually will result in a total accumulation of $100,000 immediately after the fifth payment. (a) Prepare a fund accumulation schedule showing the theoretical growth of the fund over the 5-year period. (b) Give all of the entries that would appear in the accounts for the increases in the property acquisition fund balance for the first three years.

10-14. The Dobb Company insured the life of its president for $100,000. Annual premiums of $4,200 are paid beginning July 1, 1977. A dividend of $600 is to be paid annually beginning July 1, 1978. Cash surrender value after the second year is $2,200; after the third year, $4,460. The president died January 1, 1980, and a premium refund of $1,500 is made in addition to the face value of the policy. If Dobb Company closes its accounts on December 31, give the required entries in the accounts for the years 1977-1980.

10-15. In 1970, the Cragen Appliance Corporation purchased for $78,000 ten acres adjoining its manufacturing plant to provide for possible future expansion. From 1970-1980 the company paid $20,000 in taxes and $30,000 in special assessments. In 1980 it sold one half of the land for $87,000 and erected a building at a cost of $300,000 on the other half. The company books on December 31, 1980, show a "plant" account balance of $341,000. Give the journal entries to correct the accounts.

PROBLEMS

10-1A. The Roger Corp. and the Martin Corp. each have 150,000 shares of no-par stock outstanding. Water's Ltd., acquired 25,000 shares of Roger stock and 60,000 shares of Martin stock in 1976. Changes in retained earnings for Roger and Martin for 1980 and 1981 are as follows:

	Roger Corp.		Martin Corp.
Retained earnings (deficit), January 1, 1980 ..	$140,000		$(20,000)
Cash dividends, 1980	(30,000)		0
	$110,000		$(20,000)
Income before extraordinary items		$20,000	$ 80,000
Extraordinary gain		30,000	20,000
Net income, 1980	50,000		100,000
Retained earnings, December 31, 1980	$160,000		$ 80,000
Cash dividends, 1981		$(20,000)	
Market value of stock dividends issued — 7,500			
shares (transferred to share capital section) .		(30,000)	(50,000)
			$ 30,000
Net income (loss), 1981	(60,000)		(10,000)
Retained earnings, December 31, 1981	$100,000		$ 20,000

Instructions:

Give the entries required in the accounts of Water's Ltd., for 1980 and 1981 to account for its investments.

10-2A. J. Takashi owns 800 shares of Gino Inc., acquired on May 1, 1977, for $30,000. During 1980 and 1981, the following transactions took place with respect to this investment:

1980

Mar. 1 Received cash dividend of 50¢ per share and stock dividend of 25%.

Oct. 15 Received stock rights offering the purchase of 1 share at $70 for every 5 shares held. At this time each share was quoted ex-rights at $95 and rights were quoted at $5 each; share cost was apportioned on this basis. Rights were exercised.

1981

Mar. 1 Received a cash dividend of 50¢ per share and a stock dividend of 20%.

Dec. 5 Received stock rights offering the purchase of 1 share at $68 for every 5 shares held. At this time each share was quoted ex-rights at $78 and rights were quoted at $2 each; share cost was apportioned on this basis. Rights were sold at $3, less brokerage charges of $75.

Instructions:

(1) Give journal entries to record the foregoing transactions.

(2) Give the investment account balance as of December 31, 1981, including shares and costs in support of this balance.

10-3A. On January 1, 1977, Shaw, Ltd., purchased 100,000 shares of Squires Corporation common stock for $600,000. At the time, Squires had 400,000 shares authorized and issued. You are given the following information:

(a) Squires Corporation asset values at January 1, 1977, are as follows:

	Book Value	Market Value
Net current assets	$1,250,000	$1,250,000
Land	350,000	350,000
Buildings (10-year remaining life)	900,000	700,000
	$2,500,000	$2,300,000

(b) Squires Corporation reported income for 1977 of $400,000.

(c) On February 1, 1978, Squires paid a dividend of $1 per share.

(d) Squires Corporation reported income for 1978 of $350,000.

Instructions:

Give the necessary journal entries to record the above information. (Assume income is earned evenly throughout the year.)

10-4A. The following balances appeared in the ledger of the Fleming Company on December 31, 1978:

Investment in Ace Co. Common, par $100, 250 shares	$24,000
Investment in Ace Co. 6% Preferred, par $100, 50 shares	$ 3,950

The Fleming Company uses the first-in, first-out method in accounting for share transactions. In 1979, 1980, and 1981, the following transactions took place relative to the above investments:

1979

Jan. 20 Holders of Ace Co. 6% preferred were given the right to exchange their holdings for an equal number of Ace Co. common, and the Fleming Co. made such exchange. Common shares on the date of exchange were quoted on the market at $120 per share.

Dec. 29 Received cash dividends of $3 per share on Ace Co. common.

1980

July 30 Received additional shares of Ace Co. common in a 4-for-1 stock split. (Par value of common was reduced to $25.)

Dec. 28 Exercised option to receive one share of Ace Co. common for each 40 shares held in lieu of a cash dividend of $1 per share held. The market value of Ace Co. common on the date of distribution was $50 per share. Dividend revenue was recognized at the value of the shares received.

1981

July 1 Received a stock dividend of 10% on Ace Co. common.

Oct. 15 Received warrants representing right to purchase at par 1 share of Ace Co. common for every 4 shares held. On date of warrants issue, the market value of shares ex-rights was $37, and the market value of rights was $3; cost of the shares was allocated on this basis.

Oct. 31 Exercised 440 rights identified with the first lot of shares acquired and sold remaining rights at $2.50 per right less brokerage charges of $30.

Dec. 31 Sold 660 shares of Ace Co. common at $43 per share less brokerage charges of $330.

Instructions:

(1) Prepare journal entries to record the transactions in Ace Co. holdings.

(2) Prepare a schedule showing the balance of Ace Co. Common Shares held by Fleming Company on December 31, 1981.

10-5A. The Tong Co. has the following securities on hand on January 1, 1980.

Investment in North Co. 6% Preferred, par $60, 75 shares	$ 2,700
Investment in Ontario Iron Common, 500 shares	$30,250

During 1980, the following transactions were completed relative to investments.

Jan. 24 Purchased 150 shares of Wyler Co. common for $8,400.

Feb. 1 Received a cash dividend of 50¢ and stock dividend of 10% on Ontario Iron common.

Apr. 12 Purchased 200 shares of Wyler Co. common for $14,000.

May 20 Received the semi-annual dividend on North Co. 6% preferred.

July 1 Wyler Co. common was split on a 2-for-1 basis.

Aug. 11 Received a dividend of $2 on Wyler Co. common.

11 Received a cash dividend of 50¢ and a stock dividend of 10% on Ontario Iron common.

Oct. 10 Sold 200 shares of Wyler Co. common for $9,100 and also sold the 75 shares of North Co. 6% preferred for $5,000.

28 Received rights on Wyler Co. common to subscribe for additional shares as follows: 1 share could be acquired at $40 for every 4 shares held. On this date Wyler common was selling for 48 and rights were selling at 2; share cost was apportioned on this basis.

Nov. 15 Sold all of the Wyler rights for $815.

Dec. 20 Received a special year-end dividend on Ontario Iron common of $3.

Instructions:

(1) Assuming the use of first-in, first-out for assigning costs to sales, give journal entries to record the foregoing transactions. (Give calculations in support of your entries.)

(2) Give the investment account balance as of December 31, 1980, including the number of shares and costs comprising such balances.

10-6A. Transactions of Merrill Machines, Inc., during 1980 included the following:

Jan. 15 Purchased 600 units of Joel Co. preferred and common at $60 per unit: each unit consists of one share of preferred and two shares of common. No market costs are available. Brokerage charges were $540.

Feb. 10 Received a 20% stock dividend on the common shares.

Feb. 15 Sold all the preferred for $16 per share less brokerage charges of $420.

Mar. 10 Received stock rights permitting the purchase of one share at $14 of common for every 5 shares held. On this day, rights were being traded at $1 each and shares were being traded ex-rights at $19 per share.

Mar. 21 Exercised 1,000 rights pertaining to the shares acquired on January 15, and sold remaining rights at $1 less brokerage charges of $6.

June 30 Received a stock dividend of 82 shares of $25 per preferred on the common shares held. On the date of distribution the common was selling for $20 and the preferred for $30. Because Merrill keeps its share records on the fifo method, it is necessary to allocate cost according to the different lots held.

Aug. 15 Sold the shares acquired on March 21 plus 300 shares from the holdings acquired on January 15 at $22 less brokerage charges of $225.

Dec. 15 Redeemed the preferred shares at a call price of $35.

Instructions:

(1) Give journal entries to record the foregoing transactions. (Give computations in support of your entries.)

(2) Give the investment account balance on December 31, 1980, and the shares and costs making up this balance.

10-7A. Each of the two parts of this problem is independent of the other. Prepare solutions for each of the following requirements.

Part I

On January 1, 1981, Todd Corporation made the following investments:

1. Todd acquired, for cash, 80% of the outstanding common shares of Meadow Corporation at $70 per share. The shareholders' equity of Meadow on January 1, 1981 consisted of the following:

Common shares, par value $50	$50,000
Retained earnings	20,000

2. Todd acquired, for cash, 70% of the outstanding common shares of Van Corporation at $40 per share. The shareholders' equity of Van on January 1, 1981 consisted of the following:

Common shares, par value $20	$60,000
Contributed surplus	20,000
Retained earnings	40,000

After these investments were made, Todd was able to exercise significant influence over the operations of both companies. An analysis of the retained earnings of each company for 1981 is as follows:

	Todd	Meadow	Van
Balance, January 1, 1981	$240,000	$20,000	$40,000
Net income (loss) from own operations	104,600	36,000	(12,000)
Cash dividends paid	(40,000)	(16,000)	(9,000)

Instructions:

(1) What entries should have been made in the accounts of Todd during 1981 to record the following?
   (a) Investments in subsidiaries
   (b) Parent's share of subsidiary income or loss
   (c) Subsidiary dividends received
(2) At what amounts should these investments be shown on Todd Corporation's separate entity (non-consolidated) balance sheet as at December 31, 1981?

(AICPA adapted)

Part II

The North Salem Company has supplied you with the following information regarding two investments that were made during 1981:

On January 1, 1981, North Salem purchased, for cash, 40% of the 500,000 shares of voting common stock of the Yorktown Company for $2,400,000, representing 40% of the net worth of Yorktown. Yorktown's net income for the year ended December 31, 1981 was $750,000. Yorktown paid dividends of $0.50 per share in 1981. The market value of Yorktown's common shares was $14 per share on December 31, 1980. North Salem exercised significant influence over the operating and financial policies of Yorktown. Any difference between purchase cost and the fair value of Yorktown's net assets is attributable to depreciable assets that have 10 years of useful life remaining.

On July 1, 1981, North Salem purchased, for cash, 15,000 shares, representing 5% of the voting common stock of the Mahopac Company for $450,000. Mahopac's net income for the six months ended December 31, 1981 was $350,000 and for the year ended December 31, 1981 was $600,000. Mahopac paid dividends of $0.30 per share each quarter during 1981 to shareholders of record on the last day of each quarter. The market value of Mahopac's common stock was $32 per share on January 1, 1981 and $34 per share on December 31, 1981.

Instructions:
(1) As a result of these two investments, what should be the balance in the investment's account for North Salem at December 31, 1981?
(2) As a result of these two investments, what should be the income reported by North Salem for the year ended December 31, 1981?   (AICPA adapted)

10-8A. During your December 31, 1981 audit of Rich Corporation, you find the following items in the account summarizing the investment in Musket Motors & Co. common shares:

ACCOUNT   Investment in Musket Motors & Co. Common Shares

DATE		ITEM	DEBIT	CREDIT	BALANCE	
					DEBIT	CREDIT
1981						
Jan.	1	Purchased 5,000 shares at $30	150,000		150,000	
Mar.	31	Cash dividend		3,000	147,000	
June	30	Share of net income for first half of 1981	20,000		167,000	
Nov.	10	Received stock rights		16,700	150,300	
	30	Cash dividend		5,000	145,300	
Dec.	30	Exercised stock rights to purchase 1,000 shares at $34 ..	40,680		185,980	
	31	Share of net income for second half of 1981	18,000		203,980	

After inquiry, the following additional data were obtained.
(a) Musket Motors & Co. net income for the first and second halves of 1981 was $400,000 and $450,000 respectively.
(b) Broker's fees of $2,500 on the original purchase were recorded as an expense.
(c) The dividend of March 31 represented a distribution of earnings from the second half of 1980.
(d) The dividend of November 30 was $1 per share; 70¢ per share represents earnings and the balance represents a liquidating dividend.
(e) Musket Motors & Co. offered its shareholders the opportunity to subscribe to new shares at $34 per share up to 50% of their holdings. At distribution date, stock rights were selling for $5. Rich Corporation was informed that 10% of share cost was applicable to rights.

Instructions:
(1) Give the individual entries for each correction required in the Musket Motors & Co. investment account on December 31, 1981, to bring this account in conformity with generally accepted accounting principles.
(2) Give the corrected balance for the investment account on December 31, 1981, and the shares and costs making up this balance.

10-9A. Transactions of Coleman Service Co. in securities during 1981 were as follows:

Feb. 10 Purchased 1,000 shares of Harper, Inc., common for $37,000.

Mar. 15 Purchased 9,000 shares of Fisher Co. preferred for $72,000.

Oct. 24 Sold 500 shares of Harper, Inc., common for $15,000.

The fair market value of Fisher Co. preferred and Harper, Inc., common on December 31, 1981, the date of the annual audit, was $7 and $25 per share respec-tively. The president of the company recommends that the cost balance in the invest-ments account be retained because the investments are in reality long-term and the declines in market values seem to be temporary. The auditor counters that since one half of the Harper, Inc., common has been sold during the year and since the invest-ment in Fisher Co. is in preferred shares, the investments appear to be current assets rather than long-term investments.

Instructions:

(1) Give journal entries to record any valuation adjustments that would be made if the auditor's recommendations are followed.

(2) Give journal entries to record any valuation adjustments that would be made if the president's recommendations are followed.

(3) Give journal entries to record any valuation adjustments that would be made if the Harper, Inc., common is identified as long-term, but the decline is felt to be permanent. The Fisher Co. shares are still classified as a current asset.

10-10A. Investo Ltd. is a small investment company which has a December 31 year-end. At the beginning of 1978, the subsidiary ledger of investments includes the following two cards:

A Co Ltd. — bonds:	nominal value	$10,000
	cost (including accrued interest)	$ 9,990
	purchase date	Dec. 31, 1977
	interest rate	8%
	due date	Oct. 1/1979
	payment dates for interest	Apr. 1 and Oct. 1
B Co Ltd. — common stocks:	quantity	10,000 shares
	cost	$49,000
	purchase date	July 1/1977

During 1978 the company had the following transactions:

(1) On July 1, B Co. Ltd. declared a stock dividend of 100%. This stock dividend was distributed on July 15 to all shareholders recorded as at July 1.

(2) On July 1, Investo Ltd. bought some more bonds of A Co Ltd. These bonds, which had the same characteristics as those previously described, had a nominal value of $10,000. The company paid $10,380 including accrued interest.

(3) On August 1, Investo Ltd. received from B Co. Ltd. one right for each common share it owned. These rights could be used to buy one common share at the price of $2.25 before July 31, 1979. On August 1, the rights had a market value of $.45 each and the shares had a market value of $2.70 each.

(4) On October 2, the company sold the following investments:

— bonds of A Co. Ltd.:	par value	$10,000
	selling price	9,500
— rights of B Co. Ltd.:	quantity	one half of the rights owned
	selling price	$.50 each
— shares of B Co. Ltd.:	quantity	one fourth of the shares owned
	selling price	$3.10 each

(5) On December 15, B Co Ltd. declared a dividend of $.20 per share on all its shares. This dividend was paid on December 20 to all shareholders recorded as at November 30, 1978.

(6) Investo Ltd. received all payments for dividends and interest.

Instructions:

Determine the total income provided by these two investments, including gains or losses on sales. Your schedule must show in detail the various sources of this income. Show all calculations.

NOTE: 1. The company uses the weighted average method to determine the cost of any investment sold.

2. The company amortizes any premium or discount on a straight-line basis.

(SMA adapted)

10-11A. On December 31, 1981, a four-payment fund is set up to redeem $30,000 of preferred shares. The fund is guaranteed to earn 6% compounded annually, and must generate enough income to enable the company to retire the shares after the fourth payment. The annual instalments paid to the fund trustee are $6,857.75. The first deposit is made immediately.

Instructions:

(1) Give the journal entries in connection with the fund for the years 1981 and 1982. (Assume the company keeps its books on the calendar year basis.)

(2) Suppose that on December 31, 1985, the fund balance of $30,000 consisted of $8,000 cash and $22,000 in securities. The securities are sold for $24,000. Give all of the journal entries that would be made to sell the securities, retire the $30,000 of preferred shares, and liquidate any balance in the fund account.

10-12A. During the course of the audit of the Harlen Lee Company, which closes its accounts on December 31, you examine the life insurance policies, premium receipts, and confirmations returned by the insurance companies in response to your request for information. You find that prepaid insurance on December 31, 1980 was $3,000, and in 1981 the company had paid premiums on the life of the president, Harlen Lee, as shown below:

Sole Owner and Beneficiary	Face of Policy	Annual Billed Premium 1981	Cash Dividend Used to Reduce Premium	Annual Premium Date	Cash Surrender Value December 31 1981	1980
1. Harlen Lee Company	$100,000	$2,500	$700	June 30	$32,000	$30,000
2. Dorothy Lee, wife of Harlen Lee	50,000	1,600	300	Sept. 30	15,000	14,000
3. Harlen Lee Company	100,000	3,600	800	April 1	22,000	21,000

Instructions:

(1) Prepare all of the journal entries required for the year 1981.

(2) What balances relating to these insurance policies would appear on the balance sheet prepared on December 31, 1981?

10-13A. The analysis on page 403 relates to the Craig Corporation investment account:

Craig Corporation
Analysis of Investments
For Year Ended December 31, 1981

Date		Debit	Credit
	(1)		
	Ace Tool Company Common Shares		
1981			
Mar. 15	Purchased 1,000 shares at $25 per share	$ 25,000	
June 28	Received 50 shares of Bymore Sales Company common stock as a dividend on Ace Tool Company common (memorandum entry in general ledger).		
Sept. 30	Sold 50 shares of Bymore Sales Company common at $14 per share		$ 700
Oct. 31	Awarded 500 shares of Ace Tool Company common to selected members of Craig's management as an incentive award and accounted for as employee compensation		12,500
	(2)		
	Mascot, Ltd., Common and Preferred Shares		
Mar. 15	Purchased 600 units of common and preferred shares at $36 per unit. Each unit consists of one share of preferred and two shares of common stock	21,600	
Apr. 30	Sold 300 shares of common at $13 per share		3,900
June 28	Received 900 common stock rights. Each right entitles the holder to purchase one share of common for $12 (memorandum entry in general ledger).		
Sept. 30	Exercised 450 common stock rights to acquire 450 shares of common at $12 per share	5,400	
Sept. 30	Sold remaining 450 common stock rights at $4 per right		1,800
	(3)		
	Standard Service, Corp., Common Shares		
Mar. 15	Purchased 10,000 shares at $17 per share	170,000	
Oct. 31	Received dividend of 75¢ per share		7,500
	(4)		
	Kevin Instruments, Ltd., Common Shares		
Mar. 15	Purchased 4,000 shares at $28 per share	112,000	
Apr. 30	Purchased 2,000 shares at $30 per share	60,000	
June 28	Received dividend of 40¢ per share		2,400
	(5)		
	Other Investment		
Oct. 31	Reacquired 1,600 shares of its own (Craig) outstanding common shares at $14 per share with the Intention of retiring them	22,400	

Additional information follows:

(a) The fair market value for each security as of the 1981 date of each transaction follows:

Security	March 15	April 30	June 28	Sept. 30	Oct. 31
Ace Tool Company common	$25				$42
Bymore Sales Company common			$ 8	$14	
Mascot, Ltd., preferred stock	20				
Mascot, Ltd., common stock	10	$13	15*	16	
Mascot, Ltd., common stock rights			3	4	
Standard Service, Corp., common stock .	17				
Kevin Instruments, Ltd., common stock ..	28	30			
Craig Corporation common stock					14

*Ex-rights

(b) Standard Service, Corp., has only one class of shares authorized and there were 30,000 shares of its common stock outstanding throughout 1981. Craig's cost of its investment in Standard was not materially different from its equity in the recorded values of Standard's net assets; recorded values were not materially different from fair values (individually or collectively). Standard's net income from the date of acquisition of Craig's investment to December 31, 1981, was $336,000. There were no intercompany transactions requiring elimination.

(c) Kevin Instruments, Ltd., has only one class of shares authorized and there were 40,000 shares of its common outstanding throughout 1981. Craig's cost of its investment in Kevin was not materially different from its equity in the recorded values of Kevin's net assets; recorded values were not materially different from fair values (individually or collectively). Kevin's net income from the date of acquisition of Craig's investment to December 31, 1981, was $120,000. There were no intercompany transactions requiring elimination.

(d) All other investments of Craig are widely held, and Craig's percentage of ownership in each is nominal (5% or less.)

(e) At December 31, 1981, Craig Corporation had 98,400 shares of its $10 par value common shares outstanding. The balance in the premium on common shares account was $100,000.

Instructions:

Prepare necessary adjusting journal entries classified by each of the securities analysed in (a) through (e) to properly adjust the investment account. Identify each security by type (preferred, common, rights, etc.) as well as by company. Schedules supporting calculations should be in good form and either included as part of the journal entry explanation or properly cross-referenced to the appropriate journal entry. (Ignore brokers' fees, transfer and income taxes.)   (AICPA adapted)

10-14A. King Oil Company, to maintain closer ties with associated companies in the oil business, decided to purchase holdings of common shares in several companies. The following is a list of activities associated with these acquisitions during 1979.

Feb. 15, 1979 — Acquired 75,000 shares of Lub Oil Co. at $8 per share representing 70% of the outstanding shares. At date of acquisition the book value of Lub Oil Co.'s net assets was $800,000. Assets were considered to have fair values equal to recorded book values.

April 13, 1979 — Acquired 130,000 shares of Richman Refineries at $11 per share representing 65% of the outstanding shares. The purchase price corresponds to King's proportionate interest in underlying book values.

May 17, 1979 — Acquired 50,000 shares of Discovery Co. Ltd. at $6 per share, representing 2% of the outstanding shares.

June 30, 1979 — Lub Oil Co. announced a loss of $40,000 for the first six months of 1979.

June 30, 1979 — Richman Refineries announced earnings of $110,000 for the first six months of 1979 and declares a dividend of 15¢ per share.

August 15, 1979 — Dividend received from Richman Refineries.

Oct. 11, 1979 — Dividend of 5 cents per share received from Discovery Co. Ltd. with a Statement of Earnings for the six months ending September 30th indicating net earnings of $50,000.

Dec. 31, 1979 — Lub Oil Co. announced a loss for the year of $35,000.

- Richman Refineries announced earnings for the year of $190,000, including an extraordinary gain of $30,000.
- Discovery Co. Ltd. announced earnings for the nine months ending December 31 of $80,000.

Instructions:

(1) Investments in shares can be accounted for using either the equity method or the cost method. Distinguish between the two methods, indicating under what circumstances each method should be used.

(2) Prepare journal entries to record the above transactions in the accounts of King Oil Company assuming use of the equity method of accounting where appropriate.

(3) For external reporting purposes, how should King Oil Company account for its long-term investments? (SMA adapted)

10-15A. During your audit of the 1981 financial statements of Longwood, Corp., you find a new account titled Miscellaneous Assets. Your examination reveals that in 1981 Longwood, Corp., began investing cash in securities and the corporation's accountant entered all transactions believed related to investments in this account. Information summarized from the miscellaneous assets account appears below:

Longwood Corp.
Information Summarized from
the Miscellaneous Assets Account
For Year Ended December 31, 1981

Date		Folio	Debit	Credit
	Compudata Common Shares			
1981				
Mar. 31	Purchased 500 shares at 48	CD	$24,000	
July 31	Received cash dividend of $2 per share	CR		$ 1,000
July 31	Sold 100 shares at 60	CR		6,000
Nov. 15	Pledged 100 shares as security for $4,000 bank loan payable February 15, 1982	CR		4,000
Nov. 30	Received 150 shares by donation from shareholder whose cost in 1974 was $10 per share	JE	1,500	
	Standard Atomic Common Shares			
Mar. 31	Purchased 900 shares at 26	CD	23,400	
June 30	Received dividend (25¢ per share in cash and 1 share Standard Atomic preferred for each 5 shares common owned)	CR		225
	Standard Atomic Preferred Shares			
June 30	Received 180 shares as stock dividend on Standard Atomic common	MEMO		
July 31	Sold 80 shares at 17	CR		1,360
	Other			
Dec. 29	Paid 1982 rental charge on safe deposit box used for investments	CD	35	
	Total		$48,935	$12,585

All security purchases include brokers' fees, and sales are net of brokers' fees and transfer taxes when applicable. The fair market values (net of brokers' fees and transfer taxes) for each security as of the 1981 date of each transaction were:

Security	3/31	6/30	7/31	11/15	11/30
Compudata common	48		60	$61^1/_4$	62
Standard Atomic common	26	30			
Standard Atomic preferred		$16^2/_3$	17		

Instructions:

Prepare a work sheet to distribute or correct each of the transactions entered in the miscellaneous assets account. Ignore income tax in your solution. Formal adjusting entries are not required. Make separate entries for each transaction; do not combine adjustments. In addition to columns for entries in the miscellaneous assets account, the following column headings are recommended for your work sheet:

Adjustments to Distribute and Correct Items Entered
in the Miscellaneous Assets Account

Miscellaneous Assets Debit (Credit)	Investments Debit (Credit)	(Gain) Loss from Sale of Investments	(Revenue) from Dividends and Interest	Other Accounts Name of Account	Debit (Credit)

(AICPA adapted)

11 INTANGIBLE ASSETS

The term *intangible assets* is used in accounting to denote long-term property items not having physical characteristics. From a strictly legal point of view, such assets as shares, bonds, and claims against customers may be regarded as intangibles. In accounting, however, the term is generally restricted in use to include such items as patents, copyrights, trademarks, franchises, leaseholds,[1] and goodwill.

Intangible assets derive their values by affording special rights or advantages expected to contribute to the earnings of a business. Special rights contributing to earnings may be found, for example, in the ownership of patents; special advantages contributing to earnings may arise from the skill of employees, the ability of management, the desirable location of a business, and good customer relationships — all of which are elements of a company's goodwill.

The intangible assets designation is perhaps unfortunate since it has contributed to a general misunderstanding of the nature of these assets and of their accounting treatment. Mere physical existence does not affect an item's economic significance. A factory building about to be razed may be reported on the balance sheet at little or no value despite its massive physical dimensions. On the other hand, a patent without physical qualities could be the most valuable property item owned by a company. Intangible assets, no less than tangible properties, require a full accounting.

---

[1]The subject of leases, including leaseholds and leasehold improvements, is treated in Chapter 15.

VALUATION OF INTANGIBLE ASSETS AT TIME OF ACQUISITION

In general, valuation for intangible assets should follow the standards employed for tangible assets. Intangible assets should be recorded at cost. Cost should include all expenditures specifically related to the development or the purchase of the assets. When an intangible asset is acquired in exchange for an asset other than cash, the fair market value of the asset exchanged or that of the intangible asset, whichever is more clearly determinable, should be used to record the acquisition. When shares of stock or bonds are issued in exchange for an intangible asset, the fair market value of the securities issued or the intangible asset acquired should be used in recording the exchange. When several intangible assets or a combination of tangible and intangible assets are acquired for a lump sum, amounts must be allocated to the individual assets in some equitable manner, normally on the basis of the relative market values of the individual assets acquired.

Costs are reported for intangible assets only when expenditures can be specifically related to their acquisition. For example, no value should appear in the accounts for a franchise acquired without cost or for a company's goodwill developed internally over a period of years. But when an intangible asset without an accountable cost makes a significant contribution to the earnings of a business, reference on the balance sheet to this right or advantage by means of a note may be appropriate.

VALUATION OF INTANGIBLE ASSETS SUBSEQUENT TO THE TIME OF ACQUISITION

The subject of accounting for intangible assets subsequent to their acquisition has received wide attention. The costs of intangible assets have been charged off in many different ways. The process of assigning the costs of intangible assets to operations in a systematic manner is called *amortization*. Amortization is recorded by a debit to an expense account and a credit to the asset account or to an asset valuation account.

The terms of existence of certain intangible assets are limited by law, regulation, contract, or economic factors. The terms of existence of other intangible assets are not limited and the periods of their usefulness are indefinite or indeterminate. The cost of a limited-life intangible asset historically has been assigned to revenue according to an estimate of its useful economic life. The cost of an intangible asset having no limited term of existence and no indication of limited life at the time of acquisition has generally been carried forward until it appeared that any benefits would be of limited duration or that there was no longer any contribution to revenue. At that time, the cost of the asset was either assigned to revenue over the period of the remaining estimated life or written off, not uncommonly to retained earnings thus by-passing the income statement.

In 1973 the Accounting Research Committee issued Section 1580 of the *Accounting Recommendations* on business combinations, and made the following observation:

> In the opinion of the Committee, however, goodwill does not have a limitless life, and therefore, amortization of goodwill should have the same theoretical recognition as is presently afforded depreciation of tangible assets. Goodwill existing at the acquisition gradually disappears and may, or may not, be replaced by new goodwill. Furthermore, goodwill is a cost which is incurred in anticipation of future earnings, and should be amortized by systematic charges to income over the periods of those future earnings in order to produce a proper matching of costs against revenue. The straight-line method of amortization should be applied. An analysis of all pertinent factors should normally enable the company to assess a reasonable estimated life of such goodwill. However, the period of amortization should not exceed forty years.[2]

Thus, the Committee established a maximum amortization period for goodwill. Strictly speaking, Section 1580 of the *Accounting Recommendations*, as it relates to intangibles, only applies to goodwill. Factors to be considered in estimating the useful lives of intangible assets include:

a. Legal, regulatory, or contractual provisions may limit the maximum useful life.
b. Provisions for renewal or extension may alter a specified limit on useful life.
c. Effects of obsolescence, demand, competition, and other economic factors may reduce a useful life.
d. A useful life may parallel the service life expectancies of individuals or groups of employees.
e. Expected actions of competitors and others may restrict present competitive advantages.
f. An apparently unlimited useful life may in fact be indefinite and benefits cannot be reasonably projected.
g. An intangible asset may be a composite of many individual factors with varying effective lives.[3]

A company should evaluate periodically the estimated life selected for each intangible asset to determine whether current events or circumstances warrant a revision of the original estimated lives. When a change is indicated, the amortization plan may be modified as described earlier for tangible assets. Thus, a change in the period of usefulness of an intangible asset would be recognized by an increase or a decrease in the rate of amortization for the remainder of the asset life. When a revised life for an intangible asset is indicated, this should not exceed forty years from the original date of acquisition. Under some conditions, a significant reduction in the unamortized cost of an intangible asset may be warranted. If such reduction is material, it may be reported as a separate component of income from operations and

[2]*CICA Handbook: Accounting Recommendations*, Section 1580, "Business Combinations" (Toronto: Canadian Institute of Chartered Accountants, 1973), par. 57.
[3]*Opinions of the Accounting Principles Board, No. 17*, "Intangible Assets" (New York: American Institute of Certified Public Accountants, 1970), par. 27.

disclosure made of the effects of the transaction, or it may qualify as an extraordinary item. Moreover, if periodic reviews are made of the estimated future benefits of recorded intangible assets, the need for recognizing these unusual write-offs would be minimized.

Intangible assets subject to amortization are reported on the balance sheet at unamortized cost or at original cost less accumulated amortization. If an intangible asset is reported at a value other than cost, full information concerning the valuation should be provided. The periodic charge for amortization is reported as a manufacturing cost or as an operating expense depending upon the nature of the contribution made by the intangible asset.

Because of their relationship to certain intangible assets, research and development costs are discussed in the next section. Additional accounting problems related to specific intangibles are then discussed in the remaining sections of this chapter.

RESEARCH AND DEVELOPMENT COSTS

Enterprises often engage in research and development activities designed to discover new products or processes, or to improve existing ones. Historically, there has been considerable diversity in accounting for research and development (R & D) costs. Expenditures for general research have frequently been recorded as part of manufacturing overhead, more specifically as the cost of keeping abreast of current technological advances. On other occasions, especially when research was directed toward particular product improvements, research costs have been deferred and amortized.

A major factor in the decision to defer or expense R & D costs is the extent to which current research costs can be identified with specific future benefits. If a current research expenditure has a definite causal relationship with identifiable future benefits, accounting theory would suggest deferral. On the other hand, where no measurable cause and effect relationship can be determined, the current expensing of research costs is more appropriate.

In 1974, the Financial Accounting Standards Board issued Statement No. 2 dealing specifically with the accounting treatment for research and development costs. The FASB recognized the need for more uniform treatment of costs relating to research and development activities. It also recognized the uncertainty of future benefits of research costs and the difficulty in measuring the cause and effect relationships of such costs. As a result, the FASB concluded that all costs associated with research and development activities should be charged to expense when incurred.[4] Costs of R & D activities conducted under contractual arrangements are not covered by Statement No. 2. Nonetheless, the Statement has both standardized and simplified accounting practice in this area.

---

[4]*Statement of Financial Accounting Standards No. 2*, "Accounting for Research and Development Costs" (Stamford, Conn.: Financial Accounting Standards Board, 1974), par. 12.

The accounting treatment of R & D costs is also the subject of Section 3450 of the *Accounting Recommendations*, issued in 1978. In general, the Committee requires that research and development costs be charged as an expense of the period in which they are incurred. Development costs, however, may be deferred where the development relates to a product or process that is technically and commercially feasible with adequate resources being available for its completion. In circumstances that meet the criteria for deferment the Committee requires deferral of the development costs to the extent that recovery out of related future revenues is reasonably assured. The Committee acknowledges that it may be difficult to determine the appropriate period over which deferred development costs should be amortized. In the event uncertainties relating to technological and economic obsolescence may make it necessary to use an arbitrary amortization period, the Committee suggests a relatively short period. In most cases, however, the estimates of future sales or use that justified deferment should also permit determining a satisfactory amortization period.

To differentiate research costs from development costs, Section 3450 includes the definitions set forth below. In addition, the Section lists activities that typically would be (1) included in research, (2) included in development and (3) excluded from research and development. These lists should help to distinguish research costs and development costs, and to differentiate both from other similar costs.

> *Research* is planned investigation undertaken with the hope of gaining new scientific or technical knowledge and understanding. Such investigation may or may not be directed toward a specific practical aim or application.
>
> *Development* is the translation of research findings or other knowledge into a plan or design for new or substantially improved materials, devices, products, processes, systems or services prior to commencement of commercial production or use.[5]

In common with FASB Statement No. 2, Section 3450 does not apply to research and development activities conducted for others under contract or to activities that are unique to extractive industries. The recognition of all research and many development costs as current period expenses modifies the accounting treatment given certain intangibles, e.g., patents, as explained in later sections.

IDENTIFIABLE INTANGIBLE ASSETS

Intangible assets may be divided between those assets identified with a specific right or type of activity, and those assets not specifically identified but which are regarded as related to the enterprise as a whole. The latter

---

[5]*CICA Handbook: Accounting Recommendations*, Section 3450, "Research and Development Costs" (Toronto: Canadian Institute of Chartered Accountants, 1978), par. .02.

are generally lumped together and designated as *goodwill*. Managements involved in the purchase of a company carefully value all tangible assets as well as all identifiable intangible assets. An amount paid on the purchase of a company exceeding the sum of the fair values of net identifiable assets is normally recorded as goodwill.

Patents

A *patent* is an exclusive right granted by government to an inventor enabling the inventor to control the manufacture, sale, or other use of the invention for a specified period of time. The Federal Government, through the Department of Consumer and Corporate Affairs issues patents which are valid for seventeen years from the date of issuance. Patents are not renewable although effective control of an invention is frequently maintained beyond the expiration of the original patent through new patents covering improvements or changes. The owner of a patent may grant its use to others under royalty agreements or the patent may be sold.

The issuance of a patent does not necessarily indicate the existence of a valuable right. The value of a patent stems from whatever advantage it might afford its owner in excluding competitors from utilizing a process resulting in lower costs or superior products. Many patents cover inventions that cannot be exploited commercially and may actually be worthless.

Patents are recorded at their acquisition costs. When a patent is purchased, it is recorded at the new owner's purchase price. When a patent is developed through company-sponsored research, the accounting treatment falls under that which would apply to research and development costs. Only patent licensing and related legal fees are included as its costs. All related experimental and developmental expenditures, along with the cost of models and drawings not required by the patent application, are considered R & D costs and should be accounted for as such.

The validity of a patent may be challenged in the courts. The cost of successfully prosecuting or defending infringement suits is regarded as a cost of establishing the legal rights of the holder and may be added to the other costs of the patent. In the event of unsuccessful litigation, the litigation cost, as well as other patent costs, should be written off as a loss.

Patent costs should be amortized over the useful life of the patent. The legal life of a patent is used for amortization only when the patent is expected to provide benefits during its full legal life. The economic or useful life of a patent is usually much shorter than its legal life because of obsolescence. New and more efficient inventions or changes in demand for certain products may result in loss of patent value; processes developed by competitors sufficiently different to qualify as new inventions, yet so similar to a company's own process as to destroy the economic advantages enjoyed through patent protection, may also result in the loss of patent value. In some instances, the useful life of a patent is expressed in terms of productive output rather than in years, and cost is assigned to operations on the basis of units produced.

The classification of the charge for patent amortization depends upon the nature and the use of the patent. A charge for a patent used in the manufacturing process would be recognized as a manufacturing cost. A charge for a patent used in shipping department activities would be recognized as a selling expense.

Copyrights

Copyrights are exclusive rights granted by the Federal Government permitting an author or an artist to publish, sell, or otherwise control literary, musical, or artistic works. With certain exceptions, the right to exclusive control is issued for the lifetime of the author plus 50 years. Copyrights, like patents, may be licensed to others or sold.

The cost assigned to a copyright consists of those charges required to establish the right. When a copyright is purchased, the copyright is recorded at its purchase price.

The useful life of a copyright is generally considerably less than its legal life. The cost of a copyright may be amortized over the number of years in which sales or royalties can be expected, or cost may be assigned in terms of the estimated sales units relating to such rights. However, since the cost of obtaining a copyright is usually nominal it is often charged to expense when incurred. A copyright acquired by purchase should be recorded at cost which would then be subject to amortization.

Franchises

A *franchise* is a contract, giving exclusive rights to perform certain functions or to sell certain products or services. The rights may be granted for a specified number of years or in perpetuity; in certain instances, the rights may be revoked by the grantor.

The cost of a franchise includes any sum paid specifically for a franchise as well as legal fees and other costs incurred in obtaining it. Although the value of a franchise at the time of its acquisition may be substantially in excess of its cost, the amount recorded should be limited to actual outlays. When a franchise is purchased from another company, the amount paid is recorded as the franchise cost.

When a franchise has a limited life, its cost should be amortized over that limited life. When the life of a franchise can be terminated at the option of the granting authority, the cost is best amortized over a relatively short period. The cost of a perpetual franchise which appears to be of continuing economic value should probably be amortized over a maximum period of 40 years.

A franchise may require that periodic payments be made to the grantor. Payments may be fixed amounts or they may be variable amounts depending upon revenue, utilization, or other factors. These payments should be recognized as charges to periodic revenue. When certain property improvements are required under terms of the franchise, the cost of the improvements should be capitalized and charged to revenue over the life of the franchise.

Trademarks and Trade Names

Trademarks and *trade names*, together with distinctive symbols, labels, and designs, are important to all companies that depend upon a public demand for their products. It is by means of these distinctive markings that particular products are differentiated from competing brands. In building up the reputation of a product, relatively large costs may be involved. The Federal Government offers legal protection for trademarks through their registry with the Registrar of Trademarks in Ottawa. Prior and continuous use is the important factor in maintaining the registration of a particular trademark. The right to a trademark is retained as long as continuous use is made of it. Protection of trade names and brands that cannot be registered must be sought in the common law. Distinctive trademarks, trade names, and brands can be assigned or sold.

The cost assigned to a trademark consists of those expenditures required to establish it, including filing and registry fees, and expenditures for successful litigation of the trademark. When a trademark is purchased, it is recorded at its purchase price.

Even though the legal life of a trademark is not limited, the trademark cost is frequently amortized over a relatively short period on the theory that changes in consumer demand may limit its usefulness.

Organization Costs

In forming a corporation, certain expenditures are incurred including legal fees, promotional costs, share certificate costs, underwriting costs, and incorporation fees. The benefits to be derived from these expenditures normally extend beyond the first fiscal period. Further, the recognition of these expenditures as expenses at the time of organization would commit the corporation to a deficit before it actually begins operations. These factors support the practice of recognizing the initial costs of organization as an intangible asset.

Expenditures relating to organization may be considered to benefit the corporation during its entire life. Thus, when the life of a company is not limited, there is theoretical support for carrying organization costs as an intangible asset indefinitely or for amortization over a maximum period of forty years. On the other hand, it may be argued that the organizational and start-up costs of a business are of primary benefit during the first few years of operation. Beyond that point, these costs generally become insignificant in terms of impact on the success or failure of the enterprise. These reasons have led to the widespread practice of writing off organization costs within a relatively short period, generally five years, from the date of incorporation.

It is sometimes suggested that operating losses of the first few years should be capitalized as organization costs or as goodwill. It is argued that the losses cannot be avoided in the early years when the business is being developed, and hence it is reasonable that these losses should be absorbed in later years. Although losses may be inevitable, they do not generally carry any future service potential. To report these losses as intangible assets would result in the overstatement of assets and owners' equity. This practice cannot be condoned.

A related question deals with so-called developmental stage companies which are trying to establish a new business. In order to clarify the accounting and reporting practices for developmental stage enterprises, the FASB in the United States issued *Statement of Financial Accounting Standards No. 7*. The FASB concluded that the accounting practices and reporting standards for developmental stage companies should be no different than for other companies. The same set of generally accepted accounting principles should govern the recognition of revenues and the determination of costs as expenses or assets for both developmental stage enterprises and established operating enterprises.[6]

GOODWILL

Goodwill is the most intangible of intangible assets. It is generally regarded as the summation of all the special advantages, not otherwise identifiable, related to a going concern. It encompasses such items as a good name, capable staff and personnel, high credit standing, reputation for superior products and services, and favorable location.

On the one hand, goodwill is a familiar concept; at the same time, it has not yet been precisely defined. There is, however, general agreement about certain characteristics of goodwill:[7]

1. Goodwill relates to a business as a whole and, accordingly, is incapable of separate existence and of being sold apart from the identifiable assets of the business.
2. Individual factors that may contribute to goodwill are not susceptible to

---

[6]*Statement of Financial Accounting Standards No. 7*, "Accounting and Reporting by Development Stage Enterprises" (Stamford, Conn.: Financial Accounting Standards Board, 1975), par. 10.

[7]FASB Discussion Memorandum, "An Analysis of Issues Related to Accounting for Business Combinations and Purchased Intangibles" (Stamford, Conn.: Financial Accounting Standards Board, 1976), par. 148.

independent valuation by any method or formula. Their values can be determined only as aggregate in relation to a business as a whole.
3. The future benefits of goodwill recognized in a business combination may have no relationship to the costs incurred in the development of that goodwill. Goodwill may exist in the absence of specific costs to develop it.

Another matter on which there is general agreement is the rule that internally generated goodwill should not receive accounting recognition. Thus, goodwill in accounting is purchased goodwill. It is the excess of purchase cost over the fair value of identifiable assets acquired, net of any liabilities assumed. It is recognized directly in a purchase of assets business combination, but only indirectly in a purchase of shares combination as part of the process of preparing consolidated financial statements.

It should also be noted that in accounting goodwill is often related to the ability of a business to earn above-normal earnings on identifiable assets employed. Above-normal earnings means a rate of return greater than that normally required to attract investors into a particular type of business.

Valuation of Goodwill

Goodwill is recorded in the accounts only when it is acquired by purchase, usually in a business combination, or otherwise established through a business transaction. The latter condition includes recognition in connection with the reorganization of a corporation, a partial purchase of a business, or a change of partners in a partnership. Recognition under these restricted circumstances assures an objective approach to the valuation of goodwill. To permit the recognition of goodwill on the basis of judgment and estimates by owners and other interested parties would encourage potential abuse and misrepresentation. Goodwill reported on the balance sheet arises from a purchase or a contractual arrangement calling for its recognition.

In the purchase of a going business, the actual price to be paid for goodwill usually results from bargaining and compromises between the parties concerned. A basis for negotiation in arriving at a price for goodwill normally involves the following steps:

1. Projection of the level of future earnings.
2. Determination of an appropriate rate of return.
3. Current valuation of the net business assets other than goodwill.
4. Use of projected future earnings and rate of return in developing a value for goodwill.

Projection of the Level of Future Earnings. Past earnings ordinarily offer the best basis upon which to develop a specific value for goodwill. However, it is not these past earnings but projected future earnings that are being purchased. In considering past earnings as a basis for projection into the future, reference should be made to earnings most recently experienced. A sufficient number of periods should be included in the analysis so a representative measurement of business performance is provided.

In certain instances, it may be considered necessary to restate revenue and expense balances to give effect to alternative depreciation or amortization methods, inventory methods, or other measurement processes considered desirable in summarizing past operations. Unusual or infrequently occurring and extraordinary gains and losses which cannot be considered a part of normal activities should be excluded from past operating results. Depending on the circumstances, these items may include gains and losses from the sale of investments and land, buildings, and equipment; gains and losses from the retirement of debt; and losses from casualties.

The normal earnings from operations should be analysed to determine their trend and stability. If earnings over a period of years show a tendency to decline, careful analysis is necessary to determine whether this decline may be expected to continue. There may be greater confidence in possible future earnings when past earnings have been relatively stable rather than when widely fluctuating.

Any changes in the operations of the business which may be anticipated after the transfer of ownership should also be considered. The elimination of a division, the disposal of substantial property items, or the retirement of long-term debt, for example, could materially affect future earnings.

The normal earnings of the past are used as a basis for estimating earnings of the future. Business conditions, the business cycle, sources of supply, demand for the company's products or services, price structure, competition, and other significant factors including inflation, must be studied in developing data making it possible to convert past earnings into estimated future earnings.

Determination of an Appropriate Rate of Return. The existence of above-normal earnings, if any, can be determined only by reference to a normal rate of return. The *normal earnings rate* is that which would ordinarily be required to attract investors in the particular type of business being acquired. In judging this rate, consideration must be given to such factors as money rates, business conditions at the time of the purchase, competitive factors, risks involved, enterpreneurial abilities required, and alternative investment opportunities.

In general, the greater the risk entailed in an investment, the higher the rate of return required. Because most business enterprises are subject to a considerable amount of risk, investors generally expect a relatively high rate of return to justify investment. A long history of stable earnings or the existence of certain tangible assets that can be easily sold reduce the degree of risk in acquiring a business and thus reduce the rate of return required by a potential investor.

If goodwill is to be purchased, it should be looked upon as an investment and must offer the prospect of sufficient return to justify the commitment. Special risks are associated with goodwill. The value of goodwill is uncertain and fluctuating. It cannot be separated from the business as a whole and sold, as can most other business properties. Furthermore, it is subject to rapid deterioration and may be totally lost in the event of business sale or liquidation. As a result, a higher rate of return would normally be required on the purchase of goodwill than on the purchase of other business properties.

Current Valuation of Net Business Assets Other than Goodwill. Because goodwill is associated with the earnings that cannot be attributed to a normal return on identifiable assets, the ultimate valuation of goodwill depends upon the valuation of business properties. In appraising properties for this purpose, current market values should be sought rather than the values reported in the accounts. Receivables should be stated at amounts estimated to be realized. Inventories and securities should be restated in terms of current market values. Land, buildings, and equipment items may require special appraisals in arriving at their present replacement or reproduction values. Intangible assets, such as patents and franchises, should be included at their current values even though, originally, expenditures were reported as expenses or were reported as assets and amortized against revenue. Care should be taken to determine that liabilities are fully recognized. Assets at their current fair market value less the liabilites to be assumed provide the net assets total that, together with estimated future earnings, is used in arriving at a purchase price.

Use of Projected Future Earnings and Rate of Return in Developing a Value for Goodwill. A number of methods may be employed in arriving at a goodwill figure. Several of these will be described. Assume the following information for Company A:

Net earnings after adjustment and elimination of unusual and extraordinary items:

1977	$140,000
1978	90,000
1979	110,000
1980	85,000
1981	115,000
Total	$540,000

Average net earnings 1977-1981: $540,000 ÷ 5 = $108,000.
Estimated future net earnings, $100,000.
Net assets as appraised on January 2, 1982, before recognizing goodwill, $1,000,000. (Land, buildings, equipment, inventories, and receivables, $1,200,000; liabilities to be assumed by purchaser, $200,000.)

The average net earnings figure of $108,000 for the five-year period 1977-1981 was used in arriving at an estimate of the probable future net earnings. It is assumed the prospective buyer after analysing the assembled data concludes future earnings may reasonably be estimated at $100,000 a year.

Capitalization of Average Net Earnings. The amount to be paid for business may be determined by capitalizing expected future earnings at a rate representing the required return on the investment. Capitalization of earnings, as used in this sense, means calculation of the principal value that will yield the stated earnings at the specified rate. This is accomplished by dividing the earnings by the specified rate.[8] The difference between the amount to be paid for the business as thus obtained and the appraised values of the individual property items may be considered the price paid for goodwill.

If, in the example, a return of 8% were required on the investment and earnings were estimated at $100,000 per year, the business would be valued at $1,250,000 ($100,000 ÷ .08). Since net assets, with the exception of goodwill, were appraised at $1,000,000, goodwill would be valued at $250,000. If a 10% return were required on the investment, the business would be worth only $1,000,000. In acquiring the business for $1,000,000, there would be no payments for goodwill.

Capitalization of Average Excess Net Earnings. In the above method, a single rate of return was applied to the earnings in arriving at the value of the business. No consideration was given to the extent the earnings were attributable to net identifiable assets and the extent the earnings were attributable to goodwill. It would seem reasonable, however, to expect a higher return on an investment in goodwill than on the other assets acquired. To illustrate, assume the following facts:

	Company A	Company B
Net assets as appraised	$1,000,000	$500,000
Estimated future net earnings	100,000	100,000

If the estimated earnings are capitalized at a uniform rate of 8%, the value of each company is found to be $1,250,000. The goodwill for Company A is then $250,000, and for Company B, $750,000 as shown:

	Company A	Company B
Total net asset valuation (earnings capitalized at 8%)	$1,250,000	$1,250,000
Deduct net assets as appraised	1,000,000	500,000
Goodwill	$ 250,000	$ 750,000

These calculations ignore the fact that the appraised value of the net assets identified with Company A exceed those of Company B. Company A, whose earnings of $100,000 are accompanied by net assets valued at $1,000,000,

---

[8] This may be shown as follows: P = principal amount or the capitalized earnings to be computed; r = the specified rate of return; E = expected annual earnings. Then, $E = P \times r$, and $P = E \div r$.

would certainly command a higher price than Company B, whose earnings of $100,000 are accompanied by net assets valued at only $500,000.

Satisfactory recognition of both earnings and asset contributions is generally effected by (1) requiring a fair return on identifiable net assets, and (2) viewing any excess earnings as attributable to goodwill and capitalizing the excess at a higher rate in recognition of the degree of risk that characterizes goodwill. To illustrate, assume in the previous cases that 8% is considered a normal return on identifiable net assets and that excess earnings are capitalized at 20% in determining the amount to be paid for goodwill. Amounts to be paid for Companies A and B would be calculated as shown here.

	Company A	Company B
Estimated net earnings	$ 100,000	$ 100,000
Normal return on net assets:		
Company A — 8% of $1,000,000	80,000	
Company B — 8% of $ 500,000		40,000
Excess net earnings	$ 20,000	$ 60,000
Excess net earnings capitalized at 20%	÷ .20	÷ .20
Value of goodwill	$ 100,000	$ 300,000

	Company A	Company B
Value of net assets offering normal return of 8% . . .	$1,000,000	$ 500,000
Value of goodwill, excess net earnings capitalized at 20%	100,000	300,000
Total net asset valuation	$1,100,000	$ 800,000

Number of Years' Purchase. Behind each of the capitalization methods just described, there is an implicit assumption that the superior earning power attributed to the existence of goodwill will continue indefinitely. The very nature of goodwill, however, makes it subject to rapid decline. A business with unusually high earnings may expect the competition from other companies to reduce earnings over a period of years. Furthermore, the high levels of earnings may frequently be maintained only by special efforts on the part of the new owners, and they cannot be expected to pay for something they themselves must achieve.

As the goodwill being purchased cannot be expected to last beyond a specific number of years, one frequently finds payment for excess earnings stated in terms of *years' purchase* rather than capitalization in perpetuity.[9] For example, if excess annual earnings of $20,000 are expected and payment is to be made for excess earnings for a five-year period, the purchase price for

---

[9]Calculation of goodwill in terms of number of years' purchase will yield results identical to the capitalization method when the number of years used is equal to the reciprocal of the capitalization rate. Payment for five years' earnings, for example, is equivalent to capitalization earnings at a 20% rate (1 ÷ .20 = 5). Payment of four years' earnings is equivalent to capitalization at a 25% rate (1 ÷ .25 = 4).

goodwill would be $100,000. If the excess annual earnings are expected to be $60,000 and the payment is to be made for four years' excess earnings, the price for goodwill would be $240,000.

The years' purchase method has the advantage of conceptual simplicity. It is related to the common business practice of evaluating investment opportunities in terms of their *payback period* — the number of years expected for recovery of the initial investment.

Present Value Method. The concept of number of years' purchase can be combined with the concept of a rate of return on investment. Excess earnings can be expected to continue for only a limited number of years, but an investment in these earnings should provide an adequate return, considering the risks involved. The amount to be paid for goodwill, then, is the discounted or present value of the excess earnings amounts expected to become available in future periods.

To illustrate the calculation of goodwill by the present value method, assume the earnings of Company A exceed a normal return on the net identifiable assets used in the business by $20,000 per year. These excess earnings are expected to continue for a period of five years, and a return of 8% is considered necessary to attract investors in this industry. The amount to be paid for goodwill, then, may be regarded as the discounted value at 8% of five instalments of $20,000 to be received at annual intervals. Present value tables may be used in determining the present value of the series of payments. The present value of 5 annual payments of $1 each, to provide a return of 8%, is found to be $3.9927.[10] The present value of five payments of $20,000 each would then be calculated as $20,000 × 3.9927 = $79,854.

It may be noted that the calculation of goodwill by the present value method, using a five-year period and an 8% return, produced approximately the same result as would have been obtained by purchasing four years' excess earnings, or by capitalizing these earnings at 25%. The principal advantage of the present value method is the explicit recognition of the anticipated duration of excess earnings together with the use of a realistic rate of return. Thus it focuses on the factors most relevant to the goodwill valuation.

Implied Goodwill

When a lump sum amount is paid for an established business and no explicit evaluation is made of goodwill as illustrated in the preceding section, goodwill may still be recognized. In this case the identifiable net assets require appraisal, and the difference between the full purchase price and the fair value of net identifiable assets can be attributed to the purchase of goodwill.

---

[10] See Table IV on the inside back cover.

Failure to recognize the payment for goodwill separately may result in attaching this cost to identifiable assets and thus result in their over-valuation. If this cost is attributed to depreciable assets, the periodic depreciation charges and net income, as well as financial position, may then be misstated.

When shares are issued in exchange for a business, the fair value of the shares determines the consideration paid for the assets. Care must be exercised so that what in effect represents a discount on the shares is not reported as goodwill. For example, assume a company exchanges 100,000 shares of common stock, par $10, selling on the market at $7^{1/2}$, for a business with assets appraised at $800,000 and liabilities of $200,000. The acquisition should be recorded as follows:

Assets	800,000	
Goodwill	150,000	
Discount on Common Shares	250,000	
Liabilities		200,000
Common Shares, $10 par		1,000,000

If the discount is not recognized and goodwill is established at $400,000, both assets and shareholders' equity will be misstated.

The entry given above recognizes the exchange as a *purchase*. Not all exchanges are recognized in this manner. As indicated in an earlier chapter, under certain conditions the issuance of shares in exchange for the owners' equity in the net assets of a company is recognized as a *pooling of interests*. In applying this concept, the company issuing the shares reports the net asset balances at the same amounts previously reported. No changes to reflect current market values for property items are made and no additional intangible assets are recognized. The increase in net assets is accompanied by an increase in the shareholders' equity, and in certain instances this increase is recorded in the invested capital and retained earnings accounts at the same amounts previously reported. The Accounting Research Committee has been concerned that the pooling of interests method might not be fair and realistic in its application to certain combinations, and in Section 1580 of the *Accounting Recommendations*, it severely restricts use of the pooling concept. The only criterion that permits the use of pooling is the rare inability to identify one of the combining companies as the acquirer.[11]

Adjustment of Goodwill after Acquisition

The amortization of goodwill is also governed by Section 1580 of the *Accounting Recommendations*. As indicated earlier in this chapter, Section 1580 requires straight-line amortization of goodwill over a maximum period

---

[11]*CICA Handbook: Accounting Recommendations*, Section 1580, "Business Combinations" (Toronto: Canadian Institute of Chartered Accountants, 1973), par. 21.

of forty years. In some cases goodwill may have a measurable life less than forty years and in such circumstances the amortization period selected should be based upon this shorter life.

Some accountants have suggested that goodwill should be written off immediately after acquisition. Justification for this treatment is presented below.

1. Goodwill is not a resource or property right that is consumed or utilized in the production of earnings. It is the result of expectations of future earnings by investors and thus is not subject to normal amortization procedures.
2. Goodwill is subject to sudden and wide fluctuations. That value has no reliable or continuing relation to costs incurred in its creation.
3. Under existing practices of accounting, neither the cost nor the value of non-purchased goodwill is reported in the balance sheet. Purchased goodwill has no continuing, separately measurable existence after the combination and is merged with the total goodwill value of the continuing business entity. As such, its write-off cannot be measured with any validity.
4. Goodwill as an asset account is not relevant to an investor. Most analysts ignore any reported goodwill when analysing a company's status and operations.[12]

This position has consistently been rejected by the committees of both the CICA and the AICPA. Thus, the lump-sum write-off of goodwill and other intangible assets is strongly discouraged. In opposing the arbitrary write-off of goodwill or any other intangible asset, it can be maintained that asset and owners' equity balances are misstated and the ratio of earnings to owners' equity is distorted. Earnings thus appear to be more favorable than is actually the case as a result of this conservative practice.

INTANGIBLE ASSETS ON THE BALANCE SHEET

When a single long-term asset classification is given on the balance sheet, tangible and intangible asset subheadings should be provided and summaries developed for each group. When separate classifications are given for tangible and intangible assets, the intangible asset classification usually follows the tangible asset classifications. Each intangible asset should be listed separately. If an intangible asset has been acquired for consideration other than cash, disclosure should be made of the properties or securities exchanged and the data used in arriving at the original cost assigned to the asset. Disclosure should also be made of the valuation procedures employed for intangible assets subsequent to their acquisition.

Intangible assets as they might appear on the balance sheet follow:

---

[12]George R. Catlett and Norman O. Olson, *Accounting for Goodwill*, Accounting Research Study No. 10 (New York: American Institute of Certified Public Accountants, 1968). The authors of this research study recommended the write-off of goodwill immediately upon acquisition.

Intangible assets:

Goodwill, at cost less amortization on 40-year basis ..	$220,000	
Licences, at costs less amortization based on estimated useful lives	18,000	
Patents, acquired through issue of 12,000 shares of common stock with a market value of $12.50 per share and reported at such value, less amortization based on an estimated useful life of 10 years	107,500	$345,500

1. What are the characteristics that distinguish intangible assets from tangible assets?

2. How would a trademark worth $5,000,000 be reported on the balance sheet if (a) the trademark were purchased for $5,000,000 or (b) the trademark gradually became identified over the years as a company symbol?

3. What factors should be considered in estimating the useful lives of intangible assets?

4. How are research costs and development costs defined?

5. How are identifiable intangible assets more similar to tangible assets than to the intangible asset, goodwill?

6. (a) What items enter into the cost of a patent developed by a business? (b) What factors should be considered in establishing a schedule for amortizaton of patent cost?

7. What costs are capitalized as (a) copyrights, (b) franchises, (c) trademarks?

8. How should the following assets be amortized: (a) copyrights; (b) franchises; (c) trademarks; (d) organization costs?

9. (a) What items are normally considered to compose the organization costs of a company? (b) Would you approve the inclusion of the following items: (1) common stock discount; (2) first-year advertising costs; (3) first-year loss from operations?

10. How should development stage enterprises report (a) their organization costs and (b) any operating losses?

11. (a) Under what conditions may goodwill be reported as an asset? (b) The Radcliff Company engages in a widespread advertising campaign on behalf of new products, charging above-normal expenditures to goodwill. Do you approve of this practice? Why or why not?

12. What factors should be considered in estimating the future earnings of a business in order to develop a fair valuation of goodwill?

13. Give four methods for arriving at a goodwill valuation, using estimated future earnings as a basis for these calculations. Which method do you think would give the most relevant valuation of goodwill?

14. The transactions that result in recording goodwill are primarily related to the acquisition and merger of companies. Describe an accounting method for recording such mergers that has eliminated the need for recognizing goodwill.

15. Wells, Inc., has valuable patent rights that are being amortized over their legal lives. The president of the company believes these patents are contributing substantially to company goodwill and recommends patent amortization be capitalized as company goodwill. What is your opinion of this proposal?

16. What are the major arguments for writing off goodwill immediately after acquisition? What effect would an immediate write-off of goodwill have on a company's ratio of earnings to owners' equity?

17. The Rory Corporation purchased the Stardust Club for $500,000 which included $100,000 for goodwill. Rory Corporation incurs large promotional and advertising expenses to maintain Stardust Club's popularity. The Rory Corporation controller feels that amortization of the purchased goodwill in the same periods that heavy expenses are incurred to maintain the goodwill in effect creates a double charge against income of the period. Do you agree?

EXERCISES

11-1. The Beacon Corporation purchased land, a building, and a franchise for the lump sum of $150,000. A real estate appraiser estimated the building to have a resale value of $90,000 (75% of the total worth of the land and building). The franchise had no established resale value.

The estimated useful life of the franchise on the acquisition date was 20 years. After 15 years, Beacon Corporation management decided that the franchise would be of economic value for an additional 30 years.

(a) Give the journal entry to record the acquisition of the assets.
(b) Give the journal entry to record the amortization of the franchise in the sixteenth year, assuming straight-line amortization.

11-2. The Qualis Co. applied for and received numerous patents at a total cost of $14,450 at the beginning of 1976. It is assumed the patents will be useful during their full legal life. At the beginning of 1978, the company paid $3,750 in successfully prosecuting an attempted infringement of these patent rights. At the beginning of 1981, $12,000 was paid to acquire patents that could make its own patents worthless: the patents acquired have a remaining life of 15 years but will not be used.

(a) Give the entries to record the expenditures relative to patents.
(b) Give the entries to record patent amortization for the years 1976, 1980, and 1981.

11-3. Flex Corporation acquired the following assets at the beginning of 1977. (1) Give the entries to record the acquisition of the assets. (2) Give the entries for the amortization for 1977, if any. (3) In each case justify the useful life estimated.

(a) Paperback copyright to a best-seller novel in exchange for 240 shares of Flex Corporation stock; $50 par, common stock selling for $224 per share.

Paperback sales of the novel are estimated to be 500,000 copies in 1977, 300,000 in 1978, 100,000 in 1979, 20,000 in 1980, and no sales thereafter.
(b) A fast foods franchise in exchange for one acre of prime real estate. Franchises of this type are selling for $100,000 cash. The land was purchased 10 years ago for $5,000. The franchise has an unlimited life as long as Flex Corporation maintains the quality standards of the grantor, but its cost will be amortized over 40 years.
(c) Enoc Enterprises for $425,000 cash. Net identifiable assets of Enoc Enterprises are fairly valued at $375,000. The purchased goodwill is expected to grow every year as Flex Corporation plans to expend substantial resources for advertising and other promotional activities.

11-4. (1) Which of the following activities of the All-World Aerodynamics Corporation would be considered research and development activities?
(a) Testing of electronic instrument components during their production.
(b) Development of a new, more efficient wing design.
(c) Construction of a prototype for a new jet model.
(d) Start-up activities for the production of a newly developed jet.
(e) Study of the possible uses of a newly developed fuel.

(2) Which of the following costs are considered research and development costs of the **current period**?
(a) The portion of the president's salary allocable to research and development activities.
(b) The cost of a market research study.
(c) Costs of a pension plan for employees engaged in research and development activities.
(d) Current period depreciation taken on the company's laboratory research facilities.

11-5. The Bronco Mfg. Co. was incorporated on January 1, 1981. In reviewing the accounts in 1982, you find the organization costs account appears as follows:

ACCOUNT Organization Costs

ITEM	DEBIT	CREDIT	BALANCE DEBIT	BALANCE CREDIT
Discount on common shares issued .	62,400		62,400	
Incorporation fees	2,500		64,900	
Legal fees relative to organization ...	14,100		79,000	
Stock certificate cost	4,000		83,000	
Cost of rehabilitating building acquired at beginning of 1981 and estimated to have a remaining life of 10 years	48,000		131,000	
Advertising expenditures to promote company products	12,000		143,000	
Amortization of organization costs for 1981, 20% of balance of organization cost (per board of director's resolution)		28,600	114,400	
Loss for 1982	36,000		150,400	

Give the entry or entries required to correct the account.

11-6. In analysing the accounts of Oliver's, Ltd., in an attempt to measure goodwill, you find pretax earnings of $200,000 for 1981 after debits and credits for the items listed below. Land, buildings, and equipment are appraised at 50% above cost for purposes of the sale.

Depreciation of land, buildings, and equipment (at cost)	$30,000
Special year-end bonus, to president of company	10,000
Gain on sale of securities	18,000
Gain on revaluation of securities	6,000
Write-off of goodwill	60,000
Amortization of patents and leaseholds	25,000
Income tax refund for 1979	8,000

What is the normal pretax earnings balance for purposes of your calculations?

11-7. The appraised value of net assets of the Cassidy Co. on December 31, 1981, was $100,000. Average net earnings for the past 5 years after elimination of unusual or extraordinary gains and losses were $16,500. Calculate the amount to be paid for goodwill under each assumption given below:

(a) Earnings are capitalized at 15% in arriving at the business worth.
(b) A return of 9% is considered normal on net assets at their appraised value; excess earnings are to be capitalized at 15% in arriving at the value of goodwill.
(c) A return of 12% is considered normal on net assets at their appraised value; goodwill is to be valued at 5 years' excess earnings.
(d) A return of 10% is considered normal on net identifiable assets at their appraised value. Excess earnings are expected to continue for 6 years. Goodwill is to be valued by the present value method using a rate of 12%. (The present value of 6 annual payments of $1 providing a return of 12% is $4.1114. See Table IV.)

11-8. Because of superior earning power, Hanks & Co. is considering paying $301,915 for the Sage Proprietorship with the following assets and liabilities:

	Cost	Fair Market Value
Accounts receivable	$120,000	$110,000
Inventory	70,000	75,000
Prepaid insurance	5,000	5,000
Buildings & equipment (net)	85,000	150,000
Accounts payable	(80,000)	(80,000)
Net assets	$200,000	$260,000

Estimated future earnings are expected to exceed normal earnings by $13,800 for four years. Hanks & Co. uses the present value method of valuing goodwill. Hanks is willing to purchase Sage if the normal rate of return for Sage exceeds 10%. Should Hanks & Co. purchase Sage Proprietorship? (Use present value table.)

11-1A. On January 10, 1973, the Banks Company spent $12,000 to apply for and obtain a patent on a newly developed product. The patent had an estimated useful life of 10 years. At the beginning of 1977, the company spent $9,000 in successfully prosecuting an attempted infringement of the patent. At the beginning of 1978, the company purchased for $25,000 a patent that was expected to prolong the life of its original patent by 5 years. On July 1, 1981, a competitor obtained rights to a patent which made the company's patent obsolete.

Instructions:
Give all of the entries that would be made relative to the patent for the period 1973-1981, including entries to record the purchase of the patent, annual patent amortization, and ultimate patent obsolescence. (Assume the company's accounting period is the calendar year.)

11-2A. In your audit of the accounts of Flagg Corporation for the year ending September 30, 1981, you found the following items in connection with the company's patents account:

(a) The company had spent $102,000 during the fiscal year ended September 30, 1980, for research and development costs and debited this amount to its patents account. Your review of the company's cost records indicated the company had spent a total of $123,500 for the research and development of its patents, of which only $21,500 spent in its fiscal year ended September 30, 1979, had been debited to Research and Development Expense.

(b) The patents were issued on April 1, 1980. Legal expenses in connection with the issuance of the patents of $14,280 were debited to Legal and Professional Fees.

(c) The company paid a retainer of $7,500 on October 5, 1980, for legal services in connection with an infringement suit brought against it. This amount was debited to Deferred Costs.

(d) A letter dated October 15, 1981, from the company's lawyers in reply to your inquiry as to liabilities of the company existing at September 30, 1981, indicated that a settlement of the infringement suit had been arranged. The other party had agreed to drop the suit and to release the company from all future liabilities for $16,000. Additional fees due to the lawyers amounted to $590.

(e) The balance of the patents account on September 30, 1981, was $96,000. No amortization had been recognized on the patents for the fiscal year ended September 30, 1981.

Instructions:
(1) From the information given, prepare correcting journal entries as of September 30, 1981. (Assume an estimated life for the patents of 17 years from date of issuance.)
(2) Give the entry to record amortization on patents for the year ended September 30, 1981.

11-3A. Transactions during 1981 of the newly organized Brook Corporation included the following:

Jan. 2 Paid legal fees of $5,000 and share certificates costs of $1,600 to complete organization of the corporation. Organization costs will be amortized over 40 years.

15 Hired a clown to stand in front of the corporate office for two weeks and hand out pamphlets and candy to create goodwill for the new enterprise. Clown cost $800; candy and pamphlets, $500.

Apr. 1 Patented a newly developed process with the following costs:

Legal fees to obtain patent	$11,200
Patent application and licensing fees	400
Total ⁚..	$11,600

It is estimated that in five years other companies will have developed improved processes making the Brook Corporation process obsolete.

May 1 Acquired both a licence to use a special type of container and a distinctive trademark to be printed on the container in exchange for 600 shares of Brook Corporation common stock selling for $80 per share. The licence is worth twice as much as the trademark, both of which may be used for 6 years.

July 1 Constructed a shed for $50,000 to house prototypes of experimental models to be developed in future research projects. The shed has a 10-year life and will be depreciated on a straight-line basis.

Dec. 31 Salaries for an engineer and a chemist involved in product development totalled $75,000 in 1981.

31 Amortized all intangible assets. Brook Corporation takes a full year's amortization in the year of acquisition of intangible assets.

Instructions:

(1) Give journal entries to record the foregoing transactions. (Give explanations in support of your entries.)

(2) Present in good form the "Intangible assets" section of the Brook Corporation balance sheet at December 31, 1981.

11-4A. The Aurora Corp. in considering acquisition of the Cherryhill Company assembles the following information relative to the company.

Cherryhill Company
Balance Sheet
December 31, 1981

Assets	Per Company's Accounts	As Adjusted by Appraisal and Audit
Current assets	$120,000	$115,000
Investments	40,000	35,000
Land, buildings, and equipment (net)	349,000	325,000
Goodwill	80,000	80,000
	$589,000	$555,000
Liabilities and Shareholders' Equity		
Current liabilities	$ 18,750	$ 18,750
Long-term liabilities	200,000	200,000
Capital stock	200,000	200,000
Retained earnings	170,250	136,250
	$589,000	$555,000

An analysis of retained earnings discloses the following information:

	Per Company's Accounts	As Adjusted by Appraisal and Audit
Retained earnings, January 1, 1979	$144,450	$118,250
Add net income, 1979-1981*	61,800	54,000
Deduct dividends, 1979-1981	(36,000)	(36,000)
Retained earnings, December 31, 1981	$170,250	$136,250
*After loss on sale of assets in 1981	$ 61,200	$ 66,000

Instructions:
(1) Calculate the amount to be paid for goodwill, assuming that earnings of the future are expected to be the same as average normal earnings of the past 3 years, 8% is accepted as a reasonable return on net assets other than goodwill as of December 31, 1981, and average earnings in excess of 8% are capitalized at 15% in determining goodwill.
(2) Give the entries in the accounts of the Aurora Corp., assuming purchase of the assets of the Cherryhill Company and responsibility for its liabilities on the basis indicated in (1). Cash is paid for net assets acquired.

11-5A. East Coast Industries, Inc., assembles the following data relative to the Atlantic Corp. in determining the amount to be paid for the net assets and goodwill of the latter company:

Assets at appraised values (before goodwill)	$850,000
Liabilities	320,000
Shareholders' equity	$530,000

Net earnings (after elimination of extraordinary items):

1977	$ 90,000
1978	72,000
1979	97,000
1980	95,000
1981	101,000

Instructions:
Calculate the amount to be paid for goodwill under each of the following assumptions:
(1) Average earnings are capitalized at 16% in arriving at the business worth.
(2) A return of 12% is considered normal on net assets at appraised values; goodwill is valued at 5 years' excess earnings.
(3) A return of 14% is considered normal on net assets at appraised values; excess earnings are to be capitalized at 20%.
(4) Goodwill is valued at the sum of the earnings of the last 3 years in excess of a 10% annual yield on net assets at appraised values. (Assume that net assets are the same for the 3-year period.)
(5) A return of 10% is considered normal on net identifiable assets at their appraised values. Excess earnings are expected to continue for 10 years. Goodwill is to be valued by the present value method using a 20% rate. (Use present value table.)

11-6A. The Rocca Company is considering the acquisition of the assets and business of the Holiday Corporation as of June 30, 1981. The Rocca Company is willing to pay the appraised value of the net identifiable assets of Holiday plus a reasonable amount for goodwill. The net assets other than goodwill are appraised at $2,600,000 on June 30, 1981.

All-inclusive income statements prepared by the Holiday Corporation show the following pre-tax income for the four years preceding the proposed acquisition:

Year Ending June 30	Pretax Income
1978	$345,000
1979	382,000
1980	375,000
1981	385,000

Similar operating results are expected in the future except for the following items:

(a) A review of Holiday Corporation accounting records reveals that equipment acquired in July, 1976, at a cost of $300,000 has been depreciated on a straight-line basis with a 20-year useful life and no estimated salvage value. This equipment was included in the appraisal of net tangible assets at a current value of $452,000. Company engineers estimate that the equipment will probably be retired with an estimated salvage value of $40,000 in approximately 16 years.

(b) Holiday had been paying $15,000 per year in interest charges on bonds that were redeemed at a gain of $16,000 on June 30, 1981. Funds for bond retirement were provided by sale in June, 1981, of the company's Consumer Products division for $500,000. This division had constant losses of approximately $30,000 annually.

(c) Normal maintenance on the equipment of Holiday Corporation has been inadequate by approximately $19,000 annually.

Both parties agree that a return of 14% before tax is normal on assets employed in the type of business engaged in by Holiday Corporation. Earnings in excess of this amount are expected to continue for another 5 years but since there is less certainty about excess earnings, a return of 20% is considered reasonable for an investment in above-normal pretax earnings.

Instructions:
Prepare a summary showing how the amount to be paid for goodwill of the Holiday Corporation is determined using the present value method of calculating goodwill. (Use Appendix A present value table.)

11-7A. Sorenson Manufacturing Corporation was incorporated on January 3, 1976. The corporation's financial statements for its first year's operations were not examined by a CA. You have been engaged to examine the financial statements for the year ended December 31, 1981, and your examination is substantially completed. The trial balance at December 31, 1981, appears on the following page.

Sorenson Manufacturing Corporation
Trial Balance
December 31, 1981

Cash	37,000	
Accounts Receivable	42,500	
Allowance for Doubtful Accounts		500
Inventories	38,500	
Machinery	75,000	
Equipment	29,000	
Accumulated Depreciation		10,000
Patents	85,000	
Prepaid Expenses	10,500	
Organization Costs	29,000	
Goodwill	24,000	
Licensing Agreement No. 1	50,000	
Licensing Agreement No. 2	49,000	
Accounts Payable		147,500
Deferred Credits		12,500
Capital Stock		300,000
Retained Earnings, January 1, 1981	27,000	
Sales		668,500
Cost of Goods Sold	454,000	
Selling and General Expenses	173,000	
Interest Expense	3,500	
Extraordinary Losses	12,000	
	1,139,000	1,139,000

The following information relates to accounts that may yet require adjustment:

(a) Patents for Sorenson's manufacturing process were purchased January 3, 1981, at a cost of $68,000. An additional $17,000 was spent in December, 1981, to improve machinery covered by the patents and debited to the patents account. Depreciation on fixed assets has been properly recorded for 1981 in accordance with Sorenson's practice which provides a full year's depreciation for property on hand June 30 and no depreciation otherwise. Sorenson uses the straight-line method for all depreciation and amortization.

(b) On January 3, 1980, Sorenson purchased two licensing agreements that were then believed to have unlimited useful lives. The balance in the licensing agreement No. 1 account includes its purchase price of $48,000 and expenses of $2,000 related to the acquisition. The balance in the licensing agreement No. 2 account includes its $48,000 purchase price and $2,000 in acquisition expenses, but it has been reduced by a credit of $1,000 for the advance collection of 1982 revenue from the agreement. In December, 1980, an explosion caused a permanent 60% reduction in the expected revenue-producing value of licensing agreement No. 1 and in January, 1982, a flood caused additional damage that rendered the agreement worthless.

A study of licensing agreement No. 2 made by Sorenson in January, 1981, revealed that its estimated remaining life expectancy was only 10 years as of January 1, 1981.

(c) The balance in the goodwill account includes (1) legal expenses of $16,000 incurred for Sorenson's incorporation on January 3, 1980, and (2) $8,000 paid January 15, 1981, for an advertising program that is expected to increase Sorenson's sales over a period of 3 to 5 years following the disbursement.

(d) The balance in the organization costs account properly includes costs incurred during the organizational period. The corporation has exercised its option to amortize organization costs over a 60-month period beginning January, 1980, for income tax purposes and wishes to amortize these costs for accounting purposes in the same manner. No amortization has yet been taken.

Instructions:

Prepare the journal entries in 1981 required by the information given. (Note: Licensing Agreement No. 1 is amortized after explosion damage loss is determined.)   (AICPA adapted)

11-8A. Your new client, Nu-Mode Company, is being audited for the first time. In the course of your examination, you encounter in the ledger an account titled "Intangibles," which is essentially as below:

Intangibles

July 2, 1980 Goodwill	10,000	Dec. 31, 1981 Amortization	500
Jan. 2, 1981 Patent	8,500	Dec. 31, 1982 Amortization	4,000
May 1, 1982 R and D	19,200		
June 30, 1982 Bond discount	6,000		

By tracing entries to the journal and other supporting documents, you ascertain the following facts:

(a) The July 2, 1980 entry was to recognize Nu-Mode's superior earning power. While other companies were earning a 12% return on assets, Nu-Mode earned 15% on assets in each of the last three years. The entry was:

Intangibles — goodwill 10,000
    Retained earnings   10,000

(b) The Jan. 2, 1981 entry was to recognize the purchase of a recently developed patent which is being amortized over its legal life. The economic life is expected to be the same.

(c) The Dec. 31, 1981 Amortization was debited to Amortization expense and credited to Intangibles-patent.

(d) The R and D was made up of two items, $15,000 paid to Market Research Inc., for market studies conducted for Nu-Mode and $4,200 was spent on an advertising campaign as a result of the market research report. Sales since the beginning of the campaign rose sharply and were continuing strong at year-end.

(e) The company issued $100,000 par value 10-year, 8%, bonds at 94; the bond discount was entered in the Intangibles account. The December 30 entry for payment of the semi-annual interest was a debit to Interest expense and a credit to Cash for $4,000.

(f) Amortization on Dec. 31, 1982 was as follows:

R and D amortized over 4 years......................	$3,200
Patent (see (b) above)	500
Bond discount amortized over 10 years	300
	$4,000

Amortization expense was debited for the $4,000.

Instructions:

Make necessary correcting entries for Nu-Mode's accounts as at December 31,

1982, assuming that the accounts have been adjusted but not closed for the year.

(CGA adapted)

11-9A. A friend of yours is negotiating for the purchase of the Manufacturing Company Limited, a private company. As a consultant to your friend, you have examined the accounting records and have compiled the following pertinent data:

Manufacturing Company Limited
Assets and Liabilities
at date of acquisition

	Book Value	Estimated Fair Market Value
Cash and Receivables	$100,000	$ 90,000
Inventories (LIFO)	70,000	110,000
Plant and Equipment (Net)	520,000	700,000
Research and Development	——	60,000
	$690,000	$960,000
Current Liabilities	$100,000	$100,000
Long-Term Debt	200,000	200,000
	$300,000	$300,000

Manufacturing Company Limited
Revenues and Expenses

Revenues

Total revenues reported during last five years	$3,520,000
Budgeted revenues for the next year	740,000

Expenses

Total operating expenses, excluding depreciation and income taxes, during the last five years	1,710,000
Budgeted operating expenses for the next year (excluding depreciation & taxes)	360,000
Estimated portion of the current value of inventories not reflected in the LIFO valuation over the last five years	35,000

Depreciation has averaged $70,000 per year during the last five years; it is budgeted at $75,000 for the next year, computed on the original cost of the assets. The estimated annual increase in depreciation on the basis of the current fair value of depreciable assets should amount to $25,000.

The estimated current value of research and development is based on a study of the costs incurred on developing a new product. These costs were incurred and charged to expense during the last two years. The new product was introduced at the end of the current year and the development cost might properly be amortized over a period of ten years.

The buyer, your friend, has studied the above data and believes they provide a sound basis for arriving at a fair offering price for the shares. He has agreed that the company's average experience over the last five years and the budget for the next year provide the basis for a reasonable estimate of average annual earnings for the next five years. Income taxes may be estimated at 50% of average estimated net income. The buyer states that he considers an after-tax return of 12% on net assets a normal return for a company in this industry.

Instructions:

(1) Make an estimate of the Manufacturing Company Limited unrecorded goodwill on the basis of each of the following approaches:

   (a) The sum of estimated superior earnings for the next five years,

   (b) Superior earnings capitalized at 12%,

   (c) The present value of average superior earnings expected over the next five years at 12%,

   (d) Capitalization of the first $10,000 of expected average superior earnings at 25%.

(2) Assuming that there are 20,000 common shares of Manufacturing Company Limited outstanding, recommend to the buyer a range of price per share that he might reasonably be willing to pay for the shares. Explain the reasoning used to arrive at your recommendation. (SMA adapted)

11-10A. The major shareholder of Kanam Corporation is about to retire and wishes to sell a substantial portion of his stock in the company. In order to establish a fair offering price for the shares, you have made a systematic estimate of the current fair value of the stock. Kanam Corporation is a private company; common shares are closely held and have not been offered on the market.

The following data summarizes the company's operating history for the past five years:

Year	Profit Before Income Taxes
1976	$169,700
1977	149,500
1978	137,700
1979	184,700
1980	146,400
	$788,000

The company has 50,000 shares of common stock outstanding. At the end of 1980, a review of the records indicates that a building is undervalued by $120,000 and items of machinery and equipment are undervalued by $42,000. In both cases, the undervaluation is due to excessive amounts of depreciation charged to expense in 1980 and prior years on a straight-line basis. The building was purchased near the end of 1960 with an estimated life of 25 years. The items of machinery and equipment were purchased early in 1977 with an estimated life of 8 years.

Included in operating income for 1979 is an amount of $45,000 collected as damage for infringement of a patent owned by the company. Legal expenses of 1979 included an amount of $5,000 which represented legal fees incurred in connection with the infringement of the company's patent.

It is agreed that a rate of return of 12% on average shareholders' equity is considered to be a normal rate of return in this business and that average superior earnings should be capitalized at 20%.

The earnings performance of the company during the last five years is considered a fair indication of future earnings of the company. Income taxes which have averaged 50% of reported net profit during the past five years, are not expected to change in the future.

Instructions:

(1) Compute an adjusted average earnings figure for the five-year period ending in 1980.

(2) Compute an estimate of the current fair value of the Kanam Corporation common shares at the end of 1980. Assume that the average adjusted shareholders' equity was $500,000 and that the adjusted shareholders' equity at December 31, 1980 amounts to $632,900.

(SMA adapted)

12 CONSOLIDATION AND EQUITY ACCOUNTING

According to law, control of a corporation is determined by ownership of a majority (more than 50 per cent) of its issued and outstanding voting shares. In such circumstances, assuming an intercorporate investment, the investee corporation becomes a subsidiary of the investor or parent corporation. As separate legal entities, both corporations prepare their own financial statements; however, for external reporting purposes the parent would most likely present consolidated financials. This is because external financial reporting is based on "a presumption that consolidated statements are more meaningful than separate statements and that they are usually necessary for a fair presentation when one of the companies in a group directly or indirectly has a controlling financial interest in the other companies.[1] In rare circumstances, one or more subsidiaries may be excluded from the consolidation and be accounted for as unconsolidated subsidiaries under either the cost or the equity method, as applicable.

Consolidated financial statements present the financial position, results of operations and changes in financial position for a parent company and its one or more subsidiaires as if the group were a single entity. The parent and subsidiary corporations, although separate legal entities, are considered to be components of one economic unit or entity for financial reporting purposes. Consolidated financial statements may be briefly described as

[1]*Accounting Research and Terminology Bulletins — Final Edition*, "No. 51, Consolidated Financial Statements" (New York: American Institute of Certified Public Accountants, 1961) par. 1.

combined statements that have been modified by the elimination of reciprocal items; they are "produced by aggregating the financial statements of one or more subsidiary companies on a line-by-line basis (i.e., adding together corresponding items of assets, liabilities, revenues and expenses) with the financial statements of the parent company (related by common share ownership) eliminating intercompany balances and transactions, and providing for any minority interest in a subsidiary company."[2]

A large number of Canadian public or distributing corporations present consolidated financial statements in their annual reports. Of the 325 survey companies reviewed in the CICA publication, *Financial Reporting in Canada*, 299, or 92 per cent, indicated the existence of one or more subsidiaries in 1978 financials[3] The discussion that follows is intended to provide only a basic introduction to the preparation of consolidated financial statements. This topic is considered in greater depth in more advanced university courses and their equivalent offered by professional accounting associations.

BUSINESS COMBINATIONS AND INTERCORPORATE INVESTMENTS

The essential characteristic that identifies an intercorporate investment is the presence of two separate legal entities: (1) an investor corporation, and (2) an investee corporation. Intercorporate investments only give rise to business combinations when the investor and investee corporations come under common ownership and control in a parent and subsidiary relationship. A purchase of shares combination is therefore both a business combination and a long-term intercorporate investment.

A business combination occurs when two or more corporations, or unincorporated entities, come under common ownership or control. Thus, the substance of a business combination is simply common ownership or control of the economic entity that emerges from the combination. The accounting treatment of a business combination is determined by classification of the combination as either a purchase or as a pooling of interests[4] In a purchase of shares combination, this distinction will determine the amount to be recorded in the parent corporation's investment account.

For accounting purposes, when a business combination is classified as a purchase, the valuation of that which is acquired (either the assets or the shares of another business entity) is based on cost "measured in money, or, in the event other consideration is given, at the fair value of such other consideration, or at the fair value of the property acquired, whichever is more

[2]*CICA Handbook: Accounting Recommendations, Section 1600*, "Consolidated Financial Statements and the Equity Method of Accounting" (Toronto: Canadian Institute of Chartered Accountants, 1975), par. .03.

[3]*Financial Reporting in Canada*, thirteenth edition (Toronto: Canadian Institute of Chartered Accountants, 1979), p. 28.

[4]See *CICA Handbook: Accounting Recommendations*, Section 1580, "Business Combinations" (Toronto: Canadian Institute of Chartered Accountants, 1973).

clearly evident."[5] A business combination that is classified as a purchase involves the recognition of a new basis of accountability with respect to that which is acquired. Moreover, this method of accounting for a business combination is in accordance with the cost concept as generally applied when accounting for asset acquisitions.

By contrast, when a business combination is classified as a pooling of interests, no new basis of accountability arises. Under the pooling concept, the valuation of the assets or the shares of the corporations combined or pooled is based on their existing book values, assuming these values are stated in conformity with generally accepted principles applied on a reasonably uniform basis. Except for consistency adjustments and the effect of any changes in capitalization, pooling generally results in carrying forward established book values, including contributed surpluses, retained earnings, and/or deficits of the constituent corporations to the economic entity that emerges from the combination.

Historically, in Canada, most business combinations have been accounted for as purchases.[6] Thus, in Canadian practice, pooling-of-interest accounting has been used on relatively few occasions. Moreover, effective April 1, 1974, Section 1580 of the *Accounting Recommendations* restricted use of pooling to "those rare business combinations in which it is not possible to identify one of the parties as the acquirer."[7] Given the rare application of pooling in Canada, the material in this chapter is restricted to the preparation of consolidated statements where the related business combination was accounted for by the purchase method, and to the application of the equity method of accounting.

THE BASICS OF CONSOLIDATION

The accounting records and financial statements of a parent corporation and its one or more subsidiary companies are based on the principle that each affiliate is a separate legal entity. The preparation of consolidated financial statements takes place by way of the work sheets and schedules used to assemble consolidated data.

A combined balance sheet for two or more corporations would present line-by-line the total combined amounts for cash, receivables, inventories, and so forth. The aggregation that produces a combined statement is part of the consolidation process. To consolidate, however, it is also necessary to eliminate intercompany balances and transactions, including the effects of

---

[5]*Accounting Research and Terminology Bulletins — Final Edition*, "No. 48, Business Combinations" (New York; American Institute of Certified Public Accountants, 1961), par. 8.

[6]Martin, Samuel A.; Laiken, Stanley N.; and Haslam, Douglas F. *Business Combinations in the '60s*: A Canadian Profile. London: University of Western Ontario, 1969 and Canadian Institute of Chartered Accountants, 1970.

[7]*CICA Handbook: Accounting Recommendations*, Section 1580, *op. cit.*, par. .21.

intercompany transactions, and to provide for any minority interests. The key to the preparation of consolidated financials lies in recognizing the need for eliminating all reciprocal or mirror items.

To avoid duplication or *double-counting* on consolidated statements, reciprocal items which would normally appear on the individual statements of each affiliate must be offset and eliminated. For example, an intercompany merchandise transaction would increase the sales and purchases of the corporations being consolidated, and in most cases would result in an entry under the receivables of one corporation and under the payables of the other, thus presenting a distorted picture if like items are simply combined. Therefore, it is necessary to compensate by eliminating from consolidated statements intercompany sales and purchases, receivables and payables.

Moreover, any merchandise acquired intercompany that is included in inventories should usually, in accordance with GAAP, be valued at cost, including the amount of any unrealized intercompany gain or loss pertaining thereto. On a reciprocal basis, any unrealized intercompany gain or loss included in inventories is also included in the separate entity net income or loss and the retained earnings of the vendor corporation. For purposes of consolidation, it is necessary to eliminate (1) intercompany sales and purchases, (2) intercompany receivables and payables, if any, and (3) unrealized intercompany gains or losses included in inventories. Elimination (1) above serves to eliminate the intercompany merchandise transaction(s), while elimination (3) eliminates the effect of the transaction(s). Elimination (2) serves to eliminate any resulting intercompany balances from both receivables and payables. At this point, it is sufficient to recognize that these eliminations are necessary in order to avoid duplication or double-counting. Also, it is the elimination of reciprocal or mirror items that serves to distinguish consolidated statements from combined statements.

The preparation of consolidated financial statements can become both detailed and complex, especially when there are several subsidiaries and numerous intercompany transactions. The potential complexities of consolidation can be somewhat reduced by drawing two important distinctions that serve to identify specific stages in the application of the consolidation process. First of all, there is pedagogical merit in drawing a distinction between (1) balance sheet only consolidation, and (2) the consolidation of all financial statements, including the income statement and the statement of changes in financial position. Secondly, a distinction should be made between (1) consolidation as at the date of acquisition or combination, and (2) consolidation subsequent to the date of acquisition or combination. The discussion and illustrations that follow assume consolidation in accordance with Section 1600 of the *Accounting Recommendations*.

A wide variety of methods underlie the preparation of consolidated financial statements. In practice, for obvious reasons, the detailed worksheet method not only dominates, but is clearly justified given the complex situations commonly encountered. It can be argued, however, that the worksheet method may indeed inhibit comprehension of the basics of the consolidation process. Also, more direct methods that utilize supporting schedules rather than detailed worksheets are very definitely time efficient. Once the basics of consolidation have been mastered, the transition to detailed worksheets can be accomplished with ease.

PURCHASE PRICE DISCREPANCY AND MINORITY INTEREST

The basics of consolidation rest, in part, upon a clear understanding of two unique items that generally pertain to consolidated financial statements. These items, which have no direct counterpart in separate entity financials, are (1) the purchase price discrepancy, and (2) the minority interest. The former is simply the difference, if any, between the cost of the investment and the parent corporation's pro-rata or proportionate interest in the book value of the net assets that underlie the parent's ownership of the subsidiary's voting shares.

A minority interest arises in circumstances where the parent corporation owns less than 100 per cent of the subsidiary's voting shares.

The parent corporation's investment account represents the parent's net interest in the assets and liabilities of the subsidiary corporation. Moreover, under the conventional historic cost model, the cost of the investment is unlikely to equal the carrying value of the parent's ownership interest as reflected in the separate entity accounts of the subsidiary. It is important to note that the resulting purchase price discrepancy, if any, is simply an unidentified part of the parent's total investment in the subsidiary. It therefore follows that the amount of the purchase price discrepancy is not subject to disclosure in the separate entity financials of the parent corporation. As part of the process of preparing consolidated financial statements, the parent company's investment account is offset against the shareholders' equity accounts of the subsidiary. It is at this point that the purchase price discrepancy, if any, will emerge and should be accounted for in accordance with the recommendations contained in Section 1580. Assuming the discrepancy is positive (i.e., an excess of investment cost over book value acquired), which is often the case, the purchase price discrepancy is first reduced by applicable fair value allocations to net identifiable assets, and any remaining balance is considered goodwill.

Fair value increments refer to any differences between the fair values and the recorded book values of the subsidiary's net identifiable assets as at the date of acquisition. The term *net identifiable assets* includes all the underlying individual assets of the subsidiary, except goodwill, net of any liabilities assumed. Fair value allocations then are the portions of the fair value increments that are recognized in the preparation of the consolidated statements. Section 1580 of the *Accounting Recommendations* restricts the recognition of fair value allocations and goodwill to the parent corporation's pro-rata share as at the date of acquisition, or, in other words, to the amount purchased. It follows that "the interest of any minority shareholders in the identifiable assets acquired and liabilities assumed should be based on their carrying values in the accounting records of the company acquired."[8]

If the parent corporation's interest in identifiable assets acquired and liabilities assumed, based on their fair values, exceeds the cost of the investment, the result is *negative goodwill* or an *assignable excess*. According to Section 1580, "the amounts assigned to identifiable non-monetary assets should be reduced to the extent that the excess is eliminated."[9] This requirement may involve an examination of previously assigned fair values and/or an assessment of the book values recorded by the subsidiary, which are essentially matters of judgment. In the absence of substantive evidence, it may be necessary to reduce identifiable non-monetary assets on a pro-rata basis.

In any event, the procedure involves an *investment elimination entry*. As illustrated later in this chapter, the captions and amounts for the elimination are best determined from a schedule that provides an analysis of the combined transaction.

The investment elimination entry serves several important purposes: it eliminates 100 per cent of the shareholders' equity accounts of the subsidiary and recognizes a minority interest for that portion, if any, of the shareholders' equity of the subsidiary that is not owned, directly or indirectly, by the parent corporation; it eliminates the parent's investment account; and it provides accounting recognition for any fair value allocations and goodwill. In the event of an assignable excess, the investment elimination entry serves generally similar purposes, except that there is no goodwill to be recognized and, depending on the circumstances, the carrying values of the subsidiary's identifiable non-monetary assets may have to be reduced.

When a consolidated balance sheet includes the accounts of other than wholly-owned subsidiaries, that part of the shareholders' equity of the subsidiaries that is not directly or indirectly owned by the parent corporation is shown separately and identified as minority interest. This practice is consistent with the position that each group of shareholders, the majority and the minority, holds a proportionate interest in the aggregate net assets of the subsidiary corporation. Although a minority interest is usually shown as a one line item on the consolidated balance sheet, its components, such as capital stock, contributed surplus, and retained earnings, may be disclosed in the notes to the financials.

There is no general agreement on the appropriate balance sheet classifi-

---

[8]*Ibid.*, par. .44.
[9]*Ibid.*

cation for minority interest. Possible alternative classifications include: (1) a creditor claim or liability; (2) a separate component of shareholders' equity; and (3) a separate item between total liabilities and shareholders' equity, a compromise that is often used in practice. Section 1600 of the *Accounting Recommendations* rejects disclosure of the minority interest as part of shareholders' equity.[10] Therefore, Section 1600 may be interpreted as supporting either of two balance sheet classifications: (1) a creditor claim or liability, and (2) a "what-you-may-call-it" shown between total liabilities and shareholders' equity.

Consolidated financials prepared subsequent to the date of acquisition include both a minority interest in net assets and in consolidated income, provided that one or more subsidiaries are not wholly-owned. In the context of balance sheet consolidation, the minority interest in consolidated income is subsumed within the retained earnings of the one or more subsidiary corporations. Thus, the minority interest consists of the minority's pro-rata share of the equity of subsidiaries that are not wholly-owned, and includes, as retained earnings, the minority's interest therein at date of acquisition, plus or minus accumulated earnings or losses since acquisition (measured in accordance with recommendations contained in Section 1600), less any dividends to minority shareholders.

PREPARATION OF CONSOLIDATED FINANCIAL STATEMENTS

Apart from the methodology employed, the preparation of consolidated financial statements involves three steps:

1. *Establish reciprocity* by reconciling all intercompany accounts. This step is likely to involve the adjustment of account balances for:
   (a) intercompany items in transit, and
   (b) errors in the intercompany accounts as maintained by the affiliate corporations.
2. *Eliminate reciprocals:*
   (a) the investment elimination entry
   (b) adjustments pertaining to fair value allocations;
      (i) realization of fair value allocations to current items.
      (ii) depreciation and amortization on fair value allocations to net identifiable assets of subsidiary corporations.
      (iii) realization, by way of sale or other disposition, of net identifiable assets subject to fair value allocations.
   (c) amortization of goodwill
   (d) intrastatement eliminations;
      (i) intra-balance sheet eliminations such as receivables and payables, loans to and from, and advances.
      (ii) intra-income statement eliminations such as sales and purchases, in-

---

[10]*CICA Handbook: Accounting Recommendations*, Section 1600, *op. cit.*, par. .69.

terest income and interest expense, and management fees revenue and management fees expense.

(e) interstatement eliminations which involve both the income statement and balance sheet and require that operating results be restated with a corresponding change in asset or equity items. These eliminations concern unrealized intercompany gains and losses pertaining to:

(i) merchandise inventory purchased intercompany,

(ii) fixed assets and intangible assets purchased intercompany,

(iii) bonds with original issue or acquisition premium or discount held intercompany.

3. *Consolidate non-reciprocals* by combining on a line-by-line basis similar financial statement items of the affiliate corporations, as adjusted in steps 1 and 2 above.

The first step, establishing reciprocity, confirms the starting point for the consolidation process by assuring that all intercompany accounts balance. This step is primarily concerned with the end-of-period cutoff of intercompany transactions. Cutoff problems include such possibilities as the parent corporation shipping merchandise to a subsidiary at or near its fiscal year end. In such circumstances, it is possible that the sale may be recorded by the parent but the purchase may not have been recorded by the subsidiary. Similarly, if a subsidiary declares a dividend at year end, it is indeed possible that the dividend declaration may be recorded by the subsidiary but the reciprocal side of the transaction may not have been recorded by the parent corporation. This step is essentially procedural, as also is step 3, consolidating non-reciprocals. It therefore follows that the elimination of reciprocals is the critically important step in the consolidation process. In general, the complexities here pertain to the interstatement elimination of unrealized intercompany gains and losses, such as may result from inventory and fixed asset transactions that involve parent and subsidiary corporations. Moreover, in the context of balance sheet consolidations, these eliminations are an important determinant of consolidated retained earnings.

CONSOLIDATED RETAINED EARNINGS

Eric L. Kohler defines the term *consolidated retained earnings* thus:

The combined retained earnings of all companies whose accounts are consolidated, after deducting minority stockholders' interests therein, the interest acquired by the parent company in the subsidiary companies' retained earnings existing at the date of their acquisition, and intercompany eliminations.[11]

In the context of purchase accounting, it may be useful to examine in detail the impact of consolidation on the retained earnings balances as shown in the separate entity financials of the parent corporation and its

[11]Kohler, Eric L. *A Dictionary for Accountants*. Englewood Cliffs, N.J.: Prentice-Hall, Inc., 1975.

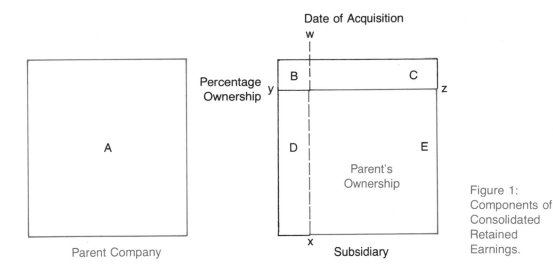

Figure 1: Components of Consolidated Retained Earnings.

subsidiaries. For illustrative purposes, assuming only one subsidiary corporation, the blocks in the following diagram represent: (1) the retained earnings balance of the parent corporation, and (2) the retained earnings balance of the subsidiary corporation.

The vertical axis (wx) of the block that represents the retained earnings balance of the subsidiary indicates the date of acquisition, while the horizontal axis (yz) indicates the parent corporation's percentage ownership. At date of acquisition, consolidated retained earnings is equal to the retained earnings balance of the parent corporation as shown on its separate entity balance sheet. Subsequent to the date of acquisition, the components of consolidated retained earnings are: (1) the retained earnings of the parent corporation, presented as block A in the above illustration, and (2) the parent corporation's pro-rata share of the change in the retained earnings of the subsidiary since the date of acquisition, presented as block E. The total amount represented by blocks A and E must then be adjusted for: (1) the realization of fair value allocations to current items, if any, (2) any depreciation and amortization of fair value allocations to the net identifiable assets of subsidiary corporations, (3) the realization, by way of sale or other disposition, of net identifiable assets subject to fair value allocations, (4) the amortization of goodwill, if any, and (5) the elimination of unrealized intercompany gains and losses. It is also possible that establishing reciprocity may encompass intercompany items in transit and errors that would impact on consolidated retained earnings. This would result, for example, if the items in transit happened to include a subsidiary dividend declaration.

The minority interest in retained earnings is not dependent upon the date of acquisition. Therefore, in figure 1, the minority interest in retained earnings is presented as blocks B and C. The amount represented by blocks B and C is determined by applying the minority's percentage ownership to the retained earnings balance as shown in the separate entity financials of the subsidiary corporation. This amount must then be adjusted for the minority interest portion of any unrealized intercompany gains and losses allocated or pro-rated between majority and minority interests. Again, it is possible that in transit items and errors may impact on the minority interest in retained earnings.

Returning again to figure 1, block D, the parent corporation's share of the subsidiary's retained earnings at date of acquisition, represents the purchased retained earnings of the subsidiary corporation. Under purchase accounting, the amount represented by block D is excluded from consolidated retained earnings. Instead it is part of the book value acquired; it is therefore eliminated against the investment account of the parent corporation as part of the investment elimination entry.

Based on the foregoing analysis, the computation of consolidated retained earnings and the minority interest in retained earnings, if any, can be summarized in the format of a schedule, as follows:

Company	Balance	Purchased Retained Earnings	Minority Interest	Consolidated Retained Earnings
Parent	XXX--			A
Subsidiary	XXX	D	B + C	E
	XXX	XXX	XXX	XXX

Adjustments and eliminations:		
Realization of fair value allocations to current items		XXX
Depreciation and amortization on fair value allocations		XXX
Realization of fair value allocations by sale or other disposition		XXX
Amortization of goodwill		XXX
Unrealized intercompany gains and losses	XXX	XXX
In transit items and errors	XXX	XXX
	XXX	XXX
Balances	XXX	XXX

Under recommendations contained in Section 1580, only the parent corporation's pro-rata share of fair value increments to the subsidiary's net identifiable assets, and only purchased goodwill are given accounting recognition. Therefore, any adjustments to current items, and adjustments for any depreciation and amortization of fair value allocations and for the amortization of goodwill, only impact on consolidated retained earnings.

The interstatement elimination for unrealized intercompany gains and losses, under recommendations contained in Section 1600, require allocation or pro-ration between majority and minority interest where an unrealized intercompany gain or loss has been recognized by a subsidiary corporation in which there is a minority interest. Depending upon their nature, in transit items and errors may affect both consolidated retained earnings and the minority interest in retained earnings.

Although a schedule in the above format may have pedagogical merit, for problem-solving purposes the same information can be presented in a more practical format, as follows:

	Consolidated Retained Earnings	Minority Interest
Retained earnings balances:		
Parent	XXX	
Subsidiary	XXX	
	XXX	
Deduct:		
Purchased retained earnings	XXX	
Minority interest	XXX——→XXX	
	XXX	
	XXX	XXX
Adjustments and eliminations:		
Realization of fair value allocations to current items	XXX	
Depreciation and amortization on fair value allocations	XXX	
Realization of fair value allocations by sale or other disposition	XXX	
Amortization of goodwill	XXX	
Unrealized intercompany gains and losses	XXX	XXX
In transit items and errors	XXX	XXX
	XXX	XXX
Balances	XXX	XXX

INTERCOMPANY TRANSACTIONS

It is not unusual for there to be numerous intercompany transactions between the constituent corporations that comprise the economic entity for which consolidated statements may be prepared. The consolidation process requires elimination of the effects of all intercompany transactions. This is necessary in order for consolidated financials to present the financial position, the results of operations, and changes in financial position of the consolidated entity with other entities outside and independent of the consolidated group of corporations. It must be clearly understood that consolidated financial statements reflect only transactions between the economic entity to which they pertain and other external entities.

In the context of balance sheet consolidation, intercompany transactions can obviously give rise to intercompany balance sheet items, such as receivables and payables, loans to and from, and advances. For consolidation purposes, the resulting balances are subject to intrastatement balance sheet eliminations which are essentially routine. For example, the following entry serves to eliminate intercompany receivables and payables in the amount of $50,000:

| Accounts payable | 50,000 | |
| Accounts receivable | | 50,000 |

This entry is strictly for purposes of consolidation. In common with all elimination entries, it is not recorded in the separate entity accounts of any of the corporations being consolidated. As an example of an intrastatement balance sheet elimination, the above entry eliminates equal amounts from the separate entity balance sheets of two of the corporations being consolidated.

Depending upon the length of the transaction cycle, intrastatement balance sheet eliminations may or may not have multi-period effects. In general, however, any multi-period effects pertaining to these eliminations should usually relate to loans, advances, and intercompany bond transactions. Moreover, the multi-period effects, if any, should cause no problem because, regardless of the length of the transaction cycle, all that is required for consolidation purposes is the elimination of year-end date of consolidation balances.

Most intercompany transactions involve the sale or other transfer of assets between the constituents that form the consolidated group of corporations. Moreover, the vendor corporation, as a separate legal entity, may indeed recognize a gain or loss as a result of intercompany transactions. Similarly, the constituent corporation that acquires assets intercompany will include any gain or loss recognized by the vendor corporation in the carrying values at which assets acquired intercompany are shown on its separate entity balance sheet.

For example, assume that a parent corporation sells land that cost $200,000 to a subsidiary corporation for $500,000. Obviously, the parent, as a separate legal entity, will report a gain on the transaction of $300,000; the subsidiary will report the land on its separate entity balance sheet at its cost, $500,000. However, the cost of the land to the consolidated entity is only $200,000. For purposes of consolidation, the intercompany gain, which is unrealized because the land is still owned within the consolidated group of corporations, must be eliminated. Thus, the carrying value of the land is reduced to the cost incurred by the consolidated entity. In the context of balance sheet consolidation, the following entry serves to eliminate the unrealized inter-company gain of $300,000:

Retained earnings	300,000	
Land		300,000

The consolidation process requires elimination of any unrealized inter-company gains or losses included in the amounts at which assets acquired intercompany are carried in the separate entity accounts of the corporations being consolidated. As an example of an interstatement elimination, the above entry restates operating results by the debit to retained earnings and reflects a corresponding change in assets, the credit to land. All interstate-ment eliminations, by definition, involve both the income statement (re-tained earnings for purposes of balance sheet consolidation) and the balance sheet. Also, without exception, interstatement eliminations always have multi-period effects. Thus, intercompany gains and losses affect both the period of the transaction and all subsequent periods until the asset acquired inter-company is sold to an entity outside the consolidated group of corporations. It follows that these intercompany transactions must be analyzed very care-fully to assure that both the transaction period's and subsequent periods' effects are properly eliminated.

To summarize, elimination of the effects of all intercompany transactions, which is a critical part of the consolidation process, may, depending upon the circumstances, require two distinct types of elimination entries: (1) intra-statement eliminations including both intra-balance sheet eliminations and intra-income statement eliminations, and (2) interstatement eliminations. Intrastatement eliminations have as their objective the elimination of inter-company balances and intercompany transactions. The interstatement elim-inations serve to eliminate any unrealized intercompany gains and losses included in the amounts at which assets acquired intercompany are reported on the separate entity balance sheets of the corporations being consolidated. From the viewpoint of the consolidated entity, gains and losses on intercom-pany transactions are unrealized until verified or confirmed by an arm's-length transaction with an entity that is external to and independent of the consolidated group of corporations, or consumed in day-to-day operations.

UNREALIZED INTERCOMPANY GAINS AND LOSSES

Although not essential, it is useful to understanding the elimination of unrealized intercompany gains and losses to draw a distinction between downstream and upstream intercompany transactions.

In a *downstream transaction* the parent company is the vendor corpora-tion whereas in an *upstream transaction* the subsidiary is the vendor. In a downstream transaction, the intercompany gain or loss is recognized on the separate entity income statement of the parent corporation, and on the separate entity balance sheet of the subsidiary as part of the carrying value of the asset(s) acquired intercompany. Conversely, the intercompany gain or loss resulting from an upstream transaction appears on the separate entity income statement of the subsidiary corporation and on the separate entity balance sheet of the parent corporation.

Section 1600 includes the following recommendations concerning the elimination of unrealized intercompany gains and losses:[12]

> Unrealized intercompany gains or losses arising subsequent to the date of an acquisition on assets remaining within the consolidated group should be eliminated. The amount of the elimination from assets should not be affected by the existence of a minority interest.
>
> Where there is an unrealized intercompany gain or loss recognized by a subsidiary company in which there is a minority interest, such gain or loss should be eliminated proportionately between the majority and minority interest in that company's income.

These recommendations are significant. First of all, they endorse 100 per cent elimination of unrealized intercompany gains and losses (1) that pertain to assets acquired intercompany, and (2) that remain within the consolidated group of corporations. This, of course, is necessary if assets are to be presented at historical cost to the consolidated entity. Secondly, in the case of upstream transactions, Section 1600 recommends allocation of the elimination if there is a minority interest in the subsidiary corporation.

In general, three specific situations trigger the elimination of unrealized intercompany gains and losses: (1) merchandise inventory purchased intercompany, (2) fixed assets and intangible assets purchased intercompany, and (3) bonds with original issue or acquisition premium or discount held intercompany.[13] It must be emphasized that eliminations for unrealized intercompany gains and losses always have multi-period effects. Thus, intercompany gains and losses affect both the period of the transaction and all subsequent periods until the asset acquired intercompany is either sold or otherwise disposed of to an entity outside the consolidated group of corporations, or consumed in day-to-day operations.

Merchandise Inventory Purchased Intercompany

The eliminations relating to inventory purchased intercompany are reasonably straightforward, especially in the context of balance sheet consolidation. Any unrealized intercompany gains or losses included in the inventory of a subsidiary corporation result from downstream sales and therefore,

---

[12]*CICA Handbook: Accounting Recommendations*, Section 1600, *op. cit.*, par. .30 and .32.

[13]Intercompany bond transactions often involve complexitites that extend well beyond the intermediate level. Since these transactions are also rare, their coverage has been omitted from the chapter.

without exception, compliance with Section 1600 requires 100 per cent elimination. However, if the vendor corporation is a subsidiary that is not wholly-owned, only the inventory account is adjusted for 100 per cent elimination; the other side of the elimination must be allocated proportionally between the majority and minority interests.

To illustrate, assume that during the year just ended Parent Corporation's sales included $200,000 of merchandise sold to Subsidiary Limited. Of this merchandise, 25 per cent still remains in Subsidiary's inventory at the end of the year. Parent Corporation marks up the merchandise it sells to Subsidiary Limited 60 per cent based on selling prices. Also, assume that during the year just ended Subsidiary Limited's sales included $100,000 of merchandise sold to Parent Corporation. The average gross profit as a percentage of Subsidiary Limited's sales is 50 per cent. Parent Corporation's inventory at year end includes 20 per cent of the merchandise acquired from Subsidiary Limited. Parent Corporation owns 80 per cent of Subsidiary Limited's common shares.

The sales of Parent Corporation to Subsidiary Limited are downstream; therefore 100 per cent of the unrealized intercompany gain included in the closing inventory of Subsidiary Limited must be eliminated for purposes of consolidation. The amount to be eliminated is $30,000 ($200,000 × .25 × .60); the following entry serves to eliminate the $30,000 unrealized intercompany gain included in the inventory of Subsidiary Limited:

Retained earnings	30,000	
Inventory		30,000

It should be noted that the amount of the unrealized gain in inventory is measured in terms of the gross margin applicable to merchandise purchased intercompany. The alternative of using net margins, while perhaps good theory, involves practical problems of expense allocation the solutions for which are arbitrary. It can also be argued that in many cases intercompany sales may be essentially marginal and therefore unlikely to generate any direct expenses except for cost of sales.

The sales of Subsidiary Limited to Parent Corporation are upstream. Compliance with Section 1600 of the *Accounting Recommendations* requires 100 per cent elimination of the intercompany gain of $10,000 (50% of $20,000) from the inventory of Parent Corporation. The other side of the elimination, however, must be pro-rated between the majority and minority interests in Subsidiary Limited. The elimination entry is presented below:

Retained earnings	8,000	
Minority interest	2,000	
Inventory		10,000

For purposes of preparing a consolidated balance sheet, no adjustment is required for unrealized intercompany gains and losses in opening inventories. Thus, in the case of an unrealized gain, for example, the elimination of the intercompany gain in the opening inventory would reduce the beginning balance in consolidated retained earnings and increase the period's consolidated net income. Since year-end consolidated retained earnings includes the sum of the beginning balance and the consolidated net income, the effect of eliminating an unrealized intercompany gain from the opening inventory cancels out in the determination of the closing balance in consolidated retained earnings. Elimination, however, is indeed relevant to both the consolidated income statement and the statement of consolidated retained earnings, as illustrated later in the chapter.

Fixed Assets and Intangible Assets Purchased Intercompany

Unrealized gains and losses on fixed assets purchased intercompany are realized from the viewpoint of the consolidated entity as a result of depreciation subsequent to the date of the intercompany transaction. For purposes of preparing a consolidated balance sheet, the elimination where fixed assets have been purchased intercompany requires (1) eliminating from the fixed asset account 100 per cent of any gain or loss recognized on the transaction, (2) elimination from accumulated depreciation of the subsequent depreciation pertaining to any gain or loss recognized on the transaction, and (3) elimination from retained earnings of the difference between the amounts determined in (1) and (2) above, which is the unrealized portion of the gain or loss, if any, recognized on the transaction. If the transaction is upstream, subsidiary to parent, the elimination in (3) above should be pro-rated between the majority and minority interest, if any.

To illustrate, assume Parent Corporation sold a machine to Subsidiary Limited at the beginning of the current period for $25,000 that on the date of sale had a net book value of $20,000 and a remaining useful life of 5 years. Parent Corporation, the vendor company, will recognize in its separate entity accounts a gain of $5,000 on the transaction. Similarly, Subsidiary Limited will record the fixed asset purchase in its separate entity accounts at its cost, $25,000, which includes the unrealized intercompany gain of $5,000 recognized by Parent Corporation.

From the viewpoint of the consolidated entity, the relevant net book value is only $20,000 and the subsequent consolidated depreciation should reflect this fact. For purposes of balance sheet only consolidation, assuming both companies use the straight-line method of depreciation, the following elimination entry would be required at the end of the year in which the intercompany transaction occurred:

Retained earnings	4,000	
Accumulated depreciation	1,000	
Plant and equipment		5,000

It should be noted that 100 per cent of the $5,000 intercompany gain included in the plant and equipment account of Subsidiary Limited ($25,000 – $20,000) is eliminated from plant and equipment. The realized portion of the gain $1,000, which is the excess depreciation recorded in the separate entity accounts of Subsidiary Limited ($5,000 divided by 5 years), is eliminated by the debit to accumulated depreciation. In this case, the un-realized portion of the gain $4,000 ($5,000 – $1,000), which will be realized over the remaining useful life of the machine, is debited to retained earnings. If the intercompany transaction had been upstream, subsidiary to parent, the $4,000 would have had to be pro-rated between the majority and minority in-terests because there is a 20 per cent minority interest in Subsidiary Limited. The required elimination entry at the end of the year would be as follows:

Retained earnings	3,200	
Minority interest	800	
Accumulated depreciation	1,000	
Plant and equipment		5,000

Assuming the machine is retained in service by Subsidiary Limited, the required elimination entries one year later and two years later, are presented below:

	One Year Later		Two Years Later	
Retained earnings	3,000		2,000	
Accumulated depreciation	2,000		3,000	
Plant and equipment		5,000		5,000

Again, 100 per cent of the $5,000 intercompany gain included in Subsid-iary Limited's plant and equipment account is eliminated. Moreover, this amount will be eliminated at the end of each subsequent period until the machine purchased intercompany is sold to an entity outside the consoli-dated group of corporations, or otherwise retired from service. Each year during the remaining useful life of the machine the realized portion of the gain increases by the amount of excess depreciation recorded in the separate entity accounts of Parent Corporation. The unrealized portion of the gain decreases each year by the same amount. If the intercompany transaction had been upstream, because there is a 20 per cent minority interest in Subsidiary Corporation, the unrealized gain at each year end, during the remaining useful life of the machine would be allocated proportionately between the majority and minority interests. If the machine should remain in service beyond its estimated useful life, the following entry would be required at the end of each year until the machine is eventually retired, scrapped or otherwise disposed of:

Accumulated depreciation	5,000	
Plant and equipment		5,000

In the case of an intercompany fixed asset transaction involving land, any gain on the transaction remains unrealized until the land purchased intercompany is sold to an entity outside the consolidated group of corporations. Each year that the land purchased intercompany is retained within the consolidated entity, 100 per cent of the unrealized gain or loss must be eliminated from the land account. For purposes of balance sheet only consolidation, retained earnings must be adjusted, and also minority interests provided the transaction is upstream and the subsidiary is other than wholly owned. If the land is subject to depletion, the consolidation eliminations are essentially analogous to what would apply if the transaction had involved depreciable fixed assets.

The consolidation eliminations for unrealized gains and losses on intangible assets purchased intercompany are similar to those that pertain to depreciable fixed assets. The unrealized intercompany gain or loss is realized by way of the annual amortization recorded by the purchasing corporation. Since separate accounts for accumulated amortization are rare, the elimination is usually for only the unrealized portion of the intercompany gain or loss. To illustrate, assume Port Corporation sold a patent to Stanley Limited realizing an intercompany gain of $10,000 on the transaction. At the date of consolidation, $4,000 of the intercompany gain had been realized as a result of the amortization charges recorded by Stanley Limited. The following elimination entry would be required for purposes of balance sheet only consolidation:

Retained earnings	6,000	
Patents		6,000

Alternatively, assuming the use of a separate account for accumulated amortization, the elimination entry would appear as follows:

Retained earnings	6,000	
Accumulated amortization	4,000	
Patents		10,000

ELIMINATION OF RECIPROCALS

Without exception, the elimination of reciprocals requires an investment elimination entry. Depending on specific circumstances, any or all of 4 additional types of adjustments or eliminations may be required: (1) adjustments pertaining to fair value allocations, (2) amortization of goodwill, (3) intrastatement eliminations, and (4) interstatement eliminations. Intrastatement eliminations cancel equal amounts from within either the balance sheets or the income statements of parent and subsidiary corporations. Interstatement eliminations involve both the income statement and balance sheet, and therefore require that operating results be restated with a corresponding

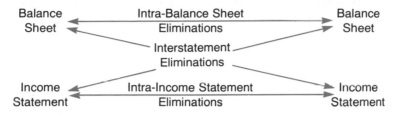

PARENT CORPORATION   SUBSIDIARY CORPORATION

Balance Sheet ← Intra-Balance Sheet Eliminations → Balance Sheet

Interstatement Eliminations

Income Statement ← Intra-Income Statement Eliminations → Income Statement

Figure 2: Intrastatement and Interstatement Eliminations

change in asset or liability items. Figure 2 illustrates the distinction between intrastatement and interstatement eliminations.

Consolidation at Date of Acquisition

Assuming purchase accounting, the preparation of a consolidated balance sheet at the date of acquisition or combination always requires an investment elimination entry, and may also require an intra-balance sheet elimination if the parent and subsidiary corporations have receivables and payables due each other. The amounts required for the investment elimination entry may be determined from an analysis of the combination transaction. The intra-balance sheet elimination, if required, is straightforward; it involves the elimination of equal amounts from the receivables and payables of the parent and subsidiary corporations.

Subsequent Consolidation

Under the purchase method of accounting, only a consolidated balance sheet is appropriate at date of acquisition. As previously noted, its preparation requires only an investment elimination entry, and possibly one intra-balance sheet elimination for any intercompany receivables and payables. Under the purchase method, it is only for purposes of subsequent consolidation that the whole range of possible adjustments and eliminations becomes potentially applicable. It should also be noted that under purchase accounting the consolidation of income statements and statements of changes in financial position would only apply for purposes of subsequent consolidation.

Subsequent to the date of acquisition or combination, the preparation of a consolidation balance sheet under purchase accounting may require, subject to specific circumstances, two types of adjustments: (1) adjustments pertaining to fair value allocations, and (2) amortization of goodwill, in addition to an investment elimination entry, and both intrastatement and interstatement eliminations, as circumstances may dictate. The adjustments pertaining to fair value allocations concern the realization of the line-by-line amounts attributed to the net identifiable assets of the subsidiary at the date of acquisition. Any amounts attributed to current items, such as receivables and inventories, are realized as the receivables are collected, or as the inventory is sold. Except in rare circumstances, these amounts should be realized in the first year subsequent to the date of acquisition or combination. The amounts attributed to depreciable assets, identifiable intangibles and long-term debt of the subsidiary corporation are realized by the depreciation and amortization adjustments required for purposes of subsequent consolidation. Fair value allocations to land remain unrealized until the land is sold outside the consolidated group of companies. Section 1580 of the *Accounting Recommendations* imposed the mandatory amortization of goodwill. More specifically, the requirement is straight-line amortization over a period not to exceed 40 years.[14]

BALANCE SHEET CONSOLIDATION

It is useful to draw a distinction between balance sheet consolidation as at the date of acquisition or combination and subsequent balance sheet consolidation. This distinction is particularly relevant in the case of purchase accounting because this is the method that should be used to account for all corporate combinations, excluding only those rare combinations where it is not possible to identify one of the corporations as the acquirer. Section 1600 of the *Accounting Recommendations* is concerned with the detailed practical application of the consolidation and equity methods of accounting under the purchase method of accounting.

Consolidation at Date of Acquisition

The preparation of a consolidated balance sheet at the date of acquisition or combination always requires an investment elimination entry. As previously noted, the amounts required for this entry may be determined from an analysis of the combination transaction. The line-by-line detail for the identifiable assets and liabilities to be shown on the consolidated balance sheet is determined by the following formula or equation.

	Parent			Subsidiary
Line-by-line Detail	=	100% of Book Value	+	100% of Book Value	±	Parents' pro-rata share of Fair Value increments

This formula is based on recommendations contained in the *CICA Handbook*. An analysis of the combination transaction provides the line-by-line amounts for the parent corporation's pro-rata share of fair value increments. This analysis also provides the amount to be recognized as goodwill, if any.

Under purchase accounting, the shareholders' equity section of the

[14]*CICA Handbook: Accounting Recommendations*, Section 1580, *op. cit.*, par. .58.

consolidated balance sheet at date of acquisition is always identical to the shareholders' equity of the parent corporation. The share capital on any consolidated balance sheet is restricted to the shares issued by the parent corporation. The share capital accounts of the subsidiary corporation(s) are eliminated as part of the investment elimination entry. To the extent that the subsidiary's shares are owned by the parent corporation, they are offset against the parent's investment account; the shares of subsidiary corporations that are not owned by the parent, including preferred shares, if any, are shown on a consolidated balance sheet as part of the minority interest. At the date of acquisition, the consolidated retained earnings or deficit under purchase accounting is always equal to the parent's separate entity retained earnings or deficit. This is because purchase accounting recognizes the operating results of the acquired corporation only from the date of the combination transaction. As stated in Section 1600, "the retained earnings or deficit of a subsidiary company at the date(s) of acquisition by the parent should not be included in consolidated retained earnings."[15] Thus, the investment elimination entry eliminates 100 per cent of the acquisition retained earnings or deficit of the subsidiary corporation(s) — the purchased portion is offset against the parent's investment account and any remaining balance becomes part of the minority interest.

The financial data shown below will be used in the following paragraphs to illustrate balance sheet consolidation at the date of acquisition or combination, assuming purchase accounting.

On June 30, Parent Corporation purchased 80 per cent of the outstanding common shares of Subsidiary Limited for $1,500,000. The individual balance sheets at that date are summarized as follows:

	Parent Corporation Book Value	Subsidiary Limited Book Value	Subsidiary Limited Fair Value
Summarized Financial Data As At Date of Acquisition			
Monetary assets	$ 200,000	$ 50,000	$ 50,000
Inventories	300,000	75,000	75,000
Investment in Subsidiary Limited (at cost)	1,500,000	——	——
Land	200,000	25,000	150,000
Other fixed assets (net)	2,500,000	850,000	1,100,000
Identifiable intangibles	800,000	——	——
	$ 5,500,000	$1,000,000	
Current liabilities	$ 100,000		
Long-term debt	400,000		
Common shares	1,500,000	600,000	
Retained earnings	3,500,000	400,000	
	$ 5,500,000	$1,000,000	

---

[15]*CICA Handbook: Accounting Recommendations*, Section 1600, *op. cit.*, par. .22.

The following steps summarize the preparation of a date-of-acquisition consolidated balance sheet: (1) analyze the combination transaction, (2) compute the minority interest, if any, and (3) assemble data for the consolidated balance sheet. A schedule analyzing the combination transaction is presented below.

Analysis of the Combination Transaction
As At Date of Acquisition

Purchase price	$1,500,000
Book value acquired (80%)	
Common shares (80% of $600,000)	$ 480,000
Retained earnings (80% of $400,000)	320,000
	$ 800,000
Purchase discrepancy	$ 700,000
Fair value allocation (per schedule below)	300,000
Goodwill	$ 400,000

Fair Value Allocation
As At Date of Acquisition

	Book Value	Fair Value	Fair Value Increment	Purchased Portion (80%)
Land	$ 25,000	$ 150,000	$125,000	$100,000
Other fixed assets . . .	850,000	1,100,000	250,000	200,000
				$300,000

Although a separate schedule to determine fair value allocations may have pedagogical merit, the line-by-line amounts for the purchased portion or parent's pro-rata share of fair value increments can be included in the analysis of the combination transaction, as follows:

Purchase discrepancy	$700,000
Fair value allocation (80%)	
Land	100,000
Other fixed assets	200,000
	$300,000
Goodwill	$400,000

The minority interest at the date of acquisition is simply the minority percentage applied to the book values at which the subsidiary's shareholders' equity is shown on its separate entity balance sheet. The schedule below supports the minority interest to be shown on the consolidated balance sheet at the date of acquisition.

Minority Interest As At Date of Acquisition

Common shares (20% of $600,000)	$120,000
Retained earnings (20% of $400,000)	80,000
	$200,000

The final step is to assemble the necessary data for the preparation of the consolidated balance sheet. The line-by-line detail for the identifiable assets and liabilities to be shown on the consolidated balance sheet at the date of acquisition is determined in accordance with the formula or equation presented on page 456. Separate schedules support the amounts for goodwill and minority interest. At the date of acquisition, the shareholders' equity accounts to be shown on the consolidated balance sheet are those of Parent Corporation. In addition, an intra-balance sheet elimination is required if there is any intercompany indebtedness. The resulting consolidated balance sheet is presented below.

Parent Corporation and Subsidiary Limited Consolidated Balance Sheet As At Date of Acqusition	
Monetary assets ($200,000 + $50,000)	$ 250,000
Inventories ($300,000 + $75,000)	375,000
Land ($200,000 + $25,000 + $100,000)	325,000
Other fixed assets ($2,500,000 + $850,000 + $200,000)	3,550,000
Identifiable intangibles	800,000
Goodwill (per schedule)	400,000
	$5,700,000
Current liabilities	$ 100,000
Long-term debt	400,000
Minority interest (per schedule)	200,000
Common shares	1,500,000
Retained earnings	3,500,000
	$5,700,000

Depending on the circumstances, two elimination entries may be required to produce a date-of-acquisition consolidated balance sheet: (1) an investment elimination entry, and (2) an intra-balance sheet elimination. In this case, only an investment elimination entry is required. On the consolidated balance sheet above, the first two amounts in parentheses combine the alike line items from the balance sheets of Parent Corporation and Subsidiary Limited; the other amounts come from the adjustments and eliminations, in this case from the investment elimination entry as follows:

Land	$100,000	
Other fixed assets	200,000	
Goodwill	400,000	
Common shares...............................	600,000	
Retained earnings	400,000	
Investment in Subsidiary Limited		$1,500,000
Minority interest		200,000
Investment elimination entry		

Subsequent Consolidation

Subsequent balance sheet consolidation requires a detailed computation of consolidated retained earnings. As illustrated earlier in the chapter, this computation can be presented in the form of a supporting schedule. Otherwise, with minor modifications, the steps required for purposes of subsequent consolidation essentially parallel those necessary for the preparation of a date-of-acquisition consolidated balance sheet, specifically: (1) analyze the combination transaction, (2) compute consolidated retained earnings, (3) compute the minority interest, if any, and (4) assemble data for the consolidated balance sheet.

<table>
<tr><td colspan="3" align="center">Parent Corporation and Subsidiary Limited
Summarized Financial Data,
One Year Following Date of Acquisition</td></tr>
<tr><td></td><td align="center">Parent
Corporation</td><td align="center">Subsidiary
Limited</td></tr>
<tr><td>Sales ....</td><td>$1,500,000</td><td>$ 800,000</td></tr>
<tr><td>Gain on asset disposal ....</td><td>5,000</td><td>——</td></tr>
<tr><td>Investment income ....</td><td>16,000</td><td>——</td></tr>
<tr><td></td><td>$1,521,000</td><td>$ 800,000</td></tr>
<tr><td>Cost of sales..................................</td><td>$ 900,000</td><td>$ 400,000</td></tr>
<tr><td>Operating expenses ....</td><td>121,000</td><td>200,000</td></tr>
<tr><td></td><td>$1,021,000</td><td>$ 600,000</td></tr>
<tr><td>Net income ....</td><td>$ 500,000</td><td>$ 200,000</td></tr>
<tr><td>Dividends paid:</td><td></td><td></td></tr>
<tr><td> Common shares............................</td><td>50,000</td><td>20,000</td></tr>
<tr><td>Earnings retained in the business ....</td><td>$ 450,000</td><td>$ 180,000</td></tr>
<tr><td>Retained earnings (opening) ....</td><td>3,500,000</td><td>400,000</td></tr>
<tr><td>Retained earnings (closing) ....</td><td>$3,950,000</td><td>$ 580,000</td></tr>
<tr><td>Monetary assets...............................</td><td>$ 150,000</td><td>$ 51,000</td></tr>
<tr><td>Inventories....................................</td><td>350,000</td><td>80,000</td></tr>
<tr><td>Investment in Subsidiary Limited (at cost) ....</td><td>1,500,000</td><td>——</td></tr>
<tr><td>Land ....</td><td>200,000</td><td>25,000</td></tr>
<tr><td>Other fixed assets (net) ....</td><td>3,000,000</td><td>1,090,000</td></tr>
<tr><td>Identifiable intangibles ....</td><td>750,000</td><td>——</td></tr>
<tr><td></td><td>$5,950,000</td><td>$1,246,000</td></tr>
<tr><td>Current liabilities ....</td><td>$ 100,000</td><td>$ 66,000</td></tr>
<tr><td>Long-term debt................................</td><td>400,000</td><td>——</td></tr>
<tr><td>Common shares...............................</td><td>1,500,000</td><td>600,000</td></tr>
<tr><td>Retained earnings ....</td><td>3,950,000</td><td>580,000</td></tr>
<tr><td></td><td>$5,950,000</td><td>$1,246,000</td></tr>
</table>

Provided the parent's percentage ownership of the subsidiary's voting shares has not changed, the analysis of the combination transaction will be the same regardless of when a consolidated balance sheet is to be prepared. For purposes of subsequent consolidation, the accumulated amortization of goodwill should be deducted from the amount of goodwill, if any, determined at the date of aquisition. Thus the schedule analyzing the combination transaction will support the amount of goodwill to be shown on the consolidated balance sheet.

The computations for consolidated retained earnings and minority interest can be conveniently combined into one supporting schedule. The adjustments and eliminations to be shown on the schedule are dependent upon specific circumstances but may include any or all of the following: (1) realization of fair value allocations to current items, (2) depreciation and amortization on fair value allocations, (3) realization of fair value allocations by sale or other disposition, (4) amortization of goodwill, and (5) unrealized gains and losses on assets acquired intercompany. In addition, depending upon their nature, in transit items and errors may impact on both consolidated retained earnings and the minority interest in retained earnings.

The Parent Corporation and Subsidiary Limited example of balance sheet consolidation at date of acquisition will now be expanded to illustrate subsequent consolidation. The individual financial statements of Parent Corporation and Subsidiary Limited one year later are illustrated on page 460. Additional information concerning intercompany events and transactions is as follows.

Additional information:

1. Subsidiary Limited's fixed assets that on consolidation are subject to fair value allocations have a remaining useful life of 10 years. Both Parent Corporation and Subsidiary Limited use the straight-line method of depreciation.
2. Goodwill recognized on consolidation is to be amortized over a period of 40 years.
3. During the year just ended Parent Corporation's sales included $200,000 of merchandise sold to Subsidiary Limited. A total of $50,000 of this merchandise remains in Subsidiary's inventory at the end of the year. Parent Corporation marks up the merchandise it sells to Subsidiary Limited 60 per cent based on selling prices.
4. During the year just ended Subsidiary Limited's sales included $100,000 of merchandise sold to Parent Corporation. The average gross profit as a percentage of Subsidiary Limited's sales is 50 per cent. Parent Corporation's inventory at year end includes 20 per cent of the merchandise acquired from Subsidiary Limited.
5. An analysis of intercompany receivables and payables indicates that Subsidiary Limited owes Parent Corporation $15,000.
6. At the beginning of the current period Parent Corporation sold a machine to Subsidiary Limited for $25,000 that on the date of sale had a net book value of $20,000 and a remaining useful life of 5 years.

The analysis of the combination transaction one year later is presented below. Except for the amortization of goodwill this schedule is identical to the one prepared at the date of acquisition. Moreover, this will always be the case provided the parent's percentage of ownership of the subsidiary's voting shares remains unchanged.

Parent Corporation and Subsidiary Limited
Analysis of Combination Transaction
One Year Following Date of Acquisition

Purchase price	$1,500,000
Book value acquired (80%):	
Common shares (80% of $600,000)	$ 480,000
Retained earnings (80% of $400,000)	320,000
	$ 800,000
Purchase discrepancy	$ 700,000
Fair value allocation (80%):	
Land	$ 100,000
Other fixed assets	200,000
	$ 300,000
Goodwill at date of acquisition	$ 400,000
Amortization (40 years)	10,000
Goodwill one year later	$ 390,000

For purposes of balance sheet only consolidation the investment elimination entry one year later is generally similar to the one prepared at date of acquisition. The only difference concerns the $180,000 change during the period in Subsidiary Limited's retained earnings ($580,000 – $400,000). Because Parent Corporation holds an 80 per cent ownership interest in Subsidiary Limited, $144,000 (80% of $180,000) is included in consolidated retained earnings. This amount is Parent Corporation's pro-rata share of the change in Subsidiary Limited's retained earnings since the date of acquisition. The minority interest is increased by $36,000 (20% of $180,000).

Land	100,000	
Other fixed assets	200,000	
Goodwill	400,000	
Common shares	600,000	
Retained earnings	580,000	
Investment in Subsidiary Limited		1,500,000
Minority interest		236,000
Retained earnings		144,000
Investment elimination entry		

It should be noted that the $236,000 credit to minority interest includes the following components:

Common shares (20% of $600,000)	$120,000
Retained earnings (20% of $580,000)	116,000
	$236,000

For purposes of subsequent balance sheet consolidation the next steps are to compute (1) consolidated retained earnings, and (2) minority interest. As previously noted, these computations can easily be combined into one schedule, as follows.

Parent Corporation and Subsidiary Limited Consolidated Retained Earnings and Minority Interest One Year Following Date of Acquisition		
	Consolidated Retained Earnings	Minority Interest
Retained earnings balances:		
Parent Corporation	$3,950,000	
Subsidiary Limited	580,000	
	$4,530,000	
Deduct:		
Purchased retained earnings	$ 320,000	
Minority interest (20% of $580,000)	116,000	$116,000
	$ 436,000	$116,000
	$4,094,000	$116,000
Adjustments and eliminations:		
Depreciation on fair value allocations:		
Depreciation ($200,000 ÷ 10)	$ 20,000	
Amortization of goodwill ($400,000 ÷ 40)	10,000	
Unrealized intercompany gains and losses:		
Inventories:		
Downstream	30,000	
Upstream	8,000	2,000
Plant and equipment	4,000	
	$ 72,000	$ 2,000
Consolidated retained earnings	$4,022,000	
Minority interest in retained earnings		$114,000
Minority interest in capital stock:		
Common shares (20% of $600,000)		120,000
Minority interest		$234,000

The purchased retained earnings, in this illustration $320,000, comes from the analysis of the combination transaction. The interstatement eliminations for unrealized intercompany gains and losses parallel the illustrations described earlier in the chapter. The schedule of consolidated retained earnings and minority interest gives rise to the following adjustments and eliminations:

Retained earnings	20,000	
Other fixed assets		20,000
Depreciation on fair value allocations to other fixed assets		

Retained earnings	10,000	
Goodwill		10,000
Amortization of goodwill		

Retained earnings	30,000	
Inventories		30,000
Unrealized gain in inventory of Subsidiary Limited		

Retained earnings	8,000	
Minority interest	2,000	
Inventories		10,000
Unrealized gain in inventory of Parent Corporation		

Retained earnings	4,000	
Other fixed assets		4,000
Unrealized gain on fixed asset transaction $5,000, net of depreciation of $1,000		

In the circumstances of the illustration an intra-balance sheet elimination is required for the intercompany receivables and payables of $15,000, as indicated by the additional information supplied on page 461.

Current liabilites	15,000	
Monetary assets		15,000
Intra-balance sheet elimination		

The final step is to assemble the data to prepare the consolidated balance sheet. The amounts to be shown for 3 items — (1) goodwill, (2) consolidated retained earnings, and (3) minority interest — are supported by the schedules used to assemble consolidated data. Except for consolidated retained earnings, the shareholders' equity section of the consolidated balance sheet is identical to the shareholders' equity section of Parent Corporation's separate entity balance sheet. The line-by-line detail for the identifiable assets and liabilities to be shown on the consolidated balance sheet is determined in accordance with the following formula:

Parent Corporation at book value	XXX
Subsidiary Limited at book value	XXX
± Parent's pro-rata share of fair value increments	XXX
± Subsequent realization of fair value increments, as applicable	XXX
+ Unrealized intercompany losses	XXX
− Unrealized intercompany gains	XXX
	XXX

Other fixed assets illustrate the application of this formula, as follows:

	Other Fixed Assets
Parent Corporation at book value	$3,000,000
Subsidiary Limited at book value	1,090,000
	$4,090,000
Fair value allocations	200,000
	$4,290,000
Subsequent realization	$ 20,000
Unrealized intercompany gain	4,000
	$ 24,000
Consolidated	$4,266,000

The consolidated balance sheet one year later is presented below.

Parent Corporation and Subsidiary Limited
Consolidated Balance Sheet
One Year Following Date of Acquisition

Monetary assets ($150,000 + $51,000 − $15,000)	$186,000
Inventories ($350,000 + $80,000 − $30,000 − $10,000)	390,000
Land ($200,000 + $25,000 + $100,000)	325,000
Other fixed assets	4,266,000
Identifiable intangibles	750,000
Goodwill	390,000
	$6,307,000
Current liabilities ($100,000 + $66,000 − $15,000)	$ 151,000
Long-term debt	400,000
Minority interest	234,000
Common shares	1,500,000
Retained earnings	4,022,000
	$6,307,000

To elaborate on subsequent consolidation, and to further explain the multi-period effects on interstatement eliminations, the Parent Corporation and Subsidiary Limited illustration will now be extended to two years after date of acquisition. The individual financial statements and additional information, are summarized below.

Parent Corporation and Subsidiary Limited
Summarized Financial Date
Two Years Following Date of Acquisition

	Parent Corporation	Subsidiary Limited
Sales	$2,376,000	$1,400,000
Investment income	16,000	
Management fees	24,000	
	$2,416,000	$1,400,000

Parent Corporation and Subsidiary Limited
Summarized Financial Date
Two Years Following Date of Acquisition

	Parent Corporation	Subsidiary Limited
Cost of sales.....................................	$1,560,000	$ 770,000
Operating expenses	156,000	230,000
	$1,716,000	$1,000,000
Net income	$ 700,000	$ 400,000
Dividends paid:		
Common shares............................	50,000	20,000
Earnings retained in the business	$ 650,000	$ 380,000
Retained earnings (opening)	3,950,000	580,000
Retained earnings (closing)	$4,600,000	$ 960,000
Monetary assets................................	$ 200,000	$ 80,000
Inventories.....................................	400,000	100,000
Investment in Subsidiary Limited (at cost)	1,500,000	
Land	200,000	25,000
Other fixed assets	3,700,000	1,445,000
Identifiable intangibles	650,000	
	$6,650,000	$1,650,000
Current liabilities	$ 150,000	$ 90,000
Long-term debt.................................	400,000	
Common shares................................	1,500,000	600,000
Retained earnings	4,600,000	960,000
	$6,650,000	$1,650,000

Additional information (in addition to information previously provided):

1. During the year just ended Parent Corporation's sales to Subsidiary Limited increased to $300,000. Subsidiary Limited's inventory purchased intercompany increased to $80,000, including $20,000 of goods purchased during the preceding year. During the current period, Parent Corporation's average markup on based selling prices increased from 60 per cent to 65 per cent.

2. During the year just ended Subsidiary Limited's sales included $200,000 of merchandise sold to Parent Corporation. At year end 25 per cent of this merchandise is still in Parent Corporation's inventory (all goods in inventory were acquired during the current period). Subsidiary Limited marks up the merchandise it sells to Parent Corporation 45 per cent based on selling prices.

3. An analysis of intercompany receivables and payables indicates that Subsidiary Limited owes Parent Corporation $40,000.

4. Because of the increased volume of intercompany transactions, and with a view toward the integration of operations, Parent Corporation decided at the beginning of the current period to charge Subsidiary Limited's management fee of $2,000 per month.

Parent Corporation and Subsidiary Limited
Analysis of Combination Transaction
Two Years Following Date of Acquisition

Purchase price	$1,500,000
Book value acquired (80%):	
Common shares (80% of $600,000)	$ 480,000
Retained earnings (80% of $400,000)	320,000
	$ 800,000
Purchase discrepancy	$ 700,000
Fair value allocation (80%):	
Land	$ 100,000
Other fixed assets	200,000
	$ 300,000
Goodwill at date of acquisition	$ 400,000
Amortization ($400,000 ÷ 40 × 2)	20,000
Goodwill two years later	$ 380,000

Parent Corporation and Subsidiary Limited
Consolidated Retained Earnings and Minority Interest
Two Years Following Date of Acquisition

	Consolidated Retained Earnings	Minority Interest
Retained earnings balances:		
Parent Corporation	$4,600,000	
Subsidiary Limited	960,000	
	$5,560,000	
Deduct:		
Purchased retained earnings	$ 320,000	
Minority interest (20% of $960,000)	192,000	$192,000
	$ 512,000	$192,000
	$5,048,000	$192,000
Adjustments and eliminations:		
Depreciation on fair value allocations:		
Depreciation ($200,000 ÷ 10 × 2)	$ 40,000	
Amortization of goodwill ($400,000 ÷ 40 × 2)	20,000	
Unrealized intercompany gains and losses:		
Inventories:		
Downstream	51,000	
Upstream	18,000	$ 4,500
Plant and equipment	3,000	
	$ 132,000	$ 4,500
Consolidated retained earnings	$4,916,000	
Minority interest in retained earnings		$187,500
Minority interest in capital stock:		
Common shares (20% of $600,000)		120,000
		$307,500

The foregoing gives rise to the following adjustments and eliminations.

Land	100,000	
Other fixed assets	200,000	
Goodwill	400,000	
Common shares	600,000	
Retained earnings	960,000	
Investment in Subsidiary Limited		1,500,000
Minority interest		312,000
Retained earnings		448,000
Investment elimination entry		
Retained earnings	40,000	
Other fixed assets		40,000
Depreciation on fair value allocations to other fixed assets		
Retained earnings	20,000	
Goodwill		20,000
Amortization of goodwill		
Retained earnings	51,000	
Inventories		51,000

Subsidiary Limited:

60% of $20,000	$12,000	
65% of 60,000	39,000	
	$51,000	

Retained earnings	18,000	
Minority interest	4,500	
Inventories		22,500
Unrealized gain in inventory of Parent Corporation		
Retained earnings	3,000	
Other fixed assets		3,000
Unrealized gain on fixed asset transaction $5,000, net of depreciation of $2,000		
Current liabilities	80,000	
Monetary assets		80,000
Intra-balance sheet elimination		

At this point, it must again be emphasized that these adjustments and eliminations are strictly for purposes of consolidation. They are not recorded in the separate entity accounts of either Parent Corporation or Subsidiary Limited. It follows, therefore, that adjustments pertaining to the realization of fair value allocations and to the amortization of goodwill must be for cumulative amounts subsequent to the date of acquisition. For purposes of balance sheet only consolidation, the interstatement eliminations for unrealized intercompany gains and losses are based on the position at the end of period date of consolidation.

It should also be noted that, for purposes of preparing a consolidated balance sheet, no elimination entry is required for unrealized intercompany gains or losses in opening inventories. This is because the effect of the elimination would be cancelled out in the determination of the closing balance of the year-end consolidated retained earnings, which includes both the sum of the beginning balance and the consolidated net income or loss.

The consolidated balance sheet two years later is presented below.

Parent Corporation and Subsidiary Limited Consolidated Balance Sheet Two Years Following Date of Acquisition	
Monetary assets ($200,000 + $80,000 − $40,000)	$ 240,000
Inventories ($400,000 + $100,000 − $51,000 − $22,500) ...	426,500
Land ($200,000 + $25,000 + $100,000)	325,000
Other fixed assets	5,302,000
Identifiable intangibles	650,000
Goodwill	380,000
	$7,323,500
Current liabilities ($150,000 + 90,000 − $40,000)	$ 200,000
Long-term debt	400,000
Minority interest	307,500
Common shares	1,500,000
Retained earnings	4,916,000
	$7,323,500

The amount shown for other fixed assets was determined as follows:

	Other Fixed Assets
Parent Corporation at book value	$3,700,000
Subsidiary Limited at book value	1,445,000
	$5,145,000
Fair value allocations	200,000
	$5,345,000
Subsequent realization	40,000
Unrealized intercompany gain	3,000
	$ 43,000
Consolidated	$5,302,000

OTHER FINANCIAL STATEMENTS

The consolidated process has traditionally been presented from a balance sheet perspective. This is certainly valid since it is indeed possible for the preparation of a consolidated balance sheet to require the whole range of consolidation adjustments and eliminations, excluding only intra-income statement eliminations. It must also be acknowledged that the consolidation of income statements has received much less attention than balance sheet consolidation; the statement of changes in financial position has been virtually ignored.[16]

For purposes of balance sheet only consolidation, operating results are subsumed within retained earnings. Therefore, income statement consolidation requires the disaggregation of the retained earnings adjustments and eliminations to the line items on the income statements and the beginning retained earnings balances affected by the adjustment or elimination. In addition, applicable intra-income statement eliminations are required.

The intercompany fixed assets transaction described on page 452 will be used to illustrate disaggregation. For purposes of balance sheet only consolidation, the required elimination at the end of the year in which the transaction occurred is repeated below.

Retained earnings	4,000	
Accumulated depreciation	1,000	
Plant and equipment		5,000

The line items on the income statements that are subsumed in the $4,000 debit to retained earnings are the $5,000 gain on asset disposal reported by Parent Corporation, and the $1,000, overstatement of depreciation expense recorded by Subsidiary Limited. Assuming the consolidation of all financials, the elimination entry at the end of the year in which the transaction occurred would be as follows:

Gain on asset disposal	5,000	
Accumulated depreciation	1,000	
Plant and equipment		5,000
Depreciation expense		1,000

Again, it must be emphasized that consolidation adjustments and eliminations are for consolidation purposes only; they are not recorded other than on the working papers or schedules used to assemble consolidated data. One year later, it is still necessary to eliminate the $5,000 intercompany gain from plant and equipment, and, by then, to eliminate $2,000 from accumulated depreciation. The $1,000 credit to depreciation expense eliminates Subsidiary Limited's current period overstatement of depreciation expense while the $4,000 debit to retained earnings which balances the elimination recognizes the impact of the intercompany transaction on the beginning of period retained earnings balances.

The several steps involved in the consolidation of all financial statements are generally similar to those that apply to balance sheet consolidation. The following steps summarize the preparation of all consolidation financials: (1) analyze the combination transaction, (2) compute consolidated net in-

---

[16]The consolidated statement of changes is prepared from the consolidated financials and other information in a manner generally similar to that described and illustrated in chapter 20. Since the objective here is to provide a basic introduction to consolidated financial statements, the consolidated statement of changes will not be covered in this chapter.

come and consolidated retained earnings, (3) compute the minority interest, if any, and (4) prepare consolidated financial statements. The computations for consolidated net income and consolidated retained earnings can be conveniently combined into one supporting schedule. This is illustrated below using the Parent Corporation and Subsidiary Limited example used earlier to illustrate balance sheet consolidation.

Parent Corporation and Subsidiary Limited
Consolidated Net Income and Consolidated Retained Earnings

	Period Ended	
	One Year Later	Two Years Later
Net income:		
Parent Corporation	$ 500,000	$ 700,000
Subsidiary Limited	200,000	400,000
	$ 700,000	$1,100,000
Dividends	$ 16,000	$ 16,000
Depreciation on fair value allocation	20,000	20,000
Amortization of goodwill	10,000	10,000
Unrealized intercompany gains and losses:		
Inventories:		
Opening		(40,000)
Closing	40,000	73,500
Plant and equipment:		
Intercompany gain	5,000	
Depreciation expense	(1,000)	(1,000)
	$ 90,000	$ 78,500
Consolidated income before		
minority interest	$ 610,000	$1,021,500
Minority interest	$ 40,000	$ 80,000
Upstream gains and losses		
Inventories	2,000	2,500 ($4,500 − $2,000)
	$ 38,000	$ 77,500
Consolidated net income	$ 572,000	$ 944,000
Dividends paid:		
Common shares	50,000	50,000
Earnings retained in the business	$ 522,000	$ 894,000
Retained earnings (opening)	3,500,000	4,022,000
Retained earnings (closing)	$4,022,000	$4,916,000

Parent Corporation accounts for its investment in Subsidiary Limited by the cost method; therefore, the dividends received from Subsidiary Limited, $16,000 (80% of $20,000), are included in Parent Corporation's separate entity net income and must be eliminated. The other items on the schedule parallel the adjustments and eliminations required to determine consolidated retained earnings for purposes of balance sheet consolidation.

The amounts shown for unrealized intercompany gains in inventories are totals resulting from both downstream and upstream transactions, determined as follows:

	Period Ended	
	One Year Later	Two Years Later
Unrealized intercompany gains in inventories:		
Downstream	$30,000	$51,000
Upstream	10,000	22,500
	$40,000	$73,500

If there is a minority interest in the subsidiary, Section 1600 of the *Accounting Recommendations* requires that any unrealized intercompany gains and losses on upstream transactions be eliminated proportionately between the majority and minority interests. This allocation impacts on the minority interest line of the consolidated income statement; it does not affect cost of goods sold. This is because the minority interest in the income of the one or more subsidiaries being consolidated is presented as a one-line item on the consolidated income statement. The consolidated income statements below and on page 473 illustrate the presentation of the minority interest.

As previously noted, income statement consolidation requires applicable intra-income statement eliminations. Those required in the example are presented below.

Period Ended One Year Later

Sales	300,000	
Cost of sales		300,000

Period Ended Two Years Later

Sales	500,000	
Cost of sales		500,000
Management fees	24,000	
Operating expenses		24,000

The final step is the preparation of the consolidated financials. The balance sheets are the same as those presented earlier in the chapter. The consolidated income statements follow:

Parent Corporation and Subsidiary Limited Consolidated Income Statement One Year Following Date of Acquisition	
Sales ($1,500,000 + $800,000 − $300,000)	$2,000,000
Cost of sales ($900,000 + $400,000 − $300,000 + $40,000)	$1,040,000
Operating expenses (per schedule)	350,000
	$1,390,000
Consolidated income before minority interest	$ 610,000
Minority interest	38,000
Consolidated net income	572,000

Parent Corporation and Subsidiary Limited
Consolidated Income Statement
Two Years Following Date of Acquisition

Sales ($2,376,000 + $1,400,000 − $500,000)	$3,276,000
Cost of sales ($1,560,000 + $770,000 − $500,000 − $40,000 + $73,500)	$1,863,500
Operating expenses (per schedule)	391,000
	$2,254,500
Consolidated income before minority interest	$1,021,500
Minority interest	77,500
Consolidated net income	$ 944,000

The consolidated amounts for operating expenses were determined as follows:

Operating Expenses

	Period Ended	
	One Year Later	Two Years Later
Parent Corporation	$121,000	$156,000
Subsidiary Limited..............................	200,000	230,000
	$321,000	$386,000
Depreciation on fair value allocation	$ 20,000	$ 20,000
Amortization of goodwill	10,000	10,000
Depreciation expense............................	(1,000)	(1,000)
Management fees expense		(24,000)
	$ 29,000	$ 5,000
	$350,000	$391,000

EQUITY METHOD OF ACCOUNTING

The equity method of accounting has already been covered in chapter 10. The objective in this chapter is to illustrate the application of the equity method using a more complex example then was possible earlier. In addition, a more complex example should facilitate a better understanding of both consolidation and the equity method of accounting.

The equity method of accounting is defined in Section 3050 of the *Accounting Recommendations*, as follows:

> The equity method is a basis of accounting for long-term investments whereby the investment is initially recorded at cost and the carrying value adjusted thereafter to include the investor's pro rata share of post acquisition earnings of the investee, computed by the consolidation method. The amount of the adjustment is included in the determination of net income by the investor and the investment account of the investor is also increased or decreased to reflect the investor's share of capital transactions and prior period adjustments applicable

to post acquisition periods. Profit distributions received or receivable from an investee reduce the carrying value of the investment.[17]

In particular, it must be emphasized that this definition requires adjustment of the investment account to include the investor's proportionate share of post acquisition earnings computed by the consolidation method. This definition differs from others that may be found in some accounting literature, and from other methods that have sometimes been referred to as the equity method. These variants of equity accounting generally do not encompass those intercompany and other adjustments that are required in the preparation of consolidated financial statements. Moreover, these variants, sometimes referred to as the simple equity method, the traditional equity method, or the old equity method, are not synonymous with and should not be used as an alternative to the equity method as defined in Section 3050.

CONSOLIDATION AND THE EQUITY METHOD OF ACCOUNTING

The difference between consolidation and the equity method of accounting concerns the degree of detail reported in the financial statements. Thus, the result of failure to consolidate is one line balance sheet disclosure, and one or two line income statement disclosure, dependent on whether the investee is reporting extraordinary items, of aggregated net amounts that would be subject to detailed disclosure in consolidated statements. Accounting for an investment under the equity method results in both the net income and retained earnings of the investor being the same as the consolidated net income and consolidated retained earnings would have been if the financial statements of the investee had been consolidated with those of the investor. The consolidation and equity method alternatives must produce the same bottom line income and retained earnings figures because under the equity method the amount reflected on the income statement by the investor is net of adjustments (1) to eliminate unrealized intercompany gains and losses, and (2) to reflect the appropriate treatment of any difference between the cost of the investment and the underlying equity in the book value of the net assets of the investee as at the date of investment. In addition, both alternatives require separate income statement disclosure of the investor's proportionate share of the investee's extraordinary items, if any, and also, separate statement of retained earnings disclosure of the investor's pro-rata share of the investee's prior period adjustments, if any. Under the equity method of accounting, dividends received from an investee corporation reduce the carrying value of the investment, and accordingly do not affect the investor's income before extraordinary items. The same income effect is accomplished under consolidation by the elimination of dividends received from the investee corporation.

[17]*CICA Handbook: Accounting Recommendations*, Section 3050, *op. cit.*, par. .03(c).

More specifically, the equity method of accounting requires adjustment of the investee's income before extraordinary items for: (1) depreciation and amortization on that part of the purchase discrepancy, if any, applicable to depreciable assets and identifiable intangibles, (2) amortization on that part of the purchase discrepancy, if any, attributable to goodwill, (3) intercompany gains and losses recorded by the investee that are unconfirmed by transactions with parties external to the intercorporate relationship, and (4) unconfirmed intercompany gains and losses recorded by the investor. It should also be noted that the adjustment of the investee's income before extraordinary items for the unconfirmed intercompany gains and losses recorded by the investor requires the elimination of an amount that does not enter into the measurement of income by the investee as a separate corporate entity. This adjustment, however, is necessary if the net income of the investor under the equity method is to be the same as the consolidated net income would have been assuming the financial statements of the investee had been consolidated with those of the investor. Section 1600 of the *Accounting Recommendations* permits separate provision in the investor's financials because adjustment against investment income might be potentially misleading given the amount reported on the balance sheet for the related investment. This separate provision alternative does not alter income before extraordinary items. The investor's unrealized gains and losses are instead charged or credited to cost of goods sold or other income statement captions, excluding only the line item investment income.

It should also be noted that the equity method of accounting is not a valid substitute for consolidation. Thus, for subsidiaries it has to be concluded that the detail disclosed by consolidation is indeed important. The alternative, remember, is aggregated net one line disclosure on the balance sheet, and one or two line disclosure on the income statement. The real issue here is the impact of these disclosure alternatives on the information content of the financial statements, and, in turn, on financial ratios. For example, consider the debt-equity ratio: under the consolidation method, investee debt is combined with that of the investor, subject to the elimination of intercompany debt; under the equity method, investee debt is netted in the one line balance sheet disclosure of the investment. Obviously, the resulting debt-equity ratio may be very different if the investee's financials are consolidated as opposed to the investment being accounted for under the equity method.

APPLICATION OF THE EQUITY METHOD

All subsidiaries should be consolidated except in rare circumstances when one or more subsidiaries may be excluded from consolidation and, instead, be accounted for by the equity method (or the cost method, depending on the circumstances). To illustrate the equity method, it will be assumed that circumstances apply to the Parent Corporation and Subsidiary Limited example that would permit the use of equity accounting.

The equity method of accounting requires the recognition of all consolidation adjustments and eliminations that impact on earnings. This is accomplished in the computation of the *equity pick-up*, which is the amount of investment income to be accrued by the investor corporation. Under the equity method of accounting, there is no counterpart for the intra-statement eliminations which are required under the consolidation alternative. This is because intra-statement eliminations do not impact on bottom-line income measurement.

The computation of the equity pick-up for the Parent Corporation and Subsidiary Limited example is presented below.

Subsidiary Limited		
Net income	200,000	400,000
Parent Corporation		
Pro-rata share (80%)	160,000	320,000
Adjustments:		
Depreciation on fair value allocation	20,000	20,000
Amortization of goodwill	10,000	10,000
Unrealized intercompany gains and losses		
Inventories:		
Downstream	30,000	21,000
Upstream (80%)	8,000	10,000
Plant and equipment:		
Intercompany gain	5,000	
Depreciation expense	(1,000)	(1,000)
	72,000	60,000
Equity pick-up	88,000	260,000

The treatment of the unrealized intercompany gains in the above schedule merits two general comments: (1) in the case of upstream transactions, the adjustment is for the investor corporation's pro-rata share of unrealized intercompany gains and losses, and (2) subsequent to the period in which the investment was made, the adjustment for unrealized intercompany gains and losses in inventories is based on the inventory change during the period, i.e., the adjustment nets the amounts that pertain to opening and closing inventories. Thus, the amounts shown for inventories in the schedule for the second year of the two-year period subsequent to the investment are determined as follows:

	Downstream	Upstream	
Closing inventory	$51,000	$18,000	(80% of $22,500)
Opening inventory	30,000	8,000	(80% of $10,000)
Adjustment	$21,000	$10,000	

The equity pick-up is recorded by Parent Corporation as follows:

Investment in Subsidiary Limited 88,000
    Equity in earnings of Subsidiary Limited 88,000
Period ended one year subsequent to the investment

Investment in Subsidiary Limited 260,000
    Equity in earnings of Subsidiary Limited 260,000
Period ended two years subsequent to the investment

Since Parent Corporation accounts for its investment by the cost method, the dividends received from Subsidiary Limited are included in income. The following entry must be made each year to transfer any dividends received from Subsidiary Limited to Parent Corporation's investment account.

Investment income 16,000
    Investment in Subsidiary Limited 16,000

A continuity of Parent Corporation's investment account under the equity method of accounting is presented below.

Investment Account (Equity Method of Accounting)	
Investment at cost	1,500,000
Equity in earnings of Subsidiary Limited	88,000
	1,588,000
Dividends	16,000
Balance one year subsequent to investment	1,572,000
Equity in earnings of Subsidiary Limited	260,000
	1,832,000
Dividends	16,000
Balance two years subsequent to investment	1,816,000

Financial statements for Parent Corporation under the equity method of accounting can now be prepared. These statements should be compared with the consolidated financials presented on pages 465, 469, 472 and 473. In particular, note that the statements show the same amounts for both net income and retained earnings. The statements should also be examined for the different degrees of detailed disclosure they provide.

Parent Corporation Income Statements		
	Period Ended	
	One Year Later	Two Years Later
Sales	1,500,000	2,376,000
Gain on asset disposal	5,000	
Equity in earnings of Subsidiary Limited	88,000	260,000
Management fees.................................		24,000
	1,593,000	2,660,000

Cost of sales	900,000	1,560,000
Operating expenses	121,000	156,000
	1,021,000	1,716,000
Net income	572,000	944,000

Parent Corporation
Balance Sheets

	One Year Later	Two Years Later
Monetary assets	150,000	200,000
Inventories	350,000	400,000
Investment in Subsidiary Limited	1,572,000	1,816,000
Land	200,000	200,000
Other fixed assets	3,000,000	3,700,000
Identifiable intangibles	750,000	650,000
	6,022,000	6,966,000
Current liabilities	100,000	150,000
Long-term debt	400,000	400,000
Common shares	1,500,000	1,500,000
Retained earnings	4,022,000	4,916,000
	6,022,000	6,966,000

APPENDIX: WORK SHEET CONSOLIDATION

Working papers provide a widely used methodology for the preparation of consolidated financial statements. Moreover, detailed work sheets to support consolidated financial statements are an obvious requirement in accounting practice. This appendix illustrates the use of working papers to prepare a consolidated balance sheet for Parent Corporation and Subsidiary Limited one year following the date of acquisition.

There is considerable variation in the format of the working papers used to prepare consolidated financial statements. In general, however, the format provides separate columns for the balance sheets (or trial balances) of the parent company and each subsidiary corporation, two columns for adjustments and eliminations, and one column to assemble consolidated data. Completion of the work sheet is mechanical; the challenge lies in determining the adjustments and eliminations to be posted to the working papers. For the example, the adjustments and eliminations are presented in journal entry form on pages 462 and 464. The completed work sheet follows.

Parent Corporation and Subsidiary Limited
Consolidated Work Sheet
One Year Following Date of Acquisition

	Parent Corporation	Subsidiary Limited	Adjustments and Eliminations Dr.	Adjustments and Eliminations Cr.	Consolidated
Monetary assets	$ 150,000	$ 51,000	$	$ 15,000	$ 186,000
Inventories	350,000	80,000		30,000	390,000
				10,000	
Investment in Subsidiary Limited	1,500,000			1,500,000	
Land	200,000	25,000	100,000		325,000
Other fixed assets (net)	3,000,000	1,290,000	200,000	20,000	4,266,000
				4,000	
Identifiable intangibles	750,000				750,000
Goodwill			400,000	10,000	390,000
	$5,950,000	$1,246,000			$6,307,000
Current liabilities	$ 100,000	$ 66,000	$ 15,000		$ 151,000
Long-term debt	400,000				400,000
Minority interest			2,000	236,000	234,000
Common shares	1,500,000	600,000	600,000		1,500,000
Retained earnings	3,950,000	580,000	580,000	144,000	4,022,000
			20,000		
			10,000		
			30,000		
			8,000		
			4,000		
	$5,950,000	$1,246,000	$1,969,000	$1,969,000	$6,307,000

QUESTIONS

1. Distinguish between a parent corporation and a subsidiary corporation.

2. What is a business combination? Explain how a business combination might also simultaneously be an intercorporate investment. In what circumstances would a long-term intercorporate investment not also qualify as a business combination?

3. Distinguish between combined statements and consolidated statements.

4. Why must reciprocal items be eliminated in the preparation of consolidated financial statements? List five examples of reciprocal items.

5. Define purchase price discrepancy. How is it treated on consolidation?

6. Distinguish between fair value increments and fair value allocations. In what circumstances, if any, might they be the same?

7. How is the minority interest determined in the preparation of a consolidated balance sheet as at the date of acquisition or combination?

8. Define goodwill and negative goodwill. How should each be treated on consolidation?

9. What purposes are served by the investment elimination entry?

10. List the alternative balance sheet classifications for minority interest. Which alternatives meet the accounting standards of the profession in Canada?

11. The preparation of consolidated financial statements involves three steps. What are they?

12. Distinguish between intrastatement and interstatement eliminations. What purposes do each serve?

13. For each of the following situations state whether the required elimination is an intrastatement or interstatement elimination:
- (a) The closing inventory of Secondary Limited includes merchandise acquired from Primary Corporation;
- (b) Primary Corporation owns 10% bonds issued by Secondary Limited. These bonds were acquired at their face value;
- (c) Primary Corporation charges Secondary Limited a monthly management fee;
- (d) Secondary Limited sells merchandise to Primary Corporation. At year end, none of this merchandise is included in Primary Corporation's inventories;
- (e) Primary Corporation sold land to Secondary Limited and realized a gain on the transaction.

14. List the specific situations that give rise to the elimination of unrealized intercompany gains and losses.

15. Distinguish between downstream and upstream intercompany transactions. How should any unrealized intercompany gains and losses on such transactions be eliminated on consolidation?

16. Describe the multi-period effects of an intercompany fixed asset transaction, assuming the asset acquired intercompany is subject to depreciation.

17. Fair value allocations recognized on consolidation impact on income measurement. Explain the impact on income measurement of fair value allocations to (a) inventories, (b) land, (c) identifiable intangibles in the first year subsequent to the date of acquisition or combination.

18. List the several types of adjustments and eliminations that may arise for purposes of balance sheet consolidation as at (a) the date of acquisition or combination, and (b) a date subsequent to acquisition.

19. The formula for determining the line-by-line detail for the identifiable assets and liabilities to be shown on a date of acquisition consolidated balance sheet is given on page 456. How would this formula be expanded for purposes of subsequent balance sheet consolidation?

20. Unrealized intercompany gains and losses in opening inventories can be ignored for purposes of balance sheet consolidation. Explain why this is valid.

21. What is disaggregation, as this term is used in the context of income statement consolidation?

22. Net income under the equity method of accounting is identical to what consolidated net income would be if the investor corporation had been consolidated rather than accounted for under the equity method. Explain why this statement is valid.

Balance sheets for Combinor Corporation and Target Limited are presented below.

| | Combinor Corporation | | Target Limited | |
	Book Value	Fair Value	Book Value	Fair Value
Current assets	200,000	210,000	30,000	28,000
Plant	150,000	150,000	90,000	90,000
Accumulated depreciation	(50,000)		(20,000)	
	300,000		100,000	
Liabilities	50,000		40,000	
Share capital	150,000		50,000	
Retained earnings	100,000		10,000	
	300,000		100,000	

12-1. Combinor Corporation purchases the net assets of Target Limited for $100,000. After this transaction Target is to wind-up.

Record journal entries as they would appear in the accounts of (a) Combinor Corporation, and (b) Target Limited.

12-2. Prepare a balance sheet for Combinor Corporation after giving effect to its purchase of Target's net assets as described in exercise 12-1.

12-3. Assume Combinor Corporation acquires 100 per cent of the share capital of Target Limited from Target's shareholders for $100,000, cash.

Prepare journal entries to be recorded by Combinor Corporation, and prepare a separate entity balance sheet for Combinor Corporation, giving effect to the share purchase transaction.

12-4. Based on the situation presented in exercise 12-3, prepare a consolidated balance sheet for Combinor Corporation as at the date of acquisition of Target Limited. Comment on this balance sheet relative to the one required in exercise 12-2.

12-5. Assume Combinor Corporation acquires the net assets of Target Limited in exchange for common shares of Combinor: par value, $50,000, fair value $100,000. After this transaction Target is to wind-up.

Prepare journal entries to be recorded by Combinor Corporation and by Target Limited, assuming the combination is to be accounted for as: (a) a purchase; and (b) a pooling-of-interests.

12-6. Canco issued additional shares of common stock in exchange for all the assets and liabilities of Queco and Ontco on December 31, 1982. Queco and Ontco then distributed their Canco shares to their shareholders and wound up on the same date. Balance sheets immediately prior to the combination are presented below.

	Canco	Queco	Ontco
Current assets	200,000	50,000	20,000
Plant assets — net	1,000,000	400,000	205,000
Total	1,200,000	450,000	225,000

	Canco	Queco	Ontco
Current liabilities	100,000	30,000	25,000
Long-term debt	300,000	100,000	100,000
Common shares (par $10)	300,000	90,000 (par $9)	50,000 (par $10)
Retained Earnings	500,000	230,000	50,000
	1,200,000	450,000	225,000

The common share exchange ratio was negotiated to be 1:1 for both Queco and Ontco.

Prepare Canco's journal entries to record the combination of Canco, Queco and Ontco.

(a) assuming pooling-of-interests accounting is used

(b) assuming purchase accounting is used and the identifiable assets and liabilities of Queco and Ontco as reported on the balance sheets above are equal to their fair values at December 31, 1982. Assume that Canco's common shares are traded at $30 on December 31, 1982.

12-7. On December 31, 1981, the condensed balance sheets of Avid Corporation and Shy Limited appear as follows:

	Avid	Shy
Monetary assets	$ 300,000	$ 200,000
Non-monetary assets	1,700,000	1,300,000
Total	$2,000,000	$1,500,000
Monetary liabilities	$ 100,000	$ 150,000
Common shares (par $10) ...	500,000	——
Common shares (par $50) ...	——	500,000
Contributed surplus	100,000	500,000
Retained earnings	1,300,000	350,000
	$2,000,000	$1,500,000

The monetary assets and monetary liabilities of both companies have fair values that are equal to their carrying values. The fair values of Avid's non-monetary assets are $2,000,000. The fair values of Shy's non-monetary assets are $1,700,000.

These two companies can effect a business combination by several different approaches. Described below are two possibilities. These two cases are completely *independent*. For each, you are to prepare the combined balance sheet at acquisition. In selecting the accounting method to be used the requirements of Section 1580 must be met.

(1) Avid issues 40,000 of its shares in return for all of the outstanding shares of Shy. The shares of Shy are cancelled and Shy ceases to exist as a legal entity. At the date of acquisition, Avid's shares are trading at $50 per share.

(2) A new company is formed to acquire all the net assets of both Avid and Shy. The new company issues 10,000 shares of its stock to Avid Corporation and 10,000 of its shares to Shy Limited. The shares are without nominal or par value. Subsequent to the combination, the shares of the new company trade at $225 per share.

12-8. Financial data for Horse Limited and Radish Limited as at December 31, 1982 are indicated below:

| | Horse Limited | | Radish Limited | |
	Book Value	Fair Value	Book Value	Fair Value
Current assets	$ 4,000	$4,500	$ 3,000	$3,000
Land	3,000	9,600	1,000	3,000
Building	10,000	9,600	7,000	6,200
Accumulated Depreciation	(3,000)	(3,200)	(1,000)	
Goodwill	1,000	9,800		
	$15,000		$10,000	
Current liabilities	$ 1,000	$1,000	$ 1,000	$1,000
Bonds payable	5,000	4,800	2,000	1,800
Common shares	6,000		2,000	
Retained earnings	3,000		5,000	
	$15,000		$10,000	

Effective December 31, 1982, Horse Limited acquires 100 per cent of Radish Limited's common shares in exchange for 800 common shares of Horse Limited, fair market value $10 per share and $2,500 cash. Prepare a consolidated balance sheet as at December 31, 1982.

(OISA adapted)

12-9. On December 31 of the current year Peerless Company Ltd. purchased 90 per cent of the shares of Sanders Company Ltd. The data reported on their separate balance sheets immediately after the acquisition are reported below. The fair value of Sanders Company's assets correspond to their carrying amounts, except for equipment, which is valued at $175,000. Prepare a consolidated balance sheet as at that date omitting captions for current assets, plant assets, etc.

Assets	Peerless Company	Sanders Company
Cash	$ 22,000	$ 8,000
Accounts receivable (net)	35,000	21,000
Inventories	143,000	46,000
Investment in Sanders Company	250,000	——
Equipment (net)	400,000	165,000
	$850,000	$240,000

Liabilities and Shareholders' Equity		
Accounts payable	$ 50,000	$ 13,000
Common shares, $10 par	500,000	150,000
Retained earnings	300,000	77,000
	$850,000	$240,000

12-10. The results of operation of Carter Company Ltd. and its wholly owned subsidiary, Duncan Enterprises Ltd., for the current year ended June 30 appear on the next page. During the year Carter sold merchandise to Duncan for $70,000; the merchandise was sold by Duncan to non-affiliated companies for $100,000. Carter's interest income was realized from a long-term loan to Duncan.

	Carter		Duncan	
Sales		$620,000		$300,000
Cost of goods sold	$420,000		$190,000	
Selling expenses	75,000		30,000	
General expenses	60,000		40,000	
Interest income	(8,000)		——	
Interest expense	——	547,000	8,000	268,000
		$ 73,000		$ 32,000

Instructions:

(a) Prepare a consolidated income statement for the current year for Carter and its subsidiary. Use the single-step form and disregard income taxes.

(b) If none of the merchandise sold by Carter to Duncan had been sold during the year to non-affiliated companies, and assuming that Carter's cost of the merchandise had been $50,000, determine the amounts that would have been reported on the consolidated income statement for the following items:
(1) Sales, (2) Cost of goods sold, (3) Net income.

PROBLEMS

12-1A. A Limited is considering a business combination with either B Limited or C Limited. Since all three companies use a calendar fiscal year, the proposed combination would take effect on December 31, 1982. Either proposed combination would be carried out by exchanges of common shares. Since the shares of A Limited are more highly favored on the stock exchange than the shares of the other two companies, a combination would result in A Limited issuing a certain number of shares in exchange for all the outstanding shares of either B Limited or C Limited. Estimated comparative information for the three companies for fiscal 1982 (before either of the proposed combinations) follows:

	A Limited	B Limited	C Limited
Assets	$10,000,000	$10,000,000	$10,000,000
Liabilities	8,000,000	7,000,000	7,500,000
Shareholders' equity	2,000,000	3,000,000	2,500,000
Number of shares outstanding........	500,000	500,000	500,000
Earnings (loss) per share	1.00	1.00	(1.00)
Market price per share	30.00	10.00	4.00
Number of shares of B Limited or C Limited required to be exchanged for one share of A Limited	——	2	5

An analysis of the fair values of the net identifiable assets of B Limited and C Limited reveals the following excess of fair values over book values:

	B Limited	C Limited
Land	$1,500,000	——
Fixed Assets	400,000	$100,000
Inventory	200,000	300,000

The estimated remaining life of B Limited's and C Limited's fixed assets are eight and ten years, respectively. In both companies, inventory turns over three times a year.

Instructions:

Based on the assumption that either proposed combination could be accounted for as a purchase or as a pooling-of-interests, compute the eight consolidated amounts for A Limited required to complete the following comparative schedule.

		Combination of A Limited		
A Limited consolidated as at December 31, 1982		with B Limited		with C Limited
Total assets	X	X	X	X
Earnings per share	X	X	X	X

Show supporting computations. (CICA adapted)

12-2A. The condensed balance sheet of Douglas Limited as of June 30, 1982 appears as follows:

ASSETS

Cash		$ 96,000
Receivables		125,500
Inventory		176,500
Prepaid expenses		19,000
		$417,000
Land	$ 50,000	
Buildings & equipment.....................................	854,500	
Accumulated Depreciation	(236,500)	668,000
Deferred Financing charges		$ 42,000
		$1,127,000

EQUITIES

Accounts payable		$ 89,800
Income taxes payable		126,200
		$ 216,000
Bonds payable, due 1982		300,000
Common shares	$250,000	
Retained earnings	361,000	$ 611,000
		$1,127,000

Effective July 1, 1982, Douglas Limited acquires 70 per cent of the outstanding common shares of Brown Corporation Limited for the following consideration:

Cash	$	50,000
Bonds of Douglas Limited due 1982		50,000
	$	100,000

The condensed balance sheet of Brown Corporation Limited as at June 30, 1982 is presented below.

	Book Value	Fair Value
Cash	$ 6,000	$ 6,000
Receivables	16,500	14,800
Inventory	25,500	30,000
Land	10,000	18,200
Buildings & equipment	100,000	110,000
Accumulated depreciation	(33,000)	(36,300)
Accounts payable	$ 10,500	10,000
Income tax payable	9,500	9,500
Common shares	50,000	
Retained earnings	55,000	
	$125,000	$125,000

Instructions:

Prepare a consolidated balance sheet for Douglas Limited and Subsidiary as at July 1, 1982. (OISA adapted)

12-3A. On June 30, 1981, Paul Corporation acquired for cash of $19 per share all of the outstanding voting common shares of Sand Corporation. Both companies continued to operate as separate entities and both companies have calendar fiscal years.

On June 30, 1981, after closing the nominal accounts, Sand's condensed balance sheet was as follows:

Assets:

Cash	$ 700,000
Accounts receivable, net	600,000
Inventories	1,400,000
Property, plant and equipment, net	3,300,000
Other assets	500,000
Total assets	$6,500,000

Liabilities and shareholders' equity:

Accounts payable and other current liabilities	$ 700,000
Long-term debt	2,600,000
Other liabilities	200,000
Share capital, par value $1.00 per share	1,000,000
Contributed surplus	400,000
Retained earnings	1,600,000
Total liabilities and shareholders' equity	$6,500,000

On June 30, 1981, Sand's assets and liabilities that had fair values different from their book values were as follows:

	Fair Value
Property, plant and equipment, net	$16,400,000
Other assets	200,000
Long-term debt	2,200,000

The differences between fair values and book values resulted in a charge or credit to depreciation or amortization on the consolidated statements for the six-month period ending December 31, 1981, as follows:

Property, plant and equipment, net	....	$500,000 charge
Other assets	....	10,000 credit
Long-term debt	....	5,000 charge
		$495,000 charge

The amount paid by Paul in excess of the fair values of the net identifiable assets of Sand is attributable to expected future earnings of Sand and will be amortized over the maximum allowable period.

During the six-month period ending December 31, 1981, Sand acquired merchandise from Paul at an invoice price of $500,000. The cost of the merchandise to Paul was $300,000. At December 31, 1981, one half of the merchandise was not sold and Sand had not yet paid for any of the merchandise.

The 1981 net income (loss) for both companies was as follows:

	Paul	Sand
January 1 to June 30	$ 250,000	$ (750,000)
July 1 to December 31	1,600,000	1,250,000

The $1,600,000 net income of Paul includes its equity in the net income of Sand.

On December 31, 1981, after closing the nominal accounts, the condensed balance sheets for both companies were as follows:

Assets	Paul	Sand
Cash	$ 3,500,000	$ 600,000
Accounts receivable, net	1,400,000	1,500,000
Inventories	1,000,000	2,500,000
Property, plant and equipment, net	2,000,000	3,100,000
Investment in subsidiary, at equity	20,250,000	—
Other assets	100,000	500,000
Total assets	$28,250,000	$8,200,000

Liabilities and shareholders' equity:		
Current liabilities	$ 1,500,000	$1,100,000
Long-term debt	4,000,000	2,600,000
Other liabilities	750,000	250,000
Share capital, par value $1.00 per share	10,000,000	1,000,000
Contributed surplus	5,000,000	400,000
Retained earnings	7,000,000	$2,850,000
Total liabilities and shareholders' equity	$28,250,000	$8,200,000

Instructions:
Prepare the condensed consolidated balance sheet of Paul Corporation and its wholly-owned subsidiary, Sand Corporation, as at December 31, 1981. Show supporting computations. Ignore income tax considerations.

(AICPA adapted)

12-4A. King Company acquired a 90 per cent interest in Edward Company on June 30, 1981 at a cost of $120,000. The difference between the cost of this investment and the book value acquired was attributable to a manufacturing formula held by Edward Company which was expected to have a useful life of five years from June 30, 1981. Condensed balance sheets of the two corporations as at December 31, 1981 are shown on the next page.

Balance Sheet

December 31, 1981

	King Company	Edward Company
Current assets	$172,800	$ 94,300
Investment in Edward Company	141,330	
Fixed assets (net)	153,600	57,500
Intangible assets		2,500
Cost of goods sold	346,000	138,100
Operating expenses	130,900	50,200
Dividends	20,000	12,000
	$964,630	$354,600
Current liabilities	$ 67,600	$ 15,600
Share capital	200,000	80,000
Contributed surplus		10,000
Retained earnings	153,800	25,000
Sales	511,100	224,000
Equity in earnings of Edward Company	32,130	
	$964,630	$354,600

The nominal account balances shown for Edward Company are for the six months ended December 31, 1981. Those for King Company relate to the full year.

King Company uses the equity method of accounting; however, adjustments to reflect the appropriate treatment of the purchase price discrepancy and to eliminate the effects of intercompany transactions have yet to be made.

On July 1, 1981, King Company sold an item of equipment to Edward Company realizing a gain of $10,000. The equipment has since been depreciated at an annual rate of 20 per cent applied to Edward's purchase cost.

In November, 1981, Edward Company sold a tract of land to King Company realizing a gain of $3,000.

The inventory of King Company on June 30, 1981, included goods purchased from Edward Company during 1981 on which Edward Company had realized a gain of $2,500.

Subsequent to the combination, Edward Company sold goods to King Company for $75,000, of which $12,000 remained unpaid as at December 31, 1981. The inventory of King Company at December 31, 1981 included $10,500 of these goods on which Edward Company had realized a gain of $2,100.

Instructions:

(1) Determine the amount of the purchase price discrepancy and the amount at which intangible assets (the manufacturing formula) would be shown on a consolidated balance sheet prepared at the date of acquisition.

(2) Determine the amounts for each of the following as they should appear in 1981 consolidated financials:

 (a) Current assets
 (b) Net fixed assets
 (c) Consolidated net income
 (d) Consolidated retained earnings
 (e) Minority interest

12-5A. The following data relate to P Company Ltd. and S Company Ltd., several years after P Company Ltd. acquired control of S Company Ltd. for $490,000 paid in cash:

Assets	P Company Ltd.	S Company Ltd.	Consolidated
Investment in S Company Ltd.	$ 670,000		
Other assets	1,700,000	$1,030,000	$2,500,000
Goodwill			40,000
	$2,370,000	$1,030,000	$2,540,000

Liabilities & Shareholders' Equity			
Bonds payable	$ 500,000		$ 350,000
Other liabilities	280,000	$ 330,000	530,000
Capital stock, no par	600,000	200,000	600,000
Retained earnings	990,000	500,000	990,000
Minority interest			70,000
Total liabilities & shareholders' equity	$2,370,000	$1,030,000	$2,540,000

On the date of the combination transaction the book values of the net assets of S Company Ltd. approximated fair values. Goodwill has not been amortized because the combination took place prior to the effective date of Section 1580. Neither company has issued any shares subsequent to the combination.

Instructions:
Answer each of the following requirements. Include supporting computations and/or explanations, as appropriate.
(a) What method was used to account for the combination transaction?
(b) Determine the percentage of shares in S Company Ltd. owned by P Company Ltd.
(c) Determine the face value of bonds issued by P Company Ltd. now held by S Company Ltd.
(d) If S Company Ltd. owes P Company Ltd. $70,000 on open account, how much does P Company apparently owe to S Company Ltd.?
(e) Reconcile the consolidated amount for Other assets with the combined total of Other assets for P Company Ltd. and S Company Ltd.
(f) How much of the Retained earnings of $500,000 currently reported by S Company Ltd. is included in the $990,000 Retained earnings shown on the consolidated balance sheet?
(g) Determine S Company's retained earnings balance on the date that P Company Ltd. acquired control of S Company Ltd.
(h) Prepare the investment elimination entry as at the date of the consolidated balance sheet.

12-6A. The Black Corporation purchased an 80 per cent interest in the voting shares of Champion Company on January 1, 1978, for $720,000. The total shareholders' equity of Champion at that time was $800,000. Since book values approximated fair values, the excess cost is attributable to goodwill which is to be amortized over the maximum period provided for in section 1580 of the *Accounting Recommendations*.

On January 1, 1979, Black purchased equipment from Champion at a cost of $15,000. Champion's net book value was $9,000. The equipment has a remaining useful life of 5 years and is being depreciated using the sum-of-the-years-digits method with no salvage value.

During 1980 Black sold $100,000 of merchandise to Champion. The selling price included a 25 per cent markup on cost. Champion still owes $17,500 on open account and 20 per cent of the goods are in Champion's inventory at December 31, 1980.

Champion sold $50,000 of merchandise to Black during 1980. The gross margin on sales to Black and to unrelated firms is equal and has not changed from previous years. Black held $36,000 of goods acquired from Champion in its opening inventory and $30,000 in its closing inventory.

Black billed Champion $5,000 for consulting services. The charge was expensed by Champion and included in sales by Black.

On November 1, 1980, Champion borrowed $30,000 from Black issuing twelve per cent, 90-day notes for $2,500 each.

The following separate entity income statements were prepared for 1980.

	Black Corporation	Champion Company
Sales	$200,000	$150,000
Cost of goods sold	130,000	100,000
Gross margin	$ 70,000	$ 50,000
Operating expenses	36,000	30,000
	$ 34,000	$ 20,000
Interest income	1,200	
Net income	$ 35,200	$ 20,000

Instructions:
Prepare a consolidated income statement for 1980.

12-7A. The individual and consolidated statements of companies P and S for the year ending December 31, 1982 are as follows:

Balance Sheets
as at December 31, 1982

	Consolidated	P Company	S Company
Cash and accounts receivable	$ 194,800	$ 70,000	$ 216,000
Inventories	244,000	80,000	180,000
Fixed assets (including land)	1,128,000	818,000	230,000
Investment in S Company		592,000	
Portfolio investments	56,000		256,000
Goodwill	28,000		
	$1,650,800	$1,560,000	$ 882,000
Accounts payable and accrued liabilities	$ 116,000	$ 138,400	$ 56,000
Dividend declared and unpaid	24,800	21,600	16,000
Mortgage bonds — 5%	290,000	400,000	90,000
Capital stock	600,000	600,000	400,000
Retained earnings	476,000	400,000	320,000
Minority interest	144,000		
	$1,650,800	$1,560,000	$ 882,000

Income Statements
Year Ended December 31, 1982

	Consolidated	P Company	S Company
Sales	$1,520,000	$1,200,000	$ 800,000
Cost of sales	806,000	720,000	560,000
Selling and administrative expenses			
including bond interest	382,200	276,400	115,000
	$1,188,200	$ 996,400	$ 675,000
	331,800	203,600	125,000
Investment income	2,000	25,600	12,000
	333,800	229,200	137,000
Income tax	179,000	112,000	67,000
	$ 154,800		
Minority interest	14,000		
Net income	$ 140,800	$ 117,200	$ 70,000
Dividends	43,200	43,200	32,000
Transfer to retained earnings	$ 97,600	$ 74,000	$ 38,000

P Company purchased its 80 per cent interest in S Company on December 31, 1977. At that time, it was decided that consolidated financials should be prepared in accordance with Section 1600 of the *Accounting Recommendations*.

Except for a difference of $100,000 between the fair value of land and its recorded book value, S Company's book values on December 31, 1977 approximated fair values. Goodwill is being amortized over a period of forty years.

P Company sells its product in part to S Company for further processing, and in part to other firms. The inventories of S Company included an intercompany markup at both the beginning and end of the year. Cash transfers are made between the companies according to working capital needs.

S Company's portfolio investments include $200,000 of P Company's bonds acquired at face value. Prior to the current fiscal period S Company had not paid dividends.

Instructions:
On the basis of the information you can develop from an analysis of the individual and consolidated statements, answer each of the following questions. Show all computations necessary to support your answers.

(a) Does P Company carry its Investment in S on the cost or equity basis? State the reasons for your conclusion.
(b) What was the balance of S's Retained earnings at the date of acquisition?
(c) Prepare a schedule analysing the combination transaction as at the date of acquisition.
(d) Prepare a reconciliation schedule which will explain clearly the difference between P Company's Retained earnings at December 31, 1982, $400,000, and the Consolidated Retained earnings at December 31, 1982, $476,000.
(e) Prepare a schedule reconciling the sum of the Cost of sales of P and S individually with the Consolidated Cost of sales. Show clearly the intercompany markup in the beginning and ending inventories of S Company and how you determined the amounts.

(f) Show the amounts of intercompany debts, excluding the bonds, and show which company is the debtor and which is the creditor in each instance.
(g) What are the components of the Minority interest on the consolidated balance sheet?   (CICA adapted)

12-8A. The individual and consolidated statements of companies X and Y for the year ending December 31, 1982 are as follows:

	X Company	Y Company	Consolidated
Cash and receivables	$ 35,000	$211,000	$200,400
Inventories	40,000	90,000	122,000
Plant (net)	460,000	140,000	635,000
Investment in Y	245,000		
	$780,000	$441,000	$957,400
Current payables	$ 70,000	$ 23,000	$ 53,000
Dividends payable	10,000	8,000	12,400
Mortgage bonds	200,000	50,000	250,000
Capital stock	300,000	200,000	300,000
Retained earnings	200,000	160,000	234,000
Minority interest			108,000
	$780,000	$441,000	$957,400
Sales...............................	$600,000	$400,000	$760,000
Cost of sales	360,000	280,000	403,000
Gross profit	$240,000	$120,000	$357,000
Operating expenses	130,000	54,000	184,000
Operating profit	$110,000	$ 66,000	$173,000
Interest income	1,800	5,000	1,800
Dividend income	11,200	-0-	-0-
Total	$123,000	$ 71,000	$174,800
Interest expense	$ 10,000	$ 3,000	$ 8,000
Provision for income taxes	56,000	34,000	90,000
Minority share			10,200
Net income	$ 57,000	$ 34,000	$ 66,600
Dividends..........................	20,000	$ 16,000	$ 20,000
Transfer to retained earnings	$ 37,000	$ 18,000	$ 46,600

X Company purchased its 70 per cent interest in Y Company several years ago. The consolidated amount of $635,000 shown for plant (net) includes a $35,000 fair value allocation determined at the date that X Company acquired its interest in Y.

X Company sells its product in part to Y Company for further processing, and in part to other firms. The inventories of Y Company included an intercompany markup at both the beginning and end of the year. Cash transfers are made between the companies according to working capital needs.

Instructions:

On the basis of the information you can develop from an analysis of the individual and consolidated statements, answer the questions below. Show clearly all computations necessary to support your answers.

(a) Does X Company carry its Investment in Y on the cost or equity basis? State the reason for your conclusion.
(b) What was the balance of Y's Retained earnings at date of acquisition?
(c) Prepare a reconciliation schedule which will explain clearly the difference

between X Company's Retained earnings at December 31, 1982, $200,000, and the Consolidated Retained earnings at December 31, 1982, $234,000.

(d) Show the amounts of intercompany debts, and show which company is the debtor and which is the creditor in each instance.

(e) Prepare a schedule reconciling the sum of the Cost of sales of X and Y individually with the Consolidated Cost of sales. Show clearly the intercompany markup in the beginning and ending inventories of Y Company and how you determined the amounts.

(f) What are the components of the Minority interest on the consolidated balance sheet?   (AICPA adapted)

12-9A. Expansion Limited has decided to adopt the equity method of accounting for its 40 per cent common share interest in Investee Limited which it acquired on July 1, 1981 at a cost of $15,000,000.

On July 1, 1981, the shareholders' equity section of Investee Limited's balance sheet appeared as follows:

Preferred shares, 8% non-cumulative, $100 par value . . . . $ 5,000,000
Common shares, $50 par value 10,000,000
Contributed surplus 8,000,000
Retained earnings 11,000,000

The only material difference between book and fair value as at July 1, 1981 were:

	Book Value	Fair Value
Land	$2,000,000	$ 3,000,000
Building (remaining useful life, ten years)	8,000,000	10,000,000
Accumulated depreciation	2,000,000	

For the year ended June 30, 1982, Investee Limited's income statement showed income before extraordinary items in the amount of $2,500,000 and a net income of $2,000,000 including a profit of $150,000 on sales to Expansion Limited. The statement of retained earnings showed that per share dividends of $8 on the preferred shares and $5 on the common shares had been paid by Investee Limited. Expansion Limited credits dividends received to its investment account.

As at June 30, 1981, Expansion Limited held inventory costing $1,200,000 on which a profit of $200,000 had been recorded by Investee Limited. One year later, Expansion's inventory included 25 per cent of the items acquired from Investee prior to July 1, 1981 and 50 per cent of the items acquired since that date.

In June, 1982, Expansion Limited sold some merchandise to Investee for $500,000 which was included in Investee's inventory as at June 30, 1982. This merchandise had cost Expansion Limited $400,000.

The 1982 summarized financial statements for Expansion Limited as a separate legal entity and before recording any equity pick-up are presented below:

Sales	$25,000,000
Cost of goods sold	15,600,000
Expenses	4,400,000
	20,000,000
Net income	5,000,000
Dividends paid	500,000
Earnings retained in the business	4,500,000
Retained earnings, July 1, 1981	25,500,000
	$30,000,000

Net monetary assets	$ 5,000,000
Inventory	8,400,000
Investment in Investee Limited	14,600,000
Fixed assets (net) ›	12,000,000
	$40,000,000
Common shares	$10,000,000
Retained earnings	30,000,000
	$40,000,000

Instructions:

(1) Prepare an income statement for Expansion Limited for the year ended June 30, 1982. Expansion Limited wishes to show the maximum amount of net income that is consistent with the accounting standards of the profession in Canada.

(2) Prepare a balance sheet for Expansion Limited as at June 30, 1982.

(OISA adapted)

12-10A. Brighton Corporation acquired 80 per cent of the 1,250 shares of $100 par value common of Solvo Corporation on July 1, 1982 for $208,600. Brighton uses the "old" equity method of accounting for its investment in Solvo.

The December 31, 1982 balance sheets for both companies appear below:

Balance Sheets
December 31, 1982

Assets	Brighton	Solvo
Cash	150,000	20,000
Accounts receivable	205,000	55,000
Notes receivable	180,000	11,000
Notes receivable discounted	(4,000)	
Accrued interest receivable	1,600	400
Dividends receivable	6,400	
Inventories	300,000	75,000
Plant and equipment	794,000	280,600
Allowance for depreciation	(260,000)	(30,000)
Investment in Solvo Corporation	217,400	
Investment in Solvo Corporation bonds	40,000	
Advance to Solvo Corporation	35,000	
Totals	$1,665,400	$412,000

Liabilities and Shareholders' Equity		
Accounts payable	220,400	54,800
Notes payable	142,000	24,200
Dividends payable		8,000
Accrued interest payable	22,100	3,900
Other accrued liabilities	7,900	3,100
Advance from Brighton Corporation		35,000
Bonds payable	600,000	85,000
Capital stock	360,000	125,000
Capital in excess of par	49,000	12,000
Retained earnings	264,000	61,000
Totals	$1,665,400	$412,000

The following information is also available:

(1) Solvo reported net income and dividends for 1982 as follows:

Net income for six months ending:
June 30	$10,000
December 31	20,000

Dividends declared:
March 31	4,000
June 30	4,000
September 30	1,000
December 31	8,000

(2) Data pertaining to 1982 intercompany sales and ending inventories were as follows:

Intercompany sales:
January 1 to June 30	$40,000	$ 95,000
July 1 to December 31	60,000	105,000
Markup on cost	20%	25%
Intercompany payable at year end	13,000	$ 5,500
Year-end inventory of intercompany purchases at FIFO cost.	$25,000	$ 18,000

(3) Sales of equipment by Brighton to Solvo during 1982 were as follows:

Date	Book Value on Brighton's Records	Price Paid by Solvo	Depreciation Method	Estimated Life
February 1	$11,000	$13,500	Double-declining balance	10 years
October 1	14,000	12,200	Straight-line	5 years

For depreciation purposes Solvo estimates salvage at 10 per cent of the equipment's cost.

(4) Brighton acquired $40,000 of the 6 per cent Solvo bonds at par value on July 1, 1982. Interest is paid each July 1 and January 1 by Solvo Corporation.

(5) On December 1, 1982, Brighton discounted $4,000 of non-interest bearing notes payable at Solvo.

(6) Brighton amortizes goodwill, if any, over the maximum period permitted by Section 1580 of the *Accounting Recommendations*.

(7) Analysis of the fair values of the net assets of Solvo at the date of acquisition indicated the following items were undervalued by:

Inventories	$ 6,250
Plant and Equipment	42,500

Depreciation expense booked by Solvo from July 1 to December 31 was $2,500. Estimated remaining life of the fixed assets is 10 years. Inventory turns over twice a year.

Instructions:
Prepare a consolidated balance sheet for Brighton and Solvo, as of December 31, 1982. You may assume that both companies made all of the adjusting entries required for separate financial statements unless an obvious discrepancy exists. Income taxes should not be considered in your solution.   (AICPA adapted)

12-11A. Padre Company, a wholesaler, purchased 80 per cent of the issued and outstanding shares of Sun, Ltd., a retailer, on December 31, 1978, for $120,000. At that date Sun, Ltd., had one class of common shares outstanding at a stated value of

$100,000 and retained earnings of $30,000. Padre Company had a $50,000 deficit balance in retained earnings.

Padre Company purchased the Sun, Ltd., shares from Sun's major shareholder primarily to acquire control of signboard leases owned by Sun. The leases will expire on December 31, 1983, and Padre Company executives estimate the leases, which cannot be renewed, were worth at least $20,000 more than their carrying value when the shares were purchased.

The financial statements for both companies for the year ended December 31, 1982, follow:

Padre Company and Sun, Ltd.
1982 Financial Statements
Balance Sheet

Assets	Padre Company	Sun, Ltd.
Cash	$ 14,200	$ 17,300
Accounts receivable	80,000	76,000
Inventories	54,800	85,600
Other current assets	15,000	18,200
Investment in Sun, Ltd.	120,000	
Notes receivable	8,000	
Land	25,000	10,500
Plant and equipment	200,000	42,000
Accumulated depreciation	(102,000)	(7,000)
Signboard leases		42,000
Amortization to date		(33,600)
Total	$415,000	$251,000

Equities

	Padre Company	Sun, Ltd.
Accounts payable	$ 35,500	$ 47,000
Dividends payable		9,000
Other current liabilities	24,500	12,000
Notes payable		8,000
Common shares	300,000	100,000
Retained earnings	55,000	75,000
Total	$415,000	$251,000

Income Statement

	Padre Company	Sun, Ltd.
Sales and other revenue	$420,000	$300,000
Cost of goods sold	315,000	240,000
Gross margin	105,000	60,000
Expenses	65,000	35,000
Net income	$ 40,000	$ 25,000

(a) Padre Company sells merchandise to Sun, Ltd., at the same prices and terms applicable to other customers. During 1982 Padre's sales to Sun totalled $100,000. Sun had $30,000 of merchandise purchased from Padre on hand on December 31, 1982, which was an increase of $10,000 over the previous year. Sun had not paid Padre for $21,000 of the merchandise and also owed Padre for a $15,000 cash advance which was in Sun's cash account on December 31, 1982.

(b) On July 1, 1979, Sun purchased a parcel of land from Padre for $10,500 cash. A building on the land was also purchased the same date from Padre for $42,000;

Sun paid $10,000 cash and gave a mortgage which called for four payments of $8,000 each plus interest at 6 per cent to be paid annually on the anniversary of the sale. Padre credits the interest paid by Sun to Interest expense. The land originally cost Padre $10,500, and Padre's net book value for the building was $30,000 at the date of the sale. Sun estimated the building had a 20-year life and no salvage value when purchased and has computed depreciation on a monthly basis.

(c) Sun declared a 9 per cent cash dividend on December 20, 1982, payable on January 16, 1983, to shareholders of record on January 2, 1983. Padre carries its investment at cost and had not recorded this dividend on December 31, 1982. Neither company paid a dividend during 1982.

Instructions:

(1) Prepare a consolidated income statement and consolidated balance sheet for Padre Company and its subsidiary, Sun, Ltd. Where applicable, apply the recommendations contained in Section 1600 of the *Accounting Recommendations*.

(2) Assume that Padre Company decides to account for Sun, Ltd. by the equity method of accounting rather than by consolidation. Calculate the equity pick-up to be recorded by Padre Company. (AICPA adapted)

12-12A. Prior to January 1, 1982, the shareholders of Big Company and Little Company approved the combination of the two companies. On January 1, 1982, 5,000 shares of Big Company common stock were issued to the Little Company shareholders in exchange for the 3,000 shares of Little Company common stock outstanding. At the date of combination the carrying values of Little Company approximate fair values. On January 1, 1982, the common shares of Big Company closed at $26.

The December 31, 1982, postclosing balance sheets of the two companies are as follows:

Postclosing Balance Sheet
December 31, 1982

	Big Company	Little Company
Cash	$ 36,400	$ 28,200
Notes receivable	22,000	9,200
Accounts receivable	20,900	21,700
Accruals receivable	13,000	3,300
Inventories	81,200	49,600
Plant and equipment	83,200	43,500
Accumulated depreciation	(12,800)	(9,300)
Investment in Little Company	130,000	——
Totals	$373,900	$146,000
Notes payable	$ 4,000	$ 12,000
Accounts payable	42,000	19,600
Dividends payable	——	4,500
Accruals payable	2,600	2,100
Notes receivable discounted	8,100	——
Capital stock, $10 par value	120,000	——
Capital stock, $20 par value	——	60,000
Capital in excess of par	108,500	20,000
Retained earnings	88,700	27,800
Totals	$373,900	$146,000

The following additional information is available:

(1) Net income for 1982 (disregard income taxes):

Big Company	$21,700
Little Company	$10,200

(2) On December 31, 1982, Little Company owed Big Company $16,000 on open account and $8,000 in interest bearing notes. Big Company discounted $3,000 of the notes received from Little Company at the bank.

(3) On December 31, 1982, Little Company accrued interest payable of $120 on the notes payable to Big Company: $40 on the notes of $3,000 discounted with the bank and $80 on the remaining notes of $5,000. Big Company did not accrue interest receivable from Little Company.

(4) During 1982 Big Company sold merchandise which cost $30,000 to Little Company for $40,000. Little Company's December 31 inventory included $10,000 of this merchandise priced at Little Company's cost.

(5) On July 1 Little Company sold equipment that had a book value of $15,000 to Big Company for $17,000. Big Company recorded depreciation on it in the amount of $850 for 1982. The remaining life of the equipment at the date of sale was ten years.

(6) Little Company shipped merchandise to Big Company on December 31, 1982, and recorded an account receivable of $6,000 for the sale. Little Company's cost for the merchandise was $4,800. Because the merchandise was in transit, Big Company did not record the transaction. Their terms of the sale were F.O.B. shipping point.

(7) Little Company declared a dividend of $1.50 per share on December 30, 1982, payable on January 10, 1983. Big Company made no entry for the declaration.

(8) Any goodwill is to be amortized over a period of thirty years.

Instructions:

Prepare a consolidated balance sheet as at December 31, 1982, assuming the use of purchase accounting. (AICPA adapted)

13 LIABILITIES AND ACCOUNTING FOR BONDS

Liabilities are obligations arising from past actions, i.e., transactions to pay sums of money, to convey certain other assets, or to perform certain services. In an economic system based largely on credit, many indications of debt will be found on the balance sheet. Most goods and services are purchased on account. Funds are borrowed from banks for working capital purposes. Large sums are provided by bond issues to finance new buildings and equipment. During the life of most obligations, interest accrues as an additional liability. Taxes accrued but not yet due appear as liabilities until paid. Employees of the enterprise are creditors until they are paid for their services.

Liabilities of a business unit must be fully recognized and properly measured on the balance sheet if both the amounts owed and the owner's equity in business assets are to be reported accurately. In presenting liabilities, appropriate distinction must be made between current and non-current items if the company's working capital position is to be accurately determined. Also, any *contingent liabilities*, those liabilities that may materialize in the event of certain acts or circumstances in the future, must be recognized.

Valuation problems arise in the measurement of payables just as they do in the measurement of receivables. In reporting receivables, it was recognized that theoretical accuracy would require reporting at present values. It was further observed that valuation accounts should be established for amounts estimated to be uncollectible and that further reductions should be recognized when receivables included finance and interest charges in their face amounts. In reporting payables, similar considerations apply. When properties, goods, or services are acquired at an amount payable at some future date, this amount may be regarded as composed of a purchase price and a charge for interest for the period of payment deferral. If determinable, an established exchange or purchase price may be used to arrive at the present value of the payable. In the absence of such a price, the present value of the payable should be determined by discounting the amount payable at an appropriate interest rate for the period payment is deferred. The acquisition, then, is recorded by a debit to the account reporting the purchase at the amount computed, a debit to the discount on the payable, and a credit to the payable at its face amount. The discount is amortized over the life of the payable as a debit to interest expense; in preparing a balance sheet, any unamortized discount is reported as a direct subtraction from the payable.

As indicated in Chapter 5, the Accounting Principles Board in Opinion No. 21 has concluded that the discounting procedure is not regarded as appropriate in all instances, and exempts from such practice payables in the normal course of business due on customary trade terms not exceeding one year.[1] Deductions should also be recognized for such items as discounts that can be anticipated in the course of settlement, and also for any finance or interest charges included in the face amounts of payables.

Not all obligations are definite in amount at the time financial statements are prepared. For example, obligations the amounts of which cannot be exactly determined include payments under certain pension plan agreements and payments under product service warranties where experience shows that liabilities do exist. Such obligations are often referred to as *estimated liabilities*.[2] Even though the exact amounts to be paid are not precisely determinable, proper matching of revenues and expenses, as well as the proper inclusion of all of the amounts owed by a business, requires that estimates of these obligations be made as accurately as possible.

It was indicated in Chapter 3 that *current liabilities* are broadly defined to include (1) all obligations arising from operations related to the operating cycle, and (2) all other obligations to be paid within a year. These liabilities make a claim against resources classified as current. Current liabilities are subtracted from current assets in arriving at *working capital*.

CURRENT LIABILITIES THAT ARE DEFINITE IN AMOUNT

Representative of current liabilities that are definite in amount and that are frequently found on the balance sheet are notes and accounts currently

---

[1]Although there is no Canadian counterpart for APB Opinion No. 21, the discounting procedure has theoretical merit that extends beyond the applications that the Opinion requires.

[2]Estimated liabilities should be distinguished from contingent liabilities. The former category includes definite obligations whose exact amounts are not determinable and must be estimated on an accrual basis. The latter category includes items for which it is not certain there is a liability, even though an amount may be known, e.g., in a pending lawsuit.

payable, current maturities of long-term obligations, cash dividends payable, deposits and agency obligations, sales taxes, payroll taxes and income tax withholdings, and liabilities under bonus agreements. Some of the problems arising in determining the balance to be reported for these items are described in the following sections.

Notes and Accounts Currently Payable

Both notes and accounts currently payable originate from the purchase of goods and services and from short-term borrowings. Notes currently payable may include notes issued to trade creditors for the purchase of goods and services, to banks for loans, to officers and shareholders for advances, and to others for the purchase of property. Accounts currently payable may consist of a wide variety of items, including obligations to trade creditors for the purchase of goods and services, obligations for the purchase of property items and securities, credit balances in customers' accounts, customers' refundable deposits, advances from officers and shareholders.

In presenting current payables on the balance sheet, it is normally desirable to classify notes and accounts in terms of their origin. Such presentation affords information concerning the sources of business indebtedness as well as the extent to which the business has relied upon each source in financing its activities.

In arriving at the total amount owed trade creditors, particular attention must be given to the purchase of goods and services at the end of the fiscal period. Both the goods and the services acquired, as well as the accompanying obligations, must be reported on the statements even though invoices evidencing the charges are not received until the following period.

Individual notes and accounts are frequently secured by the pledge of certain assets. Assets pledged may consist of marketable securities, notes receivable, accounts receivable, inventories, or property items. The pledge of an asset limits the use or the disposition of the asset or its proceeds until the related obligation is liquidated. In the event of bankruptcy, the cash realized on a pledged asset must first be applied to the satisfaction of the related obligation. A liability is *partly secured* or *fully secured* depending upon whether the value of the pledged property is less than the amount of the obligation or whether such value is equal to or in excess of the obligation. It has already been stated that reference is made to a lien on an asset by a parenthetical remark in the "Assets" section of the balance sheet. It is also desirable to provide a parenthetical remark or footnote in connection with the liability item identifying the asset pledged and indicating its present market value.

There are many kinds of notes. However, two types frequently create difficulty in recording: (1) the note with no stated interest rate, and (2) the note that is discounted. An example of each of these types is included in the following paragraphs:

1. Assume equipment is purchased on terms calling for issue of a $10,000 non-interest-bearing note for one year. If the equipment and the related obligation are recorded at $10,000, this would fail to recognize the charge for interest implicit in the deferred payment arrangement and both asset and liability balances would be overstated. If money is worth 8% per year, the asset, as well as the liability, must be recognized at a cash-equivalent value of $9,259.26 ($10,000 ÷ 1.08). The following entry should be made:

Equipment	9,259.26	
Discount on Notes Payable	740.74	
Notes Payable		10,000.00

In reporting the note on the balance sheet prior to its payment, an ajustment should be made to recognize the accrual of interest at 8% on the amount of the debt of $9,259.26 to the date of the balance sheet. The accrual of interest is recorded by a debit to Interest Expense and a credit to Discount on Notes Payable. The balance of the discount on notes payable is subtracted from notes payable in reporting the liability on the balance sheet. A similar procedure would be required if a note provided for a nominal interest rate that was substantially lower than the current market rate.

2. Assume a company discounts a $10,000 one-year, non-interest-bearing note at the bank, receiving $10,000 less a discount of 8%, or $9,200. If the amount of the discount is recognized as prepaid interest and the note is recorded at $10,000, both asset and liability balances would be overstated: interest has not been paid in advance but is still to be paid; the obligation at the time of borrowing is no greater than the amount borrowed. The following entry should be made:

Cash	9,200	
Discount on Notes Payable	800	
Notes Payable		10,000

In reporting the note on the balance sheet prior to its payment, an adjustment should be made to recognize the accrual of interest just as in the first example. However, a discount of 8% is, in effect, a charge for interest at the rate of 8.7% ($800 ÷ $9,200). The accrual of interest, then, is computed at 8.7% on the amount of the debt of $9,200 to the date of the balance sheet.

Current Maturities of Long-Term Obligations

Bonds, mortgage notes, and other long-term indebtedness are reported as current liabilities if they are to be paid within a twelve-month period. When only a part of a long-term obligation is to be paid currently, as in the case of bonds payable in a series of annual instalments, the maturing portion of the debt is reported as current, the balance as non-current. But if the maturing obligation is payable out of a special retirement fund or if it is to be retired from the proceeds of a new bond issue or by conversion into share capital, the obligation will not call for the use of current funds and therefore should continue to be listed as non-current. Reference to the plan for liquidation should be made parenthetically or by a note. The reporting of current maturities of long-term obligations is usually accomplished by way of a *reclassification entry*, that is, a work sheet entry solely for the purpose of financial statement presentation. This is in contrast with an adjusting entry that would, of course, be recorded in the normal manner.

Dividends Payable

A cash dividend declared by appropriate action of the board of directors is recorded by a debit to Retained Earnings and a credit to Dividends Payable. The latter balance is reported as a current liability. The declaration of a dividend payable in the form of additional shares of stock is recorded by a debit to Retained Earnings and a credit to Stock Dividends Distributable. The latter balance is not recognized as a liability but is reported in the "Shareholders' equity" section since it represents retained earnings in the process of transfer to share capital and perhaps also, in part, to contributed surplus.

A company with cumulative preferred shares outstanding may have sufficient retained earnings to legally declare a dividend but may fail to declare a dividend in order to preserve cash for other purposes. No liability is recognized because dividends are not payable until formal action is taken by the corporate board of directors authorizing the distribution of earnings. Nevertheless, the amount of unpaid cumulative dividends should be reported on the balance sheet. This amount may be shown parenthetically in the "Shareholders' equity" section following a description of the shares or by a note.

Deposits and Agency Obligations

Current resources of a company may include monies deposited with it and returnable to depositors, or monies collected or otherwise accumulated and payable to third parties. A company may have received deposits as guarantees of contract performance, and a current liability needs to be recognized until the deposits are returned. In other instances, companies will make payroll deductions for such items as employees' income tax, payroll taxes, insurance plans, or saving plans. These current liabilities payable to third parties need to be recognized until payments are made and the company fulfils its responsibilities as an agent.

Sales Taxes

With the passage of sales tax laws by federal and provincial governments, additional duties are required of a business unit. Laws generally provide that the business unit must act as an agent for the governmental authority in the collection from customers of sales tax on the transfers of tangible personal properties. Laws may also provide that the business unit is additionally liable for sales tax on goods it buys for its own use. Provision must be made in the accounts for the liability to governments for the tax collected from customers and any additional tax that the business must absorb.

Sales Tax Collections Included in Sales Balance. The sales tax payable is generally a stated percentage of sales. When the sales tax collections as well as sales are recorded in total in the sales account, it becomes necessary to divide this amount into its component parts, sales and sales tax payable. For example, if the sales tax is 5% of sales, then the amount recorded in the sales account is equal to sales + .05 of sales, or 1.05 times the sales total. The amount of sales is obtained by dividing the sales account balance by 1.05, and 5% of the sales amount as thus derived is the tax liability. To illustrate, assume that the sales account balance is $100,000, which includes sales tax of 5%. Sales, then, are $100,000 ÷ 1.05 = $95,238.10. The sales tax liability is then 5% of $95,238.10 = $4,761.90. The liability can also be determined by subtracting the sales figure, $95,238.10 from $100,000.00. To record the liability, Sales would be debited and Sales Tax Payable would be credited for $4,761.90.

Sales Tax Collections Recorded Separately. Frequently, the actual sales total and the sales tax collections are recorded separately at the time of the sale. The sales tax payable account then accumulates the sales tax liability. If sales tax collections are not exactly equal to the sales tax liability for the period as computed under the law, the payable account will require adjustment to bring it to the balance due. In making this adjustment a gain or a loss on sales tax collections is recognized.

Payroll Taxes and Income Tax Withheld

Social insurance and income tax legislation impose three, and in some provinces, four taxes based upon payrolls:

1. Canada or Quebec Pension Plan
2. Unemployment insurance
3. Federal and provincial income taxes
4. In some provinces, for example Ontario, health insurance premiums.

Liabilities relating to payrolls, except for the net pay due to employees, are the result of legislation, the details of which may change from year to year.[3] Deductions for income tax, Unemployment Insurance, and Canada or Quebec Pension Plan are compulsory in all provincial jurisdictions. Employ-

---

[3] While the details may have changed somewhat, payroll deductions and the related payroll taxes levied against employers are subject to more extensive coverage in John R. E. Parker, C. Rollin Niswonger, and Philip E. Fess, *Accounting Principles, Second Canadian Edition* (Toronto: Gage Publishing Limited, 1981), Ch. 11.

ers are also subject to payroll related expenses pertaining to the employers' premiums for Unemployment Insurance, Canada or Quebec Pension Plan, and Workmen's Compensation. The latter relates to legislation enacted in all provinces which pays hospital and medical expenses of workers injured as the result of an accident arising out of and in the course of employment, plus a percentage, usually 75%, of wages or salaries for the period during which an employee is unable to work because of an injury suffered on the job. No deduction is made from employees with respect to Workmen's Compensation earnings.

Liability Under Bonus Agreements

Bonuses accruing to officers, managers, or employees at the end of a period are recorded by a debit to an expense account and a credit to a liability account. Employee bonuses, even though they may be defined as a sharing of profits with the employees, are deductible expenses for purposes of income tax.

Special problems frequently arise in the computation of the amount of the bonus accruing to personnel. An agreement may provide for a bonus computed on the basis of gross revenue or sales or on the basis of earnings. When earnings are to be used, the computation will depend upon whether the bonus is based on: (1) income before deductions for bonus or income tax, (2) income after deduction for bonus but before deduction for income tax, (3) income after deduction for income tax but before deduction for bonus, or (4) net income after deductions for both bonus and income tax. Regardless of the method employed in its computation, the bonus should be reported on the income statement as an expense before arriving at the amount of income before extraordinary items, if any, or net income.

ESTIMATED CURRENT LIABILITIES

The amount of an obligation is generally established by contract or accrues at a certain rate. There are instances, however, when an obligation clearly exists on a balance sheet date but the amount ultimately to be paid cannot be determined with certainty. Because the amount to be paid is not definite does not mean the liability can be ignored or given a contingent status. Instead, the obligation must be estimated from whatever data are available. The amount to be paid in the form of income tax, for example, must be estimated in preparing both interim statements and statements at the end of the period. Although the exact amount ultimately payable is not known, the obligation is unquestioned and requires recognition. Expenditures arising from current operations, for example, the cost of meeting warranties for service and repairs on goods sold, also call for estimates when prior experience indicates there is a definite liability. Here, uncertainty as to the amount to be expended is accompanied by an inability to identify the payees as well as to determine the timing of payments; but the fact that there are charges yet to be absorbed is certain. These liabilities generally call for current liquidation and hence are classified under the current heading.

Representative short-term liabilities that are estimated in amount and are frequently found on financial statements include the following:

1. *Estimated tax liabilities*, reporting the estimated income, property, and other tax obligations.
2. *Estimated liabilities on customer premium offers*, reporting the estimated value of premiums or prizes to be distributed as a result of past sales or sales promotion activities.
3. *Estimated liabilities under warranties for service and replacements*, reporting the estimated future claims by customers as a result of past guarantees of services or product or product part replacement.
4. *Estimated liabilities on tickets, tokens, and gift certificates outstanding*, reporting the estimated obligations in the form of services or merchandise arising from the receipt of cash in past periods.

Some of the problems arising in the development of the balances to be reported for these items are described in the sections that follow.

Estimated Tax Liabilities

Estimates are required for all taxes related to current operations but not finally known at the time financial statements are prepared. Estimates may thus be called for in the case of federal and provincial income taxes, property taxes, and various other licences and fees. When governments are considering revisions in tax rates and their application, the best available information should be used in developing estimates. Not only may estimates have to be made relative to rates but also to the bases to which such rates may apply. In the case of property taxes, for example, the valuation to be assigned to properties owned may have to be estimated in arriving at an estimated tax liability.

Estimated taxes are recorded by debits to expense and credits to liability accounts. Liabilities are closed when the taxes are paid. Any difference between the amount paid and the obligation originally recognized may be reported as an expense in the period of payment.

In the case of income taxes, the amount shown as expense is based on an estimate made by the company. During the year, monthly instalment payments are required and an income tax return (or returns) must be filed no later than six months after the corporation's year end. Income tax returns and related records and documents are subject to review and assessment by taxation authorities. It is only after completion of the assessment process, which may be a lengthy period because of the possibility of appeals, that the actual income tax liability can be determined. Since the liability for income taxes is provisional rather than final, it is often described on the balance sheet as Estimated Income Taxes Payable. Similarly, the expense shown on the income statement may be described as Provision for Income Taxes.[4]

Property Taxes. Property taxes are based upon the assessed valuation of properties as of a given date. This has given rise to the view held by courts and others that taxes accrue as of a given date. Generally the date of accrual has been held to be the date of property assessment. However, accounting treatment, in general, has been to charge taxes ratably over a tax year rather than to recognize these at the time the legal obligation arises.

Property taxes have been charged against the revenue of various periods, including (1) the year in which paid (cash basis), (2) the year ending (or beginning) on the assessment (or lien) date, and (3) the fiscal year of the governing body levying the tax.

The Committee on Accounting Procedure of the AICPA in considering the various alternatives for tax accounting has suggested, "generally, the most acceptable basis of providing for property taxes is monthly accrual on the taxpayer's books during the fiscal period of the taxing authority for which the taxes are levied."[5] This would relate the tax charge to the period in which taxes provide benefits through governmental services. However, the Committee indicated that special circumstances may suggest the use of alternative accrual periods, and it concludes, "consistency of application from year to year is the important consideration and selection of any of the periods mentioned is a matter for individual judgment."[6]

Accounting for tax when accrual is made over the fiscal year of the taxing authority is illustrated in the example that follows. Assume the accounting period for the Reid Co. is the calendar year. The fiscal year for the city in which this company is located begins on July 1 and ends on the following June 30. Property taxes are assessed in March, but bills are sent out in November covering the year ending June 30 of the following year. Tax payments in equal instalments are due on December 10 and the following April 10. The Reid Co. accrues taxes in its accounts monthly in terms of the fiscal period of the governmental unit.

On July 1, 1977, the Reid Co. estimated total property tax for the year July 1, 1977, to June 30, 1978, at $1,800. On November 4 the company received a tax bill for 1977-78 of $1,842. Entries to record the monthly tax charges and tax payments are shown on page 508.

It should be noted that when the actual tax charge became known in November, an adjustment was made for charges of previous months.[7]

---

[4]Accounting for income taxes is otherwise presented in Chapter 14.

[5]*Accounting Research and Terminology Bulletins — Final Edition*, "No. 43, Restatement and Revision of Accounting Research Bulletins" (New York: American Institute of Certified Public Accountants, 1961), Ch. 10A, par. 14.

[6]*Ibid.*, par. 13.

[7]An alternative treatment would apply the adjustment over the remaining months of the fiscal year of the taxing authority.

Estimated Liabilities on Customer Premium Offers

Many corporations offer special premiums to those purchasing their products. These offers to stimulate the regular purchase of certain products may be open for a limited time or may be of a continuing nature. The premium is normally made available when the custmer submits the required number of product labels, box tops, wrappers, or certificates. In certain instances the premium offer may provide for a cash payment.

If a premium offer expires at the end of the corporation's fiscal period, adjustments in the accounts are not required. Premium requirements are fully met and the premium expense account summarizes the full charge for the period. However, when a premium offer is continuing, an adjustment must be made at the end of the period to recognize the liability that is found in the continuing costs of the offer — Premium Expense is debited and an appropriate liability account is credited. The expense is thus charged to the

TRANSACTION		ENTRY		
At the end of July, August, September, October:				
Estimated tax for 1977-78	$1,800	Property Tax Expense	150.00	
Monthly accrual, 1/12 × $1,800	150	Property Tax Payable		150.00
At the end of November:				
Amount of tax for year	$1,842.00	Property Tax Expense	167.50	
		Property Tax Payable		167.50
Amount chargeable to date				
4 × $153.50 ($1,842 ÷ 12)	$ 614.00			
Accrual recognized to date				
4 × $150	600.00			
Tax deficiency — prior periods	$ 14.00			
Add accrual for November	153.50			
Total charge	$ 167.50			
December 10:				
Payment of first instalment, 50% × $1,842 = $921,		Property Tax Payable	767.50	
chargeable as follows:		Property Tax Expense	153.50	
July-November (accrued)	$767.50	Cash		921.00
December (current period)	153.50			
At the end of January, February, March:				
Monthly accrual.		Property Tax Expense	153.50	
		Property Tax Payable		153.50
April 10:				
Payment of second instalment, 50% × $1,842 = $921,		Property Tax Payable	460.50	
chargeable as follows:		Property Tax Expense	153.50	
January-March (accrued)	$460.50	Prepaid Property Tax	307.00	
April (current period)	153.50	Cash		921.00
May and June (prepaid)	307.00			
At the end of May, June:				
Monthly amortization of prepaid property tax.		Property Tax Expense	153.50	
		Prepaid Property Tax		153.50

TRANSACTION	ENTRY		
1977:	Premiums — Bowl Sets	10,000	
Premium purchases:	Cash		10,000
10,000 sets × $1 = $10,000	Cash	240,000	
Sales:	Sales		240,000
400,000 packages × $.60 = $240,000	Premium Expense	6,000	
Premium claim redemptions:	Premiums —		
120,000 certificates, or 6,000 sets × $1 = $6,000.	Bowl Sets		6,000
December 31, 1977:			
Coupons estimated redeemable in future periods:	Premium Expense	2,000	
Total estimated redemptions —	Estimated Premium		
40% of 400,000 160,000	Claims Outstanding		2,000
Redemptions in 1977 120,000			
Estimated future redemptions 40,000			
Estimated claim outstanding:			
40,000 certificates or 2,000 sets @ $1 ... $ 2,000			
January 1, 1978 (optional):	Estimated Premium		
Reversal of accrued liability balance.	Claims Outstanding	2,000	
	Premium Expense		2,000

period benefiting from the premium plan and current liabilities reflect the claim for premiums outstanding. If premium distributions are debited to an expense account, the liability balance may be reversed at the beginning of the new period.

To illustrate the accounting for a premium offer, assume the following: Smart Foods offers a set of breakfast bowls upon the receipt of 20 certificates, one certificate being included in each package of the cereal distributed by this company. The cost of each set of bowls to the company is $1. It is estimated that only 40% of the coupons will be redeemed. Transactions and entries are as shown at the top of the page.

The balance sheet at the end of 1977 will show the inventory of premiums of $4,000 as a current asset and estimated premium claims outstanding of $2,000 as a current liability; the income statement for 1977 will show premium expense of $8,000 as a selling expense.

Experience indicating a redemption percentage that differs from the assumed rate will call for an appropriate adjustment in the subsequent period and the revision of future redemption estimates.

The estimated cost of the premiums may be shown as a direct reduction of sales by recording the premium claim at the time of the sale. This requires an estimate of the premium cost at the time of the sale. For example, in the previous illustration, the entry to be made at the time of the sale, employing the sales reduction approach, would be as follows:

Cash	240,000	
Sales		232,000
Estimated Premium Claims Outstanding		8,000

The redemption of premium claims would call for debits to the liability account. Either the expense method or the sales reduction method is acceptable and both are found in practice.

Some organizations have adopted plans for the issuance to customers of trading stamps, cash register tapes, or other media redeemable in merchandise, premiums, or cash. The accounting procedure followed will depend upon the nature of the plan. A business may establish its own plan, prepare its own stamps or other trading media, and assume redemption responsibilities. Under these circumstances, the accounting procedure would parallel that just illustrated for specific premium offers. On the other hand, a business unit may enter into an agreement for a stamp plan with a trading-stamp company. The latter normally assumes full responsibility for the redemption of stamps and sells the trading stamps for a set unit price whether they are redeemed or not. The business would report stamps purchased as an asset and stamps issued as a selling expense; the trading-stamp company would recognize in its accounts the sale of stamps, purchase of premiums, distributions of premiums, and the estimated liability for the costs of merchandise and related services identified with stamps expected to be redeemed.

Estimated Liabilities Under Warranties

Some corporations agree to provide free service on units failing to perform satisfactorily or to replace defective goods. When agreements involve only minor costs, such costs may be recognized in the periods incurred. When agreements involve significant future costs and when experience indicates a definite future obligation exists, estimates of such costs should be made. Such estimates are recorded by a debit to an expense account and a credit to a liability account. Subsequent costs of fulfilling warranties are debited to the liability account. Adjustments to the liability account will be required if experience differs from the estimates. The anticipation of costs results in appropriate charges during the period in which revenue is realized and in recognition of the obligation outstanding. To illustrate this procedure, consider the following example. Supersonic Sound, Ltd., sells compact stereo systems with a two-year warranty. It estimated that 10% of all sets sold will need repairs in the first year, and 20% will need repairs in the second year. The average repair cost is $50 per system. The number of systems sold in 1977 and 1978 was 5,000 and 6,000, respectively. Associated repairs were $28,000 in 1977 and $60,000 in 1978.

In certain cases customers are charged special fees for a service or replacement warranty covering a specific period. In such cases, a customer's advances account is credited. Expenditures in meeting contract requirements are debited to expense, and the advances balance is recognized as revenue over the warranty period. Recognition of revenue in excess of expenses

TRANSACTION			ENTRY		
1977					
Warranty Expense:			Warranty Expense		75,000	
Stereo systems sold		5,000	Estimated Liability		
Repair rate (.10 + .20)		.30	Under Warranties			75,000
Systems ultimately to be repaired		1,500	Estimated Liability		
Cost to repair each system		× $50	Under Warranties		28,000
Warranty expense		$75,000	Cash			28,000
Repairs actually made: $28,000					
1978					
Warranty Expense:			Warranty Expense		90,000	
Stereo systems sold		6,000	Estimated Liability		
Repair rate (.10 + .20)		.30	Under Warranties			90,000
Systems ultimately to be repaired		1,800	Estimated Liability		
Cost to repair each system		× $50	Under Warranties		60,000
Warranty expense		$90,000	Cash			60,000
Repairs actually made: $60,000					

indicates a profit on such service contracts; revenue less than expenses indicates a loss on such contracts. The customers' advances balance should be reported as a current liability in view of the claim it makes upon current assets.

Estimated Liabilities on Tickets, Tokens, and Gift Certificates Outstanding

Many companies sell tickets, tokens, and gift certificates that entitle the owner to service or merchandise: for example, airlines issue tickets used for travel; local transit companies issue tokens good for fares; department stores sell gift certificates redeemable in merchandise.

When instruments redeemable in services or merchandise are outstanding at the end of the period, accounts should be adjusted to reflect the obligations under such arrangements. The nature of the adjustment will depend upon the entries originally made in recording the sale of the instruments.

Ordinarily, the sale of instruments redeemable in services or merchandise is recorded by a debit to Cash and a credit to a liability account. As instruments are redeemed, the liability balance is debited and Sales or an appropriate revenue account is credited. Certain claims may be rendered void by lapse of time or for some other reason as defined by the sales agreement. In addition, experience may indicate a certain percentage of outstanding claims will never be presented for redemption. These factors must be considered at the end of the period, when the liability balance is reduced to the balance of the claim estimated to be outstanding and a revenue account is credited for the gain indicated from forfeitures. If Sales or a special revenue account is originally credited on the sale of the redemption instrument, the adjustment at the end of the period calls for a debit to the revenue account and a credit to a liability account for the claim still outstanding.

LONG-TERM LIABILITIES

Long-term financing of a corporation is accomplished either through the issuance of long-term debt instruments, usually bonds, or through the sale of additional ownership equity. The issuance of bonds instead of shares may be preferred by shareholders for the following reasons: (1) the charge against earnings for bond interest may be less than the share of earnings that would otherwise be payable as dividends on a new issue of preferred shares or on the sale of additional common shares; (2) present owners continue in control of the corporation; and (3) interest is a deductible expense in arriving at taxable income while dividends are not.

But there are certain limitations and disadvantages of financing through bonds. Bond financing is possible only when a corporation is in satisfactory financial condition and can offer adequate security to a new creditor group. Furthermore, interest must be paid regardless of the corporation's earnings and financial position. With operating losses and the inability of the corporation to raise sufficient cash to meet periodic interest payments, bondholders may take legal action by way of bankruptcy proceedings, or, depending upon the terms and conditions of the bond issue, assume control of company properties.

Bonds are purchased for both short-term and long-term purposes by corporations, principally insurance companies, banks, trust companies, and educational and charitable institutions. Because of the similarity in accounting for bonds as a liability and as a long-term investment, both sides of a bond transaction will be discussed in this chapter.

ACCOUNTING FOR BONDS

Borrowing by means of bonds involves the issuance of a number of certificates of indebtedness. Bond certificates may represent equal parts of the bond issue or they may be of varying denominations. Bonds of a business unit are commonly issued in $1,000 denominations, referred to as the *bond face, par,* or *maturity value*.

The group contract between the corporation and the bondholders is known as the *bond* or *trust indenture*. The indenture details the rights and obligations of the contracting parties and indicates the property pledged as well as the protection offered on the loan.

Bonds may be sold by the corporation directly to investors, or they may be underwritten by an investment dealer or a syndicate of dealers. The underwriters may agree to purchase the entire bond issue or that part of the issue which is not sold by the company, or they may agree simply to manage the issue on a commission basis.

Types of Bonds

Bonds may be classified in many different ways. When all of the bonds mature on a single date, they are called *term bonds*; when bonds mature in instalments, they are known as *serial bonds*. Bonds issued by private corporations may be *secured* or *unsecured*. Secured bonds provide protection to the investor in the form of a mortgage covering the company's real estate and perhaps other property, or a pledge in the form of certain collateral. A *first-mortgage bond* represents a first claim against the property of a corporation in the event of the company's inability to meet bond interest and principal payments. A *second-mortgage bond* is a secondary claim ranking only after the claim of the first-mortgage bonds or senior issue has been completely satisfied. A *collateral trust bond* is usually secured by shares and bonds of other corporations owned by the issuing company. Such securities are generally transferred to a trustee who holds them as collateral on behalf of the bondholders and, if necessary, will sell them to satisfy the bondholders' claim.

Unsecured bonds are not protected by the pledge of certain property and are frequently termed *debenture bonds*. Holders of debenture bonds simply rank as general creditors with other unsecured parties. The risk involved in these securities varies with the financial strength of the debtor. Debentures issued by a strong company may involve little risk; debentures issued by a weak company whose properties are already heavily mortgaged may involve considerable risk.

When another party promises to make payment on bonds if the issuing corporation fails to do so, the bonds are referred to as *guaranteed bonds*. A parent company, for example, may guarantee payment of bonds issued by its subsidiaries.

Obligations known as *income bonds* have been issued when business failure has resulted in corporate reorganization. These bonds require the payment of interest only to the extent that the corporation's current earnings permit. Income bonds may be cumulative or non-cumulative. If cumulative, interest that cannot be paid in one year is carried over as a lien against future earnings; if non-cumulative, no future lien arises from inability to meet interest payments.

Bonds may provide for their conversion into some other security at the option of the bondholder. Such bonds are known as *convertible bonds*. The conversion feature generally permits the owner of bonds to exchange holdings into common shares. The bondholder is thus able to exchange the claim into an ownership interest if corporate operations prove successful and conversion becomes attractive; in the meantime the special rights of a creditor are maintained.

Other bond features may serve the issuer's interests. For example, bond indentures frequently give the issuing corporation the right to call and retire bonds prior to their maturity. Such bonds are termed *callable bonds*. When a corporation wishes to reduce its outstanding indebtedness, bondholders are notified of the portion of the issue to be surrendered, and they are paid in accordance with call provisions.

Bonds may be classified as (1) *registered bonds* and (2) *bearer* or *coupon bonds*. Registered bonds call for the registry of the owner's name by the issuer. When a bond is sold, the corporate transfer agent cancels the bond certificate surrendered by the vendor and issues a new certificate to the buyer. Interest cheques are mailed periodically to bondholders of record. Bearer or coupon bonds are not recorded in the name of the owner, title to such bonds passing with delivery. Each bond is accompanied by coupons for individual interest payments covering the life of the issue. Coupons are clipped by the owner of the bond and presented to a bank for deposit or collection. The issue of bearer bonds eliminates the need for recording bond ownership changes and preparing and mailing periodic interest cheques. But coupon bonds fail to offer the bondholder the protection found in registered bonds in the event bonds are lost or stolen. In some cases, bonds provide interest coupons but require registry as to principal. Here, ownership safeguards are afforded while the time-consuming routines involved in making interest payments are avoided.

Bond Market Price

The market price of bonds varies with the safety of the investment. When the financial condition and earnings of a corporation are such that payment of interest and principal on bonded indebtedness may be assured, the interest rate a corporation must offer to market a bond issue is relatively low. As the risk factor increases, a higher interest return is necessary to attract investors. The interest rate on the bonds is known as the *bond, stated,* or *contract rate*. Although bonds provide for the payment of interest at a certain rate, this rate may not be the same as the prevailing or *market rate* for bonds of similar quality at the date of issue. Furthermore, the market rate constantly fluctuates. These factors often result in a difference between bond face values and the prices at which the bonds sell on the market.

The purchase of bonds at face value implies agreement between the bond rate of interest and the prevailing market rate of interest. If the bond rate exceeds the market rate, the bonds will sell at a premium; if the bond rate is less than the market rate, the bonds will sell at a discount. The premium or the discount is the discounted value of the difference between the contract rate and the market rate of the series of interest payments. A declining market rate of interest subsequent to issuance of the bonds results in an increase in the market value of the bonds; a rising market rate of interest results in a decrease in their market value. The bond rate corrected for the premium or the discount on the purchase gives the actual return on the bonds, known as the *effective rate of interest*. Bonds are quoted on the market as a percentage of face value. Thus, a bond quotation of 96 means the market price is 96% of face value, or at a discount; a bond quotation of 104 means the market price is 104% of face value, or at a premium.

The market price of a bond at any date can be determined by discounting the maturity value of the bond and each remaining interest payment at the effective rate of interest for similar debt on that date. Present value tables that can be used for discounting are located on the inside of the front and back covers.

To illustrate the computation of a bond market price from the tables, assume 10-year, 8% bonds of $100,000 are to be sold on the bond issue date. The effective interest rate for these bonds is 10%, compounded semi-annually. The computation may be divided into two parts:

1. *Present Value of Maturity Value:*
   Maturity value of bonds after ten years or twenty semi-annual periods = $100,000
   Effective interest rate — 10% per year, or 5% per semi-annual period:
   $PV_n = A(PVF_{\overline{n}|i}) = \$100,000(\text{Table II}_{\overline{20}|5\%}) = \$100,000(.3769) = \$37,690.$

2. *Present Value of Twenty Interest Payments:*
   Semi-annual payment, 4% of $100,000 = $4,000
   Effective interest rate — 10% per year, or 5% per semi-annual period:
   $PV_n = R(PVAF_{\overline{n}|i}) = \$4,000(\text{Table IV}_{\overline{20}|5\%}) = \$4,000(12.4622) = \$49,849.$

The market price for the bonds would thus be $87,539, the sum of the two parts. Because the effective interest rate is higher than the stated interest rate, the bonds would sell at a $12,461 discount at the issuance date.

Special adaptations of present value tables are available to determine the price to be paid for the bonds if they are to provide a certain return. A portion of such a bond table is illustrated at the top of the next page.

Note that the present value from the table of 8% bonds to return 10% in 10 years is $87,539, the same amount computed above. If the bond return or effective interest rate was 7.5%, the present value would be $103,476.

Values to the Nearest Dollar of 8% Bond for $100,000 Interest Payable Semi-annually					
Yield	8 years	8¹/₂ years	9 years	9¹/₂ years	10 years
7.00	$106,046	$106,325	$106,595	$106,855	$107,107
7.25	104,495	104,699	104,896	105,090	105,272
7.50	102,971	103,100	103,232	103,360	103,476
7.75	101,472	101,537	101,595	101,658	101,718
8.00	100,000	100,000	100,000	100,000	100,000
8.25	98,552	98,494	98,437	98,372	98,325
8.50	97,141	97,012	96,893	96,787	96,678
8.75	95,746	95,568	95,398	95,232	95,070
9.00	94,383	94,147	93,920	93,703	93,496
9.25	93,042	92,757	92,480	92,214	91,953
9.50	91,723	91,380	91,055	90,751	90,452
9.75	90,350	89,960	89,588	89,238	88,902
10.00	89,162	88,726	88,310	87,914	87,539

This table can also be used to determine the effective rate on a bond acquired at a certain price. To illustrate, assume that a $1,000, 8% bond due in 10 years is selling at $951. Reference to the column "10 years" for $95,070 shows a return of 8.75% is provided on an investment of $950.70.

BOND ISSUANCE

The issuer normally records bonds at their face value — the amount that the company must pay at maturity. Hence, when bonds are issued at an amount other than face value, a bond discount or premium balance is established for the difference between the cash received and the bond face value. This amount is added to or subtracted from the bond face value in the liability section of the balance sheet. Although undesirable, it is not uncommon for bond discount to be shown as a deferred charge on the asset side of the balance sheet rather than as a deduction from the face value of the bonds.

The investor normally records an investment in bonds at cost, which includes brokerage fees and any other costs incident to the purchase. No separate premium or discount account is therefore required. Bonds acquired in exchange for assets or services are recorded at the fair market value of such consideration. When bonds and other securities are acquired for a lump sum, an apportionment of such cost among the securities is required. Purchase of bonds on a deferred payment basis calls for recognition of both the asset and liability balances.

The purchase, as well as the issuance of bonds, when made between interest payment dates requires calculation of the accrued interest which is added to the bond price. The amount paid for accrued interest on a purchase is subtracted from subsequent interest collections in measuring interest revenue; the amount received for accrued interest on an issuance is subtracted from subsequent interest payments in measuring interest expense.

To illustrate the accounting for bond issuance, assume a 10-year, $200,000, 8% bond issue is sold at 103, on May 1. Interest payment dates are February 1 and August 1. The entries in the accounts of the issuer and the investor would be as follows:

Issuer's Accounts

May 1	Cash	210,000	
	Bonds Payable		200,000
	Premium on Bonds		6,000
	Interest Expense*		4,000
	To record issuance of bonds.		

Computation:
$200,000 × 103 = $206,000 purchase price.
Interest: $200,000 × .08 × 3/12 = $4,000   1 Feb → 1 May

Investor's Accounts

May 1	Investment in Bonds	206,000	
	Interest Revenue*	4,000	
	Cash		210,000
	To record investment in bonds.		

For convenience, a 360-day year was assumed in the illustration. A 365-day year is frequently used for governmental obligations and is increasingly used by many banks.

When bonds are issued in exchange for property, the transaction should be recorded at the cash price at which the bonds could be issued. When difficulties are encountered in arriving at a cash price, the market or appraised value of the property acquired would be used. A difference between the face value of the bonds and the cash value of the bonds or the value of the property acquired is recognized as bond discount or bond premium.

The issuance of bonds normally involves costs for legal services, printing and engraving, taxes, and underwriting. These costs should be summarized separately as issuing costs, classified as deferred charges, and charged to revenue over the life of the bond issue.[8]

Issuance of Convertible Bonds

The issuance of *convertible debt securities*, most frequently bonds, has become increasingly popular. These securities are usually convertible into the common shares of the issuing corporation generally at a specified price and at the option of the holder. These securities usually have the following characteristics:[9]

---

*As indicated in Chapter 2, the real accounts Interest Payable and Interest Receivable could have been used rather than Interest Expense and Interest Revenue. These real accounts could then be reduced when the interest payments are made or received, or they could be adjusted to their proper balances at the end of the reporting period.

[8]*Opinions of the Accounting Principles Board, No. 21,* "Interest on Receivables and Payables" (New York: American Institute of Certified Public Accountants, 1971), par. 16.

[9]*Opinions of the Accounting Principles Board, No. 14,* "Accounting for Convertible Debt and Debt Issued with Stock Purchase Warrants" (New York: American Institute of Certified Public Accountants, 1969), par. 3.

1. An interest rate lower than the issuer could establish for non-convertible debt.
2. An initial conversion price higher than the market value of the common shares at time of issuance.
3. A callable option retained by the issuer.

The popularity of these securities may be attributed to the advantages to both the issuer and the holder. The issuer is able to obtain financing at a lower interest rate because of the value of the conversion feature to the holder. Because of the call provision, the issuer is in a position to exert influence upon the holders to exchange the debt into equity capital if share prices increase; the issuer has had the use of relatively low interest rate financing if share prices do not increase. On the other hand, the holder has the advantage of the security of a debt instrument that, barring default, assures the return of investment plus a fixed return, and at the same time offers an option to transfer his or her interest to equity capital should such transfer become attractive.

Differences of opinion exist as to whether convertible debt securities should be treated by the issuer solely as debt, or whether part of the proceeds received from the issuance of debt should be recognized as equity capital. One view holds that the debt and the conversion privilege are inseparably connected, and therefore the debt and equity portions of the security should not be separately valued. The holder cannot sell part of the instrument and retain the other. An alternate view holds that there are two distinct elements in these securities and that each should be recognized in the accounts: that portion of the issuance price attributable to the conversion privilege should be recorded as a credit to Contributed Surplus; the balance of the issuance price should be assigned to the debt. This would decrease the premium otherwise recognized on the debt or perhaps result in a discount.

These views are compared in the illustration that follows. Assume 500 ten-year bonds, total face value $500,000 are sold at 105. The bonds contain a conversion privilege that provides for exchange of a $1,000 bond for 20 common shares par value $40. The interest rate on the bonds is 8%. It is established that without the conversion privilege, the bonds would sell at 96. The journal entries to record the issuance by the issuer under the two approaches follow.

Debt and Equity Not Separated

Cash	525,000	
Bonds Payable		500,000
Premium on Bonds Payable		25,000

Debt and Equity Separated

Cash	525,000	
Discount on Bonds Payable .... $500,000 (1−.96)	20,000	
Bonds Payable		500,000
Capital Arising from Bond Conversion Privilege		45,000

The periodic charge for interest will differ depending upon which method is employed. Under the first approach, the annual interest charge would be $37,500 ($40,000 paid less $2,500 straight-line premium amortization). Under the second approach, the annual interest charge would be $42,000 ($40,000 paid plus $2,000 straight-line discount amortization).

In 1969, the Accounting Principles Board in APB Opinion No. 14 stated that when convertible debt is sold at a price or with a value at issuance not significantly in excess of the face amount, "... no portion of the proceeds from the issuance ... should be accounted for as attributable to the conversion feature."[10] The Opinion stated that greater weight for this decision was placed upon the inseparability of the debt and the conversion option than upon the practical problems of valuing the separate parts. However, the practical problems are considerable. Separate valuation requires asking the question: How much would the security sell for without the conversion feature? In many instances this question would appear to be unanswerable. Investment dealers responsible for selling these issues are frequently unable to separate the two features for valuation purposes. The cash required simply could not be raised, they contend, without the conversion privilege. The question of accounting for convertible debt has not, as yet, been considered by the Accounting Research Committee. Therefore, in Canada, the separate debt and equity components of convertible debt are not given accounting recognition.

Issuance of Bonds with Share Purchase Warrants Attached

In addition to an increasing volume of convertible debt issues, bonds with detachable share purchase warrants have been issued. Because the debt instrument and the warrant are separate, they can and do trade on the market separately. Unlike convertible debt, repayment of which is uncertain, the presumption in debt with detachable warrants is that the debt will be repaid upon maturity. The decision to exercise the warrants depends upon the movement of share prices.

Because the warrants are separable from the debt instrument, a value can be assigned to the warrants based on the relative fair value of the debt security without the warrants and the value of the warrants themselves at the time of issuance. Assume the same example used in the discussion of convertible bonds except that share purchase warrants are substituted for the conversion feature: 500 ten-year bonds, total face value $500,000, are sold at 105. Each $1,000 bond is accompanied by one warrant that permits the holder to purchase 20 common shares, par value $40. Each bond without the warrant has a market value of $960, and each warrant has a market value of $90. The proceeds of $525,000 would be allocated $480,000 to the debt and $45,000 to owners' equity in the issuer's accounts as follows:

[10]*Ibid.*, par. 12.

Cash	525,000	
Discount on Bonds Payable	20,000	
Bonds Payable		500,000
Common Shares Purchase Warrants		45,000

In the preceding example, the sum of the market value for the bonds and warrants equalled the issue price of the joint offering. Market imperfections rarely provide such perfect relationships. When such relationship is not found, sales proceeds should be allocated between the two securities on the basis of their relative market values at the time of their issuance. When the purchase warrants are used to acquire shares, the proceeds received by the issuing corporation, in this case an amount equal to the par value of the shares, is credited to Common Shares and the amount allocated to equity is transferred to the account Premium on Common Shares.

BOND INTEREST — TERM BONDS

When coupon bonds are issued, cash is paid by the corporation in exchange for interest coupons on the interest dates. Payments on coupons may be made by the corporation directly to bondholders, or payments may be cleared through a bank or other disbursing agent. Subsidiary records with bondholders are not maintained since coupons are redeemable by bearers. In the case of registered bonds, interest cheques are mailed either by the company or its transfer agent. When bonds are registered, the bonds account requires subsidiary records for bondholdings by individuals and changes in such holdings. Cheques are sent to bondholders of record as of the interest payment dates.

When a transfer agent is to make interest payments, the corporation normally transfers cash to the agent in advance of the interest payment date. Since the company is not freed from its obligation to bondholders until payment has been made by its agent, it records the cash transfer by a debit to Cash Deposited with Transfer Agent and a credit to Cash. On the date the interest is due, the company debits Interest Expense and credits Interest Payable. Upon receipt from the transfer agent of paid interest coupons, or other evidence that the interest was paid, the company debits Interest Payable and credits Cash Deposited with Transfer Agent.

Amortization of Premium or Discount

When bonds are issued at a premium or discount, the market serves to adjust the stated interest rate to a market or effective interest rate. Because of the initial premium or discount, the periodic interest payments do not represent the complete revenue and expense for the periods involved. An adjustment for the periodic write-off of the premium or discount is necessary to reflect the effective interest rate being incurred or earned on the bonds. The periodic adjustment of bonds to their face value is referred to as *bond premium* or *discount amortization*.

A premium on bonds issued recognizes that the stated interest rate is higher than the market interest rate. Amortization of the premium reduces the interest revenue or expense below the amount of cash transferred. As the bond approaches the maturity date, reduction of the premium balance through amortization results in a bond investment or liability account that approaches the maturity value.

A discount on bonds issued recognizes that the stated interest rate is lower than the market interest rate. Amortization of the discount increases the amount of interest revenue or expense above the amount of cash transferred. As with the premium amortization, reduction of the discount through amortization results in a bond investment or liability balance that approaches the maturity value.

Two principal methods are used to amortize the premium or discount in the accounts of both the issuer and the investor. These are (1) the straight-line method and (2) the interest method.

Straight-Line Method. The straight-line method provides for the recognition of an equal amount of premium or discount amortization each period. The amount of monthly amortization is determined by dividing the premium or discount at purchase or issuance by the number of months remaining to the bond maturity date. For example, if a 10-year, 8% bond issue with a maturity value of $200,000 were sold on the issuance date at 103, the $6,000 premium would be amortized evenly over the 120 months until maturity, or at a rate of $50 per month, ($6,000 ÷ 120). The premium amortization would reduce both interest expense in the issuer's accounts and interest revenue in the investor's accounts. A discount amortization would have the opposite results: both accounts would be increased.

The simplicity of straight-line amortization is indeed appealing in spite of the method's deficiencies in the context of accounting theory. Nonetheless, the straight-line method of amortizing a bond premium or discount is still widely used in Canadian accounting practice. There is nothing to prevent use of the interest method as an alternative to straight-line amortization; at the same time, there are no authoritative pronouncements or legal requirements of Canadian origin that encourage use of the interest method.

Interest Method. The interest method of amortization uses a uniform interest rate based upon a changing investment or liability balance and provides for an increasing premium or discount amortization each period. In order to use this method, the effective interest rate for the bonds must first be determined. This is the rate of interest at bond issuance that discounts the maturity value of the bonds and the periodic interest payments to the market price of the bonds. This rate is used to determine the effective revenue or expense to be recorded in the accounts.

For example, as shown on page 515, $100,000, 10-year, 8% bonds sold to return 10% would sell for $87,539 or at a discount of $12,461. If the bonds were sold on the issuance date, the discount amortization for the first six months would be computed as illustrated below.

Investment balance at beginning of first period	$87,539
Effective rate per semi-annual period	5%
Stated rate per semi-annual period	4%
Interest amount based on effective rate ($87,539 × .05)	$ 4,377
Interest payment based on stated rate ($100,000 × .04)	4,000
Difference between interest amount based on effective rate and stated rate	$ 377

This difference is the discount amortization for the first period under the interest method. For the second semi-annual period, the bond carrying value increases by the discount amortization. The amortization for the second semi-annual period would be computed as follows:

Investment balance at beginning of second period ($87,539 + $377)	$87,916
Interest amount based on effective rate ($87,916 × .05)	$ 4,396
Interest payment based on stated rate ($100,000 × .04)	4,000
Difference between interest amount based on effective rate and stated rate	$ 396

The amount of interest for each period is computed at a uniform rate on an increasing balance. This results in an increasing discount amortization over the life of the bonds that is graphically demonstrated below:

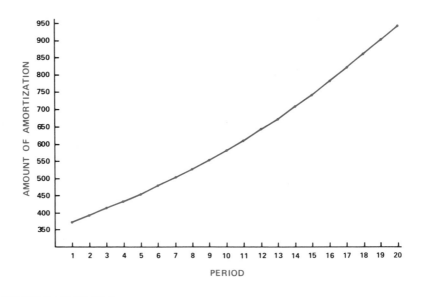

Premium amortization would be computed in a similar way except that the interest amount based on the stated interest rate would be higher than the amount based on the effective rate. For example, $100,000, 10-year, 8% bonds sold to return 6% would sell for $114,880, or at a premium of $14,880. If the bonds were sold on the issuance date, the premium amortization for the first and second six-month periods would be computed as follows:

Investment balance at beginning of first period	$114,880
Effective rate per semi-annual period	3%
Stated rate per semi-annual period	4%
Interest payment based on stated rate ($100,000 × .04)	$ 4,000
Interest amount based on effective rate ($114,880 × .03)	3,446
Difference between interest amount based on stated rate and effective rate, or premium amortization	$ 554
Investment balance at beginning of second period ($114,800 − $554)	$114,326
Interest payment based on stated rate ($100,000 × .04)	$ 4,000
Interest amount based on effective rate ($114,326 × .03)	3,430
Difference between interest amount based on stated rate and effective rate	$ 570

As illustrated, as the investment or liability balance is reduced by the premium amortization, the interest based upon the effective rate also decreases. The difference between the interest payment and the interest based upon the effective rate increases in a manner similar to discount amortization. Special bond amortization tables, such as the partial one illustrated below, may be prepared to determine the periodic adjustments to the bond carrying value.

Amortization of Premium — Interest Method
$100,000 10-Year Bonds, Interest at 8% Payable Semi-annually,
Sold at $114,880 to Yield 6%

Interest Pay-ment	A Interest Paid (4% of Face Value)	B Interest Expense (3% of Bond Carrying Value)	C Premium Amortization (A − B)	D Unamortized Premium (D − C)	E Bond Carrying Value ($100,000 + D)
				$14,880	$114,880
1	$4,000	$3,446 (3% of $114,880)	$554	14,326	114,326
2	4,000	3,430 (3% of 114,326)	570	13,756	113,756
3	4,000	3,413 (3% of 113,756)	587	13,169	113,169
4	4,000	3,395 (3% of 113,169)	605	12,564	112,564
5	4,000	3,377 (3% of 112,564)	623	11,941	111,941
6	4,000	3,358 (3% of 111,941)	642	11,299	111,299
7	4,000	3,339 (3% of 111,299)	661	10,638	110,638
8	4,000	3,319 (3% of 110,638)	681	9,957	109,957
9	4,000	3,299 (3% of 109,957)	701	9,256	109,256
10	4,000	3,278 (3% of 109,256)	722	8,534	108,534
.	.	.	.	.	.
.	.	.	.	.	.
.	.	.	.	.	.

Because the interest method adjusts the stated interest rate to an effective interest rate, it is theoretically more accurate as an amortization method than is the straight-line method. Since the issuance of APB Opinion No. 21, it is now the required amortization method in the United States. The more popular straight-line method may be used by a company if the results of using it do not differ materially from the amortization using the interest method.[11]

Accounting for Bond Interest

Entries for premium or discount amortization may be made as adjusting entries at the end of a company's fiscal year or interim period, or as each interest payment is made. The accounting entries for bond interest and first year discount amortization in both the issuer's and investor's accounts would be as follows. Assume the bonds are issued at a discount as described on page 520 and the discount is amortized by the interest method when each payment is made or received.

Issuer's Accounts

First payment:	Interest Expense	4,377	
	Cash		4,000
	Discount on Bonds Payable		377
Second payment:	Interest Expense	4,396	
	Cash		4,000
	Discount on Bonds Payable		396

Investor's Accounts

First payment:	Cash	4,000	
	Investment in Bonds	377	
	Interest Revenue		4,377
Second payment:	Cash	4,000	
	Investment in Bonds	396	
	Interest Revenue		4,396

If the bonds were sold at a premium, the investment or liability balance would be reduced over the life of the bonds to maturity value. Assume a 10-year, $200,000, 8% bond issue is sold at 103 on May 1 and is recorded as shown on page 517. Interest payment dates are February 1 and August 1, and the straight-line method of amortization is used. The following entries in both the issuer's and investor's accounts for the first year would be required.

Issuer's Accounts

Aug. 1	Interest Expense	7,846	
	Premium on Bonds Payable	154	
	Cash		8,000

---

[11]*Opinions of the Accounting Principles Board, No. 21*, "Interest on Receivables and Payables" (New York: American Institute of Certified Public Accountants, 1972), par. 15.

Computation:

Premium amortization for 3 months:
$6,000/117 = $51.28 per month
$51.28 × 3 = $153.84, or $154

Feb. 1	Interest Expense	7,692	
	Premium on Bonds Payable	308	
	Cash		8,000

Computation:

Premium amortization for 6 months:
$51.28 × 6 = $307.68, or $308

Investor's Accounts

Aug. 1	Cash	8,000	
	Investment in Bonds		154
	Interest Revenue		7,846
Feb. 1	Cash	8,000	
	Investment in Bonds		308
	Interest Revenue		7,692

When bonds are acquired as a temporary investment, investment cost is maintained in the accounts without adjustment for premium or discount amortization. Any difference between the purchase and sales price is recognized as a gain or loss at the time the investment is disposed of.

BOND INTEREST — SERIAL BONDS

When serial bonds are issued, the amortization schedule for bond premium or discount requires recognition of a declining debt principal. Successive bond years cannot be charged with equal amounts of premium or discount because of a shrinking debt and successively smaller interest payments.

Premium or discount on serial bonds may be amortized by the straight-line method or by the interest method. The straight-line procedure is referred to as the *bonds-outstanding method* and calls for decreases in the amortization schedule proportionate to the decrease in the loan balance. The interest method is as described for term bonds but is applied to a declining total debt.

Bonds-Outstanding Method

Amortization by the bonds-outstanding method is illustrated in the example that follows. Assume that bonds of $100,000, dated January 1, 1977, are issued on this date for $101,260. Bonds of $20,000 mature at the beginning of each year. The bonds pay interest of 8% annually. The company's accounting period ends on December 31; the accounting period and the bond year thus coincide. A table showing the premium to be amortized each year is developed as shown on the schedule on the next page.

	Amortization Schedule — Bonds-Outstanding Method		
Year	Bonds Outstanding	Fraction of Premium to be Amortized	Annual Premium Amortization (Fraction × $1,260)
1977	$100,000	100,000/300,000 (or 10/30)	$ 420
1978	80,000	80,000/300,000 (or 8/30)	336
1979	60,000	60,000/300,000 (or 6/30)	252
1980	40,000	40,000/300,000 (or 4/30)	168
1981	20,000	20,000/300,000 (or 2/30)	84
	$300,000	300,000/300,000 (or 30/30)	$1,260

The annual premium amortization is found by multiplying the premium by a fraction whose numerator is the number of bond dollars outstanding in that year and whose denominator is the total number of bond dollars outstanding for the life of the bond issue. As bonds are retired, the amounts of premium amortization decline accordingly.

Periodic amortization may be incorporated in a table summarizing the interest charges and changes in bond carrying values as shown below.

	Amortization of Premium — Serial Bonds Bonds-Outstanding Method					
Date	A Interest Payment (8% of Face Value)	B Premium Amortization	C Interest Expense (A − B)	D Principal Payment	E Bond Carrying Value Decrease (B + D)	F Bond Carrying Value (F − E)
Jan. 1, 1977						$101,260
Dec. 31, 1977	$8,000	$420	$7,580	$20,000	$20,420	80,840
Dec. 31, 1978	6,400	336	6,064	20,000	20,336	60,504
Dec. 31, 1979	4,800	252	4,548	20,000	20,252	40,252
Dec. 31, 1980	3,200	168	3,032	20,000	20,168	20,084
Dec. 31, 1981	1,600	84	1,516	20,000	20,084	———

Interest Method

Tables show that the bonds discussed on the preceding page were sold to return approximately 7½%. Use of this rate results in the interest charges and premium amortization shown in the table at the top of page 527.

The bonds-outstanding method of amortization provides for the recognition of uniform amounts of amortization in terms of the face value of bonds outstanding. The interest method provides for the recognition of interest at a uniform rate on the declining debt balance.

	A	B	C	D	E	F
		Interest				
	Interest	Expense	Premium		Bond Carry-	Bond
Date	Payment	(7½% of Bond	Amortiza-	Principal	ing Value	Carrying
	(8% of	Carrying	tion	Payment	Decrease	Value
	Face Value)	Value)	(A − B)		(C + D)	(F − E)
Jan. 1, 1977						$101,260
Dec. 31, 1977	$8,000	$7,595	$405	$20,000	$20,405	80,855
Dec. 31, 1978	6,400	6,064	336	20,000	20,336	60,519
Dec. 31, 1979	4,800	4,539	261	20,000	20,261	40,258
Dec. 31, 1980	3,200	3,019	181	20,000	20,181	20,077
Dec. 31, 1981	1,600	1,523*	77*	20,000	20,077	——

Title: Amortization of Premium — Serial Bonds / Interest Method

*The last payment is adjusted because the effective rate was not exactly 7½%. On the final payment the premium balance is closed and interest expense is reduced by this amount.

Amortization Procedures when Bond Year and Fiscal Year Do Not Coincide

When serial bond retirement dates do not agree with the company's fiscal year, the amortization schedule must provide for amortization other than for full annual periods. To illustrate, assume that $500,000, 5% serial bonds, dated March 1, 1977, are sold on April 1, 1977, at a discount of $35,000. Bonds of $100,000 mature on March 1 of each year. The discount should be amortized over 59 months. Assuming that the fiscal period for the issuer is the calendar year, an amortization schedule that uses *bond month-dollars* may be prepared as shown below.

Title: Amortization Schedule When Bond Year and Fiscal Year Do Not Coincide — Bonds-Outstanding Method

Year	Bonds Outstanding	Months Outstanding	Bond Month-Dollars (Months Times Bonds Outstanding)	Total Bond Month-Dollars	Fraction of Discount to be Amortized	Annual Discount Amortization (Fraction × $35,000)
1977	$500,000	9	$4,500,000	$ 4,500,000	45/175	$ 9,000
1978	500,000	2	1,000,000			
	400,000	10	4,000,000	5,000,000	50/175	10,000
1979	400,000	2	800,000			
	300,000	10	3,000,000	3,800,000	38/175	7,600
1980	300,000	2	600,000			
	200,000	10	2,000,000	2,600,000	26/175	5,200
1981	200,000	2	400,000			
	100,000	10	1,000,000	1,400,000	14/175	2,800
1982	100,000	2	200,000	200,000	2/175	400
		59		$17,500,000	175/175	$35,000

CONVERSION OF BONDS

Convertible bonds grant to the investor the right to convert debt to equity under certain conditions. The conversion privilege is granted when the bonds are sold, but as discussed earlier, the value of the conversion privilege is normally combined with the cost of the debt instrument. When conversion takes place, a valuation problem must be resolved. Should the market value of the securities be used to compute a gain or loss on the transaction? If the security is viewed as debt, then the conversion to equity would seem to be a significant economic transaction and a gain or loss should be recognized. If, however, the security is viewed as equity, the conversion is really an exchange of one type of equity capital for another, and the historical-cost principle would seem to indicate that no gain or loss would be recognized. In practice, the latter approach seems to be most commonly followed by both the issuer and investor. The carrying value of the bonds is normally transferred to become the value of the shares issued.

If the investor viewed the security as debt, conversion of the debt could be viewed as an exchange of one asset for another. The general rule for the exchange of non-monetary assets is that the market value of the asset exchanged should be used to measure any gain or loss on the transaction.[12] If there is no market value of the asset surrendered or if its value is undeterminable, the market value of the asset received should be used. The market value of convertible bonds should reflect the market value of the shares to be issued on the conversion, and thus the market value of the two securities should be similar. Before an exchange is recorded, the investment account should be brought up to date for premium or discount amortization.

To illustrate bond conversion for the investor recognizing a gain or loss on conversion, assume Carl Co. offers bondholders 40 shares of Carl Co. common shares, $25 par, in exchange for each $1,000, 8% bond held. An investor exchanges bonds of $10,000 (carrying value as brought up to date, $9,850) for 400 common shares having a market value at the date of the exchange of $26 per share. The exchange is completed three months after an interest payment date. The exchange is recorded as follows:

Cash	200	
Investment in Carl Co. Common Shares	10,400	
Investment in Carl Co. 8's		9,850
Gain on Conversion of Carl Co. Bonds		550
Interest Revenue		200

$10,000 \times .08 \times \dfrac{3\ mos}{12\ mos}$

$= \$200$

If the investor chose not to recognize a gain or loss, the journal entry would be as follows:

---

[12]*Opinions of Accounting Principles Board, No. 29*, "Accounting for Nonmonetary Transactions" (New York: American Institute of Certified Public Accountants, 1973), par. 18.

Cash	200	
Investment in Carl Co. Common Shares	9,850	
Investment in Carl Co. 8's		9,850
Interest Revenue		200

Similar differences would occur in the issuer's accounts depending upon the viewpoint assumed. If the issuer desired to recognize the conversion of the convertible debt as a significant transaction, the market value of the securities would be used to record the conversion. To illustrate the journal entries for the issuer using this reasoning, assume 100 bonds, total face value $100,000 are exchanged for 2,000 shares common shares, $40 par value, $55 market value. At the time of the conversion there is an unamortized premium on the bond issue of $3,000. The conversion would be recorded as follows:

Bonds Payable	100,000	
Premium on Bonds Payable	3,000	
Loss on Conversion of Bonds	7,000	
Common Shares		80,000
Premium on Common Shares		30,000

Computation:

Market value of shares issued (2,000 shares at $55)		$110,000
Face value of bonds payable	$100,000	
Plus unamortized premium	3,000	103,000
Loss to company on conversion of bonds		$ 7,000

If the issuer did not consider the conversion as a culminating transaction, no gain or loss would be recognized. The bond carrying value would be transformed to the share capital account on the theory that the company upon issuing the bonds is aware of the fact that bond proceeds may ultimately represent the consideration to be identified with shares. Thus, when bond-holders exercise their conversion privileges, the value identified with the obligation is transferred to the security that replaces it. Under this assumption, the conversion would be recorded as follows:

Bonds Payable	100,000	
Premium on Bonds Payable	3,000	
Common Shares, $40 par		80,000
Premium on Common Shares		23,000

The profession has not resolved the accounting issues surrounding convertible debt. Although the practice of not recognizing gain or loss in either the issuer's or the investor's accounts is widespread, it seems inconsistent with the treatment of other items that are transferred by an entity. The economy reality of the transaction would seem to require a recognition of the change in value at least at the time conversion takes place.

TERMINATION OF BONDS

Bonds always include a specified termination or maturity date. At that time, the issuer must pay the current investor the maturity or face value of the bond. Bonds may be terminated earlier than the maturity date in one of two ways: (1) the issuer may *reacquire* individual bonds on the market and retire them, or (2) the issuer may utilize the call provision frequently included in bond indentures and *redeem* all or part of the issue prior to maturity. Issuing corporations frequently finance the termination of bonds by issuing new debt securities. When the two transactions are merged into one, such financing is referred to as *bond refunding*. The following sections discuss the accounting problems for both the issuer and the investor dealing with termination of bonds.

Bond Retirement at Maturity

Most bond issues are payable at the end of a specified period. When bond discount or premium and issue cost balances have been satisfactorily amortized over the life of the bonds, bond retirement simply calls for elimination of the liability or the investment by a cash transaction. Any bonds not presented for payment at their maturity date should be removed from the bonds payable balance in the issuer's accounts and reported separately as Matured Bonds Payable; these are reported as a current liability except when they are to be paid out of a sinking fund. Interest does not accrue on matured bonds not presented for payment.

If a bond fund is used to pay off a bond issue, any cash remaining in the fund may be returned to the cash account. Appropriations of retained earnings established during the life of the issue may be returned to retained earnings.

Bond Reacquisition Prior to Maturity

Corporations frequently reacquire their own bonds on the market when prices or other factors make such action desirable. Reacquisition of bonds prior to their maturity calls for the recognition of a gain or a loss for the difference between the bond carrying value and the amount paid. This gain or loss may be termed an *early extinguishment of debt*, and is reported on the income statement. Payment of accrued interest on bond reacquisition is separately reported as a debit to Interest Expense.

When bonds are reacquired, amortization of bond premium, discount, and issue costs should be brought up to date. Reacquisition calls for the cancellation of the bond face value together with any related premium, discount, or issue costs as of the reacquisition date.

To illustrate bond reacquisition, assume $100,000, 8% bonds of Atlas, Ltd., are not held until maturity, but are sold back to the issuer on February 1, 1979, at 97 plus accrued interest. The carrying value of the bonds in both the issuer's and investor's accounts is $97,700 as of January 1. Discount amortization has been recorded at $50 a month using the straight-line method. Interest payment dates on the bonds are November 1 and April 1; accrued interest adjustments are reversed. Entries in both the issuer's and investor's accounts at the time of bond redemption would be as follows:

Issuer's Accounts

Feb. 1	Interest Expense	50	
	Discount on Bonds Payable		50
	To record discount amortization for January, 1979.		
Feb. 1	Bonds Payable	100,000	
	①Interest Expense	2,000	
	Discount on Bonds Payable		2,250
	Cash		99,000
	Gain on Bond Reacquisition		750
	To record reacquisition of bonds and payment of three months' interest.		

Computation:

Carrying value of bonds, January 1, 1979	$97,700
Discount amortization for January	50
Carrying value of bonds, February 1, 1979	$97,750
Sales proceeds	97,000
Gain on sale	$ 750

① Interest expense for 3 months:
$100,000 × .08 × 1/4 = $2,000

Investor's Accounts

Feb. 1	Investment in Atlas, Ltd., 8% Bonds	50	
	Interest Revenue		50
	To record discount amortization for January, 1979.		
Feb. 1	Cash	99,000	
	Loss on Sale of Bonds	750	
	Investment in Atlas, Ltd., 8% Bonds		97,750
	Interest Revenue		2,000
	To record reacquisition of bonds and receipt of three months' interest.		

Bond Redemption Prior to Maturity — Term Bonds

Provisions of the bond indenture frequently give the issuer the option of calling bonds for payment prior to maturity. Ordinarily the call must be made on an interest payment date and no further interest accrues on the bonds not presented at this time. When only a part of the issue is to be retired, the bonds called may be determined by lot.

The inclusion of call provisions in the bond agreement is a feature favoring the issuer. The company is in a position to terminate the bond agreement and eliminate future interest charges whenever its financial position makes such action feasible. Furthermore, the company is protected in the event of a fall in the market interest rate by being able to retire the old issue from proceeds for a new issue paying a lower rate of interest. The bond contract normally requires payment of a premium if bonds are called. The bondholder is thus offered compensation if the investment is terminated.

When bonds are called, the difference between the amount paid and the bond carrying value is reported as a gain or a loss in both the issuer's and investor's accounts. Any interest paid at the time of the call is recorded as a debit to Interest Expense or a credit to Interest Revenue. The entries to be made are the same as illustrated previously for the sale and reacquisition of bonds.

When an investor acquires callable bonds at a premium, conservatism calls for an amortization policy that prevents the bonds from being reported at more than their redemption values at the various call dates. To illustrate, assume bonds of $10,000 are acquired for $10,800 on January 1, 1978. The bonds were originally issued on January 1, 1976, and have a maturity date of January 1, 1996. The following table of redemption values is included in the indenture.

Redeemable January 1, 1981, to December 31, 1985, at 105
Redeemable January 1, 1986, to December 31, 1990, at 102$^1/_2$
Redeemable January 1; 1991, to December 31, 1995, at 101

Regular premium amortization and accelerated amortization based upon bond redemption values of $10,500, $10,250, and $10,100, are compared below:

Regular Amortization	Accelerated Amortization
$800 ÷ 18 years = $44.44 per year (1978–1996)	($10,800 − $10,500) ÷ 3 years (1978–1980) = $100 per year
	($10,500 − $10,250) ÷ 5 years (1981–1985) = $ 50 per year
	($10,250 − $10,100) ÷ 5 years (1986–1990) = $ 30 per year
	($10,100 − $10,000) ÷ 5 years (1991–1995) = $ 20 per year

If regular amortization procedures are followed in the accounts of the investor, bond redemption prior to maturity will result in a recovery of cash that is less than bond carrying value and will require recognition of a loss that nullifies in part the earnings recognized in the past. Accelerated amortization reduces the investment to its redemption value; bond redemption values are used for income measurement purposes and the need for recognition of a loss upon redemption is avoided. Obviously, bonds reported at a discount, or bonds reported at a premium reduced by normal amortization to an amount that is not greater than redemption value, require no special treatment.

Bond Redemption Prior to Maturity — Serial Bonds

When serial bonds are reacquired prior to their maturities, it is necessary to cancel the unamortized premium or discount relating to that part of the bond issue that is liquidated. For example, assume the issuance of serial bonds previously described on page 525 and amortization on the premium by the bonds-outstanding method as given on pages 525 and 526. On April 1, 1978, $10,000 of bonds due January 1, 1980, and $10,000 of bonds due January 1, 1981, are reacquired at 100½ plus accrued interest. The premium for the period January 1–April 1, 1978, relating to retired bonds affects bond interest for the current period and will be written off as an adjustment to expense. The balance of the premium from the retirement date to the respective maturity date of the series retired must be cancelled. The premium balance relating to retired bonds is calculated as follows:

```
Premium Identified with 1978: 20,000/80,000 × $336 × 9/12 = $ 63
Premium Identified with 1979: 20,000/60,000 ×   252         =   84
Premium Identified with 1980: 10,000/40,000 ×   168         =   42
Premium Identified with Retired Bonds ..................  $189
```

Instead of the above procedure, the premium amortization per year on each $1,000 bond may first be calculated and this rate applied to bonds of each period that are cancelled. The annual amortization rate per $1,000 bond is calculated as follows:

$$\frac{\$1,260 \text{ (Total Premium: Life of Bonds)}}{300 \text{ (Total \$1,000 Bonds Outstanding: Life of Bonds)}} = \$4.20$$

The premium to be cancelled may now be determined as follows:

Year	Number of $1,000 Bonds	×	Annual Amortization per $1,000 Bond	×	Fractional Part of Year	=	Total Premium Cancellation
1978	20		$4.20		9/12		$ 63
1979	20		4.20				84
1980	10		4.20				42
Premium Identified with Retired Bonds							$189

Bonds, carrying value $20,189, are retired at a cost of $20,100 resulting in a gain of $89. Payment is also made for interest on bonds of $20,000 for three months at 8%, or $400. The entry to record the retirement of bonds and the payment of interest on the series retired follows:

```
Bonds Payable .........................................  20,000
Premium on Bonds Payable .............................     189
Interest Expense ......................................     400
    Cash ..................................................         20,500
    Gain on Bond Retirement ..............................             89
```

A revised schedule for the amortization of bond premium follows:

	Amortization Schedule — Bonds-Outstanding Method Revised for Bond Retirement		
Year	Annual Premium Amortization per Original Schedule	Premium Cancellation on Bond Retirement	Annual Premium Amortization Adjusted for Bond Retirement
1977	$ 420		$ 420
1978	336	$ 63	273
1979	252	84	168
1980	168	42	126
1981	84		84
	$1,260	$189	$1,071

Bond Refunding

Cash for the retirement of a bond issue is frequently raised through the sale of a new issue and is referred to as bond refunding; the original issue is said to be *refunded*. Bond refunding may take place when an issue matures. Bonds may also be refunded prior to their maturity when the interest rate has dropped and the interest savings on a new issue will more than offset the costs of retiring the old issue. To illustrate, assume a corporation has outstanding 8% bonds of $1,000,000 callable at 102 and with a remaining 10-year term, and similar 10-year bonds can be marketed currently at an interest rate of only $6^{1}/_{2}\%$. Under these circumstances it would be advantageous to retire the old issue with the proceeds from a new $6^{1}/_{2}\%$ issue since the future savings in interest will exceed by a considerable amount the premium to be paid on the call of the old issue.

The desirability of refunding may not be so obvious as in the preceding instance. In determining whether refunding is warranted in marginal cases, careful consideration must be given to such factors as the different maturity dates of the two issues, possible future changes in interest rates, changed loan requirements, different indenture provisions, income tax effects of refunding, and legal fees, printing costs, and marketing costs involved in refunding.

When refunding takes place before the maturity date of the old issue, the problem arises as to how to dispose of the call premium and unamortized discount and issue costs of the original bonds. Three positions have been taken with respect to dispositon of these items:

1. Such charges are considered a loss on bond retirement.
2. Such charges are considered deferrable and to be amortized systematically over the remaining life of the original issue.
3. Such charges are considered deferrable and to be amortized systematically over the life of the new issue.

Although arguments can be presented supporting each of these alternatives, the Accounting Principles Board concluded that "all extinguishments of debt before scheduled maturities are fundamentally alike. The accounting for such transactions should be the same regardless of the means used to achieve the extinguishment.[13] The first position, immediate recognition of the gain or loss, was selected by the Board for all early extinguishment of debt. The Financial Accounting Standards Board considered the nature of this gain or loss and defined it as being an extraordinary item requiring separate income statement disclosure.[14] As yet, there are no Canadian counterparts for either APB Opinion 26 or SFAS No. 4. As a result, all three of the above methods find varying degrees of use in Canadian accounting practice.

BOND FUNDS

Bond indentures for term bonds frequently require the issuing company to establish a *sinking fund* to be used to retire the bonds at maturity. The annual amount to be paid into the fund is computed using compound interest tables as illustrated in Chapter 10. Bond funds may be administered directly by a corporation or by an independent trustee.

The example on pages 536-537 illustrates the accounting that may be employed when (1) information is recorded currently in the company's accounts, and (2) information is recorded at the end of the period in the company's accounts from summaries provided by a trustee. The example assumes the establishment of a fund for the retirement of bonds and gives the entries for the fund accumulation in the first year and for debt retirement in the last year.

It should be observed that when separate accounts are maintained by a trustee, assets are balanced by a *company* account summarizing the trustee's accountability to the company. This account is credited for assets received from the company as well as for net asset increases resulting from earnings; it is debited for assets applied to the purpose for which the fund was established as well as for assets transferred to the company. The *fund* account maintained by the company, in turn, reports the company's equity in the fund. This account is debited for assets transferred to the trustee and for net asset increases resulting from fund earnings; it is credited for assets applied to the purpose for which the fund was established and for the assets transferred to the company. The company account maintained by the trustee and the fund account on the company's books are *reciprocal accounts* since the credit balance in the company account is equal to the debit balance in the fund account when both sets of accounts are up to date. When a corporation

---

[13]*Opinions of the Accounting Principles Board, No. 26,* "Early Extinguishment of Debt" (New York: American Institute of Certified Public Accountants, 1972), par. 19.

[14]*Statement of Financial Accounting Standards No. 4,* "Reporting Gains and Losses from Extinguishment of Debt" (Stamford, Conn.: Financial Accounting Standards Board, 1975), par. 8.

TRANSACTION	FUND TRANSACTIONS RECORDED CURRENTLY IN COMPANY'S ACCOUNTS		
	ENTRY		
1977:			
June 30, 1977 The Powell Corporation made the first of a series of 20 equal semi-annual deposits of $40,000 to bond fund.	Bond Fund Cash .... Cash	40,000	40,000
July 6, 1977 Purchased bond fund securities for $35,750, which included accrued interest of $150.	Bond Fund Securities .... Bond Fund Revenue .... Bond Fund Cash	35,600 150	35,750
December 31, 1977 Received interest on bond fund securities, $900.	Bond Fund Cash .... Bond Fund Revenue	900	900
December 1, 1977 Paid bond fund custodian fees, $200.	Bond Fund Expenses .... Bond Fund Cash	200	200
Made second deposit of $40,000 to bond fund.	Bond Fund Cash .... Cash	40,000	40,000
To record accrued interest on bond fund securities and cash deposits, $225.	Interest on Bond Fund Securities Receivable .... Bond Fund Revenue	225	225
To record amortization of premium on bond fund securities, $100.	Bond Fund Revenue .... Bond Fund Securities	100	100
(a) To recognize bond fund revenue and expense. (b) To close bond fund revenue and expense balances.	(b) Bond Fund Revenue .... Bond Fund Expenses ..... Income Summary	875	200 675
1986 **December 31, 1986** Sold bond fund securities carrying value after entries for amortization, $1,060,000, for $1,100,000, which included accrued interest, $8,000; total proceeds were added to bond fund cash on hand on this date of $15,000.	Bond Fund Cash .... Bond Fund Securities .... Bond Fund Revenue .... Gain on Sale of Bond Fund Securities	1,100,000	1,060,000 8,000 32,000
Paid bonded indebtedness from bond fund cash, $1,000,000.	Bonds Payable .... Bond Fund Cash	1,000,000	1,000,000
Transferred bond fund cash on hand after payment of bonds to cash account.	Cash .... Bond Fund Cash	115,000	115,000
(a) To recognize bond fund income or loss. (b) To close nominal accounts relating to bond fund activities.	(b) Bond Fund Revenue .... Gain on Sale of Bond Fund Securities .... Income Summary	8,000 32,000	40,000

FUND TRANSACTIONS RECORDED CURRENTLY IN TRUSTEE'S ACCOUNTS

ENTRY IN CORPORATION'S ACCOUNTS			ENTRY IN TRUSTEE'S ACCOUNTS		
Bond Fund — A. G. Shaw, Trustee	40,000		Cash	40,000	
Cash		40,000	The Powell Corporation		40,000
			Investment in Securities	35,600	
			Interest Revenue	150	
			Cash		35,750
			Cash	900	
			Interest Revenue		900
			Expenses	200	
			Cash		200
Bond Fund — A. G. Shaw, Trustee	40,000		Cash	40,000	
Cash		40,000	The Powell Corporation		40,000
			Interest on Securities Receivable	225	
			Interest Revenue		225
			Interest Revenue	100	
			Investment in Securities		100
(a) Bond Fund — A. G. Shaw Trustee	675				
Bond Fund Expenses	200				
Interest Revenue		875			
(b) Interest Revenue	875		Interest Revenue	875	
Bond Fund Expense		200	Expenses		200
Income Summary		675	The Powell Corporation		675
			Cash	1,100,000	
			Investment in Securities		1,060,000
			Interest Revenue		8,000
			Gain on Sale of Securities		32,000
Bonds Payable	1,000,000		The Powell Corporation	1,000,000	
Bond Fund — A. G. Shaw, Trustee		1,000,000	Cash		1,000,000
Cash	115,000		The Powell Corporation	115,000	
Bond Fund — A. G. Shaw, Trustee		115,000	Cash		115,000
(a) Bond Fund — A. G. Shaw, Trustee	40,000				
Interest Revenue		8,000			
Gain on Sale of Bond Fund Securities		32,000			
(b) Interest Revenue	8,000				
Gain on Sale of Bond Fund Securities	32,000		Interest Revenue	8,000	
			Gain on Sale of Securities	32,000	
Income Summary		40,000	The Powell Corporation		40,000

administers a fund but wishes to remove fund detail from the general ledger, a separate ledger can be provided in a form similar to that employed by the trustee.

Bond fund cash is commonly used to purchase a company's own bonds. Such fund use frequently operates to support a firm market price for the issue since the corporation can enter the market whenever the market price makes retirement of the company's bonds attractive.

In the example, the bond fund assets as shown in the company's accounts or as reported to the company by the trustee at the end of 1977 are as follows:

Bond fund cash	$44,950
Bond fund securities	35,500
Accrued interest on bond fund securities	225
Total	$80,675

Bond fund revenue for 1977 is $875 and bond fund expense is $200; the difference, $675, represents the fund earnings. This amount is reported on the income statement as "Other revenue." A gain or a loss on the sale of fund securities would be recognized as other revenue or expense. The individual assets in the fund would be reported under the long-term investments heading on the balance sheet.

The foregoing illustration assumed purchase of securities other than bonds originally issued by the corporation.

When a corporation retires its own bonds through bond fund cash, the liability is cancelled, the bond fund cash account is credited, and a loss or gain on the retirement is recorded. For example, assume that the accounts of a corporation show bonds of $100,000 outstanding with an unamortized bond discount balance relating to this issue of $3,500. The company acquires and formally retires bonds with a face value of $20,000 at a cost of $19,500. The entry to record the bond retirement follows:

Bonds Payable	20,000	
Loss on Bond Retirement	200	
Bond Fund Cash		19,500
Unamortized Bond Discount . . $\frac{3500}{100000} \times 20,000 =$ . . .		700
To record bond retirement.		

Computation:

Amount paid on retirement	$19,500	
Carrying value of bonds retired: face value of bonds,		
$20,000 less unamortized discount applicable to bonds,		
$700	19,300	
Loss on retirement	$ 200	

When bonds are acquired by a trustee and kept *alive*, such bonds are sometimes carried in the accounts the same as any other investment. The trustee records the bonds at cost, collects interest on the bonds and records collections as revenue, applies accumulation and amortization procedures in calculating effective earnings, and reports a gain or a loss on the resale of bonds to outsiders. The treatment of reacquired bonds as an investment results in periodic cash transfers to the trustee representing bond interest and permits fund accumulation in accordance with scheduled requirements. Interest paid by the corporation on its own bonds is counterbalanced by interest received by the trustee. Any difference between the carrying value of the liability and the amount paid for the bonds is recognized over the remaining life of the bonds by the entries for discount accumulation and premium amortization by the corporation and by the trustee.

The treatment of bond reacquisition as an investment is not supportable in theory. Reacquired bonds, even though in the hands of a corporate agent, cannot be considered an asset by the corporation. Such bonds are, in effect, evidence of debt retirement. Reacquired bonds may be sold and thus provide additional cash, but this is also true of unissued bonds; both reacquired and unissued bonds are no more than instruments that may be used in future borrowing.

In some instances, the trustee may assume the liability for payment of the bonds. In these circumstances, the bond liability is reduced as payments are made to the trustee and no fund investment is reported on the issuer's balance sheet.

The issuance of serial bonds eliminates the need for a bond sinking fund. When a sinking fund cannot produce earnings at a rate equivalent to that paid on the bond issue, serial bonds are advantageous to the issuing corporation. In this case, cash otherwise deposited in the fund is applied directly to the retirement of debt, and the payment of interest relating to that portion of the debt is terminated.

BOND RESTRUCTURING

Economic conditions sometimes arise making it difficult for the issuer of bonds to make the cash payments required by the bond indenture. These payments include interest payments, and possibly principal payments to retire serial bonds, periodic payments into bond sinking funds, and payments at the maturity of the debt.[15] To avoid bankruptcy proceedings or foreclosure of the bonds, investors in such situations may agree to revise the original terms of the bond issue to permit the issuer to recover from financial problems. The restructuring may take many different forms. For example, there may be a suspension of interest payments for a period of time, a reduction in the interest rate, an extension of the maturity date of the debt, or even an exchange of equity securities for the debt. The principal accounting

---

[15]For a detailed discussion of the problems involved in restructuring of debt, see *FASB Discussion Memorandum*, "Accounting by Debtors and Creditors When Debt is Restructured" (Stamford, Conn.: Financial Accounting Standards Board, 1976).

question in these cases, in both the accounts of the issuer and the investor, is whether a gain or loss should be recognized upon the restructuring of the debt.

The accounting problems arising upon debt restructuring may be illustrated as follows: assume the issuing corporation has outstanding $1,000,000, 8% bonds issued at an effective interest rate of 10% with a present carrying value of $922,768. The bonds are scheduled to mature in five years. Because of financial difficulties, the company is behind in its interest payments and in payments to the bond sinking fund. In order to avoid foreclosure on the bonds, the holders of the bonds, principally large financial institutions, agree to a reduction in the interest rate to 5% per year. The current rate of interest for similar debt is 12% per year.

The present value of the restructured debt may be computed using one of at least two possible interest rates: the interest rate implied in the original debt before restructuring or the current interest rate for similar debt. If the restructuring is viewed as a new lending situation, the current rate of interest would be used. If it is viewed as a modification of an existing lending situation, the effective interest rate in the original debt instrument would be used.[16] The difference in the computed present value between these methods is illustrated as follows:

Assume the current rate of interest is used to find the present value of the restructured debt.

1. *Present Value of Maturity Value:*
   Maturity value of bonds after five years or ten semi-annual periods = $1,000,000
   Effective interest rate — 12% per year, or 6% per semi-annual period:
   $PV_n = A(PVF_{\overline{n}|i}) = \$1,000,000(\text{Table II}_{\overline{10}|6\%}) = \$1,000,000(.5584) = \$558,400.$

2. *Present Value of Ten Semi-annual Interest Payments at Current Rate:*
   Semi-annual payment, $2^1/2\%$ of $1,000,000 = $25,000
   Interest rate — 12% per year, or 6% per semi-annual period:
   $PV_n = R(PVAF_{\overline{n}|i}) = \$25,000(\text{Table IV}_{\overline{10}|6\%}) = \$25,000(7.3601) = \$184,002.$

The present value of the restructured debt using the current market interest rate is $742,402($558,400 + $184,002).

Assume the effective rate of interest of the original debt is used to find the present value of the restructured debt.

1. *Present Value of Maturity Value:*
   Maturity value of bonds after five years or ten semi-annual periods = $1,000,000
   Effective interest rate — 10% per year, or 5% per semi-annual period:
   $PV_n = A(PVF_{\overline{n}|i}) = \$1,000,000(\text{Table II}_{\overline{10}|5\%}) = \$1,000,000(.6139) = \$613,900.$

2. *Present Value of Ten Semi-annual Interest Payments at Effective Interest Rate of Original Bonds:*
   Semi-annual payments, $2^1/2\%$ of $1,000,000 = $25,000
   Effective interest rate — 10% per year, or 5% per semi-annual period:
   $PV_n = R(PVAF_{\overline{n}|i}) = \$25,000(\text{Table IV}_{\overline{10}|5\%}) = \$25,000(7.7217) = \$193,042.$

---

[16]*Ibid.*, p. 7.

The present value of the restructured debt using the effective rate of interest of the original debt is $806,942($613,900 + $193,042).

The gain in the issuer's accounts and the loss in the investor's accounts on the restructuring would be $180,366 ($922,768 − $742,402) if the current interest rate is used or $115,826 ($922,768 − $806,942) if the effective interest rate on the original debt is used.

To illustrate the entries required to record the restructuring of the debt, assume the effective rate of interest on the original debt is used to compute the present value of the restructured debt. The entries would be as follows:

Issuer's Accounts

Discount on Bonds Payable	115,826	
Gain on Restructuring of Bonds Payable		115,826

Investor's Accounts

Loss on Restructuring of Bonds Held as Investment	115,826	
Investment in Bonds		115,826

These entries would reduce the carrying value of the liability and the investment to $806,942. The larger discount would be amortized over the remaining ten years of the bond life, preferably by the interest method of amortization. Thus, in the first semi-annual period, the new interest payment would be $25,000 (2$\frac{1}{2}$% of $1,000,000) but the amount of expense or revenue, assuming the original interest rate is used and the interest method of amortization is applied, would be $40,347 ($806,942 × .05). While this amount is lower than the $46,138 ($922,768 × .05) expense and revenue before restructuring, there is less impact on income than would be reflected if no gain or loss were recognized on the restructuring and the expense and revenue were reduced by the entire difference in cash interest payments of $15,000 ($40,000 − $25,000).

Similar adjustments of present value could be made for an extension of the bond maturity date or other modification of bond terms.

The profession has not yet agreed on whether the restructuring should be viewed as a new lending situation or a modification of an existing lending situation. Practice seems to favor the latter view, which, with rising interest rates, tends to produce a lower amount of gain or loss than would be true using the former view.

CURRENT LIABILITIES ON THE BALANCE SHEET

The nature of the detail to be presented for current liabilities depends upon the use to be made of the financial statement. A balance sheet prepared for shareholders might report little detail; on the other hand, creditors may insist on full detail concerning current debts.

Current assets are normally recorded in the order of their liquidity, and consistency would suggest liabilities be reported in the order of their maturity. The latter practice may be followed only to the extent it is practical: observance of this procedure would require an analysis of the different classes of obligations and separate reporting for classes with varying maturity dates. A bank overdraft should be listed first in view of the immediate demand it makes on cash. Disclosure of liabilities secured by specific assets should also be made by a parenthetical remark or note.

The current liabilities section of a balance sheet prepared on December 31, 1977, might appear as shown below:

Current liabilities:			
Notes payable:			
Trade creditors	$12,000		
Banks (secured by assignment of monies to become due under certain contracts totalling $36,000 included in asset section)	20,000		
Officers	10,000		
Miscellaneous	2,500	$44,500	
Accounts payable:			
Trade creditors	$30,500		
Credit balances in customers' accounts	1,250		
Miscellaneous	3,500	35,250	
Long-term liability instalments due in 1978		10,000	
Cash dividends payable......................		4,500	
Income tax payable		6,000	
Other liabilities:			
Salaries and wages payable	$ 1,250		
Property taxes	1,550		
Miscellaneous liabilities	1,400		
Customer advances	7,500		
Estimated repair costs on goods sold with service warranties	2,500	14,200	$114,450

REPORTING OF BONDS ON THE BALANCE SHEET

Bond accounts are frequently very significant items on the balance sheet of both the investor and the issuer. Generally, bonds are reported in the non-current section; however, under some circumstances they may be reported as current items. The valuation and reporting problems for the investor and the issuer will be considered separately.

Reporting Bond Investments

The market value of bonds varies with changes in the financial strength of the issuing corporation, changes in the level of interest rates, and shrinkage in the remaining life of the issue. In the absence of material price declines, bonds held as long-term investments are reported on the balance sheet at their carrying value. As a result of amortization, this value approaches face value as the bonds move closer to maturity. To this extent, then, the accounting can be considered to follow a similar change that is taking place on the market as the bond life is reduced and a correspondingly lower valuation is attached to the difference between the actual rate and the market rate of remaining interest payments. Although investments are properly reported at carrying value, parenthetical disclosure of the aggregate market value of the securities makes the financial statements more informative.

A material decline in bond value, however, as a result of unfavorable developments relating to the issuer cannot be ignored. Assume, for example, that the issuing corporation has found it impossible to meet redemption fund requirements, which suggests it may have difficulties in paying off the obligation at its maturity. Even more serious, assume that there has been default on bond interest payments. These conditions may lead to a restructuring of debt as discussed earlier. However, even before restructuring occurs, if significant investment loss is indicated, there is a strong argument for recording the loss. Such loss may be established by referring to current market quotations, by an investigation of prices at which similar bonds are sold, or by special appraisal of the assets that are pledged as security on the bonded indebtedness.

Bond funds are also normally classified as long-term investments. Even when the maturity date of term bonds will occur during the next fiscal period, the fund and the liability continue to be reported as non-current items.

Data relative to bond investments might be reported as follows:

Long-term investments:		
Investment in Wilkins Co. 8% Bonds, $100,000 face value, due July 1, 1982 (reported at cost as adjusted for amortized discount)		$ 98,250
Bond retirement fund in hands of trustee, composed of:		
Cash	$ 15,000	
Shares and bonds (reported at cost; aggregate quoted market value, $240,000)	210,500	
Dividends and interest receivable	4,500	230,000

Reporting Bond Liabilities

In reporting bond liabilities on the balance sheet, the nature of the liabilities, maturity dates, interest rates, methods of liquidation, conversion privileges, and other significant matters should be disclosed. When assets have been pledged to secure a liability, full particulars of the pledge should be disclosed in the description of the obligation. This may be accompanied by identification on the asset side of the balance sheet of the specific assets pledged.

The portion of serial bonds payable within one year and other long-term debt maturing within one year should be reported as a current liability only if retirement will claim current assets. If the debt is to be paid from a bond retirement fund or is to be retired through some form of refinancing, it would continue to be reported as non-current with an explanation of the method to be used in its liquidation.[17]

Bond liabilities may be reported on a balance sheet as of December 31, 1977, as follows:

Current liabilities:		
Serial 7% debentures, instalment due May 1, 1978		$ 10,000
Long-term liabilities:		
20-year, 6% First-mortgage bonds outstanding, due January 1, 1989	$210,000	
Less unamortized bond discount	4,500	205,500
Serial 7% debentures, due May 1, 1979 to May 1, 1988, inclusive		100,000

[17]*Statement of Financial Accounting Standards No. 6*, "Balance Sheet Classification of Short-Term Obligations Expected to be Refinanced" (Stamford, Conn.: Financial Accounting Standards Board, 1975). Again, there is no Canadian counterpart for this pronouncement.

QUESTIONS

1. (a) Define liabilities. (b) Distinguish between contingent and estimated liabilities.

2. What problems arise in the proper valuation of liabilities?

3. The Cable Co. issues a non-interest-bearing note due in one year in payment for equipment. Describe the accounting procedures that should be employed for the purchase.

4. Under what circumstances would an interest-bearing note be reported at an amount that is less than its maturity value?

5. When does (a) a cash dividend become a liability and (b) a stock dividend become a liability?

6. What is the nature of a firm's liability for sales taxes?

7. The hourly wage of an employee is $3, but the total employee labor cost, including tax-related expenses, is greater than $3 an hour. Explain.

8. When the fiscal year of the taxpayer is different from that of the taxing authority, how should the taxpayer account for property taxes?

9. What information must a firm accumulate in order to adequately account for estimated liabilities on tickets, tokens, and gift certificates?

10. What factors should be considered in determining whether cash should be raised by the issue of bonds or by the sale of additional shares of stock?

11. Distinguish between (a) secured and unsecured bonds, (b) collateral trust and debenture bonds, (c) guaranteed bonds and income bonds, (d) convertible bonds and callable bonds, and (e) coupon bonds and registered bonds.

12. What is meant by bond, stated or contract rate, and effective rate? Which of these rates changes during the lifetime of the bond issue?

13. An investor purchases bonds of $100,000. Payment for the bonds includes charges for (a) a premium, (b) accrued interest, and (c) brokerage fees. How would each of these charges be recorded and what disposition would ultimately be made of each of these charges?

14. (a) Why do companies find the issuance of convertible bonds a desirable method of financing? (b) What are the usual characteristics of convertible bonds?

15. Convertible bonds provide something extra over a regular bond. That "extra" is really part of the owners' equity of the company, and part of the bond proceeds should be allocated to the shareholders' equity. What are the chief arguments against this proposal?

16. (a) What is the difference in the accounting treatment between convertible bonds and bonds issued with detachable share warrants? (b) Do you think this difference Is justified? Give your reasons.

17. Distinguish between straight-line and interest methods of bond premium amortization. What arguments can be offered in support of each method?

18. (a) Describe the bonds-outstanding method for premium or discount amortization. (b) How does this method differ from the interest method of amortization?

19. The conversion of convertible bonds to common shares by an investor may be viewed as an exchange involving no gain or loss, or as a transaction for which market values should be recognized and a gain or loss reported. What arguments support each of these views for the investor and for the issuer?

20. What is the difference between bond reacquisition and bond redemption?

21. What purpose is served by using callable bonds? What effect does a call feature have upon the amortization of a bond premium?

22. What is meant by refunding a bond issue? Why may refunding be advisable?

23. Restructuring of bond debt may be accomplishd in several ways. Why is restructuring sometimes necessary, and what are some of the more common ways it can take place?

13-1. The following notes were issued by the Sunshine Co.:

(a) Note issued to purchase machinery. Face amount $12,960; no stated interest rate; market rate of interest, 8%; term of note, one year; date of note, November 1, 1977.

(b) Note issued to bank for a cash loan. Maturity value of note, $5,000; bank discount rate, 9%; term of note, one year; date of note, October 1, 1977.

(1) Give the entries required at the time the notes were issued. (2) Give the adjusting entries required on December 31, 1977, to recognize the accrual of the interest on each note.

13-2. Total sales plus sales tax for the Geronimo Electric Company in 1977 were $99,750; 60% of the sales are normally made on account. Prepare an entry summarizing these data for 1977 if the sales tax rate is 5%.

13-3. On July 1, 1977, the Stephens Company estimated total property tax for the year July 1, 1977, through June 30, 1978, at $960. On November 7, the company received the tax bill of $1,080. One half of the tax bill is paid on December 8, 1977. Give all required entries for 1977 to record monthly tax charges and the tax payment in December.

13-4. The Melvin Co. includes one coupon in each box of cereal that it packs, 15 coupons being redeemable for a premium consisting of a toy. In 1977, the Melvin Co. purchased 6,000 premiums at 75¢, and sold 125,000 boxes of cereal at 79¢ each. 22,500 coupons are presented for redemption. It is estimated that 60% of the coupons issued will be presented for redemption. Make all journal entries required in 1977 to properly account for the above information.

13-5. In order to make a line of dish washing machines more attractive to customers, New-Way introduced a three-year warranty policy against defects. Reliability studies indicate that for each machine sold, cost of repairs will average $10. The timing of the repairs per machine are expected to be $2 in the first year of sales, $3 in the second year after sale and $5 in the third year after sale. Sales and actual warranty expenditures for the three years since introduction of the warranty plan were:

	Machines Sold	Actual Warranty Expenditures
1980	900	$1,000
1981	1,000	4,800
1982	1,200	9,700

(a) Give journal entries relative to warranty cost for each of the three years.

(b) What amount should be reported as a liability on the balance sheet at the end of each year? (CGA adapted)

13-6. The Klear Kolor Appliance Company sells color television sets with a three-year repair warranty. The sales price for each set is $550. The average expense of repairing a set is $20. Research has shown that 10% of all sets sold are repaired in the first year, 15% in the second year, and 40% in the third year. The number of sets sold were as follows: 3,000 in 1977; 5,000 in 1978; and 6,000 in 1979. Total payment for repairs associated with the warranties were $5,500 in 1977, $14,500 in 1978 and $30,000 in 1979. Sales were made on account evenly throughout the year. Sales tax is charged at 5%.

Give the entries to record sales, the liability for warranties, and the payment made in connection with warranties for 1977, 1978, and 1979.

13-7. What is the market value of each of the following bond issues? Round to nearest dollar.
- (a) 5% bond of $50,000 sold on the bond issue date; 10-year life, interest payable semi-annually, effective rate 8%.
- (b) 6% bond of $200,000 sold on bond issue date; 20-year life, interest payable semi-annually, effective rate 4%.
- (c) 8% bond of $100,000 sold 30 months after bond issue date; 15-year life, interest payable semi-annually, effective rate 6%.

13-8. The Johnson Company Ltd. needs funds to finance the building of a new plant and therefore issues $5 million of 9% bonds due in 20 years with interest payable annually. Because of market conditions at the date of issue it is expected that the bonds will yield 10% to the investor. The bonds will be issued on January 1 and the company's year end is December 31. (a) Calculate the proceeds of the bond issue. (b) Prepare journal entries to record the bond issue and the first annual interest payment in the accounts of Johnson Company Ltd. using the interest method to amortize bond premium or discount. (c) Prepare the journal entry to record the first annual interest payment using the straight-line method of amortization. (d) Explain briefly why the effective rate method produces a different interest cost than the straight-line method.

(SMA adapted)

13-9. The Riggs Co. has issued 10,000 shares of $100 par common stock. The company requires additional working capital and finds it can sell 5,000 additional shares of common at $60, or it can issue $300,000 of 10% bonds at par. Earnings of the company before income tax have been $80,000 annually, and it is expected that these will increase 30% (before additional interest charges) as a result of the additional funds. Assuming that the income tax is estimated at 45%, which method of financing would you recommend as a common shareholder? Why? (Show calculations.)

13-10. Herde Insurance decides to finance expansion of its physical facilities by issuing convertible debenture bonds. The terms of the bonds are: maturity date 20 years after May 1, 1976, the date of issuance; conversion at option of holder after 2 years, 40 shares of $30 par value stock for each $1,000 bond held; interest rate of 6% and call provision on the bonds of 104. The bonds were sold at 102. (a) Give the entry to record the sale of 1,000 bonds on July 1, 1977; interest payment dates are May 1 and November 1. (b) Assume the same condition as in (a) above, except that the sale of the bonds is to be recorded in a manner that will recognize a value related to the conversion privilege. The estimated sales price of the bonds without the conversion privilege is 98.

13-11. The NAPA Corporation issued $100,000 of 5% debenture bonds on a basis to return 7%, receiving $91,684. Interest is payable semi-annually and the bonds mature in 5 years.
- (a) What entries would be made for the first two interest payments, assuming discount amortization on interest dates by (1) the straight-line method and (2) the interest method? Round to nearest dollar.
- (b) If the sale is made on a 4% return, $104,491 being received, what entries would be made for the first two interest payments, assuming premium amortization on interest dates by (1) the straight-line method and (2) the interest method? Round to nearest dollar.

(c) What entries would be made in the accounts of the investor assuming one party obtained all the bonds and the straight-line method of amortization was used? Round to nearest dollar.

13-12. Craven Corporation purchased 8% serial bonds on April 1, 1977, for $2,000,000. The bonds mature in $400,000 lots on April 1 of each of the following years. Interest is payable semi-annually; the issue has a discount of $50,000. Assuming that Craven operates on a calendar year, prepare a table summarizing interest charges and bond carrying values by the bonds-outstanding method.

13-13. On June 30, 1977, the original issue date, Toni Taylor purchased $500,000 of 20-year, 7% convertible bonds of Moore Corporation at 104. Moore bonds are convertible to 25 shares of $20 par common shares for each $1,000 bond. The bond interest is payable semi-annually, June 30 and December 31. On March 31, 1982, Taylor converts $200,000 of the bonds. Both Taylor and Moore Corporation use the calendar year as their fiscal year and amortize the bond premium on the straight-line basis.
   (a) Record the entries for both Taylor and Moore Corporation for the conversion in the absence of a market value for the shares.
   (b) Record the entries for both Taylor and Moore Corporation if the market value of the shares was $50 at the conversion date and a gain or loss is to be recognized on the conversion.

13-14. On December 1, 1979, the Haymond Company issues 10-year bonds of $100,000 at 104. Interest is payable on December 1 and June 1 at 8%. On April 1, 1981, the Haymond Company reacquires and retires 20 of its own $1,000 bonds at 98 plus accrued interest. The fiscal period for the Haymond Company is the calendar year. What entries are made to record (a) the issuance of the bonds, (b) the interest payments and adjustments relating to the debt in 1980, (c) the reacquisition and retirement of bonds in 1981, and (d) the interest payments and adjustments relating to the debt in 1981? Round to nearest dollar.

13-15. B. Jenkins acquired $40,000 of Texacana Corp. 9% bonds on July 1, 1979. The bonds were acquired at 92; interest is paid semi-annually on March 1 and September 1. The bonds mature September 1, 1986. Jenkins' accounts are kept on a calendar year basis. On February 1, 1982, Jenkins sold the bonds for 97 plus accrued interest. Assuming a straight-line discount amortization, give the entry to record the sale of the bonds on February 1. Round to nearest dollar.

13-16. Give the entries that would be made for each of the following bond retirement fund transactions, assuming that (1) transactions are recorded only in the accounts of the corporation, and (2) the transactions are recorded in a double-entry set of accounts maintained by the trustee and are summarized in the accounts of the corporation.
   (a) Cash is transferred to the bond retirement fund trustee, $78,000.
   (b) Securities are purchased out of bond retirement fund cash, $73,000.
   (c) Income is collected on bond retirement fund securities, $8,100.
   (d) Expenses are paid out of bond retirement fund cash, $550.
   (e) All of the bond retirement fund securities are sold for $89,000.
   (f) Bonds are redeemed at maturity date out of bond retirement fund cash, $100,000.
   (g) Remaining cash in bond retirement fund is deposited in general cash account.
   (h) Nominal accounts are closed.

13-1A. The information below is selected from the accounts of Jenkins Lumber Co. for the year 1978:

Sales on account (including sales tax of 5%)	$183,750
Net income	14,500
Cash dividends (declared December 30, 1978)	10,000
Stock dividends (declared December 30, 1978)	7,000
Machinery purchased (a non-interest-bearing note was issued in payment)	20,000
Notes payable (a note for $5,000 was discounted at the bank at 9%)	$ 5,000
Marketable securities	8,000
Bonds payable	25,000
Common stock, $100 par	50,000

Instructions:

Prepare necessary journal entries to record the following transactions:

(1) Discounting the note payable.
(2) Purchase of machinery (money is worth 12% per year).
(3) Declaration of cash dividend.
(4) Declaration of stock dividend.
(5) Sales tax.

13-2A. The Super-Soap Corp. manufactures a special type of low-suds laundry soap. A package of three golf balls is offered as a premium to customers who send in two proof-of-purchase seals from these soap boxes and a remittance of $1. Data for the premium offer are summarized below:

	1978	1977
Soap sales ($1.20 per package)	$1,500,000	$1,200,000
Golf ball purchases ($2.50 per package)	$75,000	$62,000
Number of golf ball packages distributed as premiums	28,500	20,000
Estimated number of golf ball packages to be distributed in subsequent periods	1,000	3,500

Mailing costs are 26¢ per package.

Instructions:

(1) Give the entries for 1977 and 1978 to record product sales, premium purchases and redemptions, and year-end adjustments.
(2) Present "T" accounts with appropriate amounts as of the end of 1977 and 1978.

13-3A. During the year 1977, the Mass Transit Authority sold the following tokens at 25¢ each.

Month	Tokens Sold
January	20,000
February	22,000
March	23,000
April	25,000
May	30,000
June	37,000
July	38,000
August	39,000
September	26,000
October	25,000
November	21,000
December	18,000

Past experience has shown that 60% of the tokens are used in the month of sale, 30% in the following month, 5% in the next month, and 5% are rendered void after six months.

Instructions:

Give entries for 1977 to account for the tokens:
(1) Assuming a liability account is originally credited.
(2) Assuming a revenue account is originally credited.

13-4A. The following data are made available for purposes of stating the financial position of the Salt Water Corp. on December 31, 1977.

Cash in bank	$20,000
Petty cash, which includes IOU's of employees totalling $350 that are to be repaid to the petty cash fund	2,000
Marketable securities, valued at $48,900; securities valued at $25,000 having been pledged on a note payable to the bank for $20,000, reported in the accounts at cost	45,000
Notes receivable, which have been reduced by notes discounted of $10,000 that are not yet due and on which the company is contingently liable	15,500
Accounts receivable, which include accounts with credit balances of $560 and past-due accounts of $2,650 on which a loss of 80% is anticipated	34,700
Merchandise inventory, which includes goods held on a consignment basis, $1,800, and goods received on December 31, $2,600, neither of these items having been recorded as a purchase	29,600
Prepaid insurance, which includes cash surrender value of life insurance policies, $4,200	9,100
Rents paid in advance	830

Furniture and fixtures, which include fixtures that were fully depreciated and that have just been scrapped, $4,500:		
Cost	$25,000	
Accumulated depreciation	11,750	13,250

Notes payable, which are trade notes with the exception of a 6-month, $20,000 note payable to Commerce Bank on June 15, 1978	30,500
Accounts payable, which include accounts with debit balances of $675	18,100
Miscellaneous accrued expenses	3,650
Long-term notes, which are payable in annual instalments of $2,500 on February 1 of each year	10,000
Preferred 6% shares, $15 par, cumulative, on which dividends for 3 years are in arrears	45,000
No-par common shares, 40,000 shares authorized and outstanding	60,000
Retained earnings	2,730

The following data are not included in the above account balances:

(a) A special sales offer made in December will result in redemption of premiums estimated at a cost of $4,000 during the next year.
(b) Product replacement warranties outstanding are estimated to result in costs to the company of $6,000.

Instructions:

Prepare a classified balance sheet, including whatever notes are appropriate in support of balance sheet data.

13-5A. The Miracle Radio Corporation, a client, requests that you compute the appropriate balance for its estimated liability for product warranty account for a statement as of June 30, 1977.

The Miracle Radio Corporation manufactures television tubes and sells them with a six-month warranty under which defective tubes will be replaced without charge. On December 31, 1976, the Estimated Liability for Product Warranty had a balance of $510,000. By June 30, 1977, this balance has been reduced to $80,250 by debits for estimated net cost of tubes returned which had been sold in 1976.

The company started out in 1977 expecting 8% of the dollar volume of sales to be returned. However, due to the introduction of new models during the year, this estimated percentage of returns was increased to 10% on May 1. It is assumed that no tubes sold during a given month are returned in that month. Each tube is stamped with a date at time of sale so that the warranty may be properly administered. The table of percentages indicates the likely pattern of sales returns during the six-month period of the warranty, starting with the month following the sale of tubes.

Month Following Sale	Percentage of Total Returns Expected
First	20%
Second	30
Third	20
Fourth through sixth — 10% each month	30
Total	100%

Gross sales of tubes were as follows for the first six months of 1977:

Month	Amount	Month	Amount
January	$3,600,000	April	$2,850,000
February	3,300,000	May	2,000,000
March	4,100,000	June	1,800,000

The company's warranty also covers the payment of freight cost on defective tubes returned and on new tubes sent out as replacements. This freight cost runs approximately 10% of the sales price of the tubes returned. The manufacturing cost of the tubes is roughly 80% of the sales price, and the salvage value of returned tubes averages 15% of their sales price. Returned tubes on hand at December 31, 1976, were thus valued in inventory at 15% of their original sales price.

Instructions:

Using the data given, draw up a suitable working-paper schedule for arriving at the balance of the estimated liability for product warranty account and give the proposed adjusting entry. Assume that proper recognition of costs for financial accounting will be allowed for income tax purposes.   (AICPA adapted)

13-6A. The Novelties Co., Ltd., is engaged in manufacturing and wholesaling two principal products. As their accountant, you have been asked to advise management on its sales policy for the coming year.

Two different plans are being considered by management, either of which, they believe, will (1) increase the volume of sales, (2) reduce the ratio of selling expense to sales, and (3) decrease unit production costs. The following are the proposals presented.

Plan 1 — Premium Stamp Books

It is proposed that each package of Product A will contain 8 premium stamps, and each package of Product B will contain 4 premium stamps. Premium stamp books will be distributed to consumers, and when a book is filled with stamps (100 stamps), it will be redeemed by the award of a cash prize in an amount indicated under an unbroken seal attached to the book at the time of distribution. Every 10,000 books distributed will provide for prizes in accordance with the following schedule.

Number of Books	Prize for Each	Total Prizes
1	$150.00	$ 150
5	50.00	250
14	20.00	280
50	10.00	500
160	5.00	800
1,020	1.00	1,020
8,750	.40	3,500
10,000		$6,500

This schedule is fixed and not subject to alteration or modification. The cost of this plan will be as follows:

Books, including distribution cost ....$15 per 1,000 books
Stamps ....$1 per 1,000 stamps
Prizes ....$650 per 1,000 books

The premium stamp book plan will take the place of all previous advertising, and previously established selling prices will be maintained.

Plan 2 — Reduced Selling Prices

It is proposed that the selling price of Product A will be reduced by $8^1/_3\%$ and of Product B by 5% and to increase the advertising expenditures over those of the prior year. This plan is an alternative to Plan 1, and only one will be adopted.

Management has provided you with the following information as to the previous year's operations, and as to anticipated changes:

	Product A	Product B
Prior year's operations:		
Quantity sold	200,000 units	600,000 units
Production cost per unit	$.40	$.30
Selling price per unit	.60	.40
Selling expenses were 18% of sales, of which one third was for advertising. Administrative expenses were 5% of sales.		
Expected changes:		
Increase in unit sales volume:		
Plan 1	50%	50%
Plan 2	40%	25%
Decrease in unit production cost:		
Plan 1	5%	10%
Plan 2	$7^1/_2\%$	$6^2/_3\%$
Advertising:		
Plan 1	None	None
Plan 2	8% of sales	7% of sales
Other selling expenses:		
Plan 1	15% of sales	12% of sales
Plan 2	12% of sales	12% of sales
Premium book expenses:		
Plan 1	As indicated	
Plan 2	None	None
Administrative expenses:		
Plan 1	4% of sales	4% of sales
Plan 2	Same dollar amount as prior year.	

Instructions:

Prepare a schedule for submission to management comparing operations of the previous year with those under both proposed plans. (AICPA adapted)

13-7A.(1) On June 30, 1981, Crown Derby Corporation issued $100,000 of 8% ,000(payable 4% semi-annually) ten-year bonds dated June 30, at an effective interest rate of 10%. The proceeds to the company were computed as $37,689 plus $49,849 = $87,538.

10% ÷ 2 = 5%

Instructions:

(a) What do each of the first two amounts represent?
(b) Record the issue of bonds.
(c) Record the payment of interest on December 31, 1981, and amortization using the interest method.
(d) Record the payment of interest on December 31, 1981, and amortizaton using the straight-line method.

(2) An investor purchased $10,000 of the bonds on June 30, the date of issue.

Instructions:

(a) Record the purchase of bonds (round to nearest dollar).
(b) Record receipt of interest on December 31, 1981, and amortization using the interest method.
(c) Record receipt of interest on December 31, 1981, and amortization using the straight-line method. (CGA adapted)

13-8A. Sellers Products decided to issue $1,000,000 in 10-year bonds. The interest rate on the bonds is stated at 7%, payable semi-annually. At the time the bonds were sold, the market rate had increased to 8%.

Instructions:

(1) Determine the maximum amount an investor should pay for these bonds. Round to nearest dollar.
(2) Assuming that the amount in (1) is paid, compute the amount at which the bonds would be reported after being held for one year. Use two recognized methods of handling amortization of the difference in cost and maturity value of the bonds, and give support for the method you prefer. Round to nearest dollar.

13-9A. The Roman Co. acquired $20,000 of Mapleton Sales Co. 7% bonds, interest payable semi-annually, bonds maturing in 5 years. The bonds were acquired at $20,850, a price to return approximately 6%.

Instructions:

(1) Prepare tables to show the periodic adjustments to the investment account and the annual bond earnings, assuming adjustment by each of the following methods: (a) the straight-line method, and (b) the interest method. Round to nearest dollar.
(2) Assuming use of the interest method, give entries for the first year in the accounts of both companies.

13-10A. Upon inspecting the records of the Ile Corporation you find that $200,000 of 6½% first-mortgage serial bonds were authorized and dated July 1, 1974, with interest payable semi-annually. The issue was sold on October 1, 1974, at $196,950 which included accrued interest. Bonds of $20,000 mature at annual intervals; the first maturity date is July 1, 1975. Bonds are callable on any interest payment date. On

January 1, 1977, the company called in the 1979 maturities at 103. The company maintained a single account for the bond issue, and on December 31, 1977, the close of an annual fiscal period, this account showed a balance of $116,350, and appeared as follows:

ACCOUNT 6¹/₂% First-Mortgage Serial Bonds

DATE		ITEM	DEBIT	CREDIT	BALANCE DEBIT	BALANCE CREDIT
1974						
Oct.	1	Proceeds from sale of bonds		196,950		196,950
1975						
July	1	Retirement of 1975 maturities	20,000			176,950
1976						
July	1	Retirement of 1976 maturities	20,000			156,950
1977						
Jan.	1	Retirement of 1979 maturities	20,600			136,350
July	1	Retirement of 1977 maturities	20,000			116,350

Instructions:

(1) Give the correcting journal entries in the issuer's accounts as well as any adjusting entries required as of December 31, 1977. (Assume the accounts for 1977 have not been closed. Give any schedules that may be required in developing the entries.)

(2) What account balances and amounts relating to the bond issue would appear on the balance sheet as of December 31, 1977, and on the income statement for the year ending December 31, 1977?

13-11A. In auditing the accounts for the Hunsaker Corporation as of December 31, 1977, before the accounts are closed, you find the following long-term investment account balance:

ACCOUNT Investment in Corey Steel 6% Bonds (Maturity Date, April 1, 1981)

DATE		ITEM	DEBIT	CREDIT	BALANCE DEBIT	BALANCE CREDIT
1977						
Jan.	22	Bonds, $100,000 par, acquired at 102 plus accrued interest	102,850		102,850	
Mar.	10	Proceeds from sale of bonds, $50,000 par and accrued interest		53,000	49,850	
June	1	Interest received		1,500	48,350	
Nov.	1	Amount received on call of bonds, $20,000 par, at 101 and accrued interest		20,700	27,650	
Dec.	1	Interest received		900	26,750	

Instructions:

(1) Give the entries that should have been made relative to the investment in bonds, including any adjusting entries that would be made on December 31, the end of the fiscal year. (Assume bond premium amortization by the straight-line method.)

(2) Give the journal entries required at the end of 1977 to correct and bring the accounts up to date in view of the entries actually made.

13-12A. D. A. Davis Company established a bond retirement fund to retire their recently issued bonds. The fund is held by a trustee who maintains a separate record of transactions.

You obtain the following information:

1977

Mar. 31 Davis transferred $125,000 to the bond retirement fund.

Apr. 1 The trustee bought $50,000 of Jensen 6% bonds at 110, including interest. The bonds pay interest on March 1 and September 1; they mature in five years.

May 1 The trustee purchased $30,000 of Blacker Corp. 6% bonds for $28,000, including interest. Interest is paid on January 1 and July 1; the bonds mature in ten years.

Dec. 1 Sold Jensen bonds for $52,000, including accrued interest.

Dec. 1 Exchanged Blacker bonds for 2,000 shares of Peterman Corporation common stock with a market price of $15^1/_2$.

Instructions:

Give the necessary entries to record the transactions in 1977 in the accounts of both the trustee and the company. Round to nearest dollar.

13-13A. The Catalina Co. issued $1,000,000 of convertible 10-year debentures on July 1, 1976. The debentures provide for 9% interest payable semi-annually on January 1 and July 1. The discount in connection with the issue was $19,500 which is being amortized monthly on a straight-line basis.

The debentures are convertible after one year into 7 shares of the Catalina Co.'s $100 par value common stock for each $1,000 of debentures.

On August 1, 1977, $100,000 of debentures were turned in for conversion into common. Interest has been accrued monthly and paid as due. Accrued interest on debentures is paid in cash upon conversion.

Instructions:

Prepare the journal entries to record the conversion, amortization and interest in connection with the debentures as of: August 1, 1977; August 31, 1977; and December 31, 1977 — including closing entries for end of year. No gain or loss is to be recognized on the conversion. Round to nearest cent.   (AICPA adapted)

13-14A. The Arden Company issued $3,000,000 of 8% first-mortgage bonds on October 1, 1973, at $2,873,640 plus accrued interest. The bonds were dated July 1, 1973; interest payable semi-annually on January 1 and July 1; redeemable after June 30, 1978, and to June 30, 1980, at 104, and thereafter until maturity at 102; and convertible into $100 par value common stock as follows:

Until June 30, 1978, at the rate of 6 shares for each $1,000 of bonds.

From July 1, 1978, to June 30, 1981, at the rate of 5 shares for each $1,000 of bonds.

After June 30, 1981, at the rate of 4 shares for each $1,000 of bonds.

The bonds mature in 10 years from their date. The company adjusts its accounts monthly and closes its accounts as of December 31 each year. It follows the practice of writing off all unamortized bond discount in the period of bond retirement.

The following transactions occur in connection with the bonds:

1979

July 1 $500,000 of bonds were converted into shares.

1980

Dec. 31 $500,000 face amount of bonds were reacquired at 99¼ and accrued interest. These were immediately retired.

1981

July 1 The remaining bonds were called for redemption. For purpose of obtaining funds for redemption and business expansion, a $4,000,000 issue of 6% bonds was sold at 98¾. These bonds were dated July 1, 1981, and were due in 20 years.

Instructions:

Prepare in journal form the entries necessary for the company in connection with the preceding transactions, including monthly adjustments where appropriate, as of the following dates. Round to nearest dollar.

(1) October 1, 1973   (4) December 31, 1980
(2) December 31, 1973   (5) July 1, 1981
(3) July 1, 1979   (AICPA adapted)

13-15A. Zakin Co. recently issued $1,000,000 face value, 8%, 30-year subordinated debentures at 97. The debentures are redeemable at 103 upon demand by the issuer at any date upon 30-days notice ten years after issue. The debentures are convertible into $10 par value common stock of the company at the conversion price of $12.50 per share for each $500 or multiple thereof of the principal amount of the debentures.

Assume that no value is assigned to the conversion feature upon issue of the debentures. Assume further that five years after issue, debentures with a face value of $100,000 and carrying value of $97,500 are tendered for conversion on an interest payment date when the market price of the debentures is 104 and the common stock is selling at $14 per share and that the company records the conversion as follows:

Bonds Payable	100,000	
Discount on Bonds Payable		2,500
Common Shares		80,000
Premium on Common Shares		17,500

Instructions:

Do you agree with this entry? If not, prepare a correct one.   (AICPA adapted)

14 ACCOUNTING FOR INCOME TAX

Accounting for income taxes, especially the income tax of corporations, has become an increasingly complex topic for the accounting profession. A tax based upon income has traditionally been an important source of revenue for both federal and provincial governments. Although income taxes had been levied by the provinces, it was not until 1917 that the federal government first introduced taxes on income as a temporary war measure. Initially the tax rates were low and not too much attention was paid to this new tax outlay by either individuals or by businesses. However, as the services provided by governments expanded, the rates increased and the significance of income tax on personal and business decision making greatly expanded.

NATURE OF INCOME TAX

Theoretically, income tax could be viewed as either an expense of operating a business or as a distribution of income between governmental units and the owners of business entities. The private enterprise philosophy supports acceptance of the former view; income tax is a levy placed by a government on all businesses and thus they are necessary expenses of doing business within our society. As an expense, income tax can be differentiated from other expenses in the sense that income tax expense is zero if there is no income to tax. This argument, however, never succeeded as support for the theory that income tax might indeed be a distribution rather than an expense.

Because the amount of tax expense is directly related to the income earned, control of the expense is limited to tax planning that will take advantage of income tax laws so as to minimize the present value of tax outlays over the life of the business. Usually, this means taking advantage of provisions to minimize the tax payable each year. This strategy often makes the income reported for tax purposes different from that reported for accounting purposes, and this difference creates the need for an income tax adjustment in the accounts referred to as *interperiod income tax allocation*. This adjustment and its ramifications have created complex problems in accounting for income tax. In addition, adjustments referred to as *intraperiod income tax allocation* are required whenever extraordinary items or prior period adjustments arise.

Although the federal tax is the most significant income tax, provincial income taxes are also an important expense outlay. With the exception of Quebec, the provincial governments pattern their income tax laws after the federal government. This simplifies the preparation of income tax returns for businesses and permits more efficient tax planning. Although emphasis in this chapter will be on the federal tax, accounting for provincial income taxes would be handled in a similar manner with variations depending upon the particular laws involved.

Because income tax affects almost every business entity, accounting for income tax has widespread interest. The federal tax laws and regulations are complex, and specialists on income tax are usually employed to do the tax planning and tax return preparation. The purpose of this chapter is not to discuss the income tax laws specifically, except as they might have an impact on the timing of tax payments. Most problems in accounting for income tax may be divided into three categories.

1. Accounting for intraperiod income tax allocation
2. Accounting for interperiod income tax allocation
3. Accounting for loss carrybacks and carryforwards

Each of these areas will be discussed in the remainder of this chapter.

INTRAPERIOD INCOME TAX ALLOCATION

Because income tax is related specifically to income items, the reporting of income tax should be directly related to the income involved. If all income items were classified in one place on the financial statements, the income tax expense could be reported directly as a deduction against that income. However, as discussed in Chapter 4, the income statement separates operating income, from the so-called extraordinary items, if any. Both of these items usually have income tax consequences. For example, an extraordinary gain on retirement of a long-term debt would be reported for income tax purposes and a tax would be paid. Similarly, an extraordinary loss from disposing of a business segment would be deductible from other taxable income and thus the loss would reduce the income tax otherwise payable. The intraperiod income tax allocation principle requires that income tax expense or tax reduction be related to the specific classification on the financial statement involved. Prior period adjustments reported as an adjustment to retained earnings for accounting purposes and currently on income tax returns would also require intraperiod tax allocation.

Intraperiod Income Tax Allocation Illustrated

Many factors influence corporate tax rates in Canada. These include the type, size and location of the corporate operation. Rates vary depending on whether the corporation is or is not engaged in manufacturing or processing, on whether it is eligible for the small business deduction and on the provincial jurisdiction under which it conducts business. In general, the federal tax rate is 46% less an abatement for provincial income taxes of 10%. The manufacturing and processing deduction is 6% and, where applicable, the small business deduction is 21%. The rates of income taxes levied by the provinces generally range between 10% and 13%. To simplify discussion, it will be assumed in this section that the income tax rate is 45% and is constant for all income. Assume examination of Springer Corporation's financial statements and income tax return for 1980 revealed the following information before computation of applicable income tax.

Income classified as ordinary income	$290,000
Extraordinary loss from disposal of a business segment	(100,000)
Extraordinary loss from earthquake	(50,000)
Taxable income on income tax return	$140,000

Using a 45% tax rate, the income tax of $63,000 ($140,000 × .45) would be allocated as follows:

Income tax on ordinary income ($290,000 × .45)	$130,500
Income tax reduction from extraordinary loss from disposal of a business segment ($100,000 × .45).......................	(45,000)
Income tax reduction from extraordinary loss from earthquake ($50,000 × .45)...	(22,500)
Income tax payable for current year	$ 63,000

The journal entry required to record these allocations in the accounts would be as follows:

Provision for Income Tax 130,500
   Income Tax Reduction from Extraordinary Loss on
   Disposal of a Business Segment 45,000
   Income Tax Reduction from Extraordinary Loss from
     earthquake 22,500
   Income Tax Payable 63,000

The abbreviated income statement below shows how the information might be reported. Alternatively, the detail for the "Provision for income tax" section could be presented in notes to the financial statements.

The illustration demonstrates how the amount of income tax applicable to ordinary income and to extraordinary items might be disclosed. In practice, however, the breakdown shown for the provision is rarely provided. However, notes are usually included with the financial statements to provide any additional detail that might be required. Sometimes the amount of the income tax expense or tax reduction that applies to extraordinary items is included in the note rather than on the income statement and the extraordinary item(s) would be reported "net of income tax effects." Either method of disclosure is acceptable.

Springer Corporation Income Statement (Partial) For Year Ended December 31, 1980		
Income from operations before income tax		$290,000
Provision for income tax:		
Income tax currently payable	$ 63,000	
Income tax reduction from extraordinary losses	67,500	130,500
Income before extraordinary items		$159,500
Extraordinary items:		
Extraordinary loss on disposal of business segment		
(less applicable income tax of $45,000)	(55,000)	
Extraordinary loss from earthquake damage (less		
applicable income tax of $22,500)	(27,500)	(82,500)
Net income		$77,000

INTERPERIOD INCOME TAX ALLOCATION

The most complex aspect of accounting for income tax is the adjustment necessary to apply the accrual concept to income tax expense. Income tax law does not always follow generally accepted accounting principles. This is not necessarily a weakness in either tax legislation or in accounting principles. One important objective of income tax is to raise revenue for federal and provincial governments. Tax considerations, such as taxing according to ability to pay, taxing according to the benefits taxpayers receive, and taxing to depress or stimulate various portions of the economy are significantly different from the objectives accountants have for income measurement purposes. Consequently, income for tax purposes can and usually does differ from income for accounting purposes.

Permanent and Timing Differences

Differences between accounting income and taxable income can be conveniently classified as *permanent differences* and *timing differences*. Permanent differences are revenue or expense items that will never be subject to tax. Timing differences are taxable, but the timing of their recognition for accounting and for tax purposes differs. In general, permanent differences impact on income tax expense; under the allocation method, timing differences give rise to *deferred income tax*.

As a result of double digit inflation during the 1970s, the government was pressured to recognize the LIFO method of inventory costing for income tax purposes. This pressure was resisted, but in 1978 a 3% inventory allowance was introduced that provides an important example of a permanent difference; important because the inventory allowance, while deductible for tax purposes, has no counterpart for accounting purposes. The 3% inventory allowance applies to all tangible property included in inventories as at the beginning of each period. Other common examples of permanent differences include club membership dues, most intercorporate dividends, and one-half of any realized capital gains and losses, although the latter may only be deducted for tax purposes against capital gains.

ACCOUNTING ALTERNATIVES

There are two alternative methods of accounting for income tax: (1) the taxes payable method and (2) the allocation method. In the past both methods were widely used; however, accounting standards now require the allocation method, except for regulated and similar enterprises.

Under the taxes payable method, the provision for income tax or income tax expense is determined by applying the tax rate to taxable income. Thus, the amount of tax payable becomes the expense because it is taxable income that attracts the tax. While this is true, the taxes payable method is essentially cash basis accounting, whereas the conventional accounting model is essentially based on the accrual and matching concepts.

Under the allocation method, the provision for income tax or income tax expense is generally determined by applying the tax rate to the accounting income before tax adjusted for any permanent differences. Assuming income tax allocation, the formula or equation shown at the top of page 562 can be used to determine the provision or expense provided there is no reversal of timing differences on which deferred income tax may have been accumulated at a rate which differs from the current income tax rate.

Accounting income before tax ± Permanent differences × Tax rate

The allocation method is an application of accrual accounting. Income tax expense is recognized when accounting income is recognized regardless of when the tax may become payable. Thus, the allocation method provides a matching of expense and revenue in the period of accounting recognition. Accountants accept that tax allocation is an essential part of income measurement and generally accepted accounting principles are based on this view.

The data set forth below will be used to illustrate the taxes payable and allocation methods of accounting for corporate income tax. The data pertains to the first year's operation of New Company.

Accounting income before provision for income tax, per income statement	$500,000
The following items have been deducted in arriving at the above income:	
(1) Depreciation, a timing difference	90,000
(2) Interest on late instalment payments, a permanent difference .	2,000
Capital cost allowance, a timing difference	140,000
Income tax rate	45%

For purposes of the illustration, the following schedule provides the starting point. Journal entries to record income tax under both the taxes payable and allocation alternatives then follow.

Accounting income before provision	$500,000
Disallowed interest expense	2,000
Accounting income adjusted for permanent difference	$502,000
Depreciation	90,000
	$592,000
Capital cost allowance	140,000
Taxable income	$452,000

	Taxes Payable Method		Income Tax Allocation
Provision for income tax	203,400		225,900
Income tax payable		203,400	203,400
Deferred income tax			22,500

Under the allocation method, the excess of capital cost allowance $140,000, over depreciation of $90,000 gives rise to a timing difference of $50,000, that results in a deferred income tax credit of $22,500 (45% of $50,000). The taxes payable alternative permits the $22,500 to flow through to net income. The partial income statements presented below illustrate the point.

New Company Partial Income Statement	Taxes Payable Method	Income Tax Allocation
Income before provision for income tax	$500,000	$500,000
Provision for income tax	203,400	225,900
Net income	$296,600	$274,100

It should also be noted that under the allocation method, the provision for income tax can be sub-divided into its current and deferred components as follows:

Current portion	$203,400
Deferred portion	22,500
Provision for income tax	$225,900

In some future period, if depreciation should exceed capital cost allowance the result is a timing difference reversal that necessitates a debit to accumulated deferred income tax credits. In the meantime, depending on the nature and direction of specific timing differences, both deferred income tax debits and credits may be accumulated in appropriate balance sheet accounts pending the reversal of the timing differences that occasioned their recognition. Under the allocation method, deferred income tax must be recognized on all timing differences.

Historical Development

The principal of interperiod income tax allocation was recognized by the Accounting and Auditing Research Committee in Bulletin No. 10, issued in September, 1954, but the Committee then only expressed a preference for the allocation method. The alternative, the taxes payable or flow-through method, continued to be widely used in practice in spite of the Committee's expressed preference for the allocation method. As previously noted, under the taxes payable method the provision or income tax expense is based on the amount of taxes actually payable, whereas the provision or expense under the allocation method is based on the accounting income before taxes adjusted for permanent differences, which may be a very different amount than taxable income.

The Accounting and Auditing Research Committee in September, 1967, issued Bulletin No. 26 (now included in the *CICA Handbook* as Section 3470 of the *Accounting Recommendations*) with a view to extending the principle of income tax allocation and to recommending uniformity in practice. In Bulletin No. 26, the Committee concluded that "the allocation basis provides the most satisfactory method of achieving the prime objective of a proper matching of costs and revenues in the case of tax timing differences."[1] On this premise, the Committee then recommended that "income taxes should be accounted for on the tax allocation basis for all corporations with the exception of regulated and similar enterprises."[2] Allowing for this exception, the net result of Bulletin No. 26 has been to require the use of comprehensive income tax allocation for financial reporting purposes in Canada.

Comprehensive income tax allocation requires the recognition of deferred income tax on all timing differences regardless of expectations concerning their reversal. Although the total timing difference between capital cost allowance and straight-line depreciation may increase each year, depreciation on a specific asset should reverse so that in the latter part of the asset's life more depreciation should be charged in the accounts than the amount of capital cost allowance claimed for income tax purposes. However, the reversal related to an individual asset is often obscured by the excess of capital cost allowance on more recently acquired assets. Moreover, fixed asset disposals may take place before the timing difference would have otherwise reversed. As a result, numerous corporations have accumulated large deferred income tax credits on their balance sheets; in a few cases, the deferred tax credit may be the largest single item on the equities side of the statement.

Although comprehensive income tax allocation is widely accepted, there is still concern as to the true nature of the deferred amount reported on the balance sheet. If the amount is a credit, it is usually reported as a long-term deferred credit among long-term liabilities, unless it arises from transactions such as instalment sales, the related asset balance for which is reported in current assets. Accumulated deferred income tax credits, however, can be differentiated from other liabilities in the sense that no taxing authority has a reciprocal claim against the business. If the amount is a debit, it is usually reported as a long-term deferred charge after property, plant, and equipment or, depending upon its nature, as a current asset. Because the deferred tax is drawn down only when the items reverse, analysts often delete at least part if not all the amount from the liability section of the balance sheet when they are computing ratios for comparative purposes.

Interperiod income tax allocation places principal emphasis on the income statement and the proper matching of expenses with revenues. If in the future increased emphasis should be placed on the balance sheet, the attractiveness of interperiod income tax allocation may diminish and the profession may consider some form of partial allocation.

Accounting for Different Types of Timing Differences

Timing differences may be classified into the several categories listed on page 565. Examples of items for each category are also included.

---

[1] *Accounting and Auditing Research Committee, Bulletin No. 26*, "Accounting for Corporate Income Taxes" (Toronto: Canadian Institute of Chartered Accountants, 1967), par. 11.

[2] *Ibid.*, par. 12.

1. Reported accounting income before tax is less than taxable income.
    (a) Revenue deferred for accounting purposes but currently recognized for tax purposes.
        (1) Unearned income on certain types of construction contracts deferred for accounting purposes but taxable in the current period.
    (b) Expense currently recognized for accounting purposes is deferred for tax purposes.
        (1) Warranty expense accrued in advance for accounting purposes but allowed for tax purposes only when costs are incurred under the warranty.
2. Reported accounting income before tax is more than taxable income
    (a) Revenue currently recognized for accounting purposes is deferred for tax purposes.
        (1) Instalment sales method used for tax purposes but accrual method used for accounting purposes.
    (b) Expense deferred for accounting purposes is currently recognized for tax purposes.
        (1) Straight-line depreciation for accounting purposes and capital cost allowance for tax purposes.

Interperiod Income Tax Allocation Illustrated

To illustrate the accounting for interperiod income tax allocation when income tax rates are constant at 45%, assume the following data pertaining to the first three years, operations of Thompson Limited, a service business that does not maintain any inventories.

	Accounting Income Before Tax	Depreciation	Capital Cost Allowance	Warranty		Club Memberships	Taxable Income
				Expense	Payments		
1978	100,000 +	85,000 −	100,000 +	30,000 −	20,000 +	5,000 =	100,000
1979	130,000	100,000	125,000	35,000	41,000	5,000	104,000
1980	175,000	100,000	95,000	35,000	20,000	5,000	200,000

The payment of club memberships gives rise to a permanent difference. The several different kinds of timing differences should be maintained separately for computation purposes, although, within current and non-current classifications, they may be combined and netted as applicable for reporting purposes. The excess of warranty expense over warranty payments causes accounting income to be lower than taxable income. The excess of capital cost allowance over straight-line depreciation causes the opposite effect: accounting income exceeds taxable income. If the item is reversed in a particular year, accounting and taxable income are affected in the opposite direction. It should also be noted that the liability for the warranty is a current liability and therefore the related tax deferral should be shown on the balance sheet among current assets. Since the capital cost allowance-depreciation timing difference pertains to fixed assets, the related deferred income tax credit should be presented on the balance sheet as a non-current item.

The income tax expense or provision for the period is based on the accounting income adjusted for any permanent differences. The current income tax liability is based on the taxable income for the period. The difference between the income tax expense and the income tax liability is recorded as a deferred charge or a deferred credit. To illustrate, the entries below would be recorded for the years 1978-1980, based on the preceding example:

1978: Provision for Income Tax	47,250	
Deferred Income Tax — Warranty[3]	4,500	
Deferred Income Tax — Depreciation[3]		6,750
Estimated Income Tax Payable		45,000

Computation:
Income tax: 45% × $105,000 = $47,250
Deferred income tax — warranty: 45% × $10,000 = $4,500
Deferred income tax — depreciation: 45% × $15,000 = $6,750
Income tax payable: 45% × $100,000 = $45,000

1979: Provision for Income Tax	60,750	
Deferred Income Tax — Warranty		2,700
Deferred Income Tax — Depreciation		11,250
Estimated Income Tax Payable		46,800

Computation:
Income tax: 45% × $135,000 = $60,750
Deferred income tax — warranty: 45% × $6,000 = $2,700
Deferred income tax — depreciation: 45% × $25,000 = $11,250
Income tax payable: 45% × $104,000 = $46,800

1980: Provision for Income Tax	81,000	
Deferred Income Tax — Warranty	6,750	
Deferred Income Tax — Depreciation	2,250	
Estimated Income Tax Payable		90,000

Computation:
Income tax: 45% × $180,000 = $81,000
Deferred income tax — warranty: 45% × $15,000 = $6,750
Deferred income tax — depreciation: 45% × $5,000 = $2,250
Income tax payable: 45% × $200,000 = $90,000

A three-column worksheet provides a convenient methodology for the analysis that underlies the above journal entries.[4] All permanent differences are entered in columns one and two; all timing differences are entered in columns two and three. Since all differences are entered in column two, this column provides a reconciliation between accounting income before tax and taxable income. Column one provides for the adjustment of accounting income for permanent differences. Since all current period timing differences are included in column three, this column provides the amounts upon which the current period increases and decreases in deferred taxes are based.

---

[3]These accounts may be combined and only the net effect reported as long as they are both current or both non-current items.

[4]A deep debt of gratitude is owed to Brian J. Thompson, a partner of Price Waterhouse & Co., Chartered Accountants, who first brought this methodology to the attention of the Canadian author.

Assuming a constant tax rate, as is the case in the example, the provision or expense is determined from column one, the liability from column two, and deferred taxes from column three. The methodology is illustrated below:

1978	1 Accounting Income	2 Taxable Income	3 Deferred Tax
Accounting income	$100,000	$100,000	
Club memberships	5,000	5,000	
Depreciation		85,000	$ 85,000
Warranty expense		30,000	30,000
	$105,000	$220,000	$115,000
Warranty payments		$ 20,000	$ 20,000
Capital cost allowance		100,000	100,000
		$120,000	$120,000
	$105,000	$100,000	$ 5,000
Provision (45%)	$ 47,250		
Payable (45%)		$ 45,000	
Deferred:			
Warranty ($10,000 × .45) . . .			$ 4,500 (Dr.)
Fixed assets ($15,000 × .45)			6,750 (Cr.)
			$ 2,250 (Cr.)
Net income	$ 52,750		

1979	1 Accounting Income	2 Taxable Income	3 Deferred Tax
Accounting income	$130,000	$130,000	
Club memberships	5,000	5,000	
Depreciation		100,000	$100,000
Warranty expense		35,000	35,000
	$135,000	$270,000	$135,000
Warranty payments		$ 41,000	$ 41,000
Capital cost allowance		125,000	125,000
		$166,000	$166,000
	$135,000	$104,000	$ 31,000
Provision (45%)	$ 60,750		
Payable (45%)		$ 46,800	
Deferred:			
Warranty ($6,000 × .45)			$ 2,700 (Cr.)
Fixed assets ($25,000 × .45)			11,250 (Cr.)
			$ 13,950 (Cr.)
Net income	$ 69,250		

1980	1 Accounting Income	2 Taxable Income	3 Deferred Tax
Accounting income	$175,000	$175,000	
Club memberships	5,000	5,000	
Depreciation		100,000	$100,000
Warranty expense		35,000	35,000
	$180,000	$315,000	$135,000
Warranty payments		$ 20,000	$ 20,000
Capital cost allowance		95,000	95,000
		$115,000	$115,000
	$180,000	$200,000	$ 20,000
Provision (45%)	$ 81,000		
Payable (45%)		$ 90,000	
Deferred:			
Warranty ($15,000 × .45) . . .			$ 6,750 (Dr.)
Fixed assets ($5,000 × .45) . .			2,250 (Dr.)
			$ 9,000 (Dr.)
Net income	$ 94,000		

Based on the foregoing, financial statement presentations for each year would appear as follows:

Partial Income Statements

	1978	1979	1980
Income before income tax	$100,000	$130,000	$175,000
Provision for income tax:			
Current	45,000	46,800	90,000
Deferred	2,250	13,950	(9,000)
	47,250	60,750	81,000
Net income	$ 52,750	$ 69,250	$ 94,000

Balance Sheets

	1978	1979	1980
Current assets:			
Deferred income tax – Warranty	$ 4,500	$ 1,800	$ 8,550
Current Liabilities:			
Estimated income tax payable	45,000	46,800	90,000
Deferred income tax — Fixed assets . . .	6,750	18,000	15,750

Section 3470 of the *Accounting Recommendations* requires disclosure of the current and deferred portions of the income tax provision or expense, but does not specify any particular method of disclosure. One method, disclosure on the face of the income statement, is illustrated above. However, disclosure in the notes or on the statement of changes in financial position are acceptable alternatives for reporting this information.

Although not essential, a summary of timing differences provides a convenient way to maintain separate records for several different kinds of possible timing differences and, in addition, provides support for the deferred tax balances to be shown on the balance sheet. Schedules summarizing the timing differences of Thompson Limited are presented below.

Summary of Timing Differences			
1978	Balance	Change	Balance
Warranty	Nil	$(10,000) *	$(10,000)
Fixed assets:			
Excess of net book value (NBV) over undepreciated capital cost (UCC)	Nil	15,000	15,000
		$ 5,000	$ 5,000
Deferred:			
Warranty	Nil	$(4,500)	$ (4,500)
Fixed assets	Nil	6,750	6,750
	Nil	$ 2,250	$ 2,250
1979			
Warranty	$(10,000)	$ 6,000	$ (4,000)
Fixed assets:			
Excess of NBV over UCC	15,000	25,000	40,000
	$ 5,000	$ 31,000	$ 36,000
Deferred:			
Warranty	$ (4,500)	$ 2,700	$ (1,800)
Fixed assets	6,750	11,250	18,000
	$ 2,250	$ 13,950	$ 16,200
1980			
Warranty	$ (4,000)	$(15,000)	$(19,000)
Fixed assets:			
Excess of NBV over UCC	40,000	(5,000)	35,000
	$ 36,000	$(20,000)	$ 16,000
Deferred:			
Warranty	$ (1,800)	$ (6,750)	$ (8,550)
Fixed assets	18,000	(2,250)	15,750
	$ 16,200	$ (9,000)	$ 7,200

*Brackets denote debits

Although the Thompson Limited example illustrates the use of separate accounts for the warranty and fixed asset timing differences, one deferred tax account could have been used. The issue is disclosure, not the mechanics of accounting. When only one deferred tax account is used, it is necessary to separate its current and non-current components for purposes of balance sheet disclosure. As illustrated, a summary of timing differences is one way to do this.

The table presented below provides a comparison of reported net income for Thompson Limited with and without income tax allocation.

| Year | Accounting Income Before Tax | Interperiod Income Tax Allocation | | | |
| | | With | | Without | |
		Income Tax	Net Income	Income Tax	Net Income
1978	$100,000	$47,250	$52,750	$45,000	$55,000
1979	130,000	60,750	69,250	46,800	83,200
1980	175,000	81,000	94,000	90,000	85,000

Examination of the table shows that without interperiod income tax allocation the income tax expense in 1979 is almost the same as for 1978, even though accounting income before tax was $30,000 higher in 1979. Also, in 1980, net income without allocation is not significantly different from 1979's net income in spite of the reported income before tax being $45,000 higher in 1980. The results using interperiod income tax allocation are believed to provide a better matching of expense with revenue. Allocation also smoothes out differences in the amounts of reported net income.

CHANGES IN TAX RATES

If income tax rates change over time, the change in rates must be accounted for either retroactively or prospectively. In susbtance, this issue depends upon how the allocation method is applied. Two alternatives exist: (1) the deferral method, and (2) the liability method. Under the *deferral method*, the current tax rate is used to accumulate tax deferrals on current period timing differences and to determine the amount currently payable. No adjustment is made when tax rates change unless a timing difference reverses, as discussed later. Under this method, the provision or expense is determined by combining the payable and deferred amounts applicable to the reporting period. Under the *liability method*, the rate used to accumulate tax deferrals is the rate expected to be in effect when timing differences reverse. Since this future rate is uncertain, the current rate is normally used as an estimate of the future tax rate. When tax rates change, accumulated deferred tax balances must be adjusted and the resulting gain or loss forms part of the current period's provision or expense. Thus, if the rate decreases, a gain is reported on accumulated deferred tax credits, a loss on accumulated deferred tax debits, as a result of the rate change. The Accounting Research Committee in Section 3470 opted in favor of the deferral method which is now the generally accepted method in Canadian accounting practice. It should be noted that, in the absence of tax rate changes, the deferral and liability methods yield identical results.

In general, where timing differences between accounting income before income tax and taxable income reverse, therefore requiring a transfer from the deferred tax balances accumulated in prior periods, the transfer should be computed at the tax rate at which the deferrals were accumulated. Since in practice it may be difficult to identify the specific timing differences that give rise to the reversal, the transfer, according to Section 3470, "may be calculated at the effective average rate of accumulation . . . either by types of differences or in the aggregate.[5] The effective average rate of accumulation is simply the proportion that accumulated deferred tax credits and debits bear to the accumulated difference between accounting income before tax and taxable income.

The Thompson Limited example presented earlier will be used to illustrate the deferral method of income tax allocation, given a change in tax rates. The illustration is based on 1980 data and assumes a tax rate of 40% rather than the 45% rate used earlier. The three column analysis for 1980, as presented on page 568, produced the before tax totals shown below.

	Accounting Income	Taxable Income	Deferred Tax
	$180,000	$200,000	$20,000
Applicable tax rate		40%	
Payable/Deferred		$ 80,000	$ 8,250
Provision ($80,000 − $8,250)	71,750		
Net income ($175,000 − $71,750)	$103,250		

The total 1980 timing difference of $20,000 includes a $15,000 accumulation pertaining to the warranty, and a $5,000 reversal with respect to fixed assets. Since the accumulation must be recorded at the current tax rate, the result is a current deferred tax debit of $6,000 (40% of $15,000). The fixed asset reversal or drawdown should, where possible, be recorded at the rate of accumulation (in this case 45%), resulting in a non-current deferred tax debit of $2,250 (45% of $5,000). For 1980, deferred taxes therefore total $8,250. Income tax payable is determined using the current tax rate. The provision or expense of $71,750 simply combines the payable and deferred amounts applicable to 1980. In particular, it must be emphasized that a reversal of accumulated deferred tax balances precludes use of the general formula for determining the provision or expense under income tax allocation, as presented on page 562, if there is a difference between the current tax rate and either the rate of accumulation or the effective average rate of accumulation.

---

[5]CICA Handbook: Accounting Recommendations, Section 3470, "Corporate Income Taxes" (Toronto: Canadian Institute of Chartered Accountants, 1968), par. 18.

In such circumstances, the provision or expense should be determined as follows:

1. Determine the amount payable by applying the current tax rate to taxable income.
2. Determine the amount deferred by computing
    (a) current period accumulations using the current tax rate, and
    (b) reversals using either the rate of accumulation or the effective average rate of accumulation.
3. Determine the provision by combining the amounts determined in 1 and 2 above.

In general, the rate of accumulation should be used to compute reversals of deferred income taxes. However, this requires detailed information about individual timing differences such as that provided by a summary of timing differences illustrated on page 569. Where this information is not available, there is no alternative but to use the effective average rate of accumulation to compute any reversals. In most cases, any differences between the rate of accumulation and the effective average rate of accumulation are unlikely to be material.

Problem Areas in Interperiod Income Tax Allocation

Several complex questions have arisen concerning interperiod income tax allocation as it relates to specific industries and situations. For example, the equity method of accounting for investment revenue generally results in accounting income in excess of taxable income. While income from investments is subject to personal income tax only when distributed, the taxation of intercorporate distributions is a complex matter that extends beyond the scope of intermediate accounting. Nonetheless, it can be argued that if distribution never occurs, the difference is really a permanent difference rather than a timing difference.

Another question that has been discussed is whether deferred income taxes should be discounted to report the amount at the present value of expected future payments. In Section 3470 of the *Accounting Recommendations*, the Accounting Research Committee concluded that deferred income tax should not be accounted for on a discounted basis.[6]

The application of the tax allocation method to regulated industries has been the subject of extensive discussion. Although the Accounting Research Committee believes that the allocation method should be equally relevant to regulated industries, the Committee nonetheless concluded that the taxes payable method would be appropriate in the regulated utility field where only the amount of income taxes currently payable may be allowed as an

---

[6]*Ibid.*, par. 22.

element of cost for rate-setting purposes. A second exception to the allocation method relates to companies whose revenues may be determined under long-term contracts which provide for reimbursement of incurred cost that include only the taxes payable for the period. The Committee's recommendation reads, as follows:[7]

> Provided there is reasonable expectation that all taxes payable in future years will be:
> (a) included in the approved rate or formula for reimbursement and
> (b) recoverable from the customer at that time.
> the taxes payable basis would be appropriate in the rare situations referred to.
> ... In those circumstances where tax allocation principles are not applied, the matter should be fully disclosed in the financial statements with reasons therefore as well as information relating to the nature and amount of the tax effects involved.

ACCOUNTING FOR BUSINESS LOSSES

Since income tax is based upon the amount of taxable income earned, no tax is payable if a corporation experiences a loss for tax purposes. In order to provide an equitable outcome for those businesses that experience alternate periods of income and losses, income tax laws provide a way to ease the risk of loss years. This is done through carryback and carryforward provisions that permit a corporation to apply a loss occurring in one year against the income of the immediately preceding year, and any remaining balance of the loss forward for a period of five years. Thus, a corporation experiencing a loss for the current year first applies the loss to the income of the immediately preceding year and an income tax refund is claimed. Loss carrybacks result in an entry to establish a receivable for the income taxes recoverable and to reduce the loss for the current year by reflecting the tax savings arising from recovery of the prior year's income taxes. Depending on the circumstances, deferred income taxes can also be affected.

To illustrate, assume Superior Company had the following pattern of income and losses for the years 1977-1980. For simplicity, no permanent or timing differences are included in this example.

Year	Income (Loss)	Income Tax at 45%
1977	$15,000	$6,750
1978	(10,000)	0
1979	14,000	6,300
1980	(29,000)	0

The $10,000 loss in 1978 would be carried back to 1977 resulting in income taxes recoverable of $4,500. The $29,000 loss in 1980 would be carried back to the extent of the $14,000 income in 1979 resulting in income

---

[7]*Ibid.*, par. 58.

taxes recoverable of $6,300. The entry to record the income tax receivable as a result of the 1980 loss would be as follows:

```
Income Tax Refund Receivable ..............................  6,300
    Provision for income tax refund from applying loss carryback ..       6,300
```

The refund will be reflected on the income statement as a reduction of the loss before income tax as follows:

```
Loss before income tax .......................................  $29,000
Provision for income tax refund from applying loss carryback .......   6,300
Net Loss ...............................................  $22,700
```

Realization of a loss carryback is assured because a refund can only arise to the extent that there is taxable income in the immediately preceding year. The corporation is entitled to file an amended return and recover up to the amount of income tax paid in the previous year, in this example $6,300. Realization of a loss carryforward, however, is uncertain because it is dependent upon the corporation generating sufficient taxable income in the five-year carryforward period to offset the amount of the tax loss applicable to future years. In this example, the loss carryforward is $15,000 ($29,000 − $14,000) and the potential benefit upon realization is $6,750 (45% × $15,000). The uncertainty concerns the ability of the corporation to earn $15,000 of taxable income during the carryforward period, 1981 to 1985, inclusive. Any portion of the $15,000 loss carryforward that has not been used prior to the end of the 1985 tax year expires and is lost.

The tax allocation method is concerned with the accounting for income taxes, and therefore, the various elements of an accounting loss merit examination. The Superior Company example presented on page 573 included no permanent or timing differences; therefore, accounting income before income tax and taxable income for each year were, of course, equal. Now, assume that for 1980 the accounting loss of $29,000 was determined after the deduction of $4,000 depreciation, and that no capital cost allowance was claimed in 1980. Given an accounting loss, the effect of claiming capital cost allowance would be to increase the amount of the loss for income tax purposes. In this example, the 1980 accounting loss includes the following components:

```
Accounting loss before income tax ............................  $29,000

Represented by:
    Timing difference — depreciation ...........................  $ 4,000
    Loss carryback ...........................................   14,000
    Loss carryforward .........................................   11,000
                                                                $29,000
```

The loss for tax purposes is only $25,000, determined as follows:

Accounting loss before income tax	....	$29,000
Depreciation (not allowable for income tax purposes)	....	4,000
Loss for income tax purposes	....	$25,000

The resulting income statement presentation, ignoring consideration of any loss carryforward, will show a total provision for income tax of $8,100, ~~$18,000 × .45~~ including a current portion of $6,300, the refund from applying the loss carryback, and deferred income tax of $1,800 (45% × $4,000). The balance sheet will show the $6,300 income tax refund receivable as a current asset and a reduction of $1,800 in the amount of accumulated deferred tax credits. Note that the introduction of a timing difference relating to depreciation has served to reduce the loss carryforward from $15,000 to only $11,000. Since the loss carryforward is subject to possible expiration at the end of 1985 it may be prudent to keep its amount as low as possible if there is doubt that ? *see below* ① the company will earn sufficient taxable income during the five year carry-forward period to utilize the full amount of the loss carryforward.

Introduction of the timing difference relating to depreciation has also served to reduce the amount of the loss reported on the income statement. A comparison of the bottom portion of the resulting income statements is presented below.

	(1) No Timing Difference	(2) Timing Difference Depreciation
Loss before income tax	$29,000	$29,000
Provision for income tax:		
Current portion	$ 6,300	$ 6,300
Deferred income tax	——	1,800
	$ 6,300	$ 8,100
Loss	$22,700	$20,900

In each case, notes to the financial statements should disclose the existence of a loss carryforward the benefit of which has not been recorded. In case (1), the unrecorded benefit is $6,750 (45% × $15,000); in case (2), $4,950 (45% × $11,000).

The amount of the loss carryforward might be further reduced, or possibly eliminated, if Superior Company amended its 1979 capital cost allowance claim. Assume that in 1979 capital cost allowance of $5,000 was claimed, this amount being exactly equal to the depreciation recorded for accounting purposes. If Superior Company amends its 1979 tax return to reduce the amount of capital cost allowance to zero, this will increase taxable income to $19,000 ($14,000 + $5,000), and also increase the loss carryback to $19,000. As a result, the loss carryforward becomes only $6,000 rather than $11,000. This amendment alternative does not change the refund receivable; instead,

① CCA rates fixed?
How? 578
see p. be
CCA may
claimed
0 → max.
permitted by
tax laws

the deferred tax is adjusted. The purpose of amendment is simply to minimize the amount of loss carryforward.

Assuming amendment, the entry to record income taxes and a partial income statement for Superior Company would be as follows:

Income tax refund receivable	6,300	
Deferred income tax .... $9,000 x .45	4,050	
Provision for income tax		10,350

	(3) Timing Difference Depreciation Capital Cost Allowance Amended
Loss before income tax	$29,000
Provision for income tax:	
Current portion	$ 6,300
Deferred income tax	4,050
	$10,350
Loss	$18,650

Again, notes to the financial statements should disclose the existence of a loss carryforward, the benefit of which has not been recorded. In case (3), the unrecorded benefit is $2,700 (45% × $6,000).

In appropriate circumstances, the benefits relating to loss carryforwards may be recognized for accounting purposes in the period of the loss. These circumstances are examined in the paragraphs that follow.

Less Carryforward Assuming Virtual Certainty

Uncertainty is the obvious problem if the benefit of a loss carryforward is to be given accounting recognition in the period of the loss. The alternative is recognition in the period when the benefit of the loss carryforward is realized, assuming eventual realization. The Accounting Research Committee in Section 3470 of the *Accounting Recommendations* relies on the *virtual certainty* test as the standard that must be met in order to record as an asset the benefit of the loss carryforward or even a portion thereof. The virtual certainty test applies in the year of the loss and requires that all of the following conditions be met.[8]

1. The loss results from an identifiable and non-recurring cause,
2. A record of profitability has been established over a long period . . . with any occasional losses being more than offset by income in subsequent years, and
3. There is assurance beyond any reasonable doubt that future taxable income will be sufficient to offset the loss carryforward and will be earned during the carryforward period prescribed by the tax laws.

[8]*Ibid.*, par. 40.

The closing of an unprofitable division or a strike should clearly meet the first criterion. The second criterion eliminates new corporations and those with erratic performance records. The third criterion is essentially a question of professional judgment.

Assuming that the Superior Company can meet the virtual certainty test, the income tax provision for 1980 would be recorded as follows, based on case (2) since it is unlikely amendment of prior capital cost allowance claims would be considered when the conditions for virtual certainty can be met.

Income tax refund receivable	6,300	
Income tax recoverable	4,950	
Deferred income tax	1,800	
Provisions for income tax		13,050

Computations:
Income tax refund — loss carryback: 45% × $14,000 = $6,300
Income tax recoverable — loss carryforward: 45% × $11,000 = $4,950
Deferred income tax — depreciation: 45% × $4,000 = $1,800
Provision for income tax: 45% × $29,000 = $13,050

The provision will be reflected on the income statement as a reduction of the loss before income tax as shown below.

Loss before income tax			$29,000
Provision for income tax:			
Current portion		$6,300	
Deferred income tax		6,750	13,050
Loss			$15,950

The current portion of the provision for income tax includes only the refund arising from the loss carryback, $6,300. The income tax recoverable as a result of the loss carryforward, $4,950, is a timing difference; it has been recognized for accounting purposes but not for tax purposes. On the balance sheet, the income tax refund receivable should be shown as a current asset; both the income tax recoverable, $4,950, and the deferred income tax draw-down of $1,800, should be separately classified as non-current items; they should not be netted.

In the rare situation where there is no longer virtual certainty of realizing the benefit, or a portion thereof, relating to loss carryforwards, the previously recorded asset should be written off and shown on the income statement as an extraordinary item.[9] This outcome might arise occasionally where subsequent events during the carryforward period did not conform with the professional judgment inherent in the third criterion of the virtual certainty test as listed on page 576.

It should be noted that the subsequent realization of the benefit of a loss carryforward that had not previously been recorded should also be

---

[9] *Ibid.*, par. 47.

shown as an extraordinary item on the income statement(s) for the period(s) of realization.[10]

Loss Carryforwards Without Virtual Certainty

Failure to meet the virtual certainty test, which only applies in the year of the loss, denies asset recognition of the benefit of the loss carryforward. It does not necessarily deny income statement recognition of the benefit, or a portion thereof, which may be accomplished by drawing down accumulated deferred tax credits, or by the creation of deferred income tax debits. These alternatives, which need only be considered in the absence of virtual certainty, rest on two facts: (1) depreciation must be recorded annually under generally accepted accounting principles, and (2) capital cost allowance may be claimed at any amount from zero to the maximum permitted by income tax law. While other timing differences may be used to produce the same end result, the depreciation — capital cost allowance difference has by far the widest application.

Both the loss carryforward for income tax purposes and capital cost allowance have in common the ability to reduce taxable income. The former, however, expires at the end of the five-year carryforward period; the latter continues forever assuming continuity of the entity. Therefore, where deferred income tax credits have previously been recorded, "the unrecorded tax benefit of the loss carryforward should be recognized to the extent of any reductions in accumulated deferred income tax credits available in the carryforward period by claiming less capital cost allowances than depreciation recorded or by making other adjustments of a similar effect."[11] The use of this method of accounting for deferred income taxes has the effect, assuming future depreciation charges are predictable with reasonable certainty, of converting the loss carryforward into a timing difference that does not suffer a short-run expiration date. In other words, future taxable income during the carryforward period will be reduced first of all by application of the tax loss carryforward, and secondly, by claiming capital cost allowances only after utilization of the tax loss carryforward is reasonably assured.

The income statement presentation under this method of accounting for deferred income taxes is the same as that presented on page 577 which assumes virtual certainty. On the balance sheet, the $4,950 shown as a non-current asset described as income tax recoverable, assuming virtual certainty, must in the absence of virtual certainty be netted against the accumulated deferred income tax credits. Thus, for balance sheet purposes, the benefit relating to the loss carryforward must be charged against accumulated deferred tax credits rather than set up separately on the asset side of the balance sheet, as would be the case assuming virtual certainty.

Depending on the circumstances, limits may apply to the amount of loss

---

[10]*Ibid.*, par. 53.
[11]*Ibid.*, par. 45.

carryforward benefit that may be recognized by drawing down accumulated deferred tax credits. One limit is the amount of the benefit, in this case $4,950 (45% of $11,000). Two other potential limits might apply: (1) the tax effect on the amount by which depreciation during the five-year carryforward might exceed capital cost allowance, and (2) the balance in accumulated deferred tax credits. In the example, it is assumed that neither of these limits apply. In practice, the balance in accumulated deferred tax credits is most often the limit that may apply because the drawdown method does not permit creating a deferred tax debit.

Although perhaps rare, another situation arises when the conditions for virtual certainty cannot be met and there are no accumulated deferred tax credits. In such circumstances, timing differences arising in the loss period give rise to deferred tax debits. This fact may make it possible to record at least part of the benefit of the loss carryforward by not claiming capital cost allowances. Therefore, as stated in Section 3470, "the tax effects of such timing differences would be recorded in the normal manner when there was reasonable assurance that the timing differences would be reversed.[12] To elaborate, if a corporation has taxable income before any claim for capital cost allowance, it would be prudent to wipe out the taxable income by application of the loss carryforward rather than by claiming capital cost allowance. This situation is in fact partially illustrated by the comparative illustration of income statements on page 575, especially case (2) which includes a timing difference relating to depreciation.

To further illustrate, consider the following possibility.

Income before depreciation	Nil
Depreciation	$1,000
Loss before income tax	$1,000

Assuming virtual certainty does not apply and there are no accumulated deferred tax credits to drawdown, is it possible to record a deferred tax debit of $450 (45% of $1,000)? The answer according to Section 3470 is yes, provided there is reasonable assurance that the current period timing difference will be reversed in subsequent years; otherwise the answer is no. Assuming reasonable assurance, the following entry would be recorded.

Deferred income tax	450	
Provision for income tax		450

It should be noted that in these circumstances reasonable assurance only applies to timing differences in the loss period. However, the deferred tax debit that may be recorded is not constrained by the five-year carryforward period because the debit is related to a non-expiring timing difference, as distinct from the loss carryforward. More specifically, it is the anticipated reversal that is not constrained by the five-year carryforward period.

---

[12]*Ibid.*, par. 48.

TREATMENT OF LOSSES ILLUSTRATED

To illustrate the foregoing discussion, a comprehensive example follows. Assume that Loss Leader Limited has an accumulated deferred tax credit of $22,500, at December 31, 1978, as a result of claiming capital cost allowance in excess of depreciation. A summary of timing differences is set forth below.

Net book value (NBV)	$310,000
Undepreciated capital cost (UCC)	260,000
Excess NBV over UCC..	$ 50,000
Tax rate in all prior periods	45%
Deferred income tax credit.....................................	$ 22,500

First of all, to illustrate the accounting for a loss carryback, the following data pertaining to 1979 and 1980 will be used. The tax rate applicable to both years is 45%.

Example 1
Carryback Only

	1979	1980
Accounting income before tax	$ 60,000	$ 6,000
Depreciation	$ 10,000	$ 15,000
Capital cost allowance	(20,000)	(25,000)
Current period timing difference	$(10,000)	$(10,000)
Taxable income (loss)	$ 50,000	$ (4,000)

The entries to record income taxes for 1979 and 1980 are presented below, together with partial income statements.

1979

Provision for income tax	27,000	
Deferred income tax		4,500
Estimated income tax payable		22,500

1980

Provision for income tax	2,700	
Income tax refund receivable	1,800	
Deferred income tax		4,500

Computations:
Provision for income tax: 45% × $60,000 = $27,000
Deferred income tax — 1979 timing difference: 45% × $10,000 = $4,500
Estimated income tax payable: 45% × $50,000 = $22,500
Provision for income tax: 45% × $6,000 = $2,700
Income tax refund receivable — loss carryback: 45% × $4,000 = $1,800
Deferred income tax — 1980 timing difference: 45% × $10,000 = $4,500

Loss Leader Limited Partial Income Statements	1979	1980
Income before income tax	$60,000	$ 6,000
Provision for income tax:		
Current portion	$22,500	$(1,800)
Deferred income tax	4,500	4,500
	$27,000	$ 2,700
Net income	$33,000	$ 3,300

At this point, the summary of timing differences would appear as follows:

Summary of Timing Differences	Balance 12/31/78	Change 1979	Balance 12/31/79	Change 1980	Balance 12/31/80
Fixed assets: Excess of NBV over UCC	$50,000	$10,000	$60,000	$10,000	$70,000
Tax rate	45%	45%	45%	45%	45%
Deferred income tax ...	$22,500	$ 4,500	$27,000	$ 4,500	$31,500

The relevant balance sheet disclosures are presented below.

Balance Sheet Disclosures	1979	1980
Current assets:		
Income tax refund receivable		$ 1,800
Current liabilities:		
Estimated income tax payable	$22,500	
Deferred income tax	$27,000	$31,500

To extend the example, assume that Loss Leader Limited reported a loss before income tax of $80,000 in 1980, all other facts remain the same. Summary data would now appear as follows:

Example 2 Loss Exceeds Income of Preceding Year	1979	1980
Income (loss) before tax	$ 60,000	$(80,000)
Depreciation	$ 10,000	$ 15,000
Capital cost allowance	(20,000)	(25,000)
Current period timing difference	$(10,000)	$(10,000)
Taxable income (loss)	$ 50,000	$(90,000)

Since the 1980 loss exceeds the income of 1979, a loss carryforward arises. If Loss Leader Limited can meet the stringent conditions for virtual certainty the following entries would apply.

1979

Provision for income tax	27,000	
Deferred income tax		4,500
Estimated income tax payable		22,500

1980

Income tax refund receivable ... *50,000 × .45*	22,500	
Income tax recoverable ... *(90,000 − 50,000) × .45*	18,000	
Deferred income tax .... *10,000 × .45*		4,500
Provision for income tax ... *80,000 × .45*		36,000

The entry for 1979 is identical to the one presented on page 580. Since the loss in 1980 exceeds the income of the preceding year, the full amount of tax paid for 1979, $22,500, is now recorded as a tax refund receivable. The loss carryforward for tax purposes is $40,000 ($90,000 − $50,000), the benefit is $18,000 (45% of $40,000), and, under virtual certainty, the benefit is recorded as an asset. The current period timing difference of $10,000 generates a $4,500 credit to deferred income tax. The provision to be shown on the income statement is credited for $36,000 (45% of $80,000).

In the absence of virtual certainty, Loss Leader Limited should consider amending the amounts of capital cost allowance claimed or claimable in 1979 and 1980. In the circumstances of the example, this possibility would completely eliminate the loss carryforward, as illustrated below.

	1979		1980
	As Reported	As Amended	
Income (loss) before tax	$ 60,000	$60,000	$(80,000)
Depreciation	$ 10,000	$10,000	$ 15,000
Capital cost allowance	(20,000)	(5,000)	Nil
Current period timing difference	$(10,000)	$ 5,000	$ 15,000
	$ 50,000	$65,000	$ 65,000

Income tax for 1979 has already been recorded based on the as reported data above. The following entry records income tax for 1980.

Income tax refund receivable	22,500	
Deferred income tax	13,500	
Provision for income tax		36,000

By way of explanation, note that the capital cost allowance claimed in 1979 has been reduced during the current period by $15,000, and in 1980 the current period timing difference is a $15,000 drawdown. These two amounts total $30,000 to which the 45% tax rate (the rate of accumulation) is applied to determine the $13,500 debit to deferred income tax. The following schedule provides a continuity for the deferred income tax account.

	Timing Differences	45%
	Fixed Assets Excess NBV	Deferred Income Tax
Dec. 31, 1978	$50,000	22,500
1979 change	10,000	4,500
Dec. 31, 1979	$60,000	27,000
Amendment	$15,000	
1980 drawdown	15,000	
	$30,000 13,500	
Dec. 31, 1980	$30,000	13,500

Since Loss Leader Limited has accumulated deferred tax credits, the benefit of the loss carryforward can be recorded without amending the capital cost allowance claimed in 1979. Under current income tax law, Loss Leader Limited can claim in 1980 any amount of capital cost allowance from zero to the maximum applicable, presumably $25,000. Assuming the company elects to claim zero, the entry to record income tax for 1980 would be identical to that presented on page 582. The timing differences and related deferred income tax are set forth below.

	Timing Differences		45%
	Fixed Assets Excess NBV	Loss Carryforward (LCF)	Deferred Income Tax
Dec. 31, 1978	$50,000		22,500
1979 change	10,000		4,500
Dec. 31, 1979	$60,000		27,000
1980 drawdown	15,000		13,500
LCF recorded		$(15,000)	
	$45,000	$(15,000)	13,500

All three alternatives result in the same amount of net income being reported. The relevant balance sheet presentations, however, will differ depending on whether or not virtual certainty applies.

In the absence of virtual certainty, amendment of the preceding period's capital cost allowance claim, as illustrated, is one alternative which, depending on the circumstances, may or may not be combined with the drawdown alternative. In practice, however, the drawdown alternative by itself is generally preferred to avoid any tax consequences that might arise as a result of filing an amended return for the preceding year.

To illustrate the drawdown technique where limits would also apply, assume that Loss Leader Limited reported a loss before income tax of $200,000 in 1980, all other facts remain the same, except that no capital cost allowance is to be claimed in 1980. Summary data would now appear as follows:

Example 3 Loss Carryforward Exceeds Accumulated Deferred Tax Credits		
No Virtual Certainty		
	1979	1980
Income (loss) before tax	$ 60,000	$(200,000)
Depreciation	$ 10,000	$ 15,000
Capital cost allowance	(20,000)	——
Current period timing difference	$(10,000)	$ 15,000
Taxable income (loss)	$ 50,000	$(185,000)

The limits that may apply to the amount of loss carryforward benefit to be recognized in the period of the loss, given that the conditions for virtual certainty cannot be met, restrict recognition to the lesser of three amounts, determined as follows:

1. Accounting loss $200,000
   Loss carryback .... $ 50,000
   Current period drawdown 15,000
   $ 65,000
   Loss carryforward $135,000
   Potential benefit (45%) .... $ 60,750

2. Potential depreciation drawdown during carryforward period
   ($15,000 × 5) $75,000
   Potential benefit (45%) $33,750

3. Accumulated timing differences $45,000
   Deferred tax credit (45%) $20,250

Because the third limit applies, the 1980 provision in example 3 is restricted to $49,500. The following schedule supports the amount to be reported as the 1980 provision for income tax.

1980 Provision for Income Tax			
Accounting loss	200,000	Potential provision	90,000
Loss carryback	50,000	Refund receivable	22,500
Current period drawdown...	15,000	Deferred	6,750
LCF recorded	45,000	Deferred	20,250
	110,000	Provision	49,500
LCF unrecorded	90,000	Potential benefit	40,500

The entry to record the 1980 provision, together with a schedule to provide a continuity for the deferred income tax account, are presented below.

Income tax refund receivable 22,500
Deferred income tax 27,000
   Provision for income tax ...110,000 × .45............. 49,500

| | Timing Differences | | 45% |
	Fixed Assets Excess NBV	Loss Carryforward	Deferred Income Tax
Dec. 31, 1978	$50,000		22,500
1979 change	10,000		4,500
Dec. 31, 1979	$60,000		27,000
1980 drawdown	15,000	⎱ 27,000	
LCF recorded		$(45,000) ⎰	
Dec. 31, 1980	$45,000	$(45,000)	Nil

To illustrate realization of the potential benefit pertaining to the unrecorded loss carryforward, assume that in 1981 Loss Leader Limited reported income before income tax of $300,000, after deducting $25,000 for depreciation. Applicable capital cost allowances totalled $50,000, and the tax rate continued to be 45%. Summary data for 1981 would appear as follows:

	1981
Accounting income before tax	$300,000
Depreciation	$ 25,000
Capital cost allowance	(50,000)
Current period timing difference	$ (25,000)
Taxable income	$275,000

The entries[13] to record income taxes for 1981 and the related financial statement disclosures are presented below.

```
Provision for income tax ..... 300,000 × .45 .......   135,000
    Deferred income tax ........ 25,000 × .45 ......              11,250
    Estimated income tax payable ... 275,000 × .45              123,750
1981 provision for income tax

Estimated income tax payable ........................    60,750
    Deferred income tax .............................             20,250
    Extraordinary item ..............................             40,500
Application of loss carryforward to reduce estimated
    income tax payable
```

Loss Leader Limited Partial Income Statement Year Ended December 31, 1981	
Income before income tax	$300,000
Provision for income tax:	
Current portion	$ 63,000
Deferred income tax	72,000
	$135,000
Income before extraordinary item	$165,000
Realization of benefit pertaining to an unrecorded loss carryforward	40,500
Net income	$205,000

[13]These entries could be combined into a single entry.

Computations:

Current portion: $123,750 − $60,750 = $63,000
Deferred income tax: $135,000 − $63,000 = $72,000

Balance Sheet Disclosures

Current liabilities:
Estimated income tax payable $63,000
Deferred income tax 31,500

And finally, the following schedule provides a continuity for the deferred income tax account.

	Timing Differences		45%
	Fixed Assets Excess NBV	Loss Carryforward	Deferred Income Tax
Dec. 31, 1980	$45,000	$(45,000)	Nil
1981 change	25,000		11,250
	$70,000		
From unrecorded		(90,000) ⎰	20,250
Used		135,000 ⎱	
	$70,000	Nil	31,500

CAPITAL GAINS AND LOSSES

Prior to 1972, Canada did not impose a tax on capital gains, nor were capital losses tax deductible. Effective January 1, 1972, the taxation of capital gains became an important part of Canada's income tax system. The introduction of the capital gains tax, however, was not retroactive so that only gains and losses subsequent to valuation days would have income tax consequences. In the case of publicly traded shares or securities, valuation day was proclaimed to be December 22, 1971, and in relation to any other property December 31, 1971.

In general, only one-half of realized capital gains are subject to tax at the regular rates of tax applicable. The other half of a capital gain is therefore an important example of a permanent difference between accounting income before tax and taxable income. Capital losses can only be deducted or offset against capital gains. However, allowable capital losses can be carried forward indefinitely. While this is indeed significant, it does not ensure realization of the tax benefit relating to capital losses unless there is virtual certainty that sufficient taxable capital gains will be realized in the foreseeable future. In the context of capital losses, virtual certainty requires all three of the following conditions to be present:[14]

---

[14]*CICA Handbook: Accounting Recommendations, Section 3470, op. cit.,* par. 41.

1. A potential capital gain is present in unrealized form and in assets which are not essential to the future operations of the corporation.
2. The balance of the unrealized capital gain, after allowance for possible decline before disposal, is sufficient to offset the loss in question, and
3. There is satisfactory evidence of an intent to dispose of the particular assets in the foreseeable future and thus realize the potential capital gain.

Assuming these conditions can be met, the potential tax benefit relating to the capital loss would be reflected in the financial statements for the period in which the loss occurs. However, because the corporation is recognizing a tax benefit which will be realized in a future period, the benefit should be determined using the tax rates for relevant future periods, if enacted. Otherwise the current tax rate would be used. However, if applicable tax rates should change from those used to determine the benefit, the effect of the change in rates should be recognized when the rate change occurs by adjustment of both the asset account and the provision for income tax.

It must be emphasized that the virtual certainty test concerns accounting recognition of the benefit pertaining to a capital loss. For tax purposes, the benefit cannot be fully used until sufficient taxable capital gains have been realized. A capital loss, therefore, will often give rise to a timing difference that will require the recognition of deferred income tax.

A general understanding of the tax treatment of capital gains and losses is important in the application of deferred income tax accounting. As previously mentioned, only 50% of capital gains constitute taxable capital gains. Similarly, only 50% of capital losses constitute allowable capital losses. In each case, the other 50% is a permanent difference.

Dispositions of property may often involve both permanent and timing differences. To illustrate, assume that accounting income before income tax includes a gain on disposal of depreciable assets of $70,000, being the difference between the disposal price of $110,000 and the net book value of $40,000 (cost of $60,000 less accumulated depreciation of $20,000). Since the original capital cost of the asset sold was $60,000, the accounting gain of $70,000 includes a capital gain of $50,000 ($110,000 − $60,000), 50% of which is a taxable capital gain, and 50% of which is a permanent difference. For income tax purposes, the asset class must be credited with the lesser of the proceeds of disposal or the capital cost of the asset, in this case with $60,000, the capital cost of the asset. Since for accounting purposes the net book value of $40,000 must be removed from the property accounts while $60,000 must be credited to the asset class for tax purposes, the result is a $20,000 timing difference. The components of the accounting gain can be summarized as follows:

Accounting gain	$70,000
Capital gain ($110,000 − $60,000)	$50,000
Income gain ($60,000 − $40,000)	20,000
Accounting gain	$70,000
Permanent difference (50% of $50,000)	25,000
Taxable for accounting purposes under the tax allocation method	$45,000
Timing difference	20,000
Currently subject to income tax	$25,000

In the event that the property disposition might qualify for presentation as an extraordinary item, intraperiod income tax allocation would apply. The tax effects of the disposition, assuming a tax rate of 45%, would be recorded as follows:

Extraordinary Gain — Provision		
For Income Tax	20,250	
Deferred Income Tax		9,000
Estimated Income Tax Payable		11,250

Computation:
Provision for income tax: 45% × $45,000 = $20,250
Deferred income tax — depreciation: 45% × $20,000 = $9,000
Estimated income tax payable: 45% × $25,000 = $11,250

For financial statement purposes, the provision of $20,250 would be offset against the extraordinary gain of $70,000. As a result, the extraordinary gain would be shown separately on the income statement, as follows:

Income before extraordinary items	xxx
Extraordinary items:	
Gain on disposal of property net of income tax in the amount of	
$20,500 ~~20,250~~	$49,750
Net income	xxx

FINANCIAL STATEMENT PRESENTATION

The *Accounting Recommendations* require disclosure of the current and deferred portions of the provision for income tax.[15] As previously noted, this breakdown can be shown on the face of the income statement, in the notes to the financial statements, or on the face of the statement of changes in financial position.[16]

The balance sheet presentation of deferred income tax balances, which may be credits, debits, or both credits and debits, has already been covered in the discussions included earlier in the chapter. For balance sheet purposes, the key point to remember is the segregation of current and non-current

---

[15]*Ibid.*, par. 30.
[16]The statement of changes in financial position is the subject matter of Chapter 20.

items according to the classification of the assets and liabilities to which the deferred tax balances relate. Beyond maintaining the distinction between current and non-current balances, the netting of deferred tax balances is permitted. Section 3470 contemplates netting as follows: "the usual treatment would be to show the net total of the current items and the net total of the non-current items."[17]

The accounting issues involving income tax are still evolving. Although interperiod income tax allocation is being applied extensively, there are still many who doubt its usefulness, especially where the deferred tax credit on the balance sheet continues to increase in amount and the likelihood of any drawdown appears to be remote. Continual attention needs to be given to the accounting for this significant cost of doing business.

---

[17]*CICA Handbook: Accounting Recommendations, Section 3470, op. cit.*, par. 23.

1. Accounting methods used by a company to determine income for accounting purposes frequently differ from those used to determine taxable income. What is the justification for these differences?

2. What is meant by intraperiod income tax allocation?

3. Describe the entries that would be made in recognizing income tax for the period in each case below:

- (a) There are earnings from ordinary operations and an extraordinary loss that is less than such earnings.
- (b) There are earnings from ordinary operations and a credit for a correction of an error recorded directly in Retained Earnings. An amended income tax return has been filed.
- (c) There is a loss from ordinary operations, an extraordinary gain that is greater than the loss, and a debit for a correction of an error recorded directly in Retained Earnings. A claim for an income tax refund has been filed.

4. Distinguish between a timing difference and a permanent difference when accounting for interperiod income tax allocation.

5. Distinguish between the taxes payable and allocation methods of accounting for income tax.

6. What theoretical support exists for interperiod income tax allocation?

7. Distinguish between partial interperiod income tax allocation and comprehensive interperiod income tax allocation. Which method is generally accepted and why?

8. How would the balance sheet account for deferred income tax differ if a company used the liability concept of interperiod income tax allocation as opposed to the deferral method?

9. When a company grows, all liabilities grow in amount. The growth in the credit balance of deferred income tax is no different from the growth in accounts payable. Do you agree?

10. In adopting income tax allocation procedures for timing differences, what adjustments are made when (a) reported accounting income before tax is less than taxable income, and (b) reported accounting income before tax is more than taxable income? What timing differences are most commonly encountered?

11. (a) Under what circumstances would Deferred Income Tax be classified as a current liability on the balance sheet?
(b) Under what circumstances would Deferred Income Tax be classified as a current asset on the balance sheet?

12. Under what circumstances will a Deferred Income Tax credit balance be reduced to zero? Why do most companies report an increasing balance in this account?

13. How do the operating loss carryback and carryforward provisions of the Income Tax Act reduce risk for a corporation?

14. In applying the operating loss carryback and carryforward provisions, what order of application must be followed?

15. Under what conditions should the benefit of a loss carryforward be recorded on the asset side of the balance sheet?

16. (a) How would an operating loss carryback be reflected in the financial statements?
(b) How would the realization of a carryforward be reflected in the financial statements in other than the year of the loss?

17. Explain briefly how to convert a loss carryforward into a timing difference that would not be subject to an expiration date.

18. How are capital gains and capital losses treated for income tax purposes?

EXERCISES

14-1. In 1980, the Broer Co., a service company, reported taxable operating income of $120,000 and a fully taxable extraordinary gain of $30,000. Assume income tax rates for 1980 of 45% on all items. (a) Give the entry to record income tax for 1980. (b) Assuming there was a fully deductible extraordinary loss of $30,000 rather than an extraordinary gain, give the entry to record income tax for 1980.

14-2. The Alberta Corporation reported the following income items before tax for the year 1980.

Income before income tax and extraordinary items	$230,000
Extraordinary loss from disposal of a business segment	40,000
Extraordinary gain on retirement of debt	70,000

The income tax rate is 45% for all items and the extraordinary items are fully taxable. Prepare the portion of the income statement beginning with "Income before income tax and extraordinary items" for the year ended December 31, 1980, after applying intraperiod income tax allocation procedures.

14-3. Caldwell Limited uses the allocation method of reporting income tax expense. The following information relates to the fiscal year just ended:

Deferred income tax at beginning of current year	$200,000
Income before tax per income statement	600,000
Straight-line depreciation	100,000
Capital cost allowance	180,000
Income tax rate	45%

Present the entry, in general journal form, to record the income tax expense for Caldwell Limited. What is the balance in Deferred Income Tax at the end of the current year?

14-4. Taxable income of $600,000 includes the proceeds of a prior period lawsuit in the amount of $120,000, and a gain of $90,000 on the disposal of fixed assets (not an extraordinary item). In addition, the capital cost allowance claim of $200,000 exceeds straight-line depreciation by $100,000. Although highly unusual, the accounting gain on the fixed asset disposition is exactly equal to the taxable gain, which for tax purposes is not a capital gain. The retained earnings balance at the beginning of the period was $1,000,000. Dividends declared during the period total $60,000. Assume a 40% tax rate. Starting with "Income before income tax" prepare the bottom part of the Combined Statement of Income and Retained Earnings.

14-5. For each of the following items, indicate whether each is a timing difference or a permanent difference. For each timing difference, indicate whether a deferred credit or a deferred debit is more likely to result.
  (a) Capital cost allowance in excess of depreciation, $240,000.
  (b) Excess of income on instalment sales over income reportable for tax purposes, $170,000.
  (c) Fine paid for violation of a government statute, $250,000.
  (d) Royalties collected in advance of period earned, $100,000.
  (e) Provision for warranty repairs in excess of actual expenditure for current year, $70,000.
  (f) Dividend income from taxable Canadian corporations, $15,000.

14-6. Using the information given in Exercise 14-5, and assuming an accounting income of $2,450,000 adjusted for permanent differences and an income tax rate of 45%, calculate taxable income and prepare the entry to record income tax for the year. Your entry may "net" the various deferred income tax accounts into one account. Note that "accounting income" refers to statement income adjusted for permanent differences.

14-7. The Barbara Elaine Foods Corporation reports income of $155,000 on its income tax return for the year ended December 31, 1980. Timing differences between pretax accounting income and taxable income for the year are:

Depreciation in excess of capital cost allowance	$35,000
Estimated premium expense in excess of actual premiums redeemed	5,000
Earnings of a foreign subsidiary not yet remitted	10,000

The premium expense arose as a result of a product promotion by the Barbara Elaine Foods Corporation that was initiated on April 1, 1980. According to the rules, a customer could redeem 10 coupons, available in company products, for a cooking utensil set. The company estimated that $12,000 worth of premiums relating to 1980 sales would be redeemed. By year-end, only $7,000 worth of premiums had been redeemed.

The earnings of the foreign subsidiary, Alimientos de Barbara Elaine, S.A., had not been remitted by December 31, 1980, but were expected early in the following year. For purposes of this question, assume the earnings to be subject to Canadian income tax when remitted.

Assuming an income tax rate of 45%, compute the provision for income tax, deferred income tax, and estimated income tax payable. Prepare the journal entry to record these amounts. Use one deferred income tax account.

14-8. The Waltrip Co. shows reported accounting income before income tax and taxable income for 1979 and 1980 as follows:

	Accounting Income before Income Tax	Taxable Income
1979	$ 95,400	$149,400
1980	115,800	110,400

The discrepancies arose because the company, organized in the middle of 1979, wrote off against revenue of that year organization costs totalling $60,000. For income tax purposes, however, the organization costs can be written off at the rate of 10% applied to year-end balances on a declining balance basis.

Prepare the entries that would be recorded in the accounts of the company at the end of 1979 and 1980 to recognize the provision for income tax and to provide for a proper allocation of income tax in view of the differences between accounting income and taxable income. Assume an income tax rate of 45%.

14-9. The following historical financial data are available for the Mendoza Company.

Year	Income	Tax Rate	Tax Paid
1978	15,000	48%	7,200
1979	20,000	45%	9,000

In 1980, the Mendoza Company suffered a $50,000 operating loss due to an economic recession.

(a) Using the information given, calculate the refund arising from the loss carry-back and the amount of the loss available to carryforward to future periods. Assume a 1980 tax rate of 45%. Also, assume that the conditions for virtual certainty do not apply and that the company has no accumulated deferred tax credits.

(b) Prepare the entry necessary to record the refund due and the loss reduction.

(c) Using the answer from (a), prepare the bottom portion of the income statement reflecting the effect of the loss carryback on the 1980 income statement.

(d) Assuming the company had accumulated deferred tax credits that could predictably be drawn down during the carryforward period, prepare the entry necessary to record the 1980 provision for income taxes.

14-10. During 1980, Loser Limited recorded an accounting loss of $1,000,000, which was the same as the loss for tax purposes. In 1979, the company earned $500,000, and paid taxes of $160,000 on taxable income of $400,000. The difference between accounting income and taxable income in 1979 was the result of a timing difference pertaining to fixed assets. At the end of 1979, accumulated timing differences, all pertaining to fixed assets, totalled $200,000, resulting in deferred taxes of $80,000. Virtual certainty does not apply to the 1980 loss. In 1981, Loser Limited reported income before tax of $350,000, and will claim capital cost allowance in an amount equal to depreciation charges. On an after-tax basis, determine the 1980 loss and 1981 income to be reported by Loser Limited. Show supporting computations.

PROBLEMS

14-1A. The Hansen Manufacturing Co. reported accounting income before tax and taxable income for the fiscal year ended October 31, 1980, of $620,000. Income tax rates were 45%. Included in the $620,000 was a gain of $75,000 properly classified as extraordinary. Also included in taxable income was a fully deductible loss of $80,000 from the disposal of a business segment. The annual audit disclosed a $60,000 over-statement in income of the previous year which should be treated as an error and the correction reported on the statement of retained earnings. An amended income tax return will be filed. The income tax rate on the refund will be 45%.

Instructions:
(1) Prepare journal entries to record income tax using intraperiod income tax allocation procedures.
(2) Prepare the income statement for the fiscal year ending October 31, 1980, beginning with "Income before income tax and extraordinary items."

14-2A. The Krahl Corporation accrued certain revenue in its accounts in 1978 and 1979 of $6,500 and $5,000 respectively, but such revenue was not subject to income tax until 1980. Accounting income before tax and taxable income for the three-year period are as follows:

	Accounting Income Before Income Tax	Taxable Income
1978	$18,000	$11,500
1979	17,000	12,000
1980	12,000	23,500

Assume the income tax rate applicable to taxable income is 45% in each year.

Instructions:
Prepare the entries that would be made at the end of each year to recognize the provision for income tax and to provide for a proper allocation of income tax in view of the differences between accounting income before income tax and tax-able income.

14-3A. Income data for the Edwards Company, a service company, during the first five years of its operations are summarized on page 594.

	1976	1977	1978	1979	1980
Sales	$1,250,000	$1,300,000	$1,400,000	$1,400,000	$1,500,000
Cost of services provided	750,000	780,000	820,000	840,000	900,000
Gross margin	$ 500,000	$ 520,000	$ 580,000	$ 560,000	$ 600,000
Operating expenses	200,000	210,000	230,000	220,000	240,000
Income before income tax	$ 300,000	$ 310,000	$ 350,000	$ 340,000	$ 360,000

Cost of services provided includes depreciation on buildings and equipment items calculated by the straight-line method. However, for income tax purposes, the company claimed capital cost allowance providing for higher charges in the early years of asset life and correspondingly lower charges in the later years. Depreciation charges in the accounts as compared with charges recognized for income tax purposes during the five-year period were as follows:

	1976	1977	1978	1979	1980
Depreciation	$165,000	$170,000	$170,000	$175,000	$175,000
Capital cost allowance	270,000	226,000	180,000	155,000	125,000

All revenue of the company is taxable; all expenses are deductible for income tax purposes except for depreciation. Income tax rates in each year were 45% of taxable income.

Instructions:

(1) Prepare the entries that would be made by the company for the years 1976 through 1980 to record the accrual of income tax if income is debited with income tax allocable to such income.

(2) Prepare a comparative income statement for the Edwards Company for the five-year period assuming the use of interperiod income tax allocation procedures.

(3) Prepare a comparative income statement for the Edwards Company for the five-year period assuming the interperiod income tax allocation procedures were not used and charges for income tax were recognized at the amounts actually payable each year.

14-4A. The Bartholomew Company prepared the following reconciliation between taxable and accounting income for 1980:

Income per tax return	$2,750,000
Add excess of capital cost allowance over depreciation	200,000
	$2,950,000
Less: Extraordinary gain on early retirement of debt	150,000
Estimated cost of future warranties not allowable for tax purposes until actually incurred	100,000
Revenue advance taxable in period of receipt (next year)	50,000
Reported accounting income before income tax and extraordinary items	$2,650,000

A prior period adjustment for the correction of an error was debited directly against Retained Earnings. An income tax refund claim has been filed for this adjustment. Ordinary income tax rates apply.

Instructions:

(1) Assuming an income tax rate of 45%, prepare required journal entries to record income tax for 1980.

(2) Prepare the income statement for 1980 beginning with "Income before income tax and extraordinary items."

(3) Describe how accumulated deferred taxes should be shown on the balance sheet (amounts not required).

14-5A. The following data were taken from the financial statements of the Whipple Company:

Year	Accounting and Taxable Income	Tax Rate	Income Tax Paid
1977	$17,000	48%	$8,160
1978	13,000	52%	6,760
1979	(50,000)	48%	0
1980	(35,000)	48%	0

Assume that there are no accumulated Deferred Income Tax balances.

Instructions:

(1) Calculate the income tax refund due as a result of the 1979 loss.

(2) What is the amount, if any, of the loss carryforward?

(3) Assuming virtual certainty, prepare the journal entry to record the 1979 provision for income tax.

(4) How much of the 1980 loss, if any, could be carried back and how much would be a loss carryforward?

(5) In 1980, the conditions for virtual certainty that applied to the 1979 loss are no longer present. Prepare the journal entry to reflect the absence of virtual certainty.

14-6A. The following financial history shows the income and losses for McBride Corporation for the ten-year period 1971-1980.

Year	Income (Loss)	Tax Rate	Tax Paid
1971	$ 5,000	52%	$2,600
1972	6,000	52%	3,120
1973	7,000	48%	3,360
1974	(15,000)	48%	0
1975	4,000	48%	0
1976	(12,000)	50%	0
1977	10,000	50%	0
1978	20,000	45%	6,300
1979	(35,000)	45%	0
1980	40,000	45%	?

Assume that neither permanent nor timing differences exist and that because of erratic performance the conditions for virtual certainty are not present.

Instructions:

(1) For each of the loss years, calculate the income tax refund due from the loss carryback and the amount of carryforward (if any).

(2) For 1980, calculate the estimated liability for income tax showing the benefit of the loss carryforward.

(3) For 1980, prepare the entry to record the estimated income tax liability.

(4) For 1980, prepare the income statement beginning with "Income before income tax and extraordinary items."

14-7A. At December 31, 1979 the net book value of depreciable assets ($900,000) was $140,000 in excess of their undepreciated capital cost ($760,000). There were no other timing differences between accounting income and taxable income on a cumulative basis, so that the balance in the deferred income tax account at December 31, 1979 (using a 40% rate of tax up to that time) was $56,000.

The 1980 accounts indicate the following:

(1) The income statement shows income before provision for income taxes of $400,000.
(2) The following items have been included in arriving at income before income taxes:
    (a) Dividends from a subsidiary out of control period earnings $20,000 (a permanent difference).
    (b) Gain on disposal of depreciable assets of $70,000, being the difference between the sale price of $110,000 and the net book value of $40,000. Since the original capital cost of the asset sold was $60,000, the accounting gain of $70,000 includes a capital gain of $50,000 ($110,000 − $60,000). Under Canadian tax law only 50% of a capital gain is subject to tax.
(3) The following items have been deducted in arriving at income before taxes:
    (a) Interest of $2,000 on late income tax instalments (a permanent difference).
    (b) Depreciation of $90,000.
    (c) Provision for repairs to fixed asset $40,000. No expenditures were incurred during 1980.
(4) Capital allowance claimed in 1980 was $140,000.
(5) The 3% inventory allowance for 1980 is $6,750 (a permanent difference).
(6) The rate of income tax remains at 40%.

Instructions:

(a) Calculate the provision for income taxes for 1980, the net income for the year, and the balance in the deferred tax account as at December 31, 1980.

(b) Prepare a summary of timing differences.　　　　　　　　　　(OISA adapted)

14-8A. Manufacturers Limited uses the allocation method of accounting for corporate income tax. The following information pertains to the fiscal year just ended:

Income before income tax per income statement	$750,000
Expense deductions on the income statement include:	
Straight-line depreciation	100,000
Membership fees to the Island Yacht and Country Club	2,000
Provision for warranties	15,000
Capital cost allowance	180,000
3% inventory allowance	4,000

A new product was introduced during this past fiscal period and its sales totalled $300,000. This was the first product sold by Manufacturers for which a warranty was provided. Although no payments were made during the year just ended, costs were estimated to be 5% of sales and a provision was established for $15,000.

The notes to last year's financial statements disclose that Manufacturers Limited has a loss carryforward of $200,000, the benefit of which was not recorded because the company could not meet the virtual certainty test contained in Section 3470 of the *Accounting Recommendatins*. Moreover, Manufacturers Limited could not net the benefit of its loss carryforward against accumulated deferred tax credits because it was only this year that the company adopted the straight-line method of depreciation for accounting purposes.

Maximum capital cost allowances for the fiscal year just ended were $180,000. The corporation income tax rate for the current fiscal period is 45%.

Instructions:
(1) Starting with "Income before income tax," prepare the bottom portion of Manufacturers Limited's income statement for the fiscal period just ended.
(2) What is the amount of income tax payable for the current fiscal period?
(3) Prepare a summary journal entry to record the income tax applicable to the current fiscal period.

14-9A. Smoky Limited uses the allocation method of accounting for corporate income taxes. Information for the fiscal year ended December 31, 1980 follows:

Accumulated deferred income tax credits, January, 1980	$200,000
Income before income taxes and extraordinary items	600,000
Extraordinary loss	100,000
Straight-line depreciation	100,000
Capital cost allowance	180,000
3% inventory allowance	6,000
Income tax rate	40%

The extraordinary loss is a capital loss, but Smoky Limited can meet the virtual certainty test applicable to capital losses. To date, Smoky Limited has not experienced any capital gains for income tax purposes.

During 1980, Smoky Limited paid $1,500 entrance and membership fees to the Cape Island Country Club for the company's president. His monthly accounts at the club totalled $3,500 for 1980.

Also in 1980, Smoky established a provision for warranties in the amount of $30,000, for a new product. Warranty costs incurred during the year were only $20,000.

In 1979, Smoky Limited incurred a substantial loss. For accounting purposes, the benefit of the loss was fully recognized, in part, by application against the income of 1978, and in part, by drawing down accumulated deferred tax credits. For tax purposes, however, $150,000 of the loss has yet to be deducted. January 1, 1980, timing differences can be summarized as follows:

	Balance January 1, 1980	Deferred Income Taxes
Excess of net book value over undepreciated capital cost	$650,000	$260,000
Loss carryforward	150,000	60,000
	$500,000	$200,000

Instructions:
(1) Starting with "Income before taxes and extraordinary items," prepare the bottom part of Smoky Limited's income statement for the year ended December 31, 1980.
(2) Prepare a summary of timing differences showing clearly 1980 changes and year-end balances.
(3) List the amounts to be shown on Smoky Limited's balance sheet as at December 31, 1980, giving for each amount its appropriate classification.

14-10A. The following facts pertain to SOAB Limited, a manufacturing company, for the year ended December 31, 1980.

Income before income tax and extraordinary item (before reflecting gain on sale of land)	$5,390,000
Gain on sale of land (as recorded by the client but before income tax considerations)	500,000

On December 31, 1980, the company sold some land adjacent to its manufacturing facility for $1,000,000 cash. Cost of disposing of the land amounted to $50,000. The original cost of the land was $450,000. For accounting purposes, the gain qualifies for presentation as an extraordinary item. For tax purposes, the gain is a capital gain.

At December 31, 1979, the company's only depreciable fixed assets were equipment with a net book value of $2,900,000 and an undepreciated capital cost of $3,700,000. The company had reasonable assurance that, at some time in the future, taxable income would be sufficient to allow the company to claim capital cost allowances. Consequently, the company recorded deferred income tax debits of $320,000 related to this timing difference.

During 1980, the company sold equipment having an original cost and net book value of $120,000 and $10,000, respectively, for $15,000. No new equipment was acquired during the year. Depreciation and capital cost allowance amounted to $605,000 and $1,700,000, respectively.

The company has provided a general provision for inventory obsolescence of $100,000. This provision has not been allocated nor is it identifiable with individual inventory items. At January 1, 1980, inventories on hand, all tangible property, totalled $4,000,000.

An analysis of miscellaneous expenses reveals the $10,000 in membership fees were paid to luncheon and golf clubs during 1980 and foreign advertising expense incurred totalled $20,000.

The company had a loss for income tax purposes of $1,400,000 at December 31, 1979, the tax benefit of which was not reflected in the financial statements as at that date. The only timing difference that existed at December 31, 1979, related to fixed assets as indicated above.

The effective tax rate for 1980 was 40%.

Instructions:
(1) Prepare journal entries to record income tax for 1980.
(2) Prepare a summary of timing differences (continuity schedule).
(3) Prepare the financial statement presentation for the balance sheet and income statement starting with "Income before provision for income taxes and extraordinary items," for the year ended December 31, 1980.   (OISA adapted)

14-11A. The following is financial data for Loss Leader Limited.

	Situation I	Situation II	Situation III	Situation IV Year 1	Situation IV Year 2
Loss before income taxes ..	(550,000)	(550,000)	(550,000)	(500,000)	600,000
Depeciation	450,000	450,000	450,000	50,000	50,000
Capital cost allowance	200,000	200,000	——	——	100,000

At the beginning of the current year, Loss Leader Limited has a deferred credit balance of $560,000 on its accounts, all relating to an excess of capital cost allowance claimed over depreciation recorded at a tax rate of 40%. This information should be used as the starting point for each of the four unrelated situations above.

In Situation I, assume that management has met the stringent provisions for the *CICA Handbook* concerning virtual certainty.

In the remaining situations, management is unable to convince Tough CA's & Co. that the conditions for virtual certainty are present and Loss Leader Limited is finally convinced to accept Tough's position. It is anticipated in each of these situations, that the depreciation indicated will remain the same for each of the next ten years.

Instructions:

Assuming a tax rate of 40%, draft the financial statement presentation, including any notes, for each of the above situations. (OISA adapted)

14-12A. The following facts relate to Xavier Ltd., a manufacturing company.

	1977	1978	1979	1980
Income (loss before provision for income tax and extraordinary items)	$500,000	$(100,000)	$800,000	$1,300,000
Interest on deficient tax instalments (a permanent difference)	5,000	——	——	——
Dividends from taxable Canadian corporations	20,000	20,000	20,000	20,000
Depreciation	400,000	400,000	200,000	400,000
Capital cost allowance	650,000	480,000	410,000	300,000
Beginning inventories, all tangible property	——	4,000,000	3,600,000	5,000,000

At the beginning of 1977 there was a deferred income tax credit on the financial statements of $250,000, all relating to an excess of capital cost allowance claimed over depreciation recorded. The income tax rate for 1976 and all prior years was 50%.

Toward the end of 1979, the company decided to close an unprofitable division and entered into an agreement with a third party to sell certain inventories and fixed assets which it did in April, 1980. Resulting losses, to be reflected in 1979 for accounting purposes were the following, before income taxes:

To reduce inventory to net realizable value, deductible for tax purposes in 1979	$ 600,000
To reduce fixed assets to net realizable value (net book value $500,000).	200,000
Provision for employee termination settlements	300,000
	$1,100,000

Management is virtually certain that any loss carryforwards will be offset by income in amounts sufficient to utilize the benefits. The auditor is satisfied from his review that the conditions for virtual certainty have been met.

Instructions:

Prepare the financial statement presentation for each of the years 1977 to 1980 for the balance sheet and income statement starting with "Income (loss) before income taxes and extraordinary items." Also indicate the general nature of any notes to the financial statements that may be required. Assume a tax rate of 40% throughout the period. (OISA adapted)

14-13A. The following information relates to Commencement Limited, a manufacturing company that started business on January 1, 1980.

	Years Ended December 31	
	1980	1981
Income (loss) before income taxes	(150,000)	700,000
Depreciation	50,000	50,000
Capital cost allowances	——	200,000
Warranty expense (no claims were paid during 1980 or 1981).	15,000	30,000
Golf club dues	2,000	6,000
3% inventory allowance	2,000	3,000

Assume that 1980 capital cost allowance will *not* be refiled, and that a tax rate of 40% applies to both years.

Instructions:

With respect to income taxes, prepare financial statement presentations for Commencement Limited for 1980 and 1981 in accordance with recommendations in the *CICA Handbook*. State your assumptions, if any.   (OISA adapted)

15 ACCOUNTING FOR LEASES AND PENSION COSTS

One of the more interesting and challenging aspects of accounting is the need to continually adjust methods and techniques to account for changes in the type of business transactions occurring in the economy. In recent years few types of transactions have created more discussion and controversy in accounting than those involving leases and pension plans. Because of the attention devoted to these two topics by the accounting profession, they have been segregated from the other chapter material, and the latest developments are presented in this separate chapter.

LEASES

The use of leases as a means of transferring property to others has experienced enormous growth in the decades since World War II, especially during the 1960s. Indeed, much of the growth that has occurred in businesses can be attributed to the added flexibility lease financing offers both to the one transferring the property, the *lessor*, as well as the one receiving and using the property, the *lessee*.

Simple lease rental contracts have, of course, existed for many decades. Lessees frequently rented equipment for short periods of time with no intent of using it throughout the equipment's economic life. Lease payments were debited to an expense account as they were made. But as lease arrangements became more sophisticated, it became more difficult to distinguish between a rental contract and a sale and purchase of an asset. Leases were frequently non-cancellable or cancellable only with severe penalty. They contained terms that extended over the life of the asset, required the lessee to pay the costs of ownership, including taxes and maintenance, and even included options to purchase or renew the lease at bargain amounts. Since there was no recording of the implied liability arising from the lease agreement, there was increasing concern among accountants that accounting for these types of leases as simple rentals no longer described the true nature of the transaction. The legal form of the transaction was different from a purchase/sale transaction, but the substance of the transaction was frequently the same.

Leases can be classified on the basis of the economic functions they perform; thus, there are *operating* leases and *capital* or *financial* leases. Under an operating lease, the lessor retains the responsibilities of ownership and, subject to due notice, the lessee may cancel the lease. Although the lessor bears the risk of technological obsolescence, his portfolio of leased assets should permit taking advantage of economies of scale. The most common operating leases in Canada cover such assets as telephones, computers, and motor vehicles. A capital or financial lease requires the lessee to undertake a non-cancellable obligation to pay to the lessor a series of payments spread over substantially all the expected useful life of the leased asset. The payments under a capital or financial lease are intended to return the lessor's purchase price and to provide a reasonable return on investment. Since the lease is non-cancellable, it is the lessee who bears the risk of technological obsolescence.

At this point it is useful to consider the differences between (1) a purchase of assets on long-term credit terms and (2) a leasing transaction that would require the lessee to pay as rent an amount roughly equivalent to what he would have paid if he had purchased the asset and financed payment for it. An asset purchase contract results in both the asset and the debt appearing on the balance sheet, but under a lease neither appears. For this reason leasing is sometimes referred to as *off-balance sheet financing*.

Historical Development of Lease Accounting

Perhaps the earliest accounting recognition of the importance of leasing as a financial investment occurred in 1949 when the Committee on Accounting Procedures of the AICPA issued Accounting Research Bulletin No. 38, "Disclosure of Long-Term Leases in Financial Statements of Lessees." When the Accounting Principles Board and Accounting Research Division were formed in 1959, the topic of leases was one of the initial ones to be considered by the Accounting Research Division. This resulted in the publication of Accounting Research Study No. 4, "Reporting of Leases in Financial Statements."[1] The Accounting Principles Board responded to this research and continued need with four opinions on the subject spread over its brief fourteen-year history. Two of the opinions, Number 5 and Number 31, dealt with accounting for leases by lessees. The other two, Number 7 and Number 27, dealt with accounting for leases by lessors. But the profession was not satisfied with the results of these opinions. Inconsistencies developed between the accounting for lessees and lessors, and much of the opinions dealt with footnote disclosure rather than the accounting procedures themselves. Rules for requiring capitalization of leases on the balance sheet were vague, and few companies actually reported leases as assets and the accompanying liabilities.

By way of example, it should be obvious that accounting for the leasing transactions of lessees and of lessors ought to be essentially reciprocal or mirror images of each other. Under a now obsolete APB Opinion this was not necessarily the case. It has, therefore, been said that some 747s are flying the skies which are not recorded in the accounts of any company. This anomaly results from the fact that under APB Opinion No. 5 an airline may not be required to capitalize the lease pertaining to its 747s, while the manufacturer or supplier, under APB Opinion No. 7, may have no alternative but to use the *financing method* for revenue accounting purposes. Under the financing method, the leased asset is not reported on the balance sheet; instead, the aggregate rentals receivable, net of unearned lease revenue, is reported as a current asset or as an investment depending upon payment and maturity dates.

The Financial Accounting Standards Board put the topic of leases on its original topical agenda. In 1974, a comprehensive discussion memorandum on lease accounting was published by the Board. Public hearings were held and in August, 1975, an exposure draft of a proposed Statement of Financial Accounting Standards was issued. Reaction to the exposure draft was generally negative, especially in terms of the suggested criteria for distinguishing between financial and operating leases and the period of transition. As a result, the Board issued a revised exposure draft a year later and a final FASB statement was adopted in November 1976.[2]

Early in 1978, the Accounting Research Committee published an exposure draft of proposed accounting recommendations which closely followed the FASB position. This exposure draft culminated, in December 1978, with the release of Section 3065 of the *Accounting Recommendations*. The material in this chapter is based upon this section.[3]

---

[1]John Myers, *Accounting Research Study No. 4*, "Reporting of Leases in Financial Statements" (New York: American Institute of Certified Public Accountants, 1962).

[2]*Statement of Financial Accounting Standards No. 13*, "Accounting for Leases" (Stamford, Conn.: Financial Accounting Standards Board, 1976).

[3]*CICA Handbook: Accounting Recommendations, Section 3065* "Leases" (Toronto: Canadian Institute of Chartered Accountants, 1978).

Accounting for Leases — Lessee

A lessee has access to designated leased property during the term of the lease, perhaps with some specific renewal or purchase privileges. Title to the property remains with the lessor; however, many of the normal ownership responsibilities and risks may be transferred to the lessee by contract. These could include payment of such executory costs as maintenance, insurance, and taxes. Basically, all leases as viewed by the lessee may be divided into two types: operating and capital leases. Accounting for operating leases essentially requires all rental payments to be debited to expense when incurred. If rent is prepaid, it is debited to expense as the period for which the rent applies is reached. No asset for the leased property or liability for the long-term commitment is recognized on the balance sheet, and information concerning the lease is limited to disclosure by notes to the financial statements. Accounting for a capital lease essentially requires the lessee to report on the balance sheet the present value of the future lease payments, both as an asset and a liability. The asset is amortized or depreciated as though the asset has been purchased and was owned by the lessee. The liability is accounted for in the same manner as would be a mortgage on the property. The difference in the impact of these two methods on the financial statements is frequently significant.

Accounting for Operating Leases — Lessee. Operating leases are considered to be the same as simple rental agreements with debits being made annually to an expense account as payments are made. For example, assume the lease terms for manufacturing equipment were $40,000 a year on a year-to-year basis. The entry to record the payment for a year's rent would be as follows:

Rent Expense	40,000	
Cash		40,000

Rent payments are frequently made in advance. In this event, if the lease period does not coincide with the lessee's fiscal year, or if the lessee prepares interim reports, a prepaid rental account would be required to record the unexpired portion of rent at the end of the accounting period. Amortization of the prepayment should be made on a straight-line basis. In some cases, the terms of an operating lease provide for a large initial payment, and smaller annual charges in the future. Other patterns that vary from straight-line may also be encountered, including patterns with small payments in the early years and larger payments in the later years. In these instances, recording of rent expense should approximate a straight-line pattern, and differences between the actual payments and the debit to expense would be reported either as Prepaid Rent or Rent Payable. For example, assume the terms of the lease were $70,000 rent each year for the first two years of a five-year lease, with annual payments for the last three years reduced to $20,000 a year. The total lease payments for the five years would be $200,000, or $40,000 a year on a straight-line basis. The required entries in the first two years would be as follows:

Prepaid Rent	30,000	
Rent Expense	40,000	
Cash		70,000

The entries for each of the last three years would be as follows:

Rent Expense	40,000	
Prepaid Rent		20,000
Cash		20,000

Even though a lease is accounted for by the lessee as an operating lease, users of financial statements need to be informed as to the nature of the agreement if the amounts involved are significant. Disclosure standards for operating leases are stated in Section 3065 of the *Accounting Recommendations* as follows:

> Disclosure should be made of the future minimum lease payments, in the aggregate and for each of the five succeeding years under operating leases. The nature of other commitments under such leases should also be described.[4]

Section 3065 further states that

> It may be desirable to disclose the amount of operating lease rentals included in the determination of net income, the basis of determination of any contingent rentals, type of property leased, remaining term of the lease, existence and terms of renewal options and to segregate minimum rentals, contingent rentals, and sub-lease revenue.[5]

Accounting for Capital Leases — Lessee. Capital leases are considered to be more like a purchase of property than a rental. Consequently, the accounting for capital leases requires entries similar to those required for the purchase of an asset with long-term credit terms. The amounts to be recorded as an asset and a liability should represent the present value of future minimum rental payments, including the present value of any *bargain purchase*[6] or other guarantee of the residual value[7] made by the lessee, and any penalty required to be paid by the lessee if the lease is not renewed at the end of the lease term. The minimum rental payment would not include payments representing executory costs such as insurance, maintenance, or taxes paid by the lessee plus any profit thereon. These latter costs are considered period costs, and would be recorded as Lease Expense when paid or accrued. The

---

[4]*Ibid.*, par. 32.

[5]*Ibid.*, par. 33

[6]A provision allowing the lessee, at his or her option, to purchase the leased property for a price which is sufficiently lower than the expected fair value of the property at the date the option becomes exercisable when that exercise of the option appears, at the inception of the lease, to be reasonably assured. *Ibid.*, par 3e

[7]The use of the term residual value will be discussed on page 616.

lease term used to establish minimum rental payments is the fixed non-cancellable term of the lease plus all periods covered by *bargain renewal* options,[8] or renewal periods for which failure to renew the lease imposes penalty provisions so severe that renewal appears reasonably assured. The lease term does not, however, extend beyond the date a bargain purchase option becomes exercisable. The recommended discount rate to be used by the lessee is the lessee's *incremental borrowing rate*, the rate that, at the inception of the lease, the lessee would have incurred to borrow, over a similar term and with similar security, the funds necessary to purchase the leased asset.[9] However, if the interest rate implicit in the lease is known by the lessee, and this rate is lower than the lessee's incremental borrowing rate, then this lower rate must be used.

For example, assume Buehner Corporation leases equipment from Universal Leasing Company with the following terms:

Lease Period: Five years, beginning January 1, 1981. Non-cancellable.
Rental Amount: $40,000 a year plus $3,000 a year executory costs. Payable in advance.
Incremental Borrowing Rate of Lessee: 8%
Expected Residual Value of Equipment at End of Lease Period: None

Because the rental payments are payable in advance, the formula to find the present value of the lease is the annuity-due formula described in Appendix B. The present value for the Buehner lease would be $172,484[10] computed as follows:

$$PV_n = R(PVAF_{\overline{n-1}|i} + 1)$$
$$PV_n = \$40,000(\text{Table IV}_{\overline{4}|8\%} + 1)$$
$$PV_n = \$40,000(3.3121 + 1)$$
$$PV_n = \$172,484 \qquad 172,485.07$$

The journal entry to record the lease at its inception would be as follows:

1981

Jan. 1	Leased Equipment Under Capital Leases	172,484	
	Obligations Under Capital Leases		172,484[11]
1	Lease Expense	3,000	
	Obligations Under Capital Leases	40,000	
	Cash		43,000

---

[8] A provision allowing the lessee, at his or her option, to renew the lease for a rental which is sufficiently lower than the expected fair rental of the property at the date the option becomes exercisable that exercise of the option appears, at the inception of the lease, to be reasonably assured. *Ibid.*, par 3f.

[9] *Ibid.*, par. 30.

[10] All computations of present value in this chapter will be rounded to the nearest dollar. This will require some adjustment at times to the final figures in tables to balance the amounts.

[11] It is also possible to record the liability at the gross amount of the payments ($200,000) and offset it with a discount account. The net method is more common in accounting for leases by the lessee and will be used in this chapter.

Leased equipment, however, cannot be recorded at a value greater than its fair market value. If, in the above example, Buehner Corporation is able to buy the same machinery on the open market for 160,000, then this is the maximum value that can be recorded as Leased Equipment Under Capital Leases. The amount of the liability would similarly be adjusted, and the interest rate used to amortize the debt would be increased.

Although the asset and liability balances are the same at the inception of the lease, they seldom remain the same during the lease period. The asset value should be amortized in accordance with the lessee's normal depreciation policy over the asset's life. [12] The liability should be reduced each period so as to produce a constant rate of interest expense on the remaining balance of the obligation. The lessee's incremental borrowing rate is generally the constant interest rate for the lessee under the provisions of Section 3065. Table 1 on page 608 shows how the $40,000 payments (excluding executory costs) would be separated between payment of the obligation and of interest expense to produce this constant rate of return. If the normal company depreciation policy for this type of equipment were straight-line, the required entry at December 31, 1981, for amortization of the asset would be as follows:

```
1981
Dec. 31  Amortization Expense on Leased equipment ......   34,497
                 Accumulated Amortization of Leased Equipment
                 Under Capital Leases .......................        34,497
```

Computation:
$172,484 ÷ 5 = $34,497

Similar entries would be made for each of the remaining four years. Although the credit could be made directly against the asset account, the use of a contra asset account provides disclosure information concerning the original lease value and accumulated amortization to date.

Another entry is required at December 31 to record the accrual of the interest expense for the year. As indicated in Table 1, the interest accrual for 1981 would be computed by applying the incremental borrowing rate of 8% against the initial present value of the obligation less the immediate $40,000 first payment [($172,484 − $40,000) × .08] or $10,599.

```
1981
Dec. 31  Interest Expense............................   10,599
                 Interest Payable on Obligations Under Capital
                 Leases ..................................        10,599
```

---

[12] Section 3065 identifies three criteria to be used to determine whether a lease is an operating lease or a capital lease. (See page 618). If the lease qualifies under the first criterion as a capital lease, the asset life should be used for amortizing the capitalized value of the leased asset. If the lease qualifies under the second two criteria, the lease term (period) should be used for amortization purposes. *CICA Handbook: Accounting Recommendations*, Section 3065 *op. cit.*, par. 17.

TABLE 1
Schedule of Lease Payments and Interest Accruals
[Five-Year Lease, $40,000 Annual Payments (Exclusive of Exectory Costs) 8% Interest]

Date	Description	Interest Expense*	Lease Payment Amount	Lease Payment Interest	Lease Payment Principal	Lease Obligation	Interest Payable
1– 1–81	Initial balance					$172,484	
1– 1–81	Payment		$40,000		$40,000	132,484	
31–12–81	Interest accrual	$10,599				132,484	$10,599
1– 1–82	Payment		40,000	$10,599	29,401	103,083	0
31–12–82	Interest accrual	8,247				103,083	8,247
1– 1–83	Payment		40,000	8,247	31,753	71,330	0
31–12–83	Interest accrual	5,706				71,330	5,706
1– 1–84	Payment		40,000	5,706	34,294	37,036	0
31–12–84	Interest accrual	2,964				37,036	2,964
1– 1–85	Payment		40,000	2,964	37,036	0	0

*Preceding lease obligation × 8%.

The December 31, 1981, balance sheet of Buehner Corporation would include information concerning the lease as illustrated below:

Buehner Corporation
Balance Sheet
December 31, 1981

Assets		Liabilities	
Land, buildings, and equipment:		Current liabilities:	
Leased equipment under capital leases	$172,484	Obligations under capital leases, current portion ...	$29,401
Less accumulated amortization of leased equipment under capital leases	34,497	Interest payable on obligations under capital leases.	10,599
			$40,000
Net value	$137,987	Long-term liabilities:	
		Obligations under capital leases, exclusive of $29,401 included in current liabilities	$103,083

The income statement would include the amortization on leased property of $34,497, interest expense of $10,599, and executory costs of $3,000 as expenses for the period. The total expense of $48,096 exceeds the $43,000 rental payment made in the first year. As the amount of interest expense declines each period, the total expense will be reduced and, for the last two years, will be less than the $43,000 payments (Table 2). The total amount debited to expense over the life of the lease will, of course, be the same regardless of whether the lease is accounted for as an operating lease or as a capital lease. If a declining balance method of amortization is used, the difference in the early years between the expense and the payment would be even larger.

Additional information concerning lease obligations in notes to the financial statements should include interest rates, expiry dates, and any restrictions placed on the lessee as a result of the lease contract.

As for operating leases, disclosure must be made of future minimum lease payments in total and for each of the five succeeding years.

TABLE 2
Schedule of Amounts Charged to Operations —
Capital and Operating Leases Compared

| | Charge to Operations — Capital Lease | | | | Charge to Operations — Operating | |
Year	Interest	Executory Costs	Amortization	Total	Lease	Difference
1	$10,599	$ 3,000	$ 34,497	$ 48,096	$ 43,000	$ 5,096
2	8,247	3,000	34,497	45,744	43,000	2,744
3	5,706	3,000	34,497	43,203	43,000	203
4	2,964	3,000	34,497	40,461	43,000	(2,539)
5	—	3,000	34,496	37,496	43,000	(5,504)
	$27,516	$15,000	$172,484	$215,000	$215,000	$ 0

The second lease payment on January 1, 1982, would be recorded:

```
1982
Jan. 1  Lease Expense .....................................        3,000
        Interest Payable on Obligations Under Capital Leases     10,599
        Obligations Under Capital Leases .................       29,401
           Cash .........................................                    43,000
```

Similar entries would be made for each year of the lease. At the end of the five years, both the asset and liability balances would be reduced to zero.

In many leases, the lessee is given the option of purchasing the property at some future date at a bargain price. When this option exists, the present value of the purchase option should be included in the capitalized value of the lease. Assume in the previous example that there was a bargain purchase option of $60,000 exercisable after five years, and the economic life of the equipment was expected to be ten years. The other lease terms remain the same. The present value of the revised lease would be increased by the present value of the bargain purchase amount of $60,000, or $40,836 computed as follows:

$$PV = A(PVF_{\overline{n}|i})$$
$$PV = \$60,000(\text{Table II}\overline{5}|8\%)$$
$$PV = \$60,000(.6806)$$
$$PV = \$40,836$$

The total present value of the lease is $213,320 ($172,484 + $40,836). This amount will be used to record the initial asset and liability. Again, the fair market value of the equipment would be the ceiling for the value of the asset.

Total present value is used when it is lower. If fair market value were $260,000 in this example, then total present value of $213,320 would be appropriate. The asset balance of $213,320 will be amortized over the asset life of ten years because of the existence of the bargain purchase option which makes the transaction in reality a sale. The liability balance will be reduced as shown in Table 3. At the date of exercising the option, the net balance in the asset

TABLE 3
Schedule of Lease Payments and Interest Accruals
[Five-Year Lease with Bargain Purchase Option of $60,000 after Five Years,
$40,000 Annual Payments (Exclusive of Executory Costs) 8% Interest]

| Date | Description | Interest Expense | Lease Payment | | | Lease Obligation | Interest Payable |
			Amount	Interest	Principal		
1- 1-81	Initial balance					$213,320	
1- 1-81	Payment		$40,000			173,320	
31-12-81	Interest accrual	$13,866				173,320	$13,866
1- 1-82	Payment		40,000	$13,866	$26,134	147,186	0
31-12-82	Interest accrual	11,775				147,186	11,775
1- 1-83	Payment		40,000	11,775	28,225	118,961	0
31-12-83	Interest accrual	9,517				118,961	9,517
1- 1-84	Payment		40,000	9,517	30,483	88,478	0
31-12-84	Interest accrual	7,078				88,478	7,078
1- 1-85	Payment		40,000	7,078	32,922	55,556	0
31-12-85	Interest accrual	4,444				55,556	4,444
1- 1-86	Purchase		60,000	4,444	55,556	0	0

account, Leased Equipment Under Capital Leases, and its related accumulated amortization account would be transferred to the regular equipment account. If the equipment is not purchased and the lease is permitted to lapse, a loss in the amount of the net remaining balance in the asset account, less any remaining liabilities, would have to be recognized by the following entry:

Loss from Failure to Exercise Bargain Purchase Option on
Capital Lease 46,660
Obligations Under Capital Leases 55,556
Interest Payable on Obligations Under Capital Leases 4,444
Accumulated Amortization of Leased Equipment Under
Capital Leases 106,660
   Leased Equipment Under Capital Leases 213,320

Computation:

Accumulated Amortization:
One half amortized after five years of a ten-year life: $213,320 ÷ 2 = $106,660
Obligation Under Capital Lease: See Table 3

If, under the conditions given, a renewal of the lease is negotiated, the lease would be considered a new one and adjustments would be made to the accounts to bring them into proper balance for the new lease terms.

Accounting for Leases — Lessor

The lessor in a lease transaction gives up the physical possession of the property to the lessee. If the transaction is considered temporary in nature, the lessor will continue to carry the leased asset as an owned asset on the balance sheet, and the revenue from the lease will be reported as it is received and earned. Depreciation of the leased asset will be debited against the revenue. This type of lease is described as an operating lease and is similar to the operating lease described for the lessee. However, the lease may have terms that in effect make the transaction similar in substance to a sale or a permanent transfer of the asset to the lessee. Under these conditions, the lessor should no longer report the asset as though it were owned, but should reflect the transfer and the future minimum rental payments as a receivable with revenue recognized according to the substance of the transaction. These types of leases may be classified as (1) *Sales-type leases* and (2) *Direct financing leases*. Sales-type lease transactions are in effect similar to a sale of property carried by the lessor at a cost lower (or in some cases higher) than the current fair market value of the property. The difference between the fair market value and the cost of the asset is referred to as the manufacturer's or dealer's profit (or loss if cost exceeds the fair market value). A second revenue exists for these leases. The difference between the gross amount of future rentals and the current fair market value of the asset is considered to be interest revenue, and is recognized over the life of the lease. Direct-financing lease transactions involve no manufacturer's or dealer's profit. They are essentially financial arrangements between a financial institution and the lessee, and only interest revenue is recognized over the life of the lease.

Thus, from the lessor's point of view, leases may be divided into three categories: operating leases, sales-type leases, and direct financing leases. As is true for the lessee, the accounting for these types of leases is usually materially different.

Accounting for Operating Leases — Lessor. Accounting for operating leases for the lessor is very similar to that described for the lessee. The lessor recognizes the payments as they are received as revenue. If there are significant variations in the payment terms, entries will be necessary to reflect a straight-line pattern of revenue recognition. To illustrate accounting for an operating lease in the lessor's accounts, assume the equipment leased by Buehner Corporation for $40,000 a year plus executory costs of $3,000 per year had a cost of $300,000 to the lessor. It is expected that the equipment has a ten-year life, with no salvage value at the end of the ten years. If the lease contract is on a year-to-year basis, it would usually qualify as an operating lease. The entry to record the first-year's receipt of rent would be as follows:

```
1981
Jan.  1 Cash  ........................................   43,000
          Rent Revenue  ..............................            43,000
```

Assuming the lessor depreciates the equipment on a straight-line basis, the depreciation entry at the end of the first year would be:

```
1981
Dec. 31  Depreciation Expense on Leased Equipment ......    30,000
            Accumulated Depreciation on Leased Equipment            30,000
```

If the rental period and the lessor's fiscal year do not coincide or if the lessor prepares interim reports, a rent received in advance account would be required to record the unearned rent revenue at the end of the accounting period.

There are no special disclosure problems on the financial statements; however, a note disclosure of the lease terms similar to those included by the lessee (page 605) is desirable. The leased property with its accumulated depreciation should be disclosed separately under the Land, Buildings, and Equipment caption on the balance sheet. If there are any initial direct costs associated with the lease, they should be deferred and allocated over the lease period.

Accounting for Sales-Type Leases — Lessor. If the lessor uses leases as an alternative means of financing its sales, there is usually a manufacturer's or dealer's profit identifiable under the lease terms. Normally, leases used to market products by manufacturers or dealers will have three identifiable values: (1) the maximum value, or gross amount of rental payments excluding periodic payments of executory costs but including any bargain purchase amount plus any unguaranteed residual value accruing to the lessor;[13] (2) the fair market value of the asset; and (3) the cost or carrying value of the asset to the lessor including any initial costs to acquire the lease. The manufacturer's or dealer's profit is the difference between the fair market value of the asset [(2) above] and the cost or carrying value of the asset to the lessor [(3) above]. If cost exceeds the fair market value, a loss will be reported. The difference between the gross rentals [(1) above] and the fair market value of the asset [(2) above] is interest revenue and arises because of the time delay in paying for the asset as provided by the lease terms. The relationship between these three values is demonstrated below.

1. Gross rentals, including bargain purchases, plus un-
   guaranteed residual value ....

   Financial Revenue
   (Interest)

2. Fair market value of leased asset ....

   Manufacturer's or
   Dealer's Profit

3. Cost or carrying value of leased asset to lessor ......

---

[13]The estimated fair value of the leased property at the end of the lease term exclusive of any portion guaranteed by the lessee or unrelated third party. *Ibid.*, par 3s and 3t.

To illustrate this type of lease, assume the equipment described on page 606 had a fair market value equal to its present value at 8% interest or $172,484, and a cost of $125,000. The three values and their related revenue amounts would be as follows:

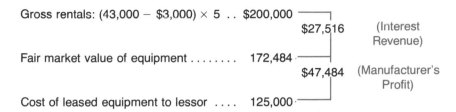

Gross rentals: (43,000 − $3,000) × 5 .. $200,000

$27,516 (Interest Revenue)

Fair market value of equipment 172,484

$47,484 (Manufacturer's Profit)

Cost of leased equipment to lessor 125,000

The interest revenue is recognized as revenue over the life of the lease so as to produce a constant periodic rate of return on the net investment of the lease in a similar manner to the recognition of interest expense on the lessee's books (see Table 1). The manufacturer's profit is recognized as revenue in the current period by including the fair market value of the asset as a sale and debiting the cost of the equipment carried in the finished goods inventory to Cost of Sales. The reimbursement of executory costs to the lessor is either credited to Miscellaneous Revenue or to the executory expense accounts involved. The entries to record this information in the lessor's accounts at the inception of the lease would be as follows:

1981
Jan. 1 Lease Payments Receivable . . . . 200,000 [14]
         Cost of Leased Equipment Recorded as Sale . . . 125,000
            Finished Goods Inventory   125,000
            Unearned Interest Revenue   27,516
            Sales   172,484
       1 Cash   43,000
            Miscellaneous Revenue (or Executory
               Expenses)   3,000
            Lease Payments Receivable   40,000
               First year lease receipts.

At the end of the first year, interest revenue would be recognized in the same amount as indicated in Table 4 and recorded as follows:

$$\left(172,484 - 40,000\right) \times .08$$

1981
Dec. 31 Unearned Interest Revenue   10,599
            Interest Revenue   10,599
               Earned Interest.

---

[14]It is also possible to record the receivable as the net difference between the gross receivable and the unearned interest revenue. The gross method is more common in accounting for the lessor and is used in this chapter.

TABLE 4
Schedule of Lease Receipts and Interest Revenue
[Five-Year Lease, $40,000 Annual Payments
(Exclusive of Executory Costs) 8% Interest]

Date	Description	Interest Revenue*	Lease Receipt	Lease Payments Receivable	Unearned Interest Revenue
1– 1–81	Initial balance			$200,000	$27,516
1– 1–81	Receipt		$40,000	160,000	27,516
31–12–81	Interest revenue	$10,599		160,000	16,917
1– 1–82	Receipt		40,000	120,000	16,917
31–12–82	Interest revenue	8,247		120,000	8,670
1– 1–83	Receipt		40,000	80,000	8,670
31–12–83	Interest revenue	5,706		80,000	2,964
1– 1–84	Receipt		40,000	40,000	2,964
31–12–84	Interest revenue	2,964		40,000	0
1– 1–85	Receipt		40,000	0	0

*Preceding lease payment receivable less unearned interest revenue × 8%.

The balance sheet of the lessor at December 31, 1981 will report the lease receivable less the unearned interest revenue as follows:

Universal Leasing Company
Balance Sheet
December 31, 1981

Assets

Current assets:
Lease payments receivable .... $ 40,000

Long-term assets:
Lease payment receivable (exclusive of $40,000 included in
   current assets)....................................... $120,000
   Less unearned interest revenue 16,917   103,083

The income statement would include the sales and cost of sales amounts yielding the manufacturer's profit of $47,484, and interest revenue of $10,599. A note to the financial statements would describe in more detail the nature of the lease and its terms.

This example parallelled the illustration of accounting for a capital lease by the lessee because it was assumed the fair market value was equal to the present value discounted at the lessee's incremental borrowing rate. This condition would not be normal, but was used to highlight the accounting entries required in the lessor's accounts. In the more normal situation, the fair market value of the equipment is known, and the interest rate must be computed from the terms of the lease. The interest rate that will discount future lease rentals, including residual value to the lessor, to the fair market value of the leased asset is referred to as the *implicit interest rate* of the lease. The method of determining this rate from the present value annuity tables is illustrated in Appendix B. Thus, if the fair market value of the above lease had been $166,796 rather than $172,484, the computation of the implicit interest rate would have been made as follows:

$$PV_n = (PVAF_{\overline{n-1}|i} + 1)$$

$$PVAF_{\overline{n-1}|i} + 1 = \frac{PV_n}{R}$$

$$PVAF_{\overline{4}|i} \quad \frac{\$166,796}{\$40,000} - 1$$

$$\text{Table IV}_{\overline{4}|i} = 3.1699$$

By moving horizontally across Table IV for n = 4, the implicit rate is seen to be 10%. If the table does not have the exact value, interpolation is required as illustrated in Appendix B.

For complex lease situations involving something besides equal annual lease payments, computation of the implicit rate of interest must be done from the present value formulas themselves. This computation is facilitated by use of a computer.

The Accounting Research Committee has recommended that the lessor use the fair market value of the leased asset to record the net receivable, and the implicit rate of interest to recognize the earned interest revenue. As indicated in the discussion of accounting for the lessee, the Committee recommended that the lessee use its incremental borrowing rate to determine the present value of the lease agreement unless it is practicable for the lessee to learn the lessor's computed implicit interest rate, and that rate is lower than the lessee's incremental borrowing rate. Thus, the amount capitalized as an asset by the lessee and the amount recorded as a net receivable by the lessor may often be different.

Accounting for Direct Financing Leases — Lessor. If the cost of the leased property and its fair market value are the same, no manufacturer's or dealer's profit exists, and the entire difference between the gross amount of the lease payments plus unguaranteed residual value and the cost is considered to be interest revenue to be recognized over the life of the lease. Usually, the lessors of direct financing leases are primarily engaged in financing operations rather than in manufacturing or dealerships. Renewals of sales-type leases are frequently considered to be direct financing leases inasmuch as no manufacturer's or dealer's profits could exist at the time of the renewal.

To illustrate the accounting for a direct financing lease, assume the cost of the leased equipment in the above example was $172,484, the same amount as the fair market value, and the purchase had been entered in the account Equipment Purchased for Lease. The entry to record the initial lease would be as follows:

Lease Payments Receivable	200,000	
Equipment Purchased for Lease		172,484
Unearned Interest Revenue		27,516

No sales or cost of sales figures would be reported. The entries for recognition of interest revenue would be the same as in the example for a sales-type lease.

Accounting for Residual Values

One of the most difficult questions in accounting for leases has involved the treatment of expected salvage or residual value of the property at the end of the lease term. Frequently, the economic life of a leased asset exceeds the initial lease term, and thus a significant economic value may still exist at the end of the initial lease term. In some leases, the lessee guarantees payment of the residual value at the expiration of the lease term which may or may not constitute a purchase of the property. For example, the lessee may agree to make up a deficiency below a stated amount in the lessor's realization, and the stated amount thus becomes a guaranteed residual value. In leases involving the guarantee of the residual value, the minimum lease payment includes the amount of the guarantee, and both the lessee and the lessor include the present value of the guaranteed residual value in the valuation of the lease. In many leases, however, no bargain purchase or guarantee of the residual value exists, and the lessor receives the benefit of the residual value at the expiration of the lease. The *Accounting Recommendations* require that lessors involved in both sales-type leases and direct financing leases add the expected unguaranteed residual value of leased property to the minimum lease payments to determine the gross investment in the lease. No consideration for possible changes in the purchasing power of the monetary unit is to be included in this estimate of residual value. The present value of the residual value computed using the new implicit interest rate is deducted from the cost, thus increasing the manufacturer's or dealer's profit by the present value of the residual value rather than by the gross amount. The difference between the gross amount of residual value plus the gross amount of minimum lease payments and their present values is recognized over the life of the lease as interest revenue. Sales for the transaction is computed by applying the implicit interest rate to the minimum lease rentals.

To illustrate this approach to accounting for residual values assume in the example of the Universal Leasing Company lease on page 606 that there was an expected unguaranteed residual value of $60,000 at the end of the five-year period with no bargain purchase option. The residual value would be added to the gross lease receivable to determine the gross investment by the lessor in the leased asset ($200,000 + $60,000 = $260,000). Because the asset now includes both the residual value and the lease receivable, a change in the account title of the asset from Lease Payments Receivable to Gross Investment in Leases is recommended. Assume the fair market value of the property with residual value was $213,320. Because the terms of the lease now include both an annuity and a future lump-sum value, the computation of the implicit interest rate is more complex and would require use of the formulas rather than the normally established tables. In this example, the implicit rate is 8%. The present value of the residual value using this rate is $40,836 ($60,000 × .6806), and the entry to record the lease initially on the lessor's would be as follows:

1981

Jan.	1	Gross Investment in Leased Assets	260,000	
		Cost of Leased Equipment Recorded as a Sale	84,164	
		Finished Goods Inventory		125,000
		Unearned Interest Revenue		46,680
		Sales		172,484

Computation:

Cost of leased equipment recorded as a sale:

Cost from finished goods	$125,000
Less present value of residual value	40,836
	$ 84,164

Unearned interest revenue:

Gross investment in lease	$260,000
Less fair market value of lease	213,320
	$ 46,680

Sales:
    Same as computation on page 606.

The manufacturer's profit in this case would be $88,320 ($172,484 − $84,164), or $40,836 (present value of unguaranteed residual value) more than the example on page 613. The annual recognition of interest revenue would also differ from the earlier example because the interest rate is applied to a higher net investment base that includes the present value of the residual amount. For example, the interest revenue for the first year would be $13,866 (Table 3) rather than $10,599 (Table 1) computed without the residual value (see page 614).

Because of the significance of the residual value in lease accounting, the estimate of its amount should be reviewed at least annually. If it is felt to be excessive and the decline is other than temporary, the accounting should be revised to reflect the changed estimate. The resulting reduction in the net investment is recognized as a loss in the period when the estimate is changed. If the residual value is felt to be too low, adjustment would result in a gain. The Accounting Research Committee has recommended that no upward adjustment be made in the estimate[14a] again demonstrating the conservative bias of accounting principle-making bodies.

[14a]*CICA Handbook: Accounting Recommendations, Section 3065, op. cit.,* par 41.

Criteria for Distinguishing Between Types of Leases

The previous sections have described the accounting entries and reporting necessary for different classifications of leases in both the lessee's and lessor's accounts. The remaining problem is how to determine which classification fits a particular lease. This is another area that has generated considerable discussion and controversy. In the Discussion Memorandum issued by the Financial Accounting Standards Board in 1974, the Board identified fourteen criteria that might be considered to have some support for lessee classification purposes. Five additional criteria were listed for possible use in classifying leases by lessors. Subsequent public hearings and correspondence disclosed that several of the criteria were overlapping and/or were embodied in other criteria. The Board considered the recommendations carefully; and in Statement No. 13, the criteria have been distilled to four criteria covering both lessees and lessors, plus two additional criteria for lessors.[15] The Canadian position, regrouping slightly, involves three criteria covering both lessees and lessors, plus the two additional criteria for lessors. Section 3065 provides that if a lease meets any one of the three criteria, it is considered to be a capital lease to the lessee; otherwise, it is an operating lease.[16] If it meets any one of the three criteria *and* meets both of the additional criteria for lessors, it is considered to be a sales-type or direct financing lease to the lessor depending upon the existence of a manufacturer's or dealer's profit; otherwise, it is an operating lease.

Criteria Applying to Both Lessee and Lessor. A lease must meet at least one of the following criteria to qualify as a capital, sales-type, or direct financing lease.[17]

1. There is reasonable assurance that the lessee will obtain ownership by the end of the lease term. This would occur when the lease provides for the transfer of title to the lessee or if the lease contains a bargain purchase option.

2. The lease term is equal to 75% or more of the estimated economic life of the leased property.

3. The present value of the minimum lease payments excluding that portion representing executory costs, such as insurance, maintenance, and taxes to be paid by the lessor, equals or exceeds 90% of the fair market value of the leased property. The lessor shall compute the present value of the minimum

---

[15]For a full discussion of the FASB's reaction to all criteria included in the Discussion Memorandum, see Appendix B of Statement No. 13.

[16]Generally, if land is involved in a lease, the lease may only be accounted for as a purchase and sale of an asset if the lease terms allow ownership to pass or there is a bargain purchase option. *CICA Handbook: Accounting Recommendations*, *Section 3065*, *op. cit.*, par. 71-73. In this chapter, it is assumed that leases do not involve land.

[17]*Ibid.*, par. 6 and 7.

lease payments using the interest rate implicit in the lease.[18] The lessee shall compute the present value of the minimum lease payments using the incremental borrowing rate unless it is practicable to learn the implicit rate computed by the lessor, and it is less than the lessee's incremental borrowing rate. In this case, the lower implicit rate should be used.

Criteria Applying Only to Lessor. In addition to meeting at least one of the above criteria, the lease must meet both of the criteria listed below in order to qualify as a sales-type or direct financing lease.

1. The credit risk associated with the lease payments receivable is normal when compared to similar receivables.
2. Unreimbursable costs to be incurred by the lessor under the terms of the lease can be reasonably estimated.

The objective of these criteria is to identify leases that are more like purchases and sales of property than like simple rentals. Thus, the accounting rules deal with the substance rather than the form of a transaction. The complexity of the criteria is dictated by the complex nature of lease terms now in existence in our economy.

Complications in Lease Accounting

The discussion of leases included in this chapter and the examples used to illustrate leases have not dealt with many of the complexities that may be encountered in accounting for the various types of leases that are currently being used. For example, a special type of lease, known as a *leveraged lease*, involves three parties — the lessee, a long-term creditor, and the lessor.[19] Several accounting problems arise with this type of lease; they are considered in paragraphs 40–47 of FASB Statement No. 13. These complex leases are beyond the scope of this introductory discussion of lease accounting.

Another type of lease is identified as a *sale-leaseback* transaction. Typical of this lease is an arrangement whereby one party sells the property to a second party, and then the first party leases the property back. Thus, the vendor becomes a vendor-lessee and the purchaser a purchaser-lessor. The accounting problem raised by this transaction is whether the vendor should recognize the profit from the original sale immediately, or defer it over the lease term. The Accounting Research Committee has recommended that if

---

[18]The computation of the implicit rate includes as part of the gross receivable any unguaranteed residual value as discussed on page 616. If there is no unguaranteed residual value of the leased property, the implicit rate will always reduce the minimum lease payments to a present value equal to 100% of the fair value of the leased property, and the lease would meet the fourth criterion for the lessor. If there is an unguaranteed residual value, the implicit interest rate will be computed using the unguaranteed residual value, but will be applied to the minimum lease payments without residual values for applying the 90% test; e.g., in the given example, the lease would not meet the 90% test: $172,484 ÷ $213,320 = 80.9%.

[19]Because of income tax considerations, leveraged leases are rarely used in Canada.

the initial sale produces a profit, it should be deferred and amortized in proportion to the amortization of the leased asset if it is a capital lease, or in proportion to the rental payments if it is an operating lease. If the transaction produces a loss because the fair market value of the asset is less than the undepreciated cost, an immediate loss should be recognized.[20]

Summary of Accounting for Leases

Accounting for leases has occupied much of the agenda for both the Canadian Accounting Research Committee and the American standards-setting bodies. Industries and companies have been concerned about accounting standards because of the extent to which they may be engaged in leases. The increase in liabilities in lessee's accounts when leases are capitalized may create debt to equity ratios that will cause a company to be in violation of long-term bond covenants. The additional debt load may also affect investor and lender decisions. The computations necessary to implement retroactively full-scale lease accounting will be difficult because of a lack of necessary information. These implementation difficulties have led to the conclusion in the United States that there be an interim transition period when accounting for leases is modified. FASB statement No. 13 does not require full retroactive application of its provisions until after a four-year transition period ended in December, 1980. This interim period provided companies the chance to make whatever adjustments may have been necessary to loan indentures and gave companies time to develop the information necessary to make retroactive adjustments to the accounts. Canadian provisions must be applied to all leases entered into after January 1, 1979, and retroactive application is encouraged. If Section 3065 is not applied retroactively, comprehensive disclosure is required in notes to the financial statements concerning the effect on net assets and income had the recommendations been applied.

PENSION COSTS

Accounting for pension costs is another area that has demanded considerable attention by accounting principle-making bodies. In 1963, the CICA published a research study, *Accounting for Costs of Pension Plans* by W. B. Coutts and R. B. Dale-Harris which was followed in 1965 by the release of Bulletin No. 21, under the same title. The recommendations contained in Bulletin No. 21 are now included in Section 3460 of the *Accounting Recommendations*, "Pension Costs."

Pension accounting is the subject of a recent study by Ross M. Skinner,

---

[20]*CICA Handbook: Accounting Recommendations, Section 3065, op. cit.*, par. 65-70.

published privately by Clarkson Gordon[21] In addition, the CICA is to publish a research study by Professor T. Ross Archibald, University of Western Ontario. Thus the topic of pension accounting is currently under study and revised, updated accounting standards can be anticipated in due course.

In March 1980, the Financial Accounting Standards Board issued Statement No. 35, *Accounting and Reporting by Defined Benefit Pension Plans*. This pronouncement concerns the plan itself, not the pension accounting of employers, and applies to both private and public sector plans. There is, as yet, no Canadian counterpart for this pronouncement.

This portion of the chapter will highlight the development of pension plans and the principal accounting problems surrounding pension plan accounting. The currently accepted methods of accounting for pension costs are presented, and areas where changes may occur are identified.

Growth of Pension Plans

The number of pension plans and the size of their investment portfolios have grown sharply in the period since World War II. As inflation has made it more difficult for government programs, such as the Canada Pension Plan, to provide employees with an adequate retirement, labor negotiations between unions and managements have often included provisions for company-sponsored pension programs. Generally, these plans have been given income tax recognition permitting corporations to deduct contributions to the plan as expenses, but allowing the employees to defer recognition of income until retirement benefits are received. Because individuals working as employees for corporations or other identified institutions had definite tax advantages in the pension plan area, additional tax provisions were enacted giving similar tax incentives to self-employed individuals or to those whose employers did not have a definite pension plan. This has led to an entire industry of individual registered retirement savings plans and has extended significantly the number of persons directly concerned about pensions.

Pension plans historically have varied widely, with many different types of plans, methods of funding, and concepts of benefits. Income tax laws include provisions to control the tax consequences of pension plans and their effect on the employer's deductions and on employee's income from pension plans. However, limited control has been exercised to protect employees from under-funded plans, termination before the benefits are available to the employees, i.e., *vesting*[22] and protection in the event the plan is terminated due to employer bankruptcy. Trustees of pension plans assumed responsibility for determining necessary contributions and for investing the portfolios

---

[21] Ross M. Skinner, *Pension Accounting* (Toronto: Clarkson Gordon, privately printed, 1980).

[22] Vested benefits are those benefits that are not contingent upon any future services by employees. These benefits are thus available to the employee should he or she leave the employer.

to meet established goals. Institutions, such as insurance companies, unions, and other associations, assumed the trustee role. Yet, very few plans were necessarily subject to independent financial audit.

At the provincial level there are various laws relating to minimum funding of plans, minimum vesting rights to employees, minimum disclosure and audit requirements, and minimum requirements for trustees of pension plans. Although these laws differ among the provinces, they nonetheless provide an important element of protection to employees covered by pension plans.

On the question of financing pension plans, at one extreme is the fully funded plan where periodic payments to a trustee are sufficient to purchase or provide for the pension benefits which have accrued to date. The opposite extreme is the unfunded plan, where the only payments are those made to retired employees. The Canada Pension Plan is one example of an unfunded plan. Most pension plans, however, are at least partially funded.

Principal Pension Cost Accounting Problems of Employers

The issues involved in accounting for pension costs are well defined. They may be summarized as follows: (1) How much should be debited to pension expense each period for current employee service performed? (2) How much should be recorded as a liability for unfunded pension costs on the employer's balance sheet? (3) How should actuarial gains and losses on pension plans be recognized on the employer's income statement? Other accounting issues connected with pension costs are either subsets of these three areas or are potentially minor in effect. Each of these three issues will be discussed separately.

Amount of Periodic Pension Cost. Most pension plans are administered by an outside trustee, one not directly connected with the employer. The plan itself identifies the benefits that will be paid to employees upon retirement based upon variables such as length of service, amount earned, accumulated contributions, and position in the company. Contributions are made to the trustee based upon accepted actuarial assumptions and legal requirements. Traditionally an employer has tended to debit to expense the actual amount contributed to the trustee. If the contributions made follow a well-defined pattern, the resulting debit to expense may be reasonable. However, if the contributions to the trustee are made somewhat arbitrarily, erratic expense patterns may arise and as a result net income may be misstated.

Contributions to the trustee usually consist of two principal items: (1) normal costs and (2) past service costs. _Normal costs_ are the current annual costs assigned under the actuarial cost method in use to years subsequent to the inception of a pension plan. They are the present value of the future increase in benefits arising from the current year's service to the company by covered employees. *Past service costs* are the costs related to the past service of employees before the adoption of a pension plan. They are the present value of the future benefits arising from services performed by employees before the pension plan was initiated. At any date subsequent to the adoption of a pension plan, a company may need to determine the total of all past normal costs plus past service costs under the pension plan. The date of such determination is identified as a *valuation date*, and the sum of these costs is defined as *prior service costs*. These costs may be illustrated by the following time line for an individual employee:

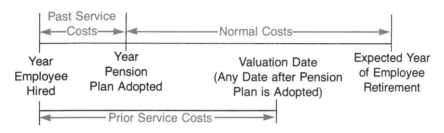

The pattern of funding these items depends upon the actuarial cost method required by the provisions of the pension plan.

Actuarial Cost Methods. There are several well-defined methods of pension costing being used; however, they can all be divided into two major classifications: (1) *accrued benefit costs methods* and (2) *projected benefit cost methods*. The accrued benefit cost method, also referred to as the *unit benefit* or *unit credit method*, identifies a distinct unit of retirement benefit with each year of credited service, and the present value of the unit can be computed at any date. The computation of past service costs under this method is easily made. The projected benefit cost methods relate the cost to the prospective benefits of a closed group of employees. Costs are computed so as to remain constant over the life of the employee. Projected benefit methods include the following:

1. Entry age normal
2. Attained age normal
3. Aggregate
4. Individual level premium

The pattern of funding under these methods is illustrated in Figure 1 on page 624. The latter two methods spread past service costs over the entire pension period rather than over just a predetermined number of years (twenty in this illustration), and thus do not provide for a separate computation of past service costs. Consistent use of any plan provides for an orderly accrual of costs for the plan.

Accrual Requirement for Pension Costs. The key recommendations

ACCRUED BENEFIT COST METHOD

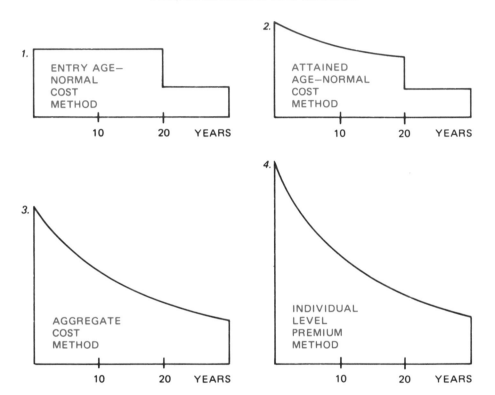

PROJECTED BENEFIT COST METHODS

Figure 1:
Annual Cost
Patterns for
a Typical
Pension Plan
Under Five
Actuarial Cost
Methods
Currently
Acceptable for
Accounting
Purposes[23]

contained in Section 3460 are that the employer charge pension costs to income in a consistent manner; and because past service costs are incurred in contemplation of future services to be rendered, that they be charged against current and future revenues rather than against prior periods. These recommendations became known as the accrual requirements for pension costs. Because funding requirements were often very loose and did not always follow one of the established methods, the practice of debiting expense for the actual contribution made was not considered acceptable. Section 3460

---

[23] William A. Dreher, "Alternatives Available Under APB Opinion No. 8: An Actuary's View," *Journal of Accountancy* (September, 1967), p. 41.

required all employers to select a basis that would provide for the accrual of pension costs, such as one of the actuarial cost methods identified above, and to use it consistently over the years. It did not have to be the method used for funding purposes; however, it could be the same method. Thus, in practice, the contribution and the accrual are frequently identical because the same actuarial cost method is used for funding and accrual purposes. If the amount funded and the amount expensed are not the same, the difference is to be recorded as a Liability Under Pension Plan or a Deferred Pension Expense depending upon the nature of its balance.

Illustration of Pension Cost Entries. To illustrate accounting for pension costs, assume the Marlowe Corporation initiated a pension plan effective January 1, 1981. The present value of the future benefits assumed earned by employees as of January 1, 1981 were separately identified as past service costs and amounted to $150,000. Assume the contribution plan required payment of these costs over a fifteen-year period plus interest on the unfunded portion at 8%. In addition, normal costs were funded each year. If normal costs in 1981 were $22,000, the total contribution for 1981 would be computed as follows:

Normal costs	$22,000
Amortization of past service costs ...*150,000 ÷ 15 years*.....	10,000
Interest on unfunded past service costs (8% of $150,000)	12,000
Total contribution	$44,000

Assume the employer decided to debit expense using the same method as used for the contribution. The entry to record the contribution and the accrual would be as follows:

Pension Expense	44,000	
Cash		44,000

Assume the employer made the decision to accrue the pension cost according to the pattern described above even though the contribution was for the normal cost only. The entry to record this situation would be as follows:

Pension Expense	44,000	
Cash		22,000
Liability Under Pension Plan		22,000

The liability would be classified on the balance sheet according to the expected contribution data. It should be emphasized that Section 3460 requires the present value of vested past service costs to be recognized as a deferred charge offset by a liability, to the extent the past service costs have not been charged to operations.

There can be cases where the amount funded could exceed the amount accrued, in which case a deferred pension expense account would be debited.

For example, assume in the previous example that the contribution for the first year was $55,000. The journal entry would be as follows:

Pension Expense	44,000	
Deferred Pension Expense	11,000	
Cash		55,000

In the above examples, the pension expense for the first year was the same regardless of how the plan was funded. Subsequent years' expense would vary according to the amount of interest on unfunded past service costs. In many cases, pension plans are written to fund past service costs by equal contributions over a specified number of years. The interest on unfunded past service costs is included in the payment and the annual contribution is computed from annuity tables. If a company expenses the same amount as funded, no asset or liability for pension costs is created on the balance sheet. However, if the company desires to expense past service costs equally, but over a number of years that differs from the number of years used for funding purposes, asset or liability balances will be created.

To illustrate these conditions, assume the past service costs for the Andrus Co. at the adoption of a pension plan is $310,500. The interest rate used in the plan is 10%. If contributions are made at the end of each year for twelve years, the amount of each contribution (rent) would be computed as follows:

$$PV_n = R(PVAF_{\overline{n}|i})$$

$$R = \frac{PV_n}{PVAF_{\overline{n}|i}}$$

$$R = \frac{\$310,500}{\text{Table IV}_{\overline{12}|\,10\%}}$$

$$R = \frac{\$310,500}{6.8137}$$

$$R = \$45,570 \qquad \text{\textit{f} } 45,570.009$$

Thus, payments of $45,570 for twelve years would liquidate the past service cost liability. If the company decides to amortize the past service costs equally over a ten-year period to pension expense, computations similar to the above would be made to determine that the annual amortization would be $50,532 ($310,500 ÷ 6.1446). Similarly, if a fifteen-year amortization is used, the annual charge would be $40,822 ($310,500 ÷ 7.6061). If the amortization period differs from the contribution period, an interest adjustment to pension expense will be necessary. If the contribution period covers fewer years than the amortization period, the trustee has funds in advance of the accrual period and a reduction in pension expense for the lower interest is necessary. If the contribution period covers more years than the amortization period, the trustee has deferred receiving funds and an addition to pension expense for the additional interest paid must be made.

The effects of these different patterns of contribution and amortization on

handwritten margin notes: 50,532.445 and 40,822.608

TABLE 5
Andrus Company
Past Service Cost Accounting
Accrual of Pension Liability
Amortization — 10 Years

Year	(A) Funding Contribution 12 Years	(B) Annuity Amortization	(C) Add Interest (10%) on Previous Liability Balance	(D) Pension Expense (B + C)	(E) Liability Increase (Decrease) (D − A)	(F) Liability Balance
1	$45,570	$50,532	$ 0	$50,532	$ 4,962	$ 4,962
2	45,570	50,532	496	51,028	5,458	10,420
3	45,570	50,532	1,042	51,574	6,004	16,424
4	45,570	50,532	1,642	52,174	6,604	23,028
5	45,570	50,532	2,303	52,835	7,265	30,293
6	45,570	50,532	3,029	53,561	7,991	38,284
7	45,570	50,532	3,828	54,360	8,790	47,074
8	45,570	50,532	4,707	55,239	9,669	56,743
9	45,570	50,532	5,674	56,206	10,636	67,379
10	45,570	50,532	6,738	57,270	11,700	79,079
11	45,570	0	7,908	7,908	(37,662)	41,417
12	45,570	0	4,153*	4,153	(41,417)	0

*Adjusted for rounding differences.

TABLE 6
Andrus Company
Past Service Cost Accounting
Accrual of Deferred Pension Expense
Amortization — 15 Years

Year	(A) Funding Contribution 12 Years	(B) Annuity Amortization	(C) Less Interest (10%) on Previous Deferred Charge Balance	(D) Pension Expense (B − C)	(E) Deferred Charge Increase (Decrease) (A − D)	(F) Deferred Pension Expense Balance
1	$45,570	$40,822	$ 0	$40,822	$ 4,748	$ 4,748
2	$45,570	40,822	475	40,347	5,223	9,971
3	45,570	40,822	997	39,825	5,745	15,716
4	45,570	40,822	1,572	39,250	6,320	22,036
5	45,570	40,822	2,204	38,618	6,952	28,988
6	45,570	40,822	2,899	37,923	7,647	36,635
7	45,570	40,822	3,664	37,158	8,412	45,047
8	45,570	40,822	4,505	36,317	9,253	54,300
9	45,570	40,822	5,430	35,392	10,178	64,478
10	45,570	40,822	6,448	34,374	11,196	75,674
11	45,570	40,822	7,568	33,255	12,315	87,989
12	45,570	40,822	8,799	32,023	13,547	101,536
13	0	40,822	10,154	30,668	(30,668)	70,868
14	0	40,822	7,087	33,735	(33,735)	37,133
15	0	40,822	3,689*	37,133	(37,133)	0

*Adjusted for rounding differences.

balance sheet accounts are illustrated in the two tables shown on page 627.

Journal entries to record the past service pension cost amortization and contribution to the pension fund may be made directly from the tables for any year included. Thus, the entry for Year 8 assuming a ten-year amortization period for past service costs would be as follows:

Pension Expense	55,239	
Cash		45,570
Liability Under Pension Plan		9,669

The entry for Year 8 assuming a fifteen-year amortization period would be as follows:

Pension Expense	36,317	
Deferred Pension Expense	9,253	
Cash		45,570

Of course, normal pension costs would be added to the amortization of past service costs to arrive at the total pension expense for the year.

Liability for Unfunded Prior Service Costs. Unfunded prior service costs are those prior pension costs, both past service costs and past-normal costs, not yet funded to the trustee. As previously noted, Section 3460 does not require reporting of this amount as a liability except to the extent of vesting. Traditionally, an employer often had only limited liability for unfunded prior service costs. In the event bankruptcy occurred, claims against the plan by the employee were usually limited to the amount of funds in the plan. Many accountants have felt that this failure to record as a liability unfunded prior service costs is a serious deficiency. They advocate reporting these unfunded prior service costs offset by a deferred charge for the portion of prior service costs not yet charged against revenue. With the tightening of funding requirements and requirements for accelerated vesting privileges, it seems likely that the definition of legal liability may be restated.

Actuarial Gains and Losses. The amount of required contributions to a pension plan is based upon many actuarial assumptions including mortality tables for employees, expected employee turnover rates, anticipated investment revenue from dividends, interest and sales of securities, amount of future compensation to be paid to employees, and vesting benefits. When these variables differ from the estimates, more or less funds are provided than planned. These differences are referred to as *actuarial gains* and *losses*. Alternative ways of accounting for these gains and losses are *immediate recognition, spreading* in a consistent manner, and *averaging* over a reasonable number of years, defined as the period expected to elapse before the next revaluation. The major objective of these methods is to avoid significant year-to-year fluctuations due to actuarial gains or losses.

Disclosure Requirements

Pension plans are of great importance to the proper understanding of both financial position and results of operations. There is a need for the adequate disclosure of such plans. The Accounting Principles Board in APB Opinion No. 8, suggested that disclosure be made in financial statements or by notes, as follows:

1. A statement that such plans exist, identifying or describing the employee groups covered.
2. A statement of the company's accounting and funding policies.
3. The provision for pension cost for the period.
4. The excess, if any, of the actuarially computed value of vested benefits over the total of the pension fund and any balance sheet pension accruals, less any pension prepayments or deferred charges.
5. Nature and effect of significant matters affecting comparability for all periods presented, such as changes in accounting methods (actuarial cost method, amortization of past and prior service cost, treatment of actuarial gains and losses, etc.), changes in circumstances (actuarial assumptions, etc.), or adoption or amendment of a plan.[24]

Since pension costs are part of employee remuneration, Section 3460 does not generally require separate line-item disclosure of the expense on the income statement, or even supplementary disclosure by way of footnote. Nonetheless, the expense for pension costs should generally comprise (1) normal or current service costs, (2) past service pension costs, and (3) adjustments arising from actuarial revaluations.[25] Where item (3) above results in a material adjustment in the period or periods in which it appears on the income statement, it should be shown separately.[26]

For balance sheet purposes, the accrual for pension cost should include (1) current and past service pension costs accrued as charges to operations, (2) the provision, if any, for vested past service benefits, and (3) any recorded adjustment resulting from actuarial revaluations; reduced in each case by amounts funded by cash payments or other consideration.[27] Any unabsorbed debit relating to past service costs should be shown on the balance sheet as a deferred charge.[28] Footnote disclosure is widely used to provide further details pertaining to pension plans, their costs, and related liabilities.

It is interesting to note that less than 60% of Canadian corporations disclose the existence of a pension plan in their financial statements.[29] In part, this low percentage may be explained by the fact that Section 3460 of the *Accounting Recommendations* imposes no disclosure requirements pro-

---

[24]*Opinions of the Accounting Principles Board, No. 8*, "Accounting for the Cost of Pension Plans" (New York: American Institute of Certified Public Accountants, 1966), par. 46.

[25]*CICA Handbook: Accounting Recommendations, Section 3460*, "Pension Costs" (Toronto: Canadian Institute of Chartered Accountants, 1968), par. 24.

[26]*Ibid.*, par. 25.

[27]*Ibid.*, par. 26.

[28]*Ibid.*, par. 27.

[29]*Financial Reporting in Canada* (13th ed.; Toronto: Canadian Institute of Chartered Accountants, 1979), p. 182.

vided a company has a fully-funded plan and all past service costs have been charged to operations.

A transitional provision contained in Bulletin No. 21, and carried forward into Section 3460, stated that where provision had not been made in the accounts in prior years, or where the actual accrual to 1965 was insufficient, any deficiency could be accounted for by a charge to retained earnings. Alternatively, such costs could be regarded as the equivalent of past service costs and therefore be amortized by charges to future operations in the manner recommended for past service costs.[30]

Accounting for pension costs is still essentially in a transition period. However, as a result of Section 3460 and its predecessor, Bulletin No. 21, there is increasing consistency in the complex and evolving area of accounting for pension plans.

---

[30]*CICA Handbook: Accounting Recommendations, Sections 3460, op. cit.,* par. 23.

APPENDIX: CLASSIFICATION OF LEASES — DECISION TREES[31]

CLASSIFICATION OF A LEASE — LESSEE

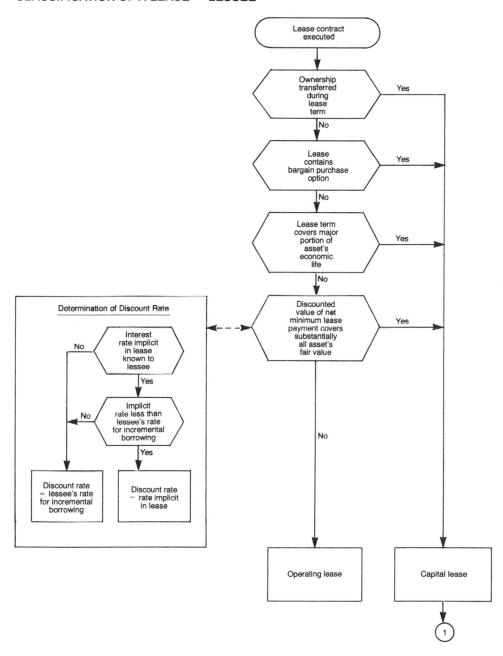

---

[31]*CICA Handbook: Accounting Recommendations, Section 3065, "Leases"* (Toronto: Canadian Institute of Chartered Accountants, 1968) Appendix B, pp. 1178-1182.

ACCOUNTING FOR A CAPITAL LEASE

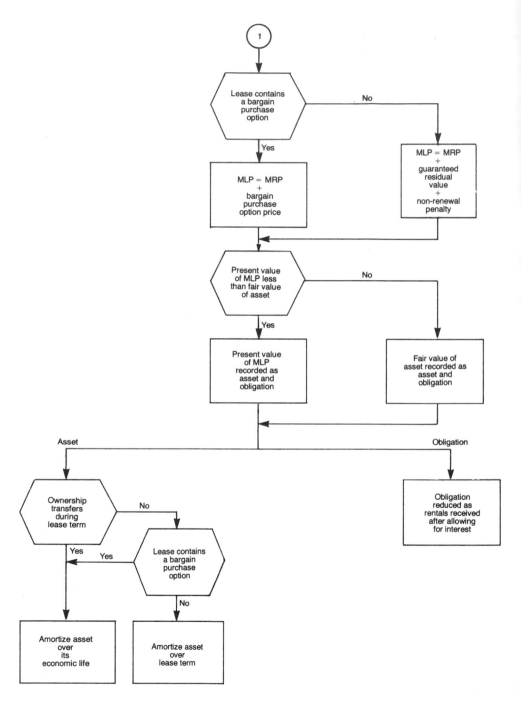

MLP = Net minimum lease payments
MRP = Net minimum rental payments called for over the lease term

CLASSIFICATION OF A LEASE — LESSOR

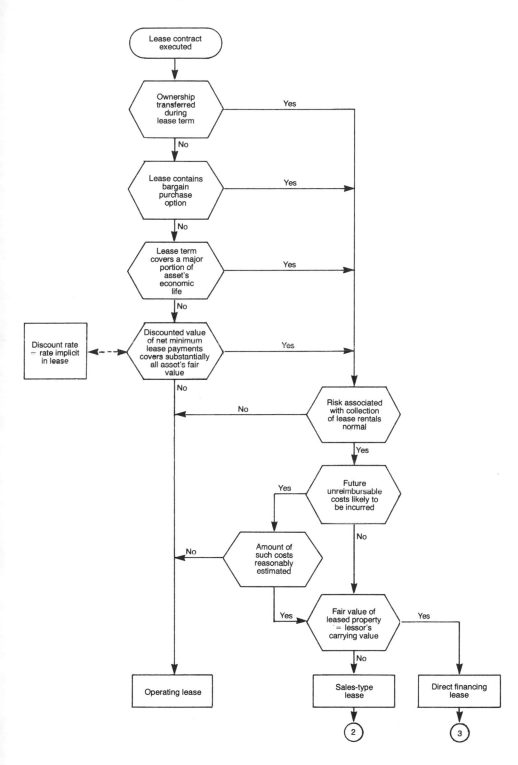

ACCOUNTING FOR A SALES-TYPE LEASE

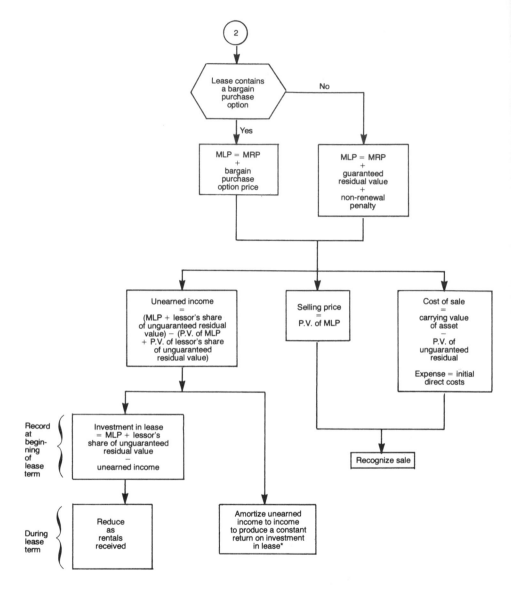

MLP = Net minimum lease payments
MRP = Net minimum rental payments called for over the lease term
P.V. = Present value

*Investment in lease for purposes of income recognition:
  (a) when income tax factors taken into consideration for accounting
       purposes = MLP + lessor's share of unguaranteed residual value − unearned income
       − deferred taxes − investment tax credit; or
  (b) when income tax factors not taken into consideration for accounting
       purposes = MLP + lessor's share of unguaranteed residual value − unearned income.

ACCOUNTING FOR A DIRECT FINANCING LEASE

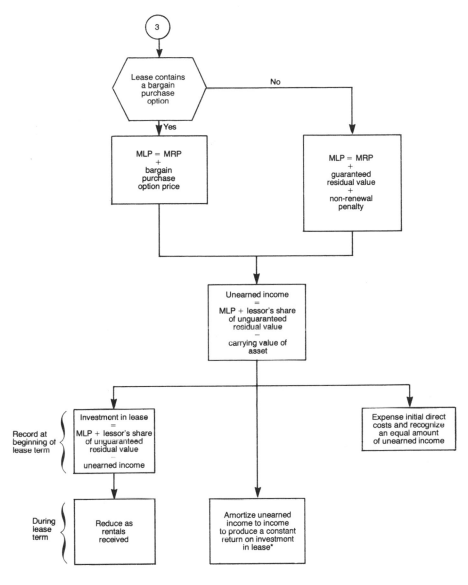

MLP = Minimum lease payments
MRP = Minimum rental payments called for over the lease term

*Investment in lease for purposes of income recognition:
 (a) when income tax factors taken into consideration for accounting
     purposes = MLP + lessor's share of unguaranteed residual value − unearned income
     − deferred taxes − investment tax credit; or
 (b) when income tax factors not taken into consideration for accounting
     purposes = MLP + lessor's share of unguaranteed residual value − unearned income.

1. Why has leasing as a means of financing and investing enjoyed such a remarkable growth rate since the end of World War II?

2. What is the basic difference between an operating lease and a capital lease from the viewpoint of the lessee?

3. If a lease defined as an operating lease requires the payment of uneven rental amounts over its life, how should the lessee recognize rental expense?

4. What disclosure would be required on the lessee's financial statements for operating leases with six-month terms?

5. What amounts should be recorded as an asset and a liability for capital leases in the accounts of the lessee?

6. Why do asset and liability balances for capital leases usually differ after the first year?

7. The use of capital lease method for a given lease will always result in a lower net income than the operating lease method. Do you agree? Explain fully.

8. If a lease contains a bargain purchase option, what entries are required in the accounts of the lessee under each of the following conditions?
    (a) The bargain purchase option is exercised.
    (b) The bargain purchase option is not exercised and no renewal of the lease is made.
    (c) The bargain purchase option is not exercised, but a renewal of the lease is obtained.

9. How does classification of leases by the lessor differ from the classification by the lessee?

10. Contrast a sales-type lease from a direct financing lease.

11. Under what circumstances would a lessor recognize an amount, greater than the difference between the gross amount of lease receivables and the cost of the asset to the lessor, as interest revenue over the lease term?

12. How would a lessor report future lease payments receivable on the balance sheet?

13. What is meant by an implicit rate of interest on a lease contract? How is it computed?

14. Unguaranteed residual values accrue to the lessor at the expiration of the lease. How should the lessor reflect these values on the financial statements during the lease term?

15. What criteria must be met before a lease can be properly accounted for as a capital lease on the books of the lessee?

16. In determining the classification of a lease, a lessor uses the criteria of the lessee plus two other criteria. What are these criteria and why are they included in the determination of the classification of lessor's leases?

17. What are the principal accounting problems relating to pension costs?

18. Define (a) normal costs, (b) past service costs, (c) prior service costs, (d) vested benefits.

19. What portion of past service costs must be reported as a liability under current accounting principles?

20. Why are past service costs considered a charge against future earnings rather than an adjustment of past earnings?

21. (a) Define actuarial gains and losses, (b) What are the three alternative ways of accounting for gains and losses? Which do you recommend?

22. What pension information should be disclosed in annual reports?

23. At present, less than 60% of Canadian corporations disclose the existence of pension plans in their annual reports. Briefly explain why this is so.

EXERCISES

15-1. The Clark Construction Company leases a bulldozer from Universal Leasing Company for $2,500 a month plus a surcharge of $5 an hour for all hours used in excess of 200 hours per month. The lease is from month to month. The bulldozer was used 198 hours in April, 205 hours in May, and 215 hours in June. Give the entry necessary to record the rent expense for each of the three months.

15-2. Wagstaff, Ltd., leases equipment on a five-year lease. The lease payments are to be made in advance as shown below.

The equipment is to be used evenly over the five-year period. For each of the five years, give the entry that should be made at the time the lease payment is made to allocate the proper share of rent expense to each period. The lease is classified as an operating lease by Wagstaff, Ltd.

January 1, 1981	$ 75,000
January 1, 1982	65,000
January 1, 1983	60,000
January 1, 1984	50,000
January 1, 1985	40,000
Total	$290,000

15-3. Smetena Smelting Company entered into a lease beginning January 1, 1981, for equipment to use in its smelting operations. The term of the lease is essentially the expected economic life of the equipment. Smetena uses straight-line depreciation on all its owned assets. The operating terms of the lease call for annual payments of $75,000 in advance plus $4,000 per year as payment for executory costs, such as taxes and insurance, for the fifteen-year period of the lease. At the end of the fifteen years, the equipment is expected to be junked. The incremental borrowing rate of Smetena is 10%. The lessor's computed implicit interest rate is unknown to Smetena.

Record the lease on the books of Smetena and give all the entries necessary to record the lease for its first year plus the entry to record the second lease payment on January 2, 1982. Round to nearest dollar.

15-4. On January 2, 1981, the Midland Company entered into a non-cancellable lease for a new warehouse. The warehouse was built to the Midland Company's specifications and is in an area where rental to another lessee would be difficult. Rental payments are $125,000 a year for ten years, payable in advance. The warehouse has an estimated economic life of twenty years. The taxes and maintenance are to be paid by the Midland Company, and they have an option to purchase the property at the conclusion of the lease for a nominal amount. Assume the cost of borrowing funds for this type of an asset by Midland Company is 8%. (a) Give the entry that should be made at the inception of the lease. (b) Give the entries that should be made for 1981 and 1982 relative to the amortization of the warehouse value assuming the warehouse value is amortized by the straight-line method.

15-5. On January 1, 1980, the Lee Company leases an asset for three years with annual payments of $143,714, payable at the beginning of each of the three years. The asset has a life of three years and the present value of the lease payments when discounted at 8% is equal to $400,000. The Lee Company closes its accounts on December 31 of each year. Provide journal entries to record the signing of the lease, all of the lease payments and year-end adjusting entries for each of the three years.

(SMA adapted)

15-6. Union Rent-All leases equipment to Lindsay Manufacturing Company. The lease is for five years and is classified as an operating lease. The lease requires advance payments of $5,000 per year. Union has a calendar year accounting period. The lease began April 1, 1981, at which time the first payment was made. The equipment has a cost of $50,000 and an economic life of twenty years. Union uses the declining balance method of depreciation (rate 10%) on all equipment owned. What entries should be made by Union Rent-All for the first year of the lease?

15-7. A-1 Leasing leases equipment to A-1 Manufacturing (an unrelated company). The fair market value of the equipment is $221,487. Lease payments, excluding executory costs, are $35,000 per year, payable in advance, for ten years. What is the implicit rate of interest A-1 Leasing should use to record this capital lease on its books?

15-8. The Northwestern Finance Company purchased a printing press to lease to the Apex Printing Company. The lease was structured so that at the end of the lease period of fifteen years Apex would own the printing press. Lease payments required in this lease were $50,000 per year, the annual payment being payable in advance. The cost of the press to Northwest was $418,335, which is also considered to be its fair market value at the time of the lease. (a) Is this lease a sales-type or a direct financing lease? Why? (b) Give the entry to record the lease transaction on the books of Northwestern Finance Company. (c) Give the entry at the end of the first year on Northwestern Finance Company's books to recognize interest revenue.

15-9. The Lind Leasing and Manufacturing Company uses leases as a means of financing sale of its equipment. Lind leased a machine to Ace Awning for $10,000 per year, payable in advance, for a ten-year period. The cost of the machine to Lind was $65,000. The fair market value at the date of the lease was $75,000. Assume a residual value of zero at the end of the lease. (a) Give the entry required to record the lease on Lind's books. (b) How much profit will Lind recognize initially on the lease, excluding any interest revenue? (c) How much interest revenue would be recognized in the first year?

15-10. The Bellows Corporation leases a machine to the Furness Company. The lease payments are $10,000 per year in advance for ten years. The machine cost Bellows

$55,000. The fair market value of the machine at the lease date is $72,942. The machine is expected to have an unguaranteed residual value of $30,000 at the end of the lease. Bellows' computed implicit interest rate on the lease is 12%. Furness Company's incremental borrowing rate is 10%. Give the entries necessary to record the lease on the books of both the lessee and the lessor at the inception of the lease.

15-11. On January 1, 1982, the Smith Corporation entered into a lease for manufacturing equipment with the Stark Company. The lease provided for $50,000 yearly payments, payable in advance. The lease term is 15 years, and has an implicit interest rate of 16%. The machine was built by Stark for $370,000. At the end of the lease, the residual value is estimated to be $32,000 and the machine will have 3 remaining useful years. Give the entry necessary to record the lease in the accounts of the Stark Company.

15-12. All-Rite Cleaners leases its dry cleaning equipment from Rite-Way Leasing Company. In each of the following cases, assuming none of the other criteria for capitalizing leases is met, determine whether the lease would be a capital lease or an operating lease. Your decision is to be based on the terms presented, considering each case independent of the others.

    (a) At the end of the lease, the market value of the equipment is expected to be $5,000. All-Rite has the option of purchasing it for $2,500.

    (b) The fair market value of the equipment is $25,000. The present value of the lease payments is $22,500 (excluding any executory costs).

    (c) All-Rite obtains the property at the end of the lease.

    (d) The economic life of the equipment is 15 years. The lease term is for 12 years.

    (e) The lease requires payments of $5,500 per year in advance, plus executory costs of $500 per year. The lease period is for three years, and All-Rite's incremental borrowing rate is 8%. The fair market value of the equipment is $17,000.

    (f) The lease requires payments of $5,500 per year in advance which includes executory costs of $500 per year. The lease period is for three years, and All-Rite's incremental borrowing rate is 8%. The fair market value of the equipment is $17,000.

15-13. The Dupont Company accrued pension costs of $25,000 for 1981. Give the entry to record pension costs for 1981 if the company funds are (a) $25,000, (b) $19,000, and (c) $28,000.

15-14. On January 1, 1981, the Golden Age Corporation institutes a pension plan for its employees. The actuary informs the company that, on this date, the past service pension liability is equal to $2,000,000. The company plans to amortize this amount to income over ten years on a straight-line basis, without regard to interest charges on any unfunded amounts of this past service pension liability. The Golden Age Corporation closes its accounts on December 31 of each year. (a) Provide the journal entries that would be required on January 1, 1981 and December 31, 1981, assuming that past service benefits are vested. (b) Provide the journal entries that would be required on January 1, 1981 and December 31, 1981, assuming that past service benefits are not vested. (SMA adapted)

15-15. The Suzuki Corporation funds its past service pension costs over fifteen years and amortizes them over ten years. Past service pension costs at the adoption of the pension plan are $360,000 and the interest rate is 10%. The corporation accountant has prepared the following four-year table accounting for past service pension costs.

Suzuki Corporation
Past-Service Pension Costs
Accrual of Pension Liability

Amortization — 10 Years

Year	Funding Contribution 15 Years	Annuity Amortization	Add Interest (10%) on Previous Liability Balance	Pension Expense	Increase (Decrease)	Liability Balance
1979	$47,330	$58,000	0	$58,000	$10,670	$10,670
1980	47,330	58,000	$1,067	59,067	11,737	22,407
1981	47,330	58,000	2,041	60,241	10,911	33,318
1982	47,330	58,000	3,332	60,000	14,000	47,318

(a) Prepare a corrected table for 1979-1982.
(b) Give the entry to record past service pension cost for 1981 assuming no entry has been made.

PROBLEMS

15-1A. Altaman Mining and Manufacturing Company leases from Wasatch Leasing Company three machines under the following terms:

Machine #1   Lease Period — ten years, beginning April 1, 1975.
                 Lease Payment — $9,000 per year, payable in advance.
Machine #2   Lease Period — ten years, beginning July 1, 1979.
                 Lease Payment — $15,000 per year, payable in advance.
Machine #3   Lease Period — fifteen years, beginning January 1, 1980.
                 Lease Payment — $12,500 per year, payable in advance.

All of the above leases are classified as operating leases.

Instructions:
Prepare the note to the 1981 financial statements that would be required to disclose the lease commitments of Altaman Mining and Manufacturing Company. Altaman uses the calendar year as its accounting period.

15-2A. As of January 1, 1976, the Sports Bazaar Inc. leased a store in a new shopping centre for a period of 6 years. The lease agreement provided that rent would be payable at the end of each year at the annual rate of 5% on gross sales up to $100,000, and 2% on any sales in excess of $100,000 per year. During the term of the lease, the contract called for minimum annual rents of $5,000. The contract further provided that if, in any one year, the rent based on sales did not equal the minimum annual rental, the minimum would be payable, but the difference paid as a result of such minimum could be applied in reduction of the next year's rent to the extent that the next year's rent exceeded the minimum for that year. Gross sales by years amounted to the following:

1976	$ 70,000
1977	90,000
1978	140,000
1979	130,000
1980	80,000
1981	110,000

Instructions:
(1) Compute the rent payable each year under the terms of the lease, showing clearly the amount available for carry-forward and the amount of carry-forward applied.
(2) Discuss the appropriate accounting treatment of any amounts paid under the minimum rental provisions of the lease.
(3) The treasurer of the Sports Bazaar Inc. proposed at the time this lease was signed that the lease contract should be capitalized. Discuss the merits of this proposal.
(4) Assume that the company followed the policy of capitalizing the lease contract at 10%. Give all journal entries in connection with the lease for 1976 and for 1978. (SMA adapted)

15-3A. The 3-N Company leased a machine on July 1, 1981, under a ten-year lease. The economic life of the machine is estimated to be 15 years. Title to the machine passes to 3-N Company at the expiration of the lease and thus the lease is a capital lease. The lease payments are $30,000 per year, including executory costs of $2,000 per year, all payable in advance annually. The incremental borrowing rate of the company is 10%.

Instructions:
(1) Record the entry in the accounts on the lessee, and give all the entries necessary to record the operation of the lease for the first year.
(2) Assume the lessor retains title to the machine at the expiration of the lease, there is no bargain renewal or purchase option, and that the fair market value of the equipment was $190,000 as of the lease date. Using the criteria for distinguishing between operating and capital leases according to the *CICA Handbook: Accounting Recommendations, Section 3065,* what would be the amortization or depreciation expense for 1981?

15-4A. The Bland Corporation entered into a lease for manufacturing equipment from the Scatter Corporation, on January 1, 1980. The terms of the lease provide for yearly payments, in advance, of $26,000 for seven years. The yearly payments include $2,400 maintenance costs. At the end of the lease, Scatter Corporation plans to reclaim the equipment which is expected to last one more year. Scatter Corporation estimated the residual value at $17,000, but did not disclose this information to the Bland Corporation. The Scatter Corporation purchased the asset at its fair market value. The interest rate implicit in the lease is 12%; the Bland Corporation's incremental borrowing rate is 16%.

Instructions:
Give all entries required to account for the lease in both the lessee's and the lessor's accounts in 1980.

15-5A. Randall Electric Company has a policy of acquiring its equipment by leasing. On January 3, 1981, the company signed a lease for a coiling machine. The lease stipulates that payments of $45,000 will be made annually for five years. The payments are to be made in advance. At the end of the five-year period, the company may purchase the machine for $20,000. Its estimated fair market value at that date is $75,000. The company's incremental borrowing rate is 8%. The estimated economic life of the equipment is eight years. Randall Electric Company uses the calendar year for reporting purposes.

Instructions:

(1) Compute the amount to be capitalized as an asset for the lease of the coiling machine.
(2) Prepare a table similar to Table 3, page 610, that shows the computation of the interest expense for each period.
(3) Give the journal entries that would be made in Randall Electric Company's accounts for the first two years of the lease.
(4) Assume on January 2, 1986, the purchase option is exercised. Give the journal entry to record the exercise of the option in Randall Electric Company's accounts.

15-6A. The Bor Company manufactures a piece of machinery at a cost of $70,000. The company is prepared to sell the equipment for a cash price of $83,499. Alternatively, it will lease the machine for a period of three years in return for an annual payment of $30,000, payable at the beginning of each year. The estimated useful life of the asset is three years and no salvage value is anticipated at the end of this period. On January 1, 1979, the Bor Company leases one machine to the Lee Company under the terms described above. Both companies use straight-line depreciation on all of their assets.

Instructions:

(1) Prepare a schedule in which you show the lease payments, the computation and amount of the Bor Company's Interest Revenue (or the Lee Company's Interest Expense) and the end of the period balance in the Bor Company's Lease Receivable (or the Lee Company's Lease Liability) for each of the three years of the lease term.
(2) Provide the journal entries that would be required for the Bor Company to record the lease in the years 1979 and 1980.
(3) Provide the journal entries that would be required for the Lee Company to record the lease in the years 1979 and 1980.
(4) Provide the original entry to record the lease in the Bor Company's accounts, assuming that the machinery would have an $18,000 residual value at the end of the lease. (SMA adapted)

15-7A. The Royal Shipbuilding Company uses leases as a method of selling its products. In 1980, the company constructed a ferry to ply the waters between Vancouver and Victoria. The ferry was leased to Sea Breeze Ferry Line on April 1, 1981, for a total lease payment of $150,000 per year for twenty years, paid annually in advance. The fair market value of the ferry on the lease date was $1,404,735. The cost of the ferry was $1,294,855. At the end of the lease period, the title to the property passes to Sea Breeze.

Instructions:

(1) From the information given above, compute the amount of financial revenue that will be earned over the lease term and the manufacturer's profit that will be earned immediately by Royal.
(2) Give the entries to record the lease in Royal's accounts. What is the implicit rate of interest on the lease?
(3) Give all the entries necessary to record the operating of the lease for the first three years, exclusive of the initial entry. Royal's accounting period is the calendar year.

(4) What would be the balance in each of the following accounts at December 31, 1983: Unearned Interest Revenue; and Lease Payments Receivable?

15-8A. The Granada Manufacturing Company both leases and sells its equipment to its customers. The most popular line of equipment includes a machine that costs $120,000 to manufacture and sells normally for $175,136. The lease terms provide for five annual payments of $42,000 each, with the first payment due when the lease is signed. The implicit rate of interest in the contract is 10% per year. Big Powder Co. leases one of these pieces of equipment on January 3, 1981. Their incremental borrowing rate is determined to be 8% per year. The equipment is very specialized, and it is assumed it will have no salvage value after five years. Assume the lease qualifies as a capital lease and sales-type lease for the lessee and lessor respectively. Also assume that both the lessee and the lessor are on a calendar year basis.

Instructions:
(1) Give all entries required in the accounts of Big Powder Co. to record the lease of equipment from Granada Manufacturing Company for the year 1981. The depreciation on owned equipment is computed once a year on the straight-line basis.
(2) Give entries required in the accounts of Granada Manufacturing Company to record the lease of equipment to Big Powder Co. for the year 1981.
(3) Prepare the Balance Sheet section involving lease balances for both the lessee's and lessor's financial statements at December 31, 1981.
(4) Determine the amount of expense Big Powder Co. will report relative to the lease for 1981 and the amount of revenue Granada Manufacturing Company will report for the same period.

15-9A. The Colton Leasing Company buys equipment for leasing to various manufacturing companies. On October 1, 1980, Colton leases a strap press to the Hermes Shoe Company. The cost of the machine to Colton, which approximated its fair market value on the lease date, was $163,590. The lease payments stipulated in the lease are $27,500 per year in advance for the ten-year period of the lease. The payments include executory costs of $2,500 per year. The expected economic life of the equipment is also ten years. The title to the equipment remains In the hands of Colton Leasing Company at the end of the lease term, although only nominal scrap value is expected at that time. Hermes incremental borrowing rate is 8% and it uses the straight-line method of depreciation on all owned equipment. Both Hermes and Colton have a fiscal year-end of September 30.

Instructions:
(1) Prepare the entries to record the lease in the accounts of the lessor and lessee assuming the lease meets the criteria of a direct-financing lease for the lessor and a capital lease for the lessee.
(2) Compute the implicit rate of interest of the lessor.
(3) Give all entries required to account for the lease in both the lessee's and lessor's accounts for the fiscal years 1981, 1982, and 1983 [exclusive of the initial entry required in (1)].

15-10A. Clyde Manufacturing Company manufactures and leases a variety of items. On January 3, 1981, Clyde leased a hydraulic left-handed skyhook to Astro Industries Co. The lease is for six years with an annual amount of $30,381 payable annually in advance. The skyhook has an estimated useful life of eight years, and was manufactured by Clyde at a cost of $130,000. The lease payment includes executory costs of $1,500 per year. It is estimated that the skyhook will have a residual value of $50,000 at the end of the six-year lease term. There is no guarantee by the lessee of this amount, nor is there any provision for purchase or renewal of the skyhook by Astro at the end of the lease term. The skyhook has a fair market value at the lease inception of $166,589. The implicit rate of interest in the contract is 10%, the same rate which Astro Industries Co. can borrow money at their bank. Astro depreciates assets on a straight-line basis.

Instructions:
(1) Give the entries required in the accounts of lessor and lessee to record the incurrence of the lease and its operation for the first year, assuming the lease meets the qualifications for a capital lease for the lessee and a sales-type lease for the lessor.
(2) Show how the lease would appear on the balance sheets of Clyde Manufacturing Company and Astro Industries Co. (if applicable) as of December 31, 1981.
(3) Assume Clyde Manufacturing Co. sold the skyhook at the end of the six-year lease for $60,000. Give the entry to record the sale assuming all lease entries have been properly made.

15-11A. The Hawkins Company adopts a pension plan on January 3, 1981. Past-service costs at that date are $250,000, and the plan calls for payment of these costs plus interest at 8% over a 20-year period. The company decides to write off past service pension costs over a 25-year period, plus interest of 8% on the unfunded portion. Interest tables are not used to equalize the annual amounts. Normal costs for 1981 and 1982 are $40,000 and $42,000 respectively and are funded each year.

Instructions:
Give the entries required in 1981 and 1982 to record pension expense and pension contributions to the fund. Show all computations.

15-12A. The Connors Corporation adopted a pension plan on January 6, 1980. Past service costs are estimated by the firm's actuary to be $427,975. The plan will be funded over fifteen years and earn an average earnings rate of 8%. Past service costs will be amortized over twelve years.

Instructions:
(1) Construct the first four years of a table showing the computation of annual past service pension expense and accrued pension liability.
(2) Prepare journal entries to record pension related transactions for 1982.

15-13A. The Andrus Company experienced actuarial gains and losses in relation to its pension plan as follows:

Year	
1	$ 7,000
2	2,000
3	(3,000)
4	(1,500)
5	4,000

Actuarial gains and losses are spread over ten years using a straight-line basis.

Instructions:
(1) Construct a table showing the spreading of Andrus Company's actuarial gains and losses for the five years.
(2) Assuming past service costs are being amortized according to Table 5 on page 627, record pension expense for Year 4. Normal costs are $125,000.

15-14A. The President of Wilcox Limited had just been discussing the 1981 financial statements with the firm's auditor. For the past several years the auditor had qualified his audit report because the president had insisted each year that only the current service portion of pension payments be shown as an expense on the income statement. Wilcox Limited was family controlled but the president was considering a public issue of the company's shares in the near future to finance much needed capital expenditure programs.

The company had been formed just before World War II. The war boom continued for the company after the war and sales increased steadily during the 1950s. In 1949, the president voluntarily instituted a pay-as-you-go pension plan which was regarded as having one of the highest benefit schedules in the country. In 1958, the company began paying into an independently administered pension fund. The payments into the fund were intended to provide for the funding of current service costs and a portion of past service costs over a thirty-year period. However, the amount of these payments varied from year to year depending on the company's ability to pay. The plan was entirely voluntary and did not entail any legal obligations for the company. In its income statement the company showed only the current service portion of its payments into the fund.

In 1960, the union successfully negotiated for a formalized pension agreement setting out details of the pension plan and specifying the annual payments which the company was to make into the independently administered pension fund. This plan recognized the existing informal plan and provided for full transfer or incorporation of existing benefits. Employee pension benefits were to be based on the number of years of employment, calculated from the date of commencement of service. The pension fund contributions were to be made by the company, and employees were to acquire a vested interest in these payments after 20 years of employment. However, this union contract did not provide for full funding of past service benefits. Each year since then the firm's auditor had urged the president to fully provide for the past service costs in the financial statements. Since the issue of Bulletin No. 21 on pension costs, the auditor had qualified his report with respect to the firm's treatment of pension costs.

At the end of 1981, the president had engaged a firm of actuarial consultants to perform an actuarial evaluation of Wilcox Limited's pension plan. They reported that, as of December 31, 1981, unfunded past service costs aggregated $14,000,000 and that an annual provision of about $1,500,000 would be required to fully cover both continuing current service costs and unfunded past service costs over a thirty-year period. Unfunded vested benefits aggregated $2,000,000.

In his discussion with the firm's auditor the president had pointed out that the actuarial evaluation did not reflect an anticipated 20% reduction in the work force when the modernization plan was implemented in a few years. The president also felt that the 3% rate of interest used by the actuary in his evaluation was not realistic and that 4% more fairly represented the rate of return that could be expected on the fund contributions. If the 4% rate of return was used, the annual provision would need to be $1,200,000 as opposed to the $1,500,000 at the 3% rate. Moreover, Wilcox Limited's legal liability under the pension plan was limited by the provision of the union contract which was due to expire in two years and the existing contract did not provide for full funding of past service costs. In view of these points the president felt that a $1,500,000 annual provision based on the actuarial evaluation was excessive. Finally, the president insisted that the firm simply would not have sufficient cash resources to pay a $1,500,000 annual contribution.

On the following Exhibit are summarized financial data of Wilcox Limited.

Wilcox Limited

Exhibit

(in thousands of dollars)

	Contributions to Pension Fund	Past Service Cost Portion	Net Income (Loss)	Year End Cash	Balance of Retained Earnings
1970	$ 800	$100	$3,500	$2,000	$12,000
1971	1,100	350	4,000	2,500	12,500
1972	700	——	1,800	1,900	10,100
1973	650	——	(600)	1,500	8,000
1974	660	——	(200)	1,300	7,800
1975	900	100	1,500	1,400	7,000
1976	870	50	2,000	900	6,500
1977	890	100	1,800	1,000	6,900
1978	900	80	2,000	1,200	7,300
1979	1,070	100	2,300	1,100	7,500
1980	1,120	100	2,000	1,400	7,200
1981	1,200	100	2,500	1,600	8,000

Instructions:

(1) Comment on the president's objection to increasing the pension contributions.
(2) Outline how the company should disclose the pension cost in the 1981 financial statements. Give your reasons.

16 ACCOUNTING FOR SHARE CAPITAL

A corporation is an artificial entity created by law that has an existence separate from its owners and, within prescribed limits, may engage in business just as a natural person. The modern corporation makes it possible for large amounts of property to be assembled under one management. Property is usually transferred to the corporation by individual owners because they believe they can earn a greater rate of return through the corporation's efficient use of the property than would be possible from alternative uses including investments. In exchange for this property, the corporation issues ownership interests in the form of shares of stock. A board of directors elected by shareholders appoints the officers who manage the use, operation, and disposition of the property. Unless the life of the corporation is limited by law, it has perpetual existence.

Corporations are the dominant form of organization in today's economy. Not only are they the major source of our national output, but they also provide the majority of employment opportunities. Accounting for corporations has become very important because of the division between ownership and management and the widespread holding of corporate securities.

FORMING THE CORPORATION

Business corporations may be created under the companies or corporation laws of any one of the ten provinces or of the Federal Government. In general, those corporations whose activities are confined to one province usually incorporate under the Act of that province, while a corporation operating in several provinces is more likely to seek federal incorporation. The choice, however, is not a question of jurisdiction; subject to licensing requirements, any corporation may carry on business in any province.

In practice, most small to medium-sized companies are incorporated at the provincial level, while the majority of large corporations are federally incorporated. According to *The Financial Post* approximately 60% of the largest manufacturing, resource, and utility corporations in Canada are incorporated federally, while Ontario, with less than 20%, ranks second.

Certain types of corporations, such as chartered banks, trust, and insurance companies, are incorporated under special legislation. In addition, there are a number of government or Crown corporations including the Bank of Canada, Central Mortgage and Housing Corporation, the Canadian Broadcasting Corporation, and Air Canada, each of which is incorporated under its own statute.

The formation of a corporation is governed by the laws of the incorporating jurisdiction. While the procedures vary depending upon the jurisdiction, in general at least three individuals must join together in applying for incorporation in most provincial jurisdictions. The federal act, the Canada Business Corporations Act,[1] permits one or more individuals, over eighteen, of sound mind and not bankrupt, to incorporate by submitting the required documentation, primarily *articles of incorporation*, to the Director, the official responsible for administration of the act.

Several of the provincial statutes use the letters patent system to grant a charter of incorporation. In the other provinces, incorporation takes place upon the registration of a memorandum of association. In either case, the incorporating documentation is usually brief with a view to providing flexibility in the operation of the corporation. The documentation is supplemented in the case of a memorandum company by articles of association, or by-laws in the case of a letters patent company. It should be noted that a corporation can exercise only those powers and perform only those functions that are consistent with its incorporating documents and the legislation under which it is constituted.

The articles of incorporation, as required under the Canada Business Corporations Act, must set forth the name of the corporation, the place within Canada where its registered office is to be located, the shares that the corporation is authorized to issue including any restrictions to the right to transfer shares, the number of directors, and any restrictions on the business that the corporation may carry on. In addition, the articles may include (1) any matter that could be included in the by-laws or, (2) any

---

[1] The Canada Business Corporations Act received Royal Assent on March 24, 1975, and has since been proclaimed in force effective December 15, 1975.

unanimous shareholder agreement. The name of the corporation must include "Limited," "Incorporated," or "Corporation" in English or French, or in abbreviated form, as its last word. Incorporation takes place pursuant to filing the articles and other required documents and being issued a certificate of incorporation.

Under the Canada Business Corporations Act incorporation is a matter of right, rather than a privilege. Provided that the incorporating documentation conforms to law, the Director has no discretion to accept or refuse the documents; he must accept them and issue a certificate of incorporation. At this point, the corporation comes into being as a legal entity separate and apart from its owners, the shareholders. By electing a *board of directors* the shareholders exercise control over the management of corporate activity. The board meets from time to time to determine corporate policies and to appoint the officers who will manage the corporation.

Expenditures incurred incidental to the formation of a corporation, such as legal fees, the fees paid on incorporation, and promotional costs, are normally charged to an intangible asset account entitled Organization Costs. Although such costs may have no realizable value upon liquidation, they are as essential as plant and equipment, for without them the corporation could not have been created. If the life of a corporate enterprise could be stated in terms of a definite period of time, the organization costs should be amortized over that period by annual charges to an expense account. However, at the time of incorporation, the life-span of most corporations is indeterminate.

There are two opposite viewpoints on the appropriate accounting for organization costs and other intangibles of indeterminate life. One extreme would consider the cost of intangibles as a permanent asset until there was convincing evidence of loss in value. The other extreme would consider the cost of intangibles as an expense in the period in which the cost is incurred. Amortization provides a practical solution to the problem as expressed in the following quotation:

> . . . Allocating the cost of goodwill or other intangible assets with an indeterminate life over time is necessary because the value almost inevitably becomes zero at some future date. Since the date at which the value becomes zero is indeterminate, the end of the useful life must necessarily be set arbitrarily at some point or within some range of time for accounting purposes?

In practice, increasing numbers of corporations are amortizing organization costs. A probable explanation may be the fact that the Income Tax Act permits a portion of organization cost to be written off over a period of years. However, when organization costs have been neither written off nor amortized they should be shown on the balance sheet as an intangible asset.

---

²*Opinions of the Accounting Principles Board, No. 17*, "Intangible Assets" (New York: American Institute of Certified Public Accountants, 1970), par. 23.

Corporations may be classified as *profit* or *non-profit*. *Profit* corporations are engaged in business or commercial activities; they depend upon profitable operations for their continued existence. *Non-profit* corporations include those organized for charitable, educational, recreational, or philanthropic purposes; they depend upon members' dues and/or upon donations and government grants for their continued existence. Profit corporations whose ownership or share capital is widely distributed are commonly referred to as *public corporations*, or as *distributing corporations*; those whose share capital is held by a small group of shareholders are often referred to as *private corporations*, (even though certain statutes no longer use this terminology) or as *corporations that restrict the transfer of shares*. Under the Canada Business Corporations Act only distributing corporations and corporations that exceed either of two size tests based on gross revenues and on assets are subject to the financial disclosure requirements. Moreover, corporations that are not subject to the disclosure requirements may dispense with the appointment of an auditor by means of an annual resolution consented to by all shareholders.

SECURITIES REGULATION

When a corporation issues shares the result is an increase in both assets and shareholders' equity, and the issuance may be termed a *primary distribution*. Except for the case of the so-called private company, shares are fully transferable. Thus, a shareholder is free to sell his shares, or a portion thereof, to any willing buyer. This type of transaction, termed *secondary distribution*, has no effect on the accounts of the corporation. The stock exchanges provide the market in which most secondary distribution takes place.

In order to issue shares a corporation must comply with a variety of statutory requirements. Each of the ten provinces has a securities act which is administered by a provincial securities commission or, in a few instances, by a branch or division of the provincial Attorney General's department. In addition, the companies acts, which include both federal statutes and separate acts in each province, impinge indirectly, as does the federal Criminal Code, on matters concerning fraud. Because of the distribution of powers between the federal and provincial governments set forth in the *British North America Act*, there is, as yet, no Canadian counterpart of the Securities and Exchange Commission in the United States.

Securities regulation statutes may include (1) the fraud prevention type of provision which establishes an agency with broad powers to ferret out and prosecute instances of fraud; (2) the so-called "blue sky" provision which confers on an agency discretionary power to determine what securities may be sold to the public, and by means of registration, the authority to pass on the suitability of persons in the stock brokerage business; and (3) the disclosure type of provision which requires an issuer to file a prospectus with a designated agency, have it cleared by the agency, and sent to prospective purchasers of the securities being offered. While securities legislation across Canada is far from uniform, the Ontario Securities Act has formed the basis of the law throughout Western Canada.

The subject of securities regulation is complex. In the Province of Ontario, for example, the Business Corporations Act and the Securities Act contain virtually identical provisions pertaining to many events, transactions, and disclosures. This pattern is significant because it provides for uniform securities regulation as applied to companies incorporated in Ontario and to companies incorporated elsewhere but using the Ontario securities markets. In general, the Securities Act imposes a prohibition as to trading in the course of primary distribution to the public until both a preliminary and final prospectus have been filed with the Ontario Securities Commission, and receipts have been obtained for each. A prospectus, or offering circular, is designed to provide information which will enable a prospective investor to form an opinion as to the merit of the shares or other securities, for example corporate bonds, that the corporation proposes to issue. As stated in the Securities Act, a prospectus shall provide full, true, and plain disclosure of all material facts relating to the proposed issue. The Securities Act is generally applicable to all corporations whose securities are listed on the Toronto Stock Exchange, or whose equity shares have been the subject of a filing under the act. Since filing is normally required before any primary distribution can take place, it follows that the Securities Act should eventually apply to almost all corporations whose securities are being traded in the Province of Ontario. In this context, the word "should" is appropriate because in general the legislation provides for both exempt securities and exempt trades. However, the new Ontario Securities Act, 1978, restricts exemptions such that the prospectus requirements now apply to virtually every distribution, both public and private, unless the specific distribution qualifies for one of the specified exemptions contained in the act. If an issue is to be sold in more than one province, clearances must be obtained in each province.

When a corporation proposes to issue shares it usually engages the services of an investment dealer who will normally underwrite the entire issue. In most cases, the underwriter guarantees the issuing corporation full payment net of a commission and assumes the responsibility for distribution. The commission or spread between the price to the public and the net proceeds to the corporation is a negotiable item. In the case of speculative issues, it is not uncommon for the underwriter to insist on contingent compensation, such as a package of options to purchase shares at a fixed price and exercisable for a period of several years, in addition to a commission. This form of compensation is termed contingent because the options will compensate the underwriter only if, during the option period, the market value of the shares rises above the fixed option price.

NATURE OF SHARE CAPITAL

An ownership interest in a corporate entity is evidenced by shares of stock in the form of certificates. A share of capital stock represents nothing more than a proportionate interest in a corporate entity. The general term applied to the shares of a corporation is *capital stock*. The classes and usually the numbers of shares that a corporation is *authorized* to issue are set forth in its incorporating documents. The term *issued* is applied to shares that have actually been issued to shareholders. A company may, under circumstances discussed later in the chapter, reacquire some of the shares it has issued. The shares remaining in the hands of shareholders are referred to as *outstanding*. For most corporations, the number of shares issued and the number outstanding should be the same.

Shares of capital stock are frequently assigned an arbitrary value, known as *par value*. The par value is printed on the share certificate, which is the evidence of ownership issued to the shareholder. Shares may also be issued without par value in which case they are known as *no-par-value* shares or as shares *without nominal or par value*. The shares issued by a company incorporated or continued[3] under the Canada Business Corporations Act are required by statute to be in registered form, and to be without nominal or par value. In general, other Canadian corporations, depending upon the laws of their incorporating jurisdictions, may issue shares with or without par values.

At one time all shares were required to have a par value. In 1917, the federal act was amended to permit the issuance of shares without nominal or par value. Subsequently, all provinces passed similar amendments. Since 1975, under legislation for federal corporations, the issue of par value shares has been expressly proscribed. Within the foreseeable future it appears that company law in Canada may perhaps reverse its one-time position by requiring all shares to be without nominal or par value.[4]

The issue of no-par-value shares was initially premised on the grounds that: (1) such shares could be sold as *fully paid* without the subscriber being perhaps contingently liable to creditors as could be the case if par value shares were issued at a discount; (2) investors would not be misled by a

---

[3]As a transitional device, continuance provides a means whereby existing corporations incorporated under the Canada Corporations Act, and certain other federal statutes, can be brought under the Canada Business Corporations Act. In general, most existing corporations must apply for a certificate of continuance within five years of the proclamation date of the Canada Business Corporations Act; if they do not do so, they will be automatically dissolved by operation of the Act. The five year transition period ended on December 15, 1980.

[4]The Canada Business Corporations Act has already provided the general model for new acts in Manitoba and Saskatchewan and similar draft legislation exists in New Brunswick and Prince Edward Island. Alberta is expected to follow these precedents. British Columbia and Ontario have amended their acts to include some provisions very similar to those contained in the Canada Business Corporations Act.

less-than-par *bargain* price; moreover, in the absence of a value appearing on share certificates they might be more likely to investigate the value of a share; and (3) assets acquired in exchange for shares would be recorded at their actual worth rather than at inflated amounts set by par values, possibly as a means of enabling shareholders to avoid any contingent liability for the discount.

It is questionable whether investors have subjected no-par-value shares to closer investigation than shares with a par value. It is also questionable whether more satisfactory valuations have been applied to properties received in exchange for no-par-value shares as compared with shares with a par value.

Rejection of the par value concept gives emphasis to the fact that a share is simply a proportionate interest in a corporate enterprise. For example, if an investor buys 1,000 shares of $1 par value in a corporation with an issued share capital of 10,000 shares, the true measure of this investment is not $1,000, but rather a 10% share in a business the value of which must, of necessity, fluctuate as the fortunes of the corporation rise and fall. In this example, it is unlikely an investor would pay exactly $1,000 for 10% of the issued share capital, nor is it likely that $1,000 would represent either the current market or liquidation value of 1,000 shares.

Many corporations issue only a single class of shares. However, there may be advantages in issuing more than one class of shares with varying rights and priorities. When a single class is issued, the shares are all alike and are generally known as *common shares*. When more than one class is issued, shares given certain preferences over the common shares have been traditionally referred to as *preferred shares*.

Although in general the distinction still applies to provincially incorporated companies, the Canada Business Corporations Act does not distinguish between preferred and common shares. Instead, it provides for the issue of more than one class of shares with the rights, privileges, restrictions, and conditions of each class to be set forth in the articles of incorporation. One class, however, must provide for the holders two specific rights similar to those traditionally identified with common shares: (1) the right to vote at all meetings of holders of that class of shares, and (2) the right to participate in distributions of both dividends and remaining assets upon dissolution of the corporation. Regardless of the fact that the Canada Business Corporations Act does not use the terms "common" and "preferred" with reference to shares, it is likely this terminology will continue to be used in practice. Moreover, since these terms provide a useful way to distinguish classes of shares, the terms will be used for this purpose in the discussion that follows.

The articles of incorporation may provide for *pre-emptive rights*, in which case new issues of shares must be offered first to existing shareholders who have the right to acquire shares in proportion to their holdings of shares of that class at the price and on the terms that shares are to be offered to others. In the absence of specific provision in the articles, the pre-emptive right does not apply to the shares issued by companies incorporated or continued under the Canada Business Corporations Act. All shareholders, of course, have the right to receive dividends declared by the board of directors.

The Canada Business Corporations Act permits any class of shares to be issued in one or more series, if authorized by the articles. A series is simply a sub-division of a class of shares. The intent of permitting the issue of shares in series is to give more flexibility to corporate financing.

Because of the increased demand for funds for investment, other types of securities have been increasingly used. Some types have both debt and equity qualities and may be converted into straight equity securities at the option of the holders. The use of these securities changes as economic conditions change, and they increase in variety as the acquisition of new funds for investment becomes more difficult.

If two or more classes of shares are issued, the special features of each class are stated in the incorporating documents and become a part of the share contract between the corporation and its shareholders. One must be familiar with the overall capital structure to understand fully the nature of the equity found in any single class of shares. Frequently, the share certificate describes the rights and restrictions relative to the ownership interest it represents, and possibly those pertaining to other securities issued. Shares represent personal property and may be freely transferred by their owners, subject to any restrictions on transfer contained in the incorporating documents.

Legal or Stated Capital

When shares are issued by a corporation, a portion or all of the capital arising from the issue may be designated *legal* or *stated capital*. In general, corporation laws provide that dividends cannot reduce corporate capital below legal capital, and may go beyond these limitations and add that legal capital cannot be impaired by the reacquisition of share capital. Creditors of a corporation cannot hold individual shareholders liable for claims against the company. But with a portion of the corporate capital restricted as to distribution, creditors can expect the absorption by the ownership group of losses equal to the legal capital before losses are applied against the claims of creditors.

Share capital accounts should be maintained so as to disclose legal capital in conformity with the law of the incorporating jurisdiction. Legal capital is defined by statute and its definition varies as between jurisdictions. Regardless of its specific definition, the concept of legal capital connotes some minimum amount of shareholder investment that cannot easily be reduced or withdrawn.[5] In general, and there are exceptions, legal capital includes the total consideration received upon the issuance of shares without nominal or par value and, in the case of par value shares, an amount equal to the par value multiplied by the number of shares issued. Separate share capital accounts are maintained for each of the classes of shares that a corporation is authorized to issue.

The Canada Business Corporations Act requires a corporation to maintain a *stated capital account* for each class and each series of shares issued. In general, the full amount of consideration received by the corporation for each share issued increases the stated capital account for shares of that class or series. If a corporation issues its own shares in payment of a dividend, the money value of the shares issued is added to the stated capital account for the dividend shares. Stated capital accounts may be reduced only in accordance with the act, and should be rare except when a corporation purchases, redeems, or otherwise acquires its own shares.

It should be noted that through the prohibition of par value shares, together with the requirement to increase the stated capital account(s) by the amounts of consideration received on the issue of shares, the Canada Business Corporations Act effectively eliminates contributed surplus except as may result from certain capital transactions or where property is donated to the corporation. No longer will a company incorporated or continued under the Canada Business Corporations Act be able to create contributed surplus from any part of the proceeds of a share issue. However, the share capital transactions of provincially incorporated companies may continue to give rise to possible increases or decreases of contributed surplus, depending upon the nature of the transactions and upon the province of incorporation.

To facilitate the issue of dividend cheques, proxy forms, and financial reports, a record of the name and address of each shareholder and the number of shares held must be maintained. In some corporations, the share capital accounts are controlling accounts and a subsidiary ledger, known as the *shareholder's ledger*, is used to provide whatever detailed information may be required.

Most large corporations, and certainly those whose shares are widely held, use the services of a registrar and a transfer agent, usually a trust company. Thus, the responsibility for keeping shareholder records, transferring the corporation's shares, and preparing official lists of shareholders as required by the corporation, is often undertaken by a trust company or companies appointed by the board of directors. If a corporation's shares are listed on a stock exchange, the regulations of the exchange ordinarily require

---

[5]Legal provisions exist that permit a corporation to reduce its capital, usually by amendment of its incorporating documents. In general, a resolution is required that must receive a stipulated majority of the votes of shareholders, the voting normally being by class of shares, and the reduction in capital may be subject to the approval of the court.

the appointment of both a registrar and a transfer agent. Most exchanges, however, allow the same trust company to hold both appointments.

Par and No-Par-Value Shares

As stated above, the issue of par value shares is proscribed for companies incorporated or continued under the Canada Business Corporations Act. In order to avoid administrative problems, the Act provides that the shares of a corporation continued under the Act will be deemed to be shares without nominal or par value, even though they may have been originally issued as par value shares. Since the Canada Business Corporations Act provides a period of five years, until December 15, 1980, during which existing corporations can apply for continuance, many federally incorporated companies may continue to have par value shares outstanding at least throughout most of 1980. Furthermore, in several provinces par value shares may still be issued by provincially incorporated companies. Therefore, a knowledge of the accounting for par values shares is not yet obsolete.

If the authorized capital of a provincially incorporated company includes par value shares, the corporation, at the time of its formation, is free to set par at any amount it chooses. The par designation is merely one method of dividing share capital into a number of units of ownership. A corporation can also change the par value of its shares, or change its par value shares into no-par shares, providing it complies with the requirements of its incorporating jurisdiction.

Generally speaking, the price at which shares can be sold by a corporation is influenced by (1) its financial condition, its earnings record, and its dividend record, (2) its potential or future earning power, (3) the availability of money for investment purposes, and (4) general business and economic conditions and prospects. The par value of its shares, if any,is not a determinant of the price at which the shares can be sold.

By definition, a premium or discount on shares can only arise if the shares have a par value. In other words, the amount of any premium or discount is determined by comparing the issue price with the par value of the shares issued.

When a provincially incorporated company is authorized to issue par value shares, the incorporating jurisdiction may permit such issue only for an amount equal to or in excess of par. An amount received in excess of par value is recorded as a premium and should be reported on the balance sheet as contributed surplus.

In certain provinces corporations may be permitted to sell shares at a discount.[6] Persons subscribing for shares at a discount fulfill their obligation

[6]Most Canadian jurisdictions do not permit the issuance of shares at a discount. A company incorporated in New Brunswick is an exception, as also are mining companies incorporated in certain provinces. However, the law in New Brunswick is expected to change, probably in the near future.

to the corporation upon payment of the agreed price. However, the law may provide that if the assets of a corporation are insufficient to meet its obligations, creditors may hold shareholders personally liable for deficiencies up to the amounts of the discount.

In some respects the problems of issuing shares at a discount is largely academic. In the first place, a corporation can set the par value of its shares at so low an amount, for example $1 per share, or even less, that the question of discount is unlikely to arise. Secondly, the problem can be avoided by issuing shares without nominal or par value.

Most Canadian corporate statutes, including the Canada Business Corporations Act, permit the payment of a commission on the issuance of shares. The net effect, of course, is similar to a discount on shares. In the event of any substantial issue of shares, it is common practice to utilize the services of an investment dealer or underwriter, and the payment of a commission is then inevitable. In contrast with a discount on shares, a commission may be accounted for as part of the organization costs of the company.

When shares are issued at a discount, cash or other assets are debited for the amount received; a discount account is debited for the amount of the discount, and the share capital account is credited for the par value of the shares. For example, if a corporation issues 20,000 shares of $25 par common stock at $22 per share, the entry to record the transaction would be as follows:

Cash	440,000	
Discount on Common Shares	60,000	
Common Shares		500,000

There are two contrasting viewpoints regarding the financial statement presentation of a discount on shares. Under one alternative, the discount is shown as a deduction from the par value of the shares issued and the difference is extended as the amount of share capital received by the corporation. The other alternative is to treat the discount as a contra contributed surplus item. Neither company law nor the *Accounting Recommendations* provide any clear answer as to which alternative should be preferred. Under no circumstances should the discount be listed on the balance sheet as an asset, nor should it be amortized as if it were an expense.

When no-par shares are issued company law generally requires the credit to share capital to be equal to the aggregate amount of the consideration received. This requirement presents no problem in the case of cash consideration. If the consideration takes the form of non-cash assets or past services, their value should be the fair equivalent of the amount the corporation would have received if the shares had been issued for cash. The responsibility for making this determination falls on the board of directors, as also does the responsibility for establishing the price at which no-par shares may from time to time be issued.

As the result of a 1978 amendment, the requirement that the credit to share capital should equal the full amount of consideration received for each share issued does not apply to certain non-arm's-length transactions.[7] When a corporation issues shares in exchange for property to a person who does not deal with the corporation at arm's-length, or in exchange for shares of another corporation, that does not deal with the issuer at arm's-length (either before the exchange or because of the exchange), any amount not exceeding the full consideration may be added to the stated capital account for the shares issued. This exclusion from the general rule also applies to shares issued pursuant to an amalgamation agreement.

When shares are issued for other than cash consideration, it is not always possible to make an objective determination of fair values in terms of the amount of cash the corporation would have received if the shares had been issued for cash. However, if shares were also issued for cash at about the same time, this cash price may provide an objective basis for the valuation of the non-cash consideration. Theoretically, the fair value of the non-cash consideration must equal the fair value of the shares issued. In the imperfect markets of practice, however, this may rarely be the case. As a practical solution, a valuation may be placed on either the consideration received or on the shares issued, the choice being dependent upon which is more objectively determinable in the circumstances.

Prior to July 1, 1965, it was possible for a federal corporation to issue no-par shares and, at its discretion, set aside part of the consideration received, in most cases not more than 25% of the proceeds, as distributable surplus rather than share capital. In spite of the fact that a federal corporation can no longer create or increase distributable surplus, such amounts as were established prior to July 1, 1965, may continue to appear on corporate balance sheets. In addition, similar provisions may still exist in some provincial companies acts.

In some cases, particularly in jurisdictions in the United States, no-par shares may be assigned a stated value per share, and the excess of the proceeds over the stated value may be credited to Excess of Issue Price Over Stated Value of Common Shares. It is readily apparent that the accounting for no-par shares with a stated value should follow the same pattern as the accounting for par value shares. From the viewpoint of Canadian company law, there should be no objection to the use of stated values provided the balance in such accounts as Excess of Issue Price Over Stated Value of Common Shares is shown in the balance sheet under the Share Capital caption.

---

[7]The Canada Business Corporations Act uses the term non-arm's-length as defined in the Income Tax Act.

PREFERRED SHARES

When a corporation issues both preferred and common shares, the preferences attaching to the preferred normally include both a prior claim to dividends and, in the event of liquidation, a claim on assets in priority to common shareholders. A dividend preference does not assure shareholders of dividends on the preferred issue but simply means that dividend requirements must be met on preferred shares before anything may be paid on common shares. Dividends do not legally accrue; a dividend on preferred, as on common, requires legal ability on the part of the corporation to make such a distribution, as well as appropriate action by the board of directors. When the board of directors fails to declare a dividend at the time such action would be called for, the dividend is said to be *passed*. Although preferred shareholders have a prior claim on dividends, such preference is usually accompanied by limitations on the amount of dividends they may receive.

When preferred shares have a par value, the dividend preference is stated in terms of a percentage of par value. When preferred shares are without nominal or par value, the dividend must be stated in terms of dollars and cents. Thus, holders of 5% preferred shares with a $50 par value are entitled to an annual dividend of $2.50 per share before any distribution is made to common shareholders; holders of $5 no-par preferred shares are entitled to an annual dividend of $5 per share before dividends are paid to common shareholders.

A corporation may issue more than one class of preferred shares. For example, preferred issues may be designated first preferred or second preferred with the first preferred issue having a first claim on earnings and the second preferred having a second claim on earnings. In other instances the claim to earnings on the part of several preferred issues may have equal priority, but dividend rates or other preferences may vary. Holders of the common shares can receive dividends only after the satisfaction of all preferred dividend requirements.

Other characteristics and conditions are frequently added to preferred shares in the extension of certain advantages or in the limitation of certain rights. Such factors may be expressed by modifying adjectives such as *cumulative* preferred, *convertible* preferred, and *callable* preferred. More than one of these characteristics may be applicable to a specific issue of preferred shares.

Cumulative and Non-cumulative Preferred Shares

Cumulative preferred shares provide that whenever the corporation fails to declare dividends on this class, such dividends accumulate and require payment in the future before any dividends may be paid to common shareholders. For example, assume a corporation has outstanding 10,000 shares of

$9 cumulative preferred shares without nominal or par value. Dividends were last paid through December 31, 1978, and the company wishes to resume payments at the end of 1981. The company will have to declare dividends on preferred for three years, or $270,000, before it may declare any dividends on its common shares. Preferred dividends on cumulative preferred shares that are passed are referred to as *dividends in arrears*. Although these dividends are not a liability until declared by the board of directors, this information is of importance to shareholders and other users of the financial statements. Disclosure of the amount of the dividends in arrears is usually made by means of a note to the financial statements.

If preferred shares are *non-cumulative*, it is not necessary to provide for passed dividends. A dividend omission on preferred shares in any one year means it is irretrievably lost. Dividends may be declared on common shares as long as the preferred receive the preferred rate for the current period. Preferred share contracts normally provide for cumulative dividends. Courts have generally held that dividend rights on preferred shares are cumulative in the absence of specific conditions to the contrary.

Convertible Preferred Shares

Preferred shares are *convertible* when terms of the issue provide that they can be exchanged by holders for some other security of the issuing corporation. Conversion rights generally provide for the exchange of preferred shares into common shares. Since preferred shares normally have a prior but limited right on earnings, large earnings resulting from successful operations accrue to the common shareholders. The conversion privilege gives the preferred shareholder the opportunity to exchange his or her holdings for shares on which the rights to earnings are not limited. In some instances, preferred shares may also be convertible into bonds. Here the investor has the option of changing his or her position from that of a shareholder to that of a creditor. Convertible preferred issues have become increasingly popular in recent years.

The decision by a shareholder as to when to convert preferred holdings into common shares is a difficult one and involves many factors including the time limitation, if any, on the conversion privilege, the relative dividend returns on common shares as compared with preferred shares, as well as other provisions related to the two classes of securities.

Callable Preferred Shares

Preferred shares are *callable* or *redeemable* when they can be called or redeemed at the option of the corporation. Many preferred issues are callable. The *redemption price* is usually specified in the original agreement and provides for payment of dividends in arrears as part of the repurchase price. When convertible shares also have a call provision, the holder frequently is given the option of converting his or her holdings into common shares. The decision made by the investor will be based on the market price of the common shares.

Asset and Dividend Preferences upon Corporate Liquidation

Preferred shares are generally preferred as to assets upon corporate liquidation. Such a preference, however, cannot be assumed but must be specifically stated in the preferred share contract. The asset preference for shares with a par value may be an amount equal to par, or par plus a premium; in the absence of a par value it is a stated amount. Terms of the preferred contract may also provide for the full payment of any dividends in arrears upon liquidation, regardless of the retained earnings balance reported by the corporation. When this is the case and there are insufficient retained earnings, or a deficit, such dividend priorities must be met from the capital relating to common shares; common shareholders receive whatever assets remain after settlement with the preferred group.

COMMON SHARES

Strictly speaking, there should be but one class of common shares. Common shares represent the residual ownership equity and carry the greatest risk. In return for this risk, common shares ordinarily share in earnings to the greatest extent if the corporation is successful. Voting rights are frequently given exclusively to common shareholders as long as dividends are paid regularly on preferred shares. Upon failure to meet preferred dividend requirements, special voting rights may be granted to preferred shareholders, thus affording this group a more prominent role in the management.

Because of legal restrictions on preferred shares, some corporations have issued two types of common shares, known as Class A shares and Class B shares. One of the two types will have special preferences or rights that the other type does not have, such as dividend preferences or voting rights. The distinction between Class A and Class B shares, then, may be similar to that normally found between a company's preferred and common issues. The use of such classified common shares has in the past been so abused that this form of corporate financing has been largely discontinued.

In addition, as previously noted, a company incorporated or continued under the Canada Business Corporations Act may issue a class of shares in series. Although different series of shares in any one class, such as common shares, may have different rights and conditions, no series can have priority in respect to dividends or return of capital over any other series of shares of the same class. The amount of variation in the rights and conditions pertaining to series of shares in any one class is dependent upon the latitude that the shareholders are prepared to give the board of directors. For example, the directors could be given the right to issue common shares in series with a different dividend rate for each series within a specified range of dividend entitlement per share.

ISSUANCE OF SHARE CAPITAL

Depending on the legal requirements of the incorporating jurisdiction, the share capital of a corporation may be authorized but unissued; it may be subscribed for and held for issuance pending receipt of cash on share subscriptions; it may be held pending the exercise of stock options or warrants; it may be outstanding in the hands of shareholders; it may be reacquired and held by the corporation for subsequent resale or other distribution; it may be cancelled by appropriate corporate action. An accurate record of the position of the corporation as a result of exchanges of property between shareholders and the corporation must be maintained in the accounts.

Subscriptions and Calls

Thus far, discussion of the issuance of shares has assumed full payment in cash, other assets, or past services, prior to issue. In most instances, such is in fact the case. It should be noted, however, that some jurisdictions permit a corporation to sell shares on the basis of subscriptions whereby the investor agrees to pay the subscription price at a future date, or in a series of instalments. In a few jurisdictions, shares may be issued subject to call; that is, partially-paid shares are issued with further payment subject to specific calls by the board of directors.

Since the policy of most securities commissions is that shares must be fully paid before they are issued, instances of partially-paid shares, calls, and even of subscriptions, are rare. Moreover, the Canada Business Corporations Act states that shares may not be issued until they have been fully paid. While this requirement precludes the issue of shares subject to call, it is still possible for a company incorporated or continued under the act to sell shares with payment on an instalment basis. However, the issue of the shares cannot take place until payment is made in full and, until then, the subscriber does not have the rights of a shareholder.

In those circumstances where a corporation undertakes to sell shares directly to investors it is possible to encounter a subscription arrangement. For example, the investor may first enter into an agreement to subscribe for shares at a specific price. The terms of the agreement may provide for a payment to accompany the subscription, with the balance to be paid subject to acceptance and an allotment of shares, or at some future date, or in instalments over a period of time. In most cases, this type of arrangement determines in advance when various payments are to be made. On the other hand, when partially paid shares that are subject to calls are issued, it is not known in advance how or when the balance is to be paid. In the case of calls, the usual procedure is to credit share capital only as calls are made and then only to the extent of each call. Thus, the full credit to share capital is not made until the issue price has been fully called.

When shares are subscribed for at par, the subscription price is debited to the asset account Share Subscriptions Receivable and credited to the share capital account Shares Subscribed. If the shares are without nominal or par value, the issue price authorized by the board of directors is used to record the transaction.

When shares are subscribed for a price above or below par, the share subscriptions receivable account is debited for the subscription price rather than par. The shares subscribed account is credited at par, and the difference between the subscription price and par is debited to a discount account or credited to a premium account, as the case may be.

After a subscriber completes his agreed payments, the corporation issues the share certificate. The shares subscribed account is then debited for the total par of the shares issued or for the total consideration in the case of no-par shares, and the share capital account is credited for the same amount.

There are two contrasting viewpoints regarding the financial statement presentation of the items subscriptions receivable and shares subscribed. One alternative would list the subscriptions receivable as a current asset and the shares subscribed as share capital. Depending upon the requirements of the incorporating jurisdiction, this alternative may be acceptable provided that the subscriptions are currently due and there is no doubt as to their collectibility. As an alternative, the subscription receivable may be shown as a deduction from the balance in the shares subscribed account. Again, depending on the requirements of the incorporating jurisdiction, this alternative should be acceptable regardless of whether the receivable is current or whether it represents an amount due at some more remote date.

Since the Canada Business Act precludes the issue of shares pending payment in full, no amounts pertaining to shares subscribed or subscriptions receivable should appear under the Shareholders' Equity caption on the balance sheet. Any amounts of cash or other assets received as partial payments for shares should therefore be shown among the liabilities, current or non-current depending upon the circumstances. The amounts received from subscribers should be credited to a liability account, Partial Payments Received on Share Subscriptions. When payment has been made in full, the

TRANSACTION	ASSUMING SHARES ARE $10 PAR VALUE		
November 1 Received cash of $10,000 and equipment valued at $20,000 in exchange for 3,000 shares.	Cash	10,000	
	Equipment	20,000	
	Capital Stock		30,000
November 1-30 Received subscriptions for 5,000 shares at 12$1/2$ with 50% down payment, balance payable in 60 days.	Share Subscriptions Receivable	62,500	
	Share Capital Subscribed ...		50,000
	Premium on Capital Stock ..		12,500
	Cash	31,250	
	Share Subscriptions Receivable		31,250
December 1-31 Received balance due on one half of subscriptions and issued stock to the fully paid subscribers, 2,500 shares.	Cash	15,625	
	Share Subscriptions Receivable		15,625
	Share Capital Subscribed	25,000	
	Capital Stock		25,000

liability account is debited for the total consideration, and share capital is credited for the same amount. It should be noted that such accounts as Share Subscriptions Receivable and Shares Subscribed, if maintained, are only memorandum records. Their balances would not appear on the balance sheet, which should reflect only the cash or other assets received from subscribers and the related liability.

Issuance of Share Capital Illustrated

The examples presented above and at the top of page 665 illustrate the entries for the sale of shares when: (1) shares have a par value; (2) shares are without nominal or par value; in each case assuming provincial incorporation. The third example assumes incorporation under the Canada Business Corporations Act.

SUBSCRIPTION DEFAULTS

If a subscriber defaults on a subscription or call by failing to make a payment when it is due, the corporation has several alternatives: (1) return to the subscriber the amount paid, (2) return to the subscriber the amount paid less any reduction in price or expense incurred upon the resale of the shares, (3) declare the full amount paid as forfeited, or (4) issue to the subscriber shares equal to the number paid for in full. The practice followed will depend upon the policy adopted by the corporation within the legal limitations set by the jurisdiction in which it is incorporated, and upon any terms in the subscription contract.

ASSUMING SHARES ARE NO-PAR VALUE			INCORPORATION UNDER CBCA		
Cash	10,000		Cash	10,000	
Equipment	20,000		Equipment	20,000	
Capital Stock		30,000	Capital Stock		30,000
Share Subscriptions Receivable	62,500		Cash	31,250	
Share Capital Subscribed ...		62,500	Partial Payments Received on		
			Share Subscriptions		31,250
Cash	31,250		Cash	15,625	
Share Subscriptions			Partial Payments Received on		
Receivable		31,250	Share Subscriptions		15,625
Cash	15,625		Partial Payments Received on		
Share Subscriptions			Share Subscriptions	31,250	
Receivable		15,625	Capital Stock		31,250
Share Capital Subscribed	31,250				
Capital Stock		31,250			

The Canada Business Corporations Act does not contemplate subscription defaults. In general, certain provincial acts permit a corporation to forfeit shares for the non-payment of either subscriptions or calls. If such should occur, the original subscriber loses all rights and therefore by law is entitled to neither a refund nor a settlement. The corporation has the option of cancelling the forfeited shares or, alternatively, of reissuing them. The usual procedure is to open a suspense account for forfeited shares pending determination of their disposition. If the forfeited shares are cancelled, a gain results in the amount of the payments received by the corporation. If the forfeited shares have a par value, the price at which they may be reissued must be sufficient that, when combined with the amounts originally received, the corporation receives at least the total par value of the shares. Any excess over the total par value may be accounted for as either a gain or as a premium, or be allocated between the two, depending upon the circumstances. In general, shares without nominal or par value may be reissued at virtually any price authorized by the board of directors. The gain, if any, resulting from transactions involving forfeited shares should be accounted for as contributed surplus rather than retained earnings.

The third alternative enumerated above conforms with the general pattern of provincial corporate statutes in Canada. Nonetheless, any of the other alternatives may be adopted as a matter of corporate policy. To illustrate this range of alternatives, assume that one subscriber for 100 shares of $10 par value capital stock with a subscription price of $12.50 defaults after making a 50% down payment. Defaulted shares are subsequently resold at $11. The entries to record the default by the subscriber and the subsequent resale of the defaulted shares would be as follows:

1. *Assuming the amount paid in is returned:*

Share Capital Subscribed	1,000	
Premium on Capital Stock	250	
Share Subscriptions Receivable		625
Cash		625

Cash	1,100	
Capital Stock		1,000
Premium on Capital Stock		100

2. *Assuming the amount paid in less the price reduction on the resale is returned:*

Share Capital Subscribed	1,000	
Premium on Capital Stock	250	
Share Subscriptions Receivable		625
Payable to Defaulting Subscriber (*payment withheld pending resale of the shares*)		625

Cash	1,100	
Payable to Defaulting Subscriber	150	
Capital Stock		1,000
Premium on Capital Stock		250

Payable to Defaulting Subscriber	475	
Cash		475

3. *Assuming the full amount paid in is declared to be forfeited:*

Share Capital Subscribed	1,000	
Premium on Capital Stock	250	
Share Subscriptions Receivable		625
Gain on Forfeited Shares		625

Cash	1,100	
Gain on Forfeited Shares	150	
Capital Stock		1,000
Premium on Capital Stock		250

4. *Assuming shares equal to the number paid for in full are issued:*

Share Capital Subscribed	1,000	
Premium on Capital Stock	125	
Capital Stock		500
Share Subscriptions Receivable		625

Cash	550	
Capital Stock		500
Premium on Capital Stock		50

SALE OF SECURITY UNITS FOR A SINGLE SUM

Corporations sometimes sell for a single sum *security units* consisting of two or more classes of securities. In recording sales of this kind, the sales proceeds must be allocated among the different issues. When a sale consists of two different securities and both have a known market value, the single sum may be allocated to the securities according to their relative fair market values. If only one of the securities has a known market value, the sales price of the other may be determined by subtracting the known value from the sales price of the unit. To illustrate, assume one share of common, par $50, is offered with each $1,000, 6% bond at $1,050. If the common shares are selling for $80 per share, this value is assigned to common and the sales price applicable to the bonds is calculated as follows:

Unit price of $1,000 bond together with 1 share of common	$1,050
Price identified with common share (market price)	80
Price identified with bond	$ 970

A discount should thus be identified with the bonds and a premium with the common shares. The entry to record the sale of 100 units would be:

Cash	105,000	
Discount on Bonds Payable	3,000	
Common Shares, $50 par		5,000
Premium on Common Shares		3,000
Bonds Payable		100,000

If market prices are known for each security, an allocation is necessary. For example, assume two shares of common, par $25, are offered with five shares of preferred, par $100, at $620 per unit.[8] If the preferred and common shares have a per share market price of $102 and $45 respectively, the allocation is calculated as follows:

Market price — preferred shares ($102 × 5)	$510
Market price — common shares ($45 × 2)	90
	$600
Cost allocated to preferred: $510/$600 × $620	$527
Cost allocated to common: $90/$600 × $620	93
	$620

The entry to record the sale of 100 units, consisting of 500 shares of preferred and 200 shares of common, at $620 per unit would be:

Cash .... *100 @ $620*	62,000	
Preferred Shares, $100 par .... *500 @ $100*		50,000
Common Shares, $25 par .... *200 @ $25*		5,000
Premium on Common Shares		4,300
Premium on Preferred Shares		2,700

100 units @ $527   *100 units @ $93*

If neither preferred nor common shares have a market price, it may be necessary to record the acquisition in a combined account until one of the securities develops a market price that can be used to separate the securities.

---

[8] A unit might sell at a price in excess of the market value of its components if the unit provided the only practical way for an investor to become a common shareholder.

SHARE CAPITAL ISSUED FOR CONSIDERATION OTHER THAN CASH

When share capital is issued for consideration in the form of property[9] other than cash, or for services, particular care is required in recording the transaction. When, at the time of the exchange, shares are sold by the corporation for cash or the shares are quoted on the market at a certain price, this price can be used in recording the consideration received and the capital increase. When means for arriving at the cash value of the securities are not available, it will be necessary to arrive at a value for the acquired consideration.

It may be possible to arrive at a satisfactory valuation of property received in exchange for shares through an appraisal by a competent outside authority. But this solution may not be available in arriving at a valuation for consideration in the form of certain services as, for example, promotional services in organizing the corporation.

Normally the board of directors is given the right by law to establish valuations for any non-cash consideration. Such values will stand for all legal purposes in the absence of proof that fraud was involved in the action. The assignment of values by the board of directors should be subject to particularly careful scrutiny. There have been instances where directors have assigned excessive values to the consideration for shares in order to avoid the recognition of a discount on the issue or to improve the company's reported financial position. When the value of the consideration cannot be clearly established and the directors' valuations are used in reporting assets and invested capital, the source of the valuations should be disclosed on the balance sheet. When there is evidence that improper values have been assigned to the consideration received for shares, such values should be restated.

Capital stock is said to be *watered* when assets are overstated and capital items are correspondingly overstated. On the other hand, the balance sheet is said to contain *secret reserves* when there is an understatement of assets or an overstatement of liabilities accompanied by a corresponding understatement of capital. These misstatements may be intentional or unintentional. The accountant cannot condone either overstatement or understatement of net assets and capital. It should be observed once more that any failures in accounting for assets are not limited to the balance sheet: the overstatement of assets will result in understatements of net income as asset cost is assigned to revenue; the understatement of assets will result in overstatements of net income as asset cost is assigned to revenue.

SHARES ISSUED IN EXCHANGE FOR A BUSINESS

A corporation, upon its formation or at some later date, may take over a going business, issuing capital stock in exchange for the properties acquired.

---

[9]Under the Canada Business Corporations Act property received as consideration for the issue of shares cannot include a promissory note or promise to pay. The Act also contains a general prohibition that precludes the corporation from making loans or guarantees in connection with a purchase of the corporation's shares.

In determining the accounting for shares issued in exchange for business assets, the fair market value of the shares, as well as the values of the properties acquired, must be considered. Frequently the value of the shares transferred by the corporation will exceed the value of the net identifiable assets acquired because of the favorable earnings record of the business acquired. If the exchange is recognized as a purchase, which is the usual accounting treatment, the value of the shares in excess of the values assigned to net identifiable assets is recognized as goodwill. On the other hand, if the exchange is recognized as a pooling of interests, neither the revaluation of assets nor the recognition of goodwill is recorded. Assets are stated at the amounts previously reported; shareholders' equity is increased by the amount of the net increase in assets.

INCORPORATION OF A SOLE PROPRIETORSHIP OR PARTNERSHIP

When a sole proprietorship or partnership is incorporated to secure the advantages of the corporate form of organization, the accounting records of the predecessor entity may be used after the changes that have taken place as a result of incorporation have been recorded, or a new set of records may be opened. The accounting procedure to be followed in each instance will be illustrated. Assume Rogers and Jones, partners who share earnings and losses in a ratio of 3:2 respectively, desire to retire from active participation in their business, and they form a corporation to take over partnership assets. The partnership balance sheet just before incorporation on March 15, 1981, appears below.

Rogers and Jones
Balance Sheet
March 15, 1981

Assets			Liabilities and Owners' Equity	
Cash		$ 8,600	Accounts payable	$12,000
Accounts receivable	$15,000		Rogers, capital	50,000
Less allowance for			Jones, capital	16,200
doubtful accounts	400	14,600		
Inventories		20,000		
Equipment	$50,000			
Less accumulated				
depreciation —				
equipment	15,000	35,000		
			Total liabilities and owners'	
Total assets		$78,200	equity	$78,200

The corporation is organized as the Raleigh Corporation and is authorized to issue 25,000 shares of no-par stock. Fifteen thousand shares are sold at $10. The corporation takes over partnership assets other than cash and assumes partnership liabilities in exchange for the remaining 10,000 shares. In taking over net assets, the corporation makes the following adjustments:

1. The allowance for doubtful accounts is increased to $1,000.
2. Inventories are recorded at their present market value of $23,500.
3. Equipment is recorded at its appraised value of $52,500.
4. Accrued liabilities of $400 are recorded.

The 10,000 shares received by the partners are divided as follows: Rogers, 7,500 shares; Jones, 2,500 shares. The cash of $8,600 is then withdrawn by the partners according to the balances remaining in their capital accounts.

TRANSACTION	ENTRY		
(a) To record revaluation of assets upon transfer to Raleigh Corporation, the net gain from revaluation and adjustments of $20,000 being credited to Rogers and Jones in the earnings distribution ratio of 3:2 respectively.	Inventories	3,500	
	Equipment	2,500	
	Accumulated Depreciation—		
	Equipment	15,000	
	Allowance for Doubtful		
	Accounts		600
	Accrued Liabilities		400
	Rogers, Capital		12,000
	Jones, Capital		8,000
(b) To record goodwill as indicated by excess of value of shares issued to partners over the appraised value of net assets transferred:	Goodwill	22,400	
	Rogers, Capital		13,440
	Jones, Capital		8,960
Value of shares issued (10,000 shares at $10, price at which shares are currently being sold) $100,000	*Excluding CASH*		
	① *Equip* 50 + 2.5 = 52.5		
Value of net assets transferred:	*Inv.* 20 + 3.5 = 23.5		
Assets .... $90,000 ①	*A/R* 14.6 - .6 = 14		
Less liabilities .... 12,400 ✓ 77,600			
Goodwill credited to partners in earnings distribution ratio .... $ 22,400	*90*		
(c) To record distribution of shares according to agreement:	Rogers, Capital	75,000	
	Jones, Capital	25,000	
Rogers — 7,500 shares valued at $10 . $ 75,000	Capital Stock		100,000
Jones — 2,500 shares valued at $10 .. $ 25,000			
(d) To record distribution of cash in final settlement of partners' claims according to balances in capital accounts:	Rogers, Capital	440	
	Jones, Capital	8,160	
	Cash		8,600
Rogers Jones			
Capital after adjustment $75,440 $33,160			
Less payment in stock 75,000 25,000			
Balance paid in cash .... $ 440 $ 8,160			
(e) To record sales of 15,000 shares at $10.	Cash	150,000	
	Capital Stock		150,000

If Original Accounts Are Retained

If the partnership accounting records are retained, entries are first made to record the revaluation of assets and adjustments to partners' interests at the date of incorporation. A revaluation account may be debited with losses and credited with gains resulting from revaluations, and the balance in this account may subsequently be closed into the capital accounts using the earnings distribution ratio. However, with relatively few changes in asset balances, gains and losses may be reported directly in the capital accounts. In recording the issuance of shares in exchange for the partners' equities, the partners' capital accounts are debited and Capital Stock is credited. Subsequent corporate transactions are recorded in the old accounts that have become the records for the newly formed corporation. The entries to record the incorporation are shown at the bottom of page 670.

A balance sheet for the corporation after the foregoing transactions is shown below:

Raleigh Corporation Balance Sheet March 15, 1981					
Assets			**Liabilities**		
Cash		$150,000	Accounts payable		$ 12,000
Accounts receivable.	$15,000		Accrued liabilities		400
Less allowance					$ 12,400
for doubtful					
accounts ...	1,000	14,000			
Inventories		23,500	**Shareholders' Equity**		
Equipment		52,500	Capital stock, no-par, 25,000		
Goodwill		22,400	shares authorized and issued .		250,000
			Total liabilities and shareholders'		
Total assets		$262,400	equity		$262,400

If New Accounts Are Opened for the Corporation

If new accounting records are opened for the corporation, all of the accounts of the partnership accounts are closed and partnership assets and liabilities are recorded on the new records. In closing the partnership accounts, entries are made to record the transfer of assets and liabilities to the corporation, the receipt of capital stock, and the distribution of shares and cash in payment of partners' respective interests. If desired, it would be possible to record the revaluation of assets and the recognition of goodwill before recording the transfer of assets and liabilities. Entries to close the partnership of Rogers and Jones may be made as shown on page 672.

TRANSACTION	ENTRY		
To record the transfer of assets and liabilities to Raleigh Corporation, the difference between claim against vendee, $100,000 (10,000 shares of stock valued at $10), and book value of net assets transferred, $57,600, representing gain on sale of business of $42,400. The gain is distributed to partners in the ratio of 3:2 as follows: To Rogers: 3/5 of $42,400 .... $25,440 To Jones: 2/5 of $42,400 .... 16,960 $42,400	Receivable from Raleigh Corporation		
	Accounts Payable	12,000	
	Allowance for Doubtful Accounts	400	
	Accumulated Depreciation — Equipment	15,000	
	Accounts Receivable		15,000
	Inventories		20,000
	Equipment		50,000
	Rogers, Capital		25,440
	Jones, Capital		16,960
To record the receipt of capital stock in payment of net assets transferred.	Shares of Raleigh Corporation	100,000	
	Receivable from Raleigh Corporation		100,000
To record distribution of capital stock according to agreement.	Rogers, Capital	75,000	
	Jones, Capital	25,000	
	Shares of Raleigh Corporation		100,000
To record distribution of cash in final settlement of partners' claims according to balances in capital accounts.	Rogers, Capital	440	
	Jones, Capital	8,160	
	Cash		8,600

The entries on the separate corporation books would be as follows:

TRANSACTION	ENTRY		
To record acquisition of assets and liabilities from Rogers and Jones.	Accounts Receivable	15,000	
	Inventories	23,500	
	Equipment	52,500	
	Goodwill	22,400	
	Allowance for Doubtful Accounts		1,000
	Accounts Payable		12,000
	Accrued Liabilities		400
	Payable to Rogers and Jones		100,000
To record issuance of 10,000 shares of stock in payment of net assets acquired.	Payable to Rogers and Jones	100,000	
	Capital Stock		100,000
To record sale of 15,000 shares of stock for cash.	Cash	150,000	
	Capital Stock		150,000

REACQUISITION AND RETIREMENT OF SHARES

A corporation may have the right to call certain classes of shares for redemption and may choose to exercise this right. In other cases, a corporation may be permitted to purchase its own shares on the market and reissue or cancel the acquired shares. Whether obtained through call for redemption or through purchase on the market, retirement of shares at a cost differing from the original amount accounted for as share capital presents accounting problems.

The reacquisition and retirement of shares cannot be considered to give rise to income or loss. A corporation in issuing shares raises capital which it hopes to employ profitably; in reacquiring and retiring shares it reduces the capital to be employed in subsequent operations. Income or loss arises from the utilization of resources placed in the hands of the corporation, not from capital transactions between the corporation and its shareholders. Since the reacquisition and retirement transaction is clearly a capital transaction, any resulting gain or loss must be excluded from income measurement and also from retained earnings. In some cases, as will be explained later, it may be necessary to reduce retained earnings; however, in no circumstances should retained earnings be increased as the result of a capital transaction.

When a corporation redeems or reacquires its own shares the cost will usually be different from the original amount accounted for as share capital. A cost allocation is obviously required for accounting purposes except where the cost is equal to the original amount accounted for as share capital. If cost is the larger of these two amounts, the *Accounting Recommendations* take the position that the cost should be allocated as follows:

1. To share capital, in an amount equal to the par, stated or assigned value of the shares;
2. Any excess, to contributed surplus to the extent that contributed surplus was created by a net excess of proceeds over cost on cancellation or resale of shares of the same class;
3. Any excess, to contributed surplus in an amount equal to the pro rata share of the portion of contributed surplus that arose from transactions, other than those in (2) above, in the same class of shares;
4. Any excess, to retained earnings.[10]

For purposes of this allocation, it should be obvious that amounts cannot be charged against contributed surplus, except to the extent that related amounts are included in the contributed surplus balance. The allocation recommended by the Accounting Research Committee, first of all requires that any gains included in contributed surplus as a result of prior transac-

---

[10]*CICA Handbook: Accounting Recommendations*, Section 3240, "Share Capital" (Toronto: Canadian Institute of Chartered Accountants, 1972), par. 15.

tions involving cancellation or resale of shares of the same class be reduced to zero. Secondly, contributed surplus should also be reduced to the extent of any amounts included therein as a result of other transactions in the same class of shares. In most cases, such amounts are likely to be premiums received by the corporation when the shares were originally issued. As regards any remaining excess of cost, there is no alternative but to charge it against retained earnings.

In the converse situation where the cost of redemption or reacquisition is less than the original amount accounted for as share capital, the difference, which is a gain, should be credited to contributed surplus.[11] Since no income can result from capital transactions, no gain arising upon the redemption or reacquisition of shares can be included in retained earnings.

The effects of these provisions are illustrated in the following examples. Assume a corporation reports the following balances related to an issue of preferred shares:

Share Capital
    Preferred shares, par $10, 10,000 shares $100,000
Contributed Surplus
    Premium on preferred shares 10,000
    Gain from redemption of preferred shares 2,000

1. Assume the corporation redeems and retires 2,000 shares, or 20% of the preferred shares at $12.50 per share. Reductions are made in the preferred share account for 2,000 shares, par $10, or $20,000, in the gain from redemption of preferred shares for $2,000, and in the premium on preferred shares for a pro rata share of the premium, 20% of $10,000 or $2,000, and the difference between the sum of these accounts and the amount paid is debited to Retained Earnings. The entry, then, is as follows:

Preferred Shares 20,000
Gain from Redemption of Preferred Shares 2,000
Premium on Preferred Shares 2,000
Retained Earnings 1,000
    Cash 25,000

2. Assume the corporation redeems and retires the 2,000 shares of preferred shares at only $9 per share. The preferred share account is reduced by the par value of the shares, $20,000, and the difference between the debit to Preferred Shares and the amount paid is credited to a contributed surplus account. The following entry is made:

Preferred Shares 20,000
    Cash 18,000
    Gain from Redemption of Preferred Shares 2,000

When shares are formally retired or cancelled there is a reduction in the corporate legal or stated capital. In general, company law permits the reduction of legal or stated capital when shares are issued subject to redemption

[11]*Ibid.*, par. 17.

and redemption is made at the price provided by terms of the share issue.

When a company incorporated or continued under the Canada Business Corporations Act redeems or reacquires its own shares, it must meet certain solvency tests as discussed later in the chapter, and it must deduct from the stated capital account for the shares redeemed or reacquired an amount determined by the following formula:

$$\text{Stated Capital before Redemption or Reacquisition} \times \frac{\text{Number of Shares Redeemed or Reacquired}}{\text{Number of Issued Shares Before Redemption or Reacquisition}}$$

This calculation corresponds with the *Accounting Recommendations* which state that "the amounts to be allocated to the share capital account should be based on the average per-share amount in such account for that class of share at the transaction date."[12] Any difference between this amount and the cost of the redemption or reacquisition should be allocated as previously described and illustrated. Since the Canada Business Corporations Act proscribes the issue of par value shares and requires the total proceeds of a share issue to be included in the stated capital account, it follows that any allocation to contributed surplus can only relate to gains included therein as a result of prior redemption or reacquisition transactions.

TREASURY SHARES

Traditionally, company law in Canada has prohibited corporations from purchasing their own common shares. At the same time, the issue of redeemable preferred shares has been permitted for many years.

With the proclamation of the Business Corporations Act on January 1, 1971, Ontario became the first Canadian jurisdiction to permit a corporation to purchase its own shares. The Canada Business Corporations Act has followed Ontario's example, and other provincial jurisdictions also permit this practice. The term *treasury shares* or *treasury stock* is used to describe a corporation's own shares that (1) have been issued as fully paid, (2) have been subsequently reacquired by the issuing company, and (3) have not been cancelled or reissued if such is permitted by the incorporating jurisdiction.

Treasury stock is not an asset. A corporation cannot own a part of itself. Treasury stock has no voting rights, it does not have the preemptive right to participate in additional issuances of shares, nor does it generally participate in cash dividends. When a corporation purchases its own shares, it is returning capital to the shareholders from whom the purchase was made.

Corporations may occasionally show treasury stock on the balance sheet as an asset. The justification for such treatment is that the shares can be

---

[12]*Ibid.*, par. 18.

reissued and are thus comparable to an investment in the shares of another corporation. The same argument might well be extended to authorized but unissued shares, which is obviously indefensible. It is generally agreed among accountants that treasury shares should not be reported as an asset.

There are many reasons a corporation may find it desirable to repurchase its own shares. A survey by the Conference Board cited seven major reasons for repurchasing shares.

1. To obtain shares for executive stock options and other compensation programs.
2. To obtain shares to be used in acquisition.
3. To improve per-share earnings by reducing the number of shares outstanding.
4. To obtain shares for conversion from other securities.
5. To invest surplus cash temporarily.
6. To support the market price of the shares.
7. To increase the rate of debt to equity.[13]

Under the Canada Business Corporations Act a corporation is prohibited from holding shares in itself or in its parent corporation. There are, however, two exceptions to this general rule: (1) it may do so as a legal representative provided that neither the parent corporation nor a subsidiary of either the corporation or its parent has a beneficial interest in the shares; and (2) it may do so by way of security for the purpose of a transaction in the ordinary course of business that includes the lending of money. Regardless of this general prohibition, as modified by the exceptions noted above, a corporation may nonetheless purchase or otherwise reacquire its own shares for various purposes such as the settlement of debts, the elimination of fractional shares, and the fulfilment of contracts. Moreover, in certain circumstances, a corporation may be compelled to purchase its own shares from a dissident shareholder. A corporation is also permitted to accept shares surrendered to it by way of donation.

It should be noted that the purchase or other reacquisition of its own shares by a corporation is subject to any constraints contained in its articles of incorporation, and to a solvency test. In general, the solvency test requires that the corporation's assets be sufficient after paying the purchase price to cover the aggregate of all liabilities and, depending upon the specific transaction, possibly also the stated capital of one or more classes of shares. For example, when the corporation is compelled to acquire shares from a dissident shareholder, the solvency test only requires that assets exceed total liabilities. On the purchase or redemption of its own redeemable shares, or where the purchase or other reacquisition relates to the settlement of debts, elimination of fractional shares or the fulfillment of a contract, the solvency test requires that assets exceed both total liabilities and the amount required

---

[13]Francis J. Walsh, Jr., *Repurchasing Common Stock* (New York: The Conference Board, Inc., 1975), p. 5.

to pay senior shareholders on redemption or liquidation. In the event of any other purchase or reacquisition of shares, the solvency test encompasses the stated capital of all classes of shares. For purposes of applying the solvency test, it is the realizable value of the corporation's assets that is relevant rather than the accounting values.

Except for shares held by virtue of the two exceptions noted previously, the Canada Business Corporations Act requires that treasury shares be cancelled or, if the articles of incorporation limit the number of authorized shares, restored to the status of authorized but unissued shares. Thus, the so-called "treasury shares" cannot be reissued as such, but instead only as a new issue of authorized shares.

Certain provincial jurisdictions still prohibit a corporation from purchasing or otherwise reacquiring its own shares, other than its own redeemable shares. Moreover, legal requirements concerning treasury shares vary widely even in those jurisdictions that permit such transactions. The accounting for treasury share transactions requires careful review of the law applicable to the incorporating jurisdiction. In general, applicable company law may require that the purchase or other reacquisition of shares serve some legitimate corporate purpose and be made without injury or prejudice to the creditors or to remaining shareholders. In some jurisdictions, the legal or stated capital of the corporation cannot be reduced by reacquisition. Accordingly, purchases are limited to a corporation's retained earnings, or in some instances to the sum of retained earnings and contributed surplus balances; thus they reduce the amount otherwise available for distribution as dividends. To illustrate the effects of such legislation, assume the capital of a corporation is as follows:

Capital stock, $10 par, 100,000 shares outstanding	$1,000,000
Retained earnings	500,000

The company can declare dividends of $500,000 and creditors will continue to be safeguarded by the shareholders' investment of $1,000,000 as reported in the capital stock account. But assume the reacquisition by the corporation of part of its outstanding shares for $400,000. If dividends of $500,000 were still permitted and were paid, protection to creditors would shrink to $600,000. With the corporation's ability to pay dividends reduced to $100,000 upon the purchase of treasury shares for $400,000, the original protection to the creditor group is assured; the sum of payments for treasury shares and dividends will not reduce net assets below the reported legal capital of $1,000,000.

Purchase of Treasury Shares

A number of different methods for recording the purchase of treasury shares have been suggested. These methods flow from two general approaches to the problem of treasury share purchases:

1. The purchase of treasury shares may be viewed as the retirement of outstanding shares. (Two transaction method).
2. The purchase of treasury shares may be viewed as giving rise to a capital element whose ultimate disposition still remains to be resolved. (One transaction or cost method)

The two approaches are described in the following sections. Descriptions are accompanied by examples illustrating the different approaches.

First Approach: Treasury Stock Purchase Viewed as Capital Retirement (Two Transaction Method). The purchase of treasury stock may be regarded as the withdrawal of a group of shareholders calling for the cancellation of capital balances identified with this group. It follows that the sale of treasury shares, if permitted by the incorporating jurisdiction, represents the admission of a new group of shareholders calling for entries to give effect to the investment by this group. Thus, there are two separate transactions that must be recorded, the purchase and the sale.

When the purchase of shares is viewed as the retirement of capital, alternate methods may be employed in reporting the reduction in the capital stock balance: (1) the capital stock account may be debited directly; or (2) a treasury stock account may be debited and the balance treated as an offset account to total shareholders' equity; this procedure preserves capital at the legal or stated amount as reported by the capital stock account. The alternate methods are illustrated on pages 680 and 681. The transactions for each case are described below.

Treasury Stock Reported as a Reduction in Capital Stock
Transaction 1:
Treasury stock is acquired at a price exceeding the original issue price. Debits are made to the capital stock and premium accounts and to retained earnings applying the allocations stated on pages 680 and 681. If treasury stock is acquired at a price less than the original issue price, a separate contributed surplus account should be credited for the difference in values.

Transaction 2:
If the treasury stock is sold at more than its par value, Capital Stock is credited at par and a contributed surplus account, Gain from Sale of Treasury Stock, is credited for the excess. If the stock is sold at less than par value, Capital Stock is credited at par and a debit for the difference is made to any contributed surplus from earlier sales or retirements of treasury stock of the same class, or to Retained Earnings.

Treasury Stock Account Used to Report Reduction in Capital Stock
Transaction 1:
When treasury stock is acquired at a price exceeding its par value, a treasury stock account instead of capital stock may be debited for the amount of the

reduction in capital stock. Debits to other paid-in capital and retained earnings balances would be made as described in the preceding section.

Transaction 2:
When the treasury stock is sold, the treasury stock account is credited for the amount at which treasury stock is carried and any difference between the sales price and the carrying amount is treated as described in the preceding section.

Second Approach: Treasury Stock Purchase Viewed as Giving Rise to Capital Element Awaiting Ultimate Disposition (One Transaction or Cost Method). The purchase of treasury shares may be viewed as an application of cash to a capital purpose that has not been finally defined or consummated. Upon the purchase of treasury shares a treasury stock account is debited for the cost of the purchase regardless of whether this cost is more or less than the original issue price. This balance is recognized as a negative shareholders' equity element that does not call for specific identification with share capital, contributed surplus or retained earnings at this time. If treasury stock is subsequently retired, the debit balance in the treasury stock account can be allocated to the appropriate equity balances as in the first approach. If the treasury stock is sold, the difference between the acquisition cost and the selling price is reported as an increase or decrease in shareholders' equity. It is the retirement or the sale of treasury stock that makes possible a determination of the effect of treasury stock transactions upon the elements of shareholders' equity. The application of this method, which is endorsed by the Accounting Research Committee,[14] is illustrated above and on page 681. The transactions in the example are described below.

Transaction 1:
When treasury stock is purchased, it is recorded at its cost regardless of whether this cost is more or less than the original issue price. In a presentation of corporate capital at this time, treasury stock, consisting of a cost unallocated as to the different capital elements, would normally be reported as a subtraction from total shareholders' equity.

Transaction 2:
If treasury stock is sold at more than its cost, Treasury Stock is credited at cost and a contributed surplus account, Gain from Sale of Treasury Stock, is credited. If the stock is sold at less than cost, Treasury Stock is credited at cost and a debit is made to any contributed surplus from either sales or retirements of treasury stock of the same class, or to Retained Earnings.

When retained earnings are restricted for dividend purposes while treasury stock is held, there are several ways these restrictions may be shown on the balance sheet. The most common are (1) as an appropriation of retained earnings, (2) as a parenthetical note in the body of the statement, and (3) as a

---

[14]*CICA Handbook: Accounting Recommendations, Section 3240* (op. cit.), par. 10.

TRANSACTION	FIRST APPROACH: TREASURY STOCK PURCHASE VIEWED AS CAPITAL RETIREMENT	
	TREASURY STOCK PURCHASE REPORTED AS REDUCTION IN CAPITAL STOCK	
1980 Issue of stock, 10,000 shares, $10 par, at 15.	Cash . . . . 150,000 Capital Stock . . . . Premium on Capital Stock	100,000 50,000
Net income for year, $30,000.	Income Summary . . . . 30,000 Retained Earnings	30,000
1981 (1) Reacquisition of 1,000 shares at 16.	Capital Stock . . . . 10,000 Premium on Capital Stock 5,000 Retained Earnings . . . . . . 1,000 Cash	16,000
(2) Sale of treasury stock at 20	Cash . . . . 20,000 Capital Stock . . . . Gain from Sale of Treasury Stock	10,000 10,000
"Shareholders' Equity" section after sale of treasury shares:	Shareholders' Equity Share capital: Capital Stock . . . . Contributed surplus: Premium on capital stock . . . . Gain from sale of treasury stock . . . Retained earnings . . . . Total shareholders' equity	$100,000 45,000 10,000 29,000 $184,000

note to the financial statements. The restriction would be reported regardless of the method used to record the purchase of the shares.

The procedures illustrated in this chapter may be modified to meet existing legal requirements relative to the status of treasury stock and to the effects upon capital balances when treasury stock is sold or retired.[15]

Acquisition of No-par Treasury Shares

Previous discussions assumed the purchase and cancellation or sale of treasury shares with a par value. When there is no par value and the capital stock account has been credited with the proceeds from shares issued at different prices, a special problem arises. Under these circumstances, the capital stock offset is usually considered to be the weighted average price at

---

[15]In practice, the cost method appears to be the preferred method for recording treasury stock. In 1974, 355 of the companies reported in *Accounting Trends & Techniques* used this approach for common stock and 67 used the two transaction method. *Accounting Trends & Techniques* (29th ed.; New York: American Institute of Certified Public Accountants, 1975), p. 244.

FIRST APPROACH: TREASURY STOCK PURCHASE VIEWED AS CAPITAL RETIREMENT		SECOND APPROACH: TREASURY STOCK VIEWED AS GIVING RISE TO CAPITAL ELEMENT AWAITING ULTIMATE DISPOSITION	
TREASURY STOCK ACCOUNT USED TO REPORT REDUCTION IN CAPITAL STOCK			
Cash	150,000	Cash	150,000
Capital Stock	100,000	Capital Stock	100,000
Premium on Capital		Premium on Capital	
Stock	50,000	Stock	50,000
Income Summary	30,000	Income Summary	30,000
Retained Earnings	30,000	Retained Earnings	30,000
Treasury Stock	10,000	Treasury Stock	16,000
Premium on Capital Stock	5,000	Cash	16,000
Retained Earnings	1,000		
Cash	16,000		
Cash	20,000	Cash	20,000
Treasury Stock	10,000	Treasury Stock	16,000
Gain from Sale of		Gain from Sale of	
Treasury Stock	10,000	Treasury Stock	4,000
Shareholders' Equity		Shareholders' Equity	
Share capital:		Share capital:	
Capital stock	$100,000	Capital stock	$100,000
Contributed surplus:		Contributed surplus:	
Premium on capital stock	45,000	Premium on capital stock	50,000
Gain from sale of treasury stock ...	10,000	Gain from sale of treasury stock ...	4,000
Retained earnings	29,000	Retained earnings	30,000
Total shareholders' equity	$184,000	Total shareholders' equity	$184,000

which the shares were originally issued. For example, assume no-par shares issued as follows:

2,000 shares @ $18	$36,000
2,000 shares @ $20	40,000
1,000 shares @ $22	22,000
5,000 shares	$98,000

Further, assume 1,000 shares are reacquired at $16.50 and are to be cancelled, as generally required by the Canada Business Corporations Act.

The transaction is recorded at the average issuing price, calculated as follows:

$98,000 (proceeds from sales) ÷ 5,000 (number of shares issued) = $19.60

The entry to record the acquisition and the reduction of stated capital would be:

Capital Stock	19,600	
Cash		16,500
Gain from Capital Stock Reacquisition		3,100

Conclusions Relative to Treasury Stock Transactions

From the discussion of treasury shares and the presentation of the different methods that may be followed when treasury stock is purchased, the current approaches may be summarized as follows:

1. Treasury stock is rarely includable as an asset on corporation balance sheets and normally does not qualify for dividends.
2. Neither gain nor loss can be recognized on the income statement relative to transactions in a company's own shares.
3. Retained earnings can be decreased as a result of capital transactions; however, retained earnings cannot be increased through such transactions.
4. In some jurisdictions, retained earnings equal to the cost of treasury stock is legally unavailable for dividends. This restriction on retained earnings is reported on the balance sheet by an appropriation of retained earnings, by parenthetical note, or by a note to the financial statements.
5. Total shareholders' equity is not affected by the method used to account for treasury stock; however, the amounts reported as contributed surplus and as retained earnings can be affected by the recording procedure followed.

QUESTIONS

1. Mark Good has been operating a small machine shop for several months. His business has grown, and he has given some thought to incorporating his business. Explain briefly the procedure for incorporation under the Canada Business Corporations Act.

2. Distinguish between the following: (a) a profit corporation and a non-profit corporation, (b) a public or distributing corporation and a private corporation, (c) primary and secondary distribution.

3. What are the basic rights of shareholders?

4. (a) Define legal capital. (b) What limitations may be placed upon the corporation by law to safeguard legal capital? (c) What is a stated capital account?

5. List the advantages and the disadvantages applying to no-par value shares as compared with par-value shares.

6. The Bailey Co. records the discount on common shares issued as organization cost and writes this balance off against periodic revenue. What objections do you have to this treatment?

7. (a) What preferences are usually granted preferred shareholders? (b) What are callable preferred shares? (c) What are convertible preferred shares? (d) Distinguish between cumulative and non-cumulative preferred shares. (e) What limitations on shareholders' rights are generally found in preferred shares?

8. Although subscriptions receivable are generally presented as an asset, the theoretical propriety of such presentation has been questioned and it has been suggested that they be treated as a subtraction item in reporting the shareholders' equity. What questions can you raise as to the general treatment and what support can you provide for the alternative presentation?

9. The Holmes Co. treats proceeds from capital stock subscription defaults as miscellaneous revenue. Would you approve of this practice?

10. (a) What alternatives may a company have when a subscriber defaults on a subscription? (b) What limits the choice between these alternatives?

11. (a) How should cash proceeds be assigned to individual securities when two different securities are sold for a single sum? (b) Would your answer differ if one of the securiites is designated a bonus? Give reasons for your answer.

12. (a) What are "secret reserves"? (b) The treasurer of your client is in favor of secret reserves as a means of achieving "balance sheet conservatism." What is your comment?

13. The Welch Company acquires the assets of the Goodman Company in exchange for 10,000 shares of its common stock, par value $10. (a) Assuming the appraised value of the property acquired exceeds the par value of the shares issued, how would you record the acquisition? (b) Assuming the par value of the shares issued exceeds the appraised value of the property acquired, suggest different methods for recording the acquisition. What factors will determine the method to be used?

14. What entries are made upon incorporation of a partnership when the original partnership books are retained?

15. The controller for the Scott Co. contends that the redemption of preferred shares at less than issue price should be reported as an increase in retained earnings since redemption at more than issue price calls for a decrease in retained earnings. How would you answer the argument?

16. Why might a corporation purchase its own shares?

17. What is the purpose of legislation limiting the purchase by a company of its own shares to its retained earnings balance?

18. The Waters Co. reports treasury stock as a current asset, explaining that it intends to sell the shares soon to acquire working capital. Do you approve of this reporting?

19. (a) Describe two approaches that may be taken in recording the reacquisition of treasury stock. (b) What are the entries in each case assuming: (1) the shares are purchased at more than par value; (2) the shares are purchased at less than par value?

20. There is frequently a difference between the purchase price and the sales price of treasury stock. Why isn't this difference properly shown as an income statement item, especially in view of pronouncements which restrict entries to Retained Earnings?

16-1. The Holt Company pays out dividends at the end of each year as follows: 1979, $75,000; 1980, $120,000; 1981, $280,000. Give the amount to be paid per share on common and preferred stock for each year, assuming capital structures as follows:

(a) 250,000 shares of no-par common; 10,000 shares of no-par, $7, non-cumulative preferred.

(b) 250,000 shares of no-par common; 10,000 shares of no-par, $7, cumulative preferred, dividends three years in arrears at the beginning of 1979.

(c) 250,000 shares of $10 par common; 15,000 shares of no-par, $7, cumulative preferred, no dividends in arrears at the beginning of 1979.

16-2. Ferris Corporation has 400,000 shares of $10 par common and 200,000 shares of $100 par, 7% preferred outstanding. The preferred is cumulative. Give the amounts paid on each share of common and preferred stock each year, assuming dividend distributions as follows: 1979, $700,000; 1980, $2,600,000; 1981, $4,000,000. There were no dividends in arrears at the beginning of 1979.

16-3. The shareholders' equity for the Folsom Corporation on July 1, 1981, is as follows:

Share capital:

Preferred shares, cumulative, no-par value, 10,000 shares outstanding, entitled upon involuntary liquidation to $20 per share plus dividends in arrears amounting to $8 per share on July 1, 1981	$185,000
Common shares, $1 par value, 90,000 shares outstanding	90,000
Premium on common shares	100,000
Retained earnings	28,000
Total shareholders' equity	$403,000

Give the amounts that would be paid to each class of shareholders if the corporation is liquidated on this date, assuming cash available for shareholders after meeting all of the creditors' claims is: (a) $150,000; (b) $250,000; (c) $320,000.

16-4. The Hunter Corporation is organized with authorized capital as follows: 30,000 shares of no-par common and 4,000 shares of 8% preferred, par $100. Give the entries required for each of the following transactions:

(a) Assets formerly owned by E. Hansen are accepted as payment for 10,000 shares of common stock. Assets are recorded at appraised values as follows: land, $30,000; buildings, $35,000; inventories, $95,000.

(b) Remaining common shares are sold at $18.50.

(c) Subscriptions are received for 2,500 shares of preferred stock at 103. A 30% down payment is made on preferred.

(d) One subscriber for 250 shares of preferred defaults and her down payment is retained pending sale of this lot. Remaining subscribers pay the balances due and the stock is issued.

(e) Lot of 250 shares of preferred is sold at 101. In accordance with corporate policy, the loss on resale is charged against the account of the defaulting subscriber, and the down payment less the loss is returned to her.

16-5. On January 1, 1981, Nance Corporation received authorization to issue 100,000 shares of no-par common stock. The stock was offered to subscribers at a subscription price of $50 per share. Subscriptions were recorded by a debit to Subscriptions

Receivable and credits to Common Stock Subscribed. Subsequently a subscriber who had contracted to purchase 500 shares defaulted after paying 50% of the subscription price. Give four methods of accounting for the default, and give the journal entry to record the default under each method.

16-6. The Athey Co. issues 20,000 shares of preferred stock and 90,000 shares of common stock, each without nominal or par value, in exchange for properties appraised at $1,200,000. Give the entry to record the exchange assuming:

(a) No price can be assigned at date of issuance to the preferred or common shares.

(b) Common stock is selling on the market at $11 per share; there was no preferred stock issued prior to this issue.

(c) Common stock is selling on the market at $10 per share; preferred stock is selling on the market at $15 per share.

16-7. $2,000,000 in Dodd Company bonds are sold at 105. The price incudes a bonus of 3 shares of Dodd Company no-par common stock with each $1,000 bond. At the time the bonds were sold, the shares were selling on the market at $23.50 per share. What entry would be made to record the sale of the bonds?

16-8. Clock, Ltd., sells 4,000 shares of its $5 cumulative preferred shares to an investment group for $460,000, giving 1 share of common stock, par $50, as a bonus with every 4 shares of preferred. The market value of the preferred stock immediately following the sale is $103 per share. What is the entry for the sale?

16-9. A balance sheet for Aston and Barker, prepared on June 30, appears below. Partners share earnings and losses in the ratio of 3:1 respectively.

Aston and Barker
Balance Sheet
June 30, 1981

Assets			Liabilities and Owners' Equity	
Cash		$ 2,000	Accounts payable	$ 5,100
Accounts receivable	$ 6,200		Aston, capital	22,500
Less allowance for			Barker, capital	17,300
doubtful accounts ..	600	5,600		
Inventories		10,300		
Equipment	$30,000			
Less accumulated				
depreciation	8,000	22,000		
Goodwill		5,000		
Total assets		$44,900	Total liabilities and owners' equity ...	$44,900

An appraisal of the assets discloses the following current values:

Inventories	$14,800
Equipment	26,000

Aston and Barker decide to incorporate as Bushnell Co.; 7,000 shares of $2 par common stock are issued to the partners in exchange for partnership assets other than cash. The corporation also agrees to assume partnership obligations. On this date the corporation stock has a market value of $7 per share. In dissolving the partnership,

Aston agrees to take 4,000 shares and Barker, 3,000 shares. The partnership cash is then appropriately divided between the partners. Give the entries to record the foregoing in the accounts of the partnership and in the new accounts of the corporations.

16-10. The Willich Co. reported the following balances related to an issue of common shares:

Common Shares, $10 par, 25,000 shares issued and outstanding $250,000
Premium on Common Shares 50,000

On June 1, 1981, and December 31, 1981, the company purchased and retired 5,000 shares at $14 and 10,000 shares at $9 respectively. Give the entries to record the acquisition and retirement of the common shares.

16-11. Assume the Willich Co. is incorporated under the Canada Business Corporations Act, and on June 1, 1981 has a balance in the stated capital account for its common shares of $300,000. Otherwise, the facts are identical to those presented in Exercise 16-10. Give the entries to record the acquisition and retirement of the common shares.

16-12. The Yoshi Company issued 20,000 shares, no-par value, at $32 and 40,000 shares at $50. During 1981, 4,000 shares were reacquired at $42. Assume treasury shares are to be carried at the weighted average price per share. Prepare the journal entry to record the reacquisition.

PROBLEMS

16-1A. The Yoko Co. was organized on May 25, 1981, and was authorized to issue 250,000 shares of no-par common stock and 10,000 shares of $4 preferred stock.

The following were the company's capital stock transactions through September 15, 1981.

June 1 Issued 50,000 shares of common stock to an investment group at $20.
June 15 Assets were obtained from Tom Co. in exchange for 75,000 shares of common stock. The assets were appraised as follows:

Merchandise inventory $300,000
Furniture and fixtures 75,000
Machinery and equipment 475,000
Land 375,000

July 1 Subscriptions were received for 100,000 shares of common stock at $25 and for 5,000 shares of preferred at $55; each class is to be paid for in two instalments, 25% on the date of subscription and 75% within 90 days.
Sept. 15 The second instalments on the common stock and preferred stock were paid in full and the stock was issued.

Instructions:
(1) Give the journal entries to record the preceding transactions.
(2) Prepare a balance sheet based on results of the preceding transactions.

16-2A. The Chambers Co., organized on April 10, 1981, was authorized to issue shares as follows:

100,000 shares of $10 par common stock
5,000 shares of 8% preferred stock with a par value of $100

Capital stock transactions through September 15, 1981, were as follows:

May 15   Subscriptions were received for 50,000 shares of common stock at $15 on the following terms: 10% was paid in cash at the time of subscription, the balance being payable in three equal instalments due on the fifteenth day of each succeeding month. *$75,000* *$225,000/installment*

June 1   All of the preferred stock was sold to an investment company for cash at $96 and stock was issued.

June 15 The first instalment on subscriptions to 48,800 shares was collected. Terms of the subscription contract provided that defaulting subscribers have 30 days in which to make payment and obtain reinstatement; failure to make payment within the specified period will result in the forfeiture of amounts already paid in.

July 15 The second instalment on common subscriptions was collected. Collections included receipt of the first and second instalment on 200 shares from subscribers who defaulted on their first instalment; however, subscribers to 250 shares defaulted in addition to subscribers already in default.

Aug. 15 The third instalment on common subscriptions was collected. Collections included receipt of the second and third instalment from subscribers to 200 shares who defaulted on their second instalment. Stock certificates were issued to fully paid subscribers.

Sept. 1 Stock in default was sold to an investment company at 13.

Instructions:
(1) Give the journal entries to record these transactions.
(2) Prepare the "Shareholders' Equity" section of the balance sheet on September 15, 1981.

16-3A. The Addison Company had the following account balances in its balance sheet at December 31, 1981, the end of its first year of operations. All shares were sold on a subscription basis, and the applicable laws permit the corporation to retain all partial subscriptions paid by defaulting subscribers.

Common Share Subscriptions Receivable	$50,000
Common Shares, $25 par	25,000
Common Shares Subscribed	75,000
Premium on Common Shares	20,000
Preferred 8% Shares, $100 par	50,000
Premium on Prefered Shares	25,000
Capital from Default on Preferred Stock (100 shares)	5,000
Preference 10% Shares, $50 par	10,000
Retained Earnings	10,000

The reported net income for 1981 was $20,000.

Instructions:
From the above data, reconstruct in summary form the journal entries to record all transactions involving the company's shareholders. Indicate the amount of dividends distributed to each class of shareholders.

16-4A. Owen and Thomas, partners, who share earnings and losses in a ratio of 3:2 respectively, wish to retire from active participation in their manufacturing business and decide to form a corporation to take over the partnership assets. The partnership balance sheet prepared on March 1, 1981, appears below.

Owen and Thomas
Balance Sheet
March 1, 1981

Assets			Liabilities and Owners' Equity	
Cash		$ 26,000	Notes payable	$ 42,000
Notes receivable		49,000	Accounts payable	80,000
Accounts receivable		60,000	Owen, capital	75,000
Inventories		70,500	Thomas, capital	87,500
Land		30,000		
Buildings	$50,000			
Less accumulated depreciation — buildings	32,000	18,000		
Machinery	$80,000			
Less accumulated depreciation — machinery	49,000	31,000	Total liabilities and owners'	
Total assets		$284,500	equity	$284,500

The partners, together with Baldwin and Casper who wish to join the new enterprise, agree to the following:

(a) The corporation shall be known as the Super Scope Company, and its authorized shares shall consist of 100,000 shares of common stock, $10 par, and 7,500 shares of preferred 7% stock, $50 par.

(b) Partnership assets other than cash are to be transferred to the corporation and the liabilities are to be assumed by the corporation. The corporation is to issue 4,000 shares of preferred stock in payment for net assets acquired. (It is assumed the shares are worth par value.) The shares are to be divided equally between Owen and Thomas, and the partnership cash is then to be withdrawn by the partners in settlement of their interests. Partnership properties other than land, buildings, and machinery are to be recorded on the corporation records at carrying values. Land, buildings, and machinery items are to be recorded at current fair values as follows:

Land	$42,000
Buildings	22,000
Machinery	32,000

(c) Baldwin will take charge of the organization of the corporation and will be allowed 2,000 shares of common stock in full payment for his services.

(d) Casper, who owns valuable patent rights, will be given 8,000 shares of common stock upon transfer of these rights to the corporation.

The Super Scope Company is incorporated on March 1 and the foregoing transactions are completed.

Instructions:

(1) Prepare the entries to record the transfer of assets and liabilities to the

corporation, and the distribution of shares and cash in the partnership accounts.

(2) Prepare the entries for separate corporation accounts.

(3) Prepare a balance sheet for the corporation as at March 1, 1981, after the foregoing transactions have been recorded.

16-5A. Hank, Ike and Jake, partners sharing earnings and losses 3:3:2 respectively, draw up the following partnership balance sheet on November 1, 1981:

Hank, Ike and Jake
Balance Sheet
November 1, 1981

Assets			Liabilities and Owners' Equity	
Cash		$ 31,450	Notes payable	$ 15,000
Accounts receivable		35,000	Accounts payable	21,400
Merchandise inventory ..		62,000	Hank, capital	40,250
Furniture and fixtures	$21,450		Ike, capital	35,000
Less accumulated			Jake, capital	31,000
depreciation —				
furniture and				
fixtures	7,250	14,200	Total liabilities and owners'	
Total assets		$142,650	equity	$142,650

The partners incorporate on this date as HIJ, Inc., with authorized capital as follows:

Preferred stock, 5,000 shares, $25 par
Common stock, 20,000 shares, $10 par

The partners agree to the following:

(a) Adjustments are to be made in asset values as follows:
  (1) An allowance for doubtful accounts is to be established at 5% of accounts receivable.
  (2) Furniture and fixtures are to be restated at present replacement cost of $30,000 less accumulated depreciation of 30% on replacement cost.
  (3) Expenses of $550 have been prepaid and are to be recognized as an asset.
(b) Partners are to be paid for their partnership interest as follows, it being assumed that stock has a value equal to its par:
  (1) 1,200 shares of preferred are to be allowed to each partner.
  (2) Remaining capital interests are to be paid for with common stock, in even multiples of 100 shares, each partner to be paid cash for his or her capital balance in excess of the highest 100-share multiple that can be issued.

The above adjustments and transactions are completed and shares not required for the settlement of the partners' interests are immediately sold for $25 in the case of the preferred shares and $10 for the common shares.

Instructions:

(1) Prepare journal entries to record the incorporation, assuming that it is to be reflected in the existing partnership accounts. No separate accounting records are to be opened for the corporation.
(2) Prepare a balance sheet for the corporation. (Assume transactions are completed on November 1.)

16-6A. Howard & Sanders Electrical Contracting Co., a partnership, and Grover Wholesale Electricians' Hardware Co., a proprietorship, have agreed to transfer the assets and liabilities of their companies on November 1, 1981, to a newly chartered corporation, Major Electrical, Inc., in exchange for Major Electrical, Inc.'s shares. The agreement provides:

(a) Preferred shares shall be issued at par value of $100 per share to each of the parties in exchange for his or her share of the net assets (assets minus liabilities) transferred to Major Electrical, Inc. Jill Grover shall receive at least 900 shares of preferred stock and Bill Howard and Joe Sanders shall receive together a total of not more than 480 shares of preferred stock. Cash shall be contributed to the companies by the respective parties or distributed by the companies to the parties to accomplish the proper net asset transfers.

(b) Common shares shall be issued in a total amount equal to the earnings expected to be contributed by the companies to Major Electrical, Inc., for the next five years to the extent that the earnings of each company respectively, based on the past three calendar years, exceed the average earnings of its industry. The common shares shall be issued without nominal or par value to the owners of the companies in the ratio of the amount that each company's average earnings are expected to exceed the average industry earnings of the company with the lesser earnings. A par value of $10 for the common shares had been considered but was rejected.

Additional information incudes the following:

(c) Trial balances at October 31, 1981, for both companies are given below.

Grover Hardware Co. and
Howard & Sanders Co.
Trial Balances
October 31, 1981

	Grover Hardware		Howard & Sanders	
Cash	17,000		20,700	
Accounts Receivable	43,000			
Allowance for Doubtful Accounts		3,000		
Inventory	63,000		3,500	
Prepaid Expenses	2,000		1,300	
Land, Buildings, and Equipment	44,000		26,000	
Accumulated Depr. — Buildings and Equip......		27,000		12,000
Accounts Payable		54,000		
Accrued Liabilities		4,000		
Deposit on Contract				2,500
Grover, Capital		75,000		
Grover, Drawing	5,000			
Howard, Capital				11,300
Sanders, Capital				7,700
Revenues		200,000		70,000
Cost of Producing Revenues	160,000		31,000	
Howard, Salary			4,000	
Sanders, Salary			3,000	
Operating Expenses	29,000		14,000	
	363,000	363,000	03,500,	103,500

(d) Howard and Sanders maintain the partnership accounts on the cash basis of accounting and Grover maintains her proprietorship records on the accrual basis. Major Electrical, Inc.'s accounts are to be maintained on the accrual basis. Items not recorded on Howard and Sanders' accounts at October 31, 1981, follow:

Accounts receivable	$20,300
Allowance for doubtful accounts	400
Unbilled contract in progress	8,000
Prepaid expenses	1,200
Accounts payable	6,200
Accrued liabilities	2,400

All accounts receivable are for jobs completed and billed. The unbilled contract in progress is for a $10,000 contract which was 80% complete and upon which a $2,500 deposit was paid to Howard & Sanders when the contract was signed. Cash payments for work on the contract to October 31, 1981, total $3,500 and were recorded in the partnership accounts as inventory. Accounts payable include $2,800 owed to Grover Wholesale Electricians' Hardware Co.

(e) The partnership agreement specified Bill Howard would receive a salary of $12,000 per year and share 60% of any earnings or loss and Joe Sanders would receive a salary of $9,000 per year and share 40% of any earnings or loss. Each partner will receive the same annual salary from the corporation.

(f) Jill Grover withdraws an amount each month from her proprietorship equal to a normal salary. Grover's annual salary from the corporation will be $15,000.

(g) Based on the past three years, Jill Grover could expect her proprietorship to earn an average of $39,000 per year for the next five years before any salary allowance with average expected sales of $600,000 per year. The industry average net income (after deducting all salaries and income tax) for electrical hardware wholesale for the next five years is expected to be 1.35% of sales.

(h) Based on the past three years, Bill Howard and Joe Sanders could expect their partnership to earn an average of $55,500 per year for the next five years before deducting partners' salaries with average expected revenues of $240,000 per year. The industry average net income (after deducting all salaries and income tax) for electrical contractors for the next five years is expected to be 7.5% of sales.

(i) The parties expect the corporation to pay income tax at an average of 40% during the next five years.

Instructions:
Complete a work sheet with the columnar headings indicated below to determine the opening account balances of Major Electrical, Inc., giving effect to the agreement to transfer the assets and liabilities and issue stock.

Your work sheet would include space to list the names of accounts followed by a pair of columns for each of the following headings:

Grover Hardware Trial Balance
Howard & Sanders Trial Balance
Grover Hardware Adjusting and Closing Entries
Howard & Sanders Adjusting and Closing Entries
Major Electrical, Inc., Opening Accounts Balances.

Prepare supporting schedules computing (1) any cash contributions or distributions necessary and preferred shares to be issued to each party and (2) the amounts of common shares to be issued to each party. Formal adjusting and closing entries and formal financial statements are not required. (AICPA adapted)

16-7A. The capital accounts of the Harris Company were as follows on June 1, 1981.

Preferred 8% Shares, $50 par, 10,000 shares issued and outstanding .	$ 500,000
Premium on Preferred Shares	10,000
Common Shares, $15 par, 80,000 shares issued and outstanding	1,200,000
Premium on Common Shares	240,000
Retained Earnings	160,000

During the remainder of 1981, the Harris Company called the preferred stock at $55 per share and then retired the shares. Also, the company reacquired 30,000 shares of common stock at $14, and 20,000 of the reacquired common shares were reissued (resold) at $20 per share.

Instructions:

(1) Give the entries to record the reacquisition and retirement of the preferred shares and the acquisition and reissue of the common shares assuming the common stock is viewed as a capital retirement and the treasury stock account is to be debited.

(2) Give the entry to record the acquisition and resale of the common shares assuming the common stock purchase is viewed as a capital element awaiting ultimate disposition.

16-8A. The shareholders' equity section of CBCA Limited's balance sheet as at October 31, 1981, appeared as follows:

Share Capital

Preferred shares, no par value, 30,000 shares issued and outstanding .	$330,000
Common shares, no par value, 30,000 shares issued and outstanding .	150,000
Retained earnings	120,000
	$600,000

The company is incorporated under the Canada Business Corporations Act, and its articles make no provision for authorized capital. On November 1, 1981, CBCA Limited reacquired, for cash, 500 preferred shares at $9 per share, and 1,000 common shares at $20 per share.

Instructions:

(1) Give journal entries to record the reacquisition of its shares by CBCA Limited.

(2) Prepare the shareholders' equity section of CBCA Limited's balance sheet for November 1, 1981, as it would appear after the reacquisition of its shares.

(SMA adapted)

16-9A. Rank Limited, incorporated in Ontario, had 1,000 shares of $100 par value common shares outstanding, originally issued at $103. On January 15, Rank purchased 20 shares of its own stock at $105. On March 1st, 10 of the treasury shares were sold at $100. Retained earnings at March 1st were $10,000, without any treasury stock transactions. However, Rank Limited follows the policy of appropriating retained earnings in its accounting for treasury stock transactions.

Instructions:

(1) Give journal entries to record treasury stock transactions.

(2) Prepare the shareholders' equity section of the balance sheet at March 1st, after giving effect to the treasury stock transactions.

(CGA adapted)

16-10A. The Hansen Company has two classes of capital stock outstanding: 8%, $10 par preferred and $50 par common. During the fiscal year ending November 30, 1981, the company was active in transactions affecting the shareholders' equity. The following summarizes these transactions:

Type of Transaction	Number of Shares	Price per Share	
(a) Issue of preferred	10,000	$14	140,000
(b) Issue of common	35,000	50	1750,000
(c) Retirement of preferred	2,000	16	32,000
(d) Purchase of treasury stock — common (reported at cost)	5,000	70	350,000
(e) Stock split — common (par value reduced to $25)	2 for 1		
(f) Reissue of treasury stock — common	5,000	45	225,000

Balances of the accounts in the Shareholders' Equity" section on November 30, 1980, were:

Preferred Shares, 50,000 shares	$ 500,000
Common Shares, 100,000 shares	5,000,000
Premium on Preferred Shares	200,000
Premium on Common Shares	1,000,000
Retained Earnings	520,000

Dividends were paid at the end of the fiscal year on the common at $1 per share, and on the preferred at the preferred rate. Net income for the year was $500,000.

Instructions:
Based upon the above data, prepare the "Shareholders' Equity" section of the balance sheet as of November 30, 1981. (Note: A work sheet beginning with November 30, 1980 balances and providing for transactions for the current year will facilitate the preparation of this section of the balance sheet.)

16-11A. Transactions of the Shrub Company during 1981, the first year of operations, that affected its shareholders' equity are given below.
(a) Sold 20,000 shares of 9% preferred, $10 par, at $14.
(b) Sold 50,000 shares of $25 par common at $27.
(c) Purchased and retired 4,000 shares of preferred stock at $15.
(d) Purchased 6,000 shares of its own common stock at $29.
(e) Sold 1,000 shares of treasury stock at $31.
No dividends were declared in 1981 and net income for 1981 was $150,000.

Instructions:
(1) Record each of the above transactions. Assume treasury stock acquisitions are recorded at cost.
(2) Give the entries for (d) and (e) assuming treasury stock acquisitions are reported as capital stock retirement.
(3) Prepare the "Shareholders' Equity" section of the balance sheet assuming treasury shares are recorded at cost and assuming retained earnings restrictions are shown by parenthetical remarks.

(4) Prepare the "Shareholders' Equity" section of the balance sheet assuming treasury shares are recorded at par value and assuming retained earnings restrictions are shown as appropriations.

16-12A. *Fedco Limited was federally incorporated a number of years ago, but elected to continue under the Canada Business Corporations Act effective December 31, 1977. In connection with its decision to apply for continuance, it was decided to remove the ceiling on the number of shares the corporation could issue, and to transfer premiums received on previous issues of par value shares into stated capital. The shareholders' equity section of the corporation's balance sheet as at December 31, 1977, before giving effect to continuance, is presented below:

Share Capital
Authorized

20,000 5% cumulative preferred shares of $50 par value, redeemable at $102 per share		$1,000,000
100,000 common shares of $10 par value		1,000,000
		$2,000,000
Issued		
10,000 preferred shares		$ 500,000
50,000 common shares		500,000
		$1,000,000
Contributed Surplus		
Premium on preferred shares	$ 40,000	
Premium on common shares	100,000	
Donated property	10,000	150,000
Retained Earnings		400,000
		$1,550,000

Assume the following events occurred in 1978:

(a) The articles of incorporation were amended on February 1, 1978, to designate the existing class of preferred shares as Class C shares, and to create two new classes of preferred shares:

    (i) 100,000 Class A shares carrying a cumulative dividend entitlement of $7 per share and redeemable on demand of the shareholder at net asset value per share, plus 10%. (Net asset value is defined at the net book value at the end of the previous quarter in which redemption is demanded.)

    (ii) Class B shares, issuable in one or more series at the discretion of the directors, but no share of any series may have a dividend entitlement of more than $12 cumulatively. None of the shares are redeemable at the election of the shareholders. The directors may at any time redeem shares of any series which have been given a dividend entitlement of $9 per share or more. The shares of any series carrying a dividend entitlement of less than $9 per share are only redeemable by special resolution of the common shareholders. Any share entitled to a dividend of $12 per share shall be redeemed no later than two years after the date of its issue. The purchase or redemption price of the shares of any series may not exceed the weighted average of the shares of that series issued before that time.

---

*Adapted from an illustration developed by Robert W. V. Dickerson, Farris, Vaughan, Wills, and Murphy, Vancouver, British Columbia.

(iii) Any shares redeemed before December 31st in any year are not entitled to a dividend in respect of that year.

(b) On March 1, 1978, 8,000 Class A shares were issued at $30 per share. 240,000 (A)

(c) Also, on March 1, 1978, the directors designated the following series of Class B shares and obtained the certificate of amendment.

Series 1 — $ 9 dividend

Series 2 — $ 8 dividend

Series 3 — $12 dividend (the articles of amendment provide that the number of shares in series 3 may not exceed 2,000 shares).

(d) On March 27, 1978, the directors issued the following Class B shares:

Series 1 — 40,000 shares at $120 each   4,800,000 (B-1)

Series 2 — 9,000 shares at $130 each   1,170,000

Series 3 — 1,000 shares at $150 each   150,000

(e) On April 15, 1978, the following shares were issued:

4,000 Class A shares at $90 per share   360,000 (A)

1,000 Class B series 1 shares at $100 per share (B-1)

$$\frac{3}{12} \times 600,000 = 150,000$$

(f) On June 30, 1978, a shareholder holding 3,000 Class A shares demanded redemption. The net asset value at the time, as defined, was $112 per share.

$112 + .10 (112)

123.20

369,600

(g) On July 31, 1978, the directors decided to redeem 4,000 Class B series shares at a redemption price of $120 per share. Stated capital is to be reduced by the weighted average of the issue price of Class B shares. (Round to the nearest dollar.)   = 480,000 $$\frac{A}{41} \times 4,900,000 = 478,049$$

(h) On August 31, 1978, the articles were amended to allow conversion of the Class C shares into common shares on a one-for-one basis. On September 30, 1978, a holder of 1,000 Class C shares elected to convert.

Throughout 1978, the corporation's liabilities were $600,000, and net income for the year ended December 31, 1978, was $75,000. No dividends were declared.

Instructions:

(1) Prepare the "Shareholders' Equity" section of Fedco Ltd.'s balance sheet as at December 31, 1977, giving effect to the corporation's continuance under the Canada Business Corporations Act.

(2) Prepare the "Shareholders' Equity" section of Fedco Ltd.'s balance sheet as at December 31, 1978.

17 SHARE CAPITAL TRANSACTIONS, CONTRIBUTED SURPLUS, AND RETAINED EARNINGS

Shareholders' equity originates from different sources which need to be clearly identified on the balance sheet. This information serves to clarify the nature of the components that comprise shareholders' equity, and also must be known to determine the amounts legally distributable by way of dividends. The two primary sources of shareholders' equity are: (1) investments by the shareholders and (2) retention of net assets resulting from earnings.

1. *Investments by the shareholders.* Net assets received by the corporation in exchange for its shares are the source of the company's invested capital. Invested capital is divided into (a) an amount forming the corporate legal or stated capital, and (b) the balance not classified as legal capital. The amount of the investment representing the legal or stated capital is reported as share capital. The balance, if any, is reported as *contributed surplus*.
2. *Retention of net assets resulting from earnings.* Changes in net assets arising from the sale of goods and services give rise to earnings and losses, which may include other realized gains and losses, and are summarized as *retained earnings*. When a portion of retained earnings is unavailable for dividends, it is referred to as *appropriated* or *reserved;* any balance is then regarded as *unappropriated* or *free*. A debit balance in retained earnings resulting from losses is termed a *deficit* and is subtracted in arriving at the total shareholders' equity.

Individual accounts should be maintained for each separate source within each of the classifications listed. For example, separate accounts should be provided for preferred shares and for common shares, for a premium on preferred shares, and for a premium on common shares, for a retained earnings appropriation related to a bond redemption fund and for a retained earnings appropriation related to the acquisition of treasury stock. In reporting the shareholders' equity on the balance sheet, individual contributed surplus and retained earnings balances are frequently combined and presented under captions that are really headings. Detail may then be provided in the notes to the financial statements. Whether reported separately or in combined form, the objective is to designate the source of the shareholders' equity. It should be noted that the individual accounts are not related to specific assets.

Although in financial statements there are variations in the amount of detail presented and in the descriptive captions employed, sources of significant amounts should be adequately disclosed. In accordance with pronouncements of the Accounting Research Committee, the shareholders' equity section of the balance sheet should be classified in the manner set forth in the following diagram. The objective of this classification is to emphasize the sources of the various components of shareholders' equity. At the same time, the financial statement presentation of shareholders' equity must conform with various legal requirements. It should be noted that the *Accounting Recommendations* are not intended to override the requirements of a governing statute.

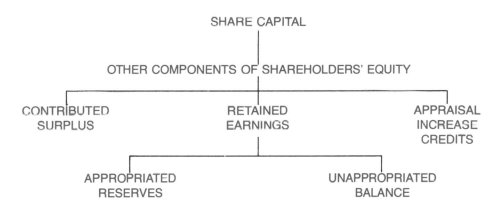

Use of the term "surplus" as a single-word designation should be avoided in financial statements. Moreover, the term "surplus" when combined with such words as "capital," "paid-in," or even "earned," can be a source of inconsistency and ambiguity in many financial statements. Since these terms are still occasionally encountered in corporate financial reports, their significance should be understood.

COMPONENTS OF SHAREHOLDERS' EQUITY

The components of shareholders' equity are set out in the above diagram. Each will be briefly described in the paragraphs that follow.

Share Capital

The nature of share capital and a wide range of transactions concerning the issue, redemption, and reacquisition of shares, comprised the subject matter of the preceding chapter. In addition, shares may be issued as a result of conversions and, in general, corporations are permitted to receive shares by way of gift or donation. Stock rights and options, and stock splits and reverse stock splits, are events and transactions that need to be understood in terms of their impact on the accounting and disclosure requirements pertaining to both the share capital accounts and to the other components of shareholders' equity. These several topics are part of the subject matter of this chapter.

In financial statements there are numerous variations in the terminology and presentation of share capital. It is not uncommon for this part of the balance sheet to be headed Capital, or Capital Stock, rather than Share Capital. Since some of the amounts received from shareholders, for example, a premium on shares, may not constitute legal capital, use of the term "paid-in capital" as a heading should be avoided.

Full particulars of authorized share capital must appear in the financial statements, including a brief description of the rights and privileges attached to each class of shares. In addition, issued share capital must be disclosed both as to the number of shares issued and the total amount of legal capital pertaining thereto. If shares have been issued since the date of the last balance sheet, this fact must be disclosed indicating both the number of shares issued and the consideration received. Other required disclosures include dividends in arrears on cumulative preferred shares, and commitments relating to shares, for example, the number of shares reserved to meet any conversion or option privileges.[1] Disclosures relating to share capital may appear on the face of the balance sheet, in notes to the financial statements, or a combination of these methods may be used.

Contributed Surplus

The contributed surplus classification is used to report (1) amounts received from shareholders that do not constitute legal or stated capital and (2) capital received from other sources, for example, donated property.

Contributed surplus from shareholders includes such items as premiums on shares, proceeds on the sale of treasury shares and forfeited shares, proceeds on the sale of donated shares, and credits resulting from the redemption or conversion of shares at less than the amounts set up as share capital. Some jurisdictions permit part of the proceeds received on the issuance of no-par shares to be excluded from legal capital. These amounts, known as distributable surplus, also constitute part of contributed surplus.[2]

[1]*CICA Handbook: Accounting Recommendations, Section 3240*, "Share Capital" (Toronto: Canadian Institute of Chartered Accountants, 1972).

[2]*CICA Handbook: Accounting Recommendations, Section 3250*, "Surplus" (Toronto: Canadian Institute of Chartered Accountants, 1968), par. .05.

Donations of property, including a corporation's own shares, are indeed rare. Also, on rare occasions, assistance may be received from a government which holds an equity position by virtue of being a shareholder.[3] In any of these rare circumstances, the amounts involved constitute capital received from the other sources and therefore form part of contributed surplus.

In most cases, contributed surplus is presented as a line item on the face of the balance sheet; the detail is then disclosed in notes to the financial statements. Alternatively, the individual components of contributed surplus may be shown as line items. Any changes in the amounts of contributed surplus since the date of the last balance sheet should be adequately disclosed.

Although it is common practice to report contributed surplus on the balance sheet as a single line item, separate accounts should be maintained to identify sources. Various sources of contributed surplus and the accounts summarizing them are listed below.

SOURCE OF CONTRIBUTED SURPLUS	INDIVIDUAL ACCOUNTS
Sale of shares at more than par value	Premium on Capital Stock
Subscription defaults resulting in forfeiture of amounts paid in	Gain on Forfeited Shares
Reacquisition or redemption of shares at less than original issue price	Gain from Capital Stock Reacquisition (or Gain from Capital Stock Redemption)
Conversion of outstanding shares into a new issue with a smaller total par value	Capital Received from Conversion of Capital Stock
Reduction in corporate legal or stated capital as a result of recapitalization	Capital from Reduction in Value Assigned to Capital Stock
Sale of treasury shares at more than cost	Gain from Sale of Treasury Stock
Donation of shares or properties or forgiveness of corporate indebtedness by shareholders	Donated Capital
Assistance from a government by virtue of its position as a shareholder	Donated Capital

Debits should be made to contributed surplus accounts only when (1) transactions may be regarded as the direct opposite of a previous transaction that resulted in a credit to contributed surplus, or (2) there is an express authorization by the board of directors for such reduction. To illustrate (1) above, the redemption and the retirement of preferred shares may properly be recorded by cancellation of the preferred stock balance as well as any premium balance relating to the original issue; all reference to contributed surplus relating to the preferred shares is thus cancelled with the redemption

---

[3]*CICA Handbook: Accounting Recommendations, Section 3800*, "Accounting for Government Assistance" (Toronto: Canadian Institute of Chartered Accountants, 1975), par. .16.

of this class of shares. To illustrate (2), authorization by the board of directors for the capitalization of a portion of a particular contributed surplus balance would call for a reduction in the contributed surplus account and an increase in the share capital account. Contributed surplus balances should not be charged with losses whether from normal operations or from extraordinary sources, nor should contributed surplus be used for the cancellation of a deficit in the absence of formal action as may be permitted or required by the incorporating jurisdiction.

As noted in Chapter 16, the Canada Business Corporations Act effectively eliminates contributed surplus except as may result from certain capital transactions, or where property is donated to the corporation. The capital transactions that may trigger contributed surplus are likely to be rare, but may occasionally arise when a corporation purchases, redeems or otherwise reacquires its own issued shares. To illustrate, assume the stated capital account of a corporation has a balance of $300,000 from the issue of 10,000 shares, and the corporation purchases 1,000 shares for $20,000. Further, assume the corporation can meet the applicable solvency test. The required reduction in the stated capital account is determined as follows:

$$\text{Stated Capital before Purchase of Shares} \times \frac{\text{Number of Shares Purchased}}{\substack{\text{Number of Issued Shares} \\ \text{Before Purchase}}}$$

$$\$300,000 \times \frac{1,000}{10,000} \qquad \$30,000$$

The purchase of the shares can now be recorded:

Capital Stock	$30,000	
Gain from Capital Stock Reacquisition		10,000
Cash		20,000
To record purchase of shares.		

It should be noted that the reduction in the stated capital account is for the average per share amount included therein. If, as may often be the case, this average per share amount is less than the price paid to purchase, redeem or otherwise reacquire shares, the resulting debit should first be charged against contributed surplus to the extent of any gains included therein as a result of capital transactions pertaining to the same class of shares, or otherwise, be charged to retained earnings. However, if the Court orders a corporation to refund to a shareholder any part of the price paid for shares, subject to the corporation meeting the applicable solvency test, the stated capital account must be reduced by the amount refunded.

When a company that continues under the Canada Business Corporations Act has contributed surplus arising from a premium on the issue of par value shares, while the amount of the premium would be deemed to be part of stated capital, it may nonetheless be shown on the corporation's balance sheet as contributed surplus. This transitional provision eliminates any need to alter existing accounts, and thereby avoids potential income tax problems.

The availability as a basis for dividends of capital not designated as legal capital depends upon the laws of the incorporating jurisdiction. In the absence of legal restrictions, contributed surplus can be used as a basis for dividends. When capital other than retained earnings is used as a basis for dividends, shareholders should be informed by the corporation concerning the source of such distribution because shareholders have the right to assume that dividends represent distributions of earnings unless they are notified to the contrary.

Retained Earnings

Retained earnings is essentially the meeting place of the balance sheet accounts and the income statement accounts. In successive periods retained earnings are increased by income and decreased by losses and dividends. As a result, the retained earnings balance represents the net accumulated un-distributed earnings of the corporation.

The retained earnings account is also affected by items defined as prior period adjustments. It should never be increased as a result of a company dealing in its own shares; however, as indicated previously, it may be decreased. In earlier times, the term "earned surplus" was widely used as the title for this balance sheet classification. The designation "retained earnings" is preferable, however, because it is more accurately descriptive.[4]

If the retained earnings account were affected only by income or losses and dividends, there would be little confusion in its interpretation. But a number of factors tend to complicate the nature of retained earnings. Among these factors are: transactions between the corporation and its shareholders affecting retained earnings; stock dividends which require the capitalization of earnings; recapitalizations resulting in transfers between retained earnings and capital stock; legal restrictions upon retained earnings to protect the shareholder and creditor groups; and contractual limitations upon the use of retained earnings for dividends. The nature of retained earnings is frequently misunderstood and this misunderstanding may lead to seriously misleading inferences in reading the balance sheet.

The earnings of a corporation may be distributed to shareholders or retained to provide for expansion. When earnings are retained, they may be appropriated so as to be reported as unavailable for dividend declaration. Appropriations, known also as reserves, are cancelled after the purpose of the appropriation has been fulfilled. When operating losses or other debits to the

---

[4]*CICA Handbook: Accounting Recommendations, Section 3250*, op. cit., par. .03.

retained earnings account produce a debit balance in this account, the debit balance, as previously noted, is referred to as a *deficit*.

On the balance sheet, the amount shown as retained earnings includes the unappropriated balance, which should be supported by a separate statement or schedule, and any appropriations. It should be noted that appropriations may be disclosed as separate line items on the balance sheet, usually under the "Retained Earnings" caption, or in notes to the financial statements.

Appraisal Increase Credits

This classification is used to report amounts relating to the adjustment of fixed asset values on the basis of an appraisal. Since the valuation of fixed assets at appraised values constitutes a departure from the cost concept, appraisal increase credits are indeed rare. According to the pronouncements of the Accounting Research Committee, an appraisal increase credit can remain on the balance sheet indefinitely, or be transferred to retained earnings in amounts not exceeding realization through sale or depreciation.[5]

SHARES ISSUED ON CONVERSIONS

Shareholders may be permitted by the terms of their share agreement or by special action of the corporation to exchange their holdings for shares of other classes. No gain or loss is recognized on these conversions because it is the exchange of one equity for another. In certain instances, the exchanges may affect only capital stock and contributed surplus; in other instances, the exchanges may also affect retained earnings.

To illustrate the different conditions, assume that the capital of the Ottawa Corporation on December 31, 1981, is as follows:

Preferred shares, $100 par, 10,000 shares	$1,000,000
Premium on preferred shares	100,000
Common shares $25 par, 100,000 shares	2,500,000
Premium on common shares	500,000
Retained earnings	1,000,000

Preferred shares are convertible into common shares at any time at the option of the shareholder.

Case 1 — Assume conditions of conversion permit the exchange of each share of preferred for 4 shares of common. On December 31, 1981, 1,000 shares of preferred are exchanged on the above basis. The amount originally paid for the preferred, $110,000, is now the consideration identified with 4,000 shares of common with a total value of $100,000. The conversion is recorded as follows:

---

[5]*CICA Handbook: Accounting Recommendations, Section 3270*, "Appraisal Increase Credits" (Toronto: Canadian Institute of Chartered Accountants, 1968), par. .02.

Preferred Shares, $100 par	100,000	
Premium on Preferred Shares	10,000	
Common shares, $25 par		100,000
Premium on Common Shares		10,000

Case 2 — Assume conditions of conversion permit the exchange of each share of preferred for 5 shares of common. In converting 1,000 shares of preferred for common, an increase in the common shares of $125,000 must be recognized although it is accompanied by a decrease in the preferred equity of only $110,000; the increase in the legal capital related to the new issue can be accomplished only by a debit to Retained Earnings. The conversion, then, is recorded as follows:

Preferred Shares, $100 par	100,000	
Premium on Preferred Shares	10,000	
Retained Earnings	15,000	
Common Shares, $25 par		125,000

Under the Canada Business Corporations Act conversions reduce the stated capital account for one class of shares, and increase the stated capital account of another class. The amount of the reduction is determined by use of the formula presented on page 700; this amount is also the increase in stated capital for the shares issued.

The problems relating to the conversion of bonds were described in Chapter 13. When either shares or bonds have conversion rights, the corporation must be in a position to issue shares of the required class. Unissued or, depending upon the laws of the incorporating jurisdiction, reacquired shares may be held by the corporation for this purpose. Detailed information should be given on the balance sheet relative to security conversion features, as well as the means for meeting conversion requirements.

DONATED SHARES

Shares may be donated to a corporation by its shareholders for various reasons, such as to raise working capital through their sale or to eliminate a deficit. Ordinarily, all shareholders participate in the donation, each donating a certain percentage of holdings so that relative ownership in the corporation remains unchanged.

Donations of shares sometimes arise where large blocks of shares were originally issued in exchange for properties of uncertain values for example, mining properties, patents, and leaseholds. Such a donation may represent a sacrifice on the part of the donors of the shares; frequently, however, it represents no more than the return of an overissue.

Assuming the assets of the corporation have been fairly valued, the sale of donated shares is recorded by a debit to Cash and a credit to Donated Capital, which is a part of contributed surplus. If assets of the corporation have been overvalued, it would be improper to recognize an increase in capital arising from the sale of donated shares. Under these circumstances, the sale price for the shares should be used as a basis for restating corporate assets and shareholders' equity.

To illustrate the latter instance, assume the Bonanza Mining Co. is formed to take over the mining properties of partners Clark and Davis and the corporation issues 10,000 shares without nominal or par value to the partners in exchange for the properties. A value of $250,000 is assigned to the properties and an entry is made for the acquisition as follows:

Mining Properties	250,000	
Capital Stock		250,000

Shortly after corporate formation, Clark and Davis donate 4,000 shares to the corporation, and the corporation sells these for $15 per share. If $15 can be regarded as a measure of the fair value of the shares exchanged for the properties, properties should be restated at $90,000 or $15 × 6,000, the number of shares actually exchanged for the properties. Upon the sale of the donated shares, then, entries should be made (1) to correct the property account and capital stock for both the overissue of shares and the property overvaluation, and (2) to record the sale of the donated shares. These entries are:

Capital Stock	160,000	
Mining Properties		160,000
Cash	60,000	
Capital Stock		60,000

The balance sheet for the corporation would now show the following balances:

Cash	$60,000	Capital stock, no-par, 10,000	
Mining properties	90,000	Shares outstanding	$150,000

When shares are donated so that a corporation may cancel a deficit, the corporation should take formal action to retire donated shares. Upon retirement Capital Stock is debited for the decrease in legal capital and contributed surplus is credited. Subject to applicable legal requirements, the deficit may then be applied against the additional contributed surplus balance.

STOCK RIGHTS AND OPTIONS

As discussed in Chapter 10, a corporation may grant rights and options to buy its shares. These grants generally arise under the following circumstances:

1. A corporation requiring additional capital may offer shareholders subscrip-

tion rights to make the purchase of additional shares attractive, or to comply with preemptive rights that may apply to existing shareholders.

2. A corporation may provide subscription rights or warrants with the issue of various classes of securities to promote the sale of these securities.
3. A corporation may offer promoters, officers, or employees subscription rights or options as compensation for services or other contributions.

Rights to purchase shares are evidenced by certificates called *options* or *warrants*. The rights enable their owners to purchase shares at a specified price or a variable price dependent upon future events. The period for exercise is usually limited. Because the rights are usually represented by separate certificates, they can have a market value and be traded on the stock exchanges, subject to any restrictions on their transferability. The rights have a value because of the difference between the exercise price of the right as compared with a higher market value for the security, either present or potential.

Rights Issued to Existing Shareholders

When rights are issued to shareholders, only a memorandum entry is made by the issuing corporation stating the number of shares that may be claimed under the outstanding rights. This information is required so the corporation may reserve sufficient shares to meet the exercise of the rights. Upon surrender of the rights and payments as specified under the terms of the rights, shares are issued. At this time a memorandum entry is made to record the decrease in the number of rights outstanding accompanied by an entry to record the issue of the shares. The entry for the issue depends upon the amount paid for the shares:

1. When the cash received on the exercise of rights is less than the par value, if any, the difference must be debited to Retained Earnings; retained earnings are permanently capitalized under these circumstances.
2. When the cash received is equal to the par value of the shares, Cash is debited and Capital Stock is credited.
3. When the cash received is more than the par value of the shares, the excess is recorded as a credit to a premium account and should be shown on the balance sheet as contributed surplus.

Information concerning outstanding rights should be reported on the balance sheet so the effects of their exercise may be ascertained.

Rights Issued with Various Classes of Securities

When rights are issued with various classes of securities as a unit, such as with debt or preferred shares, separate purchase warrants are issued to accompany the basic security. From the viewpoint of accounting theory, the issue price of the unit should be allocated between the basic security and the purchase warrants and the amount attributable to detachable purchase warrants should be classified as part of owner's equity. The value to be assigned to the warrants is the relative fair market value of the warrants in relation to the fair market value of the security without the warrants plus the fair market value of the warrants. Thus, if a market value exists for the purchase warrants at the date of issue, a separate equity account should be credited with that portion of the issue price assignable to the warrants. If the rights are exercised, the value assigned to the common shares is the value assigned to the warrants plus the cash proceeds received on the issue of the shares. If the rights are allowed to lapse because of a change in market conditions, the value assigned to the warrants should be transferred to contributed surplus.

Accounting for rights attached to a preferred issue is illustrated as follows: assume the Matson Co. sells 1,000 shares of $50 par preferred stock for $60 per share. As an incentive, Matson Co. gives the purchaser separate warrants enabling holders to subscribe to 1,000 shares of $20 par common stock for $25 per share. The rights expire after one year. Immediately following the issue of the shares the purchase warrants are selling at $5 per warrant. Assume the fair market value of the preferred shares without the warrant attached is $55. The proceeds of $60,000 should be allocated as follows:

$$\text{Value Assigned to the Purchase Warrants} \ldots \frac{\$5}{\$55 + \$5} \times \$60,000 = \$5,000$$

The entry to record the sale of the preferred shares with detachable warrants is as follows:

Cash	60,000	
Preferred Shares, $50 par		50,000
Premium on Preferred Shares		5,000
Common Share Purchase Warrants		5,000

If the rights are exercised, the entry to record the issue of common shares would be as follows:

Common Share Purchase Warrants	5,000	
Cash	25,000	
Common Shares		20,000
Premium on Common Shares		10,000

This entry would be the same regardless of the market price of the common shares on the date of issue.

If the rights in the above example were allowed to lapse, the following entry is recommended.

Common Share Purchase Warrants	5,000	
Contributed Surplus from Lapsed Warrants		5,000

Rights or Options Issued to Employees

Many corporations have adopted various plans, contracts, and other agreements giving employees the opportunity to purchase shares in their employer corporation. These plans may be part of a corporate program to secure equity capital and, at the same time, spread ownership to the employee group. They may also be intended as a form of compensation to employees for services rendered to the corporation. Depending upon the principal objectives of the corporation in initiating the plan, plans may be classified as *non-compensatory* or *compensatory*. No special accounting problems arise, if the plan is classified as non-compensatory — no compensation is recognized by the employer corporation when the shares are issued — the cash price is the issue price. If the plan is compensatory, compensation may or may not be recorded depending upon the provisions of the plan.

Except for recommending descriptive disclosures, the Accounting Research Committee has yet to issue any recommendations pertaining to stock rights or options. In the United States, the Accounting Principles Board in Opinion No. 25 identified four characteristics essential in a non-compensatory program.

1. Substantially all full-time employees who meet limited employment qualifications may participate.
2. Shares are offered to eligible employees equally or based on a uniform percentage of salary or wages.
3. The time period for exercise of an option or purchase right is limited to a reasonable period.
4. The discount from the market price of the shares is no greater than would be reasonable in an offer of shares to shareholders or others.[6]

The major accounting questions associated with compensatory plans are: (1) what amount, if any, should be recognized as compensation, and (2) what periods should be charged with the cost? Opinion No. 25 specifies that "compensation for services that a corporation receives as consideration for stock issued through employee stock option plans should be measured by the quoted market price of the stock at the measurement date, less the amount, if any, that the employee is required to pay."[7]

If a quoted market price is not available, the best estimate of the market value should be used. Most of the accounting controversy with compensatory plans has been concentrated on determining the measurement date. The AICPA Committee on Accounting Procedures has pointed out that six dates may be considered for this purpose: (1) the date of the adoption of an option plan; (2) the date on which an option is granted to a specific individual; (3) the date on which the grantee has performed any conditions precedent

---

[6]*Opinions of the Accounting Principles Board, No. 25*, "Accounting for Stock Issued to Employees" (New York: American Institute of Certified Public Accountants, 1972), par. 7.

[7]*Ibid.*, par. 10.

to exercise of the option; (4) the date on which the grantee may first exercise the option; (5) the date on which the option is exercised by the grantee; and (6) the date on which the grantee disposes of the shares acquired.[8] Additional date options are available if the purchase plan includes variable factors depending on future events; for example, a plan that awards a variable number of shares as an option with a variable option price.

The Accounting Principles Board has considered these options and has defined the measurement date as the first date on which are known both (1) the number of shares that an individual employee is entitled to receive, and (2) the option or purchase price, if any.[9] For many plans, the measurement date is the date of the option agreement. The premise here is that this is the date on which the corporation acknowledges the claim and takes action precluding any alternative use of the shares covered by the option. Dates prior to this time are not pertinent: plans calling for services are no more than proposed courses of action until services are formally recognized and the liability becomes effective. Dates after this time are not pertinent: changes in the values of the compensation award after its accrual are beyond the scope of the plan and represent matters of concern only to the grantee. Thus, a corporation should recognize compensation expense for compensatory plans unless the employee pays an amount at least equal to the quoted market price at the measurement date.

The other date for valuing an option that has received strong support from some members of the accounting profession is the exercisable date, the date on which the grantee may first exercise the option. The argument supporting this view is that prior to the exercisable date, the employee has no right to exercise the option and thus is unable to appraise its value. The rights are given with the anticipation of a rise in market and if such condition does occur, the intended compensation is realized. A difficult measurement problem exists with the exercisable date, however, since the market price at the exercisable date is unknown until it is reached. Thus, the total amount of compensation is uncertain and it would be difficult to determine compensation for the periods between the measurement date and the exercisable date. This difficulty has resulted in the rejection of this alternative.

If compensation expense is to be recognized, the remaining accounting problem is the determination of what period should be charged for the cost. Generally, the compensation should be charged to the current and future periods in which the employee performs the services for which the shares are issued. Past periods should not be adjusted. When several periods of employment are involved before the shares are issued, the employer corporation should accrue compensation expense in each period involved.

---

[8]*Accounting Research and Terminology Bulletins — Final Edition*, "No. 43, Restatement and Revision of Accounting Research Bulletins," *op. cit.*, Ch. 13, sec. B, par. 6.

[9]*Opinions of the Accounting Principles Board, No. 25, op. cit.*, par. 10b.

Illustrative Entries for Recording Compensatory Stock Options. Accounting for compensatory plans can be illustrated by the following example:

Assume on December 31, 1978, the board of directors of the Aredo Corporation authorizes the grant of non-transferable stock options to supplement the salaries of certain executives. Options permit the purchase of 10,000 shares of $10 par common at a price of $47.50. The shares are currently selling at $50. Options can be exercised beginning January 1, 1981, but only if executives are still in the employ of the company; options expire at the end of 1982. All of the options are exercised on December 31, 1981, when the shares are quoted on the market at $60.

The value of the stock options at the date of the grant (compensation expense) is determined as follows:

Market value of common stock on December 31, 1978,
10,000 shares at $50	$500,000
Option price, 10,000 shares at $47.50	475,000
Value of stock options (compensation expense)	$25,000

The terms of the grant indicate that the services are being performed for the period from the grant date to the exercisable date, or for 1979 and 1980.

The following entries are made by the corporation to record the grant of the options, the annual accrual of option rights, and the exercise of the options.

TRANSACTION	ENTRY
December 31, 1978 Grant of non-transferable stock options.	(Memorandum entry) Granted non-transferable options to executives for the purchase of 10,000 shares of common stock at $47.50. Options are exercisable beginning January 1, 1981, providing officers are in the employ of the company on that date. Options expire on December 31, 1982. Value of options on December 31, 1978 is $25,000 (market value is $500,000; option price, $475,000).

December 31, 1979
To record compensation and option credit accrual for 1979: value of stock options, $25,000; period of service covered by plan, 1979 and 1980; cost assigned to 1979: 1/2 × $25,000 = $12,500.
	Executive Compensation Expense. 12,500
	   Credit Under Stock Option Plan 12,500
	  ↑
	Show under Contributed Surplus

December 31, 1980 To record compensation and option credit accrual for 1980: 1/2 × $25,000 = $12,500.	Executive Compensation Expense. 12,500 Credit Under Stock Option Plan 12,500

December 31, 1981
To record exercise of stock options: cash received for shares, 10,000 shares at $47.50, or $475,000; par value of shares issued, 10,000 shares at $10, or $100,000.
	Cash 475,000
	Credit Under Stock Option Plan .. 25,000
	   Common Shares 100,000
	   Premium on Common Shares .. 400,000

The accrued compensation reported in Credit Under Stock Option Plan may be reported as part of contributed surplus because it will be liquidated by the issuance of shares. If options expire through a failure of employees to meet the conditions of the option or through changes in the price of the shares making exercise of options unattractive, the balance of the account should be eliminated by decreasing compensation expense in the period of forfeiture.[10]

Disclosure of Stock Options

When stock option plans are in existence, disclosure should be made as to the status of the option or plan at the end of the reporting period, including the number of shares under option, the option price, and the number of shares which were exercisable. Information on options exercised should also be provided, including the number of shares exercised and the option price.

STOCK SPLITS AND REVERSE STOCK SPLITS

When the market price of shares is high and it is felt that a lower price will result in a better market and a wider distribution of ownership, a corporation may authorize that the shares outstanding be replaced by a larger number of shares. For example, 100,000 shares of stock, par value $100, are called in and exchanged for 500,000 shares of stock, par value $20. Each shareholder receives 5 new shares for each share owned. The resulting increase in shares outstanding is known as a *stock split* or *stock split-up*. The reverse procedure, replacement of shares outstanding by a smaller number of shares, may be desirable when the price of shares is low and it is felt there may be certain advantages in increasing the price for shares. The reduction of shares outstanding by combining shares is referred to as a *reverse stock split* or a *stock split-down*.

After a stock split or reverse stock split, the capital stock balance remains the same; however, the change in the number of shares outstanding is accompanied by a change in the par value, if any, of the shares. It would normally be desirable to establish a new account reporting the nature and the amount of the shares issued. In any event, notations will be required in the subsidiary shareholders' ledger or by the registrar and transfer agent to report the change in the number of shares held by each shareholder.

Stock splits are sometimes effected by issuing a large stock dividend. In this case, the par value, if any, of the shares is not changed and an amount equal to the par value of the newly issued shares or the money value of the stock dividend is transferred to the share capital account from either re-

---

[10]*Ibid.*, par. 15.

tained earnings or from contributed surplus or, in part, from both. A further discussion of this type of stock split is included in the discussion of stock dividends presented later in the chapter.

RECAPITALIZATIONS

Corporate recapitalization occurs when an entire issue of shares is changed by appropriate action of the corporation. In some jurisdictions, recapitalizations, including changes in the legal capital, are possible by action of the board of directors and shareholders; in other jurisdictions, recapitalizations may also require the approval of creditors and administrative authorities.

A common type of recapitalization is a change from par to no-par-value shares. If the capital stock balance is to remain the same after the change, the original capital stock account is closed and an account for the new issue is opened. Any premium relating to the original issue should be transferred to some other contributed surplus account appropriately titled. If the capital stock balance is to exceed the consideration received on the original issue of the shares, a new capital stock account is credited for the value assigned to the new issue, original balances are closed, and the retained earnings account is debited for the difference. If the capital stock balance is to be reduced, the original account, as well as any premium account, is closed, a new capital stock account is credited for the value assigned to the new stock, and an appropriately titled contributed surplus account is credited for the difference.

A situation may arise in which a corporation's properties were acquired at costs that do not permit earnings under current conditions. There may also be a deficit from previous operations or a retained earnings balance insufficient to absorb a reduction in the carrying value of the property items. Yet such a reduction may be warranted by current conditions and indeed may be necessary if the corporation is to be able to report profitable operations in future periods.

Depending upon applicable company law, a corporation under such circumstances may elect to write down property items and to accompany such action with a restatement of its capital structure, eliminating the resulting deficit after the write-off. The elimination of a deficit through a restatement of invested capital balances providing, in effect, a fresh start accounting-wise for the corporation, is sometimes called a *reorganization* or *corporate readjustment*.

To illustrate the nature of a reorganization, assume the Baldwin Corporation has suffered losses from operations for some time and both current and future revenues appear to be insufficient to cover the depreciation on properties acquired when prices were considerably higher than at present. The corporation decides upon a restatement of assets and also the restatement of capital to remove the deficit and make possible the declaration of dividends upon a return to profitable operations. A balance sheet for the corporation just prior to this action is given below.

Baldwin Corporation
Balance Sheet
June 30, 1981

Assets			Liabilities and Shareholders' Equity		
Current assets		$ 250,000	Liabilities		$ 300,000
Land, buildings, and			Capital stock, $10		
equipment	$1,500,000		par, 100,000		
Less accumulated			shares	$1,000,000	
depreciation	600,000	900,000	Less deficit	150,000	850,000
			Total liabilities and		
Total assets		$1,150,000	shareholders' equity ..		$1,150,000

The reorganization is to be accomplished as follows:

1. Land, buildings, and equipment are to be reduced to their present fair market value of $600,000 by reductions in the asset and accumulated depreciation balances of $33^1/_3\%$.
2. Capital stock is to be reduced to a par value of $5, $500,000 in capital stock thus being converted into contributed surplus.
3. The deficit of $450,000 ($150,000 as reported on the balance sheet increased by $300,000 arising from the write-down of land, buildings, and equipment) is to be applied against the contributed surplus resulting from the reduction of the par value of the shares.

Entries to record the changes follow:

TRANSACTION	ENTRY		

(1) To write down land, buildings, and equipment and accumulated depreciation balances by $33^1/_3\%$.	Retained Earnings (Deficit) ...
	 Accumulated Depreciation ...
	   Land, Buildings, and Equip-
	     ment ....
		300,000
		 200,000
			
			 500,000

(2) To reduce the capital stock balance from $10 par to $5 par and to establish contributed surplus from reduction in par value.	Capital Stock, $10 par ....
	   Capital Stock, $5 par ......
	   Contributed Surplus from
	     Reduction in Par Value ....
		1,000,000	
			 500,000
			
			 500,000

(3) To apply the deficit after asset devaluation against contributed surplus from reduction in par value.	Contributed Surplus from Re-
	   duction in Par Value ....
	   Retained Earnings (Deficit) .
		450,000	
			
			 450,000

The balance sheet after the reorganization is shown below:

Baldwin Corporation				
Balance Sheet				
June 30, 1981				

Assets			Liabilities and Shareholders' Equity	
Current assets		$250,000	Liabilities	$300,000
Land, buildings, and			Capital stock, $5 par, 100,000	
equipment	$1,000,000		shares	500,000
Less accumulated			Contributed surplus from reduction	
depreciation	400,000	600,000	in par value	50,000
			Total liabilities and shareholders'	
Total assets		$850,000	equity	$850,000

Following the reorganization, accounting for the corporation's operations is similar to that for a new company. Earnings subsequent to the reorganization, however, should be accumulated in a *dated retained earnings* account. On future balance sheets, retained earnings dated as of the time of reorganization will inform readers of the date of such action and of the fresh start in earnings accumulation. The *Accounting Recommendations* require that the description of retained earnings on successive balance sheets for at least three years include the date of the reorganization.[11]

DIVIDENDS

Dividends are distributions to the shareholders of a corporation in proportion to the number of shares held by them. Distributions may take the form of (1) cash, (2) other assets, (3) evidences of corporate indebtedness, in effect, deferred cash dividends, and (4) shares of a corporation's own stock. All dividends involve reductions in retained earnings except liquidating dividends, which represent a return to shareholders of a portion or all of the corporate legal capital and call for reductions in invested capital.

Under the Canada Business Corporations Act, dividend distributions are subject to a solvency test which requires the realizable value of the corporation's assets to exceed the aggregate of both its total liabilities and the stated capital of all classes of shares. The application of a solvency test should preclude the occasional practice of declaring dividends from recent or current periods' incomes when there is a deficit.

Use of the term *dividend* without qualification normally implies the distribution of cash. Dividends in a form other than cash should be designated by their special form, and dividends declared from a source other than retained earnings should carry a description of their special origin. The terms *property dividend, scrip dividend*, and *stock dividend* suggest distributions of a special form; designations such as *liquidating dividend* and *dividend distribution of contributed surplus* identify the special origin of the distribution.

---

[11]*CICA Handbook: Accounting Recommendations*, Section 3250, *op. cit.*, par. .12.

"Dividends paid out of retained earnings" is an expression frequently encountered. Accuracy, however, would require the statement that dividends are paid out of cash, which serves to reduce retained earnings. Earnings of the corporation increase net assets and also shareholders' equity. Dividend distributions represent no more than asset withdrawals that reduce net assets and shareholders' equity.

Among the powers delegated by the shareholders to the board of directors is control of dividend policy. Whether dividends shall or shall not be paid, as well as the nature and the amount of dividends are matters the board determines. In declaring dividends, the board of directors must observe legal requirements governing the maintenance of legal or stated capital. These requirements vary among different jurisidictions. In addition, the board of directors must consider the financial aspects of dividend distributions — the corporate asset position, present asset requirements, and future asset requirements. The board of directors must answer two questions: Do we have the legal right to declare a dividend? Is such a distribution financially sound?

When a dividend is legally declared and announced, its revocation is not possible. In the event of corporate insolvency prior to payment of the dividend, shareholders have claims to the dividend as a creditor group, and as an ownership group to any assets remaining after all corporate liabilities have been paid. A dividend that was illegally declared is revocable; in the event of insolvency, such action is nullified and shareholders participate in asset distributions only after creditors have been paid in full.

The Formal Dividend Announcement

Three dates are relevant to the declaration and payment of dividends: (1) date of declaration, (2) date for determining shareholders of record, (3) date of payment. Dividends are payable to shareholders of record as of a date following the date of declaration and preceding the date of payment. The liability for dividends payable is recorded on the declaration date and is cancelled on the payment date. No entry is required on the record date, but a list of the shareholders is made as of the close of business on this date. This list identifies the shareholders who will receive dividends on the payment date. The shares sell *ex-dividend* on the day following the date of record. The purchaser of shares selling ex-dividend (shares purchased in the period between the date of record and the date of payment) does not receive the dividend.

Cash Dividends

The most common type of dividend is a *cash dividend*. For the corporation, these dividends involve a reduction in both retained earnings and cash.

A current liability for dividends payable is recognized on the declaration date; this is cancelled when dividend cheques are sent to shareholders. Entries to record the declaration and the payment of a cash dividend follow:

Retained Earnings	100,000	
Dividends Payable		100,000
Dividends Payable	100,000	
Cash		100,000

Scrip Dividends

If a corporation has retained earnings that may be used as a basis for dividend declaration but does not have sufficient funds at the time for a cash dividend, it may declare a *scrip dividend* which consists of a written promise to pay certain amounts at some future date. The corporation can thus take regular dividend action although it is temporarily short of cash. Shareholders, in turn, are provided currently with a negotiable instrument they may sell for cash if they wish. Such dividends are rare because for most corporations borrowing to pay a dividend should be a more attractive alternative.

Property Dividends

A distribution to sharcholders that is payable in assets other than cash is generally referred to as a *property dividend*. Frequently the assets to be distributed are securities of other companies owned by the corporation. The corporation thus transfers to its shareholders its ownership interest in such securities. Again, such dividends are rare.

This transfer is sometimes referred to as a *non-reciprocal transfer to owners* inasmuch as nothing is received by the corporation in return for the distribution to shareholders. This type of transfer should be recorded using the fair market value (as at the date of declaration) of the assets distributed; a gain or loss is recognized for any difference between the carrying value in the accounts of the issuing company and the fair market value of the assets.[12]

Stock Dividends

A corporation may distribute to shareholders additional shares of the company's own stock as a stock dividend. A stock dividend permits the corporation to retain within the business net assets produced by earnings while at the same time offering shareholders some tangible evidence of the growth of their equity.

A stock dividend usually involves (1) the capitalization of retained earn-

---

[12]*Opinions of the Accounting Principles Board, No. 29*, "Accounting for Nonmonetary Transactions" (New York: American Institute of Certified Public Accountants, 1973), par. 18.

ings, and (2) a distribution of common shares to common shareholders. Thus a portion of retained earnings is no longer available for distribution, and the legal capital of the corporation is increased. In recording the dividend, a debit is made to Retained Earnings and a credit to Share Capital and possibly also a credit to Contributed Surplus. A stock dividend may be viewed as consisting, in effect, of two transactions: (1) the payment by the corporation of a cash dividend; and (2) the return of the cash to the corporation in exchange for capital stock.

In distributing shares as a dividend, the issuing corporation must meet legal requirements relative to the amounts to be capitalized. If shares have a par value, an amount equal to the par value of the shares issued will have to be transferred to capital stock; if the shares are without nominal or par value, the laws of the incorporating jurisdiction may leave determination of the amounts to be transferred to the corporate directors.

Although the minimum amounts to be transferred to legal or stated capital balances upon the issuance of additional shares are set by law, the board of directors is not prevented from going beyond minimum legal requirements. For example, assume that $100 par value shares were originally issued at $120. Legal requirements may call for the capitalization of no more than the par value of the additional shares issued. The board of directors, however, in order to preserve the premium relationship, may authorize a transfer from retained earnings of $120 per share; for every share issued, share capital would be increased $100 and a premium account $20.

The subject of stock dividends has not, as yet, been considered by the Accounting Research Committee. In the United States, however, the Committee on Accounting Procedure of the AICPA, in commenting on the issuance by a corporation of its own common shares to its common shareholders, has indicated that proper corporate policy in certain situations would call for the capitalization of an amount equal to the fair value of the shares issued. The Committee pointed out:

> . . . a stock dividend does not, in fact, give rise to any change whatsoever in either the corporation's assets or its respective shareholders' proportionate interests therein. However, it cannot fail to be recognized that, merely as a consequence of the expressed purpose of the transaction and its characterization as a *dividend* in related notices to shareholders and the public at large, many recipients of stock dividends look upon them as distributions of corporate earnings and usually in an amount equivalent to the fair value of the additional shares received. Furthermore, it is to be presumed that such views of recipients are materially strengthened in those instances, which are by far the most numerous, where the issuances are so small in comparison with the shares previously outstanding that they do not have any apparent effect upon the share market price and, consequently, the market value of the shares previously held remains substantially unchanged. The committee therefore believes that where these circumstances exist the corporation should in the public interest account for the transaction by transferring from earned surplus to the category of

permanent capitalization (represented by the capital stock and capital surplus accounts) an amount equal to the fair value of the additional shares issued. Unless this is done, the amount of earnings which the shareholder may believe to have been distributed to him will be left, except to the extent otherwise dictated by legal requirements, in earned surplus subject to possible further similar stock issuances or cash distributions.[13]

However, the Committee indicated that certain circumstances would suggest that retained earnings be debited for no more than the par value of the shares or other value as required by law. The Committee stated:

> ... Where the number of additional shares issued as a stock dividend is so great that it has, or may reasonably be expected to have, the effect of materially reducing the share market value, the committee believes that the implications and possible constructions discussed ... are not likely to exist and that the transaction clearly partakes of the nature of a stock split-up. ... Consequently, the committee considers that under such circumstances there is no need to capitalize earned surplus, other than to the extent occasioned by legal requirements. It recommends, however, that in such instances every effort be made to avoid the use of the word *dividend* in related corporate resolutions, notices, and announcements and that, in those cases where because of legal requirements this cannot be done, the transaction be described, for example, as a *split-up effected in the form of a dividend*.[14]

The Committee indicated that the majority of stock dividends would probably fall within the first category stated above, suggesting debits to retained earnings of amounts exceeding legal requirements. Although reluctant to name a dividend percentage that would require adherence to this practice, the Committee did suggest that in share distributions involving the issuance of less than 20% to 25% of the number of shares previously outstanding, there would be few instances where debits to retained earnings at the fair value of additional shares issued would not be appropriate.

The following examples illustrate the entries for the declaration and the issue of a stock dividend. Assume the capital for the Bradford Co. on July 1 is as follows:

Capital stock $10 par, 100,000 shares outstanding	$1,000,000
Premium on Capital Stock	1,100,000
Retained earnings	750,000

The corporation declares a 10% stock dividend, or a dividend of 1 share for every 10 held. Shares are selling on the market on this date at $16 per share. The stock dividend is to be recorded at the market value of the shares issued, or $160,000 (10,000 shares at $16). The entries to record the declaration of the dividend and the subsequent issue of shares follow:

---

[13]*Accounting Research and Terminology Bulletins — Final Edition*, "No. 43, Restatement and Revision of Accounting Research Bulletins" (New York: American Institute of Certified Public Accountants, 1961), Ch. 7, sec. B, par. 10.
  [14]*Ibid.*, par. 11.

Retained Earnings	160,000	
Stock Dividends Distributable		100,000
Premium on Capital Stock		60,000
Stock Dividends Distributable	100,000	
Capital Stock, $10 par		100,000

Assume however, that the corporation declares a 50% stock dividend, or a dividend of 1 share for every 2 held. Also, assume that legal requirements call for the transfer to capital stock of an amount equal to the par value of the shares issued. This transfer may be made from retained earnings or from contributed surplus. Entries for the declaration of the dividend and the issue of shares follow:

Retained Earnings (or Premium on Capital Stock)	500,000	
Stock Dividends Distributable		500,000
Stock Dividends Distributable	500,000	
Capital Stock, $10 par		500,000

Under the Canada Business Corporations Act, a stock dividend increases the stated capital account of the dividend shares by an amount equal to the value of the shares issued as a dividend. Since the Act generally requires shares to be issued at fair market value, it follows that a stock dividend must be added to stated capital at fair market value. If Bradford Co. was incorporated under the Canada Business Corporations Act, the required entries would be similar to those at the top of the page except that the shares would be without nominal or par value.

Although a stock dividend can be compared to a stock split from the investors' point of view, its effects upon corporate capital differ from those of a nominal or par value split. A stock dividend results in an increase in the number of shares outstanding and in an increase in the capital, with no change being made in the value assigned to each share on the corporate records. The increase in capital stock outstanding is effected by a transfer from the retained earnings balance, retained earnings available for dividends being permanently reduced by this transfer. A stock split merely divides the existing share capital balance into more parts with a reduction in the stated or legal value related to the shares; there is no change in the retained earnings available for dividends, both the capital stock and the retained earnings balances remaining unchanged.

A stock split effected in the form of a large stock dividend is sometimes referred to simply as a stock split. This can be misleading because additional shares of shares are issued in this situation and the par value, if any, of the stock is not changed. A careful distinction should be made between a pure stock split as described earlier in this chapter and the large stock dividends discussed above.

Fractional Share Warrants. When stock dividends are issued by a corporation, it may be necessary to issue *fractional share warrants* to certain shareholders. For example, when a 10% stock dividend is issued, a shareholder owning 25 shares can be given no more than 2 full shares; holdings in excess of an even multiple of 10 shares are recognized by the issue of a fractional share warrant in this case for $1/2$ share. The warrant for $1/2$ share may be sold, or a warrant for an additional $1/2$ share may be purchased so a full share may be claimed from the corporation. In some instances, the corporation may arrange for the payment of cash in lieu of fractional warrants or it may issue a full share in exchange for warrants accompanied by cash for the fractional share deficiency.

Assume that the Miller Company in distributing a stock dividend issues fractional share warrants totalling 500 shares, par $50. The entry for the fractional share warrants issued would be as follows:

Stock Dividends Distributable	25,000	
Fractional Share Warrants Issued		25,000

Assuming 80% of the warrants are ultimately turned in for shares and the remaining warrants expire, the following entry would be made:

Fractional Share Warrants Issued	25,000	
Capital Stock, $50 par		20,000
Gain on Forfeitures of Fractional Share Warrants		5,000

Stock dividends on the Balance Sheet. If a balance sheet is prepared after the declaration of a stock dividend but before issue of the shares, Stock Dividends Distributable should be reported in the Shareholders' equity section as an addition to Capital Stock Outstanding. By the declaration of the dividend, the corporation has reduced its retained earnings balance and is committed to the increase of share capital.

Liquidating Dividends

A corporation will declare a *liquidating dividend* when the dividend is to be considered a return to shareholders of a portion of their original investments. These distributions by the corporation represent reductions of invested capital balances. Instead of actually debiting capital stock and contributed surplus balances, it is possible to debit a separate account for the reduction in invested capital. This balance is then subtracted from the invested capital balances in presenting shareholders' equity on the balance sheet.

Corporations owning wasting assets may regularly declare dividends that are in part a distribution of earnings and in part a distribution of the corporation's invested capital. Entries for such dividend declarations should reflect the decrease in the two capital elements. This information should be reported to shareholders so they may recognize dividends as representing in part income and in part a return of their investments.

Dividends on Preferred Shares

When dividends on preferred shares are cumulative, the payment of a stipulated amount on these shares is necessary before any dividends may be declared on common. When the board of directors fails to declare dividends on cumulative preferred shares, information concerning the amount of dividends in arrears should be reported parenthetically or in the notes to the financial statements. Alternatively, retained earnings may be sub-divided on the balance sheet to show the amount required to meet dividends in arrears and the free balance for other purposes. In this case retained earnings may be reported on the balance sheet in the following manner:

Retained earnings:		
Required to meet dividends in arrears on preferred shares	$40,000	
Balance	60,000	
Total retained earnings		$100,000

Dividends on No-Par Shares

Cash dividends on no-par-value shares must be expressed as a certain amount per share since there is no par value to which a percentage may be applied. Dividends on capital stock with a par value are often expressed in the same manner.

Extraordinary Dividend Distributions

In the case of common shares, a corporation may establish a policy of *regular dividends* and may provide for greater payments when warranted through *extraordinary dividends* or *extra dividends*. For example, a corporation may have a regular dividend rate of 50 cents a quarter or $2 a year per share on common stock. In a particular quarter the corporation may wish to declare a dividend of 80 cents a share. Such a dividend may be expressed as a 50-cent regular dividend plus a 30-cent extra dividend.

USE OF TERM "RESERVE"

The term *reserve* has been employed with a variety of different meanings in accounting practice. Thus the term has been used in the following ways:

1. *As a Valuation Account.* The reserve designation has been employed to report a valuation account related to a balance sheet item. For example, deductions

may be required from recorded asset values in arriving at the realizable amounts, as in the case of marketable securities, receivables, or inventories. Deductions may also be required from the cost or other value of assets in the recognition of cost expirations, as in the case of assets subject to depreciation, depletion, or amortization. When such reductions are related to current revenues, expense accounts are debited and asset valuation accounts are credited. Valuation accounts are ultimately applied against the items to which they relate. The accounts receivable valuation account is used to absorb accounts expected to be uncollectible; the property valuation account is applied against the property item when the latter is disposed of or scrapped. As suggested earlier, a term such as *allowance* should be substituted for the term reserve in designating valuation accounts.

2. *As an Estimate of a Liability of Uncertain Amount.* The reserve title has been employed to designate a liability of uncertain amount requiring an estimate. Estimates may be required for such items as unsettled claims for damages and injuries, claims under product guarantees for services and/or replacements, tax obligations, and obligations under pension plans. When these claims are related to current revenue, expense accounts are debited and liability accounts are credited. The liabilities are ultimately cancelled through payment or other settlement. Designation of the accounts in this class as *estimated liabilities* rather than as reserves would clarify the nature of the items presented.

3. *As an Appropriation of Retained Earnings.* The reserve title is used to indicate that retained earnings have been appropriated in accordance with legal or contractual requirements or as a result of legal or contractual requirements or as a result of authorization by the board of directors. The appropriation of retained earnings has no effect upon individual assets and liabilities, nor does it change total capital; amounts are merely transferred from retained earnings to special retained earnings accounts and assets otherwise available for dividend distribution are kept within the business. The appropriation balance is no guarantee that cash or any other specific asset will be available to carry out the purpose of the appropriation. Resources represented by retained earnings may have been applied to the enlargement of plant, to the increase of working capital, or to the retirement of corporate indebtedness. If assets are to be made available for a particular purpose, special action relative to asset use would be required. When the purpose of the appropriation has been served, the appropriation balance is returned to Retained Earnings.

The Accounting Research Committee has recommended that the term reserve be limited to appropriations of retained earnings and any alternative use of the term in financial statements should be discontinued.[15] The American Accounting Association Committee on Concepts and Standards Underlying Corporate Financial Statements, however, would abandon use of the term in financial statements. The Committee has maintained that although accounting terminology would be improved if the term were limited to balances includible in capital, the conflict between the general and the

---

[15]*CICA Handbook: Accounting Recommendations, Section 3260,* "Reserves" (Toronto: Canadian Institute of Chartered Accountants, 1968), par. .01.

accounting connotations of the word would still be unresolved.[16] There can be little question that greater clarity in financial statement presentation would be promoted through abandonment of the term *reserve* and the adoption of more descriptive terminology. As will be explained later, the disclosures provided by appropriations can often be accomplished by notes to the financial statements.

RETAINED EARNINGS APPROPRIATIONS

Appropriations of retained earnings may be classified as follows:

1. *Appropriations to Report Legal Restrictions on Retained Earnings*. Laws of the incorporating jurisdiction may require a company, upon reacquiring its own shares, to retain some portion of its earnings as a means of maintaining legal capital. The restriction may be recognized in the accounts by the appropriation of retained earnings.
2. *Appropriations to Report Contractual Restrictions on Retained Earnings*. Agreements with creditors or shareholders may provide for the retention of earnings within the corporation to protect the interests of specific parties and assure redemption of the securities they hold. The restriction may be indicated in the accounts by the appropriation of retained earnings.
3. *Appropriations to Report Discretionary Action by the Board of Directors in the Presentation of Retained Earnings*. The board of directors may authorize that a portion or all of the retained earnings be presented in a manner disclosing the actual use in the present or the planned use in the future of the resources represented by this part of the shareholders' equity. Discretionary action on the part of the board of directors may then be the basis for appropriations.

A number of appropriated retained earnings accounts and the purposes for which such balances are established are listed below:

ACCOUNT	PURPOSE
(1) *Appropriations to report legal restrictions on retained earnings:*	
Retained Earnings Appropriated for Purchase of Treasury Stock	To retain earnings upon the reacquisition of shares so that resources of the business and the shareholders' equity may be maintained at original legal or stated balances.
(2) *Appropriations to report contractual restrictions on retained earnings:*	
Retained Earnings Appropriated for Redemption of Bonds Retained Earnings and Appropriated for Bond Redemption Fund	To retain earnings so that resources may be available for the redemption of bonds or for transfer to a fund for bond redemption.
Retained Earnings Appropriated for Redemption of Preferred Shares Retained Earnings Appropriated for Preferred Shares Redemption Fund	To retain earnings so that resources may be available for the redemption of preferred shares or for transfer to a fund for share redemption.

---

[16]*Accounting and Reporting Standards for Corporate Financial Statements and Preceding Statements and Supplements*, Supplementary Statement No. 1 (Madison, Wisconsin: American Accounting Association, 1957), p. 20.

ACCOUNT	PURPOSE
(3) *Appropriations to report discretionary action by the board of directors in the presentation of retained earnings:*	
Retained Earnings Appropriated for General Contingencies Retained Earnings Appropriated for Possible Inventory Decline Retained Earnings Appropriated for Self-Insurance	To retain earnings in the business so that resources may be available for use in meeting possible future losses.
Retained Earnings Appropriated for Increased Working Capital Retained Earnings Appropriated for Plant Expansion	To report that resources from earnings are to be applied or have been applied to some particular business purpose and thus are unavailable for dividends.

Several specific types of appropriations are discussed in the paragraphs that follow.

Appropriations Relating to Bond Redemption

A restriction upon retained earnings arising from a contract with creditors is recorded by a debit to Retained Earnings and a credit to an appropriations account. When the restriction is removed, the appropriation is returned to Retained Earnings. To illustrate, assume that the corporation agrees to restrict retained earnings of $5,000,000 from dividend distribution during the full term of a bond issue. Entries when the loan is made and when it is liquidated follow:

Retained Earnings	5,000,000	
Retained Earnings Appropriated for Redemption of Bonds		5,000,000
Retained Earnings Appropriated for Redemption of Bonds	5,000,000	
Retained Earnings		5,000,000

When the agreement with creditors provides for the periodic appropriation of earnings during the life of the obligation, entries similar to the first entry above would be made each period.

The appropriation of retained earnings may be accompanied by the segregation of assets in a special fund for retirement of the obligation at maturity. The establishment of the fund may be voluntary or it may be required by the bond indenture. A retained earnings appropriation that is accompanied by the segregation of assets in a special fund is said to be *funded*. This practice results not only in the limitation of dividends but also in the accumulation of resources to meet the obligation. Liquidation of the obligation by means of the redemption fund and the termination of the contract with creditors releases previously existing restrictions, and the appropriated retained earnings may be returned to free status. It may be observed, however, that when proceeds from a bond issue are used for expansion purposes and when resources from profitable operations have been used to retire the bonds, the expansion has in effect been financed by earnings. Under these circumstances, the board of directors may choose to report retained earnings equivalent to the amount applied to expansion under the designation Retained Earnings Appropriated for Plant Expansion, or it may choose to effect a permanent capitalization of such retained earnings by means of a stock dividend.

Appropriations for Possible Future Losses

Appropriations of retained earnings may be authorized by the board of directors in anticipation of possible future losses. A clear distinction must be made between those possible future losses which are certain enough that they can be accrued and shown as liabilities, and those so uncertain that only disclosure of their existence is required. The Accounting Research Committee in Section 3290 of the *Accounting Recommendations*, has established two conditions that "loss contingencies" must meet if they are to be accrued Contingencies, as liabilities:

1. It is likely that a future event will confirm that an asset has been impaired or a liability incurred at the date of the financial statements.
2. The amount of the loss can be reasonably estimated.[17]

If both of these conditions are not met, but there is at least a reasonable possibility that a loss may occur, disclosure of the contingency loss should be provided in notes to the financial statements. Another form of disclosure may be through the appropriation of retained earnings with or without accompanying notes. Two examples of such appropriations are described in the next sections of the chapter: (1) appropriation for possible inventory decline; and (2) appropriation for self-insurance.

The diagram below illustrates accounting and disclosure requirements for contingent losses under conditions of uncertainty as to (1) the probability of the future event(s), and (2) estimation of the financial effects.

Probability of the Future Event(s)	Estimation of Financial Effects	
	Reasonable Estimate Possible	Estimate Not Possible
Likely	Accrue Contingent Loss	Disclose in Notes
Cannot be determined	Disclose in Notes	Disclose in Notes
Unlikely	No Disclosure	No Disclosure

---

[17]*CICA Handbook: Accounting Recommendations, Section 3290,* "Contingencies" (Toronto: Canadian Institute of Chartered Accountants, 1978) par. 12.

In general, contingent gains should not be accrued because to do so would violate the realization concept. However, when it is likely that a future event may confirm the gain, disclosure in the notes should be considered appropriate.

Appropriation for Possible Inventory Decline. When inventories are acquired in a high-price period, management may authorize that provision be made in the accounts for possible future inventory decline. Valuation accounts reducing inventory costs to a lower market are established by charges to current revenue; valuation accounts providing for inventory obsolescence, deterioration, and similar losses already incurred are also established by charges to current revenue. A provision for possible future inventory decline, however, cannot be viewed as an inventory valuation account but must be considered a part of retained earnings. Accordingly, an appropriation procedure is required. An appropriation for possible inventory decline is established by a debit to Retained Earnings, and the appropriated balance is ultimately returned to Retained Earnings; no costs or losses should be debited to the appropriation, nor should any part of the appropriation be transferred to income. A loss on inventories requires separate recognition in the period in which it occurs.

To illustrate the use of an appropriation for possible inventory decline, assume the ending inventory of Crainer Corporation has a cost valuation of $325,000 and a lower of cost or market valuation of $310,000. Officers in the corporation anticipate that inventory prices will continue to decline in the subsequent year, and that before the inventory is sold, a further decline is $30,000 in the replacement cost of the inventory can be anticipated. Selling prices of the inventory by Crainer are expected to decline in a corresponding fashion.

The following entries would be required to reflect (1) the actual decline occurring prior to the balance sheet date, and (2) the anticipated future decline by appropriating retained earnings.

Loss on Reduction of Inventory to Market	15,000	
Allowance for Inventory Decline to Market		15,000
To record actual decline in market value from cost of $325,000.		
Retained Earnings	30,000	
Retained Earnings Appropriated for Possible Future Inventory		
Decline		30,000
To approrpiate retained earnings for anticipated future inventory declines.		

The loss account in the first entry is closed through Income Summary to Retained Earnings. The allowance account is a contra inventory account on the balance sheet. The Retained Earnings Appropriated for Possible Future Inventory Decline is only a disclosure account. If prices do decline in the subsequent period, sales will be lower and income will thus be reduced. If the appropriation is no longer required at the end of the subsequent year, an entry reversing the appropriation should be made as follows:

Retained Earnings Appropriated for Possible Future Inventory Decline	30,000	
Retained Earnings		30,000
To return reserve for possible future inventory decline to un-appropriated retained earnings.		

As indicated earlier, under no conditions should the actual loss be debited to the appropriation.

Appropriation for Self-Insurance. A corporation may face certain risks but may not obtain insurance on the theory that the assumption of these risks will prove less expensive in the long run than the cost of outside protection. The Accounting Research Committee has concluded that self-insurance is in reality no insurance. The first guideline for recording contingent losses in the accounts as an expense is not met in the case of self-insurance because no asset has been impaired nor has a liability been incurred. Thus, in Section 3290, the Committee states:

> Fires, explosions and other similar perils are random in their occurrence and, since no impairment of an asset or incurrence of a liability can exist prior to the occurrence of such an event, accrual is inappropriate. Where, however, an enterprise lacks adequate insurance against a material risk that is normally insured, disclosure of this fact may be desirable.[18]

Where disclosure of the possibility of future loss may be required the appropriation of retained earnings is one acceptable method of disclosure. Actual losses incurred are charged against revenue in the period when the loss occurs. The balance in the appropriation account should be evaluated each year to determine its reasonableness relative to the risk assumed. In addition, the appropriation may be funded so that cash will be available for property replacement.

The entries on page 727 illustrate a self-insurance plan with funding for property replacement.

It should be observed that since self-insurance is simply a policy of no insurance, management, in considering such a policy, should evaluate carefully such factors as the size of the organization and how this affects risk, the protective measures available in minimizing risk, and the probable savings accruing through this action. Self-insurance should be undertaken only when a company is financially prepared to assume the full responsibilities related to its risk-bearing role.

---

[18]*Ibid.*, par. 16.

TRANSACTION	ENTRY		

Retained earnings appropriated under fire-loss self-insurance plan.	Retained Earnings ....
	  Retained Earnings Appropriated
	  for Self-Insurance Fire Loss ..
		20,000	20,000

Establishment of fund to meet self-insurance plans.	Property Replacement Fund .... Cash	20,000	20,000
Fire loss: building net book value, $15,000 (cost, $21,500; accumulated depreciation, $6,500);	Fire Loss .... Accumulated Depreciation — Buildings .... Buildings	15,000 6,500	21,500

building replacement cost, $23,500, paid $20,000 from fund and $3,500 from regular cash balance. Since the building has been replaced, there will still be a need for an appropriation for another possible fire loss; therefore, management may decide to retain the appropriation and rebuild the cash fund.	Buildings ....
	  Property Replacement Fund ..
	  Cash ....
		23,500	20,000
			3,500

Appropriations to Describe Business Purposes Served by Retained Earnings

Corporate officials may authorize appropriations to show the use of retained earnings within the business. For example, assume earnings are to be retained by a company to finance the expansion of plant facilities. Or assume resources from earnings have already been applied to plant expansion. In either instance, instead of continuing to report undistributed profits in retained earnings, which may be interpreted by shareholders as amounts available for dividends, the company may authorize transfers from retained earnings to a special account describing the utilization of earnings. Such appropriations may be carried forward indefinitely. On the other hand, in view of the permanent commitment of assets, the company may choose to effect a permanent capitalization of retained earnings by means of a stock dividend.

Objections to Appropriation Procedures

The Committee on Concepts and Standards Underlying Corporate Financial Statements of the American Accounting Association has taken issue with the general practice of earmarking retained earnings through the appropriation procedure, pointing out that such practice may serve to confuse and mislead those using the financial statements. When earnings are retained, the objectives of the retention are best explained, in the opinion of the Committee, by narrative materials included in the notes to the financial statements. There can be little objection to the position taken by the Committee, and, in practice, use of appropriations is clearly declining.

DEDUCTIONS FROM TOTAL SHAREHOLDERS' EQUITY

As previously discussed, there are two situations in which a deduction may be made from total shareholders' equity: (1) the cost of treasury shares, and (2) the accumulated changes in the valuation allowance for the marketable equity securities portfolio included in non-current assets. These may be referred to as contra equity accounts.

The first of these deductions is provided for in Section 3240 of the *Accounting Recommendations*. However, the recommendations are silent with respect to the second.

CORPORATE FINANCIAL STATEMENTS

Transactions affecting shareholders' equity have been described in this and the preceding chapter. In the remaining pages of this chapter, the financial statements for the General Manufacturing Company, a provincially incorporated company, are illustrated with special attention directed to the shareholders' equity section of the balance sheet.

The Balance Sheet

The balance sheet for the General Manufacturing Company as at December 31, 1981, is given on pages 730 and 731. The following matters deserve special attention:

1. The shareholders' equity is reported in terms of its source: (a) the amount representing legal capital; (b) the amount of contributed surplus; and (c) the amount representing earnings retained in the business.
2. The classes of capital stock are reported separately and are described in detail. Information is offered concerning the nature of the shares, the number of shares authorized, the number of shares issued, and the number of shares, if any, reacquired and held as treasury shares.
3. The capital items representing contributed surplus and retained earnings are reported in detail; when contributed surplus and appropriated retained earnings are composed of a great many items, related balances are frequently combined and reported in total on the balance sheet. Details may then be provided in notes to the financial statements.
4. In complying with legal requirements, the company has reported retained earnings equivalent to the cost of the treasury shares held as an appropriation of retained earnings. [19]

Reference is made at the bottom of the balance sheet to the notes accompanying the financial statements. (These notes appear on page 732.) This reference would also appear on other financial statements prepared by the company.

[19]Under the Canada Business Corporations Act, reacquired shares must either be cancelled or, if the number of authorized shares is limited, returned to the status of authorized but unissued shares.

Statements Accounting for the Changes in the Shareholders' Equity

Those who wish to be fully informed on the financial position and results of operations of the corporation require full information explaining the change in the shareholders' equity. When changes in contributed surplus have taken place, a *contributed statement* may be prepared. This statement reports the balances at the beginning of the period and the changes in these balances during the period as a result of such transactions as the issue of capital stock, stock dividends, the retirement of shares, and the purchase and sale of treasury shares. The contributed surplus statement for the General Manufacturing Company for the year ended December 31, 1981, is shown on page 732.

The changes in retained earnings are summarized in the retained earnings statement. In some instances, it is necessary to recognize additional changes, such as those resulting from prior period adjustments, the acquisition of treasury shares, and transfers to contributed surplus pertaining, for example, to stock dividends. Frequently the retained earnings statement is expanded to show changes in both unappropriated and appropriated balances. The statement then summarizes transfers from the unappropriated retained earnings account to accounts reporting appropriations, and also transfers from accounts reporting appropriations to the unappropriated retained earnings account.

General Manufacturing Company
Income Statement
For Year Ended December 31, 1981

Revenues:		
Sales	$1,550,000	
Other revenue	100,000	$1,650,000
Expenses:		
Cost of goods sold	$ 940,000	
Selling expense	300,000	
General and administrative expense	125,000	
Other expenses	80,000	1,445,000
Income before income tax	$205,000	
Provision for income tax	92,500	
Income before extraordinary items		$ 112,500
Extraordinary gain on extinguishment of debt, net of income tax		7,500
Net income		$ 120,000
Earnings per share.[20]		
Income before extraordinary items		$1.50
Net income		$1.64

Condensed Single-Step Income Statement

---

[20]Preferred dividend requirements are subtracted from earnings to arrive at earnings related to common shares. This computation, as well as computations for more complex capital structures, are described in the following chapter.

Assets

Current assets:

Cash on hand and on deposit		$ 55,000
Canadian Government securities (reported at cost; market value, $87,500)		86,000
Trade notes and accounts receivable	$182,600	
Less allowance for doubtful accounts	2,600	180,000
Inventories (Note 1a):		
Finished goods	$190,000	
Work in process.....................................	200,000	
Raw materials and supplies	185,000	575,000
Loans, advances, and accrued receivables		20,000
Prepayments including taxes, insurance, and sundry current items.		14,500
Total current assets		$ 930,500

Long-term investments:

Marketable equity securities (cost $124,000, less allowance to reduce valuation to market, $24,000)		$ 100,000
Fund consisting of Canadian Government securities to be used for property additions		150,000
Land held for future expansion		110,000
Total long-term investments		360,000

Land, buildings, and equipment (Note 1b):

Land, buildings, and equipment, at cost	$1,235,000	
Less accumulated depreciation	580,000	
Total land, buildings, and equipment		655,000

Intangible assets (Note 1c):

Patents, formulas, and goodwill — less amortization		120,000

Other assets:

Advance payments on equipment purchase contracts		102,500
Total assets		$2,168,000

See accompanying notes to financial statements.

Manufacturing Company
Sheet
31, 1981

Current liabilities:			
Notes and accounts payable		$ 52,500	
Estimated income tax payable		12,000	
Accrued payroll, interest, and taxes payable		23,500	
Serial debenture bonds due May 1, 1982		20,000	
Customer's deposits and sundry items		24,000	
Total current liabilities			$ 132,000
Long-term debt:			
Twenty-year 9% first mortgage bonds	$260,000		
Less unamortized discount on first-mortgage bonds	10,000	$ 250,000	
Serial 7½% debenture bonds due May 1, 1983, to May 1, 1991,			
inclusive		180,000	
Deferred leasehold revenue (Note 1d)		200,000	
Liability under pension plan (Note 2)		20,000	
Contingent liabilities (Note 3)			
Total long-term liabilities			650,000
Total liabilities			$ 782,000

Shareholders' Equity

Share capital:			
Preferred 6% shares, $100 par, cumulative, callable, 5,000 shares			
authorized and issued (Note 4)		$500,000	
No par common shares 100,000 shares authorized, 60,000 shares			
issued (treasury shares — deducted below)		500,000	$1,000,000
Contributed Surplus:			
Premium on preferred shares		$ 60,000	
Gain from sale of treasury shares at more than cost		16,000	76,000
Retained Earnings:			
Appropriated:			
For purchase of treasury shares	$16,000		
For contingencies (Note 3)	85,000	$101,000	
Unappropriated		249,000	
Total retained earnings		350,000	
Total share capital, contributed surplus and retained earnings .		$1,426,000	
Deduct: Common treasury shares, at cost (2,000 shares			
acquired at $8)	$ 16,000		
Net unrealized loss on non-current market-			
able equity securities (Note 4)	24,000	40,000	
Total shareholders' equity			1,386,000
Total liabilities and shareholders' equity			$2,168,000

General Manufacturing Company Contributed Surplus Statement For Year Ended December 31, 1981	
Balance, January 1, 1981	$60,000
Add: Increase from sale of 2,500 shares of treasury stock, common, cost $20,000, for $36,000	16,000
Balance, December 31, 1981	$76,000

The General Manufacturing Company's retained earnings statement for the year ended December 31, 1981, is illustrated below.

General Manufacturing Company
Retained Earnings Statement
For Year Ended December 31, 1981

	Retained Earnings		
	Appropriated for Purchase of Treasury Shares	Appropriated for Contingencies	Unappropriated
Balances, January 1, 1981	$36,000	$50,000	$226,500
Prior period adjustment — settlement of income tax claims for 1978 and 1979			(25,000)
Balances, January 1, 1981, as restated	$36,000	$50,000	$201,500
Return to retained earnings of earnings previously restricted through ownership of treasury shares ..	(20,000)		20,000
Retained earnings appropriated for contingencies ..		35,000	(35,000)
Cash dividends:			
Preferred shares, $6 on 5,000 shares, $30,000 ..			
Common shares, 50¢ on 55,000 shares, $27,500			(57,500)
Net income for 1981			120,000
Balances, December 31, 1981	$16,000	$85,000	$249,000

2. The company has accrued $20,000 more under the pension plan than it has paid. At December 31, 1981, the balance in the pension fund exceeds the vested benefits as of that date. No further accrual of past service cost is therefore considered necessary.

3. The company is contingently liable on guaranteed notes and accounts totalling $40,000. Also, various suits are pending on which the ultimate payment cannot be determined. In the opinion of counsel and management, such liability, if any, will not be material. Retained earnings have been appropriated in anticipation of possible losses.

4. Preferred shares may be redeemed at the option of the board of directors at 105 plus accrued dividends on or before December 31, 1983, and at gradually reduced amounts but at not less than $102^{1/2}$ plus accrued dividends after January 1, 1989.

1. List six items that may give rise to contributed surplus. Which items, if any, would not arise, if the company was incorporated under the Canada Business Corporations Act?

2. Why should retained earnings not be credited for gains arising on capital transactions, if losses from similar transactions may be debited to the account?

3. Preferred shareholders of the Beacon Corporation exchange their holdings for no-par common shares in accordance with terms of the preferred issue. How should this conversion be reported by the corporation?

4. The Walsh Co. issues 10,000,000 shares of no-par common stock in exchange for certain mineral lands. The property is recorded at $5,000,000. Shortly thereafter, shareholders donate to the corporation 20% of their shares. The shares are resold by the company at 10¢ per share. What accounting problems arise as a result of the donation and resale?

5. (a) What entries should be made in the accounts when stock rights are issued to shareholders? (b) What entries should be made when shares are issued on the exercise of rights? (c) What information, if any, should appear on the balance sheet relative to outstanding rights?

6. What characteristics are essential for a stock-option plan to be classified as non-compensatory?

7. Under what conditions would a compensatory stock option program for key executives not result in a charge to compensation expense?

8. Some users of accounting reports believe that net income is overstated on certain income statements because of the currently accepted procedure for recording employee stock options. (a) Describe how the net income may be overstated. (b) What alternative procedures would more satisfactorily match revenue and expense?

9. Define a stock split and identify the major objectives of this corporate action. What is a reverse stock split?

10. The following announcement appeared on the financial page of a newspaper:

"The Board of Directors of the Maxwell Co., at their meeting on June 15, 1977, declared the regular quarterly dividend on outstanding common stock of 50 cents per share and an extra dividend of $1 per share, both payable on July 10, 1977, to the shareholders of record at the close of business June 30, 1977."

(a) What is the purpose of each of the three dates given in the declaration? (b) When would the shares become "ex-dividend"? (c) Why is the $1 designated as an "extra" dividend?

11. Dividends are sometimes said to have been paid "out of retained earnings." What is wrong with this statement?

12. The directors of Lenox Corporation are considering the issuance of a stock dividend. They have asked you to discuss the proposed action by answering the questions below:

(a) What is a stock dividend? How is a stock dividend distinguished from a stock split: (1) from a legal standpoint? (2) from an accounting standpoint?
(b) For what reasons does a corporation usually declare (1) a stock dividend? (2) a stock split? (3) a stock split in the form of a stock dividend?

13. It has been recommended that the balance sheet maintain a permanent distinction between invested capital and retained earnings. How can such a distinction be maintained when action is taken to convert retained earnings into capital stock?

14. (a) What is a liquidating dividend? (b) Under what circumstances are such distributions made? (c) How would you recommend that liquidating dividends be recorded in the accounts of the corporation?

15. What methods can be followed in reporting dividends in arrears on preferred stock on the balance sheet?

16. (a) What criticisms have been made of the term *reserve*? (b) What position has been taken by the Canadian Institute of Chartered Accountants and by the American Accounting Association with respect to the use of the term? (c) What position would you take with respect to use of the term? What substitute terms would you employ?

17. Some of the following account titles use the term *reserve* improperly. For each account indicate (a) the proper account title, and (b) the heading under which it would appear in the balance sheet.

(1) Reserve for Contingencies
(2) Reserve for Doubtful Accounts
(3) Reserve for Possible Inventory Decline
(4) Reserve for Self-Insurance — Fire Loss
(5) Reserve for Bond Retirement
(6) Reserve for Income Tax
(7) Reserve for Undeclared Dividends
(8) Reserve for Increased Investment in Land, Buildings, and Equipment
(9) Reserve for Depletion
(10) Reserve for Redeemable Coupons Outstanding
(11) Reserve for Repairs and Replacements
(12) Reserve for Purchase of Treasury Stock
(13) Reserve for Personal Injury Claims Pending

(14) Reserve for Unrealized Building Appreciation

(15) Reserve for Sales Discounts

18. The use of appropriation accounts to disclose contingencies has declined. What method of disclosure has replaced appropriation accounts? Evaluate the disclosure methods as to their communication value for statement readers.

19. A shareholder of Barker, Inc., does not understand the purpose of the Appropriation for Bond Redemption Fund that has been set up by periodic debits to Retained Earnings. He is told that this balance will not be used to redeem the bonds at their maturity. (a) What accounts will be reduced by the payment of the bonds? (b) What purpose is accomplished by the Appropriation for Bond Redemption Fund? (c) What dispositions may be made of the appropriation?

20. Mr. Collins, President of Bolinder Corp., is concerned by Section 3290, issued by the Accounting Research Committee, that prevents his company from accruing estimated losses from self-insurance for fire losses. Assets are scattered over a wide geographical area and Mr. Collins feels the company can economically carry its own insurance risks. But he feels that revenue of each period should bear part of the fire loss, not just the periods in which the losses occur. Explain to Mr. Collins the rationale supporting the Committee's position.

21. What items are defined as contra equity accounts and deducted from the total shareholders' equity?

22. Which of the following transactions change total shareholders' equity? What is the nature of the change?

(1) Declaration of a cash dividend.

(2) Payment of a cash dividend.

(3) Retirement of bonds payable for which both a redemption fund and an appropriation had been established.

(4) Declaration of a stock dividend.

(5) Payment of a stock dividend.

(6) Conversion of bonds payable into preferred shares.

(7) The passing of a dividend on cumulative preferred shares.

(8) Donation of shares of stock by the officers.

(9) Operating loss for the period.

17-1. Capital accounts for the Kelly Co. on December 31 are as follows: **EXERCISES**

Preferred Shares, $25 par, 25,000 shares issued and outstanding	$ 625,000
Premium on Preferred Shares	31,250
Common Shares, $5 par, 200,000 shares issued and outstanding	1,000,000
Premium on Common Shares	110,000
Retained Earnings...	1,450,000

Preferred shares are convertible into common stock. Give the entry to be made by the corporation assuming 1,600 shares of preferred are converted under each assumption listed:

(a) Preferred shares are convertible into common on a share-for-share basis.

(b) Each preferred share is convertible into 8 shares of common.

(c) Each preferred share is convertible into 4 shares of common.

17-2. In your first audit of a mining company, you note the following facts with respect to its share capital transactions:

Authorized capital consists of 5,000,000 of $1 par value common stock.

All shares were issued initially in exchange for certain mineral properties. The properties were recorded in the accounts at $10,000,000.

Two million shares were received by the company as a donation shortly after incorporation and were sold immediately for cash of $3,000,000. This amount was recorded as a credit to Donated Capital.

(a) What values should be assigned to the mineral properties and shareholders' equity? Discuss. (b) Prepare any required correcting entry.

17-3. The Gividen Company needs to raise additional equity capital. After analysis of available options, the company decides to issue 1,000 shares of $100 par preferred stock with detachable warrants attached. The package of shares and warrants sells as a unit for 108. The warrants enable the holder to purchase 1,000 shares of $25 par common stock at $30 per share. Immediately following the issuance of the shares, the purchase warrants are selling at $8 per share. The market value of the preferred without the warrants is 102. What entries would be required to record the sale of the shares and subsequent use of the warrants to purchase common shares? Round answers to the nearest dollar.

17-4. The shareholders of the Johnson Co. on December 24, 1975, approved a plan granting certain officers of the company non-transferable options to buy 50,000 shares of no-par common at $8 per share. Shares were selling at this time at $10 each. The option plan provides that the officers must be employed by the corporation for the next five years, that options can be exercised after January 1, 1981, and that options will expire at the end of 1982. One of the officers who had been granted options for 10,000 shares left the corporation at the beginning of 1979; remaining officers exercised their rights under the option plan at the end of 1982. Give the entires that should be made in the accounts of the corporation at the end of each year for 1975-1982 inclusive. The market price of the shares at January 1, 1981, was $15 each.

17-5. The Luedke Co. reports its shareholders' equity as follows:

Common shares, $10 par, 750,000 shares	$7,500,000
Contributed surplus	530,000
Deficit	(880,000)
Total shareholders' equity	$7,150,000

The corporation wishes to cancel the deficit and is considering each of the possibilities listed below. Give the entries required and prepare the "Shareholders' equity" section for each assumption.

(a) Shareholders are to donate 30% of their shares to the company and these are to be formally retired.

(b) The par value of shares is to be reduced to $7.50.

(c) One new share of no-par stock is to be exchanged for each share of common stock outstanding and the legal capital for the company is to be restated at $7,150,000.

17-6. The balance sheet of the Fast Corporation shows the following:

Capital stock, $5 par value, 40,000 shares issued and outstanding	$200,000
Contributed surplus	400,000
Retained earnings...	175,000

A 25% stock dividend is declared, the board of directors authorizes a transfer from Retained Earnings to Capital Stock at par value.

    (a) Give entries to record the declaration and payment of the dividend.

    (b) What was the effect of the issue of the stock dividend on the ownership equity of each shareholder in the corporation?

    (c) Give entries to record the declaration and payment of the dividend if the board of directors had elected to transfer amounts from Retained Earnings to Capital Stock equal to the market value of the shares ($10 per share).

17-7. The capital accounts for the Dean Co. on June 30, 1981, follow:

Capital Stock, $20 par, 100,000 shares	$2,000,000
Premium on Capital Stock	725,000
Retained Earnings	3,600,000

Shares of the company's stock are selling at this time at 36. What entries would you make in each case below?

    (a) A stock dividend of 10% is declared and issued.

    (b) A stock dividend of 100% is declared and issued.

    (c) A 2-for-1 stock split is declared and issued.

17-8. On January 1, 1979, the Fast Foods Corporation floated a $10,000,000 bond issue. The bond issue agreement with the underwriters required Fast Foods to appropriate earnings of $625,000 at the end of each year until the bonds are retired. During their 1981 board meeting, the directors decided to change the company's financing policy to just short-term debt and equity, and to drop their present insurance policy in favor of a self-insurance plan. On July 1, 1981, the corporation retired the bond issue and set up their first annual appropriation for self-insurance by debiting Self-Insurance Expense for $10,000 and crediting Retained Earnings Appropriated for Self-Insurance.

    (a) Give the entries to record the periodic appropriations under the bond issue agreement for 1979 and 1980 and their cancellation in 1981.

    (b) Did the corporation use generally accepted accounting principles in setting up their appropriation for self-insurance? Explain.

    (c) If the answer to (b) is no, what entry should have been made?

17-9. A physical inventory taken by the Fisher Co. on December 31, 1981, discloses goods on hand with a cost of $860,000; the inventory is recorded at this figure less an allowance of $36,000 to reduce it to the lower of cost or market. At the same time, the company authorizes that an appropriation for possible future inventory decline of $300,000 be established.

    (a) Give the entries to be made at the end of 1981 in recording the inventory and establishing the accounts as indicated.

    (b) Give the entries in 1982 to close the beginning inventory and balances established at the end of 1981, assuming that the estimated inventory decline does not materialize and that the inventory at the end of 1982 is properly reported at cost, which is lower than market.

    (c) Give the entries in 1982 to close the inventory and other account balances established at the end of 1977 if a decline in the value of the December 31, 1977 inventory of $160,000 is to be recognized; the inventory at the end of 1978 is properly reported at cost, which is lower than its market value at this date.

17-10. The Script Co. reports appropriated retained earnings on its balance sheet at the end of 1981 at $335,000. Analysis of the account balances in support of this total discloses the following:

Reserve for contingencies — to meet estimated claims arising from damage suits in 1981 for which the company has been held to be liable	$ 45,000
Reserve for self-insurance for fire loss — to meet possible fire losses as a result of self-insurance on this contingency	40,000
Reserve for pensions — to meet estimated pension costs arising from contracts with employees	195,000
Reserve for possible declines on marketable securities — to meet possible future losses on the marketable securities	25,000
Reserve for property rehabilitation costs — to meet costs of rehabilitating plant at termination of lease in accordance with contractual requirements	30,000

(a) Which of the above items, if any, would you exclude from the appropriated retained earnings classification?
(b) State how you would classify such items, and what account title you would use.

17-11. For each of the following items, give the title of the account that would be credited and where it would be reported on financial statements.

(a) 15% stock dividend declared on common shares.
(b) Transfer to reserve for bond redemption fund.
(c) Profit-sharing bonus to employees.
(d) Gain on sale of treasury shares.
(e) Donation of land by government agency.
(f) Gain on sale of investment in securities.
(g) Premium on sale of bonds.
(h) Gain on sale of property originally acquired by exchange for capital stock.

17-12. The directors of Roof Corporation, whose $80 par value common stock is currently selling at $100 per share, have decided to issue a stock dividend. Roof has an authorization for 400,000 shares of common, has issued 220,000 shares of which 20,000 shares are now held as treasury stock, and desires to capitalize $1,600,000 of the retained earnings account balance. What per cent stock dividend should be issued to accomplish this desire?

PROBLEMS

17-1A. The board of directors of the Queen Production Co. adopted a stock option plan to supplement the salaries of certain executives of the company. Options to buy common shares were granted as follows:

		No. of Shares	Option Price	Price of Shares at Date of Grant
Jan. 10, 1978	John Hancock	75,000	16	17
June 30, 1978	Donald Norton	50,000	21	22
	Maynard Erickson	20,000		

Options are non-transferrable and can be exercised three years after date of grant providing the executive is still in the employ of the company. Options expire two years after the date they can first be exercised.

Maynard Erickson left the employ of the company at the beginning of 1980. Stock options were exercised as follows:

		No. of Shares	Price of Shares at Date of Exercise
Jan. 15, 1981	John Hancock	60,000	41
Dec. 20, 1981	John Hancock	15,000	32
Dec. 22, 1981	Donald Norton	50,000	28

Stock of the company has a $10 par value. The accounting period for the company is the calendar year.

Instructions:

Give all entries that would be made in the accounts of the corporation relative to the stock option agreement for the period 1978 to 1981 inclusive.

17-2A. The "Shareholders' equity" section of Stars, Inc., showed the following data on December 31, 1980: common stock, no par value, 100,000 shares issued and outstanding, $2,800,000; credit under stock option plan, $100,000; retained earnings, $320,000. The stock options were granted to key executives and provided them the right to acquire 20,000 shares of common stock at $30 per share. The shares were selling at $35 at the time the options were granted.

The following transactions occurred during 1981:

Mar. 31   3,000 options outstanding at December 31, 1980, were exercised. The market price per share was $42 at this time.

Apr. 1   The company issued bonds of $1,500,000 at par, giving with each $1,000 bond a warrant enabling the holder, for a one-year period, to purchase two common shares at $35. The shares were selling for $42 per share at that date.

June 30   The company issued rights to shareholders (one right on each share) permitting holders to acquire for a thirty-day period one share at $40 with every eight rights submitted. Shares were selling for $45 at this time. All but 7,000 rights were exercised on July 31, and the additional shares were issued.

Sept. 30   All shares were issued in connection with warrants issued on the sale of bonds.

Nov. 30   The market price per share dropped to $25 and options came due. Since the market price was below the option price, no remaining options were exercised.

Instructions:

(1) Give entries to record the foregoing transactions.
(2) Prepare the "Shareholders' equity" section of the balance sheet as of December 31, 1981, (assume net income of $175,000 for 1981).

17-3A. The McAllister Company has experienced several poor earnings years and has several assets in its accounts that are overvalued. It desires to revalue its assets downward and eliminate the deficit. At December 31, 1981, the company owns the following land, buildings, and equipment.

	Cost	Accumulated Depreciation	Net Book Value	Current Value
Land	$250,000	——	$250,000	$150,000
Buildings	375,000	$175,000	200,000	100,000
Machinery and equipment	175,000	75,000	100,000	75,000
	$800,000	$250,000	$550,000	$325,000

The balance sheet on December 31, 1981, reported the following balances in the "Shareholders' equity" section:

Common stock, $10 par, 100,000 shares	$1,000,000
Contributed surplus	100,000
Retained earnings (deficit)	(150,000)
Total	$ 950,000

As part of the reorganization, the common shares are to be cancelled and reissued at $5 par.

Instructions:

(1) Prepare the journal entries to record the reorganization.
(2) Give the property section and "Shareholders' equity" section of the company's balance sheet as they would appear after the entries are posted.

17-4A. The Columbia Corporation had $105,000 of dividends in arrears on its preferred shares as of March 31, 1977. While retained earnings were adequate to meet the accumulated dividends, the corporation's management did not wish to weaken its working capital position. The management also realized that a portion of the fixed assets were no longer used or useful in their operations. Therefore, the following reorganization was proposed, which was approved by shareholders to be effective as of April 1, 1977:

(a) The preferred shares were to be exchanged for $300,000 of 5% debenture bonds. Dividends in arrears were to be settled by the issuance of $120,000 in the form of 1,200 shares of $5, non-cumulative preferred stock.
(b) Common shares were to be reissued at a value of $50 per share.
(c) Goodwill was to be written off.
(d) Land, buildings, and equipment were to be written down, based on appraisal and estimates of useful value, by a total of $103,200, consisting of an $85,400 increase in accumulated depreciation and a $17,800 decrease in certain assets.
(e) Current assets were to be written down by $10,460 to reduce certain items to expected realizable values.

The condensed balance sheet as of March 31, 1977, was as follows:

Columbia Corporation
Balance Sheet
March 31, 1977

Assets		
Cash		$ 34,690
Other current assets		252,890
Land, buildings, and equipment................................	$1,458,731	
Less accumulated depreciation	512,481	946,250
Goodwill		50,000
Total assets		$1,283,830

Columbia Corporation
Balance Sheet
March 31, 1977

Liabilities and Shareholders' Equity	
Current liabilities	$ 136,860
Preferred shares, $7, cumulative, 3,000 shares*	322,470
Common shares, no-par, 9,000 shares	648,430
Retained earnings	176,070
Total liabilities and shareholders' equity	$1,283,830

*$105,000 dividends in arrears.

Instructions:

(1) Prepare journal entries to give effect to the reorganization as of April 1, 1977. Give complete explanations with each entry and comment on any possible options in recording the reorganization.

(2) Prepare a balance sheet as of April 30, 1977, assuming that net income for April was $10,320 after provision for tax. The operations resulted in a $5,290 increase in cash, a $10,660 increase in other current assets, a $2,010 increase in current liabilities, and a $3,620 increase in accumulated depreciation.

(3) In making an audit of the Columbia Corporation as of December 31, 1977, you find that the following items had been debited or credited directly to Retained Earnings during the nine months since April 1, 1977:

  (a) A debit of $14,496 arising from an income tax assessment applicable to prior years.

  (b) A debit of $7,492 resulting from a loss on fixed assets destroyed in a fire on November 2, 1977.

  (c) A debit of $13,500 representing dividends declared on common and preferred shares.

  For each of these items, state whether you believe it to be correctly debited or credited to Retained Earnings. Give the reasons for your conclusion. If the item is not handled properly, prepare the necessary correcting entry. (AICPA adapted)

17-5A. The shareholders' equity of the High Co. on June 30, 1977, was as follows:

Share capital:	
Preferred shares, no par, $4, cumulative, 20,000 shares issued, dividends 5 years in arrears	$1,000,000
Common shares, no par, 160,000 shares issued	3,200,000
	$4,200,000
Less deficit from operations	600,000
Total shareholders' equity	$3,600,000

On this date the following action was taken:

(a) Common shareholders turned in their shares and received in exchange new no-par common shares, 1 share of the new stock being exchanged for every 4 shares of the old. New shares were assigned a value of $40 per share.

(b) One-half share of the new common was issued on each share of preferred in liquidation of dividends in arrears on preferred shares.

(c) The deficit from operations was applied against the contributed surplus arising from the common stock restatement.

Transactions for the remainder of 1977 affecting the shareholders' equity were as follows:

Oct. 1   10,000 shares of preferred were called in at $55 plus dividends for 3 months. The shares were formally retired.

Nov. 10   60,000 shares of new common were sold at 42.

Dec. 31   Net income for the six months ended on this date was $170,000. (Debit Income Summary.) The semi-annual dividend was declared on preferred shares and a 50 cent dividend on common shares, dividends being payable January 20, 1978.

Instructions:

(1) Record in journal form the transactions given above.

(2) Prepare the "Shareholders' equity" section of the balance sheet as at December 31, 1977.

17-6A. The Max Co. was organized on January 2, 1980, with authorized capital consisting of 40,000 shares of $8, non-participating, no-par preferred, and 250,000 shares of no-par common. During the first two years of the company's existence, the following transactions took place:

1980

Jan. 2   Sold 10,600 shares of common stock at 8.

    2   Sold 2,600 shares of preferred stock at 108.

Mar. 2   Sold common stock as follows: 10,200 shares at 11; 2,400 shares at 12.

July 10   A nearby piece of land, appraised at $202,000 was acquired for 600 shares of preferred stock and 28,000 shares of common. (Preferred stock was recorded at 108, the balance being assigned to common.)

Dec. 16   The regular preferred and a 75 cent common dividend were declared.

   28   Dividends declared on December 16 were paid.

   31   The income summary account showed a credit balance of $204,000, which was transferred to retained earnings.

1981

Feb. 27   The corporation reacquired 12,000 shares of common stock at 9 and the shares were cancelled.

Sept. 30   The corporation sold 12,000 additional shares of common stock at $10^{1}/_{2}$.

Dec. 16   The regular preferred dividend and a 40 cents common dividend were declared.

   28   Dividends declared on December 16 were paid.

   31   The income summary account showed a credit balance of $178,000, which was transferred to retained earnings.

Instructions:

(1) Give the journal entries to record the foregoing transactions.

(2) Prepare the "Shareholders' equity" section of the balance sheet as at December 31, 1981.

17-7A. A condensed balance sheet for Ferris, Ltd., as of December 31, 1978, appears below:

Ferris, Ltd.
Balance Sheet
December 31, 1978

Assets		Liabilities and Shareholders' Equity	
Assets	$350,000	Liabilities	$ 80,000
		Preferred 8% stock, $100 par	50,000
		Common stock, $50 par	100,000
		Premium on common stock	20,000
		Retained earnings	100,000
		Total liabilities and shareholders'	
Total assets	$350,000	equity	$350,000

Capital stock authorized consists of: 500 shares of 8%, cumulative, non-participating preferred stock with a prior claim on assets, and 10,000 shares of common stock.

Information relating to operations of the succeeding three years follows:

	1979	1980	1981
Dividends declared on Dec. 20, payable on Jan. 10 of following year:			
Preferred	8% cash	8% cash	8% cash
Common	$1.00 cash 50% stock*	$1.25 cash	$1.00 cash
Net income for year	$45,000	$26,000	$34,000

*Retained earnings is reduced by the par value of the stock dividend.

1980

Feb. 12 Accumulated depreciation was reduced by $48,000 following an income tax investigation. (Assume that this was an error and qualifies as a prior period adjustment.) Additional income tax of $15,000 for prior years was paid.

Mar. 3 200 shares of common stock were purchased by the corporation at $54 per share; treasury stock is recorded at cost and retained earnings are appropriated equal to such cost.

1981

Aug. 10 All of the treasury stock was resold at $59 per share and the retained earnings appropriation was cancelled.

Sept. 12 By vote of the shareholders, each share of the common stock was exchanged by the corporation for 4 shares of no-par common which was assigned a value of $15 per share.

Instructions:

(1) Give the journal entries to record the foregoing transactions for the three-year period ended December 31, 1981.

(2) Prepare the "Shareholders' equity" section of the balance sheet as it would appear at the end of 1979, 1980, and 1981.

17-8A. On March 31, 1979, the retained earnings account of Jamison, Inc., showed a balance of $3,500,000. The board of directors of Jamison, Inc., made the following decisions during the remainder of 1979 that possibly affect the retained earnings account.

Apr. 1   Jamison, Inc., decided to assume the risk for workmen's compensation. The estimated liability for the first quarter of 1979 is $30,000. Also, a fund was set up to cover the estimated liability.

April. 30   Jamison, Inc., has not experienced even a small fire since 1942; therefore, the board of directors decided to start a self-insurance plan. They decided to start with a $100,000 appropriation.

May 15   A fire did considerable damage to the outside warehouse. It cost $90,000 to repair the warehouse.

Aug. 20   The board of directors received a report from the plant engineer which indicated that the company is possibly in violation of pollution control standards. The fine for such a violation is $200,000. As a result of the engineer's report, the board decided to set up a general contingency reserve for $200,000.

Sept. 15   The company reacquired 20,000 shares of their own shares at $29; treasury stock is recorded at cost. Due to legal restrictions, Jamison has to set up an appropriation to cover the cost of the treasury stock.

Dec. 31   The company had to pay a $200,000 fine for pollution control violations and the treasury stock was sold at $31. No workmen's compensation was paid during the year.

Instructions:
Prepare all of the necessary entries to record the above transactions.

17-9A. Accounts of the Sierra Co. on December 31, 1981, show the balances listed below:

Accumulated Depreciation — Buildings		$ 340,000
Allowance for Purchase Discounts	$ 3,000	
Bonds Payable		400,000
Bond Retirement Fund	160,000	
Buildings	1,500,000	
Capital Stock		790,000
Capital Stock Subscribed		50,000
Current Assets	960,000	
Current Liabilities — Other		325,000
Customers' Deposits		25,000
Dividends Payable — Cash		20,000
Income Tax Payable		50,000
Gain from Sale of Treasury Stock at More Than Cost		40,000
Premium on Capital Stock		30,000
Retained Earnings Appropriated for Contingencies		125,000
Retained Earnings Appropriated for Bond Retirement Fund		160,000
Retained Earnings Appropriated for Purchase of Treasury Stock.		70,000
Stock Dividends Distributable		82,000
Treasury Stock, 6,000 shares at cost	70,000	
Unappropriated Retained Earnings		186,000
	$2,693,000	$2,693,000

Instructions:
From this data prepare the Shareholders' equity section as it would appear on the balance sheet.

17-10A. The following accounts are taken from the ledger of Harris Co.

ACCOUNT Retained Earnings Appropriated for Plant Expansion

DATE	ITEM	DEBIT	CREDIT	BALANCE DEBIT	BALANCE CREDIT
1977 Jan. 1	Balance				150,000
Dec. 31			25,000		175,000

ACCOUNT Retained Earnings Appropriated for Purchase of Treasury Stock

DATE	ITEM	DEBIT	CREDIT	BALANCE DEBIT	BALANCE CREDIT
1977 Jan. 1	Balance				92,000
Apr. 1			31,000		123,000
July 1		42,000			81,000

ACCOUNT Unappropriated Retained Earnings

DATE	ITEM	DEBIT	CREDIT	BALANCE DEBIT	BALANCE CREDIT
1977 Jan. 1	Balance				750,000
Apr. 1	Appropriated for purchase of treasury stock	31,000			719,000
July 1	Appropriated for treasury stock acquisitions		42,000		761,000
Oct. 31	Preferred dividends	50,000			711,000
31	Stock dividend on common shares	200,000			511,000
Dec. 31	Appropriated for plant expansion ..	25,000			486,000
31	Net income for 1977		210,000		696,000

Instructions:
Prepare a retained earnings statement for 1977 in support of the retained earnings balance to be reported on the company's balance sheet at the end of the year.

17-11A. The shareholders' equity section of the balance sheet of Chinook Ltd., as at December 31, 1981, appeared as follows:

Share capital:
Authorized 100,000, 6% preferred shares par value $10 each 100,000
   common shares, no par value
   Issued and fully paid: 5,000 preferred shares .... $ 50,000
                       5,000 common shares 40,000
Retained earnings: 1,450,000
Total shareholders' equity $1,540,000

During 1982, the following transactions affected shareholders' equity:
(a) On January 2, the company revalued its fixed assets, thereby creating an

unrealized appraisal increase of $500,000. This amount is to be amortized over a 10-year period starting with the current year.

(b) On February 1, the company received supplementary letter patents modifying the authorized share capital as follows:

(i) The existing preferred shares will become preferred shares class A with the same rights. There will be 100,000 authorized class A preferred shares.

(ii) There will also be two new classes of preferred shares:
— 100,000 6% preferred shares class B, par value $10 each, redeemable at $11.
— 100,000 6% preferred shares class C, par value $10 each, redeemable out of capital at $11.

(iii) The number of authorized common shares will be increased to 500,000 shares which may be issued for a maximum value of $50,000,000.

(c) On Febraury 15, the company bought a building which had a market value of $208,000. To pay for it, the company gave a cheque for $10,000 plus 18,000 class B preferred shares.

(d) On April 1, the company sold 100,000 warrants at a unit price of $2. Each warrant gives the owner the right to buy one common share, on or before November 1, at a unit price of $100 each. As of November 1, 90,000 warrants had been exercised.

(e) On July 1, the company paid the following dividends:
On all outstanding preferred shares, a dividend of 6%.
On all outstanding common shares, a stock dividend of 5 class C preferred shares for each outstanding common share. No warrants were exercised prior to declaration of the stock dividend.

(f) On November 1, the company redeemed all outstanding class C preferred shares and 10,000 outstanding class B preferred shares.

(g) On December 1, the company made a 2-for-1 stock split of its common shares.

(h) Net income for the year 1982 was $250,000.

(i) On December 31, the directors created a reserve for contingent losses of $100,000.

Instructions:

(1) Prepare journal entries to record the above transactions. If no journal entry is required, explain why. Show supporting computations.

(2) Prepare the shareholders' equity section of the balance sheet as at December 31, 1982.   (SMA adapted)

17-12A. The following partial balance sheet was prepared for The Black Co. Ltd. as of June 30, 1981.

The Black Co. Ltd.
Partial Balance Sheet
June 30, 1981

Shareholders' Equity:		
Common shares — $20 par value, authorized 100,000 shares;		
issued and outstanding, 25,000 shares		$500,000
Contributed surplus:		
Premium on common shares	$ 50,000	
Retained earnings	125,000	175,000
		$675,000

During the period ended December 31, 1982, the following shareholders' equity transactions took place.

1981

July 1   The company received authorization to issue 10,000 shares, $25 par value, 8% cumulative preferred stock and these shares were offered to common shareholders at $28 per share, with each preferred share including a detachable warrant, good until June 30, 1982. Each warrant entitled the holder to purchase one share of common stock for $25 per share. On the date the warrants became issuable the common shares were selling at $27 per share.

July 15   Payment was received from common shareholders for all of the authorized preferred stock and the shares were duly allotted.

Sept. 1   The board of directors granted non-transferrable stock options for 1,000 common shares to the senior officers of the company under the following conditions:

— Common shares could be purchased for $25 per share during the six months ended December 31, 1982.

— Unexercised options would lapse at that time.

Sept. 1   The market price of common shares was $27.50 per share.

Sept. 1   The company obtained a building valued at $300,000 in exchange for 10,000 common shares.

Dec. 1   The market price for common shares was $28 per share. The perferred shareholders presented cash and warrants to purchase 8,000 common shares.

1982

June 30   During the past six months, the company's common shares sold in the range of $21 to $23 per share and preferred shareholders allowed the remaining detachable warrants to lapse.

Aug. 15   Senior officers presented cash and options for 700 common shares and the shares were issued to them.

During the latter part of the year, the market value of the common stock declined significantly and no further stock options were exercised in 1982. Net income for the 18 months ended December 31, 1982 was $215,000. No dividends were declared.

Instructions:

(1) Prepare journal entries to record the above transactions.

(2) Prepare the shareholders' equity section of the balance sheet as it would appear at the interim date, December 31, 1982.   (SMA adapted)

17-13A. The following information is from the accounts of the Frazer Department Stores Ltd. as at December 31, 1981.

6% Convertible bonds (1,000 bonds outstanding)	$1,050,000
Common shares, class A	
Authorized 1,200,000 shares, par value $10	
Outstanding 800,000 shares	8,000,000
7% Cumulative preferred shares, par value $100,	
redeemable at $108, authorized 100,000 shares,	
outstanding 75,000 shares	7,500,000
Premium on preferred shares	375,000
Premium on common shares, class A	1,600,000
Retained earnings	2,549,990

During 1982 the following transactions took place:

(a) In January, Frazer Department Stores Ltd. issued for cash 250,000 class B common shares, par value $5 at a price of $35 per share (300,000 shares authorized).

(b) During April, the company acquired a catalogue operation valued at $1,300,000, from a rival firm, in exchange for 20,000 class A common shares and 10,000 class B shares which, at the date of the transaction, were actively trading at $40 and $37, respectively.

(c) On June 1, a bondholder exercised his privilege to convert 200 of his 6% convertible bonds. The bonds are convertible at a ratio of 30 class A common shares for each $1,000 bond. On that day, class A common shares were trading at $41.50. The conversion privilege expires December 31, 1984.

(d) On June 30, the board of directors declared a dividend of $0.25 per class A common share and $0.05 per class B common share. The dividend was paid in due course.

(e) The company follows the practice of not recording any executive compensation expense from stock option plans and at September 1, options had been granted to senior executives to acquire 25,000 class A shares at the market price of $30 per share. This option expires December 31, 1983. On September 2, a senior executive exercised his option to acquire 5,000 class A shares at $30 per share.

(f) On December 1, the board of directors declared a 2% stock dividend on both classes of common shares. On December 1, class A shares were trading at $42 and class B at $40.

(g) Preferred dividends were declared and paid on December 31, 1982.

Instructions:

(1) Prepare journal entries to record the above transactions.

(2) Prepare the shareholders' equity section of the balance sheet for Frazer Department Stores Ltd. as at December 31, 1982. Include any necessary notes to the statement. Assume that the December 31, 1982 retained earnings balance is $1,800,000. (SMA adapted)

17-14A. The following trial balance was taken from the accounts of the Welcome Manufacturing Company as of April 30, 1977:

Welcome Manufacturing Company
Trial Balance
April 30, 1977
(Prior to giving effect to continuance under the Canada Business Corporations Act)

Cash	$ 310,000
Accounts Receivable	800,000
Finished Goods on Hand	500,000
Finished Goods Out on Consignment	100,000
Raw Materials on Hand	750,000
Land, Buildings, and Equipment	1,460,000
Prepaid Expenses	5,400
Sales Returns and Allowances	25,000
Administrative Salaries	65,000
Cost of Goods Sold	2,350,000
Travel Expenses	30,030
Interest Expense	10,570

Accounts Payable		$ 175,000
Notes Payable		100,000
Payroll Payable		6,000
Interest Payable on 6% Bonds		10,000
Capital Stock — 6% Preferred		1,000,000
Capital Stock — Common		1,416,000
6% Bonds, due June 30, 1985		500,000
Sales		2,500,000
Retained Earnings, December 31, 1976		520
Contributed Surplus		698,480
	$6,406,000	$6,406,000

The following transactions had been completed by the company prior to continuance under the Canada Business Corporations Act:

(a) The company has purchased various lots of its $100 par value common stock, aggregating 840 shares , at an average price of $65.50 per share, for $55,020. In recording these transactions the company has cancelled the stock certificates and debited the common stock account with the par value of $84,000 and credited the contributed surplus with the difference of $28,980 between par and the cash paid.

(b) Contributed surplus was previously credited with (1) a premium at $20 per share on 15,000 shares of common stock issued, and (2) adjustments arising from the appraisal of land, buildings, and equipment bought at a receivers' sale, $398,000.

(c) 6% bonds of the face amount of $250,000 falling due on December 31, 1983, were issued on January 1, 1959, at a 10% discount. To June 30, 1975, $16,500 of this discount had been charged against revenues and as of this date the entire issue of these bonds was retired at par and the unamortized discount debited to Contributed Surplus.

(d) A new issue of $500,000, 6% ten-year bonds was effected as of July 1, 1975, at par. Expenses incurred with respect to this issue in the amount of $20,000 were debited to Contributed Surplus.

Instructions:

Prepare a balance sheet as of April 30, 1977, in which effect has been given to such changes as may be necessary in view of the treatment accorded by the company to the transactions described above and in view of the company's continuance under the Canada Business Corporations Act effective April 30, 1977. The company is entitled to carry forward contributed surplus upon its continuance. (AICPA adapted)

17-15A. You are a senior accountant responsible for the annual audit of Desco, Inc., for the year ended December 31, 1977. The information available to you is presented on the following pages. You may assume that any pertinent information not presented has already been checked and found satisfactory.

(a) Excerpts from the December 31, 1977 trial balance are given below:

	Debit	Credit
Retained Earnings		$40,000
Allowance for Inventory Decline to Market		7,500
Capital Stock, 600 shares		60,000

(b) The accounts have not been closed but all adjusting entries which the company expects to make have been posted. Their work sheets shows a $15,000 net income for the year.

(c) Selected ledger accounts follow:

ACCOUNT   Retained Earnings

DATE		ITEM	POST. REF.	DEBIT	CREDIT	BALANCE	
						DEBIT	CREDIT
1976							
Dec.	31	Balance					52,960
1977							
Apr.	29		CR8		200		53,160
Aug.	6		CD62	160			53,000
Oct.	10		J34	10,000			43,000
Dec.	31		J40	3,000			40,000

(*Note:* The balance at December 31, 1976, agrees with last year's working papers and represents the net difference over the years between credits from the income summary account and debits for dividends.)

ACCOUNT   Allowance for Inventory Decline to Market

DATE		ITEM	POST. REF.	DEBIT	CREDIT	BALANCE	
						DEBIT	CREDIT
1977							
June	30		J19		5,000		5,000
Sept.	26		CD78	500			4,500
Dec.	31		J40		3,000		7,500

(d) Analysis of selected cash receipts.

Page	Date	Account Credited	Amount	Explanation
8	1977			
	Apr. 29	{ Capital Stock	$10,000	Sold $100 par stock ✓
		{ Retained Earnings	200	at $102
20	Oct. 10	Building	20,000	See J34

(e) Analysis of selected cash disbursements.

Page	Date	Account Debited	Amount	Explanation
62	1977			
	Aug. 6	Retained Earnings	$ 160	Freak accident to company truck not covered by insurance; repair by Doe & Co.
78	Sept. 26	{ Allowance for Inventory Decline to Market	500	Purchase of materials (X Co.) to be used on orders taken prior to June 30, 1977; $500 is price increase since June 30, 1977.
		{ Purchases	6,300	

(f) Selected entries in the general journal.

Page	Date	Entry and Explanation	Debit	Credit
19	1977			
	June 30	Inventory Loss (Income Summary)	5,000	
		Allowance for Inventory Decline to Market		5,000
		Provision voted by board of directors for estimated future price increases in materials needed to complete orders on hand. (*Note:* Orders do not represent contractual obligations.)		
34	Oct. 10	Accumulated Depreciation	50,000	
		Retained Earnings	10,000	
		Building.......................................		60,000
		Sale of main office building, moved to rental quarters downtown. (See CR20)		
40	Dec. 31	Retained Earnings	3,000	
		Allowance for Inventory Decline to Market		3,000
		Provision to value materials inventory at lower of cost or market in accordance with company pricing policy.		

Cost $30,000
Market 27,000
$ 3,000

Instructions:

Prepare in good form:

(1) Schedule of recommended correcting entries to be placed in the accounts to state the shareholders' equity accounts in accordance with generally accepted accounting principles.

(2) Statement of retained earnings for 1977.

(3) "Shareholders' equity" section of balance sheet. (AICPA adapted)

18 BOOK VALUE AND EARNINGS PER SHARE

The financial statements of a corporation are illustrated in Chapter 17 and also in Appendix A. Users of these statements are interested in certain measurements that can be developed from data concerning shareholders' equity and operating results for the period. Two measurements of particular interest are described in this chapter: (1) the *book value per share* as determined by an analysis of shareholders' equity as reported on the balance sheet, and (2) the *earnings per share* as determined by an analysis of the capital structure of the company and the operations as reported on the income statement.

BOOK VALUE PER SHARE

The *book value per share* measurement is the dollar equity of corporate capital represented by each share of stock. It is the amount that would be paid on each share assuming the company is liquidated and the amount available to shareholders is exactly the amount reported as the shareholders' equity.[1] The book value measurement is used as a factor in evaluating share value. Both single values and comparative values may be required, the latter to afford data relative to trends and growth in the shareholders' equity.

---

[1] Financial analyses frequently follow the practice of subtracting any amounts reported for intangible assets from the total reported for the shareholders' equity in calculating book value per share.

One Class of Outstanding Shares

When only one class of shares is outstanding, the calculation of book value is relatively simple; the total shareholders' equity is divided by the number of shares outstanding at the close of the reporting period. When shares have been reacquired and treasury stock is reported, its cost should be recognized as a subtraction item in arriving at the shareholders' equity, and the shares represented by the treasury stock should be subtracted from the shares issued in arriving at the shares outstanding. When shares have been subscribed for but are unissued, depending upon the provisions of the incorporating jurisdiction, capital stock subscribed may be included in the total shareholders' equity and the shares subscribed added to shares outstanding. To illustrate, assume shareholders' equity for the Moore Corporation as shown below:

Share capital:		
Capital stock, $10 par, 100,000 shares issued, 5,000 shares reacquired and held as treasury stock (see below)	$1,000,000	
Capital stock subscribed, 20,000 shares	200,000	$1,200,000
Contributed surplus		350,000
Retained earnings:		
Appropriated	$ 200,000	
Unappropriated	450,000	650,000
		$2,200,000
Less shares reacquired and held as treasury stock, at cost (5,000 shares)		75,000
Total shareholders' equity		$2,125,000

The book value per share is calculated as follows:

$2,125,000 (total capital) ÷ 115,000 (shares issued, 100,000, plus shares subscribed, 20,000, minus treasury shares, 5,000) = $18.48.

More than One Class of Outstanding Shares

When more than one class of shares have been issued, it is necessary to consider the rights of the different classes of shareholders. With preferred and common issues, for example, the prior rights of preferred shareholders must first be recognized to determine the portion of the shareholders' equity related to preferred shareholders. The preferred shareholders' equity when subtracted from the total shareholders' equity gives the equity related to common shareholders, or the *residual equity*. The preferred equity divided by the number of preferred shares gives the book value of a preferred share; the common equity divided by the number of common shares gives the book value of a common share.

The portion of the shareholders' equity related to preferred would be that amount distributable to preferred shareholders in the event of corporate liquidation and calls for consideration of the liquidation value and also the dividend rights of the preferred issue.

Liquidation Value. Preferred shares may have a liquidation value equal to par, to par plus a premium, or to a stated dollar amount. Capital equal to this value for the number of preferred shares outstanding should be assigned to preferred stock. A preferred call price differing from the amount to be paid to preferred shareholders upon liquidation would not be applicable for book value computations; the call of preferred shares is not obligatory, hence call prices are not considered relevant in the apportionment of values between preferred and common shareholders.

Dividend Rights. (1) Preferred shares may have certain rights in retained earnings as a result of dividend privileges. For example, preferred shares may be entitled to dividends not yet declared for a portion of the current year, assuming liquidation; here a portion of retained earnings equal to the dividend requirements would be related to preferred shares. (2) Preferred shares may be cumulative with dividends in arrears. When terms of the preferred issue provide that dividends in arrears must be paid upon liquidation regardless of any retained earnings or deficit balance reported in the accounts, capital equivalent to the dividends in arrears must be assigned to preferred shares even though this impairs or eliminates the equity relating to common shareholders. When preferred shareholders are entitled to dividends in arrears only in the event of accumulated earnings, as much retained earnings as are available, but not in excess of such dividend requirements, relate to the preferred shares.

The computation of book values for preferred and common shares is illustrated in the following series of examples. The examples are based upon the shareholders' equity reported by the Maxwell Corporation on December 31, 1981, which follows:

Preferred 6% shares, $50 par, 10,000 shares	$ 500,000
Common shares, $10 par; 100,000 shares	1,000,000
Retained earnings	250,000
Total shareholders' equity	$1,750,000

Example 1 — Assume preferred dividends have been paid to July 1, 1981. Preferred shares have a liquidation value of $52 and are entitled to current unpaid dividends. Book values on December 31, 1981, are developed as follows:

Total shareholders' equity		$1,750,000
Equity identified with preferred:		
Liquidation value, 10,000 shares @ $52	$520,000	
Current dividends, 3% of $500,000	15,000	535,000
Balance — equity identified with common		$1,215,000

6% × ½ yr.

Book values per share:
Preferred: $ 535,000 ÷ 10,000 .... $53.50
Common: $1,215,000 ÷ 100,000 .... $12.15

Example 2 — Assume preferred shares have a liquidation value of $52. Preferred shares are cumulative with dividends 5 years in arrears that must be paid in the event of liquidation. Book values for common and preferred shares would be developed as follows:

Total shareholders' equity $1,750,000
Equity identified with preferred:
Liquidation value, 10,000 shares @ $52 .... $520,000
Dividends in arrears, 30% of $500,000   150,000   670,000
Balance — equity identified with common....................... $1,080,000

Book values per share:
Preferred: $ 670,000 ÷ 10,000 .... $67.00
Common: $1,080,000 ÷ 100,000 .... $10.80

%×5yrs.

Example 3 — Assume preferred shares have a liquidation value equal to their par value. Preferred shares are cumulative with dividends 10 years in arrears payable in the event of liquidation even though impairing the invested capital of the common shareholders. Book values for common and preferred shares are developed as follows:

Total shareholders' equity $1,750,000
Equity identified with preferred:
Liquidation value, 10,000 shares @ $50 .... $500,000
Dividends in arrears, 60% of $500,000   300,000   800,000
Balance — equity identified with common....................... $ 950,000

Book values per share:
Preferred: $800,000 ÷ 10,000 .... $80.00
Common: $950,000 : 100,000 .... $ 9.50

%×10 yrs

The nature and the limitations of the share book value measurements must be appreciated in using these data. Share book values are developed from the net asset values as reported in the accounts. Furthermore, calculations require the assumption of liquidation in the allocation of amounts to classes of shares. Book values of assets may vary materially from present fair values or immediate realizable values. Moreover, book values of property items are stated in terms of the "going concern"; the full implications of a "quitting concern" approach would call for many significant changes in the values as reported in the accounts.

EARNINGS PER SHARE PRESENTATION ON THE INCOME STATEMENT

The term *earnings per share* refers to the amount earned during a given period on each share of common stock outstanding. It is a more useful figure than net income for comparison purposes among accounting periods because it normalizes net income across periods that may have varying capital structures. As a successful company grows, net income will naturally increase. But the investor is interested in determining if it is growing relative to the size of the company's capital structure. Investors use earnings per share figures to evaluate the results of operations of a business in order to make investment decisions. For example, by dividing the earnings per share figure into the market price per share, a *price-earnings ratio* may be computed that will permit a comparison among different companies. Thus, if Company A earns $3 per share with a $21 per share market price, and Company B earns $6 per share with a $54 per share market value, an investor can state that Company A shares are selling at seven times earnings and the shares of Company B at nine times earnings. If other things were equal between these two companies, Company A's stock should be the better buy since its market price is lower in relation to earnings than is Company B's stock.

Investors, however, may be more interested in dividends than in earnings. This information may be communicated to them by using earnings per share data to compute a *dividend payout percentage* or *payout rate*. This rate is computed by dividing earnings per share into dividends per share. Thus, if Company A in the previous example pays a dividend of $2 per share, and Company B pays $3 per share, the payout percentage would be 66²/₃% for Company A and 50% for Company B.

Earnings per share data receive wide recognition in annual reports issued by companies, in the press, and in financial reporting publications. This measurement is frequently regarded as an important determinant of the market price of common shares. The earnings per share statistic is the first and, to date, only instance where those responsible for formulating accounting principles have deemed it necessary to establish rules governing the computation and disclosure of a financial ratio. The issuance of pronouncements on earnings per share supports the view that this ratio is probably the single most quoted measure of corporate financial performance.

In 1969, the Accounting Research Committee issued Section 3500 of the *Accounting Recommendations* which includes the following comment on the need for a pronouncement.

> Because of the usefulness of earnings per share data, an increasing number of companies provide this information in their financial reports. However, there have been many differences in the methods of calculating earnings per share figures and in the manner in which they are presented. To be of maximum usefulness, such figures must be computed on a consistent basis and be presented in the most meaningful manner.[2]

The Accounting Research Committee in Section 3500 has made recommendations for the calculation and presentation of earnings per share data

---

[2]*CICA Handbook: Accounting Recommendations, Section 3500*, "Earnings per Share" (Toronto: Canadian Institute of Chartered Accountants, 1969), par. .02.

under a variety of circumstances. Where Section 3500 fails to state the procedures to be followed in specific circumstances, the accountant will have to exercise judgment in developing supportable presentations within the recommended framework.

The many problems in developing earnings per share presentations arise because of the different securities making up the capital structure of a corporaton. Many new and unique securities have been issued over the past several years. Some of these securities have elements similar to common shares, and their market price often reacts to the market price of the common shares. A principal use of earnings per share data is to enable an investor to evaluate the company's future earnings potential on a per share basis. The possible future conversion of securities, and exercise of stock options, warrants, and other rights, may materially alter earnings per share data. Because of this, modifications to the computations of earnings per share are necessary for many corporations.

Simple and Complex Capital Structures

The capital structure of a corporation may be classified as *simple* or *complex*. If a company has only common shares outstanding, or there are no convertible securities, stock options, warrants, or other rights outstanding that might have a dilutive impact on earnings per share, it is obviously a company with a simple capital structure. A single earnings per share figure is computed by dividing the net income for the period, reduced by applicable dividends on preferred shares, by the weighted average number of common shares outstanding for the period. If extraordinary items are included on the income statement, a separate earnings per share figure must be reported for the income before extraordinary items. The per share amount of extraordinary items need not be reported.

Even if convertible securities, stock options, warrants or other rights exist, the capital structure may still be classified as simple if no potential material dilution of earnings per share is likely on the conversion or exercise of these items. Potential earnings per share dilution exists if earnings per share would decrease or the loss per share would increase as a result of the conversion of securities or exercise of stock options, warrants, or other rights, based upon conditions existing at the financial statement date. In the United States, the Accounting Principles Board defined material dilution as being a decrease of 3% or more in the aggregate earnings per share figure; the Accounting Research Committee decided this should be a matter of professional judgment. If the conversion of securities or exercise of stock options, warrants, or other rights would increase earnings per share or decrease loss per share, these securities would be classified as *anti-dilutive*. Thus, if earnings per share based upon common shares outstanding was $2.45, and assumed conversion of convertible preferred shares would increase earnings per share to $2.50, the convertible preferred shares would be classified as anti-dilutive. No adjustment of earnings per share data is required for anti-dilutive securities.

If a corporation's capital structure does not qualify as being simple, it is classified as complex and two earnings per share figures may be required. The first, or *basic earnings per share* figure, is computed as if the capital structure were simple. The second, or *fully diluted earnings per share* figure, gives effect to all material, potentially dilutive convertible securities, stock options, warrants, or other rights. Fully diluted earnings per share provides for the maximum potential dilution of earnings which might occur. The term *dual disclosure* is often used with reference to the earnings per share disclosures that may be required of corporations with complex capital structures.

The general pattern of earnings per share disclosures, which depends upon the classification of a corporation's capital structure, and for the fully diluted presentation, upon the materiality of the potential dilution, is set forth in the diagram below. In very specific circumstances, as described later in this chapter, additional earnings per share disclosures may also apply.

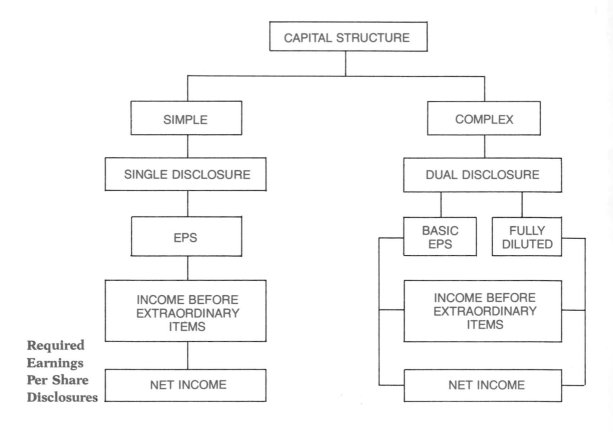

The Simple Capital Structure — Computational Guidelines

The simple capital structure calls for a single disclosure on the face of the income statement or in a note cross referenced to the income statement designated simply as *earnings per share*. The earnings per share computation presents no problem when only common shares have been issued and the number outstanding has remained the same for the entire period. Earnings divided by the number of shares outstanding gives the earnings per share. Frequently, however, consideration will have to be given to the following matters:

(1) When common shares have been issued or reacquired during a period, the resources available to the corporation have changed and this change should impact upon earnings. Under these circumstances, a weighted average for shares outstanding should be computed.

The weighted average number of shares may be computed by determining month-shares-outstanding and dividing by 12 to obtain the weighted average for the year. For example, if a corporation has 10,000 shares outstanding at the beginning of the year, issues 5,000 more shares on May 1, and retires 2,000 shares on November 1, the weighted average number of shares would be computed as illustrated below.

		Month-Shares
Jan. 1 to May 1	.10,000 × 4 months	40,000
May 1 to Nov. 1	.15,000 × 6 months	90,000
Nov. 1 to Dec. 1	.13,000 × 2 months	26,000
Total month-shares		156,000
Weighted average number of shares:		
156,000 ÷ 12		13,000

The same answer could be obtained by applying a weight to each period equivalent to the portion of the year since the last change in the number of shares occurred, as follows:

Jan. 1 to May 1	10,000 × 4/12 year	3,333
May 1 to Nov. 1	15,000 × 6/12 year	7,500
Nov. 1 to Dec. 31	13,000 × 2/12 year	2,167
Weighted average number of shares		13,000

In certain circumstances the date during the period when common shares should be considered issued for purposes of earnings per share computations may be different from the actual date on which the shares were issued. Two situations give rise to this possibility: (1) common shares issued to effect a business combination; and (2) common shares issued on conversion of senior shares, such as preferreds, or on conversion of debt. In the first situation, "the calculation of the weighted average of common shares outstanding during the period should consider the common shares as having been issued at the date from which the results of operations of the acquired business are included in the income statement."[3] When common shares are issued as a result of conversions, "the calculation of the weighted average of common shares outstanding during the year should consider the common shares as having been issued as at the date of termination of the dividend or interest obligation."[4] In general, interest accrues but dividends do not. However, the terms of the conversion privilege may alter the general rule. Thus, for example, interest may not accrue when debt is converted into common shares on any date between interest rates.

(2) When the number of common shares outstanding has changed during a period as a result of a stock dividend on common shares, a stock split, or a reverse split, recognition of this change must be made in arriving at the amount of earnings per share. In developing comparative data, recognition of equivalent changes in the common shares of all prior periods included in the statements is necessary. To illustrate these changes, assume in the above example a two-for-one stock split occurred on November 1 before the retirement of the 2,000 shares of stock. The computation of the weighted average number of shares would be changed as follows:

Jan. 1 to May 1	10,000 × 200% (two-for-one stock split) × 4/12 year	6,667
May 1 to Nov. 1	15,000 × 200% (two-for-one stock split) × 6/12 year	15,000
Nov. 1 to Dec. 31	28,000* × 2/12 year	4,667
Weighted average number of shares		26,334

*30,000 outstanding − 2,000 retired = 28,000 shares

This illustration serves to confirm that stock dividends on common shares, stock splits and reverse stock splits are exceptions to the weight-averaging requirement described above. Common shares issued to effect a business combination to be accounted for as a pooling of interests are also an exception to the weight-averaging requirement. This exception stems from the general rule that shares issued in a business combination should be considered issued as at the date from which the results of operations of the acquired (pooled) corporation are included on the income statement. It should also be noted that a stock dividend on senior shares is recognized only from the date of issue, and therefore is subject to the weight-averaging requirement.

Only by giving retroactive recognition to the above noted changes in the number of shares outstanding can earnings per share presentations for prior periods be stated on a basis comparable with the earnings per share presentation for the current period. This is because these particular changes in

---

[3] *Ibid.*, par. 21.
[4] *Ibid.*, par. 23.

shares outstanding are only changes of form rather than substance. Similar retroactive adjustments must be made even if the stock dividend or split, for example, occurs subsequent to the end of the period but before the financial statements are issued; disclosure of this situation should be made in a note to the financial statements.

(3) When a capital structure includes preferred shares, the dividend claim of preferred shareholders may have to be deducted from net income and also from income before extraordinary items in arriving at the earnings related to the common shares. If preferred dividends are non-cumulative, only the dividends declared on preferred shares during the period are deducted. If preferred dividends are cumulative, the full amount of dividends on preferred shares for the period, whether declared or not, must be deducted in arriving at the earnings or loss balance related to the common shares. If there is a loss for the period, the amount of dividends on cumulative preferred stock for the period is added to the loss in arriving at the full loss related to the common shares.

To illustrate the computation of earnings per share for a simple capital structure for a comparative two-year period, assume the following data:

Summary of changes in share capital and retained earnings:

	$6 Cumulative Preferred Shares No Par		Common Shares No Par		Retained Earnings
	Shares	Amount	Shares	Amount	
Dec. 31, 1979 Balances ..	10,000	$1,000,000	200,000	$1,000,000	$4,000,000
June 30, 1980 Issuance of of 100,000 shares of common stock			100,000	600,000	
June 30, 1980 Dividend on preferred shares					(60,000)
June 30, 1980 Dividend on common shares, 30¢					(90,000)
Dec. 31, 1980 Net income for year, including extra-ordinary gain of $75,000					360,000
Dec. 31, 1980 Balances ..	10,000	$1,000,000	300,000	$1,600,000	$4,210,000
May 1, 1981 50% Stock dividend on common shares................			150,000	800,000	(800,000)
June 30, 1981 Dividend on preferred shares					(60,000)
Dec. 31, 1981 Loss for year					(75,000)
	10,000	$1,000,000	450,000	$2,400,000	$3,275,000

(handwritten annotations: "10,000 sh. × $6" beside (60,000); "300,000 sh. × .30" beside (90,000))

Weighted average number of common shares outstanding based on December 31, 1981 subdivision of share capital:

1980: Jan. 1-June 30	200,000 × 150% (50% stock dividend in 1981) × 6/12 year 150,000	
July 1-Dec. 31	200,000 + 100,000 (issue of shares in 1980) × 150% (50% stock dividend in 1981) × 6/12 year 225,000	375,000
1981: Jan. 1-Dec. 31	300,000 × 150% (50% stock dividend in 1981) × 12/12 year	450,000

Computation of comparative earnings per share to be reported in 1981:

1980: Income before extraordinary gain ... _(360 - 75)_	$285,000
Deduct preferred dividend	60,000
Income after preferred dividend	$225,000
Add extraordinary gain	75,000
Net income identified with common shares	$300,000
Earnings per share, income before extraordinary gain, $225,000 ÷ 375,000	$ .60
Earnings per share, net income, $300,000 ÷ 375,000	$ .80
1981: Loss for year	$ 75,000
Add cumulative preferred dividends	60,000
Loss identified with common stock	$135,000
Loss per share, $135,000 ÷ 450,000	$ .30

It would be inappropriate to report earnings per share on preferreds in view of the limited dividend rights of such shares. In the case of preferred shares, however, it may be informative to indicate the number of times or the extent to which the dividend per share requirements were met. Such information should be designated as *earnings coverage on preferred shares* and in the foregoing example would be computed as follows:

300 + 60 pref. div.

1980: Earnings coverage on preferred shares, $360,000 ÷ $60,000 (cumulative preferred requirements) = 6.00 times*

1981: Earnings coverage on preferred shares. Because there was a loss in 1981, no earnings coverage on preferred shares can be computed.

*Earnings coverage on preferred shares before extraordinary gain, $285,000 ÷ $60,000, or 4.75 times.

The Complex Capital Structure — Computational Guidelines

As discussed above, complex capital structures call for a dual disclosure of earnings per share data on the face of the income statement or in a note cross referenced to the income statement: (1) basic earnings per share — a presentation which parallels the computation of earnings per share for a simple capital structure; and (2) fully diluted earnings per share — a presentation based on the assumption that all of the contingent issuances of common shares that would individually reduce earnings per share had taken place.

It should be recognized that basic earnings per share for a complex structure is not the same as primary earnings per share determined in accordance with APB Opinion No. 15.

Primary earnings per share is based upon the number of common shares outstanding plus the shares represented by common stock equivalents, securities that are in substance common shares and that have a dilutive effect on earnings per share. Although both Section 3500 and APB Opinion No. 15 may require disclosure of fully diluted earnings per share, the pronouncements contain important differences in the methods they recommend for calculating dilution on a per share basis.[5] Canadian corporations that have distributed securities in the United States must comply with Section 3500 for financial reporting purposes in Canada, and also with APB Opinion No. 15 when filing with the Securities and Exchange Commission in the United States.[6] In a few instances, Canadian corporations report earnings per share data determined in accordance with APB Opinion No. 15 on the grounds that the numbers are not materially different from what would result by applying Section 3500. At least one corporation, Genstar, provides earnings per share data determined in accordance with methods used both in Canada and the United States.

The difference between the basic and fully diluted presentations indicates the maximum extent of potential dilution through the conversion or exercise of rights that includes a call on the issuance of common shares. The objective of the fully diluted presentation "is to reflect the maximum potential dilution of current earnings per share on a prospective basis."[7] Since computation rests upon assumed conversions and assumed exercises, some of which may never take place, fully diluted earnings per share data are hypothetical. Moreover, this hypothetical data may certainly be described as conservative, perhaps even as being pessimistically conservative.

Although not a mandatory requirement, a note or schedule should be provided to accompany dual disclosure explaining the bases upon which both basic and fully diluted earnings are calculated. The assumptions made and the resulting adjustments required in developing the earnings per share data should be described in the note or schedule.

The fully diluted earnings per share statistic is hypothetical; it reflects assumptions relating to the conversion of debt and senior shares and the exercise of options, warrants and other contingent issuances. Again, the

[5]John R. E. Parker, "Income Reporting and the Canada-US Gap in GAAP" *CA Magazine*, May 1974, p. 40-41.
[6]*CICA Handbook: Accounting Recommendations, Section 3500, op. cit.*, par. 48.
[7]*Ibid.*, par. 34.

objective of the fully diluted presentation is to disclose "the maximum potential dilution of current earnings per share on a prospective basis."[8] Potential dilution results whenever the increase in the number of common shares outstanding because of assumed conversions, exercises, and contingent issuances, is not matched by an increase in the income figures of sufficient amount to maintain the original or basic earnings per share ratio. Thus, the calculation of fully-diluted earnings per share should exclude those securities whose assumed conversion, exercise, or other contingent issuance, would have the effect of increasing basic earnings per share or of decreasing a loss per share. It should also be noted that "conversion or exercise rights which do not become effective within ten years following the date of the balance sheet need not be considered as a dilutive factor."[9]

Assumed conversions should be computed using the *if converted* method. Thus, the calculation assumes conversion as at the beginning of the period, or at the date of issue of the convertible securities if issued during the current period. Similarly, options, warrants and other contingent issuances are assumed to have been exercised as at the beginning of the period or at the grant date, if later. As will be explained in detail, each individual assumption must impact on both the numerator and the denominator of the earnings per share ratio. The assumed conversion of debt, for example, has a measurable effect on earnings per share which may be determined by dividing the income or earnings adjustment by the number of shares issuable on the assumed conversion of debt. If the amount of this per share effect exceeds basic earnings per share the convertible debt would be classified as anti-dilutive and excluded from the computation of fully diluted earnings per share. Each assumed conversion and exercise should be tested individually in order to identify and exclude those securities the inclusion of which would increase earnings per share or decrease a loss per share.

Convertible Securities. In order to compute fully diluted earnings per share when convertible securities exist, adjustments must be made to both the income amount(s) and to the number of common shares outstanding. These adjustments must reflect what these amounts would have been if the conversion had taken place at the beginning of the current period or at the date of issuance of the convertible securities, whichever comes later. If the securities are bonds, the numerator is adjusted by adding back the interest expense, net of tax, to the net income and to the income before extraordinary items, if any extraordinary items are being reported; the number of common shares outstanding is increased by the number of shares that would have been issued upon the assumed conversion. If the convertible securities are shares of preferred stock, no reduction is made from income for preferred

---

[8]*Ibid.*
[9]*Ibid.*, par. 33.

dividends, as is done with the computation of earnings per share in a simple capital structure; the number of common shares outstanding is increased by the number of shares that would have been issued upon the assumed conversion. If the numerator for basic earnings per share is used as a starting point for determining the numerator for fully diluted, applicable preferred dividends have, of course, already been deducted from income, and therefore the dividend rights pertaining to convertible preferred shares must be added back. If the convertible securities were issued during the year, adjustments would be made for only the portion of the year since the issuance date. In addition, each assumed conversion should be tested to assure that its effect is dilutive rather than anti-dilutive.

The following examples illustrate the computation of fully diluted earnings per share when convertible bonds are the only potentially dilutive securities outstanding.

Summary of relevant information:

Maturity value of 8% convertible bonds	$500,000
Net income for the year	$ 83,000
Common shares outstanding (no change during year)	100,000
Conversion terms of convertible bonds . . . . 80 common shares for $1,000 bond	
Assumed tax rate	45%

Basic earnings per share

Net income	$ 83,000
Number of common shares outstanding	100,000
Basic earnings per share	$ .83

Fully diluted earnings per share

Net income		$ 83,000
Add interest on convertible bonds, net-of-tax:		
Interest, $500,000 at 8%	$40,000	
Less income tax at 45%	18,000	22,000
Adjusted net income		$105,000
Number of common shares outstanding		100,000
Additional shares issued upon assumed conversion of bonds, 500 × 80		40,000
Adjusted number of shares		140,000
Fully diluted earnings per share, $105,000 ÷ 140,000		$ .75

The adjustment to the numerator may also be determined by use of the following formula which determines a net-of-tax interest rate:

$$in = i(1 - t).$$

Where:

in = interest rate net-of-tax

i = interest rate

t = tax rate

$in = .08\,(1-.45)$

$= .044$

Applied to this example, the formula gives a net interest rate of 4.4 per cent, and resulting adjustment to the numerator of $22,000 (4.4% of $500,000).

In this example, the dilution of 8¢ per share is approximately 10 per cent of basic earnings per share. This is clearly material dilution, and therefore fully diluted earnings per share should be disclosed in a note cross referenced to the income statement, or alternatively on the face of the statement.

If the convertible bonds had been issued on March 31 of the current period, the adjustments would be made to reflect only the period subsequent to the issuance date, or $3/4$ of a year.

Fully diluted earnings per share		
Net income		$83,000
Add interest on convertible bonds, net-of-tax:		
Interest, $500,000 at 8% for $3/4$ year	$30,000	
Less income tax of 45%	13,500	16,500
Adjusted net income		$99,500
Number of common shares outstanding		100,000
Additional shares issued upon assumed conversion of bonds,		
500 × 80 × $3/4$		30,000
Adjusted number of shares		130,000
Fully diluted earnings per share, $99,500 ÷ 130,000		$ .77

If the 8% convertible bonds had been 8% convertible preferred shares issued in a prior year, the computations would be as illustrated below.

Basic earnings per share	
Net income, assuming no interest on bonds (as computed above)	$105,000
Less preferred dividends	40,000
Net income identified with common shares	$ 65,000
Number of common shares outstanding	100,000
Basic earnings per share	$ .65

Fully diluted earnings per share	
Net income assuming no interest on bonds	$105,000
Number of common shares outstanding	100,000
Additional shares issued upon assumed conversion of	
preferred shares 500 × 80	40,000
Adjusted number of shares	140,000
Fully diluted earnings per share, 105,000 ÷ 140,000	$ .75

In this latter case, the assumed conversion of preferred shares is anti-dilutive (70¢ as compared to 75¢). Thus, the preferred share conversion would be excluded, and there would be no fully diluted earnings per share to report.

The fact that the assumed conversion of preferred shares is anti-dilutive could have been determined by simply applying the anti-dilutive test. In the example, the dividends on the preferred shares are $40,000 (with no tax deduction), and the conversion terms call for the issue of 40,000 common shares. The per share effect of the assumed conversion is $1.00 ($40,000 ÷ 40,000). Since this exceeds basic earnings per share, the preferred share conversion is anti-dilutive.

Stock Options, Warrants and Other Contingent Issuances. Stock options, warrants, and similar arrangements may provide no cash yield, but have value because they offer rights for the acquisition of common shares at specified prices for possibly an extended period. Since holders clearly have a contingent call on the issue of common shares, these arrangements may be potentially dilutive.

If it is assumed that the exercise of options, warrants, or other contingent issuances takes place as at the beginning of the period or at date of issue, whichever is later, additional cash resources would have been available for corporate use. In order to compute fully diluted earnings per share when these arrangements exist, either net income must be increased to take into consideration the additional revenue such additional resources would produce, or the cash must be assumed to be used for some non-revenue producing purpose. The former approach was selected by the Accounting Research Committee and they accordingly recommended that imputed earnings, net-of-tax, on the cash receivable on the assumed exercise be included in the numerator used to compute fully diluted earnings per share. The Committee in Section 3500 takes the position that "the appropriate rate of return for imputing earnings must be a matter of judgment in each case and should be disclosed together with the dollar amount of imputed earnings after income taxes."[10]

To illustrate the computation of fully diluted earnings per share when stock options are outstanding and there are otherwise no potentially dilutive securities, assume the following data:

Summary of relevant information:	
Net income for the year	$ 92,800
Common shares outstanding (no change during year)	100,000
Options outstanding to purchase common shares	20,000
Exercise price per share on options	$ 6
Assumed earnings rate	10%
Assumed tax rate	45%
Basic earnings per share	
Net income	$92,800
Number of common shares outstanding	100,000
Basic earnings per share	$ .93

[10]*Ibid.*, par. 37.

Fully diluted earnings per share		
Net income		$92,800
Add imputed earnings, net-of-tax:		
Imputed earnings, 20,000 × $6 at 10%	$12,000	
Less income tax at 45%	5,400	6,600
Adjusted net income		$99,400
Number of common shares outstanding		100,000
Additional shares issued on assumed exercise of stock options		20,000
Adjusted number of shares		120,000
Fully diluted earnings per share, $99,400 ÷ 120,000		$ .83

In this example, the dilution of 10¢ per share is approximately 11 per cent of basic earnings per share and therefore dual disclosure would apply. If the stock options had been granted during the current period, the adjustments would be made to reflect only the period subsequent to the grant date of the options.

Fully Diluted Earnings Per Share

To illustrate the computation of fully diluted earnings per share, the data used to illustrate the computation of earnings per share for a simple capital structure (page 761) will be expanded to include the following relevant information:

1. The $6 cumulative preferred shares are convertible into common shares on the basis of 12 common shares for each preferred share.
2. The common shares issued on June 30, 1980, were part of a unit that included 6% convertible bonds with a maturity value of $100,000. The bonds are convertible into common shares on the basis of 12 common shares for each $100 bond.
3. Stock options for 20,000 common shares granted in 1979 permit the holder to purchase one common share at $5 for each option held.
4. Stock options for 10,000 common shares granted on March 31, 1981, permit the holder to purchase one common share at $9 for each option held.
5. The rate of return to be used for imputing earnings on the funds to be provided assuming the exercise of stock options is 15 per cent before income tax. Assume an income tax rate of 40 per cent.

In general, a schedule with two or three columns, three in the event extraordinary items are reported, is a useful way to organize the computation of earnings per share data. For the fully diluted computation, one additional column may be added to test for anti-dilution. In general, the numerator and denominator for basic earnings per share may be conveniently used as a starting point for the fully diluted computation.[11]

---

[11]When common shares have been issued during the current period as a result of the conversion of senior shares or debt additional information may be required with reference to basic earnings per share. As discussed later in the chapter, this situation does not lend itself to use of the basic numerator and denominator as a starting point for the fully diluted computation, except in the rare circumstances when both issue and conversion take place in the same fiscal period.

In the example below, the $9 stock options are excluded because they are anti-dilutive, their per share effect being $.81 ($8,100 ÷ 10,000 shares).

In Section 3500 the Accounting Research Committee points out that "the fully diluted earnings per share figures for the preceding period may no longer be meaningful."[12] In this example, the granting of $9 stock options on March 31, 1981, impairs the comparability of any fully diluted per share data for 1980 and 1981. The Committee recommends that "where fully diluted earnings per share figures are provided for the preceding period, the previously reported fully diluted earnings per share figures should not be recalculated for conversions of senior shares or debt, exercises of rights, warrants and options and contingent issuances which took place during the current period. Similarly, convertible senior shares, convertible debt, options, rights and warrants issued during the period should be excluded from any calculation of fully diluted earnings per share for the preceding period."[13]

	Common Shares Outstanding	Income Before Extraordinary items	Net Income	Anti-Dilutive Test
1980 basic earnings per share	375,000	$225,000	$300,000		← See p. 762
Assumed conversion of convertible bonds:				
Number of shares, 1,000 × 12 × ¹/₂ year .	6,000 ✓			
Interest net of tax, $100,000 at 3.6%* for ¹/₂ year		1,800	1,800	.30
Assumed conversion of preferred shares:				
Number of shares, 10,000 × 12	120,000			
Preferred dividends . .		60,000	60,000	.50
Assumed exercise of $5 stock options:				
Number of shares	20,000			
Imputed earnings 20,000 × $5 × 9%* . .		9,000	9,000	.45
	521,000	$295,800	$370,800	
Fully diluted earnings per share		$ .57	$ .71	

*.06 (1 − .4) = .036 or 3.6%
.15 (1 − .4) = .09 or 9%

When a loss is reported, such as is the case for 1981 in the example, any contingent issuance is anti-dilutive because the assumed conversion or exercise increases the number of common shares considered outstanding during

---

[12]*CICA Handbook: Accounting Recommendations*, Section 3500, op. cit., par. 31.
[13]*Ibid.*, par. 32.

the period for which the loss is reported. In addition, the adjustments to the numerator would decrease the amount of the loss.

Multiple Potentially Dilutive Securities

When several potentially dilutive securities exist, the combination of securities and options, warrants and other rights that produce the lowest fully diluted earnings per share should be reported. This lowest figure is the only one that meets the objective of disclosing "the maximum potential dilution of current earnings per share on a prospective basis."[14] In most cases this objective can be met by merely excluding anti-dilutive contingent issuances. In rare cases, however, the inclusion of a contingent issuance that is non anti-dilutive on an individual basis may have an anti-dilutive effect on the resulting fully diluted earnings per share. To illustrate, assume the data on page 771.

Assuming exclusion of only the anti-dilutive options, the fully diluted earnings per share is 35¢ ($114,000 ÷ 330,000). However, by excluding also the bonds, which on an individual basis are not anti-dilutive, the resulting fully diluted earnings per share is only 34¢ ($102,000 ÷ 300,000). It can certainly be argued that 34¢ reflects the maximum potential dilution, and therefore, is the amount that should be reported. On the other hand, Section 3500 is vague; it is uncertain whether the Committee intends the exclusion of anything other than securities that are anti-dilutive on an individual basis. The specific recommendation reads in part as follows:

> The calculation of fully diluted earnings per share should exclude any potential conversion of senior shares or debt, exercise of rights, warrants and options or other contingent issuances that would increase earnings per share or decrease a loss per share.[15]

There can be no doubt that the recommendation requires exclusion of anti-dilutive securities. What is confusing, however, is the inclusion in the paragraph of a concluding sentence containing the recommendation which is not actually part of the recommendation because the sentence is not in italics. This sentence states the objective of the fully diluted presentation in terms of reflecting maximum potential dilution.

Regardless of the uncertainty, the problem, while rare, is at least easy to identify. The following three steps are recommended:

1. Calculate fully diluted earnings per share excluding only those contingent issuances that are individually anti-dilutive.
2. Deduct from the numerator and denominator used in the fully diluted computation above the amounts pertaining to the least dilutive contingent issuance included therein.

[14]*Ibid.*, par. 34.
[15]*Ibid.*

Summary of relevant information:

Maturity value of 8% convertible bonds	$300,000
Net income for year	$ 90,000
Common shares outstanding (no change during year)	200,000
Conversion terms of convertible bonds ...... 100 common shares for each $1,000 bond	*= 30,000 sh.*
Options outstanding to purchase common shares	50,000
Warrants outstanding to purchase common shares	100,000
Exercise price per share on options	$ 12
Exercise price per share on warrants	$ 3
Assumed earnings rate	8%
Assumed tax rate	50%

Handwritten: 4%
50,000 × $12 × .08 (1-5)
= $24,000
50,000 sh .48
100,000 × $3 × 4%
= +12,000 .12
100,000 sh

Basic earnings per share:

Net income	$ 90,000
Number of common shares outstanding	200,000
Basic earnings per share	$ .45

Fully diluted earnings per share:

	Common Shares Outstanding	Net Income	Anti-Dilutive Test	*EPS*
Basic earnings per share	200,000	$ 90,000		*.45*
Assumed conversion of convertible bonds:				
Number of shares, 300 × 100	30,000			
Interest net-of-tax, $300,000 at 4% .... *8%(1-5)*		12,000	$.40 ✓	
Assumed exercise of options:				
Number of shares	50,000			
Imputed earnings, 50,000 × $12 at 4%		24,000	.48 ✓	
Assumed exercise of warrants:				
Number of shares	100,000			
Imputed earnings, 100,000 × $3 at 4%		12,000	.12 ✓	
	380,000	$138,000		*.36*
Deduct $12 options (anti-dilutive)	50,000	24,000		
	330,000	$114,000		*.35*
Deduct convertible bonds	30,000	12,000		
	300,000	$102,000		*.34*

3. Recalculate fully diluted earnings per share using the adjusted numerator and denominator as determined in step 2.

If step 1 results in a lower fully diluted earnings per share figure than step 3, which should be the usual outcome, there is no problem. However, a problem may exist if step 3 generates the lower amount. Logic suggests that the step 3 result is the amount at which fully diluted earnings per share should be reported. But the *Accounting Recommendations* are man-made, and therefore logic may not necessarily apply. In the context of compliance with Section 3500, the step 1 result may not only be satisfactory, but also be in accordance with the Committee's intent. In most cases, of course, any difference is likely to be immaterial. Accordingly, the problem, if one exists, is of an academic rather than practical nature.

Additional Earnings Per Share Disclosures

In two very specific situations corporations may be required to provide additional earnings per share data. These situations are: (1) where common shares have been issued during the period on conversion of senior shares or debt; and (2) where common shares have been issued subsequent to the date of the balance sheet but before the date of the auditor's report, provided the issue was (a) for cash with the proceeds used to retire senior shares or debt, (b) on conversion of senior shares or debt, or (c) in a reorganization.

The first of these situations triggers the computation of *adjusted basic earnings per share* and disclosure by a note cross-referenced to the income statement if the per share amount for adjusted basic is materially different from the basic earnings per share. The second situation gives rise to pro-forma earnings per share, including either or both *pro-forma basic earnings per share* and *pro-forma fully diluted earnings per share*. Footnote disclosure of pro-forma earnings per share data is dependent upon materiality; however, the fact that the subsequent change in capital structure has no material effect on earnings per share may be substituted for the pro-forma amount(s). In both situations, materiality is again a matter to be determined by professional judgment.

Adjusted Basic Earnings per Share. Shares issued during the period as a result of conversions are subject to the weight-averaging requirement for purposes of determining the denominator for basic earnings per share. Since the weight-averaging requirement does not apply in subsequent periods, the conversion of senior shares or debt can have an impact on future earnings per share which may not be apparent if only basic earnings per share data are provided.

Adjusted basic earnings per share is calculated as if the conversion had taken place at the beginning of the period. Thus, the denominator for adjusted basic earnings per share is not subject to the weight-averaging requirement applicable in the case of basic earnings per share. The numerator for adjusted basic earnings per share includes dividends declared during the period prior to the conversion on any senior shares that were converted, the interest expensed during the period prior to the conversion, net of income tax, on any debt that was converted.

To illustrate, assume an issue of 10,000 $6 cumulative preferred shares that have been outstanding for several years is convertible into common shares on the basis of 12 common shares for each preferred share. On April 1 of the current period, 5,000 of the preferred shares are converted after the payment of one quarterly dividend. For purposes of the basic earnings per share computation the weight-averaging requirement would apply, and only 45,000 additional shares (5,000 × 12 for ³/4 year) would be included in the basic denominator. The basic numerator would reflect the deduction of preferred dividends in the amount of $37,500 (5,000 shares at $6 + 5,000 shares at $1.50). The calculation of adjusted basic earnings per share requires that the basic numerator be increased by $7,500, the dividends paid on the converted shares, and the basic denominator by 15,000 common shares, the shares excluded from the basic denominator because of the weight-averaging requirement. With reference to the denominator, this can be diagrammed as follows:

[handwritten margin notes: 120,000 sh. ; 60,000 sh. ; $6/yr = $1.50/qtr., 4 qtrs]

```
                                   ┌── Included in Basic EPS ............  45,000
                                   │   (60,000 for ³/4 year)
Common Shares                      │
Issued on Conversion 60,000 ───────┤
(5,000 × 12)                       │
                                   └── Included in Adjusted Basic EPS ....  15,000
                                       (60,000 for ¹/4 year)
```

In the rare situation where convertible debt or shares have been both issued and converted during the same period, it may seem logical to treat the conversion as if it had taken place at the date of issue, rather than at the beginning of the period. Although Section 3500 allows for the beginning of the period of date of issue alternative with reference to fully diluted earnings per share, it fails to do so with reference to adjusted basic.[16] Logic may suggest that the date of issue should prevail over the beginning of the period where both the issue and conversion take place during the same period. Otherwise, the result is an adjustment of the denominator for adjusted basic earnings per share without any counterpart adjustment of the numerator. Since the object of the adjusted basic computation is to provide what may be a better predictor of future earnings per share than the basic computation, both the numerator and denominator should reflect the situation that will prevail next year, other things remaining equal. This viewpoint clearly justifies use of the beginning of the period rather than date of issue, if later in the rare case when issue and conversion both take place in the same fiscal period. Moreover, in future periods there can be no interest or dividend payments on securities that have been converted.

It should be recognized that the additional information conveyed by the disclosure of adjusted basic earnings per share is included in fully diluted

---

[16]*Ibid.*, par. 28.

data by definition except when issue and conversion take place in the same fiscal period. This is because the fully diluted computation requires that potentially dilutive conversions be assumed to have taken place at the beginning of the period, provided the convertible securities were issued in some prior period. Moreover, the numbers used to determine adjusted basic provide a convenient starting point for the calculation of fully diluted earnings per share.

In general, per share data can be determined very efficiently if calculated in the following order: (1) basic earnings per share, (2) adjusted basic earnings per share, if applicable, and (3) fully diluted earnings per share. The numerator and denominator for basic provide the starting point for adjusted basic, and, in turn, the numerator and denominator for adjusted basic provide a convenient starting point for the fully diluted computation. An exception to this procedure must be noted in the rare case where convertible securities are issued and converted in the same fiscal period; then the adjusted basic computation assumes conversion at the beginning of the current period regardless of date of issue while the fully diluted computation uses date of issue, if later.

Pro-Forma Earnings Per Share. Pro-forma earnings per share data should be calculated whenever common shares have been issued during the period between the year end and the date of the auditors' report, provided the issue was (a) for cash with the proceeds used to retire senior shares or debt, (b) on conversion of senior shares or debt, or (c) in a reorganization. In addition, the financial statements should include a note cross-referenced to the income statement which may either disclose the pro-forma data, or state that the subsequent change in capital structure has no material effect on earnings per share. Other issues of common shares during the subsequent events period should be excluded from the pro-forma calculations.

The objective of pro-forma disclosure is to provide per share data for the current period based on the capital structure expected to apply next year. If the subsequent change in capital structure has a material effect on earnings per share, it must follow that the predictive ability of the basic and fully dilutive disclosures has been impaired. The pro-forma data compensate for this impairment.

Issuance of common shares during the subsequent events period for any of the reasons set out above trigger the computation of pro-forma basic earnings per share. However, when common shares have been issued as a result of conversions, the calculation of pro-forma fully diluted earnings per share simply cannot arise. Since the fully diluted computation assumes potentially dilutive conversions to have taken place, it is therefore impossible for common shares issued as a result of conversions during the subsequent events period to have any impact on fully diluted earnings per share.

Earnings Per Share Presentation

When earnings of a period include extraordinary items, earnings per share amounts should be presented for both the income before extraordinary items and the net income. Section 3500 does not require reporting the per share amount of extraordinary items.

Under Section 3500 disclosure requirements can be met by means of a note or notes cross-referenced to the income statement. The available alternatives, however, include (1) disclosure on the face of the income statement, or (2) disclosure in notes to the financial statements. The first alternative is the most popular; however, a combination of statement disclosure with a note or notes is also very common.

Earnings per share data should be presented for all periods covered by the income statement. Whenever net income of prior periods has been restated as a result of a prior period adjustment, the earnings per share for these prior periods should be restated and the effect of the restatements disclosed in the year of restatement. These requirements also apply to the five or ten year financial summaries that commonly appear in corporate annual reports.

It is important that great care be exercised in interpreting earnings per share data regardless of the degree of refinement applied in the development of the data. These values are the products of the principles and practices employed in the accounting process and are subject to the same limitations as found in the net income measurement reported on the income statement.

QUESTIONS

1. Why is book value per share often a poor indicator of share value?

2. What adjustments are applied to the total shareholders' equity in computing book value per common share when there is more than one class of shares outstanding?

3. The liquidation value of preferred shares is 100 and the call price is 105. Which value should be used in computing book value for the preferred shares? Why?

4. Earnings per share computations have been receiving increased prominence on the income statement. How would an investor use such information in making investment decisions?

5. What computation may be reported for preferred shares instead of earnings per share? Why is such a computation more appropriate?

6. What distinguishes a simple from a complex capital structure?

7. What is meant by "dilution of earnings per share"?

8. What is an anti-dilutive security? Why are they generally excluded from the computation of earnings per share?

9. Dual disclosure of earnings per share is required only if the introduction of dilutive securities has a material effect. How does the profession define materiality in this case?

10. Why are earnings per share figures adjusted retroactively for stock dividends, stock splits, and reverse stock splits?

11. How are convertible securities converted during the period accounted for in computing basic and fully diluted earnings per share?

12. Compare the concept of basic earnings per share with the concept of fully diluted earnings per share.

13. Explain the formula $in = i(1 - t)$ and describe its use with reference to (a) convertible bonds, and (b) stock options.

14. How are stock options and warrants included in the computation of fully diluted earnings per share?

15. The Accounting Research Committee has stated that fully diluted per share data for prior periods may no longer be meaningful. Why is this so? Explain briefly.

16. When a loss is reported for the current period, the computation of fully diluted per share data does not generally apply. Explain.

17. In what circumstances might a corporation find it necessary to report ten earnings per share figures? List the per share figures.

18. Explain why a pro-forma fully diluted earnings per share figure is not required when common shares are issued during the subsequent events period as a result of the conversion of senior shares or debt.

19. What limitations should be recognized in using earnings per share data?

EXERCISES

18-1. As of December 31, the equity section of the McAllister, Ltd., balance sheet contained the following information: capital stock, 60,000 issued, $600,000; capital stock subscribed, 10,000 shares, $100,000; contributed surplus, $200,000; retained earnings, $900,000; treasury stock at cost, 10,000 shares, $60,000. Compute the book value per share of common stock.

18-2. The shareholders' equity of Glidden, Ltd., on December 31, 1977, follows:

Common stock, $10 par, 75,000 shares	$ 750,000
Preferred 6% stock, $25 par, 5,000 shares	125,000
Contributed surplus	75,000
Retained earnings	50,000
	$1,000,000

Compute the book values per share of the preferred and common shares under each of the following assumptions:

(a) Preferred shares are non-cumulative, callable at $30, and preferred as to assets at $27.50 upon corporate liquidation.

(b) Preferred shares are cumulative, with dividends in arrears for 6 years (including the current year). Upon corporate liquidation, shares are preferred as to assets up to par, and any dividends in arrears must be paid before distribution may be made to common shares.

18-3. Compute the weighted average number of shares outstanding for Meyers Construction Company assuming transactions in common shares occurred during the year as follows:

Date	Transactions in Common Shares	Number of Shares $10 Par Value
Jan. 1, 1977	Outstanding	16,000
Mar. 1, 1977	Issued for cash	3,200
April 1, 1977	Repurchased shares outstanding	(3,000)
June 1, 1977	Resold part of shares acquired April 1	1,400
Sept. 1, 1977	Issued in exchange for property	6,400
Dec. 1, 1977	50% stock dividend	50% of outstanding shares

18-4. The Updike Corporation had 500,000 shares of common stock outstanding at the end of 1979. During 1980 and 1981, the transactions below took place.

1980

Apr. 1 $5,000,000 of convertible bonds were converted with 25 shares issued for each $1,000 bond.

July 1 A 5% stock dividend was declared.

Oct. 1 Options to purchase 6,000 shares for $40 a share were exercised.

1981

Mar. 1 A 2-for-1 split was declared.

Aug. 1 150,000 shares were sold for $40 a share.

From the information given, compute the comparative number of weighted average shares outstanding for 1980 and 1981.

18-5. The income statement for the Braden Co. for the year ended December 31, 1981 shows the following:

Income before income tax	$660,000
Income tax	297,000
Income before extraordinary item	$363,000
Add extraordinary gain (net of income tax)	180,000
Net income	$543,000

Compute earnings per share amounts for 1981 under each of the following assumptions:

(a) The company has only one class of shares, the number of shares outstanding totalling 300,000.

(b) The company has shares outstanding as follows:
Preferred 6% stock, $50 par, cumulative, 20,000 shares; common, $25 par, 300,000 shares. Only the current year's dividends are unpaid.

18-6. The Stewart Corporation has earnings per common share of $1.51 for the period ended December 31, 1981. For each of the following examples, decide whether the convertible security would be dilutive or anti-dilutive in computing fully diluted earnings per share. Consider each example individually. The tax rate is 45%.

(a) 8¹/₂% debentures, $1,000,000 face value, are convertible into common shares at the rate of 40 shares for each $1,000 bond.

(b) $4 preferred shares are convertible into common at the rate of 2 shares of common for 1 share of preferred. There are 50,000 shares of preferred stock outstanding.

(c) Options to purchase 200,000 shares of common stock are outstanding. The exercise price is $25 per share. The corporation expects to earn a 10% return before income tax.

(d) $500,000 of 8% debentures are convertible at the rate of 20 shares of common stock per each $1,000 bond.

(e) Preferred 6% shares, $100 par, 5,000 shares outstanding, convertible into 5 shares of common for each 1 share of preferred.

18-7. On January 2, 1977, Lang Co. issued at par $10,000 of 4% bonds convertible in total into 1,000 shares of Lang's common stock. No bonds were converted during 1977.

Throughout 1977, Lang had 1,000 shares of common stock outstanding. Lang's 1977 net income was $1,000. Lang's tax rate is 45%.

No other potentially dilutive securities other than the convertible bonds were outstanding during 1977. For 1977, compute the earnings per share data that should be reported by Lang Co.

18.8. Elton Ltd. has the following capital structure:

6% first mortgage bonds, par value $5,000,000, due 1984	$5,000,000
Share capital:	
Authorized —	
1,000,000 5% cumulative redeemable preferred shares, par value $3.00 each, and 2,000,000 common shares of no par value.	
Issued and fully paid —	
500,000 preferred shares	$1,500,000
1,740,000 common shares (240,000 issued for $1,200,000 cash seven months after the beginning of the most recent fiscal year) ..	2,700,000
	$4,200,000

Elton's net income for the current year before interest and income tax of 45% is $2,500,000. Calculate Elton Ltd.'s basic earnings per share.   (CICA adapted)

18-9. The Ewing Manufacturing Company reports long-term liabilities and share-holders' equity balances at December 31, 1977, as follows:

Convertible 6% bonds (sold at par)	$ 500,000
Common stock, $25 par, 100,000 shares issued and outstanding	2,500,000

Additional information is determined as follows:

Conversion terms of bonds .... 40 shares for each $1,000 bond	
Income before extraordinary gain — 1977	$180,000
Extraordinary gain	30,000
Net income — 1977	$210,000

What earnings per share data should the company report for 1977, assuming that the income tax rate is 45%? No changes occurred in the above debt and equity balances during 1977.

18-10. The following amounts are taken from the accounts of Portage Company Limited at December 31, 1982:

Sales revenue	$420,000
Cost of goods sold	220,000
Operating expenses	88,000
Extraordinary loss on sale of foreign subsidiary	(16,800)
Prior period adjustment, collection of law suit	11,600
Dividends on common shares	24,000
Share capital, common 60,000 shares	615,000

12,000 shares were issued on May 1, 1982. Assume that income, regardless of the source, is subject to a 40% income tax rate. What earnings per share data should be reported for 1982? (CGA adapted)

18-11. Primary Company owns 80,000 shares (an 80% interest) in Secondary Company. In 1982, the reported earnings available to common shareholders of each of the two companies were as follows: (On consolidation, there were no intercompany eliminations affecting net income.)

	Primary Company (Consolidated)	Secondary Company
Net income before minority interest	$5,300,000	$2,000,000
Minority interest in Secondary Company	400,000	
Net income for the year	4,900,000	2,000,000
Deduct dividends on preferred shares	600,000	
Earnings available to common shareholders	$4,300,000	$2,000,000

The capital structures of the two companies are presented below:

Primary Company

$10,000,000 in 6% cumulative preferred shares, convertible into common shares on the basis of 5 common shares for each $100 par value preferred share.

$3,750,000 common shares (no change during 1982).

Secondary Company

$4,000,000 in 7% debentures, convertible into common at the rate of 5 common shares for each $1,000 debenture.

100,000 common shares.

Assuming a 40% tax rate, calculate 1982 basic and fully diluted earnings per share for Primary Company. (OISA adapted)

18-12. The Morton Company is planning to invest $10,000,000 in an expansion program which is expected to increase income before interest and taxes by $2,500,000. The company currently is earning $5 per share on 1,000,000 common shares outstanding. The capital structure prior to the investment is:

Debt	$10,000,000
Equity	30,000,000
	$40,000,000

The expansion can be financed by sale of 200,000 shares at $50 each, or by issuing long term debt at a 6% interest cost. The firm's most recent income statement follows:

Sales	$101,000,000
Variable cost	$ 60,000,000
Fixed Cost	30,500,000
	$ 90,500,000
Income before interest and taxes	$ 10,500,000
Interest	,500,000
Earnings before taxes	$ 10,000,000
Income tax (50%)	5,000,000
Net income after taxes	$ 5,000,000

Assuming the firm maintains its current earnings and achieves the anticipated income from the expansion, what will be the earnings per share

(a) If the expansion is financed by debt?
(b) If the expansion is financed by equity?

PROBLEMS

18-1A. The shareholders' equity for the Rice Realty and Development Company on December 31, 1981, follows:

Preferred 6% stock, $100 par, 20,000 shares	$2,000,000
Common stock, $25 par, 200,000 shares	5,000,000
Contributed surplus	500,000
Retained earnings	750,000
Total shareholders' equity	$8,250,000

Instructions:
Calculate the book values of preferred shares and common shares as of December 31, 1981, under each of the following assumptions:

(1) Preferred dividends have been paid to October 1, 1981; preferred shares have a call value of $110, a liquidation value of $105, and are entitled to current unpaid quarterly dividends.
(2) Preferred shares have a liquidation value of $110; shares are cumulative, with dividends 4 years in arrears and fully payable in the event of liquidation.
(3) Preferred shares have a liquidation value of par; shares are non-cumulative, and no dividends have been paid for the past 5 years; however, the current year's dividend has been declared.

18-2A. Transactions involving the common shares account of the French Company during the two-year period, 1980 and 1981, were as follows:

1980
Jan.   1   Balance 50,000 shares of $20 par value.
Mar. 31   Sold 10,000 shares at $27.
Apr. 26   Paid cash dividend of 50¢ per share.
July 31   Paid cash dividend of 25¢ per share, and 5% stock dividend.
Oct. 26   Paid cash dividend of 50¢ per share.

1981

Jan. 26 Paid cash dividend of 50¢ per share.
Feb. 28 Purchased 5,000 shares of treasury stock.
Apr. 30 Issued 3-for-1 stock split.
July 26 Paid cash dividend of 50¢ per share.
Oct. 26 Paid cash dividend of 50¢ per share.
Nov. 1 Sold 6,000 shares of treasury stock.

The French Company has a simple capital structure.

Instructions:

Compute the weighted average number of shares for 1980 and 1981 to be used for earnings per share computations at the end of 1981.

18-3A. The following shareholders' equity section of the balance sheet of Dry Goods Corporation Ltd. was prepared as at December 31, 1981.

$4 convertible preferred shares, $100 par, convertible into four shares of common stock	$ 100,000
Common shares, $10 par value	200,000
Premium on common shares	600,000
Retained earnings	390,000
	$1,290,000
Less: Teasury stock, 1,000 shares of common at cost	50,000
Total shareholders' equity	$1,240,000

The following transactions occurred during the fiscal year ended December 31, 1982:

Jan. 2 Received 200 shares of common stock of Dry Goods Corporation Ltd. as settlement of past-due accounts receivable of $13,000. The treasury stock is considered to be worth an amount equal to the book value of common shares at this date.

Jan. 6 Issued the 1,200 shares of the treasury stock on hand in exchange for a building valued at $70,000.

May 30 A cash dividend was declared and paid as follows: preferred, $2 per share; common, $1 per share.

June 30 One hundred shares of preferred stock were converted into common shares.

Nov. 30 A cash dividend was declared and paid as follows: preferred, $2 per share, common, $1 per share.

Dec. 31 Net income for the year was $126,000.

Instructions:

(1) Prepare journal entries to record the above transactions.
(2) Compute all data for year-end earnings per share reporting purposes.
(3) Prepare the shareholders' equity section of the balance sheet as at December 31, 1982. (SMA adapted)

18-4A. The 1981 condensed financial statements for the Brooke Corporation were prepared by the accounting department and are shown at the top of page 782.

Brooke Corporation
Income Statement
For Year Ended December 31, 1981

Sales		$10,000,000
Cost of goods sold		8,000,000
Gross profit on sales		$ 2,000,000
Expenses:		
Selling expense	$452,000	
Administrative expense	500,000	
Interest expense	48,000	1,000,000
Income from operations		$1,000,000
Income tax		450,000
Income before extraordinary items		$ 550,000
Extraordinary gain, net-of-tax		45,000
Net income		$ 595,000

Brooke Corporation
Balance Sheet
December 31, 1981

Assets	$3,500,000
Current liabilities	$1,000,000
8% Bonds, due December 31, 1988	600,000
Shareholders' equity:	
Common stock, $5 par, 250,000 shares authorized, issued and outstanding	1,250,000
Contributed surplus	400,000
Retained earnings	250,000
	$3,500,000

Instructions:

Compute earnings per share under each of the following separate assumptions (the company has a simple capital structure):

(1) No change in the capital structure occurred in 1981.

(2) On December 31, 1980, there were 150,000 shares outstanding. On April 1, 1981, 80,000 shares were sold at par and on October 1, 1981, 20,000 shares were sold at par.

(3) On December 31, 1980, there were 187,500 shares outstanding. On July 1, 1981, the company issued a 33$\frac{1}{3}$% stock dividend.

18-5A. Fast Foods Ltd. reported the comparative balances given below in the "Shareholders' equity" section of its balance sheet at the end of 1980.

1980

Mar. 1   Sold 50,000 shares of $15 par value common for $18 per share.

July 31   Sold 3,000 shares of $50 par value preferred for $60 per share.

	December 31, 1981	December 31, 1980	December 31, 1979
Preferred shares...................	$ 650,000	$ 550,000	$ 400,000
Premium on preferred shares	100,000	70,000	40,000
Common shares	4,650,000	4,500,000	3,000,000
Premium on common shares........	810,000	750,000	400,000
Paid-in capital from sale of treasury stock at more than cost	40,000	10,000	10,000
Retained earnings unappropriated	3,146,400	2,142,000	2,250,000
Retained earnings appropriated for contingencies	800,000	950,000	950,000
Total shareholders' equity........	$10,196,400	$8,972,000	$7,050,00

The following transactions involving the shareholders' equity balances occurred during 1980 and 1981.

1980

Sept. 1 Issued a 20% stock dividend on the common shares. The market price for common shares at that time was $19.
Dec. 31 Paid cash dividends of 6% on preferred shares; $2 on common shares.
Dec. 31 Net income for the year was $1,475,000, including an extraordinary gain net of tax of $75,000.

1981

Feb. 1 Sold 10,000 shares of common for $21.
May 31 Sold 2,000 shares of preferred for $65.
July 1 Split common shares 3-for-1.
Sept. 30 Purchased 6,000 shares of common for $13 to be held as treasury stock.
Dec. 1 Sold 6,000 shares of treasury stock for $18.
Dec. 31 Paid cash dividends: 6% on preferred shares; $1 on common shares.
Dec. 31 Net income for 1981 included an extraordinary loss net of tax savings of $40,000.

Fast Foods Ltd. has a simple capital structure. The call price and liquidation price of the preferred shares are both $55 per share.

Instructions:
Compute the comparative book value per share and earnings per share amounts for 1980 and 1981.

18-6A. The capital structure of the Stanley Dumont Company as of December 31, 1980 follows:

$3 Preferred shares, $50 par, 5,000 shares issued and outstanding ...	$ 250,000
Premium on preferred shares	25,000
Common shares, $10 par, 100,000 shares issued and outstanding	1,000,000
Premium on common shares	250,000
Retained earnings	725,000

On April 1, 1981, the company issued 15,000 stock options to select executives, creditors, and others, allowing for the purchase of common stock for $20 a share. The market price for the stock at this date was $15. The company expects to earn a 10% return, net of tax, on available cash resources.

There were no other capital transactions during the year. Net income for 1981 was $200,000.

Instructions:

Using the information given above, compute basic and fully diluted earnings per share.

18-7A. The following is an extract from the balance sheet of the Walker Corporation, for the year ended December 31, 1980:

7% convertible debentures	$10,000,000
Common shares, $10 par, 1,000,000 shares issued and outstanding .	$10,000,000
Retained earnings	6,750,000
Total shareholders' equity	$16,750,000

The terms of conversion state that for each $1,000 bond tendered, the corporation will transfer to the creditor 40 shares of common stock.

On June 30, 1981, the complete issue of convertible debentures was converted into common stock.

Net income for 1981 was $2,350,000. The income tax rate was 45%.

No common shares issued or repurchased during the year, other than those issued on the conversion.

Instructions:

Compute the earnings per share data that should be reported by the Walker Corporation for the year ended December 31, 1981 in order to comply with Section 3500.

18-8A. The Middleton Manufacturing Co. provides the following data at December 31, 1981:

Operating revenue...	$950,000
Operating expenses	$450,000
Income tax rate	40%
Earnings rate, net-of-tax	9%
Common stock outstanding during the entire year	25,000 shares

On January 1, 1981, there were options outstanding to purchase 10,000 shares of common stock at $20 per share. The balance sheet reports $200,000 of 8% bonds convertible into 30,000 common shares. As at December 31, 1981 none of the bonds had been converted. (Interest expense is included in operating expenses.)

Instructions:

Compute for 1981:

(1) Basic earnings per share.
(2) Fully diluted earnings per share.

18-9A. Data for the Mary Jan Cosmetics Company at the end of 1977 follow. All bonds are convertible as indicated and were issued at their face amounts.

Description of Bonds	Amount	Date Issued	Conversion Terms
10-year, 6% Convertible bonds	$ 500,000	1/1/75	60 shares of common for each $1,000 bond
20-year, 7% Convertible bonds	1,000,000	1/1/76	40 shares of common for each $1,000 bond
25-year, 6¹/₂% Convertible bonds	800,000	6/30/77	100 shares of common for each $1,000 bond

Common shares outstanding at December 31, 1976..................	800,000
Net income for 1977	$850,000
Income tax rate	45%

Instructions:

(1) Compute basic earnings per share for 1977, assuming that no additional shares of common stock were issued during the year.
(2) Compute fully diluted earnings per share for 1977, assuming that no additional shares of common stock were issued during the year.
(3) Compute basic, adjusted basic and fully diluted earnings per share assuming that the 20-year bonds were converted on July 1, 1977, and that net income for the year was $869,250.

18-10A. Several hypothetical cases are given below. For each case do your calculations according to the rules set out in Section 3500 of the *Accounting Recommendations*. In each case, the company's income for the most recent fiscal year, before bond or debenture interest and 45% income tax, was $2,500,000.

Case 1
Alpha Ltd. has had the following capital structure for several years:

6% first mortgage bonds, par value $5,000,000, due 1984	$5,000,000

Share capital:
Authorized — 2,000,000 common shares of no par value

Issued and fully paid — 1,500,000 common shares	$1,500,000

Case 2
Beta Ltd. has had the following capital structure for several years:

6% first mortgage bonds, par value $5,000,000 due 1984	$5,000,000

Share capital:
Authorized — 1,000,000 5% non-cumulative, non-redeemable preferred shares, par value $3.00 each, and 2,000,000 common shares of no par value.
Issued and fully paid —

500,000 preferred shares	$1,500,000
1,500,000 common shares	1,500,000
	$3,000,000

Beta Ltd. paid a dividend of 9¢ per preferred share during its most recent fiscal year.

Case 3
Gamma Ltd. has had the following capital structure for several years:

6% first mortgage bonds, par value $5,000,000, due 1984	$5,000,000

Share capital:
  Authorized — 1,000,000 5% cumulative redeemable preferred shares,
    par value $3.00 each, and 2,000,000 common shares of no par value.
  Issued and fully paid —

500,000 preferred shares	$1,500,000
1,500,000 common shares	1,500,000
	$3,000,000

Gamma Ltd. paid a dividend of 9¢ per preferred share during its most recent fiscal year. Four weeks after the end of that year, the company's common shares were split 2-for-1.

Case 4

Delta Ltd. has the following capital structure:

6% convertible debentures, par value $5,000,000, due 1984 (each $100 debenture is convertible into 5 common shares; no debentures were converted prior to the most recent fiscal year but 4,000 debentures were converted at the beginning of that year.)	$4,600,000

Share capital:
  Authorized — 1,000,000 5% cumulative redeemable preferred shares,
    par value $3.00 each, and 2,000,000 common shares of no par value.
  Issued and fully paid —

500,000 preferred shares	$1,500,000
1,520,000 common shares (20,000 issued during the most recent fiscal year in exchange for debentures).......................................	1,900,000
	$3,400,000

Instructions:

(1) In Case 1 calculate Alpha Ltd.'s basic earnings per share.
(2) In Case 2 calculate Beta Ltd.'s basic earnings per share.
(3) In Case 3 calculate Gamma Ltd.'s basic earnings per share.
(4) In Case 4 calculate Delta Ltd.'s fully-diluted earnings per share.

(CICA Adapted)

18-11A. On July 1, 1981, a fire completely destroyed one of the buildings of Millborn Ltd. This building, purchased January 2, 1972, cost $240,000 and had always been depreciated on a monthly basis at a rate of 5% per year. This building was insured for $100,000 and the insurance company agreed to pay that amount as an insurance settlement.

The directors of the company are uncertain about how to show this transaction in the financial statements for the year ended December 31, 1981. They are also uncertain about how to calculate earnings per share. They ask your help in these matters and have provided the following information.

(1) The income for the year, excluding the previous event but including depreciation on the building, is $125,000.
(2) All income sources are taxable at 40%. All loss items are tax deductible.
(3) During the year the company paid total dividends in the amount of $6,000 on preferred shares.
(4) On September 1, 1981, the company issued 30,000 common shares.
(5) On January 1, 1981, the shareholders' equity was as follows:

Authorized: 100,000, 6% cumulative preferred shares, par value $10 each,
each share is convertible into one common share

100,000 common shares, no par value

Issued and fully paid: 20,000 preferred shares	$ 200,000
30,000 common shares	450,000
Premium on preferred shares	20,000
Retained earnings	565,000
	$1,235,000

Instructions:

(1) Determine the gain or loss, after income taxes, on the destruction of the building.
(2) Prepare the bottom portion of the income statement starting with the amount of $125,000 given above.
(3) Determine the earnings per share data applicable in this situation.

(SMA adapted)

18-12A. The "Shareholders' equity" section of Lowe Company's balance sheet as at December 31, 1977, contains the following:

$1 Cumulative preferred shares, $25 par, convertible, 1,600,000 shares authorized, 1,400,000 shares issued, 750,000 converted to common, 650,000 shares outstanding; involuntary liquidation value, $30 a share, aggregating $19,500,000	$16,250,000
Common shares, $.25 par, 15,000,000 shares authorized, 8,800,000 shares issued and outstanding	2,200,000
Contributed surplus	32,750,000
Retained earnings	40,595,000
Total shareholders' equity	$91,795,000

On April 1, 1977, Lowe Company acquired the business and assets and assumed the liabilities of Diane Corporation in a transaction accounted for as a pooling of interests. For each of Diane Corporations' 2,400,000 shares of 25¢ par value common shares outstanding, the owner received one share of common stock of the Lowe Company.

Included in the liabilities of Lowe Company are $5\frac{1}{2}$% convertible subordinated debentures issued at their face value of $20,000,000 in 1976. The debentures are due in 1996 and until then are convertible into the common stock of Lowe Company at the rate of five shares of common for each $100 debenture. To date none of these have been converted.

On April 2, 1977, Lowe Company issued 1,400,000 shares of convertible preferred stock at $40 per share. Quarterly dividends to December 31, 1977, have been paid on these shares. The preferred stock is convertible into common at the rate of two shares of common for each share of preferred. On October 1, 1977, 150,000 shares and on November 1, 1977, 600,000 shares of preferred stock were converted into common shares.

During July 1976, Lowe Company granted options to its officers and key employees to purchase 500,000 shares of the company's common stock at a price of $20 a share. The options do not become exercisable until 1978.

Lowe Company's consolidated net income for the year ended December 31, 1977, was $9,200,000. The provision for income tax was computed at a rate of 48%. Assume an after tax earnings rate of 7% for purposes of any imputed earnings computations.

Instructions

(1) Prepare a schedule which shows for 1977 the computation of:
   (a) The weighted average number of shares for computing basic earnings per share.
   (b) The weighted average number of shares for computing adjusted basic earnings per share.
   (c) The weighted average number of shares for computing fully diluted earnings per share.

(2) Prepare a schedule which shows for 1977 the computation to the nearest cent of:
   (a) Basic earnings per share.
   (b) Adjusted basic earnings per share.
   (c) Fully diluted earnings per share.   (AICPA adapted)

18-13A. Western Limited reported a net income after taxes for 1981 of $6 million. The Company's capital structure included the following securities, all of which were outstanding throughout 1981:

Long-term debt:

Six per cent bonds, due 1984	$ 5,000,000
Four per cent 30-year bonds, due 1994 and convertible into common stock at the rate of three shares per $100, issue price, $100	$10,000,000

Shareholders' Equity:	Number of Shares Outstanding
Preferred shares, issued January 1, 1981, cumulative as dividends of $4.50, callable at $100, and convertible into common at the rate of two shares for each share of preferred, issue price $100 .	150,000
Preferred shares, cumulative as dividends at $2.50, callable at $60, and convertible into comon stock at the rate of one share for each share of preferred, issue price was $50	400,000
Common shares	1,500,000

Warrants to Purchase Common Shares:

100,000 shares at $20
200,000 shares at $52

Instructions:
Compute the earnings per share data that should be included in the financial statements of Western Ltd. if they are to conform with the recommendations contained in Section 3500 of the *Accounting Recommendations*. You may assume a 50% tax rate and 10% as an imputed earnings rate before income tax.

18-14A. The following schedule sets forth the current liabilities, long-term liabilities, and shareholders' equity of Darren Company as of December 31, 1981. The president of Darren has requested that you assist the controller in preparing figures for earnings per share computations.

Explanations of certain balances and shareholders' equity transactions during the year ended December 31, 1981 follow:

(a) The 4% convertible debentures were issued at their face value of $30,000,000 in 1960. The debentures are due in 1990 and until then are convertible into the common of Darren at the rate of 25 shares for each $1,000 debenture.

(b) The $4 cumulative, convertible preferred shares were issued in 1977. On July 1, 1981, and on October 1, 1981, holders of the preferred shares converted 80,000 and 20,000 preferred shares, respectively, into common shares. Each preferred share is convertible into 1.2 shares of common stock.

(c) On April 1, 1981, Darren acquired the assets and business of Brett Industries by the issuance of 800,000 shares of Darren common stock in a transaction appropriately accounted for as a purchase.

Current liabilities:	
Notes payable — banks	$ 4,000,000
Current portion of long-term liabilities	10,000,000
Total current liabilities	$ 14,000,000
Long-term liabilities:	
4% convertible debentures due April 15, 1990	$ 30,000,000
Other long-term liabilities less current portions	20,000,000
Total long-term liabilities	$ 50,000,000
Shareholders' equity:	
$4 cumulative convertible preferred shares, $20 par; 2,000,000 shares authorized; 1,200,000 issued and outstanding; liquidation preference $30 per share aggregating $36,000,000	$ 24,000,000
Common shares, $1 par; 20,000,000 shares authorized; 7,500,000 shares issued including 600,000 shares held in treasury	7,500,000
Contributed surplus	4,200,000
Retained earnings	76,500,000
Total paid-in capital and retained earnings	$112,200,000
Less cost of 600,000 shares of common stock held in treasury (acquired prior to 1981)	900,000
Total shareholders' equity	$111,300,000
Total long-term liabilities and shareholders' equity	$161,300,000

Additional information:

(d) Dividends on the preferred shares have been paid quarterly through December 31, 1981. Dividends paid on the common shares were 50¢ per share for each quarter.

(e) Stock options have been outstanding for several years. Each of the 25,000 options permits the holder to purchase one common share for $10. You may assume an earnings rate before tax of 10%.

(f) The net income of Darren Company for the year ended December 31, 1981, was $8,600,000. There were no extraordinary items. The provision for income tax was computed at a rate of 48%.

(g) On February 1, 1982, before the date of the auditors' report, the common shares of Darren Company were split 2:1.

Instructions:
Prepare all required earnings per share data for 1981 in compliance with Section 3500 of the *Accounting Recommendations*.

18-15A. As at December 31, 1981, the equities side of Can-Am Limited's balance sheet appeared as follows:

Can-Am Limited
Balance Sheet
December 31, 1981

Liabilities and Shareholders' Equity

Current Liabilities			$ 6,200,000
Long-Term Debt:			
Notes Payable, 8%	$ 30,000		
4% Convertible Debentures	2,500,000		
5% Convertible Debentures	2,500,000		
Shareholders' Equity:			
5% Cumulative Convertible			
Preferred Shares, Par Value $100			
Authorized, 100,000 shares			
Issued, 25,000 shares		2,500,000	
Common Shares, $1 Par Value			
Authorized 5,000,000 shares			
Issued 500,000 shares		500,000	
Contributed Surplus		2,500,000	
Retained Earnings — Beginning of Year	$2,000,000		
Net Income	1,000,000	3,000,000	8,500,000
			$20,000,000

Additional information:

(a) Options have been granted to purchase 50,000 shares of common stock at $20 per share.

(b) Warrants have been issued to purchase 100,000 shares of common stock at $25 per share.

(c) 4% and 5% convertible debentures are convertible into common stock at $25 per share.

(d) 5% cumulative convertible preferred shares are convertible at the rate of 4 shares of common for each share of preferred stock.

(e) All debt and securities were outstanding at the beginning and end of the year.

(f) The rate of return for purposes of imputing earnings should be 6%.

Instructions:

Compute all required earnings per share data in accordance with Section 3500 of the *Accounting Recommendations*. State your assumptions, if any.

18-16A. The following information relates to a Canadian company with an income tax rate of 40%:

(a) Net Income for the year ended December 31, 1977 was $2,800,000. No extraordinary terms were reported.

(b) As at January 1, 1977 there were 500,000 common shares outstanding.

(c) Share purchase warrants for 100,000 common shares issued prior to 1977 were outstanding. The warrants permit the holder to purchase one common share at $30 for each warrant held. No purchase warrants were exercised during 1977. The rate of return to be used for imputing earnings on the funds derived from the exercise of stock purchase warrants is 10% before applicable income taxes.

(d) An issue of 6% convertible debentures with a principal amount of $12,000,000 due 1982 has been outstanding for a number of years. Each $100 debenture is convertible into 3 common shares. On April 1, 1977, $8,000,000 of the outstanding debentures were converted into 240,000 common shares.

(e) An issue of 7% cumulative redeemable preferred shares in the amount of $5,000,000 has been outstanding for a number of years. There was no change in the preferred share capital during 1977.

(f) On July 1, 1977, 8% non-cumulative preferred shares in the amount of $6,000,000 were issued at par ($100). Each preferred share is convertible into 5 common shares. Dividends on these preferred shares of $4 per share were declared and paid in 1977.

(g) On January 31, 1978 (before the date of the auditors' report on the financial statements for 1977) the common shares were split on the basis of two new shares for each old one.

(h) On February 15, 1978 (before the date of the auditors' report on the financial statements for 1977), 200,000 common shares were issued for $4,400,000 cash. The proceeds from the sale of the common shares were used to redeem $4,000,000 of the 7% cumulative redeemable preferred shares at a premium of 10%

Instructions:
For the year ended December 31, 1977, calculate each of the following:

(1) Basic earnings per share.
(2) Adjusted basic earnings per share.
(3) Fully diluted earnings per share.
(4) Pro-forma earnings per share, basic and fully diluted.

19 ACCOUNTING CHANGES, CORRECTION OF ERRORS, AND STATEMENTS FROM INCOMPLETE RECORDS

When a reporting entity changes its accounting policies, adjusts its past estimates of revenues earned or costs incurred, reclassifies the presentation of items, or corrects past errors, it becomes more difficult for a user to predict the future from past historical statements. Is it better to record these changes and error corrections as adjustments of the prior periods' statements and thus increase their comparability with current and future statements, or should the changes and error corrections affect only the current and future years? Would user confidence in financial statements be shaken if the historical records were changed each year as these types of changes occurred, or should the full impact of the change be reflected only in the current and future periods?

At least three alternative procedures have been suggested as solutions for reporting accounting changes and correction of errors.

1. Adjust all prior periods' statements for the effect of the change or correction and adjust the beginning Retained Earnings balance for the cumulative amount of the change or correction (retroactive application).
2. Make no adjustment to prior periods' statements, but reflect all effects of the change only in current and future periods (retroactive application with no restatement of prior periods). Report the catch-up adjustment as it affects prior years in the current year
   a. as a special item on the income statement in a manner similar to the treatment of an extraordinary item.

b. as a direct entry to Retained Earnings in a manner similar to a prior period adjustment.
3. Make the change effective only for current and future periods. Allow no catch-up adjustment to be made. Correct errors only if they still affect the statements (prospective application).

Each of these alternative methods for reporting an accounting change or correcting an error have been used in the past, and strong arguments can be made for each alternative. Because of diversity in practice and the resulting difficulty in understandability of financial statements, the Accounting Principles Board in the United States issued Opinion No. 20 to establish greater uniformity in reporting practice.[1] Only two-thirds of the Board approved the opinion, the minimum required. This indicates the degree of divergence in views concerning this matter. The Canadian counterpart of APB Opinion No. 20 is Section 1506 of the *Accounting Recommendations*, "Accounting Changes." In addition there are brief references to accounting changes in other sections of the recommendations, especially in Section 1500, "General Standards of Financial Statement Presentation."

The Accounting Research Committee has classified accounting changes as follows:[2]

1. Change in an accounting policy.
2. A revision of an accounting estimate.
3. A correction of an error relating to prior period financial statements.

CHANGE IN ACCOUNTING POLICY[3]

As has been indicated in previous chapters, companies may select among several alternative accounting principles and the methods of their application. For example, a company may depreciate its buildings and equipment using the straight-line method, the declining-balance method, the sum-of-the-years-digits method, or other consistent and rational allocation procedure. Long-term construction contracts may be accounted for by the percentage-of-completion or the completed contract method. These alternative methods are often equally available to a given company but in most instances criteria for selection among the methods are inadequate. As a result, companies have often found it easy to justify changing from one accounting policy to another. The impact of the change on financial statements is frequently very significant.

The financial reporting of changes in accounting policy is a problem because of the flexibility that exists within generally accepted accounting

---

[1] *Opinions of the Accounting Principles Board, No. 20*, "Accounting Changes" (New York: American Institute of Certified Public Accountants, 1971).

[2] *CICA Handbook: Accounting Recommendations*, Section 1506, "Accounting Changes" (Toronto: Canadian Institute of Chartered Accountants, 1980), par. .01.

[3] The classification "change in accounting policy" includes changes in methods used to apply the policy.

principles. The consistency standard of reporting is relevant here, but it cannot, nor should it be expected to, resolve the problem of accounting changes.

In general, companies should not change accounting principles because "consistent use of accounting principles from one period to another enhances the utility of financial statements to users by facilitating analysis and understandability of comparative accounting data."[4] However, a company may change its accounting principles because of a new accounting pronouncement or legal requirement, or the change may be the result of a choice among alternative GAAPs. APB Opinion No. 20 is based on the premise that an entity should not make changes in the application of accounting principles other than to alternatives considered superior in the circumstances. While there is no direct counterpart for this premise in Canada, Section 1506 states that the "choice type of change" should only be made "if it is considered that the change would result in a more appropriate presentation of events and transactions in the financial statements of the enterprise."[5]

The Accounting Research Committee in Section 1506 recognizes that a change in the application of accounting principles may create a situation in which retroactive application is appropriate. "The new accounting policy should be applied retroactively, except in those circumstances when the necessary financial data is not reasonably determinable."[6] From among the three alternatives outlined on pages 792 and 793, the Accounting Research Committee has opted for number one: adjust all prior periods' statements for the effect of the change and adjust the beginning Retained Earnings balance for the cumulative amount of the change or correction. In addition, detailed and specific disclosure requirements are imposed in Section 1506, as follows: (1) a description of the change, (2) the effect of the change on the financial statements of the current period, and (3) when the change has been applied retroactively (which should usually be the case), the fact that the financials of prior periods that are presented have been restated and the effect of the change on those prior periods, or (4) when a change in an accounting policy has been applied retroactively but prior periods have not been restated, this fact should be disclosed together with the cumulative adjustment to the current period's opening retained earnings balance. The Accounting Research Committee recognizes that on occasion it may be extremely difficult to obtain the necessary financial data to permit retroactive application and therefore a logical and practical exception is recommended when necessary financial data is not reasonably determinable.

The cumulative effect of a change in accounting principle must usually be adjusted for the effect of interperiod income tax allocation. The change is

---

[4]*Opinions of the Accounting Principles Board, No. 20, op. cit.,* par. 15.
[5]*CICA Handbook: Accounting Recommendations,* Section 1506, *op. cit.,* par. .02.
[6]*Ibid.,* par. .11.

often from a method that was used for both tax and reporting purposes to a different method for reporting purposes. Retroactive changes in methods for tax purposes are generally not permitted. Thus, the income tax liability is usually not affected by the change; however, an adjustment is usually necessary to the deferred income tax account. For example, if a company has been using capital cost allowance as its method of depreciation for both accounting and tax purposes but changes to the straight-line method for accounting purposes, the tax effect should be reflected as a reduction in the cumulative change (prior period adjustment) and as a credit to Deferred Income Tax. If the change for accounting purposes is to a method used for tax purposes, the financial statements and the tax return would be in agreement after the change; and previously recorded amounts in Deferred Income Tax would be reversed.

Assuming retroactive application, the cumulative effect of the change is recorded directly as an adjustment to the beginning Retained Earnings balance and all prior income statement data reported for comparative purposes are adjusted to reflect the new policy. The restatement of prior year's data includes the restatement of the five or ten years earnings summaries that commonly appear in annual reports. Also, of course, any balance sheet accounts affected by the change would be restated.

To illustrate, assume Swiss Company compiles the following information concerning its change in 1981 from the completed-contract method of valuing long-term construction contracts to the percentage-of-completion method.

Year	Net Income — Completed-Contract Method	Net Income — Percentage-of-Completion Method
1976	$ 20,000	$ 40,000
1977	60,000	70,000
1978	80,000	75,000
1979	75,000	110,000
1980	90,000	85,000
Total at beginning of 1981 .	$325,000	$380,000

The retained earnings statement for 1981 would reflect the effect of the change on prior years. The example on page 796 includes an explanation of the change on the face of the statement. In practice, the explanation would usually appear in notes to the financial statements.

All prior period income statements would be adjusted to the amounts that would have been reported using the new accounting policy. If the prior statements cannot be adjusted because of inadequate data, this fact should be disclosed and the cumulative impact would be reported only on the retained earnings statement. Full disclosure of the effect of the change should be made for all periods presented. In addition, earnings per share data would be

Swiss Company Retained Earnings Statement For Years Ended December 31, 1981 and 1980	1981	1980
Retained earnings, January 1, 1981, as previously reported .	$ 900,000	$ 910,000
Add adjustment for the cumulative effect on prior years of applying retroactively the percentage-of-completion method of accounting for long-term construction contracts rather than the completed-contract method, less applicable income tax	55,000	60,000
January 1, 1981, balance as restated	$ 955,000	$ 970,000
Add net income per income statement, 1980 as restated	105,000	85,000
	$1,060,000	$1,055,000
Deduct dividends declared	100,000	100,000
Retained earnings, December 31, 1981	$ 960,000	$ 955,000

recomputed taking into consideration any impact the new income amount would have.

If comparative retained earnings statements are prepared for 1980 and 1981 as illustrated, the cumulative adjustment to beginning retained earnings for each reported year would reflect only those years prior to that particular year. Thus, in the example, the 1980 beginning retained earnings balance has been adjusted by $60,000, the difference in net income under the two methods for the years 1976-1979 ($295,000 − $235,000).

If a change in accounting principle is caused by a new pronouncement of an authoritative accounting body, the cumulative effect may be adjusted retroactively or prospectively, depending upon the transitional provisions, if any, contained in the pronouncement. In most cases, the Accounting Research Committee has not chosen to require retroactive adjustment for newly pronounced principles. However, retroactive application is often encouraged.

CHANGE IN AN ACCOUNTING ESTIMATE

Accountants must always exercise judgment in preparing financial statements to ensure a fair presentation in accordance with GAAP. Items, such as the number of years to use for depreciating buildings and equipment balances, the amount to provide for uncollectible accounts, or the amount of warranty liability to record in the accounts, are based upon estimates using the best available information at the statement date. Conditions may change in subsequent periods, and the estimate may need to be revised. The Accounting Research Committee has stated in Section 1506 that "the effect of a change in an accounting estimate should be accounted for in: (a) the period of change, if the change affects the financial results of that period only; or (b) the period of change and applicable future periods, if the change affects the financial results of both current and future periods."[7] No retroactive adjustment or restatements of prior periods are to be prepared for a change in estimate. Since a change in an estimate is considered a part of the normal accounting process, it is logical for the change to be treated prospectively.

For example, assume assets costing $30,000 are estimated initially to have a ten-year life. Depreciation of $3,000 is recorded for each of the first four years; however, in the fifth year the estimated life of the assets is changed from ten years to eight years. At the time of the new estimate, $12,000 has been accumulated in the accumulated depreciation account, and the assets have a remaining net book value of $18,000. The new annual depreciation amount will now be $4,500 ($18,000 ÷ 4 years). No separate disclosure is required for this type of change unless the amount is material or the nature of the change is rare or unusual. If desirable, separate disclosure of the change should be provided usually in a note to the financial statements.

In some instances, an accounting policy and an estimate are changed simultaneously, and the effect of the change in policy and in estimate cannot be separated. In this situation, the change is usually treated as a change in estimate rather than a change in policy.

Section 1506 provides an example: "an enterprise may change from deferring and amortizing a cost to expensing it as incurred because, as a result of new information, the future benefits of the cost have become doubtful."[8] The change to expensing as incurred is a change in policy; the change in future benefits is a change in an estimate. In the example however, the change in estimate is the reason for the new policy; therefore the effect of the simultaneous changes should be accounted for prospectively.

CORRECTION OF AN ERROR

Accounting errors can result from mistakes in computation, the failure to apply appropriate accounting principles and procedures, or the misuse or omission of certain information. When errors are discovered,[9] the accountant must be able to analyse these in determining what action is appropriate under the circumstances. This calls for an understanding of accounting standards and their application and of the system of internal control and accounting procedures as well as good judgment and skill in handling situations indicating a failure to meet such standards.

A number of special practices are usually adopted by a business unit to

---

[7]*Ibid.*, par. .24.

[8]*Ibid.*, par. .22.

[9]Section 3600.12 includes the following statement: "It is recognized that there are rare occasions when errors relating to previously issued financial statements are discovered." This ambiguous statement leaves it to the reader to determine what is rare — making errors or discovering them. Assumedly, the Committee intended to convey that making errors should be rare, and that accountants should certainly detect them when they occur.

ensure accuracy in recording and summarizing business transactions. A prime requisite in achieving accuracy, of course, is the establishment of an accounting system providing safeguards against both carelessness and dishonesty. Such a system should include orderly and integrated procedures and controls. Personnel should have well-defined responsibilites. An internal auditing staff may be established as a part of the accounting system to continuously reconcile and prove recorded data and also to evaluate information systems. Independent public accountants verify recorded data as a further means of ensuring accounting accuracy.

Despite the accounting system established and the verification procedures employed, some misstatements may enter into the financial statements. Misstatements may be minor ones having little effect on the financial presentations; others may be of a major character, resulting in material misrepresentations of financial position and the results of operations. Misstatements may arise from intentional falsifications by employees or officers as well as from unintentional errors and omissions by employees.

Intentional Misstatements

When misstatements result from intentional falsification of entries or records, the motive or motives may be: (1) to evade taxes; (2) to influence the market price of the company's securities; (3) to obtain favorable decisions by regulatory bodies; (4) to conceal the theft of cash, securities, merchandise or other assets; (5) to conceal facts that may embarrass certain parties; or (6) to improve the company's ability to borrow. When intentional misstatements arise, management personnel are often directly involved in the misstatement. Because accounting systems are usually built upon the assumptions of honest management, it is difficult to design a system to prevent this type of misstatement. Both internal and external audits can be deterrents to this type of activity.

Unintentional Misstatements

It would be impossible to offer a complete list of the misstatements that might arise unintentionally. Unintentional misstatements arise from clerical errors and omissions or from failures in the application of accounting principles. The most common misstatements include entries in the wrong customer or creditor accounts, entries in the wrong revenue and expense accounts, errors in counting and valuing inventories, errors in calculating depreciation and amortization, failures to distinguish properly between capital and revenue expenditures, and the omission of adjustments for prepaid and accrued items. These and other unintentional errors can be kept to a minimum through effective systems of internal control and satisfactory procedures for the audit and review of accounting data.

Errors are generally discovered at times when the periodic adjusting entries are being made, when an audit is being undertaken, when a business is to be sold, when a change of ownership is to be made in a partnership, when questions of taxation are to be decided, when heirs of an estate are to be satisfied, when a business is to be incorporated and shares are to be sold to outsiders, or when two or more business units are to be combined in a business combination.

Kinds of Errors

There are a number of different kinds of errors. Some errors are discovered in the period in which they are made, and these are easily corrected. Others may not be discovered currently and are reflected on the financial statements until discovered. Some errors are never discovered; however, the effects of these errors are often counterbalanced in subsequent periods and after this takes place, account balances are again accurately stated. Errors may be classified as follows.

Errors Discovered Currently in the Course of Normal Accounting Procedures. Certain errors are of a clerical nature and are discovered in the course of normal accounting processes. For example, an entry may be made that is not in balance and the entry is posted, an item may be posted to the wrong side of the account, a mistake may be made in computing an account balanced, an amount may be misstated or omitted in posting to a subsidiary ledger, or an account balance may be misstated or omitted in listing accounts or in a trial balance or on a work sheet. Such errors, when not discovered during the period, will become evident at the end of the period in the regular period-end steps of the accounting process. Errors are indicated when subsidiary account detail is not equal to the balance in the control account, when debit and credit totals on a trial balance are not equal, or when totals on a work sheet are not in balance. Normally the summarizing process points to the source of the error, and the error is readily corrected.

Errors Limited to Balance Sheet Accounts. Certain errors affect only the balance sheet accounts. For example, Marketable Securities may be debited instead of Notes Receivable, Interest Payable may be credited instead of Salaries Payable, or Prepaid Tax may be debited instead of Tax Payable. In other instances, the acquisition of a property item on a deferred payment plan may be misstated, or the exchange of convertible bonds for shares may be omitted. Such errors are frequently discovered in the period in which they are made in the course of recording subsequent transactions in the misstated accounts, or in the course of reviewing preliminary summaries and statements. When the errors are discovered currently, entries are made to correct account balances. When the errors are not discovered until a subsequent period, corrections are made at that time. However, memorandum entries should be made in the accounts to indicate which amounts were misstated so the balance sheet data may be restated when the statement is to be presented in subsequent periods for analysis purposes or for comparative reporting.

Errors Limited to Income Statement Accounts. Certain errors affect only the income statement accounts. For example, Office Salaries may be debited instead of Sales Salaries, Purchases may be debited instead of Sales Returns, or Interest Revenue may be credited instead of Dividend Revenue. The discovery of the errors in the period in which they are made calls for the correction of the revenue and expense balances. However, if the errors are not discovered in the period in which they are made, net income will still be stated correctly; in closing the accounts at the end of the period, the balance sheet accounts remaining open are accurately stated and carried into the next period. If the errors are discovered in a subsequent period, no corrections are necessary. However, memorandum entries should be made in the accounts to indicate the misstated accounts so income statement data may be restated when the statement is to be presented in future periods for analysis purposes or for comparative reporting.

Errors Affecting Both Income Statement Accounts and Balance Sheet Accounts. Certain errors, when not discovered currently, result in the misstatement of net income and thus affect both the income statement accounts and the balance sheet accounts. The balance sheet accounts are carried into the succeeding period; hence, an error made currently and not detected will affect earnings of the future. Such errors may be classified into two groups:

1. *Errors in net income which, when not detected, are automatically counterbalanced in the following fiscal period.* Net income on the income statements for two successive periods is incorrectly stated; certain account balances on the balance sheet at the end of the first period are incorrectly stated, but the account balances on the balance sheet at the end of the succeeding period are accurately stated. In this class are errors such as the misstatement of inventories and the omission of adjustments for prepaid and accrued items at the end of a period.
2. *Errors in net income which, when not detected, are not automatically counterbalanced in the following fiscal period.* Account balances on successive balance sheets are incorrectly stated until the time entries are made compensating for or correcting the errors. In this class are errors, such as the recognition of capital expenditures as revenue expenditures and the omission of charges for depreciation and amortization.

When these types of errors are discovered, careful analysis is required to determine the required action to correct account balances.

When it is discovered that an error in stating net income of the past has been counterbalanced in subsequent periods, a memorandum entry should be made to indicate the corrections required on the balance sheet and income statement in providing such presentations in the future. However, when errors of the past have not yet been counterbalanced, the Accounting Research Committee has specified that the error should be accounted for retroactively. Moreover, the financials for all prior periods presented for comparative purposes should be restated, as necessary.[10] For example, assume merchandise inventory at the end of the preceding period was materially overstated in the accounts of a corporation as the result of an error in the count; the error is corrected by a debit to Retained Earnings and a credit to Inventory. Assume a material cut-off error was made in recording sales on account at the end of the previous period; the error is corrected by a debit to Sales of the current period and a credit to Retained Earnings.

Disclosure of the nature of the error and the effect of its correction on prior period income before extraordinary items, net income, and related earnings per share amounts should be made in the period in which the error was discovered and corrected. Future financial statements need not repeat the disclosure. As indicated in earlier chapters, corporate annual reports generally provide comparative financial statements reporting the financial position and the results of operations for the current period and for one or more preceding periods. In preparing comparative statements, these should be restated to report the retroactive application of error corrections.

The paragraphs that follow illustrate the procedures applied when error corrections qualify for retroactive application. Accordingly, it is assumed that each of the errors is material and calls for correction directly to the retained earnings account summarizing past earnings. When errors are discovered, they usually affect the income tax liability for a prior period. Amended income returns are usually prepared to either claim a refund or to pay any additional tax applicable. For simplicity, the extended example on the following pages and the exercises and problems at the end of the chapter ignore the income tax effect of errors unless it is clear from the requirements that income tax should be considered.

Illustrative Example of Error Correction

The following example illustrates the analysis required upon the discovery of errors of prior periods and the entries to correct these errors.

Assume the Monarch Wholesale Co. began operations at the beginning of 1979. An auditing firm is engaged for the first time in 1981. Before the accounts are adjusted and closed for 1981, the auditor reviews the accounts, and discovers the errors summarized on pages 802 and 803. Effects on the

---

[10]*Ibid.*, par. .28.

	AT END OF 1979			
	INCOME STATEMENT		BALANCE SHEET	
	SECTION	NET INCOME	SECTION	RETAINED EARNINGS
(1) Understatement of merchandise inventory of 1,000 on December 31, 1979.	Cost of Goods Sold +	–	Current Assets –	–
(2) Failure to record merchandise purchases on account of $850 in 1979; purchases were recorded in 1980.	Cost of Goods Sold –	+	Current Liabilities –	+
(3) Failure to record merchandise sales on account of $1,800 in 1980. (It is assumed that the sales for 1980 were recognized as revenue in 1981.)				
(4) Failure to record accrued sales salaries; expense was recognized when payment was made. On December 31, 1979, $450.	Selling Expense –	+	Current Liabilities –	+
On December 31, 1980, $300.				
(5) Failure to record prepaid taxes of $275 on December 31, 1979; amount was included as miscellaneous general expense.	General Expense +	–	Current Assets –	–
(6) Failure to record reduction in prepaid insurance balance of $350 on December 31, 1979; insurance for 1979 was charged to 1980.	General Expense –	+	Current Assets +	+
(7) Failure to record accrued interest on notes receivable of $150 on December 31, 1979; revenue was recognized on collection in 1980.	Other Revenue –	–	Current Assets –	–
(8) Failure to record unearned service fees; amounts received were included in Miscellaneous Revenue. On December 31, 1979, $175.	Other Revenue +	+	Current Liabilities –	+
On December 31, 1980, $225.				
(9) Failure to record reduction in unearned rent revenue balance on December 31, 1980, $125. (It is assumed that the rent revenue for 1980 was recognized as revenue in 1981.)				
(10) Failure to record depreciation of delivery equipment. On December 31, 1979, $1,200.	Selling Expense –	+	Non-current Assets +	+
On December 31, 1980, $1,200.				

OF ERRORS ON FINANCIAL STATEMENTS

AT END OF 1980				AT END OF 1981			
INCOME STATEMENT		BALANCE SHEET		INCOME STATEMENT		BALANCE SHEET	
SECTION	NET INCOME	SECTION	RETAINED EARNINGS	SECTION	NET INCOME	SECTION	RETAINED EARNINGS
Cost of Goods Sold −	+						
Cost of Goods Sold +	−						
Sales−	−	Accounts Receivable −	−	Sales +	+		
Selling Expense +	−						
Selling Expense −	+	Current Liabilities −	+	Selling Expense +	−		
General Expense −	+						
General Expense +	−						
Other Revenue +	+						
Other Revenue −	−						
Other Revenue +	+	Current Liabilities −	+	Other Revenue −	−		
Other Revenue −	−	Deferred Revenues +	−	Other Revenue +	+		
		Non-current Assets +	+			Non-current Assets +	+
Selling Expense −	+	Non-current Assets +	+			Non-current Assets +	+

financial statements are listed before any correcting entries. A plus sign (+) indicates an overstatement in the statement section; a minus sign (−) indicates an understatement in the statement section. Each error correction is discussed in more detail in subsequent paragraphs.

(1) *Understatement of merchandise inventory.* It is discovered that the merchandise inventory as of December 31, 1979, was understated by $1,000. The effects of the misstatement were as shown below.

	Income Statement	Balance Sheet
For 1979:	Cost of goods sold overstated (ending inventory too low)	Assets understated (inventory too low)
	Net income understated	Retained earnings understated
For 1980:	Cost of goods sold understated beginning intory too low)	Retained earnings understated
	Net income overstated	Balance sheet items not affected, retained earnings understatement for 1979 being corrected by net income overstatement for 1980.

Since this type of error counterbalances after two years, no correcting entry is required in 1981.

If the error had been discovered in 1980 instead of 1981, an entry could have been made to correct the account balances so that operations for 1980 might be reported accurately. The beginning inventory would have to be increased by $1,000, the asset understatement, and Retained Earnings would have to be credited for this amount representing the income understatement in 1979. The correcting entry in 1980 would have been:

Merchandise Inventory	1,000	
Retained Earnings		1,000

(2) *Failure to record merchandise purchases.* It is discovered that purchase invoices as of December 28, 1979, for $850 were not recorded until 1980. The goods were included in the inventory at the end of 1979. The effects of the failure to record the purchases were as follows:

	Income Statement	Balance Sheet
For 1979:	Cost of goods sold understated (purchases too low)	Liabilities understated (accounts payable too low)
	Net income overstated	Retained earnings overstated
For 1980:	Cost of goods sold overstated (purchases too high)	Balance sheet items not affected, retained earnings overstatement for 1979 being corrected by net income understatement for 1977.)
	Net income understated	

Since this is a counterbalancing error, no correcting entry is required in 1981.

If the error had been discovered in 1980 instead of 1981, a correcting entry would have been necessary. In 1979, Purchases was debited and Accounts

Payable credited for $850 for merchandise acquired in 1979 and included in the ending inventory of 1979. Retained Earnings would have to be debited for $850, representing the net income overstatement for 1979, and Purchases would have to be credited for a similar amount to reduce the Purchases balance in 1980. The correcting entry in 1980 would have been:

Retained Earnings	850	
Purchases		850

(3) *Failure to record merchandise sales.* It is discovered that sales on account for the last week of December, 1980, for $1,800 were not recorded until 1981. The goods sold were not included in the inventory at the end of 1980. The effects of the failure to report the revenue in 1980 were:

	Income Statement	Balance Sheet
For 1980:	Revenue understated (sales too low)	Assets understated (accounts receivable too low)
	Net income understated	Retained earnings understated

When the error is discovered in 1981, Sales is debited for $1,800 and Retained Earnings is credited for this amount representing the net income understatement for 1980. The following entry is made:

Sales	1,800	
Retained Earnings		1,800

(4) *Failure to record accrued expense.* Accrued sales salaries of $450 as of December 31, 1979, and $300 as of December 31, 1980, were overlooked in adjusting the accounts on each of these dates. Sales Salaries is debited for salary payments. The effects of the failure to record the accrued expense of $450 as of December 31, 1979, were as follows:

	Income Statement	Balance Sheet
For 1979:	Expenses understated (sales salaries too low)	Liabilities understated (accrued sales salaries not reported)
	Net income overstated	Retained earnings overstated
For 1980:	Expenses overstated (sales salaries too high)	Balance sheet items not affected, retained
	Net income understated	earnings overstatement for 1979 being corrected by net income understatement for 1980.

The effects of the failure to recognize the accrued expense of $300 on December 31, 1980, were as follows:

	Income Statement	Balance Sheet
For 1980:	Expenses understated (sales salaries too low)	Liabilities understated (accrued sales salaries not reported)
	Net income overstated	Retained earnings overstated

No entry is required in 1981 to correct the accounts for the failure to record the accrued expense at the end of 1979, the misstatement in 1979 having been counterbalanced by the misstatement in 1980. An entry is required, however, to correct the accounts for the failure to record the accrued expense at the end of 1980 if the net income for 1981 is not to be misstated. If accrued expenses were properly recorded at the end of 1981, Retained Earnings would be debited for $300, representing the net income overstatement for 1980, and Sales Salaries would be credited for a similar amount, representing the amount to be subtracted from salary payments in 1981. The correcting entry is:

Retained Earnings	300	
Sales Salaries		300

If the failure to adjust the accounts for the accrued expense of 1979 had been recognized in 1980, an entry similar to the one above would have been required in 1980 to correct the account balances. The entry in 1980 would have been:

Retained Earnings	450	
Sales Salaries		450

The accrued salaries of $300 as of the end of 1980 would be recorded at the end of that year by an appropriate adjustment.

(5) *Failure to record prepaid expense.* It is discovered that Miscellaneous General Expense for 1979 included taxes of $275 that should have been deferred in adjusting the accounts on December 31, 1979. The effects of the failure to record the prepaid expenses were as follows:

	Income Statement	Balance Sheet
For 1979:	Expenses overstated (miscellaneous general expense too high) Net income understated	Assets understated (prepaid taxes not reported) Retained earnings understated
For 1980:	Expenses understated (miscellaneous general expense too low) Net income overstated	Balance sheet items not affected, retained earnings understatement for 1979 being corrected by net income overstatement for 1980.

Since this is a counterbalancing error, no entry to correct the accounts is required in 1981.

If the error had been discovered in 1980 instead of 1981, a correcting entry would have been necessary. If prepaid taxes were properly recorded at the end of 1980, Miscellaneous General Expense would have to be debited for $275, the expense relating to operations of 1980, and Retained Earnings would have to be credited for a similar amount representing the net income understatement for 1979. The correcting entry in 1980 would have been:

Miscellaneous General Expense	275
Retained Earnings	275

(6) *Overstatement of prepaid expense.* On January 2, 1979, $1,050 representing insurance for a three-year period was paid. The charge was made to the asset account, Prepaid Insurance. No adjustment was made at the end of 1979. At the end of 1980, the prepaid insurance account was reduced to the prepaid balance on that date, $350, insurance for two years, or $700, being charged to operations of 1980. The effects of the misstatements were as follows:

	Income Statement	Balance Sheet
For 1979:	Expenses understated (insurance expense not reported)	Assets overstated (prepaid insurance too high)
	Net income overstated	Retained earnings overstated
For 1980:	Expenses overstated (insurance expense too high)	Balance sheet items not affected, retained earnings overstatement for 1979 being corrected by net income understatement for 1980.
	Net income understated	

Since the balance sheet items at the end of 1980 were correctly stated, no entry to correct the accounts is required in 1981.

If the error had been discovered in 1980 instead of 1981, an entry would have been necessary to correct the account balances. Prepaid Insurance would have been decreased for the expired insurance of $350 and Retained Earnings would be debited for this amount representing the net income overstatement for 1979. The correcting entry in 1980 would have been:

Retained Earnings	350
Prepaid Insurance	350

The expired insurance of $350 for 1980 would be recorded at the end of that year by an appropriate adjustment.

(7) *Failure to record accrued revenue.* Accrued interest on notes receivable of $150 was overlooked in adjusting the accounts on December 31, 1979. The revenue was recognized when the interest was collected in 1980. The effects of the failure to record the accrued revenue were:

	Income Statement	Balance Sheet
For 1979:	Revenue understated (interest revenue too low)	Assets understated (interest receivable not reported)
	Net income understated	Retained earnings understated
For 1980:	Revenue overstated (interest revenue too high)	Balance sheet items not affected, retained earnings understatement for 1979 being corrected by net income overstatement for 1980.
	Net income overstated	

Since the balance sheet items at the end of 1980 were correctly stated, no entry to correct the accounts is required in 1981.

If the error had been discovered in 1980 instead of 1981, an entry would have been necessary to correct the account balances. If accrued interest on notes receivable had been properly recorded at the end of 1980, Interest Revenue would have to be debited for $150, the amount to be subtracted from receipts of 1980, and Retained Earnings would have to be credited for a similar amount representing the net income understatement for 1979. The correcting entry in 1980 would have been:

Interest Revenue	150	
Retained Earnings		150

(8) *Failure to record unearned revenue.* Fees received in advance for miscellaneous services of $175 as of December 31, 1979, and $225 as of December 31, 1980, were overlooked in adjusting the accounts at each of these dates. Miscellaneous Revenue had been credited when fees were received. The effects of the failure to recognize the unearned revenue of $175 at the end of 1979 were as follows:

	Income Statement	Balance Sheet
For 1979:	Revenue overstated (miscellaneous revenue too high)	Liabilities understated (unearned service fees not reported)
	Net income overstated	Retained earnings overstated
For 1980:	Revenue understated (miscellaneous revenue too low)	Balance sheet items not affected, retained earnings overstatement for 1979 being corrected by net income overstatement for 1980.
	Net income understated	

The effects of the failure to recognize the unearned revenue of $225 at the end of 1980 were as follows:

	Income Statement	Balance Sheet
For 1980:	Revenue overstated (miscellaneous revenue too high)	Liabilities understated (unearned service fees not reported)
	Net income overstated	Retained earnings overstated

No entry is required in 1981 to correct the accounts for the failure to record the unearned revenue at the end of 1979, the misstatement in 1979 having been counterbalanced by the misstatement in 1980. An entry is required, however, to correct the accounts for the failure to record the unearned revenue at the end of 1980 if the net income for 1981 is not to be misstated. If the unearned revenue were properly recorded at the end of 1981, Retained Earnings would be debited for $225, representing the net income overstatement for 1980, and Miscellaneous Revenue would be credited for the same amount, representing the revenue that is to be identified with 1981. The correcting entry is:

Retained Earnings	225	
Miscellaneous Revenue		225

If the failure to adjust the accounts for the unearned revenue of 1979 had been recognized in 1980 instead of 1981, an entry similar to the one above would have been required in 1980 to correct the account balances. The entry at that time would have been:

Retained Earnings	175	
Miscellaneous Revenue		175

The unearned service fees of $225 as of the end of 1980 would be recorded at the end of that year by an appropriate adjustment.

(9) *Overstatement of unearned revenue.* Unearned Rent Revenue was credited for $375 representing revenue for December, 1980, and for January and February, 1981. No adjustment was made on December 31, 1980. The effects of the failure to adjust the accounts to show revenue of $125 for 1980 were as follows:

	Income Statement	Balance Sheet
For 1980:	Revenue understated (rent revenue too low)	Liabilities overstated (unearned rent revenue too high)
	Net income understated	Retained earnings understated

When the error is discovered in 1981, Unearned Rent Revenue is debited for $125 and Retained Earnings is credited for this amount representing the net income understatement in 1980. The following entry is made:

Unearned Rent Revenue	125	
Retained Earnings		125

(10) *Failure to report depreciation.* Delivery equipment was acquired at the beginning of 1979 at a cost of $6,000. The equipment has an estimated five-year life, and depreciation of $1,200 was overlooked at the end of 1979 and 1980. The effects of the failure to record depreciation for 1979 were as follows:

	Income Statement	Balance Sheet
For 1979:	Expenses understated (depreciation of delivery equipment too low)	Assets overstated (accumulated depreciation of delivery equipment too low)
	Net income overstated	Retained earnings overstated
For 1980:	Expenses not affected	Assets overstated (accumulated depreciation of delivery equipment too low)
	Net income not affected	Retained earnings overstated

It should be observed that the misstatements arising from the failure to record depreciation are not counterbalanced in the succeeding year.

Failure to record depreciation for 1980 affected the statements as shown below:

	Income Statement	Balance Sheet
For 1980:	Expenses unerstated (depreciation of delivery of equipment too low)	Assets overstated (accumulated depreciation of delivery equipment understated)
	Net income overstated	Retained earnings overstated

When the omission is recognized, Retained Earnings must be decreased by the net income overstatements of prior years and accumulated depreciation must be increased by the depreciation that should have been recorded. The correcting entry in 1981 for depreciation that should have been recognized for 1979 and 1980 is as follows:

Retained Earnings	2,400	
Accumulated Depreciation — Delivery Equipment		2,400

Working Papers to Summarize Corrections

It is assumed in the following sections that the errors previously discussed are discovered in 1981 before the accounts for the year are adjusted and closed. Accounts are corrected so that revenue and expense accounts report the balances identified with the current period and asset, liability, and retained earnings accounts are accurately stated. Instead of preparing a separate entry for each correction, a single compound entry may be made for all of the errors discovered. The entry to correct earnings of prior years as well as to correct current earnings may be developed by the preparation of working papers. Assume the following retained earnings account for the Monarch Wholesale Co.:

ACCOUNT Retained Earnings

DATE		ITEM	DEBIT	CREDIT	BALANCE DEBIT	BALANCE CREDIT
1979 Dec.	31	Balance				12,000
1980 Dec.	20	Dividends declared.....................	5,000			7,000
		Net income		15,000		22,000

The working papers to determine the corrected retained earnings balance on December 31, 1979, and the corrected net income for 1980 are shown on page 811. As indicated earlier, no adjustment is made for income tax effects in this example.

	EXPLANATION	RETAINED EARNINGS DEC. 31, 1979 DEBIT	CREDIT	NET INCOME YEAR ENDED DEC. 31, 1980 DEBIT	CREDIT	ACCOUNTS REQUIRING CORRECTION IN 1981 DEBIT	CREDIT	ACCOUNT	
1 2	Reported retained earnings balance, Dec. 31, 1979		12,000						1 2
3 4	Reported net income for year ended Dec. 31, 1980				15,000				3 4
5	Corrections:[11]								5
6 7	(1) Understatement of inventory on Dec. 31, 1979, $1,000		1,000	1,000					6 7
8 9 10	(2) Failure to record merchandise purchases in 1979, $850 .... (3) Failure to record merchandise	850			850				8 9 10
11	sales in 1980, $1,800				1,800	1,800		Sales	11
12 13 14	(4) Failure to record accrued sales salaries: (a) On Dec. 31, 1979, $450	450			450				12 13 14
15	(b) On Dec. 31, 1980, $300			300			300	Sales Salaries	15
16 17	(5) Failure to record prepaid taxes on Dec. 31, 1979, $275		275	275					16 17
18 19 20	(6) Failure to record insurance expense on Dec. 31, 1979, $350, insurance of $700 for 1979 and 1980								18 19 20
21	being charged to 1980	350			350				21
22 23 24	(7) Failure to record accrued interest on notes receivable on Dec. 31, 1979, $150		150	150					22 23 24
25	(8) Failure to record unearned								25
26 27	service fees: (a) On Dec. 31, 1979, $175	175			175				26 27
28 29 30	(b) On Dec. 31, 1980, $225 .... (9) Failure to record rent revenue			225			225	Miscellaneous Revenue	28 29 30
31 32	on Dec. 31, 1980, $125 .... (10) Failure to record depreciation				125	125		Unearned Rent Revenue	31 32
33 34 35	of delivery equipment: (a) On Dec. 31, 1979, $1,200 .. (b) On Dec. 31, 1980, $1,200 ..	1,200		1,200			1,200 1,200	Accumulated Depr.—Delivery	33 34 35
36 37	Corrected retained earnings balance, Dec. 31, 1979	10,400				1,925 1,000	2,925	Equipment	36 37
38		13,425	13,425						38
39	Corrected net income for 1980			15,600					39
40				18,750	18,750				40
41 42 43	Net correction to retained earnings as of Jan. 1, 1981					1,000 ✓		Retained Earnings	41 42 43
44 45						2,925	2,925		44 45

---

[11]For a more detailed description of the individual errors and their correction, refer to pages 800-810.

The working papers indicate that Retained Earnings is to be decreased by $1,000 as of January 1, 1981. The reduction arises from:

Retained earnings overstatement as of December 31, 1979:
Retained earnings as originally reported $12,000
Retained earnings as corrected 10,400 $1,600

Retained earnings understatement in 1980:
Net income as corrected $15,600
Net income as originally reported 15,000   600

Retained earnings overstatement as of January 1, 1981 .. $1,000

The following entry is prepared from the working papers to correct the account balances in 1981:

Retained Earnings 1,000
Sales 1,800
Unearned Rent Revenue 125
   Sales Salaries 300
   Miscellaneous Revenue 225
   Accumulated Depreciation — Delivery Equipment 2,400

The retained earnings account after correction will appear with a balance of $21,000, as follows:

ACCOUNT Retained Earnings

DATE		ITEM	DEBIT	CREDIT	BALANCE	
					DEBIT	CREDIT
1981 Jan.	1	Balance				22,000
Dec.	31	Corrections in net incomes of prior periods discovered during the course of the audit	1,000			21,000

The balance in Retained Earnings can be proved by reconstructing the account from the detail shown on the working papers. If the net incomes for 1979 and 1980 had been reported properly, Retained Earnings would have appeared as follows:

ACCOUNT Retained Earnings

DATE		ITEM	DEBIT	CREDIT	BALANCE	
					DEBIT	CREDIT
1979 Dec.	31	Corrected balance per working papers ..				10,400
1980 Dec.	20	Dividends declared	5,000			5,400
	31	Corrected net income for 1980		15,600		21,000

In the foregoing example, a corrected net income figure for only 1980 was required; hence any corrections in earnings for years prior to this date were shown as affecting the retained earnings balance as of December 31, 1979. Working papers on page 811 were constructed to summarize this information by providing a pair of columns for retained earnings as of December 31, 1979, and a pair of columns for earnings data for 1980. It may be desirable to determine corrected earnings for a number of years. When this is to be done, a pair of columns must be provided for retained earnings as of the beginning of the period under review and a separate pair of columns for each year for which corrected earnings are to be determined. For example, assume that corrected earnings for the years 1978, 1979, and 1980 are to be determined. Working papers for the correction of account balances would be constructed with headings as shown below. Corrections for the omission of accrued sales salaries for a four-year period would appear as follows:

EXPLANATION	RETAINED EARNINGS DEC. 31, 1977		NET INCOME YEAR ENDED DEC. 31, 1978		NET INCOME YEAR ENDED DEC. 31, 1979		NET INCOME YEAR ENDED DEC. 31, 1980		ACCOUNTS REQUIRING CORRECTION IN 1981		
	DEBIT	CREDIT	DEBIT	CREDIT	DEBIT	CREDIT	DEBIT	CREDIT	DEBIT	CREDIT	ACCOUNT
Failure to record accrued sales salaries at end of:											
1977, $750	750			750							
1978, $800			800			800					
1979, $900					900			900			
1980, $625							625			625	Sales Salaries

CHANGE IN CLASSIFICATION

Comparability of financial information over time dictates the need for consistent classification in the presentation of financial statement items. How items may be combined or grouped for presentation purposes in the current period determines the classifications applicable to all periods presented. If a change in classification is made in the current period, the counterpart items in the financial statements of all prior periods presented would be reclassified to conform to the current period's presentation. In addition, the fact that reclassifications have been made should be disclosed. Thus a change in classification requires retroactive application with restatement of prior periods.

CHANGE IN REPORTING ENTITY

A change in reporting entity is specifically identified as a type of accounting change in APB Opinion No. 20. It has not been so identified by the Accounting Research Committee. Nonetheless, such a change at least merits brief consideration.

Companies sometimes change their nature or report their operations in such a way that the financial statements are in effect those of a different reporting entity. These changes include: (a) presenting consolidated or combined statements in place of statements of individual companies; (b) changing specific subsidiaries comprising the group of companies for which consolidated statements are presented; (c) changing the companies included in combined financial statements; and (d) a business combination accounted for as a pooling of interest. Section 1506 does not segregate a change in the reporting entity as an accounting change.

Because of the basic objective of preparing statements that assist in predicting future flows, it follows that the financial statements should be adjusted retroactively to disclose what the statements would have looked like if the current entity had been in existence in the prior periods. Of course, this requirement assumes that the companies acting as a unit would have made the same decisions as they did while acting alone. While this assumption is probably invalid, the retroactive adjustment will probably come closer to providing useful information for trend analysis than would statements clearly non-comparable because of the different components of the entity.

In the period of the change, the financial statements should describe the nature and reason for the change. They should also clearly show the effect of the change on income before extraordinary items, net income, and the related earnings per share amounts for all periods presented. Subsequent years' statements do not need to repeat the disclosure.

STATEMENTS FROM INCOMPLETE RECORDS

The procedures leading to the preparation of financial statements that have been applied in the preceding chapters are those required in a *double-entry system*. This is the characteristic system employed in practice and requires the analysis of each transaction in terms of debits and credits. Any set of procedures that does not provide for the analysis of each transaction in terms of double entry is referred to as a *single-entry system*.

Single-entry systems differ widely depending upon the needs of the organization and the originality of the person maintaining the system. Records found in a single-entry system may vary from a narrative of transactions recorded in a single journal, called a *daybook*, to a relatively complete set of journals and a ledger providing accounts for all significant items.

Single-entry procedures are frequently found in organizations whose activities do not warrant the employment of an accountant. Such organizations might include unincorporated retail businesses, professional and service units, and non-profit organizations. Persons acting in a fiduciary capacity, such as estate executors and trust custodians, may also limit their record keeping to single-entry procedures. When double-entry records are not maintained, a professional accountant is normally engaged at different intervals to prepare financial statements, tax returns, and any other required reports.

All of the variations of a single-entry system encountered in practice cannot be described here. A characteristic single-entry system consists of the following records: (1) a daybook or general journal, (2) a cashbook, and (3) ledger accounts showing debtor and creditor balances.

Single-entry procedures commonly take the following form. A cashbook is maintained showing all the transactions affecting cash. Instead of naming accounts to be debited or credited as a result of cash receipts and disbursements, a description of the transaction is offered and a column for the amount of cash is provided. Transactions not shown in the cashbook are recorded in a daybook in descriptive form. Whenever the account of a debtor, a creditor, or the owner is affected, attention is directed to the need for posting by indicating "dr" or "cr" before the amount. Offsetting debits or credits are not shown since accounts in the ledger are maintained only for customers, creditors, and the owner. At the end of the period, reports may be limited to summaries of customer and creditor balances. Of course, because it is single entry, there is no direct way to know if the balances are correct.

PREPARATION OF FINANCIAL STATEMENTS FROM SINGLE-ENTRY RECORDS[12]

When records do not offer a complete summary of transactions, the preparation of accurate financial statements raises a number of problems. These are discussed in the following sections.

Preparation of the Balance Sheet

When the ledger consists of account balances only for customers and creditors, the preparation of the balance sheet calls for reference to a number of different sources. Cash is reported at the balance shown in the cashbook after this figure has been reconciled with the totals of cash on hand and on deposit with the bank. Receivables and payables are summarized from the accounts maintained with debtors and creditors. Merchandise and supplies balances are found by taking inventories. Past statements, cash records, and other documents are reviewed in determining the net book values of depreciable assets. Other assets and liabilities, including accrued and prepaid items, are determined by a review of the records, including invoices, documents, and other available sources offering evidence or information concerning transactions of the past, present, and future. The owner's capital balance in

---

[12]In addition to the statements discussed in this chapter, a statement of changes in financial position could also be prepared. Discussion of this statement is deferred to Chapter 20.

a double-entry system represents an amount arrived at by combining beginning capital, additional investments and withdrawals, and revenue and expense account balances; in single-entry, capital is simply the difference between the total reported for assets less the total reported for liabilities.

Determination of the Net Income or Loss from Comparative Balance Sheet Data and Cash Summary

In the absence of revenue and expense accounts, net income may nonetheless be calculated by the single-entry method. The owner's capital at the beginning of the period is subtracted from owner's capital at the end of the period. The difference is then increased for any withdrawals and decreased for any investments made by the owner during the period. Beginning and ending owner's capital balances are taken from the balance sheets prepared at the end of the previous period and at the end of the current period. Investments and withdrawals are ascertained from owner's capital and drawing accounts maintained in the ledger, or in the absence of these, from the cashbook and other memorandum records.

To illustrate the determination of net income or loss, assume the owner's capital is reported on comparative balance sheets as follows: January 1, $20,000; December 31, $30,000. In the absence of investments or withdrawals by the owner, it must be concluded that the net income for the year was $10,000. However, assume the owner has invested $2,500 and has withdrawn $9,000 during the year. Net income is then computed as follows:

Owner's capital, December 31		$30,000
Owner's capital, January 1		20,000
Net increase in owner's capital		$10,000
Add excess of owner's withdrawals over investments:		
Withdrawals	$9,000	
Investments	2,500	6,500
Net income for the year		$16,500

Preparation of the Income Statement

A summary of the net income or loss calculated from comparative capital balances is generally inadequate. The owner needs a detailed statement of operation disclosing sales, cost of goods sold, operating expenses, and miscellaneous revenue and expense items to evaluate past success or failure and to plan future activities. Creditors may insist upon such statements. In addition, revenue and expense data must be itemized for income tax purposes.

An itemized income statement can be prepared by (1) rewriting transactions in double-entry form or (2) computing the individual revenue and expense balances by reference to cash receipts and disbursements and the changes in asset and liability balances. Obviously, little or nothing is saved by the adoption of a single-entry system if transactions are rewritten in double-entry form and posted to accounts. When the second procedure is followed, an analysis of all cash receipts and disbursements is required, unless this is already provided by special analysis columns in the cash journals. Cash receipts must be classified as: (1) receipts for goods sold for cash, (2) receipts of other revenue items, (3) collections on customers' accounts, (4) proceeds from the sale of assets other than merchandise, (5) amounts borrowed, and (6) investments by the owner. Cash payments must be classified as (1) payments for merchandise purchased for cash, (2) payments of other expense items, (3) payments on trade creditors' accounts, (4) payments for the purchase of assets other than merchandise, (5) loans paid off, and (6) withdrawals by the owner. These data, together with the data provided by the balance sheet, are used in the preparation of the income statement on an accrual basis. Obviously, the accuracy of the income statement will depend upon the accuracy of the information used in computing revenue and expense items. The procedures followed in computing revenue and expense balances on the accrual basis are illustrated in the following sections.

Sales. The amount to be reported for sales consists of the total of cash sales and sales on account. Sales are computed from the cash receipts analysis and comparative balance sheet data as follows:

Cash sales		$ 7,500
Sales on account:		
Notes and accounts receivable at the end of the period .	$1,500	
Collections on notes and accounts receivable during the period	3,000	
	$4,500	
Deduct notes and accounts receivable at the beginning of the period	2,000	2,500
Sales for the period		$10,000

Notes and accounts receivable in the foregoing tabulation are limited to those arising from sales of merchandise.

The computation of gross sales is complicated if sales discounts and returns and allowances exist, or if accounts thought to be collectible are written off. For example, assume sales data as follows:

Data from cash records:	
Cash sales	$10,000
Collections on accounts receivable arising from sales	42,000
Data from balance sheets:	
Accounts receivable at the beginning of the period	$14,300
Accounts receivable at the end of the period	12,500
Supplementary data from special analysis of records:	
Accounts written off during the period	$ 600
Sales discounts allowed customers during the period	850
Sales returns and allowances during the period	300

The supplementary data indicate that uncollectible accounts of $600, sales discounts of $850, and sales returns and allowances of $300 are to be recognized. All of these amounts must be added to cash collections in arriving at gross sales, for there must have been sales equivalent to the reductions in accounts receivable from these sources. Gross sales for the period are computed as follows:

Cash sales		$10,000
Sales on account:		
Accounts receivable at the end of the period	$12,500	
Collections on accounts receivable	42,000	
Accounts receivable written off	600	
Accounts receivable reduced by discounts	850	
Accounts receivable reduced by sales returns and		
allowances	300	
	$56,250	
Deduct accounts receivable at the beginning of the		
period	14,300	41,950
Gross sales for the period		$51,950

Failure to recognize uncollectible accounts, sales discounts, and sales returns and allowances will be counterbalanced by an understatement of gross sales. Although the omissions will have no effect on the net income balance, revenue and expense balances will not be stated accurately.

Cost of Goods Sold. The inventory balance shown on the balance sheet prepared at the end of the preceding fiscal period is reported on the income statements as the beginning inventory.

The amount to be reported for purchases consists of the total of cash purchases and purchases on account. Purchases are computed from the cash payments analysis and comparative balance sheet data as follows:

Cash purchases		$1,500
Purchases on account:		
Notes and accounts payable at the end of the period . .	$2,500	
Payments on notes and accounts payable during the		
period	5,000	
	$7,500	
Deduct notes and accounts payable at the beginning		
of the period	3,500	4,000
Purchases for the period		$5,500

Notes and accounts payable in the foregoing tabulation are limited to those arising from purchases of merchandise.

The inventory balance shown on the balance sheet at the end of the current period is reported on the income statement as the ending inventory. In the first year complete statements are prepared; an estimate of the beginning inventory must be made, if there was one, using perhaps the gross profit method of inventory valuation described in Chapter 7.

When purchase discounts and purchase returns and allowances reduce accounts payable, the computation of purchases follows the same procedure as for gross sales. The purchases balance is increased by the total purchase discounts and purchase returns and allowances since there must have been purchases equivalent to the reductions in the accounts payable from these sources.

Expense Items. An expense balance is computed from the analysis of cash payments and comparative balance sheet data. The computation of an expense item is made as follows:

Cash payments representing expense		$1,000
Add amounts not included in cash payments but to be charged to current period:		
Amount prepaid at the beginning of the period	$250	
Amount accrued at the end of the period	150	400
		$1,400
Deduct amounts included in payments but not to be charged to current period:		
Amount prepaid at the end of the period	$200	
Amount accrued at the beginning of the period	100	300
Expense for the period		$1,100

The charge for depreciation or amortization to be recognized on the income statement may be made by special analysis of balance sheet as well as cash data, if the balance sheet reflects depreciation in the asset balances. For example, assume no acquisition or disposal of property during the period and beginning and ending store furniture balances of $30,000 and $28,500 respectively. Depreciation is reported at $1,500, the net decrease in the asset account. Assume, however, the following information is assembled at the end of a fiscal period:

Data from cash records:	
Payments for store furniture, including payments on notes arising from acquisition of store furniture	$2,500
Data from balance sheets:	
Store furniture at the beginning of the period	$16,500
Store furniture at the end of the period	20,675
Instalment notes payable arising from acquisition of store furniture .	4,000

The charge for depreciation for the period is computed as follows:

Balance of store furniture at the beginning of the period .		$16,500
Add acquisitions of store furniture:		
Cash paid on acquisition of store furniture	$2,500	
Amount owed at the end of the period on acquisition of store furniture	4,000	6,500
Balance of store furniture before depreciation		$23,000
Deduct balance of store furniture at the end of the period		20,675
Depreciation of store furniture for period		$ 2,325

The charge for depreciation developed from the cash records and balance sheet data should be confirmed by computations based upon the individual property items held. The inability to confirm depreciation may indicate that property balances are not reported accurately on the balance sheet. The following analysis is made to support the charge calculated on page 819.

Property	Date Acquired	Cost	Accumulated Depreciation — Prior Years	Remaining Cost	Estimated Life	Remaining Life from Beginning of Year	Depreciation Current Year
Store furniture ...	1/4/77	$24,000	$7,500	$16,500	12 yrs.	8¹/₄ yrs.	$2,000
Store furniture ...	1/7/81	6,500	......	6,500	10 yrs.	......	325 (¹/₂ yr.)
		$30,500	$7,500	$23,000			$2,325

Other Revenue Items. Other revenue balances are computed from the analysis of cash receipts and comparative balance sheet data as follows:

Cash receipts representing revenue		$ 800
Add amounts not included in cash receipts but to be credited to current period:		
Amount prepaid at the beginning of the period	$300	
Amount accrued at the end of the period	50	350
		$1,150
Deduct amounts included in receipts but not to be credited to current period:		
Amount prepaid at the end of the period	$225	
Amount accrued at the beginning of the period	175	400
Other revenue for the period		$ 750

USE OF SINGLE-ENTRY SYSTEMS

Single entry is described here because it represents a system the accountant may encounter when called upon to prepare financial statements, audit books and records, and prepare government informational reports and income tax returns.

Among the advantages of single-entry systems are the following:

1. Record keeping is simplified and the cost of maintaining records is minimal.
2. Individuals sometimes use formal financial statements only for tax returns and occasional borrowing. When needed for these purposes, financial statements can be prepared from the single-entry records as demonstrated in this chapter.

Among the disadvantages of single-entry procedures are the following factors:

1. A trial balance offering a check on the accuracy of posting is not available.

2. Preparation of the balance sheet from miscellaneous sources and memoranda may result in omissions and misstatements.

3. Detailed analysis of transactions is necessary in arriving at a summary of operations. Misstatements of assets and liabilities, particularly failures to report assets at properly depreciated or amortized balances, affect revenue and expense balances and may result in material misstatements of net income or loss.

4. There is failure to provide a centralized and co-ordinated accounting system subject to internal control and available for satisfactory and convenient audit by accountants and officers of Revenue Canada.

---

1. Explain briefly the difference in treatments of (a) a change in an accounting policy, and (b) a change in an accounting estimate.

2. When should the effects of a change in accounting policy be shown as a restatement of prior periods? (Give examples.)

3. Describe the effect on current net income, beginning retained earnings, deferred income tax payable, individual assets accounts and asset contra accounts when:

(a) Depreciation is converted from the straight-line method to the declining-balance method.

(b) Depreciation is converted from the sum-of-the-years-digits method to the straight-line method.

(c) Income on construction contracts which had been reported on a completed-projects basis is now reported on the percentage-of-completion basis.

(d) It is determined that the warranty expenses for sales in prior years should have been 5% instead of 4%.

(e) Your accounts receivable clerk reads that a major customer has declared bankruptcy.

(f) Your patent lawyer informs you that your rival has perfected and patented a new invention making your product obsolete.

4. What is a change in classification? Give an example.

5. Name three errors that will not be counterbalanced in the following period and require corrections upon their discovery.

6. The controller for the Lopez Co. states: "The understatement of an expense in one year calls for an overstatement of the same expense in the following year even when the error is discovered; if this is not done, expense will bypass the income statement." Comment on this opinion.

7. State the effect upon net income in 1980 and 1981 of each of the following errors that are made at the end of 1980:

(a) Salaries payable are understated.

(b) Interest receivable is understated.

(c) Discount on notes payable is overstated.

(d) Unearned rent revenue is understated.

(e) Depreciation on an equipment item is overlooked.

(f) Discount on notes receivable is overstated.

(g) Interest payable is overstated.

(h) Amortization on patents acquired in 1979 is computed on the 17-year legal life instead of the 5-year useful life.

(i) A full year's depreciation is taken on items sold in June, 1980.

(j) Machinery purchased in June, 1980, was debited to the furniture and fixtures account.

8. State the effect of each of the following errors made in 1980 upon the balance sheets and the income statements prepared in 1980 and 1981.

(a) The ending inventory is understated as a result of an error in the count of goods on hand.

(b) The ending inventory is overstated as a result of the inclusion of goods acquired and held on a consignment basis. No purchase was recorded on the books.

(c) A purchase of merchandise at the end of 1980 is not recorded until payment is made for the goods in 1981; the goods purchased were included in the inventory at the end of 1980.

(d) A sale of merchandise at the end of 1980 is not recorded until cash is received for the goods in 1981; the goods sold were excluded from the inventory at the end of 1980.

(e) Goods shipped to consignees in 1980 were reported as sales; goods in the hands of consignees at the end of 1980 were not recognized for inventory purposes; sale of such goods in 1981 and collections on such sales were recorded as credits to the receivables established with consignees in 1980.

(f) One week's sales total during 1980 was credited to Gain on Sales — Machinery.

(g) No depreciation is taken in 1980 for machinery sold in April, 1980. The company is on a calendar year and computes depreciation to the nearest month.

(h) No depreciation is taken in 1980 for machinery purchased in October, 1980. The company is on a calendar year and computes depreciation to the nearest month.

(i) Customers' notes receivable are debited to Accounts Receivable.

9. Distinguish between single-entry and double-entry procedures.

10. Describe the records and the nature of recording under typical single-entry book-keeping.

11. What are the sources of information for balance sheet items when the single-entry plan is followed?

12. Distinguish between the manner in which the owner's capital balance is computed in a double-entry system as compared with a single-entry system.

13. Mary Miles has her assets appraised at the end of each year and draws up a balance sheet using such appraisal values. She then calculates the change in capital for the year and adjusts this for investments and withdrawals in arriving at the net income or loss for the year. In your opinion, does this procedure provide a satisfactory measurement of earnings?

14. State how each of the following items is computed in preparing an income statement when single-entry procedures are followed and the accrual basis is used in reporting net income:

(a) Merchandise sales
(b) Merchandise purchases
(c) Depreciation on equipment
(d) Sales salaries
(e) Insurance expense
(f) Interest revenue
(g) Rent revenue
(h) Taxes

15. Single-entry systems are obsolete and have no place in modern business. Do you agree? Explain.

19-1. The Layton Construction Company has used the completed-contract method of accounting since it began operations in 1978. In 1981, management decided, for justifiable reasons, to adopt the percentage-of-completion method.

The company had prepared the following statement reporting income for the years 1978-1980:

	1978	1979	1980
Total sales price of completed contracts	0	$1,000,000	$800,000
Less cost of completed contracts plus anticipated loss on contract in process	0	825,000	560,000
Income from operations	0	$ 175,000	$240,000
Extraordinary loss			35,000
Net income	0	$ 175,000	$205,000

Analysis of the accounting records disclosed the following income by projects was earned for the years 1978-1980 using the percentage-of-completion method of inventory valuation:

	1978	1979	1980
Project A	$125,000	$ 50,000	0
Project B	90,000	180,000	$20,000
Project C	0	20,000	80,000
Project D	0	0	(50,000)

The company continued to use the completed-contract method for tax purposes.

Give the journal entry required in 1981 to reflect the change in inventory methods. Use a 45% income tax rate.

19-2. The Sterling Sales Company decides to change from the declining-balance method of depreciation to the straight-line method effective January, 1981. From the information which follows, prepare the statement of retained earnings for 1981. Assume Sterling's claims for capital cost allowances in the past approximated the depreciation charged for accounting purposes. Also, assume a 45% tax rate.

Year	Net Income As Reported	Excess of Declining Balance Depreciation Over Straight-Line Depreciation	Direct Effect Less Tax (45%)
Prior to 1978		$25,000	$13,750
1978	$125,000	12,500	6,875
1979	109,000	15,000	8,250
1980	156,000	22,500	12,375
		$75,000	$41,250

In 1981, net sales were $380,000; cost of goods sold, $185,000; selling expenses, $95,000; and general and administrative expenses, $28,000. In addition, Sterling had a tax deductible extraordinary loss of $45,000. The balance in retained earnings as reported at December 31, 1980, was $520,000. Dividends were declared in 1981 in the amount of $35,000. Assume the fiscal year ends on December 31.

19-3. On December 31, 1981, the Pullins Company determined that heavy machinery previously thought to have a 20-year life will actually last only 12 years. The machinery was purchased nine years ago for $60,000 with an expected salvage value of $10,000. The straight-line depreciation method is used. Give the adjusting journal entry required at December 31, 1981, to account for this change in the estimated life of the machinery, if no entry has yet been made for depreciation in 1981.

19-4. The Hews Corporation purchased a patent on January 2, 1976, for $135,000. The original life of the patent was estimated to be 15 years. However, in December of 1981, the controller of Hews received information proving conclusively that the product protected by the Hews Corporation patent would be obsolete within two years. Accordingly, the company decided to write off the unamortized portion of the patent cost over three years beginning in 1981. How would the change in estimate be reflected in the accounts for 1981 and subsequent years?

19-5. The Nielson Co. reports net incomes for a three-year period as follows: 1979, $18,000; 1980, $10,500; 1981, $12,500.

In reviewing the accounts in 1982, after the accounts for the prior year have been closed, you find that the following errors have been made in summarizing activities:

	1979	1980	1981
Overstatement of ending inventories as a result of errors in count	$1,600	$2,800	$1,800
Understatement of advertising expense payable	300	600	450
Overstatement of interest receivable	250	——	200
Omission of depreciation on property items still in use	900	800	750

(a) Prepare working papers summarizing corrections and reporting corrected net incomes for 1979, 1980, and 1981.
(b) Give the entry to bring the accounts of the company up to date in 1982.

19-6. The Huntsman Manufacturing Company has been in business since 1979 and produces a single product sold with a one-year warranty covering parts and labor. An audit is made of the company's records for the first time at the end of 1981 before the accounts for 1981 are closed, and it is found that charges for warranties have not been anticipated but have been recognized when incurred. The audit discloses the following data:

Year	Sales	Warranty Expense		
		1979	1980	1981
1979	$ 900,000	$23,000	$20,000	
1980	800,000		18,000	$24,000
1981	1,100,000			29,000

The auditor decides the company should have recognized the full expense for warranties in the year in which the sales were made. She recommends the charges for warranties should be recognized as a percentage of sales and that experiences of past years should be used in arriving at such a percentage. Net incomes before correction have been as follows: 1979, $87,000; 1980, $85,000; 1981, $140,000.
  (a) What earnings would have been reported if warranty costs had been antici-pated and the percentage as calculated had been applied?
  (b) What correcting entry should be made as of December 31, 1981?

19-7. Sales salaries are reported on the income statements for 1981 at $10,700. Balance sheet data relating to sales salaries are as follows:

	January 1, 1981	December 31, 1981
Prepaid salaries (advances to sales agents) .	$250	$100
Salaries payable	700	750

How much cash was paid during 1981 for sales salaries expense?

19-8. Rent revenue is reported on the income statement for 1981 at $25,000. Balance sheet data relating to rent revenue are as follows:

	January 1, 1981	December 31, 1981
Unearned rent revenue	$4,500	$3,700
Rents receivable (delinquent rent)	400	1,650

How much cash was collected during 1981 for rent revenue?

19-9. Total accounts receivable for the Arc Canning Company were as follows: on January 1, $6,000; on January 31, $6,300. In January, $9,500 was collected on ac-counts, $600 was received for cash sales, accounts receivable of $700 were written off as uncollectible, and allowances on sales of $100 were made. What amount should be reported for gross sales on the income statement for January?

19-10. On November 1, the capital of G. T. Fisher was $3,400 and on November 30 the capital was $4,875. During the month, Fisher withdrew merchandise costing $200 and on November 25 she paid a $1,600 note payable of the business with interest at 10% for three months with a cheque drawn on her personal chequing account. What was Fisher's net income or loss for the month of November?

19-1A. A preliminary 1982 combined statement of income and retained earnings for Atlantic Limited is presented below in comparative form:

Atlantic Limited
Comparative Statement of Income and Retained Earnings
Years ended December 31, 1982 and 1981

	1982	1981
Sales	$1,200,000	$1,080,000
Costs and expense, except as detailed below	$ 641,000	$ 520,000
Interest and property tax	—	75,000
Depreciation	59,000	35,000
	$ 700,000	$ 630,000
Income before income tax	500,000	450,000
Provision for income tax (40%)	200,000	180,000
Net income	300,000	270,000
Retained earnings beginning of period	320,000	100,000
	620,000	370,000
Dividends (per share, $1.00)	50,000	50,000
Retained earnings end of period	$ 570,000	$ 320,000
Earnings per share	$ 6.00	$ 5.40

Atlantic was organized in 1980. During the year ended December 31, 1982 the company changed its method of accounting for interest and property taxes during construction from expensing such items to capitalizing them as building costs. The income for 1982 has been determined using the newly adopted accounting policy. Selected financial data follows:

	1982	1981	1980
Net income	$300,000	$270,000	$150,000
Interest and property taxes during construction	125,000	75,000	25,000
Depreciation before accounting change	50,000	35,000	30,000
Depreciation as restated	59,000	39,000	31,000

The change in depreciation may be assumed to be the same for both accounting and tax purposes.

Instructions:
(a) Prepare the Statement of Income and Retained Earnings in comparative form as it should appear in Atlantic Limited's 1982 annual report.
(b) Prepare the journal entry recorded at the beginning of 1982 to give effect to the accounting change.
(c) What was the effect of the accounting change on earnings per share for 1982, for 1981?

19-2A. AMR Limited, a Canadian company, was formed several years ago with an issued share capital of 200,000 common, which has remained unchanged since the formation of the company. The company's capital structure, in addition to the 200,000 common shares outstanding, includes the following:

8% bonds convertible into common shares on the basis of 6 shares for
each $100 bond $500,000
Options for the purchase of 20,000 common shares at $10 per share.

During 1981, the company changed its method of accounting for income taxes from the taxes payable basis to the tax allocation basis. As a result, the balance of retained earnings at August 31, 1980 is to be restated from the amount previously reported to show a retroactive charge of $250,000, representing the cumulative amount by which income taxes had been reduced at August 31, 1980. In the amount of $250,000, is $40,000 applicable to the year ended August 31, 1980, which is to be charged to earnings and included in deferred taxes in that year. The remainder is applicable to years prior to September 1, 1979.

The bottom part of AMR Limited's income statements and relevant information from its statements of retained earnings for the years ended August 31, 1981, and 1980, are presented below. (It should be noted that the 1980 statements show amounts as previously reported.)

	1981	1980
Income before income tax	$1,310,000	$1,460,000
Provision for income tax	620,000	670,000
	$ 690,000	$ 790,000
Extraordinary items:		
Gain on sale of investments net of applicable income tax	220,000	——
Loss on sale of branch plant facilities net of applicable income tax	(50,000)	——
Net income	$ 860,000	$ 790,000
Retained earnings beginning of year		$2,300,000
Net income	$ 860,000	790,000
		$3,090,000
Dividends	$ 300,000	$ 300,000
Retained earnings end of year		$2,790,000

AMR Limited is subject to income tax at a rate of 50%. In addition, the company is able to invest surplus funds to generate a return of 10% before income tax.

Instructions:
(1) Prepare the bottom part of AMR Limited's income statement and Its statement of retained earnings as they should appear in the company's 1981 annual report. It is the company's practice to present comparative financial statements.
(2) For the year ended August 31, 1981, compute the earnings per share data that should be included either on the face of the company's 1981 income statement, or in a note or notes cross-referenced to the income statement.
(3) Explain briefly why the 1981 provision for income tax of $620,000 is not exactly 50% of the reported amount of income before income tax.

19-3A. Changex Limited has decided that in the preparation of its 1981 financial statements two changes will be made from the methods used in prior years:

1. *Depreciation*. Changex has always used the declining-balance method for tax and financial accounting purposes but has decided to change during 1981 to the straight-line method for financial accounting only. The effect of this change is as follows:

	Excess of Accelerated Depreciation Over Straight-Line Depreciation
Prior to 1980	$1,300,000
1980	101,000
1981	99,000
	$1,500,000

Depreciation is charged to cost of sales and to selling, general, and administrative expenses on the basis of 75% and 25%, respectively.

2. *Bad debt expense*. In the past Changex has recognized bad debt expense equal to 1.5% of net sales. After careful review it has been decided that a rate of 2% is more appropriate for 1981. Bad debt expense is charged to selling, general, and administrative expenses.

The information below and at the top of page 829 is taken from preliminary financial statements, prepared before giving effect to the two changes:

Changex Limited
Condensed Balance Sheet
December 31, 1981
With Comparative Figures for 1980

Assets	1981	1980
Current assets	$44,069,480	$43,900,000
Fixed assets, at cost	45,792,000	43,974,000
Less accumulated depreciation	(23,761,000)	(22,946,000)
	$66,100,480	$64,928,000

Liabilities and Shareholders' Equity		
Current liabilities	$20,729,200	$23,141,520
Long-term debt	15,154,000	14,097,000
Capital stock	11,620,000	11,620,000
Retained earnings	18,597,280	16,069,480
	$66,100,480	$64,928,000

There have been no timing differences between any book and tax items prior to the above changes. The effective tax rate is 40%.

Instructions:
Compute for the items listed below the amounts which would appear on the comparative financial statements of Changex Limited after adjustment for the two accounting changes.
(a) Accumulated depreciation
(b) Deferred income tax (balance sheet amounts)

Changex Limited
Income Statement
For the Year Ended December 31, 1981
With Comparative Figures for 1980

	1981	1980
Net sales	$80,520,000	$78,920,000
Cost of sales	54,847,000	53,074,000
	$25,673,000	$25,846,000
Selling, general, and administrative expenses	19,540,000	18,411,000
	$ 6,133,000	$ 7,435,000
Other income (expense) net	(1,198,000)	(1,079,000)
Income before taxes	4,935,000	6,356,000
Provision for income taxes	1,974,000	2,542,400
	$ 2,961,000	$ 3,813,600

(c) Cost of sales
(d) Selling, general and administrative expenses
(e) Income before income taxes
(f) Provision for income taxes
(g) Current assets
(h) Current liabilities
(i) Amounts, if any, by which opening retained earnings balances must be restated
(j) Retained earnings   (AICPA adapted)

19-4A. Since you did such an outstanding job of computing various amounts which would appear on the 1981 financial statements of Changex Limited, you have been asked by your firm to continue on this assignment.

Instructions:
Prepare an income statement, statement of retained earnings, and a balance sheet for inclusion in the 1981 annual report of Changex Limited. Your financial statements are to include comparative figures for 1980. In each year, Changex declared and paid dividends in the amount of $433,200.

19-5A. Condensed Statements of Income and Retained Earnings for The Salem Company Limited for the years ended December 31, 1982, and December 31, 1981, are presented below:

The Salem Company Limited
Condensed Statements of Income and Retained Earnings
For the Years Ended December 31, 1982, and 1981

	1982	1981
Sales	$3,000,000	$2,400,000
Cost of goods sold	1,300,000	1,150,000
Gross margin	1,700,000	1,250,000
Selling, general, and administrative expenses	1,200,000	950,000
Income before extraordinary item	500,000	300,000
Extraordinary item	(400,000)	——
Net income	100,000	300,000
Retained earnings, January 1	750,000	450,000
Retained earnings, December 31	$ 850,000	$ 750,000

Presented below are four unrelated situations involving accounting changes and classification of certain items as ordinary or extraordinary. Each situation is based upon the Condensed Statements of Income and Retained Earnings of The Salem Company Limited shown above and requires revisions to these statements.

Situation A

On January 1, 1980, Salem acquired machinery at a cost of $150,000. The company adopted the 20% declining-balance method of depreciation for this machinery, and had been recording depreciation over an estimated life of ten years, with no residual value. At the beginning of 1982, a decision was made to adopt the straight-line method of depreciation for this machinery. Due to an oversight, however, the 20% declining-balance method was used for 1982. For financial-reporting purposes, depreciation is included in selling, general, and administrative expenses.

The extraordinary item in the Condensed Statement of Income and Retained Earnings for 1982 relates to shutdown expenses incurred by the company during a major strike by its operating employees during 1982.

Situation B

At the end of 1982, Salem's management decided that the estimated loss rate on uncollectible accounts receivables was too low. The loss rate used for the years 1981 and 1982 was 1% of total sales, and due to an increase in the write-off of uncollectible accounts, the rate has been raised to 3% of total sales. The amount recorded in bad debt expense under the heading of selling, general, and administrative expenses for 1982 was $30,000 and for 1981 was $24,000.

The extraordinary item in the Condensed Statement of Income and Retained Earnings for 1982 relates to a loss incurred in the abandonment of outmoded equipment formerly used in the business.

Situation C

On December 2, 1982, Salem issued 100,000 shares of its $1 par value common shares in exchange for 100,000 shares of $1 par value (100%) voting common stock of Arco Corporation in a transaction to be properly accounted for as a pooling of interests. The Condensed Statements of Income and Retained Earnings of Salem shown above do not include Arco operations. A summary of Arco's financial operations for the years 1982, 1981, and 1980 follows:

	1982	1981	1980
Sales	$600,000	$520,000	$410,000
Cost of goods sold	274,000	238,000	195,000
Gross margin	326,000	282,000	215,000
Selling, general, and administrative expenses	219,000	190,000	165,000
Net income	107,000	92,000	50,000
Retained earnings (Deficit), January 1	72,000	(20,000)	(70,000)
Retained earnings (Deficit), December 31	$179,000	$ 72,000	$ (20,000)

The extraordinary item in the Condensed Statement of Income and Retained Earnings for 1982 relates to a loss sustained as a result of damage caused by a tornado to the company's merchandise at its main warehouse in Locust City. This natural disaster was considered to be an unusual and infrequent occurrence for that geographic section of the country.

Situation D

The extraordinary item appearing in the Condensed Statement of Income and Retained Earnings for 1982 relates to a settlement between Salem and Revenue Canada, in which Salem was assessed and agreed to pay additional income taxes of $60,000 for 1981 and $340,000 for the years 1977-1980.

Instructions:

For each situation, prepare revised Condensed Statements of Income and Retained Earnings for The Salem Company Limited, for the years ended December 31, 1982, and December 31, 1981, using the worksheet format illustrated in Table 1. Each answer should recognize the appropriate accounting changes and other items outlined in the situation. Ignore income tax considerations unless indicated to the contrary. Ignore all earnings per share computations.　(AICPA adapted)

Table 1: Worksheet Format

The Salem Company Limited
Condensed Statements of Income and Retained Earnings
For the Years Ended December 31, 1982 and 1981

	Situation A		Situation B		Situation C		Situation D	
	1982	1981	1982	1981	1982	1981	1982	1981
Sales	$3,000,000	$2,400,000	$3,000,000	$2,400,000	$	$	$3,000,000	$2,400,000
Cost of goods sold	1,300,000	1,150,000	1,300,000	1,150,000			1,300,000	1,150,000
Gross margin ...	$1,700,000	$1,250,000	$1,700,000	$1,250,000			$1,700,000	$1,250,000
Selling, general, and administrative expense								
Income before extraordinary item								
Extraordinary item								
Net income	$	$	$	$	$	$	$	$
Retained earnings, January 1								
Prior period adjustment								
Retained earnings, as restated								
Net income								
Retained earnings, December 31 ...	$	$	$	$	$	$	$	$

19-6A. The first audit of the accounts for the Risenmay Corporation was made for the year ended December 31, 1981. In reviewing the accounts, the auditor discovered that certain adjustments had been overlooked at the end of 1980 and 1981, and also that other items had been improperly recorded. Omissions and other failures for each year are summarized below:

	December 31	
	1980	1981
Sales salaries payable	$1,300	$1,100
Interest receivable	325	215
Prepaid insurance	450	300
Advances from customers	1,750	2,500

(Collections from customers had been included in sales but should have been recognized as advances from customers since goods were not shipped until the following year.)

Equipment	1,400	1,200

(Expenditures had been recognized as repairs but should have been recognized as cost of equipment; the depreciation rate on such equipment is 10% per year, but depreciation in the year of the expenditure is to be recognized at 5%.)

Instructions:

Prepare journal entries to correct revenue and expense accounts for 1981 and record assets and liabilities that require recognition on the balance sheet as of December 31, 1981. Assume the nominal accounts for 1981 have not yet been closed into the income summary account.

19-7A. The Lawler Sales Co. has failed to recognize certain prepaid and accrued items in the years 1978-1981. The retained earnings account at the end of 1981 is shown below:

ACCOUNT Retained Earnings

DATE		ITEM	DEBIT	CREDIT	BALANCE	
					DEBIT	CREDIT
1978						
Dec.	31	Balance				55,000
1979		Dividends	18,300			36,700
		Net income		25,500		62,200
1980		Dividends	14,800			47,400
		Net income		24,000		71,400
1981		Dividends	20,500			50,900
		Net income		33,000		83,900

	End of			
	1978	1979	1980	1981
Prepaid expenses	$3,200	$2,500	$3,800	$5,400
Prepaid revenues		1,500	800	
Expenses payable.......................	6,000	7,500		4,200
Revenues receivable	300			400

Instructions:

(1) Prepare working papers as illustrated on page 811 to correct the retained earnings balance as of December 31, 1978, and to correct earnings for 1979, 1980, and 1981. Assume that an income tax rate of 45% applies to all years.

(2) Prepare a statement of retained earnings for the three-year period ending December 31, 1981, reporting corrected earnings.

(3) Give the entry that is required at the beginning of 1982 to correct the accounts assuming that the books are closed for 1981.

19-8A. The auditors for the Hansen Co. in inspecting accounts on December 31, 1981, the end of the fiscal year, find that certain prepaid and accrued items had been overlooked in prior years and in the current year as follows:

	End of			
	1978	1979	1980	1981
Prepaid expenses	$700	$600	$750	$1,900
Expenses payable	500	800	950	1,000
Prepaid revenues	140			420
Revenues receivable		150	125	200

Retained earnings on December 31, 1978 had been reported at $25,600; and net income for 1979 and for 1980 were reported at $9,500 and $12,250, respectively. Revenue and expense balances for 1981 were transferred to the income summary account and the latter shows a credit balance of $12,500 prior to correction by the auditors. No dividends had been declared in the three-year period.

Instructions:
(1) Prepare working papers as illustrated on page 811 to develop a corrected retained earnings balance as of December 31, 1978, and corrected earnings for 1979, 1980, and 1981. Disregard effects of corrections on income tax.
(2) Prepare a corrected statement of retained earnings for the three-year period ending December 31, 1981.
(3) Give the entry or entries required as of December 31, 1981 to correct the income summary account and retained earnings account and to establish the appropriate balance sheet accounts as of this date.

19-9A. An auditor is engaged by the Morrison Corp. in March, 1982, to examine the books and records and to make whatever corrections are necessary. The retained earnings account on the date of the audit is as follows:

ACCOUNT Retained Earnings

DATE		ITEM	DEBIT	CREDIT	BALANCE DEBIT	BALANCE CREDIT
1979						
Jan.	1	Balance				40,500
Dec.	31	Net income for year		9,000		49,500
1980						
Jan.	10	Dividends paid	7,500			42,000
Mar.	6	Premium on capital stock		16,000		58,000
Dec.	31	Loss for year	5,600			52,400
1981						
Jan.	10	Dividends paid	7,500			44,900
Dec.	31	Loss for year	6,200			38,700

An examination of the accounts discloses the following:
(a) Dividends had been declared on December 15 in 1979 and 1980 but had not been entered in the accounts until paid.
(b) Improvements in buildings and equipment of $4,800 had been debited to expense at the end of April, 1978. Improvements are estimated to have an eight-year life. The company uses the straight-line method in recording depreciation.

(c) The physical inventory of merchandise had been understated by $1,500 at the end of 1979 and by $2,150 at the end of 1981.

(d) The merchandise inventories at the end of 1980 and 1981 did not include merchandise that was then in transit and to which the company had title. These shipments of $1,900 and $2,750 were recorded as purchases in January of 1981 and 1982, respectively.

(e) The company had failed to record sales commissions payable of $1,050 and $850 at the end of 1980 and 1981, respectively.

(f) The company had failed to recognize supplies on hand of $600 and $1,250 at the end of 1980 and 1981, respectively.

Instructions:

(1) Prepare working papers for the correction of account balances similar to those illustrated on page 811, using the following columns (disregard effects of corrections on income tax):

EXPLANATION	RETAINED EARNINGS JAN. 1, 1979		NET INCOME YEAR ENDED DEC. 31, 1979		NET INCOME YEAR ENDED DEC. 31, 1980		NET INCOME YEAR ENDED DEC. 31, 1981		ACCOUNTS REQUIRING CORRECTION IN 1982		
	DEBIT	CREDIT	DEBIT	CREDIT	DEBIT	CREDIT	DEBIT	CREDIT	DEBIT	CREDIT	ACCOUNT

(2) Journalize corrections required in March, 1982, in compound form.

(3) Prepare a statement of retained earnings covering the three-year period beginning January 1, 1979. The statement should report the corrected retained earnings balance on January 1, 1979, the annual changes in the account, and the corrected retained earnings balances as of December 31, 1979, 1980, and 1981.

(4) Set up an account for retained earnings before correction, and post correcting data to this account from part (2) above. Balance the account, showing the corrected retained earnings as of December 31, 1981.

19-10A. The statements shown at the top of page 835 were prepared for Garfield, Ltd., at the end of 1981.

During January, 1982, the following facts were discovered.

(a) A 25% stock dividend, payable on February 1, 1982, was declared on December 15, 1981. No entry had been made.

(b) Accrued expenses of $105 for utilities had not been included in the adjustments at the end of 1981.

(c) On January 2, 1981, a 5-year fire insurance policy was purchased for $1,500 and debited to General Expense. No adjustment was made at the end of 1981 for the unexpired insurance.

(d) Ten-year, 6% bonds of $100,000 par were issued at 98 on June 30, 1981. The bonds payable account was credited for the amount of cash received. The interest is payable annually on June 30. No adjustments were made at the end of 1981.

(e) 7% bonds, face value $10,000, had been purchased at face value on January 2, 1981. Interest is collected semi-annually on January 1 and July 1. No adjustment for accrued interest was made at the end of 1981.

(f) The board of directors had authorized an appropriation of retained earnings of $10,000 for possible losses on damage suits at the end of 1981. No entry had been made.

(g) The petty cash fund, kept under the imprest system, had not been replenished at the end of the fiscal period. Payments had been made out of the fund as follows: $75 for General Expense and $65 for Selling Expense.

<table>
<tr><td colspan="3" align="center">Income Statement
For Year Ended December 31, 1981</td><td colspan="3" align="center">Balance Sheet
December 31, 1981</td></tr>
<tr><td>Sales ....</td><td>$257,000</td><td></td><td colspan="3" align="center">Assets</td></tr>
<tr><td>Less sales discount ....</td><td>7,000</td><td>$250,000</td><td>Cash ....</td><td>$ 40,000</td><td></td></tr>
<tr><td>Cost of goods sold:</td><td></td><td></td><td>Petty cash ....</td><td>200</td><td></td></tr>
<tr><td>Merchandise inventory,</td><td></td><td></td><td>Accounts receivable ....</td><td>97,000</td><td></td></tr>
<tr><td>January 1, 1981 ....</td><td>$ 73,000</td><td></td><td>Merchandise inventory ....</td><td>70,000</td><td></td></tr>
<tr><td>Purchases ....</td><td>170,000</td><td></td><td>Investment in bonds ....</td><td>10,000</td><td></td></tr>
<tr><td>Merchandise available for sale</td><td>$243,000</td><td></td><td>Total assets ....</td><td></td><td>$217,200</td></tr>
<tr><td>Less merchandise inventory,</td><td></td><td></td><td colspan="3" align="center">Liabilities</td></tr>
<tr><td>December 31, 1981 .....</td><td>70,000</td><td>173,000</td><td>Accounts payable ....</td><td>$ 35,000</td><td></td></tr>
<tr><td>Gross profit on sales ....</td><td></td><td>$ 77,000</td><td>Bonds payable ....</td><td>98,000</td><td></td></tr>
<tr><td>Operating expenses:</td><td></td><td></td><td>Total liabilities ....</td><td></td><td>$133,000</td></tr>
<tr><td>Selling expense ....</td><td>$ 30,000</td><td></td><td colspan="3" align="center">Shareholders' Equity</td></tr>
<tr><td>General expense ....</td><td>32,000</td><td>62,000</td><td>Capital stock, $5 par ....</td><td>$ 55,000</td><td></td></tr>
<tr><td>Operating income ....</td><td></td><td>$ 15,000</td><td>Retained earnings ....</td><td>29,200</td><td></td></tr>
<tr><td>Other revenue:</td><td></td><td></td><td>Total shareholders' equity ......</td><td></td><td>84,200</td></tr>
<tr><td>Interest revenue ....</td><td></td><td>2,300</td><td>Total liabilities and shareholders'</td><td></td><td></td></tr>
<tr><td>Net income ....</td><td></td><td>$ 17,300</td><td>equity ....</td><td></td><td>$217,200</td></tr>
</table>

Instructions:
Prepare adjusting journal entries at December 31, 1981. Disregard effects of corrections on income tax.

19-11A. You have been asked by a client to review the records of the Reardon Manufacturing Company, a small manufacturer of precision tools and machines. Your client is interested in buying the business and arrangements have been made for you to review the accounting records. Your examination reveals the following:

(a) The Reardon Manufacturing Company commenced business on April 1, 1978, and has been reporting on a fiscal year ending March 31. The company has never been audited, but the annual statements prepared by the bookkeeper reflect the following income before closing and before deducting income tax:

Year Ended March 31		Income Before Tax
1979	....	$37,800
1980	....	56,200
1981	....	53,790

(b) A relatively small number of machines has been shipped on consignment. These transactions have been recorded as an ordinary sale and billed as such.

On March 31 of each year machines billed and in the hands of consignees amounted to:

1979	....	$6,110
1980	....	none
1981	....	5,343

Sales price was determined by adding 30% to cost.

(c) On March 30, 1980, two machines were shipped to a customer on a C.O.D. basis. The sale was not entered until April 5, 1980, when cash was received in the amount of $5,800. The machines were not included in the inventory at March 31, 1980.

(d) All machines are sold subject to a five-year warranty. It is estimated that the expense ultimately to be incurred in connection with the warranty will amount to $1/2$% of sales. The company has charged an expense account for warranty costs incurred. Sales per accounts and warranty costs were:

| Year Ended March 31 | Sales | Warranty Expense for Sales Made in | | | |
		1979	1980	1981	Total
1979	$ 844,710	$680			$ 680
1980	905,000	320	$1,170		1,490
1981	1,604,110	290	1,450	$1,710	3,450

(e) A review of the corporate minutes reveals the manager is entitled to a bonus of $1/2$% of the income before deducting income tax and his bonus. The bonuses have never been recorded or paid.

(f) The bank deducts 6% on all contracts financed. Of this amount $1/2$% is placed in a reserve to the credit of the Reardon Manufacturing Company which is refunded to Reardon as finance contracts are paid in full. The reserve established by the bank has not been reflected in the accounts of Reardon. The excess of credits over debits (net increase) to the reserve account with Reardon in the accounts of the bank for each fiscal year was as follows:

1979	....	$ 2,800
1980	....	3,750
1981	....	4,960
		$11,510

(g) Commissions on sales have been entered when paid. Commissions payable on March 31 of each year were:

1979	....	$1,200
1980	....	700
1981	....	960

(h) On May 17, 1980, the building was sold to an insurance company for $890,000. Its net book value at the date of sale was $880,000.

Instructions:

(1) Present a schedule showing the revised income before income tax for each of the years ended March 31, 1979, 1980, and 1981. Make computations to the nearest whole dollar.

(2) Prepare the journal entry or entries you would present the accountant to

correct the records. Assume the accounts have not yet been closed for the fiscal year ended March 31, 1981. Disregard correction of income tax.

(3) Compute the purchase price. Your client will pay the amount of the corrected book value of the net assets at March 31, 1981, plus goodwill equal to two times the average profits before tax in excess of a 6% return on the net assets. According to the accounts the net assets were $548,250 at March 31, 1981. Extraneous gains and losses are not to be considered in the calculation of average annual profits.   (AICPA adapted)

19-12A. Mr. Brown, the proprietor of Brown's TV Shop, keeps very few records. At the beginning and end of 1981, he has made a list of his assets and liabilities as follows:

	Beginning of 1981	End of 1981
Accounts receivable	$3,000	$4,700
Accounts payable	6,000	3,000
Merchandise on hand	4,000	6,000
Cash	1,300	1,500
Store Equipment	1,900	1,900
Notes payable	-0-	1,000

Brown received cash during the year from the following sources: customers on account, $15,000; cash sales, $3,000; additional investment by Brown, $900; borrowed from bank, $1,000 (6% note dated December 1). All cash payments during the year were to merchandise creditors except the following: $3,000 paid for operating expenses; $1,000 paid for cash purchases of merchandise.

Brown purchased the store equipment last year for $2,000 and estimates that it has a 10-year service life. Of last year's receivables from customers, $240 proved uncollectible and were removed from the records. Brown estimates that 2% of this year's credit sales will not be collected. Included in receivables at the beginning of the year was a $50 account for Brown. During the year he removed the ledger sheet and tore it up.

Instructions:

On the basis of the above information, prepare an Income Statement for Brown's TV Shop for the year ending December 31, 1981. Provide supporting computations for sales and purchases.   (SMA adapted)

19-13A. The following information is obtained from the single-entry records of Wilford Clyde.

	March 31	January 1
Notes receivable	$1,200	$1,500
Accounts receivable	8,800	4,500
Interest receivable	80	100
Merchandise inventories	1,000	3,800
Prepaid operating expenses	220	250
Store equipment (net)	3,000	3,250
Notes payable	1,200	1,000
Accounts payable	2,500	3,500
Interest payable	50	30
Operating expenses payable	500	270

The cashbook shows the following:

Balance, January 1			$1,500
Receipts:	Accounts receivable	$3,600	
	Notes receivable	1,500	
	Interest revenue	200	
	Investment by Clyde	600	5,900
			$7,400
Payments:	Accounts payable	$5,200	
	Notes payable	800	
	Interest expense	150	
	Operating expenses	1,700	7,850
Balance, March 31 — bank overdraft			$ (450)

Instructions:
(1) Compute the net income or loss for the three-month period by considering the changes in the owner's capital.
(2) Prepare an income statement for the three-month period accompanied by schedules in support of revenue and expense balances.

19-14A. The following data are obtained from a single-entry set of records kept by Mary Golden, proprietor of a retail store:

	June 30	January 1
Notes receivable	$ 3,000	$ 1,000
Accounts receivable	6,000	4,000
Interest receivable	150	100
Merchandise inventories	4,400	4,000
Store equipment (net)	3,800	3,000
Notes payable	1,250	1,800
Accounts payable	4,650	3,000
Interest payable	100	200

The cashbook shows the following information:

Balance, January 1			$ 3,000
Receipts:	Accounts receivable	$10,500	
	Notes receivable	2,400	
	Interest on notes	100	13,000
			$16,000
Payments:	Accounts payable	$ 3,800	
	Notes payable	3,200	
	Interest on notes	200	
	Operating expenses	2,100	
	Withdrawals by Golden	3,000	
	Store equipment	1,000	13,300
Balance, June 30			$ 2,700

The following supplementary information is available:
(a) Accounts receivable of $250 were written off as uncollectible.
(b) Allowances of $140 were received on merchandise purchases.
(c) All notes receivable arise from sales.
(d) All notes payable arise from purchases of merchandise inventory.

Instructions:

(1) Compute the net income or loss for the six-month period by considering the changes in owner's capital.

(2) Prepare an income statement for the six-month period accompanied by schedules in support of revenue and expense balances.

20 THE STATEMENT OF CHANGES IN FINANCIAL POSITION

The primary financial statements for a business entity are those that disclose the financial position, the results of operations, and any changes in financial position. The financial position of a business at a given time is reported on the balance sheet. The operations for a given period are reported on the income statement and on the statement of changes in financial position — the funds statement. The income statement summarizes the revenues and expenses for the period and, in part, accounts for the change in retained earnings in successive periods. When there are further transactions that must be recognized in explaining the change in owners' equity, these, depending upon their nature, may be reported on the statement of retained earnings, or on a separate statement. The funds statement, on the other hand, offers a summary not only of the operations of the business but also of the financing and investing activities of the business for the period. Thus, it accounts for all changes in financial position as reported on successive balance sheets.

The funds statement has variously been referred to as *the statement of application of funds, the statement of sources and uses of funds, the source and application of funds statement, and the statement of resources provided and applied*. In reporting funds flow, it is possible to adopt a funds concept that provides for a limited recognition of financial changes or a funds concept broadened to cover all financial changes. The Accounting Research Committee recommended a broadened content for the funds statement, that the funds statement be called the *statement of changes in financial position*, and that the definition of funds be disclosed.

To simplify reference to the statement, the term *funds statement* is used in this chapter.

FUNDS DEFINED

One significant variation found in funds-flow reporting is the definition applied to the term funds. While the term has been used in different ways, the definition determines the character and form of the statement. Funds has most frequently been defined to mean working capital, and in these instances the funds statement reports financing and investing activities in terms of working capital. Defined in this manner the funds statement provides a summary of the individual sources and uses of working capital for the period. In its narrowest sense, funds has been used simply to denote cash, and a funds statement applying this concept simply provides a presentation of the individual sources and uses of cash for the period and the resulting change in the cash balance. Intermediate possibilities would define funds as net current monetary assets — current assets excluding inventory and prepaid items less current liabilities — all current monetary assets, or simply cash and temporary investments combined. In applying the alternative definitions, the funds statement would report the sources and applications of such "funds" and reconcile their change in successive balance sheets. In practice, funds reporting generally employs the working capital or cash concept, but in either case, with a broadened concept of disclosure.

THE BROADENED INTERPRETATION OF FUNDS

If the funds definitions were to be applied literally, a number of transactions involving highly significant information relative to financing and investing activities would be omitted from the funds statement and thus not available to users. For example, debt and equity securities may be issued in exchange for land and buildings; long-term investments may be exchanged for machinery and equipment; shares may be issued in payment of long-term debt; properties may be received by way of gift or donation. These transactions carry significant implications in analysing the change in financial position even though they are not factors in reconciling the change in funds defined either as working capital or cash. This suggests that in order to make the funds statement more useful, the funds interpretation should be broadened to recognize transactions such as those mentioned. The broadened view, for example, would recognize the issuance of capital stock for a property item as funds provided by the issuance of shares offset by funds applied to the acquisition of the asset.[1] Because sources and applications from such trans-

---

[1]It may be observed that this treatment requires adoption of the hypothesis that the transfer of an item in exchange or as a gift effectively provides the company with working capital or cash immediately applied to the acquisition of property, the liquidation of debt, or the retirement of capital stock.

actions are equal in amount, the remaining items reported on the funds statement will serve to reconcile the change in funds for the period. As indicated earlier, the broadened interpretation of funds, sometimes referred to as the *all financial resources* concept, was initially recommended by the Accounting Principles Board in APB Opinion No. 19, and subsequently by the Accounting Research Committee in Section 1540 of the *Accounting Recommendations* as a basis for funds statement disclosure. This interpretation is assumed throughout this chapter. It is important to recognize that the all financial resources concept can be applied on either the working capital or cash basis as illustrated in latter sections of the chapter.

NATURE OF THE FUNDS STATEMENT

The funds statement provides a summary of the sources from which funds became available during a period and the purposes to which funds were applied. An important part of the summary is the presentation of data concerning the extent to which funds were generated by income-oriented operations of the business. In addition to reporting funds provided by operations, funds inflow is also related to such sources as the sale of property items, the issuance of long-term obligations, and the issuance of capital stock. Funds outflow is related to such uses as the acquisition of property items, the retirement of long-term obligations, the reacquisition of outstanding shares, and the payment of dividends. As stated in Section 1540, the funds statement "should portray all aspects of the financing and investing activities during the period."[2]

The diagram on page 843 illustrates primary inflows and outflows.

The funds statement helps answer questions such as: What use was made of profits? How was expansion financed? Why aren't dividend payments larger in view of higher earnings? Why did cash or working capital go down even though there was a substantial income? How was bonded indebtedness paid off even though there was a substantial loss? Answers to these questions are required before the various users of financial statements can fully evaluate the operations of the business entity and the management of its resources.

USE OF THE FUNDS STATEMENT

The funds statement, although related to the balance sheet and the income statement, cannot be considered in any sense as a duplication or substitution for the other financial statements. The Accounting Principles Board, in Opinion No. 19, points out:

---

[2]*Opinions of the Accounting Principles Board, No. 19*, "Reporting Changes in Financial Position" (New York: American Institute of Certified Public Accountants, 1971), par. 5.

The funds statement is related to both the income statement and the balance sheet and provides information that can be obtained only partially, or at most in piecemeal form, by interpreting them. An income statement together with a statement of retained earnings reports results of operations but does not show other changes in financial position. Comparative balance sheets can significantly augment that information, but the objectives of the funds statement require that all such information be selected, classified, and summarized in meaningful form. The funds statement cannot supplant either the income statement or the balance sheet but is intended to provide information that the other statements either do not provide or provide only indirectly about the flow of funds and changes in financial position during the period.[3]

To illustrate the special contribution made by the funds statement, consider the needs of a prospective creditor and the means for meeting these needs. An individual, bank or other lender asked to make a long-term loan is concerned with the proposed use of the loan, ability to meet periodic interest payments on the loan, and ability ultimately to repay the loan. Balance sheet analysis will provide answers to questions relative to the cash and near-cash items on hand, the working capital of the business — its amount and composition — present long-term indebtedness, and the implications on financial position if the loan is granted. Income statement analysis will provide answers

---

[3]*CICA Handbook: Accounting Recommendations, Section 1540*, "Statement of Changes in Financial Position" (Toronto: Canadian Institute of Chartered Accountants, 1974), par. .05.

to questions relative to earnings, the ability of earnings to cover current interest charges, and the implications as to earnings and interest charges if the loan is granted. Funds statement analysis will indicate resources available in the past and the uses made of those resources, as well as the financing and investing implications if the loan is granted. Finally, funds data can be used in estimating the resources that will be generated in the future and ability to meet added indebtedness.

It is obvious that in meeting the requirements of users, funds information will be most useful if offered in comparative form for two or more years. An additional statement reporting forecasted or budgeted funds-flow data may prove of equal or even greater value. Although suggestions have been made that the latter information be made available to the external users of financial information, this practice has not yet been adopted.

FUNDS STATEMENT APPLYING DIFFERENT FUNDS CONCEPTS

Regardless of how funds may be defined, the funds statement is prepared from comparative balance sheets supplemented by explanations for individual account balance changes. The preparation of the statement calls for the steps listed below.

1. The definition to be used for "funds" is selected.
2. The funds accounts on the comparative balance sheets, are listed and totalled; the net change in funds items found here should be the same as that computed in step (3).
3. The changes in each non-fund account on the comparative balance sheets are analysed in order to classify the changes as sources or applications of funds, and the net increase or decrease arising from such changes is computed and compared with the amount determined in step (2).

To illustrate the process of analysis and the development of the funds statement applying the working capital and cash concepts, a relatively simple example will first be considered. Assume the balance sheet information for the Goodspeed Company show below and at the top of page 845.

Assets	December 31, 1980	December 31, 1979
Cash	$ 75,000	$100,000
Accounts receivable	170,000	110,000
Inventories	195,000	160,000
Prepaid expenses	10,000	20,000
Land	160,000	160,000
Buildings and equipment	130,000	——
	$740,000	$550,000

Liabilities and Shareholders' Equity		
Accounts payable	$160,000	$100,000
Accrued expenses	20,000	30,000
Long-term liabilities	80,000	100,000
Preferred shares	100,000	100,000
Common shares	320,000	200,000
Retained earnings	60,000	20,000
	$740,000	$550,000

FUNDS DEFINED AS WORKING CAPITAL

When funds are defined as working capital, balance sheet changes must be analysed in terms of their effects upon the working capital pool. Investigation of balance sheet changes for the Goodspeed Company for 1980 reveals the following:

The increase in buildings and equipment reflects funds applied to the purchase of buildings and equipment, $130,000.

The decrease in long-term liabilities reflects funds applied to the retirement of long-term liabilities, $20,000.

The increase in common shares reflects funds provided from the sale of shares, $120,000.

Retained earnings went up as a result of net income for the period. The increase in retained earnings, then, reflects funds provided, $40,000 — working capital provided through sales exceeding the working capital consumed through cost of goods sold and expenses.

The foregoing analysis indicates that funds of $160,000 were provided from operations and from the sale of common shares, and funds of $150,000 were applied to the acquisition of buildings and equipment, to the retirement of long-term liabilities, and to a net increase in funds (working capital) of $10,000.

A statement for the Goodspeed Company summarizing working capital changes for the year follows.

Goodspeed Company Statement of Changes in Financial Position — Working Capital Basis For the Year Ended December 31, 1980		
Working capital was provided by:		
Operations	$ 40,000	
Sales of common shares	120,000	$160,000
Working capital was applied to:		
Acquisition of buildings and equipment	$130,000	
Retirement of long-term liabilities	20,000	150,000
Increase in working capital		$ 10,000

	The increase in working capital is accounted for as follows:		
Working Capital Items	Dec. 31, 1980	Dec. 31, 1979	Increase (Decrease)
Current assets:			
Cash	$ 75,000	$100,000	$ (25,000)
Accounts receivable	170,000	110,000	60,000
Inventories	195,000	160,000	35,000
Prepaid expenses	10,000	20,000	(10,000)
Current liabilities:			
Accounts payable	160,000	100,000	(60,000)
Accrued expenses	20,000	30,000	10,000
Increase in working capital			$ 10,000

The funds statement shown is composed of two sections. The first section reports working capital inflow and outflow and the change in working capital for the period. The second section reports the individual changes within the working capital pool, summarizing and reconciling the individual changes with the total net change in working capital reported in the first section. Although working capital has increased by $10,000, which may be regarded as favorable, significant changes have taken place within the working capital pool which may not be similarly regarded, and the ratio of current assets to current liabilities has now changed from 3.0:1 to 2.5:1.

Instead of being prepared in two-section form, the statement may be limited to the presentation of the data in the first section and may refer to a separate supporting tabulation offering a summary of the changes in the individual working capital items.

Funds Defined as Cash

When funds are defined as cash, balance sheet account changes require analysis in terms of their effects upon the movement of cash. Cash is used in the same sense as that employed for cash recognized as a current asset — cash on hand and demand deposits in banks. The funds statement, then, describes the cash sources and cash uses and offers a reconciliation of the beginning and ending cash balances. This statement might be developed by simply classifying and summarizing cash receipts and disbursements as reported in the cash account. However, the statement is prepared to point out the broad sources and uses of cash, and such items as cash collected from customers, cash paid for merchandise, and cash paid for expenses are generally submerged in a cash-from-operations category. This information can be developed from comparative balance sheets supplemented by operating detail.

A statement for the Goodspeed Company giving effect to the cash concept is presented at the top of page 847.

Goodspeed Company
Statement of Changes in Financial Position — Cash Basis
For Year Ended December 31, 1980

Cash was provided by:			
Operations:			
Net income		$ 40,000	
Items to be added to net income:			
Decrease in prepaid expenses	$10,000		
Increase in accounts payable	60,000	70,000	
		$110,000	
Items to be deducted from net income:			
Increase in accounts receivable	$60,000		
Increase in inventories	35,000		
Decrease in accrued expenses	10,000	105,000	
Cash provided by operations		$ 5,000	
Sale of common shares		120,000	$125,000
Cash was applied to:			
Acquisition of buildings and equipment		$130,000	
Retirement of long-term liabilities		20,000	150,000
Decrease in cash			$25,000

The decrease in cash of $25,000 is the same as that reported on the comparative balance sheets.

When funds are defined as cash, the analysis of balance sheet changes is similar to that employed in the working capital example, but it must now be extended to include all working capital items except cash. A change in marketable securities is recognized as a source or an application of cash. Changes in other current assets and current liabilities related to operations are recognized by adjustments to net income. In the example, the following adjustments are required:

1. *Accounts receivable increase.* Net income is decreased since the cash receipts for goods and services sold were less than the revenue recognized in arriving at net income.

2. *Inventory increase.* Net income is decreased since purchases were greater than the charge made against revenue for cost of sales in arriving at net income.

3. *Prepaid expense decrease.* Net income is increased since the cash disbursements for expenses were less than the charges made against revenue for certain expenses in arriving at net income.

4. *Accounts payable increase.* Net income is increased since the cash disbursements for goods and services purchased were less than the charges made for these items in arriving at net income.

5. *Accrued expense decrease.* Net income is decreased since the cash disbursements for expenses were greater than the charges made against revenue for certain expenses in arriving at net income.

The cash-flow approach to the analysis of financial operations has received increasing attention in recent years.[4] The statement is readily interpreted by the reader, and it can be a highly useful tool for forecasting and planning cash flow. However, a working capital analysis may still be required to answer questions regarding effect of financial activities upon the working capital pool.

ANALYSIS OF ACCOUNT CHANGES IN PREPARATION OF FUNDS STATEMENT

As indicated earlier, the preparation of the funds statement requires comparative balance sheet information supplemented by explanations for account changes. Examples in the preceding sections were relatively simple and changes in account balances defined fund sources and applications. Ordinarily, however, more complex circumstances are encountered and it is not possible to rely on the net change in an account balance for a full explanation of the effect of that item on a company's funds flow, however defined. To illustrate, assume that comparative balance sheets report a $50,000 increase in bonds payable. Without further investigation, this might be interpreted as a source of funds of $50,000. However, reference to the liability account may disclose that bonds of $100,000 were retired during the period while new bonds of $150,000 were issued. A further analysis of the transactions affecting the liability account may reveal that a premium of $2,000 was paid on bonds retired and a discount of $7,500 pertained to the new issue. The funds statement, then, should report that funds were provided by a new issue of $142,500 and that funds were applied to retirement of an old issue of $102,000.

Decreases in non-current assets and increases in non-current liabilities and in owners' equity require analysis in determining funds provided; increases in non-current assets and decreases in non-current liabilities and in owners' equity require analysis in determining funds applied.

Fund Sources

The following examples indicate fund sources and suggest the nature of the analysis required in determining the actual amounts provided.

1. *Decreases in non-current asset accounts.* Balances in land, equipment, long-term investments, and other non-current asset accounts may decrease as a result of assets sold, thus indicating fund sources. However, an analysis of the

---

[4]See, for example, the emphasis placed on cash flows in the *Report of the Study Group on the Objectives of Financial Statements* (New York: American Institute of Certified Public Accountants, 1973) and in *Statement of Financial Accounting Concepts No. 1,* "Objectives of Financial Reporting by Business Enterprises" (Stamford, Connecticut: Financial Accounting Standards Board, 1978).

transactions accounting for each change is necessary; sale of investments at a gain, for example, provides funds exceeding the decrease in the asset account.

2. *Increases in non-current liabilities.* Balances in long-term notes, bonds, and other non-current liability accounts may increase as a result of amounts borrowed, thus representing fund sources. An analysis of the transactions accounting for each change is necessary; issuance of bonds at a discount, for example, provides less funds than the increase in the bond account.

3. *Increases in owners' equity.* Share capital balances may increase as a result of the sale of shares, thus representing fund sources. However, the amounts received for shares must be determined, for these may differ from the increases in the share capital balances. When an increase in retained earnings cannot be explained solely by the net income for the period, an analysis of the retained earnings account is necessary. An increase in retained earnings resulting from profitable operations is recognized as a source of funds; a decrease in retained earnings resulting from cash dividends is separately recognized as an application of funds.

Fund Applications

The following examples indicate fund applications and suggest the nature of the analysis required in determining the amounts applied.

1. *Increases in non-current assets.* Balances in land, buildings, patents, and other non-current asset accounts may increase as a result of the acquisitions of such items, thus representing fund uses. An analysis of transactions accounting for the change is necessary; the amount paid for patents, for example, is greater than the increase in the patents account balance when the account is reduced during the period for amortization.

2. *Decreases in non-current liabilities.* The balances in mortgage, bond, and other non-current liability accounts may show decreases resulting from retirement of obligations, thus representing fund applications. An analysis of transactions accounting for each change is necessary; the amount paid bondholders, for example, exceeds the decrease in the bonds account when a premium is paid upon bond retirement.

3. *Decreases in owners' equity.* Share capital balances may show decreases as a result of the acquisition of shares previously issued, thus representing fund applications. However, the amounts paid for reacquired shares must be determined, for these may differ from the decreases in share capital balances. When a decrease in retained earnings cannot be explained solely by a loss for the period, an analysis of the retained earnings account is necessary. A decrease in retained earnings resulting from operations at a loss is recognized as an application of funds; a further decrease resulting from cash dividends is separately recognized as an application of funds.

Changes in non-current asset and liability balances and in owners' equity account balances must be analysed and recognized as described regardless of the definition employed for funds. When the concept of funds is narrowed to cash, changes in certain current asset and current liability balances are also recognized in arriving at the amounts of funds provided and applied.

Adjustments in Developing Amounts Provided and Applied

The preceding discussion has indicated that the changes in account balances require further analysis when they fail to report the amounts of funds actually provided or applied. When there are many adjustments to be made, or when adjustments are complex, use of working papers may facilitate the preparation of the funds statement. In employing working papers, a special adjustments column is used to explain the changes in account balances in terms of the actual amounts of funds provided and applied by such changes.

The adjustments that are required in developing funds data may be classified under three headings:

1. *Adjustments to explain account changes not representing fund sources or applications.* Certain account changes may carry no funds-flow implications. For example, fully depreciated assets may have been applied against accumulated depreciation balances. Errors of prior periods may have been discovered requiring changes in property and owners' equity balances. Stock dividends may have been issued and retained earnings transferred to share capital. The foregoing items result in changes in account balances but these changes should be disregarded in reporting the flow of funds. When working papers are prepared, the adjustments made to explain such account changes do not affect the amount of funds provided or applied.
2. *Adjustments to report the individual fund sources and applications when several transactions are summarized in a single account.* The change in the balance of an account may result from funds provided by several different sources or applied to several different purposes, or from a combination of funds provided and applied. For example, the change in the land, buildings, and equipment balance may reflect funds applied to the construction of buildings and also to the purchase of equipment. The change in the bonds payable balance may reflect both funds applied to the retirement of an old bond issue and funds provided by a new issue. The change in the share capital balance may reflect both funds provided by the issue of shares and funds applied to the reacquisition and retirement of shares. When working papers are prepared, adjustments are made to report separately the different funds sources and applications.
3. *Adjustments to report individual fund sources and applications when such information is reported in two or more accounts.* The amount of funds provided or applied as a result of a single transaction may be reflected in two or more accounts. For example, certain investments may have been sold for more than cost; the gain reported in income and the decrease in the investment account must be combined in arriving at the actual amount provided by the sale. Bonds may have been issued at a discount; the increase in the discount account balance must be applied against the increase in the bond account in arriving at the actual amount provided by the issue. Preferred shares may have been retired at a premium; the decreases in share capital and in contributed surplus or retained earnings account balances must be combined in arriving at the actual amount applied to the retirement. When working papers are prepared, adjustments are made to combine related changes.

Retained Earnings is an example of an account that may be affected by all

ACCOUNT Retained Earnings

DATE		ITEM	DEBIT	CREDIT	BALANCE	
					DEBIT	CREDIT
Jan.	1	Balance				200,000
Mar.	1	Appropriation for bond sinking funds	20,000			180,000
July	10	Cash dividends	30,000			150,000
Dec.	31	Net income for the year		60,000		210,000

three types of adjustments. To illustrate, assume that a retained earnings account shows an increase for the year of $10,000. Inspection of the account discloses the information shown above.

Retained earnings was reduced by the appropriation for bond sinking fund. Although both retained earnings and the appropriated retained earnings balance show changes of $20,000, the changes are without funds significance. If working papers are prepared, the decrease in retained earnings is explained by the increase in the appropriation for bond sinking fund; the account changes are thus explained and receive no recognition in developing the funds statement. Cash dividends of $30,000 are reported separately as funds applied. This leaves $60,000 in the retained earnings account to be reported as funds provided by operations.

If certain debits or credits recognized in arriving at net income carry no funds implications, the net income figure does not report the amount of funds provided by operations. For example, assume depreciation of $20,000 is recorded in computing net income. The entry for depreciation, although representing a proper charge in arriving at net income, is without funds significance; its effects, therefore, should be cancelled. Funds from profitable operations, then, consist of $60,000, as reported, plus $20,000. If working papers are prepared, the increase in accumulated depreciation is explained by increasing funds provided by operations. To fully illustrate the nature of this adjustment, assume the following facts:

At the end of 1979, a lawyer, in establishing a new office, invests cash of $15,000 and immediately acquires furniture and fixtures for $10,000. Furniture and fixtures are estimated to have a five-year life. Condensed comparative balance sheet and income statement data for 1979–1980 appear on page 852.

Although there were no operating activities in 1979, funds of $10,000 were applied to the acquisition of furniture and fixtures and working capital changed from $15,000 to $5,000. In 1980, the income statement reported net income of $7,500 after a charge against revenue for depreciation of $2,000. However, operations provided working capital of $9,500 — fees providing working capital of $20,000 and expenses consuming working capital of $10,500. To arrive at the net increase in working capital, revenue representing working capital inflow is reduced only by those expenses involving a working capital outflow or, alternately, net income is increased by the charge for

	December 31, 1980		December 31, 1979
Working capital		$14,500	$ 5,000
Furniture and fixtures	$10,000		10,000
Less accumulated depreciation	2,000	8,000	
Capital		$22,500	$15,000
Fees received in cash or recognized as receivables		$20,000	
Expenses:			
Paid in cash or recognized as payables	$10,500		
Depreciation, recognized as reduction in furniture and fixtures balance	2,000	12,500	
Net income		$ 7,500	

depreciation involving no working capital outflow. Break-even operations would have recouped working capital equivalent to the reduction in the furniture and fixtures balance; profitable operations served to increase working capital by an amount equal to both the charge for depreciation and the reported net income.

In calculating funds provided by operations, net income must be increased for all charges that were recognized in arriving at net income from operations that involved no working capital outflow. Net income is therefore increased for such charges as depletion, depreciation of buildings and equipment items, and amortization of patents, leaseholds, bond payable discounts, and bond investment premiums. Net income must also be decreased for all credits recognized in arriving at net income that involved no working capital inflow. Net income is decreased for such items as the amortization of bond payable premiums and bond investment discounts. Any gains and losses included in net income but not related to normal operations must be identified with their particular sources; funds provided by operations are thus limited to amounts produced by normal and recurring activities.

It is also possible to classify the transactions that produce successive or comparative balance sheets using the diagram presented below. Thus, assuming funds are defined as working capital, there are (1) transactions within the current asset and current liability accounts (the working capital accounts), (2) transactions that cross the line between the current and non-current balance sheet accounts, and (3) transactions within the non-current balance sheet accounts. The funds statement, assuming funds are defined as working capital, excludes all type (1) transactions, includes all type (2) transactions, and includes *some* type (3) transactions. The type (3) transactions that are included are those involving significant financing and investing activities. Section 1540 of the *Accounting Recommendations* excludes the following type (3) transactions from the funds statement: transfers to and from reserve or appropriation accounts; stock dividends on common shares and stock splits; and appraisal adjustments to reflect the current value of assets which in conventional accounting are indeed rare.[5] Otherwise, subject to materiality, all type (3) transactions should be reported on the funds statement.

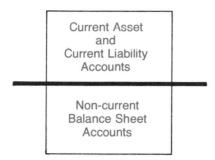

Type (1) transactions are excluded from the funds statement because funds defined as working capital have no flow implications. These transactions may change the composition or form of working capital, but not the amount. The diagram is adaptable to other definitions of funds. All that is required is the assurance that the accounts presented above the line reflect the specific definition of funds to be used.

PREPARATION OF THE FUNDS STATEMENT — FUNDS DEFINED AS WORKING CAPITAL

In the examples given earlier, funds statements were prepared directly from comparative account balances. In the following example, comparative account balances require a number of adjustments and working papers are employed in developing the funds statement. In this section it is assumed funds are defined as working capital. The modifications in working papers and in statements when funds are defined as cash are illustrated in a later section. In either case, the objective of the funds statement is to disclose all significant financing and investing activities.

Assume for Atwood, Ltd., the comparative balance sheet shown on page 855 and the supplementary data given below and on page 854.
Supplementary data:

Changes in retained earnings during the year were as follows:

Balance, December 31, 1979		$125,500
Increases:		
Net income	$ 44,000	
Appropriation for building expansion returned to		
retained earnings	100,000	144,000
		$269,500

[5]CICA Handbook: Accounting Recommendations, Section 1540, op. cit., par. .06.

Decreases:

Cash dividends	$ 12,000	
50% stock dividend on common shares	80,000	
Prior period adjustment resulting from omission of charges for depreciation on certain office equipment items	3,500	
Acquisition of treasury shares for $15,000; par value of shares, $12,000, originally issued at a premium of 2,000	1,000	96,500
Balance, December 31, 1980		$173,000

The income statement for 1980 summarizes operations as follows:

Income before extraordinary items	$36,000
Add gain on involuntary conversion of buildings	8,000
Net income	$44,000

Buildings costing $40,000 with a carrying value of $2,000 were completely destroyed in an extraordinary disaster. The insurance company paid $10,000 cash; new buildings were then constructed at a cost of $105,000.

Building expansion funds investments, cost $96,000, were sold for $102,500.

Delivery equipment was acquired at a cost of $6,000; $2,000 was allowed on the trade-in of non-similar old equipment with an original cost of $4,800 and a net book value of $2,800; and $4,000 was paid in cash. The entire loss is recognized.

Land was acquired for $108,500, the vendor accepting in payment preferred shares, par value $40,000, and cash of $68,500.

New machinery was purchased for $12,000 cash. Additional machinery and equipment was overhauled at a cost of $26,000 which extended useful life, the cost being debited to accumulated depreciation.

The amortization of patents cost and depreciation expense on buildings and equipment were recorded as follows:

Buildings	$ 5,600
Machinery and equipment	15,300
Delivery equipment	8,000
Office equipment	3,000
Patents	5,000
Total	$36,900

Office equipment was acquired for $8,000 cash.

Ten-year bonds, face value $60,000, were issued at a discount of $3,000 at the beginning of the year; discount amortization for the year was $300.

The company recognizes depreciation on machines for tax purposes by claiming capital cost allowances, and for accounting purposes by the straight-

	1980		1979	
Assets				
Current assets:				
Cash in banks and on hand	$ 59,350		$ 65,000	
Accounts receivable (net)	60,000		70,500	
Interest receivable	250		2,400	
Inventories	75,000		76,500	
Prepaid operating expenses	16,500	$211,100	12,000	$226,400
Building expansion fund investments (at				
cost)		10,000		106,000
Land, buildings, and equipment:				
Land		$183,500		$ 75,000
Buildings $290,000			$225,000	
Less accumulated depreciation 122,600	167,400		155,000	70,000
Machinery and equipment $132,000			$120,000	
Less accumulated depreciation 32,800	99,200		43,500	76,500
Delivery equipment . . . . $ 40,000			$ 38,800	
Less accumulated deprecation 26,000	14,000		20,000	18,800
Office equipment . . . . $ 34,000			$ 26,000	
Less accumulated deprecation 12,500	21,500	485,600	6,000	20,000	260,300
Patents		35,000		40,000
Total assets		$741,700		$632,700
Liabilities				
Current liabilities:				
Income tax payable	$ 10,000		$ 9,500	
Accounts payable	65,000		81,200	
Salaries payable	5,000		1,500	
Dividends payable	4,400	$ 84,400		$ 92,200
Bonds payable	$ 60,000			
Less unamortized bond discount	2,700	57,300		
Deferred income tax payable		21,000		15,000
Total liabilities		$162,700		$107,200
Shareholders' Equity				
Preferred shares	$140,000		$100,000	
Common shares	240,000		160,000	
Contributed surplus	38,000		40,000	
Retained earnings appropriated for building				
expansion			100,000	
Retained earnings	173,000		125,500	525,500
Less treasury shares, common, at par	12,000	579,000		
Total liabilities and shareholders' equity		$741,700		$632,700

line method. This depreciation timing difference caused the income tax payable on 1980 taxable income to be $6,000 less than the income tax expense based on accounting income.

In preparing a funds statement for Atwood, Ltd., the first step is to define funds as working capital. The second step is to determine the change in fund balances, in this case the working capital account balances. A schedule of changes in working capital for Atwood, Ltd., is given below:

	December 31		Increase (Decrease)
	1980	1979	
Current assets:			
Cash in banks and on hand	$ 59,350	$ 65,000	$ (5,650)
Accounts receivable (net)	60,000	70,500	(10,500)
Interest receivable	250	2,400	(2,150)
Inventories	75,000	76,500	(1,500)
Prepaid operating expenses	16,500	12,000	4,500
Total	$211,100	$226,400	$(15,300)
Current liabilities:			
Income tax payable	$ 10,000	$ 9,500	$ (500)
Accounts payable	65,000	81,200	16,200
Salaries payable	5,000	1,500	(3,500)
Dividends payable	4,400	0	(4,400)
Total	$ 84,400	$ 92,200	$ 7,800
Working capital	$126,700	$134,200	$ (7,500)

All non-fund accounts may then be analysed using the working papers illustrated on pages 858 and 859. The funds statement is taken directly from the working papers and is illustrated on page 863.

It should be noted that the working papers contain a summary working capital fund account and the other non-current or non-fund accounts, in this instance the non-working capital accounts. These are the accounts which must be analysed to determine the sources, uses, and net change in the fund balance already determined and shown above in the schedule of changes in working capital. The format of the working papers is straightforward. The first column contains the beginning balances, then there are two columns for analysis of transactions to arrive at ending balances in the fourth column. The side headings added after the account titles are those to be used in preparing the formal funds statement.

In preparing working papers, accumulated depreciation balances, instead of being reported as credit balances in the debit section, may be more conveniently listed with liability and owners' equity balances in the credit section. Similarly, negative long-term liabilities and negative owners' equity balances are separately recognized and more conveniently listed with assets in the debit section.

In developing working papers, it will normally prove most convenient to make the required analysis in the following order: (1) the change in retained earnings should be analysed, and in the process the income from ordinary operations and extraordinary items should be separately reported; (2) any extraordinary items should be related to appropriate asset or liability accounts; (3) the income statement and other supplementary data given, as well as any remaining accounts, should be reviewed to determine what additional adjustments are appropriate.

Explanations for individual adjustments recorded on the working papers for Atwood, Ltd., are given below and on pages 858–862. The letter preceding each explanation corresponds with that used on the working papers.

(a) Net income included in the ending retained earnings balance is composed of income before extraordinary items and extraordinary items. The income before extraordinary items balance will require adjustment in arriving at funds provided by operations; the extraordinary items will require separate recognition as funds provided or applied and will later be combined with other asset or liability balances in arriving at the full amounts provided by or applied to specific asset or liability items. Net income, then, is analysed and is reported by an adjustment in compound form as follows:

Funds provided by income before extraordinary items	36,000	
Funds provided by involuntary conversion of buildings	8,000	
Retained earnings		44,000

"Funds provided by income before extraordinary items" is reported on a separate line as a primary element of working capital provided from operations. Since a number of adjustments may be required in arriving at the actual amount of funds provided by operations, adequate space should be allowed after this line for these adjustments. The extraordinary items are listed below the space allowed for income adjustments. Adequate space should also be allowed after each extraordinary item for adjustments necessary to show the actual amount of funds provided by or applied to the extraordinary transaction. Additional items requiring recognition are listed after extraordinary items.

(b) The transfer of retained earnings appropriated for building expansion to retained earnings has no funds significance and the changes in the account balances are reconciled by the following entry:

Retained earnings appropriated for building expansion	100,000	
Retained earnings		100,000

(c) The cash dividends reported in retained earnings are reported separately as an application of funds by the following entry:

Retained earnings	12,000	
Funds applied to dividends		12,000

(d) The transfer of retained earnings to share capital as a result of a common stock dividend has no funds significance and the changes in the account balances are reconciled by the following adjustment:

Retained earnings 80,000

Common shares 80,000

(e) The recognition that depreciation had been omitted on certain office equipment items in prior periods is recorded by a debit to retained earnings and

Atwood, Ltd.
Working Papers for Statement of Changes in Financial Position — Working Capital Basis
For Year Ended December 31, 1980

	ITEMS	BEGINNING BALANCE DEC. 31 1979	ANALYSIS OF TRANSACTIONS DEBIT		ANALYSIS OF TRANSACTIONS CREDIT		ENDING BALANCE DEC. 31 1980	
1	Debits							1
2	Working capital	134,200			(t)	7,500	126,700	2
3	Building expansion fund invest-							3
4	ments	106,000			(i)	96,000	10,000	4
5	Land	75,000	(k)	108,500			183,500	5
6	Buildings	225,000	(h)	105,000	(g)	40,000	290,000	6
7	Machinery and equipment	120,000	(m)	12,000			132,000	7
8	Delivery equipment	38,800	(j)	6,000	(j)	4,800	40,000	8
9	Office equipment	26,000	(p)	8,000			34,000	9
10	Patents	40,000			(o)	5,000	35,000	10
11	Unamortized bond discount		(q)	3,000	(r)	300	2,700	11
12	Treasury shares, common, at par		(f)	12,000			12,000	12
13	Totals	765,000					865,900	13
14								14
15	Credits							15
16	Accumulated depreciation — buildings ...	155,000	(g)	38,000	(o)	5,600	122,600	16
17	Accumulated depreciation — machinery							17
18	and equipment.....................	43,500	(n)	26,000	(o)	15,300	32,800	18
19	Accumulated depreciation — delivery							19
20	equipment.........................	20,000	(j)	2,000	(o)	8,000	26,000	20
21	Accumulated depreciation — office							21
22	equipment.........................	6,000			(e)	3,500 ⎫		22
23					(o)	3,000 ⎭	12,500	23
24	Bonds payable........................				(q)	60,000	60,000	24
25	Deferred income tax	15,000			(s)	6,000	21,000	25
26	Preferred shares	100,000			(l)	40,000	140,000	26
27	Common shares	160,000			(d)	80,000	240,000	27
28	Contributed surplus	40,000	(f)	2,000			38,000	28
29	Retained earnings appropriated for							29
30	building expansion	100,000	(b)	100,000				30
31	Retained earnings.....................	125,500	(c)	12,000 ⎫	(a)	44,000 ⎫		31
32			(d)	80,000 ⎪	(b)	100,000 ⎬		32
33			(e)	3,500 ⎬		⎭		33
34			(f)	1,000 ⎭			173,000	34
35	Totals	765,000		519,000		519,000	865,900	35
36								36

(continued next page)

a credit to accumulated depreciation of office equipment. The correction of earnings of prior periods has no funds significance and the changes in the account balances may be reconciled as follows:

Retained earnings 3,500
    Accumulated depreciation — office equipment 3,500

	ITEMS	BEGINNING BALANCE DEC. 31 1979	ANALYSIS OF TRANSACTIONS DEBIT	ANALYSIS OF TRANSACTIONS CREDIT	ENDING BALANCE DEC. 31 1980	
37	Working capital was provided by:					37
38	Operations:					38
39	Income before extraordinary items		(a) 36,000			39
40	Add items not requiring working					40
41	capital:					41
42	Loss on trade of delivery					42
43	equipment....................		(j) 800			43
44	Amortization of patents		(o) 5,000			44
45	Depreciation expense		(o) 31,900			45
46	Amortization of bond discount		(r) 300			46
47	Increase in deferred income					47
48	tax		(s) 6,000			48
49	Deduct item not providing					49
50	working capital:					50
51	Gain on sale of investments			(i) 6,500		51
52	Involuntary conversion of					52
53	buildings		(a) 8,000			53
54			(g) 2,000			54
55	Sale of building expansion					55
56	fund investments		(l) 102,500			56
57	Issuance of preferred shares					57
58	in part payment of land		(l) 40,000			58
59	Issuance of bonds at					59
60	discount		(q) 57,000			60
61	Working capital was applied to:					61
62	Dividends			(c) 12,000		62
63	Purchase treasury stock, common			(f) 15,000		63
64	Purchase land ($40,000 paid by					64
65	issuance of preferred shares)			(k) 108,500		65
66	Construct buildings			(h) 105,000		66
67	Purchase machinery and equipment ...			(m) 12,000		67
68	Overhaul machinery and equipment ...			(n) 26,000		68
69	Purchase delivery equipment			(j) 4,000		69
70	Purchase office equipment			(p) 8,000		70
71	Decrease in working capital		(t) 7,500			71
72	Totals		297,000	297,000		72
73						73

(f) The acquisition of treasury shares, common, for $15,000 was recorded by a debit to Treasury Shares at par, $12,000; a debit to Contributed Surplus, $2,000; and a debit to Retained Earnings, $1,000. Funds applied to the acquisition of treasury shares are summarized by the following entry:

Treasury shares, common (at par)	12,000	
Contributed surplus	2,000	
Retained earnings	1,000	
Funds applied to purchase treasury shares, common		15,000

Debits to Retained Earnings of $96,500 and credits of $144,000 provide an ending balance of $173,000; fund sources and applications that were reflected in the retained earnings balance have been fully identified and given appropriate recognition.

(g) The destruction of the buildings and the subsequent insurance reimbursement produced an extraordinary gain of $8,000. This extraordinary gain was recorded as "Funds Provided by Involuntary Conversion of Buildings," in entry (a), as the result of the earlier recognition of the individual items comprising net income. Since the effect of the destruction was to provide funds of $10,000, the proceeds from the insurance company, the funds of $8,000 recognized in entry (a) may now be adjusted to show the true amount of funds provided by relating the required adjustment to the appropriate asset accounts:

Accumulated depreciation — buildings	38,000	
Funds provided by involuntary conversion of buildings	2,000	
Buildings		40,000

(h) The buildings account was increased by the cost of constructing new buildings, $105,000. The cost of new buildings is reported separately as an application of funds by the following entry:

Buildings	105,000	
Funds applied to construction of buildings		105,000

(i) The sale of building expansion fund investments was recorded by a credit to the asset account at cost, $96,000, and a credit to a gain on sale of investment. At the end of the period, the gain account was closed into retained earnings as part of income before extraordinary items. Since the effect of the sale was to provide funds of $102,500, this is reported on a separate line. The investments account balance is reduced and funds provided by operations are decreased by the amount of the gain. The following entry is made:

Funds provided by sale of building expansion fund investments	102,500	
Building expansion fund investments		96,000
Income before extraordinary items — gain on sale of investments .		6,500

(j) Delivery equipment was purchased for $6,000; $2,000 was allowed on the trade-in of non-similar delivery equipment, cost $4,800, with a net book value of $2,800; and $4,000 was paid in cash. The loss of $800 on the equipment traded was closed into retained earnings as part of income before extraordinary items. Since the effect of the trade was to apply funds of $4,000, this is reported on a separate line. The changes in the delivery equipment balance and in the balance for accumulated depreciation on delivery equipment are explained, while the funds provided by operations are increased by the loss that did not involve any current funds outflow. The following entry is made:

Delivery equipment	6,000	
Accumulated depreciation — delivery equipment	2,000	
Income before extraordinary items — loss on trade of delivery equipment	800	
Delivery equipment		4,800
Funds applied to purchase delivery equipment		4,000

(k) and (l) Land was acquired at a price of $108,500; payment was made in preferred shares valued at par, $40,000, and cash, $68,500. The analysis on the working papers is as follows: (k) the increase in the land balance, $108,500, is reported separately as an application of funds; (l) the increase in the preferred shares balance, $40,000, is reported separately as a source of funds applied to the purchase of land. The entries are:

Land	108,500	
Funds applied to purchase land		108,500
Funds provided by issuance of preferred shares in part payment of land	40,000	
Preferred shares		40,000

(m) and (n) Machinery of $12,000 was acquired during the year. Payment was made in cash and is represented by funds applied to purchase machinery; the cost of overhauling other machinery and equipment also represents the application of funds and is reported separately. The cost was debited to the accumulated depreciation account. The entries are:

Machinery and equipment	12,000	
Funds applied to purchase machinery and equipment		12,000
Accumulated depreciation — machinery and equipment	26,000	
Funds applied to overhaul machinery and equipment		26,000

(o) The changes in the patents account and in the accumulated depreciation accounts result from the recognition of amortization of the patents and depreciation on the fixed assets. Funds provided by operations are increased by the charges against earnings not involving current funds outflow by the following adjustment:

Income before extraordinary items — amortization of patents	5,000	
Income before extraordinary items — depreciation expense	31,900	
Patents		5,000
Accumulated depreciation — buildings		5,600
Accumulated depreciation — machinery and equipment		15,300
Accumulated depreciation — delivery equipment		8,000
Accumulated depreciation — office equipment		3,000

(p) Office equipment of $8,000 was purchased during the year. The entry is as follows:

| Office equipment | 8,000 | |
| Funds applied to purchase office equipment | | 8,000 |

(q) and (r) During the year, bonds were issued at a discount. The result of this transaction was to credit Bonds Payable for $60,000 and debit Unamortized Bond Discount for $3,000. The funds provided by the bond issuance of $57,000 are recognized by entry (q). Subsequently, the bond discount was amortized by reducing the unamortized bond discount account — entry (r). This decrease in the bond discount account is explained by increasing funds provided by operations by the amount of the charge against earnings not involving any current fund outflow. The entries are as shown below.

Unamortized bond discount	3,000	
Funds provided by issuance of bonds	57,000	
Bonds payable		60,000
Income before extraordinary items — amortization of bond discount .	300	
Unamortized bond discount		300

(s) The depreciation timing difference was recognized by a debit to Income Tax Expense and credits to Income Tax Payable and Deferred Income Tax. The timing difference for 1980 is $6,000 and is shown on the work sheet by an increase in Deferred Income Tax and an increase in funds provided by operations. The extra $6,000 debit to Income Tax Expense is thus added back to funds provided by operations because the extra charge against earnings did not involve any current funds outflow. The following entry is made:

Income before extraordinary items — increase in deferred income tax payable	6,000	
Deferred income tax		6,000

(t) The change in working capital is explained by the following entry:

Decrease in working capital	7,500	
Working capital		7,500

This entry explains the net change occurring in all working capital accounts, and brings the working papers into balance.

A funds statement for Atwood, Ltd., may be prepared from the working papers as shown at the top of page 863.

The funds statement should begin with a summary of the funds related to normal operations. Income or loss before extraordinary items provides a convenient starting point; net income in the absence of extraordinary items is listed. Those items reflected in this balance not requiring funds are added back while those items not providing funds are subtracted. The adjusted balance, representing funds provided by or applied to operations, is followed by any extraordinary items not related to normal and recurring events and transactions, but representing direct sources or applications of funds. Remaining sources and applications of funds are then listed to establish the net fund changes for the period.

Some persons object to the presentation of funds provided by operations in the form just illustrated. This form, they maintain, implies that depreciation generates funds. Actually, it is revenues that provide funds but the income from operations balance fails to report the full amount provided because of items such as depreciation. This objection is overcome by separately listing the individual revenues and expenses but excluding items and amounts not involving current fund inflows or outflows.

Section 1540 of the *Accounting Recommendations* adopts a very flexible position concerning the statement presentation of funds provided by opera-

| Atwood, Ltd. |
| Statement of Changes in Financial Position — Working Capital Basis |
| For Year Ended December 31, 1980 |

Working capital was provided by:
Operations:

Income before extraordinary items		$ 36,000	
Add items not requiring working capital:			
Loss on trade of delivery equipment	$ 800		
Amortization of patents	5,000		
Depreciation expense........................	31,900		
Amortization of bond discount	300		
Increase in deferred income tax..............	6,000		
	$44,000		
Deduct item not providing working capital:			
Gain on sale of investments	6,500	37,500	
Working capital provided by operations		$ 73,500	
Involuntary conversion of buildings		10,000	
Sale of building expansion fund investments		102,500	
Issuance of preferred shares in part payment of land			
(total cost of land, $108,500)		40,000	
Issuance of bonds at a discount		57,000	$283,000

Working capital was applied to:

Dividends		$ 12,000	
Purchase treasury shares, common		15,000	
Purchase land (cash paid, $68,500; preferred shares			
issued, $40,000)		108,500	
Construct buildings		105,000	
Purchase machinery and equipment		12,000	
Overhaul machinery and equipment		26,000	
Purchase delivery equipment		4,000	
Purchase office equiment		8,000	290,500
Decrease in working capital			$ 7,500

tions. This ranges from presentation as a single amount to the detailed presentation of revenue and expense items which neither provide nor use funds. The position of the Accounting Research Committee is stated as follows:

The flow of funds from, or the application of funds to, operations may be reflected as a single amount in the statement of changes in financial position. It is not considered necessary to detail revenue and expense items which do not provide or use funds. However, where it is considered desirable to provide a link between income before extraordinary items and funds from operations, the items which do not provide or use funds could be shown, either as one net amount or in detail. This reconciliation may appear on the face of the statement, in a separate tabulation or in the notes to the financial statements. There is a danger that a user of the financial statements might regard the reconciling items as sources or applications of funds, especially when the reconciliation is included on the face of the statement. Accordingly, there should be a clear indication that such items do not constitute sources or applications of funds.[6]

Special Problems

The analysis required in developing the funds statement may be simple or complex. In each instance where a non-current asset, a non-current liability, or an owners' equity account balance has changed, the question should be asked: Does this indicate a change in working capital? Frequently the answer to this question is obvious, but in some cases careful analysis is required. The following items suggest special analysis that may be required.

1. In the previous example, the claim for capital cost allowances exceeded depreciation charges. This resulted in an increase in the deferred income tax account. When charges for depreciation later exceed capital cost allowances, or when an asset with a related deferred tax liability is retired early, the deferred tax credit will be decreased by a debit to Deferred Income Tax and a credit to Income Tax Expense. This decrease in Income Tax Expense does not increase the amount of funds provided by operations nor does the decrease in Deferred Income Tax indicate that funds have been applied; therefore, the decrease in Deferred Income Tax must be recorded and funds provided by operations must be decreased by the reduction in income tax expense that did not involve current funds inflow.

2. Assume that retained earnings are reduced upon the declaration of a cash dividend payable in the following period. Declaration of the dividend has increased current liabilities and, thus, reduced working capital. Subsequent payment of the dividend will have no effect upon the amount of working capital, simply reducing both cash and the current liability. The declaration of a dividend, then, should be reported as funds applied. The reduction in working capital is confirmed in the summary of net change in working capital.

3. Assume that a long-term obligation becomes payable within a year, and requires a change to current classification. This change calls for a recognition of funds applied. The change in classification has resulted in a reduction of working capital; subsequent payment will have no effect upon the amount of working capital. The reduction in the long-term liability can be reported as "Funds applied to long-term obligations maturing currently." The change in working capital balances will confirm the reduction in working capital.

4. In previous examples, prepaid expenses were classified as current assets and therefore treated as working capital items in the analysis of the change in working capital. Prepaid expenses are sometimes listed under a separate heading or reported with non-current assets. This treatment calls for the analysis of prepaid expenses just as for other items classified as non-current, since their exclusion from the current group makes them part of the explanation for the change that took place in the current classification.

---

[6]*CICA Handbook: Accounting Recommendations, Section 1540, op. cit.,* par. .31.

Alternative Methods for Developing a Funds Statement

It is indeed possible to analyse changes in comparative balance sheets and prepare the funds statement without the use of working papers. Thus, fund changes may be determined by establishing "T" accounts to control the analysis and "T" accounts for all non-current balance sheet accounts; by the process of posting changes in these accounts the funds provided and applied during the period can be readily determined.[7]

PREPARATION OF THE FUNDS STATEMENT — FUNDS DEFINED AS CASH

When preparing a funds statement on a cash basis, one must work from financial information on an accrual basis to the cash inflows and outflows provided and applied during the period. To illustrate, if sales for the period were $80,000 as reported on the income statement and the beginning and ending accounts receivable balances were $25,000 and $20,000 respectively, the cash provided from sales would be $85,000. The beginning accounts receivable balance would have been recorded as sales during the previous period, but collected in the current period; thus, the beginning balance should be added to the $80,000 sales figure. The ending balance is included in the $80,000 amount, but will not be collected until future periods; it should be subtracted. Therefore, the net decrease in accounts receivable should be added to the reported sales figure of $80,000 to arrive at the total cash provided from sales activity during the period.

If Atwood Ltd., wishes to prepare a funds statement using a cash definition of funds, working papers would be prepared as illustrated on pages 866 and 867. Adjustments are essentially the same as those described on pages 857–862 but are supplemented by adjustments to show operations and also dividends in terms of cash. Income from operations as previously adjusted is further adjusted for the differences found in all working capital items other than cash. The entry for cash dividends (c) is adjusted for the change in the dividends payable balance in arriving at the cash applied to dividends during the period. In the illustration, entry (c) would be a debit to Retained Earnings, $12,000; a credit to Dividends Payable, $4,400; and a credit to Cash, $7,600. Entry (aa) serves the same purpose as entry (t) on page 862. The net change in cash is explained and the working papers are brought into balance by this entry. A statement of changes in financial position employing the cash concept for funds appears on page 868.

The working papers and the statement report the net amount of cash provided by operations, $70,950. When a full explanation of the cash provided by operations is desired, this can be provided by applying adjustments

---

[7]The "T" account method, using the Atwood, Ltd. example, is explained and illustrated in an appendix to this chapter.

	ITEMS	BEGINNING BALANCE DEC. 31 1979	ANALYSIS OF TRANSACTIONS DEBIT		ANALYSIS OF TRANSACTIONS CREDIT		ENDING BALANCE DEC. 31 1980	
1	Debits							1
2	Cash in banks and on hand	65,000			(aa)	5,650	59,350	2
3	Accounts receivable (net)	70,500			(t)	10,500	60,000	3
4	Interest receivable	2,400			(u)	2,150	250	4
5	Inventories	76,500			(v)	1,500	75,000	5
6	Prepaid operating expenses	12,000	(w)	4,500			16,500	6
7	Building expansion fund invest-							7
8	ments	106,000			(i)	96,000	10,000	8
9	Land	75,000	(k)	108,500			183,500	9
10	Buildings	225,000	(h)	105,000	(g)	40,000	290,000	10
11	Machinery and equipment	120,000	(m)	12,000			132,000	11
12	Delivery equipment	38,800	(j)	6,000	(j)	4,800	40,000	12
13	Office equipment	26,000	(p)	8,000			34,000	13
14	Patents	40,000			(o)	5,000	35,000	14
15	Unamortized bond discount		(q)	3,000	(r)	300	2,700	15
16	Treasury shares, common, at par		(f)	12,000			12,000	16
17	Totals	857,200					950,300	17
18								18
19	Credits							19
20	Accumulated depreciation —							20
21	buildings	155,000	(g)	38,000	(o)	5,600	122,600	21
22	Accumulated depreciation —							22
23	machinery and equipment	43,500	(n)	26,000	(o)	15,300	32,800	23
24	Accumulated depreciation —							24
25	delivery equipment	20,000	(j)	2,000	(o)	8,000	26,000	25
26	Accumulated depreciation —							26
27	office equipment	6,000			(e)	3,500 ⎱		27
28					(o)	3,000 ⎰	12,500	28
29	Income tax payable	9,500			(x)	500	10,000	29
30	Accounts payable	81,200	(y)	16,200			65,000	30
31	Salaries payable	1,500			(z)	3,500	5,000	31
32	Dividends payable				(c)	4,400	4,400	32
33	Bonds payable........................				(q)	60,000	60,000	33
34	Deferred income tax	15,000			(s)	6,000	21,000	34
35	Preferred shares	100,000			(l)	40,000	140,000	35
36	Common shares	160,000			(d)	80,000	240,000	36
37	Contributed surplus	40,000	(f)	2,000			38,000	37
38	Retained earnings appropriated							38
39	for building expansion	100,000	(b)	100,000				39
40	Retained earnings	125,500	(c)	12,000 ⎱	(a)	44,000 ⎱		40
41			(d)	80,000 ⎱	(b)	100,000 ⎰		41
42			(e)	3,500 ⎱				42
43			(f)	1,000 ⎰			173,000	43
44	Totals	857,200		539,700		539,700	950,300	44
45								45

(continued next page)

	ITEMS	BEGINNING BALANCE DEC. 31 1979	ANALYSIS OF TRANSACTIONS		ENDING BALANCE DEC. 31 1980	
			DEBIT	CREDIT		
46	Cash was provided by:					46
47	Operations:					47
48	Income before extraordinary					48
49	items		(a) 36,000			49
50	Items to be added to operating					50
51	income:					51
52	Loss on trade of delivery					52
53	equipment		(j) 800			53
54	Amortization of patents		(o) 5,000			54
55	Depreciation expense		(o) 31,900			55
56	Amortization of bond					56
57	discount		(r) 300			57
58	Increase in deferred income					58
59	tax		(s) 6,000			59
60	Decrease in accounts					60
61	receivable (net)		(t) 10,500			61
62	Decrease in interest					62
63	receivable		(u) 2,150			63
64	Decrease in inventories		(v) 1,500			64
65	Increase in income tax					65
66	payable		(x) 500			66
67	Increase in salaries					67
68	payable		(z) 3,500			68
69	Items to be deducted from					69
70	operating income:					70
71	Gain on sale of investment			(i) 6,500		71
72	Increase in prepaid operating					72
73	expenses			(w) 4,500		73
74	Decrease in accounts					74
75	payable			(y) 16,200		75
76	Involuntary conversion of					76
77	buildings		(a) 8,000			77
78			(g) 2,000			78
79	Sale of building expansion					79
80	fund investments		(i) 102,500			80
81	Issuance of preferred shares					81
82	in part payment of land		(l) 40,000			82
83	Issuance of bonds at discount		(q) 57,000			83
84	Cash was applied to:					84
85	Pay dividends			(c) 7,600		85
86	Purchase treasury shares,					86
87	common			(f) 15,000		87
88	Purchase land (cash paid,					88
89	$68,500; preferred shares					89
90	issued, $40,000)			(k) 108,500		90
91	Construct buildings			(h) 105,000		91
92	Purchase machinery and					92
93	equipment			(m) 12,000		93
94	Overhaul machinery and					94
95	equipment			(n) 26,000		95
96	Purchase delivery equipment			(j) 4,000		96
97	Purchase office equipment			(p) 8,000		97
98	Decrease in cash		(aa) 5,650			98
99	Totals		313,300	313,300		99

Atwood, Ltd.
Statement of Changes in Financial Position — Cash Basis
For Year Ended December 31, 1980

Cash was provided by:			
Operations:			
Income before extraordinary items		$ 36,000	
Items to be added to operating income:			
Loss on trade of delivery equipment	$ 800		
Amortization of patents	5,000		
Depreciation expense........................	31,900		
Amortization of bond discount	300		
Increase in deferred income tax	6,000		
Decrease in accounts receivable (net)	10,500		
Decrease in interest receivable	2,150		
Decrease in inventories	1,500		
Increase in income tax payable	500		
Increase in salaries payable	3,500	62,150	
		$ 98,150	
Items to be deducted from operating income:			
Gain on sale of investments	$ 6,500		
Increase in prepaid operating expenses	4,500		
Decrease in accounts payable	16,200	27,200	
Cash provided by operations		$ 70,950	
Involuntary conversion of buildings		10,000	
Sale of building expansion fund investments		102,500	
Issuance of preferred shares in part payment of land			
(total cost of land, $108,500)		40,000	
Issuance of bonds at a discount		57,000	$280,450
Cash was applied to:			
Pay dividends		$ 7,600	
Purchase treasury shares, common		15,000	
Purchase land (cash paid, $68,500; preferred shares			
issued, $40,000)		108,500	
Construct buildings		105,000	
Purchase machinery and equipment		12,000	
Overhaul machinery and equipment		26,000	
Purchase delivery equipment		4,000	
Purchase office equipment		8,000	286,100
Decrease in cash			$ 5,650

to individual revenue and expense items rather than to the net income balance. The operations section of the working papers will require expansion in developing this detail. The operations section of the working papers illustrated on pages 866 and 867 can be expanded as shown at the top of page 869. Adjustment (a), instead of reporting the results of operations as summarized on the income statement, lists the individual revenue and expense items. The adjustments required in developing the cash flow from operations are then applied to the individual revenue and expense balances.

Item	Analysis of Transactions	
	Debit	Credit
Cash was provided by:		
Operations:		
Sales	(a) 750,000	
Add decrease in accounts receivable	(t) 10,500	
Cost of goods sold		(a) 550,000
Add decrease in accounts payable		(y) 16,200
Deduct:		
Depreciation of building, machinery, and equipment,		
amortization of patents	(o) 25,900	
Decrease in inventories	(v) 1,500	
Selling and general expenses		(a) 146,400
Add increase in prepaid operating expense		(w) 4,500
Deduct:		
Depreciation of office and delivery equipment . . .	(o) 11,000	
Increase in salaries payable	(z) 3,500	
Other revenue — interest revenue	(a) 4,600	
Add decrease in interest receivable	(u) 2,150	
Other expense — interest expense		(a) 3,900
Deduct bond discount amortization	(r) 300	
Income tax expense		(a) 24,000
Deduct:		
Increase in income tax payable	(x) 500	
Increase in deferred income tax	(s) 6,000	
Loss on trade of delivery equipment		(a) 800
To cancel loss	(j) 800	
Gain on sale of building expansion fund investments .	(a) 6,500	
To cancel gain		(i) 6,500

Cash provided by operations as summarized above may be presented on the statement as follows:

Cash was provided by:
Operations:

Receipts	— Sales	$760,500	
	Interest revenue	6,750	$767,250
Payments	— Cost of goods sold	$538,800	
	Selling and general expenses	136,400	
	Interest expense	3,600	
	Income tax	17,500	696,300
Cash provided by operations			$ 70,950

SPECIAL OBSERVATIONS

Alternate methods may be used for the presentation of exchanges interpreted as both financing and investing activities. For example, the acquisition of land for $30,000 cash and $50,000 of capital stock may be presented as follows:

Purchase of land	$80,000	
Less capital stock issued in part payment	50,000	$30,000

The difference represents the net amount of funds and would be shown in the application section. The financing and investing aspects of the transaction are related and the net effect on funds is reported. On the other hand, it may be maintained that the issuance of shares should be reported as funds provided and the acquisition of land at the full acquisition price as funds applied. This raises the totals for funds provided and applied but does not affect the increase or decrease in funds reported for the period. This is the approach used in the chapter illustrations and is consistent with Section 1540 of the *Accounting Recommendations*.

The Accounting Research Committee in Section 1540 recognized that the form, terminology, and content of the funds statement will not be the same for every company in meeting its objectives under different circumstances. Although recognizing the need for flexibility, the Committee indicated that guidance is required for the preparation of the statement and its interpretation. Minimally, disclosures should include the items listed below:

1. funds provided from, or used in, operations;
2. outlays for purchase of non-fund assets (identifying separately such items as investments, fixed assets and intangibles);
3. proceeds from sale of non-fund assets (identifying separately such items as investments, fixed assets and intangibles);
4. conversion of non-fund debt to preferred shares or common shares;
5. issuance, assumption, redemption and reduction (by repayment of reclassification) of non-fund debt;
6. issuance, redemption, or repurchase of capital stock;
7. dividends in cash or in kind or other distributions to or on behalf of shareholders (except stock dividends and stock splits);
8. dividends paid by subsidiaries to minority interests; and,
9. increase (decrease) in funds.[8]

The Committee in Section 1540 also emphasizes that isolated statistics of working capital or cash provided from operations, especially per-share computations, should not be presented in annual reports to shareholders "in a manner which would seem to give them greater authority and prominence than conventionally computed earnings."

The funds statement is now recognized as a primary statement, one which must be audited and which is considered essential for fully reporting the activities of a business entity. Even though not specifically required for external reporting under Section 1540, the funds statement has a long history

---

[8]*CICA Handbook: Accounting Recommendations, Section 1540, op. cit.*, par. .16.

of use.[9] Many companies prepared the statement for management purposes long before actually presenting this information to external users. It is fortunate that this important statement is now readily available for all users of financial information.

APPENDIX: T ACCOUNT PREPARATION OF THE STATEMENT OF CHANGES

Of the various techniques for preparing the statement of changes in financial position, the "T" account method is perhaps the most straightforward. As implied by its name, the method uses T accounts to analyse transactions and to assemble data for preparation of the statement. The basic analyses of the method require the reconstruction of transactions which explain the net changes recorded in individual T accounts for each non-current balance sheet account.

The first published description of the "T" account method was an article by Professor William J. Vatter that appeared in the June, 1946 issue of the *Journal of Accountancy*. The steps involved, with minor variations from those proposed by Vatter, are as follows:

1. Determine the increase or decrease in working capital.
2. Open T accounts for:
    (a) Working Capital and enter an increase as a debit or a decrease as a credit.
    (b) Operations
3. Open individual T accounts for each non-current balance sheet account and enter the increase or decrease during the period in accordance with debit/credit rules.
4. Rule off the individual T accounts. A single line across the account is satisfactory.
5. From analysis of available information reconstruct the transactions which explain the increases and decreases recorded in the T accounts for each non-current balance sheet account:
    (a) The income before extraordinary items, or net income in the absence of extraordinary items, is entered in the Operations T account. The offsetting credit is to Retained Earnings.
    (b) Income statement items that do not involve a flow of working capital are recorded in the Operations T account.
    (c) Transactions that impact on current asset and current liability items are recorded in the Working Capital T account.
6. After using all available information, any differences between the increases and decreases recorded in the individual T accounts for non-current balance sheet items and the transactions reconstructed in step 5 are the result of hidden transactions. These must be explained on the basis of logical assumptions.

---

[9]While Section 1540 does not require the statement of changes, companies acts and especially securities acts typically do.

7. Foot and balance the individual T accounts for each non-current balance sheet item.
8. Transfer the balance in the Operations T account to Working Capital. This is the amount of working capital provided by operations.
9. Foot and balance the Working Capital T account. The balance in this account must equal the increase or decrease in working capital as determined in step 1.
10. Prepare the statement of changes:
   (a) The detail pertaining to working capital provided by operations is contained in the Operations T account.
   (b) All sources and applications or uses of working capital appear in the Working Capital T account.
   (c) In order to assure disclosure of all significant financing and investing activities re-examine transactions within non-current balance sheet accounts to identify any additional disclosures that may be required.

The Atwood, Ltd. example presented in the chapter will be used to illustrate the "T" account method. After step 2, the T accounts for Working Capital and for Operations appear as follows:

WORKING CAPITAL			OPERATIONS	
	7,500	DECREASE		

Step 3 requires opening individual T accounts for each non-current balance sheet item, while step 4 is purely procedural. Steps 5 and 6 are critically important because they involve the basic analysis of the "T" account method. At this point, the T accounts should appear as presented below. For convenience the transactions recorded in these T accounts are keyed by number of journal entries that summarize transaction data.

WORKING CAPITAL				OPERATIONS			
		7,500	DECREASE	(1)	36,000	6,500	(9)
(1)	8,000	12,000	(3)	(10)	800		
(7)	2,000	15,000	(6)	(14)	5,000		
(9)	102,500	105,000	(8)	(14)	31,900		
(16)	57,000	4,000	(10)	(17)	300		
		68,500	(11)	(18)	6,000		
		12,000	(12)				
		26,000	(13)				
		8,000	(15)				

BUILDING EXPANSION FUND INVESTMENTS				LAND		
	96,000				108,500	
	96,000	(9)	(11)		108,500	

BUILDINGS

	Debit	Credit	
	65,000		
(8)	105,000	40,000	(7)

ACCUMULATED DEPRECIATION — BUILDINGS

	Debit	Credit	
		32,400	
(7)	38,000	5,600	(14)

MACHINERY AND EQUIPMENT

	Debit	Credit	
	12,000		
(12)	12,000	—	

ACCUMULATED DEPRECIATION — MACHINERY AND EQUIPMENT

	Debit	Credit	
		10,700	
(13)	26,000	15,300	(14)

DELIVERY EQUIPMENT

	Debit	Credit	
	1,200		
(10)	6,000	4,800	(10)

ACCUMULATED DEPRECIATION — DELIVERY EQUIPMENT

	Debit	Credit	
		6,000	
(10)	2,000	8,000	(14)

OFFICE EQUIPMENT

	Debit	Credit	
	8,000		
(15)	8,000		

ACCUMULATED DEPRECIATION — OFFICE EQUIPMENT

	Debit	Credit	
		6,500	
		3,500	(5)
		3,000	(14)

PATENTS

	Debit	Credit	
		5,000	
		5,000	(14)

BONDS PAYABLE

	Debit	Credit	
		60,000	
		60,000	(16)

UNAMORTIZED BOND DISCOUNT

	Debit	Credit	
	2,700		
(16)	3,000	300	(17)

DEFERRED INCOME TAX

	Debit	Credit	
		6,000	
		6,000	(18)

PREFERRED SHARES

	Debit	Credit	
		40,000	
		40,000	(11)

COMMON SHARES

	Debit	Credit	
		80,000	
		80,000	(4)

CONTRIBUTED SURPLUS

	Debit	Credit	
	2,000		
(6)	2,000	—	

RETAINED EARNINGS APPROPRIATED FOR BUILDING EXPANSION

	Debit	Credit	
		100,000	
(2)	100,000		

RETAINED EARNINGS

	Debit	Credit	
		47,500	
(3)	12,000	44,000	(1)
(4)	80,000	100,000	(2)
(5)	3,500		
(6)	1,000		

TREASURY SHARES

	Debit	Credit	
	12,000		
(6)	12,000		

Supporting Journal Entries
(not required)

(1)	Operations	36,000	
	Working Capital	8,000	
	Retained Earnings		44,000
(2)	Retained Earnings Appropriated	100,000	
	Retained Earnings		100,000
	Non-working capital transaction; excluded from statement		
	(Section 1540.06)		
(3)	Retained Earnings	12,000	
	Working Capital		12,000
(4)	Retained Earnings	80,000	
	Common Shares		80,000
	Non-working capital transaction;		
	exclude from statement (Section 1540.06)		
(5)	Retained Earnings	3,500	
	Accumulated Depreciation — Office Equipment		3,500
	Error correction; exclude from statement		
(6)	Treasury Shares	12,000	
	Contributed Surplus	2,000	
	Retained Earnings	1,000	
	Working Capital		15,000
(7)	Accumulated Depreciation — Buildings	38,000	
	Working Capital	2,000	
	Buildings		40,000
(8)	Buildings	105,000	
	Working Capital		105,000
(9)	Working Capital	102,500	
	Building Expansion Fund Investments		96,000
	Operations		6,500
(10)	Delivery Equipment	6,000	
	Accumulated Depreciation — Delivery Equipment	2,000	
	Operations	800	
	Delivery Equipment		4,800
	Working Capital		4,000
(11)	Land	108,500	
	Preferred Shares		40,000
	Working Capital		68,500
	Note disclosure on statement		
(12)	Machinery and Equipment	12,000	
	Working Capital		12,000
(13)	Accumulated Depreciation — Machinery and Equipment	26,000	
	Working Capital		26,000
(14)	Operations (Amortization-Patents)	5,000	
	Operations (Depreciation)	31,900	
	Patents		5,000
	Accumulated Depreciation — Buildings		5,600
	Accumulated Depreciation — Machinery and Equipment		15,300
	Accumulated Depreciation — Delivery Equipment		8,000
	Accumulated Depreciation — Office Equipment		3,000
(15)	Office Equipment	8,000	
	Working Capital		8,000
(16)	Unamortized Bond Discount	3,000	
	Working Capital	57,000	
	Bonds Payable		60,000

(17)	Operations	300	
	Unamortized Bond Discount		300
(18)	Operations	6,000	
	Deferred Income Tax		6,000

The remaining steps, culminating in the preparation of the statement of changes, are essentially procedural. It should be noted that the acquisition of land by the issuance of preferred shares and cash provides an example of a transaction that does not in its entirety impact on working capital, but that nonetheless must be shown in full on the statement in order to assure disclosure of all significant financing and investing activities. As stated in step 10, the detail pertaining to working capital provided by operations is contained in the Operations T account; all sources and applications or uses of working capital appear in the Working Capital T account. At this point, these T accounts should appear as presented below.

WORKING CAPITAL

		7,500	DECREASE
(1)	8,000	12,000	(3)
(7)	2,000	15,000	(6)
(9)	102,500	105,000	(8)
(16)	57,000	4,000	(10)
OPERATIONS	73,500	68,500	(11)
		12,000	(12)
		26,000	(13)
		8,000	(15)
	243,000	250,500	
BALANCE	7,500		
	250,500	250,500	

OPERATIONS

(1)	36,000	6,500	(9)
(10)	800		
(14)	5,000		
(14)	31,900		
(17)	300		
(18)	6,000		
	80,000	6,500	
		73,500	
	80,000	80,000	

The statement of changes can now be prepared. In addition to the information contained in the above T accounts, re-examine transactions within the non-current balance sheet accounts to identify any additional disclosures that may be required. The resulting statement, of course, is identical to the one presented on page 863.

The "T" account method can perhaps best be described as a direct approach to the preparation of the statement of changes. With some streamlining, T accounting analysis provides a very time-efficient method for problem-solving purposes. For example, supporting journal entries are not required; postings to T accounts are all that is necessary. Moreover, depending upon the complexities involved, some of the individual T accounts may be omitted especially where the net change in an item is the result of a single transaction.

1. Describe the statement of changes in financial position. What information does it offer that is not provided by the income statement? What information does it offer that is not provided by comparative balance sheets?

2. What different concepts for funds may be applied in preparing the statement of changes in financial position? Describe the statement under each of the different fund concepts. Which approach do you support?

3. What is the "all financial resources" concept of funds? How does use of this concept improve funds statement disclosure?

4. What are the major categories of funds flows for a business entity?

5. Why must all "non-funds" account balances be analysed in preparing a funds statement?

6. Name a source of funds originating from a transaction involving (a) non-current assets, (b) non-current liabilities, (c) capital stock, (d) retained earnings. Name an application of funds identified with each group.

7. What three classes of adjustments are usually necessary in preparing the statement of changes in financial position?

8. (a) What adjustments are applied to the operating income figure when the funds statement summarizes working capital flow? (b) What adjustments are applied to operating income when the funds statement summarizes cash flow?

9. The Canadian Co. had its worst year in 1980, operations resulting in a substantial loss. Nevertheless, without the sale of property items, borrowing, or the issue of additional shares, the company's working capital increased significantly. What possible explanation can you suggest for this increase?

10. Indicate how each of the following would be reported on a funds statement assuming that funds are regarded as working capital.
   (a) Land and buildings are acquired for cash equal to 40% of the purchase price and a long-term mortgage note for the balance.
   (b) Fully depreciated machinery is written off.
   (c) Long-term notes are due within the year and their classification is changed to current.
   (d) Share capital is issued in exchange for land.

11. What alternatives exist to using working papers in developing funds statements?

12. What uses might each of the following find for a cash-flow statement?
   (a) Manager of a small laundry.
   (b) Shareholder interested in regular dividends.
   (c) Bank granting short-term loans.
   (d) Officer of a labor union.

13. Should a funds statement be audited by accountants? Give your conclusion and reasons for your conclusion.

20-1. Assuming funds are defined as working capital, use the applicable symbol to indicate those transactions which generate funds (+), those which use funds (−), and those which have no effect on funds (0).

(a) Amortization of patents .... ____

(b) Amortization of bond premium .... ____

(c) Decrease in long-term liabilities .... ____

(d) Increase in accrued wages payable .... ____

(e) Increase in trade accounts receivable............................ ____

(f) Write-off of an account receivable against the allowance account .... ____

(g) Disposal of a plant asset at a loss................................ ____

(h) Issue of a stock dividend .... ____

(i) Declaration of a cash dividend for payment in the next fiscal period .. ____

For which items, if any, would you change your answer, assuming funds are now defined as cash? (CGA adapted)

20-2. State how each of the following items will be reflected on the statement of changes in financial position if funds are defined on (1) a working capital basis, and (2) a cash basis with full disclosure of all significant financing and investing activities.

(a) Marketable securities were purchased for $20,000.

(b) At the beginning of the year, equipment, net book value $7,000, was traded for non-similar equipment costing $15,000; a trade-in value of $3,000 is allowed on the old equipment, the balance of the purchase price to be paid in 12 monthly instalments.

(c) Buildings were acquired for $75,000, the company paying $40,000 cash and signing a 6% mortgage note payable in 5 years for the balance.

(d) Uncollectible accounts of $900 were written off against the allowance for doubtful accounts.

(e) Cash of $250,000 was paid on the purchase of business assets consisting of: merchandise, $90,000; furniture and fixtures, $30,000; land and buildings, $95,000; and goodwill, $35,000.

(f) A cash dividend of $5,000 was declared in the current period, payable at the beginning of the next period.

(g) An adjustment was made increasing Deferred Income Tax by $20,000.

(h) Accounts payable shows a decrease for the period of $15,000.

20-3. Give the adjustments needed for working papers in journal entry form for a statement of changes in financial position upon analysing the following account:

ACCOUNT Retained Earnings

DATE		ITEM	DEBIT	CREDIT	BALANCE DEBIT	BALANCE CREDIT
1980						
Jan.	1	Balance				760,000
Mar.	20	Correction for error in inventory at end of 1979		15,000		775,000
June	1	Stock dividend	200,000			575,000
Aug.	5	Discount on sale of treasury shares, par $150,000, for $125,000	25,000			550,000
Dec.	5	Cash dividends	50,000			500,000
	31	Appropriated for loss contingencies	100,000			400,000
	31	Net income		75,000		475,000

20-4. The McCord Company prepared for 1980 and 1979 the balance sheet data shown below:

	December 31	
	1980	1979
Cash	$ 116,500	$ 85,000
Marketable securities	23,000	140,000
Accounts receivable (net)	120,000	115,000
Merchandise inventory	250,000	218,000
Prepaid insurance	1,500	2,000
Buildings and equipment	1,838,500	1,450,000
Accumulated depreciation — buildings and equipment	(745,000)	(665,000)
Total	$1,604,500	$1,345,000
Accounts payable	$ 204,500	$ 315,000
Salaries payable	25,000	35,000
Notes payable — bank (current)	50,000	200,000
Mortgage payable	500,000	0
Capital stock, $5 par	800,000	800,000
Retained earnings (deficit)	25,000	(5,000)
Total	$1,604,500	$1,345,000

The cash needed to purchase the new equipment and to improve the company's working capital position was raised by selling marketable securities costing $117,000 for $120,000 and by issuing the mortgage. Equipment costing $25,000 with a net book value of $5,000 was sold for $6,000; the gain on sale was included in net income. The McCord Company paid cash dividends of $30,000 during the year and reported earnings of $60,000 for 1980. There were no entries in the retained earnings account other than to record the dividend and the net income for the year. Marketable securities are carried at cost which is lower than market.

Prepare funds statements without the use of working papers:

(a) On a working capital basis.

(b) On a cash basis.

20-5. A summary of revenue and expense for the Convoy Corporation for 1980 follows:

Sales	$1,500,000
Cost of goods manufactured and sold	700,000
Gross profit	$ 800,000
Selling, general, and administrative expenses	500,000
Income before income tax	$ 300,000
Income tax	130,000
Net income	$ 170,000

Net changes in working capital for 1980 were as follows:

	Dr.	Cr.
Cash	$ 26,000	
Trade accounts receivable (net)	100,000	
Inventories		$15,000
Prepaid expenses (selling and general)	2,500	
Accrued expenses (75% of increase related to manufacturing activities and 25% to general operating activities)		8,000
Income tax payable		12,000
Trade accounts payable		35,000

Depreciation on plant and equipment for the year totalled $150,000; 70% was related to manufacturing activities and 30% to general and administrative activities.

Prepare a summary of cash provided by operations for the year showing revenues and expenses in detail.

20-6. From the following information, give the necessary adjustments in journal entry form to explain the changes in accounts listed in preparing working papers for a statement of changes in financial position for 1980.

	Dec. 31 1980	Dec. 31 1979
Land	$ 25,000	$ 40,000
Buildings	100,000	100,000
Accumulated depreciation — buildings	68,500	62,500
Machinery	39,000	45,000
Accumulated depreciation — machinery	15,500	16,000
Delivery equipment	15,000	25,000
Accumulated depreciation — delivery equipment	6,500	12,500
Tools	14,000	12,000
Patents	3,500	4,500
Goodwill	0	40,000
Discount on bonds payable	0	6,000
Bonds payable	0	500,000
Share capital	350,000	250,000
Treasury shares	22,000	0
Retained earnings appropriated for bond retirement fund ..	0	100,000
Retained earnings	179,500	180,000

ACCOUNT Retained Earnings

DATE		ITEM	DEBIT	CREDIT	BALANCE	
					DEBIT	CREDIT
1980						
Jan.	1	Balance				180,000
		Stock dividend	100,000			80,000
		Retained earnings appropriated for bond retirement fund ...		100,000		180,000
		Premium on purchase of treasury shares, par $22,000 ...	8,000			172,000
		Cash dividends	10,000			162,000
Dec.	31	Net income		17,500		179,500

The income statement reports depreciation of buildings, $6,000; depreciation of machinery, $4,000; depreciation of delivery equipment, $2,000; tools amortization, $4,000; patents amortization, $1,000; and bond discount amortization, $1,000. The income statement also reports the following:

Operating income		$ 40,000
Other revenue and expense items:		
Gain on sale of land, cost $15,000, sold for $100,000 ...	$85,000	
Gain on sale of delivery equipment, cost $10,000, net book		
value $2,000, sold for $7,000	5,000	90,000
		$130,000
Loss on scrapping machinery, cost $6,000, on which accu-		
mulated depreciation of $4,500 had been recognized ..	$ 1,500	
Goodwill written off	$40,000	41,500
Income before income tax		$ 88,500
Income tax		36,000
Income before extraordinary items		$ 52,500
Extraordinary loss on bond retirement (unamortized discount,		
$5,000 and call premium, $30,000)		35,000
Net income		$ 17,500

20-7. Information relating to Regal Co. Ltd. for the year ended December 31, 1981 is as follows:

(a) Net income for the year — $240,000.

(b) Fixed asset accounts at the year end were:

	1981	1980
Machinery and equipment	$1,160,000	$1,000,000
Buildings	580,000	500,000
Land	50,000	40,000
Construction in progress	——	150,000
	1,790,000	1,690,000
Less: Accumulated Depreciation	541,400	400,000
	$1,248,600	$1,290,000

(c) Construction in progress at December 31, 1980, included the cost to date of $40,000 for an addition to the company's main building and $110,000 for equipment in the addition. Upon completion of the addition in June 1981 the construction costs were transferred to the appropriate accounts.

(d) During 1981, equipment was disposed of as follows:

Turret lathe, purchased in 1976 for $32,000, sold for $10,000.
Punch press, purchased in 1979 for $24,000, sold for $20,000.
Dynamo, purchased in 1976 for $6,000, abandoned as useless.

The adjustments necessary to reflect the disposals have been made, with gains and losses being charged to operations. Depreciation is always provided annually on a straight-line basis at 10% on the closing balances in the fixed asset accounts.

(e) A credit of $8,000 appeared in the buildings account. This represented a refund of an amount billed twice in error during March 1981.

(f) A debit of $7,000 appeared in the accumulated depreciation account during the year. This represented the cost of two electric motors. These motors replaced two similar motors purchased 12 years ago for approximately the same cost, and which are now fully depreciated.

(g) Cost of buildings includes $14,000 architects' fees which were paid by the issue of 2,000 no par value shares of Regal Co. Ltd.

(h) The following other transactions also occurred during the year or at the year end:

    (1) Allowance for doubtful accounts increased by $2,000.

    (2) Patent rights purchased for $13,500.

    (3) Amortization of patent rights of $2,100.

    (4) Mortgage bonds converted to preference shares — $25,400.

    (5) Mortgage bonds redeemed — $38,600.

    (6) Franchise agreement acquired through issue of $11,000 mortgage bonds.

    (7) Received an income tax refund of $2,400.

    (8) Dividend of $41,200 paid by the issue of preference shares.

Prepare the funds provided by operations section of the statement of changes in financial position for the year ended December 31, 1981. Use the working capital concept of funds.

20-8. Using the information provided in Exercise 7, prepare a complete statement of changes in financial position using the working capital concept of funds.

20-9. An accounting student is having difficulty preparing a Statement of Changes in Financial Position — Working Capital Basis — for Prairie Company Limited. The student has correctly made the necessary calculations for the various items, but is unable to put the statement together. Using the student's calculations indicated below, prepare a Statement of Changes in Financial Position — Working Capital Basis — for Prairie Company Limited, as at December 31, 1980.

Proceeds from sale of equipment	$ 6,000
Proceeds from stock issue for cash	20,000
Income before extraordinary items	12,000
Purchase of land	14,000
Long-term note paid	8,000
Long-term investments sold (extraordinary item)	16,000
Amortization and depreciation	12,000
Loss on sale of subsidiary (extraordinary item)	2,000
Equipment purchases	10,000
Long-term note given for equipment	26,000
Common shares issued for land	30,000
Cash dividends declared	8,000

(CGA adapted)

20-10. The records of Browne Company Ltd. show the following information relating to balance sheet accounts.

	December 31	
Debits	1980	1981
Cash	$ 10,000	$ 11,000
Accounts receivable (net)	19,000	24,000
Inventory	52,000	50,000
Prepaid expense	3,000	4,000
Long-term investments	10,000	——
Buildings	90,000	120,000
Machinery	40,000	62,000
Patents	5,000	4,000
	$229,000	$275,000

Accounts payable	$ 12,000	$ 8,000
Notes payable — short-term (nontrade)	9,000	13,000
Accrued wages	3,000	2,000
Accumulated depreciation	40,000	39,000
Notes payable — long-term	30,000	35,000
Common shares	120,000	150,000
Retained earnings	15,000	28,000
	$229,000	$275,000

Additional data pertaining to transactions during 1981 is as follows:

(a) Net income for 1981 was $24,000.

(b) Sales of $120,000 were made on account.

(c) Amortization of patents amounted to $1,000.

(d) Purchased machinery costing $15,000; paid one-third in cash and gave a five-year interest-bearing note for the balance.

(e) Purchased machinery costing $25,000, which was paid for by issuing common shares.

(f) Collections on accounts receivable amounted to $115,000.

(g) Paid contractor $30,000 cash, for building addition.

(h) Issued common shares in payment of a $5,000 long-term note.

(i) Sold permanent investment for $12,000 cash (gain or loss reported on the income statement).

(j) Paid cash dividends of $11,000.

(k) Depreciation recorded on fixed assets was $8,000.

(l) Sold old machinery that originally cost $18,000 (one-half depreciated), for $7,000. (The loss or gain was reported on the income statement.)

Assuming funds are defined as working capital, prepare a Statement of Changes in Financial Position for Browne Company Ltd., for the year ended December 31, 1981.

(SMA adapted)

PROBLEMS

20-1A. Comparative balance sheet data for the firm of Collins and Jones are given below.

	December 31	
	1980	1979
Cash	$ 5,400	$ 3,900
Accounts receivable	8,800	10,200
Inventory	45,000	30,000
Prepaid expenses	1,200	1,700
Furniture and fixtures	25,800	16,000
Accumulated depreciation	(13,550)	(10,050)
Total	$72,650	$51,750

	December 31	
	1980	1979
Accrued expenses	$ 2,600	$ 1,900
Accounts payable	7,650	9,950
Long-term note	7,000	0
Fenley Jones, capital	20,550	19,550
Peter Collins, capital	34,850	20,350
Total	$72,650	$51,750

Income from operations for the year was $15,000 and this was transferred in equal amounts to the partners' capital accounts. Further changes in the capital accounts arose from additional investments and withdrawals by the partners. The change in the furniture and fixtures account arose from a purchase of additional furniture; part of the purchase price was paid in cash and a long-term note was issued for the balance.

Instructions:
Prepare the following (working papers are not required):
(1) A statement of changes in financial position applying the working capital concept of funds.
(2) A statement of changes in financial position applying the cash concept of funds.

20-2A. Ortiz's Optical reported net income of $12,320 for 1980 but has been showing an overdraft in its bank account in recent months. The manager has contacted you as the auditor for an explanation. The information below was given to you for examination.

Ortiz's Optical
Comparative Balance Sheet
December 31

	1980			1979	
Assets					
Current assets:					
Cash		$(1,920)			$ 9,560
Accounts receivable		8,000			2,000
Inventory		4,700			1,500
Prepaid insurance		140			390
Total current assets			$10,920		$13,450
Land, buildings, and equipment:					
Land		$25,000			$25,000
Buildings	$50,000			$50,000	
Less accumulated depreciation	30,000	20,000		28,000	22,000
Equipment	$74,500			$61,700	
Less accumulated depreciation	45,000	29,500		36,800	24,900
Total land, buildings, and equipment			74,500		71,900
Total assets			$85,420		$85,350
Liabilities and Shareholders' Equity					
Current liabilities:					
Accounts payable		$ 8,500			$ 7,000
Taxes payable		2,800			4,700
Wages payable		1,500			3,350
Notes payable — current portion		3,000			7,000
Total current liabilities			$15,800		$22,050
Long-term liabilities:					
Notes payable		21,000			23,000
Share capital		$35,000			$30,000
Retained earnings		13,620			10,300
Total shareholders' equity			48,620		40,300
Total liabilities and shareholders' equity			$85,420		$85,350

You also determine the following:

(a) Equipment was sold for $3,000; its cost was $5,000 and its net book value was $1,000. The gain was reported as Other Revenue.
(b) Cash dividends of $9,000 were paid.

Instructions:

Prepare the following (working papers are not required):

(1) A statement of changes in financial position applying the working capital concept of funds.
(2) A statement of changes in financial position applying the cash concept of funds.

20-3A. Comparative balance sheet data for Camera, Ltd., follow:

	December 31	
	1980	1979
Cash	$ 22,500	$ 40,000
Accounts receivable	60,000	50,000
Inventory	75,000	62,500
Prepaid expenses	12,500	10,000
Land, buildings, and equipment	160,000	95,000
Accumulated depreciation	(45,000)	(35,000)
	$285,000	$222,500
Accrued expenses	$ 7,500	$ 5,000
Accounts payable	52,500	42,500
Bonds payable	20,000	50,000
Share capital, at par	125,000	100,000
Contributed surplus	25,000	10,000
Retained earnings	55,000	15,000
	$285,000	$222,500

Land and buildings were acquired in exchange for share capital; the assets were recorded at $40,000, their appraised value. Equipment was acquired for $25,000 cash. Net income for the year transferred to retained earnings was $55,000; cash dividends accounted for the remaining change in retained earnings.

Instructions:

Prepare the following (working papers are not required):

(1) A statement of changes in financial position applying the working capital concept of funds.
(2) A statement of changes in financial position applying the cash concept of funds.

20-4A. The Hubbard Company presented the following comparative information:

	1980	1979
Cash	$174,000	$150,000
Accounts receivable	95,000	80,000
Inventory (lower of cost or market)	180,000	175,000
Land, buildings, and equipment (net)	315,000	350,000
Current liabilities	(210,000)	(215,000)
Bonds payable	0	(200,000)
Bond premium	0	(6,000)
Common shares, $50 par	(450,000)	(250,000)
Contributed surplus	(35,000)	(15,000)
Retained earnings	(69,000)	(69,000)

ACCOUNT Retained Earnings

DATE		ITEM	DEBIT	CREDIT	BALANCE	
					DEBIT	CREDIT
1979						
Jan.	1	Balance				69,000
		Cash dividends paid during the				
		year	10,000			59,000
		Correction of prior period inven-				
		tory understatement		20,000		79,000
		Loss (including $15,000 loss on				
		bond conversion)	10,000			69,000

Buildings, with a net book value of $80,000, were sold for $130,000 cash. Land was acquired from the proceeds of the sale for $60,000. Depreciation recorded for the year was $15,000. The bonds payable were converted to common shares on December 31, 1980, after the annual bond premium amortization of $1,000 had been recorded. The conversion privilege provided for exchange of a $1,000 bond for 20 shares. Market value of the shares on December 31, 1980, was $55 per share.

Instructions:
Prepare a funds statement applying the working capital concept of funds (working papers are not required).

20-5A. The data below were taken from the records of the Newbold Company. Income statement data for the year ended December 31, 1980, summarized operations as follows:

Income before extraordinary items	$14,650
Extraordinary loss on retirement of bonds	3,500
Net income	$11,150

Balance Sheet
December 31

	1980		1979	
Current assets		$185,200		$148,300
Land, buildings, and equipment	$100,500		$96,000	
Less accumulated depreciation	34,000	66,500	30,000	66,000
Investments in shares and bonds		32,000		35,000
Goodwill		0		25,000
Total assets		$283,700		$274,300
Current liabilities		$ 58,800		$ 43,300
Bonds payable		0		50,000
Unamortized bond discount		0		(1,250)
Preferred shares, $100 par		0		50,000
Common shares, $10 par		165,000		105,000
Contributed surplus		40,000		0
Retained earnings		19,900		27,250
Total liabilities and shareholders' equity		$283,700		$274,300

ACCOUNT Retained Earnings

DATE		ITEM	DEBIT	CREDIT	BALANCE DEBIT	BALANCE CREDIT
1980 Jan.	1	Balance				27,250
		Premium on retirement of pre-				
		ferred shares	1,000			26,250
		Cash dividends	17,500			8,750
		Net income		11,150		19,900

Fully depreciated equipment, original cost $10,500, was traded in on similar new equipment costing $16,500; $1,500 was allowed by the vendor on the trade-in. One hundred shares of Byler Co. preferred, cost $20,000, held as a long-term investment, were sold at a loss of $2,500 at the beginning of the year. Additional changes in the investments account resulted from the purchase of Carbon Co. bonds. The company issued common shares in April, and part of the proceeds was used to retire preferred shares at 102 shortly thereafter. On July 1, the company called in its bonds outstanding, paying a premium of 5% on the call. Discount amortization on the bonds to the date of call was $250. Depreciation for the year on buildings and equipment was $14,500. Goodwill was judged worthless and was written off.

Instructions:

Prepare working papers and a statement of changes in financial position applying the working capital concept of funds.

20-6A. The following information is assembled for the Window Garden Corporation.

	Balance Sheet December 31 1980		Balance Sheet December 31 1979	
Cash (overdraft in 1979)		$ 38,625		$(5,625)
Accounts receivable		82,000		95,500
Inventories		73,250		50,000
Long-term investments		12,000		27,000
Land, buildings, and equipment	$130,000		$95,000	
Less accumulated depreciation	21,500	108,500	20,000	75,000
Patents		0		35,000
Total assets		$314,375		$276,875
Accounts payable		$ 55,875		$ 49,375
Bonds payable		50,000		20,000
Premium on bonds payable		2,375		0
Preferred shares, $100 par		0		50,000
Common shares, $10 par		160,000		100,000
Premium on common shares		24,000		0
Retained earnings		22,125		57,500
Total liabilities and shareholders' equity		$314,375		$276,875

ACCOUNT Retained Earnings

DATE		ITEM	DEBIT	CREDIT	BALANCE	
					DEBIT	CREDIT
1980						
Jan.	1	Balance				57,500
Oct.	15	Cash dividends	25,000			32,500
Dec.	12	Premium on retirement of pre-				
		ferred shares	5,000			27,500
Dec.	31	Loss	5,375			22,125

Income statement data for the year ended December 31, 1980, summarized operations as follows:

Loss before extraordinary items	$4,375
Extraordinary loss on retirement of bonds	1,000
Loss	$5,375

Equipment, cost $15,000, net book value $3,000, was scrapped, salvage of $900 being recovered on the disposal. Additional equipment, cost $50,000, was acquired during the year. Long-term investments, cost $15,000, were sold for $18,250; 7% bonds, face value $20,000, were called in at 105, and new 10-year, 5% bonds of $50,000 were issued at 105 on July 1. Preferred shares were retired at a cost of 110 while 6,000 common shares were issued at $14. Depreciation on buildings and equipment for the year was $13,500. Patents, costing $35,000, were written off.

Instructions:
(1) Prepare working papers and a statement of changes in financial position applying the working capital concept of funds.
(2) Prepare a statement of changes in financial position applying the cash concept of funds.

20-7A. The Andersen Company prepared the comparative balance sheet shown on page 888 and the combined statement of income and retained earnings shown on page 889.
(a) The tax refund from correction of the inventory overstatement was received in cash during 1980.
(b) The usual annual cash dividend of $50,000 was declared on December 15, 1980, and paid on January 31, 1981.
(c) The 10% stock dividend was declared when Andersen Company stock was selling for $15 per share.
(d) Equipment costing $300,000 with a net book value of $220,000 was destroyed in an extraordinary disaster. The deferred income tax related to the difference between capital cost allowance and depreciation taken on the equipment was $35,000. This reduced the book income tax credit on the loss from $80,000 to an actual tax credit of $45,000. New equipment was purchased with cash raised by selling marketable securities, cost $150,000, for $145,000 and by taking out the mortgage for the balance due. The mortgage is due in 10 annual instalments of $20,000.

Andersen Company
Comparative Balance Sheet
December 31

	1980		1979	
Assets				
Current assets:				
Cash		$ 320,000		$ 154,000
Marketable securities (cost)	$ 90,000		$160,000	
Less allowance for decline in value of marketable securities	8,000		10,000	
Marketable securities (market)		82,000		150,000
Accounts receivable (net)		640,000		520,000
Inventories (lower of cost or market)		540,000		670,000
Prepaid expenses.....................................		6,000		8,000
Total current assets		$1,588,000		$1,502,000
Land, buildings, and equipment:				
Land		$ 50,000		$ 50,000
Buildings..	$825,000		$800,000	
Less accumulated depreciation — buildings	215,000	610,000	225,000	575,000
Machinery and equipment	$425,000		$380,000	
Less accumulated depreciation — machinery and equipment	75,000	350,000	120,000	260,000
Total land, buildings, and equipment		$1,010,000		$ 885,000
Investment in Tow Company (equity)		$ 970,000		$ 800,000
Goodwill		55,000		60,000
		$1,025,000		$ 860,000
Total assets		$3,623,000		$3,247,000
Liabilities				
Current liabilites:				
Accounts payable		$ 464,000		$ 407,000
Mortgage payable in 6 months		20,000		
Income tax payable		115,000		150,000
Accrued payables.....................................		80,000		75,000
Dividends payable		50,000		50,000
Estimated liability under service contracts (current)		65,000		60,000
Long-term liabilities:				
Mortgage payable.....................................		180,000		
Debenture bonds payable..............................	$500,000		$500,000	
Plus unamortized premium	5,500	505,500	6,000	506,000
Long-term liability under service contracts		287,500		242,000
Other long-term liabilities:				
Deferred income tax		124,000		134,000
Total liabilities		$1,891,000		$1,624,000
Shareholders' Equity				
Common shares, $10 par	$880,000		$800,000	
Contributed surplus	240,000		200,000	
Retained earnings	612,000	1,732,000	623,000	1,623,000
Total liabilities and shareholders' equity		$3,623,000		$3,247,000

Andersen Company
Income and Retained Earnings Statement
For Year Ended December 31, 1980

Income before extraordinary items		$319,000✓
Extraordinary loss on equipment (net of income tax credit of $80,000)		140,000
Net income		$179,000
Unadjusted retained earnings, January 1, 1980........................	$623,000	
Deduct: Prior period adjustment — correction of inventory overstatement, net of income tax refund of $18,000.........................	20,000	603,000
Adjusted retained earnings, January 1, 1980		$782,000
Deduct: Dividends declared..	$ 50,000	
10% stock dividend	120,000	170,000
Retained earnings, December 31, 1980		$612,000

(e) The allowance account for the decline in value of marketable securities was adjusted at year-end by a credit to the income account, Unrealized Gain on Marketable Securities.

(f) The ending inventory was written down by $50,000 to properly value the inventory at the lower of cost or market.

(g) Tow Company, in which Andersen Company holds a 35% interest, paid dividends of $600,000 and reported earnings of $800,000 during 1980. Andersen Company made an additional investment in Tow Company on December 31, 1980.

(h) A warehouse costing $200,000, with a net book value of $150,000 was destroyed by fire. The insurance proceeds were $210,000 cash. There was no tax on the gain on the old warehouse. A new warehouse costing $225,000 was built during the same year.

(i) Depreciation and amortization for 1980 were as follows:

Buildings	$40,000✓
Machinery and equipment	35,000✓
Goodwill	5,000✓
Premium on bonds payable	500✓

Instructions:
Prepare working papers and a statement of changes in financial position applying the cash concept of funds.

20-8A. Financial data for the Logan Manufacturing Co. are presented on page 890.

(a) Ten-year bonds of $100,000 had been issued on July 1, 1978, at 95. Additional 10-year bonds of $125,000 had been issued on July 1, 1980, at 94.

(b) Machinery no longer needed was sold for $7,000 in 1980; the machinery had an original cost of $13,000 and accumulated depreciation on the date of the sale totalled $5,000.

(c) Fully depreciated storage quarters were dismantled during the year; thus buildings, cost $2,000, were written off against the accumulated depreciation

Logan Manufacturing Co.
Comparative Balance Sheet
December 31

	1980		1979	
Assets				
Cash		$ 33,550		$ 65,000
Accounts receivable	$ 53,000		$ 27,625	
Less allowance for doubtful accounts	2,500	50,500	2,125	25,500
Inventories		75,000		32,000
Office supplies		5,000		1,500
Miscellaneous prepaid expenses (selling and general)		3,500		3,000
Long-term investments		115,000		20,000
Land		75,000		25,000
Buildings..	$124,500		$ 90,000	
Less accumulated depreciation	40,000	84,500	36,000	54,000
Machinery	$ 95,000		$ 75,000	
Less accumulated depreciation	44,000	51,000	40,000	35,000
Goodwill				50,000
Total assets		$493,050		$311,000
Liabilities and Shareholders' Equity				
Accounts payable		$ 23,000		$ 25,000
Miscellaneous accrued expenses (selling and general)		6,500		4,000
Income tax payable		20,000		10,000
Bonds payable	$225,000		$100,000	
Less bond discount	10,875	214,125	4,250	95,750
Capital stock, $10 par		150,000		100,000
Contributed surplus		55,000		30,000
Retained earnings		24,425		46,250
Total liabilities and shareholders' equity		$493,050		$311,000

Logan Manufacturing Co.
Condensed Income Statement
For Year Ended December 31, 1980

Sales		$218,900
Less expenses:		
Cost of goods sold (includes depreciation of machinery, $9,000, and depreciation of buildings, $6,000)	$118,000	
Selling, general, and administrative expenses	40,225	158,225
Operating income		$ 60,675
Other revenue and expense items:		
Gain on sale of investments		2,500
		$ 63,175
Loss on sale of machinery	$ 1,000	
Goodwill written off..	50,000	51,000
Income before income tax		$ 12,175
Income tax		18,000
Loss		$ 5,825

of buildings account. Long-term investments in outside companies that cost $16,000 were sold at the beginning of the year for $18,500, and additional long-term investments were subsequently made during the year. Additional capital stock was issued by the company during the year at 15 in order to raise working capital.

Instructions:
(1) Prepare working papers and a statement of changes in financial position applying the working capital concept of funds.
(2) Prepare working papers and a statement of changes in financial position applying the cash concept of funds and reporting revenue and expense detail.

20-9A. Bencivenga Company has prepared its financial statements for the year ended December 31, 1979, and for the three months ended March 31, 1980. You have been asked to prepare a statement of changes in financial position on a working capital basis for the three months ended March 31, 1980. The company's balance sheet data at December 31, 1979, and March 31, 1980, and its income statement data for the three months ended March 31, 1980, follow. You have previously satisfied yourself as to the accuracy of the amounts presented.

The balance sheet data are as follows:

	March 31, 1980	December 31, 1979
Cash	$ 87,400	$ 25,300
Marketable securities	7,300	16,500
Accounts receivable (net)	49,320	24,320
Inventory	48,590	31,090
Total current assets	$192,610	$ 97,210
Land	18,700	40,000
Buildings	250,000	250,000
Equipment	81,500	
Accumulated depreciation	(16,250)	(15,000)
Investment in 30% owned company	67,100	61,220
Other assets	15,100	15,100
Total	$608,760	$448,530
Accounts payable	$ 17,330	$ 21,220
Dividends payable	8,000	
Income tax payable	34,616	
Total current liabilities	$ 59,946	$ 21,220
Other liabilities	186,000	186,000
Bonds payable	115,000	50,000
Discount on bonds payable	(2,150)	(2,300)
Deferred income tax	846	510
Preferred shares		30,000
Common shares	110,000	80,000
Dividends declared	(8,000)	
Retained earnings	147,118	83,100
Total	$608,760	$448,530

Income statement data for the three months ended March 31, 1980, are as follows:

Sales	$242,807
Gain on sale of marketable securities (capital gain)	2,400
Equity in earnings of 30% — owned company	5,880
Gain on condemnation of land (capital gain)	10,700
	$261,787
Cost of goods sold	$138,407
General and administrative expenses	22,010
Depreciation	1,250
Interest expense	1,150
Income tax	34,952
	$197,769
Net income	$ 64,018

Your discussion with the company's controller and a review of the financial records revealed the following information:

(a) On January 8, 1980, the company sold marketable securities for cash.
(b) The company's preferred stock is convertible into common stock at a rate of one share of preferred for two shares of common. The preferred shares and common shares have par values of $2 and $1 respectively.
(c) On January 17, 1980, three acres of land were extraordinarily condemned. An award of $32,000 in cash was received on March 22, 1980.
(d) On March 25, 1980, the company purchased equipment for cash.
(e) On March 29, 1980, bonds payable were issued by the company at par for cash.
(f) The investment in the 30% owned company included an amount attributable to goodwill of $3,220 at December 31, 1979. Goodwill is being amortized at an annual rate of $480. For tax purposes, the equity in earnings, $5,880, is a timing difference.
(g) The company's tax rate is 40%.

Instructions:
Prepare in good form a statement of changes in financial position, including any supporting schedules needed, on a working capital basis for Bencivenga Company for the three months ended March 31, 1980. (AICPA adapted)

20-10A. The following schedule showing net changes in balance sheet accounts at December 31, 1980, compared to December 31, 1979, was prepared from the records of the Sodium Company. The statement of changes in financial position for the year ended December 31, 1980, has not yet been prepared.

	Increase (Decrease)
Assets	
Cash	$ 50,000
Accounts receivable (net)	76,000
Inventories	37,000
Prepaid expenses	1,000
Property, plant, and equipment (net)	64,000
Total assets	$228,000

	Increase (Decrease)
Liabilities	
Accounts payable	$ (55,500)
Notes payable — current	(15,000)
Accrued expenses	33,000
Bonds payable	(28,000)
Less unamortized bond discount	1,200
Total liabilities	$ (64,300)
Shareholders' Equity	
Common shares, $10 par	$500,000
Capital in excess of par value	200,000
Retained earnings	(437,700)
Appropriation of retained earnings for possible future inventory price	
decline	30,000
Total shareholders' equity	$292,300
Total liabilities and shareholders' equity	$228,000

Additional information includes:

(a) The net income for the year ended December 31, 1980, was $172,300. There were no extraordinary items.

(b) During the year ended December 31, 1980, uncollectible accounts receivable of $26,400 were written off by a debit to Allowance for Doubtful Accounts.

(c) A comparison of Property, Plant, and Equipment as of the end of each year follows:

	December 31		
			Increase
	1980	1979	(Decrease)
Property, plant, and equipment	$570,500	$510,000	$60,500
Less accumulated depreciation	224,500	228,000	(3,500)
Property, plant, and equipment (net)	$346,000	$282,000	$64,000

During 1980, machinery was purchased at a cost of $45,000. In addition, machinery that was acquired in 1973 at a cost of $48,000 was sold for $3,600. At the date of sale, the machinery had an undepreciated cost of $4,200. The remaining increase in Property, Plant, and Equipment resulted from the acquisition of a tract of land for a new plant site.

(d) The bonds payable mature at the rate of $28,000 every year.

(e) In January, 1980, the company issued an additional 10,000 shares of its common shares at $14 per share upon the exercise of outstanding stock options held by key employees. In May 1980, the company declared and issued a 5% stock dividend on its outstanding shares. During the year, a cash dividend was paid on the common shares. On December 31 1980, there were 840,000 shares of common shares outstanding.

(f) The appropriation of retained earnings for possible future inventory price declines was provided by a debit to Retained Earnings, in anticipation of an expected future drop in the market related to goods in inventory.

Instructions:

(1) Prepare a statement of changes in financial position for the year ended December 31, 1980, based upon the information presented. The statement should be prepared using a working capital format.

(2) Prepare a schedule of changes in working capital for the year 1980.

(AICPA adapted).

20-11A. The schedule below shows the account balances of the Relgne Corporation at the beginning and end of the fiscal year ended October 31, 1980.

The following information was also available:

(a) All purchases and sales were on account.

(b) The sinking fund will be used to retire the long-term bonds.

(c) Equipment with an original cost of $15,000 was sold for $7,000.

Debits	October 31, 1980	November 1, 1979	Increase (Decrease)
Cash	$ 226,000	$ 50,000	$176,000
Accounts receivable	148,000	100,000	48,000
Inventories	291,000	300,000	(9,000)
Prepaid insurance	2,500	2,000	500
Long-term investments (at cost)	10,000	40,000	(30,000)
Sinking fund	90,000	80,000	10,000
Land and building	195,000	195,000	
Equipment	215,000	90,000	125,000
Discount on bonds payable	8,500	9,000	(500)
Treasury shares (at cost)	5,000	10,000	(5,000)
Cost of goods sold	539,000		
Selling and general expenses	287,000		
Income tax	35,000		
Loss on sale of equipment	1,000		
Total debits	$2,053,000	$876,000	

Credits			
Allowance for doubtful accounts	$ 8,000	$ 5,000	$ 3,000
Accumulated depreciation — building	26,250	22,500	3,750
Accumulated depreciation — equipment ...	39,750	27,500	12,250
Accounts payable	55,000	60,000	(5,000)
Notes payable — current	70,000	20,000	50,000
Miscellaneous expenses payable	18,000	15,000	3,000
Taxes payable	35,000	10,000	25,000
Unearned revenue	1,000	9,000	(8,000)
Note payable — long-term	40,000	60,000	(20,000)
Bonds payable — long-term	250,000	250,000	
Common shares	300,000	200,000	100,000
Retained earnings appropriated for sinking fund	90,000	80,000	10,000
Unappropriated retained earnings	94,000	112,000	(18,000)
Capital in excess of par value	116,000	5,000	111,000
Sales	898,000		
Gain on sale of investments	12,000		
Total credits	$2,053,000	$876,000	

(d) Selling and general expenses include the following expenses:

Building depreciation	$ 3,750
Equipment depreciation	19,250
Doubtful accounts expense	4,000
Interest expense	18,000

(e) A six-months note payable for $50,000 was issued toward the purchase of new equipment.

(f) The long-term note payable requires the payment of $20,000 per year plus interest until paid.

(g) Treasury shares were sold for $1,000 more than cost.

(h) All dividends were paid by cash.

Instructions:

(1) Prepare schedules computing: (a) collections of accounts receivable; (b) payments of accounts payable.

(2) Prepare a statement of changes in financial position applying the cash concept of funds. Supporting computations should be in good form. (AICPA adapted)

20-12A. You have been contacted by the president of Boulder Company, Ltd. This cornpany has never retained the services of an accountant; all financial statements and tax returns having been prepared by the comptroller.

The president is disturbed that the net working capital and cash balances at December 31, 1980, are substantially lower than those of the previous year despite the fact that the income for 1980 before tax of $176,500 was $350,000.

You have been given the financial statements shown below and on page 890 and have satisfied yourself as to the accuracy of the figures shown.

Boulder Company, Ltd.
Comparative Balance Sheet
December 31

	1980	1979	Increase (Decrease)
Assets			
Cash in bank	$ 42,000	$129,000	$(87,000)
Accounts receivable (net of allowance for doubtful accounts)	133,000	85,500	47,500
Inventories	192,000	152,500	39,500
Land, buildings, and equipment (net of accumulated depreciation)	500,000	260,000	240,000
Deposits — utilities	4,000	3,200	800
Prepaid expenses	21,000	14,000	7,000
Total assets	$892,000	$644,200	$247,800
Liabilities and Shareholders' Equity			
Accounts payable and miscellaneous payables	$263,000	$220,850	$ 42,150
Income tax payable	176,500	61,850	114,650
Mortgage payable	——	125,000	(125,000)
Capital stock	150,000	100,000	50,000
Retained earnings	302,500	136,500	166,000
Total liabilities and shareholders' equity	$892,000	$644,200	$247,800

Boulder Company, Ltd.
Retained Earnings Statement
For Year Ended December 31, 1980

Balance, January 1, 1980	$136,500
Add net income for the year	173,500
	$310,000
Deduct dividends paid	7,500
Balance, December 31, 1980	$302,500

You also have obtained the following information:

(a) At December 31, the accumulated depreciation on fixed assets was $180,000 in 1980 and $160,000 in 1979. Machinery costing $20,000, which was one-half depreciated, was abandoned and written off in 1980. Manufacturing costs absorbed depreciation of $27,000 and selling and administrative expense absorbed $3,000.

(b) In 1980, sales were $3,300,000; cost of goods sold was $2,650,000 and selling and administrative expense (excluding taxes) was $290,000.

(c) On January 2, 1980, two insurance policies on material stored in a public warehouse were cancelled. The unexpired premiums on these policies amounted to $2,000, and refund of this amount was received from the insurance company. Insurance charged to manufacturing expense was $4,000 and to selling and administrative expense $500 for the year. Other prepaid expense write-offs were $12,000 to manufacturing expense.

(d) The balance in the allowance for doubtful accounts at each year-end was 5% of the gross amount of receivables. Write-off of receivables amounted to $2,300 in 1980.

Instructions:

(1) Prepare a statement reporting the changes in financial position accounting for the decrease in working capital.

(2) Prepare a statement reporting the changes in financial position accounting for the decrease in cash. Support this statement with details in good form showing how you arrived at cash required for sales, cost of goods sold, and expenses. (AICPA adapted)

20-13A. The comparative balance sheet for the Plainview Corporation is shown on page 897. Your working papers and other sources disclose additional information on 1980 activities:

(a) The retained earnings account was analysed as shown below.

Retained earnings, December 31, 1979		$758,200
Add net income		236,580
		$994,780
Deduct:		
Cash dividends	$130,000	
Loss on reissue of treasury stock	3,000	
10% stock dividend	100,200	$233,220
Retained earnings, December 31, 1980		$761,580

Plainview Corporation
Comparative Balance Sheet
December 31

	1980	1979	Increase (Decrease)
Assets			
Cash	$ 142,100	$ 165,300	$ (23,200)
Marketable securities (at cost)	122,800	129,200	(6,400)
Accounts receivable (net)	312,000	371,200	(59,200)
Inventories	255,200	124,100	131,100
Prepaid expenses	23,400	22,000	1,400
Bond sinking fund		63,000	(63,000)
Investment in subsidiary (at equity)	134,080	152,000	(17,920)
Land, buildings, and equipment (net) ...	1,443,700	1,534,600	(90,900)
Total assets	$2,433,280	$2,561,400	$(128,120)
Liabilities and Shareholders' Equity			
Accounts payable	$ 238,100	$ 213,300	$ 24,800
Notes payable — current		145,000	(145,000)
Miscellaneous payables	16,500	18,000	(1,500)
Income tax payable	97,500	31,000	66,500
Deferred income tax	53,900	43,400	10,500
6% Mortgage bonds (due 1992)		300,000	(300,000)
Premium on mortgage bonds		10,000	(10,000)
8% Debentures (due 2000)	125,000		125,000
Liability for estimated casualty losses ...	74,000	85,000	(11,000)
Common shares, $10 par value	1,033,500	950,000	83,500
Premium on common shares	67,700	51,000	16,700
Retained earnings	761,580	758,200	3,380
Treasury stock — at cost of $3 per share	(34,500)	(43,500)	9,000
Total liabilities and shareholders' equity .	$2,433,280	$2,561,400	$(128,120)

You noted that the client's determination of net income complied with Section 3480 of the *Accounting Recommendations*.

(b) On January 2, 1980, marketable securities costing $110,000 were sold for $127,000. The proceeds from this sale, the funds in the bond sinking fund, and the amount received from the issuance of the 8% debentures were used to retire the 6% mortgage bonds.

(c) The treasury stock was reissued on February 28, 1980.

(d) The stock dividend was declared on October 31, 1980, when the market price of Plainview Corporations' shares was $12 per share.

(e) On April 30, 1980, a fire destroyed a warehouse costing $100,000 and upon which depreciation of $65,000 had accumulated. The deferred income tax relating to the difference between capital cost allowance and depreciation on the warehouse was $12,700. The loss was debited to Liability for Estimated Casualty Losses because this is the way the company has always accounted for possible casualty losses.

(f) Building and equipment transactions consisted of the sale of a building at its net book value of $4,000 and the purchase of equipment for $28,000.

(g) In 1980, a $30,000 debit was made to accumulated depreciation for excessive capital cost allowance taken in prior years but disallowed by Revenue Canada. A tax deficiency of $16,000 was paid and debited to Deferred Income Tax.

(h) Accounts receivable written off as uncolletible were $16,300 in 1979 and $18,500 in 1980. Expired insurance recorded in 1979 was $4,100 and $3,900 in 1980.

(i) The subsidiary, which is 80% owned, reported a loss of $22,400 for 1980.

Instructions:

Prepare a formal statement of changes in financial position (working capital) for the year ended December 31, 1980. Include supporting schedules in good form.

(AICPA adapted)

20-14A. Your firm has been engaged to examine the financial statements of Lanning Company Limited for the year ended December 31, 1980. Under your supervision your assistant has prepared the following comparative balance sheet for December 31, 1980 and 1979, and the income statement for the year ended December 31, 1980.

The following additional information has been extracted from your audit work papers:

(1) During January 1980, Lanning decided to change its product mix. To accomplish this, new machinery and equipment costing $1,000,000 was purchased on February 15, 1980. The vendor supplying the machinery and equipment was paid as follows:

(a) Cash payment of $100,000.

(b) Issuance of 5,000 shares of $100 par value preferred with a fair value of $500,000.

(c) Issuance of a $400,000, 8% note secured by the machinery and equipment and payable in 20 equal annual installments, plus interest, on February 15th of each year until paid in full.

(2) The new machinery and equipment replaced dissimilar machinery and equipment, which had an original cost of $720,000, accumulated depreciation at February 15, 1980 of $504,000, and a related deferred tax liability of $24,000. The old machinery and equipment was sold for cash on December 14, 1980. No depreciation was recorded from February 15, 1980, until the date of sale.

(3) Lanning wrote off $150,000 of deferred research and development costs. The extraordinary charge for this write-off is a net of a related $72,000 deferred tax liability.

(4) Various other transactions follow:

(a) Depreciation expense for the year was $201,000.

(b) The company paid cash dividends of $300,000.

(c) The company advanced $240,000 to the corporation of which it owns 35 per cent.

Instructions:

Prepare a statement of changes in financial position based on additions to and deductions from working capital to appear in the 1980 annual report of Lanning Company Limited. (AICPA adapted)

Lanning Company Limited
Comparative Balance Sheet
December 31

Assets	1980	1979
Current assets:		
Cash	$ 326,500	$ 231,000
Accounts receivable (net).........................	621,000	614,000
Inventories	1,373,000	1,293,000
Prepaid expenses	160,000	175,000
Total current assets	$2,480,500	$2,313,000
Investment in and advances to 35% owned corporation .	$ 940,000	$ 625,000
Fixed assets:		
Land...	$ 54,200	$ 54,200
Buildings	758,000	758,000
Machinery and equipment	1,584,000	1,304,000
Allowance for depreciation	(513,000)	(816,000)
Total fixed assets	$1,883,200	$1,300,200
Deferred research and development costs	——	$ 150,000
	$5,303,700	$4,388,200

Liabilities and Owners' Equity	1980	1979
Current liabilities:		
Notes payable, bank..............................	$ 200,000	$ 250,000
Accounts payable	501,800	498,000
Accrued liabilities	187,500	271,000
Current portion of long-term debt	70,000	50,000
Income taxes payable	10,000	26,000
Total current liabilities	$ 969,300	$1,095,000
Long-term liabilities:		
6½% serial debentures payable	900,000	950,000
8% secured note payable	380,000	——
Deferred income taxes	119,000	167,000
Total long-term liabilities	$1,399,000	$1,117,000
Owners' equity:		
Preferred shares	$ 500,000	$ ——
Common shares	1,621,000	1,621,000
Retained earnings	949,400	555,200
Treasury shares, common, at cost	(135,000)	——
Total owners' equity	$2,935,400	$2,176,200
	$5,303,700	$4,388,200

Lanning Company Limited
Income Statement
For Year Ended December 31, 1980

Sales		$5,300,000
Cost of goods sold		(3,600,000)
Gross profit on sales		$1,700,000
Selling, general, and administrative expenses		(563,000)
Operating income		$1,137,000
Other Income (expense):		
Interest expenses	$ (112,000)	
Equity in the earnings of 35 per cent owned corporation	75,000	(37,000)
Net income before income taxes and extraordinary items		$1,100,000
Income taxes:		
Current	$ (480,000)	
Deferred	(48,000)	(528,000)
Net income before extraordinary items		$ 572,000
Extraordinary items:		
Gain on sale of equipment, less income taxes of $184,000		
($208,000 current less $24,000 deferred credit)	$ 200,200	
Write-off of deferred research and development costs		
less applicable deferred income tax of $72,000	(78,000)	122,200
Net income		$ 694,200

20-15A. This question concerns the various interrelationships among financial statements, accounts (or groups of accounts) among those statements, and accounts (or groups of accounts) within each statement. The following information is presented for Woods Company for the year ended December 31, 1980:

- The Statement of Changes in Financial Position.
- Selected information from the Income Statement.
- Selected information regarding the January 1 and December 31 Balance Sheets.
- Information regarding the correction of an error.
- Partially completed Balance Sheets at January 1 (prior to restatement) and December 31. The omitted account and groups-of-account balances are numbered from (1) through (16) and can be calculated from the other information given.

Statement of Changes in Financial Position

Working capital, January 1, 1980	$16,500
Add resources provided:	
Operations:	
Net loss for 1980	$ (2,885)
Adjustments not involving working capital:	
Bond premium amortization	(500)
Deferred income taxes	(200)
Depreciation expense	3,000
Goodwill amortization for 1980	2,000
Total from operations	1,415
Portion of proceeds of equipment sold representing	
undepreciated cost	10,000
Proceeds from reissue of treasury shares	11,400
Par value of common shares issued to reacquire	
preferred shares	7,500
Total resources provided	30,315

Subtract resources applied:

Purchase of land	14,715	
Current maturity of long-term bond debt	7,200	
Par value of preferred shares reacquired by issuing common shares	7,500	
Total resources applied	29,415	
Increase in working capital		900
Working capital, December 31, 1980		$17,400

Information from the Income Statement

Bad debt expense		$ 750
Bond interest expense (net of amortization of bond premium)		$ 3,500
Loss before tax adjustment		$(3,900)
Less:		
Income tax adjustment (refund due)	$815	
Deferred income taxes	200	1,015
Net loss after tax adjustment		$(2,885)

Information Regarding January 1 and December 31 Balance Sheets
The net book value of the equipment sold was two thirds of the cost of that equipment.

Selected Ratios

	January 1, 1980	December 31, 1980
Current ratio	?	3 to 1
Total shareholders divided by total liability	4 to 3	?

Information Regarding the Correction of an Error
Woods company had neglected to amortize $2,000 of goodwill in 1979. The correction of this material error has been appropriately made in 1980.

Woods Company
Balance Sheet

	January 1, 1980 (prior to restatement)	December 31, 1980
Assets		
Current assets	$22,000	$ (5)
Building and equipment	92,000	(6)
Accumulated depreciation	(25,000)	(7)
Land	(1)	(8)
Goodwill	12,000	(9)
Total assets	$ (?)	$ (?)
Liabilities and Shareholders Equity		
Current liabilities	$ (2)	$ (10)
Bonds payable (8%)	(3	(11)
Bond premium	(?)	(12)
Deferred income taxes	(4)	1700
Common shares	66,000	(13)
Contributed surplus	13,000	(14)
Preferred shares	16,000	(15)
Retained earnings (deficit)	(6,000)	(16)
Treasury shares (at cost)	(9,000)	0
Total liabilities and shareholders' equity	$ (?)	$ (?)

Instructions:

Number your answer sheet from (1) through (16). Place the correct balance for each balance-sheet account or group of accounts next to the corresponding number on your answer sheet. Show supporting computations in good form. (One account balance and the totals are shown as a question mark (?). Calculation of these amounts may be necessary to calculate the numbered balances, but is *not* required to be shown separately in your numbered answers.) *Do not recopy the balance sheets. Calculation of answers need not follow the numerical order of these blanks 1 through 16. Do not restate the January 1 balance sheet for the error.*

Hint: The computation of total equities on the January 1 Balance Sheet is a logical starting point.   (AICPA adapted)

21 FINANCIAL REPORTING AND CHANGING PRICES

Traditionally, financial statements have reflected transactions recorded in terms of the number of dollars exchanged. These statements are often referred to as *historical-cost* or *historical-dollar* statements. The primary reason for reporting transaction dollar amounts is that they are objective. Historical costs generally are based on arm's-length transactions and measure appropriate exchange values at the transaction date.

With increasing prices, that accelerated during the decade of the 70s, there has been a growing awareness of the limitations of historical-cost statements. Fluctuations in the general purchasing power of money, and significantly increased replacement costs of certain assets, make it difficult to interpret the money amounts reported in conventional financial statements. Thus, the validity of the analytical data provided by historical-cost statements has been challenged and has caused accountants to consider providing financial data reflecting price changes.

GENERAL PRICE CHANGES VS. SPECIFIC PRICE CHANGES

There are two kinds of price changes that must be clearly understood. The first deals with changes in the general price level for all commodities. In periods of rising prices this concept is generally referred to as *inflation*; it is concerned with *general price changes*. The second kind of price change relates to changes in the specific prices of particular items and therefore concerns *specific price changes*. Prices for individual items may fluctuate up or down and by differing magnitudes; the average of all specific price changes determines the change in the general price level. With respect to terminology, the accounting alternative identified with the first kind of price change is referred to as *general price-level (GPL) adjusted accounting* or simply *price-level accounting*. Accounting for the second kind of price change is referred to as *current value, current cost,* or *fair value accounting*. These distinctions are important for understanding the reporting alternatives identified in the next section.

REPORTING ALTERNATIVES

Several alternatives to financial reporting on a historical-cost basis have been proposed. The major proposals, including the currently used historical-cost basis are presented as a matrix in the diagram below.

	Historical-Cost Basis	Current Value Basis
Money Measurement	1	3
Purchasing Power Measurement	2	4

The diagram depicts two basic elements that are common to all accounting measurement models: (1) the need for a *unit of measurement* or *common denominator*, which could be either money or purchasing power units, and (2) the need for a *valuation rule*, which could be either historical cost or current value. A third basic element of any accounting measurement model is the need for a *capital maintenance concept*. The essential point about capital maintenance is the idea that income can only be recognized after capital, however defined and measured, has been kept intact or maintained.

It is important to distinguish among the four alternative measurement models depicted in the matrix diagram above. Cell 1 represents the *conventional accounting model* which is the present basis of financial statement accounting. Historical costs, representing the exchange prices of transactions, are measured in terms of money. This may be differentiated from cell 2 which maintains the historical-cost valuation rule, but changes the unit of measurement from money to purchasing power units or constant dollars, i.e., constant dollars in terms of purchasing power given a general price level. This concept, *general price-level adjustment,* is simply a refinement of the conventional accounting model; it is GAAP measured in constant dollars. Cell 3 is a significant departure from current practice and therefore would reform the conventional accounting model. While money is still the measurement unit, a new valuation rule, current value, is used. At this point, current value may be considered a generic term used to denote any alternative to historical cost, and therefore would encompass: (1) replacement cost, (2) net realizable values, (3) economic values such as the present value of future cash flows, or (4) a combination of valuation techniques. The fourth cell is a combination of the concepts incorporated in cells 2 and 3. Current values provide the valuation rule, but adjustments are also made for changes in the general price level.

This chapter discusses these alternatives. Each may be applied comprehensively to all items to produce articulated financial statements. Comprehensive application, however, is not yet practical because accounting-principles-making bodies have been unable to resolve the conceptual and implementation issues that would permit a consensus in favor of any one alternative model. While the issues involved are longstanding ones that have been debated in accounting literature for over sixty years, their serious consideration by accounting-principles-making bodies is a direct result of the double-digit inflation that dates back to the early 1970s.

For the accounting profession the decade of the 70s was a period of discussion, debate, and changed directions as regards financial reporting and changing prices. Initially the profession appeared headed in the direction of mandatory general price level adjustment. This stimulated experimentation with GPL adjustment which served to identify concerns with (1) the usefulness of price-level-adjusted financial statements, and (2) recognition that GPL adjustment might be only a partial solution to the whole problem of financial reporting and changing prices. The profession then appeared headed toward current value accounting, with or without GPL adjustment, cell 3 or 4 in the diagram on page 904. Again, this stimulated experimentation and concerns about current value accounting resulted that centred on (1) the subjectivity of current values, (2) implementation issues, and (3) a lack of consensus concerning capital maintenance. In general, these GPL adjustment and current value proposals contemplated comprehensive application. However, a lack of consensus, even within accounting-principles-making bodies created an impasse which served to stimulate selective supplementary disclosure of current value data and/or price level adjusted data confined primarily to inventories and cost of sales, and to property, plant and equipment, and depreciation. Recent pronouncements such as *FASB Statement No. 33*, "Financial Reporting and Changing Prices," and the United Kingdom and Ireland pronouncement, *SSAP 16*, "Current Cost Accounting," are examples of the profession's current position described above as selective supplementary disclosure.

THE CONVENTIONAL ACCOUNTING MODEL

The conventional accounting model, or GAAP model, has been succinctly described by Stamp as the "historical cost-realized revenue basis of determining income or value."[1] In general, historical cost is used to provide initial valuation; the recognition of subsequent value changes is determined by the realization concept which is transactions based. In the absence of a transaction, the conventional accounting model denies the recognition of value changes. In the context of reality, conventional accounting income measurement excludes value changes of the current period that have not been realized and, because of current period realization, includes value changes that in fact occurred in prior periods.

International Business Machines Corporation (IBM) provides a dramatic example of the restrictive nature of the realization concept as it applies in the conventional accounting model. A purchase of 100 shares of IBM stock in 1914 when the corporation was formed by a merger of predecessor corporations would have cost $2,750. Assuming a purchase and hold by a corporation, the conventional accounting model would retain the historical cost value of $2,750. By 1962, however, the 100 shares, increased in number by eight stock splits and twenty-five stock dividends, were worth approximately $5.5 million.[2] Their current value in 1980 might approximate $16 million. Nonetheless, assuming the original investment has been held since 1914, the conventional accounting value would still be $2,750.

The cost and realization concepts as they apply in the conventional accounting model inflict timing errors in financial statements, regardless of inflation. Timing errors result when specific price changes are not recognized for accounting purposes in the period when the changes actually take place. Accountants do not deny the reality of specific price changes, but instead have traditionally argued that only an arm's-length transaction provides an objective measurement of value changes. Inflation results from changes in the general purchasing power of money. Thus, the money measurement concept in conventional accounting gives rise to measurement unit errors because it ignores general price changes.[3]

GENERAL PRICE-LEVEL ADJUSTMENTS

As mentioned previously, transactions have been traditionally accounted for in terms of the number of dollars exchanged. Contrary to the assumption that the dollar is a stable monetary unit, money measurements represent diverse amounts of purchasing power. The dollar is an abstraction which has significance only in reference to a particular level of prices. Unless adjustments are made, the user of financial statements is likely to regard money in terms of its current general purchasing power rather than its general

---

[1] Edward Stamp, "Income and Value Determination and Changing Price Levels," *The Accountant's Magazine*, June 1971, p. 279.

[2] Thomas J. Watson, Jr., *A Business and Its Beliefs: The Ideas That Helped Build IBM* (New York: McGraw-Hill Book Company, Inc., 1963), p. 9.

[3] S. Basu and J. R. Hanna, *Inflation Accounting: Alternatives, Implementation Issues and Some Empirical Evidence* (Hamilton: Society of Management Accountants of Canada, 1975), ch. 2.

purchasing power at the time it was exchanged. Thus, the objective of general price-level adjustments is to convert all money measurements into equivalent purchasing power units or constant dollars so that a company's position and progress may be viewed in proper perspective.

To illustrate, the sum of 100 dollars and 100 pounds is an abstraction. Before proceeding with the arithmetic operation, one of the amounts must first be converted to its exchange equivalent in terms of the other. Similarly, it would seem appropriate to convert the number of dollars expended years ago for land or buildings into equivalent purchasing power units of dollars expended currently for merchandise in arriving at a meaningful asset total. This conversion of historical-dollar amounts to equivalent purchasing power units is the essence of general price-level accounting adjustment. Note that historical costs, the original exchange values, are maintained as the valuation basis, but are adjusted for general price-level changes. The basis of measurement changes from money amounts to equivalent purchasing power units or constant dollars. The restatements are accomplished by using price indexes.

Price-Level Indexes

The value or purchasing power of a monetary unit is inversely related to the price of goods or services for which it can be exchanged. Over a period of time, the prices of specific goods or services will move up or down depending upon their relative scarcity and desirability. It would be possible to adjust for specific items, but their prices may change more or less than, or in the opposite direction from, a change in the general price level. The movements of the price structure for goods and services as a whole are referred to as inflation or deflation.

The general level of prices cannot be measured in absolute terms, but the relative changes from period to period and the direction of change can be determined. To measure changes in the general price level, a sample of commodities is selected and the current prices of these items are compared with their prices during a base period. The prices during the base period are assigned a value of 100, and the prices of all other periods are expressed as percentages of this amount. The resulting series of numbers is called a *price-level index*.

Price-level indexes can be valuable aids in judging the extent of inflation or deflation. However, there are limitations in these measurements. In the first place, all price indexes are based upon a sampling process. Since all prices do not fluctuate in the same degree or direction, the selection of commodities to be included and their relative weights have important bearings on the computed values. In addition, technological improvements in the products included in the sample affect the general level of prices, but qualitative changes are difficult to measure.

Although no perfect means of measuring the changing value of money has yet been devised, indexes have been developed providing reasonable estimates of the overall change in general purchasing power. Among these are the Consumer Price Index and the GNE (Gross National Expenditure) Implicit Price Index, both of which are provided by Statistics Canada.

Each of these indexes exhibits a similar pattern of price-level change, but, since each is based upon the prices of a different group of items, the indexes report different values. Users of financial statements represent a broader interest than just consumers. Therefore, for general purpose statements adjusted for changes in the general price level, it may be logical to use a broadly based index. Because the GNE Implicit Price Index represents the most comprehensive indicator of the general price level in Canada, accounting authorities have favored recommending its use in restating financial statements for general price-level changes. The GNE Index provides price indexes in terms of annual averages beginning with 1926 and also quarterly averages from 1947. In the absence of end-of-year price-level measurements, the index for the last quarter of the year is normally used to approximate the price index at the end of the year. A summary of annual averages for the GNE index follows:

GNE Index

Year	GNE Implicit Price Index
	(1971 = 100)
1950	54.8
1955	65.0
1960	72.1
1965	79.1
1970	96.9
1971	100.0
1972	105.0
1973	114.6
1974	132.1
1975	146.3
1976	160.2
1977	171.4
1978	182.3
1979	201.1

Source: Statistics Canada, May, 1980.

From the viewpoint of shareholders and their command over goods and services, use of the Consumer Price Index for GPL adjustment purposes certainly merits consideration. This index is issued monthly, whereas the GNE Implicit Price Index is a quarterly series. Therefore, on pragmatic grounds, use of the CPI for GPL restatements avoids the delays inherent in the use of a quarterly index. The constant dollar data required under *SFAS No. 33* uses the CPI for GPL adjustment purposes. In Canada, an exposure draft issued in July 1975, and subsequently withdrawn in December 1976, proposed use of the GNE Implicit Price Index.

Effects of General Price Changes on Monetary and Non-monetary Items

In recognizing the effects of general price changes, it is necessary to distinguish between monetary items and non-monetary items. *Monetary items* are those assets and liabilities whose dollar amounts are fixed in terms of numbers of dollars regardless of changes in the general price level. All other items not representing a right to receive or an obligation to pay a fixed sum are *non-monetary*.

Monetary assets include cash as well as such items as accounts receivable, notes receivable, loans to employees, cash surrender value of life insurance, and certain marketable securities, such as bonds that are expected to be held to maturity and redeemed at a fixed number of dollars. Regardless of the changes taking place in the general price level, these balances are fixed, usually by contract, and provide for the recovery of neither more nor less than the stated amounts. Monetary liabilities include virtually all liabilities such as accounts payable, notes payable, cash dividends payable, the fixed payment amounts for accruals under pension plans, and, according to an exposure draft issued by the Accounting Research Committee in 1975, accumulated deferred income tax credits. Regardless of the changes taking place in the general price level, these balances are fixed and call for the payment of neither more nor less than the stated amounts. By holding monetary assets or liabilities, one realizes purchasing-power gains or losses which are not disclosed in conventional financial statements.

For example, assume a person placed $1,000 in cash under the mattress for "safekeeping" when the price level index was 100. If the price level were to increase to 110 (10% inflation) one year later, the individual would have suffered a purchasing-power loss because it would require $1,100 to buy the same amount of goods that $1,000 would have purchased one year earlier. On the other hand, a debt of $1,000 payable a year later, again assuming an increase in the price level to 110 from 100, would result in a purchasing-power gain. The equivalent purchasing power should be $1,100 yet the debt can be settled for the fixed amount of $1,000.

Non-monetary assets include such items as inventories and supplies; prepaid expenses; land, buildings, and equipment; and, intangible assets. These items derive their non-monetary classification because, with changes in the general price level, the money amounts at which they are reported on conventional financial statements will differ from the purchasing power resources they actually represent. Non-monetary liabilities, while few in number, would include such items as deferred revenue, advances on sales contracts, and warranties on goods sold. These items derive their non-monetary classification because, with changes in the general price level, their purchasing power equivalent will differ from the money amounts reported on conventional financial statements.[4]

The distinction between monetary and non-monetary items is not related to the current and non-current classifications used for assets and liabilities. For example, monetary assets include current assets, such as accounts receivable, and also non-current assets, such as long-term investments in bonds; non-monetary assets include current items, such as inventories and supplies, and non-current items, such as land, buildings, and equipment. Monetary liabilities include current items, such as accounts and notes payable, and non-current items, such as bonds payable; non-monetary liabilities include current items, such as advances on sales contracts, and non-current items, such as long-term sales warranties.

The difference between a company's monetary assets and its monetary liabilities is referred to as its *net monetary position*. With the number of dollars relating to monetary items remaining fixed, and reflecting current dollars regardless of the change in the price level, purchasing power gains and losses arise in response to general price changes. In any given period, the gain or loss from holding monetary assets is offset by the loss or gain from maintaining monetary liabilities. The net gain or loss for a period, then, depends upon whether a company's position in net monetary items is positive — monetary assets exceeding monetary liabilities — or negative — monetary liabilities exceeding monetary assets. Purchasing power gains and losses are associated with a company's monetary assets, monetary liabilities, and net monetary position as follows:

| | General Price Level | |
	Increasing	Decreasing
Positive Net Monetary Position	Loss	Gain
Negative Net Monetary Position	Gain	Loss

Restating Financial Statements for General Price Changes

The process of restating financial statements for general price changes involves restating the money amounts on conventional statements to equivalent purchasing power units, or constant dollars, generally in terms of the

---

[4]Ordinarily the shareholders' equity would be regarded as a non-monetary item. However, an exception may be made with respect to the equity represented by non-convertible, callable, preferred stock. When preferred shares can be retired at a fixed-dollar amount, they should be regarded as a monetary item. A comprehensive list of balance sheet items and their classification as monetary and non-monetary items, together with an explanation of the reason for classification, is given in Accounting Principles Board Statement No. 3, Appendix B, and in the exposure draft, "Accounting for Changes in the General Purchasing Power of Money," issued by the Accounting Research Committee, July, 1975, Appendix 1.

current period.[5] The formula for balance sheet restatement in terms of current year-end purchasing power units is:

$$\text{Historical-Cost Amounts for Non-monetary Assets and Liabilities} \quad \times \quad \frac{\text{Index at End of Current Period}}{\text{Index at Date Non-monetary Asset was Acquired or Non-monetary Liability Was Incurred}}$$

Non-monetary assets are generally reported on the financial statements at the number of dollars originally paid upon acquisition; non-monetary liabilities are reported at the number of dollars originally received; and non-monetary capital balances are stated at the number of dollars originally received from shareholders or accumulated from earnings and other sources. Restating these balances requires recognition of the change in the price level since the time each transaction within these groups took place. The monetary assets and liabilities state amounts recognized as representing constant dollars. These items, therefore, do not require restatement.

A number of simple examples will be given to illustrate the restatement of financial data in terms of constant dollars and to suggest the nature of the analysis afforded by these data. An extended illustration in which financial statements for successive periods are restated is presented in an appendix at the end of this chapter. In each of the examples in the following section, the activities of a company for the first year of its life are given. It is assumed in the examples that the general price level moves up evenly throughout the year and produces a 10% increase for the year.

Example 1 — Non-monetary assets are held during the year. Assume a company issues share capital of $50,000 in exchange for land valued at $50,000. The company holds the land during the year without engaging in any other activities. A balance sheet prepared in conventional form at the end of the year will show both land and invested capital at their original amounts. In preparing a balance sheet expressing financial position in terms of the price level at the end of the year, however, land and share capital will be reported as follows:

1. Land, a non-monetary asset, needs to be restated for the change in price level since its acquisition. Land, with an acquisition cost of $50,000, is expressed in constant dollars at $50,000 × 110/100, or $55,000.[6]
2. Share capital, a non-monetary item, also requires restatement so that it expresses the shareholders' investment in terms of the current price level. The share capital balance is expressed in constant dollars at $50,000 × 110/100, or $55,000.

[5]Obviously, it is possible to convert original costs to purchasing power units at a date other than the current period by using the index of whatever year is desired as the base year. However, it is usually more meaningful to convert to the current year.

[6]It is possible to use conversion rates which express the relationship of one index to another. Thus, in the example cited, 110/100 may be stated as a conversion rate of 1.10. When the restatement process is a lengthy one but requires the use of relatively few conversion factors, it is generally convenient to prepare a table of values stated in quotients and apply these values to the individual items requiring restatement.

A balance sheet restated to report assets and shareholders' equity in terms of the price level prevailing at the end of the year follows:

GPL Adjusted Balance Sheet			
	Historical Amount	Conversion Factor	Restated Amount
Land	$50,000	110/100	$55,000
Share capital	$50,000	110/100	$55,000

A comparative balance sheet for the company prepared in conventional form will show the asset and shareholders' equity balances at the end of the year to be the same as the balances at the beginning of the year. A comparative balance sheet expressed in terms of purchasing power units at the end of the year will also show account balances to have remained unchanged. In preparing adjusted comparative data, beginning balances must be updated or "rolled forward" so that they are stated in a manner permitting comparisons with the year-end statements. Updating the balance sheet does not indicate earlier balances were misstated; it is simply a means of changing the form of the information in terms of a later unit of measure. A balance sheet comparing beginning and ending balances in dollars of uniform purchasing power follows:

Comparative GPL Adjusted Balance Sheet					
	Beginning of Year				
	Historical Amount	Conversion Factor	Restated Amount	End of Year	Increase (Decrease)
Land	$50,000	110/100	$55,000	$55,000	——
Share capital	$50,000	110/100	$55,000	$55,000	——

The comparative balance sheet shows that company assets and shareholders' equity have not changed during the year. In the absence of monetary items, there has been neither purchasing power gain nor loss arising from the decline in the purchasing power of the dollar in a period of price-level advance.

Example 2 — Monetary and non-monetary assets are held and monetary liabilities are maintained during the year. Assume a company issues share capital of $75,000 in exchange for cash of $25,000 and land valued at $100,000 subject to a mortgage note of $50,000. This represents a negative net monetary position because monetary liabilities exceed monetary assets. As indicated in the diagram on page 910, in an inflationary period, this will result in a purchasing power gain. The assets are held and the liability is maintained throughout the year without any accrual of revenue or expense. A balance sheet prepared in conventional form at the end of the year shows asset, liability, and shareholders' equity balances at their original amounts. However, in preparing a balance sheet in terms of the price level at the end of the year, balances would be as follows:

1. Cash is a monetary asset, a resource of fixed-dollar amount, that has not changed with the change in the purchasing power of the dollar. The cash balance, then, is reported at $25,000.
2. Land is restated in terms of the current price level at $100,000 × 110/100, or $110,000.
3. The mortgage note is a monetary item, a legal obligation of fixed-dollar amount, that has not changed with the change in purchasing power of the dollar. The mortgage note, then, is reported at $50,000.
4. The share capital balance is restated in terms of the current price level at $75,000 × 110/100, or $82,500.
5. The shareholders' equity must be reported at an amount equal to the net assets as restated, or $85,000. With the original investment by shareholders expressed in terms of the current price level at $82,500, there has been an increase in the shareholders' equity of $2,500. Since there were no transactions during the year, the increase in the shareholders' equity indicates a purchasing power gain from the increase in the purchasing power of the company's net monetary position during the year.

A balance sheet restated to report balances in terms of the price level prevailing at the end of the year and a schedule reporting the change in shareholders' equity resulting from the purchasing power gain during the year follow:

GPL Adjusted Balance Sheet			
	Historical Amount	Conversion Factor	Restated Amount
Cash	$ 25,000		$ 25,000
Land	100,000	110/100	110,000
	$125,000		$135,000
Mortgage note payable	$ 50,000		$ 50,000
Share capital	75,000	110/100	82,500
Retained earnings	——	(see schedule)	2,500
	$125,000		$135,000

Schedule Reporting Purchasing Power Gain or Loss for Year			
	Historical Amount	Conversion Factor	Restated Amount
Excess of monetary liabilities over monetary assets at beginning of year	$ 25,000	110/100	$ 27,500
Excess of monetary liabilities over monetary assets at end of year......................			25,000
Purchasing power gain			$ 2,500

A comparative balance sheet prepared in conventional form will show asset, liability, and shareholders' equity balances as unchanged for the year. However, a comparative balance sheet expressed in terms of the purchasing power units at the end of the year shows that changes did take place. A comparative balance sheet reporting beginning and ending balances in constant dollars appears below:

Comparative GPL Adjusted Balance Sheet				
	Beginning of Year				
	Historical Amount	Conversion Factor	Restated Amount	End of Year	Increase (Decrease)
Cash	$ 25,000	110/100	$ 27,500	$ 25,000	$(2,500)
Land	100,000	110/100	110,000	110,000	——
	$125,000		$137,500	$135,000	$(2,500)
Mortgage note payable	$ 50,000	110/100	$ 55,000	$ 50,000	$(5,000)
Share capital	75,000	110/100	82,500	82,500	
Retained earnings				2,500	(2,500)
	$125,000		$137,500	$135,000	$(2,500)

Although no transactions took place during the year, the comparative balance sheet shows there was an increase in shareholders' equity. This increase resulted from a purchasing power gain identified with a financial position in which monetary liabilities exceeded monetary assets during a period of inflation.

Example 3 — Monetary assets are increased by proceeds from sale of property at year end and as a result of operations during the year. Assume a company issues share capital of $75,000 in exchange for cash of $25,000 and land valued at $50,000. The land is sold at the end of the year for cash of $60,000. Services are performed during the year resulting in operating income of $20,000; earnings accrue evenly, and at the end of the year cash is $102,500 and accounts receivable are $2,500. A balance sheet prepared in conventional form will show increases in assets of $30,000 accompanied by a corresponding increase in retained earnings. However, in preparing a balance sheet in terms of purchasing power units at the end of the year, balances are reported as follows:

1. Cash, a monetary asset, is reported at $102,500.
2. Accounts receivable is a monetary asset, a resource of fixed-dollar amount, and is reported at $2,500.
3. The share capital balance is restated in terms of the current price level at $75,000 × 110/100, or $82,500.
4. The shareholders' equity must be reported at an amount equal to total net assets, or $105,000. Since the original investment by shareholders in terms of the current price level is $82,500, there has been an increase in the shareholders' equity for the year of $22,500. Three factors explain this change: (a) the sale of land, (b) operations for the year, and (c) the change in general price level. The gain on the sale of land expressed in terms of the price level at the end of the period is $5,000 — the cost of the land in terms of

the year-end price level, $55,000 ($50,000 × 110/100), compared with a selling price at the end of the year of $60,000. The earnings from operations, $20,000, are assumed to have accrued evenly during the year and may be regarded as reflecting earnings in terms of the average price level for the year. The reported figure is adjusted to end-of-year constant dollars by the following computation:

$$\$20,000 \times 110/105 = \$20,952\,[7]$$

The purchasing power loss for the year consists of that sustained on the monetary assets held throughout the year as well as on the monetary assets that became available during the year. The computations are shown below in the Schedule Reporting Purchasing Power Gain or Loss for Year.

In reporting shareholders' equity on the balance sheet, then, share capital as restated is accompanied by retained earnings summarizing the three factors responsible for the change in shareholders' equity — the gain on sale of land, operating income, and the purchasing power loss. A statement of income and retained earnings supported by a schedule to show the computation of the purchasing power loss, and a balance sheet follow:

Income and Retained Earnings Statement for Year
GPL Adjusted

	Historical Amount	Conversion Factor	Restated Amount
Sale of land (at end of year)	$60,000	110/110	$60,000
Cost of land.................................	50,000	110/100	55,000
Gain on sale of land	$10,000		$ 5,000
Operating income (realized evenly throughout year)	20,000	110/105	20,952
Total	$30,000		$25,952
Deduct general purchasing power loss (see schedule)	—		3,452
Retained earnings at end of year	$30,000		$22,500

Schedule Reporting Purchasing Power Gain or Loss for Year

	Historical Amount	Conversion Factor	Restated Amount
Monetary position at beginning of year	$ 25,000	110/100	$ 27,500
Increase in monetary assets:			
From sale of land at end of year.............	60,000	110/110	60,000
From operations	20,000	110/105	20,952
			$108,452
Monetary position at end of year	$105,000		105,000
Purchasing power loss			$ 3,452

[7] It may be observed that if the prices rose evenly during the year, the price rise for the first half-year would be 105/100 and the price rise for the second half-year would be 110/105: the rate of increase, then, in the second half of the year is not equal to that which took place in the first half of the year.

GPL Adjusted Balance Sheet at End of Year			
	Historical Amount	Conversion Factor	Restated Amount
Cash	$102,500		$102,500
Accounts receivable.......................	2,500		2,500
	$105,000		$105,000
Share capital	$ 75,000	110/100	$ 82,500
Retained earnings	30,000		22,500
	$105,000		$105,000

Assuming the facts given, a comparative balance sheet prepared in conventional form will show an increase in shareholders' equity of $30,000. However, a comparative balance sheet expressed in terms of purchasing power units at the end of the year will show an increase in shareholders' equity of only $22,500. A balance sheet comparing beginning and ending balances in constant dollars is shown below:

Comparative GPL Adjusted Balance Sheet					
	Beginning of Year			End of Year	Increase (Decrease)
	Historical Amount	Conversion Factor	Restated Amount		
Cash	$25,000	110/100	$27,500	$102,500	$75,000
Accounts receivable ..	——		——	2,500	2,500
Land	50,000	110/100	55,000	——	(55,000)
	$75,000		$82,500	$105,000	$22,500
Share capital	$75,000	110/100	$82,500	$ 82,500	——
Retained earnings	——		——	22,500	$22,500
	$75,000		$82,500	$105,000	$22,500

The comparative balance sheet shows the change in the financial position was not as favorable as that shown on a similar statement prepared in conventional form. The gain on the sale of property, when cost and sales proceeds are expressed in purchasing power units at the end of the year, was only $5,000. The operating income, when restated in terms of the year-end price level, was $20,952, providing an increase of $25,952. However, the net increase in shareholders' equity after recognizing the purchasing power loss from holding monetary assets in a period of a price-level increase was limited to $22,500.

The foregoing examples illustrate the basic methodology of general price level accounting. A variety of simplifying assumptions concerning the timing of transactions facilitates application of the methodology. For example, sales and expenses, excluding depreciation, may be assumed to flow evenly during the year and, therefore, may be restated by using the index at the end of the year over the average index for the period. A further simplification results if GPL adjustments are reported in terms of the average price level for the reporting period. When these assumptions are combined, it becomes unnecessary to restate such items as sales, and most expenses. The constant dollar data required to comply with SFAS No. 33 can be determined using these simplifying assumptions. Their use, however, might not be considered appropriate assuming comprehensive GPL adjustment.[8]

As previously noted, an extended illustration in which financial statements for successive periods are GPL adjusted is presented in Appendix A at the end of this chapter. The simplified GPL adjustments permitted for purposes of compliance with the constant dollar disclosure requirements of SFAS No. 33 are illustrated in Appendix B.

CURRENT VALUE ACCOUNTING

Current value accounting, represented by Cell 3 in the diagram on page 904, is a generic term used to designate an alternative model to the traditional historical-cost model. Several distinctions may be made in defining current values: (1) input or entry prices, i.e., replacement costs; (2) output or exit prices, i.e., sales values; (3) net realizable values, i.e., expected sales prices less costs to complete and sell; and (4) economic values, i.e., present value of future cash flows. These distinctions are technical refinements in implementing the general approach to using current values in financial statements. In this chapter, current values will refer to the amounts required to replace specific items, i.e., replacement costs. Discussion of possible refinements is beyond the scope of intermediate accounting.[9]

Proponents of current value accounting argue that financial statements presented on a historical cost basis, even if adjusted for general price-level changes, do not adequately reflect the economic circumstances of a business. The balance sheet is deficient because only historical costs are presented which do not adequately reflect the current financial position of an entity. The income statement is deficient because charges against revenues are based on historical costs which may differ from current costs. Also, as previously explained, increases in net asset values are not recognized at the time of a change in asset value; they must await realization at time of sale. Under current value accounting, assets would be reported at their current replacement cost, thus more closely reflecting the actual financial position of a

---

[8]*Statement of Financial Accounting Standards No. 33*, "Financial Reporting and Changing Prices" (Stamford, Conn.: Financial Accounting Standards Board, 1979), par. 40.

[9]See, for example, Robert R. Sterling, *Theory of the Measurement of Enterprise Income* (Lawrence, Kansas: University Press of Kansas, 1970); Edgar O. Edwards and Philip W. Bell, *The Theory and Measurement of Business Income* (Berkeley: University of California Press, 1961); Raymond J. Chambers, *Accounting Evaluation and Economic Behavior* (Englewood Cliffs, N.J.: Prentice-Hall, 1966); James A. Largay III and John Leslie Livingstone, *Accounting for Changing Prices* (New York: John Wiley & Sons, Inc., 1976).

business entity. The impact on the income statement is uncertain. Some accountants would recognize revenues when there is evidence of an increase in net asset values; others would not recognize revenues until realized as evidenced by a sale. Also, the use of alternative capital maintenance concepts will impact on income measurement. Most accountants would agree, however, that expenses should be based on the expiration of current costs of the assets utilized, thus providing a more meaningful income measure.

Concept of Well-Offness

From an income measurement perspective, accounting income, regardless of the model used to measure it, is based on a concept of *well-offness*. As indicated in Chapter 4, this concept is widely attributed to J. R. Hicks and maintains that operating gain, often called economic income, is the amount a firm can spend during a period and still be equally well-off at the end of the period as at the beginning. Operationalized, economic income (loss) is the difference between the selling price of an item and the cost to replace that item. Alternatively, it may be viewed as the change in assets (equity change) during a period measured on a current value basis. For example, if an entity's net assets, valued in terms of current values, equaled $250,000 at the beginning of a period and $300,000 at the end of the period, given no additional investments or withdrawals, and holding the general price level constant, economic income would be $50,000.

Holding Gains or Losses

Although it could be done under the historical cost model, most current value alternatives isolate gains or losses resulting from holding assets. To illustrate, assume Current Value Company had sales of $100,000, historical cost of goods sold of $65,000, and a cost of $80,000 to replace the inventory sold. There is an operating gain of $20,000, which is the difference between the selling price and the replacement cost of the inventory. A *realized holding gain* ($15,000) represents the difference between the historical cost and replacement cost of the inventory sold. The total gross profit traditionally recognized is $35,000. However, that amount includes some *inventory profits* which will have to be reinvested if the firm is to be in an equally well-off position at the end of the period. Thus, the gross profit in an economic sense should be limited to the $20,000 operating gain.

Sales	$100,000	Operating gain
Replacment cost of inventory	80,000	Realized holding gain
Historical cost of goods sold	65,000	
Gross profit	$ 35,000	

If, in the preceding example, Current Value Company has additional inventory which is not sold but which has had a change in value, there would also be an *unrealized holding gain or loss*. Assume inventory that was not sold cost $50,000 and had a replacement cost of $70,000. There would be a $20,000 unrealized holding gain that under a current value model accountants would recognize, if not in income, in a separate revaluation account. These recognition alternatives are dependent upon the selection of a capital maintenance concept.

CAPITAL MAINTENANCE

A *capital maintenance* concept is a basic element of any accounting measurement model; this concept determines the point at which income can be recognized. As previously stated, the essential point about capital maintenance is the idea that income can only be recognized after capital, however defined and measured, has been kept intact or maintained. At least two concepts of capital maintenance are relevant in the context of an accounting measurement model, each of which may be measured in terms of either money or purchasing power units; (1) financial capital maintenance, and (2) productive capacity maintenance.[10]

The first alternative, *financial capital maintenance*, requires that capital, as at the end of the period, must exceed capital at the beginning of the period, ignoring capital transactions and dividends, in order for any income to be recognized. Assuming measurement in terms of money rather than purchasing power units, this is the capital maintenance concept that the conventional historical-cost model employs. In current value accounting, financial capital maintenance requires the recognition of holding gains in income. Again, the amount to be recognized may be measured in terms of either money or purchasing power units. When financial capital is measured in purchasing power units, income is recognized only after net assets, expressed in purchasing power units, have increased by more than the updated or rolled forward net asset balance, as at the beginning of the period, again ignoring capital transactions and dividends.

From the viewpoint of accounting theory, current value accounting alternatives should be more likely to employ the *productive capacity* concept of capital maintenance. Under this concept of capital maintenance, the increase in net assets during the period, ignoring capital transactions and dividends, must first be applied to maintaining the potential for the entity to continue

---

[10]The Accounting Research Committee's Discussion Paper "Current Value Accounting," August 1976, classifies capital maintenance concepts as (1) money maintenance, (2) general purchasing power maintenance, and (3) productive capacity maintenance. Based on the Committee's commentary and illustrations, money maintenance and general purchasing power maintenance are both financial capital maintenance with the measurement unit serving to distinguish them. Productive capacity maintenance, as the term is used by the Committee, is measured in terms of money.

to produce goods, services, or otherwise "do its thing." Income can only be recognized after this point has been reached. It should be noted that holding gains represent an increase in the value of the entity's productive capacity which must be kept intact. Therefore, under the productive capacity concept, holding gains would be segregated in a revaluation account to be reported as a separate component of shareholders' equity; they are excluded from income measurement. Since holding gains and losses constitute revaluation adjustments, only operating gains are recognized as income.

To illustrate, assume a corporation has $10,000 of net assets at the beginning of the current period and $15,000 of net assets at the end of the period, there being no capital transactions or dividends during the period. Assume further a 5 per cent increase in the general price level and that the corporation would need $12,000 of net assets at the end of the period simply to maintain its productive capacity, or, in other words, its ability to operate at the same level that was possible at the beginning of the period using $10,000 of net assets. Under each of the capital maintenance alternatives, income for the period would be determined as follows:

Financial Capital Measured in Money

$15,000 − $10,000 = $5,000

Financial Capital Measured in Purchasing Power Units

$15,000 − $10,500 = $4,500

Computation: $10,000 × 105/100 = $10,500

Productive Capacity Measured in Money

$15,000 − $12,000 = $3,000

Productive Capacity Measured in Purchasing Power Units

Not determinable[11]

Some accountants argue for retention of the conventional transactions-based realization concept within a current value accounting framework. This viewpoint can be argued to result in a hybrid capital maintenance concept: realized holding gains or losses are included in income, unrealized holding gains or losses are shown on the balance sheet as a separate component of shareholders' equity. Under this approach, current value net income equals historical-cost net income; however, the current value presentation would report separately the operating and holding components of income.

In the context of accounting theory, a transactions-based realization concept performs a more limited role in current value accounting than it does under the conventional historical-cost model. In current value accounting, it is the asset valuation rule that determines the timing for recognition of value changes and thus the period's equity change. The capital maintenance con-

---

[11]More detailed information is required to determine income on this basis. For example, current value accounting determines operating gains by matching the replacement cost at date of sale against sales revenue. Cost of goods sold measured in this manner would then have to be restated in year-end constant dollars resulting in a different income number than that shown for productive capacity measured in money.

cept allocates the equity change to determine income, and to determine the provision, if any, to maintain productive capacity. The role of the realization concept in current value accounting is therefore restricted to the measurement of operating income, as distinct from net income. In historical-cost accounting, the asset valuation rule denies the recognition of value changes and therefore the realization concept must perform this function. It can also be argued that concerns with respect to the realized and unrealized components of income confuse the broader question of liquidity with the concept of income measurement.

The diagram presented below attempts to provide a framework for organizing the complex topic of alternative accounting models.

COMMON DENOMINATOR	CAPITAL MAINTENANCE		VALUATION RULE	
Money	Money	Financial Capital	Historical Cost	
		Productive Capacity	Current Value	
			Entry Prices	Exit Prices
Constant Dollars	Constant Dollars	Financial Capital	Present Value of Future Cash Flows	
		Productive Capacity	Combination of Values	

The three vertical columns represent three basic elements that exist in any accounting measurement model. Thus, a choice must be made from the alternatives presented in each of the vertical columns. Combinations of choices flow horizontally however, the vertical and horizontal planes of the diagram are independent of each other. This does not deny the important interrelationships that exist in the combination of the vertical choices and their horizontal flow.

The conventional historical-cost model is presented across the top of the diagram: (1) common denominator — money, (2) capital maintenance — financial capital measured in money, and (3) valuation rule — historical cost. The 1976 preliminary position the Accounting Research Committee presented as a focus for continuing discussion of current value accounting may be described as follows: (1) common denominator — money, (2) capital maintenance — financial capital measured in constant dollars (by a restatement of shareholders' equity), and (3) valuation rule — combination of values.[12]

Numerous combinations are obviously possible; several are more logical

---

[12]Accounting Research Committee, Discussion Paper, "Current Value Accounting" (Toronto: Canadian Institute of Chartered Accountants, 1976), pp. 65-70. At the time of writing, the ARC's more recent position was stated in the December 1979, Exposure Draft, "Current Cost Accounting."

than others, a few may be illogical, or perhaps impossible, in the context of accounting theory. For example, productive capacity capital maintenance and the historical-cost valuation rule are considered incompatible because net asset values do not recognize holding gains or losses.

A variety of factors may be expected to influence the alternative choices and interrelationships that ultimately culminate in an accounting measurement model. FASB *Statement of Financial Accounting Concepts No. 2* has identified usefulness for decision-making as the overriding quality that makes accounting information useful.[13] Therefore, user needs in the context of decision-making must be identified as perhaps the key factor for purposes of specifying the parameters of an accounting measurement model. A cost-benefit criterion must also be considered.

CURRENT VALUE ACCOUNTING GPL ADJUSTED

The fourth cell identified in the matrix diagram on page 904 represents a combination of shifting to a current value reporting basis measured in terms of purchasing power units. This approach recognizes that adjusting for both specific and general price changes are not mutually exclusive and are not necessarily competing alternatives. Some accountants argue that this combination is conceptually the best reporting alternative. They feel adjustments must be made for both specific and general price changes.

In terms of the effect on the balance sheet, this approach is not significantly different from Cell 3. There would have to be roll-forward changes for comparative balance sheets, but the primary effect of adding GPL adjustment to current value accounting is on the income statement. The result is a further distinction among income components. For example, in the illustration referred to earlier, the following elements of income were identified:

Sales	$100,000 ⟍ Operating gain
Replacement cost of inventory	80,000 ⟨ Realized holding gain
Cost of goods sold	65,000 ⟋
Gross profit	$ 35,000

If GPL adjustments were added, assuming 10% inflation for the year, the result would be:

Sales	$100,000 ⟍ Operating gain
Replacement cost of inventory	80,000 ⟨ Real holding gain
Cost of goods sold adjusted for inflation . .	71,500* ⟨ Inflationary holding gain
Cost of goods sold at historical costs . . .	65,000 ⟋
Gross profit	$ 35,000

*($65,000 × 1.10 = $71,500)

---

[13]*Statement of Financial Accounting Concepts No. 2,* "Qualitative Characteristics of Accounting Information" (Stamford, Conn.: Financial Accounting Standards Board, 1980), par. 32.

Note that the holding gain has been broken into two parts: the real holding gain (the difference between the price-level adjusted historical cost and the replacement cost), and the inflationary holding gain (the difference between the historical costs and the price-level adjusted historical costs). In addition to the other shortcomings ascribed to the current value approach and price-level adjustments considered separately, one disadvantage of this method is the complexity, caused by combining alternatives.

CURRENT VALUE ACCOUNTING APPLIED TO DEPRECIABLE PROPERTIES

Depreciation raises several interesting questions in current value accounting. For example, should companies use the same assumptions and estimates for depreciation accounting purposes in both current value and historical-cost financial statements? To the extent the assumptions and estimates used to determine historical-cost depreciation may make allowance for the impact of inflation, then different assumptions and estimates would seem justified in current value accounting. However, it may be argued that the use of different assumptions and estimates to determine current value depreciation might permit some manipulation of income measurement. SFAS No. 33 requires that any differences in the depreciation methods and estimates used to determine the current cost depreciation be reported as supplementary information in footnote disclosures.

In its Exposure Draft, "Current Cost Accounting," the Accounting Research Committee takes the position that "the principles of depreciation as applied in historical cost financial statements apply equally to depreciation in a current cost framework."[14] An exception is then noted where "assets that have been fully depreciated in the historical cost financial statements may still be in use."[15]

One important question concerns the treatment of what is commonly referred to as *backlog depreciation*. This is the gap in accumulated depreciation that is inevitable as the replacement cost of depreciable properties increases or decreases. To illustrate, assume equipment with a four-year useful life is purchased for $3,000, and that its end-of-year replacement cost increases year-by-year to $4,000, $4,800, $6,000 and $8,000. Assuming straight-line depreciation, the tabulation presented on the next page shows the backlog that arises in years 2, 3 and 4.

In this example, it is obvious that the backlog must be credited to accumulated depreciation. The accounting issue concerns what to debit. The accounting Research Committee's Discussion Paper "Current Value Accounting," lists the following alternative treatments: (1) charge or credit retained earnings thus treating the backlog as a prior period adjustment, (2) charge or credit current income thus treating the backlog as part of the current

---

[14]Accounting Research Committee, Exposure Draft, "Current Cost Accounting" (Toronto: Canadian Institute of Chartered Accountants, 1979).
[15]*Ibid.*

	End of			
	Year 1	Year 2	Year 3	Year 4
Replacement cost	$4,000	$4,800	$6,000	$8,000
Required allowance	$1,000	$2,400	$4,500	$8,000
Depreciation based on year-end replacement cost	$1,000	$1,200	$1,500	$2,000
Beginning balance in accumulated depreciation	———	$1,000	$2,400*	$4,500*
	$1,000	$2,200	$3,900	$6,500
Backlog depreciation	Nil	$ 200	$ 600	$1,500

*Includes backlog depreciation

period's depreciation expense, or (3) adjust holding gains or losses by the amount of the backlog.[16]

Two factors should be considered in the evaluation of these alternatives: (1) capital maintenance alternatives, and (2) the separate reporting of operating income and holding gains or losses that is characteristic of current value accounting. Assuming financial capital maintenance, the second and third treatments listed both result in a charge or credit to income; in the case of number (2), a charge or credit to operating income, in the case of number (3), an adjustment of holding gains or losses. Assuming productive capacity capital maintenance, the third treatment listed bypasses both income measurement and retained earnings. If the intent of productive capacity capital maintenance is to report as retained earnings an amount available for divided distribution, as is commonly argued, then only the first two alternative treatments of backlog depreciation can be considered satisfactory. As between these two alternatives, a charge or credit to retained earnings would seem to be preferable.

It should also be noted that in the example depreciation charges have been based on year-end replacement cost values. Many accountants argue that current costs are more appropriately matched against revenues if depreciation charges are based on average replacement cost values. To illustrate, depreciation based on the second year's average replacement cost would be $1,100 ($4,400 ÷ 4); backlog depreciation would then increase to $300. While the use of average replacement cost values to determine depreciation charges may have merit for purposes of measuring operating income, the objective here can be easily thwarted by the accounting treatment of backlog depreciation.

ALTERNATIVE MODELS ILLUSTRATED

The data presented on page 925 will be used to illustrate the four alternative models depicted in the matrix diagram on page 904.

---

[16] Accounting Research Committee, Discussion Paper, *op. cit.*, p. 15.

HC Corporation
Historical-Cost Balance Sheet
As At End of Year 1

Cash	$30,000	Accounts payable	$10,000
Inventory	42,000	Share capital	55,000
Land	16,000	Retained earnings	23,000
	$88,000		$88,000

Additional information:

1. Sales at invoice prices $97,000
2. Cost of goods sold:
   - Historical cost 54,000
   - Replacement cost 58,000
3. Expenses 20,000
4. End of year 1 replacement cost data:
   - Inventory 46,000
   - Land 21,000
5. No dividends declared during year 1

Based on this data, the following preliminary income statements can be prepared.

HC Corporation
Income Statement

	Historical Cost	Current Value
Sales	$97,000	$97,000
Cost of goods sold	$54,000	$58,000
Expenses	20,000	20,000
	$74,000	$78,000
	$23,000	$19,000

At this point, the issue that must be resolved is capital maintenance. Under the conventional historical-cost model the capital maintenance concept is financial capital measured in money, and therefore, net income is $23,000. This same capital maintenance concept, when applied to current value accounting, requires the inclusion of holding gains in income. The productive capacity capital maintenance concept, measured in money, excludes holding gains from income; instead the holding gains are segregated in a revaluation account which is presented as a separate component of shareholders' equity. In the example, the holding gains are determined as follows:

HC Corporation
Holding Gains

Realized on sales ($58,000 − $54,000)	$ 4,000
Unrealized on inventory ($46,000 − $42,000)	4,000
Unrealized on land ($21,000 − $16,000)	5,000
	$13,000

Alternative current value financial statements can now be prepared using first of all financial capital and then productive capacity as the capital maintenance concept, in both cases measured in money.

HC Corporation Alternative Current Value Income Statements (measured in money)	Financial Capital	Productive Capacity
Sales	$97,000	$97,000
Cost of goods sold	$58,000	$58,000
Expenses	20,000	20,000
	$78,000	$78,000
Operating income	$19,000	
Holding gains	13,000	
Net income	$32,000	$19,000

HC Corporation Alternative Current Value Balance Sheets (measured in money)	Financial Capital	Productive Capacity
Cash	$30,000	$30,000
Inventory	46,000	46,000
Land	21,000	21,000
	$97,000	$97,000
Accounts payable	$10,000	$10,000
Share capital	55,000	55,000
Retained earnings.....................................	32,000	19,000
Revaluation		13,000
	$97,000	$97,000

During the first year, the shareholders' equity of HC Corporation increased $32,000 ($87,000 − $55,000). Since there were no additional investments by shareholders, and no dividend distributions, the equity change of $32,000 is net income under the financial capital, money measurement, capital maintenance concept. However, if HC Corporation decided to distribute a dividend of $32,000, an additional investment would be required in order for the company to continue current operations. The productive capacity capital maintenance concept argues that no income can be recognized until provision has been made for the replacement of productive capacity at year-end current values. Therefore the holding gains of $13,000 must be excluded from net income; this amount needs to be retained in order to provide for replacement, otherwise HC Corporation will be unable to continue current operations.

In current value accounting, as previously noted, the asset valuation rule determines the period's equity change which is then allocated in accordance with the capital maintenance concept. Use of historical cost for valuation purposes, coupled with the transactions based realization concept, results in an equity change for the first year of $23,000 ($78,000 − $55,000); under current value accounting the equity change, as previously noted, is $32,000. Since the historical-cost model uses financial capital measured in money as its capital maintenance concept, zero is allocated for revaluation and net income is $23,000. Although the zero allocation for revaluation is characteristic of the financial capital, money measurement, capital maintenance concept, current value accounting permits the use of productive capacity as an alternative. Under GAAP, productive capacity is not considered applicable to the historical-cost model. Under current value accounting, the use of productive capacity measured in money for capital maintenance purposes results in net income of $19,000; $13,000 of the equity change is allocated to the revaluation account.

The next issue to be resolved concerns measurement, and here the alternatives are money and purchasing power units or constant dollars. To illustrate, assume the following GPL index data:

```
Incorporation ................ 100
Average for Year 1 ........... 105   Factor 1.05
End of Year 1 ............... 110   Factor 1.10
```

GPL adjustment is much simpler when applied to current value financials rather than historical-cost statements. By definition, year-end current values are stated in year-end purchasing power units. Thus, all assets and liabilities, whether monetary or non-monetary, are already expressed in constant dollars as at the balance sheet date because this date is also the valuation date. Moreover, since the previous period's assets and liabilities were already expressed in constant dollars at the end of that period, no aging is required. Only index data reflecting general price changes for the current period are required to restate current value financial statements.[17]

For HC Corporation, the schedule on page 928 reports the purchasing power gain or loss, which is the same regardless of whether historical-cost or current value financials are being restated.

The GPL adjustment of current value financial statements also requires elimination of the inflation component otherwise included in the money amount of so-called holding gains or losses. The objective here is to show

---

[17]*Ibid.*, p. 40.

	Historical Amount	Conversion Factor	Restated Amount
Share capital	$ 55,000	1.10	$ 60,500
Sales	97,000	1.05	101,850
	$152,000		$162,350
Land	$ 16,000	1.10	$ 17,600
Purchases	96,000	1.05	100,800
Expenses	20,000	1.05	21,000
	$132,000		$139,400
Net monetary asset position at end of			$ 22,950
year	$ 20,000		20,000
			$ 2,950

only real amounts on the restated financials, regardless of capital maintenance alternatives. The real and inflation components included in the money measurement of a holding gain or increase in current values may be diagrammed, as set forth below. Note that the end of period current cost is, by definition, expressed in constant dollars.

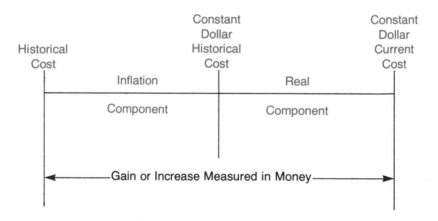

For HC Corporation, the real components of holding gains are listed below.

Real Holding Gains

Realized on sales ($60,900 − $56,700)	$4,200
Unrealized on inventory ($46,000 − $44,100)	1,900
Unrealized on land ($21,000 − $17,600)	3,400
	$9,500

The above amounts shown parenthetically are constant dollar amounts determined as follows:

	Historical Amount	Conversion Factor	Constant Dollar Historical Cost	Nominal Dollar Current Cost	Conversion Factor	Constant Dollar Current Cost
Realized on sales	$54,000	1.05	$56,700	$58,000	1.05	$60,900
Unrealized on inventory .	42,000	1.05	44,100	46,000	1.00	46,000
Unrealized on land	16,000	1.10	17,600	21,000	1.00	21,000

The nominal dollar current cost amount for cost of goods sold, $58,000, is assumed to be expressed in average purchasing power units. This amount must therefore be restated to end of period constant dollars using the conversion factor 1.05 ($58,000 × 1.05 = $60,900). Otherwise, the restated amounts shown above are self-explanatory.

Financial statements for each of the four alternative models depicted in the matrix diagram on page 904 follow. The current value financials are based on the productive capacity capital maintenance concept.

HC Corporation
Alternative Income Statements

	Historical Cost	Constant Dollar Historical Cost	Current Cost	Constant Dollar Current Cost
Sales	$97,000	$101,850	$97,000	$101,850
Cost of goods sold	$54,000	$ 56,700	$58,000	$ 60,900
Expenses	20,000	21,000	20,000	21,000
Purchasing power loss		2,950		2,950
	$74,000	$ 80,650	$78,000	$ 84,850
Net income	$23,000	$ 21,200	$19,000	$ 17,000

HC Corporation
Alternative Balance Sheets

	Historical Cost	Constant Dollar Historical Cost	Current Cost	Constant Dollar Current Cost
Cash	$30,000	$30,000	$30,000	$30,000
Inventory	42,000	44,100	46,000	46,000
Land	16,000	17,600	21,000	21,000
	$88,000	$91,700	$97,000	$97,000
Accounts payable	$10,000	$10,000	$10,000	$10,000
Share capital	55,000	60,500	55,000	60,500
Retained earnings	23,000	21,200	19,000	17,000
Revaluation			13,000	9,500
	$88,000	$91,700	$97,000	$97,000

HC Corporation
Alternative Statements of Changes in Financial Position–Working Capital Basis

	Historical Cost	Constant Dollar Historical Cost	Current Cost	Constant Dollar Current Cost
Working capital was provided by:				
Operations — Net income.......	$23,000	$21,200	$19,000	$17,000
Share capital	55,000	60,500	55,000	60,500
Revaluation providing working capital:				
Realized on sales			4,000	4,200
Unrealized on inventory			4,000	1,900
	$78,000	$81,700	$82,000	$83,600
Working capital was applied to:				
Purchase of land	16,000	17,600	16,000	17,600
Ending working capital				
	$62,000	$64,100	$66,000	$66,000

HC Corporation
Statement of Changes in Financial Position–Working Capital Basis
(Financial Capital Maintenance Measured in Money)

Working capital was provided by:	
Operations:	
Net income	$32,000
Deduct item not providing working capital:	
Unrealized holding gain on land.....................................	5,000
Working capital provided by operations	$27,000
Share capital	55,000
	$82,000
Working capital was applied to:	
Purchase of land	16,000
Ending working capital	$66,000

The statement of changes in financial position (working capital basis) is prepared from beginning and ending balance sheets, the income statement, and other information, as described and illustrated in Chapter 20. However, using alternative accounting models results in variations that merit consideration. GPL adjustment applied to either historical cost or current value financials recognizes a purchasing power gain or loss. When preparing the statement of changes, the net income or loss must be adjusted to determine working capital provided or consumed by operations for the portion, if any, of the purchasing power gain or loss that pertains to non-current monetary items.[18] In the case of current value accounting, with or without GPL ad-

___
[18]This adjustment is illustrated in Appendix A at the end of the chapter.

justment, the variations depend on the capital maintenance concept. With productive capacity maintenance, holding gains appear in a revaluation account on the balance sheet. As illustrated in the HC Corporation example, upward revaluations that pertain to current items are shown as a source of working capital. Under financial capital maintenance, holding gains are included in income. The portion that relates to non-current items is treated as an adjustment for purposes of determining working capital provided or consumed by operations. The statement of changes for HC Corporation presented on the preceding page illustrates this adjustment.

PRONOUNCEMENTS BY THE PROFESSION

At present, there are no legal or other mandatory requirements for Canadian companies to disclose information about the impact of inflation and changing prices in conjunction with conventional financial statements. This may not continue for very long because the Accounting Research Committee has issued an Exposure Draft, "Current Cost Accounting," dated December 1979. This exposure draft is an intended standard on current value accounting that, subject to a size test, would apply to all public or distributing corporations in Canada.

In September 1979, the FASB issued SFAS No. 33, "Financial Reporting and Changing Prices." SSAP 16, "Current Cost Accounting," applicable in the United Kingdom and Ireland, was issued on April 1, 1980. Subject to size tests, SFAS No. 33 and SSAP 16, will apply to 1980 financial reporting in their respective jurisdictions. More specifically, SFAS No. 33 applies to fiscal years ended on or after December 25, 1979; SSAP 16 to accounting periods starting on or after January 1, 1980.

In general, SSAP 16, more precisely ED 24, the Exposure Draft from which the pronouncement was finalized, has provided the basis for the proposals set forth in the Accounting Research Committee's Exposure Draft, "Current Cost Accounting." For this reason, coupled with the tentative nature of an exposure draft, the discussion that follows will consider SSAP 16 to be a surrogate for the Canadian Exposure Draft.

It should also be noted that there are significant differences between the FASB pronouncement, SFAS No. 33, and SSAP 16. While the differences in these pronouncements should certainly encourage experimentation, the international harmonization of accounting standards calls for eventual uniformity.

There are at least two approaches for incorporating information about changing prices into financial statements: (1) selective supplementary disclosure of information about changing prices in notes to the financial statements or elsewhere in the financial statement package, and (2) presentation of articulated current value financial statements, with or without GPL adjustment, to supplement the conventional financials. The basic position of the accounting profession is that conventional financial statements prepared in accordance with established GAAP should continue to be the reporting entity's primary financials. The recent pronouncements mentioned above may be said to illustrate both approaches: SFAS No. 33 is clearly an example of selective supplementary disclosure; SSAP 16 requires financial statement information that articulates. The Canadian Exposure Draft, while generally similar to SSAP 16, is nonetheless an example of selective supplementary disclosure; it does not propose articulated financial statements.

SFAS NO. 33

SFAS No. 33 is a disclosure orientated pronouncement that encourages experimentation and flexibility, while also giving recognition to compliance costs by simplifying the mechanics of its disclosure requirements. The disclosure requirements contained in SFAS No. 33 include two income numbers: (1) income from continuing operations adjusted for the effects of general inflation, and (2) income from continuing operations on a current cost basis, plus the following additional disclosures: (1) the purchasing power gain or loss on net monetary items, (2) increases or decreases in current cost amounts of inventory and property, plant, and equipment, net of inflation (holding gains or losses GPL adjusted), (3) the current cost amounts of inventory and property, plant, and equipment at the end of the fiscal year, and (4) a five-year summary of selected financial data including information on income, sales and other operating revenues, net assets, dividends per common share, and market price per share.[19] Although not necessarily identical, income before extraordinary items is nonetheless the Canadian counterpart of income from continuing operations.

SFAS No. 33 is an example of selective supplementary disclosure because the required restatements and adjustments only pertain to inventories and cost of goods sold, and to property, plant, and equipment and depreciation. It must also be emphasized that the Statement does not require disclosure of a "bottom-line" income number. SFAS No. 33 does require disclosure of: (1) income from continuing operations determined on both a GPL adjusted and current cost basis, (2) the purchasing power gain or loss, and (3) holding gains GPL adjusted. The important point is that there is no requirement for these disclosures to be aggregated to produce an income number. It therefore follows that SFAS No. 33 avoids having to resolve the capital maintenance issue on which, as previously noted, there is a lack of consensus within the accounting profession and even within accounting-principles-making bodies.

The constant dollar disclosure requirements contained in SFAS No. 33 may be stated in terms of the average general price level for the reporting

[19]*Statement of Financial Accounting Standards No. 33, op. cit.*, par. 29, 30 and 35.

period rather than in end of period purchasing power units. This simplifies the mechanics of compliance because it becomes unnecessary to restate such items as sales and most expenses, excluding depreciation. The methodology is illustrated in Appendix B at the end of this chapter. SFAS No. 33 also accepts LIFO cost of goods sold as the equivalent of cost of goods sold on a current cost basis, assuming no layer liquidations during the reporting period.

An illustration of formats that may be used to disclose the information required by SFAS No. 33 is presented below and on pages 934 and 935.[20]

Statement Format

STATEMENT OF INCOME FROM CONTINUING OPERATIONS
ADJUSTED FOR CHANGING PRICES
Year Ended December 31, 1979
(In thousands of dollars)

	As Reported in the Primary Statements	Adjusted for General Inflation	Adjusted for Changes in Specific Prices (Current Costs)
Net sales	$370,000	$370,000	$370,000
Cost of goods sold	275,000	275,000	275,000
Depreciation and amortization	4,000	5,310	5,900
Other operating expenses	71,750	71,750	71,750
Interest expense	5,550	5,550	5,550
Gain on sale of property...................	(300)	(110)	
	356,000	357,500	358,200
Income from continuing operations before income taxes	14,000	12,500	11,800
Provision for income taxes..................	6,000	6,000	6,000
Income from continuing operations	$ 8,000	$ 6,500	$ 5,800
Effective income tax rate — Note 1	43%	48%	51%
Other Information			
Purchasing power gain from holding net monetary liabilities during the year...................		$ 5,780	$ 5,780
Incease in specific prices (current costs) of inventories and property, plant and equipment held during the year*.....................			$ 21,400
Less effect of increase in general price level ...			20,205
Excess of increase in specific prices over increase in the general price level			$ 1,195

*At December 31, 1979, current cost of inventory was $79,500 (historical amount — $59,000) and current cost of property, plant and equipment, net of accumulated depreciation, was $101,000 (historical amount — $68,500). See Notes 1.

---

[20]Ernst & Whinney, *Inflation Accounting: Implementing FASB Statement No. 33* (Cleveland, Ohio: privately printed, 1979) pp. 8, 9 and 11.

STATEMENT OF INCOME FROM CONTINUING OPERATIONS
ADJUSTED FOR CHANGING PRICES
Year Ended December 31, 1979
(In thousands of dollars)

Income from continuing operations, as reported in the income statement		$ 8,000
Adjustments to restate costs for the effect of general inflation		
Depreciation and amortization	$(1,310)	
Gain on sale of property	(190)	(1,500)
Income from continuing operations adjusted for general inflation........................		6,500
Adjustments to reflect the difference between general inflation and changes		
in specific prices (current costs)		
Depreciation and amortization	(590)	
Gain on sale of property	(110)	(700)
Income from continuing operations adjusted for changes in specific prices		$ 5,800

Other Information

Purchasing power gain from holding net monetary liabilities during the year		$ 5,780
Increase in specific prices (current costs) of inventories and property,		
plant and equipment held during the year*		$21,400
Less effect of increase in general price level		20,205
Excess of increase in specific prices over increase in the general price level		$ 1,195

*At December 31, 1979, current cost of inventory was $79,500 (historical amount — $59,000) and current cost of property, plant and equipment, net of accumulated depreciation, was $101,000 (historical amount — $68,500).

Notes 1: SFAS No. 33 does not state that the disclosure of other information must be presented on the same schedule as income from continuing operations. While the Board's examples do present such data on the same schedule, companies may include this information in notes to the supplemental data.

Cost of goods sold is the same under each method because the company uses LIFO and there were no layer liquidations.

While the gain on the sale of property may not be material enough to warrant separate disclosure, it is shown to illustrate the treatment of such gains or losses under the different measurement approaches.

SSAP 16

SSAP 16 requires presentation of a current cost profit and loss account (income statement) and a current cost balance sheet, together with appropriate notes. The requirement to include current cost accounts in addition to historical-cost accounts or historical-cost information can be complied with by: (1) presenting historical-cost accounts as the primary financials with supplementary current cost accounts prominently displayed, (2) presenting current cost accounts as the primary financials with supplementary historical-cost accounts, or (3) presenting current cost accounts as the only financial statements accompanied by adequate historical-cost information. In contrast, both SFAS No. 33 and the Canadian Exposure Draft only require specified balance sheet information as distinct from the statement itself. Both also consider the conventional historical-cost statements to be the primary financials.

Under SSAP 16, current cost income is determined in two stages: (1) current cost operating profit (current cost income of the enterprise in the Canadian Exposure Draft), and (2) current cost profit (income) attributable to shareholders. The starting point is the historical-cost income before interest and taxes (EBIT — earnings before interest and taxes in the literature of finance). The first stage requires three adjustments: (1) the depreciation adjustment, (2) the cost of goods sold adjustment, and (3) the monetary working capital adjustment (net productive monetary items adjustment in the Canadian Exposure Draft). The first two adjustments parallel those required under SFAS No. 33 except that the FASB pronouncement separates the adjustments for depreciation and cost of goods sold into two components: (1) adjustments to historical cost to reflect the effects of general inflation, and (2) adjustments to reflect the difference between general inflation and changes in current costs. The third adjustment recognizes that monetary working capital is an integral part of the net operating assets of the entity. This adjustment represents the amount of additional or reduced resources needed for monetary working capital as a result of changes in the input or entry prices of goods and services used and financed by the entity. The Canadian Exposure Draft describes its counterpart of this adjustment as follows: "a net productive monetary items adjustment to provide for the effect of specific price changes during the period on the net productive monetary items required to support the operating capability of the enterprise." Monetary working capital is defined as the aggregate of short term trade receivables, accruals, prepaid expenses and inventories not subject to a cost of sales adjustment (inventories relating to long-term contracts and commodity dealing) less short-term payables and accruals.

The Canadian Exposure Draft also includes cash balances required for day-to-day operations and deducts short-term loans related to operating activities in its definition of net productive monetary items. The exclusion of cash balances and short-term loans from monetary working capital as defined in SSAP 16 acknowledges the subjectivity inherent in their determination. However, the pronouncement also acknowledges that it is necessary to include cash balances and short-term loans if doing so would have a material effect on current cost operating profit.

The second stage of current cost income determination recognizes the way in which the entity is financed. To the extent that net operating assets are debt financed, it can be argued that shareholders may enjoy, depending upon the direction of price changes, the double benefit of (1) holding gains from the higher current value of net operating assets, and (2) the lower purchasing power value of debt financing. SSAP 16 gives effect to this by means of a gearing adjustment (financing adjustment in the Canadian Exposure Draft). The gearing adjustment is determined by multiplying the aggregate of the current cost adjustments for depreciation, cost of goods sold and monetary working capital by the ratio net operating assets financed by borrowings to total net operating assets at current cost. Otherwise, current cost profit attributable to shareholders is determined after interest, income taxes and extraordinary items.

The example which follows is an adaptation of the illustrative example included in the Canadian Exposure Draft, "Current Cost Accounting." The adaptations are confined to minor modifications of the disclosure format.

Reconciliation of Historical Cost Income to Current Cost Income Year Ended December 31, 1979	
	'000s
Historical cost income before interest and income taxes	$23,900
Current cost adjustments:	
Depreciation	$ 5,750
Cost of goods sold	5,190
Net productive monetary items	1,333
Disposal of plant and equipment	800
	$13,073
Current cost income of the enterprise	10,827
Financing adjustment	$ 3,582
Less: Interest expense and dividends on non-participating preferred shares	4,000
	$ 418
Current cost income before income taxes	$10,409
Income taxes	8,000
Current cost income attributable to shareholders	$ 2,409
Current cost income per share	$ 0.24

Statement of Changes in Shareholders' Equity Reflecting Inventory and Property, Plant and Equipment at Current Cost Year Ended December 31, 1979	
	'000s
Opening shareholders' equity on a current cost basis	$59,800
Increase in amount required to maintain the operating capability of the enterprise, net of a financing adjustment:	
Increase in the current cost of:	
Property, plant and equipment	$ 8,950
Inventory	5,790
Net productive monetary items	1,333
	$16,073
Less: Financing adjustment	3,582
	$12,491
Current cost income attributable to shareholders	2,409
	$14,900
	$74,700
Less: Dividends on common shares	7,600
Closing shareholders' equity on a current cost basis	$67,100

Statement of Asset Values at December 31, 1979		
	'000s	
	Net Current Cost	Net Historical Cost
Inventory	$36,000	$34,000
Property, plant and equipment	$56,200	$36,700

CHALLENGE TO ACCOUNTING PROFESSION

Most would agree that the traditional accounting model has served society well. The challenge to the accounting profession is to continually modify its practices to meet the changing demands of users of financial information. Inflation and other business environmental factors have already caused several countries to adopt accounting practices which reflect changing prices; proposals for additional modification of accounting rules are also being considered. This topic is under study by the Accounting Research Committee and is the subject of an Exposure Draft, "Current Cost Accounting," dated December 1979.

The alternatives discussed in this chapter are important and certainly deserve careful consideration. Experimentation with these alternatives and further research to determine their practicality and usefulness for the future is clearly required.

APPENDIX A: COMPREHENSIVE GPL ADJUSTMENT ILLUSTRATED

PREPARATION OF FINANCIAL STATEMENTS RESTATED FOR GENERAL PRICE CHANGES ILLUSTRATED

The following information sets forth the basic procedures followed in restating financial statements in successive periods to reflect general price changes. The illustration covers operations of a company for the first two years of its life. Financial statements for the first and second years are provided in conventional formats. Financial statements are restated at the end of the first year and at the end of the second year in terms of the price levels prevailing at each of these dates.

The illustration assumes the following:

1. Price-level index numbers were:

At the time the business was formed	100
At the end of the first year	104
At the end of the second year	108

The price level rose evenly throughout each year. The average index for the first year, then, was 102; the average index for the second year was 106.

2. Sales and purchases were made evenly and expenses were incurred evenly throughout each year.
3. Inventories were valued at cost determined by the first-in, first-out method.
4. Dividends were declared and paid at the end of each year.
5. Buildings had a useful life of 10 years and depreciation was recognized at $5,000 per year.

A comparative income and retained earnings statement reporting operations of the company for the first and second years and a comparative balance sheet reporting the financial position of the company upon its organization and at the end of the first and second years prepared in accordance with the conventional historical-cost model appear below and at the top of page 940.

Comparative Income and Retained Earnings Statement		
	First Year	Second Year
Sales	$300,000	$400,000
Cost of goods sold:		
Beginning inventory	$ 55,000	$ 65,000
Purchases	200,000	280,000
Merchandise available for sale	$255,000	$345,000
Ending inventory	65,000	80,000
Cost of goods sold	$190,000	$265,000
Gross profit on sales	$110,000	$135,000
Expenses:		
Depreciation	$ 5,000	$ 5,000
Other expenses	90,000	100,000
Total expenses	$ 95,000	$105,000
Net income	$ 15,000	$ 30,000
Retained earnings at beginning of year	——	10,000
	$ 15,000	$ 40,000
Dividends paid	5,000	10,000
Retained earnings at end of year	$ 10,000	$ 30,000

Comparative Balance Sheet			
	Beginning of Business	End of First Year	End of Second Year
Assets			
Cash	$ 60,000	$ 30,000	$ 40,000
Accounts receivable	—	40,000	50,000
Inventory	55,000	65,000	80,000
Land	35,000	35,000	35,000
Buildings (net)	50,000	45,000	40,000
Total assets	$200,000	$215,000	$245,000
Liabilities			
Accounts payable	$ 20,000	$ 25,000	$ 35,000
Mortgage payable	30,000	30,000	30,000
Total liabilities	$ 50,000	$ 55,000	$ 65,000
Shareholders' Equity			
Capital stock	$150,000	$150,000	$150,000
Retained earnings	—	10,000	30,000
Total shareholders' equity	$150,000	$160,000	$180,000
Total liabilities and shareholders' equity	$200,000	$215,000	$245,000

GPL Adjusted Income and Retained Earnings Statement at the End of the First Year

An income and retained earnings statement for the first year as restated in end of the first year constant dollars, and a schedule reporting the purchasing power loss are given on page 941. The following items should be noted.

Sales. Since sales were made evenly throughout the year, the sales balance reflects the average index for the year. To restate the sales balance to constant dollars, it is multiplied by the ratio of the end-of-year index to the average index for the year.

Cost of Goods Sold. The inventory is reported on the first-in, first-out basis. Restatement of cost of goods sold to end-of-year constant dollars involves the following adjustments:

1. The beginning inventory balance reports costs incurred when the business was organized and therefore reflects the index at the beginning of the year, 100. To restate the beginning inventory to end-of-year constant dollars, it is multiplied by the ratio of the end-of-year index at the beginning of the year.
2. Purchases were made evenly throughout the year. To restate the purchases balance to end-of-year constant dollars, it is multiplied by the ratio of the end-of-year index to the average index.
3. In applying first-in, first-out, latest costs were assigned to the ending inventory. The ending inventory, then, may be regarded as composed of purchases

GPL Adjusted Statement of Income and Retained Earnings For First Year	Historical Amount	Conversion Factor	Restated Amount
Sales	$300,000	104/102	$305,882
Cost of goods sold:			
Beginning inventory	$ 55,000	104/100	$ 57,200
Purchases................................	200,000	104/102	203,922
Merchandise available for sale	$255,000		$261,122
Ending inventory	65,000	104/102	66,275
Cost of goods sold	$190,000		$194,847
Gross profit on sales	$110,000		$111,035
Expenses:			
Depreciation	$ 5,000	104/100	$ 5,200
Other expenses	90,000	104/102	91,765
Total expenses	$ 95,000		$ 96,965
Income before adjustment for purchasing power gain or loss..............................	$ 15,000		$ 14,070
Purchasing power loss (see schedule)	——		595
Net income after adjustment for purchasing power loss	$ 15,000		$ 13,475
Retained earnings at beginning of year	——		——
	$ 15,000		$ 13,475
Dividends paid	5,000	104/104	5,000
Retained earnings at end of year	$ 10,000		$ 8,475

of the current period. To restate the ending inventory to end-of-year constant dollars, it is multiplied by the ratio of the end-of-year index to the average index.[21]

Depreciation. Since the charge for depreciation represents the allocation of the cost of a property item to operations, the adjustment of the depreciation charge must be consistent with the adjustment applicable to the property item. To restate the buildings cost to end-of-year constant dollars, it is multiplied by the ratio of the end-of-year index to the index at the time the buildings were acquired, in this case the index at the beginning of the year, or 100; to restate the depreciation charge, it is similarly multiplied by the ratio expressing the general price change since the date the buildings were acquired. The charge for depreciation as restated can also be computed by applying the depreciation rate to the cost of the asset stated in terms of end-of-year constant dollars.

---

[21] When there is evidence that the ending inventory is composed of goods acquired within the last half of the year or the last quarter, the average index for such shorter period is properly applied in restating inventory.

Schedule Reporting Purchasing Power Gain or Loss For First Year	Historical Amount		Conversion Factor	Restated Amount
Net monetary position at beginning of year:				
Assets (cash)	$60,000			
Liabiliites (accounts payable and mortgage payable)	50,000	$ 10,000	104/100	$ 10,400
Increase in net monetary position during year:				
Sales		300,000	104/102	305,882
		$310,000		$316,282
Decrease in net monetary position during year:				
Purchases		$200,000	104/102	$203,922
Other expenses		90,000	104/102	91,765
Dividends....................		5,000	104/102	5,000
		$295,000	104	$300,687
				$ 15,595
Net monetary position at end of year:				
Assets (cash and accounts receivable)	$70,000			
Liabilities (accounts payable and mortgage payable)	55,000	$ 15,000		15,000
Purchasing power loss				$ 595

Other Expenses. The other expenses were incurred evenly throughout the year. To restate the other expenses total to end-of-year constant dollars, it is multiplied by the ratio of the end-of-year index to the average index.

Income before Adjustment for Purchasing Power Gain or Loss. Revenue and expense items are summarized to arrive at the income for the year before adjustment for the purchasing power gain or loss.

Purchasing Power Gain or Loss. The income and retained earnings statement is supported by a schedule reporting the purchasing power gain or loss from holding monetary assets and maintaining monetary liabilities in a period of inflation. The schedule is developed as follows:

1. The difference between the monetary assets and liabilities, net monetary position, at the beginning of the period is restated to end-of-year constant dollars.
2. Any monetary items becoming available during the year are expressed in end-of-year constant dollars and are added to or subtracted from the beginning net monetary position balance.

3. The actual monetary assets and the liabilities as of the end of the year are determined. The balance of net monetary position at the end of the year is compared with the sum of (1) and (2) above. In the example, net monetary position at the end of the year would have been $15,595 if the company had maintained its net monetary position during the period of increasing general prices; since the net monetary position is only $15,000, a loss in purchasing power for the year of $595 was sustained.

The purchasing power gain or loss is reported on the combined income and retained earnings statement, and the net income after adjustment for the gain or loss is determined.

Dividends. Dividends were declared and paid at the end of the year. The dividends balance, then, reflects end-of-year constant dollars and is reported without change.

Retained Earnings at the End of the Year. The dividends balance is subtracted from net income after adjustment for the purchasing power loss to determine the retained earnings balance at the end of the first year in terms of year-end constant dollars.

GPL Adjusted Balance Sheet at the End of the First Year

A balance sheet as restated in end-of-the-first-year constant dollars is presented below.

GPL Adjusted Balance Sheet End of First Year			
	Historical Amount	Conversion Factor	Restated Amount
Assets			
Cash	$ 30,000		$ 30,000
Accounts receivable	40,000		40,000
Inventory	65,000	104/102	66,275
Land	35,000	104/100	36,400
Buildings (net)	45,000	104/100	46,800
Total assets	$215,000		$219,475
Liabilities			
Accounts payable	$ 25,000		$ 25,000
Mortgage payable	30,000		30,000
Total liabilities	$ 55,000		$ 55,000
Shareholders' Equity			
Capital stock	$150,000	104/100	$156,000
Retained earnings	10,000*		8,475
Total shareholders' equity	$160,000		$164,475
Total liabilities and shareholders' equity	$215,000		$219,475

*See the income and retained earnings statement on page 941.

Monetary Assets. Monetary assets are reported without change.

Inventory. The ending inventory balance reflects the average index for the year. To restate this balance to end-of-year constant dollars, it is multiplied by the ratio of the end-of-year index to the average index. The constant dollar amount for the inventory on the balance sheet must be the same as that reported in arriving at cost of goods sold on the income and retained earnings statement.

Land and Buildings. Land and buildings accounts report dollar costs at the time the assets were acquired. To restate land and buildings balances to end-of-year constant dollars, these are multiplied by the ratio expressing the price-level change since the time they were acquired.

Liabilities. Liabilities, because they are monetary, are reported without change.

Shareholders' Equity. Capital stock expressed in terms of original dollar investment is restated to end-of-year constant dollars. The retained earnings balance as summarized in terms of end-of-year constant dollars on the combined income and retained earnings statement is added to the capital stock balances in arriving at shareholders' equity. If comparable assumptions and procedures have been employed in developing balances on the combined income and retained earnings statement and the balance sheet, the statements will articulate and recognition of the shareholders' equity will bring the balance sheet into balance. If the shareholders' equity is not equal to the difference between the assets and the liabilities, errors or inconsistencies are indicated, and these must be found and corrected.

GPL Adjusted Comparative Balance Sheet at the End of the First Year

A comparative balance sheet prepared in terms of end-of-first-year constant dollars is presented on page 945.

GPL Adjusted Income and Retained Earnings Statement at the End of the Second Year

A statement of income and retained earnings as restated in end-of-the-second-year constant dollars and a schedule reporting the purchasing power loss are presented on page 946. The following items should be noted:

Income before Adjustment for General Price Level Gain or Loss. In developing the income and retained earnings statement for the second year, sales, purchases, and other expense balances reflecting the average index for the year are multiplied by the ratio of the price-level index at the end of the second year to the average index for the second year. In developing cost of goods sold, the beginning inventory balance, stated at $65,000, reflecting

	Beginning of Business				
	Historical Amount	Conversion Factor	Restated Amount	End of First Year	Increase (Decrease)
Assets					
Cash	$ 60,000	104/100	$ 62,400	$ 30,000	$(32,400)
Accounts receivable				40,000	40,000
Inventory	55,000	104/100	57,200	66,275	9,075
Land	35,000	104/100	36,400	36,400	
Buildings (net)	50,000	104/100	52,000	46,800	(5,200)
Total assets	$200,000		$208,000	$219,475	$ 11,475
Liabilities					
Accounts payable	$ 20,000	104/100	$ 20,800	$ 25,000	$ 4,200
Mortgage payable	30,000	104/100	31,200	30,000	(1,200)
Total liabilities	$ 50,000		$ 52,000	$ 55,000	$ 3,000
Shareholders' Equity					
Capital stock	$150,000	104/100	$156,000	$156,000	
Retained earnings				8,475	$ 8,475
Total shareholders' equity	$150,000		$156,000	$164,475	$ 8,475
Total liabilities and shareholders' equity	$200,000		$208,000	$219,475	$ 11,475

acquisitions when the index was 102, must be adjusted to a constant dollar amount in terms of the price level at the end of the second year, 108, and hence is multiplied by 108/102; the ending inventory balance reflecting purchases during the second year is multiplied by the ratio of the index at the end of the second year to the average index for the second year, or 108/106. The charge for depreciation, reported in terms of asset cost, is multiplied by the ratio of the index at the end of the second year to the index at the date of asset acquisition, or 108/100. Revenue and expense balances are summarized to arrive at the income for the year before adjustment for the purchasing power gain or loss.

Purchasing Power Gain or Loss. The computation of the purchasing power gain or loss for the second year is made just as it was for the first year. Beginning net monetary position adjusted for monetary items becoming available to the company during the second year, expressed in terms of end-of-year constant dollars, are compared with the actual ending net monetary position. This comparison indicates a further loss of purchasing power.

Retained Earnings at the Beginning of the Year. All shareholders' equity balances expressed in terms of end-of-year constant dollars for the first year must be restated to end-of-year constant dollars for the second year. Retained

GPL Adjusted Income and Retained Earnings Statement
For Second Year

	Historical Amount	Conversion Factor	Restated Amount
Sales	$400,000	108/106	$407,547
Cost of goods sold:			
Beginning inventory	$ 65,000	108/102	$ 68,824
Purchases	280,000	108/106	285,283
Merchandise available for sale	$345,000		$354,107
Ending inventory	80,000	108/106	81,509
Cost of goods sold	$265,000		$272,598
Gross profit on sales	$135,000		$134,949
Expenses:			
Depreciation	$ 5,000	108/100	$ 5,400
Other expenses	100,000	108/106	101,887
Total expenses	$105,000		$107,287
Income before adjustment for purchasing power gain or loss	$ 30,000		$ 27,662
Purchasing power loss (see schedule)	—		954
Net income after adjustment for purchasing power loss.......................................	$ 30,000		$ 26,708
Retained earnings at beginning of year	10,000	($8,475 × 108/104)	8,801
	$ 40,000		$ 35,509
Dividends paid	10,000	108/108	10,000
Retained earnings at end of year	$ 30,000		$ 25,509

Schedule Reporting Purchasing Power Gain or Loss
For Second Year

	Historical Amount		Conversion Factor	Restated Amount
Net monetary position at beginning of year:				
Assets (cash and accounts receivable)	$70,000			
Liabilities (accounts payable and mortgage payable).	55,000	$ 15,000	108/104	$ 15,577
Increase in net monetary position during year:				
Sales..		400,000	108/106	407,547
		$415,000		$423,124
Decrease in net monetary position during year:				
Purchases		$280,000	108/106	$285,283
Other expenses		100,000	108/106	101,887
Dividends		10,000	108/108	10,000
		$390,000		$397,170
Net monetary position at end of year:				$25,954
Assets (cash and accounts receivable)	$90,000			
Liabilities (accounts payable and mortgage payable).	65,000	$ 25,000		25,000
Purchasing power loss				$ 954

earnings, then, as reported at the amount shown on the balance sheet at the end of the first year is updated to indicate its equivalent in constant dollars at the end of the second year.

Dividends. Dividends were declared and paid at the end of the year. The dividends balance, then, reflects end-of-year constant dollars and is reported without change.

Retained Earnings at the End of the Year. Having determined net income after adjustment for the general price-level change, this is increased by the beginning retained earnings balance as restated in end-of-year constant dollars and reduced by dividends to arrive at the ending retained earnings balance.

GPL Adjusted Balance Sheet at the End of the Second Year

A balance sheet at the end of the second year is presented below. Monetary assets and liabilities are reported without change. The inventory acquired during the second year is restated in end-of-year constant dollars. Land and buildings reported at dollar amounts at the time the business was organized are adjusted for the change in the general price level for the two-year period. Share capital reported on the balance sheet at the end of the preceding period is updated to report end-of-year constant dollars. The retained earnings balance as summarized in terms of end-of-year constant dollars on the statement of income and retained earnings is added to the share capital balances in arriving at the shareholders' equity. A schedule

GPL Adjusted Balance Sheet Restated End of Second Year			
	Historical Amount	Conversion Factor	Restated Amount
Assets			
Cash	$ 40,000		$ 40,000
Accounts receivable	50,000		50,000
Inventory	80,000	108/106	81,509
Land	35,000	108/100	37,800
Building (net)	40,000	108/100	43,200
Total assets	$245,000		$252,509
Liabilities			
Accounts payable	$ 35,000		$ 35,000
Mortgage payable	30,000		30,000
Total liabilities	$ 65,000		$ 65,000
Shareholders' Equity			
Capital stock	$150,000	($156,000 × 108/104)	$162,000
Retained earnings	30,000		25,509
Total shareholders' equity	$180,000		$187,509
Total liabilities and shareholders' equity	$245,000		$252,509

reconciling end-of-year retained earnings as shown on the restated balance sheet may be presented as follows:

Schedule Reconciling GPL Adjusted Retained Earnings End of Second Year	Historical Amount	Conversion Factor	Restated Amount
Retained earnings balance at beginning of second year......	$ 8,475	108/104	$ 8,801
Add item increasing retained earnings:			
Net income for year after adjustment for general price-level loss (from restated income statement)	30,000		26,708
Subtract item decreasing retained earnings:			
Dividends	(10,000)	108/108	(10,000)
Retained earnings balance at end of second year			$25,509

GPL Adjusted Comparative Statements at the End of the Second Year

A comparative statement of income and retained earnings is shown on page 950 and a comparative balance sheet prepared at the end of the second year is given on page 951.

GPL Adjusted Statement of Changes

A statement of changes in financial position for the first year as restated in constant dollars at the end of the first year is presented on page 949. This statement is prepared from GPL adjusted financial statements and other information in essentially the same way that the historical-cost statement of changes is prepared. Thus, the GPL adjusted statement of changes is not prepared by restating the historical-cost statement as is the case for both the income statement and balance sheet.

Assuming funds to be defined as working capital, the increase or decrease for the period is determined as follows:

GPL Adjusted Schedule of Changes in Working Capital For First Year	Beginning of Business	End of First Year	Increase (Decrease)
Current Assets:			
Cash	$ 62,400	$ 30,000	$(32,400)
Accounts receivable		40,000	40,000
Inventory	57,200	66,275	9,075
Total	$119,600	$136,275	
Current Liabilities:			
Accounts payable	20,800	25,000	(4,200)
Working capital	$ 98,800	$111,275	$ 12,475

The purchasing power loss reported on the income statement is $595. This amount includes a purchasing gain on the mortgage of $1,200 ($30,000 × 104/100 − $30,000), and a purchasing power loss on current monetary items of $1,795. Since this latter amount is part of the increase in working capital, only the purchasing power gain on long-term or non-current monetary items enters into the computation of working capital provided by operations.

Statement of Changes in Financial Position — Working Capital Basis For First Year	
Working capital was provided by:	
Operations:	
Net income	$13,475
Add item not requiring working capital:	
Depreciation expense	5,200
	$18,675
Deduct item not providing working capital:	
Purchasing power gain on mortgage	1,200
Working capital provided by operations	$17,475
Working capital was applied to:	
Dividends	5,000
Increase in working capital	$12,475

A statement of changes in financial position for the second year restated in end-of-second-year constant dollars is presented below. The increase in working capital was determined from the GPL adjusted comparative balance sheet on page 951.

Statement of Changes in Financial Position — Working Capital Basis For Second Year	
Working capital was provided by:	
Operations:	
Net income	$26,708
Add item not requiring working capital:	
Depreciation expense	5,400
	$32,108
Deduct item not providing working capital:	
Purchasing power gain on mortgage	1,154
Working capital provided by operations	$30,954
Working capital was applied to:	
Dividends	10,000
Increase in working capital	$20,954

The preparation of a comparative statement of changes in financial position restated in end-of-second-year constant dollars would require that the statement for the first year be rolled forward. To illustrate, the GPL adjusted schedule of changes in working capital on page 948 indicates working capital at the end of the first year of $111,275. Since this amount is stated in end-of-first-year constant dollars, it must be rolled forward to determine the increase or decrease in working capital for the second year. Thus the amount of working capital at the end of the second year, $136,509, is reduced by the rolled forward amount of working capital at the end of the first year, $115,555 ($111,275 × 108/104), to determine the increase in working capital of $20,954 reported on statement of changes for the second year.

GPL ADJUSTMENTS APPLIED TO INVENTORIES REPORTED UNDER ALTERNATIVE COST-FLOW ASSUMPTIONS

In the illustration, inventories were reflected on a first-in, first-out cost-flow assumption and the implications of this procedure were recognized in restating inventory and cost of goods sold balances. When other cost-flow assumptions are employed, restatements must be modified to recognize the

GPL Adjusted Comparative Income and Retained Earnings Statement First and Second Years					
	First Year				
	Restated to End of First Year	Conversion Factor	Restated to End of Second Year	Second Year	Increase (Decrease)
Sales	$305,882	108/104	$317,647	$407,547	$89,900
Cost of goods sold:					
Beginning inventory	$ 57,200	108/104	$ 59,400	$ 68,824	$ 9,424
Purchases	203,922	108/104	211,765	285,283	73,518
Merchandise available for sale ...	$261,122		$271,165	$354,107	$82,942
Ending inventory	66,275	108/104	68,824	81,509	12,685
Cost of goods sold	$194,847		$202,341	$272,598	$70,257
Gross profit on sales	$111,035		$115,306	$134,949	$19,643
Expenses:					
Depreciation	$ 5,200	108/104	$ 5,400	$ 5,400	——
Other expenses	91,765	108/104	95,295	101,887	$ 6,592
Total expenses	$ 96,965	108/104	$100,695	$107,287	$ 6,592
Income before adjustment for purchasing power gain or loss ...	$ 14,070		$ 14,611	$ 27,662	$13,051
Purchasing power loss	595	108/104	618	954	336
Net income after adjustment for purchasing power loss	$ 13,475	108/104	$ 13,993	$ 26,708	$12,715
Retained earnings at beginning of year	——		——	8,801	8,801
	$ 13,475		$ 13,993	$ 35,509	$21,516
Dividends paid	5,000	108/104	5,192	10,000	4,808
Retained earnings at end of year ..	$ 8,475		$ 8,801	$ 25,509	$16,708

GPL Adjusted Comparative Balance Sheet
End of Second Year

	Beginning of Business			End of First Year				Increase (Decrease)	
	Restated to End of First Year	Conversion Factor	Restated to End of Second Year	Restated to End of First Year	Conversion Factor	Restated to End of Second Year	End of Second Year	Beginning of Business to End of First Year	End of First Year to End of Second Year
Assets									
Cash	$ 62,400	108/104	$ 64,800	$ 30,000	108/104	$ 31,154	$ 40,000	$(33,646)	$ 8,646
Accounts receivable				40,000	108/104	41,538	50,000	41,538	8,462
Inventory	57,200	108/104	59,400	66,275	108/104	68,824	81,509	9,424	12,685
Land	36,400	108/104	37,800	36,400	108/104	37,800	37,800		
Buildings (net)	52,000	108/104	54,000	46,800	108/104	48,600	43,200	(5,400)	(5,400)
Total assets	$208,000		$216,000	$219,475		$227,916	$252,509	$11,916	$24,593
Liabilities									
Accounts payable	$ 20,800	108/104	$ 21,600	$ 25,000	108/104	$ 25,961	$ 35,000	$ 4,361	$ 9,039
Mortgage payable	31,200	108/104	32,400	30,000	108/104	31,154	30,000	(1,246)	(1,154)
Total liabilities	$ 52,000		$ 54,000	$ 55,000		$ 57,115	$ 65,000	$ 3,115	$ 7,885
Shareholders' Equity									
Share capital	$156,000	108/104	$162,000	$156,000	108/104	$162,000	$162,000		
Retained earnings				8,475	108/104	8,801	25,509	$ 8,801	$16,708
Total shareholders' equity	$156,000		$162,000	$164,475		$170,801	$187,509	$ 8,801	$16,708
Total liabilities and shareholders' equity	$208,000		$216,000	$219,475		$227,916	$252,509	$11,916	$24,593

cost reflected in the inventory balances as a result of the alternative assumptions. For example, using the first-in, first-out assumption, the inventory balance reports costs of the inventory in terms of most recent purchases, and accordingly the inventory is restated to the prevailing price level by applying an index expressing the general price change from the time the goods were acquired. If the last-in, first-out procedure is employed, the inventory balance may report a number of cost layers, and different indexes must be applied to express the individual cost layers in terms of the prevailing price level.

To illustrate, assume price-level changes for a two-year period as given in the illustration on page 939 and a company's inventories and costs during the first two years of its operations as follows:

	First Year	Second Year
Beginning inventory	$100,000	$120,000
Purchases	300,000	400,000
Goods available for sale	$400,000	$520,000
Ending inventory (lifo)	120,000	105,000
Cost of goods sold	$280,000	$415,000

Inventory balances and the cost of goods sold balances would be restated as follows:

	Historical Amount		Conversion Factor	Restated Amount	
First Year:					
Beginning inventory		$100,000	104/100		$104,000
Purchases		300,000	104/102		305,882
Goods available for sale		$400,000			$409,882
Ending inventory:					
Original balance	$100,000		104/100	$104,000	
First-year layer increase	20,000		104/102	20,392	
		120,000			124,392
Cost of goods sold		$280,000			$285,490
Second Year:					
Beginning inventory:					
Original balance	$100,000		108/100	$108,000	
First-year layer increase	20,000		108/102	21,176	
		$120,000			$129,176
Purchases		400,000	108/106		407,547
Goods available for sale		$520,000			$536,723
Ending inventory:					
Original balance	$100,000		108/100	$108,000	
First-year layer increase	5,000		108/102	5,294	
		105,000			113,294
Cost of goods sold		$415,000			$423,429

The inventory balance at the end of the first year was recognized as composed of two separate layers — a cost assigned to the original inventory balance and an incremental cost layer for the inventory increase for the year. The beginning cost is restated to report the change in the price level since the beginning of the year; the current cost layer is restated to report the difference between the end-of-year index and the average index for the year. The inventory at the end of the second year was recognized as composed of two layers — the cost assigned to the original inventory balance and a portion of the incremental cost related to the first year. The original cost is restated to report the change in the price level since the beginning of the first year; the incremental layer is restated to report the difference between the end-of-second-year index and the average index for the first year.

GPL ADJUSTMENTS APPLIED TO DEPRECIABLE PROPERTIES ACQUIRED AT DIFFERENT TIMES

In the illustration, there was a single acquisition of depreciable property — the acquisition of buildings when the business was formed. When depreciable properties are acquired at different times, the restatement of depreciable properties becomes more involved. The acquisition dates for individual property items must be determined and both property balances and depreciation charges must be restated to reflect price-level changes since various acquisition dates.

To illustrate, assume general price changes for a two-year period are the same as in the preceding illustration, and company purchases of depreciable properties are as follows:

Date of Acquisition	Asset	Cost	Useful Life
Beginning of first year	Building	$100,000	25 years
Middle of first year	Equipment	$ 61,200	6 years
Middle of second year	Furniture	$ 42,400	8 years

Assume depreciation charges are calculated on the straight-line basis; salvage values are negligible and are not recognized. The cost of the property items would then be adjusted at the end of the first year as follows:

Asset	Historical Amount	Conversion Factor	Restated Amount
Building	$100,000	104/100	$104,000
Equipment........................	61,200	104/102	62,400
Total	$161,200		$166,400

The charges for depreciation may be obtained by applying depreciation rates to the restated costs. On the other hand, it is possible to compute depreciation charges by applying the individual conversion factors used in restating the property items to the depreciation charges based on cost. The latter procedure is illustrated below.

Asset	Historical Depreciation Charge	Conversion Factor	Restated Depreciation Charge
Building	$4,000(1 yr.)	104/100	$4,160
Equipment	5,100(1/2 yr.)	104/102	5,200
Total	$9,100		$9,360

In determining the balances for the property items to be reported on the balance sheet at the end of the first year, the individual conversion factors are applied to the separate acquisitions and to the related balances for accumulated depreciation. These balances at the end of the first year are derived as follows:

Asset	Historical Amount	Conversion Factor	Restated Amount
Building cost	$100,000	104/100	$104,000
Accumulated depreciation	4,000	104/100	4,160
Net	$ 96,000		$99,840
Equipment cost	$ 61,200	104/102	$ 62,400
Accumulated depreciation	5,100	104/102	5,200
Net	56,100		57,200
Total	$152,100		$157,040

At the end of the second year, depreciable assets would be restated as follows:

Asset	Historical Amount	Conversion Factor	Restated Amount
Building	$100,000	108/100	$108,000
Equipment	61,200˙	108/102	64,800
Furniture	42,400	108/106	43,200
Total	$203,600		$216,000

Depreciation for the second year would be computed as follows:

Asset	Historical Depreciation Charge	Conversion Factor	Restated Depreciation Charge
Building	$ 4,000(1 yr.)	108/100	$ 4,320
Equipment	10,200(1 yr.)	108/102	10,800
Furniture	2,650 (1/2 yr.)	108/106	2,700
Total	$16,850		$17,820

At the end of the second year, cost and accumulated depreciation balances would be restated as follows:

Asset	Historical Amount		Conversion Factor	Restated Amount	
Building cost	$100,000		108/100	$108,000	
Accumulated depreciation	8,000		108/100	8,640	
Net		$ 92,000			$ 99,360
Equipment cost	$ 61,200		108/102	$ 64,800	
Accumulated depreciation	15,300		108/102	16,200	
Net		45,900			48,600
Furniture cost	$ 42,400		108/106	$ 43,200	
Accumulated depreciation	2,650		108/106	2,700	
Net		39,750			40,500
Total		$177,650			$188,460

APPENDIX B: SFAS NO. 33 ILLUSTRATED

SFAS No. 33 requires supplementary disclosure of (1) income from continuing operations adjusted for the effects of general inflation, (2) the purchasing power gain or loss on net monetary items, and (3) increases or decreases in the current value amounts of inventory and property, plant, and equipment, net of inflation (deflated holding gains)[22]. The index to be used is the consumer price index, and the minimum constant dollar information required may be measured in terms of average current period purchasing power units. This use of average index data serves to simplify the computations of the constant dollar disclosures required to comply with SFAS No. 33.

The first year information from the example presented in Appendix A, together with additional information set forth below, will be used to illustrate the disclosure requirements contained in SFAS No. 33. Additional information pertaining to inventories, land and buildings follows.

Inventories

	Units	Current Cost Per Unit	Current Cost Total
Beginning inventory	1,200	$47.00	$ 56,400
Purchases	4,000		
	5,200		
Ending inventory	1,300	52.00	67,600
Average ($47 + $52 ÷ 2)		49.50	
Average current cost of good sold	3,900	49.50	193,050

Land

	Current Cost
Beginning of year	$36,750
End of year	40,000

---

[22] As noted in the chapter, SFAS No. 33 also requires certain current cost disclosures.

(Continued)

Buildings

	Current Cost
Beginning of year	$53,000
End of year	57,000
Average	55,000
Depreciation (10%)	5,500

The following schedule restates the historical cost of goods sold into average first year purchasing power units or constant dollars.

GPL Adjusted Cost of Goods Sold
For First Year

	Historical Amount	Conversion Factor	Restated Amount
Beginning inventory	$ 55,000	102/100	$ 56,100
Purchases	200,000	102/102*	200,000
	$255,000		$256,100
Ending inventory	65,000	102/102	65,000
Cost of goods sold	$190,000		$191,100

*Assumed to be in average constant dollars

In the example, the restatement of depreciation expense is straight-forward. The historical amount $5,000 is multiplied by the conversion factor 102/100; the restated amount is $5,100.

The computation of the purchasing power gain or loss is supported by the schedule presented below.

Schedule Reporting Purchasing Power Gain or Loss
For First Year

	Historical Amount	Conversion Factor	Restated Amount
Net monetary asset position at beginning of year	$10,000	102/100	$10,200
Increase during year	5,000	102/102*	5,000
			15,200
Net monetary asset position at end of year	$15,000	102/104**	14,712
Purchasing power loss			$ 488

* Assumed to be in average constant dollars.

**This restatement rolls back the end-of-year balance to average constant dollars.

SFAS No. 33 also requires disclosure of the increases or decreases in the current cost amounts of inventory and property, plant, and equipment, net of inflation. The objective here is to eliminate the inflation component of these increases or decreases. The following schedules present the required analysis.

Increase in Current Cost of Inventories For First Year			
	Current Cost Nominal Dollars	Conversion Factor	Current Cost Average First Year Dollars
Beginning inventory	$ 56,400	102/100	$ 57,528
Purchases	200,000	102/102*	200,000
Cost of goods sold	(193,050)	102/102*	(193,050)
Ending inventory	(67,600)	102/104	(66,300)
Increase	$ 4,250		$ 1,822

*Assumed to be in average constant dollars.

Increase in Land and Buildings For First Year			
	Current Cost Nominal Dollars	Conversion Factor	Current Cost Average First Year Dollars
Beginning of year:			
Land	$36,750	102/100	$37,485
Buildings..............	53,000	102/100	54,060
Depreciation	(5,500)	102/102*	(5,500)
End of year:			
Land	(40,000)	102/104	(39,231)
Buildings (net)	(51,300)	102/104	(50,313)
Increase	$ 7,050		$ 3,499

*Assumed to be in average constant dollars.

The net book value of buildings as shown in the schedule above is equal to 90 per cent of the building's year-end current cost of $57,000 (90% of $57,000 = $51,300). The inflation component of the increases in the current cost of inventories and land and buildings are summerized below.

	Inventories	Land and Buildings	Total
Increase (nominal dollars)	$ 4,250	$ 7,050	$11,300
Increase (constant dollars)	1,822	3,499	5,321
Inflation component	$ 2,428	$ 3,551	$ 5,979

A summary of amounts restated in average first year purchasing power units or constant dollars is given at the top of the next page.

	Constant Dollar Historical Cost	Constant Dollar Current Cost
Cost of goods sold	$191,100	$193,050
Depreciation expense	5,100	5,500
Purchasing power loss	488	488
Increases in current cost:		
Inventories		1,822
Land and buildings (net)		3,499
Inventory	65,000	66,300
Land and buildings (net)	81,600*	89,544

*Land ($35,000 × 102/100)	$35,700
Buildings ($50,000 × 102/100)	51,000
	$86,700
Depreciation	5,100
	$81,600

The disclosures required under SFAS No. 33 can be presented in either reconciliation format or in statement format. Both formats are illustrated.

Statement of Income From Continuing Operations Adjusted for Changing Prices For First Year

Income from continuing operations as reported on income statement		$15,000
Adjustments to restate costs for the effect of general inflation:		
Cost of goods sold	$1,100	
Depreciation	100	1,200
Income from continuing operations adjusted for general inflation		$13,800
Adjustments to reflect the difference between general inflation and changes in current costs:		
Cost of goods sold	$1,950	
Depreciation	400	2,350
Income from continuing operations adjusted for changes in current costs		$11,540
Purchasing power loss		$ 488
Increase in current cost of inventories and land and buildings held during year*		$11,300
Effect of increase in general price level		5,979
Excess of increase in current cost over increase in general price level		$ 5,321

*At year end current cost of inventory was $67,600 and current cost of land and buildings net of accumulated depreciation was $91,300.

Statement of Income From Continuing Operations Adjusted for Changing Prices
For First Year

	As Reported in Primary Statements	Adjusted for General Inflation	Adjusted for Changes in Current Costs
Sales	$300,000	$300,000	$300,000
Cost of goods sold	$190,000	191,100	193,050
Depreciation	5,000	5,100	5,500
Other expenses	90,000	90,000	90,000
	$285,000	$286,200	$288,550
Income from continuing operations	$ 15,000	$ 13,800	$ 11,450
Purchasing power loss		$ 488	$ 488
Increase in current cost of inventories and land and buildings held during year*			$ 11,300
Effect of increase in general price level			5,979
Excess of increase in current cost over increase in general price level			$ 5,321

*At year end current cost of inventory was $67,600 and current cost of land and buildings net of accumulated depreciation was $91,300.

QUESTIONS

1. What has caused the increased interest in financial reporting and price changes?

2. Why do accountants prefer to report historical costs rather than current values in conventional statements?

3. (a) Identify three possible methods of overcoming objections to historical-cost financial statements. (b) Compare the concept of reporting current values in financial statements with the concept of restating original dollar costs for price-level changes.

4. How are general price-level indexes, e.g., the GNE Implicit Price Index, derived?

5. (a) Distinguish between monetary assets and non-monetary assets. (b) Which of the following are monetary assets?
- (1) Cash
- (2) Investment in common stock
- (3) Investment in bonds
- (4) Merchandise on hand
- (5) Prepaid expenses
- (6) Buildings
- (7) Patents
- (8) Sinking fund — uninvested cash
- (9) Sinking fund — investments in real estate
- (10) Deferred developmental costs

6. Assume a company holds property or maintains the obligations listed below during a year in which there is an increase in the price level. State in each case whether the position of the company at the end of the year is better, worse, or unchanged.

- (a) Cash
- (b) Cash surrender value of life insurance
- (c) Land
- (d) Unearned subscription revenue
- (e) Accounts receivable
- (f) Notes payable
- (g) Merchandise on hand
- (h) Long-term warranties on sales

7. If prices rise steadily over an extended period of time, indicate whether the following items would give rise to a purchasing power gain, a purchasing power loss, or neither purchasing power gain nor loss.

- (a) Owning land.
- (b) Maintaining a balance in a chequing account.
- (c) Amortizing goodwill.
- (d) Owing bonds payable.

8. Indicate whether a company gains or loses under each condition described below.

- (a) A company maintains an excess of monetary assets over monetary liabilities during a period of general price-level increase.
- (b) A company maintains an excess of monetary liabilities over monetary assets during a period of general price-level increase.
- (c) A company maintains an excess of monetary assets over monetary liabilities during a period of general price-level decrease.
- (d) A company maintains an excess of monetary liabilities over monetary assets during a period of general price-level decrease.

9. It has been suggested that although the shareholders' equity is non-monetary in character, an exception should be made in the case of the equity of preferred shareholders and this equity should be treated as a monetary item. Would you agree? Give your reasons.

10. What is the general formula for restating financial statements to reflect general price-level changes?

11. Some have suggested that the financial reporting of changing prices be limited to land, buildings, and equipment, to related depreciation charges, to inventories and cost of goods sold. Would you defend or reject such a proposal? Give your reasons.

12. Describe the restatement of inventories for general price-level changes when inventories are reported (a) on a first-in, first-out basis; (b) on a last-in, first-out basis.

13. The most time-consuming step in the restatement of accounts to report general price-level changes is the ageing of the depreciable property and the corresponding restatement of the periodic depreciation. What is meant by ageing as used here? Do you agree with this statement?

14. What special procedures are required when price-level statements are prepared for the first time for a company that has been operating for many years?

15. What are three methods of accounting for backlog depreciation?

16. What are the advantages of current-value financial statements as compared to historical-cost financial statements?

17. What is meant by capital maintenance? Identify four alternative concepts of capital maintenance.

18. What are two methods for incorporating current values into the financial statements?

19. Briefly describe the disclosure requirements of SFAS No. 33, *"Financial Reporting and Changing Prices."*

20. Under financial capital maintenance, holding gains (losses) appear on the income statement. Describe the treatment of holding gains (losses) for purposes of preparing a statement of changes in financial position.

21-1. Compute in each case below the purchasing power gain or loss assuming that assets are held and liabilities are maintained during a period in which the general price level rises by 8%.

EXERCISES

(a)	Cash	$ 50,000
	Accounts receivable	20,000
(b)	Cash	100,000
	Accounts payable	25,000
	Long-term payables	55,000
(c)	Cash	25,000
	Land	50,000
	Accounts payable	25,000
(d)	Cash	25,000
	Land and buildings	100,000
	Mortgage note payable	40,000

21-2. Assuming prices rise evenly by 9% during a year, compute the amount of the expense stated in terms of year-end constant dollars in each of the following independent cases:

(a) Expenses of $500,000 were paid at the beginning of the year for services received during the first half of the year.

(b) Expenses of $125,000 were paid at the end of each quarter for services received during the quarter.

(c) Expenses of $125,000 were paid at the beginning of each quarter for services received during the quarter.

(d) Expenses of $500,000 were paid at the end of the year for services received during the year.

(e) Expenses of $500,000 were paid evenly throughout the year for services received during the year.

In terms of year-end constant dollars, when is the best time to pay for services received in periods of rising prices?

21-3. A comparative income statement for the Panlow Company for the first two years of operations appears below.

	Results of Operations			
	First Year		Second Year	
Sales		$750,000		$900,000
Cost of goods sold:				
Beginning inventory	——		$300,000	
Purchases	$750,000		500,000	
Goods available for sales	$750,000		$800,000	
Ending inventory	300,000	450,000	400,000	400,000
Gross profit on sales		$300,000		$500,000
Operating expenses:				
Depreciation	$ 30,000		$ 30,000	
Other	240,000	270,000	350,000	380,000
Net income		$ 80,000		$120,000
Dividends		15,000		30,000
Increase in retained earnings		$ 15,000		$ 90,000

Prepare a comparative income and retained earnings statement expressing items in dollars of constant purchasing power at the end of the second year, considering the following index data and other information:

(a) Prices rose evenly and index numbers expressing the general price-level changes were:

Beginning of first year	100
End of first year	110
End of second year	140

(b) Sales and purchases were made and expenses were incurred evenly each year.

(c) Inventories were reported at cost using first-in, first-out pricing; average indexes for the year are applicable in restating inventories.

(d) Depreciation relates to equipment acquired at the beginning of the first year.

(e) Dividends were paid at the middle of each year.

(f) Assume no general price-level gain or loss in either year.

21-4. Comparative balance sheet data for Hiatt Industries, Ltd., since its formation, appear below. The general price level during the two-year period went up steadily; index numbers expressing the general price-level changes are listed following the balance sheet. Restate the comparative balance sheet data in terms of the purchasing power units at the end of the second year.

	End of First Year	End of Second Year
Cash	$ 75,000	$ 62,500
Receivables	50,000	70,000
Land, buildings, and equipment (net)*	130,000	115,000
	$255,000	$247,500

*Acquired at the beginning of the first year.

	End of First Year	End of Second Year
Payables	$ 67,500	$ 45,000
Share capital	160,000	160,000
Retained earnings	27,500	42,500
	$255,000	$247,500

Price Level Index Numbers

At the beginning of the business	112
At the end of the first year	125
At the end of the second year	140

21-5. The income statement for Bingham Oil Company is given below. Using the income statement, together with the additional data provided, prepare a GPL adjusted income statement in terms of end-of-year constant dollars accompanied by a schedule summarizing the purchasing power gain or loss for the year.

Bingham Oil Company
Income Statement
For Year Ended December 31, 19--

Sales		$990,000
Cost of goods sold:		
Beginning inventory.....................................	$ 150,000	
Purchases..	900,000	
Goods available for sale	$1,050,000	
Ending inventory	450,000	600,000
Gross profit on sales		$390,000
Operating expenses		270,000
Income before income tax		$120,000
Income tax		60,000
Net income		$ 60,000

The general price level rose evenly from 140 to 160 in the preceding year and from 160 to 200 in the current year. Sales and purchases were made evenly and expenses were incurred evenly during the year. The average index is regarded as applicable in stating inventories. All of the company's assets and liabilities, both at the beginning and at the end of the period, were classified as current and, except for inventories, monetary. Current assets were $600,000 and current liabilities were $200,000 at the beginning of the year.

21-6. On September 1, 1981, Carmen's Toy Store purchased 800 dolls at $2.50 per doll. As of December 31, 1981, Carmen's had sold three-fourths of the dolls at $6 per doll, and the doll manufacturer was selling to retailers at $3 per doll. With respect to the doll venture, how much should Carmen's Toy Store recognize as (a) operating income, (b) realized holding gain, and (c) unrealized holding gain under the current value method of accounting?

21-7. The following supplementary financial statement information is from the 1975 Annual Report of Bethlehem Copper Corporation of Vancouver, B.C.

Bethlehem Copper Corporation
Price Level Adjusted Balance Sheet
December 31, 1975 and 1974
$ 000

Assets	1975	1974	Liabilities and Shareholders' Equity	1975	1974
Cash and short term deposits	$ 60,478	$ 54,229	Current liabilities	$ 6,753	$ 3,856
Accounts receivable	995	14,378	Long term liabilities	502	480
Inventories	6,649	4,898	Accumulated provision for future taxes	2,486	1,964
Total current assets	$ 68,122	$ 73,505	Shareholders' equity	92,368	100,828
Investments	3,052	3,022			
Land, plant and equipment less accumulated depreciation	30,935	30,601			
	$102,109	$107,128		$102,109	$107,128

Bethlehem Copper Corporation
Price Level Adjusted Statement of Earnings
December 31, 1975 and 1974
$ 000

	1975	1974
Concentrate revenue	$25,548	$45,689
Operating costs	25,001	29,271
Earnings from operations	$ 547	$16,418
Interest income	4,615	6,660
Net loss resulting from effect of inflation on net monetary assets ..	(5,056)	(8,585)
Earnings before income and mining taxes	$ 106	$14,493
Provision for taxes	4,240	12,071
Earnings before extraordinary item	$ (4,134)	$ 2,422
Extraordinary item	—	1,440
Net earnings	$ (4,134)	$ 982

Bethlehem Copper Corporation
Current Value Balance Sheet
December 31, 1975 and 1974
$ 000

Assets	1975	1974	Liabilities and Shareholders' Equity	1975	1974
Cash and short term deposits	$ 60,478	$ 49,706	Current liabilities	$ 6,753	$ 3,534
Accounts receivable	995	13,180	Long term liabilities	353	371
Inventories	6,619	4,456	Accumulated provision for future taxes	1,323	918
Total current assets	$ 68,092	$ 67,342	Shareholders' equity	110,397	111,801
Investments	5,236	3,735			
Land, plant and equipment less accumulated depreciation	35,346	31,569			
Ore reserves	10,152	13,978			
	$118,826	$116,624		$118,826	$116,624

Bethlehem Copper Corporation
Current Value Statement of Earnings
December 31, 1975 and 1974
$ 000

	1975	1974
Concentrate revenue	$24,873	$40,350
Operating costs	27,441	29,675
Earnings from operations	$ (2,568)	$10,675
Interest income	4,479	5,847
Net increase in asset values during year	4,494	2,125
Earnings before income and mining taxes	$ 6,405	$18,647
Provision for taxes	4,104	10,597
Net earnings	$ 2,301	$ 8,050

Instructions:

(a) What concept of capital maintenance did Bethlehem employ in preparing its "Current Value Statement of Earnings"? How can you tell?

(b) Examine Bethlehem's balance sheet figures for current value and for price-level adjusted inventories as at December 31, 1975. What is unusual about them? Explain briefly.

21-8. Toward the end of its current fiscal year, Replacement Corporation acquired a fixed asset for $100,000. The fixed asset had a useful life of 5 years, no salvage value, and was to be depreciated on a straight-line basis with a full year's depreciation to be charged in the period of acquisition. The year-end replacement cost of this asset increased year-by-year as follows:

End of year one	$100,000
End of year two	120,000
End of year three	150,000
End of year four	200,000
End of year five	250,000

Prepare a schedule of backlog depreciation assuming depreciation expense is based on:

(a) End of period replacement cost
(b) Average replacement cost

21-9. The limitations of the historical-cost model have not escaped the attention of the accounting profession. A vast amount of literature has poured forth on this topic, and while this literature has presented a number of alternatives to the cost principle, two concepts dominate this area. These are:

(1) historical cost adjusted for general price changes, and
(2) current value accounting

A third alternative is also available. This involves combining price level adjustments with the use of current value accounting.

Assume that a company paid $100,000 for a machine on December 31, 1971. At that date the index of general prices was 100. Replacement cost as at December 31, 1982 is $350,000, and the general price index is then 200.

(a) What is the main difference between current value accounting GPL adjusted compared with historical cost adjusted for general price changes and current value accounting?

(b) Assuming productive capacity capital maintenance, determine the amount to be reported in the revaluation account for the machine under each of current value accounting and current value accounting GPL adjusted.

(SMA adapted)

21-1A. The following information was taken from the accounts of the Sessions Hardware Store during its first two years of operations:

	Useful Life	1980	1981
Beginning inventory		$150,000	$200,000
Purchases		550,000	500,000
Ending inventory		200,000	160,000
Building (acquired 1/1/80)	25 years	400,000	——
Office equipment (acquired 1/7/80)	12 years	30,000	——
Machinery (acquired 1/10/80)	8 years	16,000	——
Price index (1/1)		190	202
Price index (31/12)		202	214

Instructions:

(1) Calculate the cost of goods sold for 1980 and 1981 in terms of respective year-end constant dollars assuming a lifo inventory cost flow with average costs used for any increments. Assume the 1980 beginning inventory was purchased on January 1, 1980. Round to the nearest dollar amount.

(2) Restate depreciable assets and accumulated depreciation (straight-line, ignore salvage values) reporting the depreciation for 1980, and 1981 in terms of 1980 and 1981 year-end constant dollars respectively.

21-2A. The directors of Indexo Ltd. have adopted the policy of converting financial statement items into constant dollars starting January 1, 1982. The treasurer of the company has prepared comparative financial statements for 1981 and 1982, but the directors do not understand the meaning and the calculations of some items on these financial statements. The unadjusted comparative balance sheets are summarized as follows:

Indexo Ltd.
Comparative Balance Sheet
as at December 31

	1981	1982
Monetary assets	$110,000	$125,000
Inventories	50,000	60,000
Land	70,000	70,000
Buildings and equipment	100,000	95,000
	$330,000	$350,000
Liabilities	$ 60,000	$ 65,000
Share capital	200,000	200,000
Retained earnings	70,000	85,000
	$330,000	$350,000

The 1982 income statement is summarized below.

Indexo Ltd.
Income Statement
For Year Ended December 31, 1982

Revenues		$180,000
Cost of goods sold	$98,000	
Payroll	25,000	
Depreciation...	5,000	
Taxes	35,000	
Other expenses..	2,000	165,000
Net income..		$ 15,000

On the basis of price index data, the treasurer has made all necessary conversions and presented the following statements to the directors.

Indexo Ltd.
Balance Sheet
December 31, 1981

	Historical Amount	Conversion Factor	Restated Amount
Monetary assets	$110,000	125/100	$137,500
Inventories	50,000	125/100	62,500
Land.....................................	70,000	125/80	109,375
Building and equipment	100,000	125/80	156,250
	$330,000		$465,625
Liabilities	$ 60,000	125/100	$ 75,000
Share capital	200,000	125/70	357,143
Retained earnings	70,000		33,482
	$330,000		$465,625

Indexo Ltd.
Balance Sheet
December 31, 1982

	Historical Amount	Conversion Factor	Restated Amount
Monetary assets	$125,000	125/125	$125,000
Inventories	60,000	125/116	64,655
Land.....................................	70,000	125/80	109,375
Building and equipment	95,000	125/80	148,438
	$350,000		$447,468
Liabilities	$ 65,000	125/125	$ 65,000
Share capital	200,000	125/70	357,143
Retained earnings	85,000		25,325
	$350,000		$447,468

	Historical Amount	Conversion Factor	Restated Amount
Revenues	$180,000	125/110	$204,545
Cost of goods sold:			
From inventory	$ 50,000	125/100	$ 62,500
From purchases	48,000	125/114	52,632
Payroll	25,000	125/110	28,410
Depreciation	5,000	125/80	7,812
Taxes	35,000	125/110	39,772
Other expenses	2,000	125/110	2,272
	$165,000		$193,398
	$ 15,000		$ 11,147

Instructions:

(1) Prepare a schedule to determine the purchasing power loss during the year on monetary items.
(2) Prepare a schedule to reconcile restated retained earnings as at December 31, 1982.
(3) What is the GPL adjusted net income (loss) for 1982?   (SMA adapted)

21-3A. The income statement prepared at the end of the year for the Wagner Corporation follows:

Wagner Corporation
Income Statement
For Year Ended December 31, 19--

Sales		$350,000
Less sales discount		15,000
Net sales		$335,000
Cost of goods sold:		
Inventory, January 1	$125,000	
Purchases	180,000	
Goods available for sale	$305,000	
Inventory, December 31	120,000	
Cost of goods sold		185,000
Gross profit on sales		$150,000
Operating expenses:		
Depreciation	$ 21,250	
Other operating expenses	50,000	
Total operating expenses		71,250
Income before income tax		$ 78,750
Income tax		31,300
Net income		$ 47,450

The following additional data are available:

(a) The price index rose evenly throughout the year from 120 on January 1 to 130 on December 31.

(b) Sales were made evenly throughout the year; expenses were incurred evenly throughout the year.

(c) The inventory was valued at cost using first-in, first-out pricing; average indexes for the year are used in restating inventories. The beginning inventory was acquired in the preceding period when the average index was 122.

(d) The depreciation charge related to the following items:

	Asset Cost	Index Number at date of Acquisition	Depreciation Rate
Building	$75,000	$95	3 %
Equipment	80,000	95	12¹/₂%
Equipment	20,000	98	12¹/₂%
Equipment*	39,000	120	16²/₃%

*Acquired at the beginning of the current year.

(e) Semi-annual dividends of $7,500 were declared and paid at the end of June and at the end of December.

(f) The balance sheet position for the company changed during the year as follows:

	January 1	December 31
Current assets	$180,000	$174,700
Building and equipment (net)	120,000	137,750
	$300,000	$312,450
Current liabilities	$ 55,000	$ 35,000
Share capital	200,000	200,000
Retained earnings	45,000	77,450
	$300,000	$312,450

Instructions:
Prepare an income statement in which items are stated in end-of-year constant dollars accompanied by a schedule summarizing the purchasing power gain or loss for the year.

21-4A. Financial statements are prepared for the Ervin Co. at the end of each year in conventional form and also in general price-level adjusted form. Balance sheet data summarized in conventional and in general price-level form at the end of 1980 are given below and at the top of page 970.

	Conventional Form		General Price-Level Form (Reporting End of Year Constant Dollars)	
Assets:				
Cash		$ 23,000		$ 23,000
Accounts receivable		70,000		70,000
Inventory		105,000		106,500
Buildings and equipment.........	$120,000		$153,600	
Less accumulated depreciation ...	48,000	72,000	61,440	92,160
Land		50,000		64,000
Total assets		$320,000		$355,660

(continued)

	Conventional Form	General Price-Level Form (Reporting End of Year Constant Dollars)
Liabilities:		
Accounts payable	$ 48,000	$ 48,000
Long-term liabilities	40,000	40,000
Total liabilities	$ 88,000	$ 88,000
Shareholders' equity:		
Capital stock	$150,000	$192,000
Retained earnings	82,000	75,660
Total shareholders' equity	$232,000	$267,660
Total liabilities and shareholders' equity	$320,000	$355,660

Data from statements prepared in conventional form at the end of 1981 are given below:

Balance Sheet

Cash	$ 83,840
Accounts receivable	72,500
Inventory	125,000
Buildings and equipment	120,000
Accumulated depreciation	(56,000)
Land	50,000
	$395,340
Liabilities and Shareholders' Equity	
Accounts payable	$ 37,000
Long-term liabilities	40,000
Capital stock	150,000
Retained earnings	168,340
	$395,340

Income Statement

Sales	$1,100,000
Cost of goods sold	600,000
Gross profit on sales	$ 500,000
Operating expenses	308,000
Income before income tax	$ 192,000
Income tax	85,660
Net income	$ 106,340
Dividends	20,000
Increase in retained earnings ...	$ 86,340

The following additional data are available at the end of 1981:

(a) Price-level index numbers for the year were as follows:

January 1 150
December 31 153

The price level rose steadily during the year.

(b) Sales and purchases were made evenly and expenses were incurred evenly throughout the year.

(c) The first-in, first-out method was used to compute inventory cost; average indexes for the year are used in restating inventories.

(d) All of the land, buildings, and equipment were acquired when the company was formed.

(e) Dividends were declared and paid at the end of the year.

Instructions:

Prepare in terms of end-of-year constant dollars: (1) an income and retained earnings statement accompanied by a schedule summarizing the purchasing power gain or loss for 1981; (2) a balance sheet as of December 31, 1981.

21-5A. The comparative balance sheets and the 1982 income statement for the Price Company are given below.

Price Company
Comparative Balance Sheet
As At December 31

	1981	1982
Cash	$ 1,500,000	$ 2,000,000
Accounts receivable	2,500,000	5,000,000
Inventories	8,000,000	12,000,000
Plant and equipment (net)	18,000,000	16,000,000
Total assets	$30,000,000	$35,000,000
Current liabilities	$ 8,000,000	$ 8,000,000
Long-term debt	2,000,000	2,000,000
Common shares — no par value	5,000,000	5,000,000
Retained earnings	15,000,000	20,000,000
Total liabilities and equity	$30,000,000	$35,000,000

Price Company
Income Statement
For Year Ended December 31, 1982

Sales	$90,000,000
Cost of goods sold	$60,000,000
Depreciation expense	2,000,000
Other expenses	23,000,000
	$85,000,000
Net income	$ 5,000,000

Other information:
(a) No dividends were declared or paid by the Price Company during 1982.
(b) On December 31, 1981, the price level index was at 100. On December 31, 1982, it had risen to 120. The average for the year was 110. All plant and equipment was purchased when the price level index was at 80. The December 31, 1981 inventories were purchased when the price level index was at 95, while the December 31, 1982 inventories were purchased when the index was at 115. The common shares and long-term debt were issued when the price level index was at 80.
(c) Sales, purchases and other expenses accrued uniformly over the year, making the use of the average index appropriate for conversion of these items.

Instructions:
Prepare comparative balance sheet, 1982 income statement, and 1982 statement of changes in financial position — working capital basis for the Price Company restated in terms of constant dollars of December 31, 1982 purchasing power. Make separate calculation of any purchasing power gain or loss that took place during the year. (SMA adapted)

21-6A. To obtain a more realistic appraisal of his investment, Walter Abbott, your client, has asked you to adjust certain financial data of the Global Company for price-level changes. On January 1, 1975, Abbott invested $50,000 in the Global Company in return for 10,000 shares of common stock. Immediately after his investment, the trial balance data appeared as follows:

	Debit	Credit
Cash and Receivables	$ 65,200	
Merchandise Inventory	4,000	
Building	50,000	
Accumulated Depreciation — Building		$ 8,000
Equipment	36,000	
Accumulated Depreciation — Equipment		7,200
Land	10,000	
Current Liabilities		50,000
Capital Stock, $5 par		100,000
	$165,200	$165,200

Balances in certain selected accounts as of December 31 of each of the next three years were as follows:

	1975	1976	1977
Sales	$39,650	$39,000	$42,350
Inventory	4,500	5,600	5,347
Purchases	14,475	16,350	18,150
Operating expenses (excluding depreciation)	10,050	9,050	9,075

Assume the 1975 price level as the base year and all changes in the price level take place at the beginning of each year. Further assume the 1976 price level is 10% above the 1975 price level and the 1977 price level is 10% above the 1976 level.

The building was constructed in 1971 at a cost of $50,000 with an estimated life of 25 years. The price level at that time was 80% of the 1975 price level.

The equipment was purchased in 1973 at a cost of $36,000 with an estimated life of ten years. The price level at that time was 90% of the 1975 price level.

The lifo method of inventory valuation is used. The original inventory was acquired in the same year the building was constructed and was maintained at a constant $4,000 until 1975. In 1975 a gradual buildup of the inventory was begun in anticipation of an increase in the volume of business.

Abbott considers the return on his investment as the dividend he actually receives. In 1975 and also in 1977 the Global Company paid cash dividends in the amount of $4,000.

On July 1, 1976, there was a reverse stock split-up of the company's shares in the ratio of one-for-ten.

Instructions:
(1) Compute 1977 earnings per share of common stock in terms of 1975 constant dollars.
(2) Compute the percentage return on constant investment for 1975 and 1977 in terms of 1975 constant dollars. (AICPA adapted)

21-7A. Historical cost financial statements for Helium Corporation are given below.

Helium Corporation
Balance Sheets
For Year Ended December 31

	(000's)	
	1981	1980
Cash	$ 2,500	$ 1,040
Receivables	4,000	3,000
Inventory	8,700	8,360
Plant — net	15,200	16,000
	$30,400	$28,400
Accounts payable	$ 1,064	$ 2,400
Bonds	11,200	10,000
Deferred income taxes	4,200	4,000
Preferred stock	2,000	2,000
Common stock	4,000	4,000
Retained earnings	7,936	6,000
	$30,400	$28,400

Helium Corporation
Income Statement
For Year Ended December 31, 1981

	(000's)	
Sales.......................................		$25,200
Cost of goods sold...................	$18,800	
Depreciation	2,800	
Interest	710	
Other expenses	210	22,520
Income before taxes		$ 2,680
Income taxes...........................		400
Net income		$ 2,280

Additional Data:
(1) Purchases were acquired evenly during 1981.
(2) Dividends during 1981:

Preferred	....	$ 24,000
Common	....	320,000
		$344,000

(3) During the first quarter of 1981, Helium acquired a machine for $800,000 cash and $1,200,000 of bonds. The machine is being depreciated over five years on a straight-line basis, and a full year's depreciation was recorded in 1981.
(4) Year-end inventories were acquired evenly during the last six months in both years.
(5) Preferred shares were redeemable at $110 per $100 share.
(6) Preferred dividends were paid during the third quarter of 1981; common dividends and interest were paid on December 31.
(7) Assume other items changed evenly during 1981.

Instructions:

(a) Prepare a GPL adjusted comparative balance sheet at December 31, 1981, and a GPL adjusted statement of income and retained earnings for 1981 in last quarter 1981 constant dollars, assuming the following GPL indices.

100 at date of issue of common shares.

110 at date of issue of preferred shares, bonds outstanding at December 31, 1980, and acquisition of plant on hand at December 31, 1980.

180 3rd quarter, 1980.

200 4th quarter, 1980.

200 1st quarter, 1981.

205 2nd quarter, 1981.

215 3rd quarter, 1981.

220 4th quarter, 1981.

(b) Prepare a schedule reporting the purchasing power gain or loss on monetary items for 1981.

(c) Under what conditions would Helium have no purchasing power gain or loss during 1981?

(d) Prepare a GPL adjusted statement of changes in financial position for 1981.

(e) How would Helium's restated income be affected if deferred taxes were treated as non-monetary? Why are deferred taxes monetary?

(f) Calculate the purchasing power gain or loss based on the average price level as permitted by SFAS No. 33.

(g) Prepare in statement format the constant dollar income from continuing operations to be disclosed as supplementary information under the provisions of SFAS No. 33.   (OISA adapted)

21-8A. Coreco acquired a tract of land in 1980 at a total cost of $500,000. At that time, the general price level stood at 80. On December 31, 1986, when the general price level was 140, Coreco had a firm offer for the land of $1,000,000. The offer was refused. On December 31, 1987, Coreco received another offer of $1,350,000 for the land; at this time the general price index was 180. The offer was accepted and the transaction was completed on January 2, 1988. Mr. Avis, president, asks you if he is correct in saying that he made a $350,000 profit during 1987. He explains that he realizes that the total appreciation covered a period of almost eight years, but he feels a strict average over the eight-year period ignores the fact that some evidence of market value existed one year previously.

Instructions:

(a) Indicate how the gain on sale of land would be reported on 1987 income statements under (1) Historical cost accounting, (2) Historical cost GPL adjusted, (3) Current value accounting, and (4) Current value accounting GPL adjusted.

(b) Assuming financial capital maintenance, determine the total gain for the period the land was held that would be reported under each of the four models listed in part (a).

(c) State how each model is different from or in accord with generally accepted accounting principles.   (CGA adapted)

21-9A. Mr. Joe May has come to you and asked for an explanation of the effect of inflation on his business. You have taken the following transactions from his records in order to prepare comparative statements and to isolate some variations.

The general price index for 1981 indicated the following changes in the purchasing power of the dollar:

January 1, 1981 200
July 1, 1981 205
December 31, 1981 210

The following purchases were made:

January 1, 1981 .... 1,000 items at $3.00 per unit
July 1, 1981 .... 500 items at $3.30 per unit
December 31, 1981 .... 500 items at $3.50 per unit
January 15, 1982 .... 500 items at $3.70 per unit

Year-end inventories are valued according to the first-in, first-out method (FIFO). The company's year-end is December 31st.

Instructions:
(a) Assuming that no sales were made during 1981, determine the valuation of the year-end inventories for balance sheet purposes under each of the following methods:
   (1) historical cost
   (2) historical cost GPL adjusted
   (3) current value accounting
   (4) current value accounting GPL adjusted
(b) Assuming that the company sold 50 per cent of its inventory on December 31, 1981, at a selling price of $4.20 per unit, prepare comparative income statements using each of the following methods:
   (1) historical cost
   (2) historical cost GPL adjusted
   (3) current value accounting
   (4) current value accounting GPL adjusted
(c) Based on these comparative income statements, explain the composition of the net income amount under historical cost showing clearly the impact of general price changes, the timing of purchases, and income from sales.

(SMA adapted)

21-10A. The Forward Company began operations on January 1, 1982 with the following assets and capital:

Cash .... $ 50,000
Inventory (5,000 units @ $20) 100,000
Land 50,000
Plant and equipment 300,000

Total Assets $500,000

Common shares, no par value $500,000

The company uses the FIFO method of accounting for inventory, and straight line depreciation for plant and equipment. The plant and equipment has an estimated useful life of 10 years with no anticipated salvage value.

Transactions during 1982 were as follows:
(1) 30,000 units of merchandise were purchased on credit at $25 per unit.
(2) 25,000 units were sold for cash at $40 per unit. At this time the replacement cost of goods sold was $30 per unit.

(3) Other expenses of $120,000 were incurred and paid for.
(4) Payments on accounts payable during 1982 amounted to $700,000.
(5) Replacement cost of land, and plant and equipment increased by 50 per cent during 1982.
(6) On December 31, 1982, the replacement cost of inventories was $32 per unit.

Instructions:

(a) Prepare a 1982 Income Statement and a December 31, 1982 Balance Sheet:
  (1) using generally accepted accounting principles (ignore income tax).
  (2) using current value accounting, financial capital maintenance measured in money (ignore income tax).

(b) Some accountants argue that unrealized holding gains should be excluded from income. How would exclusion of unrealized holding gains change current value net income, as determined above?

(c) Assuming 10 per cent inflation spread evenly throughout 1982 and an even flow of transactions, prepare a current value income statement using financial capital measured in purchasing power units for capital maintenance purposes (ignore income tax). (SMA adapted)

21-11A. Keller Ltd.'s accountant has prepared four sets of financial statements on four different bases: historical cost, current value, constant dollar historical cost, and constant dollar current value. These four sets of financials are presented below in comparative format. The company was incorporated on January 1, 1981 and commenced its operations on February 1, 1981.

Keller Ltd.
Balance Sheets
as at December 31, 1981

Assets	Historical Cost	Current Value	Constant Dollar Historical Cost	Constant Dollar Current Value
Cash	$ 778,000	$ 778,000	778,000	778,000
Accounts receivable	40,000	40,000	40,000	40,000
Inventories	20,000	28,000	23,334	28,000
Land	75,000	80,000	91,306	80,000
Building	225,000	300,000	273,912	300,000
Less: Accumulated depreciation	(9,000)	(12,000)	(10,956)	(12,000)
Machinery and equipment	250,000	236,000	280,000	236,000
Less: Accumulated depreciation	(25,000)	(23,600)	(28,000)	(23,600)
	$1,354,000	$1,426,400	1,447,596	1,426,400
Liabilities and Shareholders' Equity				
Accounts payable .... $	20,000	$ 20,000	20,000	20,000
Mortage payable	190,000	190,000	190,000	190,000
Share capital	1,100,000	1,100,000	1,400,000	1,400,000
Revaluation	——	124,000	——	(1,218)
Retained earnings (deficit)	44,000	(7,600)	(162,404)	(182,382)
	$1,354,000	$1,426,400	1,447,596	1,426,400

Keller Ltd.
Income Statements
Year Ended December 31, 1981

	Historical Cost	Current Value	Constant Dollar Historical Cost	Constant Dollar Current Value
Sales	250,000	250,000	250,000	250,000
Cost of goods sold				
(See Exhibit A)	100,000	140,000	116,666	140,000
Gross profit on sales	150,000	110,000	133,334	140,000
Out-of-pocket expenses	60,000	70,000	70,000	70,000
Depreciation				
Building	9,000	12,000	10,956	12,000
Equipment	25,000	23,600	28,000	23,600
Interest expense paid				
on December 31, 1981	12,000	12,000	12,000	12,000
	106,000	117,600	120,956	117,600
Operating income or (loss)	44,000	(7,600)	12,378	22,400
Purchasing power loss	——	——	(204,782)	(204,782)
Net income or (loss)*	44,000	(7,600)	(192,404)	(182,382)

* Income taxes are ignored

Exhibit A
Cost of Goods Sold
Year Ended December 31, 1981

	Historical Cost	Current Value	Constant Dollar Historical Cost	Constant Dollar Current Value
Inventories				
January 1, 1977	——	——	——	——
Purchases				
12,000 units	$ 120,000	$ 168,000	140,000	168,000
	120,000	168,000	140,000	168,000
Less: Inventories				
December 31, 1977				
2,000 units	20,000	28,000	23,334	28,000
Cost of goods sold	$ 100,000	$ 140,000	116,666	140,000

(1) The general price index at the beginning of the year was 110.
(2) Land and building were acquired on February 15, 1981, and the general price index at that date was 115. Machinery and equipment were acquired when the general price index was 125. The general price index as at December 31, 1981, and the average index for 1981 were respectively 140 and 120. Assume that the index applicable to the sales made during the year is 125 since more sales were made during the last part of the year. Assume also that the average index (120) applies to merchandise unsold at the end of the year.

(3) The monetary assets as at January 1, 1981, amounted to $1,100,000. This amount represents the capital invested by the shareholders. There were no monetary liabilities on January 1, 1981.

Instructions:
(a) Analyse the following items and explain by means of computations how they were determined.
  (i) purchasing power loss
  (ii) revaluation account
(b) Identify the capital maintenance concept in each of the four sets of statements. For any two of the last three sets of statements, explain the reason(s) for your choice of a capital maintenance concept.
(c) Comment on the values shown for land in the comparative financial statements.

(CICA adapted)

21-12A. On January 1, 1982, the New Era Company began operations by issuing no par common shares in return for $700,000 cash. On this same date, long-term debt was issued in return for $300,000 cash, and $600,000 cash was paid to acquire a prefabricated building. This prefabricated building was erected on land which the company is allowed to use without charge. At the close of business on January 1, 1982, subsequent to recording the preceding transactions, the balance sheet of New Era Company appeared as follows:

Assets

Cash	$ 400,000
Building	600,000
Total assets	$1,000,000

Equities

Long-term debt	$ 300,000
No par common shares	700,000
Total equities	$1,000,000

The income statement for the year ending December 31, 1982, and the balance sheet as at December 31, 1982, for New Era Company are as follows:

New Era Company
Income Statement
For Year Ended December 31, 1982

Sales	$ 560,000
Cost of goods sold	$ 240,000
Depreciation expense	50,000
Other expenses	170,000
Total expenses	$ 460,000
Net income	$ 100,000

New Era Company
Balance Sheet
December 31, 1982

Assets

Cash		$ 450,000
Inventories		60,000
Building...	$600,000	
Accumulated depreciation................................	50,000	550,000
Total Assets		$1,060,000

Equities

Long-term debt	$300,000
No par common shares..................................	700,000
Retained earnings	60,000
Total Equities.......................................	$1,060,000

(1) The prefabricated building has an estimated useful life of 12 years and is being depreciated using the straight-line method. Its replacement cost on December 31, 1982 was $720,000 and the increase in value has occurred at a uniform rate throughout the year.

(2) On April 1, 1982 New Era Company purchased 100,000 units of merchandise at a cost of $3.00 per unit. On October 1, 1982, 80,000 units of this merchandise were sold for $7.00 per unit. At the date of sale, the replacement cost of merchandise was $4.50 per unit. On December 31, 1982, the replacement cost of the merchandise that is still on hand had increased to $5.00 per unit.

(3) Other expenses, paid in cash, were incurred uniformly over the year.

(4) On June 30, 1982, New Era Company declared a dividend on the common shares in the amount of $40,000. This dividend was paid on October 1, 1982.

(5) On January 1, 1982, the general price level index was 120. On April 1, 1982, the index had increased to 135. It continued to increase to 150 on June 30, 1982, and to 165 on October 1, 1982. It ended at 180 on December 31, 1982 and the average for the year was 150.

Instructions:

(a) Prepare a current value income statement for the year ending December 31, 1982, and a current value balance sheet as at December 31, 1982. Current values are defined in terms of replacement costs and all holding gains should be included in the determination of net income. Ignore income tax.

(b) Prepare a constant dollar historical-cost income statement for the year ending December 31, 1982 and a constant dollar historical-cost balance sheet as at December 31, 1982. All amounts should be expressed in constant dollars of uniform December 31, 1982 purchasing power. Ignore income tax.

(c) Assume that the current value financial statements prepared in part (a) are used to prepare current value financial statements expressed in constant dollars of uniform December 31, 1982 purchasing power. Compute the amounts for purchasing power gain or loss, depreciation expense, and cost of goods sold that would be shown on a current value — constant dollar income statement for the year ending December 31, 1982. Ignore income tax.

(SMA adapted)

21-13A. On January 1, 1982, the Advanced Company was formed with the issuance of no par common shares in return for $100,000 cash. On this same date land is purchased for $25,000 and a $40,000 prefabricated building is erected on the site. The building has an estimated useful life of ten years and comes complete with all required fixtures that are necessary to begin operations. The Company is going to sell a single product, and the remaining cash of $35,000 is used to purchase 7,000 units of merchandise at $5.00 per unit. During the subsequent year the following transactions occurred.

(1) On April 1, 1982, 4,000 units of merchandise were sold for cash at $10.00 per unit. On this date the replacement cost of the merchandise was $7.00 per unit.

(2) On July 1, 1982, an additional 4,000 units of merchandise were purchased for cash at $8.00 per unit.

(3) On October 1, 1982, 5,000 units were sold for cash at $15.00 per unit. On this date the replacement cost had increased to $9.00 per unit.

On December 31, 1982, the replacement cost of the land is $30,000, the replacement cost of the building is $50,000, and the replacement cost of merchandise is $12.00 per unit. The Advanced Company has decided to experiment with current value accounting. Income will include all holding gains that are realized while unrealized holding gains will be disclosed as a separate item in shareholders' equity. Depreciation expense will be based on end-of-year replacement cost, and merchandise is assumed to flow through the business on a FIFO basis. Other expenses, all of which were paid in cash on December 31, 1982, amount to $30,000. Income taxes are to be ignored.

Instructions:

(a) Prepare Advanced Company's income statement for the year ended December 31, 1982, using current value accounting, as defined above.

(b) Prepare Advanced Company's balance sheet as at December 31, 1982, using current value accounting, as defined above.

(c) Prepare Advanced Company's statement of changes in financial position — working capital basis using the financial statements prepared in parts (a) and (b) and the other information provided.

(d) The December 31, 1982 inventory balance contains an unrealized holding gain. Assume that the index of general purchasing power increased uniformly over the year from 145 on January 1, 1982, to 165 on December 31, 1982. How much of this unrealized holding gain reflects the decrease in the general purchasing power of the dollar, and how much represents a real holding gain?

(e) Prepare a schedule reporting purchasing power gain or loss. (SMA adapted)

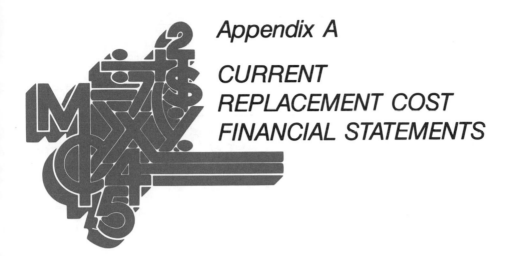

Appendix A

CURRENT REPLACEMENT COST FINANCIAL STATEMENTS

Barbecon Inc., formerly Barber-Ellis of Canada Limited, publishes an excellent annual report that is noteable because, since 1974, the company has provided supplementary current replacement cost financial statements in addition to its conventional financials.

A medium-sized manufacturing and trading company, Barbecon Inc. ranked 282nd in the *Financial Post*'s 500 for 1980. Through a group of manufacturing and trading divisions and branches, Barbecon, headquartered in Toronto, provides envelopes, printing supplies and stationery products to customers across Canada. Barbecon is listed on the Toronto stock exchange.

Barbecon is clearly in the forefront among a small group of Canadian corporations that have provided in their annual reports supplementary information concerning the effects of changing prices. The company's current replacement cost financials have been the subject of several journal articles and numerous comments in the business and financial press in both Canada and the United States.[1]

---

[1]For example, Michael O. Alexander and J. Douglas Barrington, "A Feasible Method of Current Value Accounting," *CA Magazine*, September 1975.

In Thousands of Dollars	1979	1978	1977	1976
Sales	$ 130,213	$ 104,274	$ 92,173	$ 79,83
Profit before Income Taxes	8,582	4,223	4,180	3,02
Net Earnings	4,933	2,786	2,404	1,63
Common Shares Outstanding* (December 31)	1,521,688	1,521,688	1,512,288	1,876,88
Earnings per Common Share* (dollars)	3.24	1.84(b)	1.29	.8
Dividends per Common Share* (dollars)	.90	.63	.53	.4
Total Assets	49,754	38,552	32,964	31,28
Shareholders' Equity	$ 17,136	$ 13,583	$ 11,678	$ 12,73
Current Replacement Cost Data (unaudited)				
Net Earnings	$ 2,913	$ 1,786	$ 1,535	$ 1,28
Earnings per Share* (dollars)	1.91	1.18(c)	.82	.6
Total Assets	53,294	41,393	35,541	33,44
Shareholders' Equity	$ 20,676	$ 16,424	$ 14,255	$ 14,89

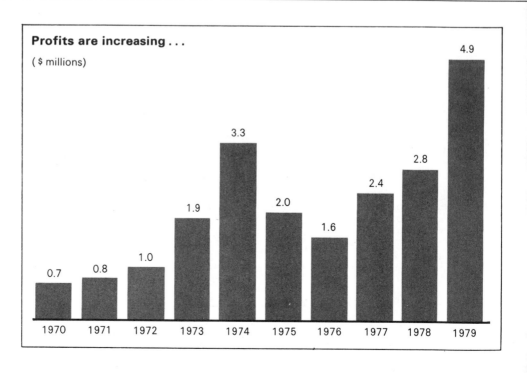

Profits are increasing . . .

($ millions)

0.7	0.8	1.0	1.9	3.3	2.0	1.6	2.4	2.8	4.9
1970	1971	1972	1973	1974	1975	1976	1977	1978	1979

1975	1974	1973	1972	1971	1970
71,122	$ 69,058	$ 49,787	$ 34,804	$ 30,680	$ 29,043
3,677	6,204	3,523	1,968	1,652	1,524
2,028	3,277	1,874	1,015	834	691
875,888	1,852,168	1,838,648	1,831,480	1,820,400	1,820,000
1.09(a)	1.77	1.02	.56	.46	.38
.53	.53	.40	.24	.18	.18
28,455	28,732	19,932	12,507	10,480	9,759
11,948	$ 10,853	$ 8,512	$ 7,353	$ 6,741	$ 6,227
1,460	$ 1,984				
.78(a)	1.08				
30,349	30,832				
13,842	$ 12,953				

* Adjusted to reflect 4 for 1 stock split in 1978

(a) Including extraordinary item of $.11 per share

(b) Including extraordinary item of $.20 per share

(c) Including extraordinary item of $.07 per share

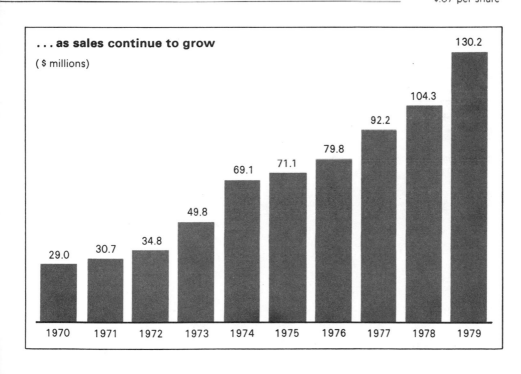

. . . as sales continue to grow

($ millions)

1970	1971	1972	1973	1974	1975	1976	1977	1978	1979
29.0	30.7	34.8	49.8	69.1	71.1	79.8	92.2	104.3	130.2

(Incorporated under The Business Corporations Act — Ontario)

Consolidated Balance Sheet
as at December 31, 1979

Assets	1979	1978
	(000's)	(000's)
Current		
Accounts receivable	**$20,193**	$15,966
Inventories	**18,897**	14,639
Prepaid expenses (Note 5)	**450**	172
	39,540	30,777
Property, plant and equipment (Note 2)	**9,578**	7,091
Unamortized excess of purchase price over fair value of net assets acquired	**636**	684
	$49,754	$38,552

On behalf of the Board of Directors

James W. Mastaway , Chairman

DK Murphy , President

See accompanying notes to consolidated financial statements.

Liabilities	1979	1978
	(000's)	(000's)
Current		
Bank indebtedness	**$15,694**	$11,867
Accounts payable and accrued liabilities	**7,520**	5,734
Income taxes	**3,119**	738
Current portion of long-term debt	**480**	507
	26,813	18,846
Deferred income taxes	**1,300**	955
Long-term debt (Note 3)	**4,505**	5,168
	32,618	24,969
Shareholders' Equity		
Capital stock (Note 4)	**608**	618
Retained earnings	**16,528**	12,965
	17,136	13,583
	$49,754	$38,552

BARBECON *Inc*

Consolidated Statement of Earnings
for the year ended December 31, 1979

	1979	1978
	(000's)	(000's)
Net sales	**$130,213**	$104,274
Costs and expenses		
Cost of products sold	**96,834**	79,503
Selling, general and administrative	**21,367**	18,047
Depreciation and amortization	**1,261**	983
Interest		
Long-term debt	**528**	553
Current debt	**1,641**	965
	121,631	100,051
Earnings before income taxes and extraordinary item	**8,582**	4,223
Provision for income taxes	**3,649**	1,735
Earnings before extraordinary item	**4,933**	2,488
Extraordinary item		
Gain on disposal of property, less related income taxes of $247,000	**—**	298
Net earnings	**$ 4,933**	$ 2,786
Earnings per share (dollars)		
(weighted average number of shares 1,521,688 ; 1978 — 1,514,792)		
Before extraordinary item	**$ 3.24**	$ 1.64
After extraordinary item	**$ 3.24**	$ 1.84

See accompanying notes to consolidated financial statements.

BARBECON *Inc*

Consolidated Statement of Changes in Financial Position
for the year ended December 31, 1979

	1979	1978
	(000's)	(000's)
Working capital provided by		
Earnings before extraordinary item	$ **4,933**	$ 2,488
Items not requiring an outlay of working capital		
Depreciation and amortization	**1,261**	983
Deferred income taxes	**345**	122
Working capital provided by operations	**6,539**	3,593
Extraordinary item		
Net proceeds on disposal of property	**—**	1,054
Proceeds on disposal of property, plant and equipment	**53**	54
Issue of common shares	**—**	68
	6,592	4,769
Working capital used for		
Expenditures for plant and equipment	**3,753**	2,718
Payment of dividends	**1,370**	949
Redemption of long-term debt	**183**	—
Decrease in long-term debt	**480**	507
Redemption of first preference shares	**10**	—
	5,796	4,174
Increase in working capital	**796**	595
Working capital at beginning of year	**11,931**	11,336
Working capital at end of year	**$12,727**	$11,931

See accompanying notes to consolidated financial statements.

Consolidated Statement of Retained Earnings
for the year ended December 31, 1979

	1979	1978
	(000's)	(000's)
Balance at beginning of year	**$12,965**	$11,128
Net earnings	**4,933**	2,786
	17,898	13,914
Dividends	**1,370**	949
Balance at end of year	**$16,528**	$12,965

See accompanying notes to consolidated financial statements.

Auditors' Report

The Shareholders,
Barbecon Inc.

We have examined the consolidated balance sheet of Barbecon Inc. as at December 31, 1979 and the consolidated statements of earnings, retained earnings and changes in financial position for the year then ended. Our examination was made in accordance with generally accepted auditing standards, and accordingly included such tests and other procedures as we considered necessary in the circumstances.

In our opinion, these consolidated financial statements present fairly the financial position of the Company as at December 31, 1979 and the results of its operations and the changes in its financial position for the year then ended in accordance with generally accepted accounting principles applied on a basis consistent with that of the preceding year.

Toronto, Ontario,
March 6, 1980.

TOUCHE ROSS & CO.
Chartered Accountants

Notes to Consolidated Financial Statements
December 31, 1979

1. Summary of significant accounting policies

a. Basis of consolidation

The consolidated financial statements include the accounts of the Company and its subsidiary company, W. V. Dawson Limitée. The 1978 comparative figures also included the accounts of Fine Papers London Limited which was amalgamated with Barbecon Inc. on December 31, 1978.

b. Inventories

Inventories are valued at the lower of average cost (determined on a weighted average basis) and net realizable value.

c. Property, plant and equipment

Expenditures for additions and major improvements are capitalized and depreciated over their estimated useful lives, generally on the diminishing-balance method at the following rates:

Buildings	5%
Machinery and equipment	20%

d. Other assets

The excess of purchase price over the fair value of net assets acquired is amortized on a straight-line basis over twenty years.

2. Property, plant and equipment

	1979			1978
	Cost	Accumulated depreciation	Net	Net
	(000's)	(000's)	(000's)	(000's)
Land.	$ 888	$ —	$ 888	$ 908
Buildings.	6,133	1,664	4,469	3,273
Machinery and equipment.	11,800	7,579	4,221	2,910
	$18,821	$ 9,243	$ 9,578	$ 7,091

3. Long-term debt

	1979	1978
	(000's)	(000's)
Term bank loan due April 1, 1983	$ 920	$1,150
5¾% sinking fund debentures due December 15, 1984	182	392
8½% sinking fund debentures due June 1, 1993	1,250	1,300
10% promissory notes	2,633	2,833
	4,985	5,675
Less current portion	480	507
	$4,505	$5,168

The 10% promissory notes are payable to Westell Financial Corporation Limited, a company beneficially owned by insiders of the Company.

Sinking fund instalments and other payments required on long-term debt to 1984 are as follows: 1980 — $480,000; 1981 — $480,000; 1982 — $2,513,000; 1983 — $280,000 and 1984 — $232,000.

The Company in 1979 redeemed $210,000 of its 5¾% sinking fund debentures and realized a gain on the transaction of $35,000.

4. Capital stock

	1979	1978
	(000's)	(000's)
Authorized		
339,960 non-voting second preference shares, par value $25 each		
5,000,000 common shares without par value		
Issued		
Nil first preference shares (1978-200 which were redeemed and cancelled in 1979)	$ —	$ 10
1,521,688 common shares	608	608
	$608	$618

5. Pension plan

The latest actuarial review of the pension plan as at December 31, 1978 determined the unfunded past service liability to be $2,256,000.

Annual amounts charged to earnings with respect to this liability will be: $273,000 to 1987; $131,000 in 1988 and 1989; and $100,000 from 1990 to 1992.

In 1979, the Company paid its 1980 past service funding requirement of $273,000 which is included in prepaid expenses.

6. Remuneration of directors and senior officers

The remuneration of directors and senior officers was $497,000 (1978 — $424,000).

7. Commitments

The Company has operating lease commitments on buildings extending over a period of fifteen years in respect of which annual payments of approximately $850,000 will be made during each of the next five years.

Supplementary
Consolidated
Financial
Statements

BARBECON Inc.

To Our Shareholders

Financial statements derive their usefulness by providing meaningful and understandable information about a company's financial circumstances. Five years ago, we faced a series of rapid cost increases that seriously compromised the ability of our traditional financial statements to perform this task. We concluded that additional financial information was necessary to operate your company. We decided that disclosure of this additional data would assist shareholders and the public at large to understand the impact that inflation was having on your organization.

In 1974, we published our first set of Current Replacement Cost Financial Statements. Since that time, the business community has come to realize that inflation imposes significant limitations on traditional financial statements that can only be remedied by some form of inflation accounting. In December 1979, the Canadian Institute of Chartered Accountants issued proposed recommendations eventually requiring large public companies to disclose the current value of their assets and to report the effect of inflation on their earnings. Barbecon's present method of reporting captures the most significant inflation adjustments recommended by these new disclosure requirements.

Our Current Replacement Cost Financial Statements differ from the traditional historical cost financial statements in two respects. As the name implies, the Current Replacement Cost Financial Statements show the current values of our company's assets and liabilities. These values are based on replacement costs. Our traditional financial statements are not based upon current values. Assets and liabilities are carried on the balance sheet at their original costs. For plant and equipment especially, this results in significant differences between the recorded values and present day values of our assets.

The second area of difference lies in the definition of profit. Our traditional financial statements use historical costs as a basis for measuring profits. When, for example, inventory is sold, the difference between selling price and the original cost of the product is reported as profit. This approach is adequate when costs are steady. However, when costs spiral, its limitations become clear. Historical cost profits fail to recognize that a portion of earnings is not available for distribution. This portion of profits represents funds that must be reinvested to replace inventory, plant, and equipment at higher current costs.

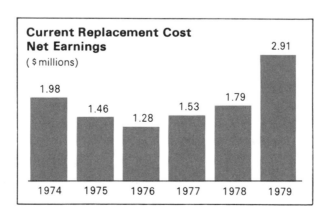

Current Replacement Cost Net Earnings

($ millions)

1.98	1.46	1.28	1.53	1.79	2.91
1974	1975	1976	1977	1978	1979

Our Replacement Cost Financial Statements recognize the necessity of financing the replacement of inventories and facilities before reporting profits. Cost of sales represents the current cost of replenishing inventory on the date of sale while depreciation represents money that must be set aside each year to fund the ultimate replacement of plant and machinery.

Our Replacement Cost Income Statement only reports profits from manufacturing and trading activities. Inflation, or price-change profits, are an illusory phenomena resulting from holding assets during times of rising prices. They are isolated, excluded from earnings, and are correctly reported as asset revaluations.

To observe the changed financial conditions that inflation creates in our company, compare our Traditional and Replacement Cost Financial Statements. 24% of our pre-tax earnings on a historical cost basis are inflationary profits. These profits have no foundation in our manufacturing and distribution operations. Although they are illusory, we are taxed on them. Our effective rate of taxation is 56%.

We are pleased to report that the company's performance is steadily improving. After removing the effects of inflation in 1979, our replacement cost earnings increased to $2,913,000. Our dividend rate is 47% of these earnings.

Your company's management believes that inflation adjusted information is the only practical basis for making sound operating and investment decisions, particularly in a year such as 1979. We urge you to review the Current Replacement Cost Financial Statements

carefully. They provide the best and most accurate financial picture of how well your company is progressing.

At Barbecon, we have observed over the past few years that inflation affects the various parts of our economy very differently. We frequently hear that "inflation in our economy is running at approximately 10%", yet we know, for example, that the price of oil is escalating at a much higher rate. The earnings of your company have been far more severely affected by inflation than the consumer price index (CPI) would have indicated. The adjacent chart shows this dramatic comparison.

David K. Murphy
President

March 6, 1980

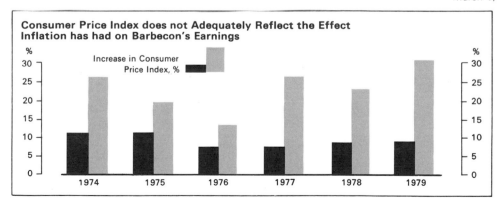

Consumer Price Index does not Adequately Reflect the Effect Inflation has had on Barbecon's Earnings

Increase in Consumer Price Index, %

1974 · 1975 · 1976 · 1977 · 1978 · 1979

(Incorporated under The Business Corporations Act — Ontario)

Consolidated Current Replacement Cost Balance Sheet
as at December 31, 1979 (unaudited)

Assets	1979	1978
	(000's)	(000's)
Current		
Accounts receivable	$20,193	$15,966
Inventories	18,922	14,663
Prepaid expenses	450	172
	39,565	30,801
Property, plant and equipment (Note 2)	13,729	10,592
	$53,294	$41,393

Liabilities		
Current		
Bank indebtedness	$15,694	$11,867
Accounts payable and accrued liabilities	7,520	5,734
Income taxes	3,119	738
Current portion of long-term debt	480	507
	26,813	18,846
Deferred income taxes	1,300	955
Long-term debt	4,505	5,168
	32,618	24,969

Shareholders' Equity		
Capital stock	608	618
Retained earnings	1,174	1,933
Revaluation account	18,894	13,873
	20,676	16,424
	$53,294	$41,393

See accompanying notes to supplementary consolidated financial statements.

BARBECON Inc

Consolidated Current Replacement Cost Statement of Earnings
for the year ended December 31, 1979 (unaudited)

	1979	1978
	(000's)	(000's)
Net sales	$130,213	$104,274
Costs and expenses		
Cost of products sold	98,285	79,919
Selling, general and administrative	21,367	18,051
Depreciation and amortization	1,830	1,373
Interest		
Long-term debt	1,641	553
Current debt	528	965
	123,651	100,861
Earnings before income taxes and extraordinary item	6,562	3,413
Provision for income taxes	3,649	1,735
Net earnings before extraordinary item	2,913	1,678
Extraordinary item		
Gain on disposal of property, less related income taxes of $247,000	—	108
Net earnings	$ 2,913	$ 1,786
Earnings per share (dollars)		
(weighted average number of shares 1,521,688 ; 1978 — 1,514,792)		
Before extraordinary item	$ 1.91	$ 1.11
After extraordinary item	$ 1.91	$ 1.18

See accompanying notes to supplementary consolidated financial statements.

BARBECON *Inc*

Consolidated Current Replacement Cost Statement of Retained Earnings
for the year ended December 31, 1979 (unaudited)

	1979	1978
	(000's)	(000's)
Balance at beginning of year	$1,933	$2,799
Net earnings	2,913	1,786
	4,846	4,585
Adjustment of accumulated depreciation to reflect current year's increase in replacement cost of plant and equipment	2,302	1,703
Dividends	1,370	949
	3,672	2,652
Balance at end of year	$1,174	$1,933

Consolidated Statement of Revaluation Account
for the year ended December 31, 1979 (unaudited)

	1979	1978
	(000's)	(000's)
Balance at beginning of year	$13,873	$10,906
Add revaluation of assets		
Inventory, December 31	25	24
Property, plant and equipment	3,570	2,527
Cost of products sold during the year	1,426	416
Balance at end of year	$18,894	$13,873

See accompanying notes to supplementary consolidated financial statements.

Notes to Consolidated Current Replacement Cost Financial Statements
December 31, 1979 (unaudited)

1. Purpose of current replacement cost accounting

The purpose of current replacement cost accounting is to give recognition to maintaining the invested capital of the business and to the current costs of earning a satisfactory return. Since the Company is viewed as a "going concern", income is not considered to have been earned without first providing for the replenishment of capital consumed in the operations. The Company maintains its productive capability by being able to replace its plant and equipment as it is used and its inventories as they are sold. The current replacement costs of inventories and of property, plant and equipment are shown on the balance sheet and earnings are determined by matching current costs with current revenues. Adjustments of the historical cost of physical assets to their current replacement costs are considered as restatements of shareholders' equity and are shown on the balance sheet under revaluation account.

The current replacement cost financial statements do not reflect the current value of the Company as a whole because the human resources and the intangible assets such as goodwill have not been included. The current replacement cost of assets is not necessarily their net realizable value should they be sold.

2. Principles of valuation

At the present time, no uniform criteria exist for the application of replacement cost accounting; accordingly, accounting policies could vary from one enterprise to another. The Company has adopted those current replacement cost accounting policies which it believes are appropriate in the circumstances.

Current replacement cost is the lowest amount that would have to be incurred in the normal course of business to obtain an asset of equivalent operating capacity.

Cash, accounts receivable and prepaid expenses
These assets are stated at their face value.

Inventories
Inventories are valued at the lower of current replacement cost and net realizable value. Current replacement cost of inventories is based on current prices for materials and conversion costs.

Property, plant and equipment

	1979			1978
	Current replacement cost	Accumulated depreciation	Net	Net
	(000's)	(000's)	(000's)	(000's)
Land	$ 1,149	$ —	$ 1,149	$ 1,169
Plant and equipment	33,201	20,621	12,580	9,423
	$34,350	$20,621	$13,729	$10,592

The current replacement costs of property and plant are based upon independent appraisals by quantity surveyors of the Canadian Institute of Quantity Surveyors or by accredited appraisers of the Appraisal Institute of Canada. Where appraisals for buildings were completed at dates other than at December 31, 1979, the appraised values were adjusted by the Non-Residential Construction Price Index developed by Statistics Canada. Land is stated at its most recent appraised value determined during the previous five years.

The current replacement cost of equipment is determined from recent suppliers prices and estimates made by those suppliers.

Provision for depreciation is computed generally on the diminishing-balance method at the following rates:

Buildings	5%
Machinery and equipment	20%

As a result of the revaluation of fixed assets in the current year, accumulated depreciation representing the expired portion of the useful lives of those assets has been increased by $2,302,000 and this amount has been charged to retained earnings.

Current and long-term liabilities
These liabilities are stated at their face value.

Cost of products sold
Cost of products sold is calculated on the basis of the current replacement cost of the items sold on the date of sale.

3. **Additional notes**

The notes to the historical cost financial statements which are numbered 1, 3, 4, 5, 6, and 7 form an integral part of these supplementary consolidated financial statements.

Appendix B

FUTURE AND PRESENT VALUE: CONCEPTS AND APPLICATIONS

A basic knowledge of future and present value concepts and techniques is becoming increasingly important in accounting. The material in this appendix is intended to: (1) provide a brief review of the basic concepts and applications of interest; and (2) present some illustrations of business problems utilizing future and present value tables.

INTEREST DEFINED

In some respects money is like any other commodity. It is a scarce resource, and a payment is generally required for its use. This payment (cost) for the use of money is *interest*. For example, if $100 is borrowed, whether from an individual, a business, or a bank, and $110 is paid back, $10 interest has, in effect, been paid for the use of the $100. Thus, interest represents the excess cash paid over the amount of cash borrowed.

Generally interest is specified in terms of a percentage rate for a period of time, usually a year. For example, interest at 8% means the annual cost of borrowing an amount of money, called the *principal*, is equal to 8% of that amount. The interest rate and the time period are assumed to be stated in common units. To illustrate, if $100 is borrowed at 8% annual interest, the total to be repaid is $108 — the amount of the principal, $100, and the interest for a year, $8 ($100 × .08 × 1). Interest on a $1,000 note for 6 months at 8%

is $40 ($1,000 × .08 × 6/12). Thus, the formula for computing *simple interest* is $i = p \times r \times t$, where:

i = Amount of simple interest
p = Principal amount
r = Interest rate (per period)
t = Time (number of periods)

The foregoing discussion relates to simple interest. Many transactions involve *compound interest*. This means the amount of interest earned for a certain period is added to the principal for the next period. Interest for the subsequent period is computed on the new amount, which includes both principal and interest. As an example, assume $100 is deposited in a bank and left for two years at 6% annual interest. At the end of the first year, the $100 has earned $6 interest ($100 × .06 × 1). At the end of the second year, $6 has been earned for the first year, plus another $6.36 interest (6% on the $106 balance at the beginning of the second year). Thus, the total interest earned is $12.36 rather than $12 because of the compounding effect. The table below, based on the foregoing example, illustrates the computation of simple and compound interest for four years. Formulas relative to common compound interest situations are provided in the next section of this appendix.

	Simple Interest			Compound Interest		
Year	Computation	Interest	Total	Computation	Interest	Total
1	($100 × .06)	$6	$106	($100.00 × .06)	$6.00	$106.00
2	(100 × .06)	6	112	(106.00 × .06)	6.36	112.36
3	(100 × .06)	6	118	(112.36 × .06)	6.74	119.10
4	(100 × .06)	6	124	(119.10 × .06)	7.15	126.25

Because of the compounding effect of interest, an adjustment of the stated annual rate of interest to its effective rate often must be made. This also requires adjusting the number of interest periods. To illustrate, 6% annual interest for 10 years compounded semi-anually would be converted to 3% for 20 periods; 12% for 6 years compounded quarterly would convert to 3% for 24 periods. A first step in working compound interest related problems is to adjust the stated interest rate to its effective interest rate for the appropriate number of periods.

FUTURE AND PRESENT VALUE COMPUTATIONS

Since money earns interest, $100 received today is more valuable than $100 received one year from today. Future and present value analysis is a method of comparing the value of money received or expected to be received at different time periods.

Analyses requiring alternative computations in terms of present dollars relative to future dollars may be viewed from one of two perspectives, the future or the present. If the future point in time is chosen, all cash flows must be *accumulated* to that future point. In this instance, the effect of interest is to increase the amounts or values over time. Examples of questions which might be answered by future value computations include:

How much will $500 deposited today at 6% annual interest amount to in 20 years?

How long would it take to accumulate a $10,000 down payment on a home if one saved $100 a month and received 5% per year on the savings?

What rate of return on an investment must be received for money to double in 20 years?

If, on the other hand, the present is chosen as the point in time at which to evaluate the alternatives, all cash flows must be *discounted* to the present. In this instance, the discounting effect reduces the amounts or values. Assuming a certain rate of interest, examples of questions using the present value approach include:

How much should be accepted today for an apartment house in lieu of rental income for the next 10 years?

How much is $5,000 due in 5 years worth today?

What lump-sum amount should be paid today for a series of equal payments of $100 a month, beginning now, for the next 5 years?

The future value and present value situations are essentially reciprocal relationships, and both are based on the concept of interest. Thus, if interest can be earned at 6% per year, the future worth of $100 one year from now is $106. Conversely, assuming the same rate of interest, the present value of a $106 payment due in one year is $100.

There are four common future and present value situations, each with a corresponding formula. Two of the situations deal with one-time, lump-sum payments or receipts[1] (either future or present values), and the other two involve annuities (either future or present values). An *annuity* consists of a series of equal payments over a specified number of periods.

Without going into the derivation of the formulas, these four situations are as follows:

1. *Future Value of a Lump-Sum Payment:* $FV = P(1 + i)^n$

    This may also be referred to as $FV = (FVF_{\overline{n}|i})$ or simply $FV = P(\text{Table I value})$ where:

FV	=	Future value
P	=	Principal amount to be accumulated
i	=	Interest rate per period
n	=	Number of periods
$FVF_{\overline{n}|i}$	=	Future value factor for a particular interest rate and for a certain number of periods from Table I

---

[1] Hereafter in this appendix, the terms *payments* and *receipts* will be used interchangeably. A payment by one party in a transaction becomes a receipt to the other party and vice versa. The term *rent* is used to designate either a receipt or a payment.

2. *Present Value of a Lump-Sum Payment:* $PV = A\left[\dfrac{1}{(1 + i)^n}\right]$

This may also be referred to as $PV = (PVF_{\overline{n}|\,i})$ or simply $PV = A(\text{Table II value})$, where:

PV	=	Present value
A	=	Accumulated amount to be discounted
i	=	Interest rate per period
n	=	Number of periods
$PVF_{\overline{n}|\,i}$	=	Present value factor for a particular interest rate and for a certain number of periods from Table II

3. *Future Value of an Annuity:* $FV_n = R\left[\dfrac{(1 + i)^n - 1}{i}\right]$

This may also be referred to as $FV_n = R(FVAF_{\overline{n}|\,i})$ or simply $FV_n = R(\text{Table III value})$, where:

FV_n	=	Future value of an annuity
R	=	Annuity payment or periodic rent to be accumulated
i	=	Interest rate per period
n	=	Number of periods
$FVAF_{\overline{n}|\,i}$	=	Future value annuity factor for a particular interest rate and for a certain number of periods from Table III

4. *Present Value of an Annuity:* $PV_n = R\left[\dfrac{1 - \dfrac{1}{(1 + i)^n}}{i}\right]$

This may also be referred to as $PV_n = R(PVAF_{\overline{n}|\,i})$ or simply $PV_n = R(\text{Table IV value})$, where:

PV_n	=	Present value of an annuity
R	=	Annuity payment or periodic rent to be discounted
i	=	Interest rate per period
n	=	Number of periods
$PVAF_{\overline{n}|\,i}$	=	Present value annuity factor for a particular interest rate and for a certain number of periods from Table IV

Because using the formulas would be time-consuming, tables have been developed for each of the four situations. Such tables are provided inside the front and back covers of this text. Each table is based upon computing the value of $1 for various interest rates and periods of time. Future and present value computations can be made by multiplying the appropriate table value factor for $1 by the lump-sum or annuity payment (rent) involved in the problem. To illustrate, consider the question described earlier: How much will $500 deposited today at 6% annual interest amount to in 20 years? This is an example of the first situation, the future value of a lump-sum payment, and involves Table I. The table value for $n = 20$ and $i = 6\%$ is 3.2071. This value times $500, the principal amount to be accumulated, is approximately $1,064. Thus, the future value of $500 deposited now, accumulating at 6% per year for 20 years, is about $1,604.

The following examples demonstrate the application of future and present value tables in solving business problems. At least one example is provided for each of the four situations just described. Note that business problems sometimes require solving for the number of periods, the interest rate, or the rental payment instead of the future or present value amounts. In each of the formulas there are four variables. If information is given about any three of the variables, the fourth (unknown value) can be determined.

Problem 1:
Joe loans his brother $5,000 for a new car. The debt is evidenced by a note due in 4 years with interest at 8% compounded semi-annually. After 1 year, Joe runs out of cash and sells the note to a friend who discounts the note at 12% compounded quarterly. How much cash did Joe receive from his friend?

Solution to Problem 1:
This problem involves a lump-sum payment to be accumulated 4 years into the future at one interest rate, then discounted back 3 years at a different interest rate.
In many present and future value problems, a time line is helpful in visualizing the problem:

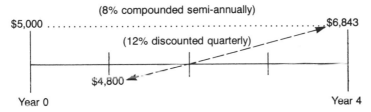

First, the $5,000 must be accumulated for 4 years at 8% compounded semi-annually. Table I is used, and the applicable formula is:

FV – P(FVF$_{\overline{n}|i}$)   where: FV = The future value of the lump sum
                                          P = $5,000
                                          n – 8 periods (4 years × 2)
                                          i = 4% effective interest rate per period
                                               (8% ÷ 2)

FV = $5,000 (Table I$_{\overline{8}|4\%}$)
FV = $5,000 (1.3686)
FV = $6,843

In 4 years, the holder of the note will receive $6,843. After Joe sells the note to his friend, the note will be worth $6,843 to the friend in 3 years. The opportunity cost of money to the friend is apparently 12% compounded quarterly. Therefore, the $6,843 must be discounted back 3 years at 12% to find the amount the friend is willing to pay Joe.
Table II is used, and the applicable formula is:

PV = A(PVF$_{\overline{n}|i}$)   where: PV = The value of the future sum discounted
                                               back three years
                                          A = $6,843
                                          n = 12 periods (3 years × 4 quarters)
                                          i = 3% effective interest rate per period
                                               (12% ÷ 4 quarters)

PV = $6,843 (Table II $_{\overline{12}|\,3\%}$)
PV = $6,843 (.7014)
PV = $4,800

The friend will pay roughly $4,800. Thus, Joe is willing to give up $2,043 ($6,843 − $4,800) in order to collect the note at the end of 1 year.

Problem 2:
Miller Sporting Goods is contemplating an investment which will require $1,250,000 capital investment and which will provide these net receipts:

Year	Estimated Net Receipts
1	$195,000
2	457,000
3	593,000
4	421,000
5	95,000
6	5,000

Miller will accept the investment only if the rate of return is greater than 10%. Will Miller accept the investment?

Solution to Problem 2:
A series of unequal future receipts must be compared with a present lump-sum investment. For such a comparison to be made, all future cash flows must be discounted to the present.
If the rate of return on the amount invested is greater than 10%, then the total of all yearly net receipts discounted to the present at 10% will be greater than the amount invested. Since the receipts are unequal, each amount must be discounted individually. Table II is used, and the applicable formula is:

PV = A(PVF$_{\overline{n}|\,i}$) where:

(1) Year = n	(2) A (Net Receipts)	(3) Table II$_{\overline{n}|\,10\%}$	(2) × (3) = (4) PV (Discounted Amount)
1	$195,000	.9091	$ 177,275
2	457,000	.8264	377,665
3	593,000	.7513	445,521
4	421,000	.6830	287,543
5	95,000	.6209	58,986
6	5,000	.5645	2,823
Total			$1,349,813

The total discounted receipts are greater than the investment; thus, the rate of return is more than 10%. Therefore, other things being equal, Miller will invest.

Problem 3:
Brothwell, Ltd., owes an instalment debt of $1,000 per quarter for 5 years. The creditor has indicated that he will accept an equivalent lump-sum payment at the end of the contract period instead of the series of payments. If money is worth 8% compounded quarterly and the first four payments have been made, what is the equivalent lump-sum payment?

Solution to Problem 3:

The equivalent lump-sum payment can be found by accumulating the quarterly $1,000 payments to the end of the contract period. Table III is used, and the applicable formula is:

$$FV_n = R(FVAF_{\overline{n}|i})$$

where:

FV_n	=	The unknown equivalent lump-sum payment
R	=	$1,000 quarterly instalment to be accumulated
n	=	16 periods [(5 years × 4 quarters) − 4 quarters already paid]
i	=	2% effective compound rate (8% ÷ 4 quarters)

$FV_n = \$1,000$ (Table III $_{\overline{16}|2\%}$)
$FV_n = \$1,000$ (18.6393)
$FV_n = \$18,639$

$18,639 paid at the end of the 5 years is equivalent to the remaining 16 payments.

Problem 4:

Mr. Robinson, proprietor of Parliament Hill Appliance, received two offers for his last deluxe-model refrigerator. Ms. Butler will pay $650 in cash. Mr. McBride will pay $700 consisting of a down payment of $100 and 12 monthly payments of $50. If the instalment interest rate is 24% compounded monthly, which offer should Robinson accept?

Solution to Problem 4:

In order to compare the two alternative methods of payment, all cash flows must be accumulated or discounted to one point in time. As illustrated by the time line, the present is selected as the point of comparison.

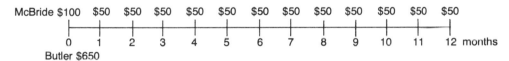

Ms. Butler's offer is $650 today. The present value of $650 today is $650.
Mr. McBride's offer consists of an annuity of 12 payments, plus $100 due today which is not part of the annuity. The annuity may be discounted to the present by using Table IV and the applicable formula:

$$PV_n = R(PVAF_{\overline{n}|i})$$

where:

PV_n	=	Unknown present value of 12 payments
R	=	$50 monthly payment to be discounted
n	=	12 periods
i	=	2% effective compound rate (24% ÷ 12 periods per year)

$PV_n = \$50$ (Table IV $_{\overline{n}|2\%}$)
$PV_n = \$50(10.5753)$
$PV_n = \$529$

Present value of McBride's payments $529
Present value of McBride's $100 down payment   100
Total present value of McBride's offer $629

Therefore, Ms. Butler's offer of $650 cash is more desirable than Mr. McBride's offer.

Problem 5:

The Angelo Company is investigating the purchase of a block of bonds. Each $1,000 bond has a stated interest rate of 12% paid semi-annually and is due in 10 years. The prevailing market rate for comparable bonds is 8%, also paid semi-annually. How much should Angelo Company pay for each bond?

Solution to Problem 5:

This problem involves finding the present value of the cash flows resulting from the purchase of a bond. A bond pays both a series of equal interest payments and the principal amount when the bond matures. To ascertain the fair price of the bond, both the series of interest payments and the future payment of the principal must be discounted to the present at the going market rate of 8% compounded semi-annually.

First the series of interest payments is discounted to the present using Table IV and the applicable formula:

$$PV_n = R(PVAF_{\overline{n}|i})$$

where:

PV_n	=	Unknown present value
R	=	$60 semi-annual interest payment
		($1,000 × .12 × $1/2$ year)
n	=	20 periods (10 years × 2 periods per year)
i	=	4% effective compound rate
		(8% ÷ 2
		periods per year)

PV_n = $60 (Table IV $_{\overline{20}|4\%}$)
PV_n = $60(13.5903)
PV_n = $815

Second, the future payment of principal is discounted to the present using Table II and the applicable formula:

$$PV = A(PVF_{\overline{n}|i})$$

where:

PV	=	Unknown present value of the principal payment
A	=	$1,000 the principal payment
n	=	20 periods
i	=	4% effective compound rate

PV = $1,000 (Table II $_{\overline{20}|4\%}$)
PV = $1,000(.4564)
PV = $456

Therefore, the price Angelo Company should pay for each bond is $815 + $456, or $1,271.

INTERPOLATION

A difficulty in using future and present value tables arises when the exact factor does not appear in the table. One solution is to use the formula. Interpolation is another, often more practical, solution. Interpolation assumes the change between two values is linear. Although such an assumption is not correct, the margin of error is often insignificant, especially if the table value ranges are not too wide.

For example, determine the table value for the present value of $1 at $4^{1}/_{2}\%$ for 9 periods. The appropriate factor does not appear in Table II. However, the two closest values are Table II $_{\overline{9}|4\%}$ = .7026 and Table II $_{\overline{9}|5\%}$ = .6446. Interpolation relates the unknown value to the change in the known values. This relationship may be shown as a proportion:

$$\frac{y}{Y} = \frac{x}{X}$$

$$\frac{5 - 4^{1}/_{2}}{5 - 4} = \frac{x}{.7026 - .6446}$$

$$\frac{^{1}/_{2}}{1} = \frac{x}{.0580}$$

$$x = .0290$$

The .0290 is the difference between the value for 5% and the value for $4^{1}/_{2}\%$. Therefore, the value needed is .0290 + .6446 = .6736. Using the mathematical formula for Table II $\left\{ PV = A\left[\dfrac{1}{(1 + i)^{n}} \right] \right\}$, the present value of $1 at $4^{1}/_{2}\%$ interest for 9 periods is .6729 $\left\{ PV = 1\left[\dfrac{1}{(1 + .045)^{9}} \right] \right\}$. The difference (.6736 − .6729 = .0007) is insignificant for many purposes.

Interpolation is useful in finding a particular unknown table value that lies between two given values. This procedure is also used in approximating the number of periods or unknown interest rates when the table value is known. The following problems illustrate the determination of these two variables.

Problem 6:
Ms. Novella leaves $600,000 to a university for a new building on the condition that construction will not begin until her bequest, invested at 5% per year, amounts to $1,500,000. How long before construction may begin?

Solution to Problem 6:
This problem involves finding the time (number of periods) required for a lump-sum payment to accumulate to a specified future amount. Table I is used and, the applicable formula is:

$$FV = P(FVF_{\overline{n}|i})$$

where:
FV = $1,500,000
P = $600,000
n = Unknown number of periods
i = 5% effective interest rate per year

$1,500,000 = \$600,000 \text{ (Table } I_{\overline{n}|\,5\%})$

$\dfrac{\$1,500,000}{\$\ \ 600,000} = \text{Table } I_{\overline{n}|\,5\%}$

$2.5 = \text{Table } I_{\overline{n}|\,5\%}$

Referring to Table I, reading down the $i = 5\%$ column:

n		Table Factor
18	=	2.4066
19	=	2.5270

Interpolating:

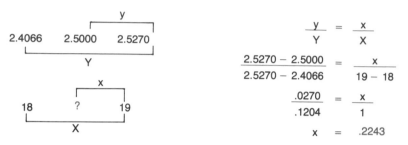

$$\dfrac{y}{Y} = \dfrac{x}{X}$$

$$\dfrac{2.5270 - 2.5000}{2.5270 - 2.4066} = \dfrac{x}{19 - 18}$$

$$\dfrac{.0270}{.1204} = \dfrac{x}{1}$$

$$x = .2243$$

The .2243 is the difference between the number of periods at table factor 2.5270 and the number of periods at table factor 2.5000. Therefore, the number of periods needed is $19.0000 - .2243 = 18.7757$. In other words, about $18^{3}/_{4}$ periods (in this case, years) are required for \$600,000 to amount to \$1,500,000 at 5% annual interest.

Problem 7:
The Newports have entered into an automobile lease-purchase arrangement. The fair market value of the leased automobile is \$5,814, and the contract calls for quarterly payments of \$570 due at the end of each quarter for 3 years. What is the implicit rate of interest on the lease arrangement?

Solution to Problem 7:
The implicit interest rate must be computed for the present value of an annuity. The present value is the fair market value of the automobile, and the payment is the lease payment. Table IV is used, and the applicable formula is:

$PV_n = R(PVAF_{\overline{n}|\,i})$ where:

PV_n	=	\$5814
R	=	\$570
n	=	12 (3 years × 4 payments per year)
i	=	The unknown quarterly interest rate

$\$5,814 = \$570(\text{Table } IV_{\overline{12}|})$

$\dfrac{\$5,814}{\$\ \ 570} = \text{Table } IV_{\overline{12}|\,i}$

$10.20 = \text{Table } IV_{\overline{12}|\,i}$

Reading across the $n = 12$ row of Table IV:

i		Table Factor
2%	=	10.5753
3%	=	9.9540

Interpolating:

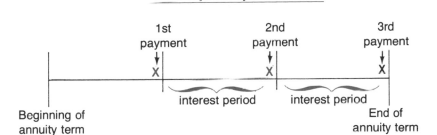

$$\frac{y}{Y} = \frac{x}{X}$$

$$\frac{10.2000 - 9.9540}{10.5753 - 9.9540} = \frac{x}{3.0 - 2.0}$$

$$\frac{.2460}{.6213} = \frac{x}{1.0}$$

$$x = .3959$$

The .3959 is the difference between the interest rate at the table factor 9.9540 and the interest rate at the table factor 10.2000. Therefore, the quarterly implicit interest rate is 3.0000 − .3959 = 2.6041%; and the annual implicit interest rate is 10.4164% (2.6041% × 4).

ORDINARY ANNUITY AND ANNUITY DUE

Annuities are of two types: ordinary annuities (annuities in arrears) and annuities due (annuities in advance). The periodic rents or payments for an *ordinary annuity* are made at the *end* of each period, and the last payment coincides with the end of the annuity term. The periodic rents or payments for an *annuity due* are made at the *beginning* of each period, and one period of the annuity term remains after the last payment. These differences are illustrated as follows:

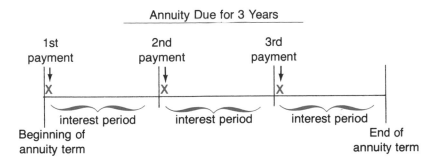

Most future and present value tables are computed for ordinary annuities; however, with slight adjustment, these same tables may be used in solving annuity due problems. To illustrate the conversion of an ordinary annuity table value to an annuity due value, consider the *future* amount of an ordinary annuity for three years (see the diagram in the middle of page 1009). This situation involves three payments; but because the first payment is made at the end of the first period, interest is earned for only two periods (3p + 2i). On the other hand, the future amount of an annuity due for three years (illustrated at the bottom of page 109) involves three payments as well as interest for three periods because the first payment is made at the beginning of the first period (3p + 3i).

As shown below, an ordinary annuity involving four payments would earn interest for three periods (4p + 3i); thus, if the fourth payment were deducted, the value would be comparable to an annuity due of 3 periods [i.e., (4p + 3i) − 1p = 3p + 3i].

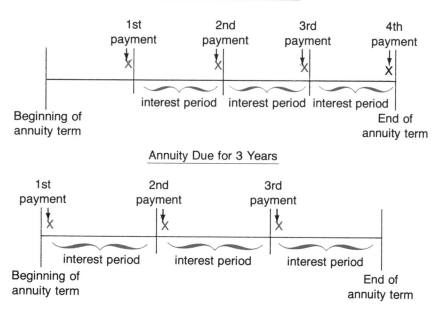

Therefore, to find the future value of an annuity due using ordinary annuity table values, simply select the appropriate table value for an ordinary annuity for one additional period (n + 1) and subtract the extra payment (which is 1.0000 in terms of the table value because the tables are computed for rents of $1.0000). The formula is $FV_n = R(FVAF_{\overline{n+1}|i} - 1)$.

For example, the table value (Table III) for the future amount of an annuity due for 3 periods at 8% is:

(1) Factor for future value of an ordinary annuity of $1 for 4 periods (n + 1) at 8%	4.5061	
(2) Less one payment	1.0000	
(3) Factor for future value of an annuity due of $1 for 3 periods at 8%	3.5061	

The situation and the underlying reasoning are reversed in converting a present value factor for an ordinary annuity to the present value factor of an annuity due. As shown in the diagrams below, the present value of an annuity due for three years involves three payments; but interest (discount) is only earned for two periods (3p + 2i). To obtain comparable interest (discount) periods, an ordinary annuity for two years is required (2p + 2i). However, one additional payment must be added to make the situations equivalent; i.e., (2p + 2i) + 1p = 3p + 2i. Consequently, to convert the present value of an ordinary annuity to the present value of an annuity due, look at the table factor for one less period (n − 1) and then add one payment (+ 1.0000). The formula is $PV_n = R(PVAF_{\overline{n-1}|\ i} + 1)$.

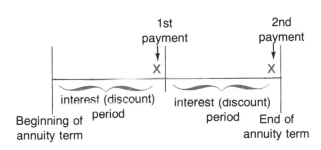

Ordinary Annuity for 2 Years

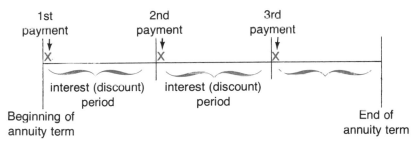

Annuity Due for 3 Years

For example, the table value (Table IV) for the present value of an annuity due for three periods at 8% is:

(1) Factor for present value of an ordinary annuity of $1 for two periods (n − 1) at 8%	1.7833	
(2) Plus one payment	1.0000	
(3) Factor for present value of an annuity due of $1 for 3 periods at 8%	2.7833	

The following problems illustrate the application of converting from ordinary annuity table values to annuity due table values.

Problem 8:

The Sampson Corporation desires to accumulate funds to retire a $200,000 bond issue at the end of 15 years. Funds set aside for this purpose would be invested to yield 6%. What annual payment starting immediately would provide the needed funds?

Solution to Problem 8:

Annuity payments of an unknown amount are to be accumulated toward a specific dollar amount at a known interest rate. Therefore, Table III is used. Because the first payment is to be made immediately, all payments will fall due at the beginning of each period and an annuity due is used. The appropriate formula is:

$$FV_n = R(FVAF_{\overline{n+1}|i} - 1) \qquad \text{where:} \quad \begin{array}{ll} FV_n & = \$200,000 \\ R & = \text{Unknown annual payment} \\ n & = 15 \text{ periods} \\ i & = 6\% \text{ annual interest} \end{array}$$

$200,000 = R(\text{Table III}_{\overline{16}|\,6\%} - 1)$
$200,000 = R(24.6725)$

$$\frac{\$200,000}{24.6725} = R$$

$8,106 = R$

Sampson Corporation must deposit $8,106 annually, starting immediately, to accumulate $200,000 in 15 years at 6% annual interest.

Problem 9:

Brigham Corporation has completed lease-purchasing negotiations. The fair market value of the leased equipment is $45,897. The lease contract specifies semi-annual payments of $3,775 for 10 years beginning immediately. At the end of the lease, Brigham Corporation may purchase the equipment for a nominal amount. What is the implicit annual rate of interest on the lease purchase?

Solution to Problem 9:

The implicit interest rate must be computed for the present value of an annuity due. The present value is the fair market value of the equipment, and the payment is the lease payment. Table IV is used, and the applicable formula is:

$$PV_n = R(PVAF_{\overline{n-1}|i} + 1) \qquad \text{where:} \quad \begin{array}{ll} PV_n & = \$45,897 \\ R & = \$3,775 \\ n & = 20 \text{ periods (10 years} \times 2 \text{ payments} \\ & \quad \text{per year)} \\ i & = \text{The unknown semi-annual interest} \\ & \quad \text{rate} \end{array}$$

$45,897 = \$3,775 \,(\text{Table IV}_{\overline{19}|\,i} + 1)$

$$\frac{\$45,897}{3,775} = 12.1581 = \text{Table IV}_{\overline{19}|\,i} + 1$$

$11.1581 = \text{Table IV}_{\overline{19}|\,i}$

Examination of Table IV for 19 periods and a factor of 11.1581 shows Table IV$_{\overline{19}|\, 6\%}$ = 11.1581. Therefore, i = 6%. The implicit interest rate is twice the semi-annual rate, or 2 × 6% = 12%.

Problem 10:
Three years remain on the lease of Nyland Food Service, Inc.'s building. The lease is non-cancelable and requires payments of $5,000 on March 1 and September 1. During February, Nyland located a new store building and asked the lessor of the old store to accept $25,000 now in full payment of the old lease. The building is very old and will not be used again. If the value of money to the lessor is 16% compounded semi-annually, should she accept Nyland's offer?

Solution to Problem 10:
The lessor must compare the $25,000 now to the value of the six remaining lease payments. The lease payments must be discounted to the present for proper comparison. Because the next payment is due now, the lease payments are an annuity due. Table IV is adjusted to find the appropriate value. The formula is:

$$PV_n = R(PVAF_{\overline{n-1}|\, i} + 1)$$

where: PV_n = Unknown present value of lease payments
R   = $5,000 per period (6 months)
n   = 6 periods (3 years × 2 periods per year)
i   = 8% (16% ÷ 2 periods per year)

PV_n = $5,000 (Table IV$_{\overline{5}|\, 8\%}$ + 1)
PV_n = $5,000 (3.9927 + 1)
PV_n = $24,964

The offer of $25,000 now is greater than $24,964, the present value of the remaining lease payments. Therefore, the lessor should accept the offer.

A

D

Funds, accounting for, 385; bond, 535; broadened interpretation of, 841; defined, 841; defined as cash, 846; defined as working capital, 845; establishment of, 383; long-term investment in, 383; redemption, 383; sinking, 383, 535

Funds flow, *illustrated*, 843

Fund sources, 848

Funds statement, 841; adjustment in developing amounts provided and applied, 850; alternative methods for developing, 865; analysis of account changes in preparation of, 848; applying different funds concepts, 844; nature of, 842; preparation of, funds defined as cash, 865; preparation of, funds defined as working capital, 853; special observations, 869; special problems in developing, 864; use of, 842; *see also* Statement of changes in financial position

_____ G _____

Gains, 123

General Accountants Associations, 8

General journal, 46; *illustrated*, 52

General ledger, *illustrated*, 49

General price index, 125

General price-level adjustments, 906 passim

General price-level changes, comparative balance sheet reporting, *illustrated*, 945; effects of, on monetary and non-monetary items, 909; restating financial statements for, 910; specific price changes vs., 903

General price-level restatements, 910-17; applied to depreciable properties acquired at different times, 953-55; applied to inventories, reported under alternative cost-flow assumptions, 950-52

General purpose statements, 84

GNE implicit price index, 908

Going concern, 28

Goods in process, 202; *see also* Work in process

Goods in transit, 205

Goods on consignment, 206

Goodwill, adjustment after acquisition, 422; calculation of, capitalization of average excess net earnings method, 419, capitalization of average net earnings method, 419, capitalization of number of years' purchase method, 420, capitalization of present value method, 421; defined, 415; implied, 421; negative, 442; valuation of, 416

Gross profit method, for estimating inventories, 246; use of, for computation of fire loss, 249; use of, for monthly inventory calculations, 248

Gross profit test, 247

Group-rate method of depreciation, 334, 341

Growth of pension plans, 621

Guaranteed bonds, 513

_____ H _____

Historical-cost, 29; statement, 903 passim

Historical development of lease accounting, 602

Historical-dollar statement, *see* Historical-cost, statement

Holding gains or losses, 918-19; realized, 918; related to purchasing power, 909; unrealized, 919

_____ I _____

Immediate recognition, 124

Implicit interest rate, 614

Implied goodwill, 421

Imprest system of cash funds, 155

Improvements, *see* Betterments

Imputed rate, 166

Income, before adjustment for general price-level gain or loss, 940, 942; importance of measuring and reporting, 115; inventories in measurement of, 203; nature of, 117

Income, before extraordinary items, 30

Income and retained earnings statement, reporting general price-level changes, *illustrated*, 940-43; restated at end of first year for general price-level changes, *illustrated*, 941; restated at end of second year for general price-level changes, 944-47, *illustrated*, 946

Income determination, *see* Income measurement

Income for accounting purposes vs. income for tax purposes, 558, 560; permanent differences, 561; reversal of timing differences, 561, 562

Income measurement, 30, 116; association, 123; matching, 123; matching method of, 119; valuation method of, 118

Income statement, 115; condensed single-step, *illustrated*, 729; contents, 129-32; current operating performance, 126; defined, 84; earnings per share presentation on, 755; equation for, 118; form of, 132; multiple-step form, 133, *illustrated*, 134; preparation from single-entry records, 815; reporting results on an all-inclusive basis, 126; single-step form, 133, *illustrated*, 135; special problems in preparation of, 125

Income statement accounts, errors limited to, 800

Income tax, accounting for, 561; Bulletin No. 26, Accounting and Auditing Research Committee, 563; interperiod allocation, 560-70; intraperiod allocation, 558-60; laws, 116; nature of, 557; provision for, 57; recording of, payable, 60; relative to income from normal operations, 132

Income tax rate changes, deferral method of accounting for, 570-72; liability method of accounting for, 570

Income tax withheld, 504

Incorporation of a partnership, 669; if new accounts are opened, 671; if original accounts are retained, 671

Incorporation of a sole proprietorship, 669

Incremental borrowing rate, 606

Indexes, price-level, *see* Price-level indexes

Indirect materials, *see* Factory supplies

Indirect method of income determination, *see* Valuation method

Inflation, component in holding gains and losses, 927; as general price changes, 903, 906

Information, accounting, users of, 2

Instalment sales method, 122

Institute of Chartered Accountants of Ontario, 7, 15, Rule 206.3, 15

Institutes of Chartered Accountants, 6

Insurance, fire, 311

Intangible assets, amortization, maximum period for, 409; on the balance sheet, 423; defined, 467; examples of, 90; identifiable, 411; purchased intercompany, 454; valuation of, at time of acquisition, 408, subsequent to time of acquisition, 408

Intentional misstatements, 798

Inter-comparability, *see* Comparability

Intercompany transactions, 447; assets purchased intercompany, 452; in consolidated financials, 447; downstream and upstream, 449; elimination entries, 448-49; gains and losses, 449; inventory purchased intercompany, 450; *see also* Unrealized intercompany gains and losses

Intercorporate investment, 437; as business combination, 438; equity method of accounting, 474-75; parent and subsidiary as separate legal entities, 438; purchase price discrepancy, 441; *see also* Consolidated financial statements

Interest on bonds, contract rate of, 514; effective rate of, 515; market rate of, 514

Internal transactions, defined, 44

Interperiod income tax allocation, 560-70; accounting for, with changes in rates, 570; accounting for different types of timing differences, 564; allocation method, 561; historical development, 563; *illustrated*, 565; problem areas in, 572; taxes payable method, 561

Intra-comparability, *see* Comparability

Intraperiod income tax allocation, 558, *illustrated*, 559

Inventories, 201; on balance sheet, 271; classes of, 201; conditional and instalment sales, 206; estimating procedures, 246; general price-level restatements applied to, reported under alternative cost-flow assumptions, 950-52; goods in transit, 205; goods on consignment, 206; perpetual-manufacturing, 63; perpetual-merchandising, 63; physical, 61; physical-manufacturing, 61; physical-merchandising, 61; segregated goods, 205; specific-goods pools, 215, *illustrated*, 217

Inventories in the measurement of income, 203

Inventory, items to be included in, 205; purchased intercompany, 450; restated for price-level changes, 944

Inventory accounts, adjusting, 61; closing, 61, *illustrated*, 62

Inventory cost methods, 207

Inventory costing, base stock method, 222; cost of latest purchases method, 221; direct costing method, 223; marginal costing method, 223; simple average of costs method, 222; specific identification of costs with inventory items, 209; standard cost method, 223; variable costing method, 223; *see also* Cost flow

Inventory decline, retained earnings appropriation for, 725

Partial periods, depreciation for, 344
Partnership, incorporation of, 669; incorporation of, if new accounts are opened, 671; incorporation of, if original accounts are retained, 671
Par value shares, 652, 656
Past service costs, 623
Patents, defined, 412
Payback period, 421
Payout percentage, 756
Payout rate, *see* Payout percentage
Payroll record, 46
Payroll taxes, 504; accounting for, 504
Pension cost accounting, amount of periodic cost, 622; prior service costs, 623
Pension costs, 620; accounting for, *illustrated*, 625-26; accrual requirement for, 623; actuarial gains and losses, 628; liability for unfunded prior service costs, 628; normal costs, 622; past service costs, 623; prior service costs, 623
Pension funding, accrued benefit costs methods, 623; actuarial cost methods, 623, *illustrated*, 624; projected benefit cost methods, 623
Pension plans, disclosure requirements of, 629; growth of, 621
Pensions, funding of, 623
Percentage-of-completion method of accounting, 122
Periodic depreciation charge, factors determining, 331
Periodic inventory system, 204
Periodic summary, 53
Permanent differences, *see* Income for accounting purposes
Perpetual inventories, adjustment for manufacturing enterprise, 63; adjustment for merchandising enterprise, 63
Perpetual inventory system, 204
Personal property, 289
Personalty, 289
Physical inventories, in a manufacturing enterprise, *illustrated*, 61-62; adjustment for manufacturing enterprise, 61; adjustment for merchandising enterprise, 61
Point of actual cash collection, 122
Point of completed production, 122
Point of sale, 121; defined, 30
Pooling of interests, 297
Post-closing trial balance, *illustrated*, 65; preparation of, 65
Posting, defined, 47
Predictive value, 33
Pre-emptive right, 377
Preferred shares, 653, 659; callable, 660; convertible, 660; cumulative, 659; dividend rights, 754; dividends on, 720; liquidation value of, 754; non-cumulative, 659-60
Premium amortization, interest method of, 521; straight-line method of, 521
Premium on shares, 656
Prepaid expense, overstatement of, 807; adjusting for, 56, *illustrated*, 57
Preparation of the funds statement, funds defined as working capital, 853
Preparing a trial balance, 53
Preparing a work sheet, 60
Price-earnings ratio, 756

Price index, 259
Price-level accounting, 32, 904
Price-level adjustments, general, 904-05
Price-level changes, fair value accounting for, 904; general vs. specific, 903-04
Price-level indexes, 907-09
Price levels, effects of changing, 125, 903
Principal pension cost accounting, problems of employers, 622
Principles, development of, by AAA, 20, by AICPA, 16, by CICA, 14, by FASB, 19, by SEC, 21; need for accounting, 5
Principles and concepts, conservatism, 27; continuity of life — the going concern, 28; entity, 29; historical-cost, 29; income measurement, 30; materiality, 31; quantifiability, 31; stable monetary measure, 32
Prior period adjustments, 127; FASB proposed standard, 127
Prior service costs, *illustrated*, 623; liability for unfunded, 628
Private corporation, 650; corporations that restrict transfer of shares, 650
Productive-output method of depreciation, 334, 340
Professional associations: AAA, 11; AICPA, 10; CGA, 9; CICA, 7; FASB, 11; FEI, 12; NAA, 13; RIA, 9; SEC, 12; SIA, 8; SMA, 8
Professions, enabling legislation, 6; regulation of, 6; regulatory legislation, 6
Proof of cash, 157; *illustrated*, 158, 159
Properties acquired at different times, general price-level restatements applied to, 953-55
Property, acquisition of, 291; disposition of, 587; valuation of, 290
Property, plant, and equipment, 288
Property damage, 311
Property dividends, 373, 715
Property items, expenditures incurred during service life of, 306
Property records, 348
Property retirements, 309
Pro-forma amounts, *see* Earnings per share
Provincial Securities Commissions, 6, 9
Public corporation, 650; *see also* Distributing corporations
Purchase commitments, losses on, 268
Purchase of property, for cash, 291; on long-term contract, 292
Purchase returns and allowances, 254
Purchasing power, affected by inflation, 906; expressed as constant dollars, 904; gain or loss, 909, 910-17, *illustrated*, 913, 915; schedule reporting, 942

Q

Qualitative characteristics, comparability, 33; consistency, 33; feedback value, 33; materiality, 33; neutrality, 33; predictive value, 33; relevance, 33; reliability, 33; representational faithfulness, 33; timeliness, 33; understandability, 35; verifiability, 35
Qualitative objectives, comparability, 25; completeness, 26; neutrality, 24; relevance, 23; timeliness, 24; understandability, 23; verifiability, 23

Quantifiability, 31
Quebec Pension Plan, 504
Quitting concern, 28

R

Raw materials, 202
Real account, 47
Real estate, interests in, 389
Real property, 289
Realization, 906; transactions-based concept, 920
Realized holding gain, 918
Realty, 289
Rearrangements, 308
Recapitalization, 711
Receivables, accounts, 164; adjustment allowance, percentage of, 169; adjustment allowance by ageing, 170; analysis of, *illustrated*, 170; anticipation of discounts and other charges in valuation of, 172; basis for doubtful accounts adjustments, 169; composition of, 163; estimated uncollectible accounts, 168; notes, 164; presentation on the balance sheet, 179; reporting at present values, 166; use of, in cash planning, 173; valuation of, 166; *see also* Accounts receivable
Reciprocal accounts, 535
Reconciliation of bank balances, 156
Recording collection of subscriptions, 663
Recording phase, of accounting records, 45; of accounting process, 45; from manual operations to electronic data processing, 52
Records, property, 348
Redemption funds, 383
Redemption of shares, 380
Registrar of trademarks, 414
Registrars, 655
Regulation of accounting profession, 6; enabling legislation, 6; regulatory legislation, 6
Relative sales value method, 225; *illustrated*, 225
Relevance, 23, 33
Reliability, 33
Renewals, 307
Reorganization, 711; *illustrated*, 712
Repairs, 307
Replacement cost, 260
Replacements, 307
Reporting entity, change in, 593, 813
Repossessions, valuation of, 270
Representational faithfulness, 33
Research and development costs, 410-11
Research Monographs, 8; *see also* Society of Industrial Accountants of Canada
Research Studies, 8; *see also* Canadian Institute of Chartered Accountants
Reserve, use of term, 720; *see also* Retained earnings appropriations
Reserved retained earnings, *see* Appropriated retained earnings
Reserves, on the balance sheet, 95
Residual value, accounting for, 616; in determining depreciation charge, 331
Retail inventory method, conventional, 253; for estimating inventories, 250
Retail-lifo, 258; procedures of, 258, *illustrated*, 259
Retail method, limitations of, 254

Retained earnings, 93, 696, 701; appropriated, 696, 701; at beginning of second year, 945; consolidated, 444; in a corporation, 93; dated, 713; restated for price-level changes at end of year, 943, 947; source of, 696, 701; unappropriated, 696

Retained earnings appropriations, 722; to describe business purposes served by retained earnings, 727; objections to appropriation procedures, 727; for possible future losses, 724; relating to bond redemption, 723; to report contractual restrictions on retained earnings, 722; to report discretionary action in the presentation of retained earnings, 722; to report legal restrictions on retained earnings, 722; for self-insurance, 726

Retained earnings statement, *illustrated*, 136, 732

Retirements, property, 309

Revenue, from long-term investment in shares, 370

Revenue expenditures, 289

Revenue-expense viewpoint, 119

Revenue from long-term investments, cost method of recognizing, 372; equity method of recognizing, 370

Revenue realization, 30

Revenue from sales, 131

Revenues, accrued, 56; deferred, 57, 91; defined by APB, 120; defined by FASB, 120; nature of, 120

Reverse stock splits, 710

Reversing the accounts, *illustrated*, 66

Reversing entries, *illustrated*, 67

Rights, stock, 704; *see also* Stock rights

Ross, Howard, 9-10

S

Sale-leaseback, 619

Sale of shares, 380

Sales, conditional, 206; on income statement, 817; instalment, 206

Sales journal, *illustrated*, 50

Sales tax, 503; collections, included in sales balance, 504; collections, recorded separately, 504

Sales-type leases, accounting for, 611

Salvage value, 331; *see also* Residual value

Schedule, reporting purchasing power gain or loss for the year, *illustrated*, 913, 915; reporting purchasing power gain or loss for first year, 942; reporting purchasing power gain or loss for second year, *illustrated*, 946

Scrip dividends, 715

SEC, *see* Securities and Exchange Commission

Second-mortgage bond, 513

Secret reserves, on the balance sheet, 668

Secured bonds, 513

Securities, acquisition of property by issuance of, 296; multiple potentially dilutive, 770; regulation, 9, 650

Securities and Exchange Commission, 12; development of principles, 21

Securities regulation, 9, 650; Business Corporations Act (Ontario), 651, 675; Exemptions, 651; National Policy Statement No. 27, 15; Ontario Securities Act, 651

Security units, 666; sale of, for a single sum, 666

Segregated goods, 205

Self-construction, acquisition of property by, 297; overhead chargeable to, 297; saving or loss on, 298

Self-insurance, retained earnings appropriation for, 726

Serial bonds, 513, 525; amortization by bonds-outstanding method, *illustrated*, 526; amortization of premium by interest method, 526; amortization procedures when bond year and fiscal year do not coincide, 527; bonds redemption prior to maturity, 531

Service-hours method of depreciation, 334, 339

Share capital, 652, 696; on consolidated balance sheet, 457; issuance of, in exchange for a business, 668; issuance of, *illustrated*, 664-65; issued for consideration other than cash, 668; nature of, 652; recording issuance of, 662; recording the subscription of, 662, 663; retirement of, 673, *illustrated*, 674; *see also* Issuance of share capital; Legal capital; Stated capital

Share subscriptions and calls, *see* Subscriptions and calls

Shareholder, rights of, 653; rights issued to existing, 705

Shareholders' equity, on balance sheet, 93; on consolidated balance sheet, 457; deduction from total, 728; restated for price-level changes, 944; statements accounting for changes in, 729

Shareholders' ledger, 48, 655

Shares, authorized, 652, 698; common, 653; ex-rights, 377; issued, 652, 698; issued on conversion, 702; nature of, 652; no-par-value of, 652, 656; outstanding, 652; par value of, 652, 656; partially paid, 663; preemptive rights, 653; preferred, 653; rights-on, 377; stated value of, 658; treasury, 675; *see also* Issuance of share capital; Legal capital; Share capital; Stated capital

SIA, *see* Society of Industrial Accountants of Canada

Simple capital structure, 757; computation of earnings per share, *illustrated*, 761-62; computational guidelines, 759-61

Single-entry systems, 815; records in, 815; use of, 820

Sinking fund, 535; method of depreciation, 334

Skinner, Ross M. *Accounting Principles: A Canadian Viewpoint*, 16

Societies of Management Accountants, 6

Society of Management Accountants of Canada, 8; Accounting Principles and Practices Committee, 8; *Cost and Management*, 8; *Research Monographs*, 8; *SMA Special Study* series, 8-9

Sole proprietorship, incorporation of, 669

Source and application of funds statement, *see* Funds statement

Special journals, 46

Specific price changes, general price changes vs., 903-04

SSAP 16, *see* Statement of Standard Accounting Practice, 16

Stable monetary measure, 32; price-level accounting, 32

Standard cost variances, 223

Stated capital, 654-55

Stated capital account, 655, 700; *see also* Canada Business Corporations Act

Statement of basic accounting theory, recommendations of AAA, 125

Statement of changes in financial position, 84, 101; cash basis, 846, *illustrated*, 868, working papers in, *illustrated*, 866-67; general price-level adjusted, 948-50; working capital basis, *illustrated*, 102, 845, working papers for, *illustrated*, 858-59; *see also* Funds statement

Statement of Financial Accounting Concepts, No. 2, 33

Statement of financial position, *see* Balance Sheet

Statement of operations, *see* Income statement

Statement of profit and loss, *see* Income statement

Statement of resources provided and applied, *see* Funds statement

Statement of retained earnings, 137; *see also* Retained earnings statement

Statement of sources and uses of funds, *see* Funds statement

Statement of Standard Accounting Practice, 16, "Current Cost Accounting," 905, 931, 935-38

Statements, accounting for changes in the shareholders' equity, 729; general purpose, 4

Stock dividends, 374; on the balance sheet, 719

Stock options, 705; disclosure of, 710; issued to employees, 707

Stock purchase plans, accounting for compensatory plan, *illustrated*, 709; compensatory, 707; non-compensatory, 707

Stock rights, 377, 704; accounting for, 378; issued to employees, 707; issued to existing shareholders, 705; issued with various classes of securities, 705

Stock split-down, *see* Reverse stock splits

Stock split-up, *see* Stock splits

Stock splits, 376, 710

Stock subscription, 662; recording 663

Stock warrants, 377; *see also* Warrants

Straight-line method of amortization, 294-95; of depreciation, 335

Subscription defaults, 664

Subscriptions, recording collection of, 663

Subsidiary company, 366

Subsidiary ledgers, 48

Sum-of-the-years-digits method of depreciation, 334, 337

Summarizing phase, of accounting process, 43, 44; compiling adjusting data, 54; preparing a trial balance, 53

Summary of accounting for leases, 620

Summary accounts, *illustrated*, 62

Supplementary schedules, to balance sheet, 98

Surplus, 95; Accounting Research Committee recommendation, 95

Systematic and rational allocation, expense recognition, 124

T

T account, preparation of statement of changes, 871

Tax, income, nature of, 557
Tax credits, deferred, 561 passim
Tax rates, 559
Taxes, on real property, 507; sales, 503
Temporary investments, 160; criteria for reporting securities as, 160
Term bonds, 513; redemption prior to maturity, 387
Termination of bonds, 530
Terminology, balance sheet, 94-97
The Accounting Review, 12; *see also* AAA
The Accounting Review Supplement, 12; *see also* AAA
The Financial Executive, 13; *see also* Financial Executives Institute
Time factor, used in decreasing-charge depreciation, 333; used in straight-line depreciation, 333
Timeliness, 24, 33
Timing differences, *see* Income for accounting purposes
Trade discounts, 208
Trade-ins, valuation of, 270
Trade names, 414
Trademarks, 414
Transaction, business, 44; defined, 44; internal, 44
Transfer agents, 655
Treasury share transactions, conclusions relative to, 682
Treasury shares, 675; acquisition of no-par, 680; defined, 675; purchase of, 677; purchase viewed as capital retirement, 678; purchase viewed as giving rise to capital element awaiting ultimate disposition, 679; two approaches of reporting share purchases, 677-80, *illustrated*, 680-81
Treasury stock, 93; *see also* Treasury shares
Trial balance, preparation of, 53, 65
Trust indenture, 512

Two transaction methods, for purchase of treasury stock, *illustrated*, 680-81
Types of leases, criteria for distinguishing between, 618; sale-leaseback, 619

U

Unappropriated retained earnings, 696
Understandability, 23, 35
Unearned revenue, failure to record, 808; overstatement of, 809
Unemployment Insurance, 504
Unintentional misstatements, 798
Unit credit method, *see* Pension funding, accrued benefit cost method
Unit depletion charge, 349
Unrealized holding gain or loss, 919
Unrealized intercompany gains and losses, 449; assets purchased intercompany, 452; inventory purchased intercompany, 450; on consolidated financials, 451-52; under equity method, 476
Use factor, used in productive-output depreciation, 333; used in service-hours depreciation, 333
Use factor methods of depreciation, 339; evaluation of, 341
Useful life, in determining depreciation charge, 332, functional factors, 332; pattern of use, 333; physical factors, 332; time factor, 333; use factor, 333

V

Valuation days, 586
Valuation of goodwill, 416; capitalization of average excess net earnings, 419; capitalization

of average net earnings, 419; current valuation of net business assets other than goodwill, 418; determination of an appropriate rate of return, 417; projection of level of future earnings, 416; use of projected future earnings and rate of return in developing a value, 418
Valuation of intangible assets, at time of acquisition, 408; subsequent to time of acquisition, 408
Valuation of inventory, 207; at cost or market, whichever is lower, 259
Valuation at market, 268
Valuation method of income determination, 118
Value of net assets, defined, 118
Verifiability, 23, 35
Virtual certainty test, 576
Voucher, 46
Voucher register, 47; *illustrated*, 51
Voucher system, 46-47

W

Warrants, 767
Watered shares, 668
Weighted average method of cost flow, 212
Well-offness, concept of, 918
Work in process, 202
Work sheet, preparation of, 60; *illustrated*, 58-59
Working capital, 500; funds defined as, 845
Working papers, for correction of account balances, *illustrated*, 811; for statement of changes in financial position, cash basis, *illustrated*, 866-67; for statement of changes in financial position, working capital basis, *illustrated*, 858-59; to summarize corrections, 810
Workmen's Compensation, 505

TABLE III

Amount of an Annuity of $1 per Period

$$FV_n = R\left[\frac{(1 + i)^n - 1}{i}\right] = R(FVAF_{\overline{n}|\,i})$$

n	2%	3%	4%	5%	6%	8%	10%	12%	16%	20%
1	1.0000	1.0000	1.0000	1.0000	1.0000	1.0000	1.0000	1.0000	1.0000	1.0000
2	2.0200	2.0300	2.0400	2.0500	2.0600	2.0800	2.1000	2.1200	2.1600	2.2000
3	3.0604	3.0909	3.1216	3.1525	3.1836	3.2464	3.3100	3.3744	3.5056	3.6400
4	4.1216	4.1836	4.2465	4.3101	4.3746	4.5061	4.6410	4.7793	5.0665	5.3680
5	5.2040	5.3091	5.4163	5.5256	5.6371	5.8666	6.1051	6.3528	6.8771	7.4416
6	6.3081	6.4684	6.6330	6.8019	6.9753	7.3359	7.7156	8.1152	8.9775	9.9299
7	7.4343	7.6625	7.8983	8.1420	8.3938	8.9228	9.4872	10.0890	11.4139	12.9159
8	8.5830	8.8923	9.2142	9.5491	9.8975	10.6366	11.4359	12.2997	14.2401	16.4991
9	9.7546	10.1591	10.5828	11.0266	11.4913	12.4876	13.5795	14.7757	17.5185	20.7989
10	10.9497	11.4639	12.0061	12.5779	13.1808	14.4866	15.9374	17.5487	21.3215	25.9587
11	12.1687	12.8078	13.4864	14.2068	14.9716	16.6455	18.5312	20.6546	25.7329	32.1504
12	13.4121	14.1920	15.0258	15.9171	16.8699	18.9771	21.3843	24.1331	30.8502	39.5805
13	14.6803	15.6178	16.6268	17.7130	18.8821	21.4953	24.5227	28.0291	36.7862	48.4966
14	15.9739	17.0863	18.2919	19.5986	21.0151	24.2149	27.9750	32.3926	43.6720	59.1959
15	17.2934	18.5989	20.0236	21.5786	23.2760	27.1521	31.7725	37.2797	51.6595	72.0351
16	18.6393	20.1569	21.8245	23.6575	25.6725	30.3243	35.9497	42.7533	60.9250	87.4421
17	20.0121	21.7616	23.6975	25.8404	28.2129	33.7502	40.5447	48.8837	71.6730	105.9306
18	21.4123	23.4144	25.6454	28.1324	30.9057	37.4502	45.5992	55.7497	84.1407	128.1167
19	22.8406	25.1169	27.6712	30.5390	33.7600	41.4463	51.1591	63.4397	98.6032	154.7400
20	24.2974	26.8704	29.7781	33.0660	36.7856	45.7620	57.2750	72.0524	115.3797	186.6880
25	32.0303	36.4593	41.6459	47.7271	54.8645	73.1059	98.3471	133.3339	249.2140	471.9811
30	40.5681	47.5754	56.0849	66.4388	79.0582	113.2832	164.4940	241.3327	530.3117	1181.8816
40	60.4020	75.4013	95.0255	120.7998	154.7620	259.0565	442.5926	767.0914	2360.7572	7343.8578
50	84.5794	112.7969	152.6671	209.3480	290.3359	573.7702	1163.9085	2400.0182	10435.6488	45497.1908